FINANCIAL MARKETS AND INSTRUMENTS
IN PRIVATE INTERNATIONAL LAW

European Union Law Series

This series brings together major works in the field of European Union Law. It features a diverse range of publications, including comprehensive handbooks designed to teach European Union Law, treaties for legal practitioners and academics, monographs on specialised topics and some of the best doctoral dissertations from across Europe. Additionally, it includes publications detailing conference proceedings on topical issues, as well as commentaries on major judgments and decisions handed down by the Court of Justice of the European Union.

P. Durand and A. Gilbert-d'Halluin (eds.), *Directive (EU) 2022/2464 as regards Corporate Sustainability Reporting (CSRD)*, 2024.

G. Marti (ed.), *European Citizenship through the Lens of EU Values*, 2025.

FINANCIAL MARKETS AND INSTRUMENTS IN PRIVATE INTERNATIONAL LAW

Augustin Gridel

Preface by Louis d'Avout

Foreword by Christine Lagarde

INTERSENTIA

Intersentia
Lefebvre Sarrut Belgium SA
Rue Haute, 139/6
1000 Bruxelles
Belgium
Email: contact@larcier-intersentia.com

Distribution for the UK, Ireland and
Rest of the World (excl. France, Belgium and Luxembourg)
Ingram Publisher Services UK
1 Deltic Avenue, Rooksley
Milton Keynes MK13 8LD
United Kingdom
Tel: +44 1752 202 301 | Fax: +44 1752 202 331
Email: ipsuk.customercare@ingramcontent.com

Distribution for France and Other Countries (excl. Ireland and the UK)
Interforum Editis
92 avenue de France
75013 Paris
France

Distribution for Belgium and Luxembourg (excl. France, Ireland and the UK)
Larcier-Intersentia
Rue Haute, 139/6
1000 Bruxelles
Belgium

Financial Markets and Instruments in Private International Law

ISBN 978-1-83970-564-9
D/2025/06040/0190
NUR 828

British Library Cataloguing in Publication Data. A catalogue record for this book is available from the British Library

ACKNOWLEDGEMENTS

This book is the English translation of a thesis defended at the Université Paris-Panthéon-Assas on the 14th of December 2021.

I would like to express my profound gratitude to professeur Louis d'Avout, whose supervision has been determining of the success of this enterprise – this study could not have had a more competent and visionary guide –, to Mrs Christine Lagarde, for the generous words she has accepted to write as a foreword of this book, and to the professors who generously accepted to sit on my jury: Sylvain Bollée, Dominique Bureau, France Drummond, Matthias Lehmann and Anne-Catherine Muller.

The preparation of the thesis benefited from a full scholarship from Université Paris-Panthéon-Assas, and from a research stay at the Institute of European and Comparative Law of the University of Oxford, where I spent one of my best years thanks to the kindness of Professors John Cartwright and Birke Häcker. I am deeply grateful to them. This research also benefited from two particularly fruitful stays at the Max Planck Institute in Hamburg and at the Hague Academy, made possible by the generosity of the Max Planck Society and the French Society of International Law.

Nevertheless, the perspective of the thesis remains that of French and European law; the book was translated into English with the hope that the reflections presented here may appeal beyond the French-speaking public.

The translation benefited from the careful proofreading of Mr Paul O'Keeffe, made possible thanks to the Fondation Panthéon-Assas, the Institut François Gény and BNP Paribas. I would like to thank them all for their generosity and dedication. All citations from French authors, books or legislation are translated from the French; any errors in translation are only imputable to me. The numeration of the paragraphs corresponds to the French version.

This book is dedicated to my parents, Jean-Pierre and Annonciade.

PREFACE

In banking and finance, transnationality permeates the day-to-day professional life and makes the dedicated lawyer an internationalist by necessity. There are good reasons for this: the intangible nature of services, the desire of operators even regulated to conquer foreign markets; sometimes because of the extraterritorial spread of local policies relating to the person of the operators or the products marketed. Although it does not always have a good reputation, private international law, with its promise of a widely understood conflict-of-laws discipline, is making inroads into the legal practice of this specialised and globalised sector.

For a young academic, it was an ambitious undertaking to systematically combine private international law with the law of financial markets and instruments. All the more so since, as Mr Augustin Gridel's methodological commitment attests from the introduction to his thesis, any good conflict-of-laws solution is developed by contemplating the domestic legal and regulatory material potentially applicable to cross-border relations. The relevant domestic law is widely publicised and, in Europe at least, consists of two equal layers, one national, the other European.

One therefore encounters the difficulty inherent in these matters, which are steeped in administrative regulation: the international applicability of public law plays a driving role, although the theory is not guaranteed, since it constitutes the dark side of the conflict-of-laws' historical development. As German academics put it, the singularity of international financial law is that it is made up of a private law of transactions and operations (contract and tort) and a public law of infrastructures and supervised operators; a largely internationalised public law, sometimes pooled by States or supranational organisations and often disregarding territories and borders. In this area of modern economic law in particular, there are macroscopic public law connecting factors – those of infrastructures, functions and systems useful to the life of the markets – which predetermine and are aligned with the microscopic connecting factors applicable to private law operations. The connecting factors applicable to infrastructures are established discreetly by public law texts or regimes: in Europe, by the MiFID directive, in particular (with regard to trading platforms). These allocation rules are also used to regulate conflicts of laws in matters of contract, insolvency and so on. With regard to cross-border takeover bids, or litigation involving aggrieved investors, the texts (Takeover

Directive, Art. 4, articulating the law of the market and the law of the issuer) or case law (*BP plc* ruling of the ECJ, for example) show that specific solutions cannot be understood without examining the technical and regulatory context of market operations.

The research mandate was, therefore, starting from a scrupulous examination of French and European regulations, never to omit conflicts of laws in public law, in other words to 'do private international law' outside the known paths of pure private law. Augustin Gridel has courageously taken up this challenge. His subject, initially limited to one aspect of the problem (the law of security interests in listed securities), has been rationally extended to explain in all its dimensions the interaction, in international matters, of the law of instruments and the law of financial markets. The law of the market must be reconciled with the law of the issuance, then with the law of the issuer when it is distinct (see the example of the aforementioned Takeover Directive), with the law of the countries of marketing and finally with that of the law applicable to the holding and settlement mechanisms. The entire work, through its logical divisions and opportune summaries in the concluding proposals, is devoted to this anatomy of international financial law and to the optimal articulation of the laws involved. The result is a 'truly comprehensive survey', as one member of the thesis jury put it.

The study is up to date with current events: the federalisation of administrative supervision is extensively covered, and the technology of distributed registers can be found here and there. The truth is that the economic and technological constraints, and consequently the regulatory environment, has changed fundamentally since dematerialisation and digitisation. As recently as fifty years ago, in the days of physical trading, things were simple because many of the relevant connections could be seen: there was a place where securities were located, and a trading venue subject to its law. Today, these connections remain, but they are no longer visible. The law of the trading platform or infrastructure has become the law of a system: a computer system backed by market rules subject to a necessarily single law. Secondly, the functions of the trading infrastructure have been split up into various institutions and systems, which is likely to increase the fragmentation of laws. In a pro-competitive and liberalising move, the lawmaker (particularly in Europe) has finally recognised the diversity of types of platforms (regulated or unregulated markets), of technologies and of the status of participants. This has shifted the focus of conflict of laws issues and made them more complex.

The originality of this book lies in the fact that it is built entirely around the study of the institutional connecting factors specific to stock market and financial matters. In a fine exposition of domestic law, the author analyses the contractual nature of 'market rules' (or system rules for mechanisms other than trading platforms), but argues that in international matters, the law of the system, a modern form of *lex mercatus* (to use a concept coined from observation of medieval markets), is not determined subjectively and voluntarily (free choice by the manager and participants), but objectively (law of the place where the system manager is established). This conclusion, which has unequal explanatory power for the law in force (see nos. 267 to 277 of the book), does not, however, have a decisive impact on the rest of the doctoral thesis.

The very principle of an institutional law is thus justified and determined by means of a a specific allocation rule, and its area of relevance is clarified in terms of the system's respective relationships with issuers and investors. The thesis then takes up classic questions and deals with them in the European and French context, not without some important notes on foreign law: the law applicable to the issuance, the regime governing public offers of securities and their marketing, the impact of the prospectus on conflicts of laws and jurisdictional issues, multi-listing and the conduct of takeover bids, etc.; to which is added the repression of market abuse.

The third and final part of the book contains other in-depth and original developments relating to the status of securities and financial contracts. The first title takes up the well-known question of the proprietary connecting factor applicable to financial securities. Contrary to some mainstream analyses (American law and The Hague Convention, in particular; the so-called PRIMA principle), Mr Gridel rebuts – with courage and a certain talent – the fragmented conflict-of-laws treatment of securities from a proprietary point of view, by refusing to consider each entry in an account with an intermediary as a relevant location of the security and proprietary rights, capable of determining the law applicable to questions of ownership. In the author's view, only a primary book entry is authentic and only transactions affecting that book entry are decisive in domestic law; this should dictate the conflict-of-laws rule applicable to proprietary issues in cross-border cases and lead to the view that the books and accounts of the central depository are equivalent to the legally relevant location of the securities. The holding and settlement systems, which tend to be intangible, constitute the technological reference environment within which securities are held and moved. Once again, these primary systems appear to be subject to their own institutional law (which also depends on the intellectual alternative of an objective or voluntary connection: the law of the account or system, or the law of the country in which the account keeper or system operator is established). The law of the primary registration system becomes, at least in part or as a matter of principle, the law applicable to the regime of ownership of registered assets. This unitary reasoning, based on the primary registration of intangible assets, is discussed at length and deserves to be considered very carefully. It has a serious chance of prevailing in the future as the technology of financial intermediation changes (distributed ledger technology, also taken into account in the book).

With the methodology he has chosen and in the field in which he has deployed it, Augustin Gridel has been a pioneer. Originally educated in private law and endowed with a solid generalist and comparative culture, he took up the challenge of climbing the regulatory mountain of financial law to reach the fundamental and technical discussions of the sector in question and offer, in terms of conflict-of-laws, a systematisation of proven or conceivable solutions. As far as doctoral theses are concerned (if we omit older works dealing, for example, with the 'admission to listing of foreign securities'), this is the first in France to have approached all the issues in an analytical way, from the bottom up; independently of public international law, which in this area prescribes so little.

The work we are about to read, which has won a number of academic and professional prizes attesting to its value, will probably give rise to others in line with technological and regulatory innovation. It will also have paved the way for a reflection on the institutional links and connecting factors applicable in international and European financial market law. In this respect, and irrespective of the fate of each of its multiple conclusions, we can expect the book to set an example.

Louis d'Avout
Professor at the Université Panthéon-Assas (Paris)

FOREWORD

If the realm of the conflict of laws has been traditionally depicted as 'a dismal swamp, filled with quaking quagmires, and inhabited by learned but eccentric professors who theorize about mysterious matters in a strange and incomprehensible jargon',[1] no less sophisticated has become nowadays the law of financial markets. In the latter, the multiplicity of actors, the heterogeneity of the legal situations and relationships which connect them one with the other and, not least, their geographical dispersion makes for a complexity which is only at par with the relevance they have gained in today's economy.

It can therefore appear a daunting task the one that Augustin Gridel has undertaken for his doctoral research, to analyse the realm of financial markets through the lens of the conflict of laws, thereby combining the subtle intricacies of these two highly technical fields. A daunting task, but a welcome one, whose results are presented in this book, that constitutes the crowning achievement of Dr. Gridel's long research and reflection [under the *magisterium* of Professor Louis D'Avout], offered in English version to the legal community of academics, private practitioners and public authorities.

The objective of Dr. Gridel's work, and one of its distinguishing features, is not to explore some specific aspects or area of the law of the financial markets, but rather to encompass the wider spectrum of legal relationships and situations which are established in the operations of those markets, and test the soundness of their regime when regarded under the conflict of laws perspective, offering proposals *de lege ferenda*, where appropriate.

In doing so, the conflictual reasoning, guided by the rigorous methods and concepts of the French doctrinal tradition of the *conflit de lois*, is preceded by an accurate overview of the substantial – national and supranational - regulation governing those relationships and situations. Substantive private laws – notably, contract and personal property law – and, to a lesser extent, public law, notably criminal law, have a key role to play in the application of financial regulation. Dr Gridel's reconstruction further factors in the analysis the administrative law underpinnings of financial markets, pointing out the similarity of their *procédé* with the one of private international law.

Far from being of academic interest only, the analysis of such relationships also has concrete policy implications. In the case of the EU, they are part and

[1] W.L. Prosser, 'Interstate Publication' (1952-1953) 51 Mich L Rev 959, at 971.

parcel of the journey towards European integration. Questions around the role that private law can play in the process of European financial sector integration, and whether private law diversity can hamper the functioning of European markets have been the subject of extensive academic scrutiny. Similarly, both the literature and institutional actors, including the European Commission, have explored the question of the eventual harmonisation of private law.

One of the many reasons why Dr. Gridel's research is valuable is because it explores, in considerable depth, the different points of connection between financial markets and national legal orders, bringing to light the legislative and administrative dimensions of their interconnection. Dr. Gridel's research also highlights the less-well understood and under-researched role that market operators and financial market infrastructures play in circumscribing the conflict of laws context in which those connections are to be understood. In his research, he also draws attention to the international status of financial contracts and the discrepancy between that status and national civil law.

It might be argued that, without a common core of basic private law rules, supra-national financial regulations are either doomed to fail on the coherence front or are destined to only unfold a fragment of their true potential. In the case of the EU, it is broadly accepted that the Union legislator lacks a general competence to harmonise private law rules. Moreover, where the EU legislator has asserted such a competence, its scope only covers those aspects of private law where national law discrepancies are considered to materially obstruct the establishment of an internal market.

This is where private international law becomes relevant, by providing a path through which those discrepancies can be negotiated. And one can only concur with the conclusion by Paul Lagarde, which Dr Gridel recalls in the very forefront of the Introduction to this book, on '*le rôle coordinateur irremplaçable de la théorie des conflits de lois*'.

I would like to conclude by praising the contribution of the work of Dr Gridel to the creation of a much needed genuinely European legal scholarship in the field of financial markets regulation, by meticulously mapping, through his research, the intersection between financial markets and private international law. One of the hallmarks of such a scholarship is the acknowledgement of the crucial role that private law as well as conflict of laws rules can play for the success of EU financial regulation. By providing the foundation for future research on the optimal degree of substantive private law harmonisation which will inform the future harmonisation agenda of policy makers and legislators, research such as the one conducted by Augustin provides a great input into the success of our common, European project.

Christine Lagarde
President of the European Central Bank

ABBREVIATIONS

EUROPEAN LEGISLATION

AIFM Directive – Directive 2011/61/EU of the European Parliament and of the Council of 8 June 2011 on Alternative Investment Fund Managers

Brussels Ia Regulation – Regulation (EU) No 1215/2012 of the European Parliament and of the Council of 12 December 2012 on jurisdiction and the recognition and enforcement of judgments in civil and commercial matters

CRD IV – Directive 2013/36/EU of the European Parliament and of the Council of 26 June 2013 relating to the taking up and pursuit of the business of credit institutions and the prudential supervision of credit institutions and investment firms

CRR Regulation – Regulation (EU) No 575/2013 of the European Parliament and of the Council of 26 June 2013 on prudential requirements for credit institutions and investment firms

CSD Regulation – Regulation (EU) No 909/2014 of the European Parliament and of the Council of 23 July 2014 on improving securities settlement in the European Union and on central securities depositories

EMIR Regulation – Regulation (EU) No 648/2012 of the European Parliament and of the Council of 4 July 2012 on over-the-counter derivatives, central counterparties and trade repositories

ESMA Regulation – Regulation (EU) No 1095/2010 of the European Parliament and of the Council of 24 November 2010 establishing a European Supervisory Authority (European Securities and Markets Authority)

Finality Directive – Directive 98/26/EC of the European Parliament and of the Council of 19 May 1998 on settlement finality in payment and securities settlement systems

Financial Collateral Directive – Directive 2002/47/EC of the European Parliament and of the Council of 6 June 2002 on financial collateral arrangements

IFD Directive – Directive (EU) 2019/2034 of the European Parliament and of the Council of 27 November 2019 on the prudential supervision of investment firms

Insolvency Regulation – Regulation (EU) 2015/848 of the European Parliament and of the Council of 20 May 2015 on insolvency proceedings

Investment Services Directive – Council Directive 93/22/EEC of 10 May 1993 on investment services in the securities field

Market Abuse Directive – Directive 2014/57/EU of the European Parliament and of the Council of 16 April 2014 on criminal sanctions for market abuse (Market Abuse Directive)

Market Abuse Regulation – Regulation (EU) No 596/2014 of the European Parliament and of the Council of 16 April 2014 on market abuse

MiFID – Directive 2004/39/EC of the European Parliament and of the Council of 21 April 2004 on markets in financial instruments

MiFID 2 - Directive 2014/65/EU of the European Parliament and of the Council of 15 May 2014 on markets in financial instruments
MiFID Regulation - Regulation (EU) No 600/2014 of the European Parliament and of the Council of 15 May 2014 on markets in financial instruments
Rome I Regulation - Regulation (EC) No 593/2008 of the European Parliament and of the Council of 17 June 2008 on the law applicable to contractual obligations
Rome II Regulation - Regulation (EC) No 864/2007 of the European Parliament and of the Council of 11 July 2007 on the law applicable to non-contractual obligations
Prospectus Regulation - Regulation (EU) 2017/1129 of the European Parliament and of the Council of 14 June 2017 on the prospectus to be published when securities are offered to the public or admitted to trading on a regulated market
Resolution Directive - Directive 2014/59/EU of the European Parliament and of the Council of 15 May 2014 establishing a framework for the recovery and resolution of credit institutions and investment firms
Regulation on the resolution of clearing houses - Regulation (EU) 2021/23 of the European Parliament and of the Council of 16 December 2020 on a framework for the recovery and resolution of central counterparties
Short Selling Regulation - Regulation (EU) No 236/2012 of the European Parliament and of the Council of 14 March 2012 on short selling and certain aspects of credit default swaps
Solvency II Directive - Directive 2009/138/EC of the European Parliament and of the Council of 25 November 2009 on the taking-up and pursuit of the business of insurance and reinsurance
SSM Regulation - Council Regulation (EU) No 1024/2013 of 15 October 2013 entrusting the European Central Bank with specific tasks concerning policies relating to the prudential supervision of credit institutions
SRM Regulation - Regulation (EU) No 806/2014 of the European Parliament and of the Council of 15 July 2014 establishing uniform rules and procedure for the resolution of credit institutions and certain investment firms under a single resolution mechanism and a single bank resolution fund
Takeover Directive - Directive 2004/25/EC of the European Parliament and of the Council of 21 April 2004 on takeover bids
TFEU -Treaty on the Functioning of the European Union
Transparency Directive - Directive 2004/109/EC of the European Parliament and of the Council of 15 December 2004 on the harmonisation of transparency requirements in relation to information about issuers whose securities are admitted to trading on a regulated market
UCITS Directive - Directive 2009/65/EC of the European Parliament and of the Council of 13 July 2009 on the coordination of laws, regulations and administrative provisions relating to undertakings for collective investment in transferable securities (UCITS)
Winding up Directive - Directive 2001/24/EC of the European Parliament and of the Council of 4 April 2001 on the reorganisation and winding up of credit institutions

SYSTEM RULES

Euronext Market Rules (Book I) – Euronext Market Rules, Book I: Harmonised Rules. Issue date: 9 November 2020.

Euronext Market Rules (Book II) – Euronext Market Rules, Book II: Special rules applicable to French regulated markets. Issue date: 2 July 2019.

Clearing Rules – LCH. SA Clearing Rules published on 6 August 2021.

Euroclear's operating rules – Operating rules of the Central Depositary, Euroclear France, Decision of 16 April 2019 on the authorisation of Euroclear France SA as a central securities depository and approval of its operating rules.

JOURNALS

Banque et droit	Revue banque et droit
Banque	Revue Banque
BJB	Bulletin Joly bourse
D.	Recueil Dalloz
Dr. et patr.	Droit et patrimoine
Dr. soc.	Revue droit des sociétés
Études Joly soc.	Études Joly Sociétés.
Europe	Revue Europe
Gaz. Pal.	Gazette du Palais
JCl. Banque crédit bourse	Juris-classeur Banque crédit bourse traité
JCP E.	Juris-classeur périodique (semaine juridique), édition entreprise
JCP G.	Juris-classeur périodique (semaine juridique), édition générale
JCP N.	Juris-classeur périodique (semaine juridique), édition notariale
JCl. soc.	Juris-classeur société traité
JCl. Eur	Juris-classeur société traité
JDI	Journal de droit international
JORF	Journal officiel (France)
OJ	Official Journal of the European Union
JPIL	Journal of private international law

Rev. CMF	Revue du Conseil des marchés financiers
RCADI	Recueil des cours de l'académie de la Haye
RDC	Revue des contrats
RDIP	Revue de droit international privé
RCDIP	Revue critique de droit international privé
RDBD	Revue de droit bancaire et de la bourse
RDBF	Revue de droit bancaire et financier
REDBF (Euredia)	Revue européenne de droit bancaire et financier
RISF	Revue internationale des services financiers
RJ Com.	Revue de jurisprudence commerciale
RTD civ.	Revue trimestrielle de droit civil
RTD com.	Revue trimestrielle de droit commercial
RTD Eur.	Revue trimestrielle de droit européen
RTDF	Revue trimestrielle de droit financier
S.	Recueil Sirey
TCFDIP	Travaux du comité français de droit international privé

INSTITUTIONS

ACPR	Autorité de contrôle prudentiel et de résolution
AIF	Alternative investment fund
AMF	Autorité des marchés financiers
CA	Cour d'appel
Cass.	Cour de cassation
CCDVT	Caisse centrale de dépôts et de virement de titres
CE	Conseil d'État
ECtHR	European Court of Human Rights
Civ.	Chambre civile (de la Cour de cassation)
COB	Commission des opérations de bourse
Com.	Chambre commerciale (de la Cour de cassation)
Cons. const.	Conseil constitutionnel

Crim.	Chambre criminelle (de la Cour de cassation)
EBA	European Banking Authority
ECB	European Central Bank
ECJ	European Court of Justice
ESCB	European System of Central Banks
ESMA	European securities and markets authority
HCJP	Haut Comité Juridique de la place financière de Paris
NCB	National central bank
RG AMF	Règlement général de l'Autorité des marchés financiers
SICOVAM	Société interprofessionnelle de compensation des valeurs mobilières
SRB	Single Resolution Board
SRF	Single Resolution Fund
UCITS	Undertakings for collective investment in transferable securities

OTHERS

Art.	Article
Ass. plén.	Assemblée plénière
Comp.	Compare
Concl.	Conclusions
Contra	Contrary to
Et al.	Et alii
Ibid.	*Ibidem*
Infra	See below
Op. cit.	*Opus citatum*
p.	Page
Supra	See above
t.	Tome
V°	*Verbo*
Vol.	Volume

TABLE OF CONTENTS

TITLE 2
THE CONNECTING FACTOR OF SYSTEMS

PART 2
THE SCOPE OF FINANCIAL MARKET LAW

TITLE 1
THE RELATIONSHIP BETWEEN FINANCIAL MARKETS AND ISSUERS

Title 2
THE RELATIONSHIP BETWEEN FINANCIAL MARKETS AND INVESTORS

PART 3
THE STATUS OF FINANCIAL INSTRUMENTS

TITLE 1
THE CONNECTING FACTOR OF SECURITIES' PROPRIETARY STATUS

INTRODUCTION

'In our opinion, these reflections should show the irreplaceable coordinating role of the conflict-of-laws theory, which today is too quickly said to be somewhat outdated and should be replaced by a substantial regulation of international relations. It is indeed possible that the conflict of laws theory has only a transitional role to play. But if the transition from the present fragmentation of legislation to future international unification were to last as long as our world does, should we be in such a hurry to bury conflicts of law?'

Paul Lagarde[1]

1. If the study of positive law is to the jurist what fieldwork is to the sociologist, in the same way, domestic law is for the internationalist the raw material of his work. We sometimes tend to forget this, simply because private international law has its own objects of study, foremost among which are conflicts of law. The latter arise from a 'founding antinomy'[2] between, on the one hand, the division of the world into distinct legal orders since, as Niboyet pointed out, 'each country must have a law adapted to its needs, and it is in diversity that true civilisation resides'[3] and, on the other hand, the existence of international private relations.[4] On the basis of this duality, private international law develops its own objectives, independent of domestic law, and sometimes contradictory: the coordination of legal orders, which is the basis of the conflict rule method,[5] the true 'medicine' for conflicts of laws,[6] and the preservation of their internal order, which is the basis of mechanisms derogating from the application of foreign law, so that international relations do not destabilise the social structure

---

1 P. Lagarde, 'Les interprétations divergentes d'une loi uniforme donnent-elles lieu à un conflit de lois?' (1964) *RCDIP*, 235.

2 The expression is by Professor d'Avout, 'La reconnaissance dans le champ des conflits de lois', *TCFDIP*, 2014–2016, pp. 215 et seq.

3 J.-P. Niboyet, *Traité de droit international privé*, vol. III, no. 1022, Paris, Sirey, 1944, p. 497.

4 In this sense, conflict of laws are a 'pure fact', an 'international reality' affecting cross-border private relations, see L. d'Avout, *Sur les solutions du conflit de lois en droit des biens*, Paris, Economica, 2006, no. 1; on this perception, see also by the same author, *L'entreprise et les conflits internationaux de lois*, RCADI, t. 398, Leiden, Brill, 2019, no. 22 and spec. n. 104.

5 P. Mayer, *Le phénomène de la coordination des ordres juridiques étatiques*, RCADI, vol. 357, Leiden, Martinus Nijhoff, 2007, p. 23.

6 As Niboyet wrote: 'The theory of conflicts, it should not be forgotten, is basically a medicine', J.-P. Niboyet, *Traité de droit international privé*, *op. cit.*

of state legal orders.[7] The discipline draws its singularity from the pursuit of its aims through a methodological approach that can move away from domestic law, either because it leads to the multiplication of points of view that are foreign to it,[8] or because it can be based on the structure of norms in order to deduce the appropriate method of resolution.[9] Nevertheless, domestic law reappears, since the methods used have in common that they are based on its analysis in order to found the rule of jurisdiction or conflict on the legal centre of gravity of the relationship in question, according to the substantive considerations that it promotes.[10] In other words, domestic law is primary in that it attempts to capture the raw fact giving rise to conflicts of law, and therefore constitutes the matrix of the conflict rules. This connection is particularly perceptible when the law of conflicts synthesises domestic law in order to constitute its own categories[11] and to give legal institutions the appropriate international connecting factor. In so doing, it casts an original eye on the legislative bodies in question, often revealing their deficiencies.[12] It is on this double exercise of synthesis and characterisation, on the one hand, and of connection, on the other hand, that the present thesis focuses in a field, financial law, where the method of the rule of conflict has not lost its vigour.

---

7 Y. Lequette, *Les mutations du droit international privé: vers un changement de paradigme?*, RCADI, vol. 387, Leiden, Brill, 2017, nos. 28 et seq. Traditionally, these two objectives were hierarchical because of the anteriority of the domestic order over the international order, see H. Batiffol, *Aspects philosophiques de droit international privé*, Paris, Dalloz, 1956, republished in 2002, spec. no. 145.

8 And in particular a point of view outside the legal orders, 'vue de Sirius', see F. Rigaux, *Les situations juridiques individuelles dans un système de relativité générale*, RCADI, t. 213, Leiden, Martinus Nijhoff, 1989.

9 This structuralist approach, theorised by Motulsky and whose scope in private international law has been considerable following the work of Professor Pierre Mayer, has produced results that are not discussed here. It should simply be noted that if the structure of norms has an influence on their methodological treatment, this influence should not be exaggerated, since the purpose pursued by the domestic rule, the set of laws in which it is inserted, or the institutional structure from which it originates may appear to be predominant. For a recent illustration of the weaknesses to which structural analysis can lead, see H. Synvet, 'La place de la décision administrative en droit bancaire' in *Mélanges en l'honneur du professeur Pierre Mayer*, Paris, LGDJ, 2015, pp. 845 et seq.

10 H. Batiffol, *Aspects philosophiques du droit international privé*, *op. cit.*, nos. 89 et seq. On this statement within the law of international jurisdiction, see E. Farnoux, *Les considérations substantielles dans le règlement de la compétence internationale des juridictions*, Paris, LGDJ, 2022. The need to study domestic law is even more apparent in order to devise appropriate substantive rules.

11 This synthesis stems from the necessary 'systematic character of domestic laws considered as a whole. This character means that a rule of detail does not often have an absolute meaning in itself because its effect can only be understood in combination with another rule [...]', cf. P. Francescakis, *La théorie du renvoi et les conflits de systèmes en droit international privé*, Paris, Sirey, 1958, para. 21; see also H. Batiffol, *Aspects philosophiques du droit international privé*, *op. cit.*, no. 8.

12 See L. d'Avout, 'Les quotas face au conflit international des lois' (2011) (56) *Revue Lamy de droit des affaires*, p. 93.

2. First views on financial markets and instruments. The concept of financial instruments is recent. However, it is based on the addition of two long-known objects: *financial securities*, i.e. shares, claims and units in collective investment undertakings, which in principle constitute financing instruments, and *financial contracts*, i.e. the contracts listed in Section C of the Annexe 1 of MiFID, whose function is to transfer risk.[13] The concept of financial instrument has the particularity of supporting, or even defining, the other concepts of financial law,[14] and as such constitutes the cornerstone of the discipline.[15] It is true that it is provided with its own regime, facilitating, according to distinct modalities depending on the securities and contracts, their circulation and the patrimonial operations of which they may be the object. Nevertheless, financial instruments were created in order to define investment services, which are activities that require authorisation from an administrative authority in order to be carried out[16] and to define the concept of financial markets, which refers to those on which financial instruments can be traded.[17] However, the converse is not true: financial instruments can be traded independently of a financial market.[18] For this reason, capital markets law could, in some respects, be presented as a branch of financial instruments law, the branch through which certain trading of financial instruments takes place.[19]

3. Although the objects that can be traded on a financial market are limited to financial instruments, the notion of financial market can nevertheless be

---

13 From the French perspective, those contracts are listed in Art. D. 211-1 A of the Monetary and Financial Code (see also Art. L. 211-1 of the Monetary and Financial Code).

14 A. Couret, H. Le Nabasque *et al.*, *Droit financier*, 3rd ed., Paris, Dalloz, 2019, no. 388; F. Drummond, *Droit financier*, Paris, Economica, 2020, no. 258; T. Bonneau *et al.*, *Droit financier*, 2nd ed., Paris, LGDJ, 2019, no. 738.

15 F. Drummond, *Droit financier*, *op. cit.*, nos. 1 and 258: 'It is around the notion of financial instruments that the texts governing the financial field are organised'. It seems to us that it is in that it underpins the other notions that the notion of financial instrument can be considered as coherent, even though they cannot be considered solely as financing instruments.

16 Art. L. 321-1 of the Monetary and Financial Code. This means that the provision of financial instruments on a professional basis inevitably triggers a set of professional obligations.

17 Art. L. 421-1 of the Monetary and Financial Code. A distinction is made between financial markets and commodity markets, see T. Bonneau *et al.*, *Droit financier*, *op. cit.*, no. 4.

18 Financial securities may be offered independently of their admission to trading on a financial market, financial contracts may be concluded over the counter.

19 As Professor Drummond writes, 'Financial markets law is first and foremost a law of assets, of those particular assets that are financial instruments', F. Drummond, 'Loi PACTE et actifs numériques', *BJB*, July 2019, No. 118 m3, p. 60.
These observations help to explain the evolution of the literature on the subject from financial market law to financial law. Financial law is both a law of financial instruments and of the means by which they are marketed, which implies a specific institutional regime. Perceiving the importance of financial instruments early on, see M. Jeantin, 'Le droit financier des biens' in *Prospectives du droit économique, Dialogues avec Michel Jeantin*, Paris, Dalloz, 1999, p. 3.

somewhat ambivalent due to the polysemy of the expression 'market'. The latter can, first of all, refer to a *sector of activity*,[20] e.g. the market for over-the-counter financial contracts, or to a set of potential clients, sometimes referred to as an outlet[21] or a 'savings market'.[22] The market can also designate a *space*, where exchanges take place, associated with a *mechanism*, whereby selling and buying interests meet.[23] This last, long-standing meaning is best illustrated by the financial markets studied here, which the legislator defines as 'a system or device within which multiple buying and selling interests expressed by third parties for financial instruments may interact'.[24]

4. Internationalisation of financial relationships. It is a well-known fact that the private relationships generated by financial markets and instruments have become largely internationalised.[25] This internationalisation takes place at several levels. First of all, it may appear independently of a financial market and result

---

20 This last meaning is similar to the concept of relevant market used in competition law, see Commission Notice on the definition of the relevant market for the purposes of Community competition law (97/C 372/03). The difference is, however, that the relevant market is intended precisely to circumscribe within a sector of activity the 'relevant' segment for assessing competition.

21 L. D'AVOUT, *L'entreprise et les conflits internationaux de lois*, *op. cit.*, no. 46.

22 A. TENENBAUM, *L'application internationale du droit boursier*, Paris, Université Paris I, 2000, no. 70. The author distinguishes it from the "market-exchange" (*ibid.*), i.e. the market from an institutional point of view (see following note).

23 See J.-J. DAIGRE, 'L'évolution de la notion de marché financier' in *Liber amicorum Jacques Malherbes*, Brussels, Bruylant, 2006, pp. 233 et seq., spec. no. 4, p. 238: 'despite these reforms, the stock market has remained what it was since the beginning of the 18th century: an organisation and a mechanism'. Buying and selling interests, also known as supply and demand, have been considered by some authors as constituting the market, see in this sense D. ROBINE, *La sécurité des marchés financiers face aux procédures collectives*, Paris, LGDJ, 2003, no. 6. This statement is based on a particularly accurate intuition: the existence of markets stems, chronologically, from the existence of merchants willing to exchange goods. People and objects inevitably precede the institutional or organisational aspect of the market. However, it seems to us that the singularity of the notion of market lies precisely in the organisation of market relations. This organisation will take place, on the one hand, through the meeting of merchants in a geographical or electronic space (it is not insignificant that they are referred to today by the notion of platform, which is precisely a meeting place) and, on the other hand, through the management of relations by an entity (public or private), which is itself most often subject to the supervision, even if passive and liberal, of a sovereign, cf. L. D'AVOUT, *L'entreprise et les conflits internationaux de lois*, *op. cit.*, no. 46: 'In a second sense, the market is a place, subject to its own rules; initially public rules of territorial application: *Ubi mercatus, ibi jus*. A modernised version of the medieval market-place is the market-institution.'

24 Art. 4(1)(19) of the MiFID 2. This is the definition of a multilateral system, common to all the definitions of the different types of financial markets, the existence of a unitary definition having been long in emerging, the doctrine having long been based on an enumeration. The legislative definition does not, however, take into account the fact that the system, and consequently the financial market, is always made up of a material element and a legal element.

25 H. SYNVET, 'L'internationalisation du droit des affaires' in *Le Code de commerce 1807-2007, Livre du bicentenaire*, Paris, Dalloz, 2007, pp. 727 et seq.

from the solicitation of French residents, by way of a public offer of financial securities or by canvassing with a view to concluding a financial contract. Conversely, French residents may solicit foreign persons either to provide them with financial instruments or to enter into financial instrument transactions with them. This first level of internationalisation of private relations requires the international application of French and European financial standards for the protection of residents to be determined,[26] and the action of the administrative authorities responsible for ensuring their application to be coordinated.

5. A second level of internationalisation arises from the admission of securities of foreign issuers to the French financial markets and the acquisition of securities admitted to the French financial market by foreign investors. The first aspect requires reconciling the 'frictions' arising from the confluence of French capital markets law and the foreign company law of the issuer.[27] This reconciliation is most often facilitated by the fact that, as Professor Synvet has shown, the rules of stock exchange law pursue an objective consistent with that of company law.[28] This does not, however, deactivate the competition between these rules. As Professor Francisco Garcimartin Alferez observed in a lecture at the Hague Academy, the resolution of conflicts of laws then requires a precise analysis not only of the delimitation of each of the laws, but also of their substantive content.[29] With regard to the acquisition of securities admitted to the French financial market by foreign investors, the problem is that of the international application

---

26 This is what some specialists in the field have been working on. In France, the reference document is the study that Professor Synvet and Ms Tenenbaum have devoted to financial instruments in the *Dalloz* international repertory, the richness of which is not, however, exhausted in the study of the rules of protection of residents, see 'Instruments financiers' in H. Synvet and A. Tenenbaum, *Répertoire de droit international*, Paris, Dalloz, 2008. However, the issue is not new. The admission to trading has often been a determining factor in the configuration of the issues in certain emblematic judgments in the field. Two examples will be given here. Firstly, in *Messagerie Maritime* (Cass. Civ., 21 June 1950, on which see the ref. in B. Ancel and Y. Lequette, *Les grands arrêts de la jurisprudence de droit international privé*, *op. cit.* comm. no. 22), the admission of the disputed debt securities to the Amsterdam stock exchange made it possible to determine that the addressees of the loan were not, in the first place, Canadian residents, and was undoubtedly instrumental in the eviction of the monetary policy rules relating to gold clauses. Then, in *Banque Ottomane* (CA Paris, 3 October 1984, *RCDIP*, 1985. 526 note H. Synvet; *JDI*, 1986. 156, note B. Goldman), the question of the characterisation of the registered office of the company was raised in order to trigger the applicability of a rule of French law on listed companies, relating to the information of shareholders. Mr Synvet, in his note under the judgment, observed early on that this rule could have been applied independently of the registered office, as a rule of protection for residents, in respect of the admission to trading of securities on a financial market located at their domicile.

27 On this type of conflict of laws, see L. d'Avout, *L'entreprise et les conflits internationaux de lois*, *op. cit.*, nos. 23–24.

28 H. Synvet, *L'organisation juridique du groupe international de sociétés*, vol. II, thesis, University of Rennes, 1979, nos. 452 et seq.

29 F. Garcimartin Alferez, *Cross-border listed companies*, RCADI, vol. 328, The Hague, Martinus Nijhoff, 2007, nos. 110 et seq.

of the rules relating to market transactions, i.e. transactions relating to financial instruments admitted to trading.[30] Market transactions, previously referred to as stock exchange transactions, are the subject of mediatised litigation[31] relating to the international application of 'stock exchange law' and questioning the State's jurisdiction in this area.[32] This is especially true for the criminal side of the rules applicable to market transactions, where the criteria used to link them have led legal scholars to question their validity.[33] In their civil aspect, if these relationships are more often studied under the angle of the international jurisdiction of the administrative authority, the question of the application of the rules of the law of the financial markets has nevertheless been summarised by Professor Synvet when he writes that 'stock exchange law imposes its respect by making it the condition of the use of the mechanism that it designs'.[34] The difficulty is, however, that, in order to impose its compliance on investors, stock market law may decide to use sanctions that only the legal system of the registered office of the company can effectively achieve, thus resurrecting, in the relationship between financial markets and investors, the necessary coordination of financial market law and the law of companies admitted to it.

6. A third level of internationalisation relates to the financial instruments themselves, and looks different with respect to securities and financial contracts. Securities have several aspects. First, their issuance most often gives rise to a conflict of laws regarding their form, which is determined by the issuer but designed for the place of marketing. The issue may also give rise to a conflict of laws whenever the *negotium* represented by the security is subject to a law different from that of the issuer: this will be the case for debt securities whose issuing is subject to a foreign law. Moreover, the determination of the law applicable to the ownership of the security raises difficulties that dematerialisation has increased and to which no solution has been satisfactorily

---

30 On this notion of market transaction, see A.-C. Rouaud, *Contribution à l'étude de l'opération de marché*, Paris, IRJS, 2010.

31 The field is full of 'mediatic cases', i.e. sulphurous disputes that sometimes cause the applicable rules to evolve. From an international perspective, the best known is undoubtedly the *Péchiney* case, which raised the question of the applicability of French law to insider trading committed on foreign financial markets. This question gave rise to the seminal article by I. Fadlallah, 'Point de vue sur l'affaire Pechiney: la localisation du délit d'initié', *RCDIP*, 1996, pp. 621 et seq.

32 On this question, see A. Tenenbaum, *L'application internationale du droit boursier*, *op. cit.* The author considers that the State has exclusive competence with regard to the organisation of stock markets, but believes that the State has 'a questionable exclusive material competence (*with regard to*) the savings market' (see *ibid.*, pp. 137 et seq.).

33 In addition to the article by Professor Fadlallah, these issues are dealt with in the broader study on the international application of criminal law, see D. Chilstein, *Droit pénal international et lois de police*, Paris, Dalloz, 2003.

34 H. Synvet, *L'organisation juridique du groupe international de sociétés*, *op. cit.*, 403.

found in French doctrine.[35] Finally, in international relations, the freedom of choice of law for financial contracts has had to be reconciled with the legislative frameworks that condition their conclusion and performance. All these problems are amplified by the superposition of these different levels of internationalisation, the development of market infrastructures, a national supervisory authority, but also the fragmentation of sources.

7. **Market infrastructures.** In its common meaning, infrastructure is defined as 'a support, an indispensable basis for the construction, maintenance or operation of a concrete or abstract structure'.[36] In the context of financial matters, the concept of infrastructure retains the same meaning: it is the indispensable basis for the existence of the financial market and is made up of various systems. In order to allow market transactions to be concluded, three distinct infrastructures are in fact necessary. The first is the financial market itself, i.e. the trading platform that allows transactions to be concluded between members and is managed by a financial market operator. The second is the clearing system, which organises a central settlement of transactions and guarantees the execution of the transaction; this system is managed by a clearing house, also called a central counterparty. The third infrastructure is the securities settlement system, which enables the delivery of financial securities traded through the market. This system is managed by the central securities depository. To these three market infrastructures, a fourth one should actually be added, consisting of the payment systems, which allow the settlement of money. Indeed, the payment systems are the condition for the functioning of the clearing system and the delivery system. The payment system used by the market infrastructures is managed by the national central banks.

8. Each of these market infrastructures is made up of two elements: on the one hand, a physical element, the computerised systems that allow, respectively, the meeting of selling and buying interests, the clearing of transactions, the settlement of cash and the delivery of securities, and on the other hand, a legal element, the rules that govern them. These system rules are drawn up by the infrastructure manager, but are not necessarily linked to the legal system of the manager's headquarters and may, in certain cases, be the subject of a choice of law. It will be shown that the connection of these systems to the manager's head office is nevertheless all the more desirable as they are likely to constitute the basis for the connection of the inter-individual transactions that these systems

---

35 In international perspective, see the synthesis of M. Lehmann, 'Financial Instruments', *Encyclopedia of private international law*, Cheltenham, Edward Elgar Publishing, 2017, p. 739.

36 See 'Infrastructure' in Trésor informatisé de la langue française.

allow.[37] In practice, the presence of an administrative authorisation required for their entry into force is likely to influence the choice of law.

9. Supervision by an administrative authority. State intervention in the legal organisation of financial markets is not new. In international law, the prescriptive jurisdiction of the State with regard to economic relations taking place on its territory has always been foreseen and has long been linked to territorial jurisdiction. Thus, in his study of the phenomenon of double taxation in tax matters, Niboyet considered, fancifully that 'each State determines, in its full sovereignty, what it deems taxable, rather like the hunter who shoots the game that flies over his domain'.[38] This jurisdiction of the State in relation to economic activities on its territory is nowadays distinguished from personal and territorial jurisdiction. It is sometimes referred to as 'market jurisdiction',[39] and refers to the jurisdiction of the state *ratione materiae.*[40] In relation to the sector of activity covered by financial law, market jurisdiction results not only in the enactment of specific legislation, but also in the establishment of an administrative authority to supervise the financial markets. This market jurisdiction is reflected in two types of jurisdiction, personal and real, which correspond to two aspects of financial market supervision by an administrative authority.

10. The personal jurisdiction of the authority is manifested by the authority's action towards all the professionals it has under its supervision. This jurisdiction is nevertheless based on a territorial criterion: the exercise of a regulated activity on the territory of the authority, which is most often characterised by a request to residents. Supervision is, first of all, aimed at the infrastructures themselves, through the supervision of managers and the approval of system rules, but in reality extends to all persons wishing to provide investment services. This is the first aspect of supervision, carried out in France by the combined action of the *Autorité de contrôle prudentiel et de résolution* and the *Autorité des marchés financiers.* The purpose of the supervision of the sector is to protect the savings of residents and to contribute to the stability of the financial system. The means

[37] See L. d'Avout, 'Les phénomènes collectifs et l'analyse macro en droit international privé' in *Mélanges en l'honneur du professeur Bertrand Ancel*, Paris, LGDJ, pp. 151 et seq., spec. nos. 21 et seq. and, by the same author, *L'entreprise et les conflits internationaux de lois, op. cit.*, nos. 152–153.

[38] J.-P. Niboyet, *Les doubles impositions du point de vue juridique*, RCADI, vol. 31, Paris, Recueil Sirey, 1931, p. 14.

[39] On the latter, see L. d'Avout, *L'entreprise et les conflits internationaux de lois, op. cit.*, nos. 155 et seq. The notion of '*competence réelle*' is already used by international criminal law when a fundamental interest of the State, understood as a public person, is at stake, and allows the deployment of criminal law across borders.

[40] *Ibid*, nos. 158. As Mr d'Avout observes, this sovereign competence has the singular property of being able to be pooled 'under the essential limit of the sufficient effectiveness of the supranational mechanisms set up for this purpose' (*ibid.*, no. 161), which is reflected in the Europeanisation of sources, as well as in the institutional mechanisms set up to monitor systemic risk.

of this supervision are provided for by the law. On the one hand, the law makes the exercise of activities relating to financial instruments conditional on authorisations given by the administrative authorities, the first of which is the approval. This approval creates a link of dependence between the supervised entities and the administrative authority, since the latter can withdraw the approval as soon as its conditions cease to be respected: the approval is a veritable umbilical cord. On the other hand, the legislator delegates the enactment of a part of the regulation, which is particularly specific and needs to be regularly revised, to the authority itself. The exercise of this supervision with regard to international operators is today part of a European framework that creates a tension between a centralised model of supervision, where an EU agency has supervisory powers but sometimes delegates the exercise of these powers to the national authorities, and the traditional decentralised model, where the European authorities help to organise coordination between the national authorities. Whichever model is chosen, private international law can provide valuable coordination tools. Niboyet had already perceived this possibility, observing that 'in every country, alongside international and administrative law, there is a branch which is constantly developing, and which is called financial law',[41] and that it is likely to give rise to 'conflicts of administrative law'.[42]

11. The second supervision, also entrusted to the *Autorité des marchés financiers*, concerns operations taking place within the authority's territory. This jurisdiction is not so much territorial as '*réel*' (*res*) in the sense given to this notion in international criminal law: the authority is competent because local savings are solicited, or because a market infrastructure is used.[43] This jurisdiction is the basis on which the authority governs the relationship of the financial market with issuers and investors. As regards issuers, the law again makes the marketing of financial securities subject to the authority's authorisation. The relationship with investors is supervised from the point of view of market transactions, i.e. the transactions of investors using the trading system. Trade monitoring may extend to off-market transactions that affect the price discovery mechanism of the trading system.

12. From an international point of view, the plurality of authorities exercising jurisdiction with the same material scope creates a real risk of conflict. It seems

---

41 J.-P. Niboyet, 'Les doubles impositions du point de vue juridique', *op. cit.*, no. 41.

42 The expression is also used by Niboyet, *ibid.*, no. 55: 'For a long time it was believed, perhaps because of its erroneous name, that private international law was limited to conflicts of private law. However, this is an absolutely false idea. Private international law is not intended to resolve only private law conflicts, but conflicts in general, whether of private or public law.'

43 The actual competence referred to here is narrower than that used by Mr d'Avout. The author refers more broadly to the overall competence of a legal order to regulate its economic market, and this competence then encompasses the two titles of competence used in the body of the text.

to us that this is exacerbated, on the one hand, by the existence of a 'solidarity of legislative and administrative competences', i.e. by the fact that the application of the local law most often entails the competence of the administrative authority[44] and, on the other hand, by the unilateral character of the determination of this global competence. As Mr d'Avout wrote: 'An administrative authority takes action, for internal and international situations, as soon as the problem posed falls within the material competence, or attribution, of the authority in question, as defined by the State to which it belongs'.[45] However, this situation is not unique to administrative authorities. The same applies when criminal jurisdiction is retained, or in matters of insolvency. In these cases, where an avatar of *forum legis* is the rule of principle, and in which a legal system considers itself to have priority jurisdiction, the coordination of the authorities involved in private international relations is most often achieved by designating a 'reference' legal system,[46] the leading one, the best placed. Coordination will then take place by unifying the title of jurisdiction. From the point of view of the forum of recognition, the latter will proceed to the self-limitation of its law and to the enactment of liberal criteria for the recognition of decisions. Penetration of the concepts of the foreign legal order will nevertheless be made possible, on the one hand, by the harmonisation of substantive legislation and, on the other hand, by taking into consideration, if not the rules of the other legal orders affected by the decision, at least their interests. Unilateralism does not necessarily rhyme with ignorance of foreign law. This means that when faced with foreign issuers and investors, administrative authorities have been able to draw on the methods of private international law in order to determine the scope of their jurisdiction and rules, and above all in order to establish effective cooperation mechanisms.[47] The administrative authorities have nevertheless been assisted in their desire for coordination by European sources of financial law.

13. European sources of financial law. European Union law has gradually taken on a decisive role in the organisation of financial markets in Europe.[48]

---

44 This coincidence is not necessary, however, and the following discussion will show that it is quite possible for an administrative authority to apply a foreign law.

45 L. d'Avout, *L'entreprise et les conflits internationaux de lois*, *op. cit.*, p. 315.

46 In the words of P. Picone, *La méthode de la référence à l'ordre juridique compétent en droit international privé*, RCADI vol. 197, The Hague, Martinus Nijhoff, 1986; P. Picone, 'Les méthodes de coordination entre ordres juridiques en droit international privé', RCADI, t. 276, The Hague, Martinus Nijhoff, 1999, pp. 128 et seq.

47 On this question, see already P.-H. Conac, *La régulation des marchés boursiers par la commission des opérations de bourse (COB) et la securities and exchange commission (SEC)*, Paris, LGDJ, 2002; see also M. Audit, 'Les autorités de régulation et le droit international privé' in *Mélanges en l'honneur du professeur Pierre Mayer*, Paris, LGDJ, 2015, pp. 43 et seq.

48 EU law is added to the two original sources, those developed by administrative authorities and market infrastructures. Some authors consider that the singularity of the sources of financial law lies precisely in the originality of their authors, see C. Granier, *Les sources du droit financier*, *op. cit.*, no. 56.

The starting point was the Commission's 1985 White Paper on completing the internal market.[49] This proposed a new approach based on liberalisation of the sector, leading to the principle of national authorisation of companies carrying out regulated activities, and mutual recognition of authorisations between Member States. In 1993, the Investment Services Directive[50] implemented this approach through the creation of a category of investment firms whose national authorisation allows them to carry out the activities subject to it in other Member States.[51] However, the Investment Services Directive does not provide for a unified regime for dealing with third country firms. This was transposed into French law in 1996 by the law on the modernisation of financial activities[52] which replaced the term 'investment firm' with the term 'investment service provider'. This latter concept of investment service providers makes it possible to add credit institutions, whose importance is central to the French financial markets, to the persons designated by the concept of investment firm.[53] From a market infrastructure perspective, the Investment Services Directive establishes an embryonic financial market regime,[54] which is considered to be the provision of a particular investment service. The liberalisation of the sector does not, however, increase competition, but leads to the gradual concentration of European financial market operators under the umbrella of the Euronext group.[55] At the same time, a directive on payment and securities settlement systems, known as the Finality Directive, harmonised in 1998 the regime and conflict of laws rules applicable to these systems, which constitute the core of

---

49 Commission of the European Communities, *Completing the Internal Market*, COM (85 final), Brussels, 14 June 1985.

50 Council Directive 93/22/EEC of 10 May 1993 on investment services in the securities field, see H. Synvet, 'La directive "service d'investissement": première lecture', *BJB*, 1993, p. 545.

51 As Professor Synvet has written, the Investment Services Directive 'is part of the construction of the large internal market, programmed by the Commission of the Communities in its "White Paper" and formalised by the Single European Act. More precisely, it contributes to the creation of a European financial area, within which companies are called upon to effectively enjoy the freedoms of establishment and provision of services granted to them by the Treaty of Rome', H. Synvet, 'La directive "service d'investissement": première lecture', *op. cit.*, no. 1.

52 Law No. 96-597 of 2 July 1996 on the modernisation of financial activities, on which see T. Bonneau (ed.), *La modernisation des activités financières*, GLN-Joly, 1996.

53 F. Drummond, *Droit financier*, *op. cit.* no. 15; H. Synvet, 'La réforme du droit français à la lumière de la directive sur les services d'investissement', *LPA*, no. 56, 8 May 1996, pp. 18 et seq.

54 Art. 1(13) Investment Services Directive.

55 On this retrospective, see F. Drummond, *Droit financier*, *op. cit.*, nos. 14 et seq. and T. Bonneau *et al.*, *Droit financier*, *op. cit.*, no. 60. On the history of the Euronext group, see P. Barban, *Les entreprises de marché*, Paris, Fondation Varenne, 2015, no. 1.
Euronext's unity, combined with the harmonisation of financial law initiated by the Investment Services and MiFID Directives, has enabled it to draw up common market rules for all these markets, supplemented by special market rules applicable to certain markets in particular.

the 'post-trade' financial infrastructure, i.e. the system for clearing, delivery of securities and payment.

14. A second step was taken in 1999 with the publication by the Commission of a Financial Services Action Plan.[56] In 2004, this resulted in a directive specifically aimed at the markets in financial instruments, known as the MiFID directive.[57] This directive profoundly changes the French market model since it aims to bring competition to the various financial markets on the territory of the Union. MiFID thus puts an end to the model based on the obligation to concentrate orders on the official market,[58] which was in force in France, and allows the creation of different 'types' of financial markets, i.e. trading systems. In addition to the regulation of financial actors and infrastructures, EU law also harmonises legislation on trading in financial instruments and market operations. Transactions in financial instruments are thus harmonised by a 2002 directive on collateral for financial instruments. Similarly, market transactions are also the subject of several directives in 2003 and 2004 on threshold crossing, public offers and market abuse.[59]

15. In response to the 2008 crisis, a new generation of legislation is emerging, both through the establishment of European regulatory authorities and through the overhaul and extension of the regulation of market infrastructures. MiFID was recast in 2013 in a directive called MiFID 2,[60] and a MiFID regulation.[61] The EU is also taking over the regulation of clearing houses and central depositories, whose statutes are harmonised by a regulation on OTC derivatives and a regulation on central securities depositories (known as the CSD regulation). This evolution of sources leaves Member States less and less room for manoeuvre:

---

56 Commission of the European Communities, Implementing *the Framework for Financial Services: Action Plan*, COM (1999) 232 final, Brussels, 11 May 1999.

57 Directive 2004/39 of the European Parliament and of the Council of 21 April 2004 on markets in financial instruments amending Council Directives 85/611/EEC and 93/6/EEC.

58 And therefore puts an end to stock exchanges, see J.-J. Daigre, 'La fin des bourses', *RDBF*, March-April 2003, no. 2, pp. 83 et seq. On the extinction of the concentration obligation, see J.-P. Bornet, 'La notion de marché dans la Directive Européenne sur les Marchés d'instruments financiers – "MIF" - du 21 avril 2004' in *Mélanges Dominique Schmidt*, Paris, LGDJ, 2005, pp. 77 et seq.

59 These are respectively: Directive 2004/109/EC of the European Parliament and of the Council of 15 December 2004 on the harmonisation of transparency requirements in relation to information about issuers whose securities are admitted to trading on a regulated market and amending Directive 2001/34/EC; Directive 2004/25/EC of the European Parliament and of the Council of 21 April 2004 on takeover bids; Directive 2003/6/EC of the European Parliament and of the Council of 28 January 2003 on insider dealing and market manipulation (market abuse).

60 Directive 2014/65/EU of the European Parliament and of the Council of 15 May 2014 on markets in financial instruments and amending Directive 2002/92/EC and Directive 2011/61/EU.

61 Regulation No 600/2014 of the European Parliament and of the Council of 15 May 2014 on markets in financial instruments and amending Regulation (EU) No 648/2012.

the Investment Services Directive was minimum harmonisation, MiFID and MiFID 2 are maximum harmonisation, and the regulations have direct effect.[62] Moreover, European legislative developments are gradually shifting the focus of decision-making on relations with third-country infrastructure managers to EU agencies.[63] The latter are developing coordination with third country legal systems, making access to European territory conditional on a method of equivalence of legislation, associated with cooperation agreements between authorities. The granting to the Commission of the power to decide on equivalence nevertheless causes a change in its *ratio legis*, making the equivalence decision an instrument of power in relations with third countries. Moreover, the crisis has increased the importance of the objective of stability of the financial system, which is added to the traditional objectives of financial law of the proper functioning of financial markets and the protection of investors. The stability of the financial system is based in particular on the prevention of systemic risk, defined by the European legislator in these terms:

> 'A risk of disruption in the financial system that could have serious repercussions for the domestic market and the real economy. All types of financial intermediaries, markets and infrastructures can be potentially systemically important.'[64]

16. Already known in financial law, systemic risk was mainly used to justify the special privileges enjoyed by payment, clearing and securities settlement systems, on the one hand, and by financial institutions on the other, in the event of the bankruptcy of their contracting party (their 'counterparty'). Since the crisis, systemic risk has been identified as a pathology, which the rules of financial law aim to prevent and, where necessary, treat. Systemic risk underpins

---

62 The objective of using a regulation is 'to establish a single set of rules for all institutions imposing certain requirements, to avoid the risk of regulatory arbitrage and to enhance legal certainty while reducing regulatory complications for market participants justifies the use of a legal basis for adopting a regulation', Recital 3 MiFID Regulation.

63 O. Girard, 'Une brève histoire des clauses d'équivalence ou l'Union européenne comme rouage clé de la régulation financière mondiale' in *Liber amicorum Blanche Sousi*, Revue Banque Édition, 2016, pp. 124 et seq.; A.-C. Rouaud, 'L'accès des pays tiers au marché européen bancaire et financier', in *Mélanges en l'honneur du professeur Gilbert Parléani*, IRJS Editions, 2021.

64 Art. 2(c) of Regulation (EU) No 1092/2010 of the European Parliament and of the Council of 24 November 2010 on Community macro-prudential oversight of the financial system and establishing a European Systemic Risk Board. The financial system referred to in this definition is made up of 'all financial institutions, markets, products and market infrastructures' (Art. 2(b) of the aforementioned regulation), and financial institutions include most of the companies subject to the supervision of the European authorities (Art. 2(a) of the aforementioned regulation. On these authorities, see below).
On the history of system risk, initially conceived by the Basel Committee, see A. Gaudemet, 'Risque de système: une perspective historique', *RTDF*, July 2010, pp. 97 et seq. On this notion, see by the same author 'Le risque de système' in A. Supiot (ed.), *Face à l'irresponsabilité, la dynamique du principe de solidarité*, Paris, Collège de France, 2018, pp. 161 et seq.

entire areas of financial legislation and is monitored at European and global level by a range of authorities. From the point of view of operators, systemic risk today justifies the enactment of prudential rules, sophisticated supervisory and default (override) schemes under the authority of a specialised administration. Their objective is to prevent the failure of the most important financial institutions, including market infrastructure managers, and, in the event of failure, to allow their activities to continue. The prevention of systemic risk also has an impact on financial instruments, and in particular on the regime for financial contracts. Financial contracts were decisive in the propagation of systemic risk in 2008 and are therefore now forced to be guaranteed by a clearing house to which a significant part of the systemic risk has been shifted.[65] Moreover, the conclusion of these contracts must be reported to central repositories that monitor the state of interdependencies between operators, as well as the risks transferred by financial contracts, in order to ensure that the lure of profit does not lead operators to take ill-considered risks.

17. Entanglement of orders and distribution of competences. The fragmentation of the sources of financial law contributes to the fragmentation of legal systems and orders. Indeed, while there are attempts at global regulation, EU law is now the main source of the discipline, and the place of national law seems residual. However, it would be misleading to think that national law only exists in the gaps left by European directives, or in the fields that European law has not yet entered. In reality, national law retains two particularly decisive powers, both from a normative and institutional point of view.[66]

18. From a normative point of view, national law retains jurisdiction whenever financial law is involved in the civil order: contract, property, tort.[67] Thus, financial contracts, when subject to French law, are subject to French contract law and may be submitted to French courts. Similarly, the proprietary status of securities is likely to be subject to French property law, and a defective prospectus may trigger the application of French tort law. Moreover, national law is always applicable when financial law is confronted with commercial law, whether it is company law or insolvency law.[68] This confrontation often turns

---

65 A. Gaudemet, 'Le risque de système', *op. cit.*, no. 27.

66 While the institutional aspect is also normative, this distinction is necessary for presentational reasons.

67 These interactions between financial law and civil law have given rise to several doctoral theses, see in particular A.-C. Muller, *Droit des marchés financiers et droit des contrats*, *op. cit.*; A. Gaudemet, *Les dérivés*, *op. cit*; A.-C. Rouaud, *Contribution à l'étude de l'opération de marché*, *op. cit.*; P. Pailler, *Le contrat financier, Un instrument financier à terme*, Paris, IRJS, 2010; J. Prorok, *La responsabilité civile sur les marchés financiers*, Paris, LGDJ, 2019.

68 The interactions between financial law and insolvency law have given rise to fewer doctrinal works (apart from the thesis by D. Robine, *La sécurité des marchés financiers face aux procédures collectives*, *op. cit.*) than those with company law, conceived from different angles, see in particular A. Pietrancosta, *Le droit des sociétés sous l'effet des impératifs financiers et*

to the advantage of financial law, which influences related fields in order to obtain the solutions necessary for the pursuit of its goals.[69] The result is a certain porosity of disciplines, which must nevertheless be clearly distinguished in order to delimit the international applicability of the various legislative bodies. These two issues will be illustrated by comparing financial law with other branches of commercial law.

19. In the first place, the confrontation between financial law and company law takes place in two distinct areas. Firstly, financial law influences the law applicable to the internal status of companies that wish to carry out financial activities. In doing so, it strengthens the links between the internal organisation of companies and their activities. Indeed, it is as if the statute to which these companies are subject were to give rise to a genuine special company law applicable to credit institutions, insurance companies and investment firms, which would supersede the distinction between companies according to their corporate form.[70] In particular, a set of prudential obligations emerges, the purpose of which is to prevent the operator from defaulting, and which is internationally applicable by virtue of its territorial location. The reason for this is that the consequences of a default will be borne by the local legal order. Financial law also has an influence on companies whose securities are admitted to trading. In fact, admission to trading triggers the application of two types of standards. The first type, from financial market law, is related to the functioning of the financial market and affects the ownership of the company, simply because

---

boursiers, Université Paris I, 1999; H. Bouthinon-Dumas, *Le droit des sociétés et le marché boursier: étude des conditions juridiques de la détermination de la valeur de la société par le marché boursier*, Université Paris-Dauphine, 2006; R. Dambre, *Les contrats financiers sur actions*, Brussels, Larcier, 2016.

In these two branches, it should nevertheless be noted that national law solutions are influenced by Union law through the applicable sectoral directives, see most recently Directive 2017/1132 of the European Parliament and of the Council of 14 June 2017 on certain aspects of company law, and Directive 2019/1023 of the European Parliament and of the Council of 20 June 2019 on preventive restructuring frameworks.

69 As Professor Bonneau observes with regard to the European sources of financial law: 'The Community imprint has thus gone beyond the strict domain of financial legislation to place these other domains at the service of the latter', T. Bonneau, 'Législation "financière" et droit communautaire', *in Le Code de commerce, 1807-2007*, Paris, Dalloz, 2007, pp. 707 et seq.

70 See already in this sense the observations of Professor Synvet: 'We thus see the emergence, under the effect of prudential regulations, of a sort of special law applicable to companies carrying on a banking activity. If we compare this with the body of rules relating to the governance of credit institutions (Art. L. 511-51 et seq. of the Monetary and Financial Code), we can see that a special legislation is being put in place, which is a derogation from ordinary company law'. H. Synvet, *D.* 2020, 2085. No doubt it can be considered that the distinction between companies according to the activities they carry out does not supersede the distinction according to their corporate form since companies, whatever their activity, must always take a particular form. However, the activity carried out actually dictates the form taken, leaving the choice of corporate form illusory.

the control of the company has an influence on the price of the traded share. The second is derived from company law, and forms a special law for listed companies whose function is most often to improve the governance of these companies.[71] Recent legislative efforts echo this distinction in order to reduce the overlapping of provisions in the Commercial Code and the Monetary and Financial Code.[72] Although it is sometimes difficult to distinguish between these two types of rules, it is necessary to do so, because the search for the applicable law depends on it, and at the same time it helps to establish it: whereas the rules contributing to the functioning of the financial market should be subject to the law of the place of listing, those relating to the internal organisation of the company should be subject to the *lex societatis*.

20. Secondly, the confrontation between financial law and insolvency law also takes place in various ways. First of all, transactions in financial instruments usually benefit from a favourable regime when insolvency proceedings are involved. However, this is only a form of hidden privilege. Financial law appears more original since it pushes for the institution of a special insolvency regime, derogating from ordinary law and applicable to credit institutions and investment firms. Moreover, the derogatory default schemes thus instituted justify *a priori* supervision of institutions under prudential obligations, which therefore appear to be the link attaching company law to insolvency law. Indeed, instituted in order to prevent the failure of operators, prudential obligations nevertheless have as their object the management of the company and are therefore inevitably linked to the law governing them. The following study will show that their international applicability echoes this double filiation.

21. Beyond these normative aspects, the competence of the national legal system also stems from the jurisdiction of its regulator[73] in the supervision of

---

[71] To the point of making admission to trading a new *summa divisio* of company law, see in this sense M.-A. Frison-Roche, 'La distinction entre sociétés cotées et sociétés non-cotées' in *Mélanges AEBF-France 1997*, Banque Editeur, 1997, pp. 189 et seq.

[72] On this overlapping, see F. Drummond, 'Code de commerce et Code monétaire et financier, ou l'enchevêtrement des Codes' in *Le Code de commerce 1807-2007, Livre du Bicentenaire*, Paris, Dalloz, 2007, pp. 95 et seq. On the elaboration of a chapter dedicated to listed companies, see F. Drummond and J. Klein, 'Pour la création d'un Chapitre X du Titre II du Livre II du Code de commerce dédié aux sociétés cotées' in *Études à la mémoire de Philippe Neau-Leduc, Le juriste dans la Cité*, Paris, LGDJ, 2018.

[73] In France, this is the Autorité des marchés financiers. The situation is different from that in other federated areas, and in particular the United States, where jurisdiction is exercised by a single regulator, the SEC. This unified jurisdiction has been criticised for hindering the trading of financial securities, whereas the decentralised jurisdiction in force in the field of company law allows for more innovation, see in this sense R. Romano, *The advantage of Competitive Federalism for Securities Regulation*, AEI Press, 2003. It seems to us, however, that the argument is unsuccessful, because the objects of competition are too different: the improvement of the legal organisation of companies is very distinct from the conditions of protection of residents, an objective with which the organisation of trading is closely linked. Decentralised competence has the advantage of allowing administrative competence

infrastructure managers established on its territory, as well as in the administration of private law relationships generated by financial law. This administrative jurisdiction with regard to private relationships is not currently rivalled by that of a European authority; it is possible that it will be gradually replaced by a change in the European legal order. These aspects imply frequent interaction with the authorities of other Member States, but also of third countries, and therefore require cooperation; the conditions for its implementation find inspiration in certain methods of private international law.

22. Private ordering and financial law. These observations are likely to qualify the idea that the financial sphere is the land of choice for private ordering, an ordering that supposedly structures private international law today.[74] It is necessary to reject the idea that financial markets are spontaneous phenomena that regulation has subsequently apprehended, either by hindering them[75] or by disciplining them.[76] From a legal point of view, financial markets are truly attached to a State and the rules governing them always find their source in State law, either directly or indirectly through legislative empowerment.[77] It is therefore difficult to perceive here the 'inversion of the relationship between law and market'.[78] This reality could be characterised when financial instruments are traded or concluded independently of the financial markets. In particular, the international standardisation of financial contracts has been seen as topical to

to be exercised as close as possible to the citizens. On this question, see lastly R. Gaspard, *La reconnaissance mutuelle en droit bancaire et financier*, Paris, Fondation Varenne, 2019, nos. 599 et seq.

74 Defending in particular the latter claim, see J. Basedow, *The Law of Open Societies*, RCADI, t. 360, The Hague, Martinus Nijhoff, 2013, part 2.

75 On this perspective from Hayek's work, see the contradiction in A. Riles, *Collateral knowledge: Legal Reasoning in the Global Financial Markets*, Chicago, Chicago University Press, 2011, p. 157.

76 As sociologists have pointed out, 'Markets are not pre-given and exogenous to regulation but rather constituted by regulation, states and non-state governance'. M. Schneiberg and T. Batley, 'Regulating or redesigning finance? Market architectures, normal accidents, and dilemmas of regulatory reform' in M. Lounsbury and P. Hisrh (eds.), *Markets on trial: the economic sociology of the U.S. financial crisis*, Research in the sociology of organizations, Bingley, Emerald Press, 2010, p. 281. B. Carruthers, 'Economy and Law', in P. Aspers and N. Dodd, *Re-imagining Economic Sociology*, Oxford, Oxford Scholarship Online, 2015, p. 137.

77 Therefore, as Ms Riles writes, 'The creation of a private sphere of transnational law beyond the reach of state authority demands the authority and institutions of the state itself.' A. Riles, *Collateral knowledge*, *op. cit.*, p. 185.

78 H. Muir Watt, *Aspects économiques du droit international privé (Réflexions sur l'impact de la globalisation économique sur les fondements des conflits de lois et de juridictions)*, RCADI, vol. 207, The Hague, Martinus Nijhoff, 2004, no. 72; see by the same author, 'La globalisation et le droit international privé' in *Mélanges Pierre Mayer*, Paris, LGDJ, 2015, pp. 591 et seq. We agree here with the contrary opinion expressed by Mr d'Avout, see *L'entreprise et les conflits internationaux de lois*, *op. cit.*, no. 9.

the emergence of a global private law, uncoupled from the state.[79] The following study will also dispel this impression: on the one hand, the status of financial instruments is just as dependent on state law as that of the financial markets, and on the other hand, the local market has an influence on the way in which the instrument is thought of and used.[80] State law will continue to dominate the normative field as long as it makes its use the condition for the legal realisation of trade.[81]

23. The singularity of financial matters is illustrated not so much by the eviction of state law as by the frequent importation of legal institutions from foreign legal systems and by the influence of professionals in the sector in the development of financial standards, both national and European and international.[82] The latter is made possible by the development of think tanks set up by specialists in the sector, both at national and international level,[83] and by the importance of professionals within interstate bodies for the unification of law.[84] The documents drawn up by these bodies constitute, if not draft

---

79 See for example in French, H. Muir Watt, 'La gouvernance privée des marchés financiers: les enjeux de la *lex contractus*', in H. Muir Watt *et al.*, *Le tournant global en droit international privé*, *op. cit.*, pp. 355 et seq., p. 358; M. Audit, 'Les dérivés de crédit à l'ombre du contrat sans loi', TCFDIP, Pedone, 2016, p. 85.

80 As Ms Riles observed during her ethnographic study in Japan: 'not only is global private law not private, it is also not global. Contrary to the technical fantasy, the pre-printed material form of ISDA documents, drafted by American and British lawyers, written in English, and laden with assumptions about market practices in the American and British markets, was literally nonsensical in the Japanese market', A. Riles, *Collateral knowledge*, *op. cit.*, p. 61.

81 Making law the infrastructure of internationalisation, see also H. Synvet, 'L'internationalisation du droit des affaires', in *Le Code de commerce, Livre du bicentenaire*, Paris, Dalloz, 2007, p. 727; K. Pistor, *The Code of Capital*, Princeton, Princeton University Press, 2019, p. 18.

82 Influence sometimes referred to as 'capture'. On this difficulty in financial law, see in French B. du Marais, 'Crise de la régulation ou capture du régulateur?' in A. Mérieux (ed.), *Rapport moral sur l'argent dans le monde 2009*, Association d'économie financière, June 2009, p. 89.

83 In France, the most significant are the 'Haut comité juridique de la place financière de Paris' and the 'Club des juristes'. The former echoes the English Financial Market Committee Law. From an international perspective, two are particularly prolific: the Basel Committee and the International Swaps and Derivatives Association (ISDA).

84 In the financial sector, one thinks of the International Organisation of Securities Commissions (IOSCO), which brings together the specialised administrations. The importance of the standards produced by this entity is such that some authors consider that 'IOSCO appears as the legislator of principle, and it is up to the States to give force to these principles on their respective territories', S. Lambert, *L'application internationale du droit financier*, thesis, Université Paris II Panthéon-Assas, 2021, no. 1309; see also in this sense B. Bréhier, 'Les nouveaux législateurs: OICV, Comité de Bâle, FSB, G20', *RDBF*, May 2015, pp. 31 et seq. On the Basel Committee, which has an indirect influence through banking legislation, see C. Feunteun, *Instruments hybrides et Accords de Bâle*, PhD thesis, Université Paris II Panthéon-Assas, 2019. It should nevertheless be noted that the global convergence of regulatory objectives does not eliminate the conflict of laws, it mitigates it.

legislation to be incorporated as such into national legal systems, at least a basis for reflection for their institutions.[85]

24. The local influence of these international projects is also due to the intense links maintained by the professionals of the sector and the administration. This is the case in France thanks to the proximity of the Treasury administration to financial sector institutions, which enables it to be particularly attentive to their needs.[86] The Treasury has a predominant place in the development of French rules. This is also the case within the EU for at least two reasons. The first is the result of comitology, i.e. the process of drafting standards by different levels of specialised committees.[87] Comitology has been conducive to the expression of the interests of the industry, the clearest manifestation of which is the Financial Collateral Directive, which is the incorporation into national law of a model law whose content was drawn up by the *International Swaps and Derivatives Association* (ISDA).[88] The second reason may be found in the links between

---

More general bodies are interested in financial issues such as the United Nations Commission on International Trade Law and the International Institute for the Unification of Private Law. On the phenomenon of capture within these two institutions, see C. Deveaux, *La fabrique du droit du commerce international*, Brussels, Larcier, 2018. From the point of view of the unification of conflict rules, the Hague Conference, when it drew up the Securities Convention, had the particularity of having given great importance to the presence of professionals in the sector.

85 Two significant recent examples can be cited here: on the one hand, the 'Basel III' project relating to prudential regulation drawn up by the Basel Committee (see T. Bonneau, *Régulation bancaire et financière européenne et internationale*, 5th ed., Brussels, Bruylant, 2020, no. 41) and incorporated into European legislation, and the IOSCO principles on market infrastructures (IOSCO and BIS, *Principles on financial markets infrastructures*, April 2012), which have also been incorporated into European law. On the porosity between *soft law* and *hard law* in financial law, see the observations of T. Bonneau, *Régulation bancaire et financière européenne et internationale*, *op. cit.*

86 The proximity of the supervisory administration and the professionals is not a French peculiarity, see in the American case, P.-H. Conac, *La régulation des marchés boursiers par la commission des opérations de bourse (COB) et la securities and exchange commission (SEC)*, *op. cit.*, ono. 118 and in the Japanese case, A. Riles, *Collateral knowledge*, *op. cit.*

87 On this phenomenon, see R. Vabres, *Comitologie et services financiers*, Paris, Dalloz, 2009.

88 ISDA has a model law on the various aspects of the regulation of financial contracts, and in particular on the compensation regime in the event of the insolvency of one of the parties to the contract. The European Commission also tends to incorporate itself the draft laws issued by international think tanks of professionals in the sector, such as the recommendations of the Basel Committee in the enactment of the various directives applicable to credit institutions, see C. Feunteun, *Instruments hybrides et Accords de Bâle*, *op. cit.*
Some authors see this as a form of extraterritoriality or consider in the same sense that 'a financial "*lex mercatoria*" is being developed which may appear as a particularly efficient mode of regulation or self-regulation of financial markets' (A. Couret, H. Le Nabasque *et al.*, *Droit financier*, *op. cit.*, no. 6). It seems to us, however, that this gives a new meaning to extraterritoriality, which does not refer to the development of sources of law outside the territory, but to the extent of the scope of application of State rules. Moreover, financial regulation is not a *lex mercatoria* at all: it is closely dependent on state law, whose blessing it constantly seeks, so that neither financial law nor finance can escape being tied to a

certain members of the EU administration and financial institutions.[89] The main advantage of this user-driven lawmaking is that it takes into account the precise expectations of the industry to ensure its international attractiveness.[90] However, several disadvantages can be noted. For example, the various claims involved are not necessarily represented, giving rise to conflicts of interest that result, if not in favouring certain professionals in the sector over others,[91] at least in overweighting their interests.[92]

25. If these methods of lawmaking do not call into question the State nature of the rules, they could be no more than a continuation of the substantive regulation of international relations by other means and, consequently, deprive conflict of laws of its purpose: if the laws designated are ultimately identical, what use are conflict rules? Several aspects nevertheless account for the divergence of the laws involved and the continued interest of the conflict method. First of all, this original elaboration of the law rarely allows for the effective unification of the rules, at most it contributes to their convergence. Moreover, when they are incorporated into national law, the contentious rules are influenced by the local conception, either because the body responsible for enacting them modifies their content, or because related rules modify their scope, or because the legislative body within which these rules are inserted modifies their interpretation.[93] Finally, even when these rules are unified at regional level, they are influenced by their implementation at national level. These observations, which show the relevance of the theories developed by specialists in comparative law, also demonstrate the

state. See P. Wautelet, 'Réglementation étatique et marchés financiers: entre autonomie et relativité' in H. Muir Watt *et al.* (eds.), *Le tournant global en droit international privé*, Paris, Pedone, 2020, pp. 341 et seq.

89 Suggesting this, see A. Gaudemet, 'Le risque de système', *op. cit.*

90 This makes it possible to put an end to a form of crisis in commercial law, for which 'the responsibility [...] lies with the legislator who intervenes in an untimely manner under the influence of a technocracy that is unaware of the realities of the business world', J. Hilaire, *Introduction au droit commercial*, Paris, PUF, 1986, p. 13. See also C. Granier, *Les sources du droit financier*, *op. cit.*, no. 749.

91 As Professor Synvet has written, 'In the real world, conflicts of interest are omnipresent. They appear at first glance when one looks at the issue of extraterritoriality. But there are also often conflicts of interest at the heart of the development of the supranational norm. Who holds the pen? The fundamental issue is that of power.' H. Synvet, 'Rapport de synthèse', *RDBF*, 2015, no. 4, pp. 41 et seq.

92 This is reflected, for example, in the privilege given, irrespective of the use of a system, to transactions in financial instruments in the event of insolvency. As Mr Synvet has written, 'The proper functioning of financial markets is not the alpha and omega of social life. Financial market law is therefore called upon to deal with other branches of law that reflect equally legitimate interests', H. Synvet, 'Droit et marchés financiers', *BJB*, November 2014, p. 517.

93 What is true for the rules is also true when the import of a foreign administrative institution is at issue: the example of the differences between the SEC and the AMF is commendable. On these differences, see the above-mentioned work by Prof. Conac.

acuity of the observations of Professor Paul Lagarde under the *Hocke* judgment, which are the epigraph to this introduction.

26. How financial law is applied internationally. Studies on this subject in private international relations have mostly focused on the relationship between the law applicable to companies whose securities are admitted to trading and the law of the financial markets.[94] They have also looked at certain aspects of the status of financial instruments offered across borders,[95] at the difficulties that financial contracts raise from the point of view of conflict of laws methods,[96] or have attempted to rationalise the international connection of securities.[97] Some authors have shown the difficulties posed by the interpenetration of stock markets and have outlined solutions;[98] others have shown the decisive influence of the action of the administrative authority in the resolution of these difficulties;[99] still others have studied the European methods of coordination between these authorities.[100] The rules of financial law were therefore most often presented as *lois de police* or administrative rules.[101] The establishment of a national supervisory authority with administrative, prescriptive and repressive jurisdiction is likely to amplify this perception, as well as the appearance of financial law rules in disputes where they seem to derogate from the normally applicable solution rather than coherently found a new category.

This perception of financial law as a set of heterogeneous and derogatory rules, which were then presented by the method of the *lois de police*, corresponded

---

94 H. Synvet, *L'organisation juridique du groupe international de sociétés*, *op. cit*; F. Garcimartin Alferez, *Cross-border listed companies*, *op. cit.*; X. Boucobza, *L'acquisition internationale de société*, Paris, LGDJ, 1998.

95 See 'Instruments financiers', in H. Synvet and A. Tenenbaum, *Répertoire de droit international*, *op. cit.*

96 J. Gavriloff, *Les méthodes du conflit de lois à l'épreuve du produit dérivé*, Université Paris Nanterre, 2020.

97 M. Ooi, *Shares and other securities in the conflict of laws*, Oxford, OUP, 2003.

98 A. Tenenbaum, *L'application internationale du droit boursier*, *op. cit*; H. Kronke, 'Capital Markets and Conflict of Law', *RCADI*, vol. 286, Martinus Nijhoff, 2000. See also, from a different and more recent angle, M. Lambert, *L'application internationale du droit financier*, *op. cit.*

99 P.-H. Conac, *La régulation des marchés boursiers par la commission des opérations de bourse (COB) et la securities and exchange commission (SEC)*, *op. cit.*

100 B. Stoeva, *La coopération entre les superviseurs financiers dans l'Union européenne*, thesis, University of Luxembourg and University of Paris II Panthéon-Assas, 2013; R. Gaspard, *La reconnaissance mutuelle en droit bancaire et financier*, *op. cit.* The latter author's work goes beyond the coordination of authorities to look at the way mutual recognition is deployed within the discipline.

101 This is echoed in the textbooks of the discipline, see e.g. D. Bureau and H.Muir Watt, *Droit international privé*, t. 2, Paris, PUF, 2017, no. 1006; B. Audit and L. d'Avout, *Droit international privé*, Paris, LGDJ, 2018, no. 1241.

well to the reality of this law at the beginning of its development.[102] Financial law has now reached a stage of maturity. The following study, in addition to taking place in a renewed legislative and institutional environment, does not limit its scope to one or other aspects of the internationalisation of the law of financial markets and instruments. By taking a synthetic look at the rules studied, it intends to renew the presentation of financial law rules by placing them, if not within bilateral conflict rules, at least within unilateral conflict rules whose unity stems not only from the links between the rules, but also from the common objective they pursue.[103] In order to constitute these conflict rules, it is therefore necessary to study, on the one hand, the connection between the infrastructures allowing the deployment of the rules governing relations between private persons. On the other hand, in order to determine the relevant categories, it is necessary to distinguish according to the objectives involved, while showing the systematic links that attach the regulation of infrastructures to that of the operations and instruments that they are intended to regulate.

27. Objective of legislative policies and configuration of the conflict of laws. When the law pursues the proper functioning of the financial market, the rules instituted may be brought together to constitute a category in the sense of private international law, which we shall refer to here, following other authors,[104] as the

---

[102] Unquestionably, when financial law consisted of three provisions of the Commercial Code and administrative regulations that did not really constitute a legislative body, the *lex mercatus* did not appear distinctly in spite of the *Manual of Stockbrokers*. It is thus not anecdotal that Professor Gaston Lagarde was able to qualify as a conventional extension of the competence of French law the former requirements of the *Chambre syndicale des agents de change* concerning the subscription and payment of shares issued by foreign listed companies, G. Lagarde, *L'émission des titres en France par les sociétés étrangères*, thesis, Poitiers, 1926, no. 89, p. 119.

[103] The rules studied here lend themselves well to the theory of assembly resulting from the work of Mr Schlurig as reported by Mr d'Avout: 'In the first stage, the potentially applicable rule of domestic law attaches itself to the concrete case, in the contemporary manner of police laws. The approach is unilateralist and casuistic. Noting then, within the same legislative order, the constant nature of these tailor-made connections of the rules of a given sector [...], experience assembles them into unilateral rules of conflict [...]. This is the second stage, which is that of synthetic unilateralism. The passage from synthetic unilateralism to bilateralism with a potentially universal vocation was then carried out according to a logic of symmetry or presumed reciprocity. L. d'Avout, 'Les phénomènes collectifs et l'analyse macro en droit international privé', *op. cit.* On this unilateral aspect of the international application of financial market law, see the comments of F. Garcimartin Alferez, *Cross-border listed companies*, *op. cit.*

[104] See already F. Garcimartin Alferez, *Cross-border listed companies*, *op. cit.*, no. 4; L. d'Avout, 'Les quotas face au conflit international des lois', *op. cit.*; from the same author, *L'entreprise et les conflits internationaux de lois*, *op. cit.*, no. 68, 163 et seq. The latter author nevertheless sees stock exchange law as a special application of the general concept of the *lex mercatus*. The notion of *lex mercatus*, when used here, refers exclusively to the law of the trading system.

lex mercatus. Its originality is, as Chemaly[105] observed early on, that it is based on the connecting factor of the negotiation system,[106] showing the links between collective interests and inter-individual situations that Professor d'Avout has endeavoured to highlight.[107] Although this connecting factor is not currently systematic within the Union, in our opinion it would gain from becoming so. In this case, financial market law concerns the relationship between investors and financial markets and applies because the mechanism of the trading platform is being used. The legal system of the financial market then usually has global jurisdiction, not only because its law has the particularity of being implemented by an administrative authority, but also because the courts of the seat of the financial market will usually have jurisdiction, either to resolve private law disputes arising from its regulation, or to challenge the administrative decisions of the market authority, or to punish those responsible for market abuse. This strict conception of the field of financial market law is obscured by several aspects.

28. Firstly, the law of the trading platform may be the connecting factor of the *lex contractus* for transactions concluded within it. However, this application of the law of the system to the transactions it allows is not specific to the financial market, but to all systems constituting market infrastructures. Because of the configuration of the relationships of the members of the system, the system rules will designate the law applicable to the transactions they allow, and will most often elect the law of the system itself. This application, which is not new, is nevertheless neither always necessary nor systematic, and is limited to the relationships of system members.

Secondly, in dealing with issuers, capital market law may apply for investor protection purposes, simply because the admission of securities to a capital market is a form of solicitation. However, these rules are usually triggered by the person making the solicitation so that the weight of internationality falls on the solicitor. The second objective traditionally assigned to financial market law, namely the protection of investors, can be recognised here and justifies separate treatment in terms of conflict of laws. Indeed, in these cases, the applicable rules, because they aim at protecting residents, obey a distinct international regime according to which local law is likely to be self-limiting

---

105 'The stock exchange, because it constitutes an organised market, constitutes, one might say, a pole of attraction for the attachment and location of the transactions concluded there [...]', See 'Bourses (de valeurs et de marchandises)', in R. Chemaly, *Rép. inter.* Dalloz, 1st ed,. 1968, no. 4. The difference with the thesis supported here is that the linkage is not made through the organisation of the market, of which the manager is the pivot, but through the mechanism constituting the market, i.e. the infrastructure itself. In practice, however, it will be seen that in the vast majority of cases the infrastructure is located at the headquarters of its manager.

106 See *ibid.*, no. 176; from the same author, 'Les phénomènes collectifs et l'analyse macro en droit international privé', *op. cit.* no. 26.

107 *Ibid.*

whenever foreign law offers equivalent protection. Whether or not local law is self-limiting, it will still apply to the liability regime that may be triggered by the conduct of the offeror: this is the inevitable price of market access. Conversely, it may be desirable in some cases to extend the application of investor protection rules to activities carried out by local companies for foreign residents in order to improve the international harmony of solutions.

29. Financial market law is influenced by the objective of preventing systemic risk, which is specific to the financial law in which it is embedded. The international deployment of regulation is therefore based on a double prism, micro and macro.[108] From the micro point of view, the system risk justifies the institution of a clearing obligation. This obliges operators to use the clearing house in order to conclude most of their financial contracts, which leads, in the vast majority of cases, to the application of the law of the clearing system to the financial contracts concluded. The application of the clearing obligation is then based, in principle, on the establishment of one of the parties to the contract on the territory of the Union, but is likely to extend to all financial contracts having an effect on the territory of the Union. This criterion has a political function, that of encouraging a global dialogue on the prevention of systemic risk. From a macro point of view, system risk justifies administrative supervision of market infrastructures, primarily clearing houses, and the correlative application of prudential and resolution legislation to these infrastructures. The criterion of connection is therefore particularly broad: the administrative authorities are competent to supervise any clearing house of systemic size that wishes to provide its services to operators established in the Union. From all points of view, the objective of preventing systemic risk, if it institutes rules binding private international relations, appears to be more closely linked to considerations close to the economic sovereignty of States and is less receptive to self-limitation. More generally, the more "macro" the approach becomes, the more private interests fade away or are integrated into political and collective considerations, which is also reflected in the equivalence method. Conflicts are then resolved alternatively through the coordination of the legislators themselves within the commands they prescribe, or in the cumulative application of the constraints imposed, which can prevent the establishment of international private relations.

30. Finally, the delivery system for securities managed by the central depository is not without impact on their regime either. It will be shown that the law of this system should apply to the entire proprietary status of the securities admitted to it. The competence of this law comes then from the one that the issuer has given up to it by entrusting it with the issued securities; it is explained by the evidential pre-eminence of the accounts that it keeps, as well as by its

---

108 The expression is borrowed from L. d'Avout, 'Les phénomènes collectifs et l'analyse macro en droit international privé', *op. cit.*

central place within the intermediation structure. Its exclusive application to the proprietary status of securities would make it possible to resolve the difficulties raised by the intermediation of securities in the conflict of laws.

These observations show that it is necessary to study international law beyond private law relationships in order to observe how market infrastructures are connected to the State (Part 1.). Indeed, this connection provides a basis for the connecting factor of other bodies of law that condition their applicability to the use of these infrastructures, and in particular to transactions between private persons concluded through trading platforms. It is also necessary to define the scope of financial market law in order to take into account cases where the law actually applies on the basis of the use of the trading platform (Part 2.). Finally, the connecting factor of market infrastructures is not only the foundation of the law of the financial market, but also of the law of financial instruments, to different extents, depending on whether securities or financial contracts are involved (Part 3.).

PART 1.

The Connecting Factor of Market Infrastructures

31. The connecting factors of market infrastructures. Today, market infrastructures are systems that have in common, on the one hand, that they are made up of a legal element, the rules of the system, and a material element, the computer system, and on the other hand, that they are managed by an infrastructure manager. For a long time, these different aspects were confused. The contemporary connecting factor of market infrastructures requires a study of the history of the French organisation of financial markets, as well as the European institutional context in which it is embedded today.

32. At first sight, the contemporary connecting factor of infrastructure managers is not very original: like legal persons under private law, these managers are connected to the legal system of their registered office. However, their uniqueness becomes apparent once it is observed that the registered office in question is their real seat, and that the law of the seat has a particularly broad scope, applying to corporate, prudential and insolvency legislation. This correlation seems to give an additional dimension to the 'universal law of private international law', according to which 'the more liberal the connecting factor, the more the field of the designated law narrows or competes with the attempts to apply third party laws'.[1] In fact, in the same way, the less liberal the connecting factor, the more the field of the conflict rule expands, making the criterion used the preferred instrument for deploying the legislative policy of the legal system designated by the conflict rule.

Another original feature of the managers is their rigorous administrative framework, which adds to their legislative attachment a real administrative connecting factor whose configuration is now on the borderline between two models. The first, which is decentralised, leaves it to the authority at the headquarters of each manager to exercise local supervision, and the national nature of this supervision is tempered by coordination mechanisms between authorities in order to deal with the cross-border exercise of the manager's activity. This traditional model, which instituted a parallelism of legislative and administrative connecting factors, is now being challenged by a second, centralised model, which, while leaving the national law of the headquarters to prevail, gives a Union body the power of administrative decision, but sometimes leaves the execution of its decisions to the national authorities, or even delegates its own decision-making power to them. This state of affairs gives rise to the need for coordination, this time between the Union's legal order and the national legal orders. These two types of connecting factors, legislative and administrative, explain, in a form of mirror image, why relations with third-country managers are also marked by this duality, with access to European territory being conditioned by various criteria, the most emblematic

---

[1] L. d'Avout, 'Suites de la jurisprudence *Centros*: les sociétés *off shore* rattrapées par le droit local de l'insolvabilité', *JCP G*, 2016, p. 519, no. 3.

of which is that based on the conditions of equivalence of foreign legislation and cooperation agreements between administrative authorities. It will be shown that this equivalence method is subject to the traditional tensions of private international law methods, between coordination of legal orders and protection of the social order of the judicial authority.

33. The affiliation of managers has an influence on the affiliation of the systems they manage. The latter are not univocally connected, some being subject to the legal order of the manager's headquarters, while others are subject to a conflict rule inspired by the law of autonomy. This duality reflects the inherent ambiguity of systems rules, the qualification of which fluctuates according to the European legal orders, and whose ambivalence is reflected in the controversial nature of French doctrine. It will be shown here that although the qualification is undoubtedly porous, the rules of French systems are today fundamentally contractual. However, their particularity is to institute an organisation that makes the application of the law of autonomy dysfunctional. They would therefore benefit from being subject to the law of their manager's headquarters, which is the legal centre of gravity of the organisation in question.

In order to carry out this demonstration, it is necessary to study the configuration of the market infrastructure connecting factor (introductory chapter) before looking at the connecting factor of managers (Title 1), then that of systems (Title 2).

INTRODUCTORY CHAPTER
THE CONFIGURATION OF THE INFRASTRUCTURE CONNECTING FACTOR

34. The current state of market infrastructure is the result of several recent distinctions: first, between the different infrastructures needed for the functioning of the financial market and, second, between the infrastructure and its manager. For a long time, these different aspects were concentrated in the statute of the stockbrokers, instituted by the State.[1] Through this, the financial market managed by the stockbrokers was already attached to the State. This legal, rather than geographical, attachment was already serving as a basis for the regulation of private relations that the infrastructure allowed. In order to observe this, it is necessary to retrace the history of French financial markets from the Middle Ages to the present day (Section 1.). The connecting factor of infrastructures has nevertheless changed, in particular because of the evolution of the institutional context, now European, in which infrastructures are embedded (Section 2.).

SECTION 1. THE CONFIGURATION OF FRENCH FINANCIAL MARKETS

The contemporary configuration of French financial markets is based on three distinctions. The first is that between the manager and the system. The second distinction is between the systems necessary for the proper functioning of the financial market: trading systems, also called trading platforms, clearing systems and securities settlement systems. The third distinction is between the different categories of trading platforms within trading systems. These three types of separation, which structure the contemporary organisation of financial markets (§ 2), are the result of the historical development of financial markets (§ 1).

---

1 As Professor Pellet writes, 'The ideal of the original self-organised market is one of the myths of liberal economic thought, whereas in reality the financial markets were not born solely of the needs of the commercial world: they were formed by the trading of public rent securities and remained for several centuries under the very close control of the States, which placed them at the service of their interests and their policies', R. Pellet, *États et marchés financiers*, Paris, LGDJ, 2017, p. 9.

§ 1. ORIGIN OF THE FRENCH FINANCIAL MARKETS

35. From '*changeurs*' (brokers) to the '*Companie des Agents de change*' (Company of Stockbrokers) (13th–18th century). The members of a financial market were historically stockbrokers, themselves 'the distant heirs of the moneychangers who set up their tables and scales in the great fairs of the Middle Ages to facilitate the payment, in bullion or cash, of obligations contracted between merchants of various origins'.[2] These money changers disappeared in particular because of the appearance, in the 13th century, of the bill of exchange. The bill of exchange, which became widespread at the end of the Middle Ages, proved to be, 'a quicker and more economical way of settling accounts'.[3] Together with the invention of scriptural money, it was the foundation of the medieval financial revolution.[4] If the bill of exchange had the effect of seeing the corporation of Parisian moneychangers abandon its honorary position in 1514, it also led to the creation and circulation of commercial bills. These were handled by the '*courratiers*'[5] or exchange brokers who 'were at the same time brokers of wholesale goods; they intervened both to facilitate the conclusion of contracts and their liquidation'.[6] Nevertheless, this new profession 'practised both by foreigners and nationals, escaped all regulation; irregularities and frauds (*ensued*)'.[7] An edict of 15 June 1572 put an end to these shortcomings by making brokers royal officers.[8] The charge, initially a means of policing private relations, also became an instrument of fiscal resources. Charges were made venal by a ruling of the King's Council

---

2 G. Boissière, *La Compagnie des agents de change et le marché officiel à la Bourse de Paris*, Paris, Rousseau, 1908, p. 1 (hereafter *La compagnie des agents de change*). The work, which is the result of the author's doctoral thesis in law, is particularly significant since this updated second edition was requested by the Chambre syndicale des agents de change itself, which, according to its representatives, 'has never ceased to consider this book, since its appearance in 1908, as the most complete and interesting work on the Compagnie des Agents de Change' (preface to the work). The other decisive work, a true 'Code des agents de change', is the *Manuel des agents de change, banque finance et commerce, contenant les lois, règlements et actes officiels qui régissent et intéressent l'exercice de leurs fonctions*, 5th ed., Paris (hereinafter *Manuel des agents de change*) which has collected and inserted, in chronological order, the texts concerning the profession of stockbroker, since its origin. We quote here the 5th edition of 1893, which will be the subject of a supplement in 1902.

3 G. Boissière, *La Compagnie des agents de change*, *op. cit.*, p. 2.

4 J. H. Munru, 'The medieval Origins of the Financial Revolution: Usury, Rentes, and Negociability' (2003) 25(3) *The International Review*, pp. 505–756, quoted by R. Pellet, *Droit financier public*, t. 1, Thémis, Paris, PUF, 2018, no. 119, p. 93.

5 According to the royal act of Philip le Bel, see *Manuel des agents de change*, *op. cit.*, p. 5.

6 G. Boissière, *La Compagnie des agents de change*, *op. cit.*, p. 3. There is already talk of liquidation, anticipating the technique of multilateral clearing.

7 *Ibid.*, p. 3. The author then shows (p. 4) that the creation of these charges was therefore independent of the tax issue. It was only after an exchange of the intermediary monopoly that a tax was introduced.

8 *Manuel des agents de change*, *op. cit.* p. 7.

on 17 May 1598.[9] The same ruling also established the brokers' monopoly of mediation, which was the premise of the monopoly of stockbrokers.[10]

36. In 1638, forty years later, an important ruling by the same Council stated that no more complaints would be received following the creation of the royal offices;[11] it also had the effect of grouping 'the brokers into a body and (*providing for*) the institution of the Syndicate responsible, under the control of the general assembly, for the care of matters concerning the common good of the company'.[12] This means that the avatars of the Chambre syndicale des agents de change are old, even if this institution was only formally created by a Conseil decree of 2 December 1786 creating a permanent committee between the general assembly and the syndic.[13] The technique of approval is not new either, since, as Mr Boissière writes, 'the same texts confirm by frequent reminders the fundamental provisions of the status of stockbroker; in particular to present a successor for approval by the royal power'.[14] As with contemporary regulations, it was not enough to comply with the prescriptions at the time of obtaining the office, it was also necessary to respect them over time, which was verified by the royal approval of the successor. The statutes of the *Compagnie des agents de change* also show the predisposition of the commercial world towards self-regulation.[15] Indeed, developing the provisions of the 1673 ordinance of commerce, the first statutes adopted the same year[16] already provided that stockbrokers 'may not exchange money or bank on their own behalf',[17] just as the manager of a financial market may not interfere in its management, or

---

9 *Ibid.*, p. 10.

10 On the meaning of this monopoly, and its international application, see *infra*, para.

11 *Ibid.*, p. 11.

12 G. Boissière, *La Compagnie des agents de change*, *op. cit.*, p. 4. The said syndicate was appointed until 1786 by the Lieutenant General of Police, when the syndicate became elected by its peers.

13 *Manuel des agents de change*, *op. cit.*, p. 96; G. Boissière, *La Compagnie des agents de change*, *op. cit.*, p. 14.

14 *Ibid.*, p. 8. However, contemporary amenity is more prefigured by the notion of burden, which has a similar function.

15 This continued throughout the 19th century, since until 1890, when a decree was issued, the conditions for executing stock exchange markets 'resulted only from the practices of the market, codified in the successive regulations of the Compagnie des agents de change, which were amended four times during the 19th century. The decree of 7 October 1890, issued in execution of the law of 28 March 1885, merely sanctioned the regulations previously in force on the Paris stock exchange by making them applicable to all exchanges. G. Boissière, *La Compagnie des agents de change*, *op. cit.*, p. 36.

16 *Ibid.*, pp. 20 et seq.

17 *Manuel des agents de change*, p. 20. Art. 1 of the aforementioned ordinance, Art. 13 of the statutes of 1684, see also G. Boissière, *La Compagnie des agents de change*, *op. cit.*, p. 9.

that stockbrokers were 'required to draw up accounts',[18] foreshadowing certain contemporary prudential obligations.[19]

37. Paradoxically, Law's system (1714–1720),[20] which created bearer bonds payable at sight in exchange for the remittance of a sum of money, caused a double injury to stockbrokers: not only did they fail under Law, but after Law, their profession suffered the bad reputation of the man who had ousted them. Indeed, on the one hand, with this system, stockbrokers lost their *raison d'être* since exchanges took place directly in Law's establishment, without intermediaries. On the other hand, Law's bankruptcy introduced a great mistrust of fiduciary money and the commercial world in general,[21] and the 'stock exchange' world in particular:[22] they lost their status of ministerial officers, could no longer announce prices aloud nor carry out forward transactions until 1774.[23] The second half of the 17th century was more favourable to them: the financial markets developed strongly thanks to the appearance of new objects of exchange, in particular shares.[24] Combined with the rise of the *Compagnie des agents de change* from 1774 onwards, Mr Boissière can write that: 'at the end of the Ancien Régime, we find the essential elements of the corporate organisation and the constitution of the financial market'.[25] The revolution marked the end of their existence: the Allarde decree of 2–17 March 1791 dissolved the corporation of

---

18 Arts. 2 and 6 of Title III of the same ordinance, Art. 15 of the statutes of 1684.

19 Or again 'that they may not be substituted in the exercise of their functions' (Art. 12 of the Statutes of 1684, Art. 5 of the Statutes of 1706), already showing here the personal nature of the approval of the providers.

20 On which see R. Szramkiewicz and O. Descamps, *Histoire du droit des affaires*, 2nd ed., Paris, LGDJ, 2013, no. 244, pp. 140–141, and R. Pellet, *Droit financier public*, t. 1, *op. cit.*, no. 174, pp. 134 et seq.

21 *Ibid.*

22 This was reflected in the edict of 1724 which, although it re-established the stock exchange, largely affected stockbrokers (out of 41 Articles, 25 were dedicated to them).

23 Date on which their status of ministerial officer is re-established. A Conseil decree of 7 August 1785 made the futures market possible only if the bills of exchange were first delivered. The forward markets were suspected of being the cause of the discrediting of royal bills, which was more likely to be due to the disarray of public finances on the eve of the Revolution (G. Boissière, *La Compagnie des agents de change*, *op. cit.*, p. 16), and another Conseil ruling of 22 September 1786 prohibited the deferment of the market for more than two months (*ibid).* See respectively these two rulings in the *Manuel de agents de change*, *op. cit.*, p. 81 and p. 93.

24 The first were those of the Compagnie des Indes and, 'alongside them, the titles of the royal lotteries, then the titles of the State debt created by the edict of 20 May 1749, and the shares of the commercial companies, which after a period of stagnation following the ruin of the System, began to form again', G. Boissière, *La Compagnie des agents de change*, *op. cit.*

25 *Ibid.* p. 18. In the same sense, J.-J. Daigre, 'L'évolution de la notion de marché financier', *op. cit.*, no. 4, p. 238: 'despite these reforms, the stock market has remained what it was since the beginning of the 18th century: an organisation and a mechanism'.

stockbrokers[26] and abolished their offices.[27] The effects of this abolition and the introduction of a system of absolute freedom for those authorised to trade on the markets were so devastating that stockbrokers were henceforth only appointed by the public authorities.[28]

38. The fortune of stockbrokers (19th century). If the 18th century was a trying time for stockbrokers, the 19th century was to be the time of their fortune. The decree of 28 Ventôse, Year IX (19 March 1801) granted the government the power to 'establish exchanges of commerce in all places [...] where it deems it appropriate'.[29] This law, which also instituted stockbrokers, was part of a legislative package aimed at providing France with various ministerial officers subject to the same constraints.[30] While they have a legal monopoly on access to the spot market, stockbrokers cannot trade on the futures market.[31] The latter are subject to legislative disgrace because of the speculation they were deemed to encourage. Nevertheless, speculation is gradually being accepted. For

---

26 *Manuel des agents de change*, *op. cit.* p. 114. However, the corporatist spirit was so intense that a free company was formed, although this did not prevent the profession from being open to all (G. Boissière, *La Compagnie des agents de change*, *op. cit.*, p. 20).

27 N. Hissung-Convert, *La spéculation boursière face au droit 1799-1914*, Paris, LGDJ, 2009, p. 44; *Contra* P.-J. Lehmann, *Histoire de la bourse de Paris*, Paris, PUF, 1998, p. 11. Technically, stockbrokers were abolished by the law of 2–17 March 1791 (Art. 2), the law of 6 May 1791 dealing only with the liquidation of their offices. The law of 8 May 1791 deals with the fundamental rules of the new status of stockbrokers.

28 This was already the case during the revolutionary period: the law of 30 Vendémiaire, Year IV (21 October 1795), repealed the law that had abolished the Compagnies and commercial associations. We refer to the developments of Mr Boissière for the details of the period.

29 Art. 1 of the law of 28 Ventôse An IX, *Manuel des agents de change*, *op. cit.* p. 207; see also the historical analysis of this law, N. Hissung-Convert, *La spéculation boursière face au droit 1799-1914*, *op. cit.*

30 This is how notaries were re-established by the law of 25 Ventôse An XI, which gave them similar characteristics: 'they are instituted for life' (Art. 2 of the law containing the organisation of the notary's office of the law of 25 Ventôse An XI), 'they are obliged to lend their ministry when they are required to do so' (Art. 3 of the same law). This analogous status helped to explain the difficulty for 19th century jurists in considering stockbrokers as merchants. This controversy gave rise to a treasure trove of sophistication which Thaller describes in his textbook, see E. Thaller, *Traité élémentaire de droit commercial*, 8th ed. by J. Percerou, Paris, Rousseau, 1931, nos. 856 et seq.
Subsequently, stockbrokers ceased to be public officials appointed for life and became public officers owning their offices by the law of 25 June 1841 (*Manuel des agents de change*, *op. cit.*, G. Boissière, *La Compagnie des agents de change*, *op. cit.)*

31 It cannot be said that they are recent, since Diderot and d'Alembert give precise details in their Encyclopaedia of the operation of the Amsterdam stock exchange, which, as early as the 18th century, had 'a conditional market, a firm market and an options market' (see 'Marché' in D. Diderot and J. Le Rond d'Alembert, *Encyclopédie du dictionnaire raisonné des sciences, des arts et des métiers*, vol. X, 1765, pp. 84–85 quoted by R. Dambre, *Les contrats financiers sur actions*, *op. cit.*, note 26, p. 28). For an account of the eventful history of the regulations preceding the law of 25 March 1885 definitively legalising the operations to which they give rise in France, see Marcadé et Pont, *Explication théorique et pratique du Code civil*, vol. 8, Paris, Delamotte et Fils, 1877, nos. 625–649, pp. 285–325.

a long time considered a public danger, as it was seen as a subversive activity, speculation was the object of a movement towards legalisation pushed by the stockbrokers. Indeed, they perceived better than others 'the great usefulness of the futures market as a support for securities pending their classification, and as a price regulator',[32] not hesitating to compare, 'the speculator to the water carrier who sells in advance the bucket of water he is going to draw from the Seine: the Stock Exchange being, in short, the river of securities'.[33] After having suffered the full force of the 1882 crash, where they stood out for their financial solidity, stockbrokers obtained their greatest victory at the end of the century: the 1885 law legalising the futures markets. This law made it possible to refine the distinction between the institution and the possible trading venues: spot markets, also called stock exchanges, were not subject to the same trading rules as futures markets.[34] Together, they constitute the institutions covered by the concept of financial market.[35]

39. From the stockbrokers' solidarity fund to the clearing house (19th–20th century). The guarantee of the transactions concluded, today ensured by the clearing house, was initially carried out by stockbrokers through several techniques:[36] the contract usually used during stock exchange transactions makes them commission agents on behalf of their clients, the latter's del credere (*ducroire*) towards the other stockbrokers.[37] This is why, in the event that their clients fail

---

32 G. Boissière, *La Compagnie des agents de change*, *op. cit.*, p. 32.

33 Boscary de Villeplaine was syndic of the stockbrokers from 14 brumaire An XI to 23 vendémiaire An XIV (*Manuel des agents de change* p. XX, reproduced by G. Boissière, *La Compagnie des agents de change*, *op. cit.*, p. 68).
The quote is taken from Mollot, *Bourses de commerce, agents de change et courtiers*, vol. I, Paris, 3rd ed., 1853, p. 16. The author was one of the councils of the stockbrokers' company.

34 Moreover, this law is especially necessary for stockbrokers since they previously bore the risk of the gambling exception (on which see *infra*, para. 456). In this market, stockbrokers are also subject to competition from behind the scenes, i.e. from brokers who do not hold a ministerial office. On this competition, see in particular the works of G. Boissière, *La Compagnie des agents de change*, *op. cit.* (for a contemporary view), N. Hissung-Convert, *La spéculation boursière face au droit 1799-1914*, *op. cit.* (for a retrospective analysis).

35 The concept of the stock exchange, which essentially refers to securities, no longer allows for the diversity of possible transactions. From the 1885 Act onwards, the concept of financial market has the comparative advantage of covering both markets.

36 In the Middle Ages, stockbrokers were also responsible for the liquidation of transactions, see P.-H. Conac, *La régulation des marchés boursiers par la Commission des opérations de bourse (COB) et la Securities and exchange commission (SEC)*, *op. cit.*, no. 221. It is difficult to know whether stockbrokers were acting as systematic internalisers or already constituted a clearing house, or whether the two roles were linked.

37 The del credere (*ducroire*) is a 'kind of guarantee commitment; more precisely, it is the name given to the stipulation annexed to distribution contracts by which an agent or commission agent guarantees the solvency of customers in return for an increase in his remuneration (known as the "ducroire" premium) and, once he has paid, subrogation in the rights of the seller with regard to the defaulting customer', see 'Ducroire' in *Vocabulaire Capitant*, 8th edition, Paris, PUF, 2007. This commitment is part of the agency contract between the agent and the principal, on which see *infra*, paras. 446 et seq.

to perform, the agents demand 'cover' (*une couverture*), i.e. the deposit of a sum of money to guarantee the final payment.[38] In this way, they concentrate all the risk of default of their own clients on their heads. In addition, stockbrokers are subject to significant capital requirements as they were initially required to provide a significant pledge to obtain their charge.[39] They therefore had to be able to absorb losses arising from the default of one of their clients: this need is also perceived by the public authorities through a particularly rigorous criminal sanction applicable in the event of default by the agent himself.[40]

40. In order to compensate for the eventual failure of a colleague, the profession has set up, like other regulated professions,[41] a solidarity fund for Parisian stockbrokers.[42] This fund aimed to compensate for the relationships between intermediaries. The latter were all the more assured of payment as the *Chambre Syndicale* 'has always acted as an intermediary to carry out without delay, on behalf of the agent, the operation that remained pending',[43] a practice that Article 55 of the decree of 7 October 1890 transforms into an obligation for the *Chambre Syndicale*. The creation of the solidarity fund for stockbrokers in 1819[44] was also the result of the establishment of a voluntary interdependence of stockbrokers in relation to the principals, 'with the sole aim of safeguarding the honour of the profession and giving the official market an unshakeable solidity'.[45]

---

38 On clearing, see our historical and contemporary developments *infra*, paras. 865 et seq.

39 Decree of 28 Ventôse Year IX (19 March 1901), see also P.-J. Lehmann, *op. cit.*, p. 11.

40 Sanction even more brutal than that of a classic trader. It is not as a defiance of the stock exchange system, but as a reflection of the trust placed in public officers such as stockbrokers. Comp. P. Barban, *Les entreprises de marché, op. cit.*, no. 1.

41 Such as notaries, lawyers, etc. It should be noted in this regard that stockbrokers are considered by some to be the equivalent of notaries in movable property: just as in the sphere of circulation, the State has 'established a control of credit operations and real estate transfers through the institution of the notary's office and the conservations of hypotheses' (G. Boissière, *La Compagnie des agents de change, op. cit.*, p. 363), it would have established a similar control over 'movable credit, given the importance it has acquired' (*ibid.*).

42 The action of the stockbrokers follows several unsuccessful experiments carried out in France in 1845 to establish the clearing of securities on a large scale, see F.-C. Jeantet, 'Le dépôt collectif de titres au porteur à la Caisse centrale de dépôt et de virement de titres', *Journal des sociétés*, 1945, pp. 161 et seq., spec. p. 163, the author referring to A. Roux, *La compensation et le virement des titres*, thèse Paris, 1930; Haas, *Le virement et la compensation des titres en Allemagne*, thèse Paris, 1932.

43 G. Boissière, *La Compagnie des agents de change, op. cit.*, p. 330.

44 A common purse had attempted to be adopted by the 1638 ruling (*ibid.*), but the attempt was aborted for various reasons, on which see G. Boissière, *La Compagnie des agents de change, op. cit.* A social fund remained, for the expenses of corporate life. It was created in two stages: first by an agreement between the stockbrokers established on the place in 1819, and then the definitive statutes were drawn up on 8 July 1922. For details of the origin, see F.-E. Mollot, *Bourses de commerce, agents de change et courtiers op. cit.*

45 G. Boissière, *La Compagnie des agents de change, op. cit.* p. 334. This solidarity was in certain circumstances singularly onerous for them, in particular during the fall of the *Union Générale* in 1882, when they took out 'a loan of 80 million to save the credit of the Place' (G. Boissière, *La Compagnie des agents de change, op. cit.*, p. 335), while the Compagnie

The fund is fed by a special contribution paid for each transaction concluded by stockbrokers, and the destination of these sums has evolved to the point of making the fund a genuine insurance mechanism.[46]

41. The solidarity fund must be clearly distinguished from the 'clearing' operation, or central liquidation, which takes place between stockbrokers. On the spot market, the price[47] is settled from agent to agent in the form of a 'green bond', then 'these green bonds are collected by the *Chambre Syndicale*, which interposes itself in order to avoid considerable and useless movements of cash',[48] which allows, 'a complete clearing embracing the totality of the negotiations settled on the same day, and in spite of this, it preserves the individuality of each of the operations'.[49] One might have thought that the stockbrokers' fund would intervene at the time of payment, with each debtor agent paying the balance owed to it, and each creditor agent receiving his balance from the fund. In fact, the *Compagnie des agents de change* had made an early arrangement with the *Banque de France*, leaving the latter to play this role, which it retained after the disappearance of the agents de change.[50] At the same time as the *Caisse Centrale de Dépôts et Virements de Titres* ('CCDVT')[51] and the *Société Interprofessionnelle*

des agents de change lyonnaise went bankrupt. However, Boissière, whose work is an ode to the corporation of stockbrokers, probably only gives part of the motivation of stockbrokers, given that, like any institution, they seek to persevere in their being; yet the colossal fortune they accumulate in times of growth, combined with their bankruptcy in times of crisis, would undoubtedly have contributed to calling into question, if not their status, then at least the monopoly granted to them by the community.

46 G. Boissière, *La Compagnie des agents de change*, *op. cit.* p. 345: 'above all, a provident and insurance fund created between the agents to cover the liabilities they may incur in the exercise of their profession, by making advances to them in critical moments or by taking their place in the event of insolvency'. If one adds to this the personal guarantees arising from the assets of each stockbroker, some authors have been able to establish that the total pledge of stockbrokers was particularly considerable: if stockbrokers were able to resist the crash of 1882, it is because few events were likely to drain them.
This is why the fund prefigures, by its functions, the appearance of both the prudential obligations reinforced since the 2008 financial crisis, but also the creation of the clearing house itself. In this respect, one could believe Boissière's contemporary words: 'There is no need to insist on demonstrating the usefulness of this institution: it prevents a temporary inconvenience, which it is possible to alleviate and the memory of which will disappear, from becoming a definitive catastrophe. It prevents the individual failure of an agent from having repercussions on several of his colleagues with whom he does business. It therefore safeguards both the interests of the public and the honour of the corporation' (*ibid.*).

47 The obligation to settle securities is not managed by the system described by Boissière; it is necessary to wait for the appearance of the first central depositories, in the middle of the 20th century, see *infra*, para. 648.

48 G. Boissière, *La Compagnie des agents de change*, *op. cit.*, p. 290. Emphasis added.

49 *Ibid.*, p. 291.

50 On the continued role of the Banque de France in payment systems, see *infra*, para. 244.

51

de Compensation des Valeurs Mobilières ('SICOVAM')[52] were created, a bilateral clearing system was set up between stockbrokers' delivery obligations. At first, this took place through internal clearing within each office,[53] then between stockbrokers through the intervention of the central clearing service of the *Chambre syndicale*.[54] It was not until 1966 and the establishment of a *Compagnie nationale des agents de change* that this 'inter-agent services' was extended to the whole of France.[55] This securities clearing function was retained by the heir to the *Chambre syndicale des agents de change*, the *Société des Bourses Françaises* ('SBF'), which this time carried out multilateral clearing of delivery obligations on the model of multilateral clearing of money settlement obligations, made possible by the existence of the central depository. The law establishing the SBF explicitly states: 'The sums and securities deposited with the specialised financial institution as collateral for clearing operations provided for in the regulation referred to in Article 6 shall be acquired by it up to the limit of the debts incurred by it as a result of these operations.'[56] The effect of this provision is to make the precursor of the market operator 'the first securities clearing house',[57] but also to confuse the clearing function with that of performance guarantee.[58]

42. The solidarity fund was not involved at the time of clearing on the futures markets, where the monthly settlement was organised by a special department of the *Chambre syndicale*,[59] within which the *Banque de France* had a similar status.[60] The 'crash' of 1882[61] and the subsequent bankruptcy of the '*Parquet de Lyon*'[62] gave the *Cour de cassation* the opportunity to examine the operation

---

52 Decree no. 49-1105 of 4 August 1949 taken for the application of Art. 26 amended of the law of 5 July 1949 and relating to the system of securities as well as to the methods of liquidation of the Caisse centrale de dépôts et de virements de titres (CCDVT). On this decree and the system set up by the CCDVT, see *infra*, para. 648.

53 This roughly prefigures systematic internalisation.

54 Who finally organised deliveries between agents taken two by two. On this question see J. Buisson, 'Les compensations entre agents de change', Chronique de la Bourse, *Banque*, 1947, p. 50.

55 M. Roussille, *La compensation multilatérale*, *op. cit.*, no. 72, pp. 43–44.

56 Art. 10(4) of Law No. 88-70 of 22 January 1988 on stock exchanges.

57 M. Roussille, *La compensation multilatérale*, *op. cit.*, no. 75, p. 46.

58 *Ibid.*,. no. 75, p. 46. This last purpose could be compared to that of the Chambre Syndicale, which, by paying its clients on behalf of the indelicate stockbroker, contributed to guaranteeing the proper completion of the transactions carried out on the stock exchange. On the evolution of the functions of the clearing house, see *infra*, para. 865.

59 Tightly regulated by the statutes of 1816 at Title IV of the *Règlement de la Compagnie des agents de change* quoted by M. Roussille, *La compensation multilatérale*, *op. cit.*, nos. 52 et seq., pp. 32 et seq. The most detailed description is given by Thaller: E. Thaller, *De la faillite des agents de change et de la liquidation de leur charge*, Imp. Larose et Forcel, 1883, pp. 206 et seq.

60 M. Roussille, *La compensation multilatérale*, *op. cit.*, nos. 52 et seq., p. 32.

61 This major financial crisis of the 19th century was – already – linked to the failure of a bank, the *Union Générale*.

62 '*Parquet*' was the name given to the Company of Stockbrokers in a given place.

and to qualify it as 'general clearing'.[63] Similar funds, called 'Liquidation' funds, appeared in order to allow the clearing of contracts on goods made on the commercial exchanges.[64] However, it was precisely for the commodity futures market that the first clearing house proper was created in 1969, and took the name 'Central Clearing Bank'. The modern clearing houses for derivatives markets appeared at the time when the future markets diversified: the clearing house for the financial futures market (MATIF), and the clearing house for the negotiable options market (MONEP).[65] In all cases, the clearing house is perfectly distinct from the market itself, and a single clearing house, LCH. Clearnet,[66] has now replaced all of these clearing houses; its status is governed by Regulation 648/2012 on OTC derivatives, central counterparties and trade repositories, known as the EMIR Regulation. Although it may have had several functions,[67] the clearing house today justifies its existence by ensuring the reliability of transactions concluded on the financial markets and by guaranteeing their settlement, i.e. their execution. The importance of this guarantee of the successful completion of transactions provided by the clearing house is considerable for the financial markets themselves, since it is also the cause of their anonymity: it is because everyone knows that the transaction will *ultimately* be executed that the counterparty risk, i.e. the risk that the co-contractor will go bankrupt, is eliminated and that, consequently, the identity of the co-contractor is no longer important.[68]

43. The emergence of the central securities depository. Once the transaction has been concluded in principle and its performance guaranteed, it is still necessary to pay in the civil sense, i.e. in the case of a contract of sale, to remit a sum of money in return for a thing. This is where central securities depositories come in. The function of delivering securities, which was reserved for financial securities only,[69] was already being performed in part by stockbrokers, but will now be carried out in full by the central securities depository. Since the clearing of cash markets only concerns the settlement of sums of money, the delivery of

---

63 Com., 28 January 1889, *DP*, I, 49, note A. Boistel. On this subject, see M. Roussille, *La compensation multilatérale*, *op. cit*, no. 54, p. 34.

64 *Ibid.*,, no. 55, pp. 34–35.

65 On these entities, see the thesis and analyses of I. Riassetto, *Les garanties des contrats à terme sur le MATIF*, Strasbourg, 1999.

66 The result of the 2003 merger of the London Clearing House and Clearnet, the Parisian clearing house.

67 See *infra*, para. 865.

68 B. Carruthers, 'Economy and Law', *op. cit.*, p. 130.

69 Financial contracts, because they are not aimed at the trading and transfer of securities, do not need to go through central securities depositories. At most, the amount of the commitments they record must be recorded in a central repository.

securities had to be simplified. Due to successive failures in 1854 and 1904,[70] this simplification only came about with the appearance of the first central depository in 1941: the *Caisse Centrale de Dépôts et Virements de Titres* ('CCDVT').[71] The existence of this particular fund was truncated/curtailed by a law of 1949,[72] whose implementing decree created the *Société Interprofessionnelle de Compensation des Valeurs Mobilières* ('SICOVAM').[73] All bearer shares can be deposited with SICOVAM through an affiliated institution,[74] which has the effect of making them fungible and transferable only by transfer to SICOVAM's accounts.[75] However, the SICOVAM system only recreates the conditions of the CCDVT with the 1981 law dematerialising securities and requiring their concentration with the central depository. Today, central depositories manage the delivery of securities through their own system, which also has an important influence on the regime of securities that are admitted to these systems.[76] However, this system needs to be co-ordinated with the payment system operated by the central bank in order to match the transfer of ownership of the securities with the settlement of the money. This settlement function is performed by an electronic platform, which considerably reduces the settlement risk, i.e. the risk of one party defaulting before having paid, but after having been paid.

44. Historical connecting factor of infrastructures. The study of the origin of the financial markets allows several observations to be made about their

---

70 Indeed, two unsuccessful attempts were made in 1854 (on the initiative of stockbrokers and entrusted to the *Banque de France*) and in 1904 (on the initiative of the *Chambre syndicale des Banquiers*) to introduce a system of transferring securities to the Stock Exchange, see J. Escarra, E. Escarra and J. Rault, *Principes de droit commercial*, t. 6, Paris, Sirey, 1936, nos. 1001–1002. The authors explain these failures as follows: 'general opinion is not yet ripe in this respect'. Indeed, by contrast, in Austria in 1872, and in Germany in 1882, *Caisses de dépôt collectif de titres*, the *Kassenvereine*, had already been created, on which see *ibid.*, nos. 994 et seq.; Haas, *Le virement et la compensation des titres en Allemagne*, thesis, Paris, 1932.

71 By the law of 18 June 1941 relating to the creation of a central securities deposit and transfer fund. On this law, see P. Didier, *Droit commercial*, t. 3, Paris, PUF, 1999, pp. 61 et seq.

72 Art. 26(1) of the Law No. 49-874 of 5 July 1949 on various economic and financial provisions.

73 Decree no. 49-1105 of 4 August 1949 taken for the application of Art. 26 modified of the law of 5 July 1949 and relating to the system of securities as well as to the modalities of liquidation of the central fund of deposits and transfers of securities (C.C.D.V.T.).

74 J. Hamel and G. Lagarde, *Traité de droit commercial*, Paris, Dalloz, 1956, no. 527, p. 647.

75 Art. 7(1) of the aforementioned decree: 'The affiliated establishments may only deliver to each other the securities paid into their current accounts or likely to be paid into them by means of a transfer made by the interprofessional body'. On this question see S. Torck, *Essai d'une théorie générale des droits réels sur choses fongibles*, Université Paris II Panthéon-Assas, 2001, no. 407.

76 To the extent that the deposit of securities with a central depository could perhaps be the basis for a new distinction within French companies, see F. Drummond, 'La société, l'actionnaire et le dépositaire central' in *Mélanges Philippe Merle*, 2012, pp. 199 et seq. On the history and importance of the central depository with regard to the status of securities, see *infra*, para. 648.

infrastructures. First, from the point of view of domestic law, it can be estimated that the three contemporary infrastructures, the trading, clearing and delivery systems for securities, were previously managed by the *Compagnie des agents de change*. The latter concentrated all the functions of the contemporary infrastructure within itself, which can be summarised as follows: trading, guaranteeing and paying. Although the three infrastructures continue to maintain close legal and economic links, reflecting the unity of these three infrastructures in the organisation of the financial markets, they are now three autonomous legal entities whose activities are subject to separate regulations and authorisations, and which may carry out activities outside the other two financial infrastructures.[77] Moreover, it is tempting to see in the contemporary market undertaking model the influence of the stockbrokers' corporation model. The similarities are striking: both make rules by which they organise the relationships between market members and with issuers; both also have a disciplinary facet with their members; both are subject to administrative supervision. However, these different aspects express less the singularity of a private or public model of the market operator[78] than the singularity of the organisation of a trading system.

45. From the international point of view, it is sometimes claimed that the connecting factor was the geographical location of the market. This statement is correct, but should be clarified by the following remark: a bond of allegiance existed between the state administration and the people in charge of the market through the status of the stockbrokers. This bond of allegiance extended to the organisation of negotiations and was the main criterion for the application of local law to the organisation of negotiations. Retrospectively, this second aspect appears to explain the traditional hold of administrative law on the matter and, consequently, the presentation of the organisation of the stock exchange. Thus, Professor Chemaly wrote in 1968:

> 'In view of the often mandatory nature of these regulations and the ever-increasing role of stock exchanges in the organisation of the financial market, it would appear that stock exchanges – and this is particularly true of securities exchanges – are tending to become semi-public services [...]. This has a twofold consequence for private international law: on the one hand, everything relating to the organisation and operation of these public markets, i.e. stock exchanges, is governed solely by French law, which applies as overriding mandatory provisions to the exclusion of any foreign law.'[79]

---

77 The clearing house can guarantee the execution of contracts that have not been concluded through a financial market. Finally, while the admission of securities to trading on a regulated market requires prior deposit with a central depository, the latter may also hold securities not admitted to trading on a regulated market.

78 Highlighting these two models, see P. Barban, *L'entreprise de marché*, *op. cit.*

79 See 'Bourses (de valeurs et de marchandise)' in R. Chemaly, *Rép. int. Dalloz*, 1968, no. 4. Even today, the presentation of the organisation of negotiations as a set of public law rules persists, see for example Mr Garcimartin Alferez who considers that 'This sector of the legal

In fact, the geographical connecting factor appeared to be rather decisive for the connecting factor of market operations, but this connecting factor took place because of the prior existence of an exchange organisation.[80] It was thus as if the administrative connecting factor of the manager was the basis for the connecting factor of the regulation of private transactions that the trading system made possible. As Professor d'Avout has written, 'This infrastructure is confronted, sooner or later, with the public order of territorial laws taking care, in addition to the systemic risks linked to the collective functioning of markets, of the typical interests of certain stakeholders in market operations'.[81] Nevertheless, the contemporary organisation of financial markets, by dissociating more radically, on the one hand, the status of the manager from the organisation of the systems and, on the other hand, the organisation of the systems from the operations that it allows to be concluded, has modified the configuration of the connecting factor of the infrastructure. It should be added here that, although there are often links of dependence between the connecting factor of the system and that of the operations it allows, this dependence is not absolute and, to the dissociation between the law of the manager and that of the system, a second dissociation may be added, between the law applicable to the operations allowed by the system, the law of the system, and the possible public order regime applicable to these operations.[82]

§ 2. THE CONTEMPORARY ORGANISATION OF FRENCH FINANCIAL MARKETS

The contemporary organisation of the French financial markets took off with the Act of 22 January 1988 which, by abrogating the status of stockbrokers, made it possible to distinguish between the financial market manager and the trading system itself (I). At the same time, the institutional environment evolved through the institution of a single regulatory authority competent to supervise both market managers and the operations permitted by the trading systems they operate (II).

---

system is characterized by a mixed nature: it encompasses rules of both a public-law and a private-law nature: a) the former are basically related to the organisation of the market; they deal with the constitution and the functioning of the capital market', F. Garcimartin Alferez, *Cross-border listed companies*, *op. cit.*, no. 69.

80 Already observe by Mr Chemaly, see *supra*, para. 27.

81 L. d'Avout, 'Les phénomènes collectifs et l'analyse macro en droit international privé', *op. cit.*

82 On the possible dissociation between the law of the system and the law of the transaction, see the example provided by the clearing of financial contracts within a clearing system, *infra*, para. 897 On the dissociation between the law of the system and the public policy regime applicable to transactions, see the example of part of the regulation of market transactions *infra*, nos. 466 et seq.

I. *Birth of Contemporary Financial Markets*

46. The rise of contemporary financial markets. From the French point of view, contemporary financial markets came into being with the law of 22 January 1988 on stock exchanges: it marked the end of the *numerus clausus* of stockbrokers,[83] and the correlative separation between access to the financial market and its ownership.[84] In retrospect, irrespective of developments in EU law, the end of the monopoly was brought about by the computerisation of quotation. The prior dematerialisation of securities[85] made continuous quotation possible and was the precondition for all the developments that led to the end of the monopoly.[86] This dematerialisation of trading venues, which already existed in part,[87] has become more systematic. The financial market 'venue' is now computerised and constitutes the material element of what EU law now calls trading platforms. In addition to this material element, i.e. the computerised systems through which buying and selling interests meet and of which the central order book is the determining element,[88] there is a legal element consisting of a body of rules governing the platform, known as trading rules or market rules. Trading is understood here as the process leading to the conclusion of an operation or transaction:[89] either a contract for the purchase or sale of financial securities or a financial contract.

---

83 This law follows the Pérouse report, M. Pérouse, *La modernisation des méthodes de cotation, d'échange et de conservation du marché des valeurs mobilières*, Paris, La Documentation française, 1980. The Compagnie nationale des agents de change was only established in 1966 with Law 66-1009 of 28 December 1966, *JORF* of 29 December 1966, p. 11622.. Stockbrokers meet in brokerage companies, which are subject to prudential obligations due to the nature of their activity, and which justify the legal monopoly still attached to their trading activity, each of these brokerage companies owning a share of the capital of the Société des bourses françaises, known as SBF, in proportion to the rights previously held as a stockbroker, See Art. 22 no. of the law of 22 January 1988 on stock exchanges, *JORF* of 23 January 1988, p. 1111. On this retrospective, P. Barban, *Les entreprises de marché*, *op. cit.*, no. 6, pp. 20 et seq.

84 Phenomenon known as 'demutualisation', on which see *ibid.*

85 *Ibid.* This is a manifestation of the intense interactions between the objects traded and the structure of the markets.

86 F. Muniesa, 'Contenir le marché, la transition de la criée à la cotation électronique à la bourse de Paris', *Sociologie du travail*, October-December 2005, vol. 47, pp. 485 et seq. From a legal point of view, the dematerialisation of financial securities took place through Art. 94(2) of the finance law of 30 December 1981, nos. 81-1160 (see *infra*, no. 652).

87 Mr Decugis already observed in 1941 that offers and requests could be made by written correspondence or even by telephone: 'The physical existence of a meeting place is therefore not essential for a market to exist in the legal sense of the term', H. Decugis, 'La loi du 28 février 1941 relative à la forme et à la négociation des actions', *Journal des sociétés*, 1941, p. 133.

88 For a description of the central order book, see J. Prorok, *La responsabilité civile sur les marchés financiers*, *op. cit.*, no. 551.

89 The definitions of market and system require that these 'interests are brought together in such a way that their meeting results in a contract, which is formed when execution takes place in accordance with the rules of the system or its internal protocols or operating

47. Different trading platforms. There are three platforms: regulated markets, multilateral trading facilities and organised trading systems.[90] These systems are not governed by the same rules, but they all have in common that they are multilateral[91] and aim to trade financial instruments. Regulated markets and multilateral trading facilities also have in common that they have non-discretionary rules,[92] i.e. the operator cannot arbitrarily alter the operation of the market.[93]

In contrast to these three systems, which constitute financial markets and whose function is to bring together multiple buying and selling interests, the 'internaliser' is a bilateral mechanism by which an investment firm directly

---

procedures', see Recital 7 of the MiFID Regulation, emphasis added; see already in this sense, T. Bonneau and F. Drummond, *Droit des marchés financiers*, *op. cit.*, no. 837-1. Other analyses of this phenomenon could have been envisaged, see Muller, *Droit des marchés financiers et droit des contrats*, *op. cit.*, no. 25. On the broader process of negotiation, see A. Couret, H. Le Nabasque *et al.*, *Droit financier*, *op. cit.*, nos. 109 et seq.

90 In the manner of the circular movement in the law of guarantee, where the use of certain guarantee is deemed excessive and leads to increased regulation by the legislator (B. Oppetit, 'Les tendances régressives dans l'évolution du droit contemporain' in *Mélanges dédiés à Dominique Holleaux*, Paris, Litec, 1990, p. 315), which prevents operators from using them, leading them to invent other ways of guaranteeing the credit they give, a circular movement is perceptible in financial market law. The emergence of one type of market leads to certain excesses in its operation, prompting the legislator to intervene by regulating access and the exercise of prerogatives on the market. These restrictive and prohibitive rules are then evaded by operators who try to use other types of platforms to avoid regulation. In still other cases, transactions take place outside any platform, over the counter. This phenomenon has not escaped the attention of the European legislator (who notes that 'under Directive 2004/39/EC, certain trading systems have developed that were not properly captured by the regulatory system. Any trading system for financial instruments [...] should in future be appropriately regulated and authorised as a multilateral trading facility or systematic internaliser'), which prompted it to create a new category of trading platform: the organised trading system (Art. 4(1)(23) of MiFID 2). The latter only allows trading in financial contracts, and has a minimal regime (see Recital 8 of the MiFID Regulation). This category has a residual purpose: it is intended to capture through it institutions that would escape the qualification of existing platforms. Its limitation is simply that it does not 'include systems where there is no real execution or organisation of transactions' (Recital 8 of the MiFID Regulation).

91 Recital 7 MiFID Regulation.

92 The concepts of 'regulated market' and 'multilateral trading facility' are aligned with each other 'to make it clear that they really do cover the same organised trading functions' (Recital 7 MiFID Regulation), in contrast to bilateral systems 'where an investment firm intervenes in each proprietary trade, even as an intermediary, without assuming any risk, between the buyer and the seller' (*ibid.*)

93 This rule does not apply to organised trading systems. However, this does not mean that the manager can trade on his own behalf within the trading system: such an option is still prohibited (Art. L. 420-2 of the Monetary and Financial Code). This rule is historical, since it was a fundamental rule for stockbrokers not to intervene in their own name in negotiations (see *infra*, para. 454; The question had been the subject of evolution, see P.-H. Conac, *La régulation des marchés boursiers par la commission des opérations de bourse [COB] et la securities and exchange commission [SEC]*, *op. cit.*, no. 221). On the other hand, such intervention on own account is possible for systematic internalisers.

contracts for the order of one of its clients.[94] In other words, the internaliser itself fulfils its client's orders instead of presenting them to the market. The process is therefore characterised by two factors: on the one hand, it matches orders directly[95] and, on the other, it can act as a co-contractor.[96] Its name derives precisely from these two aspects; it is said to be systematic because of the regularity with which it acts as counterparty to its clients' orders.[97] The distinction between internalisers and financial markets makes it possible to highlight the primary functions of the market: the collective discovery of the price of the objects that are traded there; the ability to offer each seller a buyer, and vice versa.[98] This latter purpose, also expressed by the economic notion of 'liquidity', is nevertheless linked to the former: it is through the multiplicity of sales of securities that the value of the object sold can be determined.[99] The inability to reflect a price that is acceptable or that expresses an unquestionable balance between supply and demand would indicate its irrelevance and justify the use of OTC.

48. Relationship between trading platforms and managers. The financial market is managed by the person operating it, who is referred to as a financial market manager. A distinction is made between investment firms, which operate exclusively multilateral or organised trading systems, and the market operator,[100] which is known under French law as an '*entreprise de marché*' and operates a

---

94 Art. 4(1)(20) MiFID 2. The distinction between financial markets, which are characterised by the multilateralism of the interests involved, and the systematic internaliser, which is fundamentally based on a bilateral mechanism, has been highlighted by Professor Daigre, see J.-J. Daigre, 'L'évolution de la notion de marché financier', *op. cit.*

95 Matching refers to the phenomenon of order matching in the computer system. There is no central order book and no global order matching system in the internaliser hypothesis.

96 J.-J. Daigre, 'L'évolution de la notion de marché financier', *op. cit.* This ability to intervene in negotiations is strictly prohibited for financial market managers (Art. L. 420-2 of the Monetary and Financial Code). These characteristics also explain why the management of a multilateral trading facility is exclusive of that of a systematic internaliser, so that the manager respects the philosophy underlying Art. 20(4) of the MiFID II Directive aimed at preventing conflicts of interest, cf. ESMA document, *Questions and answer on MiFID II and MiFIR market structures topics*, 14 November 2018, ESMA70-872942901-38, pp. 37–38.

97 Art. 4(1)(20) MiFID 2.

98 F. Garcimartin Alferez, *Cross-border listed companies*, *op. cit.*, no. 67: 'The two core functions of stock markets are usually summarised as (i) the provision of liquidity and (ii) accurate pricing'.

99 In this sense, systematic internalisers are an obstacle to this discovery since, in this hypothesis, it is within the intermediary's accounts that the transfers take place, and the market does not benefit from the information as to the transfer price; it may already be noted that this need to discover the price also explains why recent financial regulations provide for a trading obligation for shares admitted to trading on a regulated market or traded on a trading platform, with possible exemptions (on which see *infra*, para. 438).

100 Art. 4(1)(18) MiFID 2.

regulated market.[101] In order to satisfy its clients, a market operator will often offer several types of trading systems. This distinction between the operator and the market led to a preliminary question before the Court of Justice of the European Union[102] on whether the absorption of the manager of an organised trading system by the operator of a regulated market would confer the status of regulated market on the trading platform of the former. The Court of Justice answered in the negative, since these were two separate issues: a market undertaking may operate several trading systems, only some of which qualify as regulated markets.[103]

49. It should be added here that the function of investment firms is not limited to the management of certain financial markets. Indeed, the status of investment firm was created by the Investment Services Directive and is now governed by MiFID 2. The purpose of the former was to create a harmonised status for firms active in the investment services sector in order to enable them to exercise the European freedoms effectively, in particular the freedom to provide services and the freedom of establishment.[104] The objective was the unification of the internal market. This explains why the qualification of investment firm

---

[101] Arts. L. 412-1 et seq. of the Monetary and Financial Code. MiFID has created some confusion about the distinction between the operator and the market by stating that 'the market operator may be the regulated market itself' (Art. 4(13)°MiFID, Art. 4(18)°MiFID 2). No doubt European law takes into account the diversity of situations in the European Union, with specialists observing that 'there may be markets set up as autonomous entities that govern themselves, markets set up as entities but operated by separate groupings, and markets that have no legal personality but are owned and operated by a market undertaking' (J.-J. Daigre, 'L'évolution de la notion de marché financier', *op. cit.)* This seems to be the case in other European legal orders: if the regulated market is an autonomous entity, then there is confusion between the body that governs the market and manages it, and the financial market, which is a trading system that allows buying and selling interests to meet. Thus, even if the market is constituted within a *trust*, which seems to be the purpose of Mr Daigre's first hypotheses, the *trustees* have, in this particular hypothesis, functions equivalent to the manager of a commercial company under private law and there is indeed a distinction between the financial market, a system allowing the confrontation of opposing orders, and its manager. Admittedly, such a distinction does not involve the legal personality of private law as we understand it, but this does not mean that the market is self-exploiting. In the same way that if it constitutes the sole asset of a legal person, the market is not self-exploiting, if it is the sole asset of an unincorporated entity, it is not self-exploiting either.

[102] Case C-248/11, *Nilas*, *BJB*, ECLI:EU:C:2012:166, para. 111, p. 248, n. T. Bonneau; *Europe*, 2012, n° 5, comm. 193 F. Gazin; *Dr. Sociétés*, 2012, no. 106, p. 27, note S. Torck; *Option finance*, 2012, no. 1172, p. 27, comm. B. Zabala.

[103] It is the recognition of the system by the competent authority that gives a trading system the status of a regulated market. In France, the Minister of the Economy (Art. L. 421-6 of the Monetary and Financial Code), on the proposal of the AMF (Art. L. 421-5 of the Monetary and Financial Code; on this procedure, see P. Barban, *Les entreprises de marché, op. cit.*) It recognises the status of regulated market for a financial market by decree. See most recently the order of 5 February 2014 recognising the status of regulated market for financial instruments for the Powernext Derivatives market managed by Powernext SA.

[104] See the list of investment services established by Art. L. 321-1 of the Monetary and Financial Code.

has the function of allowing access to an activity and is independent of the legal form that these firms take;[105] it grants them a monopoly on the provision of investment services on a regular basis. This function is likely to reflect the importance of investment firms in relation to market infrastructures: on the one hand, investment firms can obtain access to market infrastructures; on the other hand, all intermediation services between the investor and the trading platform are investment services; finally, the management of certain trading platforms, multilateral and organised trading facilities, is considered an investment service.

50. Securities markets and futures markets. From the point of view of trading platforms, a distinction is still made within the various contemporary trading systems between two types of markets depending on the instruments traded: securities markets[106] and futures markets.[107] Not all trading platforms can accommodate these different instruments,[108] and it is possible for a market operator to offer only one of these two markets.[109] Securities markets are reserved for financial securities, while futures markets only allow for the conclusion of financial contracts.[110] Futures markets have developed considerably due to the growth and diversification of financial contracts. They now make it possible to transfer the risks inherent in very different objects in order to insure against variations[111] of a monetary value[112] or shareholding,[113] but also of commodities,[114]

105 For this reason, investment firms may have different legal forms in different Member States, which may or may not have legal personality. While investment firms were traditionally required to have a 'legal form appropriate' for the provision of investment services (see Arts. L. 532-2(5) and L. 532-3(2) of the Monetary and Financial Code), this requirement has disappeared. The ACPR nevertheless considered that the legal form of a simplified joint stock company was not necessarily compatible with the status of investment firm, see ACP Position 2014-P-04. On this issue, see F. Drummond, *Droit financier*, *op. cit.*, no. 549.

106 The particularity of securities lies in the duality of the markets: one is called primary, in the sense that it is the first acquisition of a security after its issue by the legal person, and the other secondary, where the securities, once acquired, can be traded.

107 Respectively the subject of Chapters 4 and 5 of the Euronext Market Rules (Book I).

108 Thus, organised trading systems cannot allow the exchange of shares, on the origin of this restriction, see F. Drummond, *Droit financier*, *op. cit.*, no. 981.

109 In practice today, only Euronext provides both markets, as it is the only market operator with a securities market.

110 This is the term in the civil law sense, see F. Drummond, 'Le contrat comme instrument financier' in *Mélanges François Terré*, Paris, PUF, 1991 pp. 661 et seq.; A. Gaudemet, *Les dérivés*, *op. cit.*, nos. 31 et seq.

111 The amplitude of the variations is referred to in finance as *volatility*. The economic use of a financial contract is precisely to insure against this volatility, so as not to suffer any depreciation. This means that one will not benefit from any appreciation.

112 Swap contract, on which see A. Gaudemet, *Les dérivés*, *op. cit.*, nos. 71 et seq.

113 Stock options, *ibid.*

114 Today, commodities are traded on the Chicago financial market and are subject to high volatility, linked to a multitude of factors – climatic and geopolitical among others – which make financial contracts on them almost indispensable.

or even of a set of shares.[115] Indeed, exactly one hundred years after exempting futures markets from the gambling exception, the legislator extended the benefit of this derogation to interest rate futures,[116] then to index and currency futures.[117] The possibilities offered by contractual freedom and human imagination give rise to almost infinite combinations of financial contracts. The existence of financial markets specialising in the exchange of securities or contracts has not prevented them from being supplied independently of the market itself.[118]

II. The Emergence of the 'Autorité des marchés financiers' *(AMF)*

51. The institution of a regulatory authority. The difficulties specific to the financial markets as an institution are increasingly distinguished from the specific problems raised by market operations, i.e. transactions carried out between private individuals using the trading system.[119] Indeed, two supervisory authorities were set up for each of these aspects: the Stock Exchange Committee created by the Act of 14 February 1942,[120] and the '*Commission des opérations de bourse*' (COB) created by an order of 28 September 1967.[121] The purpose of

115 Some index derivatives (such as the CAC 40) can be used to insure against the general devaluation of a group of securities linked to the same country.

116 Law No. 85-695 of 11 July 1985 on various economic and financial provisions.

117 Law No. 91-716 of 26 July 1991 on various economic and financial provisions.

118 As far as contracts are concerned, their OTC conclusion has been facilitated by the important contractual standardisation to which a specialised trade association, the *International Swap and Derivatives Association (ISDA)*, has made a major contribution. Nevertheless, today, OTC financial contracts must, like transactions taking place on the financial markets, be guaranteed by the clearing house because of the importance of the risk they may carry. The scope of transactions legally subject to the clearing obligation exceeds the scope of contracts concluded by a financial market alone, see *infra*, para. 870.

119 They are thus the subject of separate studies, see already very clearly in the *Répertoire Niboyet-Lapradelle*, Paris, Sirey, 1929, vol. 2, the two separate studies by Amieux at the entries 'Agent de Change' (the stock exchange institution is then still closely linked to the status of the stockbroker) and 'Bourse (opérations de)'. It was not until Mr Chemaly's study that the link between the two was made, see *supra*, para. 27; 47.

120 To which should be added, for the supervision of futures markets, the Futures Market Council. Because of their similar purpose, the two will merge to become the '*Conseil des Marchés financiers*'. The appearance of this authority put an end to the possible conflicts of interest of the *Chambre syndicale* which had, in a self-regulatory perspective, disciplinary powers (Art. 3 of the ordinance of 29 May 1816), on this point, see B. Gizard and J.-P. Deschanel, 'Déontologie financière et pouvoir disciplinaire' in *Mélanges AEBDF III*, Banque Éditeur, 2001, pp. 157 et seq., spec. p. 158; P.-H. Conac, *La régulation des marchés boursiers par la commission des opérations de bourse (COB) et la securities and exchange commission (SEC)*, *op. cit.*, no. 138.

121 Ordinance n° 67-833 of 28 September 1967 establishing a stock exchange commission and relating to the information of holders of securities and the disclosure of certain stock exchange transactions. The two institutions have now been merged into the Financial Markets Authority. On the creation of the COB, see P.-H. Conac, *La régulation des marchés boursiers par la commission des opérations de bourse (COB) et la securities and exchange commission (SEC)*, *op. cit.*, no. 23.

the former is to supervise the activities of stockbrokers and dealers in order to eliminate underground markets, and is composed of professionals from the sector.[122] The COB, inspired by the Securities and Exchange Commission (SEC),[123] is on the other hand 'responsible for monitoring the information provided to security holders and the public on companies making public offerings and on the securities issued by these companies, as well as for ensuring the proper functioning of stock exchanges'.[124] The need to monitor market operations is linked to the imperfections of a market that is not spontaneously pure and perfect. If it does become so and allows the discovery of the fairest possible

---

The distinct functions of the two bodies, the most blatant manifestation of the duality between stock market operations and the stock market institution, are nevertheless porous: this is the case for the admission of companies' securities to official listing, which was successively the responsibility of the stockbrokers' company, the stock exchange committee and then that of the Commission des opérations de bourse, only to be transferred again to the market undertaking, in a notable circularity, see Art. L. 421-14(I) of the Monetary and Financial Code. This issue is both an instrument for protecting local savings and a central element of the organisation of the stock market, since it is a condition for the latter (no admission, no market), and it clearly shows that the two orders – private transactions and institutional issues – come together.

122 This allows securities dealers to obtain not only a legal structure, but also a legal monopoly on over-the-counter trading.

123 P.-H. Conac, *La régulation des marchés boursiers par la commission des opérations de bourse (COB) et la securities and exchange commission (SEC)*, *op. cit.*, nos. 23 et seq. The COB staff even went so far as to make a trip to the United States to observe the practices and mechanisms put in place by the *SEC*, see *ibid.* The COB nevertheless differs from the *SEC* for institutional reasons: the latter is controlled by the legislative branch in the United States (*ibid.*, no. 17), on which it is closely dependent, in particular in order to limit the powers of the executive branch in a dynamic separation of powers. In addition, the interpretation of securities laws is carried out by the federal courts themselves, which are perfectly independent of the executive branch. The same is not quite true of the AMF. It is true that the COB was created to compensate for the negligence of the Treasury and to prevent the government from interfering too much in the administration of the stock market (*ibid.*, no. 23). However, it should be noted that its governance depends not on lawyers, but on administrators from the state civil service. In contrast, the advantage of the competence of European bodies in banking matters lies in the lack of complacency of European courts. As Mr Synvet writes: 'No complacency *(of the European court)* can be found with regard to the ECB. This is a far cry from the consanguinity between the Conseil d'État, the college of the ACPR and the sanctions committee, which sometimes raises doubts about the degree of objectivity guaranteed by the French repressive system'. H. Synvet, *D.* 2019. 2085. This difference in governance is significant, because the close control that Congress exercises over the *SEC* justifies the concentration of powers it enjoys (P.-H. Conac, *La régulation des marchés boursiers par la commission des opérations de bourse [COB] et la securities and exchange commission [SEC]*, *op. cit.*, no. 21). In addition, the SEC does not have a sanctions committee: at best, it can only act as a prosecuting authority.

124 Art. 1 of the above-mentioned Order. This means that the competence of the AMF in relation to prospectuses is not new. It should also be noted here that the admission of foreign securities has always been the responsibility of the Ministry of Finance.

price, it is through the institution of specific rules.[125] In particular, two kinds of information-related difficulties prevent the proper functioning of the financial market and justify the intervention of the COB.[126]

52. The first difficulty lies in the anonymity of the market, which allows an operator or a group of operators to acquire the capital of a company without declaring it, and to take control of a company without having to acquire all the shares issued by the company or to pay the control premium. These procedures affect the reliability of the price determination mechanism, and leave managers and minority shareholders in a delicate situation, from which the corporate legal mechanisms do not necessarily allow them to escape. For this reason, obligations to declare the crossing of thresholds and to file a public offer have been introduced by the Company of Stockbrokers.[127] These obligations are monitored and sanctioned by the COB.[128] The second set of difficulties lies in the evolution of stock market investors, increasingly marked by the dominant presence of institutional investors rather than that of 'small holders'.[129] Such a change exposes the often decried illusion of market atomicity, of which the stock market would have been the paradigm. Not all market players, by their very position, have the same degree of access to information, and some of them are likely to make a gain deemed illegitimate by breaking the conditions of equality between investors. Once again, such actions affect the credibility of the price determination mechanism,[130] and have been qualified as market abuse. Their prohibition has been developed through the prohibition of price manipulation, and also, with regard to the possession of privileged information, through the creation of insider trading. The prosecution of these abuses, which may be punished by criminal penalties, has also been entrusted to the COB.[131]

The role of information is not confined to the financial markets, but permeates all financial instruments law, where it has various descriptive or predictive functions.[132] The purpose of these disclosure requirements, when

---

125 It would be excessive to consider that the supervision of market rules dates from the COB. Indeed, because they involved the very purpose of price determination by the market, they were the object of the attention of the Compagnie des agents de change, which compiled the rules in their manual.

126 The central role of information in the regulation of financial markets explains the important work on this issue, see A. Sotiropoulou, *Les obligations d'information des sociétés cotées en droit de l'Union européenne*, Brussels, Larcier, 2012; J. Chacornac, *Essai sur les fonctions de l'information en droit des instruments financiers*, Paris, Dalloz, 2014.

127 P.-J. Lehmann, *Histoire de la bourse de paris*, *op. cit.*, pp. 91–92.

128 On this legislative package, see *infra*, paras. 466 et seq.

129 *Ibid.*

130 This statement has long been accepted, and is not new: it was part of the justification for prohibiting stockbrokers from acting on their behalf. Indeed, they were the recipients of *privileged* information about the state of the market.

131 On these aspects, see *infra*, paras. 541 et seq.

132 We owe this demonstration to the thesis of J. Chacornac, *Essai sur les fonctions de l'information en droit des instruments financiers*, *op. cit.*

they are intended to protect residents, is to provide investors with the means to understand the nature of the proposed instrument; this usually justifies the intervention of the regulatory authority, as in the case of prospectuses, the authorisation of which is subject to its approval. Regulatory oversight of private transactions extends beyond the financial market. At the beginning of the 21st century, the supervision of the stock exchange institution – which is exercised over both the trading system and the manager – and of market operations is entrusted to the same authority, the *Autorité des marchés financiers* (AMF).[133] A significant part of the industry is therefore subject to the authority's supervision. However, the AMF is not the only authority responsible for authorising infrastructure managers, and must work in conjunction with the '*Autorité de contrôle prudentiel et de résolution*' (ACPR).

53. The French national authorities. Paradoxically, the AMF is not the competent authority for granting market operator authorisation. Indeed, the status of regulated market manager is linked to ministerial recognition of the trading platform, in the preparation of which the AMF nevertheless has a leading role. In addition, the managers of other trading platforms may be investment firms, whose authorisation is entrusted to the ACPR, although, again, the AMF will have a role in granting authorisation. However, it will exercise direct supervision over these managers. In fact, the AMF only grants authorisation to central securities depositories,[134] since the authorisation of clearing houses is also entrusted to the ACPR.[135] The latter authority was created in 2010.[136] It was created by merging a set of French committees with separate competences for the supervision and conduct of business rules of credit institutions, insurance companies and, in some respects, investment firms.[137] In 2013, the then *Autorité*

---

[133] Law No. 2006-706 of 1 August 2003 on financial security, see P.-H. Conac, 'La fusion de la COB et du CMF' in *Mélanges AEBDF-France III*, Banque Editeur, 2001, pp. 59 et seq.

[134] Art. L. 441-1 of the Monetary and Financial Code.

[135] Art. L. 612-2 of the Monetary and Financial Code.

[136] Ruling 2010-76 of 21 January 2010 merging the banking and insurance licensing and supervisory authorities, ratified by Act 2010-1249 of 22 October 2010 on banking and financial regulation. The ACP was inspired by the proposals in the so-called 'Deletré' report (B. Deletré, J. Azoulay and P. Dugos, *Report of the advisory mission on the supervision of compliance with professional obligations towards customers in the financial sector*, July 2009).

[137] In 1984, several supervisory committees were established by the French legislature: the '*Comité de la réglementation bancaire*' (CRB), the '*Comité des établissements de crédit*' (CEC), which is responsible for authorisation, the '*Commission bancaire*' and the '*Conseil national du crédit*'. The CRB's regulatory powers and the CEC's authorisation powers were subsequently extended to investment firms, and the National Credit Council's jurisdiction was extended to securities. The first two authorities were then integrated into the *Comité consultatif de la législation et de la réglementation financière*, and the *Conseil national du crédit et du titre* into the *Comité consultatif du secteur financier*. This integration led to the creation of the *Autorité de contrôle prudentiel*, which was given not only the powers of the above-mentioned authorities, but also, for the banking sector, the powers of the CECEI

de contrôle prudentiel was given resolution powers over credit institutions,[138] in anticipation of the transposition of the Resolution Directive.[139] Since 2017, the ACPR, which is attached to the *Banque de France*,[140] has the particularity of no longer being an independent administrative authority. Indeed, it appeared to be too dependent on the *Banque de France*, of which it could be considered as a simple directorate.[141] However, it retains most of the characteristics of an independent administrative authority.[142]

54. Judicial review of authorities. The individual decisions of these authorities are subject to judicial review. As regards the AMF, the criterion for allocating appeal procedures depends on the status of the person affected: if the person is a person referred to in Article L. 621-9(II) of the Monetary and Financial Code,[143] i.e. most regulated professionals, from investment firms to infrastructure managers, the court with jurisdiction over the appeal is the *Conseil d'État*. For other persons, it will be the Paris Court of Appeal.[144] In addition to individual decisions, the AMF's administrative acts, like any other administrative act, may be appealed to the *Conseil d'État* on grounds of abuse of power. The *Conseil d'État* recently had the opportunity to include in its review of this appeal the 'opinions, recommendations, warnings and position statements' that traditionally constitute the AMF's 'doctrine'.[145] This decision, no doubt inspired by the decision of the *United Kingdom v. ECB* of the European Court of Justice,[146] 'thwarts the practice, all too common among regulators, of compelling in fact and pretending in law to limit itself to recommending'.[147] The ACPR's decisions are subject exclusively

---

and the *Commission bancaire*, and for the insurance sector, the powers of the *Autorité de contrôle des assurances et des mutuelles* and the *Comité des entreprises d'assurance*. On these authorities and their history, see T. Bonneau, *Droit bancaire*, 13th ed., Paris, Dalloz, no. 172.

138 Law No. 2013-672 of 26 July 2013 on the separation and regulation of banking activities.

139 On which see *infra*, para. 103.

140 The fact that it is attached to the *Banque de France* means that it has the resources provided by the *Banque de France* and that it is composed of staff whose employer is the *Banque de France*, see T. Bonneau, *Droit bancaire*, *op. cit.*

141 N. Mathey, 'Regulator: status of the ACPR', *RDBF*, March-April 2017, comm. No. 46.

142 T. Bonneau, *Droit bancaire*, *op. cit.*, no. 175.

143 This list concerns persons whose professional obligations are subject to supervision by the *Autorité des marchés financiers*.

144 Art. R. 631-45 I° by application of Art. L. 621-30 of the Monetary and Financial Code. The jurisdiction of the Paris Court of Appeal is explained for what seems to be a contingent reason, which is due to the success of this court in dealing with anti-competitive litigation which it has been dealing with for several years, acting as a court of appeal against the decisions of the Competition Council, see P.-H. Conac, *La régulation des marchés boursiers par la Commission des opérations de bourse (COB) et la Securities and exchange commission (SEC)*, *op. cit.*, no. 95, p. 122, note 4.

145 CE, Assemblée, 21 March 2016, *Société Fairvesta International GMBH et autres*, No. 368082.

146 Case T-496/11, *UK v. ECB*, ECLI:EU:T:2015:133. This judgment is studied *infra*, para. 245.

147 H. Synvet, *supra* note under *UK v. ECB*. The judgment concerned the ECB, but this is a frequent technique of regulatory authorities. In banking matters, the EBA has attempted, by way of guidance, to regulate the governance and supervision of retail banking products, even

to review by the *Conseil d'État*, which has jurisdiction over the decisions of the ACPR's colleges,[148] but also over appeals against the decisions of its sanctions committee.[149]

55. Articulation of the material scope of application of internal authorities. The entanglement here concerns both the material competence of the *Autorité des marchés financiers* and the *Autorité de contrôle prudentiel et de résolution*, but also the articulation between the competence of the ACPR and that of the European regulator, the ECB. With regard to the articulation of internal material competences, the interactions are governed by the Monetary and Financial Code, which states that

> 'the ACPR shall supervise the investment services business of the persons mentioned in 1° and 2°, subject to the competence of the Autorité des marchés financiers to supervise rules of conduct and other professional obligations'.[150]

In other words, the ACPR supervises investment service activities, while the AMF remains responsible for supervising conduct of business rules and professional obligations.[151] The division is more delicate during the authorisation procedure, where genuine cooperation is established between the authorities: the ACPR is responsible for granting authorisation,[152] but must forward the authorisation application to the AMF so that the latter can approve the programme of operations provided by the applicant.[153] Similarly, the coordination of a financial conglomerate is likely to require coordinated supervision by the authorities.[154] These rules explain why the ACPR and the AMF have set up a joint unit responsible for coordination.[155] The implementation of this coordination was done through an agreement between

---

though it has no competence in this area, see Case C-911/19, *FBF*, ECLI:EU:C:2021:599 (the Advocate General had concluded that the measures were invalid, but the Court validated them).

148 Art. R. 311-4 of the Code of Administrative Justice.

149 Art. L. 612-16(III) of the Monetary and Financial Code.

150 Art. L. 512-2 of the Monetary and Financial Code.

151 This also means that the ACPR does not supervise portfolio management companies, financial analysts or financial investment advisers, as these activities are subject to AMF supervision, see Th. Bonneau *et al.*, *Droit financier*, *op. cit.*, no. 222.

152 Art. L. 532-1 of the Monetary and Financial Code. This explains why the authorisation file must be sent to the ACPR (Art. R. 532-1 of the Monetary and Financial Code).

153 In certain cases, especially when the subsidiary is a direct or indirect subsidiary of an investment firm or credit institution with its headquarters in another Member State, the ACPR must consult the authority of the Member State in which the parent company is established (see Art. R. 532-5 of the Monetary and Financial Code, and the procedure in Art. 84(1) of MiFID 2). However, this is already addressing the mechanisms of intra-European cooperation.

154 Art. L. 633-1 of the Monetary and Financial Code.

155 This is a legal requirement, detailed in Art. L. 612-47 of the Monetary and Financial Code.

the authorities.[156] The French legislator has also given these two authorities the power to conclude cooperation agreements with authorities from third countries.[157] In addition to this internal and international coordination, since the introduction of a single supervisory mechanism for credit institutions in the European Union, there has been the need for coordination between the ACPR and the competent European authority, the ECB.[158]

56. Section conclusion. These developments have made it possible to trace the origin of financial markets, and to observe that market infrastructures were previously unified within the corporation of stockbrokers (*Compagnie des agents de change)*, whose administrative status gave a particular imperative to the organisation of trading. The contemporary configuration of the international connecting factor has evolved due to the dissociation between the market manager and the trading system. This dissociation takes place in the same terms between clearing houses and central depositories, on the one hand, and securities clearing and settlement systems on the other. The particularity of the contemporary connecting factor lies in the disappearance of the necessary correlation between the connecting factor of the manager and that of the system. Similarly, there are no unbreakable links between the transactions concluded by the systems and the law of the system itself. At the same time, the legal orders have gradually established specialised administrative authorities, the AMF and the ACPR, whose overlapping powers to authorise and supervise the systems operated and the transactions they allow make coordination necessary. In addition to this internal coordination, there is also coordination at the EU level.

SECTION 2. THE EUROPEAN INSTITUTIONAL CONFIGURATION

57. The two aspects of the European institutional path. The European institutional path consists of two aspects. The first is the centralisation of decision-making in monetary matters, through the original model of the European System of Central Banks. The establishment of this system was made possible by the exclusive competence of the Union over the monetary policy of the Member States whose currency is the euro,[159] and deserves to be studied for two reasons. First, because

---

156 Agreement between the *Autorité des marchés financiers* and the *Autorité de contrôle prudentiel* of 30 April 2010, concluded on the basis of Art. L. 612-49 of the Monetary and Financial Code.

157 Art. L. 632-7 of the Monetary and Financial Code.

158 Indeed, as far as credit institutions are concerned, decisions on authorisation and withdrawal of authorisation, as well as notifications of acquisition and disposal of qualifying holdings, fall within the competence of the ECB, see Article 4(1)(a) and (c) of the MSU Regulation, on which see *infra*, para. 177.

159 Art. 3(c) TFEU.

its coordination mechanisms inspired the banking supervision model applicable to infrastructure managers licensed as credit institutions. Indeed, in both cases, the supervisory model is based on the decision-making competence of the ECB, combined with a mechanism for deconcentrating its implementation. Second, because the ECB supervises payment systems. Payment systems are necessary for the proper functioning of market infrastructures, both for clearing systems and for securities settlement systems.

The second aspect of the European institutional pathway is the evolution of the coordination of authorities in matters traditionally devolved to the Member States: banking, investment services and insurance law. In this area, the Union does not have exclusive competence. However, it has been able to intervene by means of a directive on the basis of its competence to 'conciliate' legislation.[160] This conciliation has been associated at the institutional level with 'comitology', allowing regulators to meet in order to contribute to the drafting of implementing acts entrusted to the Commission in the context of harmonisation directives. However, the committees were transformed into a European supervisory authority in the wake of the subprime crisis. This institutional evolution has been accompanied by a significant delegation of powers, adding to the coordination function of the Member States' regulators a direct supervision function for certain operators, and even intervention within the markets themselves. The conciliation of legislation also served as a basis for the establishment of a European resolution authority, the Single Resolution Board (SRB), which implements resolution law in the territory of the Member States adhering to the Single Resolution Mechanism (SRM). The latter was set up as an echo of the Single Supervisory Mechanism (SSM), based on a TFEU provision on monetary policy.[161] These two hypotheses reflect initially distinct institutional solutions, with the European Supervisory Authorities continuing a decentralised model by other means, while the SSM and SRM authorities are endowed with decision-making powers. These two models are now tending to converge.

58. Influence on the connecting factor of infrastructure. These two aspects of the European institutional pathway both influence the connecting factor of market infrastructures, either in terms of their manager or in terms of the market infrastructure itself. Indeed, the European System of Central Banks has an oversight function over payment systems that has given it a central role in the coordination of payment and securities settlement systems, as well as attempting to extend its oversight to securities clearing and delivery systems. The MSU and MRU authorities are directly responsible for supervising infrastructure managers whenever they are licensed as credit institutions and may, in certain cases, be the competent authorities. In addition, some European supervisory authorities

[160] Art. 114 TFEU.
[161] Art. 127(6) TFEU.

directly supervise market infrastructure support providers, such as credit-rating agencies or trade repositories. These observations, which will be the subject of a separate study,[162] explain why it is necessary, as a preliminary step, to study the institutional mechanisms put in place in the monetary field (§ 1), before examining the evolution of supervision in the field of investment services and banking law (§ 2).

§ 1. THE EUROPEAN SYSTEM OF CENTRAL BANKS

59. The European System of Central Banks and the Eurosystem.[163] Monetary law is undoubtedly one of the first laws to have undergone a strong institutionalisation with the advent of central banks, as well as the influence of a European law in which the Union has, moreover, an exclusive competence.[164] Indeed, the institution of a single currency in Europe managed by the European System of Central Banks (hereinafter 'ESCB'), associated with the creation of a European Central Bank (hereinafter 'ECB'), definitely triggered a singular coordination of the national central banks of the Member States that adopted the single currency.

The ESCB consists of all national central banks (hereinafter 'NCBs') and the European Central Bank. However, in the Treaties, the ESCB covers two realities: in a broad sense, it refers to the ECB and all the NCBs as a whole, and in a narrow sense, to the ECB and the NCBs that have adopted the euro.[165] When the ESCB performs the latter function, it is, since the Lisbon Treaty, referred to as the Eurosystem.[166] It is only in the latter respect that the ESCB performs the four tasks assigned to it by Article 127(2) TFEU: monetary policy, issuance and overall management of the euro, management of the official foreign reserves of the Member States and promotion of the smooth operation of payment systems. The originality of the system put in place is that the central banking function is not formally entrusted to the centralised institution, in this case the European Central Bank, but to the ESCB understood as the Eurosystem.[167] As regards the ESCB in the broad sense, it does not have exclusive competence,

---

162 See *infra*, paras. 244 et seq.

163 On the history of the foundation of the monetary union, see E. Mourlon-Druol, 'History of an incomplete EMU' in F. Amtenbrink and C. Hermann (eds.), *The EU law of Economic and Monetary Union*, Oxford, OUP, 2020, nos. 2.1 et seq.

164 Since 1 January 1999, the European Union has had exclusive competence 'in the field of monetary policy and exchange rate policy for the Member States whose currency is the euro', see Art. 3(4) TFEU.

165 Opinion CON/2003/20, 19 September 2003, para. 14, [2003] OJ C 229, p. 7.

166 Art. 282(1) TFEU; Art. 1 of the Statute of the ESCB. On this name, see S. Adalid, *La Banque centrale européenne et l'Eurosystème*, Brussels, Bruylant, 2015, nos. 87–89.

167 Professor Martucci notes that the English distinction between 'central bank' and 'central banking' may be helpful here: thus, the Commission's proposal to entrust the central banking function to a Community institution was not retained, but also entrusted to the

but only co-ordination competence in foreign exchange matters. However, it should be added that the dialogue with Member States that have not adopted the euro is also conducted under the aegis of the ECB.[168]

Finally, from the point of view of sources, in addition to the provisions of the TFEU, two texts are of particular importance: the Statute of the ESCB and of the ECB, and the Guideline of the European Central Bank on monetary policy instruments and procedures of the Eurosystem (hereinafter the Guideline on monetary policy instruments and procedures).[169]

60. Functioning of the Eurosystem. The Eurosystem consists of the ECB and the NCBs whose currency is the euro. The ECB is a European institution,[170] governed by two bodies: an Executive Board, which is permanent and administers the ECB on a daily basis, and a Governing Council.[171] The Executive Board is a management body whose task is to 'implement' the monetary policy guidelines and instructions of the Governing Council.[172] The Governing Council is the decision-making body, composed of the governors of the national central banks and the Executive Board. This Council constitutes the centre of monetary power: it is the author of the normative acts governing the Eurosystem, determines

European System of *Central Banks*, showing that the central banking function is entrusted to the ESCB as a whole, see F. Martucci, 'European System of Central Banks - European Central Bank and Eurosystem - Organisation', *Jcl. Europe*, fasc. 243, 2019, nos. 7–8.

168 There is therefore no monetary equivalent of the European Banking Authority in the field of banking. Indeed, the European Central Bank succeeded the European Monetary Institute, whose mission was to prepare for economic and monetary union, and which had itself replaced the Committee of Central Bank Governors and the European Monetary Cooperation Fund, see *ibid.*

169 Guideline of the European Central Bank of 20 September 2011 on monetary policy instruments and procedures of the Eurosystem (recast) (ECB/2011/14). From a source perspective, it should be noted that this Guideline reflects more than the mere organisational power of the ECB over the NCBs that the Guidelines are intended to embody, see S. Adalid, *The European Central Bank and the Eurosystem*, *op. cit.*, no. 481.

170 A source of controversy (for details, see *ibid.*, nos. 97 et seq.), the classification as a Community institution is no longer discussed since the Court of Justice unambiguously affirmed it in its *OLAF* judgment (Case C-11/00, *Comm. v. ECB*, ECLI:EU:C:2003:395). This qualification has important consequences for the ECB's legal regime; it should simply be noted here that it also entails the jurisdiction of the Court of Justice. This jurisdiction may be extended to all contractual disputes, whether private or public, which the ECB may be called upon to hear through the inclusion of a clause in the contract in question. This clause is qualified by the Statute of the ESCB as an 'arbitration clause', it appears rather as a jurisdictional clause (the competent national courts will hear the dispute in the absence of this clause), see Art. 35 of the Statute of the ESCB.

171 A third body, the 'General Council', exists and is composed of the President and Vice-President of the ECB and the governors of the national central banks of all Member States (Art. 44(1) of the ESCB Statute).

172 Art. 12.1(2) of the ESCB Statute. The Executive Board consists of a President, a Vice-President and four members of the ECB (Art. 11.1 of the Statute of the ESCB).

the monetary policy of the Eurosystem,[173] and has real organisational and management power over the Eurosystem.[174] The originality of the system put in place lies in particular in the composition of the Governing Council, since the majority of its members come from the national central banks, even though it is an ECB body. Specialists thus observe that the Governing Council is 'neither specific to the ECB nor independent of the NCBs'.[175]

61. The NCBs, on the other hand, derive their existence from the national legal orders and, even when acting as a member of the ESCB, remain institutionally and procedurally autonomous. Nevertheless, this principle of autonomy has a residual relevance here. First, within the Eurosystem, NCBs are subject to a legal convergence requirement, which is expressed through a 'compatibility block' between European standards and national legislation.[176] Second, and most importantly, when an NCB carries out, on behalf of the Eurosystem, one of the tasks falling within the exclusive competence of the Monetary Union, it acts as a European body and cannot therefore rely on the principle of institutional and procedural autonomy.[177] However, NCBs may still act on behalf of their Member State,[178] which is why they are referred to as having dual functions:[179] depending on the function they perform, they may act as a national body or as a Eurosystem body. This functional duplication creates a duality in the regime applicable to national central banks. Indeed, when acting as a Eurosystem body, national central banks benefit from all the law applicable to Union agencies, including

---

173 Art. 12.1(1) of the ESCB Statute; see S. Adalid, *The European Central Bank and the Eurosystem*, *op. cit.*, no. 162.

174 Art. 12.3 of the ESCB Statute, see S. Adalid, *La Banque centrale européenne et l'Eurosystème*, *op. cit.* no. 285. It is possible to have an internal organisation even without a text (*ibid.*, no. 310).

175 S. Adalid, *The European Central Bank and the Eurosystem*, *op. cit.*, no. 386. The same author refuses to speak of a hierarchy within the Eurosystem, as the Governing Council, the only one with real hierarchical power, is of a hybrid composition, *ibid.*, no. 490.

176 Based on Art. 131 TFEU which states that 'Each Member State shall ensure the compatibility of its national legislation, including the statutes of its national central bank, with the Treaties and the Statute of the ESCB and of the ECB'. Professor Martucci details the compatibility block with which NCBs must comply, see F. Martucci, *L'ordre économique et monétaire*, Brussels, Bruylant, 2015, pp. 219–224; F. Martucci, 'Système européen de Banques centrales', *op. cit.*

177 The relevant basis here is Art. 14.3 of the Statute of the ESCB, which provides for the execution by NCBs of decisions taken by the ECB.

178 Art. 14.4 of the ESCB Statute.

179 F. Martucci, 'European System of Central Banks', *op. cit.*, no. 69. The authors also mention 'co-administration' and a phenomenon of 'institutional duplication', according to the different visions of European administrative law; this would in any case be an example of going beyond the classic Union law doctrine of indirect administration (S. Adalid, *La Banque centrale européenne et l'Eurosystème*, *op. cit.*, nos. 423–425).

the privileges and immunities granted to Union agencies,[180] the assessment of which is therefore left to the Court of Justice.

62. Relationship between ECB and NCBs. At first sight, the relationship between the ECB and the NCBs appears to be centripetal and centrifugal: centralisation of decision-making and decentralisation of execution. Indeed, on the surface, the ECB is the centralised decision-making body and the NCBs the decentralised implementing bodies.[181] From this perspective, the relationship between the ECB and the NCBs can be compared to the Commission's original supervisory role with regard to the application of EU law by the Member States.[182] However, the integration appears to be even deeper in that the Governing Council may decide to take over the execution of certain monetary policy decisions.[183]

However, this centralisation of decision-making does not imply a hierarchy of bodies between the ECB and the NCBs. Indeed, while there is no doubt that the ECB is the institution that gives orders to the Eurosystem,[184] it should be noted that the ECB's decision-making body, the Governing Council, is made up of a majority of representatives of the NCBs; such a constitution of the Governing Council makes it the place where monetary policy decisions

---

180 See for a contentious illustration Case C-316/19, *Commission v. Slovenia*, ECLI:EU:C:2020:1030, *Banque et droit*, uaryJanuary 2021, p. 61, note J. Chacornac; *JDI*, April 2021, var. 3, note I. Pingel.

181 This explains, for example, why the ECB itself protects the independence of the NCBs and their President, see S. Adalid, *The European Central Bank and the Eurosystem*, *op. cit.* Such a presentation can be based on Art. 12.1(3) of the Statute: 'the ECB shall have recourse to the national central banks for the performance of the operations forming part of the tasks of the ESCB'. However, this Article is misleading, as it seems to make use of the principle of subsidiarity dear to EU law. However, there is no subsidiarity in monetary matters due to the exclusive competence of the European Union (Art. 3(5) of the TFEU): subsidiarity only applies in the case of shared competence, see S. Adalid, *La Banque centrale européenne et l'Eurosystème*, *op. cit.*, no. 189. The arguments put forward for the execution of monetary policy by the NCBs would, in reality, have been based on the preservation of the jobs of NCBs' employees and the temptation for the Member States to benefit their own banking and financial sector through the retention of national central banks, see *ibid.*, no. 190.

182 This comparison is explicit in positive law, where Art. 271 d of the TFEU, which grants the ECB an action for failure to fulfil obligations against an NCB, refers precisely to the Commission's power to bring an action for failure to fulfil obligations (see Art. 258 TFEU). On this comparison, see S. Adalid, *La Banque centrale européenne et l'Eurosystème*, *op. cit.*, nos. 193–194; on the ECB's power of coercion see more generally *ibid.*, no. 386. In practice, the ECB has never brought an action for failure to fulfil obligations, which is explained by the intense collaboration of the NCBs with the ECB (*ibid.*, no. 487).

183 This is the case for fine-tuning operations, outright transactions, foreign exchange swaps and the collection of fixed-term deposits, see respectively Arts. 3.1.4(f), 3.2.4(d), 3.4.4(e) and 3.4.5(e) of Annex I to the Guideline of the European Central Bank of 20 September 2011 on monetary policy instruments and procedures of the Eurosystem (recast) (ECB/2011/14). On this point, see also S. Adalid, *La Banque centrale européenne et l'Eurosystème*, *op. cit.*, no. 444.

184 The authors observe that the ambiguity of the treaties makes it difficult to know whether the ECB carries out its tasks in its own right or on behalf of the Eurosystem, see *ibid.*, no. 94.

are taken jointly, rather than the instrument of a federal entity's policy. This control of the ECB by the NCBs is also reflected in the status of the ECB: to draw an analogy with corporate groups, the ECB is a subsidiary of the NCBs. The NCBs have paid up the capital of the ECB and still hold it.[185] It is as if, as Mr Adalid writes, the 'subsidiary (*ECB*) governs the parent companies (NCBs)'.[186] These elements make it possible to observe, as the same author writes, that 'centralisation does not mean hierarchy, just as entrusting the executive function to the NCBs does not mean decentralisation'.[187]

63. Eurosystem, credit institution and competent central bank. The recipients of the Eurosystem are credit institutions.[188] However, only some of these institutions constitute the Eurosystem's '*eligible* counterparties', i.e. persons who can be parties to monetary policy operations.[189] Indeed, the ECB establishes eligibility criteria for counterparty status, which include the fulfilment of reserve requirements,[190] and are therefore eligible for Eurosystem standing facilities and *open market* operations based on standard tenders.[191] However, elected institutions may only benefit from these services through the relevant NCB. The determination of the competent NCB is based on the Member State of incorporation of the institution, i.e. any Member State in which the institution has an establishment, head office or branch.[192] All its branches then have access to the services of the NCB of the place where they are 'established'.[193]

---

185 *Ibid.*, nos. 390–391.

186 *Ibid.*, no. 391

187 *Ibid.*, no. 489.

188 *Ibid.*, no. 259. One part of monetary law escapes the ECB, in particular the determination of the legal persons that hold an account with the ECB/NCBs: this concerns credit institutions. However, the latter were defined by a directive in 1998 (*ibid.*, nos. 136–137).

189 Art. 2.1 of Annex 1 to the Guideline on the Implementation of Monetary Policy.

190 Failure to hold minimum reserves exposes counterparties to sanctions while the very concept of minimum reserves is highly criticised, see S. Adalid, *La Banque centrale européenne et l'Eurosystème*, *op. cit.*

191 However, the ECB plays more than a counterparty role with respect to each reporting credit institution. Indeed, since the advent of non-conventional measures, the role of the ECB has evolved and plays, in addition to its role of liquidity provider to credit institutions, a role of intermediary between them when they no longer want to lend directly to each other. In these circumstances, credit institutions entrust their excess liquidity to the ECB, which then lends it back (*ibid.*, no. 335). However, while the ECB lends to some illiquid banks under these conditions, it does not lend to insolvent banks (*ibid.*, no. 341).

192 Art. 5.4 of Annex 1 to the Guideline: Counterparty bids 'must be submitted to the NCB of a Member State in which the institution has an establishment (head office or branch)'. However, there is no centralisation of minimum reserves on the account of one of the credit institution's branches: each branch must provide the minimum reserves to the NCB of the Member State in which it is established (see Art. 7.4.2 of the Guideline).

193 Art. 2.1 *in fine of* Annex 1 to the Guideline: 'An institution may access Eurosystem standing facilities and *open market* operations executed through standard tenders only through the NCB of the Member State in which it is established. If an institution has establishments (its head office or branches) in more than one Member State, each establishment has access to

Being an 'eligible counterparty' is fundamental for the credit institution, as it is the condition for responding to the ECB's liquidity tenders. These tenders allow the transfer of liquidity from the ECB to credit institutions.[194] When liquidity is tendered to counterparties, the allotment results in a contract between the NCB and the counterparty,[195] which is subject to the jurisdiction and law of the courts of the Member State in which the NCB is established.[196] In other words, the NCB's jurisdiction implies the application of its law to the liquidity contract and the jurisdiction of local courts. The centralisation of the decision at the European level is therefore without prejudice to the application of national law and the jurisdiction of the courts of the NCB's state.[197] The centralisation of the decision-making process in the Eurosystem has long had no equivalent in the EU; however, this situation has recently changed.

§ 2. FROM COMITOLOGY TO THE ESTABLISHMENT OF EUROPEAN AUTHORITIES

One will first show the context in which comitology took off (I), before observing that the European supervisory authorities are tending to move away

these operations through the NCB of the Member State in which it is established, provided that an institution's bids may only be submitted by one establishment (the head office or a designated branch) in each Member State'.

194 These contracts are fundamental from the point of view of the implementation of monetary policy, Professor Adalid observes that 'it is through these contracts that the key rate takes on a real existence, in the form of the rate at which the ECB agrees to a transfer of liquidity', S. Adalid, *La Banque centrale européenne et l'Eurosystème*, *op. cit.*, no. 348.

195 Or on a regulatory act under the applicable national law depending on the competent NCB, see *ibid.*
Thus, the Banque de France's guaranteed loan agreement goes further: the competent court is also the court of the NCB's headquarters, in this case the Paris Commercial Court. In the field of payment systems, the ECB goes even further, as it provides for the model agreement that the ECB must sign with the counterparties. This model agreement designates the applicable law and the competent court, see Art. 44 of Annex II to the Guideline of the European Central Bank of 26 April 2007 on a Trans-European Automated Real-time Gross settlement Express Transfer system (TARGET2) (ECB/2007/2).

196 Art. I-12 of Annex II to the Guideline of the European Central Bank of 20 September 2011 on monetary policy instruments and procedures of the Eurosystem (recast) (ECB/2011/14): 'The relevant contractual provisions applied by the NCB shall specify that the law governing the relevant contractual or regulatory provisions applied by the NCB and all operations resulting from such provisions (except where the cross-border use of eligible assets does not allow it) shall be that of the Member State in which the central bank is established, and that the place of resolution of the dispute shall, without prejudice to the jurisdiction of the Court of Justice of the European Union, be that of the competent courts of the Member State'. On this issue, see S. Adalid, *La Banque centrale européenne et l'Eurosystème*, *op. cit.*, nos. 449–451.

197 Including in the case of groups of credit institutions due to the rule on the determination of the competent NCB for branches.

from this model, of which they are nevertheless the heirs, to gradually join that of the European authorities set up in monetary matters (II).

I. The Rise of Comitology

64. The origin of comitology. Comitology can be defined as 'the process of adoption by the Commission of implementing measures for legislative acts, with the assistance of committees of experts from the Member States'.[198] It 'stands at the point of balance between Community and national competences, and also between the powers of the Commission and those of the Council'.[199] The first generation of committees developed with the appearance or development of the various sectoral directives on banking and insurance.[200] In addition to these first committees, there were more informal 'contact committees' for the management of collective savings schemes and financial information.[201] While the initial purpose of these advisory committees was to prepare reforms and define implementing measures, 'The establishment of these committees has also been used to settle a number of issues related to the application of Community law'.[202] These advisory committees could be made up of different

---

198 J.-L. Sauron, 'Comitologie, comment sortir de la confusion?', quoted by R. Vabres, *Comitologie et services financiers*, Paris, Dalloz, 2009, no. 2; see the definition proposed by Professor Bonneau: 'Comitology refers to the role of the various committees assisting the European Union in the drafting of European law and in the supervision of both its transposition and its application', T. Bonneau, *Régulation bancaire et financière européenne et internationale*, *op. cit.*, no. 73.
Such a definition made it possible to distinguish between two types of committee: 'those that vote on implementing measures by the European Commission, and those that assist it in drafting these measures' (R. Vabres, *Comitologie et services financiers*, *op. cit.*, no. 2). In practice, however, 'it is the same committees that for a long time fulfilled these two missions' (*ibid.*, no. 4).

199 J.-D. Nuttens, 'La "comitologie" et la conférence intergouvernementale', *RMCUE*, April 1996, no. 397, pp. 314 et seq. It will be recalled here that the institutional structure of the Union is based on the principle of institutional balance, which, without being assimilated to the idea of equality of the institutions, or separation of powers, aims rather to promote 'the institutional and existential autonomy of each of the Community institutions' (C. Blumann and L. Dubouis, *Droit institutionnel de l'Union européenne*, Paris, LexisNexis, 2019, no. 218), i.e. originally, the Parliament, the Council and the Commission.

200 For example, the Banking Advisory Committee, the forerunner of the ECB, was established by Art. 11 of the First Banking Directive adopted in 1977, and the Insurance Committee, with identical tasks, was created by a specific directive: Council Directive 91/675/EEC of 19 December 1991 setting up an Insurance Committee.

201 In the field of collective management of savings, Art. 53(1)(c) of Directive 85/611 on UCITS which created a 'contact committee', and in the field of financial information, Art. 108(d) of Directive 2001/34 contains a similar provision. On these different committees, see R. Vabres, *Comitologie et services financiers*, *op. cit.*

202 *Ibid.*, no. 7. The author quotes in this sense the article by F. Leplat, 'Marchés financiers. Comment les libertés communautaires renforent le rôle propre des autorités nationales, European Law Review n° III - The role conferred by Community law on the national laws of the Member States (2nd part)', *LPA*, 2003, no. 100, p. 3.

national actors.[203] However, in the late 1990s, the Commission recognised that Community harmonisation was insufficient and prepared a Financial Services Action Plan (FSAP),[204] which included the Lamfalussy report that created a second generation of committees.

65. The committees resulting from the Lamfalussy report. The purpose of this report was to 'speed up and make more flexible the legislative process in the securities field within the existing institutional framework'.[205] Its first contribution was to reform the advisory committees in order to distinguish between the functions of reflection on the development and application of Community law, which are now entrusted to the committees comprising only the supervisory authorities, and those of voting on implementing measures, which remain the responsibility of the advisory committees. The second contribution was to distinguish regulation into four successive levels.[206] This report led to the establishment by the European Commission of two types of committees.

66. The first type, exemplified in financial market law by the European Securities Committee,[207] was made up of representatives of national governments and a representative of the Commission. This type of committee was said to be 'hybrid' because of its institutional structure: while the Commission was in charge of the chairmanship of the secretariat and ran the machinery of the structure, 'The decision-making mechanisms [were] subject to the voting rules of the Council'.[208] In concrete terms, as Professor Vabres writes, this committee was 'directly called upon to express its views on the Commission's draft implementing measures and was the Commission's main control body for the Member States. It had the advantage of being able to decide on certain political issues 'without involving the implementation of the co-decision procedure,

---

203 R. Vabres, *Comitologie et services financiers*, *op. cit.*, no. 6.

204 Financial Services – Implementing the Framework for Financial Services: Action Plan, Doc. COM (1999) 232 final, 11 May 1999. On this plan, see already *supra*, para. 13.

205 R. Vabres, *Comitologie et services financiers*, *op. cit.*, no. 6; see also on this report, T. Bonneau, *Régulation bancaire et financière européenne et internationale*, *op. cit.*, nos. 75.1 et seq.

206 The first level is the usual legislation ('framework principles', see Final Report of the Committee of Wise Men, *The Regulation of European Securities Markets*, 15 February 2001, available on the AMF website, p. 29), i.e. the harmonisation directives, the second level is the implementing measures taken by the advisory committees, which are presented as 'detailed rules designed to adapt legislative texts to specific situations' (R. Vabres, *Comitologie et services financiers*, *op. cit.*, no. 12). The third level relates to the mechanisms for cooperation between regulatory authorities 'and should allow for convergence of national practices and measures transposing Community law' (*ibid.* The report refers to 'enhanced cooperation and networking of regulators' (abovementioned report, p. 29). The fourth relates to the Commission's action, which must be 'more vigorous' (*ibid.*), and ensure that the Member States comply with their obligations under EU law.

207 Commission Decision 2001/528/EC of 6 June 2001 establishing the European Securities Committee, [2001] OJ L 191/45.

208 R. Vabres, *Comitologie et services financiers*, *op. cit.*, no. 12.

which was generally considered too cumbersome'.[209] These aspects no doubt explain why this mechanism has been extended to certain related branches: thus, the Commission, encouraged by the Council and the Parliament,[210] has set up a European Banking Committee to replace the former Banking Advisory Committee,[211] and a European Insurance and Occupational Pensions Committee to replace the former advisory committees in these sectors.[212] As Mr Vabres writes, these new committees, which are made up of 'national administrations responsible for implementing Community law in the national system, are thus placed upstream, i.e. at the stage of drafting Community law'.[213]

67. In addition to this first type of committee, committees composed of national regulators were also set up. It was in financial markets law that a European body bringing together regulators first appeared in the form of the Committee of European Securities Regulators (CESR).[214] Its equivalent was later established for banking[215] and insurance.[216] Mr Vabres has shown the important role that CESR has gradually obtained. Indeed, from an institutional point of view, this entity became the privileged interlocutor of third-country regulators

---

209 *Ibid.*, no. 13.

210 Directive 2005/1/EC of the European Parliament and of the Council of 9 March 2005 amending Council Directives 73/239/EEC, 85/611/EEC, 91/675/EEC, 92/49/EEC and 93/6/EEC and Directives 94/19/EC, 98/78/EC, 2000/12/EC, 2001/34/EC, 2002/83/EC and 2002/87/EC in order to establish a new financial services committee structure.

211 Commission Decision 2004/10 of 5 November establishing the European Banking Committee.

212 Commission Decision 2004/9 of 5 November 2003 establishing the European Insurance and Occupational Pensions Committee.

213 R. Vabres, *Comitologie et services financiers, op. cit.* However, a distinction must be made between these committees, which were proposed by the Lamfalussy report as a continuation of the old advisory committees and whose purpose is to draw up 'retail rules' regulation, i.e. level 2, and the committees of regulators, whose purpose is to coordinate the regulatory authorities, i.e. level 3 regulation. This distinction between the levels appears, however, to be rather theoretical: in practice, Mr Vabres has shown that 'regulators, especially in the securities field, have always given impetus to Community reforms, and the introduction of the Lamfalussy mechanism has not led to a change in behaviour' (*ibid.*, no. 68).

214 For Committee of European Securities Regulators. This committee is nevertheless 'an extension of existing institutional forms', namely FESCO (Forum of European Securities Commissions), an institution which was itself the successor to the Securities Contact Committee, the creation of which was nevertheless an initiative of the regulatory authorities. On CESR's coordination methods, see B. Stoeva, *La coopération entre les superviseurs financiers dans l'Union européenne, op. cit.*, no. 168, and on the legal status of these different committees, see R. Vabres, *Comitologie et services financiers, op. cit.*, no. 14.

215 Commission Decision 2004/5 of 5 November 2003 establishing the Committee of European Banking Supervisors.

216 Commission Decision 2004/6 of 5 November 2003 establishing the Committee of European Insurance and Occupational Pensions Supervisors. However, these committees are not identical, since in both banking and insurance matters, not regulators but *supervisors* are brought together. This semantic difference stems from the fact that the latter are competent for prudential supervision – even in the case of investment firms, thus excluding the competence of CESR, *ibid.*

and, from a normative point of view, had an influence on the harmonisation of regulations.[217] The 2008 crisis and the failures it may have revealed nevertheless prompted the European legislator to introduce a new institutional organisation,[218] which was inspired by the Larosière report, commissioned by the Commission.[219]

II. The Establishment of European Authorities

68. From committees to authorities. The committees of securities, banking and insurance regulators have thus been transformed into European supervisory authorities:[220] the European Securities and Markets Authority,[221] the European Banking Authority[222] and the European Insurance and Occupational Pensions Authority.[223] The composition of their decision-making bodies is directly inspired

---

217 *Ibid.* nos. 71–74 (role of CESR) and no. 295 (on the influence of comitology on harmonisation).

218 P.-H. Conac and V. Caillat, 'De CESR à l'ESMA: le Rubicon est franchi', *BJB*, 2010, pp. 500 et seq. The authors consider that 'even if CESR has done a considerable amount of good technical work, the *Lamfalussy* process is a failure' (*ibid.*, no. 5) because of the failure of the alleged benefits: flexibility, speed and harmonisation have not been up to the challenges. This possibility of failure had nevertheless been envisaged by the Lamfalussy report itself, which considered that European authorities should be created (*Lamfalussy Report*, *op. cit.*, p. 52).

219 'The High-Level Group on Financial Supervision in the EU', chaired by Jacques de Larosière, Report, Brussels, 25 February 1999.

220 The appearance of these authorities marks for the authors the end of the so-called 'deregulation' phenomenon, see in this sense, A.-C. Muller, 'La sécurisation du secteur bancaire et financier', *RDBF*, 2014, pp. 66 et seq.

221 Regulation (EU) No 1095/2010 of the European Parliament and of the Council of 24 November 2010 establishing a European Supervisory Authority (European Securities and Markets Authority).

222 Regulation (EU) No 1093/2010 of the European Parliament and of the Council of 24 November 2010 establishing a European Supervisory Authority (European Banking Authority).

223 Regulation (EU) No 1094/2010 of the European Parliament and of the Council of 24 November 2010 establishing a European Supervisory Authority (European Insurance and Occupational Pensions Authority).
These regulatory authorities continue to interact through committees. For example, they meet in a Joint Committee of European Supervisory Authorities, notably to promote a cross-sectoral approach to regulation. In addition, there is the European Systemic Risk Board (ESRB), which has the specific task of monitoring macro-prudential risk, known as systemic risk, because its realisation would be likely to render not only certain credit institutions insolvent, but the entire financial infrastructure causing systematic failures. The distinction between micro prudential supervision, for which the European regulatory authorities are responsible, contributes to macro supervision, and vice versa: see on this point Th. Bonneau, *Régulation bancaire et financière européenne et internationale*, *op. cit.*, no. 81, note 225 and the references. On systemic risk, see *supra*, para. 16.
The ESRB is itself part of the European System of Financial Supervisors (ESFS) which also contributes to a cross-sectoral approach, and includes, in addition to the ESRB, the ECB and the competent authorities of the Member States, see Art. 2(2) of the ESMA Regulation; see on this system T. Bonneau, *Régulation bancaire et financière européenne et internationale*, *op. cit.*, nos. 102–103.

by the former committees of regulators, but their remit has been extended, their institutional structure has been strengthened and their powers have been increased. ESMA will be presented here, bearing in mind that the authorities are organised in a similar way,[224] before distinguishing it from the European authorities set up under the Banking Union, which are not a continuation of the committees.

69. ESMA. ESMA, the successor to CESR, has taken over most of the functions of CESR,[225] which are nevertheless constantly being expanded.[226] From an institutional point of view, ESMA is an EU body with legal personality[227] which 'enjoys the most extensive capacity granted to legal persons under national law'.[228] ESMA's central governance body is the Board of Supervisors. The Board of Supervisors is essentially made up of the chairpersons of the national authorities who, moreover, are the only ones with voting rights.[229] However, the Board of Supervisors elects the chair of ESMA and only the members of the Board of Supervisors are able to constitute the ESMA Board. This means that even in the composition of the European authority, national authorities are quite simply at the heart of the power, as they remain materially competent to supervise, control and enforce their own financial market.[230]

70. The formal relationship between ESMA and national authorities is expressed in several ways, such as the centralisation of information at the ESMA level, or consultation during the development of technical standards.[231] Two aspects will be considered here in the context of this study: on the one hand, the direct relationship that ESMA may have with a national operator and, on the other

224 J.-P. Kovar, 'Les autorités européennes de surveillance: Organes des régulateurs nationaux, agences européennes ou autorités européennes de régulation?', *RDBF*, July-August 2011, no. 4.

225 This is literally one of ESMA's tasks (Art. 8(1)(l) ESMA Regulation).

226 The European regulation establishing ESMA has already been amended twice since 2010: once to coordinate its action with that of the supervisory authorities, the other to give it competence to develop technical standards for AIFM, see Art. 4(4- of Directive 2011/61/EU of the European Parliament and of the Council of 8 June 2011 on Alternative Investment Fund Managers. The objective is to 'promote convergence of supervisory arrangements in the area of assessment of remuneration policies and practices' (Recital 27 of the Directive).

227 Art. 5(1) ESMA Regulation.

228 Art. 5(2) ESMA Regulation. This provision shows that, even when acting in its own name, ESMA's capacity must be assessed according to the national law of the court before which it acts. This means that, even from an institutional perspective, it is subject to the conflict of laws mechanisms.

229 This is precisely the 'Director of the national public authority competent for the supervision of financial market participants in each Member State, who shall attend in person at least twice a year' (Art. 40(1)(b) ESMA Regulation).

230 This can be seen in the budget allocated to ESMA, which is 40 million, while that of the French authority alone (AMF) exceeds 120 million.

231 On this point, see R. Vabres, 'Institution de l'Autorité européenne des marchés financiers et élaboration des normes techniques', *RTDF*, 2010, no. 3, pp. 64 et seq.

hand, the dispute resolution function. Indeed, ESMA contributes to the respect of EU law through a set of mechanisms by which it can investigate the measures taken by a national competent authority[232] in order to encourage the authority to modify its application of EU law, in particular with regard to the operators under its supervision.[233] In the event that the national authority is recalcitrant to ESMA's advice, ESMA can intervene itself to take individual measures against an operator that does not comply with EU law.[234] Such a decision will then prevail over that of the normally competent national authority.[235] However, this prerogative of ESMA is conditional on a lengthy procedure requiring the intervention of the Commission itself,[236] which makes this competence of ESMA both *ad hoc* and highly subsidiary.

71. ESMA's most significant competence with respect to Member State authorities lies rather in the resolution of disputes between national authorities. Indeed, while the latter are at the core of ESMA's governance, symmetrically, ESMA has a dispute resolution competence between the authorities themselves, but only for cross-border situations.[237] The dispute resolution procedure starts with a mandatory mediation before ESMA[238] and, if unsuccessful, results in ESMA itself taking the decision instead of the national authority.[239] In this context, decisions taken by ESMA are of particular importance for the coordination of authorities within the EU. However, to date, no 'binding mediation' has been issued on the basis of Article 19(3) of the ESMA Regulation.[240]

72. These observations make it possible to state that national authorities retain, until now, the main competence for financial supervision. This also

---

232 Art. 17(2) ESMA Regulation.

233 Art. 17 ESMA Regulation.

234 Art. 17(6) ESMA Regulation. This power of ESMA to take an individual measure directly against an actor normally subject to its national authority also exists in cases of urgency, see Art. 18(4) ESMA Regulation.

235 Art. 17(7) ESMA Regulation and Art. 18(5) ESMA Regulation.

236 Art. 17(4) and (5) ESMA Regulation.

237 Art. 19 ESMA Regulation.

238 Art. 19(2) ESMA Regulation.

239 Art. 19(3) ESMA Regulation, decision taken by a simple majority of the members of the Supervisory Board (see Art. 44(2) ESMA Regulation). This measure may be appealed by the appellant before the Appeals Committee, a joint body of the European Supervisory Authorities (Arts. 58, 59 and 60 of the ESMA Regulation), on which see R. Vabres, 'La commission de recours des autorités européennes de surveillance', *BJB*, January 2012, pp. 4 et seq.; here, we will simply note an originality: the appeal may be exercised by the authorities involved in the proceedings as well as by the institution that is the subject of the decision. The decision of the Appeals Committee may be challenged before the Court of Justice of the Union (Art. 60 of the ESMA Regulation). The institution of this mechanism has its origin in the difficulties faced by national authorities during the crisis, see B. Stoeva, *La coopération entre les superviseurs financiers dans l'Union européenne*, *op. cit.*, no. 635.

240 The only mediation that took place resulted in an amicable resolution between the authorities, see ESMA Annual Report, 2016, p. 39. The case concerned the interpretation of the UCITS Directive 2009/65.

explains why, if ESMA can 'establish contacts and administrative arrangements with supervisory authorities' from outside the EU, this should be done 'without prejudice to the respective competences of Member States'.[241] Thus ESMA is an associate member of IOSCO, which does not give it voting rights, whereas national authorities are ordinary members.[242] As Ms Tenenbaum has already observed, this situation is changing, not so much because of the binding mediation that has been instituted, which tends to give ESMA a competence that it did not have before, but because ESMA's function is no longer limited to the coordination of national authorities.[243] Indeed, ESMA has direct supervisory powers over credit rating agencies and trade repositories,[244] in addition to being able to exercise direct powers over investment firms under the Short Selling Regulation.[245] However, the 'transformation of the European legal order'[246] underway is less about the existence of direct intervention powers relating to market operations, as these powers remain limited and subsidiary – and this is the condition for their delegation[247] – than about the direct administrative attachment of certain operators to the European authorities themselves. In this respect, the authorities set up in the field of banking are undoubtedly the greatest upheaval.

73. European banking supervision. The European Banking Authority has the same status as ESMA in terms of legal capacity and composition. Its relationship with national competent authorities is also similar to that maintained by ESMA.[248] The originality in the banking field comes rather from the institution of European

---

241 Art. 33(1) ESMA Regulation.

242 Art. 30 of the IOSCO Statutes.

243 A. Tenenbaum, 'L'Autorité européenne des marchés financiers: une autorité nouvelle au service d'une mutation de l'ordre juridique européen?', *Mélanges en l'honneur du professeur Pierre Mayer*, Paris, LGDJ, 2015, pp. 847 et seq.

244 Art. 55(1) EMIR.

245 See *infra*, para. 515. It should be noted here that the granting of direct supervisory powers to ESMA when it had only been established on the basis of the approximation of laws (Art. 114 TFEU) has been the subject of significant litigation, on which see below. B. Stoeva, *La coopération entre les superviseurs financiers dans l'Union européenne*, *op. cit.*, no. 729; R. Vabres, 'Le système européen de supervision: état des lieux et perspectives', *RDBF*, January 2020, study 3, spec. nos. 25–27; F. Martucci, 'Les pouvoirs de l'Autorité européenne des marchés financiers à l'épreuve du droit constitutionnel de l'Union', *Revue des affaires européennes*, 2014, p. 19.

246 In the words of A. Tenenbaum, 'L'Autorité européenne des marchés financiers: une autorité nouvelle au service d'une mutation de l'ordre juridique européen?', *op. cit.*

247 Case C-270/12, *UK v. European Parliament and Council*, known as *ESMA* judgment, paras. 45-53.

248 The EBA can investigate the violation of EU law by a nationally competent authority, impose its opinion if the violation is proven (Art. 17 of the EBA regulation, on which see G. Hardy, *L'européanisation de la surveillance bancaire*, *op. cit.*, nos. 1034 et seq.), has the same exorbitant prerogatives in case of emergency (Art. 18 of the EBA Regulation) and has a competence to settle disputes between authorities in a cross-border situation (Art. 19 of the EBA Regulation).

authorities that exercise supervision over all operators themselves. Indeed, above a certain threshold, operators are no longer under the supervision of national regulators, themselves coordinated by the EBA, but directly under the control of the European regulator, which has the task of directly supervising investment firms and credit institutions established on the territory of the Union.[249] This European regulator is, for supervisory aspects, the ECB's Supervisory Board,[250] a body distinct from the Governing Council which is responsible for monetary issues[251] and, for resolution aspects, the Single Resolution Board. These two bodies are the central organs of the Banking Union, which does not mean the union of credit institutions, but, on the one hand, the bringing together under the head of single institutions for the territory of the Union of tasks previously exclusively devolved to national supervisory authorities and, on the other hand, the institution of a single resolution mechanism under the supervision of the Single Regulatory Board (SRB).[252] In other words, there has been a shift, at least in part, from a decentralised organisation of banking supervision to centralisation under the aegis of the ECB, where the EBA nevertheless retains a role both in the ECB's dealings with the authorities of other Member States and in certain aspects of the single supervisory mechanism.[253]

74. The imperfection of the Community legal order lies notoriously in the fact it does not carry out its own commands. This makes it necessary to use

---

249 This is why the basis on which the Union has relied to establish these authorities, Art. 114 TFEU, has been the subject of institutional litigation, see *ESMA* judgment above.

250 It may seem curious that it is not the EBA. This would be explained for the following reasons: 'In favour of the ECB, the text of Article 127(6) itself, the ECB's moral authority and the role it played in the negotiations were pleaded. The EBA had the stigma of the way it conducted stress tests (the DEXIA case is a good example: the collapse of this bank followed shortly after a favourable stress test).' J.-V. Louis, 'Conclusion' in F. Martucci (ed.), *L'Union bancaire*, Brussels, Bruylant, 2016, p. 248. The article referred to by the author comes from the TFEU and is the basis of the MSU Regulation. This basis is nevertheless debatable, see the views reported by F. Martucci, 'Union bancaire, la méthode du "cadre": du discours à la réalité', *op. cit.*, p. 27.

251 Based on the model of monetary union, where the ECB was already central, the Germans would apparently have preferred the formula 'integrated financial framework' (E. Jarry, 'L'union bancaire reste un point sensible pour l'Allemagne', *Reuters.com*, 28 June 2013 quoted by F. Martucci, 'Union bancaire, la méthode du "cadre": du discours à la réalité' in F. Martucci [ed.], *L'Union bancaire*, *op. cit.*, p. 13). This awkwardness was noted by Ms Sousi: 'we note how unfortunate the name is, because it leads lay citizens to think that it is a union of banks..., worse, an agreement between them!' (B. Sousi, 'La reconnaissance mutuelle, victime collatérale de l'Union bancaire', *D.*, 2012, p. 2531).

252 On which see *infra*, paras. 193 et seq.

253 See *infra*, para. 200. The distinction between financial supervision, where ESMA acts simply as an overarching authority with a coordinating role, and the banking system, where a single regulator exists for certain entities, is correct in principle, but needs to be qualified in terms of the way it is applied: not only does ESMA sometimes supervise certain entities directly, but the ECB, even when it does so directly, has to apply the law of the authority where the institution is headquartered, and must coordinate under the aegis of the EBA with regard to Member States not party to the SSM.

powerful homogenisation tools in order to avoid fragmented and diversified implementation of Union law,[254] without going against the principle of institutional autonomy according to which Member States are free to organise the implementation of Union law as they wish.[255] These homogenisation tools have now evolved, and the time has come to rationalise legislative production and adopt 'Systems of action whose aim is to ensure obedience by the subjects of Community and Union law'.[256] The European agencies, by acting as guardians of the national regulatory authorities, seem to fulfil this role. Professor Adalid notes that the Eurosystem is part of this trend.[257] However, the institution of the Single Supervisory and Resolution Mechanism and the agencies it creates are not part of a completely identical dynamic, which leads us to make some observations on the competence exercised by national authorities.

75. European political organisation and the notion of competence. The mere mention of European federalism is controversial, since it would imply that sovereignty resides not in the member states of the Union, but in the federal body. This perception reduces the notion of federation to a 'superposition' of legal orders, which conceives the relationship between the Member States and the European Union as a hierarchical one.[258] However, the research of Professor Beaud[259] has made it possible to dissociate the analysis of the federation from that of the state and sovereignty. The author's thesis can be summarised as follows: 'the federation is not a state; it is a political form that is autonomous from the latter, and does not have to concern itself with bringing together its constituent elements, the first of which is sovereignty.'[260] The influence of the federal phenomenon on the conflict of laws has already been studied.[261] This is why we would simply like to add here that the approach adopted by Mr Beaud

---

254 S. Adalid, *La Banque centrale européenne et l'Eurosystème*, *op. cit.*, no. 186 for the reference to Professor Azoulai who makes this point.

255 *Ibid.*, no. 187.

256 Expression of Mr Azoulai, quoted by S. Adalid, *La Banque centrale européenne et l'Eurosystème*, *op. cit.*, no. 188.

257 *Ibid.*

258 Mr Beaud believes that this French perception of federalism goes back to Georges Scelle, see O. Beaud, 'La répartition des compétences dans une Fédération. Essai de reformulation du problème', *Jus Politicum*, no. 16, p. 190; it has the disadvantage of making it very difficult to study federalism because of the 'Calhoun dilemma', see O. Beaud, *Théorie de la Fédération*, 2nd ed., Paris, PUF, 2009, pp. 39 et seq.

259 *Ibid.* The author does not consider the Union to be a federation, O. Beaud, *Le pacte fédératif*, Paris, Dalloz, 2022, pp. 463 et seq. It nevertheless borrows some of its mechanisms from this political form.

260 This formulation of Beaud's thesis is taken from Professor Carcassonne's review (Guy Carcassonne, *Le Monde*, 29 February 2008) and is considered by the author as a perfect summary, see O. Beaud, 'La répartition des compétences dans une Fédération. Essai de reformulation du problème', *op. cit.*, p. 180.

261 J. Heymann, *Le droit international privé à l'épreuve du fédéralisme européen*, Paris, Economica, 2010; Y.-E. Le Bos, *Renouvellement de la théorie du conflit de lois dans un contexte fédéral*, Paris, Dalloz, 2010.

is compatible with the distinction made between power and competence, by keeping the power at the level of the Member State, and allows an analogy between the situation of the international determination of the courts and that of the administrative authorities. It seems to us that jurisdiction can be used to designate both aspects; here we will assimilate it to competence. Indeed, within the federation, the important issue is less the question of sovereignty ('Who ultimately has the power?'), than that of competence, i.e. the delimitation of the 'field of application of the power'[262] Power is understood here as the legal functions of the State (legislative, executive and jurisdictional power), whereas competence concerns, according to Professor Combacau's demonstration, the 'field of application of the rules'.[263] Commenting on this aspect, Mr Beaud writes:

> 'The opposition is therefore clear between the concept of state power, the rights and powers of the state, and competence, which draws the contours of the exercise of this power, determines the sphere in which the power is exercised, determines a kind of perimeter. Competence would be a kind of boundary instrument if we were to use a spatial metaphor.'[264]

The question of the distribution of competences thus comes down to studying 'the reciprocal delimitation of federal and federated competences'[265] or, as Mr Beaud puts it, 'who does what?'[266] In a federal perspective, as Mr Beaud writes, 'Competence only determines the contours and boundaries of the action of the federal power and the federated authorities'. However, one can clearly see the similarity with the concept of competence generally used in private international law,[267] for example in the law of international jurisdiction:[268] in

---

262 The expression is borrowed from Professor Combacau, 'Conclusions générales', in Société française de droit international, *Les compétences de l'État en droit international*, Paris, Pedone, 2005, p. 314.

263 *Ibid.* Mr Combacau writes: 'the use of the word competence is thus reserved for the designation of the legitimate field of application of what the powers allow to be done in the spatial jurisdiction, the temporal sphere, the material domain in which they can legally be deployed' (*ibid.*, p. 307). On this notion of competence in public law and European Union law, see G. Hardy, *L'européanisation de la surveillance bancaire*, *op. cit.*, nos. 99–101.

264 O. Beaud, 'La répartition des compétences dans une Fédération. Essai de reformulation du problème', *op. cit.*, p. 204.

265 M. Bridel, *Précis de droit constitutionnel et public suisse*, vol. I, p. 170, note 1 quoted by O. Beaud, 'La répartition des compétences dans une Fédération. Essai de reformulation du problème', *op. cit.* p. 188.

266 *Ibid.*

267 P. Mayer, 'Droit international privé et droit international public sous l'angle de la notion de compétence', *RCDIP*, 1979, pp. 1 et seq. P. Mayer, *Choix d'articles de Pierre Mayer*, Paris, LGDJ, 2015, pp. 21 et seq.

268 Private international law has not waited to observe that the question of jurisdiction goes beyond the simple question of legislation, which seems to exhaust the distribution of jurisdiction for some constitutionalists, see O. Beaud, 'La répartition des compétences dans une Fédération. Essai de reformulation du problème', *op. cit.*, pp. 194 et seq. It

the same way that there are several courts likely to be internationally competent, there are several entities likely to exercise the same power, and it is necessary to 'prevent the conflict of jurisdictions by attributing to each of the authorities a field of action'.[269] This understanding of 'conflicts' of jurisdiction is presented in identical terms when conflicts between administrative authorities are at issue,[270] and already foreshadows that the solutions of the one may serve as a source of inspiration for the other.[271]

76. Indeed, the simultaneous exercise of this competence by two administrative authorities for the same cross-border operation, or for the supervision of the same activity, is likely to create conflict of laws. Such a conflict does not exist in the same terms in domestic law, since the legal system rarely grants an identical material scope of application to its authorities, and when it does, it usually provides for an allocation criterion.[272] Thus, when the competence of the AMF is discussed in domestic law, it is most often when the authority's action seems to exceed the scope of the mission that has been assigned to it; more rarely because it would encroach on the *competence* of another administrative authority,[273] for example the ACPR[274] or the *Banque de France*. The material scope of the administrative authorities does not in principle overlap. There is therefore no real conflict of jurisdiction. It is therefore more accurate, in these

should also be noted that the distinction between power and jurisdiction in the federal framework first appeared in the writings of *Dicey* (*ibid.*, p. 187), the founder of English constitutionalism, who was also and above all the founder of the famous English treatise on private international law.

269 *Ibid.*, p. 205.

270 The concept of competence in matters of conflict of administrative authorities is therefore not the one sometimes used in public international law to delimit the freedom of a State to regulate the behaviour of its subjects, but the one used in private international law, based on the idea of selection. As Mr Combacau has already observed, this notion of jurisdiction in the sense of public international law is better referred to as power, see J. Combacau, 'Conclusions générales', *op. cit.*, at 314.

271 This is the case of the *forum legis* solution, proposed *infra*, para. 190.

272 See, however, the notorious counter-example of market abuse, which can be punished by the criminal or administrative authorities.

273 This is different from the question of determining the international jurisdiction of courts. Indeed, given the existence of a large number of courts, an internal division of jurisdiction was already necessary. Thus, there were already rules in the internal order, which are known to have been sometimes projected as such into the international order. Such rules do not exist for administrative authorities.

274 For an illustration, see the supervision of compliance with the rules on derivatives transactions, which is entrusted to the ACPR (Art. L. 612-1(II)(1) and (2) of the Monetary and Financial Code) and the AMF (Art. L. 621-18-6 of the Monetary and Financial Code). Aware of this overlap, the authorities issued a joint press release detailing the articulation of these powers, see *Dr. Sociétés* 2013, alerte 57; *BJB*, 2013, no. 9, p. 387. On this overlap from an internal point of view, see *supra*, para. 57.

internal hypotheses, to consider that the AMF does not have the right, or the power, to do or not to do something.[275] As Professor Pierre Mayer writes:

> 'The distinction between activities that fall within the powers of an organ or authority and those that are excluded is only relevant to the concept of competence if it results from the existence of a plurality of organs or authorities and the distribution of powers between them.'[276]

In the context of the supervision of financial institutions in general, and of market infrastructures in particular, this distribution of competences is based on the rules of the Treaty on the Functioning of the European Union by which the Member States confer competences on the Union.[277] It is known that this treaty goes so far as to grant exclusive competences to the Union, notably in monetary matters, the exercise of which is entrusted to a European institution, the ECB. However, even in the maximalist case of exclusive competences, these competences remain *allocated* by the Member States. This has several consequences. On the one hand, Member States are likely to challenge the ECB's competence when its exercise appears to exceed the boundaries of the competence conferred on it.[278] This is why the assertion by some authors that the adoption of the single currency simply reflects the will of certain States to exercise in common a sovereignty that they retain[279] appears particularly

---

275 See P. Mayer, 'Droit international privé et droit international public sous l'angle de la notion de compétence', *op. cit.*

276 P. Mayer, 'Droit international privé et droit international public sous l'angle de la notion de compétence', *RCDIP*, 1979, pp. 1 et seq. P. Mayer, *Choix d'articles de Pierre Mayer*, Paris, LGDJ, 2015, pp. 21 et seq.

277 This is where the particularity of nascent or aggregative federations comes into play, see O. Beaud, *Théorie de la Fédération*, *op. cit.*, p. 183.

278 See e.g. *United Kingdom v. ECB*, *supra*, references no. 5 and our comments *infra* n° para. 245. This judgment was followed by another decision on the same theme in 2017. On the whole, see F. Martucci, 'La BCE, une autorité monétaire suprême?', *RDBF*, July 2018, pp. 62 et seq. In this case, it was precisely from this angle that German individuals challenged the ECB's exercise of its prerogatives. Mr Martucci summarises the issue perfectly in these terms: 'the Constitutional Court was […] seized of an action brought by individuals and political groups alleging a violation of fundamental rights since the ECB's disregard of its mandate would call into question the assent given by the Bundestag to the Maastricht Treaty and would therefore constitute a violation of the right to vote enshrined in the Basic Law' (*ibid.*; see also S. Adalid, *La Banque centrale européenne et l'Eurosystème*, *op. cit.*) Non-conventional measures are only possible even in the event of a crisis if the objective of price stability is respected, since the ECB has made this objective the condition for its second function of supporting the economic policies of the Member States. More generally, the allocation mechanism is one of the two facets, together with loyal cooperation, of the principle of European institutional balance, see *ibid.*, no. 120.

279 See in this sense F. Martucci, *L'ordre économique et monétaire*, *op. cit.*, no. 4: 'The Member States of the European Union are holders of monetary sovereignty, which is understood as the supreme power. By creating the euro, they decided to exercise jointly the powers that make up monetary sovereignty'. Recall the definition of federation given by Samuel

accurate. On the other hand, the existence of an exclusive competence of the Union means that the decision-making body is then an agency of the Union and, above all, that its judge is the Union court. However, in the absence of exclusive Union competence, decision-making power is not necessarily unified, and the division of competences between the Member States and the Union may be more subtle, showing new patterns of coordination.[280] Whether this distribution of competences is based on a decentralised or centralised model, it is always part of a form of federalism, which is sometimes imperfect, and reflects different visions, which require the institution of coordination mechanisms between legal orders.

77. **Conclusion of the section.** At the end of this section, the European institutional set-up has been clarified between the model of the European System of Central Banks, applicable to monetary matters, and the model of the European Supervisory Authorities and the competent authorities under the ESM, applicable to banking and financial matters. These institutions required a brief presentation because of their influence on the status of market infrastructures and their managers, and to show that the relationship between centralised and decentralised models is subject to a wide range of nuances, independent of the basis on which they are established.

78. **Conclusion of the chapter.** The study of the history of market infrastructures has shown how three types of dissociation have gradually emerged. First, the dissociation between the different infrastructures necessary for the functioning of the market, the trading, clearing and settlement systems, and between the trading systems themselves, which are not uniform. Secondly, the separation between the infrastructure manager, which has its own status, and the infrastructure itself, which is subject to an independent attachment. These different aspects of financial market infrastructure are subject to administrative supervision, which has the particularity of being able to intervene in a national or European framework, the function of the European authorities not being limited to the coordination of national authorities, but

---

Pufendorf, 'Confederation [...] consists of several peoples, without ceasing to be distinct states, uniting for ever for the purpose of their mutual preservation and defence, making the exercise of certain parts of sovereignty depend on their common consent' quoted by O. Beaud, *Théorie de la Fédération*, *op. cit.*

280 A certain surprise, however, arises from the fact that the basis adopted has no bearing on the degree of centralisation and concentration adopted: the monetary scheme derives from an exclusive competence of Article 3 TFEU; the scheme instituted in the field of banking is based on Art. 127(6) TFEU, whereas the centralisation of competences in the field of finance is based on Article 114 and the approximation of legislation that it allows. As Professor Vabres has already observed, 'Community law [...] is a branch of law where positivism is sometimes pushed to its limits, but where there is a multitude of institutions whose functioning and role are not clearly understood by the law'. R. Vabres, 'Le système européen de supervision: état des lieux et perspectives', *op. cit.*, no. 1.

being likely to exercise direct supervision of managers or their systems. Having made these preliminary observations, it is now possible to study the status of manager.

TITLE 1
THE CONNECTING FACTOR OF MANAGERS

79. European managers of financial infrastructures are licensed under the law of their registered office. This affiliation dictates not only the local application of company law, but also of prudential and insolvency law. The particularity of infrastructure managers is that they are subject to an administrative connecting factor, which may be with the authority of a Member State, according to a decentralised coordination model, or directly with an EU agency, according to a centralised model (Chapter 1). As a matter of principle, the provision of access to a market infrastructure on the territory of the Union triggers the applicability of European law; by way of exception, it is possible for certain third-country operators to be subject only to the law of their headquarters. This limitation of European law is then based on the equivalence method. However, it should be noted that this method is not the only mechanism for self-limitation of local law and that the objectives of substantive law may lead to the eviction of all forms of self-limitation of European law when the provision of clearing services on its territory is at stake (Chapter 2).

CHAPTER 1
THE CONNECTING FACTOR OF EUROPEAN MANAGERS

80. Duality of European managers. From the foregoing, it should be noted that there are three market infrastructure managers: trading platform managers[1] (investment firms and market operators), whose statutes are subject to MiFID 2, clearing houses or central counterparties, which are subject to EMIR, and central securities depositories, which are subject to CSD Regulation.[2] Although there are differences in the status of managers, they all share the common feature of being subject to a dual connecting factor. First, these managers are subject to a national legislative connecting factor. This is done through their registered office, which is understood to be their real seat, and has a particularly broad scope (Section 1).

Secondly, managers are subject to an administrative connecting factor. The latter reflects the designation of the administrative authority competent to approve the manager and the supervision to which the latter is subject in the exercise of his or her activity. Until recently, there was a parallelism of connecting factors. Indeed, the administrative connecting factor for managers was also the registered office. This criterion, which stemmed from a decentralised model based on a division of administrative powers between the authorities of the Member States, was based on mutual recognition. This model is now being challenged by a centralised model, where the decision is taken by an EU agency, whose legal order is therefore primarily competent to assess all administrative aspects of the managers status. The particularity of this centralised model is twofold: on the one hand, it can be deconcentrated, restoring to the national authorities part of their competence and, on the other hand, the existence of an administrative connecting factor to an EU agency does not call into question the manager's legislative connecting factor, resulting in the competent authority applying the law of the manager's headquarters (Section 2).

---

1 Also referred to as financial market managers.

2 Support function providers, such as trade repositories, rating agencies, or data reporting investment firms are therefore excluded from the scope of this study. However, their administrative affiliation will be studied for comparison purposes.

SECTION 1. THE LEGISLATIVE CONNECTING FACTOR

81. Scope. The foregoing discussion has shown that the status of managers was inspired by that of investment firms, which is explained in particular by the prior existence of the European statute for investment firms and the fact that investment firms can manage trading platforms. In order not to make the discussion more cumbersome, this inspiration, and the similarity of the resulting rules, justify that the rules relating to investment firms are those on which the following developments are based. However, one difference must be noted. The connecting factor of investment firms is made up of two aspects: the organisational rules, which are the 'internal status' of the firms, and the conduct of business rules, which constitute the external aspect of the status of the firms and relate to their relations with their clients.[3] With the exception of OTF market managers, infrastructure managers are not subject to these rules of conduct in their relations with their members, even when the latter may have the status of investment firm, in the case of NMS market managers.[4] It is therefore only the organisational rules that are the subject of this section.[5]

82. Origin of the legislative connecting factor through the head office (*siège réel*). Under French law, infrastructure managers are legal persons under private law. Their legislative connecting factor is through their registered office. The particularity is, however, that their registered office must coincide with their actual office, and that this coincidence is controlled by the administrative authority. The latter makes this one of the conditions for approval.[6] This requirement originated in the Investment Services Directive,[7] where authorisation was granted only after the authority had verified that the registered office and the 'head office' of the investment firm coincided.[8] This condition emerged following the bankruptcy of the Bank of Credit and Commerce International (BCCI), a credit institution authorised in Luxembourg, but whose main activities, as well as its decision-making centre, were located in England. The bankruptcy of this credit institution revealed the importance of the coincidence of the statutory and head office in a sector where the location of the governing bodies most often

---

3 R. Vabres, *Comitologie et services financiers*, *op. cit.*, p. 379.

4 Art. L. 424-2 of the Monetary and Financial Code. On this aspect, see *infra*, para. 137.

5 The international status of conduct of business rules applicable to investment firms will be considered in the context of access of investment firms to the territory of other Member States, see *infra*, paras. 137 et seq.

6 These conditions are specified in Commission Delegated Regulation (EU) 2017/1943 of 14 July 2016 supplementing MiFID 2.

7 The Second Banking Directive, from which the Investment Services Directive draws its inspiration, did not require the coincidence of the registered and head offices as a condition for authorisation.

8 This condition was then extended by Directive 95/26 of 29 June 1995, known as the 'post BCCI' Directive (see Directive 95/26/EC of the European Parliament and of the Council of 29 June 1995).

dictates the location of the activity.[9] The underlying idea is that institutions must carry out their activity primarily in the country in which they have established their registered office. This implies, on the one hand, that Member States do not authorise companies that seek to evade the stricter standards in the Member State where they operate and, on the other hand, that the company actually operates in its home Member State, or else it loses the authorisation. The conditions for authorisation also impose a set of so-called prudential rules. It will be shown that the function of the head office has several original features linked to the authorisation of which the entity is the subject. First of all, its function with respect to company law is not primarily the protection of third parties, but the application of local rules of the organisation of the legal person (§ 1). Indeed, the protection of third parties is ensured by the application of prudential rules in connection with authorisation (§ 2). Moreover, infrastructure managers are not necessarily subject to ordinary insolvency law. Indeed, in order to preserve the infrastructures they manage, they may benefit from a special insolvency regime: resolution (§ 3).

§ 1. SEAT THEORY AND COMPANY LAW

83. Corporate affiliation and registered office. The criterion of the real seat is the traditional one for legal persons in continental European countries. In France, it is defined as the 'seat of effective management',[10] presumed to be the statutory seat. The absence of a European agreement on this issue in the Treaties,[11] and the subsequent absence of an intergovernmental convention and European regulation, have left the criterion for connecting companies to the discretion of the legal systems of the Member States. The Court of Justice, through its interpretation of the freedoms of movement (specially the art. 49 of TFEU), has nevertheless condemned Member States using the criterion of the real seat and

9 The outsourcing of activities is limited under administrative supervision, see *infra*, para. 116.

10 Cass., Ass. plén., 21 December 1990, *Roval*: 'But whereas the connection to a State, to which Art. 26 of the 1966 Convention refers in order to prohibit discrimination, is none other than nationality, which, for a company, results, in principle, from the location of its real seat, defined as the seat of effective management and presumed to be the seat of the company's statutes'. In *Roval*, as in *Daily Mail*, the question of the determination of the *lex societatis* comes into play in support of a question of the applicability of tax law. Comp. the German definition of the real seat: the 'place where the fundamental decisions of the board of directors are effectively transposed into individual management decisions', cf. B. Audit and L. d'Avout, *Droit international privé*, Paris, LGDJ, 2018, no. 1209. The Court of Justice of the European Union also considers that the real seat of a company is 'the place where its place of management is situated', Case C-210/06, *Cartesio*, ECLI:EU:C:2008:723, para. 50, and EU law generally defines it as the place of central administration, see e.g. Art. 13(2) of the CRD IV.

11 See nevertheless Art. 58 of the Treaty on the Functioning of the EEC.

has consequently imposed, to a certain extent, the criterion of incorporation.[12] In so doing, the obligation within the conditions for authorisation to make the real seat and the registered office coincide runs counter to European case law on the establishment of companies, but also to that applicable to the change of seat during the life of the company. Indeed, the conditions of the authorisation must be permanently respected in order to continue the exercise of the authorised activity. One explanation for the contradiction between sectoral law and the case law of the Court of Justice could be that the particular risks borne by infrastructure managers require the application of the real seat in order to protect third parties. It will be shown here that this explanation is unsatisfactory, since the function of the real seat at the time of incorporation of the company is less to protect third parties (external order of the company) than to apply the local rules of the organisation of the company (internal order of the company).

84. Rejection of the interest of third parties as a basis for the real seat. The use of the real seat criterion in company law is generally justified from the point of view of the protection of third parties. In the French perspective, this function is deduced from the wording of Article 1837 of the Civil Code. Indeed, third parties could be misled by the dissociation between the statutory seat and the real seat, and the objective is then to allow them to rely on local law. Two issues in particular traditionally fall under the *lex societatis* and are detrimental to third parties if they are unaware of the content of the *lex societatis*: on the one hand, the capacity of the company and the powers of representation of its organs; on the other hand, the misconduct of the director.[13] However, these issues can be resolved by the application of local law without recourse to the real seat.

85. Registered office and powers of the directors. The application of the law of the real seat to the capacity of the company is intended to favour the validity of the contract. The cases referred to are those in which the contracting party was unaware of the existence of a foreign *lex societatis* which could hinder the company's capacity to contract, or the absence of the manager's power of representation, whereas the company appeared to be run by local representatives and the business activity was carried out on local territory. There are two possibilities to overcome this difficulty.

---

12 For a retrospective of this case law, see L. d'Avout, 'Commentaire comparé' in *Les Grands Arrêts de la jurisprudence de l'Union européenne*, Paris, PUF, 2016, no. 60, p. 299.

13 In the past, it was possible to invoke the absence of share capital, but the evolution of the rules on capital has made this rarely necessary. Similarly, the possible non-existence of the company is likely to harm third parties, but the hypothesis appears too exceptional to be the basis for the rule.

The first is to apply to these issues a law known to both parties, such as the law of the contract.[14] However, such a solution comes up against two obstacles. Firstly, unless the *lex contractus* corresponds to the domicile of the contracting party, it will be less easy for the latter to verify the content of this law than it would be to ask the director of a foreign company to prove that he can commit the company according to the legal system of its seat.[15] Moreover, it seems difficult in any case to deny the effectiveness of the *lex societatis* to the powers of the directors once it is considered applicable. Indeed, the powers of the director are at the frontier of the internal and external orders of the company, orders which often follow opposite logics. The powers of directors constitute a sort of link between these two orders of the company, causing a tension between the application of the *lex societatis* and the law in which the activity takes place. However, the principled application of the *lex societatis* should prevail for a simple reason: the law that applies to the powers of the director should be the law that empowered him or her, and this law is necessarily the law that established the legal personality. Moreover, this logic can claim a certain effectiveness since the legal system of the seat is that of the debtor, i.e. the one where the attempts to execute the disputed transaction will in principle take place. These reasons may have guided the position of the Court of Cassation when it decided to apply the *lex societatis* to the powers of the director.[16]

A second solution consists in tempering the effects of the *lex societatis*, either by recourse to the doctrine of appearances,[17] or by the law of civil liability. The latter will undoubtedly make it possible to compensate under local law for the damage suffered through ignorance of the foreign law, but will not lead to the validity of the contract, which is the element sought by the party deceived by the existence of a restrictive foreign *lex societatis*. The doctrine of appearance may be more effective, however, by creating a substantive exception to the applicability of foreign provisions restricting the company's

---

14 Two difficulties nevertheless remain: on the one hand, it will necessarily be necessary to adapt the foreign corporate form in order to determine whether its functional equivalent conditions the legal person's ability to contract and, on the other hand, the risk of non-recognition of the validity of the contract by the legal system of the registered office whose regulations have been ignored, and which will generally be the debtor's seat. Nevertheless, these two difficulties also exist under the real seat criterion.

15 If the law of the deed is applied, it will also be necessary to adapt the foreign corporate form in order to determine whether its functional equivalent determines the legal person's ability to enter into contracts.

16 Cass. com., 21 December 1987, pourvoi no. 85-13.173.

17 H. Synvet, note under the above-mentioned judgment, spec. pp. 408–409. On this solution, see also R. Crône, 'La loi applicable aux pouvoirs des dirigeants de sociétés étrangères', *TCFDIP*, 1998-2000, pp. 243 et seq.; H. Gaudemet-Tallon, 'Autorisation des cautionnements, avals et garanties dans les contrats internationaux: pour une "ignorance excusable de la *lex* societatis"', in *Le Code de commerce 1807-2017, Livre du bicentenaire*, Paris, Dalloz, 2007, pp. 751 et seq.

capacity or the powers of the director to conclude the act.[18] It is not necessary to go through the real seat test to protect a third party against the application of a *lex societatis* that he is not familiar with.

86. Registered office and tort of the director. In the case of a tort from the director, the application of the law of the real seat is intended to make it possible to hold the director civilly liable. This approach is nevertheless paradoxical for two reasons. The first is that the French concept of *faute séparable des fonctions* makes it very difficult to hold the director liable.[19] The second is linked to the qualification of the manager's fault: in the external order, it is expressly characterised as tortious.[20] This means that the tort of the director towards third parties to the company should not be subject to the *lex societatis*. Indeed, the application of local law aims at enabling the country affected by the disorder to remedy it and should therefore be based on the law of the place of the damage. The question is obviously more delicate when the liability of the director is engaged by the partners. In this case, the application of the *lex societatis* appears more difficult to avoid since it is at the heart of its field: relations between corporate bodies. The virtue of the criterion of the real seat is felt here since it makes it possible to make the place where the management is located coincide with the applicable organisational rules and creates a real preponderance of the place where the possible mismanagement should be assessed. Such a criterion makes the law applicable to the liability of the director predictable and avoids interference from other laws.[21] However, it is once again precisely in the internal order that the real seat test shows its value.

87. Function of the real seat and company organisation. The absence of the need to apply the law of the real seat in order to protect third parties at the time of incorporation of the company[22] indicates that its function is not to be sought in

---

18 See already in this sense *ibid.*, and the author's proposals which we support: on the one hand, to characterise the appearance and excusable ignorance of the contracting party and, on the other hand, to limit the hypotheses where this material exception could be invoked. See also the recent proposals to adopt in French law the criterion of incorporation, which are accompanied precisely by an exception in this sense, HCJP, *Rapport sur le rattachement des sociétés*, 31 March 2021, p. 22.

19 The precision of the definition of separable fault comes from the *Seusse* decision, Com., 20 May 2003, No. 99-17.092, on which see Y. Guyon and M. Buchberger, 'Responsabilité civile des dirigeants', *JCl. soc.*, June 2017, fasc. 132-10, spec. no. 51.

20 Cass. com., 8 March 1982, no. 79-10.412, (judgment rendered on the basis of the former Art. 1382 of the Civil Code). On this question, see Y. Guyon and M. Buchberger, 'Responsabilité civile des dirigeants', *op. cit.*, spec. no. 3.

21 Considering that French law could disregard a foreign law which would not allow the partners to sue the director, see D. Cohen, 'La responsabilité civile des dirigeants en droit international privé', *RCDIP*, 2003, p. 585, no. 35.

22 In the event of a change of registered office during the life of the company, the protection of third parties appears more significant. One solution may be to apply the *lex societatis* of the original company to commitments entered into with third parties before the change.

the external order of the company, but rather in its internal order: its purpose is to link the rules of organisation and management of the company to the place where the effective management is carried out.[23] This observation is reinforced by several aspects.

88. Real seat and jurisdictional competence. The function of the real seat with regard to the internal order is also continued in the jurisdictional field[24] where the exclusive jurisdiction of the courts of the registered office[25] allows, at least in intra-Community relations,[26] the application of local rules.[27] However, the jurisdiction of the courts of the registered office is limited to the internal order of the company, in order to guarantee the unity and proper functioning of the

23 See already in this sense on the function of the registered office: 'The law of incorporation or the law of the real seat would retain the function for which they were conceived, namely the organisation, free from any direct intervention by the public authorities, of relations between private interests meeting within the company'. H. Synvet, *L'organisation juridique du groupe international de société, op. cit.*, no. 21.

24 The first historical function of the registered office was to determine a competent court: 'The definition of domicile given above (§ 353) is based on the relations of the natural life of man, and consequently it cannot be applied to juridical persons. Nevertheless, it may be necessary to artificially assign to juridical persons a domicile similar or analogous to that of natural persons, especially when it is a question of determining the jurisdiction to which they are subject. In most cases, the relationship between the juridical person and the land removes all uncertainty [...]; but uncertainty may exist in the case of industrial undertakings whose operation does not apply to a specific place or covers very large areas, for example, in the case of railways, steam navigation, or the construction of bridges over rivers whose two banks have different jurisdictions or legislation, and sometimes do not even belong to the same State. In such cases, it is appropriate to assign a domicile to the legal person in the very act of incorporation (e.g. the statutes of the German railway company); if this precaution is neglected, the judge must artificially determine where the centre of the company is. (F.-C. Savigny, *Traité de droit romain, t. VIII*, reprinted in Panthéon-Assas, 2002, pp. 68-69).

25 Art. 24(2°) of the Brussels I *bis* Regulation. This provision, already included in the Brussels Convention (Art. 16, 2), is the result of a long tradition of doctrine and case law in France, see note Francescakis under the *Robert Peugeot* judgment (Civ. 1re, 17 June 1958, *RCDIP* 1958, pp. 705 et seq., see spec. p. 712).

26 Because of the scope of application of the Brussels I *bis* Regulation itself. The Court of Cassation refuses to retain such exclusive jurisdiction in relations with third countries, and reverts to the ordinary law, i.e. the application of the defendant's domicile (Art. 42 of the Code of Civil Procedure), see Cass. com., 15 March 2011, no. 09-72027.

27 This is what seems to justify, for Mr Synvet, this coincidence of *forum* and *jus*: 'The major interest of the exclusive jurisdiction thus provided for is to make the applicable law and the competent court coincide for the questions referred to in the Community text: the effectiveness of the monopoly of the *lex societatis*, which is justified by the concern to ensure the unity of the internal status of the company, presupposes that its application is reserved for the courts of the country of the registered office.' H. Synvet, 'Société' in *Répertoire de droit international*, no. 95; in the same sense, U. Magnus and P. Mankowski, *Brussels I*bis *Regulation*, Köln, Otto Schmidt, 2015, no. 39, p. 571.

legal personality[28] and the decisions of its organs.[29] By granting legal personality and providing for exclusive jurisdiction of its courts over the internal status of the company, the legal order of the seat guarantees its full control over the legal person.[30] Moreover, approval makes it possible to overcome the disadvantage sometimes noted in the rule of jurisdiction which refers the definition of the registered office to the private international law of the court seized,[31] which, according to some authors, would have the consequence of making the concentration of disputes 'illusory'[32]

Exclusive jurisdiction will not be retained if the object of the application is not primarily the annulment of a corporate decision, but if it is made in a subsidiary manner in order to limit the powers of representation of a director and to obtain the annulment of an act with the external order.[33] On the other hand, there is no doubt that it will be used when the main issue is a decision of a corporate body. Thus, the Court of Justice has held that the partial validity of

---

28 Dicey, Morris and Collins, *The Conflict of Laws,* 15th ed., London, Sweet&Maxwell, 2012, nos. 11–380.

29 Thus, the Court of Justice, when interpreting the scope of this rule of jurisdiction, considers that 'the essential objective of that article [...] is to centralise jurisdiction in order to avoid contradictory decisions as regards the existence of companies and the validity of the decisions of their organs', see Case C-372/07, *Hassett*, ECLI:EU:C:2008:534.
This basis was also identified by the Jenard Report (Jenard Report, [1979] OJ C 59/1) However, the justifications given by the author of the report are not convincing, as the existence of the register is not necessary for the validity of the decisions of the organs or the granting of the legal person status. For a critique, see D. Fernández Arroyo, 'Compétence exclusive et compétence exorbitante dans les relations privées internationales', RCADI, The Hague, Martinus Nijhoff, 2006, pp. 102-103.

30 Nevertheless, an avatar of this exclusive jurisdiction can be found within non-personalised groupings through the regime granted to the jurisdiction clause, and in particular *trusts* where the clause has the same function as the exclusive jurisdiction in company matters, see Art. 25(3) and (4) of the Brussels I *bis* Regulation.

31 Even though the regulations contained a definition: Art. 63 of the Brussels Ia Regulation locates companies where their registered office, central administration or principal place of business is located. However, as this is an alternative possibility, in reality it would not have allowed the establishment of a unitary jurisdiction either. See H. Gaudemet-Tallon, *Compétence et exécution des jugements en Europe*, Paris, LGDJ, 2015, no. 110, p. 119.

32 D. Fernández Arroyo, 'Compétence exclusive et compétence exorbitante dans les relations privées internationales', *op. cit.*, p. 103. The author considers in general that 'exclusive and exorbitant fora, vestiges of an outdated international law, should be limited or even eliminated' (*ibid.*, p. 246).

33 See in this sense the aforementioned *Hasset* judgment and Case C-144/10, *BVG*, ECLI:EU:C:2011:300. In these two judgments, the corporate competence intervenes incidentally, and is used to prevent the payment of a contract which the company considers that it was not concluded in a lawful manner, according to its own statutes, because the corporate body which concluded the contract did not have the power to do so.

a decision of a general meeting evicting a minority shareholder ('squeeze out')[34] falls within the exclusive jurisdiction of the registered office.[35]

89. Real seat and corporate law objectives. The function of the real seat can also be explained in the light of the different objectives pursued by the internal and external orders of the company. The purpose of legislation relating to the internal order of the company is the proper functioning of the legal person, which includes the unity of the legislation applicable to relations between the bodies of the legal person.[36] This function explains the presumption established between the statutory seat and the real seat. Indeed, in order for the rules of the organisation of the legal person to be applied correctly, it is necessary that this coincides with the statutory seat, which determines the country granting legal personality. This function of the real seat corresponds to the purpose of company law, which is to provide a legal organisation for private persons in order to facilitate civil and commercial relations, and not, as a matter of principle, to protect third parties. However, this organisation is based on a legislative policy, the legitimacy of which derives from the fact that the country of the real seat is the one which bears the effects not only of the company's dysfunctions, but also of its possible failure. This last aspect takes on new importance when confronted with market managers, and justifies certain specific rules, instituted precisely in order to protect third parties.

---

34 This institution is also known in French law, but mainly in stock exchange law (see *infra*, para. 484) and in insolvency law, see F.-X. Lucas and D. Poracchia, 'L'expropriation de l'associé qui ne finance par la restructuration de la société en redressement judiciaire' in *Etudes en la mémoire de Philippe Neau-Leduc*, Paris, LGDJ, 2018, p. 629.

35 Case C-560/16, *E.ON Czech Holding*, ECLI:EU:C:2018:167, *supra*. This decision is all the more remarkable since the dispute concerned the assessment of the consideration granted to the minority shareholders as a result of the *squeeze-out* (i.e. a question determined by the *lex contractus*), whereas, according to the Czech company law applicable to this question, the minority shareholder's recourse was powerless to annul the meeting decision.

36 In his observation of US law, Professor Muir Watt put it best: 'The cross-border operation of the business corporation would be hampered if it were to be subject to conflicting obligations. In this respect, the "internal affairs" of the corporation represent a necessarily unitary category; to disaggregate them among different laws would risk destroying a complex and interlocking balance of rights and obligations designed to function as a whole.' (H. Muir Watt, 'Economic Aspects of Private International Law', *op. cit.*, no. 48). The author also observes that the test for incorporation in the United States still has the problem of 'determining the domain of that law, particularly in relation to that of various third state police laws' (*ibid.*, no. 46).

§ 2. SEAT THEORY AND PRUDENTIAL LAW

90. Source. While managers are all subject to prudential rules, their sources are particularly fragmented.[37] This fragmentation takes on a singular dimension for investment firms, which now have their own set of rules after having been subject to the prudential rules of credit institutions for a time.[38] We will focus here on the details of the prudential rules applicable to investment firms and credit institutions, since the latter are the most accomplished example of a prudential legislative package and the model on which the prudential rules applicable to infrastructure managers are based.

---

37 See:

- for market operators, see Arts. 45 to 47 (governance) of MIFID. European regulations do not set capital requirements, but from a French perspective, see Art. L. 421-11 II, and the Order of 2 July 2007 on the minimum capital, own funds and internal control of market undertakings.
- for investment firms, in the IFR on prudential requirements for investment firms, see Arts. 9 et seq. (capital), Art. 43 (liquidity requirement), Arts. 51 et seq. (remuneration policy), and in the DTI Directive, Arts. 26 et seq. on internal governance.
- for clearing houses, in EMIR, Arts. 27 (governance), 16 (financial resources), and 30 (supervision).
- for CSDs, in Regulation CSD 27 and 28 (governance) and 47 (capital requirement).

38 Originally, the prudential rules applicable to investment firms had their sources in MiFID 2, with the exception of the prudential rules on capital requirements which were governed by the Directive of 26 June 2013 relating to the taking up and pursuit of the business of credit institutions and the prudential supervision of credit institutions and investment firms (applicable by reference from Art. 15 of MiFID 2). This directive applicable mainly to credit institutions, better known by its acronym CRD IV (Capital Requirement Directive), is supplemented by Regulation (EU) No 575/2013 of the European Parliament and of the Council of 26 June 2013 on prudential requirements for credit institutions and investment firms, known as the CRR (Capital Requirement Regulation), and the whole is referred to as the 'CRD IV package'. This regulation incorporated into European law the international commitments made in the context of the Basel Committee's Basel III reform (on this committee, see *supra*, note under para. 23). In addition to these two legislative instruments, there is the Solvency II Directive 2009/138, to which reference is often made for the definition of certain fundamental concepts, such as own funds. These requirements, designed for systemic credit institutions, have nevertheless proved to be excessive since 85% of investment firms do not hold client funds or securities and therefore do not present a systemic risk. This is why the European Union has enacted a new 'package', applicable only to investment firms and consisting of the IFD Directive of 27 November 2019 on the prudential supervision of investment firms (known as the IFD Directive) and the IFR Regulation of 27 November 2019 on the prudential requirements applicable to investment firms (known as the IFR Regulation). However, the enactment of the latter package has not severed the links between investment firms and the CRD IV package, not only because it is frequently referred to, but also because supervisors may subject investment firms to the CRD IV package whenever the importance of the investment firm justifies it: either its failure could lead to systemic risk, or it is a clearing member, i.e. a member of a clearing system, or because of the importance of its activities for the Union or the financial system [Art. 5(1) of the IFD Directive].

91. Function of prudential rules. Prudential rules refer to certain rules applicable to companies[39] wishing to engage in certain regulated activities and whose access is restricted to obtaining authorisation as an insurance company, credit institution or investment firm.[40] The purpose of these rules is to prevent, as far as possible, the failure of those subject to them[41] because of the particular risks they bear: 'credit risk, market risk, operational risk and settlement risk'.[42] One of the most enlightening indications of this function is the sanctioning of prudential rules, which does not end with the administrative responsibility of the person subject to them, but can lead to the triggering of a resolution procedure against him.[43] However, this procedure causes both the crucifixion of the legal person and its resurrection in only two days.[44]

92. This function sheds light on the relationship between prudential rules and company law. Indeed, the use of rules that are traditionally part of company law is only a means for prudential rules to achieve their ends. They will sometimes use 'internal control' rules that are not directly concerned with the relationship between corporate bodies. At other times, it is the very way in which the regulated activity is carried out, or the management of the infrastructure that will constitute their object. This is why it is simplistic to consider that prudential rules are limited to the regulation of capital.[45] It seems to us that it is also necessary to include the specific organisational requirements applicable, as well as the supervision of the investment firm: these rules serve the same purpose, the 'prudent' management of the company, and are applied according to the same criterion, that of the place of establishment of the entity. In this sense, prudential rules can be defined by reference to the rules applicable to credit institutions,

[39] French investment firms must be legal entities (Art. L. 531-4 of the Monetary and Financial Code), without any particular corporate form being imposed. Traditionally, investment firms were required to have a 'legal form suitable for the provision of investment services' (Arts. L. 532-2(5) and L. 532-3(2) of the Monetary and Financial Code), but this requirement has disappeared. The ACPR nevertheless considered that the legal form of a simplified joint stock company was not necessarily compatible with the status of investment firm, see ACP Position 2014-P-04. On this issue, see F. Drummond, *Droit financier*, *op. cit.*, no. 549.

[40] In this sense, they can be seen as the internal status of professional rules, which also have an external aspect: the rules of good conduct applicable in their relations with clients. The latter body of rules does not, however, have an identical spatial scope of application, see paras. 137 et seq.

[41] See already in this sense, F. Drummond, *Droit financier*, *op. cit.*, no. 585. Professor Bonneau considers that his standards also have the function of improving the liquidity of institutions, see T. Bonneau, 'La norme prudentielle', *RDBF*, May 2015, pp. 36 et seq.

[42] Art. 1(a) of the Regulation on prudential requirements. These risks do not quite overlap with those faced by the financial infrastructure, which is explained by the fact that the perspective of the credit institution is different.

[43] Art. 27 of the Resolution Directive; Art. 18(1) of the CCP Resolution Regulation.

[44] For a presentation of the resolution procedure, see *infra*, paras. 103 et seq.

[45] Comp. B. Stoeva, *La coopération entre les superviseurs financiers dans l'Union européenne*, *op. cit.*

with which the ECB is responsible for ensuring compliance under the single supervisory mechanism:

> 'The requirements for credit institutions to have robust governance arrangements, including requirements for good repute, knowledge, skills and experience necessary for the performance of the functions of those charged with the management of credit institutions, risk management processes, internal control mechanisms, remuneration policies and practices, and effective internal capital adequacy assessment procedures, including models based on internal ratings.'[46]

We shall first study the content of the prudential rules, which reveals a form of special company law (I). This explains, on the one hand, the function of the seat as a connecting factor in prudential matters and, on the other hand, their originality, which consists in taking into account, within the material solution that they develop, the internationality of the activity of the person who is subject to them (II).

I. Content of the Prudential Rules

93. Capital regulation. As the acronym CRD (Capital Requirements Directive) suggests, prudential rules refer mainly to rules on capital, and more generally own funds.[47] Own funds are the resources of the company and are divided into two categories: 1 and 2, the former being the strongest resources.[48] Capital is

---

46 Art. 4(1)(e) of the SSM Regulation.

47 And, in the case of systemic investment firms, additional 'capital buffers' that may be required, see Arts. 129 et seq. of CRD IV.

48 Own funds are defined by the European legislator as 'the sum of Tier 1 and Tier 2 own funds', (see Art. 4(1)(118) of the Regulation on prudential requirements; for the details of Tier 1 capital, see Art. 62 of the CRR). This distinction between own funds stems from a Basel agreement (see C. Feunteun, *Hybrid instruments and Basel agreements*, *op. cit.*, no. 37), and the different categories of own funds are defined by reference to the Directive 2009/138 on the solvency of insurance institutions (known as Solvency II), see Art. 4(1)(103), (104) and (105) of the CRR. Within the Solvency II Directive, own funds are then divided into basic own funds, i.e. the excess of assets over liabilities, and subordinated liabilities (Art. 88 of the Solvency II Directive) and ancillary own funds, i.e. '(a) the unpaid share capital or initial fund which has not been called up; (b) letters of credit and guarantees; (c) any other legally binding commitments received by insurance and reinsurance undertakings' (Art. 89 of the Solvency II Directive). It should be added for mutuals that: 'In the case of a mutual or mutual-type association with variable contributions, ancillary own funds may also comprise any future claims which that association may have against its members by way of a call for supplementary contribution, within the following 12 months'. These determination rules can be altered, see details of the Article.
This distinction between basic and ancillary own funds does not cover Tier 1 and Tier 2 capital in the prudential requirements regulation, but it does make it possible to determine them (for the details of their determination, reference is made to Article 93 of Directive 2009/38, which defines the characteristics and factors to be used to classify own funds by tier). Here, it is sufficient to note that own funds are not constituted by share capital,

only one component of own funds, but an integral part of Tier 1 own funds.[49] Capital requirements are developed not only on the basis of the investment services provided, but more importantly on the basis of the risks taken.[50] As Professor Drummond writes:

> 'The idea is that the firm's own funds must be sufficient to cover the risks to which it is exposed in its business: the requirement is expressed as a ratio, with the numerator being the capital or certain categories of capital, and the denominator being the risks, or certain types of risks.'[51]

The factors determining own funds *ratios* are designed to prevent the entity from failing by enabling the company to absorb any losses.[52] For this reason, own funds are not the common pledge against which creditors can be paid, and in whose function share capital has sometimes been identified. Indeed, in the event of default, the protection of third parties is ensured by other means, in particular for clients who have entrusted securities to an investment firm, by the securities guarantee mechanism to which investment firms are required to adhere.[53] The concepts that make up the regulation of own funds are derived from other bodies of law: company law and accounting law.[54] While company law is always the law of the seat, the accounting rules applicable to investment firms may alternatively be derived from the regulation of the French accounting

but that their determination is closely linked to the latter. However, share capital and its component, the shares, are concepts at the heart of company law. Moreover, the use of hybrid instruments based on a combination of shares and bonds to constitute equity capital (on the latter, see C. FEUNTEUN, *Instruments hybrides et Accords de Bâle*, *op. cit.*, nos. 49 et seq.) further increases the close links with share capital.

49 These are capital instruments, share premium accounts related to capital instruments, retained earnings, other accumulated comprehensive income, other reserves and funds for general banking risks, see Art. 26 CRR.

50 See respectively Art. 29(1) and (2) of the CRD IV and Art. 9 of the IFD Directive. This requirement is based in French law in Art. L. 532-2,(2) of the Monetary and Financial Code.

51 F. DRUMMOND, *Droit financier*, *op. cit.*

52 Thus, the minimum initial capital of investment firms, while in principle seven hundred and fifty thousand euros (Art. 9(1) IFD Directive, see previously Art. 28(2) CRD IV), may be reduced to seventy-five thousand euros depending on the investment services provided, and whether or not the investment firm holds funds or securities belonging to its clients, see Art. 9(1) IFD Directive. Previously, the absence of a minimum capital requirement could be compensated for by taking out liability insurance to cover risks arising from their professional negligence (see Art. 31(2)(a) and (b) CRD IV). In the latter case, a requirement is added on the spatial scope of the insurance, which must extend to the entire territory of the Union, which clearly showed that the prudential rules instituted were intended to protect all third parties located in the Union.

53 In French perspective, see Art. L. 532-2(6) of the Monetary and Financial Code.

54 See already in this sense, F. PELTIER, 'L'agrément et le contrôle prudentiel' in *La modernisation des activités financières*, *op. cit.*, p. 121. The author considers that prudential supervision is based on the development of a financial accounting order.

standards authority (*Autorité des normes comptables*) or from the accounting rules drafted by the European Commission.[55]

94. Organisational requirements. The organisational requirements of a company are usually laid down in the corporate form and the articles of association. They are intended to ensure the proper functioning of the company. The organisational requirements applicable to investment firms are somewhat ambiguous as to their function. Indeed, within this title retained by Article 16 of MiFID 2, one can distinguish two types of rules, those which genuinely relate to the internal organisation of the investment firm, and those relating to the relationship of the investment firm with its clients. The organisational requirements referred to here are those that are part of the prudential rules, i.e. those that aim to prevent the failure of the firm through the management of the risks generated by the activity. Like the regulation of equity capital, they are most often a function of the risks taken.

95. Organisational requirements relate, first of all, to the legal organisation of the company and can be divided into two types of rules. The first are governance rules, the best known of which is the so-called four-eyes rule, applicable as a condition of authorisation. This rule, which was introduced in German law following the bankruptcy of the *Herstatt Bank*,[56] consists of entrusting the management of the authorised company to at least two managers of the necessary good repute.[57] In addition to this long-standing rule, since the 2008 crisis, the governance rules applicable to credit institutions and investment firms of significant size have been extended.[58] These rules cover the management structure, the composition of the management body and, in certain cases, the establishment of specific committees.[59] The legal organisation of the company is also subject to systems and procedures aimed at controlling the risks taken by the investment firm, which are similar to compliance rules.[60] The organisational requirements also concern the physical organisation of the company. They establish a rule of proportionality between the company's programme of

---

55 The rules applicable to the accounts of investment firms are those of credit institutions.

56 M. Storck and I. Riassetto, 'La règle des quatre yeux en matière bancaire et financière' in *Mélanges en l'honneur de Jean-Jacques Daigre*, Paris, Lextenso, 2017, p. 783.

57 The rule is applied differently depending on whether the company is an insurance company, an investment company or a credit institution, see *ibid.* The directors themselves must have 'at all times the good repute, knowledge, skills and experience necessary to perform their duties', see Art. L. 533-25 of the Monetary and Financial Code.

58 Significant importance is constituted by a corporate or consolidated balance sheet in excess of EUR 5 billion, see Art. 104 of the Order of 3 November 2014 on the internal control of firms in the banking, payment services and investment services sector subject to supervision by the ACPR. The applicable rules are those set out in Articles 88 to 81 of the CRD IV (by reference to Art. 9(1) of the MiFID 2).

59 Art. L. 511-89 of the Monetary and Financial Code. On these aspects, see F. Drummond, *Droit financier*, *op. cit.*

60 F. Drummond, *Droit financier*, *op. cit.*, nos. 598 et seq.

operations, a concept that is close to the corporate purpose, and the means provided for in order to achieve it.[61] All these rules are based on two ideas: on the one hand, that the solvency of the company will be better safeguarded if it is better organised and, on the other hand, that since the administrative supervisory authority is not in a position to control everything, this control must partly rest on the company itself.[62]

96. Control of the company. The regulation of the control of the investment firm focuses on the ownership of the capital. These rules establish control of the direct and indirect shareholders of the investment firm.[63] Article L. 532-2(3) of the Monetary and Financial Code specifies that 'the Authority shall assess the status of these shareholders in the light of the need to ensure the sound and prudent management of the investment firm'.[64] As Professor Drummond writes, 'The formula is sufficiently vague to allow the authority to check the good repute and financial soundness of the holders of a qualifying holding [but also to verify that] supervision will not be hampered by capital and control links',[65] particularly in the case of a group.[66] Indeed, in the event of a change in qualifying holdings, the national authority must verify 'Whether the group to which [the investment firm] will belong has a structure which allows for effective supervision, effective exchange of information between competent authorities and determination of the allocation of responsibilities between competent authorities'.[67]

97. The purpose of shareholder control by the authority is similar to that of foreign investment control: to enable the authority to refuse the acquisition of French investment companies by international groups that might interfere with the local order. The difference lies, however, in the fact that the aim is not so much to protect the company whose acquisition is sought as to protect its customers and the sector of activity in which it operates. The sanction of control of the shareholding by the authority also recalls the control criterion sometimes used by French private international law at the beginning of the 20th century.[68] This criterion made it possible to refuse to recognise a legal person constituted

---

61 Art. 7(2) of MiFID 2. See all the information required by the AMF, AMF Instruction-2014-01.

62 See already in this sense, F. Drummond, *Droit financier, op. cit.*, no. 30; 598.

63 Art. 10(1) of MiFID 2, transposed in Arts. L. 532-2(3) and R. 532-8-1 of the Monetary and Financial Code.

64 Art. L. 532-2(3) of the Monetary and Financial Code.

65 F. Drummond, *Droit financier, op. cit.*

66 This is why the ACPR must give an advisory opinion on this issue in matters of financial concentration, see Art. L. 612-21 and 22 of the Monetary and Financial Code.

67 Art. 13(1)(d) MiFID 2.

68 For a retrospective, see L. Lévy, *La nationalité des sociétés*, Paris, LGDJ, 1984, para. 151 et seq. W.L. Craig, *La société sous contrôle étranger*, Paris, thesis, Paris II, 1981, para. 22, pp. 110 et seq., see especially on the 1914-1918 war and its aftermath, para. 22.3.

in France but controlled by a foreign shareholder.[69] As Professor Henri Mazeaud observed, 'When the national interest is at stake, judges can, if they wish it, resurrect the notion of control.'[70] The control criterion would condemn the legal person to fictitiousness, and prevent it from pursuing its activities in France, in the same way that the withdrawal of authorisation makes it impossible for the company to provide investment services.

II. International Regime of Prudential Rules

98. Material content of the rules. The particularity of the prudential rules regime is to take into account the internationality of the activities carried out by the investment firm within its substantive conditions of application. This is due to a combination of three elements: prudential rules are a function of the investment services provided by firms; the activity of investment firms is largely cross-border; and the directives establishing these prudential rules were also intended to implement the freedom of establishment and the freedom to provide cross-border services. Three examples are given here. For example, the size of the investment firm, which is a condition for many prudential rules such as the level of capital required or the establishment of committees within the company's organisation, is assessed on the basis of accounting rules which can be consolidated at group level.[71] Similarly, the submission of the investment firm regime to the more stringent prudential rules of credit institutions may be triggered by the 'importance of the cross-border activities of the investment

69 See significantly in this sense the circular of the Garde des Sceaux of 29 February 1916 (*JORF*, 2 March 1916, *JDI*. 1916, p. 701; *RDIP*, 1916, p. 366, spec. p. 368): 'The legal forms with which the company is clothed, the place of its principal establishment, all the indications to which private law attaches in order to determine the nationality of a company are inoperative when it is a question of determining, from the point of view of public law, the real character of this company; it must be assimilated to subjects of enemy nationality when its management or its capital is known to be wholly or mainly in the hands of enemy subjects, for in such cases, behind the fiction of private law, the enemy personality itself is concealed, alive and kicking. This circular concerns the application of the law of 22 January 1916 and the decree of 28 February 1916 (*JORF*, 2 March 1916, *RDIP*, 1916, p. 364) relating to the declaration of the property of subjects of enemy powers. The circular was an opportunity for the Garde des Sceaux to specify that 'this law is a police and security law which obliges all those who live in the territory'. (*RDIP*, p. 368).

70 Commentary on the paper by H. Batiffol, 'La nationalité des sociétés', *TCFDIP*, Paris, 1970, p. 79. The author considers that 'Mr Batiffol was a bit hasty in throwing it overboard' (*Ibid.*). It is true that the eminent civilist had a general propensity to prefer French law to others, which was reflected in his bold proposals to attach extra-contractual obligations to the *lex fori*. On this proposal, see H. Mazeaud, 'Conflits de lois dans le domaine de la responsabilité civile délictuelle et quasi-délictuelle', *RCDIP*, 1934, pp. 376 et seq., and the developments he devotes to the question in his textbook, H. and L. Mazeaud, *Traité de la responsabilité civile*, vol. 3, 4th ed., Paris, Sirey, 1938, paras. 2335 et seq. On this question, see also the vigorous criticism of P. Bourel, *Les conflits de lois en matière d'obligations extracontractuelles*, Paris, Sirey, 1961, pp. 20-22.

71 Arts. 7 and 8 of the IFD Directive.

firm'.[72] Finally, the monitoring of capital control of investment firms is mainly due to the vigilance of foreign control, over which the head office authority will necessarily have less control.

99. Role of the real seat criterion. Within the European Union, the prudential rules are applicable by virtue of the authorisation, and are therefore those of the head office. This means that any branch established in another Member State remains subject to the prudential rules of the head office of the company to which it belongs, and not to the law of the place of establishment.[73] A review of the prudential rules suggests that there are three reasons for this application of the law of the seat. Firstly, prudential rules are closely linked to the company law to which they relate by their purpose. They are therefore more effective when they are formulated by the legal system of the registered office: they are then more easily articulated with the body of rules above them and within which they are inserted, thus avoiding 'friction' between the laws.[74] Secondly, the legal system of the seat is the one in which the main activities of the investment firm are carried out, where the effects of its insolvency will be the most intense. It therefore has a predominant legitimacy: most third parties affected by the possible bankruptcy or disorganisation of the company are located there. This is especially true since the violation of prudential rules by the authorised entity is likely to trigger its resolution.[75] Thirdly, the application of prudential rules of the country of the seat is explained by a particularity of authorised investment firms: they are subject to supervision by an administrative authority. This supervision is more effectively carried out by the authority in the best position, that of the head office, which will be in a better position to monitor compliance with the rules of its own legal system.[76]

---

72 Art. 5(1)(c)(ii) of the IFD Directive.

73 Under the Investment Services Directive, conduct of business rules allowed for the application of certain prudential rules, leading to harmful overlaps, see *infra*, paras. 141 et seq. In relations with third country branches, the solution is to apply the rules of establishment of the place where the branch is established, see *ibid.*

74 As stated in Recital 55 of MiFID 2 with regard to the governance rules established by MiFID, these 'are purely functional and are intended to lay down rules to achieve a certain result independently of the national company law applicable to an institution in each Member State. Therefore, the definitions should be without prejudice to the overall allocation of competences under national company law'. Similarly, Art. 57 of the Resolution Directive states that public support of own funds is only possible 'in accordance with national company law', making it clear that prudential legislation is rooted in company law.

75 Art. 27 of the Resolution Directive; Art. 18(1) of the CCP Resolution Regulation.

76 This link between the prudential rules and the authority controlling them indicates the other function of the registered office: the designation of the competent administrative authority for the purpose of supervising the entity, see *infra*, para. 115.

§ 3. SEAT THEORY AND INSOLVENCY LAW

100. Registered office and insolvency. The coincidence of the head office and the statutory seat means that the insolvency criterion, based on the centre of main interests, is definitely aligned with the head office criterion. Nevertheless, infrastructure managers have the particularity of being subject to a special insolvency regime which gives a remarkably large share to the legislation of the seat (II). In order to observe this, however, it is first necessary to indicate the conditions that allow infrastructure managers to be subject to it (I).

I. Material Scope of the Resolution

101. Material scope of the resolution and the infrastructure manager. The coincidence of the registered office and the head office has another consequence on the legislative connecting factor of market operators: the latter will necessarily be subject to the insolvency law of their registered office. The particularity is, however, that infrastructure managers are not necessarily subject to ordinary insolvency law, but to a special insolvency regime, known as resolution,[77] which stems from the transposition of the Resolution Directive. The latter was adopted at a time when the insolvency of credit institutions and the consequent realisation of systemic risk had left the realm of academic hypothesis.[78] After attempting to prevent failures through new regulations on prudential requirements,[79] the legislator decided to introduce a resolution regime which is basically a favour to certain institutions. Under certain conditions, these institutions can escape from normal insolvency procedures for a public interest reason: the stability of the financial system.[80] The primary objectives of resolution are 'to ensure the continuity of critical functions, to avoid adverse effects on financial stability and to protect the resources of the state'.[81] Two separate regimes have been established: the first is applicable to credit institutions and investment firms, while the second is applicable to clearing houses. In other words, financial market managers and central securities depositories only benefit from the

---

77 This is an anglicism. In English law, the notion of 'resolution' refers to regimes that prevent insolvency.

78 If this was a textbook hypothesis, the crash of 1882 and the bankruptcy of the Lyon public prosecutor's office (see *supra*, para. 44 for a good example) clearly show that the systemic risk was known. However, the particularity is that the risk of it spreading beyond borders appears much greater today.

79 See 'CRD IV Package', *op. cit.*, no. 92.

80 On the particularity of banks and the justification of a special insolvency regime, see J. Armour, 'Making Bank resolution credible' in N. Moloney, E. Ferran and J. Payne (eds.), *The Oxford Handbook of Financial Regulation*, Oxford, OUP, 2017, pp. 453 et seq.

81 Recital 41 of the CCP Resolution Regulation. See in the same sense Art. 31 of the Resolution Directive.

resolution regime if they are licensed as investment firms or credit institutions, respectively.[82] In other cases, they are subject to the Insolvency Regulation.

102. The explanation for this baroque scope is linked to the particular place occupied by the clearing house since the 2008 crisis. Indeed, following the crisis, several measures were taken by the EU legislator to reduce systemic risk. The first was to institute a derogation regime allowing for a tailored treatment of the insolvency of credit institutions and investment firms, of which the Resolution Directive is the result. The second was to require persons established in the EU to clear financial contracts, even those concluded over-the-counter, with a central counterparty. The consequence of this obligation was to concentrate a significant part of the system risk on CCP,[83] making them a 'key node'[84] of financial stability. However, the regime developed by the Resolution Directive, if it could be applicable, as national legislators sometimes impose the status of credit institutions on clearing houses,[85] did not appear perfectly adequate.[86] A tailor-made regime was therefore established for clearing houses[87] in order to take into account their particularities, which lie in particular in their interposition between clearing members for each transaction.

103. Even if the other market infrastructure managers do not interfere with their members, it seems to us that all market infrastructure managers should benefit from the resolution regime. Indeed, the insolvency of a financial market operator or a central depository would lead to the interruption of the systems they manage.[88] It could be argued that this is especially true for

---

82 More specifically, they must be investment firms established with a capital of more than EUR 730,000 (see Art. 28(2) of the CRD IV, applicable by reference to Art. 2(1)(3) of the Resolution Directive).

83 Recital 4 of the CCP Resolution Regulation. Observing already the process at work, see A. Gaudemet, 'Les obligations de négociation et de compensation', *RDBF*, Jan. 2013, p. 65, and spec. p. 67. Some authors have considered that such a transfer of risk to the clearinghouse is an overestimation of the capacity of a clearinghouse to reduce system risk, see M. Roe, 'Clearinghouse Overconfidence' (2013) 101 *California Law Review* 1641. Other authors consider that an appropriate resolution regime is precisely what allows the system risk borne by the clearinghouse to be captured, see J. Braithwaite and D. Murphy, 'Improving resolvability: partial property transfers and central counterparties' (2019) 14(4) *Capital Markets Law Journal*431.

84 Recital 3 of the CCP Resolution Regulation.

85 This is always the case, see Arts. L. 440-1 and D. 440-2 of the Monetary and Financial Code.

86 On this issue, see A. Sotiropoulou, 'Reflections on proposed CCP resolution tools', *RTDF*, 2018, no. 2/3, pp. 62 et seq.; T. Bonneau, *Régulation bancaire et financière européenne et internationale*, *op. cit.*, p. 399; J. Braithwaite and D. Murphy, 'Improving resolvability: partial property transfers and central counterparties', *op. cit.*

87 Regulation (EU) 2021/23 of the European Parliament and of the Council of 16 December 2020 on a framework for the recovery and resolution of central counterparties.

88 See in this sense T. Bonneau, 'Difficultés financières', *RDBF*, January 2015, com. 27; T. Bonneau, 'Redressement, résolution et infrastructures de marché', *RDBF*, January 2016, marker 1; T. Bonneau, *Régulation bancaire et financière européenne et internationale*, *op. cit.*, p. 331.

central depositories since their system is subject to a legal protection that has no equivalent in positive law, except for the one granted to the clearing system.[89] In other words, the malfunctioning of the securities settlement system caused by the insolvency of its manager would also lead to a crisis whose magnitude cannot be ignored.[90] However, trading systems also are of critical importance, both because their operation is the condition for the liquidity and exchange of the securities of all issuers that have admitted their securities to them, and because of the links between the operation of the various market infrastructures. Even the European legislator admits that trading platforms have a critical function for financial stability,[91] and therefore justify the institution of a resolution regime. It is therefore likely that all market infrastructures will eventually be subject to resolution regimes.[92] However, resolution does not entirely displace ordinary insolvency law.

104. Resolution and general insolvency law. Resolution law can be described as a special insolvency law. This special character is explained by the fact that the insolvency of the banking institution would jeopardise the public interest, and is manifested, first of all, in the fact that the possible rescue of the entity in difficulty is carried out by an administrative authority, whose decisions enjoy a very protective status, extending the competence already given to the administrative order in prudential matters.[93] This special character is also perceptible in the means given to the competent authority: it has four resolution instruments at its disposal, under which it can bail out the entity, sell some of its activities, separate its assets or transfer the part of the credit institution best able to continue its activity to a new entity.[94]

---

89 On the protection afforded to transactions concluded through these systems, see *infra*, para. 747.

90 See in this sense, Recital 12 of the Resolution Directive.

91 Recital 87 of the CCP Resolution Regulation. Critical functions are defined as 'activities, services or operations the interruption of which is likely, in one or more Member States, to lead to disruption of services essential to the real economy or to disturb financial stability by reason of the size or market share of the institution or group, its internal and external interdependence, its complexity or the cross-border activities it carries out, with particular attention to the substitutability of such activities, services or operations' (Art. 2(1)(35) of the Resolution Directive)

92 See D. D'Ambra and M.-A. Frison-Roche, 'La résolution bancaire entre droit commun des procédures collectives et droit commun de la régulation' in *Mélanges en l'honneur de Jean-Luc Vallens*, Paris, Lextenso, 2017, pp. 293 et seq., spec. p. 294: 'These technical solutions (*of the resolution*) could inspire the law applicable to other 'crucial operators' than banks', see also *ibid.*, p. 303.

93 On administrative competence in prudential matters, see *infra*, para. 115 (decentralised model) and para. 180 (centralised model); on the administrative competence in resolution matters, see *infra*, para. 149 (decentralised model) and para. 193.

94 Resolution is technically defined by the Directive as the use of a resolution instrument (of which there are four: divestment of the institution's activities, use of a bridge institution, asset segregation, internal bail-in, see Art. 37(2) of the Resolution Directive), in order to achieve one of the objectives of resolution (of which there are five: ensuring the continuity

Resolution law is similar to ordinary insolvency law in several respects. Firstly, the latter directly draws on to the former since, on the one hand, not all banks will necessarily benefit from a resolution decision[95] and, on the other hand, the least solvent activities of the entity in resolution are wound up through a classic liquidation procedure.[96] Secondly, the resolution solutions are similar in their guidelines to those currently proposed by the law on companies in difficulty: on the one hand, the financial burden of the resolution must be borne primarily by the shareholders,[97] then by the creditors[98] and, on the other hand, the resolution is based on a double principle of anticipating difficulties and planning.[99] To this end, the Resolution Directive proceeds in three stages:[100] first, when the institution is not in difficulty,[101] then when the

of the critical functions of the entity, avoiding serious adverse effects on financial stability, including to market infrastructures, and maintaining market discipline, protecting state resources by minimising the use of exceptional public financial assistance, protecting depositors and investors, and protecting client funds and assets, cf. Art. 31(2) of the Resolution Directive).

95 For an illustration, see J.-C. Cabotte, 'Aspects de compétences des différentes autorités en matière de gestion de crises bancaires' in *Le traitement des difficultés des établissements bancaires et institutions financières*, Paris, LexisNexis, 2017, pp. 151 et seq.

96 Indeed, the 'residual', i.e. original, entity is wound up under a normal insolvency procedure (Art. 37(6) Resolution Directive). However, this procedure can only be triggered at the initiative of the resolution authority (Art. 86(1) of the Resolution Directive). On the articulation of the insolvency and resolution procedure, see spec. Art. 86(2) of the Resolution Directive.

97 Art. 34(1) of the Resolution Directive.

98 Art. 34(2) of the Resolution Directive. The Directive provides, under certain conditions, for the possibility to 'convert' claims, i.e. to transform them into shares. These two procedures nevertheless require certain measures to protect creditors and shareholders, on which see A. Sotiropoulou, 'Sharesholders' and creditors' protection in bail in' in *Le traitement des difficultés des établissements bancaires et institutions financières, op. cit.*, pp. 267 et seq.

99 In this sense, Professor Robine considers that the Resolution Directive only improves the common law, see D. Robine, 'La création des mécanismes de résolution sous l'influence de la crise financière', *op. cit.*

100 This three-stage presentation is borrowed from A.-C. Muller, 'Regards sur la directive Résolution', *BJB*, December 2015, no. 112z0, spec. pp. 579 et seq. It should be noted that simultaneously with the 'first stage' of resolution, when the institution is *in bonis*, it is also subject to the preventive measures provided for by the regulation on prudential requirements (the so-called 'CRD IV package'), which provide in particular for verification of compliance with prudential requirements notably through 'stress tests'. These tests are also linked to the second stage of the Resolution Directive, since they make it possible to realise whether the institution is no longer complying with certain prudential requirements, which triggers the early intervention measures provided for by the Resolution Directive.

101 Where the institution is still *in bonis*, the Resolution Directive first requires each institution to maintain and update annually a recovery plan setting out how it would recover from a significant deterioration in its financial position (Art. 5 of the Resolution Directive; recovery plans allow for the adoption of early intervention measures, which are similar to reorganisation measures, see spec. Art. 30 of the Resolution Directive). Secondly, the directive allows the resolution authorities, once the recovery plan has been obtained, to remove obstacles to resolvability in order to ensure that, if necessary, the authority can proceed to resolution. The powers granted to the authorities in this context can be

institution 'breaches, or is likely to breach in the near future' the prudential requirements normally applicable to it,[102] and finally when it is in 'actual or foreseeable' difficulty.[103] If the conditions for resolution are met, the resolution authority's control becomes total: the governing body is divested,

---

particularly intrusive (this can go as far as requiring the sale of assets, see Art. 17(5)) even though the institution is *in bonis*: Professor Prüm considers that 'this is an exorbitant power, particularly intrusive, since the institution in question is still in perfect health, but will nevertheless be forced to make changes likely to profoundly modify its legal or operational structures, the scope of its activities, the level of risks it has decided to take, and even to lead to a separation of functions deemed critical' (A. Prüm, 'Le nouveau cadre européen du traitement des faillures à vol d'oiseau', *RDBF*, 2014, no. 6, p. 94, spec.no. 20). The reason for these exorbitant prerogatives is that the authorities now want to ensure that institutions are not 'too big to rescue'.

102 Art. 27 of the Resolution Directive. The Resolution Directive then gives the group and the authorities of the group and its subsidiaries the power to adopt a set of measures. This second stage already carries its share of radical prerogatives offered to the authorities since it allows them to dismiss, individually or collectively, the managing members (Art. 28 of the Resolution Directive; Art. 29 allows the appointment of a temporary administrator and Art. 30 provides for the coordination of these measures at group level). The existence of such a prerogative undoubtedly explains why one of the key measures of this second phase, the decision to provide intra-group financial support, is left to the sovereign appreciation of the shareholders, and why, consequently, the powers of the authorities are strictly framed: intra-group financial support may be encouraged by the authority under certain conditions (Art. 19(3) of the Resolution Directive; the fear undoubtedly stems from the fact that intra-group financial support will have the consequence of impoverishing one institution in the group to the benefit of another, see T. Bonneau, 'Le traitement administratif des entreprises bancaires et financières', *RDBF*, November 2014, pp. 77 et seq., spec. no. 6), and without the possibility of repression (Art. 19(4) of the Resolution Directive).

103 This third stage is that of the resolution itself. If the principles of resolution have strong similarities with the law of collective proceedings (see Art. 34 of the Resolution Directive), but appear more radical for all the third parties affected by the resolution (there is, literally, a price to pay to allow the resolution, and it is the creditors who will bear it), the conditions for triggering the resolution nevertheless differ from those of the insolvency procedure. They meet three cumulative conditions (Art. 32(1)(a), (b) and (c) of the Resolution Directive; for the case of financial undertakings belonging to a group, see Art. 33(4) of the Resolution Directive). Firstly, the failure must be proven or foreseeable (Art. 32(4) Resolution Directive; the gradation between these two states has consequences in terms of regime: the impairment/conversion obligation is thus only possible if the entity is no longer viable, see Art. 59(3)(b) Resolution Directive and, for the assessment of viability, Arts. 59(5) and 61 Resolution Directive) Secondly, there must be no reasonable alternative prospects or private measures to remedy the situation. Thirdly, the resolution must be necessary in the public interest. The latter is defined in Art. 32(5) of the Resolution Directive. The European legislator did not want to leave too much room for manoeuvre in the assessment of standards. It should be noted that the conditions for resolution are relaxed in the context of groups of companies, where the parent company may be subject to resolution if its subsidiaries, which are institutions subject to the Resolution Directive and have entered into resolution, to the extent that 'their failure threatens an institution or the group as a whole, or the insolvency law of the Member State requires groups to be treated as a whole and the resolution measure in respect of the entity (*the parent enterprise*) is necessary for the resolution of one or more of its subsidiaries [...] or to the resolution of the whole group', see Art. 33(4) of the Directive.

the appointment of new managers is closely controlled by the authority.[104] More generally, the Resolution Directive provides that the powers of resolution authorities cannot be restricted or conditioned by the approval of a public or private authority.[105] Most importantly, it becomes possible to put in place a resolution plan,[106] the preparation and execution of which is the core of the resolution process.[107]

II. Resolution and Legislation of the Registered Office

105. Universality and territoriality of bankruptcy law. As a special insolvency regime, resolution does not escape the traditional tensions of insolvency law when confronted with international relations. Two traditional perceptions are opposed, between a universal and unitary approach and a territorial and plural approach. According to the first theory, 'a defaulting debtor can only be the subject of one proceeding at a given time (principle of the unity of bankruptcy) and this proceeding must take effect in all States where he has assets (principle of the universality of bankruptcy)'.[108] From the point of view of direct jurisdiction, this theory, based on the substantive approach of bankruptcy law, gives priority jurisdiction to the court of the debtor's domicile,[109] and implies, from the point of view of the effects of foreign judgments, 'recognition as automatically as possible of the decision of this court (with exclusive jurisdiction), with all the effects that a *lex concursus* attaches to it, which is by the same token also unique'.[110] According to the opposite theory, bankruptcy can only have territorial effects, i.e. limited to the territory of the court that pronounced it. It will therefore be necessary to open as many bankruptcy proceedings as there are territories in which the bankrupt possesses assets (the principle of plurality of bankruptcies), and the recognition of foreign judgments therefore appears to be thwarted.

As Mr Synvet writes, while both conceptions are excessive and outdated, 'the intelligence of these systems remains useful, in that it allows an overview of the possible solutions, with their justifications and concrete consequences'.[111] The

---

104 Art. 28 of the Resolution Directive. Indeed, of the two, the resolution authority appoints a temporary administrator (Art. 29). One will recognise here prerogatives known from insolvency law: the Resolution Directive specifies that, when there is a resolution, the Member States must put the resolution authority in a position to manage the institution directly or indirectly (Art. 72 of the Resolution Directive).

105 Art. 63(2) of the Resolution Directive.

106 Art. 10 of the Resolution Directive.

107 Not surprisingly, this is where coordination of authorities is most crucial. As resolution planning is a central element of resolution, it is logical that coordination of authorities is established in the preparation, planning and implementation of resolution decisions.

108 See 'Faillite' in H. Synvet, *Répertoire de droit international*, Paris, Dalloz, 1998, no. 11; see also D. Bureau and H. Muir Watt, *Droit international privé, op. cit.*, no. 1081.

109 Designated by the centre of main interests in the Insolvency Regulation, see Art. 3(1).

110 See 'Faillite' in H. Synvet, *Répertoire de droit international, op. cit.*

111 *Ibid.*, no. 10.

law of resolution borrows largely from the universalist theory of bankruptcy, but tempers its solutions by decorrelation of the competent authority and the applicable law, and the application of local law in all cases where the latter proves to be the predominant centre of gravity of the legal institution in question.[112] These solutions do not date from the Resolution Directive: they were already included in the Winding up Directive, which constitutes the backdrop on which the resolution mechanisms are deployed.[113]

106. The adoption of the directive on the reorganisation and winding up of credit institutions. The European Union has been dealing with the prevention and failure of credit institutions since 2001, through the Winding up Directive. The universal bankruptcy scheme introduced is inspired by the mutual recognition of authorisations and the prudential supervision model that it generates. Indeed, the Winding up Directive is a continuation of Directive 2000/12 of the European Parliament and of the Council of 20 March 2000 relating to the taking up and pursuit of the business of credit institutions. The latter marked the consolidation of the mutual recognition method for the authorisation of credit institutions. Under this method, the supervision of the institution and its branches established in the territory of other Member States was subject to the authority of the head office of the institution. In this context, the European legislator considered that 'it would be particularly inappropriate to abandon the unity which the institution forms with its branches when it is necessary to adopt reorganisation measures or to open winding-up proceedings'.[114] The entry into force of the Insolvency Regulation, from which the banking sector was excluded, made it necessary to treat the banking sector separately. This is why the Winding up Directive covers all credit institutions established in the EU, but also branches of institutions from third countries if they have two branches in two EU Member States.[115] The Resolution Directive has extended the solutions to investment firms in order to align their material scope of application.

107. Universal application of the law of the seat. The current pattern is that of centralisation within the legal system of the home Member State of reorganisation

---

112 This lack of coincidence of the need for *forum* and *jus* in a matter where it is customary to do so merits further discussion, which will be devoted to it in the study of these detailed solutions, see *infra*, para. 758.

113 The Directive 2001/24/EC of the European Parliament and of the Council of 4 April 2001 on the reorganisation and winding-up of credit institutions, hereinafter 'the Winding up Directive', is still in force, and the Resolution Directive has extended its solutions in two ways: firstly, by extending its material scope, previously restricted to credit institutions, to investment firms (Art. 1(3) of the Winding up Directive) and, secondly, by considering that any resolution instrument constitutes a reorganisation measure (Art. 117 of the Resolution Directive amends Art. 1(3) and Art. 2(7) of the Winding up Directive in this sense).

114 Recital 4 of the Winding up Directive.

115 Each branch then benefits from independent treatment within the meaning of the Directive, see point 22 and Article 8 of the Winding up Directive. In these cases, we are back to territorial bankruptcies.

and possibly liquidation measures.[116] The applicable law is then that of the State which issued the authorisation,[117] i.e. the law of the registered office, the application of which is entrusted to the administrative and/or judicial courts of the same Member State. Article 3 of the Winding up Directive states that

> '1. The administrative or judicial authorities of the home Member State alone shall be empowered to decide on the implementation of one or more reorganisation measures in a credit institution, including branches established in other Member States,.
>
> 2. The reorganisation measures shall be applied in accordance with the provisions of the laws, regulations and procedures applicable in the home Member State, unless otherwise provided in this Directive.'

The head office authorities therefore have exclusive competence for the reorganisation and winding-up measures of the institution and its branches.[118] The host Member States, i.e. those where the branches are located, must recognise the measures taken by the home Member State, including with regard to third parties, without the need to obtain an exequatur.[119] As Mr d'Avout writes, this is a radical illustration of 'the "jurisdiction/recognition" pairing, which is fairly classic in international matters and is decisive for the articulations made (jurisdiction restricted to one State or a small number of States, covering the administrative decision and the judicial remedies; recognition in all the other States concerned and doomed to passivity)'.[120] This system should allow for the unitary and universal treatment of reorganisation and possibly liquidation in order to guarantee the equality of creditors in the latter case.[121] However,

116 B. Audit and L. d'Avout, *Droit international privé*, *op. cit.* The internal functioning of the credit institution does not fall within the scope of the directive, the European legislator observing that the *lex societatis* corresponds in any case to the law of the Member State of origin, see in this sense Recital 8 of the Winding up Directive, according to which: 'Certain measures, in particular those which affect the operation of the internal structure of credit institutions or the rights of directors or shareholders, do not need to be covered by this Directive in order to have full effect in the Member States insofar as, in applying the rules of private international law, the applicable law is that of the home State.'

117 Art. 3(2°) (reorganisation measures) and 10 (liquidation) of the Winding up Directive.

118 Art. 3(1°) (reorganisation measures) and 9 (winding up) of the Winding up Directive. The term exclusive competence appears in Recitals 6 and 16, which explain its necessity because of the equal treatment of creditors.

119 Art. 3(2°) paras. 2 and 3 of the Winding up Directive. This Article has been implemented extensively, see Case C-85/12, *Landbanski*, ECLI:EU:C:2013:697. Prof. Kleiner (*D.* 2014, 249) considers, on the one hand, that the disputed measures did not fall within the scope of the Directive and, on the other hand, that their retroactive nature disqualified them from the scope of Article 3.

120 L. d'Avout, 'L'articulation des droits et des procédures dans un espace fédéralisé', *op. cit.*, p. 18.

121 Recital 16 of the Winding up Directive.

the European legislator seems to have foreseen the radical nature of the power given to the law of the institution's registered office and has taken care to 'temper'[122] these solutions by the specific application of the law of another Member State when the effects of the reorganisation or winding-up procedure 'conflict with the rules normally applicable to the economic and financial activity of the credit institution and its branches in the other Member States'.[123]

108. Tempering. The Directive thus considers it necessary to limit the scope of the law applicable to the measure, whether it is a reorganisation or liquidation measure. There are two ways of limiting the law of the seat: either the institution in dispute is made subject to a law other than the law of bankruptcy, or the scope of the law of bankruptcy is materially limited. Both techniques are used here. Firstly, the effects of the reorganisation or winding-up measure are no longer subject to the law of the home Member State, but to the law normally applicable to the affected institution.[124] This is notably the case for securities settlement systems which remain subject to their own law in case of insolvency.[125] This first tempering is also present in the Resolution Directive, which provides that the transfer of assets and its effects are subject to the law of the place where the assets are located,[126] without however giving jurisdiction to the courts of that State to challenge the measure.[127] Secondly, the law of the seat is also limited in its substantive scope so that the measures it takes 'shall not affect'[128] certain institutions which have in common the protection of the contracting party or

122 The term is used several times in the French version of the Directive itself (Recitals 23 and 24).

123 Recital 23 of the Winding up Directive.

124 This is particularly the case for contracts of employment (Art. 24 and Art. 20(a) of the Winding up Directive), contracts relating to immovable property (Art. 20(b) of the Winding up Directive –Art. 20(b) also regulates the conflict of classification relating to the determination of the movable or immovable nature of the thing in question by applying the law of the immovable property), rights in immovable property, ships or aircraft which require registration in the register of the State. It also regulates the conflict of characterisation linked to the determination of the movable or immovable nature of the thing in question by applying the law of the immovable property), rights in immovable property, ships or aircraft which require registration in a public register (Art. 20(c) of the Winding up Directive) or pending proceedings (Art. 32 of the Winding up Directive). A similar situation concerns netting arrangements and repurchase agreements, although their special status, which also contains a material limitation outside of the resolution, deserves its own development, see *infra*, para. 893.

125 sRecitals 25 and 26 of the Winding up Directive. These solutions are implicitly included in the scope of a general article on the exclusion from the scope of the reorganisation and winding-up measure, see Art. 24 of the Winding up Directive.

126 Art. 66(1) of the resolution. Some authors see in this article the setting up of '(a) system of mutual recognition of transfers of shares, property titles, assets, rights and liabilities operated by a resolution authority', J. Morel-Maroger, *Banque et droit*, October 2015, no. 163, pp. 56 et seq.

127 Art. 66(3) of the Resolution Directive.

128 This is the verb used in Art. 22(1) and Art. 23(1) of the Winding up Directive.

of credit: this is the case of the real rights of third parties,[129] retention of title or set-off, which remain respectively subject, in the event of insolvency, to the law which is normally applicable to them, *the lex contractus* or *the lex situs.*[130] While these solutions effectively temper the scope of the law of the seat of the establishment, they in no way limit the exclusivity of the legislative jurisdiction granted to the law of the registered office.

109. Conclusion of the section. Like all legal persons, infrastructure managers are attached to the legal system of their registered office. Their particularity, however, is that the connecting factor is that of the head office and that, in addition to the application of company law, it entails the application of prudential rules. Although the purpose of these rules is to apply company law, their purpose is to prevent the insolvency of the persons they cover. These observations have made it possible to qualify the role of the real seat in the protection of third parties, not only because other sets of legislation may protect them by virtue of the local establishment of the institution, but also because, in the context of market managers and, more broadly, of banking and financial institutions, this function is mainly carried out by prudential rules. The interaction of these two sets of rules and the coincidence of their criteria for application means that company law appears to be the trunk from which certain branches develop, such as insolvency law and prudential law. Inevitably, these branches are based on concepts defined by company law, such as capital securities, partners, or legal personality, in the same way that company law concepts are themselves based on those derived from civil law, such as contract or claim. These observations remind us of the interdependence of rules and the systemic nature of law. They show that the consistent application of legal requirements is not better served by applying liberal connecting factor criteria. They also suggest that the application of substantive European law will necessarily have to be coordinated with applicable national rules as long as Member States retain competence

---

129 Art. 21 of the Winding up Directive.

130 The original law, *lex concursus* or law of reorganisation, remains applicable to the action for nullity or unenforceability of the contractual or real prerogative. In French law, this means, for example, that the nullities of the suspect period can be applied. However, even this reservation is limited by a general provision protecting acts which the *lex contractus* renders 'unassailable', i.e. which in particular cannot be subject to nullity or unenforceability, including in the event of insolvency, see Art. 30 of the Winding up Directive – the provision speaks of 'prejudicial acts' and requires that this act be subject to the law of a Member State other than the one of origin (on this issue see also Recital 28 of the Winding up Directive). On these aspects, studied under the prism of the detailed solutions of the Insolvency Regulation and in the light of them, see *infra*, para. 913.
It should simply be noted here that the foreign law, if it is applied by the forum, should follow the procedural regime of the foreign law in European insolvency proceedings on which see F. Mélin, 'L'application d'une loi étrangère devant les procédures européennes d'insolvabilité' in *Mélanges en honneur Jean-Luc Vallens*, Paris, Lextenso, 2017, pp. 331 et seq.

in company law and civil law. However, the legislation applicable to market managers has one particularity: it is subject to supervision by an administrative authority, whose designation appears to be particularly significant.

SECTION 2. ADMINISTRATIVE CONNECTING FACTOR

110. The existence of centralised and decentralised models. Authorisation establishes a close connection between the administrative authority competent to grant authorisation and the authorised entity, a connection which explains why one can speak of a genuine *administrative connecting factor* similar to the legislative connecting factor. Administrative connecting factor refers to the criteria and process by which one or more administrative authorities are designated to authorise an infrastructure manager to carry out its activity. It justifies its existence on the grounds that 'the protection of the financial system depends, first and foremost, on the quality of the professionals who intervene in the markets in the context of providing investment services to their clients or carrying out market activities'.[131]

The result is administrative supervision of compliance with the conditions under which authorisation was granted, and in particular the prudential rules to which the manager is subject. The authority thus designated has only *executive* powers, but no legislative powers.[132] In this sense, if prudential rules are a meeting point of company law and insolvency law,[133] they are also a meeting point of administrative law and EU internal market law. The administrative connecting factor of infrastructure managers is modelled on that of investment firms. According to the latter, the exercise of their activity is conditional on an administrative authorisation granted by the authority of the Member State in which their registered office is located. This national authorisation nevertheless allows them, thanks to the mutual recognition mechanism, to carry out their activity on the territory of the other Member States. Following other authors,[134]

---

131 F. Drummond, *Droit financier, op. cit.*, no. 542; F. Peltier, 'L'agrément et le contrôle prudentiel', *op. cit.*, no. 253.

132 See from the point of view of the ECB, G. Hardy, *L'européanisation de la surveillance bancaire, op. cit.*, no. 75.

133 See *supra*, paras. 93 et seq.

134 This distinction is often used, but centralisation can sometimes refer to decision-making (see in this sense L. d'Avout, 'L'articulation des droits et des procédures dans un espace fédéralisé', *op. cit.*, p. 17), or to administrative cooperation. This last hypothesis is the case of the above-mentioned thesis by Ms Stoeva. The author shows that, in financial matters, the Union is divided between two models of cooperation between authorities, a decentralised cooperation and a centralised cooperation. The statement is correct and we agree with the author. However, it seems to us that, from the point of view of administrative competence, cooperation is secondary and dependent on a prior question, which is that of the author of the administrative decision. This reality explains our approach, which is not based on the

this model can be described as decentralised. In fact, it does not lead to the 'centralisation of the decision-making process'[135] in an EU agency, but keeps it within each Member State. This model is still in force today (§ 1). However, it is being challenged by a centralised model where approval is granted directly by an EU agency for the territory of the entire European Union. This model, which is in force in related fields, is likely to be extended to the administrative connecting factor of European infrastructure managers (§ 2).

§ 1. THE DECENTRALISED MODEL

111. Singularity of authorisation. The administrative connecting factor of market managers is always based on an authorisation, i.e. an authorisation to carry out the activity. The role of administrative authorisations in economic matters is not new.[136] It is an expression of the State's juridiction in economic matters[137] which is reflected in a network of administrative authorisations.[138] Authorisation is nevertheless somewhat ambiguous because of the two meanings it can have. Indeed, authorisation can mean, alternatively, 'delegating a part of the authority that one possesses oneself', or 'consenting to what one would have the right to prohibit'.[139] In French administrative law, authorisation is generally connected to the second meaning, since it is traditionally presented 'as a police instrument instituted with the aim of preventing the exercise of certain freedoms from disturbing public order'.[140] However, a study of French positive law today shows that administrative authorisations have distinct functions that can be connected to these two meanings.[141] Thus, while approval is an authorisation issued by the administration in order to carry out an economic activity, it nonetheless

modalities of cooperation, but on the question of the centralisation of the administrative decision. It is a nuance with regard to the colleges of authorities, which are as much a tempering of the decentralisation of the administrative decision as a mode of centralised cooperation.

135 According to Recital 10 of the SRM Regulation.

136 French law has long known the mechanism of prior authorisation in economic matters since, from the promulgation of the Commercial Code until the law of 24 July 1867, public limited companies have been subject to the administrative authorisation regime (B. Tricot, 'L'agrément administratif des institutions privées', *D.* 1948. 25) and from the law of 1867 onwards, this authorisation regime 'was maintained or subsequently re-established for certain insurance companies, whether or not they were in the form of limited companies'. (*Ibid.* The author cites in a note the decree-law of 14 June 1838).

137 On which, see *supra*, para. 9.

138 B. Tricot, 'L'agrément administratif des institutions privées', *op. cit.*: 'More than the adage that denies it a monopoly on the public good, the contemporary State is inspired by the other that nothing that concerns the general interest is foreign to it.'

139 A. Lalande, *Vocabulaire technique et critique de la philosophie*, 3rd ed., Paris, PUF, 2010, see 'Autorisation'.

140 L. Seurot, *L'autorisation administrative*, doctoral thesis, University of Lorraine, 2013, no. 1.

141 *Ibid.*

grants its holder 'a privileged situation which entails, in return, obligations and control'.[142] This explains why, as Professor Seurot puts it, 'approved institutions are subject to certain statutory and technical conditions, compliance with which is ensured by the supervision of the Administration. This control ranges from the simple right to be kept informed to the right to approve or even give instructions'.[143] In financial law, the activities subject to authorisation are the provision of investment services,[144] or access to a securities trading, clearing or settlement system.

112. The advent of a horizontal division of powers based on domicile. The existence of national authorisation traditionally meant that the provision of an investment service in France required authorisation from the French authority.[145] However, the desire to unify the EU's internal market changed this, as national authorisation was seen as an obstacle to the completion of the internal market. The choice was then made to enshrine a decentralised model, which is characterised by a distribution of administrative competences based on the registered office: the authority of the Member State of the registered office is the one competent to issue the authorisation.[146] This explains why today, if the authorisation is national, the prudential supervision to which it gives rise extends to all the Member States in which the company carries out its activity. As Mrs Tenenbaum has said, 'a national supervisory authority cannot now disregard the international aspect of the infrastructures and operators it supervises and claim that its action and the exercise of its powers are limited solely to the geographical territory of the State which established it'.[147]

This is why the national competent authority to grant authorisation is required to cooperate with the authorities of other Member States, according to different procedures depending on the managers, either because the entity requesting authorisation is part of a group present in other Member States or because it carries out its activity on the territory of other Member States and its supervision requires an exchange of information (I). This decentralised

---

142 *Ibid.*, p. 27.

143 *Ibid.*

144 The specificity of the authorisation of investment firms, compared to that of insurance or credit companies, is that the authorisation is given specifically for certain investment services only. For this reason, if an investment firm exceeds its authorisation, it may be subject to an administrative sanction (Art. L. 621-15 referring to Art. L. 621-14 of the Monetary and Financial Code) and may incur civil liability. On this issue, see F. Drummond, *Droit financier*, *op. cit.*

145 For the risk of criminal sanctions, see Arts. L. 573-1(1) and L. 573-7 of the Monetary and Financial Code.

146 In France, this is the ACPR, see Art. L. 532-1 of the Monetary and Financial Code. However, the AMF is closely involved in the procedure, as it approves the programme of operations provided by the investment firm.

147 A. Tenenbaum, 'La disparition de l'exigence de territorialité en matière de compétence des autorités de contrôle à l'épreuve du droit des marchés dérivés?', *RDBF*, July 2015, p. 74, no. 1.

connecting factor has two consequences. The first is that the manager's access to the territory of other Member States is permitted on the basis of the mutual recognition of authorisations. Where an investment firm is involved, the price of easy access to the territory of another Member State is, however, that if the firm has a branch there, it must comply with the local rules of conduct. The latter will be the basis for liability (II). The second consequence is to institute a decentralised treatment of the resolution of infrastructure managers who are subject to this regime (III).

I. Administrative Connecting Factor to a Member State

113. Function of the head office. In the administrative order, the function of the head office as a connecting factor is to designate the competent authority to grant accreditation on the one hand and to supervise the accredited entity on the other. However, the competence of the authority entails the competence of the entire legal order: its law will apply to the conditions of the authorisation[148] and to the authorisation procedure.[149] The competent courts in the event of a dispute with the authority will be those of the legal system that decided on the authorisation.[150] These elements are based on different grounds. Indeed, the basis for the application of local law to the conditions of authorisation is to be found in the function pursued by the organisational rules. On the other hand, the application of the law of the authority to the authorisation procedure is explained by reasons of good organisation of the administration. Finally, the courts competent to rule on administrative decisions are those designated by the legal order that established the administrative authority. The competence of the administrative order of the seat of the operator is not limited to the protection of local public order, but must also ensure the protection of European order insofar as the authorisation granted allows the operator to provide access to the system it operates in other Member States. The existence of this control partly explains

148 See in French law for investment firms Art. L. 532-2 of the Monetary and Financial Code.

149 However, it should be noted that this application of the local procedure is tempered by the unification of the procedure at European level by Implementing Regulation (EU) 2017/1945 of 19 June 2017 laying down technical implementing standards with regard to notifications by and to applicant or authorised investment firms.

150 Art. R. 621-45(I) of the Monetary and Financial Code states that 'appeals against individual decisions taken by the AMF relating to authorisations or sanctions concerning the persons and entities mentioned in II of Article L. 621-9 shall be brought before the Conseil d'État, in accordance with the procedures laid down in the Code of Administrative Justice'. The persons referred to in Art. L. 621-9(II) of the Monetary and Financial Code are in fact all financial actors, since the purpose of this Article is to determine the operators towards whom the AMF has a prudential supervisory role. The doctrine concludes from Article R. 621-45(I) that 'the two-month time limit provided for in the Administrative Justice Code is therefore applicable to individual AMF decisions relating to authorisations or sanctions' (E. Guillaume and L. Coudray, 'Autorités de régulation' in *Répertoire du contentieux administratif*, Paris, Dalloz, 2010, no. 57).

the function of the 'real seat' ('*siège reel*' i.e. of the head office), which is to enable the authority of the seat to exercise its control over the authorised entity when the latter is likely to operate in other Member States, which makes it necessary to establish the decision-making centre on the territory of the authority.[151]

114. Outsourcing. However, a difficulty exists for the exercise of supervision by the competent authority when the infrastructure manager outsources its activity to another Member State or a third country, either to a third party or to another member of the group within which the infrastructure manager operates.[152] In order to avoid this situation, outsourcing is closely monitored by legislation and controlled by the competent authority.[153] This control can lead to the withdrawal of the authorisation if the outsourcing affects key aspects of the business.[154] In particular, ESMA considered that outsourcing could not concern the key functions of management and business managers, internal control, IT systems control infrastructure, risk control or the compliance function.[155] With regard to trading platforms,[156] outsourcing may not involve the design, control and supervision of the operation of the trading system, the suspension or withdrawal of trading or the implementation of trading halt measures on the markets.[157] Furthermore, outsourcing may not be an obstacle to the authority's exercise of supervision, which presupposes that, where the investment firm is not established in the EU, cooperation agreements exist and are effective.[158]

151 See explicitly in this sense Recital 46 of MiFID 2 (which is an identical repetition of Recital 4 of the Investment Services Directive).

152 Outsourcing is defined as 'any arrangement, in whatever form, between an investment firm and a investment firm whereby the investment firm takes over a process, service or activity that would otherwise have been the responsibility of the investment firm itself', see Art. 2(3) of the Commission Delegated Regulation (EU) 2017/565 of 25 April 2016. On this issue, see HCJP report on the accessibility of the French market by UK banking and financial institutions in a post-Brexit environment, 7 November 2017, p. 31.

153 Art. 35 EMIR; Art. 30 CSD Regulation.

154 See for example Recital 44 of the Delegated Regulation 2017/565.

155 ESMA, 'Opinion, General principles to support supervisory convergence in the context of the United Kingdom withdrawing from the European Union', 31 May 2017, ESMA42-110-433, spec. paras. 31 et seq. See in the more specific context of trading platforms, ESMA, 'Opinion to support supervisory convergence in the area of secondary markets in the context of the United Kingdom withdrawing from the European Union', 13 July 2017, ESMA70-154-270, paras. 17 et seq. See from a banking perspective EBA, Guidance on outsourcing, 25 February 2019 (EBA/GL/2019/02), O. Bernardi and C. Feunteun, 'L'externalisation sera-t-elle un cheval de troie britannique?', *RISF*, 2019, no. 3-4, pp. 119 et seq.; G. Hardy, *L'européanisation de la surveillance bancaire*, *op. cit.* para. 1106.

156 For investment firms, see ESMA, 'Opinion to support supervisory convergence in the area of investment firms in the context of the United Kingdom withdrawing from the European Union', 13 July 2017, ESMA35-43-762, and HCJP Report cited above, pp. 35-36.

157 ESMA, 'Opinion to support supervisory convergence in the area of secondary markets in the context of the United Kingdom withdrawing from the European Union', *op. cit.*

158 See in particular Art. 32 of the Delegated Regulation (EU) 2017/565 and Art. 16(5) MiFID 2.

115. Authorisation and cooperation. The possibility for companies to offer their services on the territory of other Member States also has an impact on the supervision of the manager and makes European cooperation necessary when monitoring compliance with its conditions. The purpose of cooperation is therefore the exchange of information and, in certain cases, requests for on-site checks and investigations. The private international law issues raised by cooperation on prudential matters are nevertheless similar to those raised by cooperation on market abuse, in particular because the former has been modelled on the latter,[159] and they will therefore be dealt with jointly.[160] The following developments will examine how the connecting factor and the coordination it entails takes place for financial market managers (A), clearing houses (B), and central securities depositories (C).

A. Financial Market Managers

116. Administrative connecting factor of market operators. The notion of market operator is directly connected to the quality of the trading platform it operates, a regulated market. In France, in order to qualify as a market operator, the operator must obtain a singular administrative authorisation: recognition of the trading platform as a regulated market by a decree published by the Minister of the Economy,[161] which is issued on the basis of a proposal by the AMF[162]. Once the platform is recognised as such, the operator becomes a market operator and is therefore subject to AMF supervision. Although the procedures for connecting a platform to the AMF are different from those for investment firms, the result is the same: the market operator is connected to the authority of its head office, quite simply because, to obtain this status, 'its head office and effective management must be established on French territory'.[163]

117. The group of market operators. The particularity of a large number of market operators in Europe is that they are part of the same group, Euronext,[164] whose lead holding company is in the Netherlands.[165] As each subsidiary has the status of a market operator, the supervision of the group is carried out by the authority of the head office of each subsidiary. However, the coordination of

---

159 N. Cazenave, 'La perspective d'une autorité nationale de supervision', *Banque et droit*, special issue, February 2020, pp. 26 et seq.

160 See *infra*, paras. 546 et seq.

161 Art. L. 421-6 of the Monetary and Financial Code. See lastly the order of 5 February 2014 granting the status of regulated market for financial instruments to the Powernext Derivatives market managed by Powernext SA.

162 Art. L. 421-5 of the Monetary and Financial Code.

163 Art. L. 421-2 of the Monetary and Financial Code.

164 On the history of this group, see *supra*, para. 13 and references.

165 This has not always been the case, and the existence of the Euronext group in the United States has required transatlantic coordination, see P. Barban, *Les entreprises de marché*, *op. cit.*

this supervision is the subject of an agreement between the authorities,[166] which is regularly updated to take account of changes in the structure of the group,[167] and whose purpose is to 'define the manner in which they intend to exercise their responsibilities for the coordination of the regulation and supervision of Markets and Benchmark Administrators on a cooperative basis with a view to ensuring a common regulatory approach'.[168] The authorities intend to consult on any 'matters of common interest', covering both aspects relating to the internal functioning of the administrator,[169] and those specific to the trading system itself: its management arrangements, but also the rules governing the trading system.[170] Consultation takes place through the establishment of various committees, which take decisions by consensus[171] whenever a subject has a significant regulatory impact on the markets.[172] The committees set up by the cooperation agreement on supervision of the Euronext group are a special forum for exchanging information.[173]

118. Connecting factor of investment firms. Investment firms are subject to authorisation by the authority of their registered office. In France, this is the '*Autorité de contrôle prudentiel et de résolution*'.[174] The fact that an investment firm is connected to the authority of a Member State sometimes requires

---

166 However, this agreement is only 'a declaration of intent (*which*) does not give rise to any rights that may be invoked or any obligations' (Art. 2.3). These agreements have been described as 'the formalisation of possible administrative practices', S. Lambert, *L'application internationale du droit financier, op. cit.*, no. 1201. On the status of this agreement in international law, see R. Bismuth, *La coopération internationale des autorités de régulation du secteur financier et le droit international public*, Brussels, Bruylant, 2011, no. 312.

167 See lastly, the Cooperation Agreement between: *Autoriteit financiële markten* ('AFM' – Netherlands); *Autorité des marchés financiers* ('AMF' – France); Central bank of Ireland ('CBI' - Ireland); *Comissão do mercado de valores mobiliários* ('CMVM' – Portugal); Financial conduct authority ('FCA' – United Kingdom); *Finanstilsynet* ('FSA' – Norway); Financial services and markets authority ('FSMA' – Belgium), concerning the coordination of the regulation and supervision of the European regulated markets of the Euronext group and Euronext N.V. and the Euronext benchmark administrators, *JORF*, 20 February 2020, no. 43, NOR: AMFP2003959X. On a previous version of this agreement, the substance of which remained largely the same, see T. Bonneau, 'Contrôle du groupe Euronext', *RDBF*, November 2010, no. 6, comm. 236; B. Stoeva, *La coopération entre les superviseurs financiers dans l'Union européenne, op. cit.*, nos. 560 et seq.

168 Art. 1(4) of the above agreement.

169 From the modalities of its governance to its control, through its legal structure, see Art. 3.2.1 to 3.2.3 of the above-mentioned agreement.

170 Art. 3.2.4 of the above agreement.

171 Art. 4.2 of the above agreement.

172 Although the Euronext group takes the initiative in assessing materiality, it is nonetheless the chairmen's committee that is *ultimately* responsible for determining whether a transaction is material.

173 Arts. 1.5 and 2.2 of the above agreement.

174 Art. L. 532-1 of the Monetary and Financial Code. The AMF is nevertheless closely involved in the procedure, since it approves the programme of operations provided by the investment firm.

cooperation with the authorities of other Member States, particularly in the case where the firm is a subsidiary of a company authorised in another Member State. Indeed, in this case, MiFID 2 provides for a consultation mechanism prior to the granting of an authorisation, the function of which is to enable the authority to obtain the information necessary to grant the authorisation.[175] This consultation can take place according to the bilateral model established by MiFID 2, whereby each competent authority designates a contact point to respond to requests for information.[176] This request for information is made possible, on the one hand, by harmonising confidentiality requirements[177] and, on the other hand, by regulating the use that can be made of the information requested.[178] Finally, the possibility of mediation before ESMA makes it possible to remedy a lack of cooperation from the requested authority.[179]

119. The case of groups. The issue of supervision of groups of investment firms is the subject of more elaborate regulations than those governing market operators[180] and helps to temper the drawbacks of the decentralised model. Its source is no longer MiFID 2, but the IFD Directive.[181] In the case of a group of investment firms, the authority of the head office of the parent investment firm in the EU is given a specific power:[182] that of carrying out 'supervision on a consolidated basis or monitoring compliance with the capital adequacy test'.[183] The monitoring of compliance with the capital adequacy test allows small groups to escape supervision on a consolidated basis.[184] The notion of 'consolidated basis' is borrowed from accounting law where consolidation refers to the practice of aggregating accounting data by a company to analyse the activities of the group as a whole. In relation to supervisory requirements, it refers to the consolidated position, i.e. 'the position resulting from the application of the requirements of this Regulation (to a group of institutions) as if that undertaking, together with all the investment firms, financial institutions, ancillary services undertakings and tied agents in the group of investment firms, formed a single investment firm'.[185]

---

175 On this aspect, see B. Stoeva, *La coopération entre les superviseurs financiers dans l'Union européenne*, *op. cit.*

176 Art. 81(1) MiFID 2.

177 Art. 76 MiFID 2.

178 Art. 81(3) MiFID 2.

179 Art. 82 MiFID 2.

180 The reason for this is that it draws its inspiration from the regulation of the prudential supervision of groups of credit institutions, see Recital 30 of the DTI Directive.

181 On the solutions of this directive, see C. Feunteun, 'Refonte du régime prudentiel européen des entreprises d'investissement', *RDBF*, November 2019, comm. 211.

182 Art. 46(1) of the IFD.

183 *Ibid.*

184 Recital 30 of the IFD, see Art. 8 of the IFR.

185 Art. 1(11) of the IFR.

In order to designate the competent authority on a consolidated basis, a number of cascading jurisdictional rules have been established. They are based on the structure of the group.[186] Jurisdiction is in principle given to the parent enterprise if it is authorised, either as an investment firm or as a credit institution.[187] If this is not the case, the Directive provides for several subsidiary solutions[188] which can nevertheless be set aside by agreement between the various authorities concerned.[189] The competent authority is then designated as the authority on a consolidated basis, or group supervisor. The group supervisor may, where appropriate, set up a college of supervisors,[190] consisting of the supervisory authorities of the subsidiaries and, where appropriate, third country supervisory authorities if they meet confidentiality requirements equivalent to those laid down in the Directive.[191] While the college of supervisors is a privileged place for the coordination of authorities, in particular in order to facilitate requests for information, its establishment does not, however, apparently call into question the final word of the voice of the group supervisor who alone adopts the decisions taken.[192] At most, it should be noted that the supervisor's decisions relating to the functioning of the college may be challenged before the EBA.[193]

B. Clearing Houses

120. Connecting factor of clearing houses. Clearing houses are also linked by an authorisation to the authority of their head office.[194] The particularity is, however,

---

186 In this respect, the IFD refers to the definitions set out in the CRR Regulation, which in turn refers to Directive 2002/87/EC of the European Parliament and of the Council of 16 December 2002 on the supplementary supervision of credit institutions, insurance undertakings and investment firms in a financial conglomerate.

187 Art. 46(2) of the IFD.

188 If the holding company is not authorised, but there is an authorised subsidiary in the same state, the authority of the registered office of this subsidiary is the authority on a consolidated basis (Art. 46(3) DTI Directive), otherwise the size of the largest investment firm (assessed by its balance sheet total) may be the criterion for designation, see Art. 46(4) and (5) DTI Directive.
These mechanisms are inspired by the banking model, on which see B. Stoeva, *La coopération entre les superviseurs financiers dans l'Union européenne, op. cit.*

189 Art. 46(6) of the IFD.

190 Art. 48(1) of the IFD.

191 Art. 48(5) of the IFD.

192 Art. 48(6) of the IFD. Approving this model, see B. Stoeva, *La coopération entre les superviseurs financiers dans l'Union européenne, op. cit.*, para. 430. It should be noted that the model is not identical in the area of resolution, where the EBA's field of intervention is not limited to the functioning of the college, see *infra*, para. 161.

193 Art. 48(7) of the IFD. This competence of the EBA rather than ESMA appears curious and is undoubtedly the mark of the banking regulator's experience in prudential matters. However, it echoes the competence of the EBA within resolution colleges, see *infra*, para. 162.

194 Art. 14 of the EMIR.

that when the head office authority grants authorisation, a procedure requires it establishes a college of European authorities. One of the functions of the latter is to give its opinion to the head office authority on the granting of authorisation, and this college will subsequently be involved in all decisions taken by it.[195] This college is established by the head office authority of the clearing house, which has a central role in its operation.[196] It is made up of members of the CCP Oversight Committee (a body of ESMA),[197] the supervisory authorities of the members of the clearing system operated by the CCP, as well as the authorities of the market infrastructure managers connected to the CCP and, finally, the members of the European System of Central Banks, which have supervisory jurisdiction over the clearing system itself.[198] The functioning of the college is subject to the authority of the home Member State, but is distinct from that known for groups of investment firms because of the existence of an embryonic form of co-decision. Indeed, authorisation cannot be granted if all members of the college oppose it. The head office authority can then only appeal to ESMA.[199] Furthermore, during supervision, the home authority is likely to receive an injunction from ESMA, in order to verify that the clearing house still complies with the conditions of the licence.

Two observations are necessary here. Firstly, the presence of a college does not change the administrative connecting factor of clearing houses. They remain subject to the authority of their head office: although the latter may be constrained by the college when granting authorisation, it is nevertheless the authority that originates the decision, and its administrative order will be the one competent to contest the decision. Moreover, the headquarters authority alone has the power to decide on the withdrawal of the authorisation. Secondly, the particular legitimacy enjoyed by the headquarters authority, which is not only based on the principle of subsidiarity, but stems from the fact that its

---

195 Art. 18(1) of the EMIR.

196 See Art. 4 of Commission Delegated Regulation (EU) No 876/2013 of 28 May 2013 supplementing Regulation (EU) No 648/2012 of the European Parliament and of the Council as regards technical regulatory standards for colleges of central counterparties. The home Member State authority plays the role that ESMA may play in colleges of supervisors of investment firms subject to the ESM, see Art. 21 of Regulation 1095/2010. On the ESM, see *infra*, para. 177.

197 On which, see Art. 24a of the EMIR.

198 The members of the college are listed in Art. 18(2) of the EMIR. On the European System of Central Banks see *supra*, para. 61, and on the competence they exercise over clearing systems, see *infra*, paras. 244 et seq.

199 Art. 17(4) paras. 3 and 4 of the EMIR. On this point, see already B. Stoeva, *La coopération entre les superviseurs financiers dans l'Union européenne*, *op. cit.*, no. 587. In favour of such a co-decision process, see S. Lambert, *L'application internationale du droit financier*, *op. cit.*, no. 937.

legal order is the one that will be most affected by the possible insolvency of the chamber.[200]

C. Central Securities Depositories

121. Connecting factor of depositories. Central securities depositories are authorised by the authority of their head office. Certain authorities, known as 'relevant authorities', must nevertheless be involved in the granting of the authorisation and the supervision of the CSD.[201] The first relevant authority is 'the authority responsible for the oversight of the securities settlement system operated by the central depository in the Member State whose law applies to that system'.[202] Indeed, this authority will not necessarily be the authority of the seat because of the possible dissociation between the law applicable to the securities settlement system and the law of the seat of the depositary. The authorities concerned are also the central banks which, in the Union, 'issue the most relevant currencies in which settlement takes place',[203] it being noted that the Regulation applies to central securities depositories established in States not belonging to the monetary union. Finally, the last authority concerned is, where applicable, the central bank providing the cash settlement function for the exchange of securities within the settlement platform.[204] However, this cash settlement function is not necessarily performed by a central bank. Indeed, the CSD Regulation only encourages a central bank to be the settlement agent 'in order to avoid settlement risks due to the insolvency of a settlement agent'.[205] If this is not the case, it is possible for the CSD to either offer this service itself or to designate one or more authorised credit institutions for this purpose.[206] In this case, the bank licensing authority has the sole power to grant the authorisation to the central depository, although it must also consult the authorities concerned by the granting of the central depository authorisation. The main difference in the process in place for the authorisation of central depositories, apart from the

---

200 As perfectly expressed in Recital 52 of EMIR: 'Where a CCP is at risk of insolvency, the Member State in which the CCP is established may have to assume the bulk of the resulting fiscal responsibility. The authorisation and supervision of that CCP should therefore be entrusted to the competent authority of that Member State'. On this link, see also B. Stoeva, *La coopération entre les superviseurs financiers dans l'Union européenne, op. cit.*, no. 580.

201 Art. 12(1) CSD Regulation.

202 Art. 12(1)(a) CSD Regulation.

203 Art. 12(1)(b) of the CSD Regulation.

204 Art. 12(1)(c) CSD Regulation. The Regulation encourages a central bank to be the settlement agent 'in order to avoid settlement risks due to the insolvency of a settlement agent' (Recital 44 CSD Regulation), see Art. 40 CSD Regulation. If this is not the case, it is possible for the CSD to either offer this service itself or to designate one or more authorised credit institutions for this purpose (Art. 54(3) CSD Regulation).

205 Recital 44 CSD Regulation, see also Art. 40 CSD Regulation.

206 Art. 54(3) of the CSD Regulation. On this aspect, see B. Stoeva, *La coopération entre les superviseurs financiers dans l'Union européenne, op. cit.*, no. 618.

absence of an institutional consultation process comparable to that set up for the supervisory colleges of clearing houses, lies in the absence of possible opposition from the authorities concerned by the authorisation to the decision to authorise the institution.[207]

The existence of an international group of central securities depositories, Euroclear, and the absence of supervisory colleges made it necessary to establish a memorandum of understanding between authorities.[208] This has the same status as the one studied for the supervision of the Euronext group, and specifies the division of tasks between the authorities of the various subsidiaries,[209] and the authority of the Belgian parent entity,[210] in addition to providing for information exchange mechanisms under the aegis of a designated coordinator, the Belgian central bank.[211]

II. Access to the Territory of Other Member States

122. Solicitation and access to the territory of other Member States. In European financial law, access to the territory of another Member State by an entity subject to administrative authorisation is most often achieved through mutual recognition. This has the effect of setting aside the public law rules governing access to the host Member State's market, and the associated control by the host Member State's administrative authority. However, mutual recognition operates in a different way depending on whether the issue is access to a market infrastructure or the provision of an investment service. This second case creates a tension between the objectives of European financial law of internal market integration and investor protection. In order to resolve it, it is necessary to use the concept of solicitation. Here, solicitation has the meaning that it has in common parlance, namely 'the action of soliciting something from someone, of pressing in order to obtain something'.[212] As Mr d'Avout has written, 'the act of soliciting the public' is 'the cause and measure of the applicability of local law',[213] and access by investment firms to the territory of other Member States is an illustration of this.

---

[207] See in favour of the establishment of a supervisory board, *ibid.*, nos. 621 et seq.

[208] Memorandum of understanding on the co-operation framework for the oversight/supervision of Euroclear SA/NV (ESA), *JORF*, 14 November 2012. On this agreement, see B. Stoeva, *La coopération entre les superviseurs financiers dans l'Union européenne, op. cit.*, no. 635 and T. Bonneau, 'Conclusion d'un accord entre diverses autorités européennes en vue de la supervision du groupe Euroclear', *RDBF*, July 2010, no. 4, comm. 163.

[209] Art. 5.4 of the above-mentioned Memorandum of Understanding and spec. Art. 3.1.12 for the MFA.

[210] Art. 3.1 of the above-mentioned Memorandum of Understanding.

[211] Arts. 5.2 et seq., spec. 5.3 of the above-mentioned Memorandum of Understanding.

[212] See 'Sollicitation' in *Trésor informatisé de la langue française.*

[213] L. d'Avout, 'L'entreprise et les conflits internationaux de lois', *op. cit.*, no. 79.

However, the solicitation criterion is only subsidiary to the access to foreign territory; the objective here is to preserve the logic of integration of the internal market (A). Nevertheless, it underpins the logic of the international applicability of the rules of conduct applicable to the exercise of the activity, which are indissociable from the access to foreign territory.[214] Indeed, these rules, applicable to the relationship between the investment firm and its clients, constitute the necessary premise for the investment firm's liability. The application of local law to the liability regime appears to be the inevitable counterpart of the limitation of local law on access to the territory (B).

A. Access to the Territory of Other Member States and Mutual Recognition

123. Mutual recognition and access to infrastructure. Mutual recognition has its origins in the case law interpretation of the freedom of movement of goods under primary law. This served as a model for the mutual recognition of authorisations subsequently introduced by European regulations, particularly in the area of investment firms.[215] However, as Professor Régis Vabres and Mr Roger Gaspard have shown, the mutual recognition imposed by the case law in the name of primary law does not have the same function as that resulting from secondary law. In the first case, 'its main purpose is to invalidate obstacles to European freedom of movement'[216] and 'in no way prejudges the division of competences between the Member State of origin and the host Member State'.[217] On the other hand, in the second case, secondary legislation 'implements a genuine division of competences between the Member States and entrusts the exercise of these competences primarily to the home Member State'.[218] The

214 H. Muir Watt, 'L'entrave à la prestation transfrontière de services' in *Mélanges Béguin*, Paris, LexisNexis, 2005, pp. 545 et seq.

215 As the Commission itself admits, see White Paper on completing the internal market, COM (85) 310, 14 June 1985, para. 102: 'A comparison can be made between the approach taken by the Commission following the ruling in the "Cassis de Dijon" case with regard to industrial and commercial products and the action to be taken now with regard to insurance, home savings contracts, consumer credit, collective investment schemes, etc.'; see also in this sense R. Gaspard, *La reconnaissance mutuelle en droit bancaire et financier*, *op. cit.*, nos. 2 and 12.

216 *Ibid.*, no. 9.

217 R. Vabres, *Comitologei et services financiers*, *op. cit.*, p. 282.

218 R. Vabres, *Comitologie et services financiers*, *op. cit.*, p. 282. These quotations are taken up by R. Gaspard, *La reconnaissance mutuelle en droit bancaire et financier*, *op. cit.*, Mr Gaspard thus showed in the first part of his thesis that mutual recognition, based on the freedom of movement of the original law of the Union, had precisely the function of prohibiting cumulation of regulation. In the second part of his thesis, the author considers that this prohibitive function is supplanted in the area of the 'financial passport', in particular the prospectus, by a distributive function of regulatory competence. For the difference in the way the two methods identified by the author are deployed, see *ibid.*, nos. 385–390. The idea that mutual recognition proceeds to a distribution of the legislative competence of public law rules was already supported, see e.g. H. Muir Watt, 'L'entrave à la prestation transfrontière de services', *op. cit.*

Second Banking Directive[219] owes its fame precisely to the fact that it was the first European text to explore this new method, which was taken up by the Investment Services Directive and, subsequently, by all the rules relating to the status of infrastructure managers. It is therefore not surprising that secondary legislation implements a division of competences based on mutual recognition, applicable both to managers and to investment firms operating on non-regulated markets. Nevertheless, we would like to show here that the logic of primary law also permeates, in secondary law, certain rules applicable to the Member States where the infrastructure managers are located, on which the need to allow investment firms from other Member States to access the services provided by these managers weighs (1). It will then be shown, on the one hand, that mutual recognition does not completely eliminate the logic of the conflict of laws, which appear in the conditions of its implementation and, on the other hand, that mutual recognition presents some singularities when it concerns the particular administrative authorisation that constitutes the authorisation (2).

1. *Access to Services Provided by the Infrastructure Manager*

124. Principle. Secondary European legislation establishes a genuine *right of access* to infrastructure for which the Member States to which the managers are connected are accountable. Secondary law seems to adopt the logic of primary law established in the area of free movement of goods. More specifically, these prerogatives of authorised entities show the desire for total integration of market infrastructures within a single market. In particular, two access rights are granted to certain authorised entities: access to infrastructure by investment firms and access to infrastructure by other managers.

125. Firstly, MiFID 2 allows access for investment firms to the services provided by infrastructure managers. This access is given concrete form by the positive obligation on Member States to allow access to investment firms from other Member States.[220] It is as if the existence of legal obstacles to the

[219] Second Council Directive 89/646/EEC of 15 December 1989 on the coordination of laws, regulations and administrative provisions relating to the taking up and pursuit of the business of credit institutions.

[220] Arts. 36 and 37 of MiFID 2. However, while the Member States have a positive obligation, the infrastructure manager is only subject to an obligation of means with regard to the members of the infrastructure in providing physical access to the computerised system. See clearly in this sense, in a case where there was a breakdown of the computerised system causing damage to a member, CA Paris, 13 February 2013, no. 10/17571, *RDBF*, January 2014, no. 1, note A.-C. Muller; Cass. com., 6 il April 2001, *Popovici c/Sté des bourses françaises,* now Euronext Paris, T. Bonneau, *RDBF*, March 2002, study 100016. This obligation originates from Art. 15(1) of the Investment Services Directive. Paragraph 2 of the same Article marked the definitive end of the numerus clausus that limited the number of market members in France through the system of charges for stockbrokers.

implementation of this right of access were considered a barrier.[221] However, there is a curious exception to this rule: managers who may have the status of investment firms, i.e. managers of non-regulated markets (MTF and OTF), are not subject to it. It seems to us, however, that primary law could be used to fill this legislative gap in order to eliminate a rule that creates an obstacle to the access of an investment firm to a multilateral or organised trading facility, or even establishes a restriction of competition.[222] Secondly, this same logic is applied to the relationship between market infrastructure managers themselves, whether for identical infrastructures, as is the case between central counterparties,[223] or between different types of infrastructures, such as access by central counterparties and central securities depositories to the system managed by market managers.[224]

---

221 It is true that the manager himself may, in some cases, refuse access, but in these cases the guarantees required to become a member of the market are involved, see Art. L. 421-17 of the Monetary and Financial Code, based on the former Article 42(3) of the MiFID Directive, on which see F. Drummond, *Droit financier*, *op. cit.*, no. 575.
Some authors see this obligation on the manager of a regulated market as the mark of the public service mission exercised by the market undertaking (see *ibid.*, n. 972). It seems to us, however, that it is rather a mark of the influence of European law, and in particular of the objective of integration of the internal market.

222 Indeed, the first type of non-discriminatory barrier identified in *Cassis de Dijon* is supplemented by a second type, which may have appeared not in the area of the movement of goods, but in financial law, where access to the activity is sometimes subject to certain restrictions, see R. Gaspard, *La reconnaissance mutuelle en droit bancaire et financier, op. cit.* This second type of obstacle also concerns a measure that is indiscriminately applicable, although it would not necessarily be contrary to the legislation of origin. For these other indiscriminately applicable rules, the qualification of obstacle would lie in the substantial solution they advocate: the prevention, for a foreign operator, of *de facto* access to the regulated economic segment (which is why it would always be possible for the Member State concerned to restrict the conditions for exercising the regulated economic activity, but not access to an activity, see 'The rules of the Member States', *op. cit.* For an illustration of this type of obstacle in the area of investment services, in the *Alpine Investment* judgment, in the banking area, in the *CaixaBank* judgment, and in the insurance area, in the *Commission v. Italy* judgment, on which see R. Gaspard, *La reconnaissance mutuelle en droit bancaire et financier, op. cit.*, nos. 66 et seq.) It was noted that it was close to the definition of the restriction of competition as formulated in Article 101 TFEU. Thus, after observing that 'the question raised, which technically falls within the scope of freedom of establishment, also concerns competition', Mr Synvet noted, in his observations under the *CaixaBank* judgment (*D.*, 2006, 155), that 'it is moreover remarkable that the main French banks associated themselves in the proceedings with the French government to defend the regulatory prohibition on remuneration; it is doubtful that their main concern was consumer protection or the encouragement of medium- or long-term savings'. See also R. Gaspard, *La reconnaissance mutuelle en droit bancaire et financier, op. cit.*, nos. 68–69. The independence of these two concepts, the intrinsic obstacle and the restriction of competition, is based on the idea that freedom of movement would be illusory if national rules effectively prevented access to the market.

223 Art. 7 EMIR; see also the interoperability agreements between CCPs in Arts. 51 et seq.

224 Art. 8 EMIR and Art. 53 CSD Regulation. See also from the point of view of market managers, Arts. 35 and 36 MiFID Regulation.

126. Limitations. This right of access to an infrastructure is, however, limited. The first is related to the operators of multilateral and organised trading facilities. As the provision of access to this platform is an investment service, it is treated as such and subject to the conditions of mutual recognition of authorisations.[225] This treatment is not perfectly identical since the investment firm will not have to wait for the notification procedure to operate in the desired territory. The notification by the administrative authority of its seat is sufficient. This seems to indicate a desire to treat market infrastructures differently.[226] The second limitation is specific to central securities depositories, for which the exercise of their activity on the territory of another Member State is subject to the same conditions as investment firms.[227]

2. *Mutual Recognition of Authorisations*

127. Existence of a notification procedure. Mutual recognition of authorisations is not automatic, but subject to a notification procedure. The triggering of the notification procedure shows the penetration of conflict-of-laws methods within mutual recognition, simply because the notification criterion is based on the location of the service in a territory. It will nevertheless be shown that the use of location criteria from private international contract law appears to be out of step with the objective pursued by mutual recognition. This difficulty in developing an appropriate criterion for triggering the procedure stems from the tension inherent in the objectives of MiFID 2 (a). It will then be argued that the object of mutual recognition is not the foreign regulation but, on the one hand, the decision of the foreign administrative authority and, on the other hand, the supervision of the authority of the home Member State, which leads to some observations on the regime of this recognition (b).

a. The Conditions of Access to the Territory of Another Member State

128. Condition of access. Once authorisation has been obtained, it becomes possible for authorised firms to carry out their activities on the territory of another Member State without recourse to another authorisation.[228] Such cross-border operations, if they truly constitute a right of the authorised firms, are

---

[225] B. Stoeva, *Cooperation between financial supervisors in the European Union, op. cit.*

[226] This is reflected in a CESR paper, see CESR, 'The Passport under MiFID. Recommendations for the implementation of the Directive 2004/39/EC', May 2007, CESR/07-337, spec. no. 56, p. 12 and Recommendation no. 12.

[227] Recitals 22 and 23 and Art. 23 CSD Regulation.

[228] This also applies to investment firms operating a non-regulated market, see Art. 34(6) and (7) MiFID 2. The role of authorisation is all the more important because the host Member State authority has insignificant powers under any procedure. Indeed, the procedure to be followed by investment firms is not the same if they wish to provide investment services

subject to three conditions: compliance with the conditions of its authorisation in the home Member State, obtaining an authorisation in that same home State covering the activities that the firms wishes to carry out in another Member State, and finally compliance with two formal conditions.

The first relates to the notification of the investment firm to its home competent authority: the notification must not only identify individually the Member State in which it intends to operate or establish a branch, but must also provide 'a programme of operations, including an indication of the investment service(s) it intends to provide'[229] and, finally, indicate the intention of the investment firm to use a tied agent within the Member State. Two remarks are necessary here. First, the investment services in question may not exceed the material scope of the activities for which the firm has been authorised.[230] Secondly, the notification appears here as a formal element of the investment firm's intention to solicit foreign residents, and therefore allows the firm to be held liable.[231] The second formal condition is the communication by the home Member State authority to the host Member State authority, i.e. the one referred to in the notification.[232] Only then, after a period of two months,[233] can the investment firm provide the services for which it has been authorised.

129. Implementation of the notification procedure. However, two difficulties have arisen in relation to the notification procedure. The first was the question of who is responsible for the notification obligation between an investment firm and its branch when the latter is the establishment acting under the freedom to provide services.[234] The rule was interpreted strictly, and it is up to the investment firm itself to notify its home authority of its branch's intention to operate in another Member State under the freedom to provide services.

The second difficulty relates to the material criteria for triggering the notification procedure. This issue first arose in the area of banking, but is

---

through the establishment of a branch, or through the freedom to provide services, the structure of the prerogatives granted to the investment firm does not change: the home Member State truly retains control over the investment firm in both cases.

229 Arts. 34(2) and 35(2) MiFID 2.

230 This condition, which is constant in European regulations, is reminiscent of one of the conditions of the theory of acquired rights that Pillet developed during the 'major cases arising from the irregular life of Russian companies in France', where the author wrote that 'it was necessary to bow to the evidence that if an acquired right must be respected, conversely, *a company cannot have more rights in France than in its own country of origin*' ('Notice biographique de Pillet par Niboyet' in *Mélanges Antoine Pillet*, Paris, Recueil Sirey, 1929, p. 13, emphasis added).

231 In the same way that it appears to be a formal element of the issuer's intention to solicit foreign residents, see *infra*, para. 422.

232 On the formal aspects of this notification between authorities, see B. Stoeva, *La coopération entre les superviseurs financiers dans l'Union européenne*, *op. cit.*, no. 86.

233 *Ibid.*, no. 72.

234 Interpretative Communication of the European Commission of 30 June 1997 [1997] OJ C 209/6.

now being addressed in the same terms for investment firms. Following the Second Banking Directive establishing the mutual recognition mechanism, the notification procedure was triggered by the provision of the service 'in the territory of another Member State under the freedom to provide services'.[235] The question arose as to whether credit institutions 'passively' providing their service to clients located in the territory of another Member State were subject to the notification procedure. The European Commission issued a communication interpreting the notification procedure by basing the location of the service on the customer's territory only if the institution provides the service characteristic of the contract there.[236] The Commission concludes that sending representatives upstream or downstream of the service provided does not trigger the localisation of the service abroad, even if it involves the conclusion of acts prior to the provision of the service, and that the customer's move also deactivates the notification procedure. In any case, the *ratio* of the Commission's interpretation is always based on a geographical move: either of the persons providing the service or of the service itself.

130. Several criticisms of this interpretation have emerged. The first was the excessive number of notifications. Mr Roeges then proposed a reduction of the material scope of application of the notification procedure to only those activities aimed at 'consumers of financial services'.[237] According to the author of this proposal, the criterion for triggering this procedure should no longer be based on the characteristic service, but should be inspired by the criterion used by the Rome Convention for consumer contracts.[238] A second criticism relates to the inadequacy of the criterion for services provided at a distance.[239] Indeed, the Commission's criterion was developed at a time when services provided at a distance, in particular by electronic means, were very little developed. Mr Partsch therefore considers that notification should take place as soon as the objective of the notification procedure is under consideration, i.e. whenever 'a credit institution plans to develop an activity under the freedom to provide services to its territory and therefore to the population living there'.[240] The author

---

235 The disputed provision is now included in Art. 39(1) of the CRD IV. The question arises in the same terms for investment firms, see already art. 18 of the Investment Services Directive, now Art. 34(2) of MiFID 2. From the banking point of view, see B. Stoeva, *La coopération entre les superviseurs financiers dans l'Union européenne, op. cit.*, para. 76.

236 Interpretative Communication of the European Commission of 30 June 1997 [1997] OJ C 209/6. At the same time, the Commission based the notification procedure for insurance companies on the location of the risk. On this issue, see L. Roeges, 'Quelques réflexions sur le cadre légal pour la libre prestation de services bancaires et financiers', *REDBF (Euredia)*, 2000, no. 2, pp. 149 et seq.

237 *Ibid.*, p. 152.

238 *Ibid.*

239 P.-E. Partsch, *Droit bancaire et financier européen, t. 1, Cadre général - Les établissements de crédit*, 2nd ed., Brussels, Larcier, no. 1024.

240 *Ibid.*

deduces from this, as does the Commission in its interpretation directive, that the movement of the customer to the Member State of the institution should not therefore trigger the notification procedure.[241]

It seems to us that the idea retained by Mr Partsch should prevail: the notification procedure should be applicable whenever its purpose is at stake.[242] However, it is necessary to base this objective on a clearly identifiable material criterion. Therefore, the Commission's proposal to base the notification procedure on the criterion of the location of contracts is not convincing. This criterion was designed to identify the applicable contract law in the absence of a choice of law by the parties. However, on the one hand, this criterion often proves to be unsuitable for locating financial services and, on the other hand, more fundamentally, it appears to be out of step with the objective pursued by the notification procedure. The purpose of the notification procedure is to enable the host Member State authority to know which operators are operating on its territory so that it can, in certain cases, monitor their activities and possibly protect its residents.[243] In these circumstances, the relevant criterion will never be one based on the location of the contract, which is irrelevant to the objective pursued by the notification procedure. The Commission, as well as Mr Partsch, are aware of this when they consider that the arrival of the customer on the territory of the establishment should deactivate the obligation to notify. Indeed, this is based on the fact that the decisive criterion is in fact the solicitation of the customer. This should be the criterion for considering the notification procedure to be applicable.[244]

131. Notification and mutual recognition. The penalty for failure to notify, or for notification that does not comply with the formal requirements, is particularly severe, since it entails failure to recognise the foreign authorisation and, consequently, a ban on providing an investment service on French territory.[245] This sanction tempers the assertion in European regulations that authorisation

---

241 *Ibid.*, no. 1025.

242 See already in this sense in a related field, G. Parléani, 'La localisation des services financiers' in *Mélanges en l'honneur de Jean Stoufflet*, Paris, LGDJ, 2001, p. 279, no. 5.

243 *Ibid.*, no. 1024.

244 This is why it seems to us, as Ms Stoeva considers (B. Stoeva, *La coopération entre les superviseurs financiers dans l'Union européenne, op. cit.*, para. 77), that publicity in another Member State should always trigger the notification procedure, since it is unquestionably a form of solicitation.

245 This solution can be deduced by analogy. In a similar matter subject to a similar procedure (Art. L. 511-23 of the Monetary and Financial Code), the Conseil d'Etat has ruled that a credit institution from another EU Member State that notifies the French authority directly, instead of its competent administrative authority, can only receive a prohibition on carrying on business on French territory from the French authority, see CE, 14 June 2010, no. 305671. On the other hand, notification by the home Member State authority leads to the benefit of mutual recognition within two months of the notification, even if the host Member State does not acknowledge receipt, see Art. 35(6) of MiFID 2.

granted by a national authority has a Community-wide scope of application.[246] In fact, authorisation retains its national scope of application, but its recognition is considerably facilitated by EU law, due to the material harmonisation of the conditions for obtaining it.

b. Purpose and Regime of Mutual Recognition of Authorisations

132. Purpose of recognition. Mutual recognition of authorisations is sometimes referred to as a 'passport for actors', which is distinguished from 'product passports' in that, in the first case, mutual recognition leads to a person being able to carry out his activity in another Member State, while in the second case it allows the marketing of a financial instrument in another Member State. What these two expressions of mutual recognition have in common is that they allow the avoidance of overlapping administrative regimes through a division of competences made possible by the prior harmonisation of authorisation conditions. The 'actor passport', or more precisely, the mutual recognition of authorisations, nevertheless has certain specific features linked to the purpose of the recognition.

133. When used in secondary legislation in financial matters, the subject matter of mutual recognition is not a foreign administrative regulation, as may have been the case in relation to the movement of goods, but usually an administrative decision: this is the case, for example, with the approval of the prospectus. In the context of authorisation, the purpose of mutual recognition is different because of the purpose of the authorisation itself, which concerns not a document but a person. The purpose of the authorisation has an impact on the purpose of mutual recognition, which is duplicated. The mutual recognition consists of the administrative decision to grant authorisation, but also, and above all, of the supervision of the foreign supervisory authority. Indeed, the singularity of approval of persons amongst administrative authorisations is precisely that it is subject to continuous control by a specialised administrative authority. It is this control that appears to be the most significant aspect of the authorisation. It is therefore the absence of this control by the authority of the place where the activity is carried out in the host Member State which is the most original element of the mutual recognition of authorisations and which explains the central place of national regulators in the mutual recognition process. This is why, when mutual recognition concerns an authorisation, the need for harmonisation of the conditions of the authorisation is compounded by the need for trust between the supervisory authorities.

---

[246] Comp. in relation to prospectuses, *infra*, para. 347.

This is also why, as Mr Synvet writes, mutual recognition 'can flourish whenever sufficient trust is established between national regulators'.[247] However, it must be added that it can *only* flourish on this condition. Here, just as the designation of a foreign law by a bilateral conflict rule is only possible when the legal orders involved share a certain 'community of law', mutual recognition is only conceivable from a certain degree of homogeneity of the law of the forum and the foreign law, which extends to a necessary cooperation of the authorities. In other words, the legislator's restraint in applying its own rules is not only 'because a foreign rule is applicable and is deemed satisfactory',[248] but also because the control of the authority is also deemed satisfactory *and* capable of effective cooperation.

134. Regime. When used in secondary legislation on administrative authorisation, mutual recognition has the effect of making the administrative supervision of the investment firm entirely subject to a single authority for the territory of the Union, that of its head office, which supervises the application of the local rules of organisation. It does not lead to the dispensation of the authorisation, but forces Member States to recognise the validity of the one already granted.[249] The most original aspect of the mutual recognition method, as used in secondary legislation, is the drastic limitation of local administrative action. In this sense, the system of recognition undoubtedly goes beyond a simple taking into account of foreign law,[250] and even goes beyond the bilateral conflict rule in its reception of foreignness since the foreign regime is fully accepted by way of recognition, without the local authority having been the instrument of it: the forum cannot play on the qualification or use the corrective mechanisms.[251]

---

247 H. Synvet, 'L'internationalisation du droit des affaires', *op. cit.*, no. 7. The author thus observes: 'An example is provided by the two mutual assistance and mutual recognition agreements concluded between the Commission des opérations de bourse and the American Commodity Futures Trading Commission on 6 June 1990 (Bull. COB, no. 237, June 1990, pp. 37 et seq.), which open up the possibility for intermediaries authorised in their country of origin to market financial futures instruments to investors in the other State, and to receive the corresponding funds.' (*ibid.*).

248 H. Synvet, 'L'internationalisation du droit des affaires', *op. cit.*, no. 7.

249 Depending on how it is interpreted, the exemption is alternatively a form of exemption, i.e. self-limitation, or of exoneration, i.e. it is part of the taking into consideration.

250 Comp. L. d'Avout, 'L'entreprise et les conflits internationaux de lois', *op. cit.*, no. 318. However, there is more of a difference in degree than in kind between the application of a foreign law and its simple consideration. On this question see S. Bollée, 'La prise en considération des lois de polices étrangères dans le Règlement Rome I' in *Mélanges en l'honneur du professeur Bertrand Ancel*, Paris, LGDJ, 2017, pp. 203 et seq.

251 This is why it seems excessive to consider that the European rules designating the competent authority for prospectus or authorisation to carry on an activity are bilateral conflict rules (see in this sense R. Gaspard, *La reconnaissance mutuelle en droit bancaire et financier européen*, *op. cit.*, nos. 394–398). From the point of view of the authority, the question of foreign law only arises insofar as it necessarily recognises the foreign administrative decision and the regime associated with it; the rule of apportionment of legislative and administrative

The protection of the interests of the host Member States is therefore not based on its own authority, but on that of the Member State of origin,[252] which is therefore placed in a singular situation of hegemony vis-à-vis the professional.

However, there are two exceptions to this limitation on local action. The first is where the competent authority of the host State identifies an irregularity in the obligations which are under the control of the authorities of the home State. In this case, if the home state authority does not respond effectively to the information provided by the host state authority, the latter may prohibit the foreign company from continuing to provide services on its territory.[253] This option has already been exercised by the AMF.[254] A second exception is where a foreign company is guilty of an irregularity with regard to a rule whose observance is directly supervised by the host Member State authority, in particular where a branch is established.[255] The issue here is the rules of conduct. These rules, in addition to determining the modalities for imposing administrative sanctions on the investment firm, also determine whether it is liable to civil law.

B. Access to the Territory of Other Member States and Applicable Rules of Conduct

135. The price of market access. It should be noted at the outset that the conduct of business rules in question apply only to relations between investment firms and their clients. Infrastructure managers are not subject to them in their dealings with their members, even where the latter may have investment firm

competence laid down by European law does not lead to the authority using the bilateral conflict rule. If it does, it is because of other rules, e.g. the application of the law of the registered office to certain preliminary issues.

252 This hypothesis is not unprecedented in EU law, see on the subject of resolution *infra*, para. 152.

253 Art. 86(1) of the MiFID 2. Comp. in banking matters, Art. 41 of the CRD IV where this power has been replaced by the referral to the EBA, see B. Stoeva, *La coopération entre les superviseurs financiers dans l'Union européenne*, *op. cit.*, no. 94. However, the banking example has shown that these powers can be crucial, see the contentious illustration of *icesave* in the area of supervision of the liquidity of the banking establishment, *ibid.*, nos. 94 and 98. Some authors have proposed the introduction of the effects criterion in order to delimit the competences of the authorities (see K. Pistor, 'Host Dilemma: Rethinking EU Banking Regulation in Light of the Global Crisis', *ECGI Finance WP n° 286/2010*, 28 June 2010). However, it seems to us that such a criterion, which is too vague as such, faces uncertain implementation and risks leading to the cumulative application of regulations.

254 AMF decision of 29 July 2016, *Roderer Limited*, and AMF press release of the same day available on its website. On this decision, see the comments of A. Tenenbaum, *Banque et Droit*, September 2016, pp. 39-40; and, by the same author, 'Les autres sources du droit européen des contrats: incidence du droit matériel européen des sociétés et des marchés financiers', *Revue des contrats*, March 2017, pp. 149 et seq.

255 Art. 86(2) MiFID 2.

status.[256] This is because, as Professor Drummond writes, '"market members" are not the manager's clients; the manager does not act on their behalf'.[257] However, as the author observes, this statement is not accurate for certain trading systems, especially organised trading systems, where the manager may intervene on its own behalf when its member consents, transforming the member into a true client and thus triggering the application of the conduct of business rules.[258] Moreover, in the case of central securities depositories, the situation is likely to evolve as distributed ledger technology may eliminate the need for intermediation in securities settlement services.[259] Finally, these conduct of business rules are still relevant in the relationship between investment firms and their clients:[260] their violation gives rise to civil liability for the investment firm.[261] This is especially important since, as Ms Drummond observes: 'Civil liability is the only way for the client to obtain compensation for the damage caused by the investment firm's failure; other civil sanctions are very rarely imposed'.[262] These rules thus appear to be the price of the market access granted by the approval.[263] We will try to show here that their international applicability echoes this: depending on the weighting of the company's location, the law of the place where the activity is carried out, which always has jurisdiction under the liability regime,[264] is likely to extend its scope to the rules of conduct that make it possible to assess the existence of a fault.

136. Sources and function of conduct of business rules. The conduct of business rules applicable to the relationship between investment firms and their clients were for a long time based on case law and linked to the general or special law of contracts.[265] Today, conduct of business rules also have their sources in the professional law applicable to investment firms in return for authorisation.

---

256 Art. L. 424-2 of the Monetary and Financial Code, see *supra*, para. 50.

257 F. Drummond, *Droit financier*, *op. cit.*

258 *Ibid.*, no. 982.

259 On this aspect, see *infra*, paras. 740 et seq.

260 As such, they are likely to apply whenever a member of a trading, clearing or settlement or delivery system conducts a transaction for a retail client.

261 In addition to its administrative and even criminal liability, see F. Drummond, *Droit financier*, *op. cit.*, no. 719.

262 F. Drummond, *Droit financier*, *op. cit.*

263 This situation is not specific to investment services, see the numerous examples given by L. d'Avout, 'L'entreprise et les conflits internationaux de lois', *op. cit.*, nos. 76 and seq. It should be added here that the rules applicable between investment firms as market members and market infrastructures may also engage the civil liability of the investment firm vis-à-vis its clients, see *infra*, para. 255.

264 Because of the criterion of connecting the law of tort to the place of the damage, see *infra*, para. 427.

265 See the illustrations given by F. Drummond, *Droit financier*, *op. cit.*, no. 646.

They are derived from MiFID 2.[266] While prudential rules constitute the 'internal order' of the professional status of investment firms, conduct of business rules with clients are their 'external order'. Their function is to protect clients against the investment firm which, because of its situation, could be led to behave unfairly. Therefore, the content of conduct of business rules depends on the types of clients:[267] professional clients, and retail clients.

137. Purpose and sanction of conduct of business rules. Conduct of business rules may govern various aspects of the investment firm's relationship with its clients. They establish pre-contractual obligations of the professional towards his client: information, advice or warnings. The rules of conduct may also apply to the execution of the contract, such as the best execution obligation, which requires the investment firm to execute the client's order on the best possible terms for the client,[268] or the rules governing the firm's remuneration, or the obligation to report to the client on the execution of the order.[269] Violation of conduct of business rules entails both the administrative liability of the investment firm vis-à-vis the supervisory authority of its head office and its civil liability vis-à-vis its client. In both cases, however, the conduct of business rules applicable to the cross-border relationship must be identified. In order to determine them, European law has successively relied on two solutions: after having applied to the rules of conduct the law of the place where the service is provided (I), it now bases the localisation of the applicable rules on the mode of access to the territory of the clients (II).

1. *The Law of the Place Where the Service Is Provided*

138. Sources and principle. In the Investment Services Directive, the conflict of laws rule governing conduct of business rules referred to the law of the Member State where the investment service is provided.[270] This state was then responsible for implementation and enforcement,[271] ousting the jurisdiction of the home

---

266 These rules, set out in a section entitled 'Rules of good conduct', are listed in Arts. L. 533-11 et seq. of the Monetary and Financial Code. For a synthetic presentation, see J. Prorok, *La responsabilité civile sur les marchés financiers*, *op. cit.*, paras. 63 et seq.; F. Drummond, *Droit financier*, *op. cit.*, nos. 646 et seq. and references.

267 Recital 104 MiFID 2.

268 Art. 27 MiFID 2.

269 Art. 26(1) MiFID 2.

270 Art. 11(2°) of the Investment Services Directive. Such a criterion is in line with the idea of localisation of the rules of conduct according to the place where the activity is carried out.

271 *Ibid.* For a contentious illustration see CA Paris, 15th ch. B, 30 June 2006, *Sté Morgan Stanley & Co International Ltd and Sté Morgan Stanley Dean Witter Inc. c/ SA LVMH*, RG no. 04/06308, on which see the analysis of J. Prorok, *La responsabilité civile sur les marchés financiers*, *op. cit.*, no. 492 and the references cited. The Court of Appeal then considered that the Investment Services Directive only established the exclusive jurisdiction of the law of origin in matters of organisation, and that it did not therefore prevent the application

state authority. It would probably have been simpler to apply the law of the seat of the investment firm to this issue. This would have given jurisdiction to the authority of the home Member State, allowing the unity of the internal and external status of the investment firm. This would also have ensured that the trade-friendliness of the Investment Services Directive would be respected by allowing the investment firm to act in a similar way with all its clients across the EU. Finally, this would have avoided a breach of the rules of conduct to be adopted towards clients, all of whom are EU citizens, although some would benefit from rules that are more favourable to them depending on their location. However, the objective of protecting investors, which is the basis of the conduct of business rules, made it difficult to apply the law of the place of business.

The application of the law of the place where the service was provided was probably a compromise between the law of residence of the client and the law of the investment firm. This rule was also based on the idea that the place where the service is provided designates the legal system affected by the relationship in question, which is therefore competent to govern it: since the rules for the protection of clients are closely linked to the service provided, they are part of the socio-cultural environment of the latter. The preference for intra-Community trade, which permeated the Investment Services Directive, gave way here to the protection of clients.[272] Moreover, by making the rules of the Member State where the service is provided applicable, this criterion obliges private operators to adapt to the rules of conduct of the Member States on whose territory they wish to trade. Finally, the importance of this conflict rule can be tempered since the Directive sets out the 'minimum' content of conduct of business rules;[273] so as to make non-harmonised conduct of business standards residual.

139. Limitation of the rule. The application of the law of the place where the service is provided had several weaknesses. The first was that it did not provide a criterion for determining the place of supply of the investment service, leaving it to each national authority to determine the location of the service provided. This indeterminacy was compounded either by the possible development of separate criteria for different investment services,[274] or by the use of the characteristic performance criterion, which resulted in a different criterion being applied

---

of French rules on tort liability to the bank's conduct. It also ruled out the application of Art. 49 EEC on the freedom to provide services. On this issue see also R. Gaspard, *La reconnaissance mutuelle en droit bancaire et financier*, *op. cit.*

272 The reversal of this question in the MiFID and MiFID 2 directives makes it possible to temper the idea that client protection is central to them, see *infra*, para. 147.

273 Art. 11 of the Investment Services Directive.

274 See for example the criteria proposed by A. Tenenbaum, *L'application internationale du droit boursier*, *op. cit.*, no. 376.

depending on the service provided.[275] This solution made it very difficult to determine the applicable rules.[276] As the competent authority was that of the host Member State, it was most often inclined to consider that the service was provided to the customers, allowing the application of its own law and making the place where the services are provided an avatar of the residence of the customers.[277] This choice was further justified by the objective of these rules, which is the protection of customers.[278] Therefore, the application of the law of the place of their residence was inevitable.

The second weakness of the rule was related to its scope, as the conduct of business rules applicable to clients listed in the Investment Services Directive were intended to cover certain prudential rules internal to the status of investment firm.[279] The Commission noted that host Member State authorities applied, in addition to 'national conduct of business and advertising rules [...], a number of requirements relating to organisational structure or of a prudential nature (holding of client funds) when services are provided to domestic investors'. This overlapping of prudential regimes hinders cross-border provision of services, in particular for brokerage/trading services.[280] The reason for this overlap is that prudential rules and conduct of business rules are linked: the former are, inter alia, a function of the risks taken in dealing with clients, showing that these bodies of rules are two sides of the same coin, the professional status of investment firms. The experience of the Investment

---

275 For an illustration of this attempt, see G. Parléani, 'La localisation des services financiers', *op. cit.*, nos. 16 et seq.; H. de Vauplane and J.-P. Bornet, *Droit des marchés financiers*, 3rd ed., Paris, Litec, 2001, no. 1243; and, more recently, *Rapport du HCJP relatif à l'accessibilité du marché français par les établissements bancaires et financiers britanniques dans un environnement post-Brexit*, 7 November 2017, pp. 6 et seq.

276 D. Guinaudeau, 'Succursales: loi applicable et supervision au titre de la directive concernant les Marchés d'instruments financiers (MIF)' in *Mélanges AEBDF V*, 2008, pp. 231 et seq.

277 The Commission notes in this respect that following the Investment Services Directive, while Member States used a wide variety of criteria to locate investment services, the criteria employed generally resulted in the application of the law of the host Member State, see point 3.2 of the Communication from the Commission to the European Parliament and the Council - Upgrading the Investment Services Directive (93/22/EEC)/* COM/2000/0729 final */.

278 See in this sense, D. Guinaudeau, 'Succursales: loi applicable et supervision au titre de la directive concernant les Marchés d'instruments financiers (MIF)', *op. cit.*, p. 237.

279 The conduct of business rules were based on Art. 11(1°) of the Investment Services Directive (now transposed in Arts. L. 533-11 et seq. of the Monetary and Financial Code) and included provisions on conflicts of interest and internal procedures.

280 Point 3.2 of the Communication from the Commission to the European Parliament and the Council – Upgrading the Investment Services Directive (93/22/EEC)/* COM/2000/0729 final */. See also the Commission Communication of 14 November 2000, entitled "The application of conduct of business rules under Art. 11 of the ISD" (COM[2000] 722 final). On the latter Communication in particular and this topic in general, see H. Synvet and A. Tenenbaum, 'Instruments financiers', *op. cit.*, no. 131; D. Guinaudeau, 'Succursales: loi applicable et supervision au titre de la directive concernant les Marchés d'instruments financiers (MIF)', *op. cit.*

Services Directive has therefore led the Commission to change the criterion for the application of conduct of business rules and to base it on a material criterion: the mode of access to the territory of the Member State.

2. *Freedom to Provide Services and Establishment*

140. MiFID 2 criterion. Where an investment firm hopes to provide investment services abroad, it may do so under the freedom to provide services, or by establishing a branch in the Member State concerned. This distinction is the one on which the criterion of the law applicable to the conduct of business rules is based today: in the first case, the conduct of business rules will be those of its registered office, while in the second, it will be those of the place where the branch is established. This solution, already included in Article 32(7) of MiFID, is now included in Article 35(8) of MiFID 2[281] which states:

> 'It shall be the responsibility of the competent authority of the Member State where the branch is located to ensure that the services provided by the branch within its territory comply with the obligations laid down in Articles 24, 25, 27 and 28 of this Directive and Articles 14 to 26 of Regulation (EU) No 600/2014, as well as by the measures adopted in accordance with those provisions by the host Member State if it is authorised to do so under Article 24(12).'

Articles 24, 25, 27 and 28 of MiFID 2 are all part of the same section on investor protection and deal respectively with the general principles of investor protection and client information, the assessment of the adequacy and appropriateness of client information, the best execution obligation and the rules for handling orders with clients. All conduct of business rules applicable to clients are therefore subject to the law of the branch's establishment.[282] The reason given by MiFID 2 is the proximity of the branch to the host Member State authority, which is therefore 'best placed to detect and bring to an end breaches of the rules applicable to transactions carried out by the branch'.[283] Two difficulties have arisen under MiFID, from which this provision derives: one relating to the concept of branch, the other relating to the provision of investment services by a branch to clients located in another Member State. These difficulties have not both been satisfactorily resolved by MiFID 2.

---

281 This solution has been transposed to Art. L. 532-18 of the Monetary and Financial Code.

282 See in French perspective Art. L. 532-18(2) of the Monetary and Financial Code. Comp. H. Synvet and A. Tenenbaum, 'Instruments Financiers, *op. cit.*, Art. 134, who consider that a distinction should be made according to the services: 'The same localising element cannot be retained for all the services provided. This element should vary depending on whether the service is order reception and transmission, order execution, portfolio management or placement and underwriting. The execution of transactions, the location of the account or the investor's place of residence are all locational factors to be taken into account.'

283 Recital 90 MiFID 2. See already in this sense Recital 32 of the MiFID.

141. Establishment and branch. The distinction proposed by MiFID 2 between the freedom to provide services and the establishment of a branch leaves two gaps between these modes of cross-border provision: tied agents and permanent representative offices.[284] Tied agents are subject to a specific provision treating them as a modality of the freedom to provide services, subject to the provision of a set of information to the host Member State authority.[285] The treatment of these two forms of establishment in another country should nevertheless be aligned with that of branches.[286] Indeed, the *ratio legis* of the MiFID 2 distinction is based on the idea that local rules should apply from the moment a form of permanent establishment exists. The reason why the trader acting under the freedom to provide services can rely on the conduct of business rules of his head office is precisely the temporary nature of the activity carried out within the foreign legal order.[287]

Admittedly, the Court of Justice has held that the temporary nature of the activity pursued under the freedom to provide services does not prevent the investment firm from 'equip himself with some form of infrastructure in the host Member State (including an office, chambers or consulting rooms) in so far as such infrastructure is necessary for the purposes of performing the services in question'.[288] However, the distinction with the freedom of establishment is made as soon as a 'stable and continuous' activity[289] is carried out in the host Member State. These elements no doubt make it possible to observe that the distinction between freedom to provide services and freedom of establishment is sometimes simply a matter of degree. However, the adjective 'permanent' attached to representative offices is not misleading: it is indeed a question of the provider carrying on a stable and continuous activity. Similarly, the presence of a tied agent[290] is not incidental, but is usually the first step in establishing a

---

284 B. Stoeva, *La coopération entre les superviseurs financiers dans l'Union européenne*, *op. cit.*, paras. 145 and 152.

285 Art. 34(2) and (5) MiFID 2.

286 The definition of a branch can be modelled on the definition of secondary establishment in Art. R. 123-40 of the Commercial Code, according to which 'a secondary establishment within the meaning of this section is any permanent establishment, distinct from the registered office or the principal place of business and managed by the person required to be registered, an agent or a person with the power to enter into legal relations with third parties'.

287 Case C-55/94, *Gebhard*, ECLI:EU:C:1995:411. On this judgment see B. Stoeva, *La coopération entre les superviseurs financiers dans l'Union européenne*, *op. cit.*, para. 74

288 *Gebhard* judgment, cit., para. 27.

289 *Gebhard* judgment, cit., para. 28.

290 A tied agent is defined by Art. 4(1)(29) MiFID 2 as 'any natural or legal person who, under the full and unconditional responsibility of a single investment firm on whose behalf it acts, promotes to clients or potential clients investment and/or ancillary services, receives and transmits instructions or orders from clients in respect of financial instruments or investment services, places financial instruments or provides advice to clients or potential clients in respect of such instruments or services'.

business, which is reflected in the fact that the investment firm is responsible for the actions of the tied agent, and that the tied agent must disclose the investment firm it represents prior to any transaction with a client.[291] This is why tied agents are assimilated to branches by MiFID 2.[292] Finally, from the point of view of the contracting party, the continuous presence of the interlocutor in the territory in question necessarily gives the impression of local presence. It is therefore fortunate that the rules of conduct of the place of this continuous presence prevail.

142. Branch and clients located in other Member States. While MiFID 2 addresses the problem of clients located in the territory of the branch, there was some ambiguity in the case of clients residing in the territory of other Member States. The notion of 'services provided by the branch within its territory' had to be interpreted. One solution proposed by the *British Bankers Association* was to make all dealings with customers, even if they were located in other Member States, subject to the law of the Member State of the branch, provided that the contract was concluded with the branch's representatives.[293] This solution was criticised, and the *British Bankers Association* then proposed locating the service by means of the characteristic performance criterion, developed by private international contract law, and already used to trigger the applicability of the notification mechanisms relating to the exercise of an activity in the territory of another Member State. Nevertheless, this criterion did not allow the applicable law to be designated with certainty, in particular because, as Professor Vabres observed, 'it is not always easy to identify what falls within the scope of the characteristic performance and what belongs to related steps or services'.[294] Moreover, the use of this criterion appears all the more awkward as it was designed to locate the socio-economic environment of the contract,[295] whereas the rules of conduct are a set of rules triggering the tort and administrative liability of the provider.

143. The Commission was ultimately asked to distinguish between three regimes:[296] either the client is resident in the territory of the branch, in which

---

291 Art. 29(2) MiFID 2.

292 Art. 35(2) MiFID 2.

293 B. Stoeva, *La coopération entre les superviseurs financiers dans l'Union européenne*, *op. cit.*, no. 162; R. Gaspard, *La reconnaissance mutuelle en droit bancaire et financier*, *op. cit.*, para. 343.

294 R. Vabres, *Comitologie et Services Financiers*, *op. cit.*, para. 428.

295 On the development of this criterion, see Y. Lequette, *Les mutations du droit international privé: vers un changement de paradigme?'*, RCADI, t. 387, The Hague, Martinus Nijhoff, 2017, nos. 63 et seq.

296 European Commission, 'Supervision of Branches under Mifid', Brussels, 18 June 2007, MARKT/G/3/MV D(2007) 2386.
See also on this issue, CESR, 'Protocol on the supervision of branches under MiFID', Ref. Cesr/07-672, October 2007, updated in October 2009. From the point of view of the sources, this protocol shows the importance of the committees of regulators even before the

case the rules of the establishment of the branch apply,[297] or the client of the branch is resident in the territory of the head office of the investment firm, in which case the applicable conduct of business rules and the competent authority are those of the head office,[298] or the client of the branch is resident in the territory of another Member State, in which case a distinction must be made on a case-by-case basis.[299] In the third case, in the absence of agreement between the competent authorities, the Commission suggests that operators should be given the choice between the applicability of the rules of the host or the home state, in the same way that branches may decide to transmit the information arising from *reporting* obligations to the home or host authority,[300] or to give jurisdiction to the authority of the host Member State.[301]

The Commission's interpretation of MiFID is contradictory in more than one respect: on the one hand, while the residence of clients is ignored when the service was provided under the freedom to provide services, it is omnipresent when the service was provided through a branch and, on the other hand, the analogy with the *reporting* obligations fails to convince since they have very different objectives.[302] Mr Vabres proposed to draw inspiration from the Hague Convention on the Law Applicable to Agency Contracts of 14 March 1978, and in particular from the criterion applicable in the absence of choice of law, which provides for the application of the law of the investment firm.[303]

144. Critical analysis. The evolution of the criteria for identifying the law applicable to conduct of business rules shows the penetration of the logic of conflict of laws. Indeed, the presupposition of the reasoning of the British Banking Association and the European Commission is always to link the investment service to a territory. Therefore, both institutions try to identify the centre of gravity of the relationship governed by the conduct of business rules, and are led to 'locate' financial services. The analysis is relevant because it is partly based on the purpose of the conduct of business rules: since the rules are designed to protect customers, the residence of the customer should be the determining criterion for their location. The application of local law on the

establishment of European supervisory authorities, see R. Vabres, 'L'influence des comités européens des régulateurs sur le droit des services financiers', *REDBF (Euredia)*, 2007/2008, no. 3, pp. 294 et seq. See also on this issue, B. Stoeva, *La coopération entre les superviseurs financiers dans l'Union européenne*, *op. cit.*, no. 162; R. Gaspard, *La reconnaissance mutuelle en droit bancaire et financier*, *op. cit.*, no. 344.

297 European Commission, 'Supervision of Branches under Mifid', no. 8(a).

298 *Ibid.*, no. 8(b).

299 *Ibid.*, no. 8(c).

300 Art. 25 MiFID.

301 R. Gaspard, *La reconnaissance mutuelle en droit bancaire et financier*, *op. cit.*, no. 344.

302 See B. Stoeva, *La coopération entre les superviseurs financiers dans l'Union européenne*, *op. cit.*, no. 162 and references.

303 R. Vabres, *Comitologie et services financiers*, *op. cit.*, p. 381. This Convention is discussed in detail *infra*, para. 451.

basis of economic presence has a long tradition in private international law.[304] However, this criterion is flawed in two respects.

First of all, even if the function of protecting residents were to apply exclusively to the domestic rule, it should be noted that in international matters other elements must be taken into account in order to establish a connecting factor.[305] In particular, the protection of clients may be seen to be limited when the client himself solicits an investment firm established in another legal order. As Mr d'Avout writes, a distinction must be made 'between fortuitous presence and conscious participation in the local market'[306] and the application of local law in this case 'could be criticised on the basis of individual expectations, where the actor had no way of anticipating the effect of his conduct in a territory other than that in which he acted'.[307] Unquestionably, it makes sense to apply the rules of conduct of the provider's headquarters so that the weight of internationality rests on the person who initiated the solicitation. This criterion is precisely the one used by the MiFID Regulation in relations with third countries.[308] It would benefit from being retained here, under certain conditions. Indeed, a second aspect appears to be decisive in the localisation of conduct of business rules: the objectives of the legislative package in which they are inserted, which aim at coordinating European legal orders in order to unify the internal market.

145. In other words, from an international perspective, MiFID 2 conduct of business rules are not solely geared towards the protection of residents, as evidenced by the fact that in the event of access to another Member State through the exercise of the freedom to provide services, the conduct of business rules applicable are those of the head office. There is undoubtedly a tension between the objective of the conduct of business rules, which is the protection of investors, and that of MiFID 2, which promotes the unification of the internal market, a tension that is reflected in the diversity of criteria proposed in the case of the branch. Nevertheless, it seems to us that this difficulty can be resolved by a unitary and predictable criterion. Indeed, the authors of MiFID 2 wished to get rid of the systematic application of the rules of conduct of the clients' domicile resulting from the Investment Services Directive. However, the objective of protecting clients makes it impossible to find the opposite solution of locating conduct of business rules at the head office of the investment firm. A balance

---

304 L. d'Avout, 'L'enteprise et les conflits internationaux de lois', *op. cit.*, nos. 72 and seq.; see also *ibid.*, no. 171: 'With such a territorial regulation of the market, whether sectoral or trans-sectoral, sometimes echoing the corporatism of yesteryear, France exercises its competence to police and structure individual and collective economic relations, its market competence.'

305 As Lerebours-Pigeonnière wrote, 'the analysis of domestic law is necessary, but it is not always sufficient', Y. Loussouarn, 'L'œuvre de Lerebours-Pigeonnière', *JDI*, 1954, p. 892.

306 L. d'Avout, 'L'entreprise et les conflits internationaux de lois', *op. cit.*, no. 75.

307 *Ibid.*

308 See *infra*, para. 208.

can be struck by applying the conduct of business rules of the branch's place of establishment as a matter of principle, tempered by a material exception whenever the branch initiates the solicitation. In the latter case, the rules of conduct of the customer's domicile would apply. Such a criterion has the dual advantage of predictability and balance between the objectives under consideration: it limits the multiplication of laws, while basing it, when it occurs, on the conduct of the investment firm.[309]

146. Relationship with the Rome II Regulation. As the liability of an investment firm which violates these rules of conduct arises outside a contractual breach, it is to be expected that it will be qualified as extracontractual.[310] The law applicable to its liability must therefore be sought under the Rome II Regulation. A priori, one might be tempted to select the law of the seat of the investment firm subject to the rules of conduct whose violation is alleged. It would suffice to locate the damage there, a criterion retained by Article 4 of the Rome II Regulation, leading to the application of the law of the rules of conduct to the entire liability regime which derives from them. This solution has a twofold advantage: it preserves the balance that the national legislator may have wished to establish between the standard of conduct required of professionals and the associated liability regime and, by giving precedence to the operative event, is in line with the French legal tradition.[311] This solution nevertheless has the serious disadvantage of denying the choice made by the European legislator when it instituted, as a connecting factor, the place of the damage rather than that of the event giving rise to it.

---

309 This criterion is also likely to explain the host member authority's willingness to regulate the advertising of foreign investment firms on its territory, and therefore offers a unitary criterion for application. It is in line with an observation made by Ms Tenenbaum according to which: 'the State could only impose rules of conduct to target activities with a sufficient link to its territory [...] it would be appropriate for the interests of the States least concerned to be sacrificed to the one most interested in the situation', A. Tenenbaum, *L'application internationale du droit boursier*, *op. cit.*, p. 277.

310 The recent case law of the Court of Justice seems to make the need for interpretation of a contract the point of delimitation of contractual and tortious qualifications, at least on the basis of the Brussels Ia Regulation (Case C-59/19, *Wikingerhof GmbH*, ECLI:EU:C:2020:950; see *infra*, para. 397). The existence of a contract between the parties, which will be the case in the hypothesis studied here, does not necessarily lead to a contractual qualification of the liability action.

311 French case-law gave precedence to the law of the territory in which the event giving rise to the dispute took place, see P. Bourel, *Les conflits de lois en matière d'obligations extracontractuelles*, *op. cit.*, at p. 48: 'Whether the event giving rise to these obligations is unlawful or lawful, and whether it gives rise to rights to reparation, to recovery or to restitution, in all cases the source of the obligation is identical: it consists of a juridical fact to which the legislator attaches certain consequences, without regard to any consideration of the will of the parties. This commonality of origin of obligations in tort and quasi-contractual matters thus justifies, in private international law, the application of a single law, that which governs the juridical fact, the cause of the legislative intervention. See L. d'Avout, 'Que reste-t-il du principe de territorialité des faits juridiques', *D.* 2009, 1629, no. 2.

A solution that is more respectful of the Rome II Regulation exists without calling into question the selection of rules of conduct designated by sectoral law. It is sufficient to equate the rules of conduct with the rules of conduct and safety in Article 17 of the Rome II Regulation, according to which: 'Account shall be taken, as a matter of fact and in so far as is necessary, of the rules of safety and conduct in force at the place and on the day when the event giving rise to liability' occurred. The comparison does not seem extravagant in view of the broad interpretation that the European legislator suggests for the rules of conduct.[312] In this case, the source of the liability and its regime would have to be separated. On the one hand, the source of liability would be the conduct of business rules of the investment firm's headquarters as a matter of fact insofar as these rules are designated by MiFID 2. On the other hand, the liability regime remains subject only to the law of the place of the damage. Such dissociation between the source and the regime of liability is already familiar,[313] and simply presupposes a coherent articulation which will be carried out under the law of the damage.

III. The Administrative Treatment of the Resolution

147. Links between the Prudential Supervisory Authority and the resolution authority. We have already seen the conditions under which resolution law could be applicable to infrastructure managers:[314] we must now look at the conditions under which the administrative implementation of resolution would take place. Indeed, one of its singularities compared to ordinary insolvency law is that its implementation is entrusted to an administrative authority and not to a judicial authority.[315] The reason given is the reputation of the former for

---

312 Recital 34 of the Rome II Regulation.

313 See in this sense M.-A. Moreau-Bourlès, *Structure du rattachement et conflits de lois en matière de responsabilité civile délictuelle*, Paris, typed thesis, 1985. The author shows the 'lack of adaptation' (*ibid.*, pp. 27 et seq.) and even the 'perversity' of a single connecting factor (*ibid.*, pp. 122 et seq.), and then proposes to distinguish between the sources and the regime, the former being subject to the place where the act occurred, and the latter to the law of the place where the harm was suffered. See in particular the statement of the proposed rules *ibid.*, p. 827. See O. Boskovic, *La réparation du préjudice en droit international privé*, Paris, LGDJ, 2003. The author, considering that reparation of harm constitutes an autonomous category of the source of liability, proposes to apply to it the connection of the place of reparation, the only 'connection which makes it possible to embrace the complexity of the category' (*ibid.*, p. 292). On this question, see also J. Knetsch, 'La réparation du dommage extracontractuel en droit international privé' in *Mélanges en l'honneur du professeur Bertrand Ancel*, Paris, LGDJ, 2018, pp. 979 et seq.

314 See *supra*, para. 103.

315 Art. 3 of the Resolution Directive. While this is undeniably a restriction, a certain diversity remains since the authority designated within the Member State may be a ministry as well as an independent administrative authority, with the limitation that the functioning of the authority must exclude conflicts of interest (Art. 3.5 of the Resolution Directive). These

greater responsiveness and efficiency,[316] in particular because they can impose administrative sanctions on institutions.[317] Another reason is undoubtedly the possible nationalisation, even if only temporarily, of the institution in resolution procedure and, therefore, the commitment of public funds whose use is traditionally decided by the administration.[318] In addition, resolution law was conceived as an echo of prudential supervision: the links maintained by prudential law and resolution law at the legislative level are perpetuated at the administrative level. These links between the administration of prudential rules and resolution rules take the form of cooperation in three stages. Firstly, it takes place at the stage of preventing the failure of the institution. Indeed, the aim of the supervisory rules also corresponds to the aim of the early intervention measures of the resolution authority. Cooperation then takes place, as Mr Fernandez-Bollo writes:

> 'At the most important moment, namely the assessment of the situation where an institution is no longer able to resolve its difficulties itself: this is the nodal point of articulation between supervision, which, following the institution continuously, is responsible for recognising when this moment of failure has been reached, and resolution, which must then take charge of the decision whether or not to intervene with the rescue tools available to it.'[319]

Finally, as the result of resolution is the perpetuation of the critical functions of the failing bank, cooperation still takes place at the end of the resolution since the institution is destined to return to the control of the Prudential Supervisory Authority.[320] Given this attachment to prudential supervision, it is not surprising that resolution law mimics its mechanisms: thus, this law proceeds from an administrative connecting factor, that of the head office

---

requirements can be explained by the considerable prerogatives of the resolution authority. We will give just one example: when the bridge institution is set up, it is owned (partially or entirely) and controlled by the resolution authority (Art. 40 of the Resolution Directive): its prerogatives even allow it to appoint the managers (Art. 41 of the Resolution Directive). The purpose of this operation is nevertheless to sell the bridge institution which is not designed to last (Art. 41(3)(a) and (c) of the Resolution Directive).

316 A.-C. Muller, 'Regards sur la directive Résolution', *op. cit.*, p. 578; T. Bonneau, 'Le traitement administratif des entreprises bancaires et financières', *op. cit.*

317 In addition to any criminal sanctions that may be applicable (Art. 110 of the Resolution Directive). The Directive also harmonises the types of penalties to be imposed, and the circumstances to be taken into account (Arts. 111 et seq. of the Resolution Directive).

318 This is not unique to Western systems, see the example given by Ms Riles concerning the bankruptcy of LTCB and its nationalisation by the Japanese authorities, A. Riles, *Collateral Knowledge, op. cit.*, p. 204.

319 E. Fernandez-Bollo, 'L'impact de l'Union bancaire sur la coopération en matière de contrôle bancaire', *Banque et droit*, special issue, February 2020, pp. 12 et seq.

320 *Ibid.*

authority,[321] but tempers the exercise of this jurisdiction by the institution of a supervisory college.[322]

148. The presence of this college, while it is a matter of principle for clearing houses, only comes into play in the case of groups for institutions subject to the Resolution Directive. The reason for this is simple: the institution of this college is intended to facilitate cross-border resolution decided by the head office authority. The institution of a college is, in our opinion, the condition for a universalist type of insolvency procedure which, decided by the head office authority, nevertheless has its effects on the entire territory of the Union. In the same way that the law of the seat gave way to the law of the place of realisation of certain assets, the home authority involves the authorities of the other Member States in order to make the chosen plan acceptable and to ensure that its decisions are properly implemented on their territory. However, in the case of the resolution of clearing houses, the college questions the pre-eminence of the decision of the head office authority simply because, in the event of disagreement within the supervisory college, ESMA is likely to take the decision in place of the authorities. We will first look at the concentration of jurisdiction on the home authority (A) before looking at how colleges of authorities temper the exercise of that power in the resolution and clearing house directives (B).

A. Centralisation of administrative jurisdiction of home authority

149. Jurisdiction of home authorities. Within the Resolution Directive, the main ground of jurisdiction is based on the existence in the territory of the authority of a personified entity,[323] i.e. a subsidiary or the parent company. Therefore, branch authorities do not have jurisdiction over the resolution: while they are not completely ignored,[324] they will not be part of the resolution college.

150. Group coordination. This jurisdiction of the head office authority explains why, while the Directive strongly encourages joint decision-making by the competent authorities on the treatment of resolution at group level,[325]

---

321 The latter is not necessarily the authority responsible for prudential supervision, and if it is, it should not be subordinate to it.

322 The presence of a similar scheme dispenses with two separate studies: we will focus on the model resulting from the banking resolution, indicating the possible divergences with that of the clearing house.

323 The expression is used by L. D'Avout, 'L'articulation des droits et des procédures dans un espace fédéralisé', *op. cit.*, p. 20. As the author writes, 'Any international insolvency regime starts in principle from the first legal level, which is the legal person' (*ibid.*, p. 18).

324 They may indeed be consulted in certain cases, see e.g. Art. 13(2) of the Resolution Directive.

325 Thus, resolution at group level can be initiated by the supervisory authority on a consolidated basis, i.e. the authority competent for the supervision of the group (Art. 92 of the Resolution Directive), or by the authority of a subsidiary (Art. 91 of the Resolution Directive). Comp.

the Directive still allows the home authority of the subsidiary to reject the adopted plan, and to unilaterally put in place a resolution plan for the subsidiary established on its territory.[326] It should simply be noted that, even in this case, the competent authority is then obliged to take into account the potential impact in other Member States.[327]

The need to propose a coordinated treatment of the group is justified by the fact that the proven failure of one entity of the group is likely to make the failure of other entities of the group foreseeable,[328] making a plan for the whole group desirable. As in prudential matters, a specific competence is given to the 'consolidated supervisor', as determined by the CRR.[329] However, due to the links between subsidiaries, branches and the parent, and the unequal financial situation of each of these entities, the initial scheme of the Resolution Directive, whose entry points were alternatively the subsidiary or the group head, is not necessarily the most likely to produce the expected results. This is why Directive 2019/879 amending the 2014 Resolution Directive changes this state of affairs by introducing new entry points into the group through 'resolution entities' and 'resolution groups',[330] so as to be able to deal with the group from different angles, depending on the state of the entities and the links between them. Such a mechanism, stemming from the proposals of the Financial Stability Board,[331] is likely to allow for the establishment of resolution plans for subgroups within the international group and, as Mr d'Avout observes, 'will probably facilitate the switch of non-systemic or otherwise detachable entities to national winding-up procedures'.[332]

It should be recalled here that the competent resolution authority has two types of prerogatives: on the one hand, the powers of resolution, which have the function of placing the entity under the exclusive control of the authority

within the Insolvency Regulation, L. d'Avout, 'Le traitement des groupes de sociétés: entre formalisme et réalisme' in F. Jault-Seseke and D. Robine (eds.), *Le nouveau règlement Insolvabilité: quelles évolutions*, Issy-les-Moulineaux, Joly Editions, 2015, p. 129.

326 Art. 92(4) of the Resolution Directive. Mr d'Avout describes this prerogative of the head office authorities as a 'possible right of secession' of European subsidiaries, see L. d'Avout, 'L'articulation des droits et des procédures dans un espace fédéralisé', *op. cit.*, p. 31.

327 Art. 87(e), (f), (g), and (h) of the Resolution Directive. This obligation is not only a cosmetic one, since if it is not sufficiently taken into account by the administrative authority, the decision can be challenged in court.

328 E. Susset, 'De quelques particularités de la résolution des groupes transfrontaliers', *RDBF*, November 2014, pp. 106 et seq.

329 Art. 2(1)(37) of the Resolution Directive refers to Art. 4(1)(41) of Regulation No 575/2013 of the European Parliament and of the Council on prudential requirements for credit institutions and investment firms (hereinafter the Prudential Requirements Regulation). On the designation of the authority in this case, see *supra*, para. 121.

330 Art. 83(a) and b of the Resolution Directive.

331 E. Susset, 'De quelques particularités de la résolution des groupes transfrontaliers', *op. cit.*, no. 12.

332 L. d'Avout, 'L'articulation des droits et des procédures dans un espace fédéralisé', *op. cit.*, p. 25.

by allowing the takeover, the transfer of shares and the replacement of the management, and, on the other hand, the instruments of resolution which allow it to clean up the institution by liquidating what needs to be liquidated, and by saving the rest. These resolution instruments are exorbitant and allow the institution in resolution to divest its activities, to use a bridge institution, to separate its assets and to resort to its internal bailout. These powers are likely to affect several types of persons: on the one hand, the institution in resolution and the group of which it is a part, and on the other hand, the institution's co-contractors and creditors, who are likely to see their contractual relations and their claims considerably affected. However, the possibility for the latter to seek redress appears to be singularly limited.

151. Centralisation and limitations of remedies. Member States, which have a simple option to allow judicial review prior to the resolution measure,[333] are obliged to introduce the possibility of appeal against any decision to adopt a crisis prevention measure,[334] and to allow for an appeal against such a measure.[335] However, the possibilities of appeal against administrative decisions are drastically restricted. The restrictions appear both at the level of private international law and domestic law, substantive and procedural.[336]

152. Firstly, restrictions appear within the solutions of conflict of laws and international jurisdiction, which all lead to the centralisation of measures within the legal order of the seat. Indeed, it has been observed that the implementation of certain resolution measures was occasionally subject to local law.[337] However, the implementation of these measures under the law of the place where they are executed does not mean that their validity is subject to that law. Thus, when resolution measures are carried out on the territory of another Member State, shareholders, creditors and affected third parties 'do not have the right to prevent, contest or annul the transfer by virtue of provisions of the law of (that) Member State'.[338] The principle of resolution powers and instruments remains subject to the law of the resolution authority,[339] whose courts are the only ones with jurisdiction to exercise recourse. The consequence is that where a resolution decision, by reorganising the institution, has the effect of transferring contracts, any jurisdiction clause contained in the contract will be rendered ineffective to

333 Art. 85(1) of the Resolution Directive.

334 Art. 85(2) of the Resolution Directive.

335 Art. 85(3) of the Resolution Directive.

336 See S. Adalid, *La Banque centrale européenne et l'Eurosystème*, *op. cit.*, no. 580, on the limited admissibility of appeals against the ECB, which therefore has wide margins for manoeuvre.

337 See *supra*, para. 110.

338 Art. 66(3) of the Resolution Directive.

339 Art. 66(6) of the Resolution Directive.

prevent anyone from challenging the jurisdiction of the court of the seat of the resolution authority.[340]

153. Secondly, the restrictions on remedies relate to the regime of the remedy and its effect. On the one hand, the court will have to base its 'own assessment on the complex economic analyses of the facts made by the resolution authority'.[341] Such a rule, which deprives the claimant of the possibility of a second analysis, is likely to considerably reduce the protection of shareholders. The legislation specifies that their protection, as well as that of creditors, takes place through the valuation rules, which would therefore justify the restriction of remedies.[342] On the other hand, even if the appeal is successful, it will not lead to the annulment of the decision. Indeed, Article 85(4)(b) of the Resolution Directive states:

> 'The annulment of a resolution authority decision shall not affect administrative acts adopted or transactions entered into subsequently by the resolution authority on the basis of the annulled decision. In this case, the remedies [...] shall be limited to the compensation of the losses suffered by the applicant as a result of that decision or measure.'[343]

---

340 See the successive judgments of the English courts, at first instance, *Goldman Sachs International v. Novo Banco*, Queen's Bench Division, Commercial Court, 7 August 2015, [2015] EWHC 2371 (Comm), note H. Synvet, *D.* 2015, 2145, on appeal (2016) EWCA Civ 1902, and most notably by the *Supreme Court*, (2018) UKSC 34, spec. no. 21 for comments on the conflict of laws, and spec. para. 27 on the international jurisdiction of the court, where Lord Sumption considers that the reorganisation decision cannot be isolated from the legislative package to which it belongs: 'an administrative act [...] does not occur in a legal vaccum. In this legal scheme, it cannot make sense for the courts of another member state to give effect to a 'reorganization measure' but not to other provisions of the law of the home state affecting the operation of a 'reorganization measure'.

341 Art. 85(3) of the Resolution Directive, transposed in Art. L. 613-31-18 of the Monetary and Financial Code. The Article, which is very frank, states that 'The judge's assessment shall be based on the complex economic evaluations of the facts made by the resolution college'. Mr Synvet comments on the provision as follows: 'One will appreciate the way in which the judge is dissuaded from undertaking economic analyses that are too complex for him', H. Synvet, *D.*, 2015, 2145. Compare. 'It is with some hesitation that the judge sets foot in the field of dealing with credit institutions' failures, where he feels like an intruder', J.-L. Vallens, 'La défaillance des établissements de crédit et le recours au juge', *RDBF*, 2014, p. 91. Mr Synvet observes that the French remedy jurisdiction is not clearly identified, see H. Synvet, 'Principe de légalité et résolution bancaire' in *Mélanges en l'honneur de Jean-Jacques Daigre*, Paris, Lextenso, 2017, spec. no. 25. This provision is not included in the resolution of clearing houses, where it is specified that 'the court shall base its own assessment on the economic assessments of the facts made by the resolution authority' (Art. 74(5) of the Resolution of Clearing Houses Directive).

342 Recital 63 of the SRM Regulation.

343 Art. 85, b of the Resolution Directive. See in the same sense Art. 74(5) of the Resolution of Central Counterparties Directive.

As Mr Synvet summarises, 'there can be illegality without nullity'.[344] Illegality, on the other hand, may allow the administrative authority to be held liable for tort. In addition to these substantive restrictions, there are procedural restrictions, particularly in the conditions under which an appeal can be made. As a matter of principle, the appeal does not suspend the decision of the first instance and, above all, any suspension of the execution of the measure is subject to a simple presumption that the measure is contrary to public policy.[345] This shows the importance of the decisions of the empowered authority and, consequently, of the criteria of jurisdiction on which its prerogatives are based. This centralisation of jurisdiction at the headquarters of the resolution authority has a consequence on the resolution funding mechanism: it is national in nature, funded by the credit institutions of the headquarters of the resolution authority, except in the case of group resolution, where a mutualisation is possible.

154. The European system of funding arrangements. The Resolution Directive creates a European funding system[346] consisting of the establishment, within each Member State, of a resolution fund, financed by the credit institutions on the basis of the deposits of their clients,[347] and which, in the case of group resolution, may be pooled with the national funds of the member institutions of the group.[348] The other aspect of the European system of funding arrangements is the ability of national funds to borrow from each other.[349] The resolution fund, while it may be managed by the same administrative entity as the deposit guarantee scheme, is nevertheless distinct from it.[350] The latter have in common that they are both considered by the Directive as State aid,[351] and may be used in the context of resolution.

155. Resolution funds. National resolution funds are created by the Resolution Directive in anticipation of the expenses incurred by each Member State in resolution. The fund has two distinct functions: one to support resolution

---

344 H. Synvet, *D.*, 2015, 2145.

345 Art. 85(4) of the Resolution Directive.

346 Art. 99 of the Resolution Directive.

347 The amount must cover 1% of the covered deposits of the authorised institutions. The implementation of the deposit criterion has been subject to some criticism in the context of the single resolution fund. Indeed, in the centralised model, the different resolution funds are mutualised, and the use of the deposit volume criterion is likely to force French banks, whose customers' deposits are not placed in current accounts, but in life insurance and savings books, to make a disproportionate contribution: they provide more than 30% of the contribution to the SRF while representing only 20% of bank deposits, see A. Gosset-Grainville, 'Coopération et souverainetés', *Banque et Droit*, February 2017, special issue, pp. 71 et seq. Case T-149/18, *Arkéa Direct Bank and Others v. ECB*, ECLI:EU:T:2020:393.

348 Art. 101(1)(g and Art. 107 of the Resolution Directive.

349 Art. 106 of the Resolution Directive.

350 Art. 100(2) of the Resolution Directive.

351 Recital 47 of the Resolution Directive.

and the other to compensate. In its first function, the fund appears to be the resolution authority's wallet: it can guarantee the assets or liabilities of the institution, grant it loans,[352] acquire some of its assets, provide contributions to a bridge institution.[353] However, it is in its second function that the fund comes close to the deposit guarantee scheme since it can be used as compensation in two cases: either to pay compensation to shareholders or creditors who would have been better treated by an insolvency procedure,[354] or to compensate the loss to the institution subject to resolution of the resolution authority's decision to exclude certain creditors from the scope of the write-down or conversion of creditors when the internal bail-in instrument is applied.[355]

156. Deposit guarantee schemes.[356] Deposit guarantee schemes establish deposit guarantee funds. These schemes were harmonised in Europe by a Directive of the European Parliament and of the Council of 30 May 1994,[357] which was recast at the same time as the resolution legislation was enacted.[358] The funds are financed by contributions from their members, i.e. the credit institutions that must join a deposit guarantee scheme in order to obtain their authorisation.[359] The funds established have an indemnity function: they are intended to guarantee customer deposits[360] up to one hundred thousand euros[361] in the event of the resolution of the affiliated credit institution.[362] In this case, the deposit guarantee funds can be called upon to absorb the depreciation and conversion of claims that

---

352 These first two uses of the fund can be extended, in most cases, to its subsidiaries, to a bridge institution or to an asset management structure of the institution.

353 See respectively Art. 101(1)(a) to (d) of the Resolution Directive.

354 In which case, the shareholders or creditors are entitled to payment of the difference by the resolution fund, see spec. Art. 75 and Art. 101(1)(e) of the Resolution Directive.

355 Art. 101(1)(f) of the Resolution Directive and, for the exclusion of certain creditors from the write-down and conversion of claims, see Art. 44(3) to (8); see also Recitals 73 to 77). The legislator therefore considered that the burden of this decision should not fall on the institution subject to resolution, but be borne by the resolution fund.

356 In the United States, the institution of a guarantee fund took place following the default of a market member. The stock market regulator then created a specific guarantee fund, over the management of which it has jurisdiction, see P.-H. Conac, *La régulation des marchés boursiers par la Commission des opérations de bourse (COB) et la Securities and exchange commission (SEC)*, *op. cit.*, no. 213.

357 Directive 94/19/EC of the European Parliament and of the Council of 30 May 1994 on deposit guarantee schemes.

358 See now Directive 2014/49/EU of the European Parliament and of the Council of 16 April 2014 on deposit guarantee schemes (recast), hereinafter the Deposit Guarantee Scheme Directive.

359 Art. 10(1), para. 2 of the Deposit Guarantee Scheme Directive. Institutions may, however, choose the scheme to which they wish to be affiliated, and change it: in which case the contributions of their last twelve months will be transferred to the new scheme, see Art. 14(3) of the Deposit Guarantee Scheme Directive.

360 A range of persons are therefore excluded from this system, including public authorities, investment firms, credit institutions, etc., see the list in Art. 5(1).

361 Art. 6(1) of the Deposit Guarantee Scheme Directive.

362 Art. 11(1) and (2) of the Deposit Guarantee Scheme Directive.

may affect customer deposits when the internal bail-in instrument is applied.[363] The scope of the guarantee offered by each fund corresponds to the customer deposits of the credit institutions affiliated to it, plus the customer deposits of branches established in another Member State.[364] As for branches of institutions from third countries, there are two possibilities: either their home country has equivalent legislation, in which case affiliation is not necessary, or this is not the case and they must affiliate to a scheme existing in the territory where they are established.[365] The deposit guarantee scheme is still largely national today, and determined by the head office of the credit institutions.[366]

B. Tempering from Colleges

157. The colleges of resolution authorities in the Resolution Directive and the Resolution Regulation applicable to clearing houses have in common that they constitute tempering to unilateral decision making by the head office authority by instituting a multilateral consultation on all aspects of the resolution, and in particular when drawing up the plan. The directive and the regulation are nevertheless different, because in the context of banking resolution, in the absence of consensus, the authority of the parent company's head office can always override the recommendations of the college. This authority then deprives itself of a universal procedure for handling the resolution, showing the inseparable links between the universalist character of a corporate group insolvency procedure and its collegial implementation by the affected countries. In the context of the resolution of clearing houses, the universalist procedure is systematically preserved, at the cost of the possible constraint of the authority of the seat of the house by an authority of the Union, showing here the limits of the decentralised model.

---

[363] Art. 109(1) Resolution Directive. In this case, both the resolution fund and the deposit guarantee fund can be called upon, and their respective participation is specified, see Art. 109(3) Resolution Directive.

[364] Art. 14(1) of the Deposit Guarantee Scheme Directive (see also Recital 9). A branch is defined as 'a place of business situated in a Member State which constitutes a part without legal personality of a credit institution and which directly carries out, in whole or in part, the operations inherent in the business of a credit institution', Art. 2(10) of the Deposit Guarantee Scheme Directive. The modalities of the clients of the branches are worth mentioning: the deposits will be reimbursed by the deposit guarantee scheme of the host Member State on behalf of the scheme of the home Member State (Art. 14(2)); it must therefore provide the reimbursement in accordance with the instructions of the home Member State scheme (*ibid.*).

[365] Art. 15 of the Deposit Guarantee Scheme Directive.

[366] This is likely to change as a result of the Commission's projects, on which see F. Barrière, 'L'Union bancaire, une œuvre inachevée', in *Mélanges en l'honneur de Jean-Patrice et Michel Storck*, Paris, Dalloz, 2021, pp. 133 et seq.

158. The two stages of coordination of authorities.[367] Group resolution is defined by the Resolution Directive alternatively as the application of a resolution measure at the level of a parent enterprise, or as the coordinated application of resolution measures and the exercise of subsequent powers.[368] To this end, the Directive proposes a two-step approach.[369] In the first stage, a dialogue between the competent authorities is established through a college of resolution authorities,[370] of which a group of authorities affected by the resolution and with jurisdiction in this respect or in the context of supervision[371] are members, but which have in common that they are the authority of the head office of a subsidiary.[372] This college is not a decision-making body, but constitutes 'a platform facilitating decision-making by the national authorities',[373] in order to achieve the orderly resolution of the group in difficulty. There are two possibilities at this level: either the college reaches a plan within four months,[374] or it does not.

If the college reaches a joint decision[375] on the preparation of a plan, this means that at least some authorities[376] have agreed to adopt and implement a

---

[367] On this issue, see L. D'AVOUT, 'L'articulation des droits et des procédures dans un espace fédéralisé', *op. cit.*, pp. 20-22; N. AYMERIC, 'La résolution bancaire – Aspects transfrontières', in *Le traitement des difficultés des établissements bancaires et institutions financières*, Paris, LexisNexis, 2017, pp. 195 et seq.

[368] Art. 2(1)(42) of the Resolution Directive.

[369] This method has been transposed to Art. L. 613-20-6 of the Monetary and Financial Code, which is the seat of group coordination when the ACPR is the supervisor on a consolidated basis.

[370] Art. 88(1) of the Resolution Directive.

[371] Art. 88(2) of the Resolution Directive. The college may include representatives of third countries (Art. 88(3) Resolution Directive).

[372] With the exception of the EBA, see the list of the composition of the college given by Art. 88(2) of the Resolution Directive. The supervisory authorities of branches are thus excluded, but may be consulted, see e.g. Art. 13(2) of the Resolution Directive.

[373] Recital 98 of the Resolution Directive. The authorities ultimately retain jurisdiction for the treatment of the subsidiary established on their territory.

[374] Art 8(2) of the Resolution Directive. The notification chain for coordination is governed by Art. 81 of the Resolution Directive: the institution in difficulty notifies the authority with jurisdiction, which then notifies the whole network of authorities and the resolution system. The directive also governs the modalities of the decision of the resolution authority (Art. 82 of the Resolution Directive), which must then notify all (Art. 83); all notified actors are subject to professional secrecy (Art. 84 of the Resolution Directive).

[375] On this joint decision-making process, see L. D'AVOUT, 'L'articulation des droits et des procédures dans un espace fédéralisé', *op. cit.*, p. 21.

[376] It is possible for the authority with jurisdiction of a subsidiary to reject the group resolution plan, which may still be implemented, except for the measures provided for by the subsidiary of the authority that rejected the plan, which will then adopt a local resolution plan (Art. 8(5) of the Resolution Directive). If the plan is likely to contravene the resolution plan at group level, the mediation measure and possibly a binding decision by the EBA may take place. However, the authority with jurisdiction may still object to the decision if it considers it to be an encroachment on the budget of its Member State (Art. 13(9)). L. D'AVOUT notes in this respect that such a 'local veto right', insofar as it is motivated by the 'financial stability of the Member State', can 'virtually be implicated by the failure of

plan.[377] In order to promote the success of the resolution college, the European legislator has allowed the competent authorities that make up the resolution college[378] to seek the assistance of a specialised body, the EBA, in reaching an agreement within the resolution college.[379] This prerogative must nevertheless be exercised when the plan is drawn up:[380] the aim is to allow the authorities to reach a conciliation.

If the college does not adopt a plan within the time limit, the consolidated supervisor takes its own decision[381] and each competent authority adopts a local resolution plan.[382] In order to avoid the confusion of decisions at group level that such a situation is likely to generate, the European legislator has allowed each competent authority[383] to refer to the EBA in order to contest the measures adopted by another competent authority.[384] The referral is then suspensive of the contentious administrative decision,[385] and the authority whose plan is contested will have to comply with the EBA's decision,[386] unless it considers that it is an encroachment on the budget of its Member State.[387] This binding mechanism can also be requested by the competent authorities when obstacles to resolvability are removed.[388]

159. From the point of view of the EBA, it should be noted that, if it is seized, it benefits from possibilities of intervention on two distinct bases: either as a conciliation procedure during the elaboration of the resolution plan, or as an administrative jurisdiction in case of absence of a joint decision of the authorities.

---

any entity of importance actually established in the Member State of its headquarters and oppose intra-group financial support weakening the local establishment', see L. D'AVOUT, 'L'articulation des droits et des procédures dans un espace fédéralisé', *op. cit.*, p. 22.

377 However, it is still possible that a subsidiary does not withdraw from the plan during its execution in order to proceed with an individual resolution of its subsidiary.

378 Only authorities with their own jurisdiction can refer to the EBA, see Art. 8(7) of the Resolution Directive.

379 Art. 8(2) of the Resolution Directive. The Article refers to Art. 31 of the same Directive.

380 Art. 8(3) para. 2 Resolution Directive: 'The EBA cannot be seized after the expiry of the four-month period or the adoption of a joint decision.'

381 Art 8(3) para. 1 of the Resolution Directive.

382 Art. 18(7) of the Resolution Directive.

383 These are only the authorities with jurisdiction in respect of a subsidiary or parent, see Art. 8(7) of the Resolution Directive.

384 See Art. 8(3) para. 2 of the Resolution Directive for the parent company, and Art. 8(4) para. 2 for the subsidiaries.

385 Mr d'Avout sees in this rule a mechanism of 'lis pendens or stay of proceedings', see L. D'AVOUT, -L'articulation des droits et des procédures dans un espace fédéralisé', *op. cit.*. The stay of proceedings seems to us to be a more appropriate expression, since the contentious decision does not necessarily have to have the same object as the decision before the requesting authority for it to be possible to challenge it.

386 Art. 8(3) para. 2 of the Resolution Directive for the parent company, and Art. 8(4) para. 2 for subsidiaries.

387 Art. 13(9) of the Resolution Directive.

388 Art. 18 of the Resolution Directive.

In the first case, it acts as a specialised body providing a non-binding conciliation forum,[389] in the second case, it acts, it seems, in the manner of an authority administering a coercive decision to those who have referred the matter to it.[390] However, these remedies are provided for administrative authorities only; for the institutions subject to resolution, and for third parties, it is necessary to appeal to a national court.

160. The College of the CCP Resolution Regulation.[391] In the CCP Resolution Regulation, the issue of the college is not specific to a group of institutions, but to the resolution of the clearing house itself. The need for a college arises from the consequences of the resolution on the clearing members and on the monetary and financial stability of the Union. These two aspects explain the constitution of the college. The college is composed of resolution authorities from the headquarters of the clearing members,[392] the central banks whose currencies are affected by the resolution.[393] This first difference, linked to the distinct configuration of the resolution of the clearing house which has its effects on the whole territory of the Union, explains that the authority of the head office of the central counterparty is not fully sovereign during the reduction of the preparation of the recovery plan,[394] of the resolution,[395] of the reduction or elimination of the obstacles to resolvability.[396] In fact, just as in prudential matters, the home authority may be challenged on the granting of authorisation if the majority of the college disagrees and refers the matter to ESMA, in resolution matters, if the majority of the members of the college disagree with the head office authority, its proposed joint decision may be challenged before ESMA, which may, where appropriate, impose the content of the decision. This limitation of the jurisdiction of the home authority does not, however, call into question private international solutions concerning the scope of the applicable

389 The Resolution Directive refers in these cases to Art. 31(c) of the EBA Regulation. This Article, which is entitled 'coordination function', allows the EBA to conduct 'non-binding conciliation procedures at the request of the competent authorities or on its own initiative'.

390 The Resolution Directive then refers to Art. 19(3) of the EBA Regulation. It is striking that, in this second case, the intervention of the EBA does not follow the classic dynamic of Art. 19 of the Resolution Directive, which normally calls for conciliation before moving on to a binding decision if conciliation fails. There are two possible explanations: on the one hand, conciliation could have already taken place, in different aspects, when the EBA was asked for its specialised advice and, on the other hand, the time limits of the resolution probably do not allow for such a long procedure at the very moment when a decision has to be adopted.

391 On this regulation, see T. Bonneau, 'Bref aperçu du règlement du 16 décembre 2020 relatif au redressement et à la résolution des contreparties centrales', *RDBF*, May 2021.

392 Article 4(2)(c), (d) and (e) of the CCP Resolution Regulation.

393 Art. 4(2)(i), (j) and (k) of the CCP Resolution Regulation.

394 Art. 11(5) of the CCP Resolution Regulation.

395 Art. 14(6) of the CCP Resolution Regulation.

396 Art. 17(7) of the CCP Resolution Regulation.

law of the home authority, or the centralisation of the means of appeal against any decision taken.

C. Relations with Third-Country Resolution Authorities

161. Current patterns. Relations with third countries take place at several levels and are not based on a principle of reciprocity or symmetry. Firstly, it is necessary to know whether an agreement has been concluded by the Commission with the third countries.[397] If such an agreement has been concluded, it is to this agreement that reference must be made. In the absence of an agreement in force, the Resolution Directive provides for a set of mechanisms, which differ depending on whether the parent institution subject to resolution is located in the EU and has subsidiaries or branches abroad or, conversely, whether the institution subject to resolution is located in a third country and has subsidiaries or branches in the EU.

162. Parent establishment in the territory of the Union. In the first case, a distinction must be made between subsidiaries and branches. In principle, branches established in the territory of third countries are subject to the scope of application of the Resolution Directive.[398] It will therefore be necessary for resolution authorities to seek recognition and enforcement of their decision at the place of establishment of the branch. However, the Directive provides that with regard to the powers of authorities in relation to 'assets, rights, shares and other property situated in a third country',[399] the competent authority must ensure that its decision is capable of being enforced. If it is not, it should not be made; if the decision is already made, it should be considered nul and void.[400] The provision, which is original, is likely to apply to all decisions that the competent authority may take in respect of the branch's assets and liabilities in respect of the legal person to which it belongs. Nevertheless, the Resolution Directive is not applicable to subsidiaries established abroad, which requires close cooperation with the authorities of the headquarters of the subsidiaries in order to achieve a global group resolution.[401]

163. Parent establishment in the territory of a third country. In the second case, the question arises as to whether the foreign decision on the resolution of the group will be recognised. In order to take this decision, the competent

---

397 This mechanism could be a useful inspiration for the resolution of certain conflicts of law in the field of public bids, see *infra*, para. 510.

398 Art. 1(e) of the Resolution Directive.

399 Art. 67(1) of the Resolution Directive.

400 Art. 67(2) of the Resolution Directive.

401 Professor Synvet wonders whether a parent company can still be considered resolvable 'when it controls significant subsidiaries outside the European Union, each of which falls under the jurisdiction of different authorities' (H. Synvet, 'L'union bancaire européenne – Présentation', *RDBF*, 2014, no. 4, file 24).

authorities for the subsidiaries established in the Union come together in a college of European resolution authorities,[402] which has the same functions as the one already studied: it must lead to a joint decision which is then executed by each national competent authority.[403] In the absence of a joint decision, each authority takes a position on the recognition or non-recognition of the procedure;[404] however, the grounds for refusal of recognition or execution of the third country resolution procedure by national authorities are limited.[405] In case of refusal, the national resolution of the branch can take place under certain conditions:[406] this is a return to the previous state of international insolvency, where each country where a branch is located would liquidate it territorially.

164. Summary. In the light of these developments on the decentralised model, it can be observed that it entails the application of a whole paradigm. The national administrative connecting factor is tempered by bilateral or even multilateral cooperation under the aegis of agreements between authorities and colleges of authorities, where the European supervisory authorities are likely to mediate. Once established in prudential matters, the decentralised model extends in the same way in the case of resolution, manifesting at the administrative level the links already observed at the legislative level. It is not surprising that this decentralised vision, which corresponds to that of private international law, may have wished to borrow some of the latter's criteria in order to perfect its coordination techniques in the case of access by an administrator to another Member State or the localisation of conduct of business rules. Nevertheless, it was observed that the objectives pursued between private international contract law and measures conditioning access to a foreign territory were too dissimilar, and that this coordination was better pursued by the material criterion of solicitation.

§ 2. THE CENTRALISED MODEL

165. Centralised models and managers. Supervisory and default models are centralised when they give jurisdiction to an EU agency to grant authorisation and exercise supervision of the authorised entity or to decide on resolution and its implementation. Initially confined to the monetary field, the centralised model has now penetrated banking law and is already affecting certain providers supervised by financial market law, such as rating agencies. From the point of view of market managers, this centralised model is already positive law: on the

---

402 The college is original in that it is chaired by the European institution with the most assets see Art. 89(3) of the Resolution Directive.

403 Art. 94(2) of the Resolution Directive.

404 Art. 94(3) of the Resolution Directive.

405 See the five grounds for refusal listed exhaustively in Art. 95 of the Resolution Directive.

406 Art. 96 of the Resolution Directive.

one hand, the banking model is applicable to central counterparties and central securities depositories established in the euro area whenever they are licensed as credit institutions and, on the other hand, the European System of Central Banks supervises the clearing systems managed by the clearing houses.[407] It should be noted, however, that even when the centralised model is applicable, it does not completely crowd out the decentralised model based on mutual recognition,[408] which persists on its periphery, not only to ensure the coordination of the competent European agencies with the authorities of the States that have not adhered to centralisation,[409] but also because the techniques instituted permeate the relations with third States.

166. Reasons for extension. Several observations are necessary here regarding the extension of the centralised model to market infrastructure managers. The first is the link between prudential law and insolvency law that has already been discussed. In fact, two aspects must be distinguished. Firstly, the argument of the burden of insolvency has been used to justify the centralisation of decisions at EU level. Indeed, the transfer of prudential executive jurisdiction to the ECB 'is the counterpart of the possibility given to the European Stability Mechanism (ESM) to directly recapitalise credit institutions in difficulty, without increasing the public debt of the Member States to which they belong'.[410] In other words, because EU

---

407 One could probably add that the study of banking is desirable here because the two systems of supervision, banking and financial, have the same objective of stability of the financial system, T. Bonneau, 'Union bancaire et Autorité européenne des marchés financiers' in F. Martucci (ed.), *L'Union bancaire*, Brussels, Bruylant, 2016, pp. 223 et seq.

408 On this crowding out, see B. Sousi, 'La reconnaissance mutuelle, victime collatérale de l'Union bancaire', *op. cit.* Some authors consider that this crowding out shows the tension between the objective of prevention of systemic risk, which justified the institution of a centralised administrative jurisdiction at the level of the Union, while the principle of subsidiarity justified in part mutual recognition (S. Lambert, *L'application internationale du droit financier*, *op. cit.*, nos. 480–481). However, it seems to us that, from the point of view of jurisdiction, the principle of subsidiarity can act in both directions by considering, on the contrary, that an agency of the Union is better placed to supervise systemic institutions or institutions whose activity is deployed on a cross-border basis.

409 See B. Stoeva, *La coopération entre les superviseurs financiers dans l'Union européenne*, *op. cit.*, no. 50. In addition, 'all powers not expressly attributed to the ECB by the SSM Regulation continue to be allocated according to the mutual recognition method' (G. Hardy, *L'européanisation de la surveillance bancaire*, *op. cit.*, no. 68). On the persistence of mutual recognition between the ECB and authorities that are not members of the SSM / SRM, see *infra*, no. 199.

410 P.-E. Partsch, *Droit bancaire et financier européen, t. 1*, *op. cit.*, nos. 71 and 96 et seq. See also R. Gaspard, *La reconnaissance mutuelle en droit bancaire et financier*, *op. cit.*, no. 630; G. Hardy, *L'européanisation de la surveillance bancaire*, *op. cit.*, no. 47.
The ESM is a body set up to lend to national governments so that they have the means to bail out national credit institutions. Indeed, a vicious circle was set up during the 2008 crisis, which saw Member States bail out their national banks by issuing debt, acquired by local banks (G. Hardy, *L'européanisation de la surveillance bancaire*, *op. cit.*, no. 69). However, the discount attached to the debt issued led to a deterioration of the bank's funds, which then had to be bailed out again (R. Gaspard, *La reconnaissance mutuelle en droit bancaire*

funds are used in case of insolvency, the EU should exercise supervisory powers to prevent insolvency. However, the argument appears artificial. As Mr Gaspard has shown, the intervention of the European Stability Mechanism in order to recapitalise a credit institution is in fact very subsidiary to the state bailout, so that the pre-eminence given to the Union legal order has a more theoretical basis than one might think.[411] Therefore, the objective of the SRM Regulation to 'break the link between State and bank' so that 'the place of establishment (is) no longer a criterion'[412] does not appear to be fully achieved. One could conclude that, for once, banking law may not be the model for financial law. This is especially true since the arguments that have been used to extend the monetary model to the banking model are those of the links between monetary law and bank supervision, and these arguments are inoperative in financial matters.[413]

---

et financier européen, op. cit.) However, by borrowing from the ESM, national governments continued to add to their debt burden. The European mechanism could provide a way out of this impasse on condition that European credit institutions could borrow money directly from it (*ibid.*, no. 629). However, Germany only accepted the possibility of adding a 'direct recapitalisation instrument' to the ESM if the supervision of these institutions would be subject to a European body. As Mr Partsch writes: 'The starting point is the bargaining between the Latin countries and Northern and Germanic Europe on the possibility given to the ESM to support banks directly without aggravating the public debt of the Member State concerned in exchange for the introduction of European prudential supervision within Euroland with the Single Supervisory Mechanism', P.-E. Partsch, *Droit bancaire et financier européen, t. 1, op. cit.* See also G. Hardy, *L'européanisation de la surveillance bancaire, op. cit.*, no. 46.

411 The ESM is endowed with capital provided exclusively by the Member States, and the Member States will not be liable beyond the capital they have provided (Art. 8 ESM Treaty and R. Gaspard, *La reconnaissance mutuelle en droit bancaire et financier européen, op. cit.*) Moreover, in order to have access to recapitalisation, credit institutions cannot apply directly to the ESM, but must go through the State where they are based. Moreover, the latter must prove that it is not in a position to recapitalise the institution itself, at the risk of jeopardising its financial stability, see Art. 3.2, a of the *Guideline on Financial assistance for the Direct Recapitalisation of Institutions.* This provision has been criticised, as 'a country that recognises that it is financially incapable of rescuing one of its institutions would inevitably see its access to the market closed' (V. Catillon, 'L'instrument de recapitalisation directe du MES', *RISF*, 2017, no. 1, p. 41, especially p. 46). Even if recapitalisation is granted, it is in fact determined by a sharing protocol which determines the respective contribution of the State and the ESM, the latter only intervening as a complement (Art. 9 of the *Guideline on Financial assistance for the Direct Recapitalisation of Institutions*). This means that the Union's involvement is subsidiary. Above all, even when it intervenes, it is of intergovernmental origin. This contrasts with the competence granted to the ECB.

412 Recital 19 of the SRM Regulation. This objective is undoubtedly in line with the policy of avoiding too much interaction between financial institutions and the Member States on whose territory they are established, in particular in order to combat the 'vicious circle' between the banking crisis and the sovereign debt crisis, see F. Martucci, 'Union bancaire, la méthode du "cadre": du discours à la réalité', *op. cit.*

413 Apart from the idea that the ECB would be more appropriate because it is itself a bank (G. Hardy, *L'européanisation de la surveillance bancaire, op. cit.*, no. 740), an idea that appears more peremptory than anything else, it should be noted here that the main argument in support of the centralisation of prudential jurisdiction in the hands of the ECB often lies within the links maintained by monetary policy and prudential law. At least this is

167. Furthermore, even if the burden of insolvency is not really borne by the Union, another reason related to insolvency that could justify centralisation could nevertheless be its capacity to affect all Member States and thus generate a systemic risk. The importance of cross-border activity and its systemic nature thus justify in the banking model the direct supervision of the ECB. Nevertheless, we believe that the question of the appropriateness of the resolution regime must be dissociated from that of centralisation. It is certain that the failure of certain market infrastructures is likely to affect the entire territory of the Union, *a fortiori* because any investment firm established on the territory of the Union can have access to them,[414] and that their resolution requires coordination that is all the more important because the activity of market managers is highly concentrated in the hands of a few groups of companies. However, on the one hand, a distinction must be made according to the market infrastructures likely to affect the entire territory of the Union[415] and, on the other hand, the need for a resolution regime does not make it necessary for its implementation to be centralised by an agency of the Union: the decentralised resolution regime studied above is proof of this.

168. Secondly, centralisation may have been justified by the poor coordination of cross-border institutions and differences in supervisory cultures during the 2008 crisis.[416] The SRM Regulation is intended to address the shortcomings of a

---

what the members of the ECB say. Mr Padoa-Schioppa considered already at the time of the introduction of the euro: 'The novelty constituted by the abandonment of the coincidence between the area of competence of monetary policy and the area of competence of banking supervision', quoted *ibid.*, no. 32. More recently, Mr Coeuré has argued that 'monetary union and banking union are symbiotic and constitute the logical extension of the Maastricht Treaty, both historically and politically', B. Coeuré, 'Why the Euro Needs a Banking Union', ECB, Speech, Conference Bank funding - Markets, Instruments and Implications for Corporate Lending and the Real Economy, Frankfurt am Main, 8 October 2012, cited by G. Hardy, *L'européanisation de la surveillance bancaire*, *op. cit.* On the incompatibility of a single currency and national banking supervision, and the links between EMU and SSM see *ibid.*, nos. 32 et seq. First of all, this decorrelation between monetary policy and banking supervision did not pose any difficulty during the first decade of its implementation, and exists in foreign law (e.g. in the United States, see E. Fernandez-Bollo, 'L'impact de l'Union bancaire sur la coopération en matière de contrôle bancaire', *op. cit.) There* is in fact nothing 'symbiotic' between monetary policy and prudential supervision: the origin of the *subprime* crisis is not to be found in the European banking market, but in its interdependence with the US market. Finally, the granting of prudential jurisdiction to the ECB was granted precisely after having ensured a Chinese wall between the functions of monetary policy and prudential supervision (see G. Hardy, *L'européanisation de la surveillance bancaire*, *op. cit.*, no. 628, even if this wall seems to be defective see *ibid.*, no. 670).

414 See *supra*, para. 125.

415 Both because not all of them affect the entire territory of the Union, or present a systemic risk (we are thinking here of organised trading systems or settlement systems which are sometimes very much anchored in a single Member State).

416 Unambiguously decried by Recital 5 of the SSM Regulation, see also A. Prüm, 'L'Union bancaire européenne et les autorités de surveillance nationales', *RDBF*, July-August 2014, pp. 74 et seq.

national and unilateral response to international difficulties.[417] In other words, institutions with cross-border activity would be more effectively supervised by a European agency; here we find the principle of subsidiarity. However, it is not certain that the difficulties observed invalidate the decentralised model. Rather, they are an incentive to improve it. In this respect, the question could be resolved by the institution of the colleges associated with the possible intervention of the European authorities as a third party, without altering the national designation of the author of the administrative decision. The decentralised model is undoubtedly more respectful of the autonomy of the Member States. Moreover, this model has not proved dysfunctional to date. Therefore, before abandoning it, it would have been preferable to wait until it had been established that it could be undermined for reasons that 'unification of the decision-making process' is really likely to resolve.

169. Thirdly, in banking matters, centralisation would constitute a bulwark against the phenomenon of 'regulatory capture', i.e. the undue influence of banks on the drafting and implementation of regulations concerning them, and forbearance, i.e. the suspicious leniency of the competent national authorities for the 'national champions'.[418] There seems to be a point of contact here between centralisation of the administrative decision and resolution. An alternative solution could have been to get rid of national champions, which are the points of attachment of systemic risk, and to settle for smaller players, which can be supervised locally without risking complacency because of their size, and whose

---

417 See explicitly Recital 9 of the SRM Regulation in this sense.

418 J.-V. Louis, 'Conclusion', *op. cit.* A.-C. Muller, 'La sécurisation du secteur bancaire et financier', *op. cit.*: 'In 2008, the financial crises showed the limits of cooperation between national authorities. The supervision of international groups is difficult. The existence of a link between sovereign debt and moral hazard resulting from implicit state support is a risk factor for the banking and financial system. This is why the ECB has been entrusted with the supervision of the banking sector.' Canadian law as interpreted by its Supreme Court (Supreme Court of Canada, 2011, 3 SCR 874 § 80) seems to us to be wiser in considering that, in the words of Mr Bismuth: 'the ability of the provinces to act effectively in concert for the regulation of a given activity constitutes an important criterion in order to justify the incompetence of the federal level if the latter had aims in the matter', R. Bismuth, 'L'Union Bancaire ou les imperfections de la fédéralisation de la régulation financière au sein de l'Union Européenne. Quelques réflexions à l'aune d'une comparaison des modèles fédéraux américain et canadien' in F. Martucci (ed.), *L'Union bancaire*, Brussels, Bruylant, 2016, p. 57. Such a criterion seems to have guided the reflection on monetary matters, where the cooperation of the Member States seemed insufficient, see S. Adalid, *La Banque centrale européenne et l'Eurosystème, op. cit.*, no. 26.
Some authors also argue for a *forbearance* of ESMA, see F. Martucci and R. Vabres, 'Rapport sur la faisabilité de la consécration par le législateur de l'Union d'une procédure de forbearance faisant intervenir l'Autorité européenne des marchés financiers', *RTDF*, December 2018, no. 4, pp. 3 et seq.

failure is unlikely to cause systemic risk.[419] Moreover, such a dismantling would promote competition. As it stands, however, resolution law is likely to encourage the creation of universal banks, which are dear to the French model.[420]

170. Diversity of models and private international law. These different models of centralisation leave room for a certain diversity. Firstly, because the accomplishment of the tasks assigned to the Union gives rise to different forms of mutualisation of decision-making and de-concentration of their execution.[421] It seems to us that in the same way that the institution of colleges of authority could appear as the tempering of decentralisation, the important de-concentration of the implementation of monetary and banking supervision decisions appears as the first tempering of the centralisation of the decision, to which we must add the place occupied by the national authorities within the decision-making body.[422] Secondly, because the granting of administrative jurisdiction does not necessarily

---

419 Compare H. Synvet, 'Principe de légalité et résolution bancaire', *op. cit.*, no. 35: 'Banking resolution is the offspring of systemic banking. The latter is itself the result of an objective alliance between the temptation to concentrate inherent in financial capitalism and the propensity of the public authorities to promote "national champions". This is how we end up with a legal regime which, behind the cloak of the best intentions, denies the values of a state of law and freedom.'

420 A.-C. Muller, 'Regards sur la directive Résolution', *op. cit.* The author nevertheless notes that the prerogatives of the authorities with regard to resolvability are likely to curb the increase in the size of banks. The author also considers that the piling up of authorities would not be likely to allow resolution in the time allowed or necessary. The adoption of the SRM Regulation undoubtedly makes it possible to remedy this criticism by unifying the decision-making process. Of course, the criticism remains valid for groups of institutions with entities on the territory of non-participating Member States and, above all, on the territory of third countries. In practice, these institutions will be the most important and therefore those whose failure would have the most negative consequences. However, on the one hand, time will tell whether the coordination provided for by the Resolution Directive constitutes an obstacle to resolution and, if so, non-participating Member States may be pushed to join the Single Resolution Mechanism, disarming the criticism. Recent experience gives hope for the efficiency of the decentralised model, see J.-C. Cabotte, 'Aspects de compétences des différentes autorités en matière de gestion de crises bancaires', *op. cit.* On the other hand, the Resolution Directive makes it possible to unify at the European level the interlocutors of third States, which makes it possible to conclude uniform agreements on the territory of the Union with third States, in addition to mandating an institution which will have all the more room for manoeuvre as it will act on behalf of the Union.

421 As Professor Prüm writes, 'the sophisticated governance involved in these supervision and resolution mechanisms, based on a subtle division of competences between the Union and its Member States, is a first in European Union law'. A. Prüm, 'Le nouveau cadre européen du traitement des faillures à vol d'oiseau', *RDBF*, 2014, no. 6. The statement may be qualified in that, in certain respects, this governance is prefigured by the scheme in force in monetary matters. Nevertheless, for a clear distinction between the two, see G. Hardy, *L'européanisation de la surveillance bancaire, op. cit.*, nos. 72 et seq.

422 On this question see S. Lambert, *L'application internationale du droit financier, op. cit.* The author considers that there is a certain tension between colleges of authorities and centralisation within a federal authority. However, the question is not only one of better coordination of authorities, but also of which courts have jurisdiction to challenge the decision that may be taken.

imply the uniformity of the applicable law, leading the Union agencies to apply the law of the Member States. These two aspects explain the twofold interest of this study from a private international perspective.

171. The first interest is to show the absence of a necessary coincidence between the competent authority and the applicable law, and to observe the mechanisms that can ensure a good coordination of the application of local law by the European authority. The most common mechanism is to proceed with de-concentration, leaving it to the local authority to apply its own law. When the European authority itself exercises its prerogatives, Mr Synvet has proposed, not without humour, to institute a mechanism of preliminary referral to the national legal order.[423] It seems to us that the idea should be taken seriously and that such a mechanism would benefit from being put in place.

172. The second interest is related to international jurisdiction. As the case law of the Union stands, the determination of the jurisdiction of the courts depends precisely on whom *ultimately* has to take the administrative decision. This rule, clearly stated in the *Berlusconi* judgment,[424] means that any devolution of the tasks entrusted to the Union Agency has no effect on the court with jurisdiction, which will always be that of the Union. The rule is traditional in that it is up to the courts of the legal order that established the authority that issued the decision to annul it.[425] This rule also has the advantage of allowing the concentration of litigation in a single court and ensuring the uniform application of Union law. However, these two arguments are not convincing. The first rule, derived from public international law, is correct in interstate relations. Nevertheless, it loses its force within a federal space, where a federal agency can receive a command from a court of a Member State insofar as the federal pact provides for this. It is therefore the advantage conferred by this rule of uniform application of Union law that justifies the jurisdiction given to the Court of Justice. However, this justification loses its force once it is observed that the law applied is not uniform since it is the law of the seat of each establishment. This justifies the fact that the conflict of jurisdiction can be resolved by another rule, that of *forum legis*, which consists in giving jurisdiction to the court whose law is applied. Not only is the institution of this rule possible and desirable, but it is already present in certain aspects of the centralised model.

---

423 Mr Synvet writes: 'There is thus a tendency for the Court to leave the bed of European law to extend its jurisdiction to provisions of national law [...] Everyone knows that the judges of the Court of Justice are omniscient. However, some ill-intentioned people will wonder whether a new preliminary ruling mechanism should not be instituted, this time for the benefit of the national judge...', H. Synvet, *D.*, 2019, 2009 observations on the *Berlusconi* judgment on which see *infra*, para. 186.

424 This judgment is discussed *infra*, para. 186.

425 Another solution would lead to the courts of one State ordering the organs of another State order, and would therefore violate international law.

These different lines of thought will be explained by studying the centralised models of supervision (I) and failure (II).

I. Centralised Models of Supervision

173. Diversity of centralised models. Centralised models of supervision can be analysed from two perspectives: on the one hand, their degree of concentration and, on the other hand, the place of national authorities in the decision-making body. There is no correlation between the two, nor even with the jurisdiction granted to the Union to carry out its mission.[426] For example, the centralisation model for rating agencies[427] refers to absolute concentration, with ESMA having sole jurisdiction and ousting the national authorities,[428] but its decision-making body is actually made up of members of the national authorities. It has all the prerogatives traditionally attributed by EU law to the authorities of the home and host Member States. This includes, in addition to granting authorisation and monitoring prudential requirements,[429] investigative powers[430] and sanctioning powers,[431] which ESMA uses.[432] These direct supervisory powers are worth noting: not only is ESMA relinquishing its role as coordinator of national authorities, but more importantly the ESMA Regulation explicitly envisages extending them to market infrastructures.[433]

174. However, it seems to us that this absolute centralisation is only possible under three conditions. The first is that the entities have a truly cross-border activity on the entire territory of the Union, so that the principle of subsidiarity does not prevent it. The second condition is that the number of entities to be supervised is low, as ESMA will otherwise not have the means to carry out this supervision[434] and Member States are not attracted by the prospect of significantly increasing their contribution to ESMA's budget, when they already have a national regulator. The third condition is that the activity

---

426 See *supra*, note under para. 93.

427 This model is also applicable to trade repositories, see F. Drummond, *Droit financier*, *op. cit.*

428 Regulation No 1060/2009 of the European Parliament and of the Council of 16 September 2009 on credit rating agencies.

429 Art. 14 CRA Regulation – technically, the Regulation refers to 'registration' with ESMA.

430 Art. 23c and d of the above-mentioned Regulation on CRAs.

431 Art. 23e of the Regulation on CRAs.

432 See ESMA's sanction decisions on its website.

433 Art. 81(3) of the ESMA Regulation states: 'With regard to the issue of direct supervision of institutions or infrastructures with pan-European reach, the Commission shall, taking into account market developments, prepare an annual report on the appropriateness of conferring further supervisory responsibilities on the Authority in this field.' See for an illustration the Commission's proposal for a Regulation: Doc. COM(2017) 536 final, Brussels, 20 September 2017.

434 It should be recalled that ESMA's budget is 40 million, while that of the AMF alone is 120 million.

is not sufficiently sensitive for Member States to relinquish their administrative jurisdiction entirely. In this respect, the long-standing existence of Member State supervision will make it more difficult to transfer this jurisdiction until a characteristic failure has occurred.

The conditions for this centralisation model do not appear to be fully met for infrastructure managers: market operators are relatively numerous; central securities depositories and multilateral and organised trading facilities are often very national; clearing houses carry out an activity that is sensitive for the Member State of establishment. However, the centralised model is applicable to infrastructure managers as soon as they have a banking licence, and it is possible that the centralised model could be extended to other infrastructure managers as soon as it is deconcentrated, imposing here the study of the single supervisory mechanism.

175. The ECB and the single supervisory mechanism. Arguments about centralisation resulted in the abandonment of the 'old triptych'[435] which underpinned the construction of a European banking law: 'harmonisation of the essentials; mutual recognition of authorisations; home state authority',[436] which 'implied that while the key elements of the legislation were adopted in Brussels, the power of decision with respect to each individual credit institution remained within the states'.[437] Instead, a single supervisory mechanism was established, defined as 'the financial supervisory system consisting of the ECB and the national competent authorities of the participating Member States', under which all decision-making powers previously vested in national authorities are vested in the ECB.[438] Several observations are necessary here. Firstly, this jurisdiction devolved to the ECB is restricted to the Member States of the euro area and to

---

435 H. Synvet, 'European Banking Union. Presentation', *op. cit.*, p. 60.

436 *Ibid.*

437 *Ibid.*

438 In addition, the ECB has investigative and sanctioning powers with regard to the largest credit institutions. The ECB is thus in charge of the tasks traditionally entrusted to the home authority, from the authorisation of the institution to the supervision of its obligations (see Art. 4(1) of the SSM Regulation), up to the evaluation of acquisitions and disposals of qualified holdings in these institutions; these competences can be explained by the guarantee of neutrality that the ECB offers for taking decisions that may represent delicate political stakes, see in this sense E. Wymeersch, 'The Single Supervisory Mechanism or "SSM", Part One of the Banking Union', European Corporate Governance Institute (ECGI) – Law Working Paper no. 240/2014, 21 February 2014, no. 7. The ECB is also the competent authority in case of opening a branch in another Member State. It therefore has all the powers traditionally vested in the authorities of the home and host Member States, see Art. 4(1)(b) of the SSM Regulation. Finally, it should be noted here that the ECB has long campaigned for prudential jurisdiction, see F. Martucci, 'Union bancaire, la méthode du "cadre": du discours à la réalité' in F. Martucci (ed.), *L'Union bancaire*, *op. cit.* The author also considers that it is the need to preserve the euro that 'was the catalyst for the Europeanisation of banking supervision' (*ibid.*, p. 21).

those wishing to participate in the framework of enhanced cooperation,[439] and is without prejudice to the tasks carried out by the ECB in monetary matters.[440] The decision-making body within the SSM is therefore not the ECB's Governing Council, but its Supervisory Board, which is composed of one representative of each national authority, plus a Chairperson, a Vice-Chairperson, both appointed by the European Council on a proposal from the ECB, and four representatives of the ECB appointed by the Governing Council.[441]

176. Second, the material scope of Article 4.1 of the SSM Regulation, which is the seat of ECB competence, is not exhaustive. This is clarified by Recital 28 of the SSM Regulation, which excludes from the ECB's competence both aspects relating to the spatial scope (third country operators), but also material issues. Within the latter, however, a distinction must be made between those that are simply unrelated to prudential obligations, such as the supervision of payment services and financial markets, and those that are of a hybrid nature, in particular 'the prevention of the use of the financial system for the purpose of money laundering and terrorist financing, as well as consumer protection',[442] to which rules of conduct between banks and their customers should probably be added. These three aspects therefore fall within the exclusive national jurisdiction of the supervisory authorities, where mutual recognition is always likely to come into play. This time, it will be the ECB that will be encouraged to 'cooperate fully with national authorities'.[443] These aspects are not unrelated to prudential requirements. As Professor André Prüm points out: 'while their main purpose is not strictly prudential, the rules in question undoubtedly have a prudential dimension'.[444]

---

439 Art. 7 of the SSM Regulation. See on this question, J.-V. Louis, 'Coopération rapprochée, un nouveau mode de coopération renforcée?' in *L'identité du droit de l'Union européenne, Mélanges en l'honneur de Clause Blumann,* Droit de l'Union européenne Series, Brussels, Bruylant, 2015, p. 216 and F. Martucci, 'Union bancaire, la méthode du "cadre": du discours à la réalité', *op. cit.*

440 Art. 25(2) of the SSM Regulation. The ECB Governing Council issued a decision on 27 September 2014 on the implementation of the separation of monetary policy and prudential supervision functions (ECB/2014/39). However, not only does this separation of functions not appear to be fully effective (see G. Hardy, *L'européanisation de la surveillance bancaire, op. cit.*, no. 658), but the very principle of entrusting prudential supervision to a central bank is discussed, see E. Ferran, 'Institutional Design for Financial Market Supervision: The Choice for National Systems', *University of Cambridge Faculty of Law, Legal Studies Research Paper Series 14-15*, 15 April 2014; T.H. Tröger, 'The Single Supervisory Mechanism – Panacea or Quack Banking Regulation?' (2015) 15 *European Business Organization Review*, p. 449.

441 Art. 26(3) and (5) of the SSM Regulation.

442 Recital 28 of the SSM Regulation.

443 Recital 29 of the SSM Regulation.

444 A. Prüm, 'L'Union bancaire européenne et les autorités de surveillance nationales', *Revue de Drot bancaire et financier*, 2014, No. 4, para. 9. These remarks follow from Recitals 15, 28, 29 and Art. 1(5) of the SSM Regulation. The case of consumer protection is probably explained by the American example, on which see *infra*, para. 183.

177. Thirdly, it should be noted, on the one hand, that the unification of the administrative decision has not led to the unification of the applicable law and, on the other hand, that the ECB has only an implementing power.[445] Although the ECB has no legislative power, it is not without normative possibilities. Indeed, the ECB's power of execution is manifested in two elements: normative execution, i.e. the power granted to the ECB to specify legislation by issuing general norms, and material execution, i.e. the power to take individual decisions or to carry out operations.[446] The first power is specified in Article 6.7 of the SSM Regulation, according to which 'the ECB shall adopt and make public a framework for organising the practical arrangements for the implementation of this Article'[447] The second leads to the exercise of supervision of systematic institutions, combined with the possible pre-emption of jurisdiction. These observations make it advisable to study the particularities of the ECB's implementing powers: the deconcentration to which it is subject (A), and the lack of coincidence with the legislative jurisdiction (B). These two aspects make it possible to formulate some remarks on the determination of the court with jurisdiction (C).

A. Distribution of Administrative Jurisdiction

178. Allocation criterion. There are several types of relationships, but in order to establish them accurately, it is first necessary to consider the criterion for the allocation of supervision between the ECB and the national supervisory authorities.[448] This allocation is in principle based on the size of the credit institution, according to the criteria set out in the SSM Regulation and based on the economic importance threshold of the institution at national level.[449] On the face of it, the allocation criterion seemed to be devoid of any hierarchy of authorities, since it was based on subsidiarity,[450] explicitly favouring a form of coordination.[451] However, the implementation of this criterion is left to the ECB, which, through the inclusion of the institution in a list maintained by it, unilaterally decides to remove an entity from the supervision of the authority

---

445 G. Hardy, *L'européanisation de la surveillance bancaire*, *op. cit.*, no. 373.

446 The titles of these powers used by the doctrine (see *ibid.*, no. 412 and references) are misleading, because the substantive power of execution has of course a normative scope.

447 On this aspect, see *ibid.*, no. 415.

448 While it was envisaged that the ECB would supervise and control all credit institutions in the EU, Germany strongly opposed such a scenario, leading to the compromise solution outlined here. On this point, see T. Bonneau, 'L'union bancaire européenne. Introductory remarks', *RDBF*, July-August 2014, pp. 62 et seq., spec. no. 6.

449 Art 6(4°) of the SSM Regulation.

450 In the sense that the most significant institutions will be better supervised by a more important institution while the others may continue to be supervised by the national authority (see also in this sense, G. Hardy, *L'européanisation de la surveillance bancaire*, *op. cit.*, no. 766), it is in fact a more vertical relationship that seems to be established between the ECB and the national supervisory authorities of the countries party to the SSM.

451 This is the title of Art. 6 of the SSM Regulation.

of its registered office.[452] However, the ECB can include an institution on this list even when the national threshold is not crossed,[453] in particular because of the importance of its cross-border activities[454] and the litigation has shown that the ECB has a significant margin of discretion.[455] This control of the ECB[456] over the allocation criterion leads to its control over the competence of national supervisory authorities.[457] Even more impressive is the power of the ECB to substitute itself for the national authority if 'this is necessary to ensure a consistent application of high supervisory standards'.[458] As Professor Jean-Philippe Kovar writes, 'while the organisation of prudential supervision of credit institutions in the European Union has traditionally been based on horizontal cooperation between national authorities, the SSM establishes a form of vertical cooperation

452 Art. 49 of the SSM Regulation.

453 See the criteria in Art. 57(1) of the SSM Regulation.

454 Art. 6(4) SSM Regulation.

455 A major dispute arose over the application of Art. 6(4) of the Regulation to a German public law bank established under local law. The ECB had unilaterally decided to classify the bank as important and to remove it from the scope of supervision of the national authority and include it in its own supervision without taking into account the 'special circumstances' of Art. 6(4). In this case, the bank argued that the ECB's decision-making jurisdiction only concerned the most important institutions, the national authorities retaining their jurisdiction for the other institutions (para. 32), see CJEU, 8 May 2019, C-450/17 (T122-15), *Landeskreditbank v. ECB*, ECLI:EU:C:2019:372, spec. paras. 55 and 56 on the ECB's margin of appreciation). *In fine*, the Court considers that 'the ECB may at any time, on its own initiative after consulting the national competent authorities, or at the request of a national competent authority, decide to exercise directly itself all relevant powers in respect of one or more credit institutions referred to in that Article 5(4)', *ibid.* On the first instance judgment and the appeal judgment see, inter alia, S. Adalid, 'Le MSU, nouveau sous-système de droit de l'Union européenne', *RAE*, 2017, no. 2, pp. 363 et seq.; F. Boucard, 'Supervision of smaller institutions: Articulation of the competences of the ECB and the national competent authorities', *RDBF*, July 2017, no. 4; J.-P. Kovar and J. Lasserre Capdeville, 'Clarification by the EU General Court of the division of competences within the Single Supervisory Mechanism', *Revue Banque*, July/August 2017, no. 810, pp. 86-88; A. Pazzola, 'The Role of the European Central Bank in the Single Supervisory Mechanism: A New Paradigm for EU Governance' (2018) 43(1) *European Law Review*, pp. 3–23; T. Samin and S. Torck, 'Rejection by the General Court of the EU of the appeal lodged by a German bank against the ECB's decision qualifying it as a significant entity', *RDBF*, September 2017, no. 5, pp. 31-35; F. Annunziata, 'European Banking Supervision in the Age of the ECB' (January 2020) *European Business Organization Review*, pp. 545 et seq.; M.L. Escudero, 'Le contrôle juridictionnel de la Cour de justice dans le domaine de l'Union bancaire', *Cahiers de droit européen,* April 2020, pp. 549 et seq. M. Prek and S. Lefèvre, 'Le contentieux de la surveillance prudentielle des établissements de crédit devant le tribunal de l'Union européenne', *Journal de droit européen*, 2019, pp. 99 et seq.

456 Some authors speak of 'pre-emption of jurisdiction', see L. d'Avout, 'L'articulation des droits et des procédures dans un espace fédéralisé', *op. cit.*, p. 23; G. Hardy, *L'européanisation de la surveillance bancaire*, *op. cit.*

457 See already in this sense, J.-P. Kovar, 'La BCE et les autorités nationales de surveillance' in F. Martucci (ed.), *L'Union bancaire*, *op. cit.*, p. 236. This argument is made in support of the idea that the national authorities are merely the delegates of the ECB, see G. Hardy, *L'européanisation de la surveillance bancaire*, *op. cit.*, no. 77.

458 Art. 6(5)(b) SSM Regulation.

between its components'.[459] However, the term 'vertical cooperation' should not be misleading:[460] the SSM Regulation is in fact a hierarchical version[461] of the centralised model,[462] simply because it is the ECB that has decision-making powers in any case.[463] The Court of Justice had the opportunity to make this particularly clear in the *Landeskreditbank* judgment, where it described the jurisdiction exercised over all institutions subject to the SSM as 'exclusive'.[464] The only real qualification of this hierarchy is the composition of the Supervisory Board.

179. Interaction of authorities. This division of responsibilities results in constant interaction between the ECB and national authorities, even when the ECB is directly supervising large institutions. Indeed, its interaction with the national authorities continues, since the latter prepare the draft decision on authorisations and acquisitions of qualifying holdings,[465] and are consulted in the event of the withdrawal of an authorisation when they do not formulate the draft withdrawal themselves.[466] This bottom-up procedure is contrasted with another,

---

459 J.-P. Kovar, 'The ECB and national supervisory authorities', *op. cit.*

460 This expression borders on an oxymoron, since cooperation implies a form of equality, whereas verticality rather means obedience. However, Mr Kovar (*ibid.*) notes the existence of an obligation on the part of the ECB: that of communicating information obtained by it on certain legal or natural persons in the context of its own investigative powers (Art. 21(2) of the SSM Framework Regulation).

461 See already in this sense A. Prüm, 'L'Union bancaire européenne et les autorités de surveillance nationales', *op. cit.*, no. 7: 'It is no longer a question [...] of organising relations between equal parties, but of supporting and completing a clearly hierarchical organisation based on the authority and responsibility of the ECB. What until now appeared to be the essential tool for a shared approach becomes an instrument for a policy dictated from above.' Compare F. Martucci, 'Union Bancaire, la méthode du "cadre": du discours à la réalité', *op. cit.*, p. 40, which evokes 'some of the characteristics of a hierarchical power'.

462 See already in this sense, T. Bonneau, 'L'union bancaire européenne. Introductory remarks', *op. cit.*, no. 4.

463 Art. 4(10) of the SSM Regulation: 'The ECB shall, in accordance with paragraph 3 of this Article, have *exclusive competence* to carry out the following tasks for prudential supervisory purposes in relation to all credit institutions established in the participating Member States.' (Italics added.) This last argument is precisely the one on which the Court of Justice relies to establish the predominance of its competence over any other authority when appealing against ECB decisions, even if they are taken on the basis of a national preparatory act subject to local law, see *infra*, para. 186. Recall Professor Prüm's assertion that the SSM 'is based on a centralised and hierarchical organisation dominated by the ECB' (A. Prüm, 'Le nouveau cadre européen du traitement des faillures à vol d'oiseau', *op. cit.*, no. 8).The perception of the German Constitutional Council that the SSM did not give powers over all credit institutions has not been sustained, see G. Hardy, *L'européanisation de la surveillance bancaire*, *op. cit.*, no. 487.

464 Para. 38 of the *Landeskreditbank* judgment.

465 Art. 14(2) to (4) and Art. 15(2) and (3) of the SSM Regulation.

466 Art. 14(5). However, the teams set up to carry out these acts are composed of staff from different Member States, see Art. 39(2) of the SSM Regulation, and on this aspect, see G. Hardy, *L'européanisation de la surveillance bancaire*, *op. cit.*, no. 80.

top-down procedure: that concerning the least important institutions.[467] In these cases, although the national authorities are in principle the only competent authorities, they are still subject to the ECB's regulations, guidelines and general instructions and to the ECB's supervision.[468] Furthermore, national authorities must notify the ECB of draft key decisions, on which the ECB may issue an opinion or even request the national authority to further assess specific aspects of the procedure.[469]

This division of jurisdiction has been criticised, on the one hand, because it would prevent the need for proximity necessary for the exercise of supervision and, on the other hand, because it would constitute a brake on legislative innovation.[470] However, neither of these arguments is fully convincing. First, the SSM Regulation does not abolish national authorities, which remain competent for institutions whose size does not, as a matter of principle, justify the jurisdiction of the ECB. The issue of proximity therefore seems to have been taken into account. Secondly, the question of legislative innovation appears to be of little relevance since, precisely, the SSM Regulation allows the applicability of local law.[471]

B. Legislative Jurisdiction

180. The ECB has no legislative jurisdiction. The applicable law is designated by the seat of the institution and enacted by national legislators within the limits of the harmonisation directives.[472] It is true that the legislation is largely derived from the Union. However, both the directives and the regulations leave room for national options or discretions,[473] to which must be added the national provisions

---

[467] These expressions of bottom-up and top-down procedures are borrowed from V. di Bucci, 'Some questions concerning judicial review of the Single Supervisory Mechanism' in *Liber amicorum A. Tizzano, From the ECSC Court to the Court of the Union, The Long Journey of European Justice*, Torino, Giappichelli, 2018, pp. 316 et seq.

[468] Art. 6(5)(a) and (c) of the SSM Regulation.

[469] Art. 6(7)(c) of the SSM Regulation.

[470] R. Gaspard, *La reconnaissance mutuelle en droit bancaire et financier européen, op. cit.*

[471] This criticism could otherwise have been compared to the criticism that legislative competition between the federated states is conducive to legislative innovation, see for an application to American company law, R. Romano, *The Advantage of Competitive Federalism for Securities Regulation, op. cit.* The author, reporting the benefits of legislative competition in American corporate law, deplores the existence of a federal jurisdiction in the area of financial securities (*securities law*) which sclerotizes regulation and hinders trade.

[472] See *supra*, paras. 83 et seq.

[473] A. Gourio and M. Gillouard, 'Les options ou discrétions nationales en matière prudentielle' in *Liber Amicorum Blanche Sousi,* Paris, RB Éditipn, 2016, pp. 77 et seq.; J.-V. Louis, 'L'Union bancaire, un processus incomplet?' in *Liber Amicorum Blanche Sousi, op. cit.*, 2016, pp. 153 et seq., pp. 155-158; M. Lehmann, 'Single Supervisory Mechanism Without Regulatory Harmonisation? Introducing a European Banking Act and a "CRR Light" for Smaller Institutions', *EBI Working Paper Series*, 2017, pp. 8 et seq.

resulting from the transposition of the directives,[474] and the issues excluded from the SSM Regulation, but having an influence on it.[475] This lack of coincidence between the authority with jurisdiction and the applicable law is undoubtedly a new phenomenon,[476] as it is rare to 'unify the control before unifying the law'.[477] This dissociation is sometimes perceived as a flawed situation, which should only be transitory and lead to substantial unification. On the contrary, it seems that legislative jurisdiction should continue to be exercised by the Member States. Such an assertion makes it necessary to determine clearly what is within the scope of administrative jurisdiction, which is subject to European law, and what belongs to legislative jurisdiction and is subject to national law.

181. Legislative jurisdiction and consumer protection. The case for national legislative jurisdiction can be illustrated by an American example reported by Mr Gaspard.[478] In the United States, the diagnosis made after the subprime crisis explained the failure of prudential regulation by the jurisdiction given to the federal body, the Office of the Comptroller of the Currency (OCC) to protect consumers from abusive loans and mortgages. Indeed, attempts by the federal states to force certain national banks to apply federal regulations were thwarted by the OCC, which relied on a Supreme Court ruling allowing it, under certain conditions, to pre-empt legislative jurisdiction.[479] Through this pre-emption, the OCC sought to prevent the application of local regulations, which would have provided better consumer protection, in favour of the application of federal law.[480] This attitude was heavily criticised after the crisis, and the US legislature itself considered, through the Dodd Frank Act, that 'state law… was the pioneer in consumer protection', and therefore gave it more jurisdiction. At the same time, the OCC was reformed and its administrative jurisdiction over consumer protection was transferred to an independent, specialised agency within the US

474 On this aspect in the context of the SSM, see A. Witte, 'When Does National Law Transpose a Directive' in *ECB Legal Conference 2016*, 6 October 2016, pp. 247 et seq.

475 See on the material scope of the SSM *supra*, para. 178.

476 The reason for this can be found in the basis of the SSM Regulation, which is based on Art. 127(6) TFEU. This Article does not allow the Union to exercise normative power, which is why the ECB applies national law. On this issue, see F. Martucci, 'Union Bancaire, la méthode du "cadre": du discours à la réalité', *op. cit.*, spec. p. 30. On this basis of the SSM, see G. Hardy, *L'européanisation de la surveillance bancaire*, *op. cit.*

477 R. Vabres, 'Autorité bancaire européenne et Union bancaire' in F. Martucci (ed.), *L'Union bancaire*, *op. cit.*, p. 192. The author even considers that 'a European body in charge of implementing national law is a bit unnatural'.

478 R. Gaspard, *La reconnaissance mutuelle en droit bancaire et financier*, *op. cit.* Comp. M. Lehmann, 'Single Supervisory Mechanism Without Regulatory Harmonisation? Introducing a European Banking Act and a "CRR Light" for Smaller Institutions', *op. cit.*

479 Barnett Bank of Marion County, *N. A. v. Nelson*, Florida Ins. Comm'r (94-1837), 517 U.S. 25 (1996). This decision establishes a preemption test whereby, as Gaspard writes, 'states could regulate national banks only if such regulation did not prohibit or substantially interfere with the exercise by national banks of their powers' (*ibid.*).

480 This was notoriously the case in New York State, see *ibid.*

Federal Reserve. Indeed, another criticism of the OCC was that its remit was too broad, with prudential obligations and consumer protection, leading it to shift from the latter to the former. A similar movement took place in the UK.[481]

This foreign example makes it possible to account for the singularity of legislative jurisdiction, and to refine the understanding of the principle of subsidiarity when it is involved. In some sectors, particularly consumer protection, the needs are not identical from one Member State to another, and local specificity is better protected by the exercise of the Member State's legislative jurisdiction. It seems to us that this is not a specificity of consumer protection. Indeed, the same is true for prudential requirements, but for different reasons.

182. National legislative jurisdiction and prudential requirements. Banking models differ between and even within Member States. It might be argued that the main difference lies in the size of the credit institution and that the allocation criterion established by the ECB is therefore remarkably appropriate. However, such an assertion should be nuanced. Indeed, the local legal culture also influences the capital structure of the bank. What is there in common between a national mutual bank, whose size obliges it to be included in the ECB's jurisdiction list, a national bank of international scope, and a public bank managed by a more or less autonomous local authority? Not much, apart from the possibility of being subject to the administrative jurisdiction of the ECB. Under these conditions, the Union is not necessarily the best placed to legislate in areas where national culture is so important. This is all the more true as it is already clear that the exercise of administrative jurisdiction by the ECB does not take into account national particularities: the example of the Livret A litigation,[482] as well as the disproportionate contribution of French banks to the single resolution fund are significant examples.[483]

---

481 *Ibid.*, no. 614.

482 An example illustrating the importance of local legal culture is given by Mr Gosset-Grainville (A. Gosset-Grainville, 'Coopération et souverainetés', *op. cit.*, p. 17) through the inclusion of savings funds from the Livret A in the ECB's calculation of the leverage ratio of each banking institution. Indeed, under the terms of the legislation on the Livret A, the funds collected by the banks only pass through their balance sheet and are then managed by the Caisse des dépôts. However, 'the ECB has tried to impose the inclusion of the entire amount in the calculation of the leverage ratio of French banks, thus heavily penalising them'. The French banks nevertheless challenged these measures and won their case before the Court of Justice (see in particular Case T-733/16, *Banque Postale v. ECB*, ECLI:EU:T:2018:477). For an illustration of the different composition of national banking sectors within the EU, see J.-G. de Tocqueville, A. Bonzom and C. Feunteun, 'Focus sur la réforme CRR2', *RDBF*, November 2019, study 15, spec. no. 9.

483 French banks provide more than 30% of the contribution to the SRF, although they only represent 20% of bank deposits, which can be explained by French investment traditions, see *supra*, note under para. 156.

This first observation is coupled with another relating to both the legislative process and the exercise of legislative jurisdiction. Indeed, the European rules on prudential obligations are, to a large extent, imported from the various Basel agreements.[484] Catherine Feunteun has shown that these agreements were designed by and for large international banks.[485] However, their scope of application is extended to all credit institutions through European regulations. Moreover, this regulation contributed to the systemic crisis caused by the subprime crisis.[486] These remarks tend to show that more weight should be given to the local legal culture in the exercise of legislative jurisdiction, and that this is therefore better provided by the national order. It is to be welcomed that this is still the case in the SSM Regulation.[487]

183. Some authors in favour of complete uniformity of rules point out that national options or discretions are likely to distort competition,[488] applying different rules to players operating in the same sector. However, the French experience tends to show the opposite: the uniform application of European legislation is likely to penalise, inevitably, dissimilar banking models. Far from allowing competition, it distorts it according to the particular model for which

---

484 This is in particular the case of Regulation (EU) No 575/2013 of the European Parliament and of the Council of 26 June 2013 on prudential requirements for credit institutions and investment firms, see C. Feunteun, *Hybrid Instruments and the Basel Accords*, *op. cit.*

485 *Ibid.*, nos. 74 et seq.

486 *Ibid.*, p. 166.

487 Comp. M. Lehmann, 'Single Supervisory Mechanism Without Regulatory Harmonisation? Introducing a European Banking Act and a "CRR Light" for Smaller Institutions', *op. cit.*, p. 8.

488 See among others, M. Lehmann, *ibid.*; G. Lo Schiavo, 'The ECB and its application of national law in the SSM', in G. Lo Schiavo (ed.), *The European Banking Union and the Role of Law*, Cheltenham, Edward Elgar Publishing, pp. 177 et seq., spec. p. 193; L. Arranz, 'Level playing field: towards a more uniform application of banking legislation', in *ECB Legal Conference*, 6 October 2016, pp. 260 et seq.
The metaphor used is always the same: that of a football game where the teams are not subject to the same rules (it is taken from the following contribution: S. Lautenschläger, 'Single Supervisory Mechanism – Single Supervisory Law?, Keynote speech by Sabine Lautenschläger, Member of the Executive Board of the ECB and Vice-Chair of the Supervisory Board of the ECB, at the Workshop of the European Banking Institute (EBI) hosted by the ECB, Frankfurt, 27 January 2016) The comparison seems inappropriate to us, as it does not take into account the difficulties specific to the particularities of national banking sectors.
The European doctrine is generally unfavourable to this dissociation between legislative and administrative jurisdiction, see G. Hardy, *L'européanisation de la surveillance bancaire*, *op. cit.*, no. 265 and references. For these authors, the solution to these problems always lies in the unification of the applicable law (see among others, M. Lehmann, 'Single Supervisory Mechanism Without Regulatory Harmonisation? Introducing a European Banking Act and a "CRR Light" for Smaller Institutions', *op. cit.*, pp. 17 et seq.), and to a 'dynamic' reading of the treaty in such a way as to 'go beyond' or 'bypass' the letter and the spirit in which they were drafted; all this in order to allow the achievement of constantly expanding objectives, see for example G. Hardy, *L'européanisation de la surveillance bancaire*, *op. cit.*, nos. 162 et seq.

it is designed. It should be added here that the European experience of recent decades has been based on the existence of national legislative divergences. It is difficult to understand how the institution of a centralised supervisor, which does not owe its existence to the correction of distortions of competition, should change this state of affairs. One should rather focus on the coordination of its executive action with that of local supervisors, which leads to a clear distinction between what is of the order of the *lex auctoris*, and likely to be standardised under the aegis of the ECB's executive jurisdiction, and what is of the order of the legislative jurisdiction.[489] The preparatory acts for authorisation and the assessment of acquisitions and disposals of qualifying holdings are good examples. Both are subject to national law as *lex auctoris*.[490] The application of the *lex auctoris* here is justified by considerations of convenience for the authority. For this reason, it has little imperative force and it is likely that the ECB will introduce a gradual standardisation of the preparatory acts of the various national competent authorities. Indeed, the role of the national authority is essentially transitional, since while it continues to receive the different information transmitted by the credit institution, it must then mainly use this information to prepare the acts enabling the ECB to implement its decision, on the basis of the law of the authority's seat.

C. Court's Jurisdiction

From the point of view of Court's jurisdiction,[491] two issues arise, depending on whether a bottom-up procedure is involved, in which the national authority prepares any decisions taken by the ECB, or a top-down procedure, in which the act taken by the national authority is preceded by intervention by the

489 See e.g. on the difficulty for the ECB to overrule national law transposed contrary to Union law, V. di Bucci, 'Some Issues Concerning Judicial Review of the Single Supervisory Mechanism', *op. cit.* K. Banks, 'Incorrect Implementation of EU Directives: What Effects for the ECB and the CJEU, and What Mechanisms for Rectification?', G. Hardy, *L'européanisation de la surveillance bancaire*, *op. cit.*, nos. 270 et seq.

490 Art. 14 SSM Regulation; Art. 15 SSM Regulation. Indeed, in the same way as for investment firms (see *supra*, para. 99), these acquisitions and disposals must be notified to the supervisory authority, which has a right of opposition, see Art. 23 of the CRD IV.

491 There is an administrative mediation procedure, which makes it possible to ask an administrative review board to carry out an internal review which may lead to the repeal of the contentious decision (see Art. 24(11) of the SSM Regulation). This request is optional and does not affect the right of the person concerned to refer the matter directly to the EU courts, or to refer it to them following the decision of the Review Board if the applicant is not satisfied. On this commission, see C. Brescia Morra, 'Nature and role of the ABoR', *ECB Legal Confrence 2019*, pp. 335 et seq.; R. Smits, 'The ECB and the rule of law', *ECB Legal Confrence 2019*, pp. 350 et seq.

ECB in the form of an opinion or guidance.[492] The single basis for Court's jurisdiction nevertheless justifies treating these two procedures together.

184. The basis for imputability. The question arose as to which court had jurisdiction over bottom-up procedures where the procedure is first submitted to a national authority and then forwarded to the ECB. The dispute centred on the jurisdiction of the Court of Justice to assess the preparatory acts of the national authority subject to local law in a bottom-up procedure. The Court of Justice then expressed its exclusive jurisdiction over the entire process leading to the adoption of the ECB decision, including its national aspects.[493] There were two reasons for this choice. Firstly, because the ECB has ultimate jurisdiction to take the contentious decision under the SSM system.[494] This idea is known as the 'imputability' or 'author of the act' thesis. It consists of giving jurisdiction to the courts of the seat of the authority to which the contested decision is attributable,[495] and is based on Articles 263 and 267 of the TFEU. Secondly, because the devolution of litigation would lead to a prejudicial divergence of assessment.[496] This decision invites several remarks.

185. Firstly, the question arises as to whether the solution can be extended, by analogy, to authorisation. In the case of authorisation, too, the draft decision is prepared by the national authority[497] and then submitted to the ECB, which alone has jurisdiction to take the authorisation decision.[498] The full jurisdiction of the ECB is even more evident with regard to the withdrawal of authorisation, since 'the ECB may withdraw the authorisation on its own initiative'[499] and the role of the national authority is limited to mere 'consultation'.[500] However, such a statement should be nuanced since, in the case of authorisation, the national authority retains the power to refuse *ab initio* the request for authorisation made to it, which deprives the ECB of its decision-making power:[501] the decision is then taken exclusively by the national authority.[502] Following the imputability theory promoted by the Court of Justice, the decision to refuse authorisation

---

492 On these two aspects, see V. di Bucci, 'Some questions concerning judicial review of the single supervisory mechanism', *op. cit.*

493 Case C-219/17, *Berlusconi*, ECLI:EU:C:2018:502.

494 The Court refers to 'the exclusive decision-making competence of the Union institution' (para. 48).

495 On this thesis and its development in EU law, see G. Hardy, *L'européanisation de la surveillance bancaire, op. cit.*, no. 279.

496 Paras. 49 and 50 of the above-mentioned judgment.

497 Art. 15(3) SSM Regulation.

498 Art. 15(4) SSM Regulation.

499 Art. 15(5) SSM Regulation.

500 *Ibid.*

501 Art. 14(2) of the SSM Regulation. This nuance has already been noted by Professor A.-C. Rouaud in his above-mentioned note, p. 66.

502 Compare G. Hardy, *L'européanisation de la surveillance bancaire, op. cit.*, no. 284.

should therefore be challenged before the courts of the seat of the authority that took the refusal decision.

186. Secondly, this decision leads to the jurisdiction of national courts in top-down procedures in which national authorities have jurisdiction, insofar as the ECB has not pre-empted this jurisdiction. Indeed, in these cases, the author of the decision is the national authority. At most, it can be observed, on the one hand, that the validity of any ECB guidelines addressed to the national authority may be challenged in the national proceedings through the preliminary ruling procedure and, on the other hand, that the ECB's instructions addressed to the national authorities may be challenged directly before the Court of Justice when the acts carried out are in the context of instructions to assist the authorities in carrying out the ECB's tasks.[503] Finally, a hybrid situation exists where a national authority exercises its investigative powers on the instructions of the ECB.[504] In this case, Mr di Bucci considers that a distinction must be made between the general nature of the investigation and its specific nature. In the first case, the national courts have jurisdiction, but will have to make a reference for a preliminary ruling in order to challenge the validity of the act, whereas in the second case, the specific nature of the instruction entitles the person concerned to challenge its validity directly before the EU court.[505]

187. Thirdly, the basis of imputability leads to the Court of Justice having to interpret national law in order to review the legality of the ECB's action[506] and, if necessary, to annul the ECB's decision on the grounds of the violation of national law by the competent authority under the preparatory act.[507] While it is accepted that national law should be interpreted as it was conceived by its authors, i.e. according to the canons of the national legal order and its case

---

503 Art. 6(3); see V. di Bucci, 'Some questions concerning judicial review of the single supervisory mechanism', *op. cit.*

504 Art. 9(3) para. 3

505 V. di Bucci, 'Some questions concerning the judicial review of the single supervisory mechanism', *op. cit.*, p. 323.

506 Either in the context of assessing the transposition into national law of the provisions referred to in the directives applicable to credit institutions, or in the context of a legislative option left by a regulation. This situation is not unique; it is already the case when the Court of Justice is confronted with an arbitration clause designating it (see Art. 272 TFEU), but also in matters relating to trademarks, on these aspects see M. Prek, 'Mutual judicial deference? The delineation of the (interpretative) competence of European and national courts in the judicial review of ECB acts based on national law', *ECB Legal Conference*, December 2019, pp. 129 et seq. M. Prek and S. Lefèvre, 'The EU Courts as "national" courts: National law in the EU judicial process' (2017) 54(2) *Common Market Law Review*, pp. 369 et seq.

507 As Mr di Bucci observes, 'this prospect should encourage the ECB, including the Administrative Review Commission, to carefully check the legality of the procedure before the ACN before the adoption of the final act', V. di Bucci, 'Some questions concerning the judicial review of the Single Supervisory Mechanism', *op. cit.*

law,[508] a first difficulty arises when there is uncertainty as to the content of national law. Mr Synvet has suggested the introduction of a new preliminary ruling mechanism for the benefit of the national court.[509] This solution, which is balanced and familiar to European law, appears to be effective. A second difficulty is where national law is contrary to European law, either because it appears to be in contradiction with primary law, or because it was originally derived from a directive and has been incorrectly transposed. This difficulty makes it necessary to determine the extent of the Court of Justice's prerogatives when it is called upon to assess national law and, in particular, the question of whether the Court can set aside such law when it does not appear to be in conformity with the European law from which it derives, or even with its own constitutional law. While some authors believe that the Court of Justice has such powers,[510] it seems to us that this difficulty, as well as the previous one, could be resolved by a solution that is both simpler and more respectful of the distribution of powers within the Union between the Member States and the European bodies.

188. The *forum legis* solution. Rather than seeking palliatives to the difficulties caused by the basis of imputability, another solution would be to base the jurisdiction of the court on the legislation applied – a basis of jurisdiction known in private international law as *forum legis*. This basis of jurisdiction, which undoubtedly originated in insolvency law[511] and is now spreading to other areas of private law,[512] is particularly suitable where local public policy is intensely affected.[513] It is therefore not surprising that it is so present in criminal

---

508 See in this sense, Case T-133/16, *Caisse régionale de crédit agricole mutuel Alpes Provence v. ECB*, para. 84: 'Insofar as the interpretation of a provision of national law is at issue, it should be recalled that, pursuant to settled case law, the scope of national laws, regulations or administrative provisions must be assessed in the light of the interpretation given to them by the national courts.' This aspect leads to the question of the status of national law before the Court of Justice, on which we refer to the developments of M. Prek and S. Lefèvre, 'The EU Courts as 'national' courts: National law in the EU judicial process', *op. cit.*, pp. 371 et seq.

509 See his comments under the *Berlusconi* judgment cited *supra*, para. 174.

510 V. di Bucci, 'Some questions concerning judicial review of the single supervisory mechanism', *op. cit.*, p. 327 (the author considers that the Court of Justice should also be able to carry out constitutionality review); M. Prek, 'Mutual judicial deference? The delineation of the (interpretative) competence of European and national courts in the judicial review of ECB acts based on national law', *op. cit.* A. Kornezov, 'The Application of National Law by the ECB – A Maze of (Un)answered Question', *ECB Legal Conference 2016*, 6 October 2016, pp. 242 et seq.

511 See *infra*, para. 913.

512 See for a recent illustration in European private international law, Arts. 22 and 26(1)(a) and (b) of Council Regulation 2016/1103 of 24 June 2016 implementing enhanced cooperation in the area of jurisdiction, applicable law, recognition and enforcement of judgments in matrimonial matters.

513 Ms Greil thus defends a *forum legis* based on the applicability of '*lois de police*' when they closely affect a state interest. B. Achinard-Greil, *Lois de police et conflits de juridictions*, thesis, Université Lyon III, 2017, pp. 276 et seq.

law.[514] The *forum legis* would allow the jurisdiction of local courts to be based on administrative law.

This solution is the most consistent with the implementation of the principle of subsidiarity that the European legislator wished to put in place when distributing executive jurisdiction between national authorities and the ECB. It gives jurisdiction to the best-placed courts, and makes it possible to get rid of the two difficulties encountered here, since the interpretation of national law would be made by its natural interpreter, who is best able to understand the body of law in which the transposed directive is inserted. Moreover, the national court, as the ordinary court of law of the European Union, is the one normally competent to set aside a contentious transposition. The uniform application of the regulation would be preserved by the mechanism of the preliminary ruling, as has always been the case. It may be argued that *forum legis* faces an insurmountable obstacle: Articles 263 and 267 of the TFEU, according to which the Court of Justice alone has jurisdiction to review the validity and interpretation of acts of the Union's bodies. However, the Treaties can be amended, *especially* because the particular configuration of the SSM changes the situation. Moreover, the Court of Justice itself has already recognised the jurisdiction of national courts over Union acts in cases involving applications for suspension of operation or interim measures concerning national acts adopted on the basis of Union acts.[515]

189. Another advantage of the *forum legis* is that it unifies the jurisdictional competence when an appeal against an ECB decision and possible sanctions taken by national authorities are at stake. Indeed, the ECB, when it wishes to impose a sanction on an entity it supervises, has two means at its disposal which are governed by distinct procedures:[516] Article 18(1) of the SSM Regulation, applicable when a Union regulation is infringed, and Regulation 2532/98, applicable when an ECB act is infringed. However, these two means do not give the ECB the possibility to sanction entities, including those it directly supervises, when they violate national law. In this case, it must call upon the services of the national authorities so that they themselves take the appropriate sanctions.[517] It is clear that the imputability theory leads to a dead end when it results in the possible submission of an appeal against a sanction decision administered by

[514] See *infra*, para. 526.

[515] Certain conditions are nevertheless provided for, see V. Di Bucci, 'Some questions concerning judicial review of the single supervisory mechanism', *op. cit.*, p. 325 and the two judgments cited, Joined cases C-143/88 and C-92/89, *Zuckerfabrik Süderdithmarchchen and Others*, ECLI:EU:C:1991:65; Case C-465/93, *Atlanta Fruchthandelsgesellschaft and Others*, ECLI:EU:C:1995:369.

[516] However, these tend to converge, see G. Hardy, *L'européanisation de la surveillance bancaire*, *op. cit.*, no. 323.

[517] Art. 18(5) of the SSM Regulation. On this aspect, see also V. Di Bucci, 'Some questions concerning judicial review of the single supervisory mechanism', *op. cit.*, p. 324.

a French authority, in application of French law, against an entity established in France, to the Court of Justice, which will be hard-pressed to proceed with the proper administration of justice when all the arguments raised are aimed at the violation of French law. The same applies when the ECB exercises its own investigative powers: these must be exercised according to the applicable national law, i.e. according to the place where the investigation is carried out.[518] Again, the court best placed to assess the legality of the exercise of these investigative powers is the court whose law is applicable. The *forum legis* is the safest basis for allowing the proximity of the dispute to the judge in these cases, and the proper administration of justice that this allows.

190. Commenting on the Court of Justice's review of ECB acts implementing a national act, and the potential possibility for the applicants or the judge to raise the unconstitutionality of the applicable national law, Mr di Bucci writes: 'This situation seems to us to be fundamentally different from that of the judge who has to apply a foreign law by virtue of his own rules of private international law: the judge of the Union is not a foreign judge in relation to the legal orders of the Member States and these legal orders are not foreign to him'.[519] Without doubt, the European judge is not completely unaware of national legal orders, and there is an ever-increasing interaction between national and European law. However, this should not necessarily lead to an endless extension of the prerogatives of the European judge, to the standardisation of substantive law, or to the granting of decision-making powers to Union agencies, but rather to a reflection on how best to coordinate the legal orders. The age-old science of private international law is likely to offer valuable tools here as long as the Union continues to keep separate legal communities together. This even seems to be the vocation of the European Union: *in varietate concordia.*

II. The Centralised Failure Model

The institution of a centralised model requires a distinction between the internal (A) and external (B) relationships of the Single Resolution Mechanism.

A. Internal Relationships

191. Scope of the SSM and SRM. The Single Resolution Mechanism (SRM) was introduced to counter the 'growing risk of financial fragmentation'[520] revealed by the crisis that preceded it. For the Member States participating in the SRM,

---

518 Art. 9(1) and (2) of the SSM Regulation. Regretting this state of affairs, see G. Hardy, *L'européanisation de la surveillance bancaire*, *op. cit.*, no. 301.

519 V. di Bucci, 'Some questions concerning judicial review of the single supervisory mechanism', *op. cit.*

520 Recital 1 of the SRM Regulation.

it consists of the unification of the resolution decision-making process within a Single Resolution Board (SRB) and the pooling of national funds within a single European resolution fund.[521] The SRM is therefore at the crossroads between the Resolution Directive and the SSM.

192. Firstly, the SRM is closely linked to the SSM, whose scope it should 'mirror',[522] due to the link between supervision and resolution in the SRM Regulation.[523] This mechanism is manifested through direct references: the SRB has direct jurisdiction over the entities supervised by the ECB;[524] the SRB's jurisdiction gives it all the powers devolved, under the Resolution Directive, to national authorities;[525] the suspension or termination of its cooperation with the SSM by a Member State whose currency is not the euro entails the suspension

521 Similarly, the European Deposit Guarantee Fund has the function of preserving a minimum amount of deposits so that, in the event of a crisis, depositors can be reimbursed.

522 Recital 22 of the SRM Regulation.

523 Such a statement appears questionable, as it denies the particularities of the case. Indeed, there are many sectors where the existence of a regulated activity, even under the supervision of a regulatory authority, falls under the general insolvency law. The need for resolution must therefore be distinguished from the need for uniqueness in its decision-making process. Resolution is mainly justified by the consequences that the failure of an institution would have on financial stability. The unification of the decision-making process has more ambiguous reasons: from a legal point of view, because of the particular difficulties posed by the failure of institutions integrated into a group established on the territory of several Member States, but also from a political point of view, because of the link maintained by each Member State and its banking sector, which is likely to give rise to a moral hazard biasing the state decision.

524 Art. 7(2)(a) of the SRM Regulation.

525 The SRB therefore has all the powers relating to resolvability (from its assessment to the prerogatives it implies, see Arts. 10 and 11 of the SRM Regulation), early intervention and resolution. In the latter case, the SRB not only draws up resolution plans, but also resolution decisions. In these cases, the SRB is only obliged to consult the national competent authorities when drawing up the resolution plan (Art. 8(2) of the SRB Regulation), which in turn must consult the national authorities of significant branches (Art. 9(2) of the SRB Regulation). The Regulation provides a detailed list of elements to be included in the resolution plan (see Art. 8(9) of the SRM Regulation). In the case of group resolution, certain additions are necessary (see Art. 8(11) of the Merger Regulation), in particular the question of the identification of third countries where the group has establishments. The SRB also has the power to impose simplified requirements on institutions whose failure would not be likely to cause 'significant adverse consequences for the financial system or pose a threat to financial stability' (Art. 11 of the SRM Regulation; the conditions are nevertheless listed by the Regulation and the criteria for these conditions are also determined, see Art. 11(3) and (8) of the SRM Regulation). As the direct authority of the institutions, the SRB therefore has the necessary means of coercion to ensure that its decisions are complied with by those to whom they are addressed: it can itself administer fines and periodic penalty payments (Arts. 38 and 39 of the SRM Regulation). The SRB may carry out general investigations (Art. 35 of the Merger Regulation), which allow it to conduct both hearings it deems necessary (Art. 40 of the Merger Regulation) and inspections on the premises of establishments without having to notify the establishment concerned, or even obtain prior authorisation from the authority of the participating Member State (Art. 36 of the Merger Regulation). On the contrary, the latter must assist the SRB officers.

or termination of the coverage of entities established in that Member State by the SRM Regulation.[526] In these circumstances, cooperation between the SRB and the ECB is necessary: it involves the exchange of information, which can be done through consultation,[527] or through unilateral communication required by the Regulation[528] at all stages of resolution: under resolvability,[529] early intervention,[530] and above all resolution. In addition to this need for constant consultation and exchange of information, the jurisdiction of the SRB may be conditioned by an assessment made by the ECB. Two significant examples can be given. The first is that one of the conditions for resolution itself, i.e. the actual or foreseeable nature of the failure, should be determined as a matter of principle by an ECB assessment.[531] The second is that certain resolution powers are conditional on the ECB's assessment of them:[532] this is the case as soon as the entity's own funds are concerned, e.g. when writing down or converting claims into own funds.[533]

193. Secondly, the Resolution Directive is the backbone on which the SRM solutions are built. On the one hand, as the Single Resolution Mechanism is applicable to euro area Member States and certain other participating Member States, the coordination solutions between authorities of the Resolution Directive remain applicable with authorities of States that are not members of the SRM. The SRM Regulation itself provides that the SRB *is* the national resolution authority for the purposes of the Resolution Directive in the external relations of the SRM with non-participating Member States and third countries, for which the SRB will always be the interlocutor.[534] Moreover, when exercising its supervisory and resolution powers directly, the SRB is the competent authority of the Resolution Directive in the internal relationship of the SRM,[535] thus making direct use of its powers under the Resolution Directive. On the other hand, in many respects, the SRM Regulation only specifies the rules where the directive left room for

---

526 Art. 4(2) of the SRM Regulation.

527 See e.g. Art. 8(2) of the Solvency Regulation which provides for consultation of the ECB in the preparation of the resolution plan.

528 The ECB must therefore communicate to the SRB any changes that would make it necessary to revise or update the resolution plan (Art. 8(12) of the SRB Regulation); at the same time the SRB must send the resolution plans and any updates and revisions to the ECB (Art. 8(13) of the SRB Regulation).

529 Art. 10(1) of the SRM Regulation.

530 Art. 13 of the SRM Regulation.

531 Art. 18(1) of the SRM Regulation. If the ECB does not provide this assessment within three days of the SRB's request, the SRB may carry out the assessment itself. On the status of this act, which cannot be challenged by the person it concerns, see Case T-281/18, *ABLV Bank v. ECB*, ECLI:EU:T:2019:296, and the note by V. Michel, *Europe*, July 2019, comm. 266.

532 See e.g. Art. 18(4) of the SRM Regulation.

533 Art. 21(1) of the SRM Regulation. Again, in the absence of information from the ECB within three days, the SRB is then free to carry out the assessment itself, see Art. 21(2) of the SRM Regulation.

534 Art. 32(1) of the SRM Regulation.

535 Art. 5 of the SRM Regulation.

manoeuvre, or even repeats the solutions of the Resolution Directive.[536] However, national law is not completely ousted since it remains applicable when national authorities are competent under the Resolution Directive. In many respects, the division of competences of the SRM is similar to that of the SSM.

194. Two differences should nevertheless be underlined: the SRB's decision-making procedures leave less room for the votes of Member States;[537] the ultimate decision does not belong to the SRB. Indeed, while the SRB is the body that

536 The most important issues are the following: in the SRM Regulation, the objectives of resolution, the general principles governing resolution or the order of priority of claims are the same (see respectively Arts. 14(2°) 15 and 17 of the SRM Regulation). Indeed, the nature of the Resolution Directive does not allow the SRB to use it as it stands, so it was necessary to repeat its content. This possibility offered in the SRM is closely linked to the basis on which the SRM was adopted: Art. 114 TFEU on the approximation of laws relating to the internal market. There is, however, a distinction between approximation as it has always taken place by way of directive, and the standardisation that the SRM Regulation allows. This 'maximalist approximation' appears possible for some because of the qualification of financial stability by the Court of Justice as an 'overriding objective', see Case C-370/12, *Pringle*, ECLI:EU:C:2012:756, para. 135. This objective is one of the main objectives pursued by the SRM. This basis also helps to explain why it is credit institutions that contribute to the SRF: Art. 114 TFEU cannot require States to increase their financial contribution. On these issues, see the opinion of the Legal Service of the Council (Council of the Union, Opinion of the Legal service no. 13524/13, spec. no. 56 and F. Martucci, 'Union bancaire, la méthode du "cadre": du discours à la réalité', *op. cit.*, p. 31).

537 The SRB, based in Brussels (Art. 48 of the Council Regulation), is an *ad hoc* agency created by the Council Regulation, with legal personality, a 'specific structure adapted to its tasks' (Art. 42 of the Council Regulation) and a model that 'differs from all other agencies in the Union' (Art. 31 of the Council Regulation; the SRB is financed by compulsory contributions from the institutions subject to the Regulation, see Art. 97). Its composition is, however, at first sight reminiscent of that of the ECB (Art. 32 of the Council Regulation; on the composition of the ECB, see *supra*, para. 62): a representative of the authority of each Member State sits on the ECB with one vote; in addition, there are four permanent members, a vice-president and a president (Art. 43(b) of the Council Regulation; the latter are appointed by decision of the Commission, after a hearing by the SRB and the European Parliament and approval by the European Parliament, see Art. 56(6) and (7) of the Council Regulation). All these members meet at least twice a year in plenary session. These sessions are where decisions are taken on the direction and policy of the SRB. In addition to the plenary session, there are executive sessions where only the permanent members, the representatives of the authorities of the Member States concerned by the decisions taken, sit. However, resolution decisions are taken in executive sessions (see Art. 55 of the SRM Regulation on decision-making procedures), in an environment where the representatives of the Member States will not necessarily be in the majority. Moreover, in the absence of consensus, the decision is taken by a simple majority of the permanent members of the SRB (Art. 55 of the SRM Regulation; Mr d'Avout considers that the function of this provision is to 'stimulate consensus', L. d'Avout, 'L'articulation des droits et des procédures dans un espace fédéralisé', *op. cit.*, p. 23). This means that the votes of the Member States are not preponderant in the decision-making of the resolution. The effort to ensure the democratic legitimacy of the SRB is perhaps best illustrated by the necessary approval by the European Parliament when appointing its members, or by the hearings before the national parliaments (Art. 46 of the SRM Regulation). Neither the ECB's track record in these hearings nor the location of the SRB in Brussels, as close as possible to the Commission (Art. 48 of the SRM Regulation), is reassuring.

decides on the preparation of the resolution mechanism and its implementation, it is not the body that takes the resolution decision. *In the end*, it simply transmits its draft to the Commission. The Commission may raise objections and advise the European Council on whether to approve or reject the resolution package.[538] However, the European Council is the only one to assess whether the public interest is sufficiently at stake to justify a resolution, and is therefore the sole decision-maker.[539] This submission of the SRB to the European Council is reinforced by the way in which the members of the SRB are appointed.[540]

195. The single resolution fund (SRF). The single resolution fund is the aggregation, within the Member States of the SRM, of the resolution funds whose constitution is required by the Resolution Directive. As a decisive means of action by the resolution authority, it is understandable that the 'financing of the fund is of paramount importance for the credibility of the SRB'.[541] Nevertheless, it obeys the same rules of operation and use as the national resolution funds: it is therefore held[542] and administered[543] by the SRB, its financing is ensured by the credit institutions which are affiliated to it,[544] its use obeys the same purposes as the national resolution funds,[545] its relationship with the national deposit guarantee schemes is identical.[546] The real particularity of the SRF compared to the national funds lies in the fact that its application triggers the automatic competence of the SRB. However, the application of certain resolution instruments requires the use of the SRF, resulting in an extension of the SRB's basic powers.

---

538 Indeed, immediately after the adoption of a resolution plan, the SRB must transmit it to the Commission which has twenty-four hours to approve it or raise objections 'on the discretionary aspects of the resolution scheme' or on the amount requested from the SRF, see Art. 18(7)(a) and (b) of the SRM Regulation.

539 Twelve hours after receiving the draft, the Commission submits to the Council its proposal to approve, object to or modify the plan adopted by the SRB. The most important discretionary aspect, over which the Council is sovereign, is the assessment of the public interest character that would justify the resolution. If the Council, acting by a simple majority, refuses to consider that the public interest is at stake, the resolution is refused and the credit institution is wound up in accordance with national insolvency law, see Art. 18(8) of the SRM.

540 See previous note. The Commission also has a permanent observer in the plenary and executive sessions of the SRB, see Art. 43(3) of the SRM Regulation. In plenary sessions, observers are present in principle in the case of the Commission and the ECB (Art. 43(3) of the SRM Regulation), at the initiative of the SRB for the EBA (Art. 51(3) of the SRM Regulation). In the case of executive sessions, observers are only invited at the initiative of the SRB (Art. 53(1) of the SRM Regulation).

541 Recital 107 of the SRM Regulation.

542 Art. 67(3) of the SRM Regulation.

543 Art. 75(1) of the SRM Regulation.

544 Art. 69(1) of the SRM Regulation. The amount is 1% of the deposits covered. It should be added that within the SRM, all authorised institutions are obliged to contribute to the SRF only: *no more* diversity of funds.

545 Art. 76 of the SRM Regulation.

546 Art. 79 of the SRM Regulation.

196. Division of tasks. Significantly, the SRM Regulation does not refer to a division of powers between the SRB and national authorities, but to a division of *tasks*. This division is simple: the competence of the SRB is direct and in principle for institutions subject to ECB supervision,[547] for cross-border groups[548] and for any resolution involving recourse to the SRF.[549] Other institutions are subject to the national resolution authority. These developments allow several remarks. First, the SRB's jurisdictional titles are linked to groups, large institutions, or the ECB's prior choice to exercise supervision. The rationale for the three titles of competence is to be found within the principle of subsidiarity: European bodies are best placed to intervene when the situation goes beyond the borders of a single Member State. The advantage of giving the SRB unitary jurisdiction over groups is to put an end to the difficulties that the coordinated treatment by the Resolution Directive was likely to create, in particular between the divergent interests of the State of the head of the group and those of the State in which the subsidiary is located,[550] despite the possibility of resolution subgroups within the group. Nevertheless, in the banking and financial framework targeted by the resolution, the disadvantage is that these titles of jurisdiction risk absorbing all situations, since credit institutions and investment firms nowadays most often operate across borders. In other words, the jurisdiction of national authorities is likely to be very residual. This is undoubtedly where the ambiguity of the subsidiarity principle lies.

Secondly, even in the rare cases where the national authority has jurisdiction, this jurisdiction may appear to be a simple delegation of the SRB, since the latter can always issue a warning to the competent authority of a participating

547 Whether institutions are automatically subject to ECB supervision, or by preemption of national competence by the ECB, see Art. 7(2)(a)(i) and (ii) and the references to the SSM Regulation.

548 Art. 7(2)(b) of the Merger Regulation. The institution of a specific authority for cross-border groups undoubtedly shows the irreducibility of international issues to national difficulties. Such an institution is reminiscent of the intuition of the substantive rule to give international problems their own response. On reflection, the SRB's own jurisdiction over cross-border groups is rather reminiscent of the specialised chambers within the courts. Their particularity is not the existence of their own solutions, but on the one hand, the determination of the applicable law and, on the other hand, within this, the simple consideration in the substantive rules of the existence of the group.

549 Art. 7(3) of the SRM Regulation.

550 As Mr Synvet says on the subject of resolvability: 'We can also see the limits of the unilateral approach to the failure of large international banking groups. This is the problem of resolvability: should the group as a whole be considered, or the local subsidiary? The interests of the State of the head of the group and those of the State in which the subsidiary is located are likely to diverge', H. Synvet, 'Rapport de synthèse. L'extraterritorialité du droit en droit bancaire', *RDBF*, July 2015, p. 41; see also L. d'Avout, 'L'articulation des droits et des procédures dans un espace fédéralisé', *op. cit.*, p. 23.

Member State, and replace it if it deems it necessary.[551] As Mr d'Avout writes: 'In particular, the technique of pre-emption is used here, which is typically federal and known in the United States of America. The federal agency has priority jurisdiction, but this may remain latent and not be exercised in many cases. In these cases, the national authorities act as a kind of delegate of the federal power and under its control.'[552] At most, it can be observed that the resolution function will not necessarily exhaust those exercised by the national authorities.[553] This means that the configuration of the relationship between the SRB and the national authorities is similar to that of the SSM, even if it is exercised in the name of 'loyal cooperation'.[554] Therefore, the SRM Regulation provides in its Recital 120 that the competent court to hear an appeal against a resolution decision depends on the author of the decision, following the example of what is known in prudential supervision.[555]

B. External Relationships

197. External relationships. It is in the external relationships of the SRM that the solutions of the Resolution Directive recover their authority. These relationships are of two types: those that the SRM maintains with non-participating Member States, and with third countries. In the first case, cooperation is therefore achieved

---

551 Art. 7(4) of the SRM Regulation. The SRM Regulation thus uses a euphemism when it states that the function of the SRB is to guarantee the consistent application of the SRM, Art. 7(1) of the SRM Regulation; see in French perspective Arts. L. 612-1 and L. 613-34 of the Monetary and Financial Code, and the observations of E. Susset, 'Le régime français de prévention et de gestion des crises bancaires après la transposition de la directive sur la résolution bancaire' in *Le traitement des difficultés des établissements bancaires et institutions financières*, Paris, LexisNexis, 2017, pp. 91 et seq.

552 L. d'Avout, 'L'articulation des droits et des procédures dans un espace fédéralisé', *op. cit.* The author continues: 'Evocation mechanisms allow the federal agency to take over the conduct of a case; upward and downward referrals ensure cooperative functioning in the vertical relationships between federal and subordinate state authorities.'

553 In the same way that NCBs may act outside the Eurosystem, the resolution jurisdiction of a participating Member State may be attributed to an authority exercising other functions than resolution, which makes it likely to act outside the SRM scheme (this is the case of France, which has entrusted the resolution competence to the Autorité de contrôle prudentiel, see *supra*, paras. 5 et seq). Under these conditions, the analysis of functional duplication can probably be transposed to national resolution authorities (see *supra*, para. 63), depending on the function they pursue, they can act as a national body or as a body of the SRM. However, the SRM mechanism differs from the Eurosystem in the composition of the decision-making body: whereas the ECB Governing Council is composed of a majority of NCB representatives, the SRB executive session will, depending on the scope of the groups affected by a resolution, have a majority of members from European appointments.

554 See spec. Art. 31 of the SRM Regulation entitled '*cooperation within the SRB*', which in fact refers to the modalities by which the SRB exercises its powers over the national authorities.

555 On these aspects, see A. Sotiropoulou, 'Le contrôle juridictionnel des décisions du Conseil de résolution unique', *BJB*, November 2020, pp. 57 et seq.

through the techniques studied in the decentralised model,[556] and through those decided by a memorandum of understanding which *must* be signed by all the authorities: the ECB, the SRB, the national resolution authorities of the participating States and those of the non-participating States.[557] In the second case, the SRM merely amends the solutions of the Resolution Directive. In any case, all authorities outside the SRM have in common that the SRB will be the single point of contact in both cases,[558] and both call on the EBA.

198. The EBA as the central body for external reporting to the SRM. The relationship between the SRM and the EBA can be analysed from the executive, normative and dispute settlement angles. Indeed, the particular and hierarchical function of the SRB in the order of the participating countries does not affect its relations with the non-participating Member States, which constitute functional equivalents for the SRB in a scheme based on horizontal cooperation. This is why the EBA, whenever the coordinated treatment of a group requires coordination with an authority in a State that does not participate in the SRM, retains for the SRB the two functions that it exercises under the Resolution Directive: conciliation and binding mediation. Moreover, from a normative point of view, the EBA retains the power to draw up technical and implementing standards that the SRB will have to adopt.[559] Finally, from an executive point of view, the EBA is the competent authority for concluding non-binding cooperative framework agreements with third countries,[560] which are to be included in the closer cooperation relations that the SRB may conclude on behalf of the participating Member States with third countries.[561]

199. Coordination with third countries. As regards third countries, the solutions of the Resolution Directive, combined with those of the SRM Regulation, result in three types of agreements being concluded with third countries: firstly, the coordination agreement negotiated by the Commission on behalf of the Union, secondly, the non-binding framework cooperation agreement negotiated by the EBA on behalf of all EU resolution authorities, and thirdly, the closer cooperation agreement negotiated by the SRB on behalf of the Member States participating in the SRM.

The coordination agreement negotiated by the Commission is the basic agreement on which the conditions for the recognition and enforcement of third-country proceedings are based.[562] In the absence of such an agreement, the solutions of the Resolution Directive are applicable. However, the

556 See *supra*, para. 167.
557 Art. 30(7) of the SRM Regulation. On its content, see recital 38 of the SRM Regulation.
558 Art. 32(1) of the SRM Regulation.
559 Art. 5(2) of the SRM Regulation.
560 Art. 97(2) of the Resolution Directive.
561 Art. 32(4) of the SRM Regulation.
562 Art. 33(1) of the SRM Regulation.

particularity of the SRM is that the authority sitting in the European resolution college on behalf of the participating Member States is the SRB; at the same time, it is also the SRB that decides, on behalf of the participating Member States, whether or not to recognise the third country procedure: the national resolution authorities must then execute the decision adopted by the SRB.[563]

Finally, there is also the question of the applicability of a SRB resolution decision to an undertaking subject to the law of a third country, which is at the borderline of recognition of decisions and conflict of laws. One thinks in particular of the case of depreciation or conversion of claims.[564] The solution adopted by the SRM Regulation is in line with that of the Resolution Directive: the targeted institution must then prove that the targeted claim can be written down or converted, either because of the terms of the contract, or because of international agreements, or 'any other relevant considerations'.

200. Conclusion of the section. At the end of this section, the administrative connecting factor of infrastructure managers to an authority is clarified: it is not uniform. While until now infrastructure managers were connected to the authority of their head office, they are now likely to be directly connected to an EU authority once they become a credit institution. This paper has tried to show that the reasons that led to the establishment of a centralised regime were probably not destined to be extended to all market managers, and that it is therefore possible that the two models will continue to coexist.

The decentralised model has succeeded in adapting to the cross-border nature of the activities carried out by infrastructure managers and to their inclusion within a group of companies. This coordination can be based on two supports: the traditional one of the agreement between authorities and the more modern one of the college of authorities. In the latter case, the European supervisory authorities may be called upon to perfect this coordination, which makes it possible to temper the distinction between the centralised and decentralised models. The originality of the decentralised model is nevertheless that it calls on criteria from private international contract law when it comes to characterising access to the territory of other Member States and the applicability of national conduct of business rules. However, it seemed to us that these criteria were inoperative here and that these two aspects should be based on the concept of solicitation, which alone can resolve the tension between the objectives, relevant here, of integration of the internal market and protection of investors.

This section has also made it possible to observe that the centralised connecting factor modifies the way in which the rules are applied: if these national rules are applied by a European body, this application is overseen

563 Art. 33(2), (3), and (4) of the SRM Regulation.
564 Art. 12(17) of the SRM Regulation.

by the Court of Justice. Such dissociation of the competent authority and the applicable law does not pose any major difficulties, and even seems desirable, since the Member States are best placed to take account of the specific characteristics of their banking sector in their applicable legislation. At most, this dissociation requires the European authority to rely on national authorities. On the other hand, the Court of Justice appears less well placed to oversee the action of a European body when the application of national law is at issue. In our view, jurisdiction here would be better based on *forum legis*.

Analysing the centralised and decentralised models of resolution, Mr d'Avout observes: 'A difference of degree rather than of kind opposes these two schemes which both bear the distinctive sign of federalism: they are supranational legal solutions, implying the intervention of supranational institutions in the European interstate space.'[565] The statement perfectly captures the federal character of both centralised and decentralised models, which do not exhaust the possible models.[566] It also accounts for the small apparent difference between the institution of a college of authorities under the aegis of a national authority of a Member State, but whose dissension will allow

---

565 L. D'AVOUT, 'L'articulation des droits et des procédures dans un espace fédéralisé', *op. cit.*, p. 18.

566 Other federative models are possible, see for the United States and Canada: R. BISMUTH, 'L'Union bancaire ou les imperfections de la fédéralisation de la régulation financière au sein de l'Union européenne. Some reflections in the light of a comparison of the American and Canadian federal models', *op. cit.*, pp. 49 et seq. The author shows that the different federal models can be explained by the different dynamics of the US trade clause in the face of internal market integration in Europe.
Other models are also possible within the Union, and the establishment of an EU agency can be the basis for very different models. Community law specialists consider that the creation of an EU agency corresponds to a consolidation of loyal cooperation through integration into an agency (S. ADALID, *La Banque centrale européenne et l'Eurosystème*, *op. cit.*, no. 58). This consolidation would take place through networking, which requires both a national regulatory authority and a European agency; these are all sectoral variations of the Community method (*ibid.*,no. 63, p. 68). Under these conditions, it is easier to understand why some people have compared this system to the European Competition Network, where the distribution is based on a model of concurrent jurisdiction between the Commission and the national authorities, the former being able to decide to arrogate an investigation to itself (A. PRÜM, 'L'Union Bancaire Européenne et les Autorités de Surveillance Nationales', *op. cit.*, no. 5; in the same sense, F. MARTUCCI, 'Union bancaire, la méthode du 'cadre': du discours à la réalité', *op. cit.*). However, there are several important differences that limit the comparison. First, because of the configuration of the European competition network, which has two consequences. The first is the nature of what is at stake: these are administrative authorities acting as prosecuting authorities, which is not at all the case for the competent agencies under the SSM or the SRM. The second is the ad hoc nature of competition cases, whereas the supervision carried out by the authorities under the prudential or resolution requirements is permanent, in a non-contentious supervision logic. Secondly, unlike the Commission in the context of the European Competition Network, the ECB and the SRB have significant powers with regard to the national authorities, which therefore have a real hierarchical link: basically, in the context of the SSM or the SRM, the national authorities act on behalf of the European agency (Mr Martucci also points out this particularity, see *ibid.*)

the intervention of a Union body, and the existence of a Community decision-making body, which deconcentrates the execution of the latter to the national authorities. It seems to us, however, that this difference, however slight, is not only a question of degree, but of kind, simply because it determines the competent legal order. Indeed, the type of model used determines the competent jurisdiction in the event of a dispute. It may be considered that the application of European law by the national authorities also requires the intervention of the Court of Justice, but this is limited to the interpretation of European rules and has no direct bearing on the assessment of the legality of the administrative decision. Moreover, although the composition of the European decision-making body is representative of the authorities of the Member States, the voice of the authority of the Member State of origin is largely diluted and less attention is paid to national particularities.[567]

Finally, it should be noted that no institutional architecture will prevent crises from occurring, not only because the integrity and competence of the people who make up the decision-making bodies will always be the determining element of quality supervision, but also because the quality of supervision is never an absolute bulwark against the existence of crises. At most, it can prevent some crises and limit the effects of others: this is already a useful contribution.

201. Chapter conclusion. This chapter has explored the connecting factors of infrastructure managers in all its aspects, both legislative and administrative. It has been observed that the legislative connecting factor of infrastructure managers is made through the head office, and has a particularly broad scope since it entails the application of company law, prudential law and insolvency or even resolution law. For each of these laws, the criterion of the seat has a distinct function: for company law, to allow the application of local rules of internal organisation, for prudential law, to prevent the insolvency of the person it governs and, for insolvency law, to allow the legal system which is required to bear the effects of bankruptcy to decide on the modalities, from the ordering of privileges to the payment of creditors. Nevertheless, some infrastructure managers have the particularity of being subject to a special insolvency regime, resolution; it has been shown that this regime would benefit from being extended to all infrastructure managers. In these cases, resolution law institutes an insolvency model that is highly universalist, but which moderates its effects by sometimes applying the law of the legal institution that it covers, making it possible to give effect to the law of legal orders that are also affected by insolvency.

---

567 This is illustrated by the litigation of French banks against ECB decisions relating to the particularities of national banking law, see A. Gosset-Grainville, 'Coopération et souverainetés', *op. cit.* The author thus considers in this respect that 'for international cooperation to be acceptable, including in times of crisis, regulators must listen to the States'.

The administrative connecting factor of managers is not uniform and depends on whether they are part of a decentralised model, where the location of the manager's head office dictates the jurisdiction of the Member States' administrative authority, or a centralised model, where administrative jurisdiction is exercised directly by an EU agency. In the latter case, this jurisdiction may nevertheless be devolved and exercised by national authorities according to distribution criteria relating to the size of the establishment, unless the Union Agency decides otherwise. What both models have in common is that they do not affect legislative jurisdiction: even where an EU agency has jurisdiction, it must apply national law. The difference, however, lies in the jurisdiction to assess the authority's decision, since the basis of jurisdiction is that of the author of the act. This basis causes difficulties as the Court of Justice is not best placed to interpret national law. Legislative jurisdiction is best exercised by the Member States, and jurisdiction would benefit from being based on *forum legis*, giving jurisdiction to the courts whose law is applicable. Failing that, a mechanism for preliminary rulings from the Court of Justice to national courts would be desirable. The decentralised model coordinates authorities through memoranda of understanding and colleges of authorities, where the possible involvement of European supervisory authorities stimulates cooperation between them. The originality of this model is that it uses criteria from private international contract law to determine the applicability of access procedures to other Member States. It has been shown that these criteria, based on clumsy attempts to locate activity, are powerless to pursue the objectives of internal market integration and investor protection, which are better served by the concept of solicitation. In particular, the concept of solicitation should determine the triggering of the notification procedure applicable to the exercise of activity in another State and the identification of the conduct of business rules applicable to the relationship between the investment firm and its client.

CHAPTER 2
DEALING WITH THIRD COUNTRY MANAGERS

202. The existence of exceptions to the application of EU law. As a matter of principle, the provision of access to a market infrastructure by an operator on the territory of the Union requires, on the one hand, the establishment of a personalised entity and, on the other hand, the authorisation of the latter by an authority of a Member State. These two aspects entail the correlative application of European legislation as well as the competence of the local authorities.[1] By way of exception, it is possible for the foreign operator to provide its service in the Union without establishing a subsidiary, either by setting up a branch or by acting under the freedom to provide investment services. Access to the territory of the Union by these two means does not take place in the same way depending on the market infrastructure (Section 1). This access is nevertheless always likely to be based on the method of equivalence of legislation. This method aims to facilitate cross-border relations between private persons. It is therefore subject to the tension inherent in the objectives of private international law, between coordination of legal orders and preservation of the social order of the forum (Section 2).

SECTION 1. ACCESS TO THE TERRITORY OF THE UNION

In principle, the relationship with the legislation of third countries is identical: national authorisation is required in order to provide services within the Union.

---

1 Thus, MiFID 2 applies to investment firms and market operators established in the EU (Art. 1(1) of MiFID 2), as well as to 'third country firms providing investment services or performing investment activities through the establishment of a branch in the EU' (*ibid.*; this scope is more precise than that of MiFID, on which see D. Guinaudeau, 'Succursales: loi applicable et supervision au titre de la directive concernant les marchés d'instruments financiers [MIF]', *op. cit.*, p. 231*)* The criterion for the spatial application of the directive is therefore, in principle, the establishment within the EU of an institution that falls into the category of investment firm or market operator. The provision of access to a financial market on the territory of the Union triggers the applicability of MiFID 2. See in the same sense Art. 1(2) of EMIR and Art. 1(1) of CSD Regulation.

However, it is through the exceptions to this principle that the singularities of each market infrastructure are felt.[2] This is why we will successively study the access to the European territory of financial market managers (§ 1), central counterparties (§ 2), and foreign central depositories (§ 3).

§ 1. FOREIGN TRADING PLATFORM OPERATORS

The complexity of dealing with the legislation of foreign financial market managers stems, on the one hand, from the fragmentation of sources and, on the other, from the dual status of trading platform managers. In the case of investment firms, MiFID 2 leaves room for a system where the provision of an investment service on EU territory is largely determined by national authorisation, unless an equivalence decision has been obtained (I). In the case of regulated market operators, two distinct equivalence decisions coexist depending on the regime in question: a French regime if the foreign manager wishes to solicit the French public, and a European regime if the foreign manager hopes to be able to benefit from the favourable treatment granted by EMIR to financial contracts concluded on a market recognised by the Union (II).

I. Third Country Investment Firms

203. The principle of authorisation. Although partly harmonised by MiFID 2, the regulation of relations with third country investment firms is national in nature. Member States are therefore free to require the third country firm to have an establishment on their territory in order to provide investment services.[3] If such an obligation exists, it can take two forms: subsidiary or branch. In the first case, the subsidiary is subject to the regime laid down in European legislation and does not require any further development. The second case, the establishment of a branch, benefits from a special regime.[4] Authorisation is also required here, and entails supervision by the local authority,[5] but its benefit is more limited:

---

2 The influence of substantive legislation on the conditions of equivalence is not specific to market infrastructures, but to all financial institutions that can benefit from equivalence, see the study by A.-C. Rouaud, 'L'accès des pays tiers au marché européen bancaire et financier', *op. cit.*

3 Art. 39(1) MiFID 2.

4 Resulting from Arts. 39 to 42 of MiFID 2 and transposed in Art. L. 532-48 and 50 of the Monetary and Financial Code.

5 On this supervision, see ESMA, 'MiFID 2 Supervisory Briefing, ESMA35-43-1493', 6 February 2013, ESMA35-43-1493.

it cannot be recognised by the other Member States,[6] and therefore does not allow the branch to carry out its activity within the other Member States. The authorisation is nevertheless conditional on three aspects.

Firstly, the company wishing to establish a branch must be authorised in its home legal system for the activities it wishes to carry out and be subject to supervision by a supervisory authority. In addition, the foreign company must be a member of an approved investor compensation scheme, or one that is recognised – i.e. considered equivalent – in accordance with Directive 97/9 on investor compensation schemes.[7] Finally, the legislation of its home legal order must be at least equivalent to that of the Union in the fight against money laundering,[8] which is assessed by each Member State.[9] Secondly, authorisation leads to the application of European prudential legislation for investment firms.[10] Thirdly, the authority of the head office of the third country firm must have concluded a cooperation agreement with the authority of the place where the branch is established, which extends to tax matters.[11]

204. The conditions of this authorisation are based on the conditions of mutual recognition within the Union: the establishment of the branch requires prior authorisation in the home Member State and cooperation between authorities. This condition shows, independently of the equivalence method, that the relationship between countries is conditioned here by an equivalence of rules and institutions. It is necessary that the foreign country also subjects the investment services sector to administrative authorisation and supervision. This condition also shows that the foreign licensing regime is at least partially recognised. However, it is not considered fully equivalent, or sufficient, and therefore justifies the cumulative application of local prudential legislation in its internal (capital, governance, internal control) and external (conduct of business rules) aspects, as well as supervision by the local authority. In practice, this has the effect of subjecting the branch to the jurisdiction of the legal system of its place of establishment, and confirms the function pursued by the prudential rules.[12]

205. The jurisdiction of the legal system of the place of establishment. Several aspects point to the jurisdiction of the legal system of the place of establishment

---

6 Art. 39(1) and (2) of the MiFID 2; J.-B. Poulle, 'Les entreprises de pays tiers', *RDBF*, November-December 2014, no. 9. On the draft directive as regards third countries, see T. Bonneau, 'Les entreprises de pays tiers et le marché européen bancaire et financier', *RDBF*, May-June 2013, p. 11, and spec. on this point no. 14.

7 Art. 39(2)(a) MiFID 2.

8 Art. 39(2)(f) MiFID 2.

9 In France, the list of these countries is set by an order of the Ministry of the Economy, see Art. L. 532-48(II)(1) of the Monetary and Financial Code.

10 Art. 41(2) of MiFID 2 transposed into Art. L. 532-50 of the Monetary and Financial Code.

11 Art. 39(2)(d) and (e) MiFID 2.

12 See *supra*, para. 93.

of the branch.[13] First, this is apparent from three elements of conflict of laws. Firstly, the supervisory law will interfere with the foreign company law in its relation to the organisation of the branch. The latter will have to be reconciled with local requirements, not only because they are subject to control by the administrative authority of the place of the branch, but above all because compliance with these requirements is a condition for doing business. However, the interference is unlikely to create a conflict of laws, since it will usually take the form of additional orders regarding the organisation of the company. It is true that company law itself provides for the application of some of its provisions to branches of any foreign company wishing to carry on an activity, even if unregulated, in the territory of the Union. However, these rules are then of a publicity nature and aim at providing third parties with the information they would normally have on the company if it were registered within the Union.[14] However, prudential law is not limited to the enactment of advertising rules, but intervenes in the very organisation of the branch. Moreover, local prudential law does not stop at the borders of the branch, but also interferes in the organisation of the foreign company on which the branch depends;[15] prudential law ensures compliance here by making it a condition for access to the sector of activity.[16] Secondly, the presence of the branch leads to the application of local rules of conduct: the law applicable to the civil liability of the investment firm for the services it provides will be that of the branch's head office. Thirdly, the presence of the branch leads to the application of French bankruptcy law in a territorial version: the insolvency proceedings are then limited to the assets located in France.[17]

The jurisdiction of the legal system of the place of establishment of the branch is also perceptible from the point of view of the conflict of jurisdictions. Indeed, the presence of this branch will serve as a basis for the jurisdiction of the French courts in the event of a dispute, in application of common French law ('*droit commun français*') on international jurisdiction and the case law

---

13 P.-J. Cusset, 'Les succursales de pays tiers dans le cadre du Brexit', *RISF*, 2019/1, pp. 19 et seq.

14 From Arts. 36 to 39 of Directive 2017/1132 on certain aspects of company law. The information in question relates in particular to the law applicable to the company, the articles of association and the instrument of incorporation, and above all the sensitive question of who can bind the company vis-à-vis third parties (see spec. Art. 37).

15 Art. L. 532-50(I) of the Monetary and Financial Code. Comp. the banking regime (Art. L. 511-41 of the Monetary and Financial Code), where the prudential law will be self-limiting by an exemption decision of the ACPR whenever, in addition to the prior existence of an equivalence decision and a cooperation agreement between authorities, the parent firm assumes without restriction the commitments made by its branch.

16 To use Mr Synvet's formula, *supra*; para. 5.

17 See also L. d'Avout, *Sur les solutions du conflit de lois en droit des biens, op. cit.*, no. 274, on bankruptcy from the perspective of real status, as regards the universality seized within the limit of the special connection of the property. This is a manifestation of the proven role of the principle of effectiveness for the author.

known as the 'main stations' (*'théorie des gares principales'*), according to which the foreign company may be summoned to the head office of the branch when it is a matter of a transaction handled within the branch's jurisdiction.[18] The establishment of a branch is therefore not a trivial act, and this restrictive regime explains the existence of exceptions for companies from third countries wishing to provide services on the territory of a Member State.

206. Exceptions to the jurisdiction of the place of provision of the service. An investment firm may provide an investment service to a person established in the EU without having to establish a branch there, and therefore obtain authorisation, in three circumstances. The first is where the provision of the investment service has been solicited by the EU resident client. This idea, also known as reverse solicitation or reverse marketing, was very clearly taken up by Article 42 of MiFID 2. This unilateral limitation of European legislation is doubly restricted: the initiative must come solely from the client,[19] and it must be limited to the provision of the service requested or to 'a relationship specifically linked to the provision of that service', so that 'the initiative of these clients does not entitle the third-country firm to market new categories of investment products or services to these clients through intermediaries other than the branch, where national law requires its establishment'.[20] This exception is intended to avoid penalising foreign firms that simply respond to requests from European clients without having solicited them. It shows that the objective of investor protection itself has its limits.

The second exception, of French origin,[21] concerns a specific investment service, that of concluding transactions in financial instruments on his own account, either on a trading platform or over the counter, with a French credit institution or investment firm trading on own account. This exception aims to 'preserve so-called inter-dealer transactions by avoiding a drying up of counterparties of French institutions in the event of Brexit'.[22] This exception

[18] Y. Loussouarn and J.-D. Bredin, *Droit du commerce international*, *op. cit.*, no. 297, spec. fn. 2. The Brussels I bis Regulation, which is inapplicable here since the foreign company is not deemed to be domiciled in the EU if it does not have its registered office there, does not give jurisdiction in principle to the courts of the place of establishment of the branch. It is only by exception that the latter has jurisdiction, i.e. for certain specific contracts: consumer contracts, employment contracts and insurance contracts (see Arts. 17(2), 20(2) and 11(2) of the Brussels Ia Regulation respectively).

[19] One technique used by some foreign firms was to target European clients, while having them sign a document stating that the service provided was at their sole initiative. ESMA has had the opportunity to clarify that such a practice does not qualify for *reverse solicitation*, which is assessed objectively, see ESMA, 'Reminder to firms of the MiFID II rules on "reverse solicitation" in the context of the recent end of the UK transition period', 13 January 2021.

[20] Art. 42 MiFID 2 transposed in Art. L. 532-51 of the Monetary and Financial Code and Art. 46(5)(3) of the MiFID Regulation.

[21] Art. L. 532-51 of the Monetary and Financial Code.

[22] F. Drummond, *Droit financier*, *op. cit.*

shows that the development of restrictive criteria requires the means to achieve one's ambitions, and the particularly political nature of the connecting factor used here. The third exception to authorisation is where the investment firm is registered by ESMA after the regulation in its home jurisdiction has been declared equivalent.[23] This exception, which concerns only services provided to professional clients and eligible counterparties,[24] requires some elaboration on the equivalence mechanism.

207. **Equivalence.** Access to the European territory based on the equivalence of the home legislation relies on a double mechanism: on the one hand, a decision of equivalence of the foreign legislation and, on the other hand, a registration with ESMA.[25] The equivalence decision is based on the Commission's analysis of the foreign legal system, and in particular of the existence of several sets of rules. Firstly, the foreign legal system must provide for authorisation and ongoing supervision by the competent authority.[26] Secondly, the foreign legal system must also have rules equivalent to the investment firm statute, both as regards the applicable prudential regime (capital requirements, governance, organisational requirements) and the external reporting of the investment firm, i.e. the conduct of business rules.[27] The existence of a market abuse regime must also be proven.[28]

208. In order to obtain an equivalence decision, the foreign legal system must still provide, in a spirit of reciprocity, 'an effective equivalent system for the recognition of investment firms authorised under the legal regimes of third countries'.[29] The equivalence decision has a certain precariousness as the Commission must verify 'the persistence, for the third country concerned, of the conditions on the basis of which an equivalence decision'[30] is granted.

---

23 Art. 46 MiFID Regulation.

24 Listed in Annex II of MiFID 2.

25 The Commission's equivalence decision is the first condition for a third country firm to be included in the register maintained by ESMA, which means that if this decision is withdrawn, the third country firm is no longer entitled to conduct business even if it is registered by ESMA, Art. 47(4°) MiFID Regulation.

26 Art. 47(1)(a) MiFID Regulation.

27 Art. 47(1)(b), (c), and (d) MiFID Regulation.

28 Art. 47(1)(e) MiFID Regulation.

29 Art. 47(1) MiFID Regulation. This reciprocity condition exists in the same terms for other market infrastructures (Art. 25(9) CSD Regulation and Art. 25(6) CSD Regulation). However, it is not inherent to all equivalence regimes, see A.-C. Rouaud, 'L'accès des pays tiers au marché européen bancaire et financier', *op. cit.*, no. 9.

30 Art. 49(4°) MiFID Regulation. Moreover, the Commission was able to clarify that a 'Commission equivalence empowerment does not confer on third countries the right to have their framework assessed or to receive an equivalence determination, even if those third countries are able to demonstrate that their framework meets the relevant criteria', Communication from the Commission, Equivalence in Financial Services, 29 July 2019, (COM/2019/349 final), p. 8.

Moreover, it must be accompanied by a cooperation agreement with ESMA.[31] Once equivalence has been granted, third country firms must register with ESMA in order to operate under the freedom to provide services. In addition to verifying the existence of an equivalence decision and cooperation agreements, ESMA verifies that the authorisation held by the investment firm in its home country covers the services it wishes to provide in the EU.[32] ESMA cannot oppose the inclusion in its register if the conditions are met, but it can decide to withdraw it if the foreign firm 'has clearly harmed the interests of investors or the proper functioning of the markets',[33] or 'has seriously infringed the provisions applicable to it in the third country'.[34] In both cases ESMA must have 'solid reasons, based on written evidence'[35] of the infringements in question and must have unsuccessfully approached the third country authority within 30 days prior to the authorisation.[36]

209. Equivalence has a number of implications for the prerogatives of the registered firm. First, if the third country investment firm already has a branch, it will be 'entitled to provide the services and activities covered by its authorisation to eligible counterparties and professional clients [...] in other EU Member States without establishing new branches'.[37] In other words, equivalence gives Community-wide scope to the authorisation granted at the location of the branch.[38] However, equivalence does not allow the provision of services to retail customers under the freedom to provide services. The foreign company will have to establish a branch in the EU, which will be subject to supervision

31 Art. 47(2) MiFID Regulation.
32 Art. 46(2)(c), which refers to Art. 47(2°) of the MiFID Regulation for details.
33 Art. 49(1)(a) of the MiFID Regulation.
34 Art. 49(1)(b) MiFID Regulation.
35 The requirement to state reasons brings ESMA closer to a quasi-judicial body, in the same way as the clerk of the commercial court with regard to the RCS.
36 These criteria make the withdrawal process inappropriate for the speed of the matter: from the time the information reaches ESMA until it obtains written evidence of the infringements, a significant period of time has already elapsed; the need to wait until the competent authority of the third country does not take appropriate action, coupled with the requirement of a 30-day waiting period after the foreign authority has been informed to withdraw the registration. It would have been more appropriate to provide for an interim mechanism that allows for a temporary suspension of the registration from the moment ESMA obtains the necessary evidence until the moment the measures taken by the foreign authority have been deemed appropriate. ESMA would then reinstate the person suspended from registration, or, if the foreign authority has not taken measures deemed appropriate, the temporary suspension would become final. While the assessment of the appropriateness of the measures taken by the foreign authority is left to ESMA, which arguably further increases its powers, it should be noted that this is already the case in the current procedure.
37 Art. 47(3°) MiFID Regulation. The home Member State of the branch and the host Member State are then encouraged to establish 'proportionate cooperation arrangements to ensure [...] an appropriate level of investor protection' (*ibid.*).
38 Conversely, the absence of equivalence or its withdrawal subjects the foreign company to national regimes, see Arts. 46(4) and 54(1) of the MiFID Regulation.

by the host Member State authority.[39] Furthermore, the equivalence decision has a remarkable impact on the competent jurisdiction in case of a dispute with the client established in the EU. Indeed, the foreign provider will not be able to deprive him of 'the possibility of submitting any dispute relating to those services or activities to the court or arbitration tribunal of a Member State'.[40] The EU legislator's intention here is to prevent the exclusive concentration of litigation at the foreign service provider's headquarters by paralysing the sometimes liberal regime of jurisdiction clauses. Finally, in the absence of equivalence, it is always possible for the foreign company to provide its services on the territory of the Member States by multiplying the branches on the territory of each.

II. Third Country Regulated Market Operators

The provision of access to a regulated market in the EU is not covered by MiFID 2. Regulation is national in origin. However, the paradox is that there are Commission equivalence decisions on third country regulated markets which are made on the basis of EMIR and MiFID 2.

210. Providing access to a foreign regulated market in France. The prohibition on a foreign trading platform operator, or one of its members, from providing access to its trading platform stems from Article L. 423-1 of the Monetary and Financial Code, which states:

> 'The public may not be solicited, in any form whatsoever and by any means whatsoever, directly or indirectly, for transactions on a foreign market for financial securities other than a regulated market of a State party to the Agreement on the European Economic Area, negotiable futures contracts or any financial products, unless the market has been recognised in accordance with conditions laid down by decree and subject to reciprocity.'

The conditions for recognition of the foreign market are detailed by the AMF.[41] The AMF explicitly states that recognition is only necessary if a non-professional client is likely to be solicited by the market operator or one of its members.[42] Conversely, recognition is not required where market members are professional clients acting on behalf of professional clients, or 'on behalf of non-professional clients who have not been solicited (by the member itself or by any other intermediary)'.[43] The reason for this tolerance is to be found

---

39 Art. 47(3°), para. 2 of the MiFID Regulation. The conditions are those of Art. 39 MiFID 2, see *supra*, para. 205.

40 Art. 46(6) MiFID Regulation.

41 AMF Instruction, 'Procedure for the recognition of foreign markets', DOC-2019-05, 18 April 2019.

42 *Ibid.*, p. 2.

43 *Ibid.*

in the protection objective attached to the conditions for recognition. Indeed, the purpose of these conditions is to ensure that the instruments traded on the foreign market and the foreign legislative framework within which the latter is embedded are no less protective for investors. However, professionals are precisely supposed to know the risks they take when trading on foreign financial markets, making such safeguards superfluous.

211. When a request for recognition is made, the AMF bases its decision on the 'equivalence of the foreign market's investor protection, security, supervision and oversight rules with those of European regulations',[44] and in particular on the requirements relating to the equivalence of the technical operation of the foreign trading platform, the existence of foreign legislation on the legal operation of the market and the oversight of its manager.[45] In addition, a cooperation agreement with the foreign authority is required.[46] If recognition is granted by the Minister of the Economy, members of the foreign market that are not established in the European Union or the European Economic Area and that wish to solicit French residents to trade on the recognised foreign market still need to be approved by the ACPR.[47]

The recognition of foreign markets has two consequences: first, the French public, i.e. persons resident in France, can be solicited to buy instruments traded on these markets; and second, the French market operator can enter into agreements with the foreign operator whereby members of one of these markets are admitted as members of the other market and vice versa.[48]

212. The existence of Commission decisions on the equivalence of regulated markets. The Commission's decisions on the notion of 'equivalent regulated market' are based on the EMIR Regulation and MiFID 2. Under EMIR, the function of the concept of a third country equivalent market is to ensure that financial contracts traded on it are not considered as OTC financial contracts and therefore subject to the clearing obligation of EMIR. Indeed, the application of such an obligation would lead to a double clearing: the one provided for by the legislation applicable to the foreign financial market where the financial contract was concluded, and the one applicable to the European headquarters.[49] For this reason, the EMIR Regulation provides for the European Commission to take decisions on the equivalence of foreign regulated markets, which are assessed

---

44 *Ibid.*

45 The possible existence of a Commission equivalence decision under MiFID 2 is likely to be provided.

46 Instruction cited above, p. 4.

47 Art. D. 423-3 of the Monetary and Financial Code.

48 Art. 513-3 AMF General Regulation.

49 On the connecting factor of the clearing obligation under EMIR, see *infra*, paras. 864 et seq.

on the basis of the legislation applicable under MiFID 2.[50] In the context of MiFID 2, the concept is used in Article 25.4 to limit the information obligations of investment firms towards their clients when certain investment services (order execution and reception/transmission of orders) performed on foreign markets are involved.[51] This diversity invites two observations.

First, while the existence of separate equivalence decisions for operators trading on the same markets may seem inconsistent, this duality is justified by the different objectives pursued by these decisions. Decisions taken on the basis of the EMIR regulation are intended to limit the constraints inherent in systemic risk, whereas French equivalence decisions are intended to protect residents. Therefore, the conditions for equivalence are not identical: the rules of financial market law relating to investor protection and the existence of an agreement between authorities are not necessary in order to obtain the Commission's equivalence decision; these conditions are, on the other hand, decisive for the decision of the French bodies.

Secondly, the objective pursued by the decisions taken on the basis of Article 25.4 of MiFID 2 also appears to protect residents: information on instruments traded on foreign financial markets is made less necessary because investor protection is comparable. Under these conditions, it would be desirable to unify the effects of the equivalence decisions of MiFID 2 and Article L. 423-1 of the Monetary and Financial Code, especially since the French legislator already attaches consequences to the former from the point of view of the regime attached to the holding of financial securities by non-residents.[52]

§ 2. FOREIGN CENTRAL COUNTERPARTIES (CCPS)

213. Distinction within foreign CCPs. The provision of a central clearing service within the EU is conditional on the existence of a CCP authorisation. Exceptions to this recognition are based solely on the equivalence method, and their scope

50 See Art. (2)(7) and (2a) of the EMIR Regulation, and the numerous decisions taken by the Commission on this basis, on which see T. Bonneau, 'Notion de marché équivalent', *RDBF*, May 2017, comm. 142, pp. 77 et seq.

51 For an example of a decision made on this basis, see Commission Implementing Decision 2017/2318 of 13 December 2017 on the equivalence of the legal framework and supervisory arrangements for financial markets in Australia pursuant to Directive 2014/65/EU of the European Parliament and of the Council.
The French legislator attaches a consequence to this equivalence decision, which allows foreign owners of equity securities of French companies whose securities are admitted to trading on these markets declared equivalent to benefit from the provisions of Art. L. 228-1 of the Commercial Code, under which any intermediary may be registered on their behalf.

52 They can benefit from the provisions of Art. L. 228-1 of the Commercial Code, under which any intermediary may be registered on their behalf.

is limited by the objective of preventing system risk. Indeed, EMIR distinguishes two types of CCPs from third countries. The first are non-systemic (category 1) CCPs. In this case, the equivalence method follows the conditions already studied for investment firms: the Commission verifies the equivalence of the foreign legislation,[53] a cooperation agreement must have been signed with ESMA,[54] and the CCP must register with ESMA. In contrast, systemic (category 2) CCPs are treated differently. First, in order to grant equivalence, three conditions are added: systemic CCPs are subject to European prudential legislation applicable to CCPs,[55] plus requirements that may be imposed by the central bank whose currency is used for clearing financial instruments,[56] as well as the exercise of direct oversight by ESMA granting it enquiry and general investigative powers.[57] Secondly, ESMA may also consider that 'the systemic importance of a CCP or some of its clearing services is of such magnitude that the CCP should not be recognised for the purpose of providing certain clearing services or activities'.[58] In this case, the foreign CCP would have to establish itself in the EU if it wishes to continue to operate in the EU, in which case the Commission may establish an implementing act for the transitional period.[59]

§ 3. FOREIGN CENTRAL SECURITIES DEPOSITORIES (CSDS)

214. A CSD established in a third country wishing to provide its service in the EU has two access routes. The first one is based on the equivalence method, according to which it can directly provide its service in the EU territory by free establishment of service or by setting up a branch. In this case, the legislation of its home legal system and the supervision it is subject to must have been declared equivalent by the Commission,[60] and cooperation agreements must have been concluded between the home authority, the authority of the host Member State where the activity under the freedom to provide services is carried out or where the branch is established, and ESMA.[61] It can then obtain recognition from ESMA, allowing it to offer its services. The second route for the third country CSD is to enter into an agreement with a CSD established in the EU, referred

[53] Art. 25(6) EMIR.
[54] Art. 25(7) EMIR.
[55] Art. 25(2*ter*)(a) of the EMIR.
[56] These prerogatives are laid down in Art. 25(2*ter*)(b)(i) to (iv) of EMIR.
[57] Art. 25f (information requests) and gf (general investigative powers) of the EMIR.
[58] Art. 25(2)(c) of the EMIR.
[59] *Ibid.*
[60] Art. 25(9) CSD Regulation.
[61] Art. 25(10) CSD Regulation.

to as 'CSD links'.[62] This route, however, requires approval from the authority of the CSD's headquarters,[63] and the agreement is subject to certain mandatory provisions.[64]

215. Section conclusion. At the end of this section, it is clear that infrastructure managers are able to provide their services within the EU without being subject to the requirements of EU law as long as their home legal order is equivalent and there is a cooperation agreement between authorities. However, on the one hand, there are competing exceptions to the equivalence method in order to allow self-limitation of EU law and, on the other hand, the equivalence method is subject to different implementations depending on the different market operators, reflecting the influence of the objectives of the legislation whose equivalence is being sought.

SECTION 2. EQUIVALENCE AND OBJECTIVES OF PRIVATE INTERNATIONAL LAW

216. Equivalence method. Equivalence is a method based on an overall assessment by an administrative authority of the legal system and supervisory authorities of the foreign legal order. It leads to the self-limitation of the local law, and the consequent acceptance of the legislative and administrative jurisdiction of the foreign legal order with regard to the services provided in the territory of the administrative authority declaring equivalence. A relatively recent development within the EU, the equivalence decision is 'initially a voluntary, decentralised and national procedure',[65] which nevertheless benefits from European coordination through the Commission's committees. The centralisation of decisions at the Commission appears with the Prospectus and Transparency Directives, where it is necessary to ensure the equivalence of foreign accounting standards.[66] As this

---

62 Art. 48 of the CSD Regulation (see also Recital 34). This possibility does not exist for CCPs: in order to be able to enter into an interoperability agreement between CCPs, it is necessary to have been recognised, or to be authorised in the Union - the agreement itself is also subject to authorisation by the authorities (Art. 54 of the EMIR).

63 Art. 48(2) CSD Regulation.

64 In particular, from the conflict of laws point of view, the obligation to specify the law applicable to each aspect of the contract (Art. 48(3) CSD Regulation) and, from the substantive point of view, the obligation to provide for a 'delivery against payment' mode of settlement (Art. 48(7) CSD Regulation), or to specify certain aspects of the transfer (Art. 48(8) CSD Regulation).

65 O. Girard, 'Une brève histoire des clauses d'équivalence ou l'Union européenne comme rouage clé de la régulation financière mondiale' in *Liber amicorum Blanche Sousi*, Paris, RB Édition, 2016, p. 124.

66 On this issue, see *ibid.*, p. 235; T.-B. Wei, 'The Equivalence Approach to Securities Regulation' (2007) 2 *Northwestern Law Journal of International Law and Business*, pp. 255 et seq., spec. p. 263; S. Lambert, *L'application internationale du droit financier*, *op. cit.*, no. 971.

centralisation has now been achieved, we would like to show that equivalence follows the dialectic of the objectives of private international law: desirable in that it allows the coordination of legal orders and, consequently, the development of cross-border private relationships (§ 1), it is nevertheless likely to be crowded out or to compete with the objectives of the legislative bodies of the forum whose equivalence is sought (§ 2).

§ 1. THE OBJECTIVE OF COORDINATION OF LEGAL ORDERS

217. Equivalence and mutual recognition. The equivalence method is reminiscent in some respects of mutual recognition, of which it appears to be a projection in relations with third countries. In the same way that mutual recognition presupposes prior harmonisation of the conditions for authorisation and supervision, the equivalence method verifies precisely the equivalence on which mutual recognition is based.[67] Equivalence is thus used 'to determine the distance between both substantive rights and administrative practices'.[68] Here we find the duality of the purpose of mutual recognition in relation to authorisation. Equivalence is systematically associated with cooperation agreements between European and foreign authorities. These developments allow two observations.

The first is that cooperation with third country authorities is often voluntary, as agreements between authorities are not binding and the desire for cooperation may clash with the national interest.[69] The advantage of cooperation under the equivalence method is that it is a condition for access to the local market, and failure to cooperate therefore leads to the withdrawal of such access.[70] Such a measure is likely to strengthen cooperation considerably, since it goes so far as to allow the authority to carry out investigations on foreign territory. The second observation relates to the holistic nature of the equivalence method, which leads to giving jurisdiction to the entire foreign legal order, without separating the legislative and administrative aspects. This deference to the entire foreign legal order is reminiscent of Professor Picone's reference to the competent legal order.[71] The role of the European forum

67 E. Bonifay, *Le principe de reconnaissance mutuelle et le droit international privé,* Paris, Institut Universitaire Varenne, 2017, no. 102.

68 S. Lambert, *L'application internationale du droit financier, op. cit.*, no. 9. The author adds: 'It is in this sense that the distinction between rules and decisions [...] fades away in favour of a method of global equivalence applied a priori and using a grid of analysis by objective or by "principles."', *ibid.*

69 M. Lehmann, 'La coopération avec les États tiers en matière bancaire et financière: la confiance n'exclut pas le contrôle', *Banque et droit,* special issue, February 2020, pp. 35 et seq.

70 See e.g. Art. 25(7) of the EMIR. On this issue, see also *ibid.* p. 38.

71 P. Picone, *La méthode de la référence à l'ordre juridique compétent en droit international privé*, *RCADI,* vol. 197, The Hague, Martinus Nijhoff, 1986; P. Picone, 'Les méthodes de coordination entre ordres juridiques en droit international privé', *RCADI,* vol. 276,

remains in the control of the effectiveness of this reference, and the possibility, if necessary, of substituting its own jurisdiction if too great a discrepancy appears.[72] As perfectly summarised in Recital 7 of the EMIR Regulation, the foreign legal system 'should be considered equivalent if it ensures that the substantial result of the applicable regulatory regime is similar to Union requirements and should be considered effective if those rules are being applied in a consistent manner.' This completeness of European regulation distinguishes it from the substituted compliance mechanisms known to US law, whereby foreign law is carved up point by point and the foreign rule is crowded out as soon as it is considered, in its individuality, to be incompatible, leading to the consequent application of the law of the forum.[73] While such a mechanism is reminiscent of the international public policy exception, the resemblance is only apparent since the latter acts *in concreto*, and is therefore more concerned with the systematic nature of the law.[74]

218. The equivalence method differs from mutual recognition precisely in that it does not presuppose the reciprocity inherent in mutual recognition; it does, however, most often make it the condition for its implementation. When it is present, its function is to allow European companies unhindered access to foreign markets.[75] The equivalence method remains basically unilateral, and the

The Hague, Martinus Nijhoff, 1999, spec. pp. 128 et seq. See E. Bonifay, *Le principe de reconnaissance mutuelle et le droit international privé*, *op. cit.* no. 435 (the author also sees in the theory of acquired rights another antecedent).

72 This is reminiscent of the mechanism of the international public policy exception.

73 On this system, see in French, S. Lambert, *L'application internationale du droit financier*, *op. cit.*, nos. 1018–1019 (illustration with the *CFTC*); in English, CFTC, -Cross-Border Applications of Swaps Provision', on the CFTC website; H.E. Jackson, 'Substituted compliance: The Emergence, Challenges, and Evolution of a New Regulatory Paradigm' (2015) *Journal of Financial Regulation*, pp. 169 et seq. J. Griffith, 'Substituted Compliance and Systemic Risk: How to Make a Global Market in Derivatives Regulation' (2014) *University of Minnesota Law Review*, pp. 1291 et seq. D. Solomon, 'Rhetoric and reality: a Historical Perspective on the Regulation of Foreign Private Issuers' (2010) *University of Cincinnati Law Review*, pp. 619 et seq.

74 It is possible that a foreign rule, taken in isolation, might be contrary to the legislative policy of the forum, but that its concrete application makes it less incompatible than its abstract apprehension would suggest, especially when it is part of a legislative package.

75 In addition to this function relating to the establishment of possible competition between European companies and those from third countries, there is a second function of reciprocity relating to the prevention of the externalisation of risks in the case of the cross-border marketing of financial instruments: 'As the service provider reraps the benefits, and the clients bear the risks of financial products, supervisors of the state of origin have little incentive to care for legal obedience of the service providers in the state of distribution. The situation is different if the risks are distributed symmetrically. The more likely it is that the risk will materialize in the firm's home state, the higher will be the willingness of the latter's financial authorities to cooperate.', M. Lehmann and D. Zetzsche, 'How does it feel to be a third country? The consequences of Brexit for Financial market Law' in E. Lein and O. Fitzgerald (eds.), *Complexity's Embrace*, Center for International Governance Innovation, 2018, pp. 105 et seq., spec. p. 114.

equivalence decision is entrusted to the Commission. These two aspects invite three remarks.

Firstly, although the equivalence decision is unilateral in principle, it nevertheless has the effect of disseminating the substantive legislation in question within the other legal orders:[76] third countries wishing their nationals to have access to the European market must bring their legislation and administrative practice sufficiently into line with that of the Union in order to obtain equivalence.[77]

Secondly, granting the power to decide on equivalence to the Commission is likely to change its functions. Indeed, the equivalence decision then becomes an instrument of power in the Union's relations with third countries[78] and of protection of the Union's interests. The Commission itself makes no secret of the fact.[79] The legal sphere appears here as a necessary but not sufficient condition for the decision on equivalence. Equivalence is political and its exercise therefore requires discretion. The question of the control of the Commission's decisions is then posed in renewed terms. Indeed, judicial control will inevitably come up against what is therefore also an act of government; yet the Commission's political responsibility for these decisions is difficult to engage before the European Parliament.[80] As some authors write, 'the risk is that, on the grounds that these decisions are both technical and

---

76 As Mr Lambert writes, the equivalence method, 'while aiming to neutralise a priori possible conflicts, is nonetheless a formidable instrument for the dissemination of dominant laws', S. Lambert, *L'application internationale du droit financier, op. cit.*, no. 280; the equivalence method is not limited to financial law and this worldwide dissemination of European legislation can be observed in other fields, see A. Bradford, *The Brussels Effect,* New York, OUP, 2020, and the presentation in French of the work by A. Jeanneau, *RCDIP*, 2021, pp. 525 et seq.

77 Mr Lambert writes that: 'The equivalence method is a political technique that is indirectly extraterritorial, or extraterritorial a priori, a kind of 'soft' extraterritoriality, which tends to eliminate conflicts over rules and control [...] The equivalence method of assessing norms and control appears to be an effective and global filtering instrument, and also an instrument of international consultation', *ibid.* The expression extraterritoriality blurs more than it clarifies; nevertheless, we agree with the observation on the international consultation promoted by the equivalence method. The author illustrates this through 'autonomous alignment' (*ibid.*, nos. 72 et seq.) as well as the diffusion of the model in Asia (*ibid.*, nos. 988 et seq.). The Swiss alignment is however not entirely autonomous, but stems from explicit injunctions by the Commission to obtain equivalence, see European Commission, 'European Commission welcomes progress in EU-Swiss relations', Press Release, 22 December 2016 (on this aspect see also M. Lehmann and D. Zetzsche, 'How does it feel to be a third country? The consequences of Brexit for Financial market Law', *op. cit.*, p. 113).

78 In the same way that the power to grant a visa to a prospectus is an instrument of power for the AMF vis-à-vis companies whose securities are admitted to trading.

79 See Commission Communication, Equivalence in Financial Services, *supra*, note under para. 210.

80 European Parliament, Committee on Economic and Monetary Affairs, Report on relations between the European Union and third countries in respect of the regulation and supervision of financial services, 18 July 2018 (2017/2253[INI]) and European Parliament resolution of

political, they will be controlled neither by the Union's legislator, who has the democratic legitimacy, nor by the supervisory authorities, who have the technical competence to do so'.[81]

Thirdly, in the absence of an equivalence decision, national regimes revert to being applicable and the latter are, it seems, naturally subject to attempts at regulatory competition,[82] favoured by their jurisdiction over the modalities of access of third-country companies to their territory.[83]

219. Equivalence and the conflict rule method. By verifying the equivalence of the foreign legal order, this method leads to solutions known to the conflict rule method by applying a foreign law in the territory concerned. Equivalence may thus appear as an avatar of the 'community of law' necessary for the bilateral method to flourish. Admittedly, there are significant differences: there is no actual application of the foreign law by the forum, but a self-limitation of the local law and a correlative reception of the foreign law;[84] the regulation in question does not concern private relationships to which Savigny limited the conflictual method. However, equivalence and the 'community of law' have the same function: they are the basis on which the local application of foreign law is possible.

§ 2. THE INFLUENCE OF SUBSTANTIVE LAW OBJECTIVES

220. Investor protection objective. While the same method is used for the different market managers, it should be noted that this is not the only method. Moreover, this method pursues different objectives for different managers, leading to a different implementation. Both aspects can be explained by the objectives of the underlying substantive law.

---

11 September 2018 on relations between the European Union and third countries in respect of the regulation and supervision of financial services (2017/2253[INI]), in particular paras. 12, 14 and 17.

81 A.-C. Rouaud, 'L'accès des entreprises de pays tiers au marché européen bancaire et financier', *op. cit.*, no. 30.

82 *Ibid.*, no. 32, the author notes in this sense the report of the ESA Joint Committee on Cross-border Supervision of Retail Financial Services, 9 July 2019 (JC/2019-22), spec. nos. 40–41; see also in this sense M. Lehmann, 'Le législateur allemand face au Brexit' *RDBF*, September 2019, no. 5, file 45, spec. no. 29.

83 For the French perspective, see A.-C. Rouaud, 'The provision of investment services in the EU by third-country firms under MiFID II and the PACTE Law', *RTDF*, October 2019, no. 3, p. 24.

84 In this sense, the regime resulting from the equivalence decision is close to that of the recognition method, see L. d'Avout, 'La reconnaissance dans le champ des conflits de lois', *op. cit.* Moreover, self-limitation is a classic mechanism for resolving conflicts of laws in business law, see L. d'Avout, 'L'entreprise et les conflits internationaux de lois', *op. cit.*

Where there are competing techniques for the equivalence method, this competition is explained by the objectives of the substantive law in question. In the case of foreign trading platform operators, the self-limitation of local law is explained by the fact that its primary objective, the protection of residents, is ensured by the foreign law. However, this objective does not prevent a trading platform manager from soliciting professional clients, provided they have the knowledge necessary to protect themselves, and from responding to solicitations from retail clients. This limitation shows that the objective of investor protection must not lead to a total hindrance of freedom of trade. This statement is also illustrated in the case of foreign central securities depositories which can enter into relationships with European central depositories without having to have equivalence. Indeed, these agreements are likely to facilitate the acquisition of foreign securities by European residents and vice versa.

The situation is more subtle in cases where the self-limitation of local law is paradoxically aimed at allowing local companies to continue to operate. This is the case of the exception instituted by France in order to allow the conclusion of transactions in financial instruments on an own account basis, the latter being necessary for the liquidity of French companies. This exception also makes it possible to observe that these different modes of self-limitation of local law are most often aimed at deactivating the prudential legislation applicable to professionals, and not that relating to the direct protection of local retail clients. The rules on the marketing of securities or canvassing thus retain their applicability, regardless of the origin of the investment firm.[85] This shows the particularly close link, which is difficult to break, between legislation on the protection of savings and the domicile of the persons solicited.

221. Systemic risk prevention objectives. The absence of a derogation from the equivalence method in the case of CCPs' access to the territory of the Union shows, on the other hand, that the objective of the law that governs them is above all the protection of systemic risk rather than the protection of investors. The introduction of a special regime for systemic CCPs, as called for by the AMF,[86] also appears to be the retaliation of the ECB, which had clumsily attempted to impose their location on the territory of the Union, even though it had no regulatory competence over clearing systems.[87] It seems to us, however, that the pursuit of systems risk prevention also leads to the elimination of the equivalence method: the more the foreign CCP is considered as systemic, the more this method is avoided in favour of the application of European law and the supervision of the European authority. This mechanism therefore reconciles the

[85] On these rules, see respectively *infra*, paras. 337 et seq. and *infra*, paras. 830 et seq.

[86] AMF, 'Third countries: what equivalence for post-trade infrastructures?', 2 May 2017.

[87] Case T-496/11, *United Kingdom v. ECB*, ECLI:EU:T:2015:133. The ECB then established a cooperation agreement with the English central bank, see F. Drummond, *Droit financier*, no. 1007, note 1. On this judgment, see *infra*, para. 245.

European approach with that of the United States, which stems from the Dodd-Frank Act. The latter requires clearing houses from third countries wishing to clear transactions of US companies to submit directly to local supervision.[88] Indeed, the Dodd-Frank Act already provided for the competence of the American authority to put under regulatory supervision not only operators, but also foreign supervisory authorities, all at their own expense.[89] However, protection against systemic risk does not hide two other significant issues: competition and sovereignty.

The question of competition arises when the legislation of the foreign clearing house is less demanding in terms of prudential rules, and in particular capital requirements.[90] The interests of the Union therefore lead to the refusal of access to foreign central counterparties whose legislation is equivalent, but not identical. Such a solution is worthy of approval: clearing houses are crucial companies,[91] necessary for the proper functioning of the EU internal market, and the equivalence of foreign clearing houses would lead to the decline of local companies for reasons specific to the constraints imposed by the legal system itself; this would mean organising unfair competition on EU territory, to the detriment of local companies.[92] However, in the long run, not having a clearing house attached to one of the Member States of the European Union would mean losing the means of its own financial independence.[93] Here

---

88 A. Caillemer du Ferrage, 'Les enjeux de l'extra territorialité du droit financier', *RDBF*, November 2015, p. 95.

89 Mr Caillemer du Ferrage explains: 'The US law certainly gives the Commodity Futures Trading Commission (CFTC) the power to exempt a foreign clearing house from registration if the CFTC considers that the clearing house is subject to "comparable" supervision in its home state. However, in addition to the fact that this option has never been used to date, the DFA immediately imposes certain conditions on this exemption from registration - starting with the fact that the CFTC must first have been granted the power to conduct investigations and inspections directly at the foreign clearing house. The CFTC may even require the preparation of accounts in US GAAP to facilitate its audits. And if the national regulator of this clearing house wanted to find out what the results of these investigations or requests for information had been, the DFA requires it to sign a contract with the CFTC beforehand, in which it undertakes to indemnify the CFTC in full for any expenses and damages that may arise in the course of legal proceedings relating to the information concerned. The price of DFA's "comparability" is therefore a submission to the controls of the American regulator.' (A. Caillemer du Ferrage, 'Les enjeux de l'extra territorialité du droit financier', *op. cit.*, n° 10).

90 In concrete terms, Mr Caillemer du Ferrage reports that European clearing houses are required, due to European regulations, to ask for guarantees which are 40% higher than those of American clearing houses, see *ibid.*

91 On this notion, see M.-A. Frison-Roche, 'Réguler les "entreprises cruciales', *D.*, 2014, 1556.

92 On the fact that the rules on margin calls may give rise to significant international divergences, see S. Lambert, *L'application internationale du droit financier*, *op. cit.*

93 The issue has not escaped the European Council, see Recital 60 of the EMIR regulation: "the European Council agreed that the Union should defend its interests and values more assertively and in a spirit of reciprocity and mutual benefit in the Union's external relations and take initiatives in order, inter alia, to ensure greater market access for European business

the question of sovereignty appears,[94] explaining the political aspect of the limitation of local law, and showing the links maintained by the institution of market infrastructure and the collective interest of the Union. The latter, however, is already clear within the conditions of equivalence, through the need for reciprocity.[95]

The relationship between competition and sovereignty has been modified by the Brexit. As a result, the main European clearing house has withdrawn from the Union. Indeed, the vast majority of clearing of financial contracts on euro rates takes place in the United Kingdom, i.e. by an institution that is not subject to European law and supervision. In these conditions, granting equivalence also means not giving oneself the means to have a European clearing house. The difficulty is, of course, that economic efficiency makes the clearing service less costly according to the size of the contracts cleared. In other words, the marginal cost of clearing is decreasing; the existence in the same area of several clearing houses offering the same service will result in an increase in the cost of clearing for European operators who would be forced to use a clearing house established in the Union. In short, everything happens here as if the monopolistic tendency inherent in the economic model of certain infrastructures contradicts the objective of European 'strategic autonomy'.

222. Conclusion of the section. At the end of this section, it appears that the equivalence method is a technique of self-limitation of local law, having links with mutual recognition, and having the function of giving jurisdiction to the foreign legal order with which equivalence is sought. The substantive objectives of the legislation in question, both the protection of systemic risk and European sovereignty, are nevertheless likely to crowd out the equivalence method. Other objectives, such as investor protection, allow for the enactment of other self-restriction techniques, such as those based on the notion of solicitation.

223. Chapter conclusion. The above discussion has shown that market infrastructure managers can provide their services within the EU without being subject to local legislation. Where this access is provided by means of the equivalence method, it has been noted that this method is subject to the traditional tensions inherent in the objectives of private international law. The function of this method is to allow the coordination of legal orders through the self-limitation of local law; however, it is likely to be discarded when the

---

and to strengthen regulatory cooperation with our main trading partners. Mr Caillemer du Ferrage mischievously notes that in the text, the interests of the Union precede the values, A. Caillemer du Ferrage, 'Les enjeux de l'extra territorialité du droit financier', *op. cit.*

94 A. Pertriaux, 'Chambre de compensation: entre la souveraineté et le marché', *Revue Banque*, April 2020, p. 34.

95 See *supra*, para. 210.

objectives of the body of law of the forum are incompatible with the acceptance of foreign norms, or when coordination is better ensured by the enactment of substantive criteria of self-limitation.

224. Conclusion of the title. This first title has shown that European market infrastructure managers are subject to two types of connecting factors. The first, legislative, leads to the market infrastructure manager being subject to the legislation of its registered office, which covers company law, prudential law and insolvency law. However, the function of the registered office is not the same depending on the body of legislation in question: whereas in the case of company law it is aimed at applying the organisational rules of the place where the activity is carried out, in the case of prudential law it is aimed at protecting third parties. In the case of insolvency, the function of the registered office is both to ensure universal treatment of bankruptcy and, where appropriate, to protect the European legal order from the realisation of the systemic risk. In these cases, the particular legitimacy of the legal order of the head office stems from the fact that it is the one that *ultimately* bears the effects of the manager's insolvency.

The second, administrative, connecting factor depends on two distinct models: one decentralised to the administration of the Member State where the manager has its headquarters, which is traditional and still predominant, and the other, centralised to an EU agency, which is applicable as soon as the manager is subject to a banking authorisation. Each of these models entails the jurisdiction of the administrative order of the body granting the authorisation. The particularity of the centralised model is, however, that it breaks the parallelism of the c between competent authority and applicable law, and it has therefore been possible to propose methods of coordination between the European legal orders based on certain mechanisms known from private international law, such as *forum legis*. The decentralised model also requires coordination between competent authorities when an operator wishes to provide its services on the territory of another Member State, whether in terms of triggering the notification procedure or locating the conduct of business rules. It was found that the criteria used here of private international contract law were ineffective, and that the internal market integration and investor protection objectives of the legislative package in question were better served by the concept of solicitation.

Market infrastructure managers from third countries cannot, in principle, provide their services within the EU without being subject to EU legislation and supervision. However, the EU proceeds to the self-limitation of its law in different hypotheses according to the foreign systems in question, in particular whenever the foreign legislation and supervision are declared equivalent to that of the EU. This method of equivalence has as its function the coordination of legal orders in order to allow relations between private persons, and is therefore subject to the tension inherent in the objectives of private international law: it is likely to be competed with or crowded out by the objectives and interests of the European legislative bodies whose equivalence is sought.

TITLE 2
THE CONNECTING FACTOR OF SYSTEMS

225. Regime of the notion of system. Market infrastructures are systems, which have in common that they consist of a legal element, the rules of the system, and a physical element, the computer system. The most emblematic systems are trading systems, referred to as trading platforms, of which the topical example is the regulated market and whose lower forms are multilateral trading facilities and organised trading systems. This classification as a trading platform has a number of consequences: not only does it entail the application of a specific regime for its manager and for the members of the system, as provided for in MiFID 2, but it also entails a special regime for investors. In fact, the qualification of a regulated market makes applicable, for those who make use of this infrastructure, the legislative package constituted by the Transparency, Takeover and Market Abuse Directives, i.e. it dictates the regime to which investors wishing to conclude market transactions are subject.[1] This explains why, from an international point of view, the connecting factor of the trading platform to the regulation of market operations is possible.

A specific regime is also attached to the qualification of a system within the meaning of the Finality Directive, i.e. to the qualification of clearing, securities settlement and money settlement systems. Indeed, the Finality Directive gives transactions using these systems a definitive character: collective proceedings can no longer call into question the operation.[2] However, the use of the latter systems can be imposed. This is, first of all, the case for people who wish to use the financial market, including the issuer. If the issuer wishes to admit its securities to trading on a financial market, it is obliged by the market rules to deposit them with a central security depository (CSD). The use of these systems can also be imposed independently of the use of a financial market: private persons wishing to conclude an OTC financial contract subject to the clearing obligation will thus have to use a clearing house.[3] This shows the extremely strong link between the systems and the transactions regime, which explains

1 The classification of other trading platforms also entails the application of the market abuse regime, but not necessarily that of the takeover bid regime, which, while it may be applicable, is not under the same conditions; on market transactions, see *infra*, paras. 466 et seq.

2 On this regime see *infra*, paras. 746 et seq.

3 On this obligation, referred to as clearing, see *infra*, paras. 864 et seq.

why the international connecting factor of the former is likely to dictate that of the latter. Indeed, in the vast majority of cases, the transaction's connecting factor will be that of the system; in one case, however, that of certain contracts relating to a credit risk, the system will designate the application of a law which is – relatively – foreign to it.[4] However, even in this singular case, it is still the system that designates the law applicable to the transaction.

These observations show the fundamental nature of the connecting factor of these systems, which depends, according to the system, on MiFID 2 or the Finality Directive. Despite this importance, from the French point of view, the characterisation of system rules, and particularly those of regulated markets, is paradoxically still the subject of controversy. The French doctrine oscillates between the characterisation of public and private regulatory acts. In both cases, the authors most often refuse to describe these rules as contractual. No doubt the independence that characterisations are likely to obtain from the point of view of private international law makes it possible to temper the regrettable consequences of such uncertainty.

However, the conflict of laws echoes this duality by providing, on the one hand, the seat of the manager as a connector factor for 'the public law governing trading within the systems of a regulated market',[5] while, on the other hand, it institutes a contractual conflict rule for the rules of payment, clearing and delivery systems.

This presentation suggests that the system rules of regulated markets would not be contractual, as the applicable conflict rule implies. In contrast, the other system rules would be contractual and logically subject to an avatar of the law of autonomy. In contrast to this presentation, we would like to show that in reality, all the rules drawn up by system operators are contractual (Chapter 1), but that their particularities and their importance make the connecting factor resulting from private international contract law dysfunctional, as it is most often unsuitable for organisation-contracts, and that they should all be subject to the law of the seat of their manager (Chapter 2).

4 Relatively speaking, because the foreign law in question will provide for the same derogation regime resulting from the Finality Directive. On this hypothesis, see *infra*, paras. 887 et seq.
5 Art. 44(4) MiFID 2.

CHAPTER 1
THE NOTION OF SYSTEM

226. Diversity of systems. In the context of market infrastructures, the notion of system refers to four varieties: trading systems, clearing systems, securities settlement systems and payment systems.[1] These systems have distinct regimes depending on their purpose, which requires a closer look at their respective functioning (Section 1), before showing that they have in common that they are contracts (Section 2).

SECTION 1. MARKET INFRASTRUCTURE SYSTEMS

The different systems will be presented according to their sources. Indeed, while the law on trading systems originates from MiFID 2 (§ 1), the law on payment, clearing and settlement systems originates from the Finality Directive (§ 2). However, there is no common regime for the supervision of systems (§ 3).

§ 1. TRADING SYSTEMS

227. Notion of trading systems. Among the different varieties, trading systems are the most important in that they constitute the financial market in the strict sense of the term: they organise trading and determine the price of transactions. It should be noted that there are different ways of matching orders and, consequently, different categories of trading platforms: regulated markets, multilateral trading facilities and organised trading systems.[2] Despite this diversity, the unity of the notion of trading platform stems from the fact that they always constitute a multilateral system. MiFID 2 defines the latter concept as 'a system or arrangement within which multiple third-party buying and

---

1 Also referred to as 'interbank settlement systems', see Art. L. 330-3 of the Monetary and Financial Code. These payment systems also constitute a market infrastructure in the sense that, without them, the financial market could not function, which explains why they have the same contractual nature as all systems, and the same regime as securities clearing and settlement systems.

2 See *supra*, para. 49.

selling interests in financial instruments may interact'.[3] In addition to this first criterion, which is based on the system's function, there is a second criterion that is specific to the manager's role in these negotiations.[4] Indeed, for a market to be qualified as a 'multilateral system', case law states that the manager must not intervene in a personal capacity in the negotiations.[5] This common function of organising the negotiations and the manager's independence, however, leaves a great deal of room for the different ways of organising the negotiations, which is reflected in the scope of these rules.

228. The area of trading rules. The regulation of the organisation of trading has a broad scope[6] and several functions. The first function of trading rules is the organisation of relations between market members: this includes both the method of order issuance,[7] the trading cycle in the central order book,[8] and

---

3 This is similar to the US definition, which defines 'the exchange' as 'a market place or facilities for bringing together purchasers and sellers of securities or for otherwise performing with respect to securities the functions commonly performed by a stock exchange', Section 3(a)(1), 15 US Code, 78(c)(a)()1). The SEC later clarified that an 'exchange' would be any organisation that 'brings together the orders for securities of multiple buyers and sellers', SEC, 17 CFR § 240.3b-16 - Definitions of terms used in Section 3(a)(1) of the Act. On this question, see S. Lambert, *L'application internationale du droit financier*, *op. cit.*

4 P. Barban, 'Précisions relatives aux devoirs d'Euronext et au pouvoir normatif des entreprises de marché', note under AMF sanct., 4 December 2015, *Sociétés Euronext Paris SA et Virtu Financial Europe LTD*, *BJB*, April 2016, pp. 164 et seq.

5 He 'acts without assuming any risk and without committing his own capital in the conclusion of transactions carried out within this system' (Case C-658/15, *Atlanta Fruchthandelsgesellschaft mbH and others v. Bundesamt für Ernährung und Forstwirtschaft*, ECLI:EU:C:2017:870). This criterion, which originated in the case law, is based on Recital 6 of MiFID 1 (the notion of multilateral system was precisely intended to distinguish them from bilateral systems managed by systematic internalisers) and, from a French perspective, on Art. L. 420-2 of the Monetary and Financial Code. It should simply be added here that systematic internalisers, being in direct contact with their clients, are subject to the best execution obligation (and to all the rules of conduct), see F. Drummond, *Droit financier*, *op. cit.* On the localisation of conduct of business rules, see *supra*, paras. 137 et seq. Comp. J.-J. Daigre, 'L'évolution de la notion de marché financier', *op. cit.* no. 4, p. 238. The author considers that until the Investment Services Directive, the stock market remained both an organisation, which was expressed in the concentration and intermediation obligations, and a mechanism, that of price determination, whereas the financial markets resulting from the MiFID are merely systems for 'confronting multiple buy and sell orders' (*ibid.*, no. 3, p. 248). It seems to us, however, that there is more continuity than rupture, not so much because the concentration obligation has reappeared in a new form, but because financial markets still require the organisation of multiple relationships: between market members, between market members and the manager, between the issuer and the manager. This organisation is precisely the purpose of the trading system rules.

6 The articles quoted here are taken from Chapter 4 of the Market Rules for the securities market. For futures markets, see Chapter 5 of the Euronext Market Rules (Book I), which deals with trading rules for derivatives.

7 Arts. 4201 et seq. of the Euronext Market Rules (Book I).

8 Arts. 4301 et seq. of the Euronext Market Rules (Book I)

the market mechanisms.[9] The latter include the matching of orders,[10] on which the formation of contracts concluded through the trading system[11] depends, but also the securing of trades,[12] off-book trading, the reporting of trades and the publicity given to them.[13] In this respect, the trading rules also impose clearing and settlement obligations on market members.[14] All of these elements have in common that they dictate the behaviour of market members in terms of the ways in which they can contract with each other. The second function of the trading rules concerns the relationship between market members and the market operator. This relationship, like Janus, has two faces. The first is that of a commercial relationship: the market operator is a commercial company, and the members are its clients.[15] The second face is disciplinary: the market company can sanction the member.[16] Significantly, these two faces of the relationship are the subject of separate chapters within the market rules.[17] The third function of the trading rules concerns relations with issuers: they deal with both the conditions of admission and the methods of dissemination of securities.

From a legal point of view, however, this is where the role of the trading system ends. The system does not execute the transaction it has formed, nor does it make the payment required for the transaction, nor does it ensure the settlement of the securities if the transaction is an exchange of securities. All these different services are performed by the clearing, payment and securities settlement systems, which have in common that they are subject to a special regime stemming from the Finality Directive.

---

9 See for their entirety Section 4.4 of the Euronext Market Rules (Book I).

10 Arts. 4401 et seq. of the Euronext Market Rules (Book I).

11 Challenging the idea that order matching gives rise to the formation of a contract in French law, see A.-C. Muller, *Droit des marchés financiers et droit des contrats*, *op. cit.*

12 Which aims to combat price volatility, Arts. 4403 et seq. of the Euronext Market Rules (Book I)

13 Arts. 4502 and 4503 of the Euronext Market Rules (Book I).

14 Art. 4601/1 and 4601/2 of the Euronext Market Rules (Book I).

15 This makes their relationship contractual, and subject to the *lex contractus* of the contract between them.

16 In this sense, it is the heir to the Chambre syndicale des agents de change, see *supra*, paras. 38 et seq. This disciplinary aspect is often raised by authors in order to disqualify contractual analysis. It seems to us, on the contrary, that these two aspects of the relationship between the operator of a system and its members may have a contractual source: the system operator derives its disciplinary prerogatives from collective adherence to the rules of the market. It is in this sense that we can agree, at least in part, with Mrs Méadel's remarks: the disciplinary nature of the relationship between the market undertaking and its members reveals a facet of the stock market organisation, see J. Méadel, *Les marchés financiers et l'ordre public*, *op. cit.*, pp. 380 et seq. (however, in our opinion, it cannot be reduced to this).

17 See Chapter 2 on membership, Chapter 8 on rules of conduct in addition to membership obligations, and Chapter 9 on sanctions.

§ 2. SYSTEMS GOVERNED BY THE FINALITY DIRECTIVE

The systems governed by the Finality Directive are the payment, clearing and settlement systems for securities. We will first present these different systems (I), before looking at the ways in which they are coordinated (II).

I. Payment, Clearing and Settlement Securities Systems

229. The notion of system in the Finality Directive. These three systems have been harmonised at European level through Directive 98/26 on settlement finality in payment and securities settlement systems, the so-called Finality Directive.[18] This directive covers securities settlement, clearing and payment systems and their participants,[19] and provides a unitary definition of a system: a formal agreement,[20] agreed between three or more participants, with common rules and standardised procedures for the execution of transfer orders between participants.[21] Transfer orders are defined by the Directive as transfers of securities or cash.[22] The notion of agreement refers to the contractual record,[23] while the notion of formality refers to the fact that the contract must be in

---

18 This title comes from the English title of the directive 'on settlement finality in payment and securities settlement systems'. On this directive, see P. Bloch, 'La directive 98/26/CEE concernant le caractère définitif du règlement dans les systèmes de paiement et de règlement des opérations sur titre' in *Mélanges AEDBF-France II*, Paris, Revue Banque Édition, pp. 49 et seq.
The rules laid down by this directive have largely been transposed into Arts. L. 330-1 et seq. of the Monetary and Financial Code.

19 Art. 1 of the Directive Purpose. The scope of the Directive also extends to collateral provided in connection with operations of Member States or the European Central Bank in their capacity as central banks, see Art. 1(c)2nd indent of the Finality Directive.

20 The notion of agreement seems to qualify the relationship between the participants and Euroclear as a *contract*. See in this sense, D. Servais (ed.), *L'intégration des marchés financiers*, Brussels, Éditions de l'Université de Bruxelles, 2007, no. 1015; O. Partsch-Bobricheff, 'Analysis of the current legal framework for clearing and settlement services in the European union', *Euredia*, 2005/1, pp. 46–47.

21 Art. 2(a) of the Finality Directive, taken up by Art. L. 330-1(I) of the Monetary and Financial Code.

22 Art. 2(i) of the Directive Purpose.

23 D. Servais (ed.), *L'intégration des marchés financiers*, *op. cit.*, no. 1015. The authors write that 'by the notion of formal agreement, the Directive intends to refer to a contract, i.e. an agreement of will creating rights and obligations on the part of the parties', and observe that the choice of contract is even clearer in certain translations ('The choice of French terms [...] may seem less fortunate than, for example, the Dutch wording of the text [overeekomst, i.e. not "agreement", but "convention"]'). The explanation for this hesitation is linked to the concern to cover all systems likely to be exposed to systemic risks, regardless of their form, whether contractual or regulatory. See also in this sense, C. Keller, 'Regulation of payment systems – some reflections on article 22 of the statute of ESCB', *Euredia*, 2001-2002, no. 3, p. 459.

writing and accessible to its recipients.[24] This definition has two significant consequences. Firstly, by basing the concept of a contract on that of a system, the latter is thus distinguished from technical platforms enabling the interface between the operations carried out within it, both for payments and for the settlement of securities. This interface can take place through interconnection agreements, which link infrastructures together (for example, a clearing house must be able to access different trading platforms), or interoperability agreements, which link infrastructures of the same nature together.[25] In both cases, these interfaces do not constitute systems.[26]

Secondly, the contractual characterisation of the concept of a system has consequences in terms of private international law, which will be studied in the next chapter, but which must be briefly presented here. Although systems are contracts, they are not subject to the Rome I Regulation, but to an avatar of the contractual conflict rule, provided for by the Finality Directive itself, according to which the law applicable to the system is that of a Member State chosen by the participants from the country of their registered office.[27] This choice of law has consequences in terms of formalities. Indeed, the Member State whose law is applicable must then notify the ESMA of the system.[28] It is only once this notification has been made that the contract on which the system is based can be qualified as such within the meaning of the Finality Directive, and benefit from its particularly protective regime for the transactions carried out under it. Transactions that have become final in the system become irrevocable and can no longer be cancelled, even in the case of the insolvency of a participant.[29]

---

24 D. Servais (ed.), *L'intégration des marchés financiers*, *op. cit.*, no. 1016. The authors consider that the notion of formality reflects the fact that the contract 'must present a certain degree of written documentation making it easily accessible to participants, supervisory authorities or courts and tribunals. This agreement therefore most often takes the form of a settlement agreement or a *rule book*'.

25 F. Drummond, *Droit financier*, *op. cit.*

26 As expressed in Art. 2(a) of the Finality Directive itself: 'an agreement concluded between interoperable systems does not constitute a system'; see also in this sense Art. L. 330-1(I)(4°) of the Monetary and Financial Code. This clarification was added by Directive 2009/44/EC of the European Parliament and of the Council of 6 May 2009.

27 Art. 2(a) of the Finality Directive. In the absence of a choice of law, the applicable law would be the law of the State where the settlement body – national central bank or central securities depository - providing the characteristic service is located. See already in this sense, P. Bloch, 'La directive 98/26/CEE concernant le caractère définitif du règlement dans les systèmes de paiement et de règlement des opérations sur titre', *op. cit.*, p. 70.

28 Before the CSD Regulation came into force, the notification was addressed to the Commission.

29 On which see *infra*, para. 746. It should be noted here that a difficulty arose when transfer orders were carried out from system to system, as they no longer fell within the scope of the Finality Directive; the difficulty was resolved by an extension of this regime with the entry into force of the EMIR Regulation (see spec. Art. 87(1)).

230. Payment systems. Payment systems 'enable the transfer of funds governed by formal standardised procedures and common rules for the processing, clearing or settlement of payment transactions'.[30] Payment systems allow both payments within credit institutions and payments between credit institutions. Payment systems can therefore be set up by commercial banks themselves, according to the scheme provided for in the Finality Directive.[31] From a French perspective,[32] a distinction is made between the retail payment system, which concerns mass payments, but of a small amount, and the large-value payment systems.

231. The former are concentrated in the 'CoRe' (Compensation Retail) system, managed by a specialised company whose shareholders are French credit institutions.[33] There is sometimes confusion between payment systems and clearing systems. This is due to historical and legal reasons. In fact, interbank payment was once carried out within a bank clearing house,[34] before being based on payment systems that were autonomous from the clearing mechanism. Payment was made after the intervention of a multilateral clearing.[35] However, the analogy of the net asset value technique used should not lead to an assimilation of the systems: only payment systems have the function of making payments between their members.

232. The latter are managed by the national central banks, each of which has its own payment system. The particularity of the national central banks' payment systems is that they have accounts in 'central bank money' and are linked to each other through an interoperability system set up by the Eurosystem, TARGET2. The latter allows real-time settlements to be made between each national payment system. Access to the payment systems of the national central banks is reserved for credit institutions, and the purpose of the TARGET2 platform is precisely to allow bulk payments between credit institutions.[36] TARGET2,[37]

---

30 Art. 2(6) SEPA Regulation.

31 On the diversity of systems concerned by the directive, see P. Bloch, 'La directive 98/26/CEE concernant le caractère définitif du règlement dans les systèmes de paiement et de règlement des opérations sur titre', *op. cit.*, pp. 54–55. The author notes that the directive does not distinguish between systems that manage small and large payments, and justifies this approach by the fact that in both cases the existence of multilateral clearing gives rise to a systemic risk, justifying the protection of the system (on the relationship between systemic risk and the Finality Directive, see *infra*, para. 746).

32 On the history of French payment systems, see M. Roussille, *La compensation multilatérale*, *op. cit.*, nos. 35 et seq.; T. Bonneau, *Droit bancaire*, *op. cit.*, nos. 1057 et seq.

33 The STET company, see *Banque de France* website.

34 This is still reflected today in the term 'interbank settlement system' used by the legislator to designate payment systems, see e.g. Art. L. 330-3 of the Monetary and Financial Code.

35 M. Roussille, *La compensation multilatérale*, *op. cit.*

36 Retail payments are governed by the SEPA Regulation.

37 Guideline of the European Central Bank of 5 December 2012 on a Trans-European Automated Real-time Gross settlement Express Transfer system (TARGET2) (recast) (ECB 2012/17). The acronym TARGET stands for 'Trans-European Automated Real-time Gross settlement Express Transfer system'. TARGET 2 is the second version of the payment system, see S. Adalid, *La Banque centrale européenne et l'Eurosystème*, *op. cit.*, nos. 278–280.

like the payment systems of national central banks, uses 'central bank money',[38] settles in real time (thus eliminating default) and enables payments throughout the European economic area; it is currently the most widely used service.[39] However, although it is sometimes referred to as a system by some authors,[40] TARGET2 is not a payment system in the sense of the Finality Directive. It is merely a unified platform for the interaction of payment systems held by each national central bank.[41] Only the latter are systems within the meaning of the Finality Directive.[42]

233. Clearing system. Clearing systems are those in which CCPs carry out the physical operations necessary for clearing, and at the end of which the CCP interposes itself between the participants in order to effect the transaction.[43] The clearing system is therefore not a payment system, even though multilateral clearing leads to a form of payment, nor is it a securities settlement system: eventually, the clearing system sends a transfer order to the central depository, which is the only one to move the securities. This does not prevent the clearing house from allowing its clearing system to benefit from the favourable regime of the Finality Directive.[44]

234. Securities settlement system. The securities settlement system[45] is the one through which the central depository moves, by debit and credit, the securities accounts opened in the name of its members.[46] In France, there are two settlement systems: the historical, generalist system managed by Euroclear, and a second system, ID2S, which deals exclusively with negotiable debt securities and has the particularity of using *blockchain* technology. These two settlement

---

38 It should be recalled that scriptural money issued by commercial banks is only a secondary currency, on this issue, see T. Kokkola (ed.), *The payment system*, Frankfurt am Main, ECB, 2010, pp. 151-152; see in French, B. Courbis and B. Sousi, 'L'euro, réalité monétaire dès 1999', *D.*, 1997. B. Sousi, 'L'euro, réalité monétaire dès 1999', *D.*, 1997, 309. If it allows them to regulate relations with their clients, it does not allow them to regulate other banks. The assimilation of scriptural money issued by commercial banks to central bank money for banks stems precisely from a convertibility mechanism which allows each customer to see his claim converted into central bank money, see V. Malassigné, *Les titres représentatifs*, *op. cit.*, nos. 845–846.

39 S. Adalid, *La Banque centrale européenne et l'Eurosystème*, *op. cit.*

40 *Ibid.*, no. 278.

41 Art. 1(2) of the ECB Guidelines: 'TARGET2 is legally structured as a set of multiple RTGS systems'.

42 Art. 3.2 of the ECB Guidelines: 'Each TARGET2 component system is a designated system under the relevant national legislation implementing Directive 98/26/EC' of the ECB Guidelines.

43 These aspects are discussed in more detail *infra*, paras. 880 et seq.

44 Art. 1.3.1.4 of the LCH. SA Clearing Rules.

45 The name is a misnomer since, within settlement, the central depository only manages the delivery part. In fact, the ESES France system handles the delivery of *securities*, while *monetary* settlement is carried out by the Eurosystem's payment services, managed in France by the *Banque de France*.

46 Art. R. 211-6 of the Monetary and Financial Code.

systems have in common that they delegate the settlement function to the T2S (*Target 2 Securities*) platform.

In addition to the favourable rules established by the Finality Directive in order to avoid the disruption of the *lex concursus*,[47] the CSD Regulation has instituted a set of measures in order to avoid settlement failures in the securities settlement system.[48] First, Regulation CSD unifies the settlement of securities for transactions across financial markets (settlement must take place no later than the second business day after trading).[49] Secondly, the transfer of securities is concomitant with the transfer of cash on a 'delivery versus payment' basis.[50] Thirdly, the CSD has disciplinary powers against participants who do not respect the delivery deadline, ranging from financial penalties to the suspension of the participant's access to the system. Finally, if the participant does not deliver the securities within four days, the central depository will itself have to buy back the securities on the market in order to deliver them.[51]

II. Systems Coordination

235. Links between systems. Each system is operated by a separate manager, but they have close links with each other. For example, the clearing systems send transfer orders to the securities settlement system. Above all, the payment systems are the condition for the proper functioning of the other two. First, the securities settlement system relies on the concomitant settlement of cash by the payment system. Secondly, payments between clearing participants resulting from the balance calculated by the clearing system are settled through the payment system.[52] Finally, the links with the trading system appear upstream, since it is the latter that sends orders to the clearing system. In practice, however, two systems require special coordination: the payment system and the securities settlement system. Indeed, they must ensure the payment and settlement of securities at the same time. A special platform has been set up for this purpose: T2S (Target 2 Securities).

---

47 On which see *supra*, paras. 746 et seq.

48 See Art. 7 of the CSD Regulation; Art. 5.1 and 5.2 of the Euroclear operating rules. See also the summary by F. Drummond, *Droit financier*, *op. cit.*

49 Art. 5(2) CSD Regulation. As soon as the custodian is aware of the execution, it must record the trade in its accounts, and 'this accounting entry will constitute a book entry and will entail the transfer of ownership' (Art. 570-3 AMF General Regulation).

50 Art. 39(7) CSD Regulation.

51 Art. 7(2) and (3) of the CSD Regulation. However, whenever the transaction is cleared, this buy-in procedure will be carried out by the clearing house, see Art. 7(10)(a) of the CSD Regulation. The proceeds of financial penalties are not allocated to the CSD and must 'where possible, be allocated to non-defaulting clients as compensation and should in no case become a source of income for the CSD concerned'.

52 Art. 2.2.3.3 of the clearing rules and LCH.Clearnet Instruction n° IV.4-2 'Cash payment'.

236. Participants in the settlement platform. Like most European CSDs, Euroclear has outsourced the settlement function[53] to the T2S platform, which is owned by the Eurosystem[54] and managed by its Governing Council.[55] None of the participants in Euroclear's settlement system has a direct contractual relationship with T2S: they have a contractual relationship only with Euroclear, which allows them to be users of the T2S platform.[56] Euroclear, like other European CSDs, is party to the *T2S Framework Agreement.*[57] The relationship between Euroclear and T2S is governed by this agreement, to which each central securities depository wishing to access T2S and the members of the Eurosystem, i.e. the national central banks, are party. This agreement, which governs all aspects of the relationship between the CSD and the T2S platform, is subject to German law.[58] It provides for a sophisticated four-stage mediation procedure in the event of a dispute,[59] the failure of which allows for referral to the European Court of Justice.[60] At the same time, all national central banks outside the euro area have also signed a contract with the Eurosystem, which is also subject to German law,[61] including an almost identical mediation mechanism, which, in the event of failure, also leads to the possibility of referral to the Court of Justice

---

53 The title of this function can be confusing: here, settlement refers to the settlement of cash, while settlement refers to financial securities.

54 Art. 14.1 of the ECB Guideline of 18 July 2012 on TARGET2-Title (recast) (ECB/2012/13): 'The T2S business application is fully owned by the Eurosystem.' This outsourcing of the settlement platform is apparently linked to the reluctance of some Central Banks to allow Central Depositories to manage central bank money accounts, even though this was apparently already the case under the ESES system in force before T2S. Indeed, in order to allow for more security, the introduction of a European platform made it necessary to use dedicated cash accounts in central bank money, see *Payment and Market Infrastructure in the Digital Age,* Banque de France Publication, 2018, p. 237. While the T2S platform belongs to the Eurosystem, its governance is inclusive of the different participants, see *ibid.* p. 255.

55 Art. 4(1) of the Guideline of the European Central Bank of 18 July 2012: 'The Governing Council shall be responsible for the direction, general management and control of T2S.'

56 *Payment and Market Infrastructure in the Digital Age, op. cit.* p. 254. As users, however, they are involved in the governance of T2S.

57 Available on the ECB's website at https://www.ecb.europa.eu/paym/target/t2s/profuse/shared/pdf/T2S_Framework_Agreement_Schedules.pdf.
In order to be a party to such an agreement, a CSD must nevertheless comply with a set of eligibility criteria determined by the ECB, on which see ECB Decision of 16 November 2011 laying down detailed rules and procedures for the implementation of the criteria for access to TARGET2-Securities services by CSDs (ECB/2011/20).

58 Art. 54 of the T2S Framework Agreement.

59 Art. 42 T2S Framework Agreement. The need to go through four separate stages of mediation before being able to go to court makes the provision likely to be a real obstacle to going to court, and therefore contrary to Art. 6 ECHR.

60 Art. 43 of the T2S Framework Agreement. The title of the article, 'Arbitration', is in this sense remarkably clumsy, whereas the purpose of the stipulation is precisely to recall the modalities of the referral to the Court of Justice.

61 T2S Currency Participation Agreement, see Art. 36 referring to German law 'with the exception of its conflict of laws principles', and Art. 37 for the mediation mechanism.

of the European Union.[62] This coordination between the different systems leads to two observations. The first is that it is based on private law contracts concluded between the national central banks and the managers, which is reflected in the choice of law clause. The second is that the prevalence of German law, in the name of the location of the ECB in Frankfurt, shows that there is more than just a political issue to the headquarters agreements of the Union bodies: the law of the headquarters will apply to most of the private relationships that the Union Agency will have thereafter.[63]

237. The functioning of the platform. The T2S platform is a sophisticated interface which interacts, on the one hand, with the securities settlement system operated by the CSDs and, on the other, with the payment system (TARGET2) operated by the Eurosystem. The Eurosystem provides the settlement service through the application of T2S platform standards by the CSDs' security settlement system and the NCBs' payment systems. As a result, the T2S platform, which is neither a security settlement system nor a payment system, determines the three moments of settlement: the matching of instructions, the conclusion of the transaction and the movement of accounts.

First, when a participant in the Euroclear security settlement system issues an instruction, i.e. a transfer order within the meaning of the Finality Directive,[64] this instruction is considered to have entered the Euroclear securities settlement service only 'when its parameters are successfully checked by T2S'.[65] If this is the case, the instruction becomes irrevocable.[66] It is therefore the T2S platform that actually matches the instructions corresponding to the bilateral transactions, and determines the irrevocability of the instruction.[67] Secondly, it is also T2S that checks whether the matched

---

62 See respectively Arts. 37 and 47 for the mediation mechanism and the referral to the Court of Justice. Curiously, the Icelandic commercial bank and the Icelandic Central Bank will have to refer the matter to the Frankfurt Court (see Art. 47 cited above).

63 See already in monetary matters *supra*.

64 Art. 6.1.1 of the Euroclear Operating Rules.

65 Art. 6.1.1 of the Euroclear operating rules. The reverse is true for cash instructions, i.e. instructions entered into the relevant central bank's system, determined by the central bank's own rules (*ibid.*). The CSD Regulation (Art. 39(2°)) requires the CSD to ensure 'that each securities settlement system it operates defines the times of entry and irrevocability of transfer orders'.

66 This is what makes the ESES system special compared to its predecessors: the irrevocability of instructions on a continuous basis, see A.-C. Rouaud, 'Le moment du transfert de titres financiers négociés sur le marché réglementé', *RTDF*, December 2009, pp. 110 et seq.

67 Art. 6.1.9 of the Euroclear operating rules. The same article specifies that it is necessary to establish 'on the one hand, the agreement of the participants on the terms of the transaction and, on the other hand, their commitment to deliver the financial securities or to settle the cash related to this transaction'. Once these instructions are qualified as 'already matched' within T2S, they become irrevocable. It should be noted, however, that in practice, instructions arrive in Euroclear systems pre-matched due to a matching already established by the clearing house. As the Banque de France points out, 'instructions arrive pre-matched

transaction, also known as 'tied', can be untied. To do so, it verifies that the participant who is to deliver the securities has sufficient securities provision and that the acquiring participant has sufficient cash provision.[68] Indeed, participants have dedicated cash accounts in central bank money on the T2S platform, 'which interact with the cash accounts opened by participants in the TARGET 2 platform'.[69] In the event of insufficient provision, either in securities or in currency, the transaction is put on hold.[70] On the other hand, if the provisions are sufficient, the transaction takes place and acquires a final character, i.e. the character of 'finality' within the meaning of the Finality Directive.[71] Thirdly, and finally, the T2S platform handles the transfers on securities accounts at the same time as cash accounts.

238. Coordination of systems and applicable law. The purpose of the Finality Directive is to give finality to the transactions concluded through the systems it governs. This finality, which gives the Directive its name, prohibits the transaction carried out within the system from being challenged, even by judicial means. However, this finality is determined by applying the law of the system.[72] T2S is not a system within the meaning of the Finality Directive. From a securities perspective, the settlement system is the one governed by the Central Securities Depository, whose applicable law, while it may be that of the seat of any of the participants in the system, is in practice that of its operator.

---

in the settlement system. However, the majority of transactions originating from organised markets are cleared by a central counterparty [...], in which case the central counterparty sends to the central depository pairs of instructions that are already technically matched (or even cleared if the central counterparty offers the clearing function) and therefore do not need to go through the matching module of the settlement system', *Payment and Market Infrastructure in the Digital Age*, *op. cit.*, p. 237.

68 *Ibid.*

69 *Payment and market infrastructure in the digital age*, *op. cit.*, p. 257. This TARGET 2 platform is separate from T2S: it is the payment systems platform run by the Eurosystem. Participants transfer central bank money from the TARGET 2 platform to their dedicated accounts in T2S, which will be 'automatically repatriated by T2S at the end of the day to the cash accounts in TARGET2', *Payment and Market Infrastructure in the Digital Age*, *op. cit.* The use of this dedicated account in central bank money makes it possible to centralise on a single cash account.

70 It may then be partially untied, unless the participant objects (Art. 6.1.16 of the Central Depository Rules).

71 Art. 6.1.1 of the Euroclear Operating Rules.

72 This is why it does not seem correct to consider that '"finality" is an undefined technical concept', or that it 'would be of a more fundamental nature (than transfer of ownership and settlement) since it aims at fixing the very existence of rights (whatever their legal nature)'. See H. de Vauplane and P. Bloch, 'Loi applicable et critères de localisation des titres multi-intermédiés dans la Convention de La Haye du 13 décembre 2002', *JDI*, 2005, pp. 3 and seq., spec. no. 57. The 'finality', or more precisely in French, the finality of a transfer, is a legal concept that characterises the transfer of ownership within the securities settlement system and of payment within the payment system.

239. In this context, the general principles developed by the Eurosystem Governing Council[73] are better understood. According to these principles, the securities accounts of CSD users remain legally assigned to each custodian;[74] the distinction between the use of the system and the ownership of the system accounts is therefore clear. Moreover, the modification of the balance of these securities accounts can only be made within the T2S platform.[75] Finally, the law applicable to the transfer and its enforceability against third parties is that of the central depository of the securities account.[76] This last principle has a significant consequence as to the finality of the transaction made on T2S. Indeed, while the Finality Directive has made it possible to agree on the principle of finality of transactions recorded by the systems, the moment of finality remains subject to the different national laws governing the said systems – both from the point of view of payment systems and from the point of view of securities settlement systems. However, the different national laws most often refer the question of the moment of finality of the transaction to the rules of the central depository.[77] For this reason, the national central banks that are parties to T2S have concluded an agreement with the central securities depositories that are parties to T2S in order to standardise the moment of finality.[78] This agreement is subject to German law.[79] This is also the reason why national central banks have developed the habit of maintaining financial collateral for each other due to the complexity of the transfer of the security subject to financial collateral.[80] This complexity stems in

---

73 ECB, *General principle of Target2-Securities*, T2S-07-0132-tracked, available on the ECB's website: https://www.ecb.europa.eu/paym/target/t2s/profuse/shared/pdf/T2S_AG_meet4_aob.pdf?0dc079ccd42f59392810de2c96912ebd.

74 Principle 2 of the above-mentioned general principles.

75 Principle 6 of the above-mentioned general principles.

76 Principle 7 of the above-mentioned general principles: 'Principle 7: T2S shall require participating CSDs to be designated under the Settlement Finality Directive (SFD) in their respective jurisdiction. Participating CSDs will have to be designated as securities settlement systems under the SFD and notified by the competent national authority to the European Commission in order to benefit from protection under the SFD. Consequently, transfer orders processed in T2S will acquire adequate protection under the relevant laws and rules of the individual CSDs that are designated under the SFD. Furthermore, the proprietary aspects and the finality of transfers of securities will be determined in accordance with the laws of the country in which the CSD that has opened the securities accounts is located.'

77 In France, for example, Art. L. 330-1(III) para. 3 of the Monetary Code refers the definition of irrevocability to the operating rules of the central depository, and clearly specifies this aspect: 'In the case of systems linked by an interoperability agreement, each system determines in its own rules the moment of entry into its system and the moment of irrevocability in order to coordinate the rules of all the interoperable systems concerned. Unless the rules of all systems linked by interoperability agreements expressly provide otherwise, the rules on the moment of introduction and the moment of irrevocability of one system shall not be affected by any rules of the other systems with which it is interoperable.'

78 Collective Agreement, 22 March 2018, available on the ECB's website: https://www.ecb.europa.eu/paym/target/t2s/profuse/shared/pdf/collective_agreement.pdf

79 Art. 13 of the above-mentioned Collective Agreement of 22 March 2018.

80 S. Adalid, *La Banque centrale européenne et l'Eurosystème*, *op. cit.*

particular from the intertwining of intermediation systems and will be further explored in the study on financial securities.[81]

240. Multilateral character of systems. While all Finality Directive systems have a multilateral character, this does not express the same thing in the context of trading systems. The plurality of participants in the system gives, according to the authors of the contracts linking central depositories and national central banks to T2S, a multilateral character to the T2S platform.[82] This multilaterality is not specific to the T2S platform, but to all systems which always have in common that they bring together a multitude of participants in the system managed by the operator, and therefore give rise to an interest of their own in the community thus established. However, it should be noted that this multilateral character is distinct from that of trading systems. In the case of settlement, which can be extended to all systems subject to the Finality Directive, the multilateral character resides in the links between the participants in the platform, as the 'material negative actions' of some participants are likely to have consequences for the others, despite the absence of a direct contractual relationship. The qualification of multilateral is a way for the platform manager to impose on each participant the consideration of the collective interest of the participants, and thus to increase the responsibility of the participant in the context of a bilateral contract between each participant and the platform manager.

241. Of course, such a mechanism also exists within the trading rules: a single contract binds each participant to the market operator, and collective discipline, as reflected in the market rules, is necessary to ensure the smooth functioning of the financial market. However, MiFID 2 has a different purpose when it attributes this multilateral character to the trading system. Indeed, this multilateral character is constitutive of the price-making mechanism: the interaction within the system of 'multiple third-party buying and selling interests in financial instruments',[83] gives a collective dimension to financial markets.[84]

---

81 See *infra*, paras. 668 et seq.

82 See respectively Arts. 4 and 3 of the *T2S Framework Agreement and the T2S Currency Participation Agreement* which states that 'the Parties acknowledge that T2S is multilateral in character in that it aims at facilitating European post-trading integration by supporting cash and securities settlement in Central Bank Money, thereby combining the interests of Participating CSDs, Central Banks and all other T2S Actors. The Parties agree that actions that would have a material negative impact on any of the CSDs participating in T2S or would not be in line with the aim of achieving securities settlement in Central Bank Money are incompatible with the Multilateral Character of T2S'.

83 Art. 4(1)(19) MiFID 2 defines a multilateral system as 'a system or arrangement in which multiple third-party buying and selling interests in financial instruments may interact'.

84 On the collective dimension of markets, see the observations of A.-C. Muller, *Droit des marchés financiers et droit des contrats*, *op. cit.*, among others, no. 40 (on the collective dimension at the time of the formation of private law contracts): 'If the reduced influence of the wills in the determination of the conditions of the transaction does not, in itself, make it possible to exclude the qualification of the transaction as a contract, it nevertheless testifies

This additional dimension of multilaterality is especially true for order-driven markets, such as the French markets.[85] As Professor Rouaud puts it:

> 'Instead of the intermediaries themselves seeking a counterparty and concluding the transactions two by two, the set of orders produced by the buying intermediaries is confronted with the set of orders produced by the selling intermediaries in order to determine an equilibrium price allowing the execution of the largest possible number of orders. The multilateral character is therefore not only due to the large number of operators, but also to the way in which transactions are formed.'[86]

In contrast, payment and delivery systems, even when interacting within the settlement platform, never express multiple interests, but bilateral transfer orders aimed at the execution of an already concluded transaction. This question is, however, independent of whether the different systems express more than the interest of their members[87] and, in particular, whether their operation is of general interest.[88] The latter aspect is expressed through the supervision of the systems.

§ 3. SUPERVISION OF SYSTEMS

242. Supervision of payment systems. The supervision of payment systems is one of the tasks of the ECB.[89] The content of this task was specified in Article 22 of the Statute of the European System of Central Banks, which gives the ECB a particularly broad regulatory power. On the one hand, from a spatial point of view, the ECB's jurisdiction to issue regulations extends to the relationship between the Union's payment systems and third countries. On the other hand, from a material point of view, this Article 22 surreptitiously extends the task regarding payment systems to clearing systems by considering that:

---

to the particular, collective conception which permeates the formation of the transaction', no. 210 (on the public and collective nature of the pre-contractual period in the case of public bids); n° 392 (on the collective nature of the relationship established in the presence of a clearing house).

85 On the history of order-driven markets and their evolution in France, see A.-C. Rouaud, *Contribution à l'étude de l'opération de marché*, *op. cit.* On price-driven markets, and in particular the evolution of the London Stock Exchange, see *ibid.*, nos. 58 et seq.

86 *Ibid.*, no. 46. Price-driven markets are also multilateral systems, but do not have this singularity, see *ibid.*

87 On the two conceptions of the market's interest, see the synthesis proposed by P. Barban, *L'entreprise de marché*, *op. cit.*

88 On this question, see *ibid.*, nos. 309 et seq. It is nevertheless possible that the difference in the administrative authorisation required to qualify as a regulated market may indicate that the operation of these particular markets is closer to the general interest.

89 Art. 127(2) TFEU. It has sole jurisdiction to exercise this supervision, see F. Martucci, *L'ordre économique et monétaire*, *op. cit.*, nos. 68 et seq.

> 'The ECB and the national central banks may grant facilities, and the ECB may make regulations, to ensure efficient and sound clearing and payment systems within the Union and with third countries.'[90]

This second extension raised the question of the extent of the prerogatives that national central banks derive from the Statute of the ESCB with regard to the supervision of securities settlement systems. The issue has given rise to a controversy which is now reflected in positive law.[91] Indeed, securities settlement systems are subject to supervision by the *Banque de France*,[92] acting as a member of the Eurosystem, while the professional obligations of

---

[90] On this Art. 22, see S. ADALID, *La Banque centrale européenne et l'Eurosystème*, *op. cit.*, no. 217; F. MARTUCCI, *The economic and monetary order*, *op. cit.*, no. 70; C. KELLER, 'Regulation of payment systems – some reflections on article 22 of the statute of ESCB', *Euredia*, 2001-2002, no. 3 and T. KOKKOLA (ed.), *The payment system*, *op. cit.*

[91] Two theses have clashed (on these see also D. SERVAIS (ed.) *L'intégration des marchés financiers*, *op. cit.*, nos. 54 et seq.) The first, defended in particular by Mr Christoph Keller (C. KELLER, 'Regulation of payment systems – some reflections on article 22 of the statute of ESCB', *op. cit.*), according to which the supervisory powers of the ECB and the national central banks are limited exclusively to payment systems: it is to the latter that the Treaty on the Functioning of the European Union and Article 22 of the ESCB statute refer. A second argument extends the powers of the ESCB to SSSs, since Article 22 also refers to 'clearing systems', and since these 'systems would pose systemic risks identical in all respects to payment services, to which, moreover, securities settlement systems are closely linked' (*ibid.*). It is understandable why the ECB was attracted by the second thesis (see the ECB's opinion of 15 July 2005 [CON/2005/24] requested by the Ministry of Finance of the Czech Republic on a draft law on the integration of financial market authorities, para. 14, cited by D. SERVAIS (ed.), *L'intégration des marchés financiers*, *op. cit.*, no. 61, note 37. In the same sense, Professor Martucci deduces from the tasks defined in Art. 127(2°) of the TFEU 'a lato sensu monetary jurisdiction [which] now extends to the operation of payment and settlement systems, as well as to banking and financial supervision', F. MARTUCCI, *L'ordre économique et monétaire*, *op. cit.*, Indeed, not only does such an analysis increase the scope of the ECB's prerogatives, but the two types of systems are identical and both raise a systemic risk of the same magnitude: it is no coincidence that both types of system are covered by the same Finality Directive. However, the ECB does not have jurisdiction over systemic risk, and if it did, its scope would have to be limited as the concept is liable to infinite ramifications. Mr Keller's thesis not only follows an orthodox interpretation of the texts, but also takes into account the fact that the substance of the services offered by these two types of system is radically different. It is no coincidence that it was adopted in the *UK v. ECB* judgment.
Finally, this problem of jurisdiction regarding the supervision of payment systems is independent of the question of the creation by the ECB of an interoperability system for the settlement function. Mr Adalid thus regrets that the act of creation of T2S 'does not address this problem of jurisdiction at all' (S. ADALID, *La Banque centrale européenne et l'Eurosystème*, *op. cit.*, no. 217, note 938). This is easily explained: the T2S platform is not a payment system.

[92] Art. L. 141-2(II) of the Monetary and Financial Code. Supervision may be accompanied by control measures: documentary checks may be carried out, as well as requests for information from the securities settlement service manager, see Art. L. 141-5(III) of the Monetary and Financial Code.
It should be noted that the Banque de France's supervisory jurisdiction over securities settlement services is carried out in the same way as for payment services.

the central depository are subject to supervision by the Autorité des marchés financiers.[93] The AMF is only competent in respect of the authorisation it gives to the CSD: it checks that the conditions under which the authorisation was granted are still met.[94] In other words, Article 22 of the ESCB had indeed been interpreted particularly broadly, to the point of giving national central banks the authority to supervise securities settlement systems.

243. The *UK v. ECB* judgment.[95] This interpretation has, however, arguably been undermined by the *UK v. ECB* judgment. This judgment concerns a decision, entitled 'Eurosystem Oversight Framework', in which the ECB imposed the geographical location of CCPs operating in euro-denominated products in the territory of countries that had adopted that currency. The ECB considered that:

> '[CCPs] should be legally established in the euro area, with full management and operational control and responsibility for all core functions performed from the euro area.'[96]

Such a decision put the entire UK securities clearing business at risk. The UK therefore challenged the ECB's act. The substantive issue before the General Court was whether the ECB had been empowered by the EU legislator to regulate the activity of infrastructures such as central counterparties involved in securities clearing. The interpretation of Article 22 of the ESCB was therefore central, and in particular the question of whether this provision referred only to the clearing phase prior to payments organised by clearing houses (net settlement payment systems) or also to securities clearing systems. Based on the definition of 'payment system' in the SEPA Directive, which excludes payment transactions within a payment or securities settlement system,[97] the Court ruled that:

> 'A payment system within the meaning of Article 127(2) TFEU falls within the field of funds transfer. Therefore, while such a definition is likely to include the "liquidity" side of clearing operations, the same is not true of the "securities side of central clearing operations", as such securities, while they may be assessed as being the subject of a transaction giving rise to the transfer of funds, do not in themselves constitute payments.'[98]

---

93 Art. L. 621-9(II) of the Monetary and Financial Code.
94 In this sense, it only applies Art. 20(3) of the CSD Regulation.
95 Case T-496/11, *UK v. ECB*, ECLI:EU:T:2015:133.
96 Point 6 of the supervision framework.
97 Arts. 4, 6 and 3(h) of Directive 2007/64/EC. See paras. 93 to 95 of the *United Kingdom v. ECB* decision.
98 Para. 97 of the *UK v. ECB* decision.

The Court added that, while 'the existence of very close links between payment systems and securities clearing systems cannot be denied',[99] 'the existence of those links cannot suffice to justify the recognition by the ECB of implicit powers to regulate securities clearing systems'.[100] This solution is remarkable and deserves approval. The thesis defended by the ECB, and supported by some authors, constantly extends the jurisdiction of the institution on the basis of functional considerations that do not establish a precise title of jurisdiction and, consequently, circumscribe the administrative action. It can be deduced from this that if clearing systems are themselves outside the ECB's jurisdiction, the same applies *a fortiori* to the supervision of the securities settlement system.

As a result of this ruling, the supervision of clearing and settlement systems is removed from the jurisdiction of the ESCB. The primary supervision is that exercised by the system manager.[101] In this sense, the latter is, in the words of Ms Drummond, an infra-regulator.[102]

244. Supervision of trading systems. Trading systems are not formally subject to general supervision by an administrative authority. However, the jurisdiction exercised under the prevention of market abuse or the short-selling regime is similar. Indeed, both the manager and the market members have certain obligations to inform the AMF about the transactions carried out by the system,[103] resulting in indirect supervision of the system itself, and allowing the manager to be qualified as a 'relay of the regulator in the exercise of supervision'.[104] However, this supervision no longer serves the same purpose: as it relates to transactions, its purpose is to put the AMF in a position to pursue

---

99 Para. 106 of the *UK v. ECB* decision.

100 Para. 107 of the *UK v. ECB* decision.

101 For trading platforms, see Art. L. 420-9(I) of the Monetary and Financial Code; for clearing systems, see Art. 541-19 of the AMF General Regulation.

102 F. Drummond, *Droit financier*, *op. cit.*, no. 1031. The expression is used in relation to clearing houses; in our opinion, it applies to all managers. It should be added here that the presence of an 'infra-regulator' is indicative of the reason why 'infra-law' has in fact often become the most decisive factor for managers. This helps to explain why even an AMF press release, which in theory has no normative legal effect, can now be reviewed by the administrative order (CE, Assemblée, 21 21 march March 2016, *Société Fairvesta International GMBH et autres*, see *supra*, note under para. 56). Such a solution is not isolated: it is thus that the press release indicating the ECB's key rate is likely to be subject to a legality review by the CJEU. On this issue, see S. Adalid, *La Banque centrale européenne et l'Eurosystème*, *op. cit.*

103 See, for example, in the case of trading platforms, the obligation to report an anomaly (Art. L. 420-9(II) of the Monetary and Financial Code); in the case of central clearing systems, there is a general obligation to report cleared transactions (Art. 541-24 of the AMF General Regulation); in the case of central depositories, they inform the AMF on a daily basis of the balances of the accounts that they maintain and of pending securities settlement transactions (see Art. 560-9 to 560-12 of the AMF General Regulation).

104 F. Drummond, *Droit financier*, *op. cit.*, no. 967. The author expressly refers to trading platform managers in this way.

possible breaches,[105] and not to enable the ESCB to supervise financial stability. However, the result is the same: the system is closely supervised by the authority, which has access to all the information necessary for its broad mandate.

245. Section conclusion. At the end of this section, it appears that market infrastructures are based on systems, consisting of rules designed to allow their members to interact in order to conclude transactions. However, these systems are also called upon to coordinate with each other in order to ensure the smooth functioning of financial markets. This coordination is done by concluding contracts between the system managers. However, the purpose of each system tends to distinguish them, not only because they are likely to be subject to their own regime, but also because the function pursued justifies separate supervision. We would now like to show that these systems are private law contracts.

SECTION 2. THE CONTRACTUAL NATURE OF SYSTEMS

246. System rules. The function of system rules is to govern access and operation, membership and status of members and, finally, the prerogatives of the system operator.[106] These rules have the particularity of being subject to 'clarifications', issued unilaterally by the manager in the form of 'instructions'. The purpose of the instructions may be both legal (clarification of a market rule) and material (details of an aspect relating to the computer system). In practice, although they are widely publicised,[107] the system rules most often consist of the repetition of applicable legislative and regulatory provisions,[108] which sometimes makes it more difficult to identify the rules actually issued by the manager himself.

---

105 Thus, the prerogatives that the competent authority exercises directly on the trading system are explained with a view to preventing market abuse, or the short selling regime: this is the case of the suspension or deregistration of admitted financial instruments (Art. 69(2)(m) and (n) MiFID 2), or the injunctions it may issue to 'require any person to take steps to reduce the size of the position or exposure' (Art. 69(2)(o) MiFID 2; these Articles are transposed in Art. L. 420-10(I) of the Monetary and Financial Code).

106 In the case of the rules for trading and delivery of securities, the relationship with issuers and the status of securities must be added.

107 Art. L. 411-10 para. 5 of the Monetary and Financial Code sets out the publication obligation, the details of which are set out in Art. 511-13 of the AMF General Regulation: the publication must be made on the market undertaking's website. According to the latter Article, the market undertaking must also make available the mechanisms for settling transactions, clearing rules and the rules of the securities settlement system used if they are not already made public.

108 These come from a variety of sources: national – the Monetary and Financial Code and the AMF General Regulation – and European. The distinction between the two is blurred by the fact that national regulation is itself often of European origin (directives).

The addressees of the system rules are primarily its members, who are also referred to as members, and for whom the status of investment firm is required, unless equivalent safeguards are provided.[109] In the case of securities trading or settlement rules, the addressees of the rules are also the issuers. The legislator has specified that the relationship between the members of the system and its manager is contractual in nature.[110] In fact, when concluding the membership contract, the members of the system contractually undertake to comply with its rules. However, as Professor Daigre points out, a distinction must be made between 'the market rules and the contractual relationship that is established between the market undertaking and its members'.[111] Until recently, authors distinguished, within trading systems, the rules of the regulated market, qualified as public regulation, from the rules of other trading systems, on which there was an agreement as to their contractual nature.[112] Today, the elements distinguishing the status of market rules from that of other trading systems have disappeared; the doctrine now refuses to qualify market rules as contractual, without qualifying them as a regulatory act of public law, emphasising the ambiguity of their situation.[113]

On the contrary, it seems to us that the rules of the system are specific contracts: the existence of administrative supervision or a dedicated regime

---

109 See, for example, in the case of regulated markets, Art. L. 421-17 of the Monetary and Financial Code.

110 Art. L. 421-18 para. 2 of the Monetary and Financial Code.

111 J.-J. Daigre, 'Conséquences du transfert d'un marché réglementé à l'égard des professionnels', note under Paris, 5 October 2001, *JCP* E, 2002, 889, p. 958. See T. Bonneau, 'De l'inutilité du droit contractuel pour assurer le respect des règles de marché', *RTD com.*, 1999, pp. 257 et seq.

112 On this retrospective, see J.-B. Lenhof, 'Les règles de marché à l'épreuve du temps' in *Mélanges en l'honneur du professeur Paul Le Cannu*, Paris, LGDJ, pp. 181 et seq. A. Couret, H. Le Nabasque *et al.*, *Droit financier*, *op. cit.*, nos. 67 et seq.

113 Professor Bonneau once defended the characterisation of regulatory acts in public law in a famous article (T. Bonneau, 'De l'inutilité du droit contractuel pour assurer le respect des règles de marché', *op. cit.*). After recalling the public nature of rules issued by authority in the private era (*ibid.*, no. 8), the author endeavours to extend this qualification to all market rules (*ibid.*, nos. 12 et seq.). In contrast to this perception, Mr Neau-Leduc argued that market rules constituted private law regulation of contractual origin (P. Neau-Leduc, *La réglementation de droit privé*, Paris, Litec, 1998), a qualification which has since been further developed by Mr Rosa (F. Rosa, *Les actes de réglementation privée*, Paris, Thèse Paris I, 2011). The issue has been studied again by Mr Barban, according to whom the ambiguity of this qualification reflects the ambiguity of the market manager model within the French system; other authors have in this sense qualified these rules as 'hybrids' (J. Méadel, *Les marchés financiers et l'ordre public*, *op. cit.*, pp. 394 et seq.) is based on an intuition that seems to us to be correct: it reveals the duality of Euronext's task, which is both a commercial company governed by private law, whose members are its clients, and a quasi-disciplinary one, since it assesses the (broadly understood) behaviour of the member in order to grant it that status. This qualification is still debated, and authors generally refuse to decide, see e.g. A. Couret, H. Le Nabasque *et al.*, *Droit financier*, *op. cit.*, nos. 67 et seq.; T. Bonneau *et al.*, *Droit financier*, *op. cit.*, no. 479 (this passage is written by Mrs Rouaud); F. Drummond, *Droit financier*, *op. cit.*, no. 932).

is not such as to call into question this contractual nature. Everything here originates from an agreement of will between private persons,[114] whose disputes will in principle be settled before the judicial courts, without the notions of public power, administrative police or public service being taken into account. We shall endeavour to demonstrate this contractual nature by observing that neither the presence of legislative enabling (§ 1), nor the approval of the rules of the system[115] (§ 2), should disqualify it. Moreover, certain arguments specific to negotiation systems alone also deserve to be rejected (§ 3).

§ 1. LEGISLATIVE ENABLING

247. Rejection of the argument relating to legislative enabling. One of the arguments relating to the qualification of a regulatory act of public law stems from the legal obligation[116] for the manager to draw up these rules, and to establish their content. Two clarifications appear necessary. The first is that this obligation, described as 'legislative enabling'[117] has its source in the European regulations,[118] and that it is simply an obligation on the operator to operate the system in question, and not an enablement given by law. This is evidenced by the fact that system operators have never needed to be legally enabled to issue system rules, which are a condition for the operation of the system and are necessarily established as such.[119] The second is that the law imposes on other organisations the task of drawing up rules without, however, qualifying them as public law.[120] Indeed,

---

114 Art. 1101 Civil Code.

115 Art. L. 421-10 (regulated market rules), Art. L. 424-2, Art. L. 425-2, Art. L. 440-1 and Art. L. 441-1 of the Monetary and Financial Code.

116 At the time, this provision was introduced by Art. 42(I) para. 1, Law of 2 July 1996, now codified in Art. L. 421-10 of the Monetary and Financial Code.

117 T. Bonneau, 'De l'inutilité du droit contractuel pour assurer le respect des règles de marché', *op. cit.* We put the expression in inverted commas, because it is clearly connoted: the author is trying to bring the situation of the market undertaking closer to that of an administrative authority that would be enabled by law to take certain regulatory measures. It should already be noted that legislative enabling will subsequently be enacted by Mr Rosa as a criterion for identifying private law regulation.

118 See for example Art. 51 MiFID 2.

119 Before MiFID 2 came into force, multilateral trading facilities and organised trading facilities were not 'obliged' to establish rules, and did so anyway.

120 Other matters are subject to legislative enabling: for example, Law no. 65-557 of 10 July 1965 establishing the status of co-ownership of built-up buildings, which enables co-owners to issue co-ownership regulations. However, Art. 8(I°) of the aforementioned law explicitly declares it to be conventional, even though it must, by legal prescription, determine a considerable number of issues. Mr Bonneau's argument as to the obligation by law to conclude a contract seems all the weaker as the law provides for the obligation to conclude numerous contracts (e.g. the purchase of a car implies the conclusion of an insurance contract), and the law is often prolix in determining the clauses that must be included in contracts, and those that are prohibited (abusive clauses): this is the case for employment contracts, insurance contracts, and many adhesion or consumer contracts.

the legislator does not give managers the power to design these standards, but, in the words of an author, 'seems to acknowledge the capacity of these actors to develop standards'.[121]

'Legislative enabling' makes it all the more difficult to qualify market rules as an act of public regulation since, according to the case law of the French Constitutional Council, on which some authors nevertheless rely, this devolution is only possible 'on condition that this enabling concerns only measures of limited scope both in terms of their field of application and their content',[122] and that the person to whom the regulatory power is devolved is a legal person under public law.[123] It is true that the Constitutional Council was able to allow a private law company to exercise regulatory power in its decision of 28 July 1989 on the *Comité des Bourses de valeur*,[124] but this was a professional body, admittedly governed by private law, but with an ordinal vocation,[125] i.e. an institution far removed from a private-law commercial company such as the contemporary market company.[126]

---

121 C. Granier, *Les sources du droit financier*, *op. cit.*, no. 394.

122 Cons. const., 17 January 1989, DC no. 89-248, Recital 15; formula taken up in subsequent decisions: Cons. const., 14 January 1992, DC no. 91-304, Recital 12; Cons. const.,., 1 July 2001, DC no. 2001-497, Recital 6; Cons. const., 12 August 2004, DC no. 2004-504 of 12 August 2004, Recital 40. Mr Bonneau relies on the first decision, which concerned the *Conseil Supérieur de l'Audiovisuel*. The scope of this decision was broader. On this question, see P. Barban, *Les entreprises de marché*, *op. cit.*, no. 158. On the scope of this decision, see L. Favoreu and L. Philip, *Les grandes décisions du Conseil constitutionnel*, 18th ed., Paris, Dalloz, 2016, para. 8, p. 108. The interest of these decisions has been renewed in the context of the relationship between the sanctioning power of administrative authorities and the *ne bis in idem* rule, (see Cons. Const., 5 August 2015, DC no. 2015-715, spec. no. 66).

123 It should be noted that the Constitutional Council only had the opportunity to clarify this rule after the publication of Mr Bonneau's article, cf. Cons. const., 12 August 2004, DC no. 2004-504, Recital 40: 'Considering, secondly, that by virtue of Article 21 of the Constitution and subject to Article 13, the Prime Minister exercises regulatory power at national level; that, however, these provisions do not prevent the legislator from entrusting *a State authority* other than the Prime Minister with the task of laying down norms enabling a law to be implemented, provided that this empowerment concerns only measures of limited scope in terms of both their scope and their content'. Italics added.

124 Cons. const., 28 July 1989, DC no. 89-260.

125 The law expressly described the institution as a 'professional body with legal personality' (Art. 5 of Law no. 88-70 of 22 January 1988).

126 It must be considered that the inclusion of a professional body with legal personality among the persons liable to such devolution was an exception to the rule laid down in previous decisions according to which only a legal person governed by public law may be the recipient of a legislative empowerment.
It should be added that the solutions of foreign law converge. Indeed, United States law has long required administrative authorisation for a market undertaking to operate a securities exchange (see P.-H. Conac, *La régulation des marchés boursiers par la commission des opérations de bourse [COB] et la securities and exchange commission [SEC]*, *op. cit.)* As in France, such authorisation is subject to certain requirements, many of which relate to the enactment of market rules (Art. 6(b)(1) et seq. of the *Securities Exchange Act*, which can be

248. Scope of legislative enabling. The existence of legislative enabling is not linked to the public or private nature of the rules, but is explained in the light of their purpose. In fact, the rules of the system are, according to the expression of Professor Paul Didier, 'organisational contracts':[127] they conceive the functioning of the system in all its aspects, in the same way that the articles of association of a company arrange the functioning of the legal person, or that the rules of a co-ownership ensure the organisation of the building. Two differences must nevertheless be emphasised. The first is that in French company law, in the absence of articles of association, the law most often provides a body of suppletive rules for the functioning of the legal person. Here, without a system rule, the infrastructure is dysfunctional and no suppletive rules are enacted, hence the need to place the obligation to establish these rules on the system operator. The second is that the function of the co-ownership rules is to govern the use of the common parts of the building, the distribution of service charges and certain aspects of the collective life that the building gives rise to, whereas the system rules are not limited to the relationship between the members and the operator, but are aimed at operating the system itself. These two characteristics explain the presence of a legislative enabling which reflects the need for the operator to issue these rules in order to allow the operation of the infrastructure in question. This legislative enabling now serves as the basis for the qualification of private law regulation of market rules. This qualification, which has been adopted by the case law,[128] deserves to be traced back to its origin.

249. Private law regulation. This concept appeared in French positive law as early as 1991: a decision of principle[129] handed down in the field of social law qualified the company's internal regulations as a 'regulatory act of private law'.[130] Professor Neau-Leduc made the first effort to systematise the concept.[131] The author considers that the power to enact a regulatory act of private law comes from the agreement by which 'private persons make compulsory a collective decision-making mechanism in the organisation of their relationship, under

---

accessed on the New York Stock Exchange website), and to the various rules that market managers must provide. Such an enablement, although it orignates from federal law, does not in any way imply that these rules are public.

[127] In the words of Professor P. Didier, 'Brèves notes sur le contrat organisation' in *Mélanges en l'honneur de François Terré,* Paris, Dalloz, 1999, pp. 636 et seq.

[128] T. Com. Paris, 16th ch., 14 September 2012, *BJB*, April 2013, p. 192, note J.-J. Daigre.

[129] Cass. soc., 25 September 1991, *Bull.*, V, no. 381.

[130] This concept has been developed within this special law to explain certain specific phenomena within it, from the nature of collective agreements to the power of the employer over the employee.

[131] The latter distinguishes between private law regulatory power and private law regulatory act, and then demonstrates that this concept, which originated in labour law, existed in other parts of private law. Mr Neau-Leduc sees, for example, in the co-ownership regulations another manifestation of this private law regulation, and Mr Rosa sees in sports law multiple manifestations of private law regulation.

the sole constraint of respecting the rules of public order. They empower a private authority to issue regulations that are immediately binding on their community'.[132] The separation of powers is, for the author, likely to explain why private law regulation has a contractual basis.[133] Indeed, interpreting a decision of the Constitutional Council,[134] Mr Neau-Leduc considers that the Council 'condemns the exercise by private persons of regulatory prerogatives of public power',[135] and that the legislator has no 'vocation to modify the nature of relations between private persons'.[136] However, for the author, and this is a fundamental difference with administrative regulation of unilateral origin, private law regulation is simply a contractual mode of organisation of private relations, which allows him to characterise market rules, such as those of compensation, as private law regulation.[137]

250. A second investigation of private regulatory acts has taken place more recently penned by Professor Rosa. The author sees in the factors of expansion of private regulatory acts the removal from the empire of administrative law of certain parts of it.[138] However, Rosa differs from Neau-Leduc in that he considers that private regulation, while it may have a contractual origin, may also be unilateral.[139] Nevertheless this unilateral character of rulemaking does not detract from the fact that compliance is ensured by the contractual adherence of the members.[140] Mr Rosa however refers to the contract as 'the natural mode'

---

132 P. Neau-Leduc, *La réglementation de droit privé*, *op. cit.*, no. 333, p. 203.

133 As Mr Revet writes, 'The ability to establish a regulatory power is indeed inherent to the freedom of association and to the freedom of convention', T. Revet, preface in P. Neau-Leduc, *La réglementation de droit privé*, *op. cit.*.

134 Cons. const., 17 January 1989, DC no. 89-248.

135 P. Neau-Leduc, 'À propos de la réglementation des marchés financiers' in *Mélanges Michel Cabrillac*, Paris, Dalloz/Litec, 1999, no. 17, p. 506.

136 *Ibid.*, no. 18, p. 507.

137 P. Neau-Leduc, 'Nature et régime des sanctions prévues par les entreprises de marché et les chambres de compensation' in *Mélanges AEDBF IV*, 2004, p. 291.

138 For the author, this can be seen in the end of the principle of order concentration in financial market law.

139 In the same way, administrative regulation is not necessarily unilateral and can originate from a contract. However, the contractual origin of an act is not specific to private regulation, since the author attempts to show that administrative regulation can also come from a contract. Indeed, Mr Rosa shows that, if for its own reasons, administrative law has long rejected any possibility of hybridization between the regulatory technique and the contract, it is not the same in private law, where the advent of a regulation of conventional structure is not only conceivable, but is often the very standard on which private law regulation is based. However, the non-exclusive character of the qualification of private law regulation of contractual origin comes from administrative law, where 'the unilateral nature of the act cannot be set up as a criterion of qualification of regulatory act'. F. Rosa, *Les actes de réglementation privée*, *op. cit.*, no. 441, p. 243.

140 See P. Neau-Leduc, 'A propos de la réglementation des marchés financiers', *op. cit.*, no. 19, p. 508: 'market operators, expressly qualified as commercial companies, are, without any possible dispute, legal persons under private law. They nonetheless exercise a real regulatory power, necessarily of private law, a power to unilaterally issue standards of a general nature'.

of the act of private regulation.[141] The author identifies a private law regulation on the basis of two cumulative criteria: state enabling and regulatory scope characterised by automatic and immediate effect.[142] If the second criterion is missing, the author proposes to speak of acts with quasi-regulatory effect.[143] Thus, in labour law, the breeding ground for private law regulation, Mr Rosa observes that unilateral acts of the employer, whether they are individual or collective in scope, use 'the same procedure: that of implementing a contractual prerogative, via the enactment of a unilateral act',[144] and concludes that the contract is 'the basis of all acts with quasi-regulatory effect'.[145]

251. Whether one refers to the doctrinal analyses of Mr Neau-Leduc or Mr Rosa, it should be noted that private law regulation is most often of contractual origin, and that the presence of a legislative enabling makes it possible to identify it.[146] Mr Rosa links two regime elements to the notion: private regulation acts contribute to shaping the sectoral public order,[147] and explain the existence of exorbitant prerogatives.[148] Four things should be added here. The

In the same sense, Mr Rosa sees, for example, the company's internal rules as a unilateral regulatory act of private law. However, a distinction must be made between unilateral acts, unilateral commitments and contracts (M. Fabre-Magnan, *Droit des obligations (t. 1), op. cit.*, nos. 742 et seq.). Indeed, as some contracts may be unilateral, it is possible to see in these phenomena a duality of unilateral contracts (one party issuing a unilateral contract regulating its platform, the others a unilateral contract of acceptance), in the manner of cross-promises of sale and purchase, on which see for example P. Malaurie, L. Aynès and P. Stoffel-Munck, *Droit des obligations*, 9th ed, Paris, LGDJ, 2017, no. 447. However, it is not certain that such an analysis captures the singularity of private law regulation.

141 F. Rosa, *Les actes de réglementation privée, op. cit.*, no. 440, p. 242.

142 It seems to us, however, that automatic and immediate effect should rather be an aspect of the regime of private law regulatory acts.

143 They are manifested in labour law by all acts taken in the sole interest of the employer, and not in the realisation of collective interests, the seal of which is set by legislative enabling.

144 F. Rosa, *Les actes de réglementation privée, op. cit.*, no. 261, p. 134. The author continues as follows: 'This is so true that the employer's unilateral act with a collective purpose can only be invoked against workers who are bound to him by an employment contract' (*ibid.*).

145 *Ibid.*, no. 265, p. 136.

146 Unquestionably, legislative enabling is an element common to the various forms of private law regulation identified by the authors, in particular the collective agreement and the co-ownership regulations. In the case of condominium regulations, the enabling would be tacit. Mr Rosa makes a strong analogy with the co-ownership regulations. The effect of the latter is explained for the author by its purpose: to ensure the harmonisation of the occupation of the building (Art. 8 of the Law of 10 July 1965), which gives a political function to the condominium regulations (according to the expression of Mr J.-L. Aubert). The author observes a quasi-regulatory effect of the co-ownership regulations, as they do not create real obligations (F. Rosa, *Les actes de réglementation privée, op. cit.*, no. 921). The author sees an implicit enabling by the legislator (*ibid.*, no. 923).

147 *Ibid.*, no. 1404.

148 *Ibid.*, no. 1544. It will be seen that both characteristics can be observed here since market rules constitute rules of professional conduct engaging the administrative responsibility of those they subject, but also because the person entrusted with the drafting of the rules has exorbitant prerogatives in this context, see e.g. the power given to the market undertaking to cancel transactions *infra*, para. 265.

first is the uselessness of the public nature of market rules to ensure compliance. The system operator has all the necessary prerogatives to sanction the offending member, up to and including exclusion. The only difficulty is to ensure that the operator exercises them correctly, and it is here that the law must oblige the system operator to act in the interest of the market, and not only in his pecuniary interest. The second concerns the dual purpose of system rules compared to other acts of private regulation. Indeed, the system rules do not only organise the status of the community constituted by the market members and the operator, but also the operating rules of the computer system. When the system operator enacts this second set of rules, he does so as the owner of his property, and his special position vis-à-vis the system members is derived from the prerogatives he holds over them. The third is that, even in public law, the administrative contract remains a contract despite the regulatory power of the public person.[149] It is therefore in vain that a public law qualification would take the market rules out of the contractual orbit. The fourth is that the system rules can be brought closer to the contract of adhesion; their special character and importance nevertheless make it difficult to interfere with the regime of the contract of adhesion. Indeed, the function of this regime, which aims to protect the member, is ensured, on the one hand, by the body of special rules provided for in the Monetary and Financial Code and, on the other, by the approval of the AMF.

§ 2. APPROVAL OF THE *AUTORITÉ DES MARCHÉS FINANCIERS*

252. Rejection of the approval argument. A second argument relating to the 'control and approval' of trading rules is raised in order to qualify them as a regulatory act of public law.[150] It seems that this gives approval a scope unknown to other administrative authorisations in financial law. Indeed, the *Autorité des Marchés Financiers* is called upon to examine other documents. One need only think of the prospectus, which cannot be analysed as a public document simply because it is approved by an independent administrative authority. Admittedly, there are two major differences between these two hypotheses: on the one hand, the prospectus is not a body of rules, but a set of financial documents intended to give a true reflection of the state of its issuer and, on the other hand, the

---

149 J. Waline, *Droit administratif*, Paris, Dalloz, 2020, no. 463.

150 Raising this argument today, for example, see F. Drummond, *Droit financier*, *op. cit.* At the time of Mr Bonneau's writing, the argument could have been more easily rejected because of the private nature of the approving authority. As Mr Neau-Leduc wrote, 'the impact of such approval, emanating from a private authority, cannot have any repercussions on the private nature of the rules in question' (P. Neau-Leduc, 'A propos de la réglementation des marchés financiers', *op. cit.*, no. 19). However, the Conseil des marchés financiers has been replaced by the AMF (see *supra*, paras. 53 et seq.). Despite developments in the field, this perception is still shared, see P. Barban, *Les entreprises de marché*, *op. cit.*, nos. 154 et seq. and 249 et seq. the author excludes the argument of approval as the law stands.

Autorité des Marchés Financiers does not approve the content of the prospectus, but verifies its formal consistency.[151] However, the concept of approval of the prospectus is also the one used in European law.[152] Approval, on the other hand, is an administrative authorisation which entails approval of substantive rules, and does not alter the private nature of the operator:[153] while examining the substance, it is still an administrative authorisation. Similarly, approval is not intended to replace the rules issued by the market operator with rules written by the administration itself, or whose seal of approval would be affixed. The function of the approval of market rules is explicitly given by the legislator: it is to verify 'their compliance with the applicable legislative and regulatory provisions, as well as their proportionality to the objectives pursued'.[154] It seems excessive to deduce from this function of verification of the rules pursued by the approval a change in the nature of the latter.[155] The notion of approval must be interpreted in the light of its function and of European law, and not conceptually in the manner of French administrative law,[156] *a fortiori* given that it is in fact similar to judicial homologation.

253. Approval and professional status of the rules. However, approval has an administrative effect: it allows the AMF to hold administratively liable persons who disregard the rules of the system.[157] Indeed, approval has the effect of giving market rules the status of professional rules. However, this status does not replace the contractual qualification, but is additional to it. This coexistence has several implications. The first is that the parties to the Market Rules continue

---

151 On this approval, see *infra*, nos. 347 et seq.

152 Art. 1(1) of the Prospectus Regulation.

153 Of course, authorisation is not about these documents, but about the person providing them.

154 Art. L. 421-10, para. 3 of the Monetary and Financial Code. Approval here is similar to judicial homologation of agreements between the parties.

155 C. Granier, *Les sources du droit financier*, *op. cit.*, no. 418. For an illustration, see AMF, 4 December 2015, *Sociétés Euronext Paris-Vertu Financial Europe LTD*, SAN-2015-21.

156 This conceptual and French approach is nevertheless adopted by certain specialists, first and foremost Ms Drummond, see F. Drummond, *Droit financier*, *op. cit.*, no. 932. The author relies on the case law relating to 'medical' collective agreements and the case of regional hospital agencies. The former, concluded between social protection bodies, professional trade unions and the State, are contracts to which ministerial approval gives the scope of a unilateral regulatory act; the author shows that a recent trend inevitably leads the Council of State to consider them as contracts with regulatory content and effect. This is even more obvious in the case of regional hospitalisation agencies, where the unprecedented qualification of conventional administrative act was retained (CE, 14 January 1998, *Syndicat départemental Interco* 35 CFDT, AJDA, 1999, p. 164, note J. Petit). These rulings lead Ms Drummond to give the approval of market rules the effect of a regulatory qualification, see F. Drummond, *Droit financier*, *op. cit.* If the conceptual approach were not to be adopted, it should nevertheless be noted that one element distinguishes these approvals from the one under discussion here: the approving body is ministerial, whereas in the case of market rules it is a mere administrative authority.

157 C. Granier, *Les sources du droit financier*, *op. cit.*, no. 416.

to be contractually liable to each other. The second is that the contractual characterisation limits administrative liability on this basis to the persons who have adhered to it. The third is that it is undoubtedly possible for the client, insofar as he suffers damage, to engage the civil liability of the market member in the event of a violation of these rules. Indeed, the disregard of the rules applicable between market members and infrastructures is likely to engage the civil liability of the member towards its clients. This case law, which was developed in relation to the failure to provide collateral for stockbrokers when concluding financial contracts on the financial markets,[158] has been extended to cases involving short selling.[159] This last aspect does not, however, call into question the contractual qualification. Indeed, the ordinary law of tort allows for liability to be incurred by a third party on the basis of the violation of contractual standards.[160]

§ 3. CONTRACTUAL REGIME FOR NEGOTIATION RULES

254. Contractual freedom. Before rejecting the arguments based on the incompatibility of the negotiation rules with the regime stemming from ordinary contract law, we shall reject the argument that the market rules are opposed to the contractual freedom of the parties.[161] Indeed, Mr Rosa considers that the market operator cannot choose its co-contractor, because the market rules would require it to respond favourably to a member or issuer meeting the established criteria.[162] However, this is not the case: the market operator itself sets the criteria for access to its trading platform; it is simply prohibited from discriminating between people on the basis of their origin. This interference with contractual freedom is explained by the objective of European integration, which is to not create a distinction according to the place of establishment of the person making the request. This interference is also explained by competition law, which requires the manager of an essential infrastructure to not create undue distortion within the sector of activity. It seems to us that this interference is compatible with contractual freedom, which is not rejected in principle, but is reduced in scope. Indeed, the market operator has broad discretion not only in the choice of criteria, but also in their interpretation, so that it is excessive

158 See *infra*, paras. 865 et seq.

159 Cass., com., 7 March 2018, no. 16-15821.

160 See lastly, Cass., ass. plén., 13 January 2020, no. 17-19.963.

161 M. Fabre-Magnan, *Droit des obligations (t. 1)*, *op. cit.*, no. 64: freedom of contract includes 'the freedom to choose one's contracting party. The Cour de cassation has occasion to recall this and specifies that this freedom implies the possibility of not giving reasons for the choice of one contractor rather than another, and even the possibility of not communicating the criteria according to which this choice is made'.

162 F. Rosa, *Les actes de réglementation privée*, *op. cit.*, no. 1083.

to consider that it does not choose its co-contractors at all.[163] In the same way, Mr Rosa considers that the rules in question cannot be qualified as contractual rules, because the market operator can be sanctioned in case of non-use of its prerogatives. However, this sanction is not related to the market rules, but to the particular administrative authorisation that constitutes the recognition of the regulated market. This recognition is the functional equivalent of authorisation, and this sanction is specific to any person authorised for an investment service who does not use the prerogative granted to it by the authorisation.[164]

255. The market rules regime. The authors challenging the contractual qualification consider that it is incompatible with the contractual regime. Two arguments are raised: the first relates to the prerogatives of the contracting operator towards its co-contractors, while the second relates to the relations of the contracting operator with third parties.

256. The power to modify the rules. The argument relating to the exorbitant nature of the prerogatives of the market operator vis-à-vis its co-contractors lies in the power to unilaterally modify the rules.[165] One author thus believes that this power would create a significant imbalance falling under the former Article L. 442-6(I)(2°) of the Commercial Code, now codified in Article L. 442-1(I)(2°), requiring the liability of the author of the significant imbalance and the judicial annulment of the clause. However, there is no evidence of a significant imbalance. The author makes an analogy here with what is considered unfair in a consumer contract,[166] namely the unilateral modification of the contract. Such an analogy must be rejected, as the *ratio legis* of the two institutions is distinct: the relationship is not the same in consumer matters as between professionals. On the one hand, the manager is in charge of an essential infrastructure whose preservation is his responsibility and justifies this power of unilateral modification. On the other hand, the approval of the rules by the financial markets authority, by establishing a presumption of legality, makes the hypothesis put forward by the author all the less convincing.

257. The unilateral modification of market rules is based on the situation of the operator of a system: it is the operator who manages the trading platform and to whom the members have contractually entrusted the power to modify them in the collective interest of the trading system. However, contractual public policy does not prohibit such a power being entrusted to a co-contractor. This

---

[163] Moreover, its own immediate pecuniary interest is to increase the number of market members and issuers, since it is paid as a percentage of the volume of transactions carried out on the platform, and their increase is likely to increase said volume.

[164] See, for example, Art. 8(a) of MiFID and MiFID 2, codified in Art. L. 532-6 of the Monetary and Financial Code.

[165] P. Barban, *Les entreprises de marché*, *op. cit.*, no. 142.

[166] Art. L. 212-1 of the Consumer Code. However, the point could probably be made more forcefully in the new Art. 1171 of the Civil Code on contracts of adhesion.

idea is even the basis of private law regulation, i.e. the possibility for a group of people to proceed, by contract, to the modalities of their organisation. It is true that the market operator is likely to change the rules to its own advantage. Nevertheless, the competitive situation between the financial markets encourages the market operator not to grant itself advantages to the detriment of its members. Moreover, on the one hand, the financial market authority must approve these rules, which makes it possible to control the conflict of interest inherent in the company's situation and, on the other hand, the status to which it is subject obliges it to act with 'diligence, loyalty, neutrality and impartiality, respecting the integrity of the market',[167] which makes it possible to engage its administrative responsibility[168] or even civil liability.[169] Finally, it should be added that the law of contracts already allows one of the contracting parties to unilaterally fix certain decisive elements of the contract, first and foremost the price;[170] the power of a contracting party over the content of the contract is no longer a problem in principle, but is rather controlled *a posteriori* in order to avoid abuse.

258. The perpetual maintenance of the listing contract. The second argument, relating to the perpetual maintenance of the listing contract, concerns the relationship with issuers. Relying on the case law (the *Radiall* litigation),[171] some have tried to demonstrate that the contract for admission of securities to trading can make an issuer 'A "prisoner" of the market: its will is insufficient to obtain a delisting of the securities'.[172] However, the argument is no more convincing since the issuer, when it admits its securities to trading, knows the conditions for exit, which, although limited, are nonetheless present, so that the co-contracting parties are free to set conditions for termination of the contract.

259. Extracontractual prerogatives vis-à-vis third parties. Another argument against the contractual character of market rules is that they are applied to third parties, thus contravening the relative effect of contracts.[173] This rule states that no one can be made a creditor or debtor under a contract to which he was neither party nor represented. However, it seems to us that this is not the case in

167 Art. 512-2 of the AMF General Regulation.

168 See for an illustration, see AMF sanct., 4 December 2015, cit.

169 On the basis of Art. 1194 of the Civil Code, which allows for the incorporation of professional rules relating to the performance of the contract into the contractual standards.

170 Art. 1164 Civil Code, see F. Terré *et al.*, *Les obligations*, *op. cit.*

171 On this dispute, see P. Barban, *L'entreprise de marché*, *op. cit.*, nos. 144 et seq. and references.

172 *Ibid.*

173 Art. 1199, formerly Art. 1165 of the Civil Code. The relative effect is nevertheless likely to be tempered since, since 'the binding force of the contract comes, not from the promise, but from the value which the law attaches to this promise, it is perfectly permissible for the legislature or even the courts to decide, in order to satisfy this or that imperative, to extend the circle of persons obliged beyond those who have concluded the contract', see F. Terré *et al.*, *Droit des obligations*, Paris, Dalloz, 2018, no. 670, who refers on this question to Kelsen's article, 'La théorie juridique de la convention', *Archives de philosophie du droit*, 1940, pp. 33–76.

positive law. And, in order to be convinced of this, we will take up the distinction elaborated by Mr Barban between the prerogatives that can be exercised with regard to issuers who have not concluded a contract with the market operator, and those with regard to investors who are not members of the regulated market.

260. Third-party issuers. Some issuers may have their securities admitted to trading without having concluded an admission agreement with the market operator. The source of this possibility is Article L. 421-14(II) para. 2 of the Monetary and Financial Code, according to which equity or debt securities[174] already admitted to trading on a regulated market of a European Union Member State may be admitted to another market without the issuer's consent. However, the article specifies that 'in this case, the market operator shall inform the issuer, who shall not be under any obligation to inform the market operator'. This provision is based on the assumption that the obligations between the issuer wishing to have its securities admitted to the regulated market and the market operator managing the market have a contractual basis, since the issuer that has not entered into a contract is not subject to any obligations other than those contained in its contract for admission to trading.[175]

However, one author concludes that 'disclosure requirements are only part of the requirements that the issuer must fulfil under Article L. 421-14(I) of the Monetary and Financial Code. This is why market rules must impose additional constraints on the issuer, in order to ensure that listed securities comply with legal and regulatory obligations'.[176] The author cites in this sense Article 6.6 of Book I of the Euronext rules as well as Article 6.10 of the same rules relating to the principal of equal treatment between all shareholders.[177] However, this obligation to treat all shareholders equally[178] actually stems from MiFID[179] and is a common rule for all European regulated markets. This

174 Units or shares in collective investment schemes are therefore excluded from this rule.

175 This included the possibility for its securities to be admitted to another regulated market without its consent.

176 P. Barban, *Les entreprises de marché*, *op. cit.*, no. 146.

177 Art. 61003/1 of the Euronext Market Rules (Book I). In reality, this is less a question of the principle of equal treatment of shareholders (on the meaning of which see *infra*, para. 471) than a rule relating to the protection of investors making use of the financial market (cf. the use of the principle of equal treatment in the context of public offers, *infra*, para. 485).

178 It is true that it is present in the market rules, but only because the latter recall the applicable regulations. This is one of the conditions set out in Art. L. 421-10 of the Monetary and Financial Code for their approval by the Financial Markets Authority.

179 Art. 15(6°) MiFID (now Art. 18(8°) MiFID 2) for an issuer whose securities are admitted to trading on a regulated market, and whose securities are admitted 'without the issuer's consent' to a multilateral or organised trading facility (to use the words of MiFID above), Art. 40(5°) MiFID (now Art. 51(5°) MiFID 2) in the case of a regulated market In the latter case: 'An issuer shall not be obliged to provide the information required under paragraph 3 directly to a regulated market which has admitted its securities to trading *without its consent*.' Italics added. 'Directly', because in reality the issuer has already indirectly provided the information, by being already linked to another regulated market, the operator of

rule, by ensuring that shareholders will always be treated equally regardless of the place of admission to trading, allows securities to be listed on another EU regulated market without the issuer's consent. Without going so far as to suggest that the rules of EU regulated markets are fungible, they all respect a minimum level of harmonisation allowing for this multiple listing option within the EU without any additional obligation for the issuer. In other words, without the existence of this rule, the issuer's consent would have been required precisely in order to impose an obligation on him that the rules of the trading platform on which his instrument was admitted did not stipulate.[180] This is an illustration of the freedom-responsibility pair.

261. The market operator can even less compel the issuer that is not at the origin of the admission of its securities on its market, since the delisting of the securities on its own trading platform would have no direct effect on the admission to trading of the securities on the main trading venue. Only the market operator managing this trading venue will be able to effectively compel the issuer, and it will only be able to do so by virtue of the issuer's adherence to its

---

which may cooperate with the third regulated market. The information in paragraph 3 is that 'regulated markets shall establish and maintain effective arrangements to monitor compliance by issuers of securities which are admitted to trading on the regulated market with the requirements of Community law concerning initial, periodic and specific disclosure requirements'.

180 This is true throughout European financial law at different levels. Two examples are given here. The first concerns the Transparency Directive, which creates a number of disclosure obligations in financial matters, but only imposes them on the issuer if it has itself applied for admission of its financial securities, otherwise these disclosure obligations are incumbent on the person who has applied for admission of the financial securities (see e.g. Arts. 19 and 21 of the above-mentioned Directive). The second is Art. 19 of the Market Abuse Regulation which provides for certain information obligations of the issuer in order to prevent market abuse and facilitate its repression. Para. 4 of this Art. 19 conditions its applicability only to issuers having 'sought or approved the admission of their financial instruments' to a financial market: no consent to admission, no applicability of the legal provisions themselves.
This assessment is also reinforced when we look at the conditions under which the issuer can be held liable for defective information towards the purchaser of a financial security under English law. Two financial practices are therefore a source of difficulties: that which consists of grouping certain financial securities in an asset pool, the ownership of which is disseminated in the form of securities admitted to trading – this is the case, for example, with *depositary receipts* – and that which consists of creating financial securities the value of which is derived from other financial instruments (what some people refer to as derivative financial securities). In these cases, the liability of the issuer of the primary securities for the dissemination of defective information will only be accepted insofar as the issuer of the primary security had consented to the listing. See very clearly *Schedule 10A, paragraph 1(1)* of the *Financial Services and Market Act (Liability of Issuers) Regulations 2010*. As Mr Prorok writes, '[i]n other words, the issuer of the underlying security can only be liable to investors in the complex securities if it has consented to the admission to trading of the complex securities; otherwise, only the person who issued the complex securities can be liable to those investors, but only for the information it provides itself, not for that provided by the issuer of the underlying securities'. J. Prorok, *La responsabilité civile sur les marchés financiers*, LGDJ, Paris, 2019, no. 306.

local market rules. This perception is reinforced by an analysis of the provisions applicable to other financial markets. Indeed, what is true for European regulated markets among themselves is also true for financial markets attached to the same legal order: if a financial security were to be traded on a multilateral trading facility, or on an organised trading facility, French law explicitly states that the issuer would have no disclosure obligation towards these entities.[181] It is therefore incorrect to say that the market operator can impose obligations on third party issuers in the name of market rules. However, this statement does not prejudge the application of the relevant rules to non-member investors.

262. Non-member investors. Some authors consider that the decision-making power of the market operator is imposed on non-member investors who have purchased securities. The application of the Market Rules to these non-member investors is therefore incompatible with their contractual qualification.[182] This would be particularly true of the decision to suspend or delist securities, on the one hand, and to cancel transactions on the other.[183] However, two arguments contradict this statement.

Firstly, neither of these two decisions is exercised against non-member investors. Indeed, the decision to suspend and delist securities is exercised against the securities and primarily affects the issuer, while the decision to cancel transactions is aimed at relations between market members. However, issuers and market members are bound to the manager by a contract. Investors can undoubtedly be affected by these decisions. Nonetheless it is a feature of the economic interdependence of operators that the relations of one affect the prerogatives of the other. A subcontractor is likely to be affected by the prerogatives that the principal derives from his relationship with the main contractor; however, it has never been argued that the service contract was not a private law contract. These effects are undoubtedly particularly radical for securities holders in the case of the suspension or cancellation of the securities.

---

181 'When a financial instrument [...] is admitted to trading on a regulated market and is also traded on a multilateral trading facility *without the issuer's consent*, the issuer is not subject to any financial reporting obligations towards the operator of the facility.' Italics added. Art. L. 424-4 para. 2 of the Monetary and Financial Code for multilateral trading facilities, Art. L. 425-7 para. 2 of the Monetary and Financial Code for organised trading facilities.

182 Mr Barban writes that 'both the suspension and delisting decisions affect investors who are not contractually bound to the market operator', P. Barban, *Les entreprises de marché*, *op. cit.*, no. 147.

183 Other elements may be the reason for delisting. In the context of a regulated market, suspension may also be motivated by suspicions of market abuse (Art. 4403/3 of the Market Rules). Suspension and delisting of securities are not specific to the rules of regulated markets. The rules of Alternext Growth, a multilateral trading facility managed by Euronext, provide for the possibility of temporarily suspending the listing of an issuer's securities in the event of a breach of its obligations (Art. 7.3.1.(iv) of the Euronext Growth rules), but also the possibility of delisting (Art. 7.3.1.(iv) of the Euronext Growth rules), and provides for the application of the rules of the Euronext regulated market with regard to delisting of securities (Art. 7.3.1.(vi) of the Euronext Growth rules).

These developments allow two observations. First, as regards the jurisdiction of the law of the trading system, the manager's prerogatives over the trading of the security derive from the jurisdiction that the issuer has relinquished to it by admitting its securities.[184] In the same way that in property law, the *lex situs* determines the conditions of transfer of the property rights, the legal order of the market determines, on the one hand, the conditions of admission, listing and withdrawal of the security and, on the other hand, the conditions of conclusion of the transactions of which the security is likely to be the object. Secondly, in the same way that a tenant, if he is a third party to the co-ownership rules, is not a third party to the building,[185] the holder of a security admitted to trading, if he is a third party to the market rules, is not a third party to the trading system. He is necessarily subject to the 'infrastructure constraints'[186] linked to the mode of trading of the security held. However, the analogies borrowed from property law should not be misleading: the jurisdiction exercised by the trading system does not derive from any situation of the security at the place of listing, but exclusively from the original jurisdiction of the law of the issuer, and stops at the time of trading.[187]

263. Secondly, both these faculties originate not in the negotiation rules but in the law.[188] The trading rules merely reiterate the legal solutions, which are intended to ensure the proper functioning of the trading system. In the case of suspension or delisting of securities, the manager's decision-making power is aimed at preventing market abuse, violation of takeover bids regulations, or the short-selling regime.[189] The function of this cancellation power is to protect the trading system against distortions produced by obvious material errors of market members when submitting their orders. Truly differentiated from the civil law of

---

184 For a reminder of the phenomenon at work in the area of securities settlement, see *infra*, no. 664.

185 The expression is inspired by a formula of Professor Atias who considers that tenants are 'third parties to the agreement', but not 'third parties to the building', C. Atias, *Droit civil, Les biens*, 11th ed., Paris, LexisNexis, 2011, p. 306.

186 L. d'Avout, 'L'entreprise et les conflits internationaux de lois', *op. cit.*, nos. 163 et seq.

187 On the effective transfer of the title and the law applicable to its property status in general, see *infra*, paras. 570 et seq.

188 In the case of suspension and delisting of securities, this is covered by Art. L. 420-10(I) of the Monetary and Financial Code. These prerogatives could have had a purely contractual basis, stemming from the listing contract with the issuer. The situation is more delicate with regard to the cancellation of transactions. The legal basis for this prerogative was Art. L. 421-16-1(I) of the Monetary and Financial Code, which was repealed by Order 2016-827 of 23 June 2016. Nevertheless, Art. 514-4 of the AMF General Regulation still provides that 'the market rules shall provide for the conditions under which the market operator is empowered to cancel one or more transactions or, in exceptional cases, manifestly erroneous or irregular transactions'.

189 Art. L. 420-10(I) of the Monetary and Financial Code.

contracts (*droit commun des contrats*),[190] the implementation of this prerogative is done in a distinct way for securities[191] and contracts.[192] Nevertheless it has in

---

190 Until recently, private contract law did not allow the contracting parties to cancel their contract or to transfer to a third party this option, which is devolved to the judge, who alone can observe that one of the conditions of validity is missing. The co-contracting parties could only *terminate* their contract by mutual agreement, with the possibility of *a posteriori* judicial review. Today they can cancel it by mutual agreement, cf. Art. 1178 of the Civil Code.

191 The basis for this is Article 4403/3 of the Euronext Market Rules (Book I). This is common to all regulated markets managed by Euronext within the EU. Article 4403/3 distinguishes between cancellations that take place at the initiative of the market operator or following a request from 'one of the counterparties', i.e. not the originator, but the market member. In the first case, recorded transactions may be cancelled if they were made '(i) in breach of these rules, in particular those relating to the functioning of a fair, orderly and efficient market; or (ii) under incorrect trading conditions; or (iii) as a result of an obvious material error'. Furthermore, the market operator, when cancelling on its own initiative, may cancel transactions made on the central order book, but also those resulting from trading outside the central order book: block trades come to mind. In the latter case, if a market member requests the cancellation of a trade, the cancellation can only be made if the trade was concluded at an aberrant price, or 'on the basis of explanations provided by the member concerned'.

192 The Market Rules distinguish between the cancellation by the market operator of a transaction 'made or intended' (Art. 5403/1 of the Market Rules), and that made in error, concerning 'certain Derivative Instruments' (Art. 5403/2 of the Market Rules). In both cases, the conditions for cancellation may be set out in the national market rules or in the trading procedures, which do not seem to distinguish between them. As far as Euronext Paris is concerned, the Book II rules are silent and it is the trading procedures that govern the issue, which themselves refer to a Euronext instruction (Art. 3.5 of the trading procedures). The only instruction on this subject is Instruction 4-02. This instruction provides for the invalidation of a trade made at an 'unrepresentative price' (see Instruction 3.03, cited above) and sets out the procedures for determining whether prices are representative (Instruction 3.04, cited above). The Instruction also provides for the possibility of cancellation on a broader basis, explicitly recalling the terms of Art. 4403/3 of the Market Rules (Instruction cited above, no. 3.05: 'In addition, in accordance with Rule 4403 and/ or Rule 5403, the Relevant Euronext Market operator reserves the right to declare a trade invalid if it determines, in its absolute discretion, that such a trade does not permit the fair, orderly and efficient operation of the market.'). Finally, the Instruction provides for the possibility of a cancellation resulting from the request of a market member on the basis of a non-representative price; consequently, such a request is subject to the same modalities concerning the evaluation of a non-representative price as if the initiative came from the market operator. In this case of a request from a market member, the procedural terms considerably limit the scope of the request: the request is limited to an extremely short period of time – operators have thirty minutes to contact the market operator – and is not free of charge (they must pay two hundred and fifty euros per order issued, up to a maximum of two thousand and five hundred euros per day, cf. instructions nos. 13 and 14. If the request is made on the basis of an obvious error in a securities transaction, the sum is as high as five thousand euros, up to a maximum of fifty thousand euros per day. This means that the charge is significant and allows the procedure to be initiated only for amounts that are also significant.) Finally, there is another possibility of requesting cancellation by a market member, but which is only possible on the securities market, and that is again manifest error (Instruction cited above, no. 3.11). The exclusion of transactions in financial contracts from the scope of cancellation for manifest error at the request of a member probably stems from the fact that it is more difficult to determine what a manifest

common with the former that it can take place at the initiative of the manager or the member and that it can be justified by the aberrant price at which the order was transmitted. This substantive condition is reminiscent of the civil law lesion,[193] thus making it less alien to the spirit of French contract law.[194]

264. Conclusion of the chapter. At the end of this chapter, it appears that market infrastructures are based on systems, made up of rules designed to enable their members to interact in order to conclude transactions. However, these systems are also called upon to coordinate with each other to ensure the smooth functioning of the financial markets. This coordination is achieved by means of contracts between system managers. However, the purpose of each system tends to set them apart, not only because they are likely to be subject to their own regime, but also because the function pursued justifies separate supervision. At the same time, it has been argued that these systems are fundamentally contracts. Neither the legal obligation to establish system rules nor approval has the effect of modifying the contractual nature of the rules. The obligation to establish rules, while it is an element in the identification of acts of private regulation, above all justifies its existence in that systems cannot function without rules, and therefore contributes to the characterisation of the concept of system. The purpose of approval is not to alter the contractual nature of system rules, but to give them the status of professional rules. This status enables the regulatory authority to hold system members administratively liable in the event of a breach. Lastly, the regime of trading rules is not incompatible with ordinary contract law, but rather has the characteristics of a special contract.

---

error means in the context of financial contracts. The cancellation of transactions concerning financial contracts is not a textbook case; the ombudsman of the Financial Markets Authority reports having been petitioned on this subject, the report is available on the ombudsman's blog, see https://www.amf-france.org/blogs/blog-mediateur/Ordre-de-bourse-ex-cut----un--cours-aberrant----Euronext-peut-annuler-la-transaction-dans-des-cas-exceptionnels0, last access on 23 July 18).

193 See the former Art. 1118 of the Civil Code which enshrined lesion, while requiring textual support in the special law. Although the principle is no longer enshrined in the general regime, the special law of contracts has retained this mechanism, the best known example being that of the sale of real property which allows rescission for lesion if the seller has been harmed by more than seven twelfths of the price (Art. 1674 of the Civil Code). The desire for a general application of lesion was nevertheless largely tempered by the adage in the old law that the hazard drives out lesion.

194 It is interesting to note that American case law has reached similar results in the area of civil liability, but at significantly lower thresholds (see J. Prorok, *La responsabilité civile sur les marchés financiers*, *op. cit.)* The Supreme Court judges have created a system of presumption in this area, leading to the possibility of a liability action under such favourable conditions that some specialists have wondered 'if the information, even when it is defective, is reflected in the price, why not dispense with the notion of *reliance* and simply consider that the investor paid too much (or received too little) for the purchase or sale of a security in view of the overvaluation or undervaluation of the price?'

CHAPTER 2
THE APPLICABLE CONFLICT RULES

The rules of conflict are not identical from one system to another: while regulated markets are connected to the law of the seat of their manager, the systems subject to the Finality Directive use a connecting factor based on the law of autonomy. Such a criterion, designed for exchange contracts, does not allow an adjusted connecting factor of organisational contracts. This is one of the reasons why, on the one hand, trading systems should all be subject to the law of the seat of their manager (Section 1) and, on the other hand, the connecting factor of systems subject to the Finality Directive appears unsatisfactory (Section 2).

SECTION 1. THE LAW APPLICABLE TO TRADING SYSTEMS

We will present here the solution of the MiFID 2 Directive, applicable only to regulated markets (§ 1), before showing the reasons which push for its analogical extension to all trading systems (§ 2).

§ 1. THE APPLICATION TO REGULATED MARKETS OF THE LAW OF THE SEAT OF THE MANAGER

265. The MiFID 2 solution. Article 44(4) of the MiFID 2 Directive[1] contains a conflict rule for regulated markets which states:

> 'Without prejudice to any relevant provisions of Regulation (EU) No 596/2014 or of Directive 2014/57/EU, the public law governing the trading conducted under the systems of the regulated market shall be that of the home Member State of the regulated market.'

1 Taken from Art. 36(4) MiFID.

The home Member State of the regulated market is defined by Article 2(55)(b) of MiFID 2 as 'the Member State in which the regulated market is registered or, if under national law it has no registered office, the Member State in which the head office of the regulated market is situated'. This ambivalent rule requires several clarifications.

The first relates to the criterion used. At first sight, one might consider that the particular administrative authorisation to which the regulated market is subject, distinct from other financial markets, and which Article 44(4) seems to refer to as 'registration', is equivalent to a legislative connecting factor to the legal order of the administration that granted it.[2] In other words, from the French point of view, the notion of registration would correspond to ministerial recognition, which is equivalent to a legislative connecting factor to French law. However, this interpretation must be rejected. In reality, the notion of registration does not refer to the administrative decision, but to the notion of *registered office*, i.e. it refers to the notion of registration of the legal person. This interpretation is confirmed by the use of the criterion of central administration in Article 2(55)(b) of MiFID 2 to designate the seat of groups without legal personality, i.e. without a *registered office*. However, as the regulated market is a variety of trading system, the rule demonstrates some confusion between the operator and its system. This confusion, already present in the MiFID 2 definition of regulated market, stems from the diversity of the organisation of regulated markets in Europe. Since the Court of Justice had the opportunity to clearly distinguish the system from the market operator, it must be deduced, in accordance with what is suggested by Article 2(55)(b) of MiFID 2 to which Article 44(4) of the same directive refers, that it is the market operator that is covered by the latter rule. The seat of the market operator is therefore the connecting factor for regulated markets.

The second clarification relates to the 'public law' characterisation of the trading rules. This is a reference to the German model, where the market operator is a public law body.[3] The German doctrine extends the public law characterisation to the rules of the organisation of the trading system issued by the public body,[4] while it reserves the private law characterisation for

2 In this sense, B. Audit and L. d'Avout, *Droit international privé*, *op. cit.*, no. 1059, who consider that 'administrative approval is equivalent to a connection to a whole legal order'; see also L. d'Avout, 'Les phénomènes collectifs et l'analyse macro en droit international privé' in *Mélanges en l'honneur du professeur Bertrand Ancel*, Paris, LGDJ, 2018, no. 26; L. d'Avout, 'L'entreprise et les conflits internationaux de lois', *op. cit.*, no. 176.

3 K. Deckert, *La sollicitation publique des investisseurs en droit communautaire, français et allemand*, *op. cit.* The author quotes BörsG, § 2 para. 1.

4 Distinct from the organisation of a market operator, which under French law is a legal entity whose organisational arrangements are subject to the Commercial Code and the Monetary and Financial Code.

market operations only.[5] This reference to the German model is particularly unfortunate for three reasons. First, it maintains an administrative perception of the financial market itself, whereas MiFID has had the effect of making the market a private law model.[6] Secondly, the public nature of the organisation should not influence the contractual nature of the organisation's rules, *a fortiori* given that the European regulated markets are largely managed by a group of private law trading companies, which itself develops the trading rules within the limits established by law and under the supervision of the supervisors.[7] Finally, the scope of trading rules is no longer the status of intermediaries, but a set of elements far removed from the traditional domain of public law, since these rules regulate price setting, the trading cycle, the currency of the latter, the matching of orders and other aspects relating to the modes of formation of private contracts.

266. Restricted material scope. Curiously, the rule in Article 44(4) of MiFID 2 is restricted to regulated markets. Such a limitation of the scope could have been explained by the specific features of the regulation of market transactions on regulated markets, whether it be the regulation of threshold crossings or the obligation to file a public offer. However, these requirements do not reflect the solution adopted for two reasons: multilateral trading facilities are likely to have identical mechanisms that are simply triggered at different thresholds;[8] organised trading facilities only allow the conclusion of financial contracts, making these particularities inoperative in the latter case. Similarly, the Market Abuse Regulation applies equally to all three categories of trading systems.[9]

It could be argued that this restriction is due to prudential obligations or specific constraints arising from Title III of MiFID 2, and covers Article 44. However, these obligations also exist, but to a lesser extent, for other financial markets: their managers are subject to prudential rules specific to investment firms. MiFID 2 also provides for rules on the suspension or delisting of financial instruments and other rules specific to the system operated.[10] This is also the reason why the restriction of the solution of Article 44(4) MiFID 2 cannot find a satisfactory basis in the difference of manager. The real explanation for the rule probably lies in the historical distinction between the 'official list' and the 'free market', a distinction that is still reflected today in the special administrative authorisation required to obtain regulated market status.

267. However, there is now no longer a difference in kind between regulated markets and other multilateral trading facilities, but mainly a difference in

---

5 Recall the former French system as presented by Mr Chemaly *supra*, para. 47.

6 See on the private model P. Barban, *Les entreprises de marché*, *op. cit.*, para. 192.

7 See *supra*, paras. 13 and 119.

8 See *infra*, note under para. 490.

9 Art. 2(1) of the Market Abuse Regulation, on which see *infra*, para. 524.

10 Arts. 31 and 32 MiFID 2.

degree. This is reflected in the constraints imposed on issuers admitting their securities to trading and on market members during trading. On the other hand, the rules on investors (trading and market abuse) are tending to be homogenised, regardless of the financial market in question. It seems to us that this alignment of the regime stems from the fact that, in these cases, the objective of financial market law is to ensure that the market functions properly, and in particular to preserve the quality of the price discovery mechanism. For this reason, the trend in the future will continue to be the gradual broadening of the material scope of the rules on market transactions.[11] Therefore, in our view, there is no reason to distinguish between different financial markets in order to make an international connecting factor of their trading rules.

§ 2. THE LAW APPLICABLE TO OTHER TRADING SYSTEMS

268. Two possible solutions. MiFID 2 did not provide for a conflict rule applicable to multilateral trading facilities and organised trading facilities. Two solutions are therefore possible. The first is to extend the rule in Article 44(4) of MiFID 2 by analogy and apply the law of the seat of the operator to all trading systems. The second is to take seriously the contractual characterisation of system rules and to subject them to the Rome I Regulation. It seems to us that the first solution should prevail, for several reasons. The first reason stems from the above developments: there is no reason to distinguish between trading systems, which all have the same purpose, the proper functioning of the market they operate, and are concerned with the same object, negotiations between market members. Moreover, the criterion of the manager's headquarters deserves approval: it is the centre of gravity of the financial market since, on the one hand, all members and issuers have a link with it, on the other hand, it operates the trading platform and, finally, it is the originator of these rules. In addition, the market operator will inevitably offer its trading system to issuers and investment firms in the location of its head office. This gives the organisation in question a particularly strong foothold at the market operator's headquarters. The latter will be the competent legal authority for the protection of investors who may be solicited, and whose *lex societatis* will apply to the status of issuers who have admitted their securities to trading.

---

11 Since the regulation of company share buy-backs depends on the Market Abuse Regulation, it already covers all financial markets (see Arts. 2.1 and 5 of the Market Abuse Regulation). The Short Selling Regulation applies to regulated markets and multilateral trading facilities (see Art. 1 and Art. 2.1 of the Short Selling Regulation); the exclusion of organised trading facilities is due to the fact that no financial securities are traded there. On the scope of application of these two regulations, see respectively *infra*, paras. 513 and 515.

269. Singularity of the systems in terms of conflict of laws. The second reason is the difference in function between contractual classification in domestic law and in private international law. In this case, it does not mean application of the contractual regime, but submission to the connecting factor of the Rome I Regulation. The latter is singularly unsuited to negotiation rules. This can be explained, it seems, by a distinction made in domestic contract law between exchange contracts and organisational contracts.[12] Indeed, the law of autonomy was designed to solve the difficulties caused by the localisation of exchange contracts for which it was sometimes difficult to determine a preponderant legal centre of gravity for the contractual relationship. Traditionally, the law of autonomy justified its existence by the doubt it removed as to the place of legal establishment, and by the legal certainty it gave to the contracting parties by expressly designating the applicable law; the liberal nature of this connecting factor being tempered by the possible application of mandatory rules.[13] The situation is not the same when an organisational contract is involved,[14] for at least three reasons.

Firstly, the predominant legal location of the contract will most often be the headquarters of the organisation, i.e. the place where the organisation's decision-making centre is located.[15] There is little doubt as to the location of the organisation in question. As the physical element of the financial market has been dematerialised, and the location of computer servers is not a satisfactory criterion, it does not enjoy the support that other organisations may have. To take two similar examples already developed, the building is undoubtedly a privileged link in the co-ownership regulations, and legal personality in the articles of association. However, the legal centre of gravity of the financial market has not shifted.

270. Secondly, organisational contracts do not tolerate the interference of a foreign law within the organisation, making the overriding mandatory

---

12 On the basis of this distinction with ancient roots see F. Chénedé, *Les commutations en droit privé*, Economica, 2008. It should be added here that, as Professor Paul Didier has observed, the notion of organisational contract is not the same as that of multilateral contract: 'No doubt many organisational contracts are multilateral contracts. But companies or associations may comprise only two partners or members, not to mention the marital community, which our laws and morals require to be exclusively bilateral. And conversely, exchange contracts may well be collective contracts, as is the case when several people sell or buy the same property.' P. Didier, 'Brèves notes sur le contrat organisation', *op. cit.*, pp. 636–637.

13 Y. Lequette, *Les mutations du droit international privé: vers un changement de paradigme?*, RCADI, vol. 387, 2017, no. 63.

14 In this sense, it is not anecdotal that a number of organisational contracts are expressly excluded from the scope of application of the Rome I Regulation (Art. 1(2)), such as partnership contracts, matrimonial property regimes, or trusts.

15 This most often corresponds to the legal centre of gravity of the activity. A difficulty arises as soon as the organisation is decentralised, see in this respect the difficulties caused by the *blockchain*, see *infra*, paras. 740 et seq.

rules method (*lois de police*)[16] of little use. Indeed, the singularity of the law applicable to the internal relations of an organisation is the condition for its proper functioning.[17] This is why the application of a foreign law to an element of the internal organisation of the financial market, whether in the rules of negotiation applicable between market members, or in the disciplinary relations maintained by the market operator and the market, never arises. Here, the law of the financial market is not in competition with others.

271. Thirdly, some contractual organisations are of crucial importance to the legal order in which they are located, and do not stand up well to legislative remoteness. Their interest goes beyond that of their members and is of use to the legal order itself. This is the case for system rules in general, and for negotiation rules in particular, although the statement should be nuanced according to the negotiation system in question. This is why the exercise of choice of law, while possible in principle, will be likely to be thwarted whenever an administrative authority exercises supervision over the organisation in question. This is the case for negotiation rules: the manager is encouraged to submit these rules to French law, at the risk of being refused the approval necessary for their entry into force. It is easy to see the artifice to which the law of autonomy leads here, and it would be distressing to return[18] to the use of a public law characterisation or to the tutelage of an administrative authority in the exercise of the choice of law because private international law would be unable to take account of the singularity of certain contractual organisations.[19]

272. Finally, as Mr d'Avout has already pointed out, the connecting factor of organisations constitutes a support point for the legislative attachment of inter-individual situations, allowing the articulation of individual situations and the collective interest of the organisation. The author thus writes: 'the legal phenomena triggered around these organisations expose superimpositions of regimes; as if inter-individual relations (subject to their own law) could be attached to or detached from organisations which themselves come under a

16 See the observations of Mr d'Avout on personified organisations: 'Within the entity governed by the law that has been assigned to it, emancipating the relationship between two members (through the effect of a shareholders' agreement, for example) by subjecting it to an arbitrary law of allegiance risks, once again, giving rise to artificial conflicts and seeing the law of the bilateral relationship supplanted by the standards of public policy specific to the collective organisation', L. D'AVOUT, 'Les phénomènes collectifs et l'analyse macro en droit international privé', *op. cit.*, no. 23. In fact, it may be thought that any organisation, whether contractual or legal, does not tolerate the interference of a mandatory rule within its internal statute, see the organisation of collective proceedings *infra*, para. 914.

17 The unique application of the law of the organisation is sometimes ensured by the exclusivity of the jurisdiction of local courts, see in company law *supra*, para. 90.

18 See *supra*, para. 47 and the presentation of the old French system by Mr Chemaly.

19 L. D'AVOUT, 'Les phénomènes collectifs et l'analyse macro en droit international privé', *op. cit.*, no. 2: 'The collective is not the monopoly of public law, if public law is still clearly distinct from private law, so that private international law had to take it into account.'

singular legal regime of collective essence'.[20] In these cases, organisations may constitute a propitious support for the projection, by the legal order to which they are attached, of its legislative policy because of the set of issues that they make it possible to deal with through a single attachment.[21] These developments lead to two observations.

First of all, although not all systems result in the application of the law of the system to transactions concluded within it,[22] it should be noted that the law of the trading system is precisely the basis for part of the legislation relating to market operations, which it is difficult to imagine being deactivated by the manager's choice of law as regards system rules.[23] The regulation of market operations will most often make the use or allocation of the trading system the trigger for its material and international application. Under these circumstances, the connecting factor of market rules to the legal order of the manager's seat, which is the predominant legal order, contributes to the harmonious resolution of conflicts of law arising from market operations. This is why we agree with Mr d'Avout's observation that: 'The best possible use of *electio juris* is that which arbitrates conflicts of law by designating a legal system objectively endowed with a pre-existing (and strong) title of jurisdiction.'[24]

Secondly, it is possible that the legal order to which a system is attached wishes to use its importance for those who use it to impose a legislative policy that is not directly related to the field of system rules. This is the case today with the US interbank clearing system, the use of which for transactions prohibited by the US leads to the application of US sanctions.[25] This use is contested, and some authors consider that it is an extraterritorial connecting factor, even contrary to public international law.[26] On the contrary, it seems to us that the connecting factor of the system to the legal order is narrow, and that it is

---

20 *Ibid.*, no. 27.

21 Some authors believe that the function of these market infrastructures is precisely to unify the law applicable to a set of commercial relations. See J. Basedow, '*The Law of Open Societies*, *op. cit.*, no. 141, who sees the emergence of clearing houses in this sense, among others.

22 The rules of the clearing system provide in certain cases for the application of a foreign law to the contracts being cleared, see *infra*, no. 887. There is no absolute link of dependence between the law of the system and the law of the transactions concluded. *Contra* F. Drummond, *Droit financier*, *op. cit.*, no. 932, who considers that the approval of system rules has the effect of making 'the law of the regulator competent to approve the system rules the law applicable to the transactions carried out, cleared or settled by the system'.

23 It will be shown in the second part that the law of the trading system would be better served as the sole criterion for linking all legislation relating to the crossing of thresholds, public offers, etc. (see *infra*, paras. 466 et seq.)

24 L. d'Avout, 'Les phénomènes collectifs et l'analyse macro en droit international privé', *op. cit.*

25 See United States District Court, Southern District of New York, *US v. BNP*, Statement of Facts, 28 June 2014, nos. 34 et seq.

26 In this sense, M. Audit, R. Bismuth and A. Mignon-Colombet, 'Sanctions et extraterritorialité du droit américain: quelles réponses pour les entreprises françaises?', *JCP G*, 12 January 2015, pp. 37 et seq.

not unforeseeable that a country would not want the payment infrastructures subject to its protection to be used to violate its most imperative regulations.[27]

273. The relationship with foreign trading systems. These developments on the rationale for using as a connecting factor the manager's headquarters for negotiation rules extend their rationality to relations with foreign negotiation systems. Indeed, when a foreign organisational contract is involved, the question of its international treatment arises less in terms of applicable law than in terms of recognition. The example of companies has been studied at length, so we will not return to it. Instead, we would like to emphasise that relations with foreign negotiation systems are also based on recognition.[28] Admittedly, this recognition takes place under the condition of having equivalent substantial rules.[29] Nevertheless, the method used is significant and shows, it seems, that the development of foreign organisation will make it increasingly difficult to subject them to the conflict rule method, without making it easier to reason from the perspective of recognition of foreign decisions. The explanation probably lies in the fact that organisational contracts are not soluble within the distinction between rules and decisions, that partially fund the distinction between those two methods (conflict rule and recognition), simply because the development of contractual organisation gradually brings them closer to the notion of a legal order, requiring 'en bloc' recognition. The latter must therefore be recognised or ignored as such.[30] Indeed, there is probably more a difference in degree than in kind between an organisation and a legal order. In the same way that the sophistication of a contractual whole can lead to a real organisation,[31] the organisational contract can, from a certain degree of sophistication, be considered as an imperfect legal order.[32] The relationship with foreign negotiation systems echoes this.

---

27 See L. d'Avout, *D.*, 2014, 1967, obs. under *United States of America v. BNP Paribas SA*.

28 See *supra*, paras. 209 and 212.

29 See *supra*, para. 210.

30 See S. Lambert, *L'application internationale du droit financier*, *op. cit.*, 1408; comp. B. Haftel, *La notion de matière contractuelle en droit international privé*, thesis. Université Panthéon-Assas, 2008, no. 543, which considers the organisational contract to be in general conformity with the purpose of the principle of autonomy.

31 Through pre-contracts, framework contracts, dispute resolution clauses, etc., the company is able to provide the best possible service.

32 S. Romano, *L'ordre juridique*, *op. cit.*, para. 33, spec. no. 5, p. 105: 'Perfect or imperfect institutions', where the author states that 'from an analogous point of view, we can distinguish *perfect institutions, which are always original* and which may be simple or complex, *from imperfect ones, which are based on others*, not only of presupposition, *but of coordination or subordination.*; but they are merely coordinated with the former or are not entirely subordinate to them. [...]'. Emphasis added. On the same page, the author notes, significantly, institutions with or without personality: 'It is still of some interest to our research to distinguish between institutions which, for one thing or another, are endowed with juridical personality, and those which are devoid of it. The former have their own power to which their members, whether individuals or institutions, remain subject, and

274. Section conclusion. Regulated markets are linked to the country of their registered office. This objective connecting factor (as distinct from subjective connecting factor) should be approved. It reflects the centrality of the country of the operator in the location of the system, and should be extended by analogy to all trading systems. Indeed, if systems are contracts, they are nevertheless organisational contracts, a category for which the law of autonomy sometimes shows its limits. Above all, in the case of systems, far from resolving the conflict of laws, the law of autonomy is likely to increase them whenever it is used to designate a legal order distinct from that of the manager. It will therefore create a disjunction between the law applicable to inter-individual situations, for which the 'preponderant legal order'[33] will not necessarily allow its legislative policy to be paralysed by the choice of a separate law.

SECTION 2. THE LAW APPLICABLE TO PAYMENT, CLEARING AND DELIVERY SYSTEMS FOR SECURITIES

275. The conflict-of-laws rule of the Finality Directive. Payment, clearing and delivery systems for securities are subject to the conflict rule in Article 2(a) of the Finality Directive, which states that:

> '*(a system is)* governed by the legislation of a Member State chosen by the participants; however, participants may only choose the legislation of a Member State in which at least one of them has its registered office.'

This rule is consistent with the contractual analysis of the systems adopted by the Finality Directive itself since it is an avatar of the conflict-of-laws rule in contractual matters. However, this rule has two differences with the rule of the Rome Convention and the Rome I Regulation: the designation of the applicable law is doubly limited since it must be both the law of a Member State and that of one of the participants in the system. This double limitation, which is reminiscent of the limited freedom of choice of law in American law, where the designated law must be related to the contract,[34] is explained by the substantial harmonisation achieved by the Directive. Indeed, the freedom of choice of law can flourish insofar as it leads to the application of a law that has transposed the rules of the Directive itself, and in particular those

---

which represents the basis of their organisation. The latter, on the contrary, do not have such a power.' The perfection of the legal order does not, however, affect its subordination to the state legal order.

33 In the words of B. Achinard-Greil, *Lois de police et conflits de juridictions*, *op. cit.*, no. 10.

34 Restatement Second on the Conflict of Laws, 1971, para. 187.

relating to the preservation of the effects of insolvency proceedings against the transactions of a participant. From the point of view of the European legislator, freedom of choice therefore appears to be artificial, since it is only possible insofar as it adopts its own prescriptions: the selection of the law of a third State, even that of a participant, is prohibited. From the manager's point of view, European law is marked by a favourable regime that conditions the advantages of the service it offers to its participants; it is hard to understand why it would want to free itself from it.

276. For the application of the law of the manager's headquarters. It therefore seems that the developments related to the organisational character of trading systems can be extended to all systems, and that a unitary and objective conflict rule linking trading systems to the manager's headquarters would be more appropriate. This is all the more true since the regime established by the Finality Directive undoubtedly makes the contracts constituted by the systems special contracts (*contrats spéciaux*), and probably even more crucial for the legal order in which they are inserted. Moreover, like the negotiation system, the systems of the Finality Directive are themselves a possible support for the transactions concluded in them.[35] This will be demonstrated in the third part: the law applicable to the clearing system already constitutes the legislative support for the vast majority of financial contracts that make use of this infrastructure. The unfortunate thing is, however, that despite its fundamental importance, the securities settlement system does not constitute the proprietary connecting factor of financial securities; this leads to a profound dysfunction of the conflict of laws solutions.

277. Conclusion of the chapter. At the end of this chapter, we have shown that regulated markets are subject to the legal order of the manager's registered office and that this connecting factor would benefit from being extended to all trading systems and Finality Directive systems, the latter being subject to an avatar of the conflict-of-laws rule in contractual matters. This extension is justified firstly because the system rules are organisational contracts and the manager's registered office is the legal centre of gravity of these organisations. It is also justified because of the crucial importance of these contracts for the legal order in which these organisations are embedded and, secondly, because these organisations constitute the privileged support of the legislative policy of the prevailing legal order with regard to the inter-individual transactions that these systems make possible.

[35] This is especially true of the securities settlement system, which should constitute the linkage of the property status of financial securities; the clearing system, on the other hand, is more inclined to allow for a dissociation of the law applicable to the transactions concluded therein, see *infra*, para. 887.

278. Conclusion of title. We have shown that the systems on which market infrastructures are based are, from a legal point of view, contracts whose function is to organise the relationships of this community composed of the members of the system, the manager and, where applicable, the issuers whose securities are admitted to it. While each system has its own function, which justifies a specific regime, their coordination is necessary to allow the smooth functioning of the financial market and, in particular, to neutralise the risk of settlement failure. As each system is connected to a legal order, their international coordination is carried out by a contractual organisation under private law under the aegis of the European System of Central Banks. This organisation, without being a system, allows the articulation of national systems. Their importance justifies the supervision of an administrative authority, but this is exercised in a different way depending on the system in question. However, their connecting factor is not uniform: regulated markets are connected to the legal system of the headquarters of their manager, while payment, clearing and securities settlement systems are connected to the legal system they designate, with certain reservations. Nevertheless, the connecting factor based on the conflict rule from contract law is not suitable for systems. Indeed, system rules are organisational contracts, a category of contract for which the choice of law appears unsuitable. The manager's registered office is their legal centre of gravity. Moreover, these contracts are of crucial importance for the legal order in which these organisations are inserted. Finally, they are the privileged support of the legislative policy of the preponderant legal order as regards the inter-individual transactions that these systems allow to be concluded.

279. Conclusion of the first part. This section has allowed us to immerse ourselves in the organisation of the financial markets in order to observe the ways in which infrastructures are linked. The introductory chapter showed how the financial markets had historically been linked to the State legal order, and then how their development made it possible to distinguish between the manager of the trading system, the trading system and the securities clearing and settlement systems and, finally, to diversify the trading systems, giving rise to modern infrastructures. It has been observed that these infrastructures are now part of an interlocking supervisory system at national and European level.

These introductory observations have made it possible to study the international status of infrastructure managers, which is divided into a legislative and an administrative connecting factor. The legislative connecting factor of managers is through the head office, and gives formidable force to the legislation of the seat, which extends beyond company law to prudential and insolvency law. The particular configuration of market managers has made it possible to refine the understanding of the function of the registered office for each of these laws: while it aims to apply the rules of organisation of the place where management is exercised, the application of the criterion of the registered office in the case of prudential law really aims at the protection of third parties. Finally, in the case of insolvency, the real seat criterion reflects the legitimacy of the legislative policy of the legal order which is predominantly affected by the entity's failure. In the latter case, infrastructure managers are subject to a special insolvency regime constituted by resolution law. The latter is based on a universal application of the bankruptcy law of the seat, tempered by the application of foreign laws to certain institutions, including, significantly, systems constituting market infrastructures.

The originality of the infrastructure managers' connecting factor also lies in the fact that they are the subject of a genuine administrative connecting factor. It has been shown that there is a tension between two models, one decentralised to the administration of the Member State where the manager has its headquarters, which is traditional and still in the majority, and the other, centralised to an EU agency, which is applicable as soon as the manager is subject to a banking licence. Each of these models entails the competence of the administrative order of the body granting the authorisation. The particularity of the centralised model is, however, that it breaks the parallelism of the connecting factors between competent authority and applicable law, and it has therefore been possible to propose methods of coordination between the European legal orders based on certain mechanisms known from private international law, such as *forum legis*. The decentralised model also requires coordination between competent authorities when an operator wishes to provide its services on the territory of another Member State, whether in terms of triggering the notification procedure or locating the rules of conduct. It was found that the criteria of private international contract law were ineffective, and that the objectives of internal market integration and investor protection of the legislative package in question were better served by the concept of solicitation.

Market operators from third countries cannot in principle provide their services on EU territory without being subject to EU legislation and supervision. However, the EU proceeds to the self-limitation of its law in different hypotheses depending on the foreign systems involved, in particular whenever foreign legislation and supervision are declared equivalent to that of the EU. This method of equivalence has as its function the coordination of legal orders in order to allow relations between private persons, and is therefore subject to the tension inherent in the objectives of private international law: it is liable to be competed with or crowded out by the objectives and interests of the European legislative bodies whose equivalence is sought.

The connecting factor between systems is not unequivocal. The systems that make up market infrastructures are now based on a material element, the computer tool that enables transactions to be concluded between members, and a legal element, the system rules themselves. The latter are private law contracts organising the relationships between their members and, where applicable, organising the conditions for the admission of issuers' securities.

However, their sources are divided into two legislative instruments, MiFID 2 and the Finality Directive. The former, applicable to trading systems, connects regulated markets to the law of the headquarters of their operator, and is silent on the law applicable to other trading systems. The second, applicable to payment, clearing and settlement systems, establishes a contractual conflict rule. However, it seemed to us, on the one hand, that the differences in the regimes of the systems do not justify a difference in treatment in terms of conflict of laws and, on the other hand, that the objective connecting factor to the law of the seat of the operator appeared preferable to any other.

It has been observed that the regime attached to each of these systems also dictates the regime of the transactions that make use of them. Nevertheless, it is necessary to delimit, according to the systems in question, the scope of the different bodies of private law legislation that are based on these systems. Their international scope of application can usefully be deduced from the objective they pursue. Before examining the status of financial instruments, we will look at the status of financial markets: it is necessary to define the scope of the law in order to identify the cases where it is truly applied on the basis of an objective specific to the trading platform.

PART 2.
The Scope of Financial Market Law

280. From the foregoing, it should be noted that the financial market is a multilateral trading system, distinct from its operator, but that the connecting factor of the latter dictates that of the former. However, it is this system, i.e. the trading platform, and not the operator, that is likely to constitute the connecting factor of the law of the financial market. In other words, as Mr Daigre has written, if the financial market is 'an organisation and a mechanism',[1] it is the law applicable to this second aspect that forms the basis for the law of transactions between private persons who use it. However, it is necessary to delimit the hypotheses where, precisely, the law of the financial market truly aims to protect the mechanism it has instituted. Indeed, the law of the financial market is deployed in distinct ways, and according to a different regime, depending on whether its object is relations with issuers or with investors. In its dealings with issuers, this law is most often applied under its objective of investor protection and as the law of the place of solicitation. In fact, the rules which seek to protect the savings of residents could probably be integrated into a single category, the connecting factor of which would be based on a material criterion, that of the solicitation of residents. The regime of these rules would allow them to be self-limiting when the issuer's law also provides for their application and when they are equivalent. In its dealings with investors, however, the law of the financial market pursues the objective of the proper functioning of the financial market. The latter is also likely to allow for the establishment of a synthetic category, which could this time be bilateral and based on the trading platform.

281. The relationship with issuers. From the issuer's point of view, the admission of securities to trading on a financial market aims to collect savings where that market is embedded. In an inevitable movement, the legislation of the legal order within which the financial market is embedded reacts.[2] This reaction is based on three types of measures. The first relates to the securities issued. Here, the pre-eminence of the issuer's prescriptive jurisdiction as to the conditions of the issue, the form of the securities and their *negotium* is complete. This is precisely the reason why the financial market law will make the admission of securities conditional on the issuer itself amending the form of the securities and the clauses of the articles of association which may restrict their negotiability. The objective here is both the proper functioning of trading and the protection of investors.

The second measures concern the information requirements that are intended to inform investors about the issuer. These are triggered by the marketing of financial instruments to the public, independently of their eventual admission to the financial market, which is only one of the modalities; in the past, the notion of *appel publique à l'épargne* accounted for these

1 J.-J. Daigre, 'L'évolution de la notion de marché financier', *op. cit.*

2 On this aspect, see L. d'Avout, 'L'entreprise et les conflits internationaux de lois', *op. cit.*, nos. 76 et seq.

different mechanisms for soliciting the public. Admission to trading has the particularity of making the publication of some of this information periodic. Information of the same nature is sometimes required by the legal system of the issuer's registered office, and the financial market legislation may then be self-limiting when it considers the information provided under the law of the registered office to be equivalent. In the interests of reciprocity, French companies marketing their securities in these jurisdictions may also be subject only to the requirements of their headquarters.

The third measures relate to the defective information provided by the issuer regarding the financial instruments traded on the financial market. An issuer that proposes its securities on a market is likely to be held liable for defective information it has submitted to the market. However, this liability raises several difficulties: its nature, whether contractual or tortious, the competent jurisdiction to assess it and, finally, the law to which it is subject. It will be shown that although the characterisation of the liability action is marked by a certain contingency, the legal order of the market nevertheless benefits from solid jurisdiction to decide on the reparation of the damage caused. This jurisdiction is independent of the admission to trading, but stems from the solicitation to which local investors have been subjected (Title 1).

282. Relations with investors. In its relations with investors, the law of the financial market most often pursues the objective of the proper functioning of the market, which requires both the institution of rules allowing price discovery and increasing the liquidity of admitted securities.[3] It will be shown here that this objective justifies the institution of a set of rules that can be synthesised into a conflict rule, which can be rendered bilateral, according to which all rules that pursue the objective of the proper functioning of the financial market should be subject to the *lex mercatus*. The law of the financial market is indeed the best placed to ensure the proper functioning of the financial market. The difficulty encountered in the application of the law of the financial market is, however, that the enforcement of certain rules, and in particular those relating to market transactions, sometimes depends on sanctions which only the legal system of the issuer's seat can achieve. This difficulty can be overcome by the cooperation of the latter, in particular by making it a condition for access of its companies to local financial markets. The use of the trading system for the purpose of carrying out a market transaction will therefore trigger the application of the law of the trading system. However, this criterion is not sufficient to ensure the applicability of the criminal side of the regulation of market operations, particularly because some market abuse may take place through the conclusion of OTC financial contracts which, without using the trading system, nevertheless destabilise its mechanism. It will be seen that in these cases, the effect test can be applied

[3] On these two functions of the financial market, see *supra*, para. 49.

in the name of criminal law, and limited to financial contracts whose effective underlying is a financial instrument admitted to trading. Moreover, the exercise of criminal jurisdiction can be rationalised by the objective pursued vis-à-vis the infringements in question: the protection of the trading system. The AMF's administrative jurisdiction, when it is based on breaches, should obey the same rationalisation, quite simply because it supplants criminal law in this case, and should not exceed the scope of the legislation it replaces.

The objective of a well-functioning financial market is not limited to market operations, but also explains the application of market law to the obligations of members, quite simply because the trading system's relationship with investors is most often exercised through the market members. We have seen that the latter are contractually bound to each other and to the manager through the trading rules to which they have adhered. The legal system of the trading venue may, however, impose a significant number of additional obligations on them in order to ensure the proper functioning of the system and compliance with the regulation of market operations; it does not, however, go so far as to govern their contractual relations with their clients (Title 2).

TITLE 1
THE RELATIONSHIP BETWEEN FINANCIAL MARKETS AND ISSUERS

283. Presentation. Considering the relationship of issuers with financial markets restricts the scope of the law applicable to them in two ways. First, it restricts the scope to securities only: the issuer will solicit a financial market in order to collect the savings necessary for its own investments. Secondly, the only laws involved are, on the one hand, the law applicable to the issuer, most often the *lex societatis* or, where applicable, the law of the unincorporated group, and, on the other hand, the law of the financial market. The latter will then aim at protecting its residents, and will most often apply as the law of the place of solicitation.[1] It might be tempting to combine all the laws protecting residents into a unilateral conflict rule. This commonality of function would allow the development of a single criterion of application, the solicitation of residents, and a specific regime under which local laws are self-limiting whenever the law of the issuer provides equivalent protection. As it stands, however, this rule does not reflect positive law. Firstly, the idea behind it has penetrated the European legal order so well that it often gives global jurisdiction to the issuer's legal order as regards marketing rules which are nevertheless aimed at protecting residents. Secondly, the proposed regime could only be applicable to '*a priori*' protection rules, i.e. those relating to marketing. Indeed, the *ratio legis* of liability rules, which contribute to the protection of residents through reparation for their damage, does not lend itself well to self-limitation: it is up to the legal system whose residents have been cheated to provide redress. Moreover, the relationship between issuers and financial markets is not limited to the protection of residents. Thus, when the admission of securities to the trading platform is in question, the law of the financial market pursues the objective of the proper functioning of the market as

[1] There is no proper equivalent, in French, to the concept of securities regulation, see H. Synvet, *L'organisation juridique du groupe international de sociétés*, *op. cit.*, note 860, p. 354: 'We use the expression "stock exchange law" only reluctantly, as it is too restrictive: we are referring here to all the rules which require companies to provide information without being part of their status, whether they apply because of their listing on the stock exchange, a public offering or the dissemination of securities among multiple hands (but does not the Commission des opérations de bourse extend its authority beyond the financial markets?) We will also speak of "laws on the protection of savings", being aware that the most classic company law also pursues this end. Ideally, we would like to find an equivalent to the American "Securities Regulation".'

well as the protection of residents. Conflict of laws must therefore be examined in the light of the issuer's different relationships with the financial markets.

284. Conflict of laws. If one were to present superficially the conflict of laws relating to the issue and marketing of securities, one would readily say that they are resolved in opposite directions: the issuance would be the preserve of the law of the issuer, and the marketing that of the law of the financial market on which the securities are admitted. However, the solutions to the conflict of laws show a greater subtlety. Indeed, if the issuer's law is sovereign as to the conditions of the issue and the *negotium* issued, this sovereignty precisely makes it possible, on the one hand, to designate another law as to the regime of this *negotium* and, on the other hand, to take into account substantial solutions enacted by its environment as to the form of the securities. The first possibility takes into account the solutions applicable to debt securities, and thus requires a careful delimitation of the domain of the law of the bond contract and the law of the issuer, it being understood that certain prescriptions of the *lex mercatus* are applicable as soon as a significant modification of the voting power of the shareholders is involved. The second hypothesis is precisely the one on which the law of the financial market intends to operate, by imposing on the issuer certain conditions of form for the securities that it wishes to admit, as well as the suppression of statutory clauses likely to restrict the negotiability of the securities. The financial market law therefore applies here by obliging the issuer, in connection with the admission of the securities to trading, to comply with certain substantial solutions. The issuer will have to comply with them, regardless of whether the issue is subject to the indisputable jurisdiction of the law of the issuer and regardless of the law applicable to the acts of marketing the securities. Here, Mr Synvet's assertion that 'stock exchange law imposes compliance by making it a condition for the use of the mechanism it designs'[2] appears to be especially accurate (Chapter 1).

On the other hand, within the Union, the information obligations triggered by the marketing of financial securities in France will most often be deactivated because of their submission to the law of the issuer's seat, whose prescriptions will be recognised as equivalent; it will be shown, however, that the administrative authority of the market should retain a power to control the obligations provided. Moreover, since marketing operations are not limited to the admission of securities to trading, the law of the issuer may reappear through the law of autonomy (Chapter 2).

Finally, when the issuer's liability for defective information disseminated is at stake, the law of the financial market still retains a title of application because of the combination of the issuer's tortious conduct on its territory and the solicitation of its residents. However, this application must be articulated with that of the law of contract (Chapter 3).

---

2 H. Synvet, *L'organisation juridique du groupe international de sociétés*, *op. cit.*, no. 471, p. 403.

CHAPTER 1
THE ISSUE

285. The issue of a financial instrument. The expression 'issue' is borrowed from monetary law. This borrowing is undoubtedly explained by the fact that, like money, financial instruments constitute intangible assets, circulate, are liable to be recorded in an account and allow for payment.[1] However, French authors do not always designate the same thing, and refer indistinctly to the issue of a security, a share, or even the creation of a security.[2] All these expressions are not equivalent, however, and two clarifications are necessary with regard to the purpose of the issue and its process.

286. First, according to French law, the object of the issue is the *negotium*, i.e. the share, debt or unit of a collective investment scheme.[3] However, the issue results in the creation of an *instrumentum*,[4] the security, which accounts for the *negotium* issued. It is only by metonymy that we speak of the issue of

---

1 So much so that they are included in certain monetary aggregates, the origin of which comes from the difficult distinction between money and liquid assets. What distinguishes money, however, is its character as a universal payment, see S. Adalid, *La Banque centrale européenne et l'Eurosystème, op. cit.*, nos. 14 and 201. The distinction between the two, it seems, lies in the fact that only money is invested with a general liberatory power on the territory of the person who instituted it and binding on those who reside there. As Professor Dominique Carreau puts it, only money 'as a result of the decision of the *de jure* or *de facto* sovereign power, receives liberatory power and circulates in the territory where this supreme authority is exercised', see D. Carreau, *Souveraineté et coopération monétaire et internationale*, Paris, Cujas, 1970, p. 30. On the contemporary monetary issue on the territory of the Union, see F. Martucci, *L'ordre économique et monétaire de l'Union européenne, op. cit.*, nos. 33 et seq.

2 Mr Trébulle believes that issuance is a process, which begins with the formation of a contract and is completed with the creation and issuance of the security, but believes that 'these two steps are of equal importance in the overall process; they follow one another, and it is only through the completion of the second that the operation will be completed. The creation of the security is inseparable from the conclusion of the contract'. F.-X. Trébulle, *L'émission de valeurs mobilières*, Paris, Economica, 2002, no. 485.

3 Older authors were not mistaken and did not refer to the issue of securities, which the terminology of the time might have suggested, but to the issue of shares and the issue of bonds. For an illustration, see Y. Loussouarn and J.-D. Bredin, *Droit du commerce international, op. cit.*, no. 327.

4 It would perhaps be more accurate to speak of a medium rather than an *instrumentum*, as in monetary law, in order to highlight the particular function that the instrument is called upon to play here. Here too, the financial instrument is the 'instrument that materialises the units' (R. Libchaber, *Recherche sur la monnaie en droit privé*, Paris, LGDJ, 1992, no. 85).

securities.[5] Today, securities are made manifest in the form of a book entry, the regime of which differs from traditional instruments in several ways: it is necessary for the materialisation of the *negotium* in order to allow its transfer, its regime allows for easier circulation, and its holding is accompanied by a presumption of ownership.[6] These elements explain why it is sometimes difficult to distinguish the *instrumentum* from the *negotium*, but the resolution of conflicts of law makes it necessary, 'and if the search for the applicable law depends on this distinction, it helps at the same time to establish it: by becoming aware of the fact that one aspect of the phenomenon would not reasonably be subject to the same law as another, one is led to specify what each of these entities consists of'.[7] It should be added, however, that the situation is made more complex when the issuer places its securities with an intermediary who, in turn, issues securities offering identical prerogatives to those of the securities it holds.[8] This frequent case, which is that of depositary receipts, makes it necessary to clearly identify who the issuer of the security is, and what prerogatives are actually offered by the security.[9] Since depositary receipts are a variety of debt securities, the conflict of laws rules studied here are applicable to them.

287. Secondly, the process of issuance is subject to various meanings. In the case of negotiable instruments, but the point can be extended by analogy to securities, Professor Goldman distinguished between the creation of the security, which marks the creation of the right, its issue, which manifests the putting into circulation to the first beneficiary, and the circulation itself, when the first

5 In French law, several theories have sought to conflate or distinguish between *instrumentum* and *negotium*, on which see the summary by V. Malassigné, *Les titres représentatifs*, *op. cit.* Evoking the ownership of financial securities seems to us to reflect a metonymy of the same order. As Mr Jeantet writes about the refusal to qualify the CCDVT as the owner of the securities deposited there: 'ownership (*of the securities*) being then nothing other than the private exercise of a bundle of rights which are, precisely, reserved to the depositors'. The author already mentions the distinction: 'Should a distinction be made in this case between the *instrumentum*, the paper and the number it bears, and the rights attached to the share? We shall see that this must be considered. But here this distinction is not useful.' F.-C. Jeantet, 'Le dépôt collectif de titres au porteur à la Caisse centrale de dépôt et de virement de titres', *Journal des sociétés*, 1945, pp. 161 et seq.

6 This last characteristic accounts for the possessory function, in French law, of securities, see V. Malassigné, *Les titres représentatifs*, *op. cit.*, nos. 257 et seq.

7 Pierre Mayer was referring here to the monetary phenomenon and the distinction between unit of account and unit of payment, see preface to C. Kleiner, *La monnaie dans les relations privées internationales*, Paris, LGDJ, 2010.

8 These securities are defined by Art. 2(45) of MiFID 2. On these securities, see F. Drummond, *Droit financier*, *op. cit.*, no. 332; A. Couret and H. Le Nabasque, *Droit financier*, *op. cit.*, no. 1869. For an analysis of these securities, see C. Coupet, *L'attribution du droit de vote dans les sociétés*, Paris, LGDJ, 2015, nos. 164 et seq.; see V. Malassigné, *Les titres représentatifs*, *op. cit.*

9 V. Malassigné, *Les titres représentatifs*, *op. cit.*, nos. 513 et seq.

beneficiary disposes of it.[10] This distinction is reminiscent of the primary and secondary markets. The former corresponds to the first marketing of the security between the issuer and the investor, while the latter is "the place", the space, where securities are exchanged between investors. The creation of the security would therefore be this stage prior to the first circulation. This thesis was taken up by Professor Trébulle, for whom these two aspects constitute the issue. The latter is then presented as a contract, offered by the company, accepted by way of subscription, and of which the creation of the security constitutes the completion.[11] This presentation avoids the pitfall of overemphasising the institutional aspect of the issue, and has the advantage of showing that the issue is part of a contractual process that encompasses both aspects: in French law, an issue without marketing is not valid.[12] However enlightening this presentation may be, it will not be used here. From an international perspective, it would seem more appropriate to adopt a strict concept of issuance, which here refers to the process leading to the creation of a share or a debt represented by a security, clearly distinguished from its marketing, i.e. its delivery to the first beneficiary. The reason is simple: these rules have different functions and are therefore likely to be subject to different laws.[13]

288. The rules relating to marketing, although they are most often the responsibility of the issuer, are nevertheless not preponderantly linked to the issue

10 Thus, Professor Berthold Goldman considers that: 'Rigorously, a distinction should be made between: the creation of the security; its issuance, the act by which the person who created it hands it over to the first beneficiary (e.g., to the taker of the bill of exchange, or to the subscriber of the share or bond); and finally, its circulation, which begins at the moment when the first beneficiary relinquishes it to a new holder, the endorsee or the holder. But the issue is both the final operation of creation and the first act of circulation, – so that there is no disadvantage in dividing the life of the security into these two phases alone.' B. Goldman, 'Conflicts of Laws in Negotiable Instruments', *International Bar Association*, Martinus Nijhoff, The Hague, 1950, Annex 1, p. 6. The distinction elaborated by Goldman was not widespread. Thus, during the negotiations of the Geneva Convention on Negotiable Instruments, the English representative, in an exchange worthy of a Beckettian dialogue, 'asked if there was a difference between the words "issued" and "created". The President replied that there was no difference.' *Proceedings of the 1930 Geneva Conference*, p. 455.

11 F.-G. Trébulle, *L'émission de valeurs mobilières*, *op. cit.*

12 Self-ownership of the share capital can therefore only take place by share buy-back (on the rules surrounding this, see *infra*, para. 513). However, there is not necessarily a link between issue and contribution: it is thus possible for the issuer to give the contributor securities already issued, see H. Le Nabasque, 'La fin de la connexion apports/capital' in *Quel avenir pour le capital social?*, Colloque CRDF Paris I, Paris, Dalloz, 2004, pp. 103 et seq.

13 It is true that in some cases there may be an issue without the security being marketed: this is the case with treasury shares. However, on the one hand, treasury shares result from the acquisition by the company of shares that it had previously marketed and, on the other hand, this hypothesis is residual and is only admitted by exception, quite simply because it blurs the capital structure of the company. Moreover, debt securities bought back by the issuing company do not lead to the same result, since they are then extinguished by confusion.

of the security, but to the protection of its recipients,[14] and therefore explain the application in principle of the law of the place of solicitation.[15] On the other hand, the notion of issue is part of the delimitation of securities and financial contracts, which is reflected in the conflict of laws solutions: where the latter are subject to the private international law of contracts, the issue, associated with the regime of securities and the characteristics of the *negotia* represented, is at the origin of the elaboration of specific rules for shares and debts represented by a security.[16] These rules have a double function, firstly to protect the issuer itself: the issue of financial securities is a risky operation, and not all corporate forms are designed to support such operations; the rules relating to the designation of the bodies competent to authorise issues reflect this. This first function explains why, until recently, the prohibition of such issues was included in the general law of companies.[17] The other function, which is now residual, was specific to the protection of the recipients: the provisions relating to the protection of the body of bondholders, which are not specific to all company forms, also show this.

Finally, if the issuance is the process leading to the creation of the *negotium*, it must be carefully distinguished from the content of the *negotia* issued. This distinction is particularly important in the case of debt securities, where the law of the issuer may be dissociated from the law applicable to the issued bond. The possibility of such dissociation requires the determination of the basis for the jurisdiction of the law of the issuer.

289. Basis of the jurisdiction of the law of the issuer. It is often said that the law of the issuer has pre-eminent jurisdiction because it is the law under which the *negotium* was originally constituted, i.e. the law of the source of the rights represented by the securities. In matters of securities, it constitutes the *lex creationis*. The pre-eminence of the *lex creationis* is not specific to rights represented by financial instruments alone: since Niboyet in France, it has been an antiphon in the law of conflict of laws in relation to intangible property. Indeed, the author already proposed that debt should be subjected to the law of

---

14 Some issues are nevertheless porous, at the borderline between issuing and marketing. In addition, the purpose of certain prohibitive issuer rules – for example, the prohibition of certain companies from issuing financial securities – is similar to the purpose of the rules on the marketing of financial securities, which generally aim to protect the recipients of the securities. Mr Trébulle gives a good account of the importance of the recipients of securities in the issuance process, see F.-G. Trébulle, *L'émission de valeurs mobilières*, *op. cit.*

15 See *infra*, paras. 337 et seq.

16 See H. Synvet and A. Tenenbaum, 'Instruments financiers', *op. cit.*, nos. 6-7. Similarities are however perceptible, which probably explains why, for the sake of clarity, some authors refer to the 'issuance' of financial securities, see T. Bonneau *et al.*, *Droit financier*, *op. cit.*, no. 881. Mr Chacornac shows that the notion of issuance also explains why financial contracts do not trigger a collective information obligation, see J. Chacornac, *Les fonctions de l'information en droit des instruments financiers*, *op. cit.*, nos. 180 et seq.

17 Previously Art. 1841 of the Civil Code repealed by Order 2019-1067 of 21 October 2019. The prohibition is now set out in Art. L. 412-1 of the Monetary and Financial Code.

their source: 'The debt exists only because the law of the debt created it, just as tangible property exists only insofar as the *lex rei sitae* permits it. The latter plays the role of the former, and vice versa.'[18] Niboyet's analysis could be extended to all intangible property. As Mr d'Avout writes:

> 'Whatever the specificities of each intangible property, whether named or unnamed legal creations, the starting point of the analysis is commonly that of the submission of the property to its own law of constitution [...]. This law determines the objective characteristics of the property right in question and, consequently, the prerogatives that it can offer to its holder. The empire of the law of the source may also extend to voluntary transactions of assignment or grant by way of security undertaken in relation to the property in question.'[19]

Thus, in the same way that the *lex creationis* of the debt can restrict the conditions under which it is transmitted, in particular because it determines its validity, the *lex creationis* of the *negotia* represented by the securities is the only one that can determine the validity of the rights issued. This rule was expressed by the Court of Cassation in the *Royal Dutch* case:

> 'The obligations of the company towards its shareholders are governed by the national law of that company, in this case Dutch law, from which it follows that this law alone determines, irrespective of the country in which the securities are held, the conditions under which the status of shareholder is acquired, retained and lost.'[20]

This solution has the advantage of clarifying the distinction between the *instrumentum*, the security, and the *negotium*, the right represented by the security. When the law of the source cancels the share, by ricochet, the *instrumentum* which represented it becomes the proof of a right which is no longer there; the prerogatives attached to the form of the security disappear, and its evidential function is fully highlighted. This was particularly clear when bearer shares were evidenced in France by a paper medium: the latter lost all value from the moment the represented shares were cancelled. In the same way, the registration of a cancelled share in an account no longer has any evidential value, let alone acquisitive value. This solution, expressed as regards shares, nevertheless leaves some ambiguity, on the one hand, as regards the fate of debt securities and, on the other hand, as regards the actual basis of the jurisdiction of the *lex creationis*. In the case of debt securities, the *lex creationis* is that designated by the contract of issue. Indeed, it is the latter which gives rise to the claim, and not the law of the issuer. However, the law of the issuer

---

[18] J.-P. NIBOYET, *Traité de droit international privé*, t. IV, no. 1296, p. 670.

[19] See 'Biens' in L. D'AVOUT, *Répertoire de droit international*, Paris, Dalloz, no. 75.

[20] Civ. 1re, 17 October 1972.

continues to have *primary* jurisdiction in several aspects governed by the issue of the security, which is reflected in the conflict of laws rule developed by Professor Synvet in the draft reform of French securities law. Although this rule was not adopted, it does summarise the positive law according to which:

> 'The law of the issuer shall determine the financial securities that may be issued, the conditions of their issue and cancellation, and the form they may take.'[21]

290. The primacy of the issuer's law can be seen in its ability to cancel debt instruments that are validly subject to a foreign law. This observation makes it possible to affirm that the pre-eminence of the issuer's law does not stem from the fact that it is the source of the rights represented (i.e. the *lex creationis*), but from the fact that it is at the origin of the issue itself, and of the conditions under which the securities may be issued. Here, the issuer's jurisdiction is similar to that of the country on which the capacity of persons depends. In the same way, it comes into play before the conflict of laws relating to the *negotium* issued, and pursues an identical function according to which the protection of the company itself, of its shareholders, or of the persons to whom the disputed securities are addressed may be sought. The respect of this pre-eminence by the other countries originates from two elements. First, for a reason of proximity: the law of the issuer is objectively the best placed to determine the conditions of issue of securities of legal persons which it has itself instituted and, independently of the existence of a legal person, of contracts organising a grouping subject to its authority. A contrary solution would moreover make international harmony of solutions impossible. The second element is based on the principle of effectiveness. Indeed, the law of the issuer is the law of the place of payment: it will be difficult to obtain payment of the obligations arising from the instrument if the latter contradicts the prescriptions it has laid down.[22] This title of jurisdiction based on payment is so significant that it traditionally justified the submission of the debt themselves to the law of the debtor's domicile.[23]

This pre-eminence of the issuer's law does not mean, however, that it *must* be applied to all aspects of the *instrumentum* and of the *negotium*, but that its requirements cannot be overridden. Its substantial liberalism may therefore allow the issuer to designate another law to govern certain aspects of the *negotium*, from its regime to the means by which it may be represented. This

---

21 H. Synvet and A. Tenenbaum, 'Instruments financiers', *op. cit.*, no. 12.

22 This seems to be the element that underpins the reasoning of the above-mentioned *Royal Dutch* judgment. It is noted by Mr Batiffol who observes that all the rules of the legal system of the registered office must be applied if they so provide, even if they result from public law legislation independent of company law, see *ibid.*, p. 523.

23 This question is explored further in the context of bills of exchange, where there is also a possible dissociation between the law of creation of the instrument (that of the drawer) and the law of payment (that of the drawee), see *infra*, paras. 596 et seq.

legal basis is the origin of the possibility to subject the debts represented by the securities to a foreign law, in practice that of the source of the *negotium*, and designated as such in the contract of issue. The law of autonomy then makes it possible to make the regime of the obligations coincide with the legal order where the investors are domiciled. In the case of shares, however, the jurisdiction of the *lex societatis* seems to be invariable. An attempt will be made here to determine the reasons for this constancy. It will also be shown that the form of securities is more closely linked to the *lex creationis* than to the law of the issuer, and that the *lex creationis* should therefore determine the conditions of form of the *negotia* it governs.

291. Articulation of the law of the issuer and the law of the financial market. This foray into the foundations of the issuer's law jurisdiction now makes it possible to understand why capital market law cannot be applied authoritatively to either the terms of issue or the form of the securities. Nevertheless, it is always possible for the issuer to implement the material solutions prescribed by the *lex mercatus* (financial market law, i.e. the law of the trading venue) itself. The latter makes this a condition for admission to trading. Furthermore, the issuer may subject the form of its securities to a foreign law, in particular the law applicable to the issued *negotium* with which it is closely connected (Section 1). The law of the financial market, on the other hand, does not apply to any aspect of the issued *negotium*, except in case of the issuer's desire to match the regime of the issued debts with the law under which investors are solicited. This does not mean, however, that capital market law is indifferent to the prerogatives offered by the issued securities, as these are likely to trigger the application of the regulation of market transactions as soon as a significant change in the 'voting power'[24] of the shareholders is involved (Section 2).

SECTION 1. THE CONDITIONS OF ISSUE AND THE FORM OF THE SECURITIES

From the foregoing, it can be deduced that the law of the issuer is particularly mandatory with regard to the conditions of the issue. The statement, which is correct, nevertheless requires the determination of the scope of questions covered by these conditions (§ 1). The form of the securities should nevertheless not necessarily be subject to the law of the issuer, but to the *lex creationis* of the *negotium* (§ 2).

[24] In the words of Mr Chacornac, see *infra*, para. 473.

§ 1. THE CONDITIONS OF THE ISSUE

The law of the issuer applies to the terms of issue as the law applicable to the organisation of the company.[25] Two sets of rules included in the terms of issue can be distinguished: one relating to the ability to create financial securities[26] and the other relating to the consideration required for the allocation of the *negotium*. This consideration raises the question of the determination of contributions and their regime.

292. The ability to create securities. Although the rules on the ability to create securities are closely linked to the issuing organisation, two types of norms can be distinguished: those relating to restrictions on issuance, which allow only certain entities to issue securities, and those relating to the competence of the organs, which designate the organ within the authorised entities that is able to decide on the issue. First of all, the restrictive rules of the issue are obviously part of the conditions of the issue. The legal system of the issuer may wish to restrict the entities able to issue financial securities in order to reserve this option for those organisations that offer the most security to the recipients of the securities, whether through the rules governing the share capital or those concerning the governance of the organisation. This 'ability to create' securities is therefore determined by the law of the issuer: thus, there is a prohibition in principle on the issuance of financial securities by French companies, which is only exceptionally lifted.[27] Secondly, the rules governing the competence of the

---

25 This basis has long been perceived thanks to the international issue of debt securities, where the freedom of choice of law obliged to dissociate what was of the order of the bond issue, and subject to the option of a choice of law, from what related to the law of the issuer. Prof. Loussouarn and Bredin write that 'the company, on pain of nullity in its own country, must observe the mandatory provisions laid down by the organic law relating to the issue', Y. Loussouarn and J.-D. Bredin, *Droit du commerce international*, *op. cit.*, no. 327. The authors add: 'It is only insofar as the *lex societatis* does not lay down imperative prescriptions that the parties can be recognised as having a certain degree of autonomy in the choice of the applicable law.' (*ibid.*). The authors rely on a distinction made by Pillet concerning 'mandatory laws and optional laws' (*ibid.*), the latter corresponding to suppletive rules while the former would be the rules of public order. Such a discourse is undoubtedly marked by excessive unilateralism. Rather, it is necessary to determine the rules of the issue which are part of the "organic law" and which will always be subject to the *lex societatis*, from those which relate to aspects belonging to the domain of the law of the contract, and which will only be applicable insofar as the law of the registered office is elected as the law of the contract.

26 The expression is borrowed from Goldman, who prefers it to capacity, because although the notion of capacity is 'more precise and more technical, [...] (*it*) is not exactly appropriate for public or private entities, when considering whether or not they can issue negotiable instruments (shares, bonds, etc.)'. B. Goldman, 'Conflit de lois en matière d'instruments négociables', *op. cit.*, p. 6.

27 Art. L. 411-1 of the Monetary and Financial Code (formerly Art. 1841 of the Civil Code). The authorisation for joint stock companies is given by Art. L. 228-1 of the Commercial Code, for associations by Art. L. 213-8, and for certain unincorporated group by Art. L. 251-7. Finally,

bodies able to decide on the issuance of securities relate to the conditions of the issue. This is the heart of the issuer's internal functioning, the preserve of the law of organisation. It is here that the influence of the purpose of the issue on the conditions of the issue is most apparent: thus, within French companies, the bodies authorised to issue equity securities are not the same as those authorised to issue debt securities.[28]

293. Rules for determining contributions and their regime. The conditions of the issue may also extend to the determination of the consideration required for the granting of the *negotium* and the resulting regime. This question does not really create a difficulty in the case of debt securities or units in collective investment undertakings where the consideration required is always a sum of money which must be fully paid. It is more difficult in the case of share issues, where the consideration is in the form of a contribution. Indeed, the contribution, if it can be made in cash, can also be made in the form of services or know-how, or in kind. In the two latter cases, the *lex societatis* is likely to provide for mechanisms to verify the value of the contributions,[29] which condition the effectiveness of the capital increase and, consequently, of the issue itself.[30] The purpose of these verification rules is to avoid overvaluation of the contributions, in order to protect the integrity of the share capital, the amount of shares issued as consideration[31] and, correlatively, to avoid dilution of the rights of the other shareholders. The *lex societatis* therefore applies here again as the law of internal organisation. This observation invites two remarks.

---

it is in their capacity as undertakings for collective investment that they may issue financial securities (Art. L. 211-3 of the Monetary and Financial Code). A similar restriction applies, for example, to the issuance of a bill of exchange, see Art. L. 511-5 of the Commercial Code.

28 For 'sociétés anonymes', the extraordinary general meeting has sole authority to decide on capital increases, although it may delegate this authority to the board of directors or the management board under certain conditions (Art. L. 225-129 of the Commercial Code), whereas, as a matter of principle, the issue of bonds may be decided by the board of directors unless otherwise provided for in the articles of association or decided spontaneously by the ordinary general meeting (Art. L. 228-40 of the Commercial Code).

29 See for public limited companies, Art. L. 225-147 of the Commercial Code.

30 Art. L. 225-147 para. 3 of the Commercial Code: 'If the meeting approves the valuation of the contributions and the granting of special benefits, it shall record the completion of the capital increase.'

31 Comp. H. Synvet, 'Société', *op. cit.*, no. 91, who deduces the application of the *lex societatis* from 'Article 1832 of the Civil Code, which makes the existence of contributions a constitutive element of the partnership contract, and Article 1843-2 of the same code, which links the extent of each partner's rights in the capital to the amount of his contributions'. These elements do not seem to us to determine exactly the basis for the application of the *lex societatis* and, therefore, make it difficult to determine their scope. After having considered that the contribution is a constituent element of the partnership contract and necessarily subject to its law, Mr Synvet admits that the promise of contribution is on the other hand likely to be subject to foreign law (*ibid.*, no. 93).

294. The first relates to the links between the *lex mercatus* and the *lex societatis*. Indeed, the law of the financial market is likely to assist in the determination of the value of contributions. Whenever the contribution in kind consists of securities giving access to the capital or monetary instruments traded on a regulated market, the board of directors may decide to deactivate the corporate rules for the verification of contributions. The price established by the regulated market will then be valid provided that it is weighted at the average price at which these securities or instruments were traded on one or more regulated markets during the three months preceding the date of the effective realisation of the contribution.[32] Two interpretations of this rule are possible. The first would be that the deactivation of the *lex societatis* is not explained here by a desire to reconcile with the *lex mercatus*, but by the convergence of the objectives of company law and capital markets law, the latter being better able to fulfil the function pursued by the former. Another interpretation is simply that the *lex societatis* applies a factual element determined by the financial market.

295. The second remark relates to the extension of the scope of the *lex societatis* to the regime of contributions. Indeed, company law also regulates certain aspects of the regime of contributions in kind, in particular the transfer of ownership,[33] as well as the obligations of the contributor.[34] Two conflicts of laws then arise: one with the law of the contribution of property, the other with the law of the contribution contract if there is one.[35] Mr Synvet observes, with regard to the transfer of ownership, that this will be subject, for tangible property, to the *lex rei sitae*,[36] and that the French corporate provision is therefore inapplicable to property situated abroad. On the other hand, the author refuses to apply the law of the contract to the contributor's obligations, considering that the *lex societatis* is the only competent law.[37] In reality, it seems

---

32 Art. L. 225-147-1(I)(1°) of the Commercial Code. It is regrettable that this reference to the price determined by the *lex mercatus* is restricted to regulated markets rather than to all financial markets. On the other hand, the discretion left to the competent corporate body is equivalent to approval, since the stock market value of an equity security may be altered by media pollution and is not necessarily the most conclusive value.

33 Art. 1843-1 Civil Code. See H. Synvet, 'Société', *op. cit.*

34 As Mr Synvet writes: 'In French law, a contribution in kind is a transfer of ownership, except in the particular case of a contribution in the form of a right to use the property. And the transfer of ownership is concomitant with the registration in the trade and companies register or the increase in capital", ', H. Synvet, 'Société, ', *op. cit.*, no. 93. On the particular regime of the opposability of the property contributed, see Art. 1843-3 of the Civil Code.

35 On the existence and regime of the contribution contract, distinct from the partnership contract, see M. Buchberger, *Le contrat d'apport*, Paris, Ed. Panthéon-Assas, 2011.

36 And for intangible property, to the *lex creationis*, see *supra*, para. 291.

37 H. Synvet, 'Société', *op. cit.*, no. 93: 'In the absence of case law, the *lex societatis* has jurisdiction in principle. The contribution is in fact the vehicle for the entry of new partners into the company, and this 'aggregation' necessarily falls within the law governing this company. Consequently, a French "société anonyme" will not be bound until its extraordinary general meeting has approved the contribution in kind under the terms of

to us that neither of these two aspects, transfer of ownership and obligations of the contributor, will in principle be subject to the *lex societatis*. Nevertheless, they may both be subject to an identical response from the corporate order in order to ensure its effectiveness.

296. Contribution and transfer of ownership. As regards the transfer of ownership, this is, at least for tangible things, subject to the *lex situs*. The pre-eminence of the country of situation will lead to the application of its own law, unless it decides to restrict it by taking the view that the transfer of ownership of contributed property to a company should be governed by the *lex societatis*. The only possible response of the *lex societatis* is not to try to interfere with the transfer of the contribution, but to attach the ownership of the shares issued to the effective and irrevocable transfer of the contributed property. Indeed, the ownership of the shares falls under the *lex societatis*.[38]

297. Contribution and obligation of the contributor. The obligations of the contributor may be subject to the *lex societatis* or to the *lex contractus* of the possible contribution contract. A first argument in favour of the *lex societatis* stems from the fact that the contribution takes place at the time of incorporation of the company, and that the Rome I Regulation excludes from the domain of the law of contract 'questions governed by the law of companies and other bodies, corporate or unincorporated, such as the creation, by registration or otherwise, legal capacity, internal organisation or winding up of companies and other bodies, corporate or unincorporated'.[39] However, the Rome I Regulation refers to the granting of legal personality, i.e. 'the organic aspects of such companies'.[40] However, contributions do not constitute the attribution of legal personality under French law, and cannot therefore be excluded from the

---

Article L. 225-147 of the Commercial Code. However, a promise to contribute, subject to its own law, is perfectly conceivable. On the other hand, the obligations of the contributor, as set out in Article 1843-3 of the Civil Code, cannot escape French law as long as the beneficiary company is governed by French law. This does not mean that a foreign law cannot usefully govern certain aspects of the contract [...]: reference to a foreign law may be tantamount to use of the margin of freedom left by the suppletive nature of part of French law.' In reality, it seems to us that the spatial application of Art. 1843-3 of the Civil Code, and Art. L. 225-147 of the Commercial Code cannot be put on the same level, because the basis of the *lex societatis* is different.

38 See in this sense, European Group for Private International Law, Art. 5(f) of the draft law applicable to company law, Milan, 2016. This is the application, in relation to actions, of the rule more generally applicable to debts under French law. Indeed, the law applicable to the debt determines its ownership and the possible multiplication of this ownership when the debt is held in *trust*, see Cass. com., 13 September 2011, no. 10-25.533.

39 Art. 1(2)(f) of the Rome I Regulation. However, it is questionable whether, because the contribution is constitutive of the company, it can be excluded from the domain of the *lex societatis*. Indeed, the Rome I Regulation specifies that 'incorporation, by registration or otherwise' is excluded from the scope of the law of contract.

40 Case C-25/18, *Kerr*, ECLI:EU:C:2019:376, spec. paras. 33–34.

scope of the law of the contract on this basis.[41] Moreover, the obligations of the contributor cannot be placed on the same level as the verification obligations incumbent on the company and which condition the issue of shares, since the contributions do not relate to the internal organisation of the issuer. In reality, if it is true that the *lex societatis* should still apply to the contributor's obligations, it is because it is the best way to preserve the integrity of the share capital in which the contribution is made. We must therefore approve the old case law solutions[42] and the contemporary doctrinal projects ruling in this direction.[43] Unfortunately, as the law stands, unless there is a generous interpretation of the Rome I Regulation which would lead to the inclusion of the company's capital structure in the internal functioning of the company, everything depends on the existence of a choice of law in the contribution contract.[44] The *lex societatis* may nevertheless always, as in the case of transfer of ownership, make the acquisition by the contributor of ownership of the shares issued subject to the final fulfilment of his contractual obligations. Such a clause may usefully be inserted in the articles of association and is likely to ensure the protection of the company.

§ 2. THE FORM OF THE SECURITIES

There is no international consensus on the law applicable to the form of securities. It seems to us, however, that the law of the issuer has an indisputable pre-eminence here (I). However, in the same way that the issuer's law allows the issuer to subject certain *negotia* to a foreign law, it may also decide to allow the issuer to subject the form of its securities to a foreign law and, in particular, to the law of the *negotium* issued with which the form of the securities is

---

41 See 'Rome I Regulation: Contractual obligations', in S. Francq, *Répertoire de droit international*, Paris, Dalloz, 2013, no. 38: 'Contracts concluded between the company and third parties do fall within the scope of the Regulation, as do preliminary contracts concluded with a view to creating a company.'

42 In a case where a cash contribution had not been fully paid, the question arose as to which law to apply to the payment of the remainder: the Tribunal de la Seine ruled in favour of the *lex societatis* in a judgment of 15 April 1891, see *Clunet*, 1891. 920 and Y. Loussouarn and J.-D. Bredin, *Droit du commerce international, op. cit.*, no. 329.

43 GEDIP, Art. 5(d) of the *aforementioned* draft law applicable to companies, bringing within the scope of the *lex societatis* 'the internal functioning, organisation and capital structure'; cf. C. Gerner-Beuerle, F. Mucciarelli, E. Schuster and M. Siems, 'Making the Case for a Rome V Regulation on the Law Applicable to Companies' (2020) 39 *Yearbook of European Law*, pp. 459 et seq.

44 In the absence of an express choice of law, the obligations of the contributor will be subject to the *lex societatis* as *lex contractus*. This is because the characteristic performance of the contribution contract is the provision of the shares by the company, which therefore leads to the application of the law of the registered office, which moreover has the closest relationship to the legal relationship in question. If there is a contribution agreement with a choice of law, the obligations of the contributor will be subject to the designated law. At most, the *lex societatis* can be used as a mandatory law if it is to be described as such.

closely connected. This option is based, on the one hand, on the substantial liberalism of the law of the issuer, which is observed in the case of French legislation and, on the other hand, on an articulation of the law of the issuer and the law of the *negotium* (II).

I. The Law Applicable to the Form of the Securities

298. Positive solutions to the conflict of laws. The French conflict of laws rule, which subjects the form of securities to the law of the issuer, is mainly the result of doctrinal interpretation of the case law. The solution is deduced from a decision of the commercial chamber of the Court of Cassation of 13 February 1967.[45] The decision, which was not directly concerned with the law applicable to the form of securities, comes in the form of a preliminary question. In fact, the judgment concerned the direct claim by a client of securities deposited by his banker, in bankruptcy, with the SICOVAM (the French CSD back then), on the basis of Article 12 of the decree of 4 August 1949 which allows a proportional distribution of the securities found when the total number of the latter was lower than the total number of securities of the same category deposited in the bankrupt institution.[46] The difficulty lies in the fact that the securities were foreign. Professor Loussouarn concludes his note by saying that the Supreme Court 'implicitly, but certainly, recognises that the *lex societatis* is competent to determine the forms of shares whose issue is authorised'.[47] This rule is challenged in foreign law, and particularly in English law, by other criteria. In practice, the question of the law applicable to the form has often been examined from the point of view of the negotiability of the security, an element determined by its form. Thus, the English judges in *Macmillan* were divided between applying the *lex fori*, which is applicable because negotiability would be a question of characterisation necessarily subject to the *lex fori*, and applying the

---

45 Cass. Com., 13 February 1967, *Bull civ.*, no. 67, *RCDIP*, 1968, 52, note Y. Loussouarn, rejecting the appeal against CA Paris, 2 December 1963, *D.*, 1965, 377, concl. Bertrand, *Banque*, 1965, 185, note Marin, *RTD com.*, 1964, 642, note Houin (very critical), *RCDIP*, 1966, 40, note Y. Loussouarn; see also Y. Loussouarn and J.-D. Bredin, *Droit du commerce international*, *op. cit.*, no. 353.

46 See the note by Mr Loussouarn cited above; this technique still exists and is often referred to as 'drawing on the mass', on which see V. Malassigné, *Les titres représentatifs*, *op. cit.*; on the French system of intermediation, see para. 651.

47 See H. Synvet, 'Société', *op. cit.*, no. 95 where the author considers that 'the securities thus issued must take one of the forms provided for by the lex societatis' (see already in this sense. Niboyet who considered that 'only the law of the debt can determine whether a debt is bearer and, when it is bearer, cause it to lose this character for the future', J.-P. Niboyet, *Les conflits de lois relatifs à l'acquisition de la propriété sur les meubles corporels à titre particulier*, Paris, Sirey, 1912, p. 470).

lex loci actus, which is more generally competent for the form of legal acts, and in particular as the law of the place of negotiation.[48]

299. Criticism of the English solutions. The two solutions appear to be deplorable, the first because it is both unpredictable (the law applicable to the form will depend on which court is eventually petitioned) and unrelated to the rules of negotiation, while the second was conceived in situations where the place of negotiation was the place of delivery, whereas this dissociation is frequent today. The English doctrine, through the voice of Mrs Maisie Ooi,[49] taken up by the authors of *Dicey and Morris*, is now trying to amend the reasoning. The authors consider that the ownership of the rights arising from the instrument is subject both to the law "governing the instrument" and to the law of the place where the instrument was located when it was delivered to him.[50] The same

48 Macmillan, (1996) 1 WLR 387, 400 (on this issue, see M. Ooi, 'The ramifications of fragmentation in the choice of law for shares', *JPIL*, August 2016, pp. 411 et seq). Thus, Slaughton LJ states: 'Then a question arises as to which system of law is to determine an instrument is negotiable. One might have thought that in principle this should be the *lex fori*, since one is still at the stage of choosing a *lex causae*. Dicey and Morris at p. 1420 appear to suggest otherwise, and to prefer the law of the place where negotiation is said to have occurred. I find this a difficult question, and we do not need to decide it. By English law, whether as the law of the forum or the law of the place of alleged the negotiation, the share certificates are not negotiable; so English law is not applicable. By New York law they may be negotiable; but New York is not the forum nor the place of alleged negotiation', Macmillan, (1996) 1 WLR 387, p. 400. The judge refers to the 12th edition of Dicey and Morris. Auld LJ was convinced by the rule in Dicey and Morris, which had already been applied at first instance (see *ibid.*, p. 406).
Macmillan's solution has nevertheless become a precedent. *Re Harvard Securities Ltd (in liq.) & Anor* (1998) B.C.C. 567. The decision also concerns the problem of a priority difficulty in respect of financial securities. One of the fundamental questions raised by the judgment is to determine the negotiability of certain US shares. The English judge then relied on the *Macmillan* judgment, and considered that this question was one of qualification, subject to the law of the forum: 'The position with the regard to the US shares is somewhat more complicated because, in light of the back endorsement, it is necessary to decide whether they are negotiable instruments or not, in order to determine the applicable law. In my judgement, the question of whether the US certificates are negotiable should be determined under English law: that is the *lex fori*, and, more importantly, in light of the view of Staughton and Auld LJ, it is the place where the certificates are situated', J. Neuberger, para. 571.
The English solution is all the more surprising since, focused on the question of applying the *lex rei sitae* to shares as intangible movables ("things in action"), and giving the place of incorporation as the *situs*, English law could have usefully drawn inspiration from the field of the *lex rei sitae*, which subjects to the *lex situs* the question of qualification as immovable or movable, as well as all the rights, obligations and documents associated with this qualification:
'Rule 128 - The law of a country where a thing is situated (*lex situs)* determines whether
(1) the thing itself is to be considered an immovable or a movable; or
(2) any right, obligation, or document connected with the thing is to be considered an interest in an immovable or in a movable.'

49 See M. Ooi, *Share and other securities in the conflict of laws*, *op. cit.*, no. 5.32-5.34.

50 Dicey, Morris, and Collins, *The Conflict of Laws*, 15th ed., London, Sweet and Maxwell, nos. 33-837, 33R-376 and 33-389.

authors consider that, in the case of shares, the law governing the instrument is the law of the issuer. However, the formulation expressed by the English doctrine is not fully satisfactory. By restricting itself to shares, where the law of the *negotium* always corresponds to that of the issuer, it does not make it possible to determine which law 'governs the instrument' when the two do not coincide, for example, in the case of debt securities issued by a French company and subject, by virtue of the contract of issue, to English law.[51]

300. The possible application of the *lex creationis*. First of all, it should be remembered that the pre-eminence of the law of the issuer cannot be ignored. This is the case, for example, when French law declares the securities issued negotiable, since only the issuer recognises the person holding the financial security as the holder of the share or debt issued; conversely, foreign securities negotiated in France are subject to the regime of the law that issued them,[52] including the conditions for changing their form.[53] Indeed, negotiability can be

---

51 Moreover, because of the origin of the judgments that gave rise to the contested rule, English doctrine remained focused on the sole question of negotiability instead of examining, more broadly, the law applicable to the form of securities, a category which contains, in addition to the rules relating to negotiability, that applicable to the very mechanism of representation of the right by a security, and the prerogatives then attached to the possession of the evidentiary instrument.

52 See already in this sense, H. Rousseau, 'La forme des actions et la caisse centrale de dépôts et de virements de titres', *JCP* 1944, I, 410, no. 5. The author, analysing the scope and purpose of the law of 3 February 1943 (on which see *infra*, para. 648), which requires shareholders to register their shares or deposit them with a centralizing body, wrote: 'For those who know French capitalism, which is so keen to keep its investments and its wealth secret, it would be foolhardy to expect full success from persuasion. Recourse to coercion is inevitable, and the legislator has not failed to do so. But by this very fact it was necessary to abandon the idea of subjecting the shares of foreign companies to the new regime. The coercive procedures instituted by the law are ineffective against the owners of shares in foreign companies by the simple fact that these companies, which have their registered office abroad, escape the prescriptions of French law outside French territory.'

53 It should be noted that the law applicable to the form of securities also extends to the possibility and conditions under which the form of the security may be changed from registered to bearer and vice versa. The conversion from one form to the other should depend exclusively on the law that governed the issue, because governing the conversion of the form of a security is still governing the form of the security. In this sense, the law of the register for registered securities must be set aside, as Bartin recommended (see E. Bartin, *Principes de droit international privé*, t. III, Paris, Domat-Montchrestien, 1935, para. 378, pp. 54–55). From a French perspective, this means for example that Art. L. 228-1 para. 4 of the Commercial Code, according to which: 'Notwithstanding any agreement to the contrary, any owner whose securities are part of an issue comprising both bearer and registered securities has the option of converting his securities into the other form', is applicable to French companies, regardless of the form of holding used. Moreover, this makes it possible to apply one and the same law to this issue, where the law of the relevant securities account where the book entry is made may be different from the place of the register where the registered securities are registered.

revoked by the issuer as well as granted.[54] This is not a theoretical hypothesis: French law, in the event of dispossession of a certificated bearer security, has been able to oblige French issuers, when notified of the dispossession, to suspend the negotiability of the security.[55] This explanation is in line with a more general rule of private international law according to which it is up to the law that has established a condition to define the consequences of its violation.[56] However, this application of the issuer's law is not a necessity: it is possible that the issuer's law makes it possible to apply another law to the form of these securities. This is particularly justified in the case where the *negotium* is itself subject to a foreign law, because of the close links between the form of the securities and the *negotium* represented.[57] In the latter case, it is preferable to apply the *lex creationis* to the form of the securities, i.e. the law of the contract of issue. The application of the *lex creationis* to the form of the securities is similar to the conflict rule applicable more generally to claims.[58]

301. How the *lex creationis* is applied. There are two possibilities: either the law of the issuer imposes a defined form on all financial securities, irrespective of the place of issue or the *negotium* represented, in which case there is no doubt that this form must be respected on pain of incurring the sanctions provided for by the law of the issuer, which may go as far as the nullity of the securities issued; or the issuer's law is self-limiting, materially by applying only to a particular security (equity securities), or spatially by applying only to issues to local investors. In the latter case, the liberalism of the issuer's law will allow the application of a foreign law to the form of the securities.[59] The question of the articulation of the law of

---

54 See already in this sense, M. Ooi, *Shares and other securities in the conflict of laws*, *op. cit.* However, the author only considers shares.

55 See *infra*, para. 640.

56 See in the field of marriage, Cass. civ., 6 March 1956, *veuve Moreau*, see B. Ancel and Y. Lequette, *Les grands arrêts de la jurisprudence française de droit international privé*, 5th ed., Paris, Dalloz.

57 On the one hand, French company law does not allow all companies to issue shares: only joint stock companies can do so and benefit from the regime of Articles L. 228-1 et seq. of the Commercial Code. The *negotium* is therefore attached to a particular corporate form. Furthermore, the form of the share has an impact on it: the benefit of a double voting right is thus sometimes conditional on the share being in registered form (Art. L. 225-123 of the Commercial Code). These observations show the influence that the *instrumentum* can have on the *negotium* and vice versa.

58 Indeed, Art. 14(2) of the Rome I Regulation provides that: 'The law which governs the debt which is the subject of the assignment or subrogation determines the assignability of the debt, the relationship between the assignee or subrogated party and the debtor, the conditions under which the assignment or subrogation may be relied on as against the debtor and the nature of the performance made by the debtor.' Transposed to financial securities, there is no doubt that the notion of "law governing the debt' refers to the law applicable to the *negotium* issued, rather than to the law of the issuer.

59 See H. Synvet and A. Tenenbaum, 'Instruments financiers', *op. cit.*, no. 16, who consider that if a foreign law can apply to the form, it is only 'to the extent permitted by the law of the issuer'.

the issuer and the *lex creationis* is then likely to be addressed in two ways. The first is to subject the form of the securities to the *lex creationis*, in the form of a bilateral conflict rule, reserving the possible applicability of the prohibitive rules of the law of the issuer as an overriding mandatory rule. Since the *lex creationis* is contractual here, the conflict rule will leave the possibility for the issuer to designate the applicable law, since proper use of the *electio juris* clause can only be made by designating the law of the issuer or the law of the *negotium*, and not another law. The second is to retain the application of the law of the issuer to the form of the securities, but to make use of the renvoi mechanism in order to allow the application of the *lex creationis* to the form of the securities where the law of the issuer will allow it. The following developments will show that this is the case in French law.

II. Criteria for the Application of French Law

302. Determining the criteria for the application of French law. The issue at stake here is to know to what extent a French company wishing to issue securities to foreign investors may subject the form of its securities to foreign law. The applicability of French rules is determined by Article L. 211-3 of the Monetary and Financial Code, which makes securities 'issued in French territory and subject to French law' subject to French forms. Two criteria appear: issuance in France, and submission of the security to French law. This second criterion for subjecting financial securities to French law does not pose any difficulty: it is deemed to have been met when the issuer has its registered office in France.[60] On the other hand, the first criterion for the location of the issue in France is not linked to the issuer's registered office. Although the Commercial Code is silent on the criterion for the location of the issue,[61] an old circular nevertheless stated:

> 'French securities are understood to mean: securities issued by a public or private legal person in France and denominated in francs. Foreign securities are understood to mean: securities issued by a public or private legal person abroad as well as securities issued by a public or private legal person in France when these securities are denominated in a foreign currency.'[62]

---

60 H. Synvet and A. Tenenbaum, 'Instruments financiers', *op. cit.*, nos. 82–83.

61 The Commercial Code mentions the case of a foreign issue by a French company when it excludes, as a matter of principle, the provisions relating to the mass of issues subject to foreign law, see *infra*, para. 319.

62 Circular of 31 May 1968 on foreign accounts in francs and foreign securities records, issued in application of Decree no. 68-481 of 29 May 1968 and Order of 30 May 1968, *OJ*, 2 June 1968, pp. 5375–5376.

The currency of the contract of issue thus became the instrument of its localisation. This criterion, designed by the circular to allow authorised intermediaries to manage foreign securities on behalf of residents without authorisation from the *Banque de France*, did not prosper. Most authors have taken two approaches to the criterion for determining the location of the issue: those who consider that only issues offered to the French market are located in France, according to a criterion based on the recipient of the securities, and those who focus on the nature of the issue, i.e. the location of the material operations that make up the issue process.[63] In order to decide this question, it is necessary to identify the purpose of these rules of form.

303. Purpose of the French form rules. Three objectives guide the French rules on the form of securities. The first, traditional and overriding, is the protection of the holder of the security.[64] The related rules are primarily intended to protect French residents, and could therefore be limited to issues by French companies soliciting French residents. The difficulty lies, however, in the fact that some of the rules on form sometimes pursue objectives specific to tax law. This is the second objective. The dematerialisation of securities was intended to enable the tax authorities to control certain monetary flows in order to extract the tax.[65] The third objective of the form rules is to enable the issuer to keep track of the securities issued, so as to know how many securities are in circulation.[66] French issuers are indeed required to inform their shareholders on a monthly basis of the 'total number of voting rights and (*the*) number of shares making up the company's capital if they have varied from those previously published'.[67] This knowledge of the number of shares issued, which is necessary for the proper

[63] As H Synvet and A. Tenenbaum write, 'for the latter group of authors, if the offer and acceptance are located abroad, as well as the making available of the funds and the first book entry, then these are securities issued abroad, the nationality of the issuer, the subscribers and the currency of the issue being factors that are irrelevant to this location' (H. Synvet and A. Tenenbaum, 'Instruments financiers', *op. cit.*, no. 86).

[64] This is also the case for the form rules for negotiable instruments, see *infra*, para. 604. The rules of form of securities are part of the more general function of rules of form, see B. Audit and L. d'Avout, *Droit international privé*, *op. cit.*

[65] As Paul Didier writes, 'very quickly savings showed a sustained preference for bearer securities. There is no mystery in this preference: a portfolio of bearer securities more easily escapes the curiosity of the tax authorities than a portfolio of registered securities. But precisely for this reason, legislators made numerous efforts throughout the first half of the 20th century to persuade savings to invest in registered securities. In vain: tax incentives, double voting rights, simplification of the securities regime, nothing was successful', see P. Didier, *Droit commercial t. 3*, Paris, PUF, 1993, p. 61. On the dematerialisation law, see *infra*, para. 652.

[66] For a recent illustration of the importance of accounting in the internal functioning of the company, see A. Gaudemet, 'Comptabilité des titres financiers en rétention et droit de participer aux assemblées générales d'actionnaires', *Bull. Joly. Sociétés*, June 2020, pp. 6 et seq.

[67] Art. L. 233-8(II) of the Commercial Code. The information is only due before each Annual General Meeting (AGM) for unlisted companies.

functioning of the issuer and in particular the Annual General Meeting (AGM), is facilitated by dematerialisation. The accounting of securities is ensured by a single authentic register, kept by the issuer, or an account holder authorised for this purpose or by the central depository. The existence of securities subject to a foreign form, and possibly materialised, will therefore have to be recorded in the register; the application of a foreign law does not constitute an obstacle to the pursuit of this objective.

304. If one insists on the first objective of protecting the purchaser, one will retain the narrower connecting factor of the place of solicitation, i.e. the solicitation of French investors will lead to the submission of the financial securities to French form rules, while the solicitation of foreign investors will make it possible to submit the securities issued to foreign law. If one insists on the second objective specific to tax law, one would be tempted to extend the scope of application of the rules on the form of securities. However, it seems to us that the place of solicitation of the securities issued should prevail, for several reasons. The first is that it is not the function of the French tax administration to monitor and control the assets of foreign residents.[68] The second reason is that such a constraint leads to an unreasonable scope of application of French standards in that they become an obstacle to the collection of foreign savings. The third reason is that the purpose of issuing abroad, and in particular of choosing a foreign law, is to give the foreign investor the feeling of protection that comes from knowing the law under which the acquisition is made. In this sense, the very objective assigned to the rules of form – the protection of the person solicited – is in favour of the possibility of subjecting to foreign law the forms under which a French company is prospecting for investors, *a fortiori* when the issue is subject to that law.[69]

305. Two objections can undoubtedly be made to the reasoning here: on the one hand, the traditional rule applicable to form, *locus regit actum*, designates the place of subscription of the financial instrument and, on the other hand, the plurality of places of solicitation does not allow for the identification of a single place. First of all, while it is true that forms are generally governed by the place where the contract is signed, this rule of conflict is generally explained by the favouring appearance and convenience, as well as by the predictability of such a

---

68 It is true that the interests of the tax administration would be better protected by an extensive conception of these formal rules. However, it seems to us that the protection of these interests should rather be achieved through cooperation agreements with foreign tax authorities.

69 This argument therefore tempers the theoretical possibility of a threefold dissociation between the law of the issuer, the *lex contractus* of the contract of issue, and the rules of form of the securities.

choice for the parties.[70] These two reasons combine, in the case of cross-border issues, to allow the issuer to extend the *lex contractus* of the issuance contract to the forms of the debt securities through which it solicits foreign investors. Indeed, this choice is predictable, and the appearance of the security then corresponds to the law governing the regime of the right issued. Secondly, the plurality of the places of solicitation does not constitute an obstacle here because of the conditions under which the selection of the applicable law is made: the extension of the *lex contractus* to the conditions of form makes it possible to identify a single law, the one selected by the issuer with a view to marketing its securities on the prospected foreign market.[71]

306. Intervention of the *lex mercatus*. At the end of these developments, it should be noted that the law of the financial market does not impose its application to the securities that it admits to trading on its system. Instead, the financial market law imposes on the issuer the respect of material rules, sanctioned by a set of measures that can go as far as the suspension or even the delisting of the securities.[72] The clearest sign that the law of the financial market takes into account the primacy of the law of the issuer is that it requires the issuer to comply with its requirements, both in terms of the rules governing its internal organisation and those relating to the issuance of securities.[73]

Secondly, it solves the difficulties related to the form of the securities by requiring their admission to the central depository system.[74] The latter will, in one way or another,[75] dematerialise the securities, the admission of which will assume that they have been stipulated as bearer securities, unless the issuer retains the maintenance of the account in which the security is held.[76] Moreover, the central depository will take care of the accounting of the securities and will allow the transfer by a simple transfer from account to account within the system it manages. All this explains the particular attraction of the law of the central depository's securities settlement system as regards the

---

70 P. Louis-Lucas, 'La distinction du fond et de la forme dans le règlement des conflits de lois' in *Mélanges offert à Jacques Maury*, t. 1, *Droit international privé et public*, Paris, Dalloz/Sirey, p. 175, spec. p. 177. On this question, see also *infra*, paras. 616 et seq.

71 See H. Synvet, 'L'internationalisation du droit des affaires', *op. cit.* Observing the conditions of Art. L. 211-4 of the Commercial Code, the author deduces that '*a contrario*, French companies are authorised to adopt the traditional bearer form when the issue takes place abroad [...]. All in all, a bond placed abroad by a French issuer may look quite different from its domestic counterpart, not because the ordinary law regime is flawed, but because it is necessary to deal with other financial practices'.

72 Art. 6901 of the Euronext Market Rules (Book I). On this issue, see also A. Tenenbaum, *L'application internationale du droit bousier*, *op. cit.*, pp. 386 et seq.

73 Arts. 6201 and 6203 of the Euronext Market Rules (Book I).

74 Art. 3 CSD Regulation.

75 Either by directly maintaining the authentic register, or by immobilising the securities issued by the issuer and determining ownership through its register, see *infra*, paras. 658 et seq.

76 F. Drummond, *Droit financier*, *op. cit.*

proprietary status of the securities issued,[77] and the corresponding restriction of the issuer's competence as regards the form of the securities.

Thirdly, the *lex mercatus* (i.e. the law of the trading system) will deactivate the transfer restrictions arising from the *lex creationis* by making the admission of the securities conditional on the removal of any statutory clauses restricting transfers of shares, or clauses in the contract of issue having the same effect for debt securities. This shows the great lucidity of the law of the financial market with regard to the different laws involved. It is aware of the powers of these laws and does not try to fight them on their own ground, but makes compliance with certain solutions a condition for the use of the trading system. The purpose of these conditions is not to protect the users, but rather to protect the trading system, which could not function properly if the securities were not perfectly 'liquid'. The notion of liquidity[78] uses a metaphor more often used for money to mean the ease with which the object can be exchanged.[79] In the context of financial markets, the liquidity of the security means that it can be traded at any time. Liquidity is both economic and legal: there must be a minimum of supply and demand,[80] and the transfer must be legally irrevocable, rapid and unconstrained.

307. Section conclusion. If the conditions of the issue are subject only to the law of the issuer, this law does not necessarily extend to the obligations of the contributor, nor to the regime of transfer of ownership of the object of the contribution; this law nevertheless ensures its effectiveness by making compliance with its prescriptions the condition for the ownership of the securities issued. Nor does the law of the issuer necessarily apply to the form of the securities, which may be subject to a third law and, in particular, to the law of the *negotium* issued. Faced with the law of the financial market, the issuer is obliged, through the accession agreement, to respect certain material solutions

---

77 However, the choice of this form does not lead to the dissemination of *instruments*: precisely, the issue of securities with a central depository results in the centralisation of securities with a single depository. It will be seen, however, that as the law stands, the presence of a central depositary, while it modifies the applicable conflict of laws rule, does not necessarily lead to the application of a single law, see *infra*, nos. 676 et seq.

78 Defined by the French-language on-line dicrionary as the 'character of what flows'. This metaphor is not isolated; in the same lexical register, the market rules speak of 'free float' to designate the share of the company's issued securities that must be traded in order to justify admission to trading.

79 This is not by chance, since financial securities can be substituted for money in certain respects: for example, they can be remitted to the central bank in lieu of cash (see *supra*, note under para. 287) and are used as collateral for refinancing operations (see *infra*, note under para. 746).

80 This is why there must be a minimum of 'free float', but also why there are 'market makers' whose function is to trade in the security to keep it alive, so that an accurate monetary value can be attached to the security. The more a security is traded, the more secure its market value can appear. On liquidity agreements binding the issuer, see T. Bonneau *et al.*, *Droit financier*, *op. cit.*, no. 1023.

likely to guarantee the negotiability of the securities: the removal of statutory clauses, such as approval clauses, likely to restrict the free negotiability of the securities, but also the deposit of the securities admitted to trading in the systems of a central depositary.

SECTION 2. CONFLICTS OF LAWS SPECIFIC TO THE ISSUED *NEGOTIUM*

308. The *negotia*. If the *instrumentum* is subject to conflict of laws, this is also the case for *negotia*. We know that the Monetary and Financial Code allows for the representation of different rights by securities. Thus, Article L. 211-1(II) of the Monetary and Financial Code provides: 'Financial securities are: 1. capital securities issued by joint-stock companies; 2. debt securities; 3. units or shares of collective investment undertakings.' The *lex mercatus* interacts differently with each regime. We will study this intervention successively on shares[81] (§ 1), debt securities (§ 2), and units or shares of collective investment undertakings. (§ 3).

[81] In financial matters, the French legislator is increasingly replacing the notion of share with that of capital security. This concept appeared for the first time in the General Regulations of the Conseil des bourses de valeurs and was taken up by the legislator in the law of 2 July 1996 aimed at modernising financial activities (P. Le Cannu, 'Réflexions sur l'apport de la loi du 2 juillet 1996 au droit des sociétés', *Bull. Joly*, 1996, p. 796; see also the retrospective of this notion by A. Couret, H. Le Nabasque, *et al.*, *Droit financier*, *op. cit.*, no. 650). At a time of diversification of shares, the expression 'capital security', which emphasises the fact that the share is a fraction of the share capital, has the advantage of being able to designate all the different types of shares, even if the traditional share, which confers the fullness of the company's prerogatives, remains the model from which all the others are derived (T. Bonneau and F. Drummond, *Droit des marchés financiers*, *op. cit.*, no. 96; M. Saad, *La notion de titre de capital*, Université Paris I Panthéon-Assas, 2016, no. 2). However, the notion of capital security has the disadvantage of contributing to the confusion between the share and its evidential instrument, the financial security. This disadvantage is a major one when one wishes to study carefully the conflicts of laws specific to the *negotium*. We will therefore use here the notion of share which, despite the diversity of existing types of shares, retains a perceptible conceptual unity, in particular, in that the share is a fraction of the share capital, and that it registers its owner within the general meeting, from which certain prerogatives common to all shareholders derive. On the fact that the share constitutes a share of the share capital which distinguishes it from other financial securities, see the above-mentioned thesis by Mr Saad, reproduced by A. Couret, H. Le Nabasque *et al.*, *Droit financier*, *op. cit.*, no. 401, note 3. In English law, the emphasis is sometimes placed on the particular prerogatives that they grant: some, following Pennington, consider that the share is defined by particular prerogatives ('bundle of rights and obligations'), while others consider that the share represents 'a participation right in the enterprise', L. Gullifer and J. Payne, 'Introduction', in *Intermediation and Beyond*, *op. cit.*, p. 5; see also, for a thorough discussion, *Corporate finance Law: principles and policy*, 2nd ed., Oxford, Hart, 2015, no. 3.2.1).

§ 1. THE SHARE

309. Basis of the jurisdiction of the *lex societatis*. The *lex societatis* applies to the shares as the *lex creationis* of the *negotium*, in the same way as the *lex contractus* of the contract of issue applies to the debt evidenced by the debt security. The *lex societatis* has an invariable jurisdiction over the shares, as does the law of the issuer over the terms of the issue. One might be tempted to explain this jurisdiction of the *lex societatis* by the fact that shares always have their source in a contract that is necessarily subject to it: the articles of association.[82] It would be as if the articles of association were the framework contract at the origin of the shares, of which any issue contracts specific to each category of share would only be contracts of application. It seems to us, however, that the argument undermines itself: by recalling the fundamentally contractual relationship of the shareholders to the legal person or grouping, it allows a dissociation according to the shares, a dissociation favoured by the existence in French company law of a large variety of shares. Adding an additional type from a foreign legal system to their list seems all the easier since the '*dépeçage*' is a well-known feature of international contracts, and this possibility is already available for debt securities; the borderline between the former and equity securities is tenuous.[83]

310. However, it seems to us that there are two reasons why shares must be subject to the *lex societatis*. The first is material and results from the principle of equal treatment of shareholders.[84] It will no doubt be argued that French law itself has a large number of exceptions to this principle; however, French law is the sole arbiter of the possible distance between the different categories of shares, allowing the concept to retain a unitary regime, which can be seen in the unalterable nature of certain political prerogatives. The second reason is conflictual: the shareholders constitute the founding community of the company, and the unity of the law applicable to their status conditions the proper functioning of the company. Here we find the argument of the legislative unity necessary for the internal functioning of organisations, but this argument undoubtedly gains additional strength when a legal person is involved. In this case, the country establishing the legal person has an unavoidable power to determine the composition of its organs and, in particular, the members of the AGM, which are crucial to its operation. This inseparable link between the

82 For a contractual analysis of the commitment evidenced by shares, see F. Nizard, *Les titres négociables*, Paris, Economica, 2003, nos. 277 et seq.

83 F.-X. Lucas, 'La distinction des titres de capital et des titres de créance' in A. Couret and H. Le Nabasque (dir.), *Quel avenir pour le capital social?*, Paris, Dalloz, 2004, pp. 21 et seq.

84 On the function of this principle, see *infra*, para. 471.

shareholding and the legal person explains the dependency between the law applicable to the share and the law applicable to the legal person.[85]

311. Scope. A number of aspects follow from this original jurisdiction and the impossibility of derogating from it. First of all, as the Court of Cassation expressed it perfectly in its *Royal Dutch* judgment, the *lex societatis* alone has jurisdiction to determine shareholder status.[86] This is why it is also the only one able to determine the conditions under which this status is obtained, as well as the political[87] and pecuniary[88] prerogatives resulting from the share. Secondly, the *lex societatis* is free to leave it up to the shareholders to specify the conditions under which they wish to be associated and, consequently, to

---

85 This is all the more true since the disappearance of the legal personality makes it possible, as a counterpoint, to engage the responsibility of the shareholders by virtue of another law, that of the collective procedure; the French legal action in insufficiency of assets is the most striking emanation of this. This observation allows two remarks. Firstly, the legal fiction of legal personality is said to create a 'veil' between the shareholder and the company's assets, so that if the shareholder holds a share of the company's capital, he is not the owner of the company's assets and has no real right over the assets (In English law, although the existence of legal personality also prevents the shareholder from owning the company's assets, the notion of real right nevertheless reappears in order to designate the various prerogatives that the shareholder has against the company: income, fraction of the capital, and voting rights, 'an intangible property right in the company made up of income, capital and voting rights', see M. Ooi, *Shares and other securities in the conflict of laws*, *op. cit.*, no. 3.10). Conversely, the disappearance of the legal person makes it possible, under certain conditions, to seek the liability of the shareholder for acts carried out by the legal person. Secondly, it will be suggested here that the law of the collective proceedings, if it acts as such, can also take advantage of the basis of the law of tort, since it aims to allow the legal system affected by the fault of the shareholders to determine the reparation.

86 See *supra*, para. 291.

87 Political prerogatives, and in particular the right to vote, manifest the intrinsic link between the share and legal personality. It is therefore not surprising that the *lex societatis* has the sole competence to determine the existence, the modalities and the effective exercise of the right to vote. Two types of difficulties may arise: one relating to the identification of non-resident shareholders owning their shares through an intermediary, the other relating to groups of companies. The first difficulty, which has less to do with the field of *lex societatis* than with its reconciliation with contemporary methods of shareholding, has been resolved by granting intermediaries the possibility of attending and voting at general meetings (on this point, see the developments of H. Synvet and A. Tenenbaum, 'Instruments financiers', *op. cit.*, no. 109; C. Coupet, *L'attribution du droit de vote dans les sociétés*, *op. cit.)* The second difficulty arises from the possibility open to certain companies to issue shares or debts enabling them to acquire shares or debts of another company, whether a subsidiary or a parent company (Art. L. 228-93 and 94 of the Commercial Code; on this option, see A. Couret, H. Le Nabasque, *et al.*, *Droit financier*, *op. cit.*, nos. 551 et seq.) In the latter case, whatever the case, the conflict can only be resolved by the cumulative application of the two *lex societatis*: the competent bodies according to the registered office of each company will have to give a prior ruling before the issue of these securities.

88 The application of the *lex societatis* then extends to the conditions of the amount and form of the dividends that it wishes to pay to its shareholders; conversely, it is applicable to the limitation of the company's rights with respect to the shareholders, in particular with respect to the repayment of the securities in the event of non-payment of the capital (Y. Loussouarn and J.-D. Bredin, *Droit du commerce international*, *op. cit.*, no. 332).

allow the articles of association, depending on the corporate form, to decide on the conditions determining the ownership of the shares, the restrictions on the transfer of the shares, or the methods of exercising the prerogatives resulting from the share.[89] This freedom left to the articles of association, based on the unwavering competence of the *lex societatis* with regard to shares, gives rise to two observations.

The first is that this freedom has been perceived by the financial market legislator. This is why it requires the issuer wishing to admit its shares to trading to amend several elements of its articles of association, in particular any approval clauses or clauses restricting the transferability of shares. Here, the *ratio legis* is identical to the one pursued by the rules on the form of securities: it is a matter of allowing the trading system to function smoothly.

The second is that the contract for the issue of shares is closely linked to the articles of association, which triggers various delimitation issues as to the scope of these two acts. First of all, the contract of issuance may give rise to agency relationships affecting the functioning of the legal personality, for example in the case where the shares are held in trust.[90] In this case, the scope of the *lex societatis* must be strictly limited to relations between corporate bodies, on the understanding, on the one hand, that 'relationships between settlors and trustees fall [...] within the scope of the *lex contractus*'[91] and, on the other hand, that the *lex societatis* will be likely to preclude any contractual provision in the representation contract that might interfere with 'the legal status of the partner in relation to the company'.[92] Secondly, the issue contract may also constitute a marketing act. All marketing clauses, even if they are included in an identical instrument, may be included within the material scope of the Rome I Regulation. They will therefore be subject to the common private international law of contracts and to the interferences that choice of law has – both in the principle of free determination of the applicable law, in particular in relations with consumers, and in the possible laws applicable to marketing.[93]

---

[89] It is also because it is the *lex creationis* of the share that the *lex societatis* authorises or prohibits the conversion of shares into debt claims - it is known that in French law, shares cannot be converted into debt claims (Art. L. 228-91 para. 5 of the Commercial Code); comp. H. Synvet and A. Tenenbaum who see this as a rule specific to the issue, 'Instruments financiers', *op. cit.*, no. 14.

[90] This is the assumption of the CJEU judgment in Case C-272/18, *TvP v. VKI*, ECLI:EU:C:2019:827.

[91] *Ibid.*, para. 40.

[92] In the words of Mr Chacornac, note cited above. The author also describes perfectly the distinction with the situation of a possible bondholder: 'While the bondholder is an incidental actor of company law, who sinks into its constraints a loan contract of a particular kind, the partner is the essential actor of company law, whose exercise of rights is the oil of the company mechanism.' (*ibid.*)

[93] See *infra*, paras. 337; 829.

312. Consideration of the *lex mercatus*. The *lex mercatus* does not apply, as a matter of principle, to the share regime. However, far from ignoring it, the former conditions the application of some of its own rules on the latter. Indeed, not only is the ownership of shares taken into consideration by the rules on threshold crossing and public offers, but also the details of their prerogatives, simply because these rules base their applicability on the 'voting power'[94] of shareholders. They require the holder of the voting power to declare its threshold or even to file a public offer. Moreover, the *lex mercatus* ensures its effectiveness by depriving a shareholder who does not comply with the rules of voting power, thus interfering with the share regime, of his voting rights. This second aspect explains the need for capital market law to be consistent with the *lex societatis.*[95]

§ 2. THE DEBT

313. Choice and scope of the law of the contract. Debt securities traditionally represent a contract for the lending of money[96] between the issuer and the

---

94 On this notion, theorised by Mr Chacornac, see *infra*, para. 473.

95 The difficulties arising from this coordination are discussed in more detail *infra*,paras. 466 et seq.

96 Defending the contractual qualification of the transaction, see F. Nizard, *Les titres négociables*, *op. cit.*
The characterisation of a *loan contract* as a *sum of money contract* could nowadays be discussed. Indeed, the configuration of the loan contract traditionally lies in the uniqueness of the lender. However, although it is possible to issue debt securities individually, it is most often within a group of creditors likely to exercise their rights in common that the bondholders are registered, which is reflected in French law by the group of bondholders. No doubt this character also exists in certain sophisticated loan contracts where several lenders join together to provide the sum necessary to finance a project of the issuer; what appears to be the principle for debt securities is nevertheless the exception in the case of loans. In addition, although loan contracts can be transferred, they cannot be transferred with the same ease as debt securities and do not benefit from the same regime when transferred. Finally, it is not certain that this characterisation takes into account the variety of debt securities issued: those giving access to capital are thus irreducible to a simple money lending contract. Finally, from the point of view of private international law, it leads to two inappropriate results. Firstly, from the point of view of conflict of laws, the characterisation as a loan contract leads to the application of the law of the domicile of the owner of the debt security in the absence of a choice of law. Indeed, the Court of Justice has had occasion to hold that 'in a credit agreement concluded between a credit institution and a borrower, the provision of services consists in the remittance to the latter of a sum of money by the former in exchange for remuneration paid by the borrower, in principle, in the form of interest' (Case C-249/16, *Kareda*, ECLI:EU:C:2017:472, paras. 34–38, spec. para. 36). In relation to the issue of debt securities, it is indeed the owner of the security who, by providing the sum of money, provides the characteristic service. Secondly, from the point of view of determining the competent court, this classification leads to depriving the parties to the contract of issue of a special contractual forum: by classifying the contract of issue as a loan contract, it becomes a contract for the provision of a service, for which it will be very difficult to determine the place where the service is provided (see *infra*, para. 404).

holder of the security.[97] The following study is based on this type of debt. Although it represents the most frequent contract, the category of debt securities is nevertheless residual and is intended to accommodate 'all securities issued collectively which represent a claim against the issuer provided that it is not the right conferred by an obligation'.[98] In these various cases, the solutions proposed here may be extended by analogy. Pecuniary loan contracts are subject to the choice of law option of the Rome I Regulation. This choice will most often be between the law of the issuer and the law of the place where the securities are mainly marketed.[99] As the contract of issue is usually drawn up by the issuer, it is the latter who will designate the applicable law.[100] This solution, which is an old one,[101] faces three types of difficulties relating to the law of the contract.[102] The first, already studied, is the borderline with the conditions of issue and the form of the securities. We have seen that the law of the bond contract cannot be extended to the conditions of the issue itself, since the prohibitive rules to which the issuer is subject by virtue of its *lex societatis* always remain applicable,[103] but

---

97 On the notion of debt security, see A. Couret, H. Le Nabasque *et al.*, *Droit financier*, *op. cit.*, no. 664. The situation is more complex in contemporary positive law, since alongside debt securities issued by fungible stock there are now negotiable debt securities, issued individually, which are essentially used for short-term money lending (see A. Couret, H. Le Nabasque *et al.*, *Droit financier*, *op. cit.)* In addition, pecuniary claims do not exhaust the category of debt securities, which also includes complex or hybrid debt securities, which may give access to capital or give the right to the allocation of debt securities, but also derivative securities, see *ibid.* Finally, it is not certain that all debt securities represent a contract. For example, the contractual nature of fungible Treasury bonds (OATs) is disputed (M. Audit, 'L'État français s'endette-t-il par contrat? A la recherche de la nature juridique des obligations assimilables du Trésor [OAT]', *Revue des contrats*, September 2018, pp. 462 et seq. F. Nizard, *Les titres négociables*, *op. cit.*, nos. 252 et seq.)

98 F. Drummond, *Droit financier*, *op. cit.*

99 The latter may nevertheless impose its law, see the American example where the *Trust Indenture Act* requires the application of local law to debt securities marketed there, S. Lambert, *L'application internationale du droit financier*, *op. cit.*, no. 223; report on the imposition of local law by the Swiss, Luxembourg and Belgian regulators on contracts allowing the 'distribution' of units of UCIs (e.g. Swiss, Luxembourg and Belgian), *ibid.*, no. 236.

100 The lack of choice of law would lead to an unfortunate result if a bond issue were to be treated as a monetary contract regardless of the particularity of the issue. Indeed, the Court of Justice had the opportunity to state that the characteristic performance of a loan contract was the lending of the money. Here, this makes the law of the investor's domicile applicable to the contract, whereas the application of a single law to all securities resulting from the same issue is likely not only to facilitate the management of these contracts by the issuer, but also to allow the equality of investors for an identical bond issue. On this point, see *supra*, para. 368.

101 It is stated without ambivalence in the *Messageries Maritimes* judgment, Cass., 1re civ., 21 June 1950, B. Ancel and Y. Lequette, *Les grands arrêts de la jurisprudence française de droit international privé*, *op. cit.*, comm. no. 22).

102 While there is no doubt that the *lex contractus* governs the conditions of formation of the obligation and its regime (remuneration, payment and guarantees of the bondholders, see Arts. 10 and 12 of the Rome I Regulation), it must be reconciled with the related categories.

103 E.g. Art. L. 211-2 of the Monetary and Financial Code, see *supra*, paras. 291 et seq.

that the form of the securities can be subject to it according to the freedom left by the law of the issuer.

The second difficulty is linked to the interweaving of the contract of issue and the *lex societatis* in its external relations. This is particularly true in the case of creditor protection in the event of a merger of the issuing entity, where the conflict of laws is resolved in favour of the *lex societatis* of the absorbed company.[104] Indeed, this law, because it is applicable to the dissolution of the legal entity, will also govern its effects, in particular those relating to the protection of creditors.[105] EU law nevertheless provides in this case for a substantive rule[106] offering to the owners of debt securities, under certain conditions,[107] a special protection under the terms of which "the holders of securities, other than shares, to which special rights are attached shall enjoy, within the acquiring company, rights at least equivalent to those they enjoyed in the company being acquired [...]'.[108] However, this provision is limited to a particular category of debts, those to which special rights are attached, among which debt securities giving access to capital play an important role. This category therefore leads to the third difficulty, which arises from cases where the law of the bond contract affects the internal organisation of the company. This last aspect will be the focus of our attention because it is here that the *lex mercatus* is likely to intervene, under the regulation of market transactions, in support of the *lex societatis*. We will first look at cases where the debt, which is more complex than a simple loan of money, allows access to capital (I), and then at the provisions governing the contract of issue and affecting the internal organisation of the company (II).

I. Debts Giving Access to Capital

314. Internal classification of securities giving access to capital. Securities giving access to capital are complex securities, one of the particularities of which is that they can give access to capital, particularly by exchange, conversion or

104 Case C-483/14, *KA Finanz*, ECLI:EU:C:2016:205.

105 As Mr Chacornac writes in his above-mentioned note, 'in the final analysis, the law of the absorbed company continues to determine the creditor protection regime, according to a teleological rather than a literal argument, which finds a convincing justification in the need to secure the forecasts of third parties, who would otherwise risk seeing a legal hazard added to the economic hazard resulting from a restructuring operation'.

106 Originally from the article of Directive 78/855/EEC (the so-called 'Merger Directive') and now included in Art. 101 of the Company Law Harmonisation Directive 2017/1132.

107 Art. 101 of Directive 2017/1132 limits this protection in cases where 'the modification of those rights has been approved by a meeting of the holders of those securities, where national law provides for such a meeting, or by the holders of those securities individually, or if those holders have the right to have their securities redeemed by the acquiring company'.

108 Art. 101 of Directive 2017/1132.

redemption.[109] These securities therefore have a hybrid nature: these claims against the company always carry with them the possibility of their holder becoming a shareholder. The Court of Cassation had the opportunity to rule on their characterisation in its decision in *Métrologie*.[110] It stated that the rules applicable to these complex securities, as long as the latter have not been transformed and including if their transformation into shares is inevitable, were those derived from the law of obligations, and those derived from company law. However, a legislative act from 24 June 2004, now codified in the Monetary and Financial Code, assimilates securities that may give access to capital to the category of equity securities.[111] Some scholars believe that this reform is not likely to call into question the case law, while observing that the scope of the case law has been reduced to a minimum due to the unification of the regime for complex securities.[112]

315. Law applicable to securities giving access to capital. From an international point of view, however, the classification of securities giving access to capital is decisive for the solution of the conflict of laws. If, as in domestic law, these securities are assimilated to capital securities, the *lex societatis* is the only one applicable to any bond loan whose repayment can be made in shares and, in general, to the regime of all issues of securities giving or capable of giving access to capital. On the other hand, if one retains, at least for the purposes of conflict of laws, the characterisation of debt securities, a more subtle solution is possible.[113] The contract of issuance may then be subject to a choice of law on the part of

---

109 On conversion, see A. Couret, 'La notion juridique de conversion' in *Mélanges offerts à Pierre Vigreux*, Toulouse, Université des sciences sociales de Toulouse I, 1981, p. 219; F.-X. Lucas, 'La distinction des titres de capital et des titres de créances', in *Quel avenir pour le capital social?*, *op. cit.* Note that this prerogative can sometimes be left to the discretion of an event or a third party, see D. Poracchia, 'Remarques sur la titularité du droit de convertir des obligations en action', *RTDF*, 2015, no. 1/2, p. 107.

110 Cass. com., 13 June 1995, *Bull. civ.*, IV, no. 181, p. 168; *Rev. Sociétés*, 1995, 736, note P. Didier; *JCP* E, 1995, I, 712, note Y. Guyon; *Bull. Joly sociétés*, 1995, 855, para. 305, note A. Couret; *RDBB*, 1995, 148, obs. M. Germain and M.-A. Frison-Roche. *Adde*. P. Le Cannu, 'Obligations remboursables en actions: les enseignements de l'arrêt Métrologie International', *BJB*, 1995, para. 50, p. 251, F. Peltier, 'A propos de la nature juridique de la créance présentée par l'ORA. Réponse à P. Le Cannu', *BJB*, 1996, para. 3, p. 23.

111 Art. L. 212-1 A of the Monetary and Financial Code.

112 A. Couret, H. Le Nabasque *et al.*, *Droit financier*, *op. cit.*, no. 539. On the other hand, as the majority of the rules relating to the regime of complex securities are governed by the same articles, 'it will only be necessary to turn to the rules applicable to named primary securities (bonds or shares) to fill the gaps left open by the legislator' (*ibid.*). In any event, the equation made by the ordinance of 24 June 2004 is open to criticism since it does not allow the legal nature of these complex securities to be taken into account, see in the same sense, F. Drummond, *Droit des marchés financiers*, *op. cit.*, no. 94, who describe the connection of these securities as 'neither fair nor fruitful'.

113 It should be recalled here that a different characterisation is possible for the purposes of private international law.

the issuer. In the event of a choice, the scope of the *lex contractus* is nevertheless limited upstream and downstream by the *lex societatis*.

The scope of the *lex contractus* is limited upstream because the *lex societatis* is applicable to the rules on the conditions of the issue, both as regards the entities entitled to issue the securities and the body competent within the organisation to decide on the issue. The scope of the *lex contractus* is also limited downstream because, even if securities giving access to capital are considered as debt securities, the conditions of access to capital are also determined by the *lex societatis*. The application of the *lex societatis* results first of all from the sources of the regulation: securities giving access to capital are governed by Articles L. 228-91 et seq. of the Commercial Code, within a chapter specific to securities relating to joint stock companies; these companies are French companies. The application of the *lex societatis* is also deduced from the exclusion from the scope of the Rome I Regulation of matters relating to the internal functioning of the company. Access to the company's capital by a person from outside the company appears to be a modality of the company's internal functioning, if only because it determines membership of the most important body, the AGM, and because access to the company's capital is closely linked to control of the company. Thus, there is no doubt that the conversion clause itself will be subject to the *lex societatis*.[114]

This second characterisation, subsuming securities giving access to capital within debt securities, seems appropriate in private international law. It respects the legal nature of the *negotium*, which is indeed a claim irreducible to the share as long as it has not been transformed.[115] It is no coincidence that this orthodox position was favoured by the Cour de cassation in its *Metrology* decision. The Commercial Code itself treats holders of securities giving access to capital as bondholders: they are therefore subject to the regulations governing the group of bondholders. This characterisation provides a balanced solution for issuers wishing to solicit foreign investors. If the issue is subject to the law of their domicile, foreign investors retain the advantages of local law as long as they remain under the bond issue regime. On the other hand, they are

[114] Another reason is the equality between the different groups of bondholders who have in common that they are subject to the same body of public policy rules regarding access to capital. Differences between bondholders may of course result from the provisions of the contract of issuance, but the choice of law made in the contract should not be able to affect either the public policy provisions of the *lex societatis* applicable to access to capital or the provisions of the articles of association.

[115] As the doctrine states, 'many securities that can give access to capital are first of all bonds', see J.-J. Daigre and P. Pailler, 'Commentaire de l'ordonnance n° 2009-15 du 8 janvier 2009', *Rev. sociétés*, 2009, p. 37, no. 17; see more generally M. Saad, *La notion de titre de capital*, *op. cit.*

subject to the *lex societatis* from the moment they access the capital, including the terms of accession.[116]

316. Consideration by the *lex mercatus*. From a financial perspective, securities giving access to capital are considered together with equity securities, almost interchangeably, since for the applicability of threshold and takeover regulations only the voting power is relevant.[117] However, in the context of securities giving access to capital, a material distinction determines the applicability of the regulation. French law distinguishes between the case where access to capital is given by conversion, exchange or redemption of the bond by a share already issued, and the case where the issuer has to carry out a capital increase.[118] The distinction may seem too subtle in the sense that, from the point of view of capital market law, in both cases the bondholder has the voting power to obtain control. Nevertheless, in this case, it is probably less a difference in kind between the means of access to capital than a difference in degree that justifies the criterion for applying the regulation. Indeed, crossing a threshold or obtaining control will not be immediate if it is necessary for the bondholder to wait for the capital increase in order to obtain the additional shares. This capital increase requires the bondholder to wait for the AGM[119] or the decision of the delegated body. However, such an increase can be refused, which identifies the major difference between these two ways of access to capital: the latter is a right of claim against the issuer, whereas the former faculty vested in the bond is realised independently of the issuer. Another explanation offered for this rule is related to the clarity of the information sent to the market.[120]

---

116 No doubt one could object that such a solution leads to an excessive dismemberment of the bond contract. However, this criticism can be tempered by the distinct temporality under which the different laws apply.
See H. Synvet and A. Tenenbaum, 'Instruments Financiers, *op. cit.*, no. 18: 'As soon as it is a question of aggregating new members to the partnership or increasing the participation of certain partners, the mechanism which allows for enlargement cannot escape the jurisdiction of the law which governs both the partnership contract and the legal person.'

117 It is undoubtedly in this limited perspective that the assimilation made by Art. L. 212-1 A of the Monetary and Financial Code.

118 Art. L. 233-9(I)(4°) of the Commercial Code and Art. 223-11(II)(1°) of the AMF General Regulation. On this issue, see A. Couret, H. Le Nabasque *et al.*, *Droit financier*, *op. cit.*, nos. 543–545.

119 Except in cases of delegation.

120 A. Couret, H. Le Nabasque *et al.*, *Droit financier*, *op. cit.*, no. 545: 'If "potential" capital securities were included in the numerator, the denominator would logically have to be changed as well, as it would vary depending on the declarant; this would make the information sent to the market illegible.' The argument was raised by J.-F. Biard, 'Consultations publiques', *RDBF*, January 2009, 35.

II. Bond Issue Regime

317. Issue contract and bondholders group. The selection of the law applicable to the contract of issue may have an impact on the organisation of the company when a legal or contractual mechanism allows creditors to group together in order to influence corporate decisions. In such cases, the bond issue regime may have an influence on the internal organisation of the company: this is the case with French law on the '*masse des obligataires*' – bondholders group.[121] This deactivates in principle the provisions relating to the '*masse*' of 'loans issued abroad by French companies'.[122] This limitation does not put an end to all difficulties, in particular in the case where a foreign company submits the issue contract to French law: the option being then contractual, the issue contract may specify the application of the provisions relating to the 'masse'.[123] It is difficult to understand why foreign bondholders who have chosen French law should be deprived of the means that French law offers to adapt its relationship with the debtor.[124] Symmetrically, when a French company opts to include the provisions relating to the 'masse' in a cross-border issue, it should be able to contractually adjust the collective organisation of bondholders. Finally, the criterion of foreign issuance should be based on the solicitation of non-resident investors.

The bond issue regime is nevertheless likely to be affected by foreign debt restructuring mechanisms, which may be applied because of the choice of law of the bond contract. This is particularly true of schemes of arrangement, which are borrowed from English law and are frequently used in international trade. Although the withdrawal of the United Kingdom from the European Union may restrict their use, it was a more profound manifestation of the development of restructuring law, which is set to grow even more, and of which schemes were only one form of implementation. It is therefore necessary to consider the influence of capital market law on the bond issue regime when it provides for the possibility of a restructuring procedure.

318. Schemes of arrangement. A scheme of arrangement is a judicially enforced agreement between the bondholders and the company.[125] As summarised by Professor Payne:

---

121 Arts. L. 228-46 et seq. of the Commercial Code.

122 Art. L. 228-90 of the Commercial Code.

123 On this point, see H. Synvet and A. Tenenbaum, 'Instuments financiers', *op. cit.*, no. 25.

124 *Comp.* M. Audit, S. Bollée and P. Caillé, *Droit du commerce international et des investissements étrangers*, *op. cit.*, no. 493.

125 Part 26 of the Companies Act 2006. Section 895(1) of the Companies Act defines scheme of arrangement as 'a compromise or arrangement between a company and its creditors, or any class of them, or its members, or any class of them'. Like the 'masse des obligataires', the *scheme of arrangement* is, at least in part, derived from English company law.

> 'The English scheme of arrangement [...] is a flexible tool for reorganising a company's capital structure. Schemes of arrangement can be used in a wide compromise or arrangement between a company and its creditors or members about anything which they can properly agree amongst themselves. It is common to see both member-focused schemes and creditor-focused schemes. In practice, the most common schemes are those which seek to transfer control of a company, as an alternative to a takeover offer, and those which restructure the debts of a financially distressed company with a view to rescuing the company or its business'.[126]

This presentation makes it possible to understand the fundamental difficulty presented by schemes, which is to be the subject of a conflict of characterisation, between the laws of bond contracts,[127] the *lex societatis*, the *lex concursus* and, in the case where the company has admitted its securities to trading, the *lex mercatus*. It should be noted, however, that the question does not arise in the same way depending on whether a scheme between the company and the bondholders or between the company and the shareholders is involved. In the latter case, the scheme is often used in order to avoid the English regulation of tender offers,[128] and English law restricts its application to English companies only. However, the use of the scheme will trigger the threshold crossing and takeover legislation of the place of listing if English companies admit their securities to a foreign financial market. It is, however, in relation to the bondholders of a foreign company that schemes have caused the most difficulties. It will first be shown that, where they have a debt restructuring function, schemes are instruments relating to the prevention of insolvency, and should therefore be included in this category. Consequently, it is only insofar as they contribute to the objective pursued by the law of the seat of insolvency that they are likely to be recognised by the latter (A). This characterisation makes it necessary to distinguish between elements which, although affecting

---

126 J. Payne, 'Cross-border schemes of arrangement and forum shopping' (2013) *European Business Organisation Law Review*, pp. 563 et seq.

127 The *scheme of arrangement* can also take place with the shareholders, but there is no longer any doubt that it is applicable under English company law only, see *ibid.*, p. 568.

128 Indeed, in the case where the bidder wishes to obtain all of the capital, schemes of arrangement make it possible to obtain all of the capital as soon as 75% of the shareholders agree, whereas the 90% threshold is necessary under public offer law to obtain the squeeze-out (on this point in French law, see *infra*, para. 484 and in English law, see J. Payne, *Schemes of arrangement: Theory, Structure and Operation*, Cambridge, CUP, 2014, nos. 3 et seq. as to the scheme of arrangement used as a public offer, and spec. no. 3.7.2 on the advantages in terms of the threshold). Schemes differ from takeover law in that they are not addressed to the shareholders, but to the company, which is then the privileged interlocutor, and that they usually do not aim to obtain sole control of the company, but the entire capital. Such a situation, which makes hostile takeovers impossible, makes it less necessary to protect minority shareholders. On this aspect, see J. Payne, 'Schemes of arrangement, takeovers and minority shareholder protection' (April 2011) *Journal of corporate law*, p. 67.

restructuring, fall within the remit of the *lex societatis* and, where applicable, the *lex mercatus* (B).

A. Scheme and Restructuring Law

319. Scheme and debt restructuring. An old institution of English law that risked being in escheat,[129] the scheme of arrangement has become very popular due to the development of restructuring law. This law, described as a 'pre-insolvency proceeding', has the function of modifying the state of a company's debt (readjusting the 'capital structure of the company'[130]) before it becomes insolvent. It is a truism to state that French bankruptcy law, gradually evolving into the law of companies in difficulty, is now trying to intervene earlier and earlier in order to prevent bankruptcy rather than to implement it. This trend leads to consensual agreements between creditors and the company rather than the institution of an insolvency procedure, which always remains, nevertheless, a possibility. Such agreements have the advantage of not divesting the debtor and therefore encourage managers to resort to them at a time when insolvency can still be avoided. Renegotiation may be aimed at extending the loan repayment period, reducing the interest, forgiving the debt, or converting the debt into capital.[131] However, recourse to contract law alone, in that it requires unanimity of the creditors to succeed, may not be sufficient and a state procedure may be necessary.[132]

---

[129] On its history, see J. Payne, *Schemes of arrangement: Theory, Structure and Operation*, *op. cit.*, no. 1.2.

[130] Restructuring procedures have been described as 'a legal framework that allows firm to readjust their capital structure well before they are in fact insolvent', H. Eidenmüller, 'Contracting for a European insolvency regime' (2017) 18 *European Business Organisation Law Review*, pp. 273 et seq., spec. p. 274; see in the same sense, I. Merovach and A. Walters, 'The Characterization of Pre-insolvency Proceedings in Private International Law' (2020) 21 *European Business Organisation Law Review*, pp. 855 et seq., spec. p. 861. *Comp.* Art. 2(1)(1) of the Directive 2019/1023 of the European Parliament and of the Council of 20 June 2019 on preventive restructuring frameworks.

[131] I. Merovach and A. Walters, 'The Characterization of Pre-insolvency Proceedings in Private International Law', *o. cit.*, p. 862. This last point is of course the one that is likely to trigger the application of company law and the *lex mercatus*, see *infra*, para. 329.

[132] Two particular difficulties exist: the 'hold out' and the 'free rider'. The first refers to the case where a minority creditor attends the negotiation, but blocks its continuation in order to obtain a personal benefit, while the second refers to the creditor who refuses to participate in the renegotiation, believing that the waiver of the other creditors of their prerogatives will enable him to obtain full payment of his claim. However, the bond contract may provide, a priori, for means to resolve these difficulties through collective action clauses and significant penalties if a creditor leaves the negotiation or refuses to participate. These clauses will not always be sufficient, however, and it is in this context that a state procedure, administrative or judicial, may be necessary. On this issue, see I. Merovach and A. Walters, 'The Characterization of Pre-insolvency Proceedings in Private International Law', *op. cit.*, p. 862.

From this point of view, the scheme has three advantages: firstly, it leaves a lot of room for the will of the parties secondly, once it has been judicially approved,[133] it is very difficult to evade; finally, its conclusion is facilitated by the rules that govern it: the majority rule set at seventy-five percent of the votes cast[134] makes it possible to impose the restructuring plan drawn up by the scheme on recalcitrant minority creditors. This rule, which results in a bondholder's rights being altered without his or her consent, is tempered by the supervision of schemes by the English courts, whose function is precisely to ensure a balance between the majority and minority shareholders.[135] Two questions of private international law have arisen from the perspective of the English courts: can foreign companies make use of the scheme of arrangement? If so, what effect are such arrangements likely to have abroad?[136] These two questions are subject to a prior difficulty, that of the articulation of the scheme with the Insolvency Regulation.

320. Scheme of arrangement and insolvency. English courts base the applicability of schemes of arrangement on their insolvency legislation.[137] This legislation allows them to deal with the insolvency of unregistered companies, within which the English subsume foreign companies, provided that several

133 The English write that 'schemes of arrangement are sanctioned by Courts', i.e. the English courts have the power to unilaterally modify schemes of arrangement.

134 Companies Act 2006, s. 899(1). The vote is assessed by *class*, i.e. by the group of bondholders of each issue, and not globally. This rule is now weakened by the indirect holding system, which makes it difficult to establish this majority per class, see J. Payne, 'Intermediation and Bondholder schemes of arrangement', in *Intermediation and beyond*, 2018, Oxford, Hart, pp. 175 et seq. The author advocates abolishing this class majority rule, considering that its purpose of protecting the minority shareholders can just as well be ensured by court supervision, see J. Payne, 'The role of court in debt restructuring' (2018) *Cambridge Law Review*, pp. 124 et seq.
This rule is considered to be one of the sources of the attraction of schemes of arrangement. Thus, Messrs Synvet and Ferrand observe that: 'This option to amend a contract by majority vote, which under French law can only take place in the context of safeguard, accelerated financial safeguard or receivership proceedings, could be very attractive to certain French companies. Would it not allow them, without having to resort to collective proceedings, the effects of which, in particular in terms of image, can be disastrous, to free themselves from the law of mutual consent and in this way obtain concessions that they have not been able to obtain in the context of normal commercial negotiations?', H. Synvet and N. Ferrand, 'L'accueil en France des *schemes of arrangement* de droit anglais', *RDBF*, January-February 2014, pp. 10 et seq.

135 Some authors believe that this supervision should precisely lead to the ousting of the majority rule, in particular in order to alleviate the difficulties caused by the system of indirect holding of securities, see J. Payne, 'Intermediation and bondholders schemes of arrangement', *op. cit.*

136 Asking questions in this respect, see J. Payne, *Schemes of arrangement: Theory, Structure and Operation*, *op. cit.* See also on this second aspect from the French point of view, H. Synvet and P.-N. Ferrand, 'L'accueil en France des *schemes of arrangement* de droit anglais', *op. cit.*

137 J. Payne, *Schemes of arrangement: Theory, Structure and Operation*, *op. cit.*

conditions are met.[138] However, the English courts have interpreted these conditions particularly broadly, considering that the fulfilment, even if it is possible, of one of them allows them to hear the scheme. Such a liberal criterion inevitably made it necessary for the English courts to restrict the conditions of their jurisdiction.[139] Three new conditions were then laid down by the judges: firstly, that proof of a link with the United Kingdom be established, for example through the presence of assets in the territory; secondly, that the pronouncement of a possible insolvency could have advantages for the parties; and thirdly, that the Court have some form of jurisdiction over the persons interested in the distribution of the company's assets. The last two conditions do not relate to the spatial delimitation of the English legislation, but to the possible effectiveness of the measures taken. In fact, only the first condition, whose particularly broad wording is reminiscent of the wording of the exception clause, is intended to give the schemes an international scope of application; the other two, while they affect the international scope of application of the schemes, are specific to their material scope of application and apply indiscriminately to foreign and local companies.

321. The difficulty lies in the fact that even this condition has been interpreted very liberally: the mere choice of English law for the bond issue, combined with the existence of a jurisdiction clause, is sufficient to justify the applicability of the schemes of arrangement and the jurisdiction of English courts, even though the company has neither its registered office, nor the centre of its interests, nor even any assets on English territory.[140] This interpretation could have been challenged by the application of the Insolvency Regulation. However, firstly, schemes have not been included by the English government within the national proceedings subject to the Insolvency Regulation and, secondly, the English courts have refused to consider that only companies that are eligible for English insolvency proceedings under the Insolvency Regulation can benefit from the scheme.[141] In addition, English courts have often refused to consider schemes as proceedings subject to the Brussels I Regulation for reasons of substantive

138 Insolvency Act 1986, s. 221(5).

139 These were developed by Knox J in *Re Real Estate Development Co* [1991] BCLC 210, spec. 217, and subsequently confirmed in *Re Rodenstock GmbH* [2011] EWHC 1104 (Ch); [2012] BCC 459 at para. 21.

140 See on this point the *Rodenstock* judgment cited above, at para. 29. It seems that the presence of a choice of court clause was decisive, in particular in the light of Arts. 23 and 24 of the Brussels I Regulation.

141 See on this point J. Payne, *Schemes of arrangement: Theory, Structure and Operation*, *op. cit.*, no. 7.2.3.1; J. Payne, 'Cross-border schemes of arrangement and forum shopping', *op. cit.*, p. 575. The arguments, notably based on the anteriority of English insolvency legislation, are nevertheless very weak; it would have been better to consider that the Insolvency Regulation does not intend to govern schemes, which is now made possible by recital 16 of the Insolvency Regulation, negotiated in order to escape the broadening of the scope of the Regulation reflected in its Recital 10, see L. d'Avout, *JDI*, October 2016, chron. 10.

scope: either because schemes do not constitute a 'dispute', and therefore the decision rendered would not be of a judicial nature,[142] or because they fall within the exclusion provided for by the Regulation as regards 'bankruptcies, compositions and other similar proceedings'.[143] When accepting the application of the Regulation, the English courts took the view that schemes should not be subject to the jurisdiction of the defendant's domicile, but to Articles 23 and 24 on the voluntary prorogation of jurisdiction.[144] However, the acceptance of the Regulation as a basis was only linked to the desire to give their judgment the

142 See in this sense J.-J. KUIPERS, 'Schemes of arrangement and voluntary collective redress: a gap in the Brussels I Regulation' (2012) *Journal of Private International Law*, pp. 225–249. Messrs Synvet and Ferrand observe that, from the French point of view, 'The French conception of the jurisdictional act has always been broad, and goes beyond the framework traced by the existence of a dispute', and that 'the text of the Regulation does not refer to the notion of "judgment", but to the more open notion of "decision", of which Article 32 gives a very broad definition', see H. SYNVET and P.-N. FERRAND, 'L'accueil en France des *schemes of arrangement* de droit anglais', *'p. cit.*

143 Art. 1(2)(c) of the Brussels I Regulation. This was the reasoning in *Re DAP Holding NV* [2005] EWHC 2092 (Ch); [2006] BCC 48. The argument can be based on the rather broad definition given by the Court of Justice in its judgment *Gourdain v. Nadaler* of 22 February 1979 (Case 133/78: ECR 1979, I, p. 733), delivered under the auspices of the Brussels Convention, which excluded from the material scope of application 'proceedings based, under the various laws of the contracting parties, on the cessation of payments, insolvency or impairment of the debtor's credit, involving intervention by the judicial authority leading to compulsory and collective liquidation of assets or, at the very least, supervision by that authority'. It is difficult to understand why, in these circumstances, the UK government has refused to include schemes in the procedures subject to the Insolvency Regulation - some authors point to a loophole in the EU legislation. However, it is doubtful that the European legislator wished to leave a gap between the material scope of the Brussels I Regulation and the Insolvency Regulation, so that what does not fall within the scope of one should be considered included in the scope of the other (see already in this sense, H. SYNVET and P.-N. FERRAND, 'L'accueil en France des *schemes of arrangement* de droit anglais', *op. cit.*, no. 10). It seems to us that schemes fall within the scope of Brussels I precisely because there are two arguments against qualifying schemes as insolvency proceedings.
The first, technical argument is simply that the Insolvency Regulation applies to 'collective proceedings based on the insolvency of the debtor which entail the partial or total divestment of the debtor and the appointment of a liquidator' (Art. 1(1) of the Insolvency Regulation). However, schemes do not have the effect of divesting the debtor or appointing a liquidator (see already in this sense, H. SYNVET and P.-N. FERRAND, 'L'accueil en France des *schemes of arrangement* de droit anglais', *op. cit.)* The second argument relates to qualification and is developed *infra*, para. 324.

144 Art. 2 Brussels I Regulation.

best chance of being recognised in the Union.[145] This attitude contributed to the phenomenon of British Bankruptcy tourism.[146]

322. Characterisation of restructuring procedures. This difficult characterisation of the scheme of arrangement is linked to the broader characterisation of procedures aimed at restructuring the company's debt. Two theories have focused on establishing a criterion for distinguishing between the procedures of the Insolvency Regulation and the restructuring procedures.[147]

The first, defended by Professor Eidenmuller, is to consider that the characteristic of insolvency proceedings is to be 'fully collective'.[148] This characteristic can be explained by the function of these proceedings, which is to resolve 'the common pool problem',[149] i.e. the existence of conflicting interests in a pool of assets which is nevertheless common to all creditors: the debtor's assets. This difficulty can only be resolved by the institution of a coercive state

---

145 See very clearly in this sense J. Payne, *Schemes of arrangement: Theory, Structure and Operation*, *op. cit.*, no. 7.3.3. English judges do not hesitate to call on foreign experts in order to find out the chances of their judgment being recognised abroad when the "points of contact" with the United Kingdom are in fact very weak. The whole reasoning has nevertheless been approved by the doctrine, in that the English courts thereby offer foreign companies a sophisticated mechanism unknown to the national law of the foreign company, see in this sense, J. Payne, *Schemes of arrangement: Theory, Structure and Operation*, *op. cit.*, no. 7.4. On the reception of schemes of arrangement in French law, see H. Synvet and P.-N. Ferrand, 'L'accueil en France des *schemes of arrangement* de droit anglais', *op. cit.*

146 On which see from an English perspective in French, P. Burbidge, 'British Bankruptcy Tourism. L'Angleterre comme paradis de la faillite et les propositions de réforme du Règlement 1346/2000 sur les procédures d'insolvablité' in *Mélanges en l'honneur du professeur Paul Le Cannu*, Paris, LGDJ, 2013, pp. 587 et seq.

147 Tracing these two theories, I. Merovach and A. Walters, 'The Characterization of Pre-insolvency Proceedings in Private International Law', *op. cit.*, pp. 875–876.

148 H. Eidenmüller, 'What is an insolvency proceeding?'(2018) *American Bankruptcy Law Journal*, pp. 92 et seq. The author gives two converging definitions: 'Proceedings are fully collective in that sense if individual claim enforcement of all creditors is impeded, e.g., by a stay or by the possibility of rights modifications'; 'A proceeding is fully collective if it attempts to solve a common pool problem by, in one form or another, restricting individual rights enforcement by all the creditors of a debtor, e.g., by a stay or by the power to modify claims non-consensually.' If the procedure is fully collective, the universal nature of the procedure should be immediately recognised in other States. However, according to the author, neither schemes of arrangement nor, for example, safeguard proceedings can be qualified as fully collective proceedings, which is why they are not qualified as insolvency proceedings by the Insolvency Regulation.
This collective nature of the proceedings can also be seen as the technical basis for the application of the *lex fori concursus*. As Mr d'Avout writes, it is 'the collective nature of bankruptcy proceedings, the "multilateral effect of insolvency law" which justifies the search for a common law for the treatment of difficulties', see L. d'Avout, 'Sens et portée de la *lex fori concursus*', *Annuaire sud-américain de droit du commerce international (DeCITA)*, 2009, p. 40.

149 H. Eidenmüller, 'What is an insolvency proceeding?' On this difficulty within collective proceedings, see S. Block-Lieb, 'Fishing in Muddy Waters: Clarifying the Common Pool Analogy as Applied to the Standard for Commencement of a Bankruptcy Case' (1993) 42 *The American University Law Review*, p. 337.

procedure that takes into account the interests of all creditors. This procedure subordinates the legitimate interests of each creditor to their collective interest, which is spectacularly demonstrated by the cessation of individual lawsuits or the continuation of existing contracts; we know that this function is also at the basis of the universalist model of insolvency procedures.[150] The consequence of this first theory would be to exclude from the scope of the Insolvency Regulation all procedures that do not take into account all creditors.[151]

The second theory is that insolvency law and restructuring law have distinct domains, based on different foundations. The domain of insolvency would be the realisation of assets for the benefit of creditors in order to resolve the difficulty of conflicting interests in a common pool of assets and to prevent the destructive race to the bottom that creditors might engage in. On the other hand, restructuring law would have the function of instituting judicially sanctioned agreements between the stakeholders to agree on the distribution of the future income generated by the debtor among the creditors. Therefore, with such a distinct function, restructuring law would be closer to contract and company law and should, on the one hand, depart from the principles governing insolvency law[152] and, on the other hand, from a private international point of view, be subject to the Brussels I bis and Rome I Regulations.

323. However, both theories have the common disadvantage of ignoring the predominant links between preventive and collective procedures, which place the latter in the continuity of the former and often lead to confusion of functions. This is notoriously the case with 'Chapter 11' in US law, which allows both solvent and insolvent companies to be placed under its jurisdiction.[153] From the French point of view, the safeguard and judicial recovery procedures (*'sauvegarde et redressement judiciaire'*) are a good example of this ambiguity: both are considered as insolvency procedures for the purposes of the Insolvency Regulation, yet their function, as their name indicates, is to restore the company rather than to liquidate it. The difficulties of a company are always subject to a gradation, of which the different procedures are only reflections.[154] However, the two theories presented seem to us to deny this deep-seated unity; they would

150 See *supra*, para. 107.

151 This would be contrary to the will of the legislator, see Recital 14 of the Insolvency Regulation.

152 As some authors have written, 'The separate domains theory does more than merely address the policy dilemma of cross-border characterization', I. Merovach and A. Walters, 'The Characterization of Pre-insolvency Proceedings in Private International Law', *op. cit.*, p. 876.

153 *Ibid.*

154 Report. I. Merovach and A. Walters, 'The Characterization of Pre-insolvency Proceedings in Private International Law', *op. cit.*, p. 879: '[...] insolvency and restructuring law are on a continuum. We know that it is notoriously difficult to prove that a debtor is "insolvent" or "likely insolvent" or "viable" at any given moment in time because distress is fluid rather than static [...]. The "viable business in need of restructuring" may without intervention deteriorate into the "non viable business that ought to be liquidated."'

merit further development beyond the scope of this chapter, so we will limit ourselves here to two arguments.[155]

324. Firstly, the theory of 'fully collective' proceedings gives the illusion that there are no conflicting interests among the creditors in the restructuring proceedings. In reality, in all these proceedings, it is the collective nature of the relationship in question, and the inherent limits to the resolution of these difficulties by contract law alone, which justify the institution of specific procedures. In these cases, the limitation of the rights of certain creditors is justified by the collective interest of all creditors. In this sense, it does not matter whether all the creditors are concerned, the problem of the 'common pool', even if it is phrased differently, is nevertheless the same: it justifies precisely the enactment of a state procedure[156] for the benefit of the debtor. Moreover, this theory leads to radical distinctions between procedures that are nevertheless very similar.[157]

325. Secondly, the separate domains theory seems to deny that the reason why creditors are encouraged to negotiate is precisely because of the privileges they will obtain in insolvency. However, these links between restructuring and insolvency proceedings do not end there: failure to comply with the plan laid down in the restructuring proceedings will most often trigger the liquidation proceedings, in the same way as the violation of a prudential rule triggers the application of resolution law. This last observation calls for an analogy between restructuring law and resolution law: they have in common the desire to preserve the functioning of the company's activities.[158] However, resolution law bases its applicability, including as a preventive measure, on the criterion of the registered office (which also is the COMI thanks to prudential rules) rather than a choice of law, and this ground of jurisdiction is independent of the particularities justifying the special resolution regime. Moreover, these two theories agree on the function assigned to insolvency law, which is exhausted in the management of the difficulty caused by the conflicting interests of creditors in a common pool of assets. However, insolvency law is more than a sophisticated liquidation technique: it also institutes an ordering of payment priorities, in which local

---

155 See *ibid.*, pp. 877 et seq.

156 *Ibid.*, p. 879: 'Pre-insolvency (restructuring) proceedings, too, address holdout and free rider problems.'

157 Accelerated financial safeguard is thus excluded from the scope of collective proceedings, whereas safeguard proceedings would be included; see on this question the observations of *ibid.*, p. 882.

158 This commonality of function explains why Art. 1(2) of the Restructuring Directive 2019/1023 excludes from its material scope the entities covered by the resolution.

public policy manifests itself in its fullness, making this branch of law both insusceptible to choice of law, or to total legislative uniformity.[159]

326. It is therefore basically up to the insolvency law to decide on the treatment of restructuring proceedings; as such, their exclusion from the Insolvency Regulation should not blindside us. However, not all jurisdictions have such sophisticated preventive mechanisms, and it is in this context that the law of the seat of insolvency will have an interest in recognising foreign restructuring proceedings to the extent that they further its own objectives. As Professor Payne has already observed, forum shopping does not necessarily pose a difficulty here, and may be beneficial to the debtor.[160] Two remarks should be made.

The first is that the scheme is, like traditional insolvency proceedings, a *favour* to the debtor. As Professor Lucas writes, 'the evil from which the debtor suffers is his excessive indebtedness and certainly not the collective procedure opened against him, which is a remedy'.[161] However, offering such a benefit is a question of legal policy, which it is up to the forum of the debtor in difficulty to decide. The common trend in European legal systems is nevertheless to prevent insolvency rather than to achieve it,[162] so that the assistance of a foreign court in implementing this prevention will most often be welcomed.[163] From the French point of view, it would therefore seem appropriate to offer holders of debt securities representing bonds subject to French law, in addition to the provisions relating to the '*masse des obligataires*', those relating to the accelerated safeguard financial procedure.

The second is that the foreign scheme will necessarily be subject to scrutiny by the legal system of the debtor's seat, not only at the time of recognition of the *scheme*, but also, if insolvency proceedings are opened, in respect of the acts of the suspect period. Two factors can make this scrutiny strict. Firstly, the fact that the debtor is approaching insolvency: in this case, the initiation of insolvency proceedings might have been preferable, and it is up to the forum of the debtor's seat to determine the legal policy to be followed between preventive restructuring and collective proceedings. Secondly, the existence of

---

159 Proposing the institution of uniform insolvency regimes, subject to a choice of law within the company's statutes, see H. Eidenmuller, 'Contracting for a European insolvency regime', *op. cit.*

160 J. Payne, 'Cross-border schemes of arrangement and forum shopping', *op. cit.* It should be added here that not allowing the use of foreign restructuring procedures in a legal system that does not have an effective one leads to the absurd situation where the debtor changes its centre of main interests in the foreign legal system, see for an illustration.

161 F.-X. Lucas, *Droit de la faillite*, Paris, PUF, 2021, no. 78.

162 The entry into force of Directive 2019/1023 on preventive restructuring is therefore not anecdotal in this respect.

163 The German courts have had the opportunity to refuse recognition of a foreign *scheme* from time to time, within a body of case law that is nonetheless favourable to them, see J. Payne, 'Cross-border schemes of arrangement and forum shopping', *op. cit.*

instruments equivalent to the foreign restructuring procedure in the legal order where the centre of the debtor's main interests is located may strengthen the scrutiny over a foreign restructuring. Indeed, one may wonder why a foreign procedure was used.

B. The Influence of the Law of the Financial Market

327. Schemes, *lex societatis* and *lex mercatus*. Two other difficulties posed by the hybrid nature of schemes are related to conflict of laws. The first difficulty relates to the domain of the law of the contract since the schemes modify the bond financing contract and the modifications do not explicitly fall within the Rome I Regulation's enumeration of the domain of the law of the contract.[164] The difficulty faced by the English judges is to try to bring into the domain of the law of the contract issues that their legislator has nevertheless included, on the one hand, in company law[165] and, on the other hand, in insolvency law,[166] i.e. two issues excluded from the domain of the law of the contract in the Rome I Regulation.[167] In order to delimit, irrespective of the origin of the regulation, what should fall under the *lex contractus* of the contract of issue, the following criterion could be used: as long as the scheme remains within the limits of the debt arrangement between the company and the creditors, the law of the contract may prevail. In support of this criterion, it will be argued, as observed by Messrs Synvet and Ferrand, that the modification of the contract effected by the scheme:

> 'It could also be suggested that a rider to a contract, including by means of a Scheme of Arrangement, may be a consequence of the total or partial non-performance of (the) original obligations.'[168]

On the other hand, as soon as the scheme affects the share capital or the relationship between the corporate bodies, it may encroach on the domain of the *lex societatis* and be denied any recognition by the legal order of the registered office.[169] This will be particularly the case where the scheme inserts clauses for the conversion of debts into shares in the bond contract, or even proceeds directly to such a conversion in violation of the conditions under which it is permitted by the issuer's law. These aspects will then leave the

---

164 Bounded by Art. 12(1) of the Rome I Regulation.
165 Now listed in Part 26 of the Companies Act 2006.
166 Insolvency Act of 1985.
167 Art. 1(2) of the Rome I Regulation. See already in this sense, H. Synvet and P.-N. Ferrand, 'L'accueil en France des *schemes of arrangement* de droit anglais', *op. cit.*, no. 23.
168 H. Synvet and P.-N. Ferrand, "L'accueil en France des *schemes of arrangement* de droit anglais", *op. cit.* The authors refer in the italicised part to Art. 12(1)(c) of the Rome I Regulation.
169 Comp. *ibid.*, no. 22.

domain of the law of the bond contract, and of the restructuring procedure, and be subject to the *lex societatis* alone. Furthermore, the scheme will trigger the intervention of the *lex mercatus*, and in particular the legislation on threshold crossing and takeover bids, as soon as the voting power of the shareholders is significantly modified. This will be the case in particular when the scheme has the effect of allowing the conversion of bonds into shares, i.e. giving access to the capital,[170] or when the return for the largesse granted by the bondholders lies in the pledging of the company's equity securities.

§ 3. SHARES AND UNITS IN A COLLECTIVE INVESTMENT UNDERTAKING

328. Presentation. The particularity of this third category of financial securities comes from their issuer, the collective investment undertakings. The latter are institutions whose purpose is to make the savings collected from investors grow. The advantage for the investor is twofold: firstly, he entrusts a specialist with the management of his savings and, secondly, the pooling of capital makes it possible to generate a return that he would not have been able to obtain alone. There are two types of collective investment schemes: undertakings for collective investment in transferable securities (UCITS) and alternative investment funds (AIF).[171] UCITS have a risk-spreading obligation,[172] which most often involves an investment diversification strategy to avoid, as far as possible, the risks involved in investing.[173] This is why UCITS units can be marketed to non-professionals, which is not always the case for AIFs.

What UCITS and AIFs have in common, however, is that they can be structured with or without legal personality. Those with legal personality are organised in the form of a company, a '*société anonyme*' or a '*société par actions simplifiée*' in French law, but may have the particularity of having

---

170 On the nature of these securities giving access to capital, see A. Couret, H. Le Nabasque *et al.*, *Droit financier*, *op. cit.*, nos. 526–530.

171 In certain cases, AIFs may collect savings from non-professional investors, see A. Couret, H. Le Nabasque *et al.*, *Droit financier*, *op. cit.*, On the financial strategies of UCITS, see *ibid.*

172 Directive 2009/65/EC of the European Parliament and of the Council of 13 July 2009 makes the risk spreading strategy one of the constituent elements of UCITS, see Art. 1(2)(a).

173 On this question, see J. Prorok, *La responsabilité sur les marchés financiers*, *op. cit.*

variable capital.[174] Those without legal personality are called 'funds',[175] and are analysed in French law as a co-ownership,[176] whose members only have shares. Whether the undertaking is personified or not, the holders of shares or units in collective investment undertakings have in all cases reduced non-pecuniary prerogatives which, where they exist, do not allow them to participate in the life of the company.[177] The latter is in fact organised around two entities: the management company and the asset custodian. The management company is both the entity that initiates the formation of the collective investment scheme,[178] whether or not it is a legal entity, and the entity that appoints the scheme's custodian. It is also the management company that will draw up the fund rules or the articles of association of the company created.[179] It is the central and governing body of the collective investment undertaking, regardless of its form, without being formally included in the internal functioning of the undertaking. Moreover, the depositary's function is not limited to the custody of assets. Indeed, the depositary's mission is 'above all, to continuously monitor the regularity of transactions carried out by the UCITS, and therefore by the SICAV ("*Société d'Investissement a Capital Variable*" – "Investment Company with Variable Capital" or "Open-ended Investment Company") or the management company'.[180]

---

174 The distinction is explained by the distinct purpose of these organisations: where, as a matter of principle, UCITS will collect savings from non-professional investors in order to grow the savings in the same way as the market, AIFs are so-called "alternative" in the sense that they do not necessarily attempt to replicate the performance of the market, and that they are intended for professionals, see Art. L. 214-4 para. 1 of the Monetary and Financial Code (UCITS); L. 214-24-25 of the Monetary and Financial Code (AIF).
Even in the case of joint stock companies, these shares are referred to indiscriminately as units or shares in collective investment undertakings (see for UCITS Art. 3(b) of Directive 2009/65).

175 The difficulty here is that the term 'fund' is polysemous and can also refer to any collective investment scheme, see A. Couret, H. Le Nabasque *et al.*, *Droit financier*, *op. cit.*, no. 846.

176 Art. L. 214-8 of the Monetary and Financial Code. Depending on whether they are UCITS or AIFs, the titles of the funds are likely to be diversified: mutual fund, general purpose investment fund, etc. On the analysis of FCPs, see A. Couret, H. Le Nabasque *et al.*, *Droit financier*, *op. cit.*, no. 913, and V. Malassigné, *Les titres représentatifs*, *op. cit.*, no. 454.

177 As Mr Malassigné writes, 'They are in effect deprived of the right to demand payment from the debtors of the assigned debts, to grant them a period of grace or to grant them a debt remission. Nor can they appoint the auditor who is responsible for ensuring that the transactions carried out on behalf of the fund are properly accounted for. They do not even have the right to appoint and dismiss the management company which is entitled to manage the fund, nor, moreover, to give an opinion on its management', V. Malassigné, *Les titres représentatifs*, *op. cit.*, no. 466. The authors further observe that the difference between SICAVs and FCPs ('*Fonds Commun de Placement*' – 'Open-ended Collective Investment Fund') is minimal today, see A. Couret, H. Le Nabasque *et al.*, *Droit financier*, *op. cit.* no. 909.

178 Art. 214-8-1 para. 1 of the Commercial Code.

179 *Ibid.*

180 A. Couret, H. Le Nabasque *et al.*, *Droit financier*, *op. cit.*, no. 905.

329. Application of the *lex societatis* to the shares of the collective investment undertaking. The simple name of units and shares of undertakings for collective investment would seem to allow for an analogy with shares, and therefore to apply to the latter the law of the undertaking which gave rise to them. However, units and shares in collective investment undertakings present a double originality which could lead to the rejection of an analogy with shares: on the one hand, they provide their holder with almost no power to participate in the collectivity of the undertaking and, on the other hand, they can be issued by non-personalised entities. However, the weakness of the political rights is not such as to reverse the legal qualification of a share: thus, shares without voting rights do not lose their qualification as shares. The *lex societatis* will therefore apply to the issue and regime of *negotia* issued by the investment company.

330. Application of the law of fund regulation to units of non-personalised undertakings. Nevertheless, the issue is more complex when the issuing entity is not a legal person. Indeed, the status of non-personalised groupings does not, in principle, follow that of companies. For these particular groupings, the doctrine considers that 'the applicable law will be determined according to the contractual qualification or the status of the assets'.[181] Indeed, the Rome I Regulation applies to the contract organising the relationship between the partners,[182] i.e. the fund rules, and the assets will be governed by the law of their location. In the case of non-personalised collective investment undertakings, this means that the law applicable to the relationship between the holders themselves and between the holders and the fund will be the law of the fund rules. This law will also extend to units of non-personalised undertakings. Indeed, these units have their source in the contract between the holders and the fund, so that the law governing it should prevail. The law of the fund rules, which is the law of the issuer of the units, is the law that will govern the very possibility of issuing these units. This law will also govern other aspects: the form they may take; their regime, in particular the question of the prerogatives offered to the holder in pecuniary terms (for example, the terms of the obligation to redeem the units by the fund); and finally the extra-pecuniary prerogatives, such as the request for information on management. The importance of this law no doubt explains why its control can take place through administrative supervision.

---

[181] B. Audit and L. d'Avout, *Droit international privé*, *op. cit.*, no. 1190; see also H. Synvet, 'Société', *op. cit.*, no. 2: 'As long as the company remains a simple contract, it is subject to the conflict of laws rules applicable to contractual obligations, i.e., to date, the Rome Convention of 19 June 1980.'

[182] The exclusion of groups provided for in the Rome I Regulation seems to apply only to incorporated companies or associations, see Art. 1(2)(c). The draft law applicable to companies submitted by the European Group for Private International Law seems, on the other hand, to extend to unincorporated entities (Art. 1) and suggests applying to the latter 'the law of the country [...] under which it has been formed' (Art. 3).

331. Influence of administrative supervision. Administrative supervision may interfere with this freedom of choice offered by the Rome I Regulation.[183] A distinction must be made here between mutual funds established by UCITS and AIFs. In the case of UCITS, two separate approvals are required to establish a common fund:[184] firstly, that of the management company and, secondly, that of the common fund itself.[185] The management company must have its head office in the same place as its registered office, and may only apply for authorisation as a management company to the authority of its registered office.[186] However, once authorised, the management company may apply for authorisation of the collective investment undertaking to the authority of its choice, without having to establish a management company locally.[187] In this case, the AMF General Regulation itself does not explicitly require the application of French law to the fund rules when examining them,[188] or even the drafting of the rules in French.[189]

When it comes to UCITS, two elements tend to call into question the freedom of choice of law. The UCITS Directive is silent on this issue, but the authority's authorisation is given in view of the legal regime granted to it: this is the very meaning of the applicable French legislation.[190] This argument is reinforced by the conditions to which the fund's authorisation is subject: the French authority will have difficulty in 'examining'[191] the regulations of a fund subject to foreign law. This is all the more true since the freedom given to management companies to authorise their fund with the authority of another Member State without having to establish a local management company is likely to allow the creation of a fund subject to foreign law. However, these

183 Report on the Law Applicable to Multilateral and Organized Trading Facilities, *supra*, para. 273.

184 The case of SICAVs is slightly different: if the organs of the SICAV manage the assets themselves, the absence of a management company *ipso facto* exempts it from management company authorisation. However, if the management of the SICAV is delegated to a management company, authorisation becomes necessary, see Art. 411-6 AMF General Regulation.

185 The authorisation of the mutual fund is necessary for the marketing of the units of the fund by the management company, see Art. 5(1) of the UCITS Directive.

186 Art. 7(1)(d) of the UCITS Directive.

187 On the requirement to have the registered offices and the head office of the management company in the same place, see Art. L. 532-2(1°) of the Monetary and Financial Code. On the absence of a requirement for the registered offices of the management company and the UCITS to be in the same place within the territory of the competent authority, see Recital 20 and Art. 5(3) of Directive 2009/65.

188 Art. 411-11 AMF General Regulation.

189 Art. L. 214-23-1 of the Monetary and Financial Code. The article states that this option is conditioned and limited by the AMF General Regulation. The latter, in Art. 411-105, allows the use of a common language.

190 Thus, the section of the Monetary and Financial Code devoted to UCITS refers successively to authorisation and then to the legal regime.

191 These are the terms in which Art. 411-11 of the AMF General Regulation provides for the Authority's assessment of the fund.

arguments do not have the same force when addressed to unincorporated AIFs. Indeed, AIF management companies are not necessarily required to be authorised as management companies and may simply be registered.[192] The same applies to some AIFs, which may be neither authorised nor registered: the only regulatory constraints will then be those relating to the marketing of units.[193] Thus, from a French perspective, a French fund may be managed by a foreign management company and, conversely, a French management company may manage a foreign fund.[194] Under these conditions, the choice of the law applicable to the fund will not be disturbed.

332. Weak influence of the *lex mercatus*. With regard to the issue and regime of shares and units in collective investment undertakings, the *lex mercatus* appears to be simply inapplicable. This is in fact due to the *negotium* regime of these particular financial securities: they do not give any power to control the collective investment undertaking or even to intervene in its management. In fact, the rules on thresholds and takeover bids are no longer relevant. On the other hand, the rules on the marketing of these securities and the rules on the transfer of these securities may still apply. However, it is no longer the *lex mercatus* that is really applicable, but the laws on the protection of savings, on the one hand, and the law on the proprietary aspects of financial securities on the other.[195] In particular, the former will have an influence on the professional rules applicable to the management company when it markets a fund in a legal system other than the one in which it has its registered office.

333. Conclusion of the section. The law applicable to the *negotium* is determined by the issuer. Where the *negotium* is a share, the *lex societatis* remains invariably applicable, because the share allows access to the AGM and control of the company; it is therefore part of the internal organisation of the legal person. The legislative unity necessary for the functioning of the company therefore requires the application of the *lex societatis*, and gives it a broad scope. The prerogatives offered by equity securities are closely monitored by the law of the financial market, which makes voting power the criterion for the application of threshold crossing and public offer regulations. Debt securities can represent a variety of claims, although the archetypal claim is the claim to money. However, the issuer's financial difficulties may lead to changes in the terms of the issue, especially when restructuring procedures are used. The latter, which are part of insolvency law, may affect the issuer's organisation, in particular by modifying the issuer's

---

192 It all depends on the threshold of assets under management, see respectively Art. 3(2°) and (3°), and Art. 4(1°)(j) of the AIF Directive.

193 A. Couret, H. Le Nabasque *et al.*, *Droit financier*, *op. cit.*, no. 949.

194 Arts. L. 532-21-3 and L. 532-30 of the Monetary and Financial Code. On this issue, see I. Riassetto and M. Storck, *Les organismes de placement collectif*, t. 1, 2nd ed., Paris, Joly Editions, 2016, no. 71.

195 *Supra*, para. 334.

capital structure. Where the claims give access to capital, either through the effect of the issuance contract or through the effect of the restructuring procedure, they will have to be subject at least in part to the *lex societatis*. Above all, access to the capital of a listed company triggers the intervention of the *lex mercatus*, the requirements of which will have to be complied with by the *lex societatis* and, if it differs, by the law of the restructuring procedure.

334. Conclusion of the chapter. The issue is the subject of distinct conflicts of laws depending on whether the conditions of issue and the form of the securities are in question, on the one hand, and the regime of the *negotium* on the other. It has been shown that if the issue is the preserve of the issuer, a distinction must nevertheless be made between the conditions of issue, where the issuer's law cannot be allowed to apply a foreign law, and the form of the securities, where the issuer may decide to apply to its securities the law of the *negotium* they represent. In these cases, the law of the financial market will prescribe substantial solutions in the membership agreement to which the issuer must subscribe when it wishes to admit its securities to trading. Thus, the financial market law, aware of the primacy of the issuer's law, will make the admission of the securities conditional on the removal of any trading restrictions that the issuer may have enacted. In addition, it will require the issuer to deposit them with a central depository. The Financial Market Act does not, however, disregard the content of the admitted *negotia*, but rather takes into account the content of the negotia in the context of the regulation of thresholds and public offers. This is why the details of the prerogatives of equity securities are significant. This is also why the regime of debt securities, when they give access to capital, or when they allow the use of restructuring mechanisms to give bondholders access to capital, will be monitored.

CHAPTER 2
MARKETING

335. Definition. The marketing of financial securities, despite its importance, is curiously not subject to any general definition in French positive law.[1] In European law, only the Directive on alternative investment funds defines it as 'an offer or placement, directly or indirectly, at the initiative of the manager or on his behalf, of units or shares of an AIF which he manages, to investors domiciled or having their registered office in the Union'.[2] It can be inferred that the marketing of financial securities is understood as an offer or placement of

---

1 See already in this sense the observations of J.-J. Daigre, 'Remarques sur la commercialisation en France de produits financiers émis sur un marché étranger non reconnu' in *Liber Amicorum Blanche Sousi*, Paris, Revue Banque, 2016 no. 14. On the history of marketing conditions in France, see H. Synvet and A. Tenenbaum, 'Financial instruments', *op. cit.*, nos. 28–30.

2 Art. 4(1)(x) of Directive 2011/61/EU of the European Parliament and of the Council of 8 June 2011 on alternative investment fund managers. A concurrent definition has been established in domestic law by the Commission des Opérations de Bourse (COB) in relation to multi-manager hedge funds: 'The marketing of a fund governed by foreign law means its presentation by various means (advertising, canvassing or placement by an investment services provider) with a view to encouraging a potential investor, including a third-party manager, to subscribe to units. In this regard, any proposal to purchase or subscribe to a fund made to a potential subscriber constitutes a marketing act, except when the proposal is in response to a request from the investor for a specifically designated fund', *Bulletin Mensuel COB*, April 2003, no. 378, p. 21; this definition has been adopted by the AMF for the marketing of complex financial instruments or units or shares of UCITS or AIFs, see AMF Position no. 2010-05, 'Marketing of financial instruments'. AMF Position 2010-05, 'Marketing of complex financial instruments', document created on 15 October 2010, amended on 20 September 2013; AMF Position, 'Guide to the marketing regimes for UCITS and AIFs in France', DOC 20104-04 created on 30 June 2014 and amended on 26 June 2015 and 4 July 2016.
The issue of marketing UCITS and AIFs is carefully examined by the authority because of the special rules that apply to them and the national authorisation to which they may be subject (Art. L. 214-1-1 of the Monetary and Financial Code). These rules have now been harmonised by Directive 2019/1160 and Regulation 2019/1156, which aim to facilitate cross-border marketing (facilitation called for by the doctrine, see I. Riassetto, 'Pour une commercialisation transfrontalière sans entrave des fonds d'investissement européen', *BJB*, November 2018, pp. 60 et seq.; on the previous regime, see M. Storck and I. Riassetto, *Les organismes de placement collectif, op. cit.*, nos. 781 et seq..) The details of these solutions are not set out here because of their great specificity. See lastly, L. Suire, 'La nouvelle réglementation de la distribution transfrontalière de la distribution de fonds d'investissement', *RISF*, 2020/2, pp. 56 et seq.; M. Storck, 'Vers une amélioration de la distribution transfrontalière des organismes de placement collectif', *Revue Lamy de droit des affaires*, November 2019, pp. 14 et seq.

financial securities to investors.[3] This definition allows three remarks. Firstly, the author of the marketing acts is not necessarily the issuer.[4] Secondly, the marketing may take place without the securities being admitted to trading on a trading platform. Such admission is one of several marketing methods. Finally, marketing may be directed at the public in general or at selected investors;[5] in both cases, this function of marketing explains why it is subject, in principle, to the law of the place where its intended recipients reside. These observations lead to a clear distinction between two aspects of the marketing process: firstly, the issuer's decision to market the securities by soliciting the public and, secondly, the implementation of this decision, which is manifested in marketing acts.

336. The marketing process. While subsequent marketing acts are not necessarily the responsibility of the issuer, the initial decision to market through public solicitation is the responsibility of the issuer. This is due to the "freedom-responsibility" pairing. Indeed, the issuer, if it decides to solicit the public, will bear the information obligations that such solicitation triggers. These disclosure obligations are of two types: the prospectus, a one-off document, the preparation of which is triggered by a public offer and is subject to administrative approval, and the periodic disclosure obligations, triggered by the admission of the securities to trading.

The solicitation of the public is today done through a public offer of financial securities, which is one of the following operations:

> '1. A communication addressed in any form and by any means to persons and presenting sufficient information on the terms of the offer and on the securities to be offered, so as to enable an investor to decide to purchase or subscribe to those financial securities;
>
> 2. A placement of financial securities by financial intermediaries.'[6]

---

3 On the marketing of goods or services in private international relations, see L. D'AVOUT, *L'entreprise et les conflits internationaux de lois*, *op. cit.*

4 Including the decision to admit securities to trading, which may be requested by a person other than the issuer and without the issuer's consent; in this case, the issuer will be subject to the information obligations traditionally imposed on it, see Art. 19 of the Transparency Directive.

5 J.-J. DAIGRE, 'De la sélection discrétionnaire des investisseurs lors d'une introduction ou d'une émission en bourse' in *Mélanges AEBDF IV*, Paris, Revue Banque, 2004.

6 According to the terms of Art. 2.1(d) of the Prospectus Directive, taken up by Art. 411-1 of the Monetary and Financial Code and Art. 2(d) of the Prospectus Regulation. For a glossary of the elements that characterise a public offer, see K. DECKERT, *La sollicitation publique des investisseurs en droit communautaire, français et allemand*, thesis, Paris, Université Paris I Panthéon-Sorbonne, 2009, nos. 194–207.
This definition of a public offer of financial securities can be compared to a public offer of tokens, defined in Art. L. 552-3 para. 1 of the Monetary and Financial Code: 'A public offer of tokens consists in offering to the public, in any form whatsoever, to subscribe to these tokens.'

This particularly broad definition captures all the ways, including advertising, by which the public may be solicited to acquire financial securities.[7] The function of this concept is to trigger the obligation to draw up a prospectus.[8] This is why, as some authors have observed, a public offer does not imply any connection with a place of execution of orders.[9] There are therefore many cases where a public offer takes place without any admission of securities to trading. On the other hand, admission to trading most often leads to a public offer.[10] Indeed, admission to trading is part of a process aimed at soliciting local investors,[11] which explains why it may appear to be a particular form of public offering.[12]

337. However, there are two reasons why the concepts of admission to trading and public offer of securities should not be equated, including from the point of view of the prospectus.[13] The first reason is that admission to trading on a regulated market is subject to specific exemptions under the Prospectus Regulation.[14] The second is that only admissions to trading on a regulated

---

7 This definition is close to, but distinct from, that of civil law, see J.-J. Daigre and B. François, 'Commentaire de l'ordonnance du 22 janvier 2009 relative à l'appel public à l'épargne', *Revue des sociétés*, 2009, 1, no. 20. See also, for an assimilation, J. Chacornac, *Essai sur les fonctions de l'information en droit des instruments financiers*, *op. cit.*, nos. 80 et seq. It may be possible to compare a public offer with a unilateral commitment: this is how some authors analyse a public takeover bid or a public sale offer, see in this sense A. Viandier, *OPA OPE et autres offres publiques*, 5th edition, Paris, Francis Lefebvre, 2014, no. 21.

8 The particularly broad nature of the public offer is not unique to European law. It also exists in American law, and explains the presence of 'disclaimers', generally coupled with restrictions on access to websites, by which issuers specifically exclude American residents in order to avoid being subject to American requirements, see S. Lambert, *L'application internationale du droit financier*, *op. cit.*, no. 229.
On the other elements of the regime attached to the notion of public offer in French law, see HCJP Report on the collateral effects of the extension of the European notion of public offer of financial securities, 25 March 2019, p. 3.

9 T. Bonneau *et al.*, *Droit financier*, 1st ed., Paris, LGDJ, 2017, no. 957. As shown by its legal definition, derived from Article 2.1 d of the Prospectus Directive, taken up by Art. 411-1 of the Monetary and Financial Code. The broadness of the definition also means that the author of the prospectus is not necessarily the issuer of the security: this may be the case, for example, when a financial intermediary is asked to sell securities resulting from a private placement, or when the issuing banks appear to third parties as offerors in the context of a public offering.

10 J. Chacornac, *Les fonctions de l'information en droit des instruments financiers*, *op. cit.*

11 The author even considers it to be the most intense form of solicitation (*ibid.*, no. 179). See J.-J. Daigre and B. François, 'La société par actions simplifiée, une société pouvant faire appel au marché?', *Rev. Soc.* 2010, p. 11; J. Chacornac, *Les fonctions de l'information en droit des instruments financiers*, *op. cit.*, no. 69.

12 For the assimilation of admission to trading to a form of public offer, see J. Chacornac, *Les fonctions de l'information en droit des instruments financiers*, *op. cit.*

13 See also A. Couret, H. Le Nabasque, *Droit financier*, *op. cit.*, no. 297.

14 Art. 1(5) of the Prospectus Regulation.

market constitute, in principle, an offer to the public;[15] this will not necessarily be the case for an admission on another financial market.[16] These observations lead to a clear distinction between the marketing, solicitation and distribution of securities to the public. Indeed, the marketing of securities will not necessarily lead to solicitation of the public and, at the same time, there may be solicitation without dissemination of the securities.[17] Of these three concepts, only solicitation – and its concrete manifestations – constitutes the relevant element at the basis of the disclosure requirements, and of the derogation rules applicable to public offers.

Finally, it should be noted that the protection regime for residents in relation to the marketing of financial securities does not end with the information obligations triggered by the solicitation, but continues in the field of professional rules, both those relating to the rules of conduct[18] and to canvassing,[19] but also in the field of consumer law.[20]

338. How the law of the place of solicitation is deployed. The distinction developed within the marketing process is fruitful from the point of view of

---

15 By way of exception, it is possible that the issuer wishes to admit its securities to trading without wishing to offer them to the public: this is the case with the professional segment of Euronext, which allows admission to trading without a public offer, see *infra*, para. 360.

16 Such a reading is confirmed by Recital 14 of the Prospectus Regulation which states: 'The mere admission of securities to trading on an MTF [...] should not in itself be considered as an offer of securities to the public and is therefore not subject to the obligation to draw up a prospectus provided for in this Regulation. A prospectus should only be required where such admission or publication is accompanied by a communication constituting an "offer of securities to the public.'

17 Indeed, investors may be solicited without responding and, if they do not subscribe, the securities will not be distributed. However, in this case, there is an obligation to draw up a prospectus. It is therefore not only important that the securities be accessible, but that local investors be genuinely solicited. This point, far from being anecdotal, is not uniformly accepted. Thus, in 1964, the American legislator extended the scope of the Securities Exchange Act of 1934 to include foreign issuers 'if the orders to purchase their shares were given from the territory of the United States' (P.-H. Conac, *La régulation des marchés boursiers par la commission des opérations de bourse [COB] et la securities and exchange commission [SEC]*, *op. cit.)* The SEC then took pains to exempt foreign issuers, first by applying a threshold at which the US regulations became applicable. However, because of the low threshold (US law became applicable to foreign issuers as of 300 US resident shareholders), the SEC then accepted to receive in deposit the information communicated by foreign issuers to their home authority, while considering that these documents did not constitute a registration in the sense of US law, even if they must contain a brief description in English (see *ibid.*, no. 285, on registration in US law see *infra*, para. 360). This method cannot really be analysed as an application of the foreign law, but rather as a recognition that a foreign regulation is already applied and that this one is sufficient, i.e. equivalent, see our comments *supra*, para. 135.

18 Already studied *infra*, paras. 137 et seq.

19 Which, since they do not really relate to the relationship between the issuer and the financial markets, will benefit from being studied during the marketing of financial contracts, see *infra*, paras. 836 et seq.

20 See *infra*, para. 840.

conflict of laws. The information obligations placed on the issuer when soliciting the public have the function of protecting purchasers of financial securities by providing them with knowledge of the issuer and, where applicable, the regime of the securities issued. This descriptive function of disclosure requirements,[21] naturally makes these requirements subject to the law of the place where the persons are solicited, which corresponds to the place where the securities are marketed.[22] This law, whose function is the protection of residents, is nevertheless likely to be self-limiting whenever the issuer provides equivalent information under the law of its headquarters. The European harmonisation of information requirements has made it possible to ensure that the scope of these requirements, the content of the obligations to be provided and, where appropriate, the administrative control procedures to which the provision of this information gives rise are uniform. The question is therefore likely to shift from the distribution of legislative powers to that of determining the competent authority to control this information (Section 1). Marketing acts are diverse, and may take place by various means, such as advertising, advice, canvassing, public offer, or admission to trading. The acts themselves are not necessarily subject to the pull of financial market law, which does not apply, in principle, to the public offer, but only to the admission to trading. Indeed, if the public offer is subject to special rules, it is not because of the possible admission of the securities to trading, but because of the unity required by a contract whose addressees may be located in different legal orders (Section 2).

SECTION 1. INFORMATION REQUIREMENTS

339. The issuer has two types of disclosure obligations. The first type, which is one-off and embodied in the prospectus, is triggered by the public offering; the second type, which is periodic, is triggered by the admission of the securities to trading and lasts as long as the securities are admitted. They constitute a significant part of the cost of listing for the issuer.[23] It is therefore fortunate that European harmonisation has made it possible to unify the scope and content of these obligations. If the obligations are identical, they are most often manifested according to the requirements of the issuer's law, simply because they constitute documents relating to the company's corporate bodies, its financial status and its activities. However, these documents are initially drawn up in accordance with the *lex societatis*. This is as true for disclosure requirements arising from

---

21 J. Chacornac, *Les fonctions de l'information en droit des instruments financiers*, *op. cit.*

22 See A. Tenenbaum, *L'application internationale du droit boursier*, *op. cit.*, pp. 450 et seq. observing the application of this law in these cases before European harmonisation.

23 D. Martin, 'Le coût de la cotation' in *L'entreprise multinationale dans tous ses états*, Archive de philosophie du droit, Paris, Dalloz, 2003.

admission to trading as it is for those arising from a public offer (§ 1). In the latter case, however, the need for approval of the prospectus by an administrative authority raises an additional and different issue, namely the designation of the competent authority for the purposes of supervision. It will be shown that this should be the authority of the place of solicitation, irrespective of the law applicable to the disclosure requirements (§ 2).

§ 1. THE LAW APPLICABLE TO INFORMATION OBLIGATIONS

The disclosure requirements triggered by admission essentially contain information on the financial and accounting condition of the issuer, as well as on the regime of the securities issued. If the law of the issuer's registered office requires it to provide equivalent information, the law of the place of trading will be self-limiting, regardless of whether the obligations are those specific to securities admitted to trading (I) or those arising from the prospectus in the case of a public offer (II).

I. Obligations Arising from Admission to Trading

340. Introduction. The information requirements resulting from admission to trading are based on the Transparency Directive.[24] This directive takes its name from the fact that it harmonises information requirements that have in common that they allow a better knowledge of the issuer,[25] this knowledge improves the functioning of the financial market. As an author writes:

> 'Transparency rules in financial matters thus have an immediate objective – to make issuers transparent – which in turn serves a mediate purpose, which is the proper functioning of the financial market. Transparency, based on the dissemination of

24 Directive 2004/109/EC of the European Parliament and of the Council of 15 December 2004 on the harmonisation of transparency requirements in relation to information about issuers whose securities are admitted to trading on a regulated market (hereinafter 'the Transparency Directive'). This Directive is a recast of the European Council Directive 88/267/EEC of 12 December 1988, which was intended to define "material information on the acquisition and disposal of a major holding in a listed company.
The Transparency Directive has been transposed into the Commercial Code, the Monetary and Financial Code and, above all, into the AMF General Regulation (AMF General Regulation, Book II, Title II, Chapter II, *Periodic Information*).

25 The information provided by the issuer must be 'accurate, precise and truthful', on the origin of this legal obligation, and must include and quote the information provided by the issuer. J. Prorok, *La responsabilité civile sur les marchés financiers*, *op. cit.*, no. 177. On the function of the obligations arising from the Transparency Directive, see J. Chacornac, *Essai sur les fonctions de l'information en droit des instruments financiers*, *op. cit.*

information, serves the economic performance of the market by promoting an optimal allocation of financial resources'.[26]

This objective should have militated in favour of applying the law of the financial market. However, the disclosure requirements under the Transparency Directive are subject to the law of the issuer. This application of the law of the issuer alone is not satisfactorily explained in the case of 'ongoing obligations', i.e. relating to the regulation of threshold crossings;[27] the *lex mercatus* should also be applicable.[28] On the other hand, periodic obligations,[29] which concern the provision of half-yearly and annual reports on the organisation, management and financial state of the company,[30] can legitimately be subject to the *lex societatis*. Here they follow the trend already identified: the *lex societatis* is applicable to these obligations to the extent that they are equivalent to those required by the law of the place of negotiation. This is obviously the case within the EU, where the Transparency Directive has furthermore harmonised the content of these disclosure requirements, which consist of the provision of an annual report. This report includes 'audited financial statements, the management report' and statements to the effect that these two documents give a 'true and fair view' of the assets they represent.[31]

341. Function of periodic information. The existence of such an annual report is not specific to admission to trading, but is most often an instrument of dialogue between the corporate bodies, enabling shareholders to become aware of the state of the company or the group.[32] The admission of securities to trading does not

---

26 J. Chacornac, *Essai sur les fonctions de l'information en droit des instruments financiers*, *op. cit.*, no. 428. See F. Drummond, 'L'information des actionnaires et des investisseurs' in *Entreprise: information et rumeur*, *RJ. Com*, 2005, special issue, p. 15, spec. p. 16: 'Transparency is only a guiding principle - to use the terms of the explanatory memorandum on financial security - tending to satisfy a more noble objective: to restore confidence.' Confidence is the confidence that investors have in the reliability of the market mechanism.

27 Arts. 9 et seq. of the Transparency Directive.

28 See *infra*, paras. 472 et seq.

29 Arts. 4 et seq. of the Transparency Directive.

30 Companies whose securities are not admitted to trading have no such information obligations, with the exception of the filing of accounts with the registry, but the sanction for this is limited, and the recent declaration of the beneficial owner. Companies whose securities are admitted to trading have had access to ways of identifying their shareholders for a longer period of time.

31 Art. 4(2) of the Transparency Directive. French law specifies the content of the report, which must contain the inventory, the annual accounts, a management report (the constituent elements of which are detailed in II° of Art. L. 232-1 of the Commercial Code) and, in the appendix, a statement of the guarantees granted by the company.

32 Thus, the provision of an annual report is an obligation specific to French commercial companies, see Art. L. 232-1 of the Commercial Code. The provision is found in the title relating to 'provisions common to various commercial companies'. On the content of the annual report, see Art. L. 225-100 of the Commercial Code.

alter this function,[33] but adds another, namely that of informing investors of the state of the company so that they can decide to acquire the securities. The main difference lies not so much in the content of the report,[34] or in the possibility of its semi-annual periodicity, as in the publicity given to it: the report is no longer intended solely for the AGM, but is made available to the public.[35] Indeed, the free trading of securities on a financial market makes it necessary for investors to be able to obtain information on the state of the company before investing in it; this is a continuation of the function of the prospectus by other means.[36] Significantly, the dissemination of this information is achieved by filing it with the authority of the trading location.[37]

342. Applicable law. The reason for the dissemination of these disclosure requirements to the legal system of the place of trading is that trading on a financial market entails the ongoing solicitation of residents. The latter must therefore be protected by extensive financial information on the state of the issuer. Therefore, these disclosure requirements, if not already imposed by the law of the issuer for the information of its own shareholders, should be imposed

---

[33] The obligation to provide the annual report is based on Art. L. 232-7 of the Commercial Code, which refers to Art. L. 451-1-2 of the Monetary and Financial Code.

[34] See in counterpoint the additional obligations applicable under Arts. L. 22-10-10 et seq. of the Commercial Code. These obligations, however, relate less to the financial state of the company than to the company's operating procedures. As such, they appear to be applicable because of the size of a company whose securities are admitted to trading, and because of the admission of the securities to trading.

[35] As has been written, 'it is a succession over time of the different information necessary for public appreciation that the legislator organises', J. Chacornac, *Les fonctions de l'information en droit des instruments financiers*, *op. cit.*

[36] Mr Chacornac nevertheless considers that the function of periodic obligations resulting from admission to trading would be different, since 'information no longer serves the knowledge of the asset, but the determination of its value over time' (*ibid.*, no. 428). It seems to us that the distinction must be nuanced since, as the author himself shows, knowledge of the property is the instrument for determining its value; the evolution over time of the company makes it necessary to obtain periodic information on its changes. This is why it seems to us that periodic disclosure requirements have, at least in part, the same function as the prospectus. It is therefore no coincidence that if the issuer does not have a registered office within the EU, the competent authority for the purposes of receiving the obligations of the Transparency Directive is the one elected by the issuer for the prospectus (Art. 2(1)(i)(i) of the Transparency Directive); this consistency is explicitly desired by the EU legislator (Recital 22 of Directive 2013/50 amending the Transparency Directive).
Moreover, a similar phenomenon occurs when acquiring shares or claims of a company whose securities are not admitted to trading on a regulated market: the investment is preceded by an analysis of the corporate documents. This is why these disclosure requirements, insofar as they shed light on knowledge of the thing sold in order to protect the purchaser's consent, are part of a relationship with the ordinary law of sale and, more fundamentally, with contract law, since, as a sales document, the prospectus is likely to have an influence on consent, directly or indirectly. This is a manifestation of the 'investment atmosphere' that German doctrine has highlighted, see J. Prorok, *La responsabilité civile sur les marchés financiers*, *op. cit.*, no. 268.

[37] See thus in French perspective Art. L. 451-1-2 of the Monetary and Financial Code.

by the law of the trading location This suggestion is not new. Professor Synvet already made it in a note on the *Banque Ottomane* judgment.[38] The author observed that the case could have been settled without relying on the application of French company law, but by applying the French provisions for the protection of shareholders as overriding mandatory rules ('*lois de police*') triggered by the admission to trading on the French market. The suggestion, while old, has not lost its relevance. It is simply less apparent because of the European harmonisation of the provisions mentioned; it will be relevant whenever a company from a foreign country whose company law does not prescribe such obligations is involved.

343. This dynamic is reflected in positive law. Indeed, in intra-European relations, the law of the place of negotiation is not applicable to periodic information obligations, which are subject to the *lex societatis*. This is simply because the law of the issuer will necessarily prescribe the preparation of such information. Similarly, the law of the place of trading will, upon decision of the competent administrative authority,[39] be self-limiting in favour of the law of the third country issuer 'provided that the law of the third country in question lays down equivalent requirements or such an issuer complies with requirements of the law of a third country that the competent authority of the home Member State considers as equivalent'.[40] Otherwise, the foreign country issuer will be subject to these requirements.

The European harmonisation resulting from the Transparency Directive has the effect of making the information provided equivalent. Under these conditions, their submission to the issuer's law is a source of savings for the company, which can use the document already drawn up according to the canons of its *lex societatis* and distribute it to the authorities of the regulated markets to which it has admitted its securities, especially if the issuer has admitted its securities to several financial markets.

II. The Obligations Arising from the Public Offer

344. Function of the prospectus. The information obligations arising from the public offer lie in the preparation of a prospectus.[41] This is an information

38 H. Synvet, *RCDIP*, 1984, pp. 93 et seq.

39 This will be the one 'chosen by the issuer from among the Member States in which its securities are admitted to trading on a regulated market', Art. 2(1)(i)(i) of the Transparency Directive.

40 Art. 23(1) of the Transparency Directive.

41 Although the listing particulars were first regulated at European level in a 1980 Directive (Council Directive 80/390/EEC of 17 March 1980 coordinating the requirements for the drawing up, scrutiny and distribution of the listing particulars to be published for the admission of securities to official stock exchange listing), the current coordination scheme dates from the 2003 Prospectus Directive (Directive 2003/71/EC). The latter harmonised the conditions for the validity of the prospectus, while allowing investors in several Member States to be solicited on the basis of a single prospectus. Today, the Prospectus Regulation

document intended for potential purchasers of financial securities and containing the following elements:[42] '(a) the assets and liabilities, profits and losses, financial position and prospects of the issuer and any guarantors; (b) the rights attaching to the securities; and (c) the reasons for the issue and its effect on the issuer'.[43] These aspects show the ambiguity of the prospectus: it is both a pre-contractual sales document,[44] aimed at soliciting investors, and a document whose information is aimed at protecting investors by providing them with sufficient knowledge of the issuer in order to decide whether or not to acquire the securities.[45] These two functions traditionally contribute to the application of the same law: the law of the place where the solicited investors are established. In other words, the application of French law to the obligation to draw up a prospectus should normally take place whenever its residents are solicited. The existence of a prospectus drawn up under another law, the content of which is deemed to be equivalent, is nevertheless likely to allow the local law to be self-limiting. This is particularly the case in the European Union, because of legislative harmonisation of the scope of the obligation to draw up a prospectus and its content.

(Regulation [EU] 2017/1129) has replaced this 2003 Prospectus Directive, which, without changing the philosophy of the previous regulation, has nevertheless altered certain solutions. For a detailed history of the Prospectus Directive, see K. Deckert, *La sollicitation publique des investisseurs en droit communautaire, français et allemand*, *op. cit.*

42 The prospectus contains a registration document containing information about the issuer, which the AMF calls a 'reference document' (Art. 212-13 AMF General Regulation) and, in the case of an initial listing, a 'base document' (Art. 212-23 AMF General Regulation). In addition to this first document, there is a note on the financial securities issued (transaction note describing the characteristics of the financial transaction itself), as well as a summary (see Art. 5(3°) of the Prospectus Directive), the content and function of which have been modified to make them more important by the Prospectus Regulation, see A.-C. Muller, 'Nouveau Règlement Prospectus, des avancées, retardées à juillet 2019' (New Prospectus Regulation, progress delayed until July 2019), *Revue Lamy Droit des affaires*, 2019, no. 132, p. 16.

43 Art. 6(1) of the Prospectus Regulation.

44 The French doctrine seems to consider that it is indeed a pre-contractual information document, see in this sense F. Drummond, 'L'information des actionnaires et des investisseurs', *RJ com*, 2005, special issue, *colloquium of the Association Droit et commerce, Entreprise: l'information et la rumeur*, p. 19, who writes about the obligation to provide information on instruments offered to the public 'it is no longer the agent to whom he renders accounts, but the consumer whom he informs. This information is presented in the prospectus or in an information memorandum if the company prepares a reference document. It is pre-contractual information that is said to be 'occasional'. Its purpose is to inform the investment decision of the potential subscriber'. The English doctrine does not take a different view, see the report by Mr Paul Davies on the reform of English law on civil liability in the financial markets cited in J. Prorok, *La responsabilité civile sur les marchés financiers*, *op. cit.*, no. 285.

45 On this function, see J. Chacornac, *Les fonctions de l'information en droit des instruments financiers*, *op. cit.*

345. European scheme. Triggered by the public offer, the obligation to draw up a prospectus consists of:

> 'Publish and make available to any interested person a document intended to inform the public about the content and terms of the transaction that is the subject of the transaction, as well as the organisation, financial situation and development of the business of the issuer and any guarantors of the financial securities that are the subject of the transaction.'[46]

This obligation of principle is now derived from the Prospectus Regulation, which states that 'Member States shall not permit any offer of securities to the public within their territories without prior publication of a prospectus'[47] and that 'Member States shall ensure that any admission of securities to trading on a regulated market situated or operating within their territories is subject to the publication of a prospectus'.[48] However, 'no prospectus shall be published before approval by the competent authority of the home Member State'.[49] French law echoes this pattern: it restricts the possibility of making a public offer and requires a prospectus to be drawn up for those that can.

346. Restriction of persons entitled to offer securities to the public. French law prohibits, as a matter of principle, the public offering of financial securities.[50]

---

46 Art. L. 412-1 of the Monetary and Financial Code. The obligation to provide a prospectus prior to a public offer is well known in French law where it was introduced by Art. 3 of the law of 30 January 1907 fixing the general budget of expenditure and revenue for the financial year 1907, repealed by Art. 505 of the law no. 66-537 of 24 July 1966, see K. Deckert, *La sollicitation publique des investisseurs en droit communautaire, français et allemand*, *op. cit.*, no. 36.

47 Art. 3(1°) of the Prospectus Directive, transposed in Art. L. 412-1 of the Monetary and Financial Code. With regard to the admission of securities to trading, the transposition takes place in Art. 211-1 of the AMF General Regulation. By taking this territorial point of view ('offer of securities to the public on their territory'), the European regulations put an end to the French approach, which required French issuers making a public offer of securities abroad to prepare a prospectus (Art. 1(2) of COB Regulation No 91-02). This approach was undoubtedly inspired by the SEC's expansionist position in this area, which until 1990 also made public offers made abroad subject to disclosure requirements as soon as a simple telephone solicitation could be made to the United States, see P.-H. Conac, *La régulation des marchés boursiers par la commission des opérations de bourse (COB) et la securities and exchange commission (SEC)*, *op. cit.*, no. 290). The subsequent connection chosen by the SEC as of the 1990s, known as 'territorial', should not mask the difficulty of determining the criterion of connection to the territory, which is why the SEC was led to establish a set of criteria in order to exempt foreign issuers, see *ibid.*, no. 291.

48 Art. 3(3°) of the Prospectus Regulation, Art. 3(3°) of the Prospectus Directive.

49 Art. 20(1°) of the Prospectus Regulation, Art. 13(1°) of the Prospectus Directive. However, Art. 13(5°) of the Prospectus Directive opens the possibility to delegate the approval of the prospectus to an authority of another Member State.

50 The prohibition had its seat in general company law (Art. 1841 of the Civil Code), and is now included in Art. L. 411-1 of the Monetary and Financial Code. The prohibition is also reiterated in the special law of company, for certain types of companies, see Art. L. 223-11 (SARL), Art. L. 227-2 (SAS), L. 225-10 (GIE) of the Commercial Code.

As an exception, certain companies may make a public offer.[51] Violation of the prohibition results in several sanctions. The first is general and civil: the securities issued are cancelled, as are the contracts concluded.[52] This sanction, which is effective in the domestic order, is less effective in the international order if the companies are not French, or if the contract in question is not subject to French law. However, it could probably be applied as an overriding mandatory law with the solicitation of French residents as a connecting factor. The second sanction, a criminal one, prohibits regulated institutions from participating in public offerings.[53] Finally, if the prohibition is violated, the AMF may refer the matter to the president of the Paris court for investor protection purposes in order to put an end to the irregularity or eliminate its effects.[54] The international effectiveness of the prohibition would be even greater if it led to the administrative liability of the person who violated it, thus enabling the AMF to prosecute him or her.

347. Exemptions from the obligation to draw up a prospectus. Until the Prospectus Regulation, exemptions from the obligation to draw up a prospectus mainly concerned transactions that did not consist of a public offer, i.e. private placements.[55] The Prospectus Regulation has since expanded the notion

---

51 Which may, depending on the securities issued, be subject to additional constraints, see Art. L. 228-39 of the Commercial Code.

52 Art. L. 412-3 of the Monetary and Financial Code.

53 Art. 131-47 Criminal Code. The Criminal Code provides for a specific sanction for certain legal persons referred to in the law (Art. 131-39(6°) of the Criminal Code), but these have never been specified, making the sanction inapplicable, see C. Cardon, Q. Durand and L. Faugérolas, 'Offre au public et admission aux négociations de titres financiers sur un marché réglementé', *Etudes Joly Bourse*, Paris, Lextenso, 2019, no. 40.

54 Arts. L. 621-14 and L. 621-15 of the Monetary and Financial Code. For an illustration, see CA Paris, 28 March 1988, *D.*, 1989, jurispr. p. 116, note Decoopman.

55 A. Pietrancosta and A. Maraud des Grottes, 'La notion de "placement privé" abolished by the Prospectus Regulation of 14 June 2017?', *BJB*, January 2018, p. 60. in France, but also in other European countries (Germany, Italy, Spain, Belgium or Portugal). From the French point of view, this notion of private placement was for a long time the result of a de facto situation, in France as in Germany. The concept appeared in positive law with Directive 89/298/EC, the initial draft of which even provided for a definition; in France, Law no. 98-546 of 2 July 1998 allows the concept to appear in a vacuum, by making official the operations that do not constitute a public offering, whereas the practice had until then resulted from the position of the COB (COB, *Annual Report 1985*, pp. 92 et seq.), confirmed by case law (CA Paris, 2 November 1989, *Rev. Sociétés*, 1990, note by P. Le Cannu). The private placement mechanism is detailed in COB Regulation No 98-08 (approved by the order of 22 January 1999, *JORF*, 2 March 1999, p. 3124). On this subject see. J.-J. Daigre, 'Commentaire des aspects de droit des marchés financiers de la loi pour la confiance et la modernisation de l'économie du 26 juillet 2005', *Rev. Sociétés*, July 2006, p. 461. The concept was nevertheless anchored in Recital 5 of the Prospectus Directive, and even more clearly in the terms of Art. L. 411-2 of the Monetary and Financial Code. A doctrinal debate, dating back to the public offering, and continuing under the public offering regime, consisted in determining whether a private placement was an exception to the obligation to draw up a prospectus, as it constituted a singular public offering (the public in question being very circumscribed), or whether it was simply an offer that did not constitute a *public offering*

of public offer, ousting that of private placement. The exemptions from the obligation to draw up a prospectus now lie, on the one hand, in the aspects not covered by the material scope of the Regulation and, on the other hand, in the cases where the Regulation deactivates the obligation to draw up a prospectus. These two hypotheses are similar to those already known under the Prospectus Directive, and are applicable because of the person of the issuer (notably public persons), the addressees of the offer (qualified investors[56]), or the characteristics of the securities issued, in particular when the obligation to publish a prospectus arises from the admission to trading on a regulated market. The unification of these exemptions is welcome, as it eliminates a difficulty that was inherent in the diversity of national exemptions under the Directive. These exemptions were likely to reintroduce conflict of laws in cases where the law of the place of solicitation and the law of the seat did not coincide as regards the exemptions granted. The exemption was then subject to the law of the administrative authority competent for approval.[57]

§ 2. THE COMPETENT ADMINISTRATIVE AUTHORITY

348. Administrative approval of the prospectus. European law requires entities making a public offer to publish a prospectus,[58] which must be approved by an

---

and therefore simply fell outside the scope of the obligations arising from it. However, this debate had an important practical consequence, since the supervisory authority was not competent outside the scope of public offerings and, not surprisingly, presented the private placement as a 'transaction carried out by way of derogation. from the rules on public offerings (COB Regulation No 98-09), in order to reserve 'at least at the margin, a power of appreciation' (B. François, 'Appel public à l'épargne', *Répertoire de droit des sociétés*, Paris, Dalloz, 2006).

56 It is here that the legislator has reintroduced the hypotheses covered by private placement, see Art. L. 411-2 of the Monetary and Financial Code.

57 See, for example, in a case concerning a capital increase of a German company listed in France, where the AMF was not competent for the purposes of the prospectus, and therefore could not compel the German issuer to prepare one, Sanct. AMF, 24 November 2005, *Allianz AG and Société Euroclear France*, *BJB*, April 2006, pp. 470 et seq., note F. Martin Laprade. Another example is the exemption from the obligation to prepare a prospectus for a public offer of dividends paid to existing shareholders in the form of shares of the same class as those giving entitlement to the dividends (see Information to be disseminated in the event of a public offer or admission to trading of financial securities on a regulated market, Doc. AMF 2016-04, 21 October 2016). Under the Prospectus Directive, it was possible for one Member State to apply this exemption, while another Member State did not. R. Gaspard promotes in this case the application of the law of the home country authority as the applicable law as a matter of principle (see R. Gaspard, *La reconnaissance mutuelle en droit bancaire et financier européen, op. cit.)* It seems to us that this situation is close to the preliminary question, and that it should be decided by the *lex societatis*. As the law stands, this is not apparent since the authority of the home Member State is always the authority of the registered office.

58 Art. 3 of the Prospectus Regulation; Art. L. 412-1 of the Monetary and Financial Code.

administrative authority,[59] in France the '*Autorité des marchés financiers*'.[60] The latter verifies the formal regularity of the prospectus,[61] and not the details of the form of the securities issued, the prerogatives they offer, or the law applicable to them.[62] It expresses its approval by affixing its visa to the prospectus. The institution of this authorisation has several effects.

The first is to create a dependency link between the issuer and the administrative authority, since the issuer will have to submit to the constraints of the administrative authority in order to proceed with the offer. Although the authority cannot consider itself incompetent to approve the prospectus, it can ask for additional information,[63] or even refuse to approve it, even if it only checks its formal regularity. Such a refusal, which can be challenged before the courts of the authority's seat, is nevertheless unlikely because of the existence of detailed regulations on the content of the prospectus and the procedures for approval.[64]

The second effect of the authorisation is to create a link between the authority having granted its approval and the public offer transaction itself,

---

59 Art. 20 of the Prospectus Regulation.

60 Arts. L. 412-1 and L. 621-8 of the Monetary and Financial Code.

61 Thus, Art. L. 621-8-1 of the Financial Monetary Code states that the AMF 'shall verify whether the document is complete and comprehensible' and 'whether the information it contains is consistent'. In this regard, the Paris Court of Appeal has stated that 'the AMF's approval […] does not imply either approval of the appropriateness of the transaction or authentication of the accounting and financial information contained therein', see CA Paris, 1re ch., sect. H, 4 July 2006, no. 2006/01138. On this control, see J. Chacornac, *Les fonctions de l'information en droit des instruments financiers*, *op. cit.*, nos. 151 et seq.

62 And this is true regardless of the law designated: the AMF has thus had the opportunity to specify that 'the compatibility of the issue with the principles of Sharia does not fall within the jurisdiction of the AMF', see AMF, 'Questions and answers from the AMF on the preparation of sukuk prospectuses', AMF Position no. 2010-06, available on the authority's website. The opposite answer would have been peculiar.

63 The AMF has the power to request additional information, explanations or justifications 'concerning the situation, activity and results of the issuer and of any guarantors of the financial instruments that are the subject of the transaction' (Arts. 32(1)(a) et seq. of the Prospectus Regulation; Art. L. 621-8-1 para. 2 of the Monetary and Financial Code).
These prerogatives are the basis for a real control by the competent authority, which may require the publication of a supplement 'if significant new facts or material errors or inaccuracies within the meaning of Article 16 arise or appear after the approval of the prospectus' (Art. 24(2°) of the Prospectus Regulation and Art. 17, 2° of the Prospectus Directive). See on this subject, R. Gaspard, *La reconnaissance mutuelle en droit bancaire et financier*, *op. cit.*, no. 321.

64 Commission Delegated Regulation (EU) 2019/980 of 14 March 2019 supplementing Regulation (EU) 2017/1129 of the European Parliament and of the Council as regards the form, content, scrutiny and approval of the prospectus to be published when securities are offered to the public or admitted to trading on a regulated market.

since the authority can suspend or prohibit the public offer associated with the prospectus.[65]

The third is to allow the issuer whose prospectus has been approved to solicit local investors, but also European investors, 'provided that the competent authority of each host Member State receives the notification'.[66] Here we find the dynamics of mutual recognition of approval, but related to another administrative authorisation, the visa, and to another purpose, the prospectus. This difference in the function of the purpose of the authorisation has an impact on the criterion for determining the competent authority in intra-European relations, which is based, depending on the hypothesis, on the registered office or on the issuer's choice between the registered office and the place of solicitation. It will be shown here that the competent authority should be that of the place of solicitation[67] (I). Relations with third countries are unsurprisingly based on the equivalence method, which allows for improved coordination; once again, however, the designation of the nationally competent authority should be that of the place of solicitation (II).

I. The Competent Authority of an Issuer Established in the Union

349. Issuance of equity securities and jurisdiction of the home authority. The Prospectus Regulation distinguishes the criterion of the authority's competence according to the securities issued. The first criterion, applicable to all 'issuers of securities established in the Union',[68] is that of the registered office of the issuer. While the function of the prospectus is to protect its addressees, this rule nevertheless gives jurisdiction to the authority of the issuer's registered office

---

65 Art. 32(d) and (f) of the Prospectus Regulation. In French law, the AMF provides for its competence in Art. 213-1 and 213-2 of its General Regulation. To which must be added the link that the prospectus itself creates with its addressees. As Professor Trébulle writes, 'the prospectus will form the first legal link between the issuer and the potential subscriber. We can indeed speak of the first legal relationship, because it is by signing the prospectus that the issuer manifests itself for the first time to third parties. It is indeed through the mechanism of the offer made known to the public that the issuer will be bound.' F.-X. Trébulle, *L'émission de valeurs mobilières*, *op. cit.*, no. 86.

66 Art. 24 of the Prospectus Regulation, Art. 17(1°) of the Prospectus Directive. The term 'Community scope' is the title of Art 17 of the Directive.

67 As is already the case for periodic bonds, which, if not audited, are filed with the AMF regardless of the origin of the issuer (Art. L. 451-1-2 of the Monetary and Financial Code); such filing puts the AMF in a position to verify their formal regularity.

68 Art. 2(1°)(m)(i) of the Prospectus Regulation. This rule appears in French law in Art. L. 621-8 of the Monetary and Financial Code, as well as in Art. 212-2 of the AMF General Regulation. However, one caveat should be mentioned: it is possible for the competent authority, if the issuer so requests, to delegate the approval of the prospectus to the authority of another Member State if the latter agrees (Art. 20(8) of the Prospectus Regulation). This latter option would probably restore the prerogatives of the authority of the place of solicitation.

to monitor it.[69] This choice can be explained firstly by the unification of the applicable regulation, which makes it possible to limit the law of the place where investors are solicited. On the other hand, the choice of the authority of the issuer's registered office is due to its unitary nature: the issuer can submit to the sole jurisdiction of the authority of its registered office, without having to seek approval of its prospectus from the various authorities of the legal orders within which it wishes to disseminate it. This choice is also explained by the alignment of the issuer's company law and the disclosure requirements of the prospectus, thus reducing costs. As Professor Synvet and Ms Tenenbaum write:

> 'In the case of the prospectus, this means that the annual report, drawn up in accordance with the *lex societatis*, may be used as a reference document under the law of the same State, which will itself constitute one of the elements of the prospectus subject to approval by the authority of the country in which the registered office is located'.[70]

It should be added that at the time this criterion was introduced, the investors solicited were most often those of the issuer's registered office, the traditional connecting factor of continental European countries through the real seat constituting a strong anchoring of the company in the legal order where it is established.

350. Critique. This last argument is probably less accurate today: the liberalisation of the establishment of companies makes it possible to create an increasingly artificial link between the company's actual place of business – the place where it is effectively managed and where its activities are carried out – and its registered office. Moreover, the uniformity of the legislation on the prospectus should not necessarily deactivate the competence of local administrative authorities. Indeed, if the information required is the same, administrative monitoring practices are sometimes decisive for the consistency of the information required, and therefore for compliance with European regulations. This is all the more true as the authority most interested in protecting residents is the one of their legal order. The rule adopted means that the host Member State authority that has been duly notified cannot oppose local distribution of the prospectus.[71]

---

69 As some authors observe, 'it is thus remarkable that the competence to approve a prospectus does not depend on the location of the public offer or the market on which the securities are to be admitted', H. Synvet and A. Tenenbaum, 'Instruments financiers', *op. cit.*, no. 45.

70 *Ibid.*

71 Art. 24(1) of the Prospectus Regulation (Art. 17(1°) of the Prospectus Directive), *in fine*: 'The competent authorities of the host Member States shall not initiate any approval procedure or administrative procedure in respect of prospectuses.' Even if the information in the prospectus is deficient, the host Member State authority can do nothing except, in the

As a result, the choice of the registered office as a criterion for allocating authorities appears to be excessive in that it does too much to promote the objective of integrating the internal market, to the detriment of investor protection. This is particularly obvious when the solicitation takes place exclusively through the admission of securities to trading on the regulated market: the local authority is deprived of all *a priori* monitoring powers. Indeed, the decision to admit the securities to trading is taken by the market operator, and the prospectus is approved by the authority of the company's headquarters. As a result, for example, a foreign-registered holding company of a group whose effective management is in France, whose shares are admitted to trading on the French regulated market and whose majority of shares are held by French residents, will never be confronted with the French financial markets authority. The latter will not intervene at any stage of the process,[72] even though its geographical, linguistic and cultural proximity to the local market appears to be preponderant, and it allows the prospectus to fulfil its own function, which is to protect investors. The authority is undoubtedly not deprived of all power to intervene, particularly in the area of advertising,[73] but the bulk of its powers will only intervene *a posteriori*, after the facts, depriving the mechanism instituted by the visa[74] of effectiveness.

muted words of the Directive, 'draw the attention of its counterpart in the home Member State to the need for further information' (Art. 24(2°) Prospectus Regulation, Art. 17(2°) Prospectus Directive).

72 This statement must be qualified: the market rules sometimes provide for a mechanism for informing the authority, see Art. P. 1.1.2 of the Euronext Market Rules (Book II applicable to French regulated markets).

73 One of the innovations of the Prospectus Regulation is to give control over promotional communications relating to the offer to the public to the authority of the place where the communications are disseminated, cf. Art. 22(6) of the Prospectus Regulation. In particular, this was the AMF's doctrine, which considered it 'unavoidable that any form of advertising or commercial document should be subject to the supervision of the authorities of the host countries, which are the only ones in a position to know the local cultural codes, the distribution networks and the usual advertising methods on its national market', see AMF, 'Cross-border fund distribution in Europe: identifying barriers to entry and improving investor confidence', 19 September 2016. In addition to this, as Professor Blanche Sousi notes, 'the uncertainty of the outcome of a long and costly trial, [...] more often than not (operators) give up acting and suffer in a host state from provisions that are manifestly contrary to EU law, as they illegitimately impede the freedom of establishment or the freedom to provide services', B. Sousi, 'L'harmonisation européenne des services financiers et le juge national' in *Le juge et le droit de l'économie, Mélanges en l'honneur de Pierre Bézard*, Paris, Montchrestien, 2002, p. 200.

74 The AMF is acutely aware of this situation. The authority wrote that 'the AMF is very keen that the authority of the state in which the marketing documentation is disseminated (i.e. the host state in the case of a passported prospectus) should be able to exercise oversight over that documentation, particularly when the offer is marketed to retail investors, insofar as that authority has the proximity and knowledge of the investor base', AMF, 'The Review of the Prospectus Directive', 25 May 2016, available on the authority's website. The situation is different in the related area of marketing units in collective investment schemes, where

351. Solution. In these circumstances, the solution could be to give jurisdiction to the authority of the place where the investors are predominantly resident.[75] Such a criterion would be easily applicable when the solicitation takes place through an admission to trading – the authority of the place of trading should then have jurisdiction[76] – but is more difficult to implement when the solicitation takes place without admission to trading. In the latter case, the criterion used should be apparent and stable so that the issuer can refer to the same authority for its various issues. Several alternatives are therefore possible. The first is to revert to the head office criterion, while substituting the actual head office for the registered office, in order to re-establish a genuine link between the competent authority and the company, so that the persons most interested in the integrity of the prospectus and the authority responsible for their protection coincide.[77] However, this proposal has two disadvantages: the real seat is opaque, sometimes difficult to determine,[78] and is likely to change. The second alternative, inspired by the solution applicable to third country issuers, is to give jurisdiction to the authority of the first place of solicitation. However, it has the potential to be even more malleable for the issuer.

352. It is therefore the criterion of the issuer's registered office that appears to be the most stable and apparent in the case of a public offer without admission to trading, and should continue to prevail. While it is difficult for investors to be protected by the criterion of allocation of administrative jurisdiction, two complementary possibilities are possible. The first is for the head office authority to delegate its jurisdiction to the authority of the domicile of the investors who will be approached if their grouping within the same Member State is apparent.[79] The second is to restore the possibility for the authority to which

---

the AMF can oppose marketing and, if necessary, sanction the fund, see lastly in the case of an investment fund from a foreign country, Comm. sanct. AMF, 2 July 2019 (SAN-2019-10), *BJB*, September 2019, no. 5, p. 12 and comm. Riassetto.

75 The preponderance criterion makes it possible to avoid the argument of the geographical dispersion of investors and the illusory unity of the notion of investors' residence.

76 A criterion for coordination between authorities should be introduced when admission to trading takes place on several markets, in order to guarantee stability and predictability for the issuer. The Takeover Directive, which gives jurisdiction to the home authority if the issuer has also admitted its securities to that authority (see *infra*, para. 492), could serve as a useful model, and otherwise to the authority of the first place of listing.

77 This proposal has already been made by Mr Conac, who wrote, with regard to the draft Prospectus Directive: 'It would perhaps be appropriate, however, to reserve the case of companies whose real seat differs from the registered office, in order to submit the control of the prospectus to the authority of the real seat.' P.-H. Conac, *La régulation des marchés boursiers par la commission des opérations de bourse (COB) et la securities and exchange commission (SEC)*, *op. cit.*, no. 323.

78 In particular when the management body meets in a dematerialised manner, see L. d'Avout, 'L'entreprise et les conflits internationaux de lois', *op. cit.*, no. 89.

79 This possibility is now provided for in Art. 20(8) of the Prospectus Regulation; it was already provided for in the Prospectus Directive, see B. Stoeva, *La coopération entre les superviseurs financiers dans l'Union européenne*, *op. cit.*

the prospectus is notified to object to its local distribution if it considers that it does not meet the standards laid down by European legislation. The Prospectus Regulation currently allows the authority to take precautionary measures only after informing the home Member State authority of the irregularities and, if the latter fails to take action,[80] to require a translation of the summary of the prospectus,[81] but it cannot otherwise oppose the dissemination of the prospectus.[82] Overall, the proposed solution appears to be a less excessive compromise in favour of internal market integration.

353. The case of debt securities. The determination of the competent authority for debt securities allows a different solution. The Prospectus Regulation distinguishes between the issuance of debt securities with a nominal value of less than EUR 1,000, for which the competent authority is that of the issuer's registered office, and the issuance of complex debt securities[83] or with a denomination per unit of more than EUR 1,000, for which there is a choice. In this case, the competent authority is the one chosen by the applicant from among several options: it may be the authority of the place of the issuer's registered office, the authority of the place where the securities are admitted to trading, or the authority of the place where the securities are offered to the public.[84] The determination of the first two criteria does not pose any difficulty;[85] the third, on the other hand, is not spelled out either in the European Regulation or in French domestic law.[86] The place where the securities are offered to the public should

---

80 Art. 37 of the Prospectus Regulation.

81 Art. 27(2) of the Prospectus Regulation.

82 Art. 24 of the Prospectus Regulation.

83 I.e. 'non-equity securities giving the right to acquire any security or to receive cash upon conversion of such securities or upon exercise of the rights conferred by them, provided that the issuer of the non-equity securities is not the issuer of the underlying securities or an entity belonging to the group of the latter issuer' (Art. 2(1)(m)(ii) of the Prospectus Regulation).

84 Only in the case of the issue of debt securities or UCITS. This hypothesis is that of Art. 2(1°)(m)(ii) of the Prospectus Regulation.

85 The identification of the place of admission to trading does not really pose any difficulties; it is determined by the international connection of the financial market (see *supra*, paras. 267 et seq.). As regards the possible application of the law of the registered office, again the determination does not pose any particular difficulties and follows the observations made concerning the authority's competence with regard to an issue of capital securities (see *supra*, paras. 351 et seq.)

86 French regulations do not provide a clear answer to this question (in particular, Art. L. 621-8 of the Monetary and Financial Code, the purpose of which is to determine which transactions in financial instruments require prior approval by the AMF). However, like Art. 212-2 of the AMF General Regulation, the second paragraph of this article refers to the case of a public offer where the issuer does not have its registered office in France (the first paragraph is reserved for this case), but does not determine what is required to establish that 'the public offer is made in France', to use its terms. In both cases, the provision assumes that the transaction is carried out in France, without indicating what makes it possible to establish that it is carried out in France. As for ordinary law, which was based on Art. 1841 of the Civil Code and is now enshrined in Art. L. 411-1 of the Monetary and Financial

nevertheless be determined by the domicile of the persons solicited because of the function of the prospectus.[87] However, the originality of the criterion used does not lie in the authorities designated, but in the distinction made between debt securities and in the choice left to the issuer as to the competence of the authorities.

In the context of the Prospectus Directive, the rationale behind this option was to limit it to particularly large issues, i.e. those reserved for professionals, referred to as the 'wholesale market'.[88] To circumscribe this professional market, the criterion chosen was the amount of the nominal value of the securities, initially set at one hundred thousand euros, which was constantly lowered in the draft directives until it reached one thousand euros in the final directive.[89] This option of choice was perceived by some authors as a protectionist measure for the most important financial centres, i.e. those whose savings are most in demand,[90] allowing them to be chosen instead of the headquarters authority. Other authors have seen this as a competition between authorities.[91] This last aspect has been raised by the French government, which

---

Code, it does not resolve this issue either. Indeed, this article does not seek to determine the Member State where the securities are offered to the public: it is a prohibitive rule for public offers in France, with exceptions in the Commercial Code.

87 On this function, see *supra*, para. 346. Professor Synvet and Ms Tenenbaum believe that this solution is also justified by reasoning by analogy deduced from a publication of the Committee of European Securities Regulators (now available on ESMA's website: https://www.esma.europa.eu/sites/default/files/library/2015/11/09_798pdf.pdf question 43; accessed on 15 March 2018). The authors write thus: 'It should therefore be possible to hold that there is an offer to the public in the territory of a Member State, and therefore applicability of Directive No 2003/71/EC […], when an issuer or transferor of securities makes an offer within the meaning of Article 2.1, d) of the Directive ("communication addressed in any form and by any means to persons and presenting sufficient information on the terms of the offer and on the securities to be offered, so as to enable an investor to decide to purchase or subscribe to those securities") to persons residing in the territory of a Member State', H. Synvet and A. Tenenbaum, 'Financial instruments', *op. cit.*, no. 38.

88 According to the explanatory memorandum of the Directive, 'The pan-European operation of wholesale capital markets should be made more efficient in order to improve the integration of the European financial market'. Amended proposal for a Directive of the European Parliament and of the Council on the prospectus, Com (2002), 460 final, [January 2003] OJ C 20 E/122, spec. p. 124.

89 The explanatory memorandum of the Directive states, inter alia, that "an objective criterion based on a high denomination of the securities to be traded has been introduced to create an effective distinction between markets for professionals and the general public. Thus, the more flexible regime (i.e. the option of choice) cannot be applied to the detriment of retail investors", see Amended Proposal for a Directive of the European Parliament and of the Council on the Prospectus, Com (2002), 460 final, [January 2003] OJ C 20 E/122, spec. p. 124.

90 H. de Vauplane and J.-J. Daigre, 'Directive Prospectus. *Banque et droit*, August 2003, p. 47, spec. p. 50.

91 C. Huhne, Report on the proposal for a European Parliament and Council directive on the prospectus, COM (2001) 280 – C5-0263/2001 – 2001/0117(COD), 27 February 2002; European Economic and Social Committee, *Opinion on the proposal for a Transparency Directive*, 2002, section 4; E. Ferran, *Building an EU securities* market, Cambridge, CUP,

has criticised the resulting 'regulatory arbitrage'.[92] During the negotiations on the Prospectus Regulation, the French government considered that such freedom of choice was all the less appropriate as "the securities covered by the text are most often offered to the public in the Member State in which the issuing entity has its registered office".[93] It should nevertheless be noted that, following the government's reasoning, the relevant criterion seems to be not so much the location of the issuer's registered office as the location of the majority of the investors sought. This criterion deserves approval: there is no need to distinguish between shares and debt securities from the point of view of the prospectus, and the solution already outlined for the former is applicable here.[94]

II. The Competent Authority of an Issuer Established in a Third Country

354. Allocation criterion. Here again, a distinction must be made between the prospectus associated with an issue of equity or debt securities. In the first case, the competent authority will be that of the first place where the foreign issuer has admitted its securities to trading, or offered its securities to the public; the issuer is therefore given an initial choice, but cannot reverse it.[95] The underlying idea is

---

2004, p. 151; K. DECKERT, *La sollicitation publique des investisseurs en droit communautaire, français et allemand*, *op. cit.*, no. 377; A. PIETRANCOSTA, 'Compétence internationale de l'AMF aux fins de visa du prospectus', *Étude Joly Bourse*, no. 50. This theory was developed in the United States based on the effects of the distribution of legislative powers in the area of company law. The latter, giving rise to competition between laws, would be the source of the 'genius' of American company law. Ms Romano calls for a similar mechanism in the field of securities law, advocating the end of the SEC as a federal entity, combined with the emergence of an administrative authority for each federal state, with the possibility of the issuer electing its competent authority.

92 French Government response to the European Commission, 'Consultation paper on the review of the prospectus', 13 May 2015, Q42. The AMF has also criticised 'the generalisation of the free choice of the home Member State, which could be the State of the listing market, would create a strong incentive for regulatory arbitrage between regulators and lead to a race to the bottom in investor protection', AMF, 'The review of the Prospectus Directive', 25 May 2016 (available on the authority's website).

93 *Ibid.* The government also points out that since this choice is only possible for debt securities with a denomination per unit of more than EUR 1,000, such a rule does not promote the liquidity of the bond market. The government therefore advocated that the Member State of the registered office should also have jurisdiction over debt securities, regardless of the amount of the denomination per unit of the security concerned. We agree with this position: the distinction according to the amount of the debt security seems to us to be all the more obviously irrelevant since it has been lowered to EUR 1,000 and the threshold above which the prospectus can be drawn up is, since the Prospectus Regulation, EUR 8 million.

94 On this solution, see *supra*, para. 353.

95 Art. 2(m) Prospectus Regulation. The Prospectus Regulation allows for a change if the issuer could not initially choose the state in question.

to give the foreign issuer a permanent home Member State,[96] so that it does not change with each issue.[97] In the second case, concerning debt securities, issuers benefit from the same choice as those established on the territory of the Union, with the proviso that the authority of their home Member State is considered to be that of the first place of marketing of the securities.[98] The alignment of the authority's competence with the regime provided for the Member States is subject to the same critical observations as those developed with regard to intra-European relations.[99] It should be added that the current solution, allowing the issuer established in a third country to choose its competent authority, seems to us to accentuate the criticism of regulatory arbitrage, since the place of the first solicitation of the public may be artificially chosen, not representative of all future solicitations, and may have only a loose link with the investors solicited.

355. No correlation between competent authority and applicable law. In the case of issuers established on the territory of a third country, the competence of the elected authority does not necessarily imply the application of its law to the prospectus. Indeed, the Prospectus Directive allowed the foreign issuer to rely on its home law for the drawing up of the prospectus, under two conditions: on the one hand, its compliance with the IOSCO Disclosure Standards and, on the other hand, a decision of equivalence of the laws.[100] This equivalence decision was taken by the competent national authority. ESMA had nevertheless published a non-binding opinion on the considerations that should govern such a decision.[101] The possibility for the third country issuer to rely on its national law regarding the prospectus appeared positive, in particular because of the equivalence conditions set. However, it was unfortunate that the competent

---

96 Such an approach is reminiscent of the one adopted by Directive 2011/61/EU of the European Parliament and of the Council of 8 June 2011 on Alternative Investment Fund Managers (hereinafter the AIF Directive) through the concept of the Member State of reference, determined by a succession of connections aimed at capturing all possible marketing techniques, but always based on an objective connection criterion: that of effective marketing in a given legal order (Art. 37(4) of the AIF Directive).

97 We find the paradox that appeared for issuers established on the territory of the Member States of the Union, with a single and rigid criterion for equity securities, always ordering the competence of an authority that becomes permanent for the issuer, and the criterion chosen for debt securities.

98 That is, the same as for the issuance of equity securities, see Art. 2(1°)(m)(iii) of the Prospectus Regulation (identical article in the Prospectus Directive). From the point of view of the competent authority, the two situations are equivalent: it needs only be designated by the issuer, see Art. 215-1 of the AMF General Regulation from a French perspective.

99 See *supra*, para. 352.

100 Art. 20(1°) of the Prospectus Directive.

101 ESMA, Framework for the assessment of third country prospectuses under Article 20 of the Prospectus Directive, Opinion, ESMA/2013/317, 20 March 2013. See already, CESR, Concept paper on equivalence of certain foreign country GAAP and on description of certain third counties mechanisms of enforcement of financial information, CESR/04-509, October 2004. On this issue, see R. Vabres, *Comitology and financial services*, *op. cit.*, no. 72; R. Gaspard, *La reconnaissance mutuelle en droit bancaire et financier*, *op. cit.*, no. 521.

national authority was given total discretion to establish equivalence with the States concerned. Such a solution did not favour the 'uniform application of the directive'.[102] Above all, even though the authority could be artificially chosen, the prospectus would then acquire the right to be disseminated in other Member States, subject only to notification by the chosen authority. It would have been better to follow the example of the method used for accounting documentation.[103] Either the equivalence decision is taken by a European authority or by a joint decision of the national authorities,[104] in which case the prospectus can easily acquire an EU-wide scope, or the decision is taken unilaterally by a national authority, as was the case here, and the prospectus should not be able to be notified without a formal right of review by the authority whose investors are being solicited.

356. The Prospectus Regulation modifies this situation by using the equivalence method. Indeed, this regulation requires, on the one hand, the conclusion of a prior cooperation agreement between the authority of the Member State and the authority of the registered office of the foreign issuer[105] and, on the other hand, the establishment of a decision of equivalence of the legislation of the registered office of the foreign issuer taken by the Commission.[106] The use of the equivalence method seems particularly appropriate: while allowing the application of the foreign law and retaining the prerogatives attached to approval by a Member State authority, it gives an administrative body with specific powers in this area, the Commission, the power to ensure the quality of the foreign legislation. Without going back over the analysis of the equivalence method, it

---

102 P. Schammo, 'Marchés financiers – Emetteurs - Prospectus et admission à la négociation sur un marché réglementé', *JCl. Europe Traité*, fasc. 1025, 2014, no. 46.

103 The accounting documentation may also be subject to the foreign law of the foreign issuer. On this sensitive issue, the Commission Regulation having established a process for determining the equivalence of IFRS (*International Financial Reporting Standards)* – these are accounting standards of international origin, notably applied in the European Union. Some countries apply other standards, including the United States; far from being a purely technical issue, the *ratio legis* of the accounting nomenclature contains a whole legal policy and foreign country accounting standards, subject to an equivalence decision by the national authority. See Commission Regulation EC No 1569/2007 of 21 December 2007, [2007] OJ L 340/66. On this issue, Ms Tenenbaum and Mr Synvet rightly observe that the AMF may have considered that US documents filed with the SEC were deemed equivalent. The SEC made an equivalent decision. On the whole, see H. Synvet and A. Tenenbaum, 'Instruments Financiers', *op. cit.*, no. 41; A. Sotiropoulou, *Les obligations d'information des sociétés cotées*, *op. cit.*, nos. 318 et seq. On the considerable influence of the regulator on accounting regulations, see P.-H. Conac, *La régulation des marchés boursiers par la Commission des opérations de bourse (COB) et la Securities and exchange commission (SEC)*, *op. cit.*, p. 141.

104 The European Securities and Markets Authority did not yet exist, and it would probably have been unthinkable to give such a prerogative to CESR. However, the Commission could have fulfilled such a role, as the solution adopted by the Prospectus Regulation shows.

105 Art. 29(1°)(b) of the Prospectus Regulation.

106 Combination of Art. 29(1°)(a) and 29(3°) of the Prospectus Regulation.

should nevertheless be added that it results here in showing the independence between the competence of an administrative authority and the applicable law. This reality is often concealed by a double phenomenon well illustrated by the prospectus. Either the foreign law pursues objectives that are too distinct from the domestic law and cannot reasonably be applied without affecting local economic public policy; or, as in intra-European matters, the laws have reached a sufficient degree of fungibility to make their application perfectly equivalent. In the latter case, it does not matter whether an authority applies one law or another, and it is therefore more appropriate for it to apply the law it knows best: its own. It is in this context that the criterion of distribution of administrative jurisdiction has sometimes taken over from the conflict-of-laws rule.

357. Coordination and self-limitation. Coordination of administrative authorities in relation to prospectuses is most often achieved through self-limitation, i.e. the process by which a legal order unilaterally restricts the application of its own norms to situations with a foreign element. The limitation may come from the criterion of applicability of the rule itself, from another rule, or from a decision of the administrative authority. However, the distinction between these different forms of limitation according to the structure of the norm should not be exaggerated. Not only are decisions on exemptions, when they become frequent, likely to lead to the institution of limitation rules,[107] but in

[107] The most blatant illustration of this phenomenon is the relationship between the SEC and the COB with regard to certain public offerings made by French issuers on American territory, which suffered from contradictory orders from the legal system of origin and destination: after having made specific exemptions at the request of the COB, the SEC concluded a general agreement with the COB limiting the application of American law with regard to issuers listed on the French regulated market wishing to solicit American investors, see on the history of this issue I. Stibbe, *Les autorités administratives indépendantes et le droit du commerce international*, *op. cit.*, nos. 337–341. It is remarkable that the American law is self-limiting. This is no doubt explained by the nature of the conflicting obligations at issue: the French obligations related to the internal organisation of the French market, whereas the American obligations simply concerned the relationship between foreign issuers and the American market. This hypothesis can be compared to the *Lloyd's* cases, where the *SEC* tried to insert itself into contracts relating to the internal organisation of an English company *Lloyd's*, in application of the rules of the Securities Exchange Act (on this case, see the summary and references in H. Muir Watt, *Aspects économiques de droit international privé*, *op. cit.*, nos. 100-107). *Lloyd's* is an English insurance company which organises the meeting between underwriters and insurers. In reality, *Lloyd's* is closer to a financial market than to a company (in this sense, the Court of Appeal of the Sixth Circuit observed that 'Lloyd's is not a company; it is a market somewhat analogous to the New York Stock Exchange', *Roby*, 995 F.2d, no. 1357). *Lloyd's* is made up of persons called *Names* who have subscribed to shares in *Lloyd's*. *Names* have a role comparable to that of market members, which explains the importance of the prudential obligations and control to which they are subject: in addition to a solvency test as to the extent of the obligations for which they are guarantors, they give an irrevocable undertaking in writing to *Lloyd's*, and must appear personally in London before representatives of the *Lloyd's* Council to give an account of their understanding of the various risks and implications of their membership of *Lloyd's*, including their unlimited personal liability. The relationship between the *Names* and *Lloyd's* is governed by a contract, the *General Undertaking*. In the various *Lloyd's* cases, American *Names*

fact the enactment by the authority of a special sectoral regulation which it can modify discretionarily makes the distinction even more fragile.

358. Self-limitation may be applied in the same way in domestic and international situations: for example, when the AMF is the competent authority to approve the prospectus of a public offering on its territory, the French or foreign nature of the issuer has no bearing on the applicability of the rule. However, sometimes the material criterion used is intended to limit the application of domestic law to foreign issuers in order to encourage them to apply to the French regulated market. This is the case with the exemption from the obligation to make a public offer when listing financial securities on the professional segment of Euronext, which is intended to spare foreign companies from being subject to domestic disclosure rules.[108] The restriction of the domestic law leads in practice

---

were called upon to pay obligations for which they were guarantors, in particular because of the extent of the damage caused by asbestos and various types of pollution. Given the size of the sums involved, the American *Names* attempted to sue *Lloyd's* for breach of the *Securities Act*, claiming that they had been actively solicited, thatinformation on the risks taken had been concealed from them, and that they had been disproportionately exposed to the risks which led to their call for payment. The various disputes centred on the enforceability of the *General Undertaking*'s jurisdiction clause designating English courts and signed by the US *Names*, which the *SEC* considered unenforceable. The American courts all ended up finding the clause valid, after various analyses, most of which led to the acceptance of the jurisdiction of English law and courts under a functional *replacement* test with regard to the protection offered to American investors by English legislation which 'protects the same interests and promotes the same objectives' (as is well known, this is a frequent procedure in this area, see *supra*, para. 218). Some authors have seen this as a sign of the weakening of the regime of mandatory or overriding laws (see in this sense H. Muir Watt, *Aspects économiques de droit international privé, op. cit.*). Other authors have nevertheless approved the result of the decision while criticising the reasoning of the American decisions, in particular because the American law was simply not applicable. Thus, for Ms Julie Bédart, the market affected by the dispute was the English market, not the American market, and one of the most tangible elements of this inapplication of the American legislation is that the *SEC* had exempted *Lloyd's* from registration because this entity positively met the *accredited investor* standard of the SEC's own regulations (the author thus writes: 'It is not unreasonable to assume that an investor who is not protected *ex ante* by US disclosure regulation would not be protected *ex post facto* under the fraud provisions either.' See J. Bédart, *International conflicts of Antitrust and Securities Regulations: 'It's all about effects'*, Columbia, New-York, 2006, pp. 466–467). Indeed, it also seems to us that these decisions reflect the domain of US federal securities law rather than a deactivation of the mandatory nature of these laws. It is also possible to see in this limitation of US law a certain reluctance of the latter to intervene in what appears less as a fraudulent solicitation of US investors than as the regulation of the internal relations of a foreign organisation. This can be seen in the fact that the litigation has focused on what is similar to *Lloyd's* bylaws: its *General Understanding*. Just as the *SEC* has exempted French market members from certain US obligations, it has not applied its securities regulations to a foreign organisation.

108 See *infra*, para. 372. It also happens that the material criterion of limitation contains a geographical indication. This is for example the case in labour law where the assessment of the economic reason for a dismissal is no longer made with regard to the group of companies as a whole, but only within the limits of French territory, see P. Lokiec, 'Vers un nouveau droit du travail', *D.*, 2017, 2109.

to the acceptance of the foreign law.[109] In these cases, self-limitation is in line with its more general purpose as described by Mr d'Avout:

> 'In order to remedy inconsistencies arising from partial superimpositions of regimes and associated frictions of rules, self-limitation techniques constitute a preventive solution, manifesting a legislator's favourable disposition to the use of a legal regime offered by him in conjunction with a foreign regime.'[110]

Self-restriction most often takes the form of an exemption. It seems to have been used for the first time in the United States, where it originates from Section 5 of the Securities Act of 1933.[111] In the United States, the public offer of financial securities is prohibited as a matter of principle, unless a registration statement of the financial instruments offered is filed with the SEC.[112] Only by way of exception may the offeror be exempted from a registration statement.[113] However, the criterion for the application of registration requirements is particularly broad: it covers all companies, domestic or foreign, "whose orders to purchase their shares were given from the territory of the United States".[114]

---

109 See for other illustrations in related matters, L. D'AVOUT, *L'entreprise et les conflits internationaux de lois*, *op. cit.*, no. 113.

110 *Ibid.*, no. 108.

111 It begins as follows: 'Unless a registration statement is in effect as to a security, it shall be unlawful for any person, directly or indirectly [...]. P.-H. CONAC, *La régulation des marchés boursiers par la commission des opérations de bourse (COB) et la securities and exchange commission (SEC)*, *op. cit.*, no. 34.

112 The statement contains two documents: the prospectus, which is distributed to investors, while the second contains additional information that is available at the SEC. This distinction is intended to avoid overly voluminous prospectuses, see *ibid.*

113 Specialists in American law have observed that this 'prohibitive formulation [...] constitutes a classic technique of American law', see *ibid.* A. TUNC, 'Aspects de droits étrangers' in M. VASSEUR (ed.), *Les autorités boursières créatrices de droit*, ENAJ, 1981, p. 147.

114 P.-H. CONAC, *La régulation des marchés boursiers par la commission des opérations de bourse (COB) et la securities and exchange commission (SEC)*, *op. cit.*, no. 283; I. STIBBE, *Les autorités administratives indépendantes et le droit du commerce international*, *op. cit.* The very broad basis of Section 5 of the *Securities Act* is linked to the fact that this legislation covers *interstate* commerce, and also applies to commerce with foreign States, see Section 12(g) of the Securities Exchange Act of 1934. Aware of the excesses of such an approach, the legislature left it to the SEC to mitigate the consequences: 'The Commission may by rules or regulations or, on its own motion, after notice and opportunity for hearing, by order, exempt from this subsection any security of a foreign issuer, including any certificate of deposit for such a security, if the Commission finds that such exemption is in the public interest and is consistent with the protection of investors.' (Section 12(g)(3) of the Securities Exchange Act of 1934).
It should be noted that SEC doctrine has varied in the application of these registration requirements, going so far as to use the nationality criterion in an explicitly imperialistic manner: 'United States citizens, like citizens of the Roman Empire, carried the United States securities laws wherever they went' (E.F. GREENE, 'Reproposed SEC Rule 144a', *21 Inst. On SEC. Reg. 4* [1990], quoted by I. STIBBE, *Les autorités administratives indépendantes et le droit du commerce international*, *op. cit.*, note 102 p. 60).

For this reason, the US Congress gave the SEC the power to grant exemptions to foreign issuers.[115] The SEC then decided to exempt companies with fewer than 300 US resident shareholders from US regulation. For foreign companies that exceed this threshold, and have not actively solicited US residents, the SEC decided to make a novel conditional exemption. Indeed, the foreign company will be exempted from registration statements as long as it provides the SEC with the information given in its home country.[116] In France, the former COB, inspired by the SEC, used the same exemption technique.[117]

359. There are at least two reasons why this technique is so popular, both of which are independent of the domestic or international nature of the transactions in question. The first is the legal regime of the exemption, which reverses the burden of proof by placing it on the operator, who must prove the reasons why he can be exempted.[118] The second is that the exemption technique strengthens the authority of the institution, while allowing a subtle extension of its jurisdiction.[119] From the point of view of the authority, this allows for a high

---

115 Art. 12(g)(3) of the Securities Exchange Act, see P.-H. Conac, *La régulation des marchés boursiers par la commission des opérations de bourse (COB) et la securities and exchange commission (SEC)*, *op. cit.*, no. 283. The relationship between Congress and the SEC is particularly close since the former exercises institutional supervision over the latter, *ibid.*, no. 17.

116 *Ibid.*, no. 285. It should be noted that the solicitation criterion is also central to the regulation of American financial instruments. However, the scope of this exemption must undoubtedly be put into perspective insofar as, as Mr Conac points out, 'it is not certain that a federal court would accept jurisdiction to impose a sanction that the SEC would seek against a foreign company that had failed to apply for an exemption. Thus, the obligation to apply for an exemption, and to provide information in return, is in fact aimed less at applying US law to these companies than at facilitating US investors' access to information disseminated abroad'. P.-H. Conac, *La régulation des marchés boursiers par la commission des opérations de bourse (COB) et la securities and exchange commission (SEC)*, *op. cit.*, no. 285. The exemption is in line with one of the main functions of self-restraint in financial matters, namely to allow for multiple listings, see *infra*, para. 372.

117 The imitation with the *SEC* went as far as the minimum number of shareholders – three hundred - from which it becomes necessary to request an exemption from the application of certain stock exchange regulations, see, for the background, *ibid.*

118 As Professor Tunc put it: 'I observe a technique that is very common in the United States or in England: Section 5 (of the Securities Act of 1933) declares that the issue of securities is prohibited. The technique is classic: you put up a wall, open a few doors and put guards there', see A. Tunc, 'Aspects de droits étrangers', *op. cit.*

119 One example is the COB, which, as Mr Conac points out, 'has skilfully used its power to target the listing prospectus to improve shareholder information in the case of transactions that were beyond its control. For example, it has made the benefit of a prospectus exemption conditional on compliance with its recommendations on mergers. Thus, when the legislator granted it *de jure* a very broad regulatory power in 1985, it merely confirmed the power it had previously exercised *de facto*'. *Ibid.*, no. 43. Professor Guyon has summarised the situation for issuers in relation to the COB very well: listed companies 'were reluctant to confront head-on a body with which they had ongoing relations and whose intervention was necessary on the occasion of each public offering', see Y. Guyon, *Les autorités administratives indépendantes*, Paris, PUF, 'Les voies du droit' Series, 1988, pp. 178–179,

degree of adaptability, particularly to the diversity of international situations. However, the exemption has some decisive disadvantages from the issuers' point of view: the decision is not fully predictable; it is *ad hoc* and only applies to one transaction at a time; it is reversible. In international matters, it is as if the exemption were a stopgap measure for adjusting a scope of application that is unsuited, if not to the legislative policy pursued, at least to the pursuit of that policy in international relations.

360. Conclusion of the section. The information obligations triggered by the marketing of financial securities have the function of protecting investors, and therefore explain the particular legitimacy of the law of the place of marketing, and particularly the law of the financial market when the securities are admitted to trading. However, it has been shown that this law is likely to be self-limiting whenever the law of the issuer offers equivalent protection: this is still the case within the Union thanks to the harmonisation of substantive law. However, the competence of the law of the market arises as soon as third countries are involved. The administrative control of disclosure requirements should, however, be carried out by the authority closest to the investors being approached: it is best placed to pursue the function of the disclosure requirements. In the case of admission to trading, this authority is that of the financial market; in other cases, the difficulty of determining this authority should undoubtedly lie in the competence of the authority of the issuer's registered office, tempered by the possibility, for the authority to which a prospectus is notified, of opposing its local distribution under certain conditions.

SECTION 2. MARKETING ACTS

361. Marketing acts are not, in principle, subject to the law of the financial market, but to the law designated by the act. However, the trading rules of the platform on which the securities are admitted are indirectly applicable to all marketing acts by imposing on the issuer, under the membership agreement, certain constraints, the violation of which may lead to the delisting of its securities. These solutions will be discussed in the context of admission to trading (§ 1) and the law applicable to public offers of financial securities, the collective nature of which justifies the European legislator's deactivation of the consumer protection conflict rule (§ 2).

---

quoted by P.-H. Conac, *La régulation des marchés boursiers par la commission des opérations de bourse (COB) et la securities and exchange commission (SEC)*, *op. cit.*, no. 24. In addition, the AMF is in a particularly advantageous position vis-à-vis issuers because it can always propose a change in the law, see Art. L. 621-19(II) of the Monetary and Financial Code.

§ 1. ADMISSION TO TRADING

362. Application of the Financial Market Law. The admission of an issuer's securities to trading is a decision taken by the market operator at the issuer's request, and takes place by means of a membership agreement between the issuer and the market operator by which the issuer undertakes to comply with the rules of the trading system. These rules detail the admission process and its conditions. The admission to trading process, which is similar to a procedure,[120] is therefore governed in its entirety by financial market law, which also applies here in terms of the internal organisation of the market. Symmetrically, when delisting is initiated by the issuer itself or by the market operator,[121] it is governed by the law of the financial market.[122] On the other hand, when delisting is initiated by the issuer's shareholder, it corresponds to a market transaction and is subject, paradoxically, to the *lex societatis.*[123] There is no satisfactory explanation for this duality; it would logically be up to the law of the financial market, which has sovereignty over the conditions for admission to trading, to decide alone on the conditions for delisting.

363. Procedure for admission to the Euronext regulated market.[124] Admission is based on an admission file filed by the issuer.[125] This file must be compiled

---

[120] Relying on German doctrine, Ms Deckert observed the procedural character of the financial market itself: 'In law, the financial market seems to be a procedure for the regulation of the supply of and demand for securities by individuals, i.e. a procedure for the exchange of securities and money', see K. Deckert, *La sollicitation publique des investisseurs en droit communautaire, français et allemand*, *op. cit.*, no. 12. See also in this sense, C. Arsouze, *Procédures boursières*, Paris, Editions Joly, 2008, no. 1.

[121] Art. 6905 of the Euronext Market Rules (Book I). The grounds on which the market operator may delist a security are listed in the Market Rules, see Art. 6905(ii) of the Euronext Market Rules (Book I). The list is not exhaustive, and may include a violation of the applicable regulations, in particular the market rules (in which case the penalty is particularly heavy for shareholders), the issuer's bankruptcy, its merger, or its presence on a public list of persons contributing to money laundering. At the same time, the issuer may wish to have its securities delisted for various reasons: in order to become 'private' again, or in order to put an end to a multi-listing situation (which is the subject of a specific rule, stemming from Art. 1.4.4 of the Euronext Paris market rules), or in order to change financial markets, and move from the regulated market to a multilateral trading facility (this last hypothesis means, in France, moving from Euronext Paris to Alternext Growth). The current regulation is the result of a major dispute that led to a legislative change, see P. Barban, *Les entreprises de marché*, *op. cit.*, nos. 144 et seq.

[122] On this question, see A. Tenenbaum, *L'application internationale du droit boursier*, *op. cit.*

[123] The issuer's shareholder may decide to withdraw the shares by filing a public buy-out offer, possibly combined with a squeeze-out; it will be seen that these institutions would benefit from being subject to the *lex mercatus* (see *infra*, paras. 481 et seq.). However, from the issuer's point of view, it is not so much the difference in applicable law that is important, but rather the substantive conditions to which delisting is subject.

[124] The procedure described here is that of the only French regulated market for financial securities, which serves as a model for other financial markets.

[125] Arts. 6600 et seq. of the Euronext Market Rules (Book I).

with the help of a listing sponsor,[126] who verifies the integrity of the file and acts as a 'point of contact' with Euronext. The file must contain the necessary legal documents (e.g. the approved prospectus[127]), as well as the elements needed to ensure that the issue of securities is valid under its own law.[128] Once the documentation is received, the market operator has at least 30 days to make its decision.[129] The decision to admit or refuse admission is a unilateral and discretionary act of the market operator.[130] It must be justified and notified to the applicant.[131] The Market Rules provide for certain hypotheses of refusal

[126] Art. 6204 of the Euronext Market Rules (Book I). Their functions are defined by Euronext Instruction no. 6-01, spec. no. 2 (issued pursuant to Rule 6204 of Book I of the Euronext Rules). The same instruction allows, by way of exception and for specific tasks, that the listing sponsor may not be a member of the market (no. 3.1). On the contract between the listing sponsor and the issuer, see T. Bonneau *et al.*, *Droit financier*, *op. cit.*, no. 1022.

[127] Art. 6501(iv) of the Euronext Market Rules (Book I).

[128] It is thus necessary for the Issuer to provide 'a copy of any minutes of the Issuer's corporate bodies including the resolutions approving the issue of the Notes and the application for admission to trading in respect thereof'. Art. 6501(iv) of the Market Rules. However, this rule, which applies to intra-European relationships, does not prevent the financial market operator from requesting the application of local accounting standards to companies established in the territory of a foreign State, see Art. 6503 of the Market Rules '[...] If the Issuer's registered office is outside the territory of the European Economic Area, the relevant Euronext Market Operator may request that the Issuer's financial statements be restated in accordance with the generally accepted accounting principles applicable in the State where the relevant Euronext Market Operator has its registered office and that these restated financial statements be reviewed by an auditor whose appointment it has accepted.' This is a condition that may be simply prohibitive for the foreign issuer. By way of comparison, the New York Stock Exchange market rules allow for IFRS accounting standards to be applied, see Art. 107.1: 'A company's qualification to list will be determined on the basis of financial statements that are either: (i) prepared in accordance with U.S. generally accepted accounting principles; or (ii) reconciled to U.S. generally accepted accounting principles as required by the Commission's rules; or (iii) prepared in accordance with International Financial Reporting Standards, as issued by the International Accounting Standards Board, for Companies that are permitted to file financial statements using those standards consistent with the Commission's rules.'

[129] Art. 6301 of the Euronext Market Rules (Book I). An agreement between the issuer and the market operator may lengthen or shorten this period; however, the market operator must have the time necessary to gather the regulator's observations in the case of an initial application for admission, see Art. P. 1.1.2 of the Euronext Market Rules (Book II applicable to the French financial markets). It should be added here that the pecuniary interest of the market operator does not, intuitively, go in the direction of refusing admission: the increase in the admission of securities increases the volume of transactions, and the remuneration of the market operator is dependent on this volume. Of course, the market operator has no interest in admitting to trading securities of companies with dubious solvency, since the credibility of the market it manages will ultimately be affected, thus creating an even greater lack of attractiveness. However, in an economic environment where the pressure of short-term results is intense, leaving such a decision to the market operator may appear problematic; this explains the supervision exercised by the Autorité des marchés financiers on the conditions of admission. On this subject, see P. Barban, *Les entreprises de marché*, *op. cit.*, nos. 161 et seq.

[130] Art. L. 421-14(I) of the Monetary and Financial Code.

[131] Art. 6402 of the Euronext Market Rules (Book I).

of admission, and concentrate the possible recourse before the French courts against the decision of the market operator,[132] 'except in the case of a choice of court clause or an arbitration clause'[133] contained in the membership agreement. Since market rules are commercial matters, they benefit from the regime laid down by the Brussels I bis Regulation, which allows litigants to designate the competent forum for any dispute arising from the application for admission.[134] The market operator can hardly be forced to admit the securities of an issuer because of the discretionary power it holds in this respect.[135] The monopolistic situation of the market operator would undoubtedly merit that competition law interferes here with the discretion offered to it, which is only limited by the rules it has itself enacted.[136]

364. Admission to multiple markets. It is possible for issuers to admit their securities to trading on several financial markets.[137] From the issuer's point of view, this possibility is facilitated within the EU by the harmonisation of the information required for admission. Nevertheless, multi-listing in the EU is declining for several reasons. First, as some authors have observed, the unification of the internal market makes it possible to solicit savings from another EU country without having to resort to multiple listings. Moreover, the 'rise of collective investment schemes' sometimes makes such a listing unnecessary. Lastly, the development of digital technologies is likely to allow issuance on the national market while attracting international investors.[138] However, from the point of view of relations with investors, it calls for coordination of legislation on market operations and the authorities that supervise them.[139]

---

132 Art. 6403 of the Euronext Market Rules (Book I).

133 Art. 1701(iv) of the Euronext Market Rules (Book I).

134 Art. 25 of the Brussels Ia Regulation.

135 Art. 2303/1 of the Euronext Market Rules (Book I).

136 One author has thus developed the idea of recourse to competition law as a basis for challenging the refusal of the market operator, in particular the refusal to provide a service and the abuse of a dominant position, see M. Golberg-Darmon, *Les aspects juridiques de l'introduction en bourse*, thesis, Paris II, 2000, spec. nos. 322 et seq., p. 245. On the relationship between competition law and the freedom of the market enterprise, see already *supra*, para. 256.

137 See the observations of A. Tenenbaum, *L'application internationale du droit boursier*, *op. cit.*, pp. 367 et seq.

138 These three arguments are raised by A. Couret, H. Le Nabasque *et al.*, *Droit financier*, *op. cit.* On the loss of liquidity in the case of multiple listings, see *ibid.*

139 *Infra*, paras. 466 et seq.

§ 2. THE PUBLIC OFFER OF FINANCIAL SECURITIES

365. Choice of law. The public offer is a contractual matter[140] and is subject to the Rome I Regulation. The parties may therefore choose the law applicable to the contract;[141] in practice, this choice is made by the offeror. The absence of a choice of law, which is very unlikely in practice, gives rise to two particular difficulties: the characterisation of the characteristic performance of the contract, and its possible displacement by a law that is clearly more closely connected.

366. The characteristic performance of the offer to the public. The determination of the characteristic performance of the offer of securities to the public requires a decision as to whether it is an offer to sell securities or an offer to provide services. This second assumption is based on the idea that the offer of securities to the public is for the purpose of financing the issuer and is therefore a special kind of credit agreement.[142] However, this idea should be rejected because, as the case law of the Court of Justice stands, it leads to the application of the law of the habitual residence of the offeree, and therefore breaks the unity necessary for the public offer.[143] The first interpretation, making the public offer an offer to sell securities, seems more appropriate: only this interpretation allows for the uniqueness of the law applicable to the offer, in line with the objective of

140 This is not a new finding, see thus A. Bialard, 'L'offre publique de contrat', *RTD civ.*, 1971, 750, spec. nos. 38 et seq. where the author endeavours to show that the public offer must first be analysed as a genuine offer, before considering the impact on the pollicitation regime of this particular operation; on this question, see today J. Chacornac, *Les fonctions de l'information en droit des instruments financiers*, *op. cit.*

141 It may be a link that has no connection with France (see S. Francq, 'Rome I Regulation: contractual obligations', *op. cit.*, no. 10), within the limits of Art. 4(3) of the Rome I Regulation.

142 All the more so in the case of debt securities, since this is literally a bond issue.

143 Such an analysis results in applying to the public offer 'the law of the country in which the provider has his habitual residence' (Art. 4(1)(b) of the Rome I Regulation). The provider is not, however, the person one might think. Indeed, the Court of Justice has already held that 'in a credit agreement concluded between a credit institution and a borrower, the provision of services consists in the remittance to the latter of a sum of money by the former in exchange for remuneration paid by the borrower, in principle, in the form of interest' (Case C-249/16, *Kareda*, ECLI:EU:C:2017:472, paras 34–38, spec. para. 36, *D.*, 2017, 1036, 2054, note S. Bollée). The analogical extension of the Court of Justice's solution of the credit agreement provided by a credit institution appears questionable for several reasons. On the one hand, the solution was rendered on the basis of the Brussels I Regulation, and therefore concerns international jurisdiction, not the solution of conflict of laws; moreover, the characterisation remains uncertain, since, as Mr Bollée observes in his aforementioned note, some cases seem to prefer to use the autonomous European concept, according to which the provision of services presupposes the existence of an activity in return for remuneration (Cass., civ. 1re, 1 March 2017, no. 14-25.426). On the other hand, the purpose of the solution adopted is precisely to give jurisdiction to the court of the credit institution, which coincides with that of the defendant, allowing the centralisation of a similar dispute before the same court. However, transposing this solution to the public offer of financial securities would have precisely the opposite effect: to multiply the number of competent courts and laws.

predictability set out in the Regulation.[144] Indeed, the analysis of the offer to the public as an offer to sell securities leads to the application of the law of the country in which the seller has his habitual residence,[145] i.e. the law of the offeror. However, this solution presupposes that the securities can be considered as property within the meaning of Article 4(1)(a) of the Rome I Regulation. The latter states that this notion of '"sale of goods" (*should*) be interpreted in the same way as for the application of Article 5 of Regulation 44/2001 (*Brussels I*)'.[146] However, the latter Regulation does not refer to property in general, but to goods in particular.

367. There are two possible solutions. The first is to extend the concept of sale of goods to the sale of financial securities by analogy.[147] The second is to abandon this characterisation, to resort to Article 4(2) of the Rome I Regulation, and to consider that the characteristic performance of the contract for the offer of financial securities to the public lies in the supply of the securities.[148] These two solutions have the advantage of corresponding to the *ratio legis* of the objective connecting factor of the Rome I Regulation, which is, through the socio-economic analysis of the contract, to link the contract to the legal order in which the legal relationship is predominantly situated.[149] In the absence of a choice of law, it must therefore be assumed that the law competent to govern the offer to the public is, in principle, the law of the principal's habitual residence.[150] This law may, however, be overridden by the application of a law with a manifestly closer connecting factor. It seems to us that several strong connecting links would then have to designate another legal order, which would become preponderant. This would be the case, for example, of an issuer which admits the securities it offers

---

144 Recital 16 of the Rome I Regulation states: 'To contribute to the general objective of this Regulation of legal certainty in the European judicial area, the conflict-of-law rules should be highly foreseeable.' Behind this objective of predictability, there are two distinct considerations regarding the connecting factor: on the one hand, its unitary nature (it is more predictable to have a single applicable law, rather than several whose articulation will cause necessarily less predictable frictions) and, on the other hand, the precise determination of the connecting factor obviously contributes to its predictability. These considerations also inform the exception introduced in relation to consumer contracts, see *infra*, para. 804.

145 Art. 4(1)(a) of the Rome I Regulation.

146 Recital 17 of the Rome I Regulation.

147 On this possible extension, see *infra*, para. 404.

148 It will be recalled here that characteristic performance is defined as that 'for which payment is due', see the report on the Convention on the law applicable to contractual obligations, by prof. Giuliano and Lagarde, [1980] OJ C 282/1, M.-E. Ancel, *La prestation caractéristique du contrat*, Paris, Economica, 2002, no. 8.

149 Messrs Loussouarn and Bredin have already observed that 'as pollicitation is the determining element of the contract, it is logical to admit, at least as a suppletive measure, the law of the offeror's domicile', Y. Loussouarn and J.-D. Bredin, *Droit du commerce international*, *op. cit.*, no. 327.

150 This residence will be either its registered office for legal persons or the centre of interests of the unincorporated organisation.

to the public to a trading system and a central depository located in the State in which it also solicits investors.

368. Public offer and consumer contract.[151] The particularity of the public offer within the conflict of laws system of the Rome I Regulation is that it is exempted from the interference of Article 6 of the Regulation concerning consumer contracts. This article allows consumers, under certain conditions, to be subject to the more protective provisions of the law of their domicile. Applying this rule to the public offer[152] would break the unity of the law applicable to the investment transaction, since retail customers are solicited in different legal orders.[153] This solution, which places a costly analysis on each issuer, would drastically reduce cross-border public offerings. For this reason, it was rejected by the authors of the Rome I Regulation.[154] Indeed, Article 6(4)(d) of the Rome I Regulation provides for the inapplicability of the derogation rule applicable to consumer contracts 'to the rights and obligations which constitute the terms and conditions governing the issuance or offer to the public and public takeover bids'.[155] Consequently, the public offer is always governed by the *lex contractus* chosen by the offeror, irrespective of whether the addressee is a consumer or not.[156]

---

151 On these issues, see the two leading articles by F. Garcimartin Alferez, "New Issues in the Rome I Regulation: The Special Provisions on Financial Market Contracts", *Yearbook of PIL*, 2008, p. 245; F. Garcimartin Alferez, 'The Rome I Regulation: Exceptions to the Rule on Consumer Contracts and Financial Instruments' (2009) *Journal of Private International Law*.

152 Although the concept of public offer is not defined in the Regulation, it is useful to refer to the definition provided by the Prospectus Regulation, cf. 338. See also F. Garcimartin Alferez, 'The Rome I Regulation: Exceptions to the Rule on Consumer Contracts and Financial Instruments', *op. cit.*, p. 94.

153 In the same way that a public offer, because of the plurality of its addressees, imposes a collective information obligation (J. Chacornac, *Les fonctions de l'information en droit des instruments financiers*, *op. cit.*, no. 74), it makes it necessary, as a counterpoint, to have a unity of the law applicable to the act.

154 See in this sense Recital 28 of the Rome I Regulation: 'since these *(consumer contracts)* could lead to the applicability of different laws to each of the instruments issued, thus altering their nature and preventing their fungible marketing and offer'. The need for unity of law applicable to the offer to the public is therefore the basis of the favour to the offeror. This unity is justified by the collective nature of the offer, and consequently the multitude of investors likely to respond. There is also no doubt that the underlying purpose is not so much to protect the legal security of the issuer – the issuer, through the notification of the prospectus, is in fact aware of the investors it has actively solicited – as to favour its interests. It should also be noted that the alternative would, for example, result in the offeror being subject to every local regulation on unfair terms in consumer contracts, which would create a significant burden for him.

155 The insertion of Arts. (d) and (e) within Art. 6(4) is specific to the Rome I Regulation. These two provisions did not exist in the Rome Convention, because its article on consumer contracts had a more limited material scope: it only concerned the provision of services and the sale of tangible goods.

156 The scope of the exclusion and its relationship to the provision of financial services is discussed *infra*, para. 805.

369. Public offer and *lex contractus* scope. In addition to the classical field of the law of the contract,[157] Recital 29 of the Rome I Regulation states that the law applicable to the public offer should 'include provisions governing, inter alia, the allotment of securities or shares, rights in the event of subscription, withdrawal rights and similar aspects in the context of the offer as well as the aspects referred to in Articles 10, 11, 12 and 13'. These articles refer to aspects which are not necessarily subject to the *lex contractus*, namely the conditions for the validity of the contract: consent,[158] capacity,[159] form of the act.[160] The basis for the particular scope of the *lex contractus* is the same as the exception granted by Article 6(4)(d) of the Rome I Regulation: it is to ensure 'that all relevant contractual aspects of an offer binding the issuer or the offeror to the consumer are governed by a single law'.[161] However, there are three criticisms of this solution which explain why it should be ignored. Firstly, this solution is not reiterated in the body of the Rome I Regulation, and it leads to an interpretation of the provisions at issue counter to their very letter.[162] Secondly, the 'capacity' of the issuer is excluded from the Rome I Regulation: it is a rule relating to the functioning of the company, which is necessarily subject to its *lex societatis*, which alone is competent to determine whether a company has been empowered by its legal system to make an offer to the public.[163] Thirdly, the disproportion that this provision creates between the protection of the offeror and the addressees. Indeed, by deactivating the consumer protection rule, the Rome I Regulation has already established a favourable regime for the issuer which has no equivalent. By removing the very possibility of local law protection as regards the existence of the consent of the addressees of the offer, this interpretation directive leads to an excessive solution.

370. Public offer and *lex mercatus* interference. The rules for admission to trading, insofar as they bind the issuer to the system operator, are seemingly independent of the relationships generated by the public offer. However, these rules are likely to interfere both with the methods used to disseminate the

157 Art. 12 of the Rome I Regulation.

158 Art. 10 of the Rome I Regulation.

159 Art. 13 of the Rome I Regulation.

160 Art. 11 of the Rome I Regulation.

161 Recital 29 of the Rome I Regulation, *in fine*.

162 The national and European judge, while not bound by the 'recitals' of the Regulation, may nevertheless choose to take them into consideration, see S. Lemaire, 'Interrogations sur la portée juridique du préambule du règlement Rome I', *D.*, 2008, p. 2157.

163 It is difficult to see how a French company can escape the strict regime laid down by the Monetary and Financial Code by applying a law that is foreign to the contract, the permissive regime from the point of view of the right to make a public offer, see on the prohibitive rules of the issuer *supra*, paras. 291 et seq.

securities and with the selling price of the securities.[164] This interference takes place through the constraints to which the issuer is bound by compliance with the membership agreement, and consequently with the market rules to which it is committed, and the sanction of which may result in delisting. This is why, even when the securities are distributed through an 'off-market' placement,[165] the financial market law may intervene, *a priori*, in order to ensure that the issuer will not sell the securities at a price lower than that offered by the provision of the securities to the trading system[166] ('market provision'[167]). Finally, it should be noted that the issuer may admit its securities without making a public offer.[168] The securities are then designated as the professional segment,[169] as they are intended for professionals.[170] The public offering waiver makes it possible to establish a technical listing, 'i.e. a listing that has not given rise to a fundraising or private placement followed by a listing'.[171] This possibility, which has been available to operators in France since 2007,[172] was designed to attract foreign companies to the French regulated market; in this sense, it is the preferred instrument for multi-listing,[173] in particular because of the reduction

164 The dissemination of securities is the subject of an entire chapter of the market rules applicable to French regulated markets ('Book II'), see Arts. P. 1.2.1 et seq. of the Euronext Market Rules (Book II applicable to French markets).

165 Art. P. 1.2.3. para. 1 of the Euronext Market Rules (Book II applicable to French markets).

166 See Arts. P. 1.2.3 et seq., spec. P. 1.2.3.4 of the Euronext Market Rules (Book II applicable to the French markets). These articles provide that in the case of "mixed" dissemination, i.e. partly by making the offer available to the market and partly by placing it, 'the price set for the firm price offer or the final price resulting from the open price offer may not be higher than the price charged during the placing'. Such a provision is easily understood: the aim is to protect the reliability of the price offered to the market and to guarantee its attractiveness. The influence of the law of the market can be seen more clearly in the discretion that the market operator has given itself: 'Euronext Paris [...] assesses whether the choice of these procedures is appropriate to the characteristics of the planned transaction.'

167 On this technique, see T. Bonneau *et al.*, *Droit financier*, *op. cit.*, nos. 991 et seq.

168 Listing has long been a trigger for public offering status, see Art. 72 of the Law of 24 July 1966. This explains why the doctrine considers that this derogation is infrequent in practice and must be considered as an exception: the principle of admission to trading is that it leads to a public offering of securities, whether through a market availability of the securities or through an off-market placement followed by a market listing, see T. Bonneau *et al.*, *Droit financier*, *op. cit.*, no. 984.

169 Art. P. 1.2.3. para. 1 of the Euronext Market Rules (Book II applicable to French markets).

170 From a technical point of view, it is not really a segment of the financial market, as the latter are designed to classify listed companies according to the size of their capitalisation.

171 T. Bonneau *et al.*, *Droit financier*, *op. cit.*, no. 984.

172 This is now permitted under Arts. 516-5 and 6 of the AMF General Regulation and implemented by Art. P. 1.02 of Book II of the Euronext Market Rules. P. 1.02 of Book II of the Euronext Market Rules, since the order of 7 December 2007 approving amendments to the AMF General Regulation (*JORF*, 19 December 2007, p. 20419). See B. François, 'Mise en place sur le marché réglementé d'un compartiment destiné aux admissions sans offre préalable au public', *D.*, 2008, p. 371.

173 O. Douvreleur, 'Le nouveau compartiment professionnel du marché réglementé' in *Mélanges AEDBF - France*, Paris, Banque Editeur, 2008, pp. 15 et seq.; K. Deckert, *La sollicitation publique des investisseurs en droit communautaire, français et allemand*, *op. cit.*, nos. 172 et

in disclosure requirements.[174] The law of the market applies here to the listing, and all the rules surrounding the acquisition of securities on the market apply. Here, as in the US, multi-listing is permitted by self-limiting local standards.[175]

371. Conclusion of the section. Marketing acts are in principle subject to the law of autonomy. The law of the financial market will apply precisely in this respect to the membership agreement. The latter will enable the law of the financial market to oblige the issuer to comply with certain solutions, and in particular with a specific price for the sale of the securities it admits, regardless of the law applicable to the marketing acts. Moreover, certain acts, and in particular the public offer, benefit from a preferential treatment in terms of conflict of laws, allowing the issuer to apply a single law to the public offer, without being subject to interference from the law of the domicile of the consumers who will acquire the securities.

372. Conclusion of the chapter. The function of disclosure requirements triggered by the marketing of financial securities to the public is to protect residents. This protective function explains why the law of the place of residence

seq.; L. Faugérolas and C. Cardon, 'Premier bilan du compartiment professionnel après quatre ans d'existence', *BJB*, March 2012, pp. 112 et seq. The latter authors report that in 2011, nine companies were listed on the professional segment, all of which were already listed on another regulated market. However, some believe that the professional segment is 'stagnating', see F. Martin Laprade, 'Bilan critique de la consultation publique de l'AMF sur les IPOs', *BJB*, January 2015, p. 14.

174 Whether it is a question of the prospectus (the adoption of the Prospectus Regulation was motivated in particular by the desire to encourage 'multiple listings on regulated markets', para. 5 of the Prospectus Regulation), or of periodic information, all of these simplifications are in line with the principles of the Directive.

175 H. Synvet, *L'organisation juridique du groupe international de sociétés*, *op. cit.*, p. 356. The author, after observing that French savings protection laws, in particular stock exchange laws, are triggered by the identification of their addressees ('The delimitation of their spatial scope of application is in fact dependent on the identification of their addressees, and this is inseparable from the material objectives'), notes at the bottom of the page (no. 870): 'This is an irrefutable example of the particular nature of mandatory rules. The field of the law of the forum does not result from the implementation of a conflict rule: the legislator (or his interpreter) specifies the international scope of the substantive norm in the same spirit and with the same precision as he defines its other conditions of application. Can one imagine bringing the US Rule requiring information from foreign companies with 300 US shareholders into the fold of bilateral conflict rules?) But it does not matter from the point of view of international harmony of systems: just as the *lex societatis* and local law can coexist smoothly, so there is nothing to prevent several stock exchange laws from claiming jurisdiction together'; see, on the self-limitation of certain stock exchange laws, J. Bédart, *International Conflicts of Antitrust and Securities Regulation: It's All About Effects*, *op. cit.*, p. 158: 'Furthermore, and this is a matter of significance in the international context, the limited federal corporate governance provisions on management compensation disclosure rules and the proxy requirements have been those for which the SEC has been the most likely to find foreign issuer exemptions. In addition, stock exchanges such as the NYSE, have continued to exempt foreign issuers from most corporate governance requirements.' It should be noted, however, that the self-limitation of stock exchange law here affects matters governed not by foreign stock exchange law, but by foreign *lex societatis*.

of the solicited persons should apply to these obligations, but also why the characterisation of the solicitation, which involves the delimitation of the notion of public offer, appears to be decisive. It has nevertheless been shown that European harmonisation of the scope and content of these obligations has made it possible to apply the law of the issuer to these obligations. This dynamic also continues when third state issuers are involved. It has also been shown that the presence of administrative approval, on the other hand, gives rise to different difficulties, and that the determination of the competent authority would benefit from being based on the place where the securities are admitted to trading. In the absence of such admission, the authority of the issuer's registered office should retain jurisdiction, while leaving it to the authority of the place where the prospectus is notified to suspend the public offer on its territory. The marketing documents show that admission to trading inevitably gives the law of the financial market considerable weight in determining certain aspects of the public offer, particularly the price. Indeed, the membership agreement by which the issuer undertakes to comply with the market rules enables the system operator to compel the issuer to comply with the substantive solutions it has enacted, and in particular not to offer its securities at a lower price than the one it offers to the market. Finally, the singularity of the public offer is taken into account by the EU legislator, which allows the law designated by the offeror to avoid interference from the law of residence of potential consumers.

CHAPTER 3
THE ISSUER'S LIABILITY

373. Particularities of the liability of the issuer of financial securities for defective information. The foregoing discussion has shown that the marketing of financial securities gives rise to various legal information obligations for the issuer. What they have in common is that they constitute the information on the basis of which an investor is likely to make a decision to acquire financial securities. If this information proves to be defective,[1] the investor will try to engage the liability of the issuer.[2] This liability has several particularities.[3]

The first is that there is a certain tension between the remedial function of civil liability, and the inherent randomness of investing in financial instruments. Civil liability cannot have as its effect the removal of the possibility of losing the outlay. This is why the hazard must not be remedied, at the risk of the issuer becoming the investor's insurer,[4] and this is all the more true since the occasional existence of defective information is an element whose scope may be considerably reduced by the investor's diversification strategy.[5] The existence of a hazard also means that the defective information issued is not

---

1 The term 'defective information', which is the operative event in a fault, is used because it includes both the omission of significant information and the dissemination of false information.

2 Although Art. 11 of the Prospectus Regulation allows for the liability of persons who have been involved in the preparation of the prospectus, the issuer remains 'the archetypical defendants', M. Gargantini, 'Prospectus Liability. Competent Courts of Jurisdiction and Applicable Law', *op. cit.*, no. 19.07; on the possible liability of corporate bodies and auditors, see A. Couret, H. Le Nabasque, *Droit financier*, *op. cit.*, nos. 1757 et seq.

3 The discussion that follows, as well as the investor's loss considered here, are inspired by Prorok's seminal work on civil liability in the financial markets.

4 This is noted by the Court of Justice, see e.g. the *Kolassa* judgment, para. 51: 'The devaluation of the certificates was due not to the vagaries of the financial markets, but to the management of the funds in which the money resulting from the issue of these certificates was invested, preventing, in the long term, a positive evolution in their value.' On this question, see J. Prorok, *La responsabilité civile sur les marchés financiers*, *op. cit.*

5 Indeed, the existence of a diversified portfolio allows the holder to avoid that a defective information truly affects him in the long term, see J. Prorok, *La responsabilité civile sur les marchés financiers*, *op. cit.*, nos. 393 et seq.
If the diversification strategy is a remedy for defective information and stock market uncertainties, it is nevertheless necessary to distinguish between the two: stock market uncertainties exist independently of any defective information.

necessarily the sole cause of the variations in value of the instrument.[6] In these conditions, the establishment of proof of both a certain loss and a causal link between the event and the loss suffered appears fundamental. However, as Mr Prorok has shown, these two elements can be very difficult to prove, which is why any presumptions of harm or causality will often be decisive in resolving the dispute. It is precisely on these points that the laws diverge greatly, making the resolution of the conflict of laws extremely significant.[7]

The second feature is that the defective information, by affecting a multitude of investors, 'is likely to result in mass damage, i.e. multiple individual damage to numerous victims'.[8] This characteristic stems from the fact that the financial securities were offered to the public.[9] Although mass damage is not specific to the financial markets, this characteristic is nevertheless unusual in the context of civil liability, the procedural rather than substantive conditions of implementation of which have not been designed for this type of damage.[10]

---

6 This poses eminent difficulties if it is the alteration of the share price that needs to be compensated, see e.g. P.-Y. Chabert, in 'La gouvernance dans les sociétés anonymes, un bouclier pour les dirigeants', *Rev. Lamy dr. aff*, 2009, no. 41 supplement: 'the assessment of the damage is delicate insofar as it is difficult to attribute a variation in the share price to inaccurate information or to exogenous factors that have no causal link with this information, such as, for example, macroeconomic factors (changes in interest rates by central banks or announcements of other important indicators for the markets) or announcements made by other companies in the same economic sector (which may disrupt the share price through a contagion effect). It is also important to note that, for example, the real economic impact of inaccurate information can be artificially amplified by the market's hyper-reactivity to announcements and market volatility multiplied by the leverage used by some traders. In addition, the loss of confidence that may result from the communication of inaccurate information may also lead to a disaffection for the issuer, significantly accentuating the real impact of the inaccuracy.' see J. Prorok, *La responsabilité civile sur les marchés financiers*, *op. cit.*, nos. 339 et seq.

7 J. Prorok, *La responsabilité civile sur les marchés financiers*, *op. cit.* for American law, nos. 107 et seq. for French law, nos. 177 et seq. for German law, nos. 263 et seq. for English law, nos. 284 et seq. See also the summary by M. Gargantini, 'Prospectus Liability. Competent Courts of Jurisdiction and Applicable Law', in D. Busch, G. Ferrarini and J.P. Franx (eds.), *Prospectus Regulation and Prospectus Liability*, Oxford, OUP, no. 19.05.

8 J. Prorok, *La responsabilité civile sur les marchés financiers*, *op. cit.*, no. 48.

9 In this sense, it is striking that the Court of Cassation, in its leading judgment on the issue, does not refer to the financial market in particular, but to the public offer in general: 'Whereas a person who acquires or retains securities issued by way of a public offer in the light of inaccurate, imprecise or misleading information about the situation of an issuing company loses only the chance to invest his capital in another investment or to renounce the one already made; whereas the judgment holds that the damage suffered by the shareholders cannot be analysed as the loss of opportunity to invest their savings elsewhere since it is, in reality, at least the minimum of the investment made after the truncated information brought to their attention; whereas, in so ruling, the Court of Appeal violated the above-mentioned text. Cf. Cass. com. 9 March 2010, nos. 08-21.547 and 08-21.793, *Gaudriot*, on which see J. Prorok, *La responsabilité civile sur les marchés financiers*, *op. cit.*, no. 251-252 and the references cited.

10 See the study by U. Baxi, 'Mass torts, multinational enterprise liability and private international law', *RCADI*, vol. 176, 1999, p. 305 et seq.

The third particularity is that the event giving rise to liability lies as much in the defective nature of the information,[11] as in its dissemination. What the injured investor complains about is that he invested in securities that he would not have acquired if correct information had been communicated to him.[12] From an international perspective, the operative event is rather the dissemination of information, as this is the source of the foreign investor's solicitation.

374. The damage to the investor. The fourth particularity relates to the damage suffered by the investor, and it is here that the singularity of the admission to trading of the instrument is felt. Indeed, the event giving rise to liability may cause two types of damage that of altering the investor's decision,[13] and that of altering the financial market itself. As Mr Prorok has shown, the damage of alteration of the decision is the one generally retained in Europe, whereas the damage of alteration of the market is more widespread in the litigation in the United States.[14] This damage to the financial market can be broken down into damage to the quoted price of the financial instrument,[15] or damage to the order book.[16] Nevertheless, as Mr Prorok shows, in both cases, compensation for what can be described as collective market damage 'is essentially intended to ensure the dissuasive and non-reparative function of civil liability',[17] and would, as such, be better provided for by French criminal law.[18] From a civil liability perspective, the loss for which the investor seeks compensation is always that of

---

11 It will always be easy to show the issuer's failure to comply. Thus, issuers whose securities are admitted to trading are subject to Art. 223-1 of the AMF General Regulation (on the scope of which, see J. Prorok, *La responsabilité civile sur les marchés financiers*, *op. cit.*, no. 177, note 5), requiring them to provide accurate, precise and sincere information. On these characteristics, see T. Bonneau and F. Drummond, *Droit des marchés financiers*, *op. cit.*, nos. 432 et seq.

12 See for example, from a contractual point of view, the *Profit* judgment, and from both a tort and contractual point of view, the *UMR v. KA Finanz* judgment, Cass. com., 1 March 2017, no. 14-25 426.

13 The alteration of this decision highlights what Mr Chacornac refers to as the intellectual function exercised by information, here that of the prospectus, on the investor's decision. J. Chacornac, *Essai sur les fonctions de l'information en droit des instruments financiers*, *op. cit*; J. Prorok, *La responsabilité civile sur les marchés financiers*, *op. cit.*, no. 54.

14 In the United States, it is the alteration of the stock market price that constitutes the damage to be compensated. On this issue see J. Prorok, *La responsabilité civile sur les marchés financiers*, *op. cit.*, no. 106 and following.

15 *Ibid.*, no. 56.

16 N. Spitz, *La réparation des préjudices boursiers*, Paris, Revue Banque, 2010. The author refers to a decision loss, and a condition loss, by which he means the conditions of the quotation, i.e. the stock market price; J. Prorok, *La responsabilité civile sur les marchés financiers*, *op. cit.*, no. 543.

17 J. Prorok, *La responsabilité civile sur les marchés financiers*, *op. cit.*, no. 52.

18 This function is then explained by the desire to protect the market infrastructure itself; when it comes to the issuer's liability for the damage caused to the investor, the function of the liability is then only to repair the damage suffered by the latter.

the alteration of his investment decision, and this is true in French law as well as in English and German law.

375. This statement explains the rejection of the analysis of the investor's loss as a 'pure economic loss', the localisation of which most often leads to a futile localisation of the securities 'on which' this loss would have occurred.[19] This statement also explains the rejection of the apprehension of the investor's loss as a 'ricochet' loss. This latter analysis was proposed in the light of the *Luxalpha* judgment,[20] where an open-ended collective investment fund, had lost most of its value following the *Madoff* misappropriation. Investors who had taken shares complained about the defective information they had received from the fund's manager. In his observations under the judgment, an author considers that if the investor 'suffers a financial loss, it is because the portfolio of the SICAV has lost value. Under these conditions, insofar as the fund has legal personality, it seems convincing to us to qualify the fund as a direct victim of the damage and the investor as a victim by ricochet'.[21] This analysis, although stimulating, should be rejected. Indeed, the purpose of civil liability cannot be to compensate for the loss of value of shares: investing in financial securities, even in a fund, always involves a risk, which must be borne by the holder of the securities. On the other hand, the real loss is the one complained of by the claimant, and this can be compensated: having seen his investment decision altered by the dissemination of defective information by the manager.[22]

376. This analysis of 'ricochet' damage suggests a distinction should be made between '*l'atteinte*' (which could be translated by the harm) and the damage. In this case, the harm consists of the disturbance of the public's collective perception of the issuer, through the falsity of its representation. This characteristic of the dissemination of defective information has been perfectly perceived by German doctrine when it considers that the dissemination of the prospectus creates an 'investment climate'.[23] The alteration of the decision is a consequence of this disturbance, and constitutes the damage for which compensation is legally

---

19 M. Lehmann, 'Where does economics loss occur?' (2011) 7(3) *Journal of private international law*, 2011, pp. 523 et seq. A. Tenenbaum, 'Retombées de l'affaire Madoff sur la Convention de Lugano', *RCDIP*, 2012, 45; M. Haentjens and D.J. Verheij, 'Finding Nemo: Locating Financial Losses after Kolassa/Barclays Bank and Profit', *JIBLR* 2016-6 (available via SSRN).

20 Cass. com., 7 January 2014, no. 11-24.157.

21 S. Corneloup, note above.

22 As Ms Corneloup points out (see note above): 'In his final appeal submissions and in his appeal to the Court of Cassation, however, Mr X essentially invoked the liability of UBS as manager of the Sicav for disseminating misleading information.'

23 J. Prorok, *La responsabilité civile sur les marchés financiers*, *op. cit.*, no. 268, note 26. This theory holds that the dissemination of a prospectus leads to a favourable investment climate which in turn leads to a rebuttable presumption of causality between the information contained in the prospectus and the investor's decision.

possible.[24] The authors who describe the investor's loss as a 'ricochet' loss seem to consider that the real loss is that constituted by the harm *(l'atteinte)*, of which the loss suffered by the investor is merely a consequence, a ricochet. Under these conditions, they locate the damage at the issuer's headquarters, either because it is the issuer who is misrepresented or because it is the issuer who issued the defective information.[25] However, it is the assumption that we are contesting here: the harm does not necessarily deserve compensation,[26] and it is therefore the damage that should be retained in the notion of loss, confirming that the territorial dissociation between the place of the harm and that of the damage should be resolved in favour of the location of the damage.

377. Difficulties and importance of characterisation. This last statement presupposes the resolution of a prior and decisive question: the characterisation of the issuer's liability. The difficulty is that the characterisation of the liability action against the issuer is contingent. In private international law, it may be characterised as either contractual or tortious depending on the basis that the plaintiff gives to his action (Section 1). This characterisation has important consequences both for the conflict of laws and international jurisdiction. If the action is contractual, the applicable law will most often be the *lex societatis* or the law designated by the contract of issue, while the competent courts will depend on the presence of a consumer or the existence of an attributive clause enforceable against the investor (Section 2). If, on the other hand, the action is characterised as a tort or delict, the legal system of the investor's domicile may have comprehensive jurisdiction to award damages whenever its residents have been the object of a solicitation (Section 3).

---

24 It is easy to see why the concept of abstract damage in French case law leads to absurdity, because it leads to compensation for the injury that everyone has suffered (on this case law, see J. Prorok, *La responsabilité civile sur les marchés financiers*, *op. cit.*, nos. 246 et seq.) The need to prove the concrete nature of the injury is necessary, because the damage is not, strictly speaking, constituted by this injury, but by the personal and concrete decision which may or may not have been taken.

25 If the defective information is issued by a rating agency, the location of the injury must be separated. It could just as well be considered that in matters of collective representation of the financial state of a legal person, the falsity of the representation always takes place in the mind of the person who perceives it, and therefore the real damage should be located at the domicile of the person who suffers it.

26 This is the case of neighbourhood disturbances, which constitute an injury without the French legal system granting them any compensation. It is only if the disturbance is abnormal that a civil damages claim is made.

SECTION 1. THE NATURE OF THE LIABILITY INCURRED BY THE ISSUER

378. The four difficulties of liability characterisation. The first complication is that the European characterisation of private international law, while drawing on the legal tradition of the Member States, is nevertheless autonomous. Thus, direct action, which is a tort from the point of view of EU private international law, is considered to be contractual by French law.

The second difficulty arises from the possible independence of the characterisations from the point of view of determining the rules of jurisdiction and the applicable law. If coherence is sought, it is possible that the distinct objectives of the system of jurisdiction and determination of the applicable law will lead to divergent results.[27] Nevertheless, it will be shown that the characterisation, when it is a tort, should be identical on both levels.

The third, paradoxical, difficulty is that the characterisation in tort or delict is likely to lead to the application of the law of the contract. This is particularly the case when the defective obligations are characterised as pre-contractual: Article 12 of the Rome II Regulation then designates the law of the contract. The law of the designated contract will, however, be likely to retain its own domestic characterisation of the legal issue. Indeed, the Rome I and II Regulations do not contain a special conflict-of-laws rule on liability for information provided in connection with the issue of a security.[28] The law applicable to the issuer's liability is therefore alternatively that provided for by the law of the contract of issue in the case of a contractual relationship, or that of the place where the damage occurs in the case of tort liability. This difficulty is amplified by the diversity of defective information on the basis of which a liability action may be brought: thus, while the prospectus may be characterised as pre-contractual information, the periodic disclosure obligation lends itself less easily to this.

The fourth difficulty is linked to the tension between the distribution of jurisdiction and the characterisation of the action. The division of liability

[27] T. Azzi, 'Bruxelles I, Rome I, Rome II: regard sur la qualification en droit international privé communautaire', *D.*, 2009, pp. 1621 et seq. B. Haftel, 'Entre Rome II et Bruxelles I: l'interprétation communautaire uniforme du règlement Rome I', *JDI* 2010, pp. 760 et seq. S. Lemaire, 'La qualification' in T. Azzi and O. Boskovic (eds.), *Quel avenir pour la théorie générale des conflits de lois*, Brussels, Bruylant, 2015, p. 35.

[28] This is the case, for example, in Switzerland, where the conflict rule is the law of the issuer. Art. 156 of the Swiss Private International Law Act: 'Claims arising from the issue of equity securities and loans by means of prospectuses, circulars or similar publications are governed either by the law applicable to the company or by the law of the issuing State', see H. Kronke 'Liability, Capital Markets' in J. Basedow, G. Ruhl, F. Ferrari and P. de Miguel Ascencio, *Encyclopedia of Private International Law*, 2017, p. 1135.

actions between Articles 7(1) and 7(2) of the Brussels Ia Regulation[29] was clarified by the *Kalfelis* and *Jakob Handte* judgments: matters relating to tort, delict or quasi-delict are subsidiary and, as regards the classification of the action as contractual, this is excluded where there is 'no obligation freely assumed by one party towards the other'. This last criterion 'remains the main allocation key'[30] between these articles. However, the existence of a contract between the parties does not preclude all actions in tort. The *UMR v. KA Finanz* cases[31] are an illustration of this: on the contractual level, the disappointed investor considered that the information was fraudulent, on the tortious level, he alleged that the dissemination of defective information to persons domiciled in France constituted a specific tort, located in France. This difficulty is not specific to defective information relating to the marketing of financial securities. It is found in the same terms when the defective information relates to financial contracts sold. Under English domestic law, it is thus open to the claimant to sue the counterparty to the financial contract in contract or tort, whichever is more advantageous to him.[32] French law itself echoes this possibility of cumulation outside the law of financial instruments,[33] adopting the assertion of Carbonnier according to which: 'When positive law places two legal means at the disposal of the same individual, the most elementary meaning of this double gift is cumulation.'[34]

The existence of a possible contractual action to hold the issuer liable for defective information is sometimes rejected in doctrine because of the position of the problem. Indeed, in the vast majority of cases, an investor who has acquired a security through a financial market does not receive it directly from the issuer. His seller is therefore not the one who provided the defective information. This situation of the investor is the basis generally used to justify the tort nature of the liability action against the issuer. However, this situation is not specific to the existence of the financial market and, above all, it does not constitute an obstacle to contractual characterisation (§ 1). The real obstacle lies in the intermediation system, which in some situations does not allow the investor to own the security (§ 2).

---

29 As far as international jurisdiction is concerned, it is known that the system adopted by the Brussels I recast Regulation leads to the jurisdiction, in principle, of the court of the defendant's domicile. However, the claimant may avail himself of other courts in certain cases, both in contractual and in tort matters.

30 S. Bollée, 'La responsabilité extracontractuelle du cocontractant en droit international privé' in *Mélanges en l'honneur du professeur Bernard Audit*, Paris, LGDJ, 2014, no. 12.

31 Cass. com, 1 March 2017, no. 14-25 426.

32 J. Braithwaite, *The Financial Courts: Adjudicating Disputes in Derivatives Markets*, *op. cit.*, pp. 156 et seq. and the case law cited.

33 See lastly N. Balat, 'Le cumul d'actions en droit des obligations', *D.*, 2020, 1819.

34 J. Carbonnier, obs. under Cass., civ. 1re, 19 July 1960, *RTD civ.*, 1961, 333, quoted by N. Balat, *op. cit.*

§ 1. THE POSSIBILITY OF CONTRACTUAL LIABILITY

Positive law absolutely recognises the contractual liability of the issuer for defective information, particularly in the case of an inaccurate prospectus. Indeed, there is always a contractual relationship between the purchaser of a financial security and its issuer, that arising from the *negotium* represented by the financial security itself. This will be shown (II) after having set aside the arguments against the possibility of contractual liability of the issuer (I).

I. Rejection of Arguments against Contractual Liability

379. The arguments against contractual liability. Four arguments are generally used to justify the characterisation of the liability of the authors of the prospectus in tort.[35] The first relates to the function of the prospectus, the second to the function of the liability, the third to the breach of equality between investors depending on the method of acquisition of the security, and the fourth to the most common characterisation in comparative law. This last argument is peremptory and should be rejected immediately: English law[36] and French law[37] show that actions can be either in tort or in contract. The rebuttal of the other arguments deserves further development.

380. The addressees of the prospectus. The first argument is that the addressee of the prospectus is not the investor but the 'market'. This substitution of addressee would result from two factors: on the one hand, the responsibility of the prospectus would determine the standard of behaviour expected 'in the market' and would protect market participants by ensuring the correct information provided by the authors of the prospectus. On the other hand, the liability of the authors of the prospectus would derive from a non-contractual relationship between issuers and investors; together, this would explain why the prospectus is a 'market-oriented institution and not a contract-oriented one'. The weakness of this argument lies in the definition of the market.[38] The 'market' referred to here is not the financial market in the sense of a trading platform. This is all the more clear once it is observed that a prospectus is also required when the public offer of financial securities takes place without admission to trading, and that admission to trading does not necessarily trigger the obligation to draw up a prospectus.[39] Rather, the notion of market refers to all customers of the issuer

---

35 See e.g. their synthesis: F. Garcimartin Alferez, 'The law applicable to prospectus liability in the European Union' (2011) *Law and Financial Market Review*, p. 449, spec. p. 451; M. Gargantini, 'Prospectus Liability. Competent Courts of Jurisdiction and Applicable Law', *op. cit.*, no. 19.14.

36 See *infra*, para. 399.

37 See *supra*, para. 380.

38 On the polysemy of the notion of market, see *supra*, para. 2.

39 See *supra*, para. 339.

domiciled in the territory where the financial securities are offered to the public. In this case, however, it is difficult to understand why the function of informing the 'market' should be distinct from and superior to that of informing the contracting parties. Indeed, the function of the prospectus is primarily to enable investors to obtain the information necessary for their acquisition decision.[40] The reason for this is that, as an author has already observed:

> 'Financial instruments are subject to risks of changes in the value they represent and risks of repayment of the claims they record. While such a risk is necessarily prospective, the possibility of its realisation is embedded in the legal characteristics of the instrument. [...] The description of the instrument thus constitutes primary information in the investment decision process.'[41]

This is all the more obvious because if the prospectus is defective, investors will complain that they were not able to make their investment decision properly.[42] Therefore, the issuer is responsible to investors for the information contained in the prospectus. It is because of this responsibility that, when financial intermediaries place or subsequently resell securities, they must obtain the issuer's consent to use the prospectus.[43]

381. Function of liability. Another argument lies in the idea that liability in relation to prospectuses has an institutional function, the protection of the market, and the choice of law applicable in contractual matters therefore appears to be in contradiction with such a function. This argument seems to us to confuse the function of disclosure requirements (the protection of their addressees) with that of liability, which is to compensate for the damage resulting from the dissemination of defective information. The Prospectus Regulation

---

40 H. Bouthinon-Dumas, *Le droit des sociétés cotées et le marché boursier*, Paris, LGDJ, 2007, no. 281: 'One may consider that the information disseminated on the occasion of a public offering is mainly intended to protect the interests of savers'; K. Deckert, *La sollicitation publique des investisseurs en droit communautaire, français et allemand*, *op. cit.*, no. 272. On the nature of the pre-contractual information obligation, see *supra*, para. 346.

41 J. Chacornac, *Essai sur les fonctions de l'information en droit des instruments financiers*, *op. cit.* See very clearly in this sense recital 26 of the Prospectus Regulation: 'A valid prospectus [...] shall provide sufficient information to investors to enable them to make informed investment decisions.' (See also recital 27 of the same regulation).

42 See, among many judgments, *UMR v. KA Finanz* (see *infra*, para. 380) and *Profit* (see *infra*, par. 406).

43 See, inter alia, Recital 26 of the Prospectus Regulation, which recalls that the issuer may attach to its consent conditions under which the prospectus may be used. This combination of freedom and responsibility can also be seen in the option given to issuers, with regard to the summary of the prospectus, to 'choose the information that they consider important and significant', 'provided that they present it in a fair and balanced manner' (Recital 31), even though the summary cannot, as a matter of principle, be a source of responsibility for the issuer (Recital 33). Recall the arguments already developed with regard to the classification of market rules (*infra*, para. 262).

itself simply states that the authors of the prospectus are responsible for the content of the information contained therein.[44] An author thus shows that the remedial function of liability remains intact despite its confrontation with financial information,[45] but observes that the difficulty of its implementation leads to the protective function being ensured by administrative liability, and the repressive function by criminal law.[46]

382. Origin of acquisition: notion of primary and secondary markets. Another argument is that contractual liability for the prospectus would create an unjustified distinction between those who acquired their securities on the 'primary market' or the 'secondary market', whereas the position of the participants with regard to the prospectus is the same and they suffer equally from it. It should nevertheless be pointed out that these notions of primary and secondary markets exist independently of the admission of securities to trading on a platform: they actually refer to two successive moments in the existence of the security. The so-called primary market is the one where the issue takes place, i.e. the moment when investors subscribe to the financial securities from the issuer, while the secondary market is the place where the securities are traded, i.e. the moment of 'securities circulation'.[47] These two moments are found in the same terms when securities are not admitted to trading. Indeed, it is possible for the initial purchaser to resell the acquired securities, and his buyer will then be in a similar position to one who has acquired securities on the secondary market: he will not acquire it from the issuer. At the same time, the way securities are issued on the trading platform often requires the interposition of a syndicate between the issuer and the first real investor, so that the latter will not hold the security directly from the issuer.[48] The value of these notions is therefore not to create a distinction between securities admitted to trading and others,[49] but, in the context of liability, to show the dissociation between the author of the defective information and the seller of the securities.

---

44 Art. 11 of the Prospectus Regulation (Art. 6 of the Prospectus Directive). The function is to ensure, for those countries that do not have a general liability clause (like the former Art. 1382 of the Civil Code), that they enact a statutory liability.

45 J. Prorok, *Civil Liability in the Financial Markets*, *op. cit.*

46 See the concluding remarks of J. Prorok, *La responsabilité civile sur les marchés financiers*, *op. cit.*, p. 626: 'Let us wisely accept that, in the absence of potentially effective civil liability, it is rather up to criminal and administrative liability to play their full role in order to dissuade and prevent the occurrence of damage to investors.'

47 T. Bonneau and F. Drummond, *Droit des marchés financiers*, *op. cit.*, no. 14 and 281; J. Prorok, *La responsabilité civile sur les marchés financiers*, *op. cit.*

48 This will be true whenever the syndicate has carried out an 'underwriting', i.e. it has acquired the financial securities itself, see T. Bonneau and F. Drummond, *Droit des marchés financiers*, *op. cit.*, nos. 281–284.

49 This is why the application of the law of the financial market to the question of liability for misleading prospectuses will be contested here, and why it seems to us that the treatment of the conflict of laws should be identical depending on whether or not there is admission to trading, cf. *infra*, para. 429.

383. This separation is relevant insofar as one wishes to rely on the contract of sale of the securities to render the issuer liable. The only apparently decisive question in this view is whether the investor acquires his securities directly from the issuer or whether there has been an interposition of another person in the chain of transmission of ownership of the security. If there was, the issuer, who provided the information on which the investor based his decision, is technically a third party to the transaction from the point of view of sales law: it was not the issuer who sold the disputed securities to the investor. As a result, defective information, for example that contained in the prospectus or arising from transparency obligations, constitutes a kind of 'third party fraud'.[50] This first element is the basis for a general difficulty in civil liability for misleading information from the issuer,[51] and brings the issuer's liability closer to that for a defective product.[52] It therefore brings liability for defective information closer to a special tortious/delictual liability. However, one can resist this analysis.

II. The Possibility of a Contractual Basis

The preceding discussion, by showing the dissociation between the author of the defective information and the seller of the securities, seems to make the characterisation as a tort inevitable. However, there is a contractual link between the issuer and the owner of the security (A). Once established, this contract will not necessarily allow the liability resulting from the defective information to be included in its scope (B).

A. The Two Contractual Basis

The contractual basis can be established in two ways. The first is to observe that the law of sale recognises mechanisms of contractual liability allowing

---

50 J. Prorok, *La responsabilité civile sur les marchés financiers*, *op. cit.*, no. 103 and ref. cited.

51 This difficulty is in fact specific to any defective information issued by the issuer, whether in the context of the prospectus or the periodic or content information obligations to which the issuer is subject, particularly under the Transparency Directive, on which see *supra*, para. 341.

52 This comparison with product liability has been perfectly described by Professor Sanchez Lorenzo: 'There is a clear analogy between product liability and the liability of the issuer of financial securities for prospectuses, in relation to third parties who have acquired the product in a State other than the State of issue or "manufacture". As this is a cross-border placement of financial securities, the place of marketing, the technique and the place of transmission of the product are uncertain. Nevertheless, the issuer authorises the marketing of the product in advance (public offer) and notifies the prospectus in other Member States (primary market). He assumes the economic benefit of an offer with an international dimension; he must correlatively adapt the prospectus to the requirements of the markets envisaged, assuming the risk that a third party may acquire a security and suffer damage that materialises in the current account where the investment is credited.', *JDI*, 2016, 1461, spec. p. 1463.

the direct action of the sub-purchaser against the original seller. The latter is the issuer of the security, who was the first to put it into circulation. The liability of the prospectus could therefore be subject to the law of the contract resulting from the acceptance of the offer (1). The second is to observe that the thing transmitted, the *negotium*, aggregates its holder to a contract, thus always offering a contractual basis for his action (2).

1. *The Contract Resulting from the Acceptance of the Offer*

384. The ownership transfer chain of securities traded on a financial market. This presentation of the circulation of securities highlights a contract transfer chain, each contract successively transmitting ownership of the security from the issuer to the ultimate purchaser. However, French case law[53] allows a direct action, of contractual origin, by the sub-purchaser against the initial seller in the case of ownership transfer chains. Indeed, the Court of Cassation had the opportunity to state that 'the purchaser enjoying all the rights and actions attached to the thing which belonged to its author [he has] against the repairer of this thing a contractual action based on the non-fulfilment of an obligation'[54] (in this case an obligation of information). This direct action is distinct from that of the subcontractor against the client, or that of the victim against the insurer of the person who caused the damage, and should therefore not be the subject of an analogy,[55] including in terms of the conflict of laws.[56]

385. The characterisation of the direct action. In terms of international jurisdiction, direct actions arising from chains of contracts have been classified as torts by the Court of Justice, thus giving jurisdiction to the court of the place

[53] On the basis of the *Besse* judgment: on the retrospective of this French jurisprudential saga, see M. Fabre-Magnan, *Droit des obligations (t. 1)*, *op. cit.*, nos. 546–552.

[54] Cass. com., 3 May 2006, no. 04-12683.

[55] These actions are profoundly different: the direct action in chains of contracts appears to be symmetrical to that of the subcontractor against the prime contractor. Above all, whereas the direct action arising from chains of contracts was designed with the 'objective of protecting the sub-purchaser' (G. Viney, P. Jourdain and S. Carval, *Les conditions de la responsabilité*, 4th edition, Paris, LGDJ, 2013, no. 750) the direct action arising from the law on subcontracting aims to protect the subcontractor.

[56] See, for example, in insurance matters, Art. 18 of the Rome II Regulation allows the victim to bring a direct action against the insurer 'if the law applicable to the non-contractual obligation or the law applicable to the insurance contract so provides'. From the point of view of subcontracting, the question is a source of difficulties, both in terms of international jurisdiction and conflict of laws. It should simply be noted here that after having seemed to subject the subcontractor's direct action to the law applicable to the subcontract (cf. the first *Urmet* decision, Cass. com., 19 December 2006, no. 04-18888), the Court of Cassation preferred to reason in terms of the mandatory rules. On this question, see in particular V. Heuzé, 'La loi applicable aux actions directes dans les groupes de contrats', *RCDIP*, 1996, 243 and lastly, Cass. com., 20 April 2017, no. 15-16.922.

of the damage.[57] Such a characterisation does not necessarily bind the conflict of laws characterisation. As Professors Bureau and Muir Watt point out, 'if the French court is petitioned as a judge of the tort, there is nothing to prevent it from considering that it is contractual for the purposes of determining the law applicable to the merits',[58] which it has already had the opportunity to do.[59] Nevertheless, once it has been characterised as contractual, it is still necessary to determine on the basis of which *lex contractus* the direct action is possible. One may hesitate between the law of the contract between the manufacturer and the first purchaser, or the law of the contract by which the sub-purchaser acquired the goods. Indeed, with regard to direct actions in chains of contracts, the Cour de cassation has ruled in favour of the law of the original contract to which the manufacturer is a party.[60] This solution is favoured by some legal scholars, who consider that 'it is from this law that the obligation whose breach is invoked by the plaintiff derives, and it is therefore up to the law of the contract to specify which persons are entitled to rely on this breach'.[61]

386. The law of the public offer applicable to the direct action against the issuer of the owner of the security. In the case under consideration, this would mean that the law applicable to the direct action would be the law of the contract under which the issuer has transferred the financial instrument. Is this the contract of issue, or should a distinction be made between the contract of issue and the contract of public offer of securities? Such a distinction seems necessary, whatever

57 In addition to the court of the manufacturer's domicile.

58 D. Bureau and H. Muir Watt, *Droit international privé (t. 2)*, 4th ed., Paris, PUF, 2017, no. 881.

59 Cass., civ. 3e, 16 January 2013, no. 11-13.509. In this case, the Court of Appeal had based its decision on a direct action arising from a chain of contracts on the Hague Convention of 15 June 1955 on the Law Applicable to International Sales of Goods, which implied a contractual qualification of the direct action. The appeal challenging such a characterisation where the manufacturer is established abroad, and relying on the *Jakob Handte* case law of the Court of Justice on the determination of international jurisdiction precisely in the case of a direct action arising out of a chain of contracts, is dismissed.

60 Cass., civ. 1re, 10 October 1995, *Société Paglierani*. The judgment was handed down under Art. 3 of the Hague Convention of 15 June 1955 on the law applicable to international sales of goods, in a case where the absence of a choice of law led to the application of the law of the seller's habitual residence, i.e. Italian law, as the Paglieroni company was domiciled in Italy. However, the Court of Appeal's judgment was quashed for having determined 'by application of French law, even though the company Paglierani had its habitual residence in Italy, without ruling, if necessary ex officio, on the law competent to govern [...] the redhibitory contractual action brought directly by the company OMG against that company'.

61 P. Mayer and V. Heuzé, *Droit international privé*, *op. cit.*, no. 793. The authors refer to 'the law governing the contract by which the defendant to the action is bound' (*ibid.*). Such a formula cannot, however, be transposed to an action for payment by the subcontractor against the client, where the subcontractor is no longer a defendant but a plaintiff in the action; to consider that the law applicable to the direct action is 'in principle connected with the law of the claim whose effectiveness it ensures' is likely to be generalised and therefore seems preferable (the formula is of B. Audit and L. d'Avout, *Droit international privé*, *op. cit.*, no. 986).

the security under consideration. Indeed, from the point of view of both equity securities and debt securities, the contract of issue may be dissociated from the public offer of financial securities. However, it is the law applicable to the public offer of securities, under which the subscription and the first transmission take place, which will determine the right of the owner of the security to take advantage of the direct action.

387. Admittedly, this basis may appear unsatisfactory because of the type of object for which this action was conceived: tangible movable objects.[62] However, the historical difficulty of thinking of the security as a contract, combined with its comparison with other negotiable instruments such as bills of lading, is a reality of positive law. In its judgment in *Profit*,[63] the Court of Justice compared the jurisdiction clause in the prospectus for the debt securities at issue, firstly, with the applicability of a jurisdiction clause in the context of an action by a sub-purchaser against the manufacturer and, secondly, with the jurisdiction clause contained in a bill of lading. The Court concluded that a jurisdiction clause contained in a prospectus was capable of being relied on against the owner of the financial instrument, on the basis of the applicability of the contract of issue, in particular if the latter had 'succeeded *(to the original subscriber of the financial instruments)* in the rights and obligations attaching to those instruments under the applicable national law'.[64] This reasoning, based on the idea of successive substitution[65] illustrates, as far as European substantive law is concerned, that the logic of the law of sale still permeates the analysis of the circulation of securities from the point of view of international jurisdiction: there is no reason to think that the Court of Justice does not reason in the same way in conflict-of-laws.[66]

62 Mr Vincent Malassigné considers that the model of the representative document of title is that of the representative document of title to tangible movable property, the archetype of which is precisely the bill of lading, see V. Malassigné, *Les titres représentatifs*, *op. cit.*

63 Case C-366/13, *Profit investment*, ECLI:EU:C:2016:282.

64 *Profit*, para. 36. The Court here adopts the conclusions (see paras. 49 to 56) of its Advocate General.

65 This becomes very clear when the Court tries to determine the *ratio legis of the* applicability of a jurisdiction clause in a bill of lading. It writes thus: "It is in view of this substitution relationship between the holder of the bill of lading and the shipper that the Court has held that, by the effect of the acquisition of the bill of lading, the holder is bound by the prorogation of jurisdiction (see, in this sense, *Russ*, para. 25). Conversely, where the applicable national law does not provide for such a substitution relationship, the court seised must verify the reality of that third party's consent to the jurisdiction clause (*Coreck* judgment, cited above, para. 26). C-543/10, *Refcomp*, ECLI:EU:C:2013:62, para. 36, on which see *infra*, para. 407.

66 This reality is not a French perception. Maisie Ooi herself, in her commentary on the *Secure Capital* judgment, compares the decision of the English Supreme Court with that of the Court of Justice in *Jakob Handte*, but distinguishes between them: 'There is however a fundamental difference. The Common Depository was interposed by the issuer to facilitate the transfer of the Notes to investors. It had not purchased the Notes from Credit Suisse and was not an intermediate seller. More importantly Jakob Handte was a ruling on the

2. *The Issue Contract*

388. Original contract of *negotium*. The liability of the issuer of defective information as presented above, from the point of view of the chain of transfer of ownership and the direct action, is based on the 'external' aspect of the security, i.e. on the contracts that gave rise to its transmission. However, there is always another contract, 'internal' to the security, and arising from the *negotium* represented by the instrument. As Professor Le Nabasque writes about transferable securities ('*valeurs mobilières*'):[67]

> 'From time immemorial, transferable securities ("*valeurs mobilières*") have referred to the *negotium*, i.e. to rights of claim of a particular nature (of a lender, of a partner); not to the *instrumentum*, which only allows them to be conveyed by the simplified forms of commercial law.'[68]

The object transferred is always a debt, whereby the transferee (the owner of the security) becomes the creditor of the debtor transferred (the issuer). In other words, to be the owner of a financial securities is to be the creditor of the person who issued it.[69] Moreover, on what other basis would the investor receive interest, dividends or voting rights? It is precisely these contractual prerogatives that he wished to acquire from the issuer, on the basis of the information provided by the latter. The relevant question is then to know from which contract the transferred debt arose and the link it has with the defective information. The answer is not the same for shares, debts and units in collective investment funds. The debt is derived from the contract of issue, the share from the articles of association and the unit trust from the fund rules. In fact, the *negotium* has the dual effect of placing its holder in an individual contractual relationship with the issuer, and aggregating it in a collective contractual relationship with the holders of identical *negotia*.

389. Issuing contract and contractual liability. However, the existence of this contract does not necessarily mean that the issuer can be held contractually liable for information disseminated about the securities issued. Indeed, the main function of this initial contract (contract of issuance, articles of association, fund rules) is to organise the operation of the collective body that may be established

---

sub-buyer's invocation of the court's special jurisdiction under Art. 5(1) of the Brussels Convention, where the considerations were quite different. The absence of privity between Secure Capital and Credit Suisse in the English contractual sense does not prevent the Rome Convention's application.'

67 Which are now a category of financial securities, see Art. L. 228-1 of the Commercial Code.

68 H. Le Nabasque, 'Les actions sont des droits de créance négociables' in *Mélanges Yves Guyon*, Paris, Dalloz, 2000, p. 671.

69 No doubt the artificial characterisation of co-ownership of units in collective investment funds masks this aspect in French law.

(bondholders' group relations between corporate bodies), and to describe the regime of the securities issued. Moreover, it is the public offer contract that triggers the drawing up of the prospectus, and not the issue contract, thus resurrecting the difficulty of 'third party fraud' by bringing together a disclosure obligation (the prospectus) with a contract that is not specific to it (the issue contract). The argument can nevertheless be nuanced by the close links between these three acts: the purpose of the prospectus is to describe the securities issued by the contract of issuance; the issuance and the public offering are part of the same marketing process.[70]

390. In fact, the possibility of engaging the issuer's liability on the basis of the contract at the origin of the *negotium* has been perfectly perceived in French company law. The Court of cassation has been able to admit a contractual liability action by the shareholder against the company and its directors for having disseminated false information. In this case, the Court retained the personal injury of the shareholder in the context of a contractual action based on the *lex societatis*,[71] as the law applicable to the particular debt that is the share, insofar as:

> 'The company's shareholders claimed that they had been induced to invest in and hold the company's securities by misrepresentation by management, withholding of information and misrepresentation of accounts to shareholders.'[72]

The personal nature of the damage to the shareholder, which is known to be rarely retained by case law, stems precisely from the breach of probity of the information for which the company was liable. In the context of this analysis, this judgment shows that the holder of a share may rely on the company's contract to incur its contractual liability for the defective information disseminated.

B. The Scope of the *Lex Contractus*

391. As Mr d'Avout has pointed out in relation to the designation of the forum of the contract, the application of the *lex contractus* to obligations arising from the prospectus will undoubtedly depend on 'the manner in which

---

[70] On this aspect, see *supra*, para. 293.

[71] In particular, on the basis of Art. L. 225-252 of the Commercial Code.

[72] Cass. com., 9 March 2010, nos. 08-21.547 and 08-21.793, on which see J. Prorok, *La responsabilité civile sur les marchés financiers*, *op. cit.*, nos. 247 et seq. and the references cited. The scope of application of the rule resulting from the Gaudriot judgment was restricted by Cass. com., 16 May 2018, no. 16-20.684 (FS-D), *Société CSI Finances c/ B.*

the litigant articulates his claims'.[73] Indeed, there is sometimes a certain contingency between contractual and tortious characterisations, on the one hand, because of the different function that characterisation has for the purposes of conflict of laws and determination of international jurisdiction and, on the other hand, because of the lack of systematic causality, within the conflict of laws, between the characterisation and the applicable law. Thus, a litigant who relies on the pre-contractual nature of the disclosure obligations arising from the prospectus will be subject to the characterisation of tort or delict from the point of view of both jurisdiction and conflict of laws; the applicable law will, however, be the law of the contract, even if it is putative. The solution is even more subtle, however, since the law of the contract may refer, for the determination of the existence of consent, to the law of the investor's domicile, i.e. the law that would have been applicable under the law of the tort (1). At the same time, the presence of a contract will not always be an obstacle to an action in tort (2).

1. *The Tort Characterisation of Pre-Contractual Obligations*

392. Scope of Article 12 of the Rome II Regulation. Initially considered from the point of view of jurisdiction, liability arising from the breach of pre-contractual obligations was characterised as a tort or delict by the Court of Justice,[74] a characterisation confirmed in terms of conflict of laws by the Rome I and Rome II Regulations. This characterisation as a tort or delict nevertheless entails the application of the law of the contract. Indeed, Article 12(1) of the Rome II Regulation provides that:

> 'The law applicable to a non-contractual obligation arising out of dealings prior to the conclusion of a contract, regardless of whether the contract was actually concluded or not, shall be the law that applies to the contract or that would have been applicable to it had it been entered into.'

Recital 30 of the Rome II Regulation states:

> '*(This article)* should include the violation of the duty of disclosure and the breakdown of contractual negotiations. Article 12 covers only non-contractual obligations presenting a direct link with the dealings prior to the conclusion of a

[73] Note cited above under the *Kolassa* judgment (on this judgment, see *infra*, paras. 400; 420 et seq.) However, the author refers here to the qualification for the purpose of determining the competent court. On the contingency of the characterisation in this matter, see already M.-E. Ancel, 'L'article L. 442-6-I, 5 C. com. en droit international privé', *Revue de jurisprudence commerciale*, 2009, 200.

[74] On these judgments, see H. Gaudemet-Tallon and M.-E. Ancel, *Compétence et exécution des jugements en Europe*, *op. cit.*, no. 186.

contract. This means that if, while a contract is being negotiated, a person suffers personal injury, Article 4 or other relevant provisions of this Regulation should apply.'

However, some scholars consider that this article is inapplicable to the liability of the issuer for the prospectus because there is no negotiation or contractual relationship between the issuer and the investor.[75] Both assertions are debatable.

393. The prospectus, as an advertising medium, can be considered as a form of 'negotiation'.[76] This is all the more true because in many cases the issue is not made in the hope that the securities issued will be acquired: when it takes place, negotiations have sometimes already taken place with the future purchasers. Moreover, the information included in the prospectus is precisely intended to inform future contracting parties; this is a pre-contractual information obligation of legal origin, a situation expressly covered by Recital 30 of the Regulation. Finally, as we have seen, the acquisition of equity and debt securities has the effect of creating a contractual relationship between the owner and the issuer. Article 12 of the Rome II Regulation therefore makes the liability of the author of the prospectus subject to the law of the contract of issue, which will alternatively be that of the issuer or, in the case of debt securities, that designated in the bond issued. However, the situation is not quite the same where periodic disclosure requirements arising from admission to trading are concerned. We have undoubtedly considered that they update over time the function pursued by the prospectus[77]; moreover, their publication undoubtedly has an influence on the price of securities admitted to trading, showing that the dissemination of this information encourages the purchase or sale of these securities. It should

---

75 W.-G. Ringe and A. Hellgardt, 'The International Dimension of Issuer Liability-Liability and Choice of Law from a Transatlantic Perspective' (2011) *Oxford Journal of Legal Studies*, p. 23, spec. p. 43: 'In the case of the purchase of securities, however, no negotiations between the issuer and the investor take place, and no contractual or quasi-contractual relationship exists between them.'

76 *Comp.* S. Corneloup, 'La place du règlement Rome II dans la régulation globale des marchés financiers', *Cahier de droit de l'entreprise*, November 2012, file 30 and, from the same author, 'Vers une réforme du règlement Rome II: la réparation des dommages causés par une violation du droit des marchés financiers nécessite-t-elle une règle de conflit spéciale?' in M. Douchy-Oudot and E. Guinchard (dir.), *La justice civile européenne en marche*, Paris, Dalloz, 2012, pp. 63–78; M. Lehmann, 'Proposition d'une règle spéciale dans le Règlement Rome II pour les délits financiers', *RCDIP*, 2012, p. 485; M. Lehmann, 'Prospectus liability and private international law - assessing the landscape after the CJEU's Kolassa ruling (Case C-375/13)' (2016) 12(2) *Journal of Private International Law*, pp. 318 et seq. spec, p. 338. The authors reject the idea that the prospectus is a form of trading, and that there is a contract between the issuer and the owner of the financial security due to the interposition of an intermediary. However, this ignores the existence of the contract with the issuer that results from the ownership of the financial instrument, see *supra*, paras. 386 et seq.

77 See *supra*, para. 343.

be noted, however, that they are not triggered by a public offer, and that the characterisation of a pre-contractual negotiation is therefore more tenuous. In fact, if the authors do not wish to subject the prospectus to Article 12 of the Rome II Regulation, it is because the rule it lays down is dysfunctional: it proceeds to a questionable confusion of the functions of contractual and tortious liability in private international law.[78]

394. Consent. The reference to the law of the contract made by Article 12 of the Rome II Regulation is likely to come up against, in a form of cross-fertilisation, the application of Article 10 of the Rome I Regulation on the law applicable to the absence of consent. This allows the law of the investor's domicile to reappear 'if it appears from the circumstances that it would not be reasonable to determine the effect of that party's conduct by reference to the law [of the contract]'.[79] This provision, which reflects the necessary balance between the legal order of the contract and that of the tort as soon as a lack of consent is involved, should not be such as to call into question the contractual characterisation of the action: it simply amounts to applying a different *lex contractus* to the protection of the contracting party. Indeed, it is for contract law to define the conditions of validity of the acts which it governs.

In the context of a liability action against the author of defective information, however, it is not the absence of consent that the investor is claiming, but fraud or error. However, defects in consent are not equivalent to lack of consent and are therefore subject to the *lex contractus*. It seems to us, however, that the error or fraud causes damage which could have been subject to the law of the tort. In the context of this study, it is within this legal order that the fraudulent conduct takes place (through the local dissemination of the defective information), and it is this legal order that suffers the consequences. This temptation to subject absence of consent to the law of the place of the damage is also explained by the 'curative' character[80] of this institution, the purpose of which is precisely to annul contracts because of the wrongful conduct of one of the contracting parties. The purpose of sanctioning absence of consent is to restore the situation that would have arisen without the conclusion of the contract, i.e. to repair a relationship corrupted by a fault. This extra-contractual character of absence of consent – which we support, although we are aware that it may come as a surprise – shows the ambivalence of this notion; it is well reflected in Article 1112-1 paragraph 6 of the French Civil Code which provides, in addition to the possible nullity of the contract concluded following a breach of a pre-contractual duty to inform, of which the prospectus

78 For a critique of Art. 12 of the Rome II Regulation, which goes beyond the scope of this study, see A. Gridel, 'A case for a restrictive conception of contractual characterisation: reflections from advisory obligations' *International Business Law Journal*, 2023/5, p. 539.

79 Art. 10(2) of the Rome I Regulation.

80 F. Terré *et al.*, *Les obligations*, *op. cit.*, no. 270.

is an illustration, for the extra-contractual civil liability of the person who was bound by this obligation.

From an international point of view, however, the advantage of the law of tort has to be counterbalanced by, first, the breakdown of the contractual category which would result from it,[81] second, the difficulty of characterising the location of the damage resulting from the tortious conduct and, finally, the risk that disappointed contracting parties will always plead defect of consent in order to escape the choice-of-law clause. Above all, a distinction must necessarily be drawn between pre-contractual information obligations, which are part of the rules of negotiation and are therefore subject to the field of tort liability, even if they have an influence on the eventual consent, and the validity of the consent itself. In the latter case, it will be difficult to crowd out the *lex contractus* as it has a strong title of jurisdiction. On the other hand, its extension to the pre-contractual period, i.e. to the rules of negotiation, does not seem particularly satisfactory.[82]

2. *Extra-Contractual Liability of the Co-Contracting Party*

395. The possibility of extra-contractual liability of the co-contracting issuer. The existence of a contract between the issuer and the owner of the security does not have the effect of subjecting all the events giving rise to liability to contractual liability, simply because certain events giving rise to liability are absolutely independent of the contract.[83] In order to know whether the law of the contract should be extended to the extra-contractual liability of the co-contractor, the European case law[84] imposes a method that Mr Sylvain Bollée has masterfully summarised:

---

81 B. Audit and L. d'Avout, *Droit international privé*, *op. cit.*; no. 274; the authors report that the category conflict was rather with personal law (Pillet being in favour).

82 A. Gridel, 'A case for a restrictive conception of contractual characterisation: reflections from advisory obligations', *op. cit.*

83 Mr Bollée gives the example of a contract concluded by a fertiliser manufacturer with a farmer, who are also neighbours. The former cannot stand the latter's dog and decides to poison it. In this case, as the author writes: 'The two parties are bound by a contract (of sale); however, it cannot be seriously denied that the liability incurred by the producer-poisoner, being unrelated to the contractual relationship, is of a tortious nature", see S. Bollée, 'La responsabilité extracontractuelle du cocontractant en droit international privé', *op. cit.*, pp. 119 et seq.

84 Case C-548/12, *Brogsitter*, ECLI:EU:C:2014:148, see the comments by M. Lehmann, A. Briggs, G. Cuniberti, U. Mankowski and B. Haftel published on the website of the European Commission. Haftel published on the website of the European Association of Private International Law (EAPIL) accessible from: https://eapil.org/2020/12/14/here-lies-the-late-brogsitter-ruling/ as well as the commentary by T. Lutzi and the discussion initiated on conflictoflaws.net, https://conflictoflaws.net/2020/the-cjeus-decision-in-wikingerhof-towards-a-new-distinction-between-contract-and-tort/.

> 'In concrete terms, the approach to be followed should be this one: it must be asked whether, from the point of view of the law applicable to the contract, the alleged event giving rise to liability relates to the performance or non-performance of a legal duty [...] which would not exist, or would not have the same regime, in the absence of a contract. If so, the harmful event falls within the scope of the contract and it must then be left to the *lex contractus* to govern all the consequences, including those which might be drawn from the application of a system of extra-contractual liability.'[85]

If the defective information originates in the prospectus, there is no doubt that the event giving rise to liability – the provision of inaccurate information – would not have occurred without the issue or offer to the public. However, the obligation to draw up the prospectus arises independently of the conclusion of the contract: it is triggered by the offer itself. Therefore, in the words of the Court of Justice, 'it does not appear to be essential to examine the content of the contract concluded with the defendant in order to assess the lawfulness or unlawfulness of the conduct of which the defendant is accused, since that obligation is imposed on the defendant independently of that contract'.[86] This is why it is possible to establish the jurisdiction of the *forum delicti*, in addition to that of the contractual forum. This is even more true when the defective information originates in the issuer's periodic disclosure obligations, since these take place independently of the public offering. This is true even if these obligations ensure the continuity of the function pursued by the prospectus, and could moreover be linked, if not to the public offer, at least to the issue contract.[87]

The characterisation of the action in tort enables the owner of the security to avoid several pitfalls of contractual liability by avoiding possible limitation of liability clauses and a contractual law that may be less favourable than that of the victim's domicile.[88] However, it is not certain that such an action is

---

85 S. Bollée, 'La responsabilité extracontractuelle du cocontractant en droit international privé', *op. cit.*

86 *Wikingerhof GmbH* judgment *cited above*, para. 33.

87 In order to qualify as a tort or delict, it might have been possible for the claimant to allege that the defective information constitutes an act of unfair competition, aimed at draining local savings, and to rely on Article 6 of the Rome II Regulation. Nevertheless, this Article 6, undoubtedly relevant for a possible competitor, is less useful for the injured investor, who does not complain of a competitive harm, but of an alteration of his decision, see M. Lehmann, 'Proposition d'une règle spéciale dans le Règlement Rome II pour les délits financiers', *RCDIP*, 2012, pp. 485 et seq.

88 If the tort action is based on the fraudulent nature of the defective shares, the victim, in particular if he is a consumer, will always be able to rely on the law of his domicile (Art. 10 of the Rome I Regulation). Moreover, the presence of an insurance policy inserted in the contract of issue, triggered by the devaluation of the value of the securities below a certain threshold, will be likely to justify a contractual basis.

sufficient to defeat the existence of a forum selection clause when the plaintiff is a professional.[89]

§ 2. OBSTACLES TO CONTRACTUAL LIABILITY

396. The above discussion has shown that the owner of a security has contractual claims against the issuer. Under these conditions, the obstacles to contractual liability lie in the intermediation of the ownership of the securities, i.e. in the hypotheses where the final investor is not the owner of the disputed security, but of a security which only gives its holder prerogatives against its intermediary, in the manner of *depositary receipt*.[90] This situation is different depending on whether the direct or indirect holding system is involved. However, it always has the same effect: by no longer allowing the investor, whether a professional or a consumer, to be declared the owner of the security, it prevents him from relying on the issue contract. This will be illustrated for the indirect holding system by the London Court of Appeal's *Secure Capital* ruling[91] and for the direct holding system by the Court of Justice's *Kolassa* ruling.[92]

397. *Secure Capital* ruling. In this case, *Crédit Suisse* issued debt securities in the English form of bearer notes, ie. bearer securities represented by a certificate,[93] on the basis of an issue contract also subject to English law and containing defective information. Under English law, the holder of the certificate is the sole creditor of the company. However, the certificates are not held by the final investor, but by the Bank of New York Mellon, a depository acting on behalf

89 It is possible that the choice of court clause may interfere with the jurisdiction of the forum of the tort, in particular if the sole purpose of the action appears to be to evade the jurisdiction of the chosen court. See, in the related area of compensation actions brought following a Commission decision affirming the existence of a breach of competition law, Case C-352/13, *Cartel Damage Claims (CDC) Hydrogen Peroxide SA v. Akzo Nobel NV and Others*, ECLI:EU:C:2015:33.

90 On which see *supra*, para. 288.

91 *Secure Capital SA v. Credit Suisse AG* [2017] EWCA Civ 1486. On this judgment, see, inter alia, the analysis of *Secure Capital*'s counsel, R. Cox QC, 'Are warranties in an Immobilised Bearer Note Enforceable?' in L. Gullifer and J. Payne, *Intermediation and beyond*, Oxford, Hart Publishing 2019, spec. chapter 6; in the same book, see chapter 7 and the contibution by R. Salter QC, 'Enforcing Debt Securities'; M. Ooi, 'Intermediation and its effects on investors rights' (2015) *The Law Quarterly Review* 536, p. 537; see from the same author, 'Re-enfranchising the investor of intermediated securities' (2020) 16 *Journal of private international law*, pp. 69 et seq.

92 Case C-375/13, *Harald Kolassa v.Barclays Bank plc*, ECLI:EU:C:2015:37.

93 Called 'Permanent Global Security', *Secure Capital* ruling no. 13. The name of the certificate will be kept for simplicity.

of Clearstream.[94] The latter is the Luxembourg central securities depository.[95] In this case, the purpose of admitting the securities into the system of the central depository, itself subject to Luxembourg law,[96] is precisely to solicit Luxembourg investors to sell them the disputed debt securities. The members of the system can, through a book entry mechanism, acquire the prerogatives arising from the security, but not the ownership of the security itself.[97] Secure Capital acquired some of these securities through the central depository system.

Luxembourg law grants a number of prerogatives to the person registered in the securities settlement system as a creditor, referred to as the depositor ('*déposant*'), and considers that 'the depositor has the same rights as if the securities and other financial instruments had remained in his hands'.[98] It is on the basis of this Luxembourg law[99] that *Secure Capital* sues *Crédit Suisse* for contractual liability due to the defective documentation of the transferred claim. The application of English law or Luxembourg law leads to opposite results:[100] the first, by considering that there is no contract between the two parties to the dispute, the second, by considering that there is a possible contractual action.

However, the English judges, both at first instance and on appeal, refused to apply the law of the central securities depository to the determination of the

---

94 The certificates are 'deposited with Bank of New York Mellon ('BNYM') as common depositary. It is common ground that BNYM is the bearer of the Notes which it holds on behalf of Clearstream' (*Secure Capital* judgment no. 14).

95 Such a separation is no longer possible under the CSD Regulation. Indeed, the latter Regulation provides in Section A of its Annex that the CSD must provide 'core services', which include 'initial registration of securities in a book-entry system', the 'provision and centralised maintenance of securities accounts at the highest level' as well as the 'settlement' service.

96 On the linkage of systems, see *supra*, paras. 267 et seq.

97 Except in two cases: in the event of non-payment of the scheduled interest, or in the event of closure of the system operated by *Clearstream* for 14 days. In these two cases, the person who only had a payment claim against *Clearstream* is deemed to be the owner of the security and to be in a contractual relationship with *Crédit Suisse* (*Secure Capital* judgment no. 18).

98 Art. 6, para. 1, of the Law of 1 August 2001 on the circulation of securities and other fungible instruments, *Official Journal of the Grand Duchy of Luxembourg*, 31 August 2001, no. 106, p. 2180.

99 As detailed in the judgment (para. 21): 'Secure Capital seeks to rely on Article 8(1) of the 2001 law which provides: 'the investor may exercise or arrange to exercise corporate rights attached to the securities and the rights attaching to the holding of the securities linked to the possession of the securities by producing a certificate drawn up by the relevant account holder attesting to the number of securities registered in its custody account.'

100 As Ms Maisie Ooi writes 'Secure Capital's claim was complicated by the fact that both English and Luxembourg laws could have been relevant, and the application of one or the other led to diametrically different outcomes. English law was the governing law of the Notes, and Luxembourg law, that of the Clearstream system on which the Notes had been placed. Credit Suisse succeeded because of the court's choice of English law, and rejection of Luxembourg law, as the applicable law', M. Ooi, 'Intermediation and its effects on investors rights', *op. cit.*, p. 537; see from the same author, 'Re-enfranchising the investor of intermediated securities', *op. cit.*, p. 69.

legal action, and therefore considered that Luxembourg law was not applicable. In their view, the action brought by *Secure Capital* is of a contractual nature and must therefore be governed by the law of the contract of issue, i.e. English law. However, under English law, only the holder of the security is the owner, and therefore the co-contractor; *Secure Capital*'s action is therefore dismissed. As Ms Maise Ooi observed, the solution could have been different if the law under which *Secure Capital*'s title was constituted (the *lex creationis*) had been applied to its action.[101] Indeed, in the reported case, the object exchanged within the Luxembourg central depositary system does not correspond to the ownership of the certificate, but is a separate *negotium*, in the manner of a *depositary receipt*.[102] This question, which relates to the proprietary status of the security, will be further explored below.[103] It is sufficient to note here that the tangle of national holding systems is likely to break the coherence of domestic law and, in particular, the link between the investor and the issuer, and that conflict of laws relating to the proprietary status of the security do not only lead to disputes over priority conflicts as to the ownership of the security, but also extend to the access of the final investor to the prerogatives stemming from the issue contract. This is of additional importance if the contract of issuance contains insurance policies. The intermediation of the ownership of financial securities can also occur without a central depository. This was the case in the *Kolassa* judgment.

398. *Kolassa* judgment. In this case, Mr Kolassa, an Austrian consumer domiciled in Austria, was induced to invest, through an Austrian bank, in debt securities (bearer bonds) issued by Barclays, a UK-based bank. These bonds

---

101 M. Ooi, 'Re-enfranchising the investor of intermediated securities', *op. cit.*, pp. 107 et seq.

102 The facts were unusual: the central securities depository did not act as a depositary, but only as a manager of the securities settlement system, which allowed *Crédit Suisse to* allege that the *common depositary*, the *Bank of New York Mellon*, performed this function on behalf of *Clearstream* (some legal scholars believe that in a similar situation, that of *depositary receipts*, the *depositary* should be qualified as the real owner of the share, and therefore a shareholder, see C. Coupet, *L'attribution du droit de vote dans les sociétés*, *op. cit.*, no. 164 and then no. 165 for a critique of this solution; T. Bonneau and F. Drummond, *Droit des marchés financiers*, *op. cit.)*
It is clear that in reality the depositary performs this function not for *Clearstream*, but for the person designated as the owner according to the *Clearstream* system, which becomes clearer when the central depositary performs the full range of its functions, notary, book-entry and settlement. There is no longer any doubt that the determination of the contracting partner must be left to the law applicable to the contract of issuance, but to the system of the central depository to which the issuer has delegated the management of the securities. However, even on the facts of *Secure Capital*, the London court's reasoning is questionable: it could perfectly well have considered that the issuer's only co-contractor is the one with whom the ownership of the security is located, i.e. the central depository. Instead, the English court refused to take into consideration what looks an awful lot like a foreign mandatory rule, and left the one who bears the risk without any contractual action. It is difficult to see who will take advantage of this, if not the economic bearer of the risk.

103 See *infra*, para. 670.

subsequently lost most of their value. At the time of the public offering, Barclays distributed a prospectus in Austria which allegedly contained false information that was material to Mr Kolassa's investment. In order to sue Barclays for liability, Mr Kolassa wished to rely on his status as a consumer in order to trigger the special jurisdiction rule provided for in the Brussels I bis Regulation. Again, the difficulty lay in the absence of a contractual link between Barclays and Mr Kolassa, precisely because he did not hold the debt security. As the Court of Justice explained, Mr Kolassa was not the holder of the debt security, but only of a claim against the Austrian bank which held the certificates in its own name.[104] Thus, the Court found that:

> 'Mr Kolassa could claim only the delivery of the certificates from the corresponding share of the covering assets, it being understood that those certificates could not be transferred into his name. (...) there is no contract between Barclays Bank and Mr Kolassa, for the latter is not the bearer of the bonds referred to in paragraph 14 of this judgment, those bonds being held by direktanlage.at (*the Austrian bank*) as covering assets in its own name.'[105]

This shows how significant the holding of the financial security is: it is the cause of the existence of a contractual link between the investor and the issuer. In such cases, there are two solutions: to hold the investment firm liable, for example by alleging that the latter, by not allowing the investor to be a direct co-contractor, has failed to fulfil its professional obligations relating to client protection, or to attempt to bring a tort action.

399. Conclusion of the section. We have shown that arguments that the issuer is invariably liable in tort for the defective information it has disseminated should be rejected. There are in fact two contractual claims for liability, one arising from the public offer contract and one from the issue contract. The real obstacle to the issuer's contractual liability lies in the lack of ownership of the security by the investor, who nevertheless bears the risk of devaluation of the security.

SECTION 2. SOLUTIONS IN CONTRACTUAL MATTERS

400. Applicable law. One might think that the solutions of private international law in contractual matters are likely to be of considerable advantage to the issuer, by allowing it to select the law applicable to its liability through an *electio juris* clause, and to concentrate the litigation at its seat through a choice of forum clause. The statement is undoubtedly correct from the point of view of conflict of laws. Indeed, the law applicable to contractual liability is the one provided for in

---

104 *Kolassa* judgment, para. 15.

105 *Kolassa* judgment, para. 15 and then para. 26. Italics added.

the contract.[106] However, it has been observed that if the defective information is of a pre-contractual nature, the Rome II Regulation nevertheless provides for the application of the law of the contract. The latter will extend to the consequences attached to the nullity of the contract.[107] Above all, the Rome I Regulation gives particular force to the law of the contract by deactivating the rule applicable to consumer matters. Indeed, the latter is inapplicable:

> 'Rights and obligations which constitute financial instruments, and rights and obligations which constitute the terms and conditions governing the issue or offer to the public and public takeover bids for securities, and the subscription and redemption of units in collective investment undertakings, insofar as these activities do not constitute the provision of a financial service.'[108]

By avoiding that the issuer be confronted with the law of the seat of each consumer he solicits, this rule favours cross-border issues within the Union. However, there is no equivalent of this exception in the Brussels Ia Regulation, where the solutions are less unitary. From the point of view of jurisdiction, it should therefore be noted that if the choice of forum clause is not stipulated, the forum of the issuer's domicile will be rivalled by the special contractual forum (§ 1); if it is, however, this clause is likely to be held in check by the system applicable to its validity and enforceability (§ 2) as well as by the presence of a consumer (§ 3).

§ 1. DETERMINATION OF THE SPECIAL CONTRACTUAL FORUM

401. Modalities of the option of jurisdiction. The option offered in contractual matters requires a distinction to be made between contracts. For contracts for the sale of goods,[109] or for the provision of services,[110] the competent court is defined in a substantial way: it is respectively that of the place where the goods are delivered, or the service provided. For other contracts, the competent court is that of the place of performance of the 'obligation which serves as the basis

---

106 Art. 12(1)(c) Rome I Regulation.

107 Art. 12(1)(e) of the Rome I Regulation.

108 Art. 17(1)(d) of the Rome I Regulation. On this article, see F. Garcimartin Alferez, 'New Issues in the Rome I Regulation: The Special Provisions on Financial Market Contracts', *op. cit.*; F. Garcimartin Alferez, 'The Rome I Regulation: Exceptions to the Rule on Consumer Contracts and Financial Instruments', *op. cit.* On its relationship with financial contracts and the provision of financial services, see *infra*, para. 805.

109 Art. 7(1a) of the Brussels Ia Regulation. The sale of goods presupposes a sale of tangible personal property, which is not the case in the hypotheses under consideration here.

110 Art. 7(1b) Brussels Ia Regulation.

of the claim',[111] the determination of which requires a diversion through the conflict-of-laws rule. These concepts, which must be interpreted independently of national law and independently of substantive European law,[112] give rise to different difficulties depending on the contract on which the liability action is based.

402. If it is a liability action based on the contract resulting from the acceptance of the offer to the public, the comparison with the sale of goods is possible if this contract is extended by analogy to the sale of intangible things on the basis of the identity of the mechanism for transferring ownership. However, such a solution leads to a dead end because of the absence of a link between the place of delivery of the securities, the characterisation of which varies according to the systems and is controversial in France,[113] and the liability action for defective information. At the same time, the offer to the public, which is an act of marketing, does not lend itself well to the characterisation of the provision of a service. This is why it is probably necessary to return to the criterion of the obligation that serves as the basis for the claim. The obligation in question is that of providing accurate information on the securities marketed. Its legal origin and its pre-contractual nature are not obstacles to its contractual characterisation. This obligation, which has its source in the Prospectus Regulation, is difficult to locate; it can, however, be located on the basis of the function of the duty to inform, which is to protect its addressees. Therefore, it can be located at the investor's home insofar as it has been disseminated there.[114] This is undoubtedly a favour done to the applicant. However, it is justified, on the one hand, by the legal proximity of the court of the investor's domicile to the dispute, since the investor was solicited by the dissemination of the disputed information and, on the other hand, by the possibility for the plaintiff to defeat it through a choice of court clause.

403. If it is a liability action based on the issue contract, it may be tempting to distinguish according to the *negotium* issued in order to determine in which category each type of issue falls. It seems to us that this temptation should

---

111 Art. 7(1) of the Brussels Ia Regulation.

112 It should be recalled here that the qualification here is not only autonomous from domestic law, but also from the European treaties (in particular Art. 57 TFEU on the freedom to provide services) as well as from the various sectoral directives, cf. CJEU judgment, Case C-533/07, *Falco*, ECLI:EU:C:2009:257, paras. 20 and 33, see also H. Gaudemet-Tallon and M.-E. Ancel, *Compétence et exécution des jugements en Europe*, *op. cit.*

113 See *infra*, paras. 658 et seq.

114 The diversions through the conflict of laws imposed by the *Tessili* case law does not pose any difficulty, not so much because the issue contract designates the applicable law, as because of the European source of the disputed obligation. On the difficulties nevertheless raised by the *Tessili* case law, see G. Droz, 'Delendum est forum contractus?', *D.*, 1997, 351; V. Heuzé, 'De quelques infirmités congénitales du droit uniforme: l'exemple de l'article 5.1 de la Convention de Bruxelles du 27 septembre 1968', *RCDIP*, 2000, 595; H. Gaudemet-Tallon and M.-E. Ancel, *Compétence et exécution des jugements en Europe*, *op. cit.*

be resisted because, whatever the type of *negotium* issued, there is a common function of these *negotia* in the context of a liability action: their purpose is to collect savings for the benefit of the issuer while organising the status of their holders in their relationship with the issuer. To qualify the issue contract differently, for example by bringing it closer to a contract for the provision of services, is to institute a complex casuistry. It may well be considered that the bond issue can be assimilated to a loan of money and therefore subsumed under contracts for the provision of services. However, in addition to the fact that such a comparison faces certain limits,[115] it is certain that it does not apply to all debt securities, and that its extension to equity securities will be difficult, creating an inappropriate distinction between liability actions that are nevertheless identical. Moreover, the concept of service adopted by the Court of Justice 'implies, at the very least, that the party providing the service performs a specific activity in return for remuneration'.[116] Such a definition makes it difficult to subsume the relationship at issue, which consists rather of an exchange between the parties.[117] It is therefore once again the obligation that serves as a basis for the claim that must be considered. Depending on the basis of the action, it may be the same as for the liability action based on the contract resulting from the acceptance of the public offer, or it may be, in the words of the Paris Court of Appeal, taken up by the Court of Cassation, 'the issuance of securities, on the one hand, and the subscription of these instruments having investment value, on the other'.[118]

§ 2. THE HYPOTHESIS OF THE EXTENSION OF THE COURT'S JURISDICTION

404. Validity of choice of court clauses. The presence of a choice of court clause will constitute an obstacle to the implementation of primary and special jurisdiction. While there is a certain variety of choice of court clauses,[119] those relating to the offer of financial securities most often have the effect of concentrating the dispute, when brought by the investor, at the issuer's seat. The Brussels I *bis*

---

115 See our comments *supra*, note under para. 315.

116 *Falco* judgment cited above, para. 29, confirmed by Case C-9/12, *Cormans-Collins*, ECLI:EU:C:2013:860, para. 37; Case C-196/15, *Granarolo*, ECLI:EU:C:2016:559, para. 37.

117 This seems to have been the view of the Court of Cassation in *UMR v. KA Finanz*, Cass. com., 1 March 2017, no. 14-25 426.

118 Cass. com., 17 March 2021, no. 19-13.632.

119 See C. Kleiner, 'L'élection de for en matière bancaire et financière: entre clauses asymétriques, clauses modèles et quasi réglementaires' in M. Laazouzi (ed.), *Les clauses attributives de juridiction: de la prévisibilité au désordre*, Paris, Ed. Panthéon-Assas, 2021, spec. pp. 49 et seq. On the validity of jurisdiction clauses in French law, see H. Gaudemet-Tallon and M.-E. Ancel, *Compétence et exécution des jugements en Europe*, *op. cit.*, no. 166; see also lastly J.-B. Racine, 'Les clauses d'élection de for asymétriques' in *Mélanges en l'honneur du Professeur Bertrand Ancel*, Paris, LGDJ, 2018, p. 1323.

Regulation submits the substantive validity of the choice of court clause to the court petitioned,[120] but establishes certain material criteria relating to the form of the clause. The clause must be concluded:

> '(a) in writing or evidenced with writing;
>
> (b) in a form which accords with practices which the parties have established between themselves; or
>
> (c) in international trade or commerce, in a form which accords with a usage of which the parties are or ought to have been aware and which in such trade or commerce is widely known to, and regularly observed by, parties to contracts of the type involved in the particular trade or commerce concerned.'[121]

The question of compliance with the formal rules imposed by the Brussels Regulation on the choice of court clause arose in the case of the issue of debt securities in the *Profit* judgment.[122] In this case, a German bank had issued debt securities indexed on a credit risk.[123] The prospectus for the securities in question had been approved by the Irish stock exchange authority[124] and the securities were acquired by a UK-based investment firm. This company then sold the securities to the Italian-based company *Profit*. The credit risk was realised, causing the value of the securities to collapse. *Profit* then made various claims (compensation for the loss suffered and nullity of the sale contract) before the Italian court. In this case the attribution clause was inserted not in the issue contract but in the prospectus itself. Therefore, a question arose as to the validity of the clause with regard to the form prescribed by the Brussels I Regulation. The Court of Justice replied that it was sufficient "for the contract signed by the parties when the securities were issued on the primary market to mention acceptance of that clause or to contain an express reference to

---

120 Art. 25(1) of the Brussels Ia Regulation (the Regulation itself, however, provides for a substantive condition: the clause must relate to a specific legal relationship). The consequence of this provision, when confronted with asymmetrical clauses, is that their validity is subject to several laws.

121 Art. 25(1) of the Brussels Ia Regulation.

122 Case C-366/13, *Profit investment*, ECLI:EU:C:2016:282.

123 These are 'credit-linked notes'. The function of these securities is to transfer the risk of a debtor's default, the so-called 'credit event', in this case the debtor of the issuing bank. If the debtor remains solvent, the holder of the debt security will eventually see his capital repaid with interest plus a premium, if the debtor defaults, the debt security loses all its value. On these securities, see T. Bonneau and F. Drummond, *Droit des marchés financiers*, *op. cit.*, no. 145; A. Couret and H. Le Nabasque, *Droit financier*, *op. cit.* On the credit risk, more frequently by financial contract, see *infra*, para. 871.

124 Neither the judgment nor the opinion of the Advocate General indicates whether the securities were admitted to trading on the Irish financial market.

that prospectus".[125] However, the existence of a custom in international trade is also likely to allow compliance with the rules on form.[126] Such a usage, which meets the conditions laid down by the Court of Justice,[127] has been eventually characterised by the Italian Court,[128] so that the clause inserted in a prospectus will appear, in relations between professionals, to remove some of the difficulties.

405. Transmission. In the context of the issuer's liability, an additional difficulty lies in the enforceability of the attribution clause against the holder of the security who is not the original purchaser. This issue could be resolved by subjecting the transmissibility of the clause to the *lex contractus* of the transferred debt: it is the *lex contractus* that determines the transmissibility of the rights and obligations of the contract, including the attributive clause. In the context of the issuance of securities, it would be up to the law of the *negotium* (the *lex societatis* for shares, the law of the contract of issue for debts) to determine its enforceability against the holder of the security. The Court of Justice, once attracted by such an approach,[129] has now backtracked.[130] We will limit ourselves here to two series of observations in relation to the issuance of securities.

406. The first is that the Court of Justice had the opportunity to establish a material rule of favour for share-related clauses. In its *Powell* judgment, it held that a clause inserted in the articles of association could be relied upon against a shareholder who was not one of the founders of the company,[131] even though a dispute between this new shareholder and the company itself was at issue. Litigation relating to defective information in connection with an issue of equity securities may therefore be concentrated at the company's registered office if the articles of association so provide.[132] The scope of this solution could be extended

125 Para. 51 of the *Profit* judgment.

126 If a usage of international trade is characterised, the clause may be valid in form, even if the issue contract does not contain an express reference to the prospectus.

127 See paras. 38 et seq. of the *Profit* judgment.

128 See the note by Mr Quéquigner, *above*.

129 This was one of the meanings attached to the *Tilly Russ* case, which was decided on the basis of a negotiable document of title (in this case a bill of lading). Indeed, the Court of Justice subjected the transmission of the clause to the *lex contractus*. In French perspective, see Cass., civ. 1re, 13 November 2013, no. 13-13586; on the circulation of the clause, see in general H. Gaudemet-Tallon and M.-E. Ancel, *Compétence et exécution des jugements en Europe*, *op. cit.*, no. 170.

130 Case C-543/10, *Refcomp*, ECLI:EU:C:2013:62, para. 34. For a retrospective, see M.-E. Ancel, 'Le champ personnel des clauses d'élection de for' in M. Laazouzi (ed.), *Les clauses attributives de juridiction: de la prévisibilité au désordre*, Paris, Ed. Panthéon-Assas, 2021, pp. 121 et seq.

131 Case C-214/89, *Powell*, ECLI:EU:C:1992:115.

132 S. Lambert, *L'application internationale du droit financier*, *op. cit.*, no. 326. The author considers that an exclusive clause in the articles of association precludes the jurisdiction of foreign shareholders' courts for disputes relating to the company's liability, and gives an overview of the articles of association of French companies whose securities are admitted to trading.

to include issue contracts in the relationship between the bondholder and the company, as they are similar to those between the shareholders and the company on the basis of the articles of association. In the same way that 'the shareholder gives his consent to be bound by all the provisions of the company's articles of association [...] even if he does not agree with some of these provisions or decisions',[133] the bondholder, by acquiring a debt security, is bound by the provisions of the issue contract. Moreover, it is this issue contract that binds the bondholders to the company, and on the basis of which a liability action arises in respect of the defective information provided.

407. The second observation is that the extension of the *Powell* judgement solution to debt securities, which would be coherent, is actually frustrated by the *Profit* judgment. In this judgment, the Court of Justice held that:

> 'A jurisdiction clause contained in a prospectus produced by the bond issuer concerning the issue of bonds may be relied on against a third party who acquired those bonds from a financial intermediary if it is established, which it is for the referring to verify, that (i) that clause is valid in the relationship between the issuer and the financial intermediary, (ii) the third party, by acquiring those bonds on the secondary market, succeeded to the financial intermediary's rights and obligations attached to those bonds under the applicable national law, and (iii) the third party had the opportunity to acquaint himself with the prospectus containing that clause.'[134]

The Court of Justice analyses here debt bonds from the perspective of the law of sale. It takes up previous case law[135] based on the combination of a substantive rule (to be enforceable against third parties, the holder of the security must be the successor of the original contracting party) and a conflict rule (this succession is assessed by the law of the contract of sale, it being observed that the initial clause must be valid in order to be transmitted) which leads to the cumulative application of all assignment contracts, to which the condition relating to knowledge of the prospectus is added.

This analysis leads to two unfortunate results. The first is that it may make it difficult to concentrate the litigation that the issuer wanted to ensure through the attribution clause. The successive contracts of transmission are not of his making, and it is curious that he should suffer the consequences; there is here a split in the freedom-responsibility pairing. Above all, this decision does not take into account the negotiability of the title, the function of which is

133 Para. 19 of the *Powell* judgment.

134 Para. 51 of the *Profit* judgment.

135 See the judgments cited by the Court in para. 33 of the *Profit* judgment: *Tilly Russ*, *Castelleti*, *Coreck*, *Refcomp*, on which, see the presentation of H. Gaudemet-Tallon and M.-E. Ancel, *Compétence et exécution des juges en Europe*, *op. cit.*

precisely to purge any defects affecting the ownership of the title so that its holder succeeds perfectly to the rights of the first purchaser.[136] The second is that it cuts out part of the scope of the issue contract: the procedural means by which the issuer can be sued for contractual liability.[137] These two observations explain why the enforceability of such clauses should be subject to the *lex contractus* of the *negotium* alone.

§ 3. INTERFERENCE WITH THE CONSUMER CONTRACT

408. The Brussels Ia Regulation gives jurisdiction to the courts of the consumer's domicile:

> '[Where (...)] the contract has been concluded with a person who pursues commercial or professional activities in the Member State of the consumer's domicile or, by any means, directs such activities to that Member State or to several States including that Member State, and the contract falls within the scope of such activities.'[138]

This article requires the existence of a contract, a consumer and a form of solicitation. If there is no contract, a consumer will have to sue the issuer in tort: this is the case in the *Kolassa* judgment.[139] The solicitation of the investor, for example, through advertising, or the dissemination by the issuer of the prospectus in the territory where he is domiciled should make it possible to characterise such a direction of activities. This is what the Court of Justice seemed to accept in the *Kolassa* case when it held that the characterisation of a consumer contract was possible.[140] The second condition is the characterisation of the notion of consumer. This issue will be discussed in detail in the context of the law applicable to financial contracts.[141] We will limit ourselves here to affirming the autonomy of the notion of consumer from the point of view of the conflict of laws, and from the point of view of substantive European law. Indeed, the case law considers that the notion of consumer must be

---

136 On the function of negotiability, see *infra*, para. 638.

137 M. Gargantini, 'Prospectus Liability. Competent Courts of Jurisdiction and Applicable Law', *op. cit.*, nos. 19.63 and 19.64.

138 Art. 17(1)(c) of the Brussels Ia Regulation.

139 See *supra*, para. 400. It is arguably precisely because the court of the investor's domicile should have had jurisdiction – without the artifice that the intermediary is the owner of the financial instrument while the investor bears the risk - that the Court of Justice was persuaded to give jurisdiction to the court of the investor's domicile as a forum in tort.

140 See paras. 25-35 of the *Kolassa* judgment. The reason why the Court did not finally accept it was because of the lack of ownership of the financial instrument and, consequently, the lack of a contract with the issuer (see *supra*, para. 400 and *infra*, para. 420).

141 See *infra*, para. 810.

assessed objectively, independently of his knowledge of the sector of activity, by 'referring to the position of that person in a given contract, in relation to the nature and purpose of that contract, and not to the subjective situation of that person'.[142]

The consumer jurisdiction rule thus allows the consumer to sue the issuer at his domicile when the issuer has requested it. It will defeat any choice of court clause.[143] This rule is even likely to concentrate litigation arising from a civil liability action for lack of pre-contractual information before the consumer's court.[144] As Mr d'Avout has observed, it makes it possible to create a dual system of jurisdiction, giving rise to a 'possible concentration of financial litigation between issuers, intermediaries and professional investors [and a] necessary splitting up of the litigation triggered by lay investors litigating in the country of their establishment'.[145] This solution deserves approval in that it maintains a balance between the interest of the issuer and the protection of residents of the place of solicitation.

409. Conclusion of the section. In contractual matters, the solutions of private international law are not identical in terms of conflict of laws and conflict of jurisdictions; one might even be tempted to say that they are reversed. In terms of conflict of laws, the issuer is clearly favoured: the applicable law will be the one designated by him; the presence of a consumer is not likely to hold it in check. The *lex contractus* may, however, be removed from its scope of application in the assessment of the existence of the investor's consent in favour of the law of his residence. On the other hand, as regards the jurisdiction of the courts, the issuer's interests, which lie in the concentration of litigation at its seat, are less protected. First of all, in the case of a consumer, the court of the investor's registered office will have jurisdiction where the consumer has been solicited. This solution, which aims to protect the weaker party, is not surprising, particularly as it is tempered by the existence of a solicitation by the professional. However, it is in the absence of a consumer that the solutions are more surprising. Firstly, the jurisdiction of the defendant's domicile in principle is challenged by the existence of a special contractual forum. In the context of an action for liability for defective information, the *forum* will be determined by the place where the information is disseminated, which serves as the basis for the claim. Secondly, and more importantly, the presence of a choice of court clause will not always defeat the jurisdiction of the contractual forum. Indeed,

---

142 Case C-208/18, *Petruchova*, ECLI:EU:C:2019:825. See especially para. 41 of the *Petruchova* judgment, which is part of the Court's well-established case law (see the judgments cited by the Court).

143 Art. 19 of the Brussels I *bis* Regulation, on which see H. Gaudemet-Tallon and M.-E. Ancel, *Compétence et exécution des jugements en Europe*, *op. cit.*

144 Case C-500/18, *Reliantco investments*, ECLI:EU:C:2020:264, spec. paras. 67–71.

145 L. d'Avout, 'Commercialisation de titres financiers et compétence internationale de proximité', *D.*, 2015, 770.

the rules on the validity and enforceability of the clause are likely to hamper its effectiveness. If it is inserted in the articles of association, it will make it possible, in the case of equity securities, to concentrate disputes at its seat. This solution could usefully be extended, by analogy, to the contract for the issue of debt securities; the Court's current case law nevertheless prohibits this.

SECTION 3. THE SOLUTIONS IN TORT

410. Decisive nature of the solicitation. When the plaintiff articulates his claim from a tortious point of view, the *raison d'être* of the jurisdiction of the country of the place of the damage is to remedy the disturbance that has affected him. This jurisdiction is given additional force when its residents have been the object of a solicitation. Indeed, from an economic point of view, the crossing of borders and the application of another law present a cost,[146] and this cost should be borne by the person at the origin of the solicitation.[147] It justifies the enactment of a comprehensive jurisdiction of the legal system of the place of the crime,[148] which is best placed, both from a jurisdictional and a legislative point of view, to repair the damage.[149] This jurisdiction is nevertheless tempered in two respects, on the judicial level, by the case law of the Court of Justice, which allows the victim to avail himself of the jurisdiction of the courts of the place where the event giving rise to the damage occurred in the case of complex torts, and on the legislative level, by the possibility offered by Article 17 of the Rome II Regulation

---

146 On this question and the means of private persons deployed to limit the uncertainty of the conflict of laws inherent in the crossing of borders, see the reflections of J. Basedow, *The Law of Open Societies*, *op. cit.*, RCADI, t. 360, The Hague, Martinus Nijhoff, 2013, nos. 140 and et seq.

147 This aspect was perfectly expressed by Mr d'Avout: 'Whatever its technical form, commercial action abroad thus entails an immaterial territorial presence, real or only apparent, to which is linked a practically inevitable risk of application of local law. This risk is all the more concrete as the jurisdiction of the local law is often associated with that of the corresponding territorial court (jurisdiction relating to the disturbances resulting from the local action, which may be more widely conceived). The possible jurisdiction of foreign law does not always unfold, if only because of the different ways in which it is perceived by the public. Nevertheless, there is a memorable correlation, which is already present in positive law: that of the act of soliciting the public, the cause and measure of the applicability of local law. When an entrepreneur himself takes the initiative to cross borders for professional reasons, he thereby intentionally makes himself present abroad (*purposeful availment*) and may be confronted with the imperative jurisdiction of the judges and the law of the foreign country.' L. d'Avout, '*L'entreprise et les conflits internationaux de lois*', *op. cit.*, no. 79.

148 Report B. Achinard-Greil, *Lois de police et conflits de juridictions*, thesis, University of Lyon III, 2017, no. 10, which refers to a 'global preponderance'. The author's proposal differs in that this preponderance should be assessed in the context of identifying a *loi de police* that has a strong connection to a state interest (*ibid.*, nos. 355 et seq.).

149 Art. 7(2) Brussels Ia Regulation and Art. 4 Rome II Regulation.

to take into consideration, as factual elements, the rules of safety and conduct of the place where the event giving rise to the damage occurred.

The issuer makes itself 'intentionally present abroad'[150] whenever it solicits its residents. In this sense, as observed by Mr Synvet and Ms Tenenbaum: 'Although solicitation mainly covers canvassing operations, its scope is broader. It includes, in particular, advertising operations of any kind.'[151] This notion of advertising is precisely taken up by the Court of Justice in order to characterise the damage for the purposes of determining international jurisdiction. In the case of a prospectus, notification to the competent administrative authority of the legal system where it is distributed facilitates the characterisation of the solicitation[152]; at the same time, there is no doubt that admission to trading on a local financial market constitutes a form of solicitation. In the absence of a prospectus and the admission of securities to trading, the existence of disclaimers makes it possible to restrict solicitation in a negative way.[153] These observations lead to the view that, in matters of tort, the consistency promoted by the European legislator when characterising concepts for the purposes of determining the competent court and the applicable law should be such as to give global jurisdiction to each legal system within which the dissemination of defective information took place.

411. Localisation of the investor's damage. This global jurisdiction of the troubled legal order is facilitated by the tort solutions of the law of international jurisdiction and conflict of laws: they always depend on the localisation of the damage, and more specifically on the damage suffered by the victim, in this case of the alteration of the investor's decision.[154] The difficulty is that this damage has a ubiquitous nature, which nevertheless only reflects the ubiquitous nature

---

150 L. d'Avout, '*L'entreprise et les conflits internationaux de lois*', *op. cit.*, no. 79.

151 H. Synvet and A. Tenenbaum, 'Financial Instruments', *op. cit.*, no. 59.

152 See *supra*, para. 350.

153 S. Lambert, *L'application internationale du droit financier*, *op. cit.*, no. 158: 'First point: the characterisation of dissemination in the territory: when the information consists of the dissemination of legal or accounting documentation related to the issuer or the financial product and this documentation is filed with the local supervisory authority, there is no doubt that dissemination takes place in the territory. The situation is less clear when the information is not disseminated through formal or official channels. The way in which the information is disseminated is then as important as its content. A typical example is the "disclaimer" when certain information, particularly computerised information, can be seen in the United States. These disclaimers are intended to avoid any interpretation of the information disseminated as an offer for securities or products, or even as financial advice given locally. Similarly, in the Hong Kong Special Administrative Region, the mere fact of maintaining a website in Hong Kong, even when the information provided does not constitute an offer or advice in the Western sense, may be construed as an act of marketing.'

154 See *supra*, para. 376.

of the information disseminated.[155] If upheld, this damage would lead to the jurisdiction of all the legal orders of the investors who acquired securities.[156] This is why the notion of damage could be tempered by the existence of a solicitation.[157] This solution presupposes that the concept of damage used in European private international law be interpreted in the light of the loss suffered by the investor: this appears necessary whenever the event giving rise to liability, in this case the dissemination of defective information, is dissociated from the place where the damage occurred (§ 1). This solution appears in the jurisprudence of the Court of Justice on jurisdiction in matters of tort. It would benefit from being affirmed regardless of the location of the securities (§ 2), and from being extended to the conflict of laws solutions (§ 3).

§ 1. COMPLEX OFFENCES

412. Difficulty of dissociating the event giving rise to liability room the damage. Unfortunately, financial torts cannot be reduced to simple torts whose constituent elements are located in the same legal order. More often than not, the event giving rise to liability takes place in a different territory from the one in which the damage occurs, which makes it necessary to refine the concept of damage by dissociating it from the event giving rise to liability.[158] This distinction has long been difficult in French law because of the wording of the conflict rule, which the Court of Cassation expressed in these terms: 'The law competent to govern liability in tort is the law of the place where the harmful event [fait dommageable]

---

155 See conclusions of Bobeck AG in *Löber*, para. 70: 'In the case of the tort of misrepresentation by means of an allegedly defective prospectus, the harm, in the sense of direct damage against which a person is protected, consists in having taken, on the basis of misleading information, an investment decision which he would not have taken if he had been in possession of the correct information.' Case C-304/17, *Löber*, ECLI:EU:C:2018:701.

156 However, such a solution has already been adopted in a certain context, see *infra*, para. 425.

157 This objective should not lead to altering the qualification, but to limiting its effects by the objective assigned to the rules of jurisdiction. As Professor Quéguiner has written: 'The servant nature of the procedural rule and the objective of the proper administration of justice require that the qualification of jurisdiction be made not before, but after, the qualification of the substance', J.-S. QUÉGUINER, 'Qualification et détermination de la compétence spéciale: l'exemple de la matière contractuelle', *op. cit.*

158 In this sense, the damage resulting from defective information is similar to that resulting from defamation in the press. In both cases, the tort is complex – there is a territorial dissociation between the event giving rise to the damage and the damage – and the damage is plurilocalised in all the legal orders where the defamation took place. However, the major difference lies in the plurality of persons affected by the damage: in the tort of defamation, one person is the victim of defamation, which takes place in several legal orders, whereas in the case of the emission of defective information, all investors experience the consequences of the event giving rise to damage.

occurred'.[159] The ambiguity of such a formulation was clearly apparent in the case of complex torts, since 'the expression "harmful event" is ambivalent: depending on whether one insists on the word "event" – which gives rise to the damage – or "harmful" – in the sense of damage – it may designate two different laws'.[160] The difficulty was avoided in terms of international jurisdiction, since the Court of Justice considered that the tort or delict could be understood as meaning both the event giving rise to the damage and the event of its occurrence, which allowed the victim to bring an action in either court, in favour of the victim.[161] Wishing to adopt this directive in matters of conflict of laws, the Court of Cassation nevertheless refused to establish an 'elective cumulation',[162] i.e. to leave the choice of law to the victim.[163] Such a decision led the French Court to a casuistic approach, criticised by academics.[164] Such a result undoubtedly encouraged the European legislator to adopt a clear definition of the concept of damage.

413. European private international law solution. Indeed, Article 4(1) of the Rome II Regulation gives jurisdiction to the law of the place where the damage occurred[165] and defines the concept as follows: 'damage' means any injury resulting from a harmful event, unjust enrichment, *negotiorum gestio* or

---

159 Cass. civ. 1re, 30 May 1967 (*Kieger*),. This judgment extended a rule developed by the *Lautour* judgment, see Cass. civ., 25 May 1948, on which see B. Ancel and Y. Lequette, *Les grands arrêts de la jurisprudence française de droit international privé*, *op. cit.* comm. no. 19. The latter authors rightly state that 'if there is one decision that deserves to be called a landmark decision, it is undoubtedly the *Lautour* decision' (*ibid.*, no. 1).

160 Mr Libchaber (*Defrénois* 2004. 37894, note under the *Pays-Fourvel* see Cass., civ. 1re, 28 October 2003, no. 00-18.794 and no. 00-20.065.

161 On this famous case law, *Mines de Postasse d'Alsace*, see *infra*, para. 418.

162 This system of resolution comes from German doctrine, see P. Bourel, *Les conflits de lois en matière d'obligations extracontractuelles*, *op. cit.*, no. 84: 'Cumulation here is elective, that is to say that, in German doctrine, the victim has the option of acting according to one or other of the laws which govern the place of the tort.' This has been an undeniable success; Mr Bureau thus observed (*RCDIP*, 2004, 83), that elective cumulation was taken up by the Italian law of 31 May 1995, Art. 62-1, *RCDIP*, 1996, 174; the Tunisian law of 27 November 1998, Art. 70, *RCDIP*, 1999, 382; the Venezuelan law of 6 August 1998, Art. 32, *RCDIP*, 1999, 392; and the German law of 21 May 1999, Art. 40-1, *RCDIP*, 1999, 870.

163 A substantial element that seemed to support the rule established by the Court of Justice in jurisdictional matters.

164 B. Ancel and Y. Lequette, *Les grands arrêts de la jurisprudence française de droit international privé*, *op. cit.*, comm. no. 19, spec. no. 6: 'it is difficult to see the guiding principle which today guides the high court in matters of conflict of laws relating to civil liability in tort. For a long time, it preferred legal certainty and the predictability of solutions to the realism of the settlement of the conflict. Now it prefers realism to certainty, but only in the case of a complex tort'. This case law is still applicable for disputes that occurred before the entry into force of the European legislation on 11 January 2009 (Art. 32 of the Rome II Regulation). Events occurring since then are subject to the Rome II Regulation (Art. 31 of the Regulation).

165 Regardless of the law of the place of the event giving rise to the damage or of the indirect consequences, see Art. 4(1°) of the Rome II Regulation, 'the law applicable to a non-contractual obligation arising out of a tort/delict shall be the law of the country in which

culpa in contrahendo. Such a definition prevents the different conceptions of the concept of damage in the legal orders of the Member States from unduly disturbing the unitary application of the Rome II Regulation.[166] In conjunction with Article 4(1) of the Regulation, this definition also indicates to the court how it is to circumscribe the concept of damage, which is closely linked to the content of the disputed facts,[167] in order to exclude both causal events and indirect damage.[168]

The distinction between the event giving rise to the damage and the damage itself is therefore clearer and has been taken up by European case law on international jurisdiction. When asked whether the expression 'harmful event' should refer to the court of the event giving rise to the damage or to the court of the place where the damage occurred,[169] the Court of Justice refused to decide, allowing the victim to bring the matter before one or the other.[170] This first solution, which favoured the victim, did not, however, resolve all the difficulties, particularly those relating to the place where the damage occurred. In a case where the parties, while agreeing on the place of the causal event, differed on the determination of the place where the damage occurred, the Court stated that this place was 'the place where the event which may

---

the damage occurs, irrespective of the country in which the event giving rise to the damage occurs and irrespective of the country or countries in which the indirect consequences of that event occur'.

166 A. Dickinson, *The Rome II Regulation*, Oxford, OUP, 2008, no. 3.46. Such a distortion was inevitable, in the absence of substantial unification, in the context of the application of the Brussels Convention or the Brussels I Regulation. Thus, in the famous *Fiona Shevill* judgment, the Court of Justice stated in paras. 38 and 39: '(Para. 38) On the other hand, it does not specify the conditions under which the event giving rise to the damage may be regarded as harmful to the victim, or the evidence which the claimant must adduce before the court petitioned in order to enable it to rule on the merits of the claim. (Para. 39) *These questions must therefore be decided solely by the national court seised, applying the substantive law designated by the conflict-of-laws rules of its national law*, provided that such application does not undermine the effectiveness of the Convention.' Italics added.

167 A. Dickinson, *The Rome II Regulation*, *op. cit.*, no. 3.46: 'The provision neatly sidesteps the question whether a particular injury or loss is to be regarded as legally significant, and replaces it with a broad, fact-based concept requiring identification of the consequences arising out of tort/delict [...].'

168 *Ibid.*, no. 4.29-4.30.

169 The rule in the Brussels Convention offered the plaintiff the option of jurisdiction between the defendant's court and 'the court for the place where the harmful event occurred' (Art. 5(3°) of the Brussels Convention. The provision is reproduced identically in the Brussels I Regulation – Art. 5(3°) –, and the Brussels I *bis* Regulation – Art. 7(2°)). This expression of 'harmful event', which originated in French conflict-of-laws case law, was nevertheless ambiguous in the context of complex torts, where the event giving rise to the damage takes place in one country and the damage occurs in another. In these circumstances, the expression '*fait dommageable*' seems to be able to refer alternatively to one or the other country.

170 Case 21-76, *Mines de potasse d'Alsace*, ECLI:EU:C:1976:166.

give rise to liability in tort, delict or quasi-delict resulted in damage'.[171] It then made a clear distinction between the place of the event giving rise to the damage, which it referred to as the causal event, and the place where the damage occurred.[172] Such a definition suggests that, from the point of view of international jurisdiction, the case law concept of damage is perhaps not so far removed from that of injury. This observation is reinforced by the analysis of the location of the 'true seat of the damage' in complex torts where the choice between the law of the place of commission of the tort (the operative event) and the law of the place of the damage is in fact often based on the nature of the damage.[173]

414. Dissociation between '*dommage*' *stricto sensu* and '*préjudice*'. In French liability law, some specialists in the field make a clear distinction between these two concepts:[174]

> '*À proprement parler, le dommage désigne la lésion subie (un fait brut et matériel) appréciée de façon objective au siège de cette lésion; tandis que le préjudice est la conséquence juridique et subjective de la lésion (et est donc un concept juridique) se concrétisant dans les répercussions subjectives du dommage sur la personne et/ou sur les biens de la victime.*'

Such a presentation, which is not adopted by all authors,[175] makes it possible to distinguish between damages 'which are, under certain conditions, constituent elements of civil liability'.[176] It also makes it possible to better understand, from a logical[177] and chronological point of view, the distinction between the harm (damage *stricto sensu*) to a person, property or organisation, and the

---

171 Case C-189/08, *Zuid-Chemie v. Philippo's Mineralenfabriek NV/SA*, ECLI:EU:C:2009:475, para. 26.

172 See *ibid.*: 'the place where the damage occurred cannot be confused with the place where the event which damaged the product itself took place, since this is the place where the causal event occurred. On the other hand, the place of "materialisation of the damage" [...] is the place where the event giving rise to the damage unfolds its damaging effects, i.e. the place where the damage caused by the defective product is actually manifested.'

173 As shown, inter alia, by Mr Bourel's observations on the determination of the competent court in the case of the tort of defamation: 'The victim's home represents, in the case of invasion of privacy committed by the media [...] the real seat of the damage (because of the moral and therefore immaterial nature of the injury).' P. Bourel, 'Du rattachement de quelques délits spéciaux', *RCADI*, vol. 214, The Hague, Martinus Nijhoff, 1989, no. 117. The author considers that these observations can be transposed to legislative competence (*ibid.*).

174 See the authors listed by Mr Tourneau in favour of a dissociation: P. Le Tourneau, 'Responsabilité: généralités' in *Répertoire de droit civil*, Paris, Dalloz, 2009, no. 22; G. Viney, P. Jourdain and S. Carval, *Les conditions de la responsabilité*, *op. cit.*, no. 246-1.

175 G. Viney, P. Jourdain and S. Carval, *Les conditions de la responsabilité*, *op. cit.*, no. 246-1, and the authors cited in note 1.

176 F. Terré *et al.*, *Droit des obligations*, Paris, Dalloz, 2018, no. 920.

177 P. Brun, *La responsabilité civile extracontractuelle*, Paris, LexisNexis, 2018, no. 175.

loss resulting from this harm, which is the only way to establish the damage in terms of civil liability.[178] Moreover, from an international perspective, this distinction allows 'an awareness *of a risk of further fragmentation of the factual elements of the dispute*'.[179] Indeed, in addition to the separate territorial registration of the event giving rise to the damage and the damage in the strict sense, there is the territorial dissociation of the damage and the injury, which must be distinguished from the injury by ricochet.[180]

Finally, in cases where the event, the damage and the injury are all three separate, certain factual elements are likely to be the basis for one or other of the elements constituting liability. The elements which must be the subject of the causal link will then be decisive for the location. This is particularly the case when the issuer's liability for defective information is at issue: the event giving rise to damage takes place in each legal order where the defective information was disseminated, and the investor's loss is located at his home. The solutions developed for complex torts may be excessively favourable to the investor. For this reason, the assessment of the concept of damage should probably be made by reference to the event giving rise to the damage, the dissemination of the defective information, both in terms of jurisdiction and conflict of laws.

§ 2. THE COMPETENT COURT

415. Article 7(2) of the Brussels I *bis* Regulation gives special jurisdiction to the forum of the tort, i.e. 'the court for the place where the harmful event occurred or may occur'. We have seen the reasons why, in relation to the damage

---

178 E. Farnoux, *Les considérations substantielles dans le règlement de la compétence internationale des juridictions*, *op. cit.*, no. 268.

179 *Ibid.* In the case of the issue of defective information, the cause of the damage is the defectiveness of the information, the damage is constituted by the discrepancy between the collective representation of the value of the company and its reality, while the damage is constituted by the alteration of the investor's decision to acquire, sell or retain the issuer's financial securities.

180 Some authors see an illustration of the dissociation between injury and prejudice in the case of vicarious prejudice, in particular following the *Pays Fourvel* judgment (see *supra*, para. 377). Such a presentation seems questionable to us. In this case, French tourists had travelled to Cambodia, where some of them had died following an accident. The survivors sued the travel agency and its insurance company for contractual liability under French law. The victims' relatives also sued the agency and its insurer, but as they were not bound by a contract with the agency, the basis of their action was tort. In this case, the damage in the *strict sense of the term*, the *injury*, had taken place in Cambodia where the victims died. However, such a solution to the conflict of laws is in fact explained less by this dissociation than by the singularity of the ricochet loss, which, in the words of the Cour de cassation, 'finds its source in the damage caused to the victim'. In fact, compensation for vicarious damage can only be paid insofar as the 'primary' damage is compensated. See already in this sense, among others, the observations of Mr Libchaber, note cited above under the *Pays-Fourvel* judgment.

caused to the investor's decision by defective information, the place where the harmful event occurred or is likely to occur should be interpreted in relation to the dissemination of the defective information. This jurisdictional criterion is reflected in the case law of the Court of Justice, even if it is currently limited to a casuistic approach that does not allow for predictable and balanced solutions. This is due to the origin of the position of the Court of Justice (I), and the solution it established in the *Kolassa* judgment (II). The more recent *Effectenbezitters* case law is likely to temper these results when there is an admission to trading (III).

I. The Origin of the Court of Justice's Position

416. The difficulty in determining the place of the damage in matters of issuer liability for defective information stems from the presentation of the loss. The Court of Justice considers that the damage suffered by the investor is not an alteration of his decision, but a variety of 'pure economic loss', a form of exclusively patrimonial harm. However, the Court of Justice has refused to locate pure economic loss to the victim's home, which is conceived as the centre of his property interests. In several decisions,[181] the Court has held that the scope of the provisions allowing an option of jurisdiction must be interpreted strictly, so that the duplication of the option offered by the *Mines de Potasse d'Alsace* judgment[182] does not result in the courts of the defendant's domicile being systematically given jurisdiction. It is in this sense that the Court stated in the *Marinari* judgment that:

> 'Whilst it has thus been recognised that the term 'place where the harmful event occurred' within the meaning of Article 5(3) of the Convention may cover both the place where the damage occurred and the place of the event giving rise to it, that term cannot be construed so extensively as to encompass any place where the adverse consequences can be felt of an event which has already caused damage actually arising elsewhere.'[183]

This solution was reaffirmed in the *Kronhofer* judgment, where the location of the damage was precisely at stake in the context of financial instruments whose value had considerably decreased. In this case, Mr Kronhofer, who was domiciled in Austria, had been approached by a financial investment consultancy firm established in Germany. By telephone, the company encouraged him to invest a significant amount of money in financial contracts

---

181 Rendered under the Brussels Convention, but whose solution is transposable to the Brussels I *bis* Regulation.

182 Case 21/76, *Mines de Potasse d'Alsace*, ECLI:EU:C:1976:166.

183 Case C-364/93, *Marinari*, ECLI:EU:C:1995:289, para. 14, reproduced in Case C-168/02, *Kronhofer v.Maier and others*, ECLI:EU:C:2004:364, para. 19.

for call options.[184] After concluding these contracts on the London Stock Exchange on behalf of Mr Kronhofer, the intermediaries informed him that the transaction had resulted in the loss of part of the sum he had transferred to them. It is in this context that the Court of Justice again refused to consider that the harmful event could be located at the "centre of his wealth", which is most often his home. In other words, a mere pecuniary loss does not allow the claimant to avail himself of the jurisdiction of the courts of his domicile; only the location of the causal event and the damage are relevant.

417. The solution of these judgments, handed down in financial matters, does not seem to us to be fully transposable to the issue of issuer liability. Indeed, the *Marinari* judgment related to a dispute concerning a promissory note, i.e. a variety of commercial paper. The issue was therefore very different from the liability of issuers in securities matters. The solution of the dispute is all the more explained in *Marinari* because in the case of a commercial paper, the issue of payment is fundamental, justifying in our opinion not only the jurisdiction of the law of payment in this matter, but also the jurisdiction of the court of the place where payment was refused.[185] The *Kronhofer* judgment concerns the liability of the financial intermediary. The question could be similar to the one considered here if it had been argued that the intermediary's solicitation of the investor constituted the event giving rise to liability,[186] and/or that the intermediary's partial or defective information had determined the investment and constituted the victim's actual loss. In the latter case, the refusal to establish the jurisdiction of the court of the defendant's domicile could have been analogous to the liability of the issuer, since in both cases it is a question of the influence that the Court accepts to give to the harm of alteration of the decision in the determination of the damage. In any event, the judgment is disappointing in that the absence of solicitation by Mr Kronhofer, combined with the aggressive canvassing practice of cold calling by German companies, is a circumstance that would have deserved to be discussed in particular with regard to the opportunity for the plaintiff to avail himself of the courts of his domicile.[187]

---

184 The Court of Justice notes that these financial contracts are highly speculative (*Kronhofer* judgment, para. 6).

185 On the importance of the law of payment in relation to bills of exchange, see *infra*, para. 623.

186 See in this sense E. Farnoux, *Les considérations substantielles dans le règlement de la compétence internationale des juridictions*, *op. cit.*, no. 293.

187 This was not lost on the Advocate General, para. 46 of his opinion. The existence of a cold call should, in our view, have triggered the jurisdiction of the local courts. This solution is the opposite of the one adopted by the American judges in the *cold calling* case, i.e. the solicitation of investors domiciled in the United States, which had considered that such a practice triggered the application of American stock exchange legislation, in particular the applicability of the famous Rule 10b-5, giving jurisdiction to the SEC, see *infra*, para. 838.

II. The Kolassa *Judgment*

The Court of Justice has, however, had the opportunity to develop solutions from the point of view of the court's jurisdiction in matters of tort where the dissemination of defective information by the issuer was at issue in three successive judgments, *Kolassa*, *Löber*, and *Vereniging van Effectenbezitters* (hereinafter *Effectenbezitters*). The *Löber* judgment clarifies the solutions of the *Kolassa* judgment in cases of issuer liability for the dissemination of a prospectus relating to debt securities not admitted to trading, while the *Effectenbezitters* judgment relates to a liability action against a listed issuer for dissemination of false information provided independently of a prospectus.

418. The Court's reasoning. In *Kolassa* the issue was the liability of an issuer, *Barclays*, for defective information contained in a prospectus which the issuer had notified to the Austrian authorities for dissemination on their territory.[188] An Austrian investor, who was not the owner of the security,[189] sought to invoke the jurisdiction of the court of his domicile. In this judgment, the Court of Justice refused to consider that the distribution of the prospectus in Austria was sufficient to locate the event giving rise to the offence there. Indeed, it was because of 'the place where the damage materialised' in Austria that the Court agreed to base the jurisdiction on the courts of the defendant's domicile. Two elements combined seem to have motivated such a solution: on the one hand, the fact that the account held by the investor and on which 'the damage is directly realised'[190] was held by an intermediary established in Austria, and on the other hand, the fact that *Barclays* had nevertheless 'distributed'[191] its prospectus in Austria.

This reasoning does not meet with our support. The Court of Justice begins by recalling that the concept of 'harmful event' should be interpreted strictly (because of the principle of jurisdiction of the defendant's court), and should be qualified independently (because of the diversity of the domestic laws of the Member States). It states that this category is also subsidiary, and 'includes any claim which seeks to establish the liability of a defendant and which is not related to "matters relating to a contract"'.[192] The Court of Justice then reiterates its *Kronhofer* case law,[193] and recalls that the mere pecuniary loss is

---

188 On the notification procedure necessary for the mutual recognition of administrative authorisations, see *supra*, para. 129.

189 This excluded the contractual qualification, see *supra*, para. 400.

190 *Kolassa* judgment, para. 55.

191 *Ibid.*, para. 56, although the Court notes beforehand that the causal event, i.e. the defective information contained in the prospectus, cannot as such be located at the victim's seat. The notification of the prospectus to the Austrian authorities is therefore only a factor contributing to the localisation of the damage.

192 Para. 44 of the *Kolassa* judgment.

193 On which see *supra*, para. 418.

not sufficient to trigger the jurisdiction of the courts of the claimant's domicile, but that the causal event or the materialisation of the damage must be located there, and that the criterion used must be in line with the objective of the Regulation.

419. Weaknesses in the characterisation of the causal event. The first weakness of the judgment is that it considers the causal event to be the breach of its disclosure obligations,[194] whereas it is also, and indissociably, the dissemination of the information in the investor's territory through which the issuer wished to solicit the Austrian public.[195] This can be seen even more clearly by reasoning *a contrario*: if Mr Kolassa had not been aware of the defective information that prompted him to acquire the disputed certificates, he would not have acquired them; *Barclays*' breach of its obligation to provide accurate and truthful information would have been irrelevant to him. However, the dissemination did take place in Austria through actions attributable to the issuer: notification of the Austrian authorities of the prospectus, then dissemination of the prospectus through Austrian intermediaries.[196]

420. Incorrect characterisation of the damage. The second weakness of the judgment is that it analyses the materialisation of the damage according to its interpretation of the *Marinari-Kronhofer* jurisprudence. Thus, it states that 'the said damage is realised directly on a bank account of this claimant with a bank established in the jurisdiction of these courts'. This statement, which seems to have the sole purpose of giving jurisdiction to the court of the investor's domicile, should be rejected. Firstly, it ignores the real damage, which is the alteration of the investor's decision; such damage is necessarily located at his home, where the decision was thought out and taken.[197] Secondly, it leads to a futile headlong rush to the location of securities.[198] Not only are the securities not located *a priori* with the direct intermediary,[199] and are most often located with the central depository,[200] but their location is irrelevant to the loss suffered by the investor. The Court of Justice seems to see this in the *Universal Music*[201]

---

194 Para. 53 of the *Kolassa* judgment.

195 This was the opinion of the Advocate General, whose conclusions (see para. 67) were unfortunately not followed.

196 On the distribution of a prospectus approved by a competent authority, see *supra*, paras. 347 et seq.

197 One could consider that the alteration of the decision is manifested by the movement order. However, the defective information may also have the effect of pushing the investor to keep the securities already acquired. In this case, it is clear that the decisional damage is necessarily located in the investor's home.

198 See *supra*, para. 377.

199 Unless he is the issuer and keeps the register at home in the case of *depositary receipts*.

200 See *infra*, paras. 648 et seq.; see also the desirable location *infra*, paras. 757 et seq.

201 Para. 37 of the *Universal* judgment, Case C-12/15, *Universal Music International Holding BV v.Michael Tétreault Schilling and others*, ECLI:EU:C:2016:449.

and *Löber*[202] judgments when it considers that the bank account by means of which the acquisition of the securities took place cannot, on its own, establish the jurisdiction of the forum of the tort.

421. ***Forum actoris.*** It may well be considered that the damage of alteration of the decision leads to the establishment of a real *forum actoris*; it is opposed to the objective of predictability of the regulation which aims to 'strengthen the legal protection of persons established in the Union', which implies that the defendant can 'reasonably foresee [the court] before which he may be sued'.[203] If the Court is nevertheless genuinely opposed to such a move, it would be sufficient to confront this damage with this objective, and to consider that it should only be deemed to be located at the investor's domicile when it has been effectively solicited,[204] which translates for example into the local notification of the prospectus.[205] In the latter case, as the Court of Justice itself writes:

> 'Since the issuer of a certificate which does not fulfil its legal obligations regarding the prospectus must, when deciding to have the prospectus relating to that certificate notified in other Member States, expect that insufficiently informed operators domiciled in those Member States will invest in that certificate and suffer the damage.'[206]

202 Paras. 28–31 of the *Löber* judgment, Case C-304/17, *Löber*, ECLI:EU:C:2018:701.

203 And for 'the claimant to easily identify the court he can seize', see para. 56 of the *Kolassa* judgment.

204 Under US law, a simple telephone call from the offeror is equivalent to a solicitation of the investor and the application of US law, *Europe and Overseas Commodity Traders, SA v. Banque Paribas London* 147 F 3d 118, 129 (2d Cir 1998).

205 On which see *supra*, para. 131. In the *Kolassa* judgment, solicitation was characterised by the steps taken by the issuer with the Austrian authorities (notification of the prospectus) and intermediaries. In the *Kronhofer* judgment, the solicitation was manifested even more directly by the aggressive canvassing to which Mr Kronhofer was subjected, which actually constituted the causal event of the financial intermediary's liability. In both cases, the solicitation of the investor should have led to the jurisdiction of the plaintiff's courts on the basis of the causal event.
This criterion has already been used by the French courts, for example by the Paris Court of Appeal when it considered that the authorisation to market shares in a Luxembourg fund in France constituted the causal event on which the jurisdiction of the French courts was based under Art. 5(3°) of the Brussels I Regulation. In this sense, we deeply regret the cassation of the judgment on this point, see Cass. com., 3 June 2014, no. 12-18012.

206 Para. 56 of the *Kolassa* judgment; in the same sense, see para. 35 of the *Lober* judgment. One wonders whether a slightly different factual situation would have allowed the Court of Justice to rectify its case law. Let us keep the facts of the *Kolassa* judgment, and simply modify the location of the intermediary's establishment, which would then be established in Germany. In this case, the prospectus is still distributed at the investor's home, but the investor acquires the securities through an intermediary established in Germany: the tracking account is therefore managed by the German establishment. In this case, the Court of Justice, if it wished to accept the jurisdiction of the courts of the plaintiff's domicile, would have to accept that the solicitation of the investors constitutes the causal event of the damage suffered, and/or that the damage suffered by the investor relates to the alteration of his decision. Such a factual situation would allow the Court to get rid of the materialisation

As it stands, this circumstance of the violation of legal obligations is not sufficient to establish the jurisdiction of the tort courts. It is possible that this situation will change if the author of the defective information can be shown to have had fraudulent intent. Indeed, in this case, the *Dieselgate* case law could be extended analogously.[207] This case involved the provision of defective information by a car manufacturer about a vehicle illegally equipped by its manufacturer with software that manipulated exhaust emissions data. The court granted the victims *forum actoris* on the grounds that:

> 'By knowingly contravening the statutory requirements imposed on it, such a manufacturer must anticipate that damage will occur at the place where the vehicle in question has been purchased by a person who could legitimately expect that the vehicle was compliant with those requirements and who subsequently realises that the vehicle is defective and of lower value.'[208]

Admittedly, in certain respects, this solution seems to be unadaptable: in matters of defective information relating to securities, the damage suffered, qualified by the Court as purely pecuniary, is always deemed not to be capable of founding the jurisdiction of the tort courts. However, the *forum actoris* established by the *Dieselgate* case law can be explained precisely by the fraudulent conduct of the car manufacturer. An inaccurate prospectus does not necessarily imply deceptive intent on the part of the author. If, however, it is proven that the information in question was provided intentionally in a fraudulent manner in order to siphon off the savings of residents, the *Diselgate* case law could be extended here. There is nevertheless a certain confusion in this case law as to the function pursued by civil liability, which seems to shift from the reparation of damage to the repression of the perpetrator of fraud, a repression which traditionally falls under criminal law. This is all the more apparent since, in the case of deliberately misleading information relating to securities admitted to trading, the authors of misleading information may be held criminally liable on the basis of market manipulation.[209]

422. Partial obsolescence of the system of jurisdiction. Moreover, the implicit preference of the Court of Justice for the criterion of the solicitation undoubtedly shows the obsolescence, in these cases, of the *ratio legis* of the jurisdiction of principle of the Brussels I bis Regulation: to make the cost of the internationality weigh on the plaintiff, even though it is he who was initially solicited by the

of the damage by the criterion of the location of the securities, and consequently, to spare itself the unconvincing casuistry in which it has sometimes been locked, and which has often been denounced.

[207] Case C-343/19, *Verein für Konsumenteninformation v. Volkswagen AG*, ECLI:EU:C:2020:534.

[208] *Ibid.*, para. 37.

[209] See *infra*, para. 520.

defendant.[210] In reality, the Court of Justice does not wish to transpose the *Mines de Potasse d'Alsace* case law to financial torts, as it systematically results in the jurisdiction of the court of the plaintiff's domicile.[211] In financial matters, it seems to feel obliged to do so only when all the elements constituting liability are located there: the event giving rise to the damage and the actual damage,[212] unless it is to be considered that, 'for the alleged damage to have a localising value, it is necessary to be able to justify the specific causal link which unites it to the event giving rise to the damage which occurred in a third country'.[213] Finally, it should be noted that the *Löber* judgment adds to the *Kolassa* judgment a condition for the opening of the tort forum: it is necessary that 'the other particular circumstances of the situation also contribute to conferring jurisdiction on the said courts'.[214] This gives rise to a form of cluster of indicators relating to the characterisation of the damage, manifesting a 'pointillist methodology'[215] relating to the opening of the tort forum.

This methodology can lead to an unexpected result: for example, in cases where a resident invests through a securities account held by a foreign intermediary after a foreign issuer's prospectus has been circulated locally; as a victim of defective information, this resident cannot then rely on the jurisdiction of the court of the event giving rise to the loss – that of his domicile, as the prospectus was circulated on his territory – or of the court of the place of the loss – that of his domicile, the place of his investment decision.

III. The Influence of Admission to Trading

423. Critical analysis of the solution adopted in case of admission of securities to trading. In *Effectenbezitters*, a Dutch issuer, whose securities were admitted to trading in London and Frankfurt, was sued for defective information by a Dutch shareholders' association. The Court of Justice held in this judgment that the objective of foreseeability of the Regulation does not allow the place where the

---

210 On the *ratio legis* of the principle of jurisdiction, see D. Bureau and H. Muir Watt, *Droit international privé*, vol. 1, 4th ed., Paris, PUF, 169 (three *ratio legis*, one of which is economic in nature). On a desirable evolution of the regulation on this issue, see L. d'Avout, 'Centralisation du contentieux indemnitaire contre les sociétés cotées en Europe (le reflux du *forum actoris*)', *RCDIP*, 2021, 536, spec. pp. 543 et seq.

211 Opinion of Advocate General Maciej Spzunar in Case C-12/15, *Universal Music*, ECLI:EU:C:2016:449, paras. 38–39.

212 The Court may have been influenced by other complex torts, such as press torts; however, financial torts present themselves as the symmetry of press torts. In the *Fiona Shevill* case, there is one plaintiff and a multitude of defendants. In these circumstances, it was tempting to propose locating all the damages in the victim's home: this allows for the centralisation of litigation, but also favours the victim. However, the opposite is true here: there is a multitude of claimants, but only one defendant.

213 L. d'Avout, *D.*, 2016, p. 2025, note on the *Universal* judgment cited above.

214 Para. 36 of the *Löber* judgment.

215 H. Muir Watt, see note above, *RCDIP*, 2019, p. 145.

damage materialises to be taken as 'the investment account used to purchase the securities listed on the stock exchange in another State' because 'the criteria relating to the domicile and location of the shareholders' accounts do not enable the issuer to anticipate the determination of the international jurisdiction of the courts before which it might be sued'.[216] The Court considers that:

> 'In the case of a listed company such as that at issue in the main proceedings, only the jurisdiction of the courts of the Member States in which that company has complied, for the purposes of its listing on the stock exchange, with the statutory reporting obligations can be established on the basis of the place where the damage occurred. It is only in those Member States that such a company can reasonably foresee the existence of an investment market and incur liability.'[217]

The motivation is puzzling. The legal obligations to advertise for *the purpose of listing* are of two kinds: prospectus, as listing on the stock exchange requires in principle a public offer,[218] and periodic obligations, which are made necessary by the admission.[219] In the case of the prospectus, the legal requirements are not necessarily provided at the place of listing; indeed, in the case of a listing of equity securities, they can only be submitted to the authority of the issuer's registered office.[220] Indeed, the authority of the place of listing, if it is notified of the prospectus, is not the authority responsible for its supervision.[221] This solution, which is inappropriate in the context of the designation of the competent administrative authority, is given a curious extension here, unless one considers that notification of the prospectus to the authority of the place of listing is a 'legal obligation for the purposes of listing' and makes it possible to establish the jurisdiction of local courts. The latter interpretation would be particularly welcome in the circumstances; however, it is not naturally deduced from the reasoning of the Court of Justice.

In the case of periodic disclosure requirements arising from admission to trading, the solution is different: the competent authority for the filing of such information, governed by the *lex societatis*, is that of the trading venue.[222] However, the Transparency Directive, which is the source of these periodic obligations, excludes from its scope units in collective investment funds and exempts certain issuers of debt securities.[223] The financial market authority may

---

216 Para. 34 of the judgment *Effectenbezitters*, Case C-709/19, ECLI:EU:C:2021:377. The argument is highlighted by the Advocate General, paras. 32–36.

217 *Ibid.*, para. 35.

218 For exceptions, see *supra*, para. 372.

219 See *supra*, paras. 342 et seq.

220 See *supra*, para. 351.

221 See *supra*, para. 352.

222 See *supra*, paras. 342 et seq.

223 Arts. 1 and 8 of the Transparency Directive. The case of public authority or central bank issuers is also subject to a possible exemption.

thus not have received any 'legal notice' for listing purposes on the basis of the periodic requirements. The material scope of application of the Transparency Directive, which may be relevant for determining the circumstances in which periodic information must be provided, is not relevant for determining the competent courts for civil liability. From the point of view of the rule of jurisdiction, this solution may have the effect of depriving the victim of the forum of the tort. The latter then moves from indeterminacy to non-existence.

This means that the Court of Justice goes astray when it bases the characterisation of the tort on the legal publicity resulting from the prospectus and transparency regulations. The purpose of these regulations is to designate a competent administrative authority for the purpose of controlling a document that is a condition for the marketing of securities in the context of already harmonised European legislation. If the Court had wished to rely on the substantive law in question, it was its *objective* that should have been observed, which would have led, as the Advocate General had stated, to giving jurisdiction to the court of the investor's place of business, since the purpose of these information requirements is to protect his consent by informing his decision-making.[224] It was therefore sufficient to amend the solution, which the Court considered excessive in the light of the objective of predictability of the regulation, by taking into consideration the event giving rise to the damage, i.e. the existence of a solicitation. The solutions outlined above for the absence of admission to trading remain equally relevant here. This should come as no surprise: the constituent elements of civil liability for defective information are irrelevant to admission to trading. On the other hand, admission to trading has a significant impact on the criminal liability of the author of the information, which may then be incurred on the basis of market manipulation.[225]

If the Court wished to concentrate the litigation at the place of listing, as is probably the case, did it do so correctly? The argument could, to some extent, have been admissible in the name of the principle of foreseeability dear to the Brussels I *bis* Regulation. As the Advocate General concluded in *Effectenbezitters*, when the issuer admits its securities to a foreign financial market, it 'implicitly accepts that it could be sued outside its domicile'.[226] This explains why such a place may appear, at first sight, to be a middle way between the jurisdiction of the place of the issuer and that of the investor's domicile.

424. For a return to common law ('*droit commun*'). However, the place of listing has no direct link with either the event or the damage. The latter has

224 Para. 27 of the Advocate General's Opinion.

225 See *infra*, para. 520.

226 Para. 30 of the Advocate General's Opinion. The expression 'acceptance' is clumsy: the court of the place of the tort does not have to be accepted by the defendant in order to have jurisdiction; at most, it can be said that the jurisdiction of this court is foreseeable for the issuer once it has admitted its securities there.

nothing to do with admission to trading, even though the damage may affect the listing.[227] In our view, there is confusion between the elements constituting civil and criminal liability. If damage is inflicted on the price determination mechanism, i.e. on the financial market itself, market abuse legislation will take care of the criminal punishment of the perpetrators of this disturbance[228]; the pre-eminent competence of the legal order of the financial market is only triggered when the protection of the mechanism it has instituted is directly affected. On the other hand, it seems to us that the *raison d'être* of the forum of torts is to give jurisdiction to the legal order which, having suffered damage, has an interest in seeing its rules of conduct respected and its system of reparation observed. It follows that the correct characterisation of the harmful act is to be sought in the constituent elements of the civil liability in question.

From the perspective of civil liability of the issuer for defective information, the relevant criterion is not the place where legal publicity must take place, but the place where the issuer has solicited investors; publicity – legal or commercial – is only one element of characterisation of this solicitation. The admission of securities to trading is the ultimate solicitation of investors from the place of listing; it should not be possible to avoid the jurisdiction of the courts of that place to remedy the damage caused by misleading information. This is true even more so when the securities listed there are not legally advertised.

To this first tort forum should nevertheless be added all those where a prospectus has been notified to the local administrative authority, according to the schemes implemented by the Prospectus Regulation, given that each of these disseminations is the means for the issuer to solicit a new public. The existence of an admission to trading in a single jurisdiction should not preclude the tort jurisdictions of these other jurisdictions which, foreseeable for the issuer, have an indisputable legitimacy to judge these disputes, and probably even more so given that the jurisdiction of their administrative authorities for the purpose of prospectus control has been set aside.

The solicitation criterion is the traditional illustration of the freedom-responsibility pair: the issuer is free not to seek to collect savings in other legal systems; if it does so, it must be able to be constrained by the competent local jurisdiction.

---

227 In order to realise the inappropriateness of the solutions which the jurisdiction of the court of the place of listing leads to, it is sufficient to refer to the *Profit* judgment where such a criterion would have given jurisdiction to the Irish courts, which are completely unrelated to the dispute at issue between the German issuer and the Italian investor.

228 On this argument, which also explains why the law of the financial market is not in itself relevant to govern the civil liability of the author of defective information, see *infra*, para. 429 On the repression of market abuse, see *infra*, para. 520.

§ 3. THE APPLICABLE LAW

425. Common law interpretation guideline. Article 4 of the Rome II Regulation applies to civil liability the law of the country where the damage occurs. As in the case of jurisdiction, the damage, the alteration of the investor's decision, always takes place at his domicile. Such a characterisation of the damage has the disadvantage of subjecting the issuer to the application of laws that are strictly unforeseeable for him. Two solutions are possible to temper this result; they have in common that they go against the recent trend in private international tort law to favour the damage over the event giving rise to it.

The first is to make use of Article 17 of the Rome II Regulation in order to assess fault according to the law of the place 'where the event giving rise to liability occurred', i.e. the place of the operative event. In the case under consideration here, this place is the place where the defective information was disseminated, which can be interpreted as the place of the issuer's domicile, or, where applicable, as the place where the issuer solicited the residents. It is as if the law applicable to the conditions of liability, subject to the law of the event giving rise to the liability, and the law applicable to the compensation for the damage, subject to the law of the place where the damage occurred, were dissociated.[229] This dissociation nevertheless takes place under the auspices

---

229 Defending such a dissociation, see lastly J. Knestch, 'La réparation du dommage extracontractuel en droit international privé' in *Mélanges en l'honneur du professeur Bertrand Ancel*, Paris, LGDJ, 2018, pp. 979 et seq. The proposal is attractive, and could be implemented by a rule symmetrical to that instituted by Article 17 of the Rome II Regulation leading to the consideration of the liability regime of the victim's domicile (see in this sense Recital 33 of the Rome II Regulation, on which see *ibid.*; p. 986). However, does this not reflect the difficulty of locating tort liability in a single place? The author perfectly underlines the stakes of the underlying legal policy decision: 'Do the levels of compensation practised in a country reflect societal choices which must be acquired by its nationals as soon as they travel abroad? Or, on the contrary, should one submit to a certain extent to differences in the calculation of damages on the grounds that one has taken the risk, by venturing outside national borders, of being injured in a foreign country and being compensated according to local rules' (*ibid.*, p. 992). Three counter-arguments can nevertheless be raised. The first is the principle of private international law according to which it is for the law establishing a rule to determine the consequences of its violation (*Widow Moreau* judgment, on which see *supra*, para. 302). There is nevertheless a very strong logical link here which extends even beyond purely private conflicts of law. This can undoubtedly be seen in the recent *Milivojević* judgment of the Court of Justice (see *infra*, para. 835), where the Court of Justice did not take a very positive view of the Croatian national law's desire to attach civil consequences to the violation of a European administrative law (in this sense, the note under the judgment of Mr d'Avout, see *infra*, para. 835). The second, which is close to the first, relates to the difficulties inherent in the breakdown of the law: certain legal systems provide for flexible conditions for the implementation of liability, to which a less advantageous regime corresponds; conversely, other legal systems are especially careful about the causal link and attach a more vigorous regime against the wrongdoer. It should be added here that the causal link is central to the implementation of liability on the financial markets (see J. Prorok, *La responsabilité sur les marchés financiers*, *op. cit.*, Part 1). The proposed

of the law of the place of the damage alone, and only if the competent court considers it necessary.

The second solution is more direct and consists in interpreting the concept of damage according to the place of the event giving rise to it. It has two advantages: on the one hand, the application of rules from the same law to the conditions of liability and to the regime which follows from it and, on the other hand, the bringing together of the *forum* and the *jus*, i.e. the institution of a global jurisdiction of the legal system of the event giving rise to the damage. Indeed, a similar solution is likely to be adopted in the field of international jurisdiction.[230]

It should be added here that when the solicitation is made by the admission of securities to a financial market, it will have the same consequence as in jurisdictional matters and will entail the application of the law of the market to the tort liability of the issuer.[231] Whenever the issuer nevertheless disseminates its prospectus in other jurisdictions as a result of a new issue on that financial market, the latter's laws will be likely to apply to the issuer's local liability, thus placing the cost of internationality on the issuer. These observations lead to the rejection of doctrinal proposals to apply the law of the issuer's registered office to its liability, either because liability would be an accessory to the legal obligation to disclose and the same law should therefore be applied to it,[232] or

---

dissociation risks breaking the coherence of the whole tort law. The third is specific to the links between damage as a connecting factor in conflict of laws and conflict of jurisdiction. Despite the differences in objectives, the Brussels I bis and Rome II Regulations in many cases offer the opportunity for global jurisdiction to the legal system where the damage occurs. The proposal precisely creates an interference with the jurisdiction of what becomes in matters of liability a real 'preponderant', 'reference' legal order. Comp. O. Boskovic, 'Réflexions sur le dommage en tant que facteur de rattachement en droit international privé' in *Mélanges en l'honneur de Bertrand Ancel*, *op. cit.*, pp. 263 et seq.

230 See *supra*, paras. 417 et seq.

231 This solution has already been proposed in doctrine, see H. Kronke, *Capital markets and conflict of laws*, *op. cit.*, p. 310. It is also this law that will apply to 'the rules of safety and conduct in force at the place and on the day when the event giving rise to liability occurred' (Art. 17 of the Rome II Regulation). On this issue, see M. Gargantini, 'Prospectus Liability. Competent Courts of Jurisdiction and Applicable Law', *op. cit.*, no. 19. 37.

232 W.-G. Ringe and A. Hellgardt, 'The International Dimension of Issuer Liability – Liability and Choice of Law from a Transatlantic Perspective', *op. cit.*
France has adopted such a solution for the liability of credit rating agencies (Arts. L. 544-4 and L. 544-5 of the Monetary and Financial Code), which, combined with the reference to national law made by Art. 69 and Art. 35(4) of Regulation (EU) No 462/2013 of the European Parliament and of the Council of 21 May 2013 on credit rating agencies, applies the law of the agency's registered office to its liability for its rating. While the question of liability for defective information does not arise in the same terms when issued by a CRA (the latter does not correlatively solicit the recipients of the information), the solution is a source of criticism, on which see M. Audit, 'Aspects internationaux de la responsabilité des agences de notation', *RCDIP*, 2011, pp. 581 et seq. and D.J. Verheij, *Credit rating agency liability in Europe. Rating the combination of EU and national law in rights of redress*, The Hague, Eleven International Publishing, 2020.

because a 'country of origin' principle would give it jurisdiction.[233] We will deal with both approaches together, since they lead to the same result, with the same means, and therefore incur the same criticism.

426. Rejection of the law of the statutory seat. Some authors propose to apply the law of the issuer to liability because it allows the linking of 'duties and liability'[234] to disclosure requirements that serve to improve corporate governance. However, if the duties in question are, for the authors, derived from financial market law, the latter would generally retain its application by virtue of the law of the statutory seat. It is true that the *lex societatis* has jurisdiction over the governance of the company.[235] However, the authors seem to misunderstand the function of disclosure requirements, the function of *lex societatis* in financial law and the configuration of conflicts of laws in relation to liability.

The main function of disclosure requirements is not corporate governance: if this were the case, it would be sufficient to disseminate information only to the shareholders and not to the public at large. It is of course a function of protection of future purchasers that these obligations pursue.[236] Furthermore, the law of the registered office is only applicable to disclosure requirements insofar as it is deemed to be equivalent to the law of the financial market, in order to limit the accumulation of disclosure requirements.[237] Moreover, even in intra-European relations, the competent authority for approving the prospectus is not necessarily that of the registered office.[238] The authors also misunderstand the configuration of the conflict of laws in matters of liability, where it is not a question of resolving a combination of laws, but of selecting the applicable law in a situation where several laws are in competition. Contrary to what the authors suggest, qualifying the issuer's liability as ancillary to the issuer's duties does not necessarily lead to the application of

---

[233] R. Gaspard, *La reconnaissance mutuelle en droit bancaire et financier*, *op. cit.*

[234] W.-G. Ringe and A. Hellgardt, 'The International Dimension of Issuer Liability -Liability and Choice of Law from a Transatlantic Perspective', *op. cit.*

[235] If it is true that the *lex societatis* applies to liability, it is only in cases of intra-corporate liability: in this sense it applies to the liability of the body in internal relations. See in this sense H. Kronke, 'Capital markets and conflict of laws', *op. cit.*, p. 312: 'Generally speaking, having the *lex societatis* govern liability for incorrect disclosure appears to be justified only in cases of intra-corporate litigation, i.e. if officers or shareholders of a corporation abuse their powers and violate the fiduciary duties owed to (other) shareholders by inducing them to make (further) investments on the basis of incorrect information.' The author also sees in the application of the law of the issuer a desire to put all investors on an equal footing from the point of view of liability, whereas in his mind 'I do not see a need to treat investors on different markets equally' (*ibid.*, p. 311). See by the same author, who is very critical of the analysis in terms of 'corporate governance', *Liability (Capital Market)*, *op. cit.*, p. 1135.

[236] See *supra*, para. 346.

[237] See *supra*, para. 345.

[238] See *supra*, para. 355.

the issuer's law.[239] The argument is even less convincing when they propose to apply such a rule through the exception clause of the Rome II Regulation, explaining that since the specific issue of issuer liability has not been addressed by the Regulation, it is legitimate to subvert the meaning of Article 4(3) of the Rome II Regulation.[240] This ignores the very meaning of a common law, which is intended to cover the most diverse situations when they do not fall within the scope of any special text.

427. Rejection of a special conflict rule designating the law of the regulated market. The introduction of a special conflict rule in the Rome II Regulation has been proposed by some German scholars.[241] The authors advocate the application of a single law to all 'financial torts',[242] ranging from misrepresentation in the prospectus to market abuse. This law is the law of the regulated market on which the securities have been admitted to trading.

The material scope of application of such a rule is open to criticism for several reasons. Firstly, it is difficult to understand why the authors have restricted such a rule to regulated markets, even though the illicit behaviour targeted, from inaccurate information in prospectuses to market abuse, may well affect other financial markets such as MTF and OTF. Secondly, and much more problematically, 'financial crimes' are too heterogeneous to be brought together in a sufficiently synthetic category to be governed by the law of the market: the purpose of the regulation of market abuse is to protect the trading platform itself, not investors. Thirdly, such a rule results in dissociating two comparable situations from the point of view of the elements constituting liability: defective information disseminated when the securities are not admitted to trading and when they are admitted to trading. Moreover, even in the case where the prospectus is used in the context of a regulated market, the application of the law of the financial market leads to a confusing result when the public solicited is distinct from the one where the financial securities are

---

239 The confusion created by these authors is not unique to them it can be found among others who propose to apply the law of the country of origin, see for example R. Gaspard, *La reconnaissance mutuelle en droit bancaire et financier*, *op. cit.*

240 W.-G. Ringe and A. Hellgardt, 'The International Dimension of Issuer Liability - Liability and Choice of Law from a Transatlantic Perspective', *op. cit.*, p. 55.

241 M. Lehmann, 'Proposal for a special rule in the Rome II Regulation for financial crimes', *op. cit.*

242 German Council for Private International Law, Special Commission 'Financial Market Law', Resolution of 31 March 2012, *RCDIP*, 2012, 679: 'The law applicable to a non-contractual obligation arising out of unlawful conduct on the financial market is the law of the country in which the financial instrument concerned is admitted to trading on a regulated market. In the case of multiple listings, the applicable law shall be the law of the country in which the financial instrument was acquired or sold. The same law shall apply in the case of trading outside a regulated market, unless the person claimed to be liable could not reasonably have foreseen the applicability of that law.'

admitted to trading.[243] Finally, the rule adopted in the case of multi-listing is unfortunate since it makes such a system contingent. Investors' orders must be executed by their investment services provider according to the 'best execution' principle, which obliges them to execute the order received on the regulated market where the security is cheapest.[244] The investor could then have a law applied to his share that is completely unrelated to liability issues and has no real connection with the situation. The issuer is not in a very different situation since it has not necessarily consented to the admission of its securities to a foreign market.[245]

In reality, the law of the financial market is only relevant for civil liability when it corresponds to the law of the place of the solicited investors. In contrast, it is more appropriate in the case of market abuse. The reason for this is simple: in this case, the purpose of the regulation is to protect the trading platform itself. The authors' proposal would be relevant if the loss to be compensated was not the alteration of the investor's decision, as is the case in the Union, but the compensation for the alteration of the quotation price, as is the case in the United States.[246] In this case, the concept of 'ricochet damage', which has been rejected here,[247] could be particularly useful and would explain the application of the law of the financial market to the liability of the issuer.

428. Conclusion of the section. According to the texts, the tort liability of the issuer for the information he disseminates is subject to the jurisdiction of the place of the damage,[248] i.e. the place of the victim whose decision has been altered, to which should be added the option offered by the Court of Justice of bringing proceedings before the court of the place where the event giving rise to the damage occurred, i.e. the place of the defective information. By a curious subversion, the case law of the Court of Justice no longer refers to the constituent elements of civil liability in order to determine the forum in tort, either because it makes a poor analysis of the damage in question, entangled as it is in its previous decisions, or because of its obsession with the foreseeability of the forum that may be competent for the plaintiff. It is remarkable that these solutions can lead to the deactivation of the jurisdiction of the tort forum itself. In matters of civil liability for defective information from the issuer, the existence of a financial market has no bearing on the solutions to be adopted; at most, admission to trading will make it possible to characterise the solicitation of certain investors,

---

243 This was the case, it will be recalled, in the *Profit* judgment of the Court of Justice, where all the financial securities acquired on the basis of a misleading prospectus were acquired by an Italian investor when they were admitted to trading on the Irish financial market.

244 See *supra*, para. 139 and on its location, see para. 142.

245 See *supra*, para. 262.

246 See *supra*, para. 376.

247 See *supra*, para. 377.

248 These expressions are borrowed from K and P. Picone, see *supra*, para. 12.

which is the only relevant criterion for locating the damage when fraudulent intent has not been alleged. The statement is true both for the determination of international jurisdiction and for the resolution of the conflict of laws.

429. Conclusion of the chapter. The issuer's liability for the defective information it disseminates gives rise to a singular damage, that of the alteration of the investor's decision. The difficulty of determining the legal system competent to compensate for this loss arises first of all from the difficulty of its characterisation. This depends both on the existence of a contract between the issuer and the plaintiff, which can be characterised when the investor is the owner of the securities, and on the way in which the plaintiff articulates his claims. If the action is contractual, private international law solutions lead to the application of the law of the contract, without necessarily designating the court of the defendant's domicile as competent. Indeed, the existence of an enforceable choice of court clause and the presence of a consumer both interfere with the jurisdiction of the defendant's forum; however, where the choice of court clause is likely to allow for the concentration of the dispute at the issuer's seat when the investors are professionals, the presence of a consumer will give jurisdiction to the plaintiff's seat. It is regrettable, however, that local law does not apply to the issuer's liability towards consumers.

If there is no contract, or if the claimant articulates his claim on a tort basis unrelated to the contract, the damage of alteration of the investor's decision is inevitably located at his home. This localisation of the damage does not lead to satisfactory results as it gives jurisdiction to all the investors' legal orders. It should be tempered by the existence of a solicitation, which is sometimes echoed in European case law. This solution makes it possible to restore the legislative and jurisdictional competence of the legal system solicited by the foreign issuer and affected by the disturbance, which then has a strong jurisdictional competence to determine the compensation.[249] In fact, the fact that this mass damage occurred through contractual relations cannot have the consequence of completely depriving of jurisdiction the legal system that was requested, and whose legislation may, moreover, have been self-limiting during the marketing of the securities. It will no doubt be argued that the jurisdictional competence of this order will always be active as soon as consumers are involved. This is true, but the application of the law of the contract to the resulting liability regime will not necessarily be as favourable as that of the forum. Above all, the massive nature of the damage makes it more

[249] This is the 'price' of access to the local market, see already *supra*, para. 137. Mr Lambert (S. Lambert, *L'application internationale du droit financier*, *op. cit.*, no. 1153) considers that this competence is a limitation to the mutual recognition of information and administrative approvals necessary for marketing (on which see *supra*, paras. 125 et seq., 347 et seq.) It seems to us that the jurisdiction of the local legal order to remedy a disturbance is the same whether or not there is a self-limitation of local law to the rules on marketing.

difficult to completely abandon the protection of local investors, even if they are professionals, and would justify the institution of class actions subject to local law.

430. Conclusion of the title. The relationship between issuers and financial markets gives rise to very different conflicts of law depending on whether the issue of securities, their marketing or the liability of the issuer is at issue. In the area of issuance, the law of the issuer has a particularly strong jurisdictional competence, and the law of the financial market will not apply directly to the various aspects of the issue, but will oblige the issuer to comply with certain material solutions, especially as regards the form of the securities and all the elements likely to restrict the negotiability of the securities. In this respect, the liberalism of French law also allows French companies to subject the form of their issued securities to a foreign law. The regime of the *negotia* issued will also be taken into consideration by the regulation of market operations. In these cases, the *lex mercatus* comes into play in order to preserve the equality of investors who have acquired securities of the issuer, simply because the prerogatives offered by these securities have an influence on the supervision of the issuer. For this reason, any measures to restructure the company's debt, when they lead to changes in the prerogatives of the debt securities and the capital structure of the issuer, must be carried out in harmony with the requirements of the law of the financial market.

The marketing of financial securities triggers various information obligations to which the law of the financial market is traditionally applicable in respect of the solicitation of its residents. It may, however, be self-limiting where the issuer's law offers equivalent protection. However, it is not certain that the administrative authority supervising this information should abdicate its jurisdiction in favour of mutual recognition. Indeed, the financial market authority is best placed to ensure the protection of its residents, which is both the function of these disclosure requirements and of the supervision instituted.

These information obligations triggered by the marketing of securities are likely to engage the issuer's liability. The characterisation of this liability is relatively contingent and will depend, on the one hand, on the effective ownership of the security by the plaintiff and, on the other hand, on the basis of his claim. If the liability action is contractual, the applicable law will be that of the contract, and the competent court will depend on the presence of a choice of court clause or the presence of a consumer. If the liability action is in tort or delict, the legal system of the place of the tort or delict should be able to have global jurisdiction, when its residents have been solicited, in order to make good the damage they have suffered; as the case law of the Court of Justice currently stands, this is not yet the case.

TITLE 2
THE RELATIONSHIP BETWEEN FINANCIAL MARKETS AND INVESTORS

431. In the context of a financial market, investors are the principals who, through their intermediaries, preside over market operations. Their relationship with the financial markets is the chosen domain of the *lex mercatus*. The law of the financial market has a strong application here, based on the objective it pursues: the proper functioning of the trading platform. This function of the law of the financial market makes it possible to group the rules that pursue it into a single category, the *lex mercatus*. The application of these rules is triggered by the use of the trading platform; their connecting criterion is that of the platform itself,[1] which we have endeavoured to define.[2] Such a category is likely to be included in a bilateral conflict-of-laws rule according to which:

> 'The rules relating to the operation of the financial market shall be subject to the law of the trading venue.'

Firstly, it is possible to include the rules relating to the obligations of market members towards the financial market. These rules no longer make it necessary to subject the contract concluded with their clients to the law of the market, but they continue to ensure their protection through the rules of conduct that are imposed on members (Chapter 1). The application of the *lex mercatus* is most evident in the regulation of market transactions. Although the concept of market operation has replaced that of stock exchange operation, it nevertheless continues to designate the mechanism that 'consists in the production and execution of the order on the market'.[3] The particularity of these operations is that they are subject to special regulations controlled by an administrative

---

[1] Garcimartin Alferez had already observed this possibility in relation to the law on tender offers, where he considered that the unilateral formulation did not prevent a possible 'bilateralisation' of these rules. The author nevertheless considered that this remained theoretical because of the close links between the *forum* and the *jus* and characterisation of these operations, see F. Garcimartin Alferez, *Cross-border listed companies*, *op. cit.*, no. 156.

[2] See *supra*, paras. 267 et seq.

[3] A.-C. Muller, *Droit des marchés financiers et droit des contrats*, *op. cit.*, pp. 31 et seq.; A.-C. Rouaud, *Contribution à l'étude de l'opération de marché*, *op. cit.*

authority. It will be shown that this set of rules is fundamentally aimed at constraining the people behind the market operations, so that the resulting transactions do not alter the functioning of the financial market. The objective is as much to preserve the liquidity of the securities admitted to the market as the price determination mechanism. This function explains the predominant legislative and administrative jurisdiction of the legal system of the financial market; the unfortunate fact is, however, that certain elements are unduly removed from it and entrusted to the legal system of the registered office of the listed company (Chapter 2). The regulation of market abuse is a continuation of the regulation of market transactions. It aims to prohibit certain types of trading, in the same way that short selling law prohibits certain types of trading. However, treating this regulation separately is justified because of the criminal nature of the sanctions attached to the prohibition it imposes. Indeed, the criminal nature of these provisions gives them a disproportionate international scope of application; it will be shown that this scope should be rationalised in order to target the financial markets that this regulation is intended to protect, i.e. the European financial markets (Chapter 3).

CHAPTER 1
THE INTERPOSITION OF MARKET MEMBERS

432. The functioning of the financial market relies on the financial market manager and its members. The status of managers has already been discussed.[1] It is now necessary to consider how market membership is acquired, and the relationships that members are likely to develop. Three relationships can be distinguished: with their clients, with other market members, and with the financial market manager. The regulation of these relationships does not follow a principle of symmetry: they are governed by heterogeneous sources, which do not have identical objectives, and are therefore subject to different conflicts of laws. In the past, the law of the financial market was applied indiscriminately to these different aspects. Today, it follows a twofold movement, which we will trace here. Firstly, the *lex mercatus* applies to relations with the financial market manager and to transactions concluded between market members. Its application is imperative, as it pursues the proper functioning of the financial market (Section 1). Secondly, the law of the financial market has for a long time extended to contracts concluded between members and their clients. Today, it has withdrawn from these contractual relationships, as the protection of clients is ensured by the professional status of members (Section 2).

SECTION 1. THE RELATIONSHIP BETWEEN THE FINANCIAL MARKET AND ITS MEMBERS

Access to the status of market member is decided by the market operator itself. This status gives rise to a number of obligations for which the member is accountable in order to allow the proper functioning of the financial market (§ 1). Once the status has been obtained, the market member has access to the trading system, which allows it to conclude transactions with other members. These transactions will be subject to the law of the financial market by application of the Rome I Regulation (§ 2).

---

1 See *supra*, paras. 81 and seq.

§ 1. THE STATUS OF MEMBERS

Access to the status of market member is decided by the market manager, but is nevertheless based on categories of professionals regulated by EU law (I). This status gives rise to obligations for the member towards the financial market, contributing to its proper functioning and therefore subject to its law (II).

I. Access to the Status

433. Market membership. The first source of law to which members are subject is the Market Rules, drawn up by the market manager, to which members have adhered in order to obtain access to the platform.[2] These rules govern the admission process for market members: applicants must submit an admission file,[3] on which the market manager makes a decision.[4] This decision, if positive, leads to an admission contract, by which the new member commits to respecting the market rules.[5]

The market rules distinguish between two types of members. The first are investment firms and credit institutions. The latter must be 'authorised by the competent authorities of the home country for trading activity',[6] and have 'notified the competent authority of their willingness to exercise their rights under the EEA passport in the country in which the relevant Euronext Market Operator is established'.[7] The latter are 'non-MiFID companies', i.e. companies from third countries that do not have a branch in the territory of the financial market Member State.[8] The latter must meet a number of internal organisational criteria that are similar to the conditions for authorisation.[9] They must also be authorised and supervised in their home state, or be able to 'can demonstrate that such authorisation, licensing or permission is not required'.[10] In both cases, membership is conditional on their home country having:

> '(ii) an agreement for the exchange of information and cooperation between the supervisory authorities of the country concerned and the Competent Authorities

---

[2] See *supra*, paras. 248 et seq.

[3] Art. 2302/1 of the Euronext Market Rules (Book I).

[4] Art. 2303/1 of the Euronext Market Rules (Book I).

[5] The Market Rules impose a significant number of ongoing obligations on market members. They also allow the market manager to carry out on-site inspections in order to monitor compliance, see Art. 2401/1, spec. (iv) of the Euronext Market Rules (Book I).

[6] Art. 2201(i)(b) of the Euronext Market Rules (Book I).

[7] *Ibid.*

[8] See *supra*, paras. 205 and seq.

[9] On which see *supra*, para. 205.

[10] Art. 2201(ii)(a) of the Euronext Market Rules (Book I).

or, where permitted by the National Regulations, the relevant Euronext Market Operator'.[11]

This second condition is deemed to be met when 'the legal regimes and supervisory frameworks have been recognised as equivalent by the European Commission pursuant to Article 47(1) of MiFIR'.[12] However, it is possible for the market manager to assess the adequacy of the foreign regulation itself in the absence of an equivalence decision. In the latter case, the foreign member will not be able to provide its services to European residents without being subject to the regulation of the Member State concerned,[13] but remains free to provide investment services to its own residents. On the other hand, the law of the financial market retains its application in the relationship between the member and the manager.

II. The Relationship with the Financial Market

Financial markets justify their existence by providing an 'efficient' market price. This is the result of the confrontation of 'buying and selling interests'; in other words, supply and demand. This objective of providing the most accurate price possible explains the existence of several types of obligations that have in common the pursuit of a well-functioning market. Some of these obligations apply to the market manager, others to the members.

434. Obligation of the financial market manager. By managing a trading system, the manager is at the centre of the confrontation between supply and demand, and therefore holds the information on the trading price. The confrontation between supply and demand and the resulting price dissemination are not, however, left to his discretion. Firstly, the EU legislator imposes on the manager 'tick sizes', i.e. 'the minimum permitted difference between two directly consecutive prices on the market'.[14] The objective is to avoid that trading platforms compete on the speed with which price adjustments can take place in order to gain market share. Indeed, this type of competition ultimately degrades the price formation mechanism.[15]

Second, price disclosure is achieved by subjecting financial market managers to two disclosure obligations.[16] The first is a pre-trade transparency obligation, which consists of the publication in real time of bid and offer prices and the

---

11 *Ibid.*
12 *Ibid.* On this equivalence decision, see *supra*, para. 209.
13 On the access of investment companies to the European territory, see *supra*, paras. 205 et seq.
14 F. Drummond, *Droit financier*, *op. cit.*
15 *Ibid.* and references.
16 Art. 3 MiFID Regulation.

size of trading intentions. The authority supervising the market manager may exempt it from this obligation in various cases and under certain conditions.[17] The second is a post-trade disclosure obligation, which consists in publishing in real time, insofar as the technical means allow, the price, volume and time of the transactions carried out.[18] These obligations are all the more necessary as there are different financial markets on which identical instruments are sometimes traded. These obligations lead to the reconstitution of 'a global market, to preserve an efficient price formation process and to allow for the best possible monitoring of compliance with execution obligations'.[19] While the substantive content of these obligations, which are central to price formation, is the subject of considerable debate,[20] their international application does not pose any difficulties: they are incumbent on any person operating a trading system within the EU.

435. Obligations of market members. Market members are subject to a set of reporting obligations, which apply by virtue of their status as investment firms. Depending on the case, these obligations are aimed at establishing the market price or detecting abuses. However, both objectives have in common that they allow the system to function properly.

436. Trading obligation.[21] Market members are subject to a trading obligation, a renewed but distinct form of order concentration.[22] The trading obligation requires investment firms to bring the orders they receive from their clients onto a trading system, rather than executing them otherwise.[23] This obligation applies to shares and financial contracts. In the case of shares, the trading obligation is based on Article 23 of MiFID. Firstly, it is a favourable rule

---

17 Arts. 4 and 5 MiFID Regulation.

18 Art. 6 of the MiFID Regulation.

19 F. Drummond, *Droit financier*, *op. cit.*

20 See in particular M. Roussille, B. Bréhier, P. Pailler, A.-C. Rouaud and H. Boucheta, 'MiFID 2: what transparency at any price could cost', *BJB*, November 2012, p. 496; A.-C. Muller, 'Premier bilan après un an d'application de la MIF', *RDBF*, March-April 2009, p. 59; N. Spitz, 'MiFID 2: la recomposition des lieux d'exécution', *RDBF*, November 2014, p. 121; H. Boucheta, 'MiFID 2: microstructure and transparency, the price discovery mechanism in question', *BJB*, June 2015, p. 279.

21 Negotiation here refers to the conclusion of a contract, see T. Bonneau *et al.*, *Droit financier*, *op. cit.*, no. 1258.

22 On the outdated nature of this obligation, which has become ineffective precisely because of the internationalisation of the discipline, see H. Synvet, 'Libres propos d'internationaliste sur les obligations d'intermédiation et de concentration' in *Mélanges en l'honneur de Michel Vasseur*, Paris, Banque Éditeur, 2000; on the distinct functions of the concentration and trading obligations, see P. Barban, 'Le principe de concentration au titre du dispositif MIF 2', *RISF*, 2015/3, pp. 47 et seq.

23 Indeed, investment firms had 'developed in-house client order matching systems (*crossing networks*) which, since they did not meet the definition of a 'market' under MiFID or that of systematic internalisation, were not subject to any pre-trade transparency obligation', F. Drummond, *Droit financier*, *op. cit.*

for the financial markets, which it safeguards by ensuring that 'more movements take place through regulated trading venues',[24] in order to increase supply and demand for these shares. Such an increase improves the liquidity of shares and the price discovery mechanism. It also serves the purpose of transparency requirements, which are made effective by ensuring that they are not rendered ineffective by the execution of orders outside trading systems,[25] which would prevent price disclosure.[26] The obligation to trade in shares falls on investment firms. However, there is an exemption where trading '(a) is non-systematic, *ad hoc*, occasional and infrequent, or (b) is between eligible and/or professional counterparties and does not contribute to the price-setting process'.[27]

437. From an international perspective, this rule raises two questions. The first is whether an investment firm may, where a share admitted to trading on a European financial market is also admitted to trading outside the European Economic Area, execute the orders it receives on that foreign financial market or transmit them to a member of that market. In the absence of a Commission equivalence decision on the foreign financial market, the answer is no, unless the order to be executed falls within the scope of the exemption.[28] The second question is whether a market member from a third country is subject to this obligation. The answer depends on whether he has a branch in the Member State of the market in question. If it does, it will be subject to this requirement by virtue of the national authorisation of the branch. In the absence of a branch, the market member cannot be considered an investment firm; the trading obligation could only be applicable through the market rules.[29] For this reason, the trading obligation would be best enforced by the existence of a transaction in the admitted shares, rather than by the status of an investment firm.

438. Where it concerns financial contracts, the trading obligation is based on Article 28 of MiFID. Its material scope, i.e. the determination of the financial

---

24 Recital 11 MiFID Regulation.

25 Trading systems here are multilateral trading systems, i.e. financial markets, and bilateral trading systems, i.e. systematic internalisers.

26 This last function of the trading obligations is all the more apparent as it is possible to derogate from them when the trades in question are 'non-systematic, occasional or infrequent' and do not contribute to the price discovery process, see Art. 23(1)(b) of the MiFID Regulation and Art. 2 of the MiFID Delegated Regulation 2 2017/587, which details these assumptions.

27 Art. 23(1) MiFID Regulation.

28 ESMA, 'Esma clarifies trading obligation for shares under MIFID II', 13 November 2017, note T. Bonneau, *RDBF*, January 2018, comm. 25.

29 Art. 2401(iv) of the Euronext Market Rules (Book I). This stipulation requires the market member, regardless of its origin, to provide the market operator with 'any data required under Union Law, including but not limited to the requirements imposed by: a. EU Delegated Regulation 2017/580; b. EU Delegated Regulation 2017/590; c. the National Regulation transposing Article 57 of MiFIF; and comply with any associated technical standards, data and standards as specified by Notice'.

contracts for which this trading obligation is applicable, is modelled on that of the clearing obligation, in particular because the requirements relating to the liquidity of these contracts, a condition for their conclusion on a financial market, are identical.[30] The function of this trading obligation remains the same as for shares: it aims to protect the interest of trading systems by obliging to use them and, therefore, perfecting the price discovery mechanism. This function is precisely manifested in the exemption for financial contracts that 'do not participate in price formation'.[31] The obligation to negotiate financial contracts also has its own function: to create competition between execution venues by removing the monopoly of certain platforms on the conclusion of certain categories of financial contracts.[32]

439. Reporting obligation. In order to detect market abuse, investment firms must report to their home Member State authority all transactions in financial instruments that they have executed,[33] including those executed through their branch.[34] The report is due, regardless of the mode of execution of the transaction, from the moment the transaction concerns an instrument admitted to trading, or whose underlying is admitted to trading, or which consists of an index or basket of financial instruments traded on a platform.[35] From an international perspective, the difficulty is that these obligations are also linked to investment firm status, whereas they would benefit from being triggered by market membership. The reiteration of these obligations in the Market Rules should nevertheless remedy this shortcoming.

---

30 If the trading and clearing obligations have an identical material scope (recommending this identity, ESMA, 7 February 2020, Decision 70-156-2076; on this position, see A.-C. Rouaud, *Banque et droit*, July 2020, pp. 37 and seq.), their functions are nevertheless different. Indeed, the clearing obligation, associated with trade repositories, is the only rule leading to the prevention of systemic risk (see *infra*, para. 867). If the trading obligation contributes to this, it is in an accessory way. As Mr Gaudemet writes, 'the trading obligation does not have the same purpose as the clearing obligation. The purpose of the clearing obligation is to limit system risk. The purpose of the trading obligation is to improve the transparency of OTC derivatives markets and the ability of regulators to supervise these markets. In this respect, the trading obligation is closer to the obligation to report to a trade repository than to the obligation to clear through a CCP.' A. Gaudemet, 'Les obligations de négociation et de compensation', *op. cit.*, no. 5.

31 Recital 27 MiFID Regulation.

32 Recital 28 MiFID Regulation.

33 Arts. 24 to 27 of the MiFID Regulation. On the authority receiving this information, see *infra*, para. 543.

34 Recital 15 and Art. 14 of Delegated Regulation 2017/590. On this issue, see the comments of B. Stoeva, *La coopération entre les superviseurs financiers dans l'Union européenne, op. cit.*

35 Art. 26(2) MiFID Regulation.

§ 2. CONTRACTUAL RELATIONS BETWEEN MEMBERS

440. The *ratio legis* of Article 4, 1 h of the Rome I Regulation. Negotiations between market members take the form of contracts concluded through the trading platform. These contracts are commercial in nature and are subject to the Rome I Regulation. Their particularity lies in the way they are formed. Indeed, they result from the matching by the trading platform of two opposite orders issued by two market members through their electronic access to the trading platform.[36] As some authors write, this situation implies that there is no "*instrumentum* that could provide for the stipulation of an *electio juris* clause".[37] The consequence of this configuration of the formation of contracts on the financial markets is that the subsidiary connecting factor of the Rome I Regulation, the residence of the debtor of the obligation characteristic of the contract, would systematically apply. However, this criterion would lead to the application of very different law depending on the residence of the different members, and laws which the members cannot reasonably foresee since it is impossible for them to know with which member their order will be matched.[38] The inadequacy of the subsidiary connecting factor led the negotiators of the Rome I Regulation to make a specific provision, also motivated by the desire to establish a single law for the organisation of negotiations and contracts concluded by the system.[39] This provision is enshrined in Article 4(1)(h) of the Rome I Regulation, according to which:

> 'A contract concluded within a multilateral system which brings together or facilitates the bringing together of multiple third-party buying and selling interests in financial instruments, as defined by Article 4(1), point (17) of Directive 2004/39/EC, in accordance with non-discretionary rules and governed by a single law, shall be governed by that law.'

---

36 Some authors nevertheless consider that transactions concluded by market members are not really contracts, see A.-C. Muller, *Droit des marchés financiers et droit des contrats*, *op. cit.*, nos. 39 and seq.; A.-C. Rouaud, *Contribution à l'étude de l'opération de marché*, *op. cit.*, nos. 423 et seq.

37 M. Audit, S. Bollée and P. Caillé, *Droit du commerce international et des investissements étrangers*, *op. cit.*, no. 482.

38 This situation creates a double anonymity: of the co-contracting market member, and of his client. This second anonymity is not recent, since qualified intermediaries in stock exchange transactions are required to 'maintain the most inviolable secrecy for the persons who entrust them with the negotiations', Art. 40 of the Decree of 7 October 1890, on which see 'Bourses' in R. Chemaly, *Rép. int. Dalloz*, *op. cit.*, no. 56.

39 F. Garcimartin Alferez, 'The Rome I Regulation: Exceptions to the Rule on Consumer Contracts and Financial Instruments', *op. cit.*, pp. 98–99; Art. 4(1)(h) was proposed by the Spanish delegation, F. Garcimartin Alferez, 'New Issues in the Rome I Regulation: The Special Provisions on Financial Market Contracts' (2008) *Yearbook of PIL*, p. 245, spec. p. 247.

The scope of this rule is doubly restricted: the concept of multilateral trading system excludes systematic internalisers, but also organised trading systems; the markets covered are only those that allow the conclusion of financial instruments. These clarifications are important because the definition given should make it possible to understand financial markets outside the Union. Indeed, the law designated by the Rome I Regulation is likely to be that of a third State, and it is necessary to define materially what is considered a financial market from the point of view of this Regulation.[40]

441. The stipulation in the Market Rules. The solution of Article 4(1)(h) was, however, already established by the Euronext Market Rules, which provide as follows:

> 'Any provision of these Rules relating to orders or Transactions generated, executed or deemed to be executed on the various Euronext Markets and any matter relating thereto *(shall be subject to and construed in accordance with)* French law, as far as Euronext Paris is concerned, and shall be subject to the exclusive jurisdiction of the French Courts, except in the case of an arbitration clause or agreement.'

A transaction is 'any purchase or sale of a financial instrument admitted *(to trading)*'.[41] In fact, there is no doubt that the law of the system applies to the ordering of orders, and even to the issuing of orders themselves: the regulation of tick sizes is an example.[42] It is less certain, however, that the law of the system can be extended to transactions between members, simply because these are separate contracts. Even if the market rules were to be described as a framework contract,[43] the law of the framework contract is not applicable, as a matter of principle, to implementing contracts. There is no objective connecting factor between the framework contract, the ancillary contract or the related contracts.[44] It would not seem reasonable to provide for the application of the exception clause *in abstracto* to all implementing contracts of a framework contract. The solution of Article 4(1)(h) of the Rome I Regulation is therefore particularly welcome; it is, however, not new.

---

40 The concept of equivalent market (on which see *supra*, paras. 212 and seq.) may then be used to circumscribe the contracts that may benefit from this provision.

41 Art. 1.1 of the Euronext Market Rules (Book I).

42 See *supra*, para. 436.

43 This appears questionable since the members only have a contractual 'framework' relationship with the manager.

44 F. Leclerc, 'Le contrat cadre en droit international privé' in *TCFDIP 2002-2004*, Paris, Pedone, p. 20: 'There is no doubt that framework contracts and implementing contracts are distinct contracts, and that this distinction justifies the submission of each to its own private international law rules.' See S. Corneloup, 'Choix de loi et contrats liés' in *Le règlement communautaire 'Rome I' et le choix de loi dans les contrats internationaux*, Paris, Litec, 2011, pp. 289 and seq.

442. Traditional solution. The application of the law of the financial market to contracts concluded on the market was already a solution present in the Middle Ages.[45] The development of the place of conclusion and performance of the contract as a criterion for connecting contracts even has its origins in contracts concluded on the financial markets.[46] It is as if the stock exchange organisation constituted 'a pole of attraction for the connection and location of transactions concluded there'.[47] This is often explained as an extension of the law of stock exchange organisation.[48] Some authors even consider that this law would apply

---

45 B. Ancel, *Éléments d'histoire du droit international privé*, Paris, Édition Université Panthéon-Assas, 2017, p. 104.

46 H. Batiffol, *Les conflits de lois en matière de contrat*, Recueil Sirey, 1938, nos. 309 and seq. Thus Chemaly considered that 'it is perhaps for stock exchange transactions that the idea, which is increasingly widely accepted, is best verified, according to which, in principle, the "localisation of contracts is based on their economic characteristics, conclusion and *above all execution*, rather than on the personal situation of the parties, nationality or domicile" (H. Batiffol, *Les conflits de lois en matière de contrats*, Recueil Sirey, 1938, no. 199)'. R. Chemaly, 'Bourse', *op. cit.*, no. 56. Similarly, Professor Kahn, in his doctoral thesis on *La vente commerciale internationale* (Sirey, 1961), wrote (pp. 256–257): 'The place of conclusion of the contract seems to be the one that was historically the first to be proposed. It was set out by the canonists of the twelfth century, developed by the statutists of the thirteenth, and given form by Bartole and his disciples. It is still favoured by much of modern doctrine, since the American Restatement conceives it as a general system. [...] One may wonder whether behind this principle of territoriality there is not a historical explanation that originates in the Fairs of the Middle Ages. It is in fact recognised today that the same law governed transactions concluded on the fairground, that of the place where the fair was held, which was at the same time the place where the contract was concluded. This practice is easy to understand if one recalls the state of contract law in the twelfth and thirteenth centuries. The Roman contract had almost disappeared and in its place had arisen a feudal law based on the immovable and on the division of society into social classes where the merchant, in the modern sense, was not recognised as such. It was during the Great Fairs that a certain commercial law was able to emerge thanks to the privileges granted, in particular, by the Counts of Champagne. Originally, the submission of contracts concluded during the Fair to the law and the regulations of the Fair had the meaning of a liberation from the old feudal law and the substitution of a more flexible law better adapted to commercial necessities. The predominant theory at the time was the territoriality of the law and there was a dispute as to whether the competent territorial law was that of the place where the contract was formed or that of the place where the contract was to be performed. It is therefore reasonable to assume that the theorists of the time focused their efforts on the justification to be proposed in order to achieve a desirable result: that the rules of the Fair should govern the contracts of the Fair.' The statement is now obsolete: contracts concluded by a financial market are executed at the clearing house.

47 See 'Bourses' in R. Chemaly, *Rép. int. Dalloz*, *op. cit.*, no. 29.

48 F. Garcimartin Alferez, 'The Rome I Regulation: Exceptions to the Rule on Consumer Contracts and Financial Instruments' (2009) *Journal of Private International Law*, pp. 85 et seq., spec. p. 100: 'this solution ensures that the same legal order determines the public-law aspects (organisational law) and the private-law aspects (transactional law) of the market as an institution'. B. Audit and L. d'Avout, *Droit international privé*, *op. cit.*, fn. 126, p. 1019. The authors consider that 'Article 4, 1 h of the Rome I Regulation is grafted onto this public law connection'. On the connection of market infrastructures, see *supra*, para. 267.

as an overriding mandatory law.[49] This is excessive. The application of the law of the financial market to contracts negotiated within it does not pursue any mandatory legislative policy. Its application today is explained above all by its mode of formation: it is the law known to the parties, and prior adherence to the market rules makes it foreseeable; this criterion allows the application of a single law to all contracts formed through the use of the financial market. The importance of this connection should not be overestimated. First of all, since it concerns only the contract concluded between market members, it has no impact on the contract concluded between the member and his client. Moreover, the contract concluded through a financial market will be executed with a clearing house, which will entail novation of the initial contract between the market members into two separate contracts between each of the members and the clearing house. However, these contracts with the clearing house are not subject to Article 4(1)(h) of the Rome I Regulation, but to the law designated by the rules of the clearing system.[50]

443. Conclusion of the section. The relationship between financial markets and their members is subject to the law of the market. Indeed, the trading or transparency obligations which arise from the status of the investment firm when it intervenes on a market have as their purpose the proper functioning of the financial market; its title of application here is indisputable and undisputed. Contracts concluded between market members are also subject to the law of the financial market, because of the way in which these contracts are formed: the law of the trading platform is therefore the only predictable, objective and stable connecting factor.

SECTION 2. THE RELATIONSHIP BETWEEN MARKET MEMBERS AND THEIR CLIENTS

444. The application of capital market law to the relationship between the capital market and members has never been contested. The point of controversy has always been in the application of capital market law to the relationship between market members and their clients. As Batiffol already wrote:

> 'There is no doubt that the stock exchange transaction is governed by the law of the stock exchange [...]. The real question [that the stock exchange transaction]

[49] H. Synvet, *L'organisation juridique du groupe international de société*, *op. cit.*, fn. 973, p. 394: 'The jurisdiction of the law of the exchange is sometimes seen as an illustration of the theory of location developed on a contractual basis [...]. Here we must undoubtedly go further. The law of the stock exchange necessarily applies (as a mandatory law): it could not be set aside by the will of the parties.'

[50] See *infra*, para. 887.

raises, from the point of view of conflict of laws, is that of the law applicable to the relationship between the stock exchange intermediary and his client.'[51]

In the context of the issuance of an order on a trading platform, the contract concluded between a market member and its client is a commission contract,[52] i.e. an intermediation contract subject to the 1978 Hague Convention, which allows the parties to designate the law applicable to this contract (§ 1). The law of the financial market therefore does not apply to the contractual relationship between the member and his client. Some confusion has been created in this respect, on the one hand, by the international scope of the monopoly granted to stockbrokers and, on the other hand, by the interference of the gaming exception (§ 2).

§ 1. THE LAW APPLICABLE TO AGENCY CONTRACTS

Intermediation contracts have particularities that affect the solution of the conflict of laws (I). These peculiarities do not prevent the application of the law designated by the parties to govern the agency contract and the service provided in this respect: if the Convention provides for the application of the law of the exchange, it is only to the relationship between the agent and third parties, i.e. between the market member and its other members (II).

I. The Specificity of Intermediation Contracts

445. From the point of view of conflict of laws, intermediation contracts have several special features. The first is that they give rise to three relationships: between the principal and the intermediary, between the intermediary and the third party, between the third party and the principal. Depending on the purpose of the agency – protection of the principal or of the third party – the applicable law will not be the same: the law of the contract concluded between the agent and the principal, or the law of the place where the agent acts with the third party. The second peculiarity lies in the diversity of the origins of the power of agency i.e. the authorisation given to the agent which may come from a contract, a court decision or the law.[53] This diversity explains in particular the difficulty

---

51 H. Batiffol, *Les conflits de lois en matière de contrats*, *op. cit.*, 182.

52 A.-C. Muller, *Droit des marchés financiers et droit des contrats*, *op. cit.*, no. 432. To which a del credere obligation is generally added, see *ibid.* and lastly, P. Simler, 'Pour en finir avec le débat sur la nature juridique de la clause de ducroire' in *Mélanges en l'honneur de Jean-Philippe et Michel Storck*, Paris, Dalloz, 2021.

53 On this question see A. Tomasi, 'Les conflits de lois en matière de représentation conventionnelle et l'opportunité d'une convention internationale', *RCDIP*, 1958, pp. 651 et seq.

of establishing a unitary conflict of laws regime for agency in general. The third peculiarity is that intermediation contracts – brokerage, mandate, commission, to mention only the most frequent ones – are derived from conventional agency and have not been analysed in the same way in domestic law in the Western legal systems.[54] Domestic law can be grouped into two categories.

446. The first category is based on the doctrine of separation derived from German doctrine, and in particular from Laband.[55] It makes a clear distinction between, on the one hand, the agency, i.e. the contract between the principal and the intermediary, and, on the other hand, the powers of representation, understood as the powers of the agent to contract with a third party on behalf of the principal. This doctrine of separation, which basically aims at protecting the third party, largely explains why agency has been 'atomised'.[56] While agency is an abstract element, it is nevertheless abstract to different degrees,[57] thus leading to a distinction between two categories of agency: direct agency, where the agent acts in the name and on behalf of the principal, and indirect agency, where the agent acts in its own name but on behalf of the principal. This distinction is for example significant in the case of the commission contract. The latter is a contract of indirect agency, which implies the absence of a direct legal relationship between the third party and the principal.

447. The second category is based on the doctrine of identity originating in English law[58] which implies that the intermediary is in some way the *alter ego* of the principal.[59] This doctrine, which translates into the concept of agency, aims at protecting the relationship between the principal and the intermediary,

54 See on this subject the observations of Mr Pélichet, in his 'Report' in *Actes et documents de la treizième session du 4 au 23 octobe 1976* (hereafter *Pélichet Report*), spec. pp. 12 et seq.; C. Schmitthoff, *Agency in international trade*, RCADI, vol. 129, The Hague, Martinus Nijhoff, pp. 107 et seq., spec. p. 121; see also Rabel's developments on this issue, *The Conflict of laws*, vol. III, *Ann Arbor*, 1958, pp. 123 et seq.

55 This distinction was elaborated by Paul Laband in 1866 (P. Laband, 'Die Stellvertretung bei dem Abschluss von Rechtsgeschäften nach dem Allgemeinen Deutschen Handelgesetzbuch', *Zeitschrift für das Gesamte Handelscrecht*, 1866, 204). Laband's perception would later be challenged, with the author of the Hague Convention report noting: 'Laband's extremely rational and logical construction was that of a pure jurist with little concern for commercial reality'. The doctrine of separation is incorporated in the BGB of 1896 (Art. §§164) and is the basis of the German concept of the mandate referred to as the '*Prokura*' (Arts. 48 et seq. of the German Commercial Code). The French codifications and those influenced by French law, which predate Laband's publication, do not make such a distinction, but will be receptive to it, see C. Schmitthoff, *Agency in international trade*, *op. cit.*, p. 121; *Pélichet Report*, *op. cit.*, p. 12.

56 The expression is from Pélichet, see report mentionned above.

57 In the report by Mr Pélichet, German law had thirteen types of mandate, *Pélichet Report*, *op. cit.* p. 13.

58 Dicey, Morris and Collins, *The Conflict of Laws*, *op. cit.*, rule 243, nos. 33-408 et seq.

59 This is summarised by the Latin adage *qui facit per alium facit per se*. On the theory of identity, C. Schmitthoff, *Agency in international trade*, *op. cit.*, p. 129.

the former not being bound by the acts of the latter if he exceeds the powers delegated to him.[60] Agency is therefore no longer an abstract element, but 'the very consequence of the mandate, and in theory at least, inseparable from this contract'.[61] The doctrine of identity considers that the relationship is established between the principal and the third party, the intermediary remaining outside this relationship. An exception is made, however, if the principal is not mentioned, in which case the principal may subsequently take over on his behalf the contract entered into by the intermediary if the intermediary was able to do so.[62] The third party, on the other hand, may object to such a takeover if he can prove that he wanted to contract with him alone.[63]

448. These differences led to three systems, distinct from the Hague Convention. French law, which was receptive to Laband's theory in domestic law, but did not adopt it in terms of conflict of laws, had thus applied the system of a single law resulting in the application of the same law to all the different aspects of intermediation contracts. This was the law chosen by the parties and, in the absence of a choice of law, the law of the place of performance of the contract,[64] except in the case of employment contracts.[65] In systems that have accepted a separation of the relationships specific to intermediary contracts, the conflict-of-laws solutions for contracts are applied, i.e. the law of autonomy in the internal relationships (agent and intermediary). In the absence of a choice of law, solutions have varied from country to country between the habitual residence of the intermediary, the law of the place where the intermediary is to perform his activity, or the law of the conclusion of the contract between the principal and the intermediary. As regards external relationships, the applicable law is again the law chosen by the parties. The Hague Convention is in line with the continuity of dissociation systems, but proposes solutions that break with those adopted until its advent.

---

60 *Ibid.*, p. 130.

61 *Pélichet Report*, *op. cit.* p. 15. However, English regulations have, by act of Parliament, had the opportunity to amend the *common law* doctrine, particularly in the specific sector of commercial agents (Factor's Act of 1889, on which see C. Schmitthoff, *Agency in international trade*, *op. cit.*, pp. 131 et seq.), this time protecting the third party who acted in good faith, allowing him to rely on the appearance (Factor's Act 1889, s.2(1)).

62 That is, ratification is not possible. C. Schmitthoff, *Agency in international trade*, *op. cit.*, p. 141.

63 *Ibid.*, p. 142.

64 For a description of this system, see Y. Loussouarn and J.-D. Bredin, *Droit du commerce international*, *op. cit.*, p. 712.

65 *Ibid.*, p. 724 and review.

II. The 1978 Hague Convention

449. Scope of application. The Rome I Regulation excludes from its scope the law applicable to the relationship between the agent and third parties,[66] but remains applicable to the relationship between clients and intermediaries. However, the Regulation gives priority to the application of international conventions governing conflict of laws in contractual matters[67] in force between the signatory states.[68] Conflict of laws solutions in this area are therefore governed by the Hague Convention of 14 March 1978 on the Law Applicable to Agency,[69] which provides for its application in these terms:

> 'The present Convention determines the law applicable to relationships of an international character arising where a person, the agent, has the authority to act, acts or purports to act on behalf of another person, the principal, in dealing with a third party. It shall extend to cases where the function of the agent is to receive and communicate proposals or to conduct negotiations on behalf of other persons.'[70]

The Convention therefore applies to 'the activities of intermediaries who are upstream of the actual agency',[71] i.e. those who do not have the power to sign and bind the principal, such as brokers.[72] The particularity of the commission agent, who unlike the principal acts in his own name, could undoubtedly have

---

66 Art. 1(2°)(g) of the Rome I Regulation, and Art. 1 f of the Rome Convention.

67 Art. 25(1°) of the Rome I Regulation. Art. 25(2) of the Regulation lays down a condition relating to the number of Member States that have signed it (two), which is fulfilled in this case. If the Hague Agency Convention is applicable, it is not because of a principle of speciality which would run through international law, both public and private (in this sense with regard to the Rome Convention, P. Bloch, *Banque et droit*, July-August 1993, special issue, p. 5), but quite simply because the Regulation provides for it.

68 This means that only France, Portugal and the Netherlands are bound. See e.g., for the application of the Rome I Regulation to this issue, the comments of Dicey, Morris and Collins, *The Conflict of Laws*, *op. cit.*, nos. 33–410 et seq.; see today, the comparative study of J. Kleinschmidt, 'Agency and Authority Agent' in *Encyclopedia of Private International Law*, Cheltenham, Edward Elgar, 2017, pp. 29 et seq.

69 On which see P. Lagarde, 'La Convention de La Haye sur la loi applicable aux contrats d'intermédiaires et à la représentation', *RCDIP*, 1978, 21 and Y. Loussouarn and P. Bourel, 'La Convention de La Haye sur la loi applicable aux contrats d'intermédiaires et à la représentation', *RTD com.*, 1979, 166. See also the reflections elaborated in a contemporary perspective, G. Lardeux, 'La loi applicable à la représentation conventionnelle', *RCDIP*, 2014, 513.
However, the Convention was only signed and ratified by four countries, France, Argentina, Portugal and the Netherlands, and entered into force on 1 May 1992. The rejection of the Convention by the Anglo-Saxon countries is apparently linked to the distinction elaborated by Laband, on which see the following discussion.

70 Art. 1, paras. 1 and 2 of the Hague Convention.

71 P. Lagarde, 'La Convention de la Haye sur la loi applicable aux contrats d'intermédiaire et à la représentation', *op. cit.* p. 33.

72 Art. 1, para. 2, of the 1978 Hague Convention.

created a difficulty, but this is removed by paragraph 3 of Article 1 according to which: 'The agreement applies whether the intermediary acts in his own name or in the name of the principal and whether his activity is habitual or occasional.'[73] The title and the scope of application of this Convention are explained by the use of the English concept of *agency*,[74] which is translated by the notion of "contrat d'intermédiation".[75] Finally, the Hague Convention is restricted to the sole question of contractual representation, judicial and legal representation being excluded. It is in this context that it places, from the point of view of conflict of laws, contractual representation in the context of the dissociation between internal and external relations that intermediation creates.

450. Law applicable to the relationship between agent and principal. In the relationship between the principal and the agent, the law normally applicable is 'the internal law chosen by the principal and the agent'.[76] In the absence of a choice of law, the law applicable is 'the internal law of the State where, at the time of formation of the agency relationship, the agent has his business establishment or, if he has none, his habitual residence', except in the case where the principal has his place of business or habitual residence in the State where the agent is to principally carry on his activity, in which case the law of that State shall apply.[77] However, these criteria are only applicable if the agency or intermediation contract is 'the sole purpose or the agreement' or if '(a) the creation of this relationship is the principal purpose of the agreement, or (b) the agency relationship is severable'.[78]

451. Applicable law between the principal and the third party. In the relationship between the principal and the third party, the principle is the application of 'the

[73] Mr Pélichet explains that the very choice of the title of the Convention was chosen for this reason: 'The term 'intermediary' has a broad meaning and, above all, does not cover any special legal concept, thus making it possible to include both the traditional "agent" and the "commissionaire"', *Pélichet Report*, *op. cit.* p. 11. This explains why a broker could be qualified as an intermediary within the meaning of the Convention, see CA Grenoble, 11 January 1996, *RCDIP*, 1998, p. 483, note S. Poillot-Peruzzetto, and the observations of Mrs K. Parrot, criticising the diversions via the *lege fori* qualification, K. Parrot, *L'interprétation des conventions en droit international privé*, Paris, Dalloz, 2006, no. 452.

[74] *Pélichet report*, *op. cit.* pp. 10–11.

[75] The notion of 'intermediary contract' is borrowed from Y. Loussouarn and J.-D. Bredin, *Droit du commerce international*, *op. cit.*, p. 711.

[76] Art. 5, para 1, of the 1978 Hague Convention.

[77] Art. 6, para. 2. In the case of multiple establishments of the principal or the agent, para. 3 specifies that reference should be made to 'the establishment to which the agency relationship is most closely connected'. L. d'Avout observes that the criteria used, place of action and place of business establishment, constitute 'two privileged connections of acts of business life (*which show*) the methodological sophistication to which the localising procedure has had to be subjected in order to remain faithful to its functions in conflict of laws law', see L. d'Avout, 'L'entreprise et les conflits internationaux de lois', *op. cit.*, no. 69.

[78] Art. 7 of the 1978 Hague Convention.

internal law of the State in which the agent had his place of business at the time he acted'.[79] Indeed, it is 'the agent who is obviously at the centre of the relationship between the principal and the third party'.[80] This law governs 'the existence and extent of the agent's powers' and 'the effects of the agent's acts in the actual or purported exercise of his powers'.[81] The Convention does, however, provide for the application of the law of the principal's place of residence in certain cases, in particular where the intermediary has acted on the stock exchange.[82] The *Rapporteur* of the Convention explains that this place of performance is never fortuitous and corresponds to the expectations of the parties, who will have provided for the applicability of the stock exchange regulations governing the agency.[83] The solution resulting from the Hague Convention thus preserves the application of the law of the market between its members, while leaving them free to choose another law for the relations they establish with their clients. This is a welcome solution as it would appear excessive, for example, to subject a contract concluded by a German market member with its German client to French law.

§ 2. INTERFERENCE FROM OTHER LAWS

The difficulty in accepting the application of the *lex contractus* to the relationship between market members and their clients stems from a misunderstanding of the monopoly of stockbrokers and, subsequently, that of investment firms. In the relationship with clients, this monopoly has long led to the extension of the law of the exchange to these contracts. Today, the monopoly of investment firms no longer leads to this application, but to the application of rules of conduct independently of the law of the contract. Compliance with these rules is the counterpart of the monopoly granted to these professionals (I). On the other hand, it is possible for certain specific rules to interfere with the scope of

---

79 Art. 11(1°) of the 1978 Hague Convention. While the connecting factor is the same as that of the intermediary-customer relationship, the difference lies in the moment of assessment of this connection, which is no longer the formation of the contract, but the action. Both the principal and the third party are aware of the place of business of the agent, whereas the principal may be unaware of the place where the agent has acted, see P. Lagarde, 'La Convention de la Haye sur la loi applicable aux contrats d'intermédiaire et à la représentation', *op. cit.*, 41.

80 *Ibid.*, no. 11, p. 41. Recall the application of the law of the assignor to the effectiveness against third parties in assignments of claims (see *infra*, para. 588). Such an approach leads to neither the principal nor the third party being favoured, so that it might appear neutral. In reality, it is rather a favour to the assignor and the transfer, just as it is a favour to the intermediary.

81 Art. 11 of the 1978 Hague Convention.

82 Art. 11(c) of the 1978 Hague Convention.

83 This is the report by M. Karsten, *Actes et documents*, *op. cit.*, pp. 377 et seq.

the *lex contractus* in order to protect its residents. This is the traditional case of the gambling exception (II).

I. The International Scope of the Monopoly

452. The scope of the stockbrokers' monopoly. The monopoly of investment firms originated in the monopoly of stockbrokers. At the time, the object of this monopoly was the brokerage of listed securities and it was formulated as follows:

> 'Stockbrokers alone have the right to negotiate public and other bills of exchange likely to be quoted; to negotiate bills of exchange or notes and all other negotiable papers on behalf of others and to establish their price.'[84]

From an international perspective, questions have focused on the scope of the civil sanction for the violation of the monopoly, namely the nullity of private transactions concluded.[85] Such a sanction requires, however, that the contract at issue be subject to French law. The application of the nullity imposed by French law would then be based either on the law applicable to the contract, which in the case of stock exchange transactions is the law of the place where the contract was concluded, i.e. the law of the stock exchange,[86] or on the *locus regit actum* rule, which would have subsumed the stockbrokers' monopoly into form rules. The need to enforce this civil sanction of the monopoly has justified for the doctrine the application of the law of the stock exchange not only to contracts between intermediaries, but also to contracts between intermediaries and their clients. This led to giving the monopoly an unprecedented scope, applicable both to the organisation of the stock exchange and to all stock exchange transactions, which include contracts between clients and intermediaries. As Mr Chemaly observed:

> 'The monopoly is a rule that relates directly to the state organisation of the stock market: as such, it applies to all transactions negotiated on this market and it is for French law alone, as the law governing the status of the stock market, to determine

---

84 Former Art. 76 of the Commercial Code, in force from 1807, when the Code was promulgated, to the year 2000.

85 This nullity was intended to prohibit 'coulissiers' from competing with stockbrokers. See E. Thaller, *Traité élémentaire de droit commercial*, *op. cit.*, no. 993. The monopoly was also sanctioned by criminal law, but its application did not give rise to difficulties, it was done in the manner of the mandatory rules and security laws of Art. 3 of the Civil Code, Amieux, see 'Agent de change' in *Rép. Niboyet-Lapradelle*, no. 10.

86 It is in this sense that the Lyon-Caen resolution voted by the Institute of International Law reads: 'III. The question whether a securities contract is void as having been concluded through a person other than an official intermediary must be resolved by reference to the law of the country where the contract was concluded, to the exclusion of the law of the country where enforcement is sought in court.' (*Yearbook*, *op. cit.*, p. 401)

> the extent of the monopoly of qualified intermediaries [...], but [the rule instituted by the monopoly] also constitutes, in France at least, a condition of validity of the stock market transaction. The problem is, as we can see, at the crossroads of the "imperative" organisation of the stock exchange by French law and the conflict of laws regarding stock exchange transactions.'[87]

The particularly broad scope given to this monopoly was probably explained by its function. Indeed, the monopoly granted to stockbrokers was necessary for the task entrusted to them of organising trading (like the contemporary market manager), supervising the exchange (like the regulatory authority), but also ensuring the reliability of transactions (like the contemporary post-market infrastructures).[88] These functions relating to the organisation of the market explained the existence of the professional obligations to which stockbrokers were subject. Thus, they could no longer engage in any commercial enterprise, even through an intermediary, at the risk of losing their neutrality, even though they embodied a market surveillance authority,[89] and were subject to professional secrecy. They could not reveal the name of their client, in particular in order to promote stock exchange transactions.[90] In retrospect, however, it is doubtful whether the monopoly of stockbrokers should necessarily have resulted in the application of the law of the stock exchange to the contract concluded by the intermediary and his client. Common private international law should have applied, as the nullity provided for could be applied as an overriding mandatory law.

453. The contemporary scope of the investment firm monopoly. The evolution of the stock market infrastructure means that the monopoly of investment firms

---

87 See 'Bourses' in R. Chemaly, *Rép. int. Dalloz*, *op. cit.*, no. 28.

88 See *supra*, paras. 40 et seq.

89 Thaller explains: 'The reason is simple: agents can only enforce market neutrality by refraining from participating in it. They are the ones who would make the price, if they were personally involved in speculation. The position they would take on a security would remove all impartiality. They would exert pressure on the quotation and would lend themselves to the manoeuvres of the stockbrokers. If they were to trade outside the stock exchange, they would neglect the function of high supervision with which the government has honoured them.' (E. Thaller, *Traité élémentaire de droit commercial*, *op. cit.*, no. 859).

90 E. Thaller, *Traité élémentaire de droit commercial*, *op. cit.*, no. 848, p. 609. This secrecy is shared by the equivalent of stockbrokers abroad and Savary, in his Parfait négociant (J. Savary, *Le Parfait Négociant*, Billaine, 1675, Book III, Chapter VII) notes that 'the first thing that a bank agent must observe is secrecy, which consists of a single point, which is to *see everything, hear everything and say nothing*'. Guillard writes in this regard: 'It would certainly be a lot to ask of stockbrokers to observe a duty that seemed a little too easy to the author of *Le Parfait négociant*. Diplomacy is all about this. It would be an illusion and perhaps a danger to wish for the finesse of a Talleyrand or the enigmatic speech of Varzin's Sphinx in the financiers of the Stock Exchange. But secrecy, at the Stock Exchange, can be kept without so much mystery', see V. Guillard, 'La bourse: les agents de change et les opérations de bourse dans les législations étrangères', *Journal de droit international privé*, 1877, pp. 307 et seq.

does not serve quite the same purpose. Authorisation may still have a screening function for professionals operating on the markets,[91] which is reflected in the prudential requirements for authorisation[92] and the criminal sanction for breach of the monopoly.[93] In relations with clients, the real counterpart of the monopoly enjoyed by investment firms lies above all in the imposition of rules of conduct, the international application of which has already been studied.[94] It should simply be added here that these rules are applicable regardless of the law applicable to the contract,[95] or the domicile of the client,[96] but on the basis of the professional status of the investment firm. Such an application criterion deserves approval. It ensures that professional conduct of business rules are not disabled by the choice of a foreign law. It also has the advantage of requiring investment firms to behave with the same diligence whether their clients are domiciled within or outside the EU.

II. The Gambling Exception

454. Presentation of the gambling exception. The gambling exception is a mechanism derived from Article 1965 of the Civil Code, according to which 'the law grants no action for a gambling debt or for the payment of a bet'. This provision allows a recalcitrant debtor not to have to pay a gambling debt, paralysing the creditor's action for payment, but also the debtor's possible action for recovery.[97] This rule, which does not prohibit gambling but hinders its proper functioning, is explained by the difficulty of truly prohibiting gambling

---

91 F. Drummond, *Droit financier*, *op. cit.*

92 See *supra*, paras. 93 et seq.

93 The prohibition on providing investment services without authorisation is contained in Art. L. 531-10 of the Monetary and Financial Code; the criminal sanction is set out in Arts. L. 573-1 and L. 573-7 of the same Code.

94 On the location of these rules, see *supra*, paras. 100 et seq.

95 In domestic law, certain rules of conduct, such as those governing the execution of orders, are described by the doctrine as special obligations, applicable 'to those particular contracts which are contracts for the provision of investment services, supplementing or derogating from the rules of contract law' (F. Drummond, *Droit financier*, *op. cit.*, no. 668). The explanation is attractive in that it is based on the material scope of the rule: these obligations are designed to govern certain investment services in particular, and moreover they interfere with the performance of the contract. However, it is the personal scope of application that is paramount here: these obligations are imposed on investment firms only. For this reason, they are applicable by virtue of the status of the provider and should not be included in the scope of the contract, at the risk of deactivating them by a simple choice of law.

96 This may come as a surprise given that these rules are designed to protect clients, but it is explained by the need to obtain this status in order to offer investment services to residents.

97 This double paralysis is really the originality of the mechanism introduced by the legislator of 1804. Indeed, Roman law, which was familiar with the institution, did not paralyse the action for recovery of the debtor accipiens, and allowed him, his heirs or even the magistrate ex officio to recover the sums paid on account of a gambling debt, and in the latter case, to allocate them to works of public utility. See on this point, and the references, 'Jeu-Pari' in F. Guerchoun, *Répertoire de droit civil*, Paris, Dalloz, no. 124.

by a legal rule.[98] In the mind of Portalis, there is no doubt that the deprivation of the legal effects of gambling promises is justified by the anti-social character of gambling, whose double effect, for the winner as well as the loser, is harmful: on the one hand, because the enrichment that it can provoke, based on chance, leads to ignoring the value of work in favour of idleness, and, on the other hand, because the consequences for the losers can provoke their own ruin, and that of their family.[99] This dual purpose of the gambling exception is crucial, because depending on whether one insists on one or the other, the international characterisation of the provision is likely to vary, and all the more so because this dual function of the institution is matched by the purpose that the gambling exception defeats: the respect of commitments made.

455. This rationale for the gambling exception allowed the courts to extend the application of article 1965 of the Civil Code not to stock exchange transactions in general – stock markets being spared – but to "futures markets" in particular, which in contemporary perspective designate certain financial contracts. This rule, while undoubtedly, according to Portalis, an instrument for the protection of good morals, became by a formidable subversion a means of transgressing them, making the exception of gambling a mechanism for not paying one's debts.[100] Such a provision should have had a restricted scope of application; the extension of its scope by case law, combined with the difficulty of distinguishing

As for the paralysis of the action for repayment, Portalis, after explaining the conformity of this solution with the ordinance of Moulins, which made an exception to it only for minors, declares: 'The rights of adults are consummated when things are no longer complete; the law cannot listen to them when they invoke it for the very fact in which they have disregarded it. We would add that the repentance of the miser who has voluntarily paid a gambling debt is not sufficiently favourable to awaken the attention of justice.' (P.-A. Fenet, *Recueil complet des travaux préparatoires du Code civil*, vol. 15, Paris, 1827, p. 542).

98 This is how Portalis explains the article: 'the authority, which cannot stifle passions, must not renounce the means of monitoring those who indulge in them. Since it is powerless to prevent vices, its task is to prevent crimes', Portalis, in *ibid.*, p. 540.

99 *Ibid.*, p. 540. These reasons are confirmed by a decision of the Paris Court of Appeal of 9 August 1823, where a stockbroker had knowingly taken his client's orders even though he knew that the latter had had no other intention than to play on stock exchange differences, and was therefore deprived of his action for payment against the client. Significantly, the Court justifies its decision *in fine* by writing 'that the strict enforcement of laws and regulations in this matter can alone put a brake on this immoderate ardour to enrich oneself which has seized fathers of families who, instead of devoting themselves to honest and useful professions, rush into speculations disavowed by morality, and always followed by complete ruin or scandalous fortune'.

100 E. Thaller, *Traité élémentaire de droit commercial*, *op. cit.*, 622. The author notes that this jurisprudence was immoral: 'The stock exchange became, with this jurisprudence, the unethical way to win, without the risk of losing.'

between the fictitious and the serious market,[101] led the legislator to adopt the law of 28 March 1885. Its Article 1, still applicable,[102] states:

> 'All forward contracts on public bills and other instruments, all contracts to be delivered on goods and merchandise are deemed legal. No one may, in order to avoid the obligations resulting from them, take advantage of Article 1965 of the Civil Code, even if they are resolved by the payment of a simple difference.'

However, although most European countries share the gambling exception, and have extended it to the futures markets, not all have had a similar development of case law and its criteria, and few have adopted a law as liberal as the French law of 28 March 1885. It is in this context that the first conflict of laws in stock exchange matters arose, which was taken up by the Institute of International Law[103] (A). From an international perspective, the gaming exception should be analysed as a rule for the protection of residents, and be applicable under the domicile of the principals (B).

A. The Application of the Law of the Exchange

456. State of play. At the beginning of the 20th century, the Institute of International Law mandated Professor Charles Lyon-Caen, at the Ghent session, to determine the law applicable to the gambling exception. The author submitted his report to the Florence session in 1908, at a time when positive law was in a notoriously confused state. In fact, in addition to the diversity of legislation admitting the gambling exception,[104] prohibiting it or regulating it, there was also a diversity

---

101 See on this point the analysis, before the reform, V. Marcadé and P. Pont, *Explication théorique et pratique du Code civil*, t. 8, Paris, Delamotte et fils, 1967, no. 625, pp. 297 et seq. Pont traces the origin of the ancien régime regulation (*ibid.*, no. 628), which explains the extensive interpretation of the case law, and then shows that the explanation of the criterion for distinguishing between fictitious and serious markets lies in the fairness of futures transactions between solvent capitalists, whereas fictitious markets are those for which they would have the same effect as that deplored by Portalis in relation to betting and gambling (*ibid.*, nos. 627–629). See also the analysis of E. Thaller, *Traité élémentaire de droit commercial*, *op. cit.*, nos. 974 et seq., pp. 621 et seq. and the retrospective analysis of G. Ripert and R. Roblot, *Traité élémentaire de droit commercial*, vol. II, Paris, LGDJ, 1964, no. 1896, p. 113.

102 Codified in Art. L. 211-35 of the Monetary and Financial Code.

103 For the contemporary difficulties to which the gaming exception in private international law gives rise, see L. Usunier, 'Conflits de lois et de juridictions et jeux en ligne' in M. Behar-Touchais, J. Rochfeld and A. Guillenchmidt-Guignot, *Les jeux en ligne en France et en Europe: quelles réformes trois ans après l'ouverture du marché*, Paris, Société de législation comparée, 2013, p. 530; L. Usunier, 'La dématérialisation du jeu en ligne et la territorialité de la loi française' in G. Julia (dir.) *Jeu, argent et droit*, Paris, Dalloz, 2013, pp. 157 et seq.

104 On this diversity, see A. Wahl, 'Les jeux de bourse en droit international', *JDI*, 1898, pp. 234 et seq.; V. Guillard, 'La bourse: les agents de change et les opérations de bourse dans les législations étrangères', *Journal de droit international privé*, 1877, p. 307, p. 400 and 1878, p. 146, and p. 478.

of rules of conflict of laws: the matter was highly contentious at the time.[105] In particular, two laws seem to be in dispute: the *lex loci contractus*,[106] considered by most authors as the law of the place where the contract was concluded, and the *lex fori*, i.e. the law of the court petitioned. Academics did not share a unambiguous opinion, and the case law was not unified either in France or abroad. However, the gaming exception, whose *ratio legis* has not changed,[107] does not seem to be fully attached to either of these two laws.[108]

457. The position of Professor Charles Lyon-Caen (1843–1935). It is in these conditions that the author proposes to apply as a principle 'the law of the country where a futures contract on securities has been concluded [...] even if the execution of this contract is requested before the court of a country where this exception is admitted'.[109] Charles Lyon-Caen moderates the application of this law by stating that:

> 'The foregoing provisions shall not affect the right of a State to declare applicable by express provision the rules of its law relating to futures markets to persons

105 See the extensive bibliographical references given by Amieux, see 'Bourses (opérations de)', in R. Chemaly, *Rép. int. Dalloz*, *op. cit.*

106 The era is not yet definitively converted or convinced by the law of autonomy. The location of contracts is done objectively. This will have consequences for the analysis of mandatory rules.

107 Thus, Lyon-Caen states: 'The legislator believes that he must show himself unfavourable to operations which divert from work, by making it possible to get rich without working and which can be, as experience proves, a cause of ruin and disorder.' C. Lyon-Caen, 'Rapport à l'Institut de droit international', *Annuaire de l'Institut de droit international*, 1906-1911, (reprinted 1928), vol. 5, p. 386 (hereafter *Annuaire*).

108 Moreover, the Institute's discussion seems to be hampered by the possibility of a preliminary question on the law applicable to contracts in general. This can be explained by the context: as this resolution was discussed just after another one on the law applicable to contracts in general, there is a dispute about the preliminary nature of the latter to settle Mr Lyon-Caen's resolution. This is the case of considerable authors such as Weiss, who thus states that he regrets 'that this question has been examined before the conflicts of law in respect of obligations in general have been settled, the forward contract being only one variety of contract' in *Annuaire*, *op. cit.* The reciprocal rapporteurs of the two drafts dispute the link, and consider that the matter would be mandatory in the case of securities transactions, which covers the question of the gambling exception, and suppletive for the law applicable to contracts. They are approved by other members, some of whom observe: 'Whatever one's opinion on the question of the law which should govern obligations, it has always been accepted that stock exchange transactions are subject to the law of the place of the contract. There is therefore no preliminary question.' Mr Strisower, *Annuaire*, *op. cit.*, p. 533. If the application of the law of the place of the stock exchange seems to prevail, it is nevertheless, for the authors, not necessarily by virtue of the law of the place of conclusion of the contract, but sometimes because of the mandate given to the stockbroker.

109 *Annuaire*, *op. cit.*, pp. 555–556.

domiciled in its territory, irrespective of the country in which such markets are concluded.'[110]

Charles Lyon Caen is aware that the vast majority of authors are of the opinion that the gaming exception can be invoked *ex parte debitoris*, by application of the *lex fori*,[111] although the justification for such jurisdiction is not entirely clear. It has been argued that the application of the *lex fori* is most appropriate 'When the parties to the contract are nationals of the country of that court',[112] in order to prevent nationals of that State avoiding the prohibitive norms of their country of origin. However, Lyon-Caen considers that the gambling exception is not a procedural exception, which as such would be subject to the *lex fori*, but an exception to the merits of the contractual action; he concludes that it should be subject to the *lex contractus*, which he defines as the law of the country of the conclusion of the forward contract.[113] For the author, the application of the *lex fori* is all the less appropriate since, although the notion of *ordre public* is central to the gambling exception,[114] the diversity of legislation shows that the application of the gambling exception to futures markets cannot be considered as part of the *ordre public international*.[115] Charles Lyon-Caen, convinced that not all public policy provisions need to be extended to private international relations, is led to diminish the role of the *lex fori*. However, taking into account the remarks of the other members of the Commission, Charles Lyon-Caen proposes a subsidiary provision aiming to

110 *Annuaire, op. cit.*, p. 555. In Lyon-Caen's resolution, it should be noted that the question is presented from the point of view of domestic law - which law should be applied to the gambling exception - and it is in this context that the law of the stock exchange is invoked, but is competing with others: law of the conclusion of the contract (in which case the law of the stock exchange applies), mandatory rules/lex *fori*, law of the place where the order was given (often assimilated to the domicile of the originator), not to mention the possible exceptions (law of the domicile of the litigants if they have the same, etc.).

111 Mr Lyon-Caen gives an impressive list in this respect, both in Belgian, Dutch, German, Italian, Spanish, Greek, French and Swiss law, cf. C. Lyon-Caen, *Annuaire, op. cit.*, p. 385.

112 C. Lyon-Caen, *Annuaire, op. cit.*, p. 386.

113 C. Lyon-Caen, *Annuaire, op. cit.*, p. 387. The author underlines that Brocher, Philimore and even Story also share his opinion, cf. fn. 1, p. 387.

114 As an eminent illustration of this reality, Weiss proposes to apply the *lex fori* to the validity of the futures market, 'because the *lex fori*, when it admits the exception of gambling, has a moral character, constitutes for the State an element of its culture, which cannot suffer any infringement', *Annuaire, op. cit.*

115 He is supported in this by Westlake, who states (at the 1910 Session in Paris, following Pillet's report): 'One cannot equate, in order to allow the courts to apply the gambling exception under the *lex fori*, futures markets with acts contrary to universal morality, such as the sale of negroes. This comparison would be inaccurate, as the rules on futures markets exist in countries that belong to the same plane of civilisation. To renounce the rule of the *lex loci contractus* in favour of the *lex fori* would be to ruin all private international law', *Annuaire, op. cit.*, p. 559.

oust the law of the contract, and to apply to it the law of the court petitioned if the two litigants are nationals of the same country.[116]

458. Critique by Professor Armand Lainé (1841–1908). Although he agreed on the need to apply a law to all private law contracts irrespective of their origin, Lainé nevertheless took a critical view of Charles Lyon-Caen's proposal, which he disagreed with as regards his conception of international public policy.[117] This leads him to state that:

> 'The criterion to be followed is to ascertain to what degree, to what extent the necessities of national public order require that this or that national institution or prohibition should be preserved from any alteration in its contact with foreign laws.'[118]

Lainé also considers that, in addition to the provisions of absolute public order that can be found in private law, there are other provisions that have this character because they belong to public law. According to the author, this is the case for the author of criminal and procedural laws, but also for 'the immense category of *lois de police*'.[119] He makes a clear distinction in terms of methodology:

> 'These laws are of absolute public order; they are even more so, to a greater degree, than the laws of absolute public order just mentioned, for they do not merely have the effect of precluding the application of foreign laws; they themselves

---

116 He was prompted to draw up this rule following the remarks of Messrs Brussa and Westlake, as well as Mr de Bar, *Annuaire*, *op. cit.*, p. 545. This rule recalls, on a very distinct basis, Art. 4(2°) of the Rome II Regulation, which allows, by way of derogation, the normally applicable connecting factor (the law of the damage) to be set aside in order to apply the law of the place of the common habitual residence of the litigants; this helps to show that it is a rule for the protection of local public order. The members of the Institute observe that fraud against the law would undoubtedly have made it possible to resolve this difficulty (*Annuaire*, *op. cit.*, p. 558), but Lyon-Caen states that: 'Mr de Bar admits exceptions only in the case of fraud. But in order to avoid any dispute, it is simpler to require an express provision in the law of the State of the forum, as Mr Westlake wishes.')

117 In the *Annuaire*, *op. cit.*, p. 404, Lainé correctly points out that: 'To embark on this path is to go astray, by allowing oneself to be misled by the expression 'international public order', which is false and misleading. There is no international public order in private international law, which would be a public order common to all peoples; this idea can only be found in public international law, where it can be said, for example, that the repression of piracy is of international public order. In private international law, the public policy which may be encountered in a given country by the application of foreign laws is always national [...] even when it is imposed in an absolute manner.' The author illustrates his point with divorce and the prohibition of legal proceedings for paternity, which is not accepted by his neighbours and yet is absolute public policy.

118 *Ibid.*

119 *Annuaire*, *op. cit.*, p. 405.

apply directly to everything (persons, things and legal acts) which is within the competence of our judges.'[120]

Lainé considers that, because it is a police measure, the gambling exception must be limited to the national territory and does not fall within the *lex contractus*, so that a forward contract concluded in a country that admits the gambling exception can be enforced in a country that does not. He logically concludes that the *lex fori* has jurisdiction. Lainé's reasoning is correct on one point: the gambling exception is an overriding mandatory law. However, he is less convincing in assimilating all *lois de police* to public law.[121] This leads him to analyse the question from the point of view of the state's interest, which 'leads ineluctably – with each state giving precedence to its own interests over those of the others – not only to unilateralism, which is not a defect, but to *lex forism*, which is'.[122]

B. The Law of the Principal's Domicile

459. Position of domestic law. Armand Lainé died the year after his remarks. Antoine Pillet was to follow him as rapporteur for this question at the 1910 Paris session. Pillet applies himself to an analysis of domestic law[123] which enables him to account for a confusion on the part of Lyon-Caen. Indeed, the latter uses the same expression 'futures market' to designate the place of the exchange and the private law contract made through this place.[124] In these conditions,

120 *Ibid.*

121 Pillet observed the same thing when he stated at the 1910 Session, where he was rapporteur and where he departed from his master's conceptions, that the notion of police law had two meanings, one broad and one narrow: 'All laws concerning the good police of the country, the family, etc., in short all the laws of a State; it can be restricted to the narrow sense of police regulations aimed at good order in the street, in the stock exchange, without encompassing regulations concerning the validity of contracts of a commercial nature. in short, all the laws of a State' (*Annuaire*, *op. cit.*, pp. 1010–1011).

122 P. Mayer, 'Le phénomène de la coordination des ordres juridiques', *op. cit.*, 163. This remark by Mr Mayer was addressed to the American model of private international law.

123 The position expressed by Pillet was not supported by the members of the Institute, who endorsed Lyon-Caen's project. This prompted Pillet to write a major article, even more thorough than his report, and which no doubt better explains its conclusions. It is this article which provides the account of his thinking here, A. Pillet, 'La loi de conclusion du contrat dans les marchés à terme', *Annales de droit commercial*, 1910, in *Mélanges Antoine Pillet*, Paris, Recueil Sirey, 1929, t. II, p. 67.

124 When Lyon-Caen refers to the 'forward contract', he seems to mean the forward contract and not the futures market as a place of performance. However, the fact that Lyon-Caen wants to apply to it the law of conclusion of the contract, which is not the connecting criterion proposed in the same session, and for which he seems to decide, shows that the place of performance of the contract seems to contain a specificity, and this may be linked on the one hand to the conclusion of such a contract on a public stock exchange, and on the other hand to a favour to the validity of agreements concluded in countries where the legislation is permissive.

Pillet asks two fundamental questions: 'What is indeed the law of conclusion of the contract in the futures markets? And first, what is a futures market?'[125] Pillet defines the futures market by an economic analysis of the transaction at issue[126] before analysing the transaction legally in order to circumscribe the contract covered by the gaming exception. The author then shows perfectly that this transaction does not stem from a single contract, but, because of the intermediation to which it is subject, from at least three contracts: the first two reciprocally binding each of the clients to their intermediary agent on the stock exchange, and the third between the two agents, mandated as brokers,[127] each of whom fetches the counterparty of his client from the stock exchange. The consequence of this arrangement is that the clients have no contractual links with each other,[128] which makes it impossible to apply the gambling exception directly to them.[129]

460. For Pillet, the commission contract between the client and the agent can hardly be considered as a gambling contract, but rather as a 'half of a forward contract' since there is only an offer of a bet, to which the agent does not respond.[130] The author then shows that various aspects make it difficult to believe that the law intended to apply the gambling exception to this contract between agents,[131] *a fortiori* because the gambling exception is opposed by the client at the moment when the agent claims the payment of the difference, 'so it is after the execution of the contract of mandate that it will occur'. This leads the famous internationalist to carefully analyse the intermediary-client relationship, and to observe that if the agency contract is an act of speculation in the case of the principal, it is on the other hand for the agent an 'act of his ministry', which he cannot refuse. Pillet deduces from this that the order issued by the

---

125 A. PILLET, 'La loi de conclusion du contrat dans les marchés à terme', *op. cit.*

126 'The forward contract is, as is well known, an eminently random speculation on the differences in price that a security may present during a given period, a period that the customs of trade fix, except for the possibility of postponements, between the moment when the order is given and the liquidation that follows this time.' (*ibid.*)

127 A. PILLET, 'La loi de conclusion du contrat dans les marchés à terme', *op. cit.*

128 *Ibid.*, p. 70.

129 *Ibid.*, pp. 70–71.

130 The argument is not indisputable since the agent still undertakes to find someone to meet it.

131 On the one hand, because of the commission contract itself, which has the consequence that agents 'do not represent their clients who are gambling, so that we cannot say here what we would say without difficulty if we were in civil matters, namely that things happen as if the two clients were in each other's presence' (A. PILLET, 'La loi de conclusion du contrat dans les marchés à termeÆ, *op. cit.) Secondly*, because of the way in which the agent executes the orders, since he may well conclude the offer to buy and sell with different persons in different countries (*ibid.*, p. 71). Finally, to consider that this contract is the one that the law intended to strike the gambling exception would lead to each of the agents being able to oppose the gambling exception, since 'the legal consequences of the deal stop on their head until they can defer by the rendering of accounts on the head of their client' (*ibid.*, p. 71–72).

client is the truly speculative act that the law must strike down.[132] The difficulty is nevertheless that the contract to which this order gives rise, because it will generally be concluded by correspondence, will be subject to the law of the place where it is accepted, i.e. the seat of the stockbroker. Pillet therefore proposes to consider that the contract is formed at the place where the order is issued, since the agent will be obliged to accept it.

461. This is why the most complete formulation of Pillet's doctrine is given by Thaller who, attracted by the author's analysis, believes that the overriding *ratio legis* of the gambling exception lies in the fact that 'the legislator wished to protect his citizens from the madness of the stock market, to save individual fortunes from ruin',[133] which encourages him to subject the gambling exception to the law of the domicile of the principal.[134] Pillet refused to do so on the grounds that the stockbroker could not determine the place of residence of the principal. However, the application of the law of the place where the order is given leads to results that are out of step with the purpose of the institution because of the contingency of the results it brings about and the ease with which such a connecting factor can be manipulated.[135] On the other hand, the domicile criterion solves this difficulty: it does not matter whether the person moves, the law of his or her domicile will always be applied. Above all, Pillet greatly overestimates the practical difficulty which would simply result in stockbrokers, on the one hand, requesting the domicile of their principal[136] and, on the other hand, refusing to conclude forward contracts with persons domiciled in a legal system which prohibits forward contracts, a refusal which is all the more intuitive for the stockbroker as he will never receive the profits of the forward contract, but will always suffer losses which he will not be able to pass on to the principal.

---

132 There is something surprising in observing that the solution offered here by Pillet does not lead to 'depriving the winner of a bet of action' (A. Pillet, 'La loi de conclusion du contrat dans les marchés à terme', *op. cit.*, p. 71), which is for him the purpose of the gambling, but in fact to allowing the loser not to pay. In fact, the winner will have been paid by his stockbroker, who cannot invoke the gambling exception against him.

133 E. Thaller, *Yearbook*, *op. cit.*, p. 1013.

134 This was rejected by Pillet, who thought the proposal was excellent, because of its lack of practicality, *Annuaire*, *op. cit.*, p. 1014.

135 It seems to us that the same applies here to the law of payment proposed by Batiffol. Indeed, the eminent author thinks of the gambling exception in the category within which it falls, the bet, and observes that its purpose, like insurance or loans, is *payment*. He therefore favours application of the law of the place of payment; however, the difficulty reappears: if the parties have not specified the portability or the querability of the payment, it will be unforeseeable, *a fortiori* if the rules of their domiciles prescribe distinct rules on the matter. In this case, the author is in favour of the subsidiary application of the law of the place where the contract was concluded, which in stock exchange matters amounts to applying the law of the stock exchange. Cf. H. Batiffol, *Les conflits de lois en matière de contrats*, *op. cit.*, no. 356, p. 318.

136 This is a very simple formality, even by letter.

In retrospect, the gambling exception has the originality of being a resident protection provision, applicable in the relationship between investors and the financial market. As these relationships take place through market members, it is the latter that the provision affects. Its function places it unquestionably among the *mandatory* rules: it derogates from the law of contract, and applies to all local residents. Today, its function is taken over both by the rules of conduct for investment firms and by the regulation of consumer contracts, applicable under the domicile of the consumer, which undoubtedly shows the ambivalence of rules that interfere with the performance of the contract in order to protect one of the parties.

462. Conclusion of the section. The relationship between market members and their clients is governed by a specific law, the law designated by them in their contract. This law may be subject to interference from the rules of conduct of investment firms, which apply by virtue of their status and independently of the law applicable to the contract, and from certain laws designed to protect residents against the volatility of financial contracts. The latter rules are, however, independent of the law of the financial market, and are applicable by virtue of the protection of residents in general, or consumers in particular.

463. Conclusion of the chapter. Market members enter into three types of relationship. The first is with the financial market operator and concerns a set of obligations for which they are accountable. They should be subject only to the law of the financial market, as they are pursuing its proper functioning. The second relates to contracts concluded by market members. They are subject to the law of the financial market, because this is the only objective, stable and predictable connecting factor. The third relates to clients. Here, the law of the financial market should take a back seat to the *lex contractus* designated by the parties. However, the *lex contractus* is likely to be affected by the rules of conduct applicable to the professional status of the market member and by any rules protecting residents from financial contracts.

CHAPTER 2
MARKET OPERATIONS

464. It will be shown here that the regulation of market operations pursues the objective of the proper functioning of the market. This objective should not be too radically dissociated from that of investor protection: by protecting the functioning of the financial market, regulation indirectly protects the investors who use it. From an international perspective, this objective explains why the law to be applied should, in our view, be subject to the law of the financial market, and the supervision of transactions should be entrusted to the authority of the place of listing. The legal system of the issuer's registered office may, however, have cumulative jurisdiction, depending on the circumstances – in particular where the regulation in question is aimed at protecting the internal organisation of the listed company at least as much as that of the market. The application of the law on market transactions will be studied by distinguishing between transactions aimed at supervising the issuer and those that artificially modify the securities price. In the first case, market transactions are subject to the law on threshold crossings and takeover bids (Section 1); in the second case, they are subject to the regulations on the purchase by the issuer of its own shares and on short selling (Section 2).

SECTION 1. SUPERVISION OF THE ISSUER

465. Threshold crossing and takeover bid. Threshold crossing law is a separate body of rules from takeover regulation. The former has its source in the Transparency Directive, which was adopted on the basis of the unification of the internal market, while the latter is derived from the Takeover Directive. The latter, although adopted at the same time as the financial legislative package of the Prospectus/Transparency/Market Abuse Directives established on the basis of the internal market, is a company law directive,[1] adopted on the basis of the

[1] This is the thirteenth company law directive. The gestation of this directive was particularly long, due to the rejection of the first directive by the European Parliament on 4 July 2001. A group of experts was appointed, under the chairmanship of Mr Jaap Winter, to propose a compromise text, from which the directive and the accompanying report emerged. On the genealogy of the Takeover Directive, see M. LUBY and M. MENJUCQ, 'Offres publiques d'acquisition. Directive 2004/25/EC of 21 April 2004', *J.-Cl. Soc.*, fasc. 2132, up to date on 3 September 2010, no. 1-3.

freedom of establishment.[2] However, the French transposition of the directive runs counter to this European presentation, since the regulation of threshold crossings is set out in Articles L. 233-7 et seq. of the Commercial Code, while the regulation of takeover bids is set out in Articles L. 433-1 et seq. of the Monetary and Financial Code and Articles 233-1 et seq. of the AMF General Regulation. This presentation of their origins already shows the ambivalence of these mechanisms, which appear to be on the borderline between listed company law and financial market law. It also shows that, although major holding notifications make it easier to apply takeover law, this last feature is far from exhausting their function, and in fact does not even appear to be their primary purpose.[3] It is therefore not surprising that the conflicts of laws can show divergent solutions for these two institutions.

The difficulty in distinguishing between capital markets law and company law stems from the fact that, here, the former pursues an objective that is consistent with the latter.[4] To some extent, however, this convergence erases, from a domestic perspective, the duality of the legislative policies of each discipline. From an international perspective, this duality arises either because the objectives are likely to diverge – a foreign company law, for example, is likely to be less liberal than ours – or because the means of achieving its objectives make it impossible to consider that the foreign legislative policy is equivalent to that pursued by the forum. This explains why the conflict of laws relating to the law of thresholds and the law of takeover bids, and their resolution, are neither identical nor symmetrical.

The following discussion is intended to show why, on the one hand, the regulation of threshold crossings may be subject to *both* the *lex societatis* and the *lex mercatus* (§ 1). On the other hand, the law of the financial market should, to a very large extent, take precedence in resolving conflicts of law in relation to takeover bids we will outline the means of achieving this while respecting the primacy of the *lex societatis* where this cannot be avoided (§ 2).

---

2 This directive was adopted on the basis of Art. 44 of the Treaty establishing the European Community (now Art. 50(2°)(g) of the Treaty on the Functioning of the European Union), which allows the European institutions to achieve freedom of establishment 'by coordinating to the necessary extent and with a view to making such safeguards equivalent which, for the protection of the interests of members and others, are required by Member States of companies within the meaning of the second paragraph of Article 54', whereas financial regulation is generally carried out under Art. 114 of the Treaty on the Functioning of the European Union (formerly Art. 95 of the Treaty on the Functioning of the European Union), which is devoted to 'the establishment and functioning of the internal market'.

3 As some authors write, 'the communication of information cannot be limited to the period of a takeover bid: it must be able to take place at any time, independently of any takeover bid', T. Bonneau *et al.*, *Droit financier*, 1st ed, *op. cit.*, no. 1032.

4 As Mr Synvet observed early on, see *supra*, para. 5.

§ 1. THRESHOLD CROSSINGS

466. It is instructive that the regulation of threshold crossings is included in a section on 'notifications and information' in the chapter entitled 'subsidiaries, holdings and supervised companies' of Title III of the Commercial Code on provisions common to various commercial companies. It makes it clear that the regulation of information on the supervision of companies is not specific to companies whose shares are admitted to trading on a regulated market, but rather falls under the general law on commercial companies. This is one of the reasons why the *lex societatis* is so commonly envisaged to govern such crossings. Indeed, the rules relating to the ordinary law of notifications are concerned with information owed by the company to its shareholders. They serve a purpose specific to the operation of the company and are therefore legitimately subject to the *lex societatis* (I). While the regulation of shareholding thresholds does contribute to the information of shareholders, it will be shown that it also develops a function of its own, consisting of informing investors of the place where the shares are traded, information that contributes to price discovery. This function, which is aimed at the proper functioning of the financial market, explains why the regulation of shareholding thresholds should also be subject to the *lex mercatus* (II).

I. Corporate Function of Notifications under General Company Law

467. Identification of the company's activities. Article L. 233-6, para. 1, of the Commercial Code, applicable to all commercial companies, requires that the annual report disclose, above certain thresholds, the acquisition of a stake in the capital of a French company. This information obliges the directors[5] to report on the company's activities to the shareholders, to whom the report is addressed.[6] It allows shareholders to exercise oversight over management by learning about the company's activities. This rule is applicable to companies that have 'acquired, during a financial year, a holding in a company whose registered office is in the territory of the French Republic'.[7] French law therefore imposes on a possibly foreign company an obligation to inform its own shareholders because of a participation in a French company. It would have been more consistent to attach

5 If the obligation is incumbent on the company, the penalty for its non-performance is nevertheless incumbent on the directors, see Art. L. 247-1 of the Commercial Code. The penalty is criminal: it is a fine which may be accompanied by a two-year prison sentence.

6 This function of providing information on the company's activity is even clearer when reading para. 2 of Art. L. 233-6 of the Commercial Code, since it requires an account of the activity of each subsidiary by branch of activity. This function is also apparent from Art. L. 233-15 of the Commercial Code, which requires the company's management to append the subsidiaries and holdings to the balance sheet.

7 Art. L. 233-6 of the Commercial Code.

these obligations to French companies acquiring stakes in other companies, even if they are foreign. As far as French companies are concerned, this identification of shareholdings held by one company in another can also be seen as the first step in a broader process aimed at prohibiting self-control.

468. Prohibition of self-control.[8] Another purpose of the notification of shareholdings is to prohibit cross-shareholdings and self-control. Indeed, cross-shareholdings are discouraged by French law through the combined action of Articles L. 233-12 and L. 233-13 of the Commercial Code, which require joint-stock companies with cross-shareholdings to disclose the amount of and changes in such holdings, under penalty of a fine.[9] This information must be notified to the supervised company[10] and presented to the shareholders.[11] This provision contributes to the regulation of self-control by facilitating disclosure.[12] For this reason, the trigger for the notification obligation on companies is not the crossing of a threshold, but the acquisition of control. These measures are not exclusive of the prohibition on cross-shareholdings in Articles L. 233-29 and L. 233-30 of the Commercial Code, whose civil penalty – the deprivation of the voting rights of the company in which a holding of more than ten per cent was acquired[13] – and criminal fine[14] also help to dissuade managers from carrying out such transactions. Lastly, the sanctions provided for in Article L. 233-31 of the Commercial Code, which also aim to deprive the shares of companies attempting to exercise control over their own affairs of voting rights, are crucial to the prohibition of self-control.[15] The possibly indirect nature of the control makes it irrelevant what legal form the intermediary takes. Its purpose is also likely to be to disregard the location of its registered office.[16]

469. Function of the prohibition of treasury shares. This prohibition of treasury shares has the same objectives as the former prohibition of the company's own

---

8 Some authors consider that 'self-control is not illegal, it is only regulated in its effects, which is not the sign of a prohibition, but rather of the recognition of its validity', A. Viandier, *OPA OPE et autres offres publiques*, 5th ed., Paris, Francis Lefebvre, 2014.

9 Art. L. 247-12, para. 2, of the Commercial Code.

10 Art. L. 233-12, para. 2, of the Commercial Code.

11 Art. L. 233-13, para. 3, of the Commercial Code.

12 In this sense, see *Memento Sociétés Commerciales*, Paris, Francis Lefebvre, 2017, no. 79701. Report on the function of disclosure requirements in facilitating the detection of market abuse, *infra*, paras. 543 et seq.

13 Art. L. 233-29, para. 2 of the Commercial Code; deprivation of voting rights and not nullity of the transfer, which was confirmed by Com., 3 January 1996, *JCP E*, 199, II, 808, note H. Hovasse.

14 Art. L. 247-3 of the Commercial Code.

15 Including if the participation is in fact a minority one, but constitutes an action in concert, see e.g. Com., 29 June 2010, no. 09-112.

16 *Memento Sociétés Commerciales*, *op. cit.*, no. 79281, 1°.

share buy-back.[17] On the one hand, the aim was to preserve the integrity of the company's capital in its function as a common pledge for creditors and, on the other hand, to protect the 'principle of equality of shareholders'.[18] This first function has lost its vigour since share capital no longer seems to pursue this purpose.[19] Nevertheless, it seems to us that it still supports the regulation, because of the deceptive character of a share capital that would be held by the company itself. Indeed, even if one considers that share capital is merely an 'index of solvency',[20] the publicity of a partially self-owned share capital is likely to mislead both third parties in general and future shareholders in particular about the state of the company.

The 'principle of equality of shareholders' now justifies this regulation when companies do not have their securities admitted to trading. However, it is necessary to clarify the meaning of this principle, which concerns the equal *treatment of* shareholders in the internal order of the company and justifies, for example, the provision according to which 'the reduction of capital [...] may not affect the equality of shareholders'.[21] Academics consider that this equality in the internal order is not absolute and that 'it is rather a question of equality between shares of the same class, and it is agreed that an inequality could be accepted by each of the shareholders from whom a sacrifice would be required'.[22] Similarly, when the Commercial Code provides that 'the auditors shall ensure that equality has been respected among the shareholders, members or members of the competent body',[23] the equality referred to is that relating to the verification of the distribution of dividends or the allocation of voting rights.[24] In view of the prohibition of treasury stock, the principle of equal treatment of shareholders is intended to prevent the company from favouring one shareholder to the detriment of the others by purchasing his shares at an advantageous price.[25] However, this is as much a rule relating to the equal treatment of shareholders as it is a rule relating to the conduct of the governing body, which must act in the interests of the company. Above all,

---

17 When the company has its securities admitted to trading, an additional function appears in the regulation of the repurchase of its own shares, see *infra*, para. 513.

18 A. Couret, H. Le Nabasque *et al.*, *Droit financier*, *op. cit.*, no. 1556; R. Mortier, 'Rachats d'actions ou de parts sociales', *J.-Cl. Banque crédit bourse*, 2011, fasc. 1658, no. 16; S. Torck, 'Le rachat par les sociétés cotées de leurs propres actions' (The repurchase by listed companies of their own shares), *BJB*, 2002, no. 509.

19 On this question, see generally A. Couret et H. Le Nabasque (eds.), *Quel avenir pour le capital social*, Paris, Dalloz, 2004.

20 P. Le Cannu, 'Les rides du capital social' in A. Couret et H. Le Nabasque (dir.), *Quel avenir pour le capital social?*, Paris, Dalloz, 2004, nos. 11 et seq.

21 Art. L. 225-204 of the Commercial Code.

22 P. Merle and A. Fauchon, *Sociétés commerciales*, Paris, Dalloz, 2020, no. 653.

23 Art. L. 823-11 of the Commercial Code.

24 P. Merle and A. Fauchon, *Sociétés commerciales*, *op. cit.*, no. 576.

25 S. Torck, 'Le rachat par les sociétés cotées de leurs propres actions', *op. cit.*

the prohibition of self-control is part of the broader objective of the proper functioning of corporate bodies. Indeed, by depriving the acquired shares of voting rights, the prohibition of self-control avoids two pitfalls: that the director may unduly invite himself, in the name of the company, to the general meeting; that the effectiveness of internal oversight by the true partners over the directors is diminished.

These different functions assigned to the prohibition of self-control all relate to the functioning of the company, which justifies the application of the *lex societatis*. In the case of cross-shareholdings, the seat of one of the companies in France should be sufficient to trigger the applicability of the regulation.

II. Financial Function of the Threshold Crossing Regulation

470. The contemporary regulation of shareholding thresholds is based on Articles 9 to 16 of the Transparency Directive, transposed into Articles L. 233-7 et seq. of the Commercial Code.[26] It requires that a person who crosses a certain threshold in a company whose securities are admitted to trading disclose both the amount of his acquisition and his possible intention to acquire more. This disclosure is addressed to the company itself, but also to the market authority which is responsible for making the information public. This duality of addressees reveals the dual function of the law on threshold crossings, which is corroborated by its international application. Indeed, while the function of these rules is undoubtedly to enable the company's managers and other shareholders to know the evolution of the shareholding, they also have the purpose of informing local investors about the supervision of the company, and thereby contributing to price discovery (A). This is why this mechanism has a maximum scope of application: it applies under the *lex societatis*, as well as under the *lex mercatus* (B).

A. Function of the Threshold Crossing Regulation

471. Distinction from other notifications. The threshold crossing regulation constitutes a notification relating to the control of the company. However, the configuration of the mechanism in question distinguishes it radically from the other company law notification mechanisms previously studied. Firstly, the purpose of the threshold crossing is not the acquisition of a shareholding, but its eventuality or, more precisely, to use Mr Chacornac's expression, the *voting power*.[27] For this reason, the instruments for obtaining voting rights are

---

26 That is, it is listed in the section on notifications of equity investments.

27 J. Chacornac, *Essai sur les fonctions de l'information en droit des instruments financiers*, *op. cit.*, no. 551.

taken into account in determining the threshold.[28] Secondly, the notification obligation is not on the company, but on the shareholder crossing a threshold. The content of the notification does not stop at the declaration of the acquisition: the person crossing the threshold must also declare 'the objectives he intends to pursue over the next six months', including whether he intends to increase his shareholding in the company and how he intends to act within it.[29] Thirdly, the addressee of these notifications is not only the target company, but the general public. Fourthly, failure to notify the crossing or the declaration of intent is subject to a specific sanction, which deprives the 'shares exceeding the fraction that has not been duly declared' of voting rights.[30]

472. Double function of the notification of threshold crossings. Notification of the crossing of a threshold has a dual purpose: to protect the issuer and to inform the market.[31]

473. Protection of the issuer. The first function is the protection of the issuer. More specifically, it aims at protecting the management and other shareholders. In this first aspect, the regulation of shareholding thresholds can be seen as a correlate of the obligations imposed on the issuer as a result of the admission of securities to trading. Indeed, by imposing the elimination of any approval clauses and by obliging the issuer to stipulate, at least in part, that its securities be in bearer form, the *lex mercatus* deprived the issuer of the means of knowing the shareholder base.[32] Threshold crossing regulations partially restore this knowledge by enabling the issuer to determine the 'influence of a shareholder, in terms of capital and voting rights'[33] and, consequently, to anticipate

---

28 See the list in Art. L. 233-9 of the Commercial Code.

29 Art. L. 233-7, VII°, of the Commercial Code.

30 Art. L. 233-14, para. 1, of the Commercial Code. Not to mention that managers or other shareholders as well as the financial market authority may request the total or partial suspension of the voting rights of a shareholder who has not declared his threshold (Art. L. 233-14, para. 4 of the Commercial Code). This request can only be made to the commercial court in whose jurisdiction the company has its registered office, clearly limiting this sanction to French companies and clearly enshrining, if not the crossing of the threshold, at least the provision in the *lex societatis*. A criminal sanction accompanies this civil sanction, sentencing the natural persons managing the company to a penalty of EUR 18,000.

31 J. Chacornac, *Essai sur les fonctions de l'information en droit des instruments financiers*, *op. cit.*, no. 548; R. Dambre, *Les contrats financiers sur action*, *op. cit.*, no. 291. Also believing that the regulation of threshold crossings has a dual function (market information and shareholder protection); A. Couret, H. Le Nabasque *et al.*, *op. cit.*, no. 1352; H. Synvet, 'Propos impertinents sur l'activisme actionnarial', *RDBF*, November 2020, p. 75, spec. nos. 12 and 16.

32 This statement may be qualified by the existence of identifiable bearer securities, see Art. L. 228-2 of the Commercial Code.

33 J. Chacornac, *Essai sur les fonctions de l'information en droit des instruments financiers*, *op. cit.*, no. 548.

takeovers'.[34] In this sense, the regulation of threshold crossings is in line with that of takeover bids. This issuer protection function also explains why the articles of association may reinforce the thresholds provided for by the law.[35]

This function also explains why the French legislator wished to extend the material scope of this regulation to all 'financial instrument markets admitting shares to trading that can be registered in an account with an intermediary mentioned in Article L. 211-3 of the Monetary and Financial Code',[36] i.e. persons authorised to carry out the activity of custody account holder. Admission of securities to the systems of a central depository requires registration with a custodian, unless the issuer decides otherwise.[37] The French financial markets most often require the issuer's securities to be registered with a central depository,[38] thereby making Article L. 233-7(I) of the Commercial Code applicable[39] insofar as the issuer's articles of association allow for account registration with an authorised intermediary. This last statement was unambiguously confirmed by the Court of Cassation in a ruling in *Madag*.[40]

---

34 *Ibid.* Defending such an objective of the regulation of threshold crossings, see 'Franchissement de seuil' in P.-H. Conac, *Répertoire de droit des sociétés*, Paris, Dalloz, no. 1.

35 Art. L. 233-7 III of the Commercial Code.

36 Art. L. 233-7 I of the Commercial Code. This amendment was made by Ordinance no. 2004-604 of 24 June 2004 reforming the regime for securities issued by commercial companies, see the review by P.-H. Conac, 'Franchissement de seuil' (Threshold crossing), *op. cit.* The legislator does not distinguish between a multilateral trading facility and an organised trading facility, so the criteria set out in the law apply to both types of market. However, the AMF General Regulation applies the threshold crossing regime only to multilateral trading facilities (see Art. 223-15-1 of the AMF General Regulation), leaving organised trading facilities outside the scope of threshold crossing.

37 Art. L. 211-7 of the Monetary and Financial Code.

38 See e.g. Art. 3.1.4 of the Trading Rules of Euronext Growth (formerly Alternext) of 29 May 2018, a multilateral trading facility, which requires issuers to admit their securities to a central depository, and Art. 2.1 of the Trading Rules of Euronext Access (formerly the free market and delisted securities) of 19 June 2017.

39 This concerns only the 'quantitative' declaration of the threshold crossed, and not the declaration of intent governed by VII° of Art. L. 233-7 of the Commercial Code, see T. Bonneau *et al.*, *Droit financier*, *op. cit.*, no. 1128. However, Art. 223-15-1 of the AMF General Regulation does not make such a distinction and provides for the application of its entire quantitative and qualitative mechanism 'to the organised multilateral trading facilities mentioned in Article 524–1 when a person comes to own, under the conditions set out in Articles L. 233-7 et seq. of the Commercial Code, more than half or nineteen twentieths of the capital or voting rights'.

40 Cass., com., 10 February 2015, no. 13-14778, *Bull. Joly sociétés*, 2015, 182, note H. Le Nabasque. The argument of the authors of the appeal was that registered securities (pure or administered) would not be subject to the obligation to declare the crossing of thresholds, which is provided for bearer securities only (which was the case, due to the legislator's clumsiness during the reform of the securities regime by the order of 24 June 2004, on which see P.-H. Conac, 'Franchissement de seuil', *op. cit.*). Several authors were of this opinion, in particular because the *ratio legis* of threshold crossings would have resided solely in the issuer's knowledge of its shareholder base, which the existence of pure registered or administered securities made unnecessary: see F. Martin Laprade, 'Franchissement de seuil' in *Dictionnaire Joly Bouse*, Paris, Joly, 2012, nos. 018–028; P.-H. Conac,

This case also allowed the *Conseil Constitutionnel*, when asked about the compatibility of the infringement of property rights, by depriving a shareholder who does not declare that he or she has crossed a threshold of voting rights, to specify that this deprivation is justified by a general interest, namely that of 'preventing the acquisition of hidden holdings in listed companies in order to strengthen, on the one hand, compliance with the rules ensuring fairness in relations between the company and its members, as well as between the latter, and, on the other, the transparency of the markets'.[41] The dual function pursued here could not be better summarised.

474. Protection of the financial market. The second function of the threshold crossing notification is to warn other investors of this change in control of the company. As Mr Chacornac writes, 'the identity of shareholders and the size of their respective holdings are likely to have an impact on investors' predictions regarding the value of the issuer's financial instruments'.[42] Indeed, this information, by revealing the structure of the shareholder base (concentrated, dispersed) and its evolution (static, volatile), contributes to the determination of the value of the stock,[43] thus allowing investors to evaluate their strategy according to the distribution of control of the company among the shareholders.[44] As the COB itself wrote, 'any significant change in the capital structure is also of interest to all shareholders and the public'.[45]

B. International Scope of Application

475. Relationships within the European Union. Within the European Union, the regulation of threshold crossings is subject only to the *lex societatis*. This

---

'Franchissement de seuil', *op. cit.*, no. 220, *Bull. ANSA*, no. 05-042, Legal Committee of 1 June 2005. Such an argument is based on the idea that the sole purpose of crossing a threshold is to identify shareholders, which is questionable, see *infra*, para. 476.

41 QPC, Cons. const., 28 February 2014, Madag, no. 2013-369.

42 J. Chacornac, *Essai sur les fonctions de l'information en droit des instruments financiers*, *op. cit.*, no. 548.

43 See in this sense This is also the reason why the acquisition of control is partially regulated by the *lex mercatus*, which has an influence on the price, see *infra*, para. 486.

44 J. Chacornac, *Essai sur les fonctions de l'information en droit des instruments financiers*, *op. cit.*, no. 548. Moreover, the shareholder structure can have a determining influence not only on the price of securities, but also on their 'liquidity', on the ease with which they can be sold. It also reveals the balance of power within the company: a majority shareholder is in a position to better control the managers, which has been reflected in American law, see P.-H. Conac, *La régulation des marchés boursiers par la Commission des opérations de bourse (COB) et la Securities and exchange commission (SEC)*, *op. cit.* On the other hand, a scattered shareholder base leaving room for a management in a position of strength constitutes the breeding ground for shareholder activism, on which see H. Synvet, 'Propos impertinents sur l'activisme actionnarial', *op. cit.*

45 COB, *Annual Report*, 1974, p. 40 quoted by R. Dambre, *Les contrats financiers sur action*, *op. cit.*

connecting factor results from the application of Article 9 of the Transparency Directive,[46] with Article L. 233-7 of the Commercial Code providing a rigorous transposition of this criterion. However, the market information function of the rules on major holdings militates in favour of applying the *lex mercatus regardless of* the origin of the company. This is why linking these obligations to the *lex societatis* seems insufficient.[47] The Transparency Directive undoubtedly subjects all the information obligations it institutes to the *lex societatis*. However, we have already observed that the application of this criterion to periodic disclosure obligations was justified because it reduced the cost of this obligation for the issuer. Here, the debtor of the information is not only the company, but the investor. Moreover, the cost of providing this information is very reasonable. The argument is therefore not convincing.

It is true that the European origin of the Transparency Directive makes it possible to ensure that European legal systems know of an equivalent provision applicable when their companies have their securities admitted to trading on a French financial market. Moreover, since the regulation of threshold crossings also contributes to improving the organisation of listed companies, this connecting factor is not illegitimate. In this case, however, the company should also inform the market authority of its listing location.[48] There is no doubt that the authority best placed to receive this information is the financial market authority: it is its website that market participants know about, it is the authority best placed to disseminate the information, and it is also the authority that will subsequently be called upon to monitor any takeover bid resulting from a change of control. This last aspect shows that the regulation of shareholding thresholds is at least as closely linked to the *lex mercatus*.

Although it is not the cornerstone of takeover regulation, the regulation of threshold crossings is certainly a significant support as it automatically enables the competent authority to question the intentions of a person increasing his or her share capital.[49] It may be argued that systematically applying the *lex mercatus* to this obligation multiplies the information in the event of multiple listings of the issuer's shares. However, on the one hand, it is possible to

---

46 The latter submits this regulation to the home Member State, which is defined in Art. 2(1)(i) of the Transparency Directive.

47 In the same sense, see S. Lambert, *L'application internationale du droit financier*, *op. cit.*, no. 687.

48 As is the case in France, see Art. L. 233-7(II) of the Monetary and Financial Code.

49 Indeed, on the takeover bid side, the AMF can always question a shareholder of a company listed on the French market to find out his or her intentions with regard to the possible filing of a takeover bid (Art. L. 433-1(V) of the Monetary and Financial Code and Arts. 222-22 et seq. of the AMF General Regulation). The declaration of intent applies the regulations on public bids relating to disclosure (Art. 231-36 and 37 of the AMF General Regulation), transaction reporting (Art. 231-38 to 41 of the AMF General Regulation) and trading in the target company's securities (Art. 232-14 to 20 of the AMF General Regulation). If it states that it does not want to file an offer, it cannot file one within six months.

designate a lead market so that the information is only communicated to an authority known to all[50] and, on the other hand, even if the issuer is required to provide the information to several market authorities, it will at least be the same information within the Union, thus reducing the scope of the argument.

In fact, the dual functions pursued by the regulation of threshold crossings – proper functioning of the organisation of listed companies; informing investors of the place of listing – explains the difficulty of deciding on the conflict of laws. It seems to us, however, that a binary approach is not necessary: the harmonious solution to the conflict of laws lies, in this case, in the cumulative application of the *lex societatis* and the *lex mercatus*. If, as the law stands, the *lex societatis* prevails, it is because of the sanction attached to the violation of the threshold crossing regulation; this prevalence is nevertheless neither necessary nor inevitable.

476. The corporate sanction. The application of the *lex societatis* is undoubtedly based on the idea that the legal system of the registered office is best placed to implement the civil sanction attached to the crossing of thresholds, i.e. the deprivation of voting rights. As Professor Boucobza writes, these sanctions 'are the most appropriate to compel participants to comply with the provisions of stock exchange law'.[51] Unquestionably, such a sanction affects the functioning of the company and would, as such, fall within the scope of the *lex societatis*. Mr Synvet thus writes: 'Since the sanctions provided for in the event that they [the laws governing publicity] are violated do not affect the functioning of the company, they do not fall within the scope of the *lex societatis*.'[52] However, it is necessary to dissociate the characterisation of the rule from that of its sanction.[53] If the rule's primary function is the proper functioning of the financial market, it should be subject to the law of the financial market. The question of its sanction poses distinct difficulties. However, they are not insurmountable.

First of all, the sanction for violating the threshold crossing regulation is not limited to the deprivation of voting rights. It is also possible to hold the investor administratively liable. This sanction is sufficiently comminatory to encourage compliance with the provisions of the legal system of the place of listing. Secondly, the enforcement of corporate sanctions imposed by the legal system of the place of listing is entirely possible. It is sufficient to secure the cooperation of the legal system of the registered office. Such cooperation

---

50 See the mechanism set up for public bids, *infra*, para. 492.

51 X. Boucobza, 'L'offre publique transfrontière' in *Mélanges AEBDF I*, 1997, pp. 53 et seq. The author refers to the sanction of the public bid. In this sense, the development of *a priori* sanctions, such as the declaration of non-compliance of the bid by the AMF, is even more restrictive than *a posteriori* sanctions, even if they are automatic, such as the deprivation of voting rights.

52 H. Synvet, *L'organisation juridique du groupe international de société*, *op. cit.*, no. 461.

53 Comp. A. Tenenbaum, 'La compétence internationale des autorités de surveillance des marchés financiers en matière d'offre publique', *RCDIP*, 2006, pp. 557 et seq.

can easily be established within the Union. Where the issuer is from a third country, it can be based on an agreement between administrative authorities under which the authority of the place of the registered office undertakes to request the implementation of sanctions from the legal system of the market. The system proposed here is not new. It is the one already in force in the third countries.

477. Relationship with third countries. These observations are reinforced by the application of the Transparency Directive to third country issuers. The competent legal system is the one 'chosen by the issuer from among the Member States in which its securities are admitted to trading on a regulated market'.[54] The Monetary and Financial Code, which transposed this provision,[55] extends the application of Article L. 233-7 of the Commercial Code to issuers whose securities are admitted to trading on a financial market, even if their registered office is located outside France or the European Economic Area.[56] Article L. 451-2-1 paragraph 2 of the Monetary and Financial Code nevertheless provides that:

> 'The AMF may exempt a person holding shares in a company whose registered office is located outside the territory of the European Economic Area from the disclosure requirements mentioned in I of Article L. 233-7 of the Commercial Code if it considers that the requirements to which that person is subject under the legislation of the third country applicable to him are equivalent.'

It should be noted here that the information referred to in Article L. 233-7(I) of the Commercial Code is intended solely for shareholders and is intended to protect them. In other words, it is less a rule of financial market law than a rule of listed company law. Its limitation to French companies is therefore not surprising. In the same vein, Article L. 451-2-1 paragraph 3 of the Monetary and Financial Code allows the AMF to limit the application of Article L. 233-8 of the Commercial Code. This provision is also a shareholder protection measure: it requires issuers to inform them monthly about the counting of shares and votes, unless foreign law contains an equivalent provision.[57]

---

[54] Art. 2(1)(i)(i) of the Transparency Directive.

[55] Art. L. 451-2-1 para. 1 of the Monetary and Financial Code. The provision retains the jurisdiction of the AMF when it is the competent authority for the purposes of Art. L. 451-1-2 of the Monetary and Financial Code, i.e. the authority designated by the third-country issuer to file periodic disclosure requirements.

[56] Through the application of Art. L. 451-2-1 para. 1 of the Monetary and Financial Code, which makes Art. L. 233-7(I) of the Commercial Code to issuers covered by Art. L. 451-1-2(II) of the Monetary and Financial Code.

[57] Art. L. 233-8 of the Commercial Code is made applicable to issuers from a state outside the European Economic Area by means of Art. L. 451-2-1 para. 1 of the Monetary and Financial Code.

On the other hand, the obligation to inform the financial market of the crossing of thresholds pursuant to Article L. 233-7(II) of the Commercial Code remains applicable. The threshold crossing is then calculated on the basis of French rules, independently of the foreign *lex societatis*. The same applies to the resulting rules, in particular those relating to action in concert, which are calculated on the basis of the rules governing threshold crossings.[58] It is remarkable that the French legislator has gone so far in the sophistication of the international application of threshold crossing regulations, by clearly distinguishing the information given to shareholders from that given to the market, which is, however, in domestic perspective, the same information. It seems to us that this distinction made in Article L. 233-7 of the Commercial Code perfectly illustrates the dual objectives pursued by this provision. This distinction should, in a form of symmetry, encourage the French legislator to provide for the application of Article L. 233-7(I) of the Commercial Code to French companies whose securities are admitted to trading on a foreign financial market. A literal interpretation of Article L. 233-7(I) of the Commercial Code does not stand in the way of this.[59] It would nevertheless benefit from being clarified in this sense. The consequences of the function attributed to the regulation of threshold crossings in domestic relations should be drawn here: if it is a rule of listed company law, the *lex societatis* should apply, regardless of the place of listing. This clarification could usefully be included in the company's articles of association.

478. Conclusion of the paragraph. While it is clear that most of the disclosure obligations of issuers whose securities are admitted to trading are enshrined in the sole corporate order, the same cannot be said of the financial regulation of threshold crossings, which would benefit from being subject to the *lex mercatus in* addition to the *lex societatis*. This regulation undoubtedly has corporate roots. However, the admission of a company's securities to trading on a financial market, without severing these roots, creates other, no less profound, roots, which also link the regulation of threshold crossings to a distinct body of law, that of the *lex mercatus*.[60] This additional connecting factor does not prevent the information that the shareholder owes to the French company in respect of

58 Art. L. 451-2-1 para. 1 of the Monetary and Financial Code extends the application of Art. L. 233-7 to L. 233-12 of the Commercial Code and only provides for self-limitation with regard to the provisions in the body of the text.

59 The only material restriction imposed by the rule in Art. L. 233-7 I of the Commercial Code is that the securities must be registered with a custodian account holder (see *supra*, para. 475), which is not incompatible with the admission of securities to a foreign financial market.

60 This reality is currently ignored by the connecting factor of the conflict rule. The proposal to apply the *lex mercatus* to the regulation of major holdings allows, from the point of view of the purpose of the legislative package, a better protection of issuers while preserving the interests of investors.

threshold crossings from continuing to be subject to the *lex societatis*, even where the place of listing is not located within the Union.

§ 2. TAKEOVER BIDS

479. Scope of the study. The law on public offers governs proposals to enter into contracts which, if accepted by their addressees, result in the acquisition or sale of financial securities admitted to trading, in certain cases giving the offeror control of the company sought.[61] This definition already distinguishes between two types of public offer: those whose purpose is to sell securities and those whose purpose is to acquire them. A public offer to sell (*offer publique de vente*) is similar to an offer to the public of financial securities (*offre au public de titres financiers*) in terms of its mechanism, but differs in terms of its aims, which are for the bidder either to 'divest itself from the company, or [...] to open it up by increasing the free float, and thus the capital held by the public'.[62] This type of offer does not pose any difficulties here: the *lex societatis* is not intended to interfere in this regime, which is why the takeover bid is regulated by the market manager alone.[63] It is therefore the law on takeover bids that is the subject of the following study.[64]

Takeover bids are often presented as an instrument for the protection of minority shareholders, or for the equal treatment of shareholders. This perception makes takeover law a branch of listed company law and would

---

61 This presentation is essentially the same as in the manuals of the discipline, see T. Bonneau *et al.*, *Droit financier*, *op. cit.*, no. 1014; A. Couret, H. Le Nabasque *et al.*, *Droit financier*, *op. cit.*, no. 1596. See the former definition given by Art. 1 of COB Regulation 89-03, which first defined a takeover bid as a procedure: 'A takeover bid is the procedure whereby a natural person or legal entity makes it known publicly that it intends to acquire or dispose of all or some of the securities of a company listed on the official list, on the secondary market or traded on the over-the-counter market of a stock exchange.' See also the European legislator's definition of a takeover bid, Art. 2(1)(a) of the Takeover Directive.

62 This definition is the one proposed by A. Couret and H. Le Nabasque, *Droit financier*, *op. cit.*, no. 1597. They are used in particular in the context of privatisation. This is why the takeover bid to sell is similar to the takeover bid.

63 In the sense that it applies its own law to the offer: the conditions and procedure are subject to it. Since the purpose of the offer is to sell financial securities that have already been admitted to trading, any issuer that has admitted its securities to Euronext Paris may file a dossier, not with the regulatory authority, but with the market manager. The applicable rules are taken from Book II of the Euronext market rules. The originality of this mechanism is undoubtedly that, without being a member of the financial market, the holder of financial securities will be subject to a procedure governed by the market operator, to whom he must submit his dossier directly (Art. P. 2.4.8. of the Euronext Paris rules, see also M.-B. Diethelm, *Le droit des offres publiques d'achat: une approche internationale*, thesis, Paris II, 1992, p. 338).

64 The law on takeover bids referred to in this paragraph is therefore exclusively the law on public takeover bids.

explain why the Takeover Directive subjects part of the rules on takeover bids to the *lex societatis*. Without denying the links between takeover law and company law, it will be shown that the purpose of the former is primarily to ensure the proper functioning of the financial market (I). The consequence of this primary function should be that the financial market legal order should have a global competence – legislative, administrative and jurisdictional. This is why the Takeover Directive makes an unconvincing choice when it divides the rules of takeover law between company law and financial market law (II).

I. The Function of Takeover Bids Law

The characteristics of the law of takeover bids will be presented (A) before showing that the primary function of this law is to protect the financial market (B).

A. The Characteristics of the Takeover Bid Law

480. Presentation of the takeover bid. A takeover bid can be made by purchasing or exchanging the target securities.[65] In both cases, the offer enables the offeror to take control of the target company, which makes it an instrument of choice for the merger of companies. The law on takeover bids aims precisely at regulating this acquisition of control. Like the regulation of thresholds, takeover law is only applicable when the shares of the target company are admitted to trading on a financial market. However, the material scope of the takeover law differs in that it is not necessarily applicable in all financial markets and, when it is, it is applicable under different conditions in different markets.[66] In the case of a regulated market, the application of the takeover regulation is in principle.[67] In the case of other financial markets, the regulation of takeover bids, whether optional or mandatory, is not made mandatory under the same conditions: firstly, because its very principle is subject, in France, to a request to that effect from the

---

[65] Under US law, the two are very distinct, as only the exchange offer was subject to the regulator's control. Indeed, the jurisdiction of the American regulator was based on the takeover bid, which is necessary in the case of a public exchange offer because of the increase in capital that it implies, which was not the case for the public purchase offer, see P.-H. Conac, *La régulation des marchés boursiers par la Commission des opérations de bourse (COB) et la Securities and exchange commission (SEC)*, *op. cit.*, no. 201.

[66] In French law, the regulation of takeover bids triggered by admission to trading on a regulated market remains applicable for up to three years after the issuer has delisted its securities from the said market if it has admitted them to trading on a multilateral trading facility (see Art. L. 433-5 of the Monetary and Financial Code, and Art. 231-1(4°) of the AMF General Regulation)

[67] Art. L. 433-1(I°) of the Monetary and Financial Code, which is the legacy of Art. 33 of Act no. 96-597 of 2 July 1996, the real 'founding text' of the law on takeover bids (the expression is used by P. Le Cannu, 'Offres publiques, le nouveau règlement général', *BJB*, 1997, p. 2).

financial market operator to the *Autorité des marchés financiers*[68] and, secondly, because the threshold triggering the obligation to file is significantly looser, no longer making the acquisition of control the central element for triggering the obligation to file a takeover bid.[69] In other words, the main purpose of takeover law is to safeguard the functioning of certain financial markets.

481. The obligation to file an offer. Takeover law regulates takeovers through a procedure, subject to an administrative authority, orchestrated in France by the AMF.[70] It does so firstly by making it compulsory to file a public bid when a shareholder has exceeded the threshold of thirty per cent of voting power in the company[71] or, if he or she already had more than thirty per cent, has taken an additional one per cent of what was allowed.[72] However, it is possible for several shareholders to act together and, without each having more than thirty percent of the voting power, collectively reach this threshold.[73] This is known as concerted action ('*action de concert*') and requires them to file a takeover bid.

---

68 Such a request was made by Euronext for its Alternext market, see AMF, *Annual Report 2012*, p. 79.

69 The threshold is no longer control of 30% of the voting rights, but 50%. For optional public bids, Art. L. 431-1(IV), for mandatory takeover bids, Art. L. 433-3(II) of the Monetary and Financial Code and Art. 235-2 of the AMF General Regulation.

70 In European perspective, see K.J. Hopt, 'European takeover reform of 2012/2013 - time to re-examine the mandatory bid'(2014) 15(2) *European Business Organisation Review*, pp. 143 et seq.

71 Art. 234-2 of the AMF General Regulation. The threshold was initially 33.33%, and was lowered to 30% by Law 2010-1249 of 22 October 2010. Some observers note that this 30% threshold does not prevent a takeover, however, since 'an investor is in a position to control the composition of the corporate bodies and therefore the strategy pursued with a smaller stake if the company's capital is balkanised' (A. Viandier, *OPA, OPE et autres offres publiques*, 2nd ed., Paris, Francis Lefebvre, 1993, no. 1400); for a detailed discussion of this issue, see A. Couret and H. Le Nabasque, *Droit financier*, *op. cit.* This threshold only applies to regulated markets; for other financial instrument markets, see *infra*, note under para. 486.

72 Art. 234-5 of the AMF General Regulation. This latter obligation was introduced in order to avoid 'takeovers by stock market pick-up' (COB, *Annual Report 1989*, p. 162). The provision may, at first glance, seem superfluous, given that once the 30% threshold is exceeded, the acquirer is required to file an offer under Art. 234-2 of the AMF General Regulation. However, Art. 234-5 AMF RG fills two gaps. Firstly, it states that a takeover bid launched under Art. 234-2 AMF General Regulation has lapsed because of insufficient subscriptions (pursuant to Art. 231-9(I) AMF General Regulation, if the offeror does not hold at least 50% of the capital and voting rights, its offer is deemed to have lapsed), in which case Art. 234-2 prohibits the offeror from taking a creeping stake, which would require it to re-file an offer. Secondly, Art. 234-5 of the AMF General Regulation also prevents taking a creeping stake by shareholders who have retained more than 30% of the voting power and, as such, have not been subject to the mandatory takeover bid under Art. 234-2 of the AMF General Regulation. Indeed, if it acquires more than 1% of the voting rights in less than a year, it will have to file a takeover bid. On this issue, and the influence of the PACTE Act on the criteria for combining voting rights and capital triggering the bid, see A. Couret, H. Le Nabasque *et al.*, *Droit financier*, *op. cit.*, no. 1614.

73 O. Dexant-de Bailliencourt, *Les pactes d'actionnaires dans les sociétés cotées*, Paris, Dalloz, 2012, pp. 307 et seq.

482. The public buy-out offer. The second obligation to file a bid is the so-called 'public buy-out offer', whose title expresses its main function: to allow the withdrawal of securities from trading on a regulated market.[74] The bid may be initiated by the majority shareholders, the minority shareholders or the financial market authority itself.[75] When it is imposed by the minority shareholders on the majority shareholders,[76] the public buy-out bid is unquestionably a mandatory takeover bid, the purpose of which is not so much to withdraw from the financial market as to preserve the pecuniary interests of the minority shareholders.[77] The public buy-out offer may be accompanied by a mandatory squeeze-out, whereby the majority shareholders are transferred the shares of the minority shareholders, whether or not they so wish. Indeed, the mandatory squeeze-out,[78] which can also occur at the end of a takeover bid, is a mechanism that allows the majority shareholder, when the bid succeeds in capturing ninety per cent of the capital and voting rights, to force the transfer of the minority's securities to the bidder. These two institutions are deemed to justify their existence because of 'a substantial change in the conditions under which the company is managed'.[79] Above all, they constitute a means for the issuer to delist. It would therefore be logical to make the listing and delisting of

---

[74] It is in the light of this particular purpose that the public buy-out offer is understood, and this is why, for example, it cannot be used as a 'catch-up session' (the expression is used by Mr Viandier, *OPA, OPE et autres offres publiques*, *op. cit.*, no. 1728) for shareholders who have refused to tender their shares to a takeover bid. The public buy-out offer imposed by the minority shareholders is sometimes seen as the counterpart of the squeeze-out, see for example, in the English literature, J. Payne, *Schemes of arrangement: Theory, Structure and Operation*, *op. cit.*, no. 3.3.1.

[75] Art. 236-6 AMF General Regulation.

[76] Arts. 236-1 and 236-2 of the AMF General Regulation, on the basis of the authority provided by Art. L. 433-4(I) of the Monetary and Financial Code.

[77] This is particularly true in the case of intra-group mergers. The hypothesis is then that the majority shareholder is a listed company and decides to merge with its own subsidiary, also listed. Since such an operation requires a two-thirds majority of the extraordinary general meeting of a public limited company (Art. L. 236-2, para. 2, of the Commercial Code), minority shareholders risk having an exchange ratio imposed on them that is unfavourable. In this case, they can demand a public buyout offer from the majority shareholder. This hypothesis is reported by H. Synvet, *Accès à la cote et retrait de la cote*, Cours Inédit, 2018. On the exchange ratio in listed company mergers, see H. Synvet, 'La détermination du montant de la parité d'échange dans les fusions de société cotée', *op. cit.*, p. 573.

[78] Art. 237-2 AMF General Regulation. The squeeze-out may be triggered when a takeover bid is filed, at the bidder's discretion, see Art. L. 433-4(III) of the Monetary and Financial Code. On this issue and its history, see T. Bonneau *et al.*, *Droit financier*, *op. cit.*, no. 1194; A. Couret, H. Le Nabasque *et al.*, *Droit financier*, *op. cit.*, no. 1689.
The so-called 'PACTE' Act (Act no. 2019-486 of 22 May 2019 on the growth and transformation of businesses) lowered the threshold for a majority shareholder to file such an offer from 95% of voting rights to 90% (see Art. 75(3°) of the PACTE Act amending Art. L. 433-4 of the Monetary and Financial Code). The Takeover Directive left Member States some leeway as to the threshold, which in France now corresponds to the threshold for delisting via the market rules.

[79] The expression comes from A. Viandier, *OPA OPE et autres offres publiques*, *op. cit.*

securities subject to the law of the financial market; it would be up to the latter to determine the means by which, depending on the market, this delisting could be organised.[80]

B. The Function of Takeover Bid Law

483. Alleged function of takeover law. The function most often retained for mandatory takeover bids is the equality of shareholders, which would allow the protection of minority shareholders.[81] This function is reflected in the legislation itself: the Monetary and Financial Code provides that the regulations drawn up by the AMF must aim to 'ensure the equality of shareholders and the transparency of markets'.[82] In fact, the obligation to file a takeover bid prevents the emergence of a majority shareholder from making the shares of minority shareholders 'illiquid', and the latter from being 'trapped' in their shares, i.e. from not finding a buyer. Moreover, the bidding procedure ensures that all shareholders are treated equally since the price offered is the same.[83] There is therefore no risk that the first to sell, or those with a 'control block'[84] will be better off than the smaller minority shareholders.

80 See already *supra*, no. 364.

81 This function was first highlighted by M. Trochu, 'Les offres publiques d'achat', *RTDCom*, 1967, pp. 695 et seq. A. Viandier, *OPA OPE et autres offres publiques*, *op. cit.*, no. 1; T. Bonneau *et al.*, *Droit financier*, *op. cit.*, no. 1117. The latter authors consider that the original function highlighted by Mr Trochu is now joined by others: 'The acquisition of a minority shareholding, the elimination of minority shareholders or the restructuring of debts through a public exchange offer.' (*ibid.*) This function is sometimes justified by the fact that minority rights would be limited in the context of a takeover bid. D. Schmidt, 'Les droits de minoritaires et les offres publiques', *D.*, 2007.1887, no. 10. The argument of the equality of shareholders was so seductive that it explained even according to the most eminent authors the applicability of local company law to foreign companies. Mr Synvet wrote: 'The close link in the UK system between the takeover bid and the transfer of control ensures that the regulation, insofar as it covered the offer mechanism itself, required the acquirer of control of a locally listed foreign company to treat all its shareholders equally. It thus becomes clear that a stock exchange procedure whose main basis lies in the desire to strengthen the prerogatives of minority shareholders is from time to time likely to benefit the local members of a foreign company.' H. Synvet, *L'organisation juridique du groupe international de sociétés*, *op. cit.*, no. 468. The opinion is not unique to French authors, see e.g. M. Tedjani, *Offre publique d'acquisition: l'application internationale du droit suisse*, Zurich, Schultess, 2015, no. 626 and the references in the note; however, the latter author considers, curiously, that the links with company law do not lead to the application of the *lex societatis*, but of the *lex mercatus*, see *ibid.*, no. 731.

82 Art. L. 433-1(I) of the Monetary and Financial Code.

83 Mr Viandier speaks here of 'dogma', see A. Viandier, *OPA*, *OPE et autres offres publiques*, *op. cit.*

84 That is to say, a quantity of shares allowing the control of the company. On this notion see A.-C. Muller, *Droit des marchés financiers et droit des contrats*, nos. 488 et seq. On the notion of control in case of concert, see O. Dexant-de Bailliencourt, *Les pactes d'actionnaires dans les sociétés cotées*, *op. cit.*, pp. 372 et seq.

However, this shareholder protection function assigned to takeover law must be rejected. First of all, if it were correct, it would lead to the application of takeover law to all French companies,[85] and not just to companies whose securities are admitted to trading. However, company law does not, in principle, govern takeovers; at most, it provides the corporate bodies with the means to protect themselves against them. Secondly, as some authors have observed, 'the regulation of public bids gives shareholder equality a radically different place from that reserved for it in ordinary company law'.[86] Indeed, it is no longer a question of ensuring the equality of shareholders internally, which is what the principle of their equal treatment[87] refers to, but with regard to a third party acquirer. Above all, the equality of shareholders should not prevent shareholders in different situations from being treated differently. However, this is precisely what the regulation of takeover bids leads to by requiring majority shareholders to share the control premium with all shareholders. Moreover, the equality of shareholders cannot give minority shareholders the right to sell their shares in concert with the majority shareholder. As the Court of Justice has perfectly expressed it in European Union law, but the statement applies in the same terms to French law:

> '[EU] law does not contain a general principle of law according to which minority shareholders are protected by the obligation of the dominant shareholder acquiring or exercising control of a company to offer to buy back their shares on the same terms as those agreed upon when acquiring a shareholding which confers or enhances the control of the dominant shareholder.'[88]

The reality is quite simply that company mergers, when they take place by acquisition or proper merger, are organised by contract law. The competence of company law is essentially negative here, in that it may restrict or even prohibit the possibility of transferring shares, or even deprive the possible acquisition of interest[89]; here we find the pre-eminence of the competence of the law of the issuer as regards the status of the securities and the internal organisation of the company,[90] which takes on even greater importance as soon as the acquisition in question takes place by means of an exchange of

---

85 Some authors see the takeover as the element that shows that takeover law belongs at least partiallyto company law, see A. Couret, H. Le Nabasque *et al.*, *Droit financier*, *op. cit.*, no. 2, p. 4.

86 A. Pietrancosta and J.-F. Prat, 'Offres publiques et droit des sociétés' in G. Canivet, D. Martin and N. Molfessis (eds.), *Les offres publiques d'achat*, Paris, LexisNexis, 2009, p. 143 and the references cited.

87 See *supra*, para. 471.

88 Case C-101/08, *Audiolux*, ECLI:EU:C:2009:626, *Rev. Sociétés*, 2010.,45, note G. Parléani.

89 See *infra*, para. 501 the defences of company law against public bids.

90 See *supra*, paras. 291 et seq.

securities, or the merger leads to the dissolution of the legal personality of the absorbed company.

In other words, the *lex societatis* does not have primary jurisdiction over public bids: that jurisdiction is left to contract law. It is true that contract law may coincide with the legal order of the company's seat. However, this coincidence is not a necessity.[91] On the other hand, the legal system of the place of listing contains provisions whose purpose is to interfere in the heart of the field of contract law; it ensures that they are complied with by making the takeover bid subject to control by an administrative authority. This is why these rules have so often been presented as overriding mandatory rules.[92] It seems to us, however, that in many respects these rules are intended to replace the contract law designated by the parties, since they apply to the essential aspects of contracts. It would probably be more accurate to consider that an objective connecting factor is made to the place of listing of the target: the dismemberment of the regime of contractual obligations would not produce any beneficial effect here.

This means that the situation of takeover law is profoundly different from that of threshold crossing. It is true that takeover law can improve or at least interfere with company law, but only when the latter creates obstacles to its action. In principle, there is no agreement between the objectives of these laws.[93]

484. The real function of takeover law. The real function of takeover law is both to protect investors making use of the stock market mechanism and to protect the reliability of that mechanism itself. Firstly, the protection of investors is achieved by treating them equally, regardless of the size of their acquisition; the equality of shareholders and the protection of minority shareholders that it implies are only a consequence. Secondly, the shareholder structure will influence the liquidity of the shares and the share price.[94] The reliability of the share price

---

91 See *infra*, para. 497.

92 See e.g. X. Boucobza, *L'acquisition internationale de société*, *op. cit.*; D. Bureau and H. Muir Watt, *Droit international privé*, t. 2, *op. cit.*, no. 1006.

93 This statement is contingent. If takeover bids law were to apply to companies above certain thresholds in the future, irrespective of whether they are admitted to trading, it would have to be accepted that company law takes on the task of protecting investors and that the objectives converge.

94 See P. Le Cannu, 'Offres publiques: le nouveau règlement général', *BJB*, 1997, 1, spec. p. 2, the author considers that the reform of the law on public bids is carried out 'with a view to preserving market efficiency and the liquidity of securities'; X Boucobza, 'La loi applicable à l'offre publique d'acquisition', *BJB* 1997, 3, spec. p. 7: 'The regulation of public bids seems to be attached to the stock market. Since it is intended to ensure the equality of investors and quality information, it is in fact the very organisation of the market and not the companies listed on it that is at issue'; A. Tenenbaum, 'La compétence internationale des autorités de surveillance des marchés financiers en matière d'offre publique', *op. cit.*, p. 557: 'the takeover bid is above all a specific market operation which must be carried out in accordance with

is not ensured if the investor risks being 'locked in' to the share. The market protection function is also evident in the case of a public buy-out bid, which can hardly be classified as a minority protection bid since it can be triggered by the majority shareholder, who can combine it with a mandatory squeeze-out in order to ensure the eviction of minority shareholders in a way that goes against certain cardinal principles of company law.[95]

The purpose of takeover bids is therefore not the functioning of the company's bodies, or even their relations, but the proper functioning of the financial market and the protection of investors.[96] If the rules of the takeover bid condition the acquisition of control of the company, they do so only because of the influence that such control has on the share price and its liquidity.[97] This function is confirmed by the material scope of application of this regulation. This is limited, as a matter of principle, to companies which admit their securities to a regulated market. By way of exception, takeover law may also apply to markets other than regulated markets if their managers so request from the authority of their headquarters.[98] This purpose of financial market operation also explains the intervention of an authority[99] responsible

a procedure which is part of the very organisation of the market on which it takes place'. The comments made here refer only to the French regulation of takeover bids; other legal systems attach this set of rules less to the financial market than to the protection of local investors, as in the United Kingdom and Switzerland (see *infra*, para. 508).

95 It is true that exclusion clauses are known in company law, but they are either agreed *ab initio* by the parties concerned or they are agreed upon when a partner enters the capital.

96 Comp. M. Tedjani, *Offre publique d'acquisition: l'application internationale du droit suisse*, *op. cit.*, at 19–50. The author considers that the objectives of public bids are to guarantee the functioning of the financial markets, the protection of investors and the predictability of the law, whereas the equal treatment of investors, fairness and transparency of bids are merely means.

97 It will be recalled that these are the two objectives pursued by the financial market, see *supra*, para. 49.

98 Art. L. 433-1(IV) of the Monetary and Financial Code. From a European perspective, this refers only to multilateral trading facilities: organised trading facilities do not allow for the trading of financial securities, see *supra*, para. 49. In France Euronext Growth, for example, it is 50% instead of 30% for a regulated market, see Art. 4.1 of the Euronext Growth market rules (Part II: Additional rules for the Euronext Growth Paris market managed by Euronext Paris), published on 9 November 2020.

99 The establishment of an *administrative* authority responsible for supervising the bid is not necessary: this is the case under French law, but it should be noted that this was not always the case, since the former *Conseil des marchés financiers*, which was responsible for public bids until the establishment of the AMF, was a private law body (admittedly a hybrid, see Art. 27 of Act no. 96-597 of 2 July 1996 on the modernisation of financial activities) and, on the other hand, Art. 4 of the Takeover Directive left a wide margin of freedom to Member States. Some Member States continue to use private bodies, for example the United Kingdom, where the competent authority is not the Financial Conduct Authority, an administrative authority competent for market abuse, but the Takeover Panel, a private body.

for supervising the bid,[100] whose task is to ensure what the spontaneous organisation of the market cannot achieve.

However, it would be misleading to assume that company law does not interfere with takeover law. Firstly, its cooperation is necessary in order to achieve the sanctions attached to certain requirements of takeover law: deprivation of voting rights and non-consensual transfer of shares. Secondly, company law offers ways of effectively resisting takeover bids; these are likely to interfere with their proper functioning.

II. Critical Assessment of the Distribution of Jurisdiction

French legislation on takeover bids sets out its own scope of application with regard to relations with third countries (A). Where companies have their registered office in the European Union, the division of jurisdiction relating to public bids is based on the transposition of the Takeover Directive. This directive combines the jurisdiction of the legal system of the target company and that of the financial market (B). It seems to us that the jurisdiction of the legal order of the registered office should be ousted in order to give overall jurisdiction to the legal order of the market (C).

A. Relations with Third Countries

485. Historical background. The first regulation of takeover bids took place in the regulations of the Chambre syndicale des agents de change from 1966 onwards,[101] in reaction to the first takeover bids.[102] The French legislator did not address the issue until the laws of 2 August 1989 and 2 July 1996.[103] The international scope of application of takeover bids was then particularly restricted, not by the law

---

100 Several stages take place: first the draft bid must be filed, the decision on the conformity of the bid must be obtained from the competent authority, the period during which the bid can be favourably responded to must be waited for and, finally, the bid must be closed, see A. Viandier, *OPA OPE et autres offres publiques*, *op. cit.*, nos. 1800 et seq.

101 *Ibid.*, no. 71.

102 The first takeover bids are dated according to the authors from 1959 or 1964 (P. Bézard, *Les offres publiques d'achat*, Paris, Masson, 1982, p. 25; M. Trochu, 'Les offres publiques d'achat', *RTD com.*, 1967, 695, spec. p. 687). The first takeover bid that made an impression was BSN's exchange offer for Saint-Gobain in December 1968 and January 1969, considered by many as an illustration of 'savage capitalism' (the expression is used by M. Trochu, 'Le triomphe du capitalisme sauvage, ou BSN contre Saint Gobain', *D.*, 1969, 222), on the latter see the decision of the Chambre syndicale (regulating the practice) reproduced in L. Roblin, *Les offres publiques d'achat*, Paris, Dunod, 1969, pp. 103 et seq. Other takeover bids had preceded it, see for a detailed recapitulation, *ibid.*, pp. 95 et seq.

103 Law no. 89-531 of 2 August 1989 on the security and transparency of the financial market; Law no. 96-597 of 2 July 1996 on the modernisation of financial activities.

itself, which prescribed the application of the law of the financial market,[104] but by the action of the authorities supervising the offer, which added the need for the target company to have its registered office in France.[105] Such a restriction clearly placed the law of takeover bids within the law of listed companies, and therefore left it to foreign *lex societatis* to govern them. The feeling that takeover law was linked to company law was undoubtedly reinforced by the *Holophane* judgment of 13 July 1988.[106] This decision, which formulated the connecting factor for the first time, did not even mention listing. It was all about the location of the target, and thus established:

> 'That any takeover bid for a French company is subject to French regulations on takeover bids, which apply in an identical and non-discriminatory manner to the initiators of the offers, whether French or foreign and, in this case, to the two English initiators of the offers.'

Rather than referring to the location of the target company, the case law would have been better served by connecting the law on takeover bids to the place of listing, or at any rate by mentioning the listing, since the latter is a condition for the takeover bid. However, such a formulation is also explained by the particularities of the case, where there was not a conflict between the law of the stock exchange and the law of the target company, but between two

---

104 The two relevant laws refer, for the application of the regulation of takeover bids by the authorities of the time - the Conseil des Bourses de Valeur (CBV) and subsequently the Conseil des Marchés Financiers (CMF) – to listing on the French market, in different terms: the Act of 2 August 1989 refers to companies 'whose securities are listed on the official list or on the second market', while the Act of 2 July 1996 provides in its Art. 33 that the CMF sets the rules for 'takeover bids for financial instruments traded on a regulated market.'

105 Art. 5.5.1 of the CMF General Regulation, which corresponds to that of the CBV Regulation. On the international scope of application of the latter article, see X. Boucobza, 'La loi applicable à l'offre publique d'acquisition', *op. cit.* (see in particular the uncertainty of the French regulation and the conflict between the law and the stock exchange authority, pp. 15–16); W.H. Smith, 'Le champ d'application territorial de la réglementation des offres publiques', *Rev. CMF*, 1997, no. 4, pp. 25 et seq., and, retrospectively, D. Martin, 'La compétence internationale de l'autorité des marchés financiers en matière d'offre publique', *RTDF*, 2006, p. 37, spec. no. 4. Mr Smith ('Le champ d'application territorial de la réglementation des offres publiques', *op. cit.*, p. 29) explains this twofold criterion, which is widespread in comparative law, on the one hand because the regulation of takeover bids is based on company law, which would make it difficult to apply to foreign companies, and on the other hand for reasons of effectiveness, and finally because locally listed companies are almost always listed on their home market: under these conditions, not to regulate them is tantamount to implicitly recognising the primacy of the authorities of the country of origin, which is in line with the Community dynamic. Such cumulative application was also intended to limit the overlap of applicable rules and possibly conflicts of law in the area of takeover bids. Prior to the reform, see X. Boucobza, 'L'offre publique transfrontière', *op. cit.* and also, by the same author, *L'acquisition internationale de sociétés*, *op. cit.*, pp. 258 et seq.

106 CA Paris, *Sté Emeless PLC c/Sté Thorn Emi PLC et autres*, 13 July 1988, *D.*, 1989, jur., p. 160, note P. Le Cannu, *BJB*, 1988, 715, note Y. Sexer.

lex societatis: that of the bidder and that of the target. The Court of Appeal unambiguously ruled in favour of the target's law.

486. The rule was nevertheless modified by a decree of 8 November 1989. This gave the French regulator absolute discretion in the application of the regulation of takeover bids to foreign companies.[107] However, it was customary for the authority's discretion to be exercised:

> 'Only in cases where the target company was not listed in its home country (or where the French market was the lead market) and/or probably in cases where the home country's regulations were genuinely detrimental to the interests of shareholders and did not guarantee the basic protections recognised by the French stock exchange authorities, especially where they were deficient. In cases where the French market was only a secondary market or where the regulations applicable to the offer were satisfactory, the offer remained exclusively subject to foreign law.'[108]

It was thus as if French law was applied in a subsidiary manner to the benefit of foreign companies listed in France, but whose legal system of origin did not have equivalent legislation. As Didier Martin and Florence Haas write, 'the Comité des marchés financiers [predecessor of the AMF] had finally shown a preference for linking to the law of the financial market, while leaving itself free not to apply it'.[109] However, the provisions relating to the price guarantee, the mandatory takeover bid and the mandatory squeeze-out were still reserved for French companies only. The reason given was that these provisions touched too closely on company law.[110] On the other hand, the Paris Court of Appeal, in its *Teknecomp* decision of 13 January 1998,[111] made it clear that takeover bid regulations applied regardless of the origin of the acquirer: 'the economic public policy provisions of the Act of 2 July 1996 and the General Regulations of the Financial Markets Council apply to any operator operating on a French regulated market'.[112]

---

107 See former Art. 5.5.1 of the CMF General Regulation.

108 D. Martin and F. Haas, 'La compétence internationale de l'autorité des marchés financiers en matière d'offre publique', *RTDF*, 2006, p. 37, no. 6. The authors cite in this sense, A. Viandier, *OPA, OPE et autres offres publiques*, *op. cit.*, no. 89, as well as the example of the public bid for the securities of the Ivorian company Forestière Équatoriale (CMF opinion no. 201C0888 of 18 July 2001) and the bid for the securities of the Monegasque company Europe 1 Communication (CMF opinion no. 199C0454 of 22 April 1999).

109 D. Martin and F. Haas, 'La compétence internationale de l'autorité des marchés financiers en matière d'offre publique', *op. cit.*

110 *Ibid.*

111 CA Paris, 1re ch. H, 13 January 1998, *Teknecomp Holding International BV*; *Rev. sociétés*, 1998, 572, note P. Le Cannu; *LPA*, 18 January 1999, p. 10, note A. Tenenbaum.

112 As the acquisition took place indirectly, the Court also specified that, under Art. 5-3-7 of the General Regulations of the Financial Markets Committee: 'Natural persons or legal entities acting alone or in concert shall be required to comply with the procedures defined in this chapter when, by acquiring control of a company, they come to hold, directly or indirectly,

487. Positive law. This state of affairs has not changed in the relationship between French financial market law and issuers from third countries, which constitute an island of resistance in national law to the Europeanisation of financial law. Article L. 433-1(III) of the Monetary and Financial Code refers to the AMF General Regulation for the applicability of the rules on takeover bids to companies from third countries. Article 231-1 of the AMF General Regulation states:

> 'The AMF may apply these rules, with the exception of those governing mandatory bids and squeeze-outs, to bids for financial instruments issued by companies whose registered office is located outside a Member State of the European Community or a party to the European Economic Area agreement and which are admitted to trading on a French regulated market.'

This text, which deactivates most of the rules on takeover bids, with the exception of voluntary takeover bids, is open to two criticisms. The first is that it negates the purpose of proper functioning of the financial market and investor protection pursued by the law on takeover bids. Indeed, French residents who have invested in the French financial market through the acquisition of securities issued by a company from a third country will not benefit from the French protection granted to investors and will be at the mercy of a creeping takeover. This rule is at odds with those sometimes adopted in comparative private international law. For example, in the United States, the admission of securities to trading triggers the application of takeover regulations. In fact, this country also applies these regulations, independently of any admission to trading, if the target's registered office is located in its territory, or if a certain percentage of the capital of the disputed company is held by US residents.[113] Such a scope of application reflects the fact that US takeover law is aimed as much at the proper functioning of the financial markets as at investor protection. It is nevertheless tempered by the possibility for the SEC to exempt, at its discretion, foreign companies from local law. The justification given by the SEC is not to deprive the US resident shareholder of the capital gain that the takeover bid would allow him to obtain. Indeed, the offeror might be tempted, in order to avoid the sometimes oppressive yoke of US regulation, to exclude US residents from its offer.[114] This possibility is clearly opened by the

---

a majority of the capital or voting rights of a French company whose securities are listed on the official list or on the second market or traded on the over-the-counter market, provided that the securities held by the company over which control is acquired represent an essential part of its assets.'

113 See most recently in French M. Tedjani, *Offre publique d'acquisition: l'application internationale du droit suisse*, Zurich, Schultess, 2015, nos. 74–78; S. Lambert, *L'application internationale du droit financier*, *op. cit.*, nos. 413–414.

114 This is not an academic assumption. On this issue, see E.F. Greene, A.L. Beller *et al.*, *U.S. Regulation of the International Securities and Derivatives Markets*, 12th Editions, Wolters Kluwer, para. 9.05, pp. 9–74.

SEC to the offeror. However, the offeror will have to justify the mechanisms put in place to show the absence of links with the United States.[115]

The second criticism is that an administrative authority should be entrusted with the task of deciding on the application of a regulation. The role of the authority should be limited to observing the application of the regulation and, if necessary, interpreting it.[116] Although it has been approved by the most eminent authors in that it allows for a tailored application of local regulations,[117] the example of American law should not be transposed to French law. Indeed, in the American case, on the one hand, the discretion left to the authority is the counterpart of particularly broad application criteria that are independent of the admission of securities to a financial market and, on the other hand, the SEC is accountable for its action before Congress. Moreover, the legislature is capable of devising measured criteria that correspond to the function of the regulation it has instituted: this is the case with the criterion of the place of listing. French takeover regulations should therefore be applicable whenever a foreign issuer admits its securities to trading on a French financial market where such regulations are applicable. The discretion left to the administrative authority should be limited to the use of the mechanisms most likely not to interfere with the operation of the foreign company insofar as its original legal system would object.

---

115 'The SEC reiterated that a legend or disclaimer stating that the offer is not being made into the United States, or that the offer materials may not be distributed there, is not likely to be sufficient in itself, because if the acquiror wants to support a claim that the offer has no jurisdictional connection to the United States, it will also need to take special precautions to prevent sales to or tenders from U. S. target holders', extracted from E.F. Greene, A.L. Beller *et al.*, *U.S. Regulation of the International Securities and Derivatives Markets*, *op. cit.*, para. 9.05, pp. 9–74.

116 Seduced by the action of the SEC, Mr Synvet himself seems more reserved about the opportunity to increase the powers of the French authority. The author writes: 'Secondly, it is appropriate to return to the fundamentals of French stock market law, which is based on its administrative nature. From time to time, the gallery is amused by highlighting the interests of savers or by sympathising with the misfortunes of victims of fraud. The reality, which is much more prosaic, is that most of the powers are placed in the hands of an administrative authority, which intends to have a wide margin of discretion in their exercise. The General Regulation of the Autorité des marchés financiers does not establish an abstract rule of the game. It is primarily an instrument of constraint in the hands of the regulator. It is with this proviso, which is not entirely insignificant, that the "mandatory" nature of certain takeover bids must be understood.' H. Synvet, 'Propos désenchantés sur l'affaire Sacyr-Eiffage' in *Mélanges en l'honneur de Philippe Merle*, Paris, Dalloz, 2012, pp. 669 et seq.

117 H. Synvet, *L'organisation juridique du groupe international de sociétés*, *op. cit.*, no. 460, p. 375: 'It is not to make complexity the touchstone of quality to admit that one is seduced by the Commission's efforts to ensure that the *Securities Law* has an appropriate scope. Without necessarily approving the results in detail, there is reason to approve the method used. The matter cannot be satisfied with an abstract and uniform delimitation of the field of standards taken en bloc. It requires more specific solutions, resulting from the interaction of the various factors to be taken into consideration during the linking operation.'

488. French company and third-country financial market. Financial market managers from a third country may ask the AMF to impose its mandatory bid rules if the company whose securities are acquired is French.[118] This provision was originally intended to allow managers of multilateral trading facilities to benefit from mandatory bid legislation. However, the letter of the provision allows any financial market that is not a regulated market in the EU to benefit from it. Such a rule has the merit of being consistent with the connecting factor in European law, which makes the registered office the criterion for the applicability of takeover law. However, it misunderstands the function of this law and the legal system best placed to govern the bid.

B. Intra-European Relations

489. Division of legislative competence. In order to limit the friction between company law and financial market law in the case of the separation of the registered office and the place of admission of securities, Article 4(2)(e) of the Takeover Directive separates the responsibilities of the two in the regulation of takeover bids. The following are subject to the law of the authority of the place of admission of the securities:

> 'Matters relating to the consideration offered in the case of a bid, in particular the price, and matters relating to the bid procedure, in particular the information on the offeror's decision to make a bid, the contents of the offer document and the disclosure of the bid.'

However, the *lex societatis* of the target company applies:

> 'Matters relating to the information to be provided to the employees of the offeree company and in matters relating to company law, in particular the percentage of voting rights which confers control and any derogation from the obligation to launch a bid, as well as the conditions under which the board of the offeree company may undertake any action which might result in the frustration of the bid.'

490. Allocation of administrative competence. This allocation of legislative competence is accompanied by an allocation of administrative competence: matters subject to the *lex societatis* are supervised by the financial market authority of the target's registered office, while others are subject to the market authority of the place of listing. The situation leads to the designation of a single authority where the issuer has its securities admitted to trading on the financial market where it has its registered office. Where there is a dissociation between the issuer's registered office and the place of listing, the market authority of the

---

118 Art. L. 433-3(II) of the Monetary and Financial Code.

place of listing prevails for matters not subject to company law.[119] Finally, the problem of multiple listings is resolved in favour of the authority where the securities were first admitted.[120]

These criteria deserve approval. They solve the problem of multi-listing by designating a legal authority competent for the specific aspects of the financial market;[121] by ensuring that the offer is properly conducted, the authority in charge of its supervision effectively protects the functioning of all affected financial markets. The designated authority should also, as a matter of law, take into consideration the interests of the financial markets where the securities are admitted to trading.[122] The criterion of the first place of listing, while it may seem artificial in that it will not always correspond to the market with the closest links to the company, nevertheless has the advantage of predictability and stability.[123] Moreover, the hierarchy of connecting factors corresponds to the intensity of the company's links with the various legal orders: when an issuer has its securities traded on the financial market of its registered office, this legal order has a predominant connection with the entire offer. Finally, these criteria favour the coincidence of the *lex societatis* and the *lex mercatus*, thus avoiding possible frictions or gaps in what has often been constituted as a single body of law.[124]

---

119 This had seemed almost impossible to specialists precisely because of the potential conflicts between company law and stock exchange law, W.H. Smith, 'Le champ d'application territorial de la réglementation des offres publiques', *Rev. CMF*, no. 6, 1998, p. 22. The author considers that: 'the choice of the market as a jurisdictional criterion proves to be delicate to apply, especially in view of the potential conflicts between stock exchange law and company law', because, as the author puts it, 'the interweaving of company law and bidding law is everywhere very strong, the former invariably serving as a foundation for the latter' (*ibid.*, p. 30). The author then gives an overview of various company law provisions in other EU countries that may cause conflicts with local stock exchange regulations, even if they have been harmonised by means of a directive.

120 If the multi-listing is simultaneous, the issuer may choose the competent authority (Art. 2(c) Takeover Directive). If the issuer subsequently admits its securities to the financial market of its registered office, the authority of the registered office will then be competent for all aspects of the takeover bid.

121 On the difficulties raised by multi-listing in the field of takeover bids, see F. Garcimartin Alferez, *Cross-border listed companies*, *op. cit.* A. Tenenbaum, 'La compétence internationale des autorités de surveillance des marchés financiers en matière d'offre publique', *op. cit.*; H. Synvet, *L'organisation juridique du groupe international de sociétés*, *op. cit.*

122 This consideration mechanism appears to be the minimal temperament to the granting of a "universal" jurisdiction, reminiscent of the consideration of the interests of foreign States when a resolution authority exercises a group jurisdiction, see *supra*, para. 152.

123 The idea of a 'lead market' as a connecting criterion for the *lex mercatus* in the case of multiple listings is therefore abandoned. This rule had been applied in advance by the French and Luxembourg authorities during the Mittal takeover bid for Arcelor, on which see A. Tenenbaum, 'La compétence internationale de l'autorité des marchés financiers', *op. cit.*

124 As Garcimartin Alferez writes: 'It ensures that (a) the same authorities have competence over (b) and the same law applies to both the corporate law aspects and to the bid procedure aspects.' F. Garcimartin Alferez, *Cross-border listed companies*, *op. cit.*, no. 169.

491. The rule in Article 4(2) of the Takeover Directive establishes a form of *forum legis*, whereby the market authority is competent to the extent that local law is applicable or in respect of the local establishment of the registered office (the authority is competent because the *lex societatis* is applicable).[125] Where there are several competent authorities in respect of the same bid, Article 4(4) of the Takeover Directive establishes an obligation of cooperation between them which includes the exchange of information, which is then 'covered by the obligation of professional secrecy incumbent on persons who are or have been active in the supervisory authorities receiving it'.[126] It seems to us, however, that there is a paradox in submitting to the market authority of the registered office the control of aspects of a public bid for securities traded on a foreign financial market. Would it not be more appropriate to submit the entire bid to a single authority[127]? In order to explain the reasons for this division, Mr Garcimartin Alferez writes:

> '[We] should not forget that, from the point of view of the EU lawmaker, once we have harmonized a sector of the legal system, the principle of fungibility applies. The EU lawmaker does not have an interest in applying a national law in particular, but in laying down clear-and-cut rules pointing to a national law, whichever that may be. At first sight, those criteria cater for this objective.'[128]

While it is indisputable that these criteria allow for a precise designation of the competent authorities and laws, it seems questionable to us to consider that the Union legislator does not have an interest in applying one law rather than another once the alignment of laws has taken place. The objective of coordinating legal systems is still relevant here, and is best achieved by giving jurisdiction to the legal system with the most important links to the legal situation at issue. This will be reflected here by observing that the essential

---

125 It is perhaps worth noting that some third countries provide for the application of their takeover law irrespective of the listing criteria or the origin of the target, but because of the residence of the offerees. This is traditionally the case in American law, which has led initiators of takeover bids to exclude the target's American shareholders in order to avoid the SEC's restrictive registration requirements, see P.-H. Conac, *La régulation des marchés boursiers par la Commission des opérations de bourse (COB) et la Securities and exchange commission (SEC), op. cit.*

126 This duty to cooperate also includes 'the ability to notify legal acts necessary for the enforcement of measures taken by competent authorities in connection with tenders, as well as any other assistance that may reasonably be requested by the supervisory authorities concerned for the purpose of investigating actual or alleged breaches of the rules adopted or introduced pursuant to this Directive'.

127 Comp. S. Lambert, *L'application internationale du droit financier, op. cit.*, no. 1488, who proposes a co-decision mechanism for the competent authorities in takeover matters. It seems to us, however, that such a mechanism could not operate without the prior existence of unified legislation.

128 F. Garcimartin Alferez, *Cross-border listed companies, op. cit.*, no. 170.

contractual aspects of the bid are subject to the law of the financial market, which therefore displaces the *lex contractus* normally applicable (1). On the other hand, the peculiarities of the listing, which mark the specific features of the takeover bid, are subject to the *lex societatis*. We shall endeavour here to show that, with the exception of labour law, all the institutions subject to the *lex societatis* would benefit from being governed by the legal order of the market (2).

1. *The Competence of the Financial Market Legal Order*

492. A particular contract law. In many respects, the law on takeover bids appears to be a particular contract law governed by capital market law. The scope of application of the law of the financial market is the most striking manifestation of this. Indeed, the *lex mercatus* applies to all the decisive rules of a sale,[129] concerning both the determination of the thing and its price[130]: the consideration offered, its price, the terms of the offer, the information obligations of the offeror, and even the advertising of the offer.

493. Determination of the *lex contractus*. The Takeover Directive thus crowds out part of the applicable law under the Rome I Regulation. However, there is no doubt that the contract resulting from the public bid falls within the scope of the Rome I Regulation, which allows the bidder to choose the law applicable to the contractual aspects. The Rome I Regulation precisely provides that takeover bids are treated in the same way as takeover biding of financial securities: they are not subject to the interference of consumer contracts,[131] and the EU legislator encourages a broad scope of application of the *lex contractus*.[132] It is true that takeover bids are subject to oversight by an administrative authority; however, this oversight has no apparent impact on the law applicable to the offer. In France, the AMF requires the offeror to include in its draft offer "the law applicable to the contracts concluded between the offeror and the holders

129 Admittedly, the acquisition may be effected by means of an exchange, which is more frequent because it is less currency-intensive. Nevertheless, the special law regime for public bids is irrelevant to the classification of the contract in question.

130 The adequacy of the offer price is of course central. It is present in the AMF compliance decision mentioned above, but also in any independent expert opinion on the price that the AMF may request. The importance of price is reflected in a wide variety of takeover bid rules, such as the '100%' takeover bid principle, which means that there is no ceiling on the number of shares to be acquired when a bid is launched, or the lapse threshold set out in Arts. L. 433-1-2(I) of the Monetary and Financial Code and 231-9(1°) of the AMF General Regulation. Under domestic law, these rules ensure that the bidder does not make a bid below the market price in order to collect only the shares needed to obtain control. This would allow the bidder not to actually pay the 'price' of control, which necessarily increases the share price.

131 Art. 6(4)(d) of the Rome I Regulation.

132 Recital 29 of the Rome I Regulation. On these aspects, see *supra*, para. 371.

of securities of the target company following the offer, as well as the competent courts".[133] This statement reflects the freedom of the offeror to select a law other than that of the market authority.

494. Articulation of the *lex contractus* and the *lex mercatus*. The supervision of the offer by the market authority makes it possible to ensure that the offer sufficiently protects investors, a concern made all the more important since the latter will not benefit from the protective conflict rule in consumer matters. This is why it is fortunate that the authority can request 'all appropriate justifications and guarantees'[134] when examining the draft offer. There is, however, a paradox between the possibility for the offeror to select an applicable law that is distinct from that of the authority, and the application by the authority of the law of the financial market to a set of issues at the heart of the *lex contractus*. The AMF may "ask the offeror to amend its planned offer" if the offer is likely to infringe "the principles defined in Article 231-3 [of the AMF General Regulation]". This article refers to the – particularly broad[135] – general principles of takeover bids. They are closely linked, on the one hand, to the French perception of contract law and the principles of the Takeover Directive[136] and, on the other hand, to the area reserved for financial market law by the Takeover Directive. Thus, financial market law will oversee the sensitive issue of the consideration offered by the bidder, which may be characterised by a sum of money or by the securities he offers (exchange offer). It should be noted, however, that in the latter case the difficulty lies less in the link with the *lex contractus* than with the *lex societatis*.[137] Indeed, the *lex societatis* of the offeror is likely to govern a facet of this consideration, in particular the conditions of the possible issue that the exchange will require, as well as the details of the prerogatives offered by the securities exchanged.[138] In other words, the *lex mercatus* will assess not so much

---

133 Art. 2(4)° of the AMF Instruction 2006-07 on takeover bids.

134 Art. 232-21 AMF General Regulation

135 The content of this statement is reproduced here to remind us of its scope: 'With a view to the orderly conduct of operations in the best interests of investors and the market, all persons involved in a bid must respect the free play of bids and overbids, the equal treatment and information of the holders of the securities of the persons involved in the bid, the transparency and integrity of the market, and fairness in transactions and competition.'

136 Art. 3(1) of the Takeover Directive.

137 The consideration for takeover bids does not pose any particular difficulties: the currency used will be determined by the bid and will most often correspond to the local market currency.

138 On the competence of the law of the issuer in relation to securities see *supra*, para. 291 and on this sensitive issue see H. Synvet, 'La détermination du montant de la parité d'échange dans les fusions de sociétés cotées', *op. cit.*, spec. no. 23. Since the French *lex societatis* leaves operators free to determine the amount of the exchange ratio in the case of listed companies, this has been regulated by the stock market regulator: 'Just as lava finds a new path in a volcano when a chimney is blocked, so the discretion of company law has prompted the stock market regulator to act' (*ibid.*, no. 5). The AMF has therefore gradually regulated the issue, through Instruction 2005-11 of 13 December 2005 and Position-Recommendation

the actual consideration – the securities – as their valuation,[139] especially since, if the offeror does not have its registered office in the territory of the target, the prospectus issued in connection with the takeover bid will be approved by the authority of its registered office.[140]

495. The *lex contractus*, however, retains a residual jurisdiction. It applies to contractual matters which are not subject to another law by virtue of Article 4(2)(e) of the Takeover Directive. These issues are not 'peripheral':[141] they include the validity of the contract itself, and restitution which may, where appropriate, result from a nullification of the contract.[142] Moreover, the *lex contractus* extends to all questions relating to the general regime of obligations contained in the offer. Admittedly, this could be seen as a point of friction with the *lex mercatus*, since the latter covers 'the content of the offer document'.[143] However, this is considered in conjunction with the disclosure of the offer, which makes it clear that the term 'content of the offer document' refers not to the regime of obligations but to the information that must be included in the contract. It must therefore be assumed that the *lex contractus* applies to the regime of obligations contained in the offer. The distinction between the obligations specific to the

---

2011-11 of 27 July 2011 entitled 'Contribution or merger transactions', in which the AMF requires merger auditors to prepare their reports in accordance with the technical advice of the Commission nationale des commissaires aux comptes, i.e. the technical advice on merger auditing dated 2 December 2010. Neither of these two administrative sources is included in the *lex societatis*, and therefore they will not be applied when a foreign court applies the French *lex societatis*, which leaves the actors free to determine this. This is a very concrete example of the mischief caused by the disordering of sources and the mischief caused by the increasing power of administrative law in private law matters.

139 In particular by determining the valuation methods, for example in the case of a squeeze-out, through a multi-criteria evaluation. In France, it was the COB that historically imposed this multi-criteria method, see P.-H. Conac, *La régulation des marchés boursiers par la Commission des opérations de bourse (COB) et la Securities and exchange commission (SEC)*, *op. cit.*, no. 194; today see A. Couret and H. Le Nabasque, *Droit financier*, no. 1688 and references.

140 See *supra*, paras. 351 et seq.

141 M. Fyon and P. Wautelet, 'Le champ d'application, les questions de droit international privé et le prospectus', in *La réforme de la réglementation sur les offres publiques d'acquisition*, Kluwer, 2007, no. 32. The authors believe that this peripheral aspect of the *lex contractus* explains the lack of interest in it.

142 However, national laws do not have identical solutions regarding the validity of the contract. Thus the place of fraud or economic violence differs widely according to the legal system, making the *lex contractus* in these cases truly crucial to the realisation or non-realisation of the takeover bid and its possible consequences. The same applies to restitution. For a comparison of the differences between English and German law from the point of view of restitution, see B. Häker, *Consequences of Impaired Consent Transfers: A Structural Comparison of English and German Law*, Oxford, Hart Publishing, 2013.

143 Art. 4(2)(e) of the Takeover Directive. Some authors also note that there may be a conflict with the *lex societatis* as regards the conditionality of the offer, the revocability of contributions or the problems of intervention on the markets, see H. Reynier, 'Les offres publiques internationales: répartition géographique de compétences', *RTDF*, 2006, no. 3, pp. 96 et seq.

sale and those of the general system of obligations may appear artificial, to the point that the AMF considers itself competent to govern the nature of the offer and the suspensive conditions that it may contain.[144]

The systematic links between the rules of contract law should be respected, if not through a special rule applying to the contract resulting from the public bid the law of the place where the target is listed, then at least a choice of law in favour of the target.

2. *The Field of the Law of the Registered Office*

496. Article 4(2)(e) of the Takeover Directive makes 'company law matters' and 'corporate law matters' subject to the law of the registered office. In both cases, the registered office is that of the target company, not that of the offeror; the latter connecting factor has apparently always been rejected in comparative private international law.[145] If one has to choose between these two laws, there is no doubt that it is up to the target company's corporate law to define, for example, the rules of conduct of the corporate bodies or the percentage of voting rights that gives control. It will be shown that these so-called company law issues would benefit from being subject to the legal order of the market in the context of a takeover bid (a). On the other hand, the application of the employment law of the target's registered office deserves full approval (b).

---

[144] The AMF General Regulation contains a section entitled 'Nature of offers and conditions precedent' (Arts. 231-8 et seq. of the AMF General Regulation). The issue of lapsing offers provides an illustration of this point. France has already seen a bid that lapsed due to an unfavourable decision by the regulator on merger control: D. Carreau and H. Létréguilly, 'Offres publiques: OPA, OPE, OPR', *Répertoire de droit des sociétés*, Paris, Dalloz, spec. nos. 17 et seq. However, this issue is regulated by the AMF General Regulations (Art. 231-9 for the lapse threshold, Art. 231-11 for merger control).

[145] However, the *lex societatis* of the offeror may intervene from time to time, for example with regard to the exchange ratio in a merger. This is determined according to the offeror's *lex societatis*, which may be less generous than that granted according to the standards of the target's legal system. In France, this causes difficulties, because the method used was imposed by recommendation of the COB, on this point see the presentation and critical analysis of this misuse of power by P.-H. Conac, *La régulation des marchés boursiers par la Commission des opérations de bourse (COB) et la Securities and exchange commission (SEC)*, *op. cit.*, no. 194, for the evolution of the question, see H. Synvet, 'La détermination du montant de la parité d'échange dans les fusions de sociétés cotées', *Mélanges en l'honneur du professeur op. cit.*, spec. no. 23. Mr Synvet rightly notes that this baroque construction of French law, in which the stock market regulator intervenes in a matter that is foreign to him, causes singular difficulties in international relations, to the detriment of French operators who are not protected by their *lex societatis* (cf. the observation made on the system of oversight of professional authorities by public authorities: 'the French system displays the complexity of a baroque construction', P.-H. Conac, *La régulation des marchés boursiers par la commission des opérations de bourse [COB] et la securities and exchange commission [SEC]*, *op. cit.*, no. 155).

a. So-Called Company Law Issues

497. Derogations from the obligation to file a bid. The Takeover Directive has harmonised the obligations to file a public bid,[146] while leaving Member States room for manoeuvre as regards derogations from the obligation to file a bid. Against this background, the Takeover Directive subjects derogations from the obligation to file a public bid to the *lex societatis*, with the consequence that the very principle of filing a mandatory public bid is subject to the authority of the registered office.[147] This derogation from the obligation to file a bid should nevertheless be subject to the law which institutes this obligation, which is necessary for the proper functioning of the whole; however, it is the law of the financial markets which does this.[148] It may well be that the application of the law of the registered office does not lead to very different results when the company comes from a European legal system with an identical statute of limitations applicable according to the same criteria. However, on the one hand, Member States have different ways of implementing this obligation and, on the other hand, the obligation to make a bid is controlled by the authority whose law is applicable: it is up to the authority of the market to determine its implementation and to assess any derogations.[149]

498. Percentage of voting rights giving control. The concept of control is likely to vary according to the corporate form adopted,[150] which probably explains why the *lex societatis* is especially qualified to determine the percentage of voting rights conferring control. More than the percentage of voting rights itself, it is the very way in which control is obtained that is subject to the *lex societatis*: thus, the

---

146 Art. 5 of the Takeover Directive.

147 See for an illustration where the AMF rightly declared itself incompetent to implement the obligation to file a takeover bid for a Luxembourg company listed on the French regulated market, CA Paris, 1 July 2021, no. 20/08354; Com., 30 august 2023, no. 21-21.850.

148 It should be noted that, from a material point of view, the obligation to file a public bid may well apply to a private company whose shares are not admitted to trading, but which controls a French company whose shares are admitted to trading. In this case, the mere acquisition of control of the listed company's shareholder triggers the obligation to file a public bid, *especially* if the shares in question constitute the essential assets of the company whose change of control has been confirmed (on this last point, see Art. L. 433-4(IV) of the Monetary and Financial Code and the observations of D. Martin and F. Haas, 'La compétence de l'Autorité des marchés financiers en matière d'offre publique', *op. cit.* p. 45). This is the advantage of being able to ask the competent authority for a waiver of the obligation to file a takeover bid, see for example the waivers requested by the family shareholders of Hermès when they contributed their shares to a holding company to counter a possible increase in LVMH's capital, Decision no. 211/C/0024 of 7 January 2011, *Rev. Sociétés*, 2011, 364, note F. Martin-Laprade.

149 Report on the exemption of the prospectus *supra*, para. 349. It should be added that the situation is moreover less satisfactory as soon as third country issuers are involved, see *supra*, para. 489.

150 See e.g. France, where the notion of control is not the same for *sociétés en commandite par actions* and *sociétés anonymes*.

'*action de concert*' is also subject to the law of the place of the registered office, and is controlled by the market authority of the place of the target company.[151] However, in the same way that accounting law has a distinct understanding of the concept of control,[152] it would be possible for the *lex mercatus* to provide for its own concept of control, which would trigger the obligations it has laid down for companies seeking admission to trading on a market it governs.

499. Defences against public bids. The possibility of defences against takeover bids constitutes a challenge to the very merits of certain so-called "unfriendly" public bids. Such bids are not the result of negotiations between the management of the target company and the management of the offeror, but are the sole initiative of the offeror. This mistrust may seem curious.[153] In fact, the addressees of the bid, i.e. the shareholders of the target company, often derive significant added value from the bid, while remaining free to refuse it.[154] Managers, on the other hand, are not so free, being generally in a situation of conflict of interest which justified until recently a limitation of their powers in principle.[155] As Professor Alain Pietrancosta and Mr Jean-François Prat write:

> 'Thus, it would essentially be up to the shareholders and them alone to decide sovereignly on the merits of a takeover bid for which they are the exclusive recipients, despite the legal and factual obstacles (asymmetry of information, transaction costs linked to their dispersion, etc.), to the intelligence and efficiency of their collective action. The only defence would ultimately lie in the protection

---

151 Art. L. 433-3(I) of the Monetary and Financial Code. This is manifested by the inclusion of the rules on concerted action in the Commercial Code (Arts. L. 233-10 and L. 233-10-1). Some authors would like to extend this institution, which is specific to the law of listed companies, to ordinary company law, see F. Martin Laprade, *Concert et contrôle*, Joly sociétés, 2007. On these articles and the action de concert, see O. Dexant-de Bailliencourt, *Les pactes d'actionnaires dans les sociétés cotées*, *op. cit.*, p. 231 et seq. (the author shows the difficulties of the French approach in relation to Community developments) and pp. 260 et seq.

152 In fact, accounting law retains several notions of control depending on the applicable French or IFRS standards, see F. Saby, *La notion de contrôle en droit comptable*, Master 2 thesis, directed by H. Synvet, 2019.

153 A. Maikol, 'Il n'y a pas d'OPA inamicale', *RF gest.*, September-October 1989, p. 113 quoted by A. Pietrancosta, *Le droit des sociétés sous l'effet des impératifs financiers et boursiers*, thesis, Paris I, no. 666.

154 It is therefore not surprising that the only legitimate 'defences' are those put in place by the shareholders themselves when drafting or amending the articles of association, since they do not concern the external takeover bid, but the terms and conditions by which they agreed to become shareholders.

155 See the version of Art. L. 233-32 of the Commercial Code prior to the law of 29 March 2014. On this justification, see A. Pietrancosta, *Le droit des sociétés sous l'effet des impératifs financiers et boursiers*, *op. cit.*, nos. 666 et seq.

provided by stock market regulation itself (control of information and prices, respect for equal treatment), without any need for private reinforcements.'[156]

Such a view does not yet correspond to positive law. In all their diversity,[157] the defences against takeover bids, whether they aim to gain time[158] or to defeat the offer,[159] are in the vast majority of cases derived from corporate techniques.[160] What they have in common is that they are based on the behaviour of the manager. Company law is best placed to define the lawfulness of the conduct of the governing body. Traditionally, it is up to company law to regulate the disjunction between the interests of the director and those of the shareholders.[161] Thus, French law, after having limited the power of directors during a public bid,[162] now allows them to 'take any decision whose

156 A. Pietrancosta and J.-F. Prat, 'Offres publiques et droit des sociétés', *op. cit.*, p. 123 (already in this sense, A. Pietrancosta, *Le droit des sociétés sous l'effet des impératifs financiers et boursiers, op. cit.)* The same authors nevertheless observe that, in the United States, the justification for 'poison pills' comes from the profit that the shareholders of the target would make from a negotiation carried out by its managers, who are therefore legitimate in using means that force the negotiation, see *ibid.*, no. 682.
This undoubtedly explains the historical hostility of the SEC and the COB towards anti-takeover measures, on which see P.-H. Conac, *La régulation des marchés boursiers par la Commission des opérations de bourse (COB) et la Securities and exchange commission (SEC)*, *op. cit.*, nos. 199–202.

157 See the typology of anti-takeover defences used here, D. Martin and N. Molfessis, 'Offres publiques d'acquisition - Les défenses anti-OPA' in G. Canivet, D. Martin and N. Molfessis, *Les offres publiques d'achat, op. cit.*, pp. 573 et seq. A. Pietrancosta, *Le droit des sociétés sous l'effet des impératifs financiers et boursiers, op. cit.*, no. 687.

158 For example, by challenging the declaration of conformity, by acquiring stakes in certain regulated sectors of activity requiring prior administrative authorisation/concentration control, or in companies established in foreign countries with cumbersome regulations on takeover bids, such as the United States, but also by the existence of double voting rights (which the bidder will automatically obtain, unless the articles of association provide otherwise, if it has the patience to remain a shareholder for two years).

159 Through the search for allies, the counter-offer (the so-called 'Pacman' defence), the sheltering of a strategic asset (for example, by using organisational mechanisms under foreign law – see the example of Renault-Nissan reported by D. Martin and N. Molfessis, 'Takeover Bids – Anti-takeover defences', *op. cit.*, no. 1286), or the acquisition of assets with a considerable increase in the target's debt (which is therefore less attractive), or, symmetrically, the transfer of the coveted assets, or even the exceptional distribution, but also offer warrants and, finally, the granting of shares to the employees, the latter being deemed to be more attentive to the company's long-term future. Beforehand, the potential target can insert change of control clauses in all contracts it enters into. These techniques are commonly used, see the panorama by H. Segain and S. Devaux, 'Anti-takeover defences within French CAC 40 and CAC NEXT 20 companies. Panorama 2017/2018', *RTDF*, no. 2/3, p. 22.

160 Arts. L. 233-32 et seq. of the Commercial Code.

161 This argument leads Mr Garcimartin Alferez to qualify this issue as a corporate one, see F. Garcimartin Alferez, *Cross-border listed companies, op. cit.*, no. 174.

162 Until the Act of 29 March 2014, these rules modified the organisation of the company by limiting the prerogatives of directors and by extending the powers of the AGM for the duration of the offer period (Art. L. 233-32(I) of the Commercial Code, which transposes

implementation is likely to cause the bid to fail [...].'[163] Two limits are set: that of the company's interest, and that of the articles of association.[164] The broadening of the notion of corporate interest nevertheless gives managers more room for manoeuvre.[165] The articles of association still allow shareholders to limit the powers of directors during the bid period, by making decisions likely to frustrate the bid subject to authorisation by the AGM, or by suspending the delegations granted by the AGM before the bid.[166]

500. It is as if we were dealing with a case of alteration of the company's operation due to the listing, which therefore falls within the scope of listed company law.[167] It seems to us, however, that if this were true, the intervention of the market regulator, even if it is the one of the registered office, would not be so frequent.[168] The only reason why the law on defences against public bids

---

Art. 9 of the Takeover Directive; this rule is also referred to as 'board neutrality'). The aim was to neutralise any actions by directors that might have the effect of frustrating the bid (Art. L. 233-32(III); on this rule, see, inter alia, the critical comments of E. Wymeersch, 'Les défenses anti-OPA après la treizième directive' in *Mélanges en l'honneur de Jean Stoufflet*, Paris, LGDJ, 2001, p. 397, and, on the other hand, the more measured observations of A. Pietrancosta, 'Loi n° 2006-837 du 31 mars 2006 relative aux offres publiques d'acquisition: des "options" françaises', *RTDF*, June 2006, pp. 5 et seq.) These rules were intended to facilitate the bid. However, they could be deactivated when the legal system from which the bidder comes does not have similar rules in order to preserve equality of arms. This is what has been referred to as the 'reciprocity clause': takeover bids are only encouraged between countries that obey identical rules of good conduct (see in particular on this subject D. Martin and N. Molfessis, 'Offres publiques d'acquisition – Les défenses anti-OPA', *op. cit.*) From a private international point of view, one might be tempted to see here the premises of the community of law allowing the bilateral method to flourish. Without being very far from this scheme, it seems rather that the reciprocity clause simply aims to encourage recalcitrant countries to transpose these rules of good conduct, at the risk that their operators may not benefit from them. In other words, this reciprocity rule is related to public international law, which the very notion of reciprocity suggests.

163 Art. L. 233-32(I) of the Commercial Code.

164 Art. L. 233-32(I) of the Commercial Code.

165 A. Gaudemet, 'La loi PACTE et le droit des offres publiques', *BJB*, July 2019, pp. 40 et seq.

166 Art. L. 233-33(I) of the Commercial Code.

167 As Mr Viandier writes, it is here that 'the stock exchange procedure affects the social mechanism', see A. Viandier, 'Offres publiques et droit des sociétés' *Gaz. Pal*, 3 May 1988, p. 247. It is striking that the vast majority of the examples taken by the eminent author are in fact only concerned with the means of defence against takeover bids. This is where company law is really affected, and where the special company law needed by listed companies mainly lies.
See on this question M. Tedjani, *Offre publique d'acquisition: application internationale du droit suisse*, *op. cit.* The author simply observes that this part of the regulation is 'related to company law', without however analysing that this is the real core of the application of the *lex societatis*, in particular because he sees a vast majority of the rules of the public bid as company law rules.

168 For example, the AMF sets certain thresholds, such as those that neutralise clauses that restrict voting rights (Art. L. 233-38 of the Commercial Code), or paralyse certain prerogatives of managers (see Art. L. 233-39 of the Commercial Code). One may nevertheless wonder whether it is relevant to give a corporate competence to an authority whose purpose is not

is subject to the *lex societatis* is that the latter traditionally governs the behaviour of the company's bodies. It should be pointed out that the jurisdiction of the *lex societatis* only has primacy when the liability of the director is engaged in the internal order. In the case of takeover, the conduct of the director affects the external order, especially the legal order of the market: this is why the market can impose rules of conduct on any director of a foreign company whose securities are admitted to trading on its territory.[169] The disregard of such rules would not only entail his administrative responsibility towards the market authority, but would also constitute a tort towards third parties and, in particular, towards the author of the offer.[170] Here, the jurisdiction of the law of the financial market would in fact be expressed under the general law of civil liability: the damage then takes place on the financial market, since it consists in the impairment of the liquidity of the securities or of the price determination mechanism set up by the trading platform.

501. Shareholders' agreements. The Takeover Directive encouraged Member States to neutralise clauses restricting transfers of shares in order to facilitate the liquidity of the shares and thus enable the public bid to succeed. France transposed this rule with regard to statutory clauses,[171] but offered French companies the option of neutralising or not the same clauses contained in shareholders' agreements,[172] thus making it possible to defend against takeover bids by extrastatutory means.[173] The law designated by the shareholders' agreement is most often the law of the company.[174] As Mr d'Avout writes:

---

the establishment of distributive justice within commercial companies, but the protection of the savings of the residents of the legal system that instituted it. For a critique of the AMF's intervention in company law, see H. Synvet, 'La détermination du montant de la parité d'échange dans les fusions de sociétés cotées', *op. cit.*, spec. no. 13, p. 577.

169 These rules could even govern conflicts of interest between the majority and minority shareholders of the target insofar as the behaviour of the former would affect the price. Considering nevertheless that this is a corporate issue, see F. Garcimartin Alferez, *Cross-border listed companies*, *op. cit.*, no. 174.

170 Regarding the fault of the company director in the external order, see *supra*, para. 88.

171 Art. L. 233-34 of the Commercial Code. Such a rule could appear superfluous since market rules make admission to trading conditional on the deletion of such clauses in the articles of association.

172 Art. L. 233-35 of the Commercial Code. The same option is provided for extrastatutory clauses restricting voting rights, Arts. L. 233-36 and 37 of the Commercial Code.

173 This position was adopted after the drafting of Mr Jean-François Lepetit's report preceding the transposition. However, an extrastatutory defence is not hidden, as shareholders' agreements are published as part of the prospectus required for an IPO. On the limits of shareholders' agreements in the event of an offer, see O. Dexant-de Bailliencourt, *Les pactes d'actionnaires dans les sociétés cotées*, *op. cit.*, no. 177.

174 In the absence of a choice of law – unlikely in practice - the criterion of the domicile of the debtor of the characteristic performance of the shareholders' agreement may point to a law that has little to do with the company or stock exchange law insofar as the shareholder is foreign. In addition, it may be very difficult to determine *the* relevant characteristic benefit, either because of the absence of a *characteristic* benefit in a shareholders' agreement

'Within the entity governed by the law assigned to it, emancipating the relationship between two members (through the effect of a shareholders' agreement, for example) by subjecting it to an arbitrary law of allegiance risks, once again, giving rise to artificial conflicts and seeing the law of the bilateral relationship supplanted by the public policy standards specific to the collective organisation.'[175]

The existence of a choice of law in the agreement is nevertheless irrelevant, simply because the lawfulness of clauses restricting the transfer of shares in the event of a takeover bid may be considered not to fall within the scope of the law of contract. In fact, if the international applicability of these rules is difficult to determine, it is because they are at the crossroads of three laws: *lex contractus*, *lex societatis* and *lex mercatus*. The application of the *lex contractus* should be ruled out. Indeed, these clauses affect the internal functioning of the company and, in particular, when they are stipulated with a view to a takeover bid, the question of its takeover. These issues do not fall within the scope of the *lex contractus*.[176] It should no doubt be noted that these rules still have their source in company law, and that the application of the *lex societatis* is therefore not in doubt. How could it be otherwise when they so closely affect the functioning of the company?

It seems to us, however, that the rules on the lawfulness of clauses restricting the transfer of shares, while they may incidentally affect the operation of the company, are in fact primarily aimed at ensuring that the bid runs smoothly, as this is part of the more general framework of the proper functioning of the financial market. The reason for the illegality of these clauses is to be found in the liquidity that the securities must present in order to establish a market price and to allow for the possible realisation of a takeover bid. This is why the *lex mercatus* is justified in asserting its jurisdiction, if necessary as a mandatory rule. That said, their realisation will depend on the court petitioned, and in particular on whether a court of the Union is petitioned, on which the applicability of the Rome I Regulation depends. In the latter case, if it is

---

containing several benefits, or because of the perfectly reciprocal nature of the benefits in question. The singularity of the situation could lead one to disregard the characteristic benefit and to resort to the criterion of the closest links (Art. 4(4°) of the Rome I Regulation). However, this last criterion is difficult to apply. If the emphasis is placed on the acquisition of control regulated by the agreement, the *lex societatis will be* applied (X. Boucobza, *L'acquisition internationale de sociétés*, *op. cit.*, no. 439; O. Dexant-de Bailliencourt, *Les pactes d'actionnaires dans les sociétés cotées*, *op. cit.)* Such an analysis will undoubtedly be strengthened by observing the prerogatives implemented, whether they are related to the governance of the company or to the exercise of voting rights. On the other hand, if these prerogatives are to be linked to a strategy regarding the financial terms of exit from the capital, they should undoubtedly be seen as being more closely linked to the *lex mercatus*, particularly because of the choice made by Art. 4(2)(e) of the Takeover Directive.

175 L. d'Avout, 'Les phénomènes collectifs et l'analyse macro en droit international privé', *op. cit.* B. Audit and L. d'Avout, *Droit international privé*, *op. cit.*, no. 1232.

176 Art. 1(2)(f) of the Rome I Regulation.

a tribunal from financial market's country, it will be able to give effect to the mandatory rules of its legal order.[177] If it is a judge of the Union other than that of the place of listing, and in particular the judge of the registered office, he will be likely to take into account, or even apply, the mandatory rules of the place of listing.[178]

b. Labour Law

502. The interference of labour law. Since a takeover bid is formally a share acquisition operation, by way of purchase or exchange, employment law should remain outside the issues raised by the bid. However, the Court of Cassation rejected such an approach very early on, considering that:

> 'While it is true that the sale, regularly concluded between private individuals, of shares or units in a company constitutes, as a general rule, a private property transaction to which the provisions of the Labour Code are not applicable, the situation is different in the case where the negotiated transfer of part of the share capital is used as a means of placing the company operating a business under the dependence of another company [...]. If, therefore, it has knowledge of this, which necessarily occurs when the negotiation is carried out by the head of the company, the management is obliged [...] to provide information about it and to consult the works council.'[179]"

From this decision and the rationale behind it comes the modern regulation of the Labour Code, which requires the consultation of the works council of the target in the case of a public bid. Indeed, according to the information

177 Art. 9(2) of the Rome I Regulation.

178 Art. 9(3) of the Rome I Regulation. The article allows the application of the mandatory rules of the place of performance of the obligations of the contract insofar as these laws render the performance of the contract illegal. The restrictive covenants of a share transfer are indeed 'obligations arising out of the contract' constituted by the shareholders' agreement, and the laws relating to public bids make their performance unlawful. However, their place of performance should not be located by the shares that are the subject of the clause, which would lead to a dead end (as O. Dexant-de Bailliencourt, *Les pactes d'actionnaires dans les sociétés cotées*, *op. cit.*, no. 39), but by the law whose mandatory legislative policy is affected and which enacted the laws in question, i.e. the law of the place of listing or the *lex societatis* of the target company.

179 Cass. crim., 2 March 1978, *Haulotte*, no. 76-92008. The works council was renamed, by order no. 2017-1386 of 22 September 2017, the social and economic committee. We will continue to use here the former, less cumbersome, name of works council, which has the advantage of coinciding with the European nomenclature creating, by means of a directive, a European works council (Directive no. 94/45/EC of 22 September 1994 governing the establishment of a European works council).
The aforementioned order also had the effect of modifying the order of the articles, initially Arts. L. 431-1 et seq. of the Labour Code, which have now become Arts. L. 2325-1 et seq. and have been moved to Arts. L. 2312-11 et seq. of the same Code.

obligations, the works council is convened at the time when the information becomes public, and then discusses with its employer, which allows it to know, among other things, whether the offer has been solicited or not.[180] It is also the recipient of all the documents that must be sent to the shareholders' AGMs, which enables it to have a more informed opinion on the merits of the takeover bid.[181] Above all, the works council is the legal creditor of information obligations on the offeror itself, which must send it, within three days of the publication of the offer, an information note concerning its employment policy,[182] but also reveal to it the industrial and financial policy of the companies concerned by its offer for the twelve months that follow.[183]

503. Rule of the Takeover Directive. The Takeover Directive makes this regulation from company law subject to the law of the registered office.[184] We will restrict ourselves to threes remarks here. The first is that the law of the target's registered office does not apply to the provisions concerning the information to be provided to the employees of the bidding company.[185] The second is that

---

180 Art. L. 2312-42 of the Labour Code.

181 Pursuant to Art. L. 225-100-3 of the Commercial Code, applicable to companies whose securities are admitted to trading, this report must explain the significant elements in the event of a takeover bid.

182 This is a note provided to the AMF when the draft offer is filed so that it can give its approval (Art. L. 621-1(IX) of the Monetary and Financial Code), which the Committee can request under Art. 2312-44 of the Labour Code.

183 This information is provided during the hearing of the offeror (Art. 2312-43, para. 2, of the Labour Code). Far from being anecdotal, the works council can take legal action to have the offeror comply with these requirements on the basis of Art. 2312-46(II) of the Labour Code. See for example a legal action by works councils to obtain the cancellation of the offer, CA Paris, 1re ch., 27 October 1993.

184 Art. 4(2)(e) of the Takeover Directive. Professor Langlois' article, although written before the recodification, inspired the presentation here, see P. Langlois, 'Droit boursier et droit du travail', in G. Canivet, D. Martin and N. Molfessis, *Les offres publiques d'achat*, *op. cit.*

185 This exclusion can be explained by the configuration of the conflict of laws, where the law of the place of listing and the law of the *target's* registered office compete. No law competes with the law of the offeror's registered office. However, the offeror is subject to a particularly derogatory regulation where stock exchange law takes precedence over the principles of company law. Indeed, as the acquisition project of the bid is often fraught with consequences for the bidding company, such a decision obviously falls within the remit of the works council as established by Art. L. 2312-12, para. 1, of the Labour Code. Nevertheless, the combination of the necessary confidentiality required by a proposed public bid, together with the absence of any obligation of professional secrecy/confidentiality for works council members, led the legislator to provide for an express exemption from the obligation to consult the works council in the event of a public bid (Art. L. 2312-14 of the Labour Code). The legislator was inspired here by Art. 8(2) of Directive 94/45/EC of 22 September 1994 governing the establishment of a European works council, which prescribes, in particular in this type of case, the need to provide for derogations from the obligation to consult the works council. See on this question, P. Langlois, 'Droit boursier et droit du travail', *op. cit.*, pp. 156–157; D. Carreau and H. Létréguilly, 'Offres de l'entreprise', *op. cit.*, pp. 156-157; H. Létréguilly, 'Droit boursier et droit du travail', *op. cit.*, pp. 156–157. H. Létréguilly, 'Offres publiques: OPA, OPE, OPR', *op. cit.*, no. 161 (the authors also consider that 'not

the scope of the rules of Article 4(2)(e) of the Takeover Directive does not stop at the information of the employees, but encompasses the entire information consultation process. Its mechanism constrains the offeror: French law thus allows the works council to summon the management of the offeror within one week of the filing of the public bid with the AMF.[186] However, the hearing, which is strictly regulated by the Labour Code, is subject to highly effective sanctions, in particular that of paralysing the voting rights attached to the shares of the company subject to the bid that the company holds, this prohibition extending to the companies that control it or that it controls.[187] The third point is that the application of the criterion of the registered office to corporate law is explained by the fact that it most often corresponds to the connection of the economic activity.[188] However, it is possible that the decorrelation between the registered office and the economic activity of the company may call into question the use of this criterion. Nevertheless, it will retain its force as long as the sanction for the violation of the provisions of the Labour Code lies in the paralysis of the shareholders' prerogatives. These aspects are not, however, obstacles to the possibility of a global competence of the legal order of the financial market.

---

seizing the works council prior to the launch of the bid obviously limits the risks of insider trading'); T. Lefranc, 'Offres publiques d'acquisition', *J.-Cl. Soc.*, fasc. 2133, 4 April 2014, no. 44.

186 Art. 2312-43, para. 1, of the Labour Code.

187 Art. 2312-48 of the Labour Code.

188 Until the second half of the 20th century, such an application of the criterion of the registered office may appear traditional; social issues were, for the greatest authors, subject to the *lex societatis*, following the example of the collective representation of employees (see in this sense the note by P. Francescakis under the *Wagons-lits* judgment, 'Lois d'application immédiate et droit du travail: l'affaire du comité d'entreprise de la Compagnie des Wagons-lits', *RCDIP*, 1974, 273; today, see B. Ancel and Y. Lequette, *Les grands arrêts de la jurisprudence française de droit international privé*, *op. cit.*, 2006, no. 5, p. 493). It was only in application of the theory of the mandatory rules that this institution was removed from the corporate category, and that it was preferred, in the words of the Conseil d'État, to the law of the 'principal place of exercise of its activities as an employer in France' (CE, 29 June 1973, *RCDIP*, 1974, 344 concl. Questiaux).

Mr Pataut considers that collective representation would in fact not be a mandatory rule, but a set of territorial rules, i.e. rules which provide for 'the exclusion of foreign law, on the one hand; the sole consideration of facts constituted in the territory of the forum, on the other hand', and whose international application is therefore derived 'from public law methods, those which govern tax law or nationality law' (E. Pataut, 'Relire "Compagnie des Wagons-lits" La représentation collective des salariés dans l'espace international' in *Liber amicorum en hommage à Pierre Rodière*, Paris, LGDJ, 2019, pp. 387 et seq, spec. p. 398). It should simply be noted that international tax law is far from indifferent to what happens abroad, and most often adapts taxation by coordinating with what has already been levied by the foreign administration. Similarly, nationality law is not always indifferent to the granting of a nationality by another legal order (one only has to look at the German model in relation to dual nationals whose nationality is granted by a non-EU state to be convinced).

C. The Possibility of a Global Competence of the Legal Order of the Market

The basis for the jurisdiction of the legal order of the registered office is the effectiveness of the sanctions it can enforce. In other words, there is no necessity for the jurisdiction of the registered office (1). Under these conditions, the global jurisdiction of the legal order of the market is not only possible, it is desirable (2).

1. *The Basis for the Jurisdiction of the Legal System of the Registered Office*

504. The preceding discussion has shown the primacy of the jurisdiction of the legal order of the market. How then can the broad jurisdiction left to the legal system of the registered office be explained? The answer, it seems to us, lies in the sanctions attached to the regulation of takeover bids. When they consist of the deprivation of voting rights or the authoritative transfer of shares, they are closely related to the functioning of the company, and justify the competence of the market authority of the registered office.[189] The criterion of the registered office is justified in order to ensure that the corporate legal system does not resist an injunction, the non-compliance of which implies the use of corporate sanctions that only it is able to implement.[190]

However, this competence of the legal system of the registered office is not satisfactory. Firstly, because certain cardinal rules of takeover law, such as the obligation to make a bid, do not give rise to any corporate sanctions. Secondly, because the authority's proximity to the regulation should not be assessed on the basis of the sanction but on the basis of the rule itself: in this sense, the market authority of the place of listing is best placed to assess the violation of a market rule and to decide, if necessary, on its sanction. Thirdly, because it is sufficient, in order to escape the domain of the *lex societatis*, either to enact sanctions that are independent of the internal functioning of the company, or

---

[189] This explains the preference given to the registered office criterion in the application of English takeover law, see W.H. Smith, 'The Territorial Scope of Takeover Regulation', *op. cit.*, p. 31. For a detailed discussion of the arguments in favour of subjecting takeover law to the legal system of the target's registered office, see W.H. Smith, 'Le champ d'application territorial de la réglementation des offres publiques', *Rev. CMF*, no. 7, pp. 9–11.

[190] Whether it is a question of modifying the operation of certain bodies, such as directors who must obtain the authorisation of the general meeting in order to carry out acts that might cause the bid to fail (Art. L. 233-32 of the Commercial Code, stemming from Art. 9 of the Takeover Directive, the triggering of which is subject to a reciprocity clause), or the deprivation of voting rights in the event of the acquisition of shares in violation of the obligation to file a public bid. See, in more muted terms, M. Tedjani, *Offre publique d'acquisition: application internationale du droit suisse, op. cit.*, no. 138: 'This solution also has the advantage of avoiding the problems associated with the recognition of foreign decisions, and their inadequacy in the system where they are to be implemented.'

to secure the cooperation of the legal system of the registered office when such a sanction is provided for.

This co-operation will be facilitated where the legal system of the registered office has a takeover law with identical objectives. In such situations, cooperation between authorities is necessary to ensure that the two legal orders do not trigger the cumulative application of their legislation, one on the basis of the seat of the listed company, the other on the basis of the listing on its territory. In the case of multiple listings, the criteria used by the Takeover Directive remain relevant.[191] However, the principle of effectiveness requires that jurisdiction be left to the home jurisdiction if, in the absence of cooperation, it provides for the application of its takeover rules irrespective of the place of listing. If the registered office legal system does not have any rules on takeover bids, it is likely to regard them as infringing its conception of corporate public policy, or even as an undue intrusion by the legal system of the place of listing into what is the preserve of the registered office legal system: the prerogatives of the corporate bodies. However, far from being a legal policy decision,[192] the ignorance of these stock exchange mechanisms by the legal order of the registered office is rather due to a lesser degree of sophistication of local financial legislation:[193] the history of French regulation shows how long it took before the need for a specific regulation of takeover bids was realised.[194] In other words, the development of the financial market has the consequence of perfecting its legislation where the apparent liberalism, far from being a genuine legislative policy, stems rather from the inexperience of the legal order in regulating the sector of activity in question. In these circumstances, the legal system of the registered office is likely to carry out the sanctions administered by the financial market authority of the place of listing, *a fortiori* since these were known and accepted by the issuer who was able to select the place where it chose to admit its securities to trading.

---

191 On these criteria, see *supra*, para. 492.

192 It would be different if the legislator had, on the contrary, formalised this absence of a mandatory takeover bid, buy-out or squeeze-out mechanism. See, for example, B. Haftel, 'Les normes auto-limitées en droit international privé' in *Mélanges en l'honneur du professeur Bertrand Ancel*, LGDJ, Paris, 2018, spec. translation p. 864.

193 Report on insider trading by Mr Fadlallah, who considers insider trading to be a *sophisticated* offence, requiring a maturity of stock market regulations, I. Fadlallah, 'Point de vue sur l'affaire Péchiney. La localisation du délit d'initié', *RCDIP*, 1996, pp. 626 et seq.

194 The regulation of non-voluntary bids dates from the law of 2 August 1989, and that of the squeeze out from the law no. 93-1444 of 31 December 1993 (see no. *supra*, para. 487).

2. *The Articulation of the Jurisdiction of the Place of Listing with that of the Registered Office*

505. Proposal. These considerations lead to the proposal that French takeover law should apply to any company listing its securities on a French financial market that is subject to these regulations.[195] However, a distinction must be made between the situation of companies established on European territory, where the overall jurisdiction of the market's legal system would only be possible by revising the Takeover Directive, and that of companies from a third country. In the latter case, it is necessary to provide, on the one hand, for a rule for selecting the competent legal system in the event of multiple listings and, on the other hand, for a self-limitation of French regulations in the event that the legal system of the target's registered office provides for the application of its takeover regulations to all companies established on its territory and listed on another financial market. The Swiss legislator has already introduced such a conflict rule through the law of 28 September 2012.[196]

506. Presentation of Swiss law.[197] Swiss law made the application of takeover law subject to the cumulative criteria of being based and listed in Switzerland. Such a linkage resulted in shareholders being deprived of Swiss takeover regulation in an emblematic case where the target, whose activity and effective organisation were located on Swiss territory, had nevertheless been incorporated in Liechtenstein.[198] In these circumstances, the supervisory authority decided that 'investor protection justified the application of the effective seat principle'.[199] Subsequently, in order to avoid positive conflicts of law, Swiss case law developed a complex casuistry around the closest connections, the unpredictability of which

---

195 It is more difficult to envisage the application of French takeover law to French companies whose securities are only admitted to trading on a foreign financial market, even if the latter does not provide for it. The objective would then be to protect French investors and would require ensuring that a percentage of the capital is held by French residents. However, as the material scope of French takeover law is restricted to certain French financial markets, it is difficult to consider that takeover law is really aimed at protecting residents in general.

196 On the proposal of the COPA, the Swiss equivalent of the AMF. The amendment is included in the draft on insider trading, and the communication on the law is very brief (Message on the amendment of the Stock Exchange Act of 31 August 2011, FF 2011 6340).

197 This presentation of Swiss law is based on a comparative reading of the Swiss laws of 1995, 2013 and 2015, as well as on M. Tedjani, *Offre publique d'acquisition: application internationale du droit suisse*, *op. cit.*

198 SFBC decision of 30 September 1999 in the case of *LVMH Moët Hennessy Louis Vuitton and Tag Heuer Internatoinal SA*, *Bull. CFB*, 2000, 39, p. 25, para. 4. On this case, see M. Tedjani, *Offre publique d'acquisition: application internationale du droit suisse*, *op. cit.*

199 *Ibid.* and ref. In the same year the decision was taken to subject the supervision of market intermediaries to the criterion of the effective seat (*ibid.*, no. 578). The application of the Swiss stock exchange regulation is motivated by the protection of local investors.

prompted the Swiss legislator to reform its conflict rule.[200] The new rule no longer mentions the registered office and is based exclusively on the criterion of listing,[201] while providing for its self-limitation in the following terms:

> 'If Swiss law and foreign law apply simultaneously to a takeover bid, the provisions of Swiss law may be waived: a. if the application of Swiss law conflicts with foreign law, and b. if foreign law guarantees equivalent investor protection to that provided by Swiss law.'

507. Advantages of the Swiss rule. Such a rule requires the self-limitation of local regulation[202] in cases where a foreign law, declaring itself applicable regardless of the criterion, would already ensure the same objective. It is not to make complexity the touchstone of quality to admit to being seduced by the efforts of the Swiss legislator.[203] By ensuring the application of local regulations to companies whose securities are listed on a Swiss stock exchange, the rule also avoids conflicts of law that may arise from the simultaneous application of two sets of laws. The virtue of this rule lies in its nuance: refusing to apply if another regulation with the same objectives applies, it undoubtedly shows the way forward in this matter. The other advantage is that it avoids two excesses: leaving the application of the regulation to the pure discretion of the regulatory authority; excluding its expertise. Here, the Swiss authority has a legal obligation to apply Swiss regulation if the company is primarily listed in Switzerland. Only

---

200 For a summary of this casuistry, see *ibid.*, no. 574. This succession of amendments has the advantage of having shown the dysfunctional nature of the incorporation criterion in stock market matters.

201 Art. 125 of the Financial Market Infrastructure Act of 19 June 2015 (literally taking over Art. 22(1) and (1a) of the Federal Act of 24 March 1995 on Stock Exchanges and Securities Trading, as amended by the Act of 1 May 2013) retains the place of listing: 'The provisions of this Section (5) and Arts. 52 and 53 shall apply to public takeover bids for the securities of companies:
a. which have their registered office in Switzerland and all or some of whose securities are listed in Switzerland;
b. which have their registered office abroad and all or part of whose equity securities are principally listed in Switzerland.'

202 The other limitation of the Swiss regulation is specific to Swiss domestic law: companies listed in Switzerland may opt out of the obligation to file a takeover bid if the control threshold is exceeded (set in Switzerland as a matter of principle at 33.3%), or to raise the threshold for triggering the obligation (up to 49.9%).

203 The formula is borrowed from H. Synvet, *L'organisation juridique du groupe international de sociétés*, *op. cit.*, no. 460, p. 375 - the author refers to the efforts of the SEC to limit the ascendancy of the American stock exchange rules in order to reach an acceptable solution. It should be noted here that the Swiss legislature has succeeded in learning from the mistakes of the case law, which initially reacted legitimately to the unsuitability of the incorporation criterion in takeover law, but did not give in to the hegemonic recommendations of the group of experts it had commissioned for the reform, This was rejected by the Swiss Federal Chambers (the local parliament) because of the conflict of laws that such a criterion would cause.

by way of exception may the regulator waive the application of Swiss rules in cases where it can use its knowledge of the specific rules of the takeover bid to determine whether the foreign law offers a sufficient degree of equivalence in terms of investor protection.

508. It should be added that this rule may be further refined if the home jurisdiction applies its takeover law to the head office of the company and if it does not provide the same level of investor protection as Swiss law. As it stands, the Swiss legal system will apply its takeover rules cumulatively, as the conditions for self-limitation are not met. In our view, however, it is too late to act – in practice, only the regulations of the home legal system will be effectively complied with, since its sanctions will be the most effective.[204] The solution to this difficulty is to refrain from admitting to local markets the securities of companies whose home legal system would apply cumulatively with the regulation of the place of listing without guaranteeing equivalent investor protection. This refusal should extend to legal systems that refuse to assist in the enforcement of sanctions imposed by the market authority. Such a measure may seem particularly radical.[205] However, in practice it is rare and is likely to encourage the establishment of rules protecting the financial markets in the various legal systems and the conclusion of cooperation agreements. This means that such a rule would promote the coordination of legal systems.

509. Conclusion of the paragraph. The international scope of application of takeover bids is unsatisfactory, both in intra-European relations and in relations with third countries. By not applying to companies from third countries, French legislation is singularly out of step with the purpose of takeover law. This law, which in many respects appears to be a special contract law, aims to ensure the proper functioning of financial markets and the protection of investors. It uses corporate sanctions only because of their effectiveness. The legal system of the market is therefore in the best position not only to apply its legislation to takeover bids for securities admitted to trading on its territory, but also to ensure that they are monitored by its market authority. The statement is equally true

---

204 Some Swiss authors also observe that it will be difficult to impose the suspension of voting rights if the target's company law does not provide for such a sanction, see M. TEDJANI, *Offre publique d'acquisition: application internationale du droit suisse*, *op. cit.*

205 Considering that it would be disproportionate to make the admission of a foreign issuer's securities conditional on the presence, in the legal system of origin, of a compulsory takeover bid mechanism, see W.H. SMITH, 'The territorial scope of takeover bid regulation', op. *cit.* We know that such a method exists in relations with infrastructure managers from third countries (see *supra*, paras. 209 et seq.), as well as in relation to the prospectus requirement (see *supra*, para. 358). It is true that the purpose of the takeover bid is not to prevent system risk, which is partly the purpose of the equivalence method when certain third-country infrastructures are involved. However, the requirement of an agreement with the foreign authority is also implemented when the equivalence method is used in relation to third country prospectuses; the function of the regulation of the prospectus is to protect local investors, a function that is not unrelated to that pursued by takeover bid law.

whether the securities are issued by companies from third countries or by those established in the EU.

510. Conclusion of the section. Threshold crossing law and takeover law each have their own functions; they are linked to each other and pursue the objective of the proper functioning of the financial markets. For a long time, they have been part of company law. However, it is time to accept that their function is now distinct from that of company law, even though they may contribute to the pursuit of a company law objective. The consequences of this must be drawn in terms of their international scope of application and the *lex mercatus* must be applied to the law of thresholds and the law of takeover bids. At the same time, the law on threshold crossings continues to pursue an objective relating to the functioning of the corporate bodies and should be subject to the cumulative application of the *lex societatis*.

SECTION 2. ARTIFICIAL PRICE DISTORTION

The Financial Market Law provides for special regulation when certain transactions have a negative impact on the price formation mechanism. This regulation, which aims to protect the financial market mechanism, is subject to the law of the Financial Market (*lex mercatus*) and the supervision of the market authority. This is the case for share buybacks (§ 1) as well as for short selling (§ 2).

§ 1. SHARE BUY-BACK BY THE COMPANY

511. A company's share buy-back is the operation whereby the company acquires its own shares from its shareholders.[206] This transaction, insofar as it involves a shareholder and the company, and the company's shares, is fundamentally a matter of the relationship between the corporate bodies, and thus of the company's internal functioning. While logically governed by the Commercial Code,[207] the conditions for share buybacks are also based on European company law.[208] French law still prohibits share buybacks as a matter of principle,[209]

---

206 As the authors observe, the term 'buy-back' is not exact, but 'the term nevertheless suggests the idea of a return to a previous situation, and in particular the return of the securities to the issuing company', S. Torck, 'Le rachat par les sociétés cotées de leurs propres actions', *op. cit.*, fn. 1.

207 See spec. Arts. L. 225-206 et seq. of the Commercial Code. On the objectives pursued by this regulation, see *supra*, para. 471.

208 Art. 82 of Directive 2017/1132 of the European Parliament and of the Council of 14 June 2017 on certain aspects of company law.

209 Art. L. 225-206(I) of the Commercial Code.

but authorises them in certain cases, whether or not the company's shares are admitted to trading.[210] In the latter case, this operation directly affects the stock market price and justifies the intervention of a specific regulation. This regulation pursues an objective of both listed company law and financial market law, which explains the cumulative application of these rules.[211]

From the point of view of listed company law, French regulations provide for a special set of rules facilitating share buybacks. Its scope is restricted, in principle, to French companies whose securities are admitted to a regulated market. However, it is also available to companies whose securities are admitted to a 'multilateral trading facility subject to the provisions of II of Article L. 433-3 of the Monetary and Financial Code'.[212] The latter article refers to the possibility for an unregulated financial market manager to obtain the application of mandatory takeover bid regulations to securities admitted to trading on its platform.[213] In other words, in order for a multilateral trading facility operator to offer to French listed companies certain share buyback facilities, it must first apply to its home authority to set up a mandatory takeover bid procedure.

512. While the principle of this regulation originates in the Commercial Code, its enunciation is organised by Article L. 451-3 of the Monetary and Financial Code, which refers its details to Article 241-1 of the AMF General Regulation. The jurisdiction of financial market law becomes clearer and more fundamental once it is observed that share buybacks constitute market abuse in principle, and that it is only by way of derogation that the company is authorised to do so.[214] Not only does the Market Abuse Regulation list the purposes to which share buybacks are subject,[215] but it also requires the issuer to inform the listing authority 'of each transaction relating to the buy-back programme, including the information specified in Article 25(1) and (2) and Article 26(1), (2) and (3) of Regulation (EU) No 600/2014'.[216] The latter information is the information for which investment firms are accountable to the financial market authority in relation to the detection of market abuse.[217] Financial market law is therefore likely to restrict the possible freedom granted by the law of the company.[218]

---

210 Art. L. 225-206(II) of the Commercial Code.

211 In this sense, these rules are not in competition with each other unless the negative view of the legal order of the registered office conflicts with the possible prohibition of the legal order of the market.

212 Art. L. 225-209 of the Commercial Code.

213 See *supra*, para. 486; 490.

214 Art. 5 of the Market Abuse Regulation.

215 Art. 5(2) of the Market Abuse Regulation.

216 Art. 5(3) Market Abuse Regulation.

217 See *supra*, para. 437.

218 As some authors write: 'It is clear that the approach and logic of company law and stock market law are at odds with each other. While the former promotes the freedom of share buybacks, the latter harbours a genuine suspicion of them which leads it, on the one hand,

There is therefore no doubt about the competence of the financial market law regarding the purchase of shares by a company that has admitted its securities to it. The law must ensure that a delicate balance is struck between the advantages of this mechanism (increased liquidity of admitted securities; attractiveness of this mechanism for the issuer) and the disadvantage of artificially distorting the share price. Deciding on this balance, on which price formation and the proper functioning of the financial market depend, is unquestionably a matter for the law of the financial market.

§ 2. SHORT SELLING

513. Regulation of short selling. Short selling refers to a sales contract in which the seller does not have, at the time of the conclusion of the contract, the goods that he undertakes to deliver at the time of execution.[219] These transactions make it possible, in particular, to speculate on the downward price of the object of the contract. When these contracts concern a security admitted to trading, or an instrument which is indexed on such securities, they are likely to alter the integrity of the price by causing it to fall.[220] This is why the EU legislator has enacted a regulation governing this practice. To this end, the Regulation makes two types of distinction: short and long positions, covered and uncovered positions. The short position is defined as:

> 'A position resulting from either of the following shall be considered to be a short position relating to issued share capital or issued sovereign debt: (a) a short sale of a share issued by a company or of a debt instrument issued by a sovereign issuer; (b) entering into a transaction which creates or relates to a financial instrument other than an instrument referred to in point (a) where the effect or one of the effects of the transaction is to confer a financial advantage on the natural or legal person entering into that transaction in the event of a decrease in the price or value of the share or debt instrument.'[221]"

---

to judge them as inherently dangerous for the proper functioning of the market and, on the other, to designate among the various purposes that may be pursued through share buybacks those that appear to be inoffensive to the market, and therefore legitimate.' A. Couret, H. Le Nabasque, *et al.*, *Droit financier*, *op. cit.*, no. 1574.

219 Art. 2(1)(b) of the Short Selling Regulation also includes within short selling the case where the seller is the owner of the property in question by virtue of a loan, which does not appear to be entirely accurate, see T. Bonneau, *Régulation bancaire et financière européenne et internationale*, *op. cit.*, no. 254.

220 Recital 1 of the Short Selling Regulation. For a critical analysis of this statement, see J. Payne, 'The regulation of short selling and its reform in Europe' (2012) 13 *European Business Organisation Law Review*, pp. 413 et seq.; E. Howell, 'Regulatory Intervention in the European Sovereign Credit Default Swap Market' (2016) 17 *European Business Organisation Law Review*, pp. 319 et seq.

221 Art. 3(1) of the Short Selling Regulation.

514. The long position is defined by the reverse, i.e. holding a share, or entering into a transaction to benefit from an increase in the price or value of the share.[222] It is with these concepts that the Regulation defines the notion of an uncovered position, which is the position of a person when the sale contract is not used to cover:

> '(a) the risk of issuer default, where the natural or legal person holds a long position in the sovereign debt of the issuer to which the sovereign credit default swap is linked; or (b) the risk of a decrease in the value of the sovereign debt, where the natural or legal person holds assets or has incurred liabilities, including but not limited to financial contracts, a portfolio of assets or financial obligations, the value of which is correlated to the value of the sovereign debt.'[223]

These different concepts are the basis for several obligations. First, net short positions considered to be large, whether in equities or sovereign debt, must be notified to the competent authorities and, in the case of the former, published.[224] Secondly, uncovered short sales of equities or sovereign debt are simply prohibited, as are uncovered sovereign default swaps.[225] The penalty for these obligations is administrative liability for those who enter into such contracts.[226] Parties are discouraged from entering into such contracts, or from not notifying their positions, because of the financial and administrative consequences of doing so, even though the exercise of their activity is dependent on administrative approval.[227]

515. Scope of application. The Regulation provides for its international applicability in relation to the admission of a financial instrument to an EU trading venue. This follows from the material scope of the Regulation, which is applicable:

> 'to derivatives [...] that relate to a financial instrument (*admitted to trading on an EU platform*), or to an issuer of such a financial instrument, including such derivatives when traded outside a trading venue'.[228]

---

222 Art. 3(2) of the Short Selling Regulation.

223 Art. 4(1) of the Short Selling Regulation.

224 Arts. 6 and 7 of the Short Selling Regulation.

225 Arts. 12 and 13 of the Short Selling Regulation.

226 See in French perspective, Art. L. 621-15 of the Monetary and Financial Code. This is also what emerges from the sanctions provided for by all Member States, on which see ESMA, 'List of administrative measures and sanctions applicable in Member States to infringements of Regulation on short selling and credit default swaps', 1 January 2021, available on the authority's website.

227 See for a transatlantic illustration, A. Gaudemet and H. Boucheta, 'Reform of the OTC derivatives markets in the United States and the European Union: the new structure requirements', *BJB*, May 2011, no. 5, pp. 339 et seq., spec. no. 22.

228 Art. 1(b) of the Regulation Short selling.

Such a scope of application gives a particularly broad reach to the Short Selling Regulation, since it applies to financial contracts traded outside a financial market, and without necessarily leading to the acquisition of the financial security. However, this feature is not unique to the short-selling regulation. Indeed, the calculation of the threshold on which the regulation of threshold crossing and mandatory takeover bids is based also applies to financial contracts concluded outside the financial market, even if they only offer a simple share lending facility.[229]

The international scope of this regulation is explained by its material scope and the protection it intends to give to the price of securities admitted to trading. The protection of the mechanism established by the financial market is at stake. However, it is less a question of protecting against a system risk, even though the devaluation of all securities admitted to trading may be such a risk, than of ensuring that short sales do not interfere with price determination. It should therefore not be surprising that the Regulation covers any contract that makes use of the mechanism it protects. The difficulty, however, lies in the implementation of the sanctions it lays down. These are administrative in nature and require the cooperation of the authorities of the registered office of the operators involved in the disputed transaction.

516. Section conclusion. Both the company buy-back of its own shares and the prohibition of short selling are regulated by the financial market law because of the consequences they have on the price of the security admitted to trading. Financial market law applies whenever the protection of the mechanism it establishes is at stake; its international scope of application is closely linked to this material scope of application. These developments have confirmed the legitimacy of the law of the financial market to apply to transactions permitted by the use of its trading system which, if they contribute to its existence, must not have the effect of altering its functioning.

517. Chapter conclusion. The objective of market transactions law is the smooth functioning of the financial market. First of all, it is the right law to regulate the supervision of the issuer, i.e. the law of thresholds and takeover bids. Since they affect the functioning of the company, they were for a long time wrongly considered to be part of the *lex societatis* alone. However, the two sets of rules are not identical and it should be possible to introduce specific solutions for each of them. While the *lex mercatus* is in fact the best placed to govern takeover law, and the market authority the best placed to apply it, it should be possible to apply the *lex societatis* cumulatively to the regulation of threshold crossings by French companies whose securities are admitted to trading abroad. This should lead, on the one hand, to a change in the criterion used by the Transparency and

[229] See *supra*, para. 473.

Takeover Directives and, on the other hand, to aligning the scope of application of takeover law with respect to companies from third countries with the scope of application of the law on threshold crossings. The objective of ensuring the proper functioning of the financial market is less ambiguous when the rules in question are designed to prevent artificial price distortion. In such cases, the application of financial market law and the competence of the market authority are not in doubt.

CHAPTER 3
MARKET ABUSE

518. Definition. Market abuse is nowadays based on the Market Abuse Regulation[1] and covers two offences: insider trading and market manipulation.[2] The former is defined as follows:

> 'Insider trading arises where a person possesses inside information and uses that information by acquiring or disposing of, for its own account or for the account of a third party, directly or indirectly, financial instruments to which that information relates [...].'[3]

The Regulation adds that recommending a transaction to a third party on the basis of inside information constitutes insider trading.[4] Insiders are persons who receive inside information.[5] There are two types of market manipulation: dissemination of false information[6] and price

1 Regulation (EU) No 596/2014 of the European Parliament and of the Council of 16 April 2014 on market abuse.

2 Prohibited by Arts. 14 and 15 of the Market Abuse Regulation. Some authors make the illicit disclosure of privileged information an autonomous offence of insider trading, see F. Drummond, *Droit financier*, *op. cit.*, no. 1081.

3 Art. 8(1) of the Market Abuse Regulation, and Art. L. 465-1 of the Monetary and Financial Code. On the legislative genesis of insider trading, see I. Fadlallah, 'Point de vue sur l'affaire Péchiney. La localisation du délit d'initié', *RCDIP*, 1996, pp. 626 et seq. The offence was first identified and punished in the United States through the so-called '10b-5' rule (so called because it was adopted in application of section 10b of the Securities and Exchange Act). However, both the legislator and the US regulator were careful not to define insider trading precisely in order to facilitate its repression. On the history of Rule 10b-5 and insider trading in the United States, and on the extension of the material scope of the offence and insider misconduct, see P.-H. Conac, *La régulation des marchés boursiers par la Commission des opérations de bourse (COB) et la Securities and exchange commission (SEC)*, *op. cit.*, no. 59, p. 74 and no. 62, pp. 79 et seq.

4 Art. 8(2) Market Abuse Regulation. The following three Articles (9, 10 and 11) aim at establishing the materiality of the facts and their possible derogations.

5 Art. 8(3) of the Market Abuse Regulation. The Regulation retains a broad concept of persons who can be qualified as insiders, since it always refers to any person "who holds inside information and who knows or ought to have known" that the information was privileged (Art. 26 of the Market Abuse Regulation). On the particularly broad assessment of the notion of inside information, see P. Pailler and T. Bonneau, 'The precise nature of Inside information in European and French case law', *RTDF*, no. 2015, no. 3.

6 Art. 10 of the Market Abuse Regulation and Art. L. 465-3-2 of the Monetary and Financial Code.

manipulation,[7] i.e. behaviour aimed at distorting the price of an instrument.

519. Scope of application of French criminal law. The application of French criminal law is based on unilateral and abstract criteria that give it a particularly broad international scope. However, as Donnedieu de Vabres has already written, 'it is paradoxical to want to resolve the conflict of criminal jurisdictions without considering the purpose of criminal law, which is prior to and superior to States'.[8] Taken seriously by Professor Chilstein, this assertion led the author to draw on the mandatory rules method in order to define the international scope of application of the so-called 'accessory' criminal law, which includes market abuse.[9] In short, the idea is to align the scope of the offence not with the jurisdictional criteria of French criminal law, but with the purpose of the offence.[10] This approach is similar to that of identifying the interest protected by the offence[11] in order to deduce its scope of application in the area.[12] It was proposed in financial matters by Professor Fadlallah following the *Péchiney* case, in which the French authorities prosecuted French citizens for insider trading in a French company whose securities were listed in the United States.

The discussion that follows is in line with this analysis. The criminal characterisation of market abuse gives it an unreasonable scope of application when it has the effect of allowing French legislation to punish any market abuse occurring on the financial markets of third countries on the grounds that certain facts constituting the offence could be linked to French territory. One would simply want to add to this reasoning that market abuse has the

---

7 Art. 12 of the Market Abuse Regulation and Art. L. 465-3-1 of the Monetary and Financial Code. Manipulation of benchmark indices is also prohibited (Art. L. 465-3-3 of the Monetary and Financial Code).

8 H. Donnedieu de Vabres, *Les principes modernes de droit pénal international*, Paris, Sirey, 1928, republished in Panthéon-Assas, 2004, p. 134.

9 D. Chilstein, *Droit penal international et lois de police, op. cit.*

10 *Ibid.* at 742: 'In our view, greater emphasis should be placed on the rational scope of application of criminal laws in space on the basis of a refined analysis of their content and purpose. This is why we have proposed to transpose into international criminal law a method borrowed from private international law – the method of mandatory rules – which consists precisely in determining the field of application of laws in space according to their purpose.'

11 The identification process can be complex, see S. Fernandez, *Essai sur la distribution des compétences en droit pénal international*, Fondation Varenne, 2016, nos. 204 et seq.

12 The protected interest approach dilates rather than joins the approach initiated by Mr Chilstein, which, by stopping at 'accessory criminal law', does not allow for a satisfactory distribution of jurisdiction, see S. Fernandez, *Essai sur la distribution des compétences en droit pénal international, op. cit.* Ms Fernandez also questions the basis of mandatory rules, observing that in criminal matters, the principle of legality of offences and penalties prevents the judge from 'discovering' a mandatory rule, and that it is impossible for the French judge to apply a foreign mandatory rule. However, it seems to us that this does not call into question the use of the most significant aspect of the mandatory rule method: the delimitation of the scope of application of the norm by examining the legislative policy it pursues, or, in criminalist rhetoric, the interest it protects, the legal good it incorporates.

particularity of being easily subsumed within the '*competence réelle*'. This jurisdiction, which is based on Article 113-10 of the French Criminal Code, allows for the punishment of offences that affect the fundamental interests of the Nation. It is on this basis that counterfeiting, for example, is punished. It will be shown here that '*competence réelle*' is the best way to account for the jurisdiction of French law in matters of market abuse, in particular because it takes into account the purpose of the offence in question, and in particular that the law of market abuse is part of the regulation of the functioning of the market. This is also why the law of market abuse can be subsumed within the conflict rule outlined here, according to which the law applicable to the rules governing the functioning of the financial market is that of the trading platform. This rule should be extended to the administrative enforcement of market abuse. However, the '*competence réelle*' is not sufficient to pursue the Market Abuse Regulation's stated objective of protecting all European financial markets; it will always benefit from being supplemented by personal jurisdiction (Section 1). The dematerialisation and internationalisation of the facts constituting market abuse, in addition to rendering territorial jurisdiction artificial, makes cooperation between administrative authorities particularly necessary, which should be encouraged and whose regime should be inspired by that of judicial cooperation (Section 2).

SECTION 1. PURPOSE OF ENFORCEMENT AND JURISDICTIONAL CRITERIA

In order to demonstrate this, it will first be shown that the objective pursued by the prohibition of market abuse is the protection of European financial markets (§ 1). This objective explains why French criminal legislation should be restricted to the criminalisation of market abuse committed on European financial markets (§ 2). The international jurisdiction of the AMF should not exceed this scope either (§ 3).

§ 1. OBJECTIVES OF THE PROHIBITION OF MARKET ABUSE

520. Gradual emergence of market abuse. Market abuse is a relatively recent offence. The first to appear is market manipulation through the offence of altering prices in the former Article 419 of the Criminal Code, as drafted by the law of 3 December 1926.[13] Insider trading, which originated in the

13 Repressed by the former Art. 419 of the Criminal Code. This offence is the predecessor of price manipulation, see in this sense, M. Tomasi, 'Vers un renouveau de la lutte contre les manipulations de cours' in *Mélanges AEBDF-France IV*, p. 444. The author observes that

United States,[14] was introduced in France in the wake of the law of 24 July 1966.[15] However, some authors believe that the real birth of this offence dates from the beginning of its administrative repression with the entry into force of Law no. 89-531 of 2 August 1989,[16] which gave the former Commission des Opérations de Bourse [predecessor of the AMF] the power to supervise and sanction the standards it had previously issued.[17] From that date onwards, the criminal offences of market abuse, often referred to as 'stock market offences'

---

this text is also the legislative ancestor of modern competition law, underlining precisely 'the kinship between acts of stock market manipulation and anti-competitive practices on the goods and services markets' (*ibid.*). Mr Tomasi also notes that the material scope of application was undoubtedly both broader and more precisely formulated, as it was in line with the reprehensible behaviour: the offence of price manipulation could take place either 'by means of fraudulent procedures', or 'by exercising or attempting to exercise an action on the market with the aim of obtaining a gain which would not be the result of the natural play of supply and demand'. On this subject, see also J. Chacornac, *Les fonctions de l'information en droit des instruments financiers*, *op. cit.*, nos. 743 et seq. On the comparative history of price manipulation in French and American law, see P.-H. Conac, *La régulation des marchés boursiers par la Commission des opérations de bourse (COB) et la Securities and exchange commission (SEC)*, *op. cit.* The author observes that Art. 419 of the Criminal Code was nevertheless only applicable to manipulation of the price of public securities and could not be applied to private securities, see Crim., 30 June 1885, *D. P.* 1886.1.839.

14 Its origin is the interpretation of rule 10-b-5 of the SEC regulation in 1942, see J. Bédart, *International conflicts of Antitrust and Securities Regulations: 'It's all about effects'*, *op. cit.*, pp. 155 et seq.; J. Chacornac, *Les fonctions de l'information en droit des instruments financiers*, *op. cit.*, no. 748.

15 Law no. 70-1203 of 23 December 1970 inserts an article 10-1 in order no. 67-833 of 28 September 1967. This ordinance is the one that gave birth to the COB (see *supra*, para. 53), which is now codified in the Monetary and Financial Code under the provisions of Art. L. 465-1. However, the 1967 Order was already aware of the offence, since company directors and other insiders designated by the COB were required to register their shares and declare each acquisition (Art. 8 of the 1967 Order), and these provisions were punishable by law (Art. 11 of the 1967 Order). The contribution of the 1970 Act was to transform insider trading into an *a posteriori* sanction, at the request of the COB, which was overwhelmed by the declarations that the law imposed on insiders (Foyer: report on behalf of the Commission des lois before the Ass. p. 6, quoted by I. Fadlallah, 'Point de vue sur l'affaire Péchiney. La localisation du délit d'initié'», *op. cit.*, p. 627). This means that, as Mr Fadlallah writes, insider trading was born with the COB (*ibid.*); it is easier to understand why it is the extension of the COB's prerogatives in 1989 that leads to the full deployment of this offence.

16 Relating to the security and transparency of financial markets. This law also enabled the COB to adopt the regulation sanctioning insider trading (Reg. no. 90-08 on the use of privileged information, approved by order of 17 J uly 1990, *Bull COB*, no. June 1990, no. 237).

17 Prior to this, Law no. 85-1321 of 14 December 1985 had given the COB the power to issue standards. As of 1989, the COB became a 'policeman, judge and legislator of stock exchange law' (D. Schmidt, Summary report 'The stability of power and capital in joint-stock companies', *RJ com*, no. special issue, November 1990, p. 184). This law followed the scandal of the Péchiney affair, see F. Martin Laprade, 'Contentieux boursiers: abus de marché et autres manquements', *Rép. de droit des sociétés*, Paris, Dalloz, 2017, nos. 2 et seq.

(*délits boursiers*),[18] prosecuted by the judicial courts, and the administrative repression of the *Autorité des marchés financiers* against administrative failings coexist. The justification for this dual mechanism lies in the inadequacy of criminal law enforcement which, as Professor Conac writes, 'is necessary because it allows the most reprehensible behaviour to be punished by prison sentences [but] it is insufficient because not all reprehensible behaviour justifies a criminal sanction.'[19] Consequently, administrative repression is also explained by the fact that the regulation of market abuse contributes to the proper functioning of the financial markets; however, it appears that this is better ensured, on a daily basis, by a specialised independent administrative authority than by the judicial authority.

European law took up the issue in 1989 with a European directive covering only insider trading.[20] It was not until a second directive, in 2003, that market abuse was extended beyond insider trading: market manipulation was added, and the category of market abuse was created.[21] However, this directive was repealed in 2014 by a regulation, which defines market abuse and organises the means of its administrative repression, and a directive, which aims to harmonise criminal repression.[22]

521. Justification for criminal prosecution. As Ms Drummond has already observed, the reason for the repression of market abuse is that it 'undermines what the European legislator calls "market integrity": these are the only breaches that alter, in the sense that they corrupt, the functioning of the market'.[23] They

---

[18] This qualification is for example retained by D. Martin *et al.*, *Les abus de marché*, Paris, Lexis Nexis, 2013, no. 10; A. Lepage, P. Maistre du Chambon and R. Salomon, *Droit pénal des affaires*, Paris, LexisNexis, 2018, no. 1023.

[19] P.-H. Conac, *La régulation des marchés boursiers par la Commission des opérations de bourse (COB) et la Securities and exchange commission (SEC)*, *op. cit.*, no. 85.

[20] Directive 89/592/EEC on the coordination of regulations on insider dealing.

[21] Directive 2003/6/EC of the European Parliament and of the Council of 28 January 2003 on insider dealing and market manipulation (hereafter the former Market Abuse Directive). On the regime instituted by its transposition into French law, see on the former regime, D. Martin *et al.*, *Les abus de marché*, *op. cit.*

[22] This was transposed by Law 2016-819 of 21 June 2016 reforming the market abuse system.

[23] F. Drummond, *Droit financier*, *op. cit.*, no. 1081. The author also writes: 'In a more prosaic way, these infringements are to the market what cheating is to gambling: it is a matter of one participant securing a privileged position for himself by using information that the others do not have, or of distorting the rule which, in this case, requires that the price of a financial asset be expressed by the free play of supply and demand.' (*ibid.*)
In this sense, certain justifications provided by the Market Abuse Regulation must be rejected. The prohibition of market abuse is not justified on the grounds that the conduct in question would prevent 'transparency' (Recital 7 of the Market Abuse Regulation) or contribute to 'significant systemic risks' (Recital 20 of the Market Abuse Regulation). Market abuse is only remotely related to systemic risk, and market transparency is mainly ensured by the disclosure requirements for issuers.

corrupt it by the imbalance and unfairness[24] of the offending behaviour: insider dealing violates the requirement of equal access to information,[25] and price manipulation disturbs the normal formation of the stock market price.[26] As an author writes, market abuse has the particularity of causing psychological effects that 'undermine investor confidence and lead them to turn away from the markets',[27] in addition to undermining, from an economic point of view, the reliability of the financial market mechanism.[28] However, the importance of financial markets for the European economy justifies the use of criminal sanctions, in particular in order to show 'a stronger social disapproval than administrative sanctions'. Indeed, 'The establishment of criminal offences [...] sends a signal to the public and to potential perpetrators that the competent authorities take such behaviour very seriously [...].'[29]

522. Objectives and international scope. The above discussion has two consequences. Firstly, as the aim of the prohibition of market abuse is to protect European markets, its scope of application must be restricted to the latter, i.e. to financial markets whose managers have their registered office on the territory of a Member State.[30] This limitation is all the more important as these criminal rules are on the borderline between the administrative organisation of the market and

---

24 J. Chacornac, *Les fonctions de l'information en droit des instruments financiers*, *op. cit.*, nos. 742–743.

25 *Ibid.*, nos. 746 et seq.

26 *Ibid.*, nos. 768 et seq.

27 F. Drummond, *Droit financier*, *op. cit.*, no. 1082. The psychological consequences of insider trading have been highlighted by J. Chacornac, *Les fonctions de l'information en droit des instruments financiers*, *op. cit.* A. Tehrani, *Les investisseurs protégés en droit financier*, *op. cit.* Recital 24 of the Market Abuse Regulation takes up this idea by considering that '(*investor confidence*) is in turn based on the assurance that investors will benefit from the same conditions and will be protected against the misuse of inside information". See CA Paris, 30 March 2010, no. 2009/12248, where the Court recalls that one of the purposes of the prohibition of insider trading is to ensure that "all investors have been placed on an equal footing, that none of them has found himself in an advantageous position from which he would have benefited to the detriment of those who were unaware of the inside information'.

28 This is why the comparison made by some authors between price manipulation and competition law, the purpose of which is also to ensure the establishment of a market mechanism, is particularly accurate, see in this sense M. Tomasi, 'Vers un renouveau de la lutte contre les manipulations de cours', *op. cit.*; J. Chacornac, *Les fonctions de l'information en droit des instruments financiers*, *op. cit.* no. 743. In this sense, it is not by chance that the repression of infringements of competition law and financial market law is linked to the same thing: the effects on the market.

29 Recital 6 of the Market Abuse Directive.

30 Art. 1 of the Market Abuse Directive specifically states that 'the minimum rules on criminal sanctions' are intended to 'ensure the integrity of the Union's financial markets'. Member States are nevertheless free to provide for stricter rules, and since the *Péchiney* judgment, the Court of Cassation has held that the regulation is applicable regardless of the location of the market, see most recently Crim., 1 April 2020, no. 19-82223, no. 29, *BJB*, May 2020, p. 21, note A. Pietrancosta.

the repression of criminal behaviour. This is particularly evident in the scope of the derogations granted. Indeed, it would be difficult to justify the criminalisation of an investment firm carrying out a market sounding on a financial market of a third State which does not comply with the rules of Article 11 of the Market Abuse Regulation. Similarly, the incrimination of a French issuer buying back its shares traded on a financial market in a third country for purposes that are not covered by Article 5 of the Market Abuse Regulation appears to be largely excessive. This means that there is no doubt that it is only the European financial markets that are targeted by the Market Abuse Regulation. However, it does not matter whether the European market in question is a regulated market or a multilateral or organised trading facility: the effect of the insider dealing or price manipulation will be to affect the price disclosure mechanism and investor confidence in that mechanism. It is therefore welcome that the prohibition of market abuse is no longer limited to regulated markets.[31]

Secondly, these objectives call for the conduct to be punished irrespective of the location of the facts constituting the offence. Only the effect on the financial market should count. In this sense, it is irrelevant whether the person who initiated the insider dealing was located on the territory of the Union, or whether he disseminated the inside information on the territory of a third State. The link with the market does not derive from the place of the constitutive event, but from the admission to trading of the instrument to which the inside information relates.[32] Similarly, the connection of price manipulation to the market stems from the fact that the price of the affected instrument is determined by the market, and that this price disclosure mechanism is corrupted by the manipulation.[33] Unfortunately, both aspects run up against the territorial application criteria of French criminal law.

§ 2. CONFRONTATION WITH THE CRITERIA OF CRIMINAL JURISDICTION

The influence of the objectives identified on the scope of application of the regulation of market abuse should lead to getting rid of the territorial application of French criminal law on market abuse, which leads to artificial

---

31 F. Drummond, *Droit financier*, *op. cit.*, nos. 1092 et seq.

32 As Ms Drummond writes, 'the real focus of regulation is the instrument concerned by the conduct at issue, not so much in terms of the nature of that instrument as in terms of its connection to the protected market', F. Drummond, *Droit financier*, *op. cit.*, no. 1092.

33 This second aspect is well understood by the US courts. Indeed, in a judgment in which a price manipulation was alleged on a security admitted to trading in Germany, the American court ruled that its *anti-fraud* regulation based on section 10-b of the Securities Exchange Act (on which see *infra*, para. 538) was not applicable, see Court of Appeals, no. 11-397-cv (2d Cir. August 15, 2014), *Parkcentral Global Hub Ltd. v. Porsche Automobil Holdings SE.*

and excessive interpretations (I). Their repression would be better ensured under the '*competence réelle*'(II).

I. The Territorial Application of French Criminal Law to Market Abuse

523. French criminal law is applied according to its own criteria, the implementation of which implies a global competence of the French repressive order, in accordance with the requirements of the Market Abuse Directive (A). Their application, based on territorial jurisdiction, comes up against the fact that the offence was committed in foreign territories. This obstacle leads to an artificial localisation of the constitutive acts on the affected financial market (B).

A. Criteria for the Application of French Criminal Law

524. *Forum legis.* Criminal law, when confronted with foreign elements, presents certain particularities. The first is often underlined by the expression of 'solidarity of legislative and jurisdictional competences'. It seems to us to be more accurate to consider that French criminal law determines the jurisdiction of French courts. As Professor Lombois wrote, 'in international criminal law, the determination of the law must necessarily precede the determination of the judge'.[34] The jurisdiction of French courts is always based on the application of French criminal law. The basis of the *forum legis* will have been recognised. This appears inevitable as soon as the fundamental interests of the national community are affected. As a result, in criminal matters, the rules of legislative jurisdiction fulfil a function of 'global connection to a repressive order'.[35]

525. Territorial jurisdiction. The second particularity is that the scope of application of French criminal law is expressed in a unilateral and abstract form. Its fundament is Article 113-2 paragraph 1 of the Criminal Code, the basis for the territorial jurisdiction of French law, according to which:

---

[34] C. Lombois, *Droit pénal international*, Paris, Dalloz, 1971, no. 11. In the same sense I. Fadlalah, 'Point de vue sur l'affaire Péchiney. La localisation du délit d'initié', *op. cit.*, p. 623: 'If there is no breach of French criminal law, the criminal courts are incompetent.' The author relies on Bouzat's *Traité théorique et pratique de droit pénal*, no. 1539. Contemporary doctrine regularly reaffirms this presentation: See V. Malabat, 'Libres propos sur les conflits de lois en matière pénale' in *Droit répressif au pluriel, Liber amicorum en l'honneur de Renée Koering Joulin*, Limal, Anthemis, 2015, pp. 527 et seq. Either he establishes its jurisdiction and proceeds to its application; or he rejects this jurisdiction and his office stops. The author adds in a note that 'Legislative jurisdiction may, *by exception*, derive from jurisdictional competence (see ss 189). But this situation has the sole effect of substituting the assessment of jurisdictional competence for that of legislative competence'. Emphasis added.

[35] The expression comes from S. Fernandez, *Essai sur la distribution des compétences en droit pénal international*, *op. cit.*

'French criminal law is applicable to offences committed in the territory of the Republic. The offence is deemed to have been committed in the territory of the Republic if one of its constituent acts took place in that territory.'[36]

This jurisdiction is inspired both by Article 3 of the Civil Code and by the conflict rule in matters of tort.[37] Indeed, the basis of jurisdiction is partly identical: the legal system affected by the criminal disorder is best able to remedy it. The reparation is nevertheless accompanied by a repression inherent in the criminal nature of the provisions in question. As Merle and Vitu write: 'The penal reaction is a defence reflex of the social organism against acts that disturb it.'[38]

526. Other grounds of jurisdiction. However, it is possible for French criminal law to obtain jurisdiction irrespective of the commission on French territory of the facts constituting the offence. This is first of all the case when the perpetrator or the victim of the alleged offence is French.[39] This is also the case when the interests of the State itself are affected.[40] These two jurisdictions, personal and '*réelle*', are said to be 'extraterritorial' in the sense that the facts constituting the offence did not take place on French territory.[41] However, they do not follow an identical regime. Indeed, whereas '*réelle*' jurisdiction is special, i.e. it can only be

---

36 The basis for this jurisdiction is usually explained by the principle of sovereignty: both because the offence would be an attack on the authority of the State, but also because it is the place where the attack on the interests that a given law enforcement system protects occurs. In the alternative, other arguments assert the strength of territorial jurisdiction: it would facilitate the proper administration of justice (because it is the place where the clues, evidence and witnesses necessary for prosecution are located), the court of the place where the act in question took place would be best able to assess the importance of the disturbance to public order, and finally, it would be only there that the penitential aspect of the sentence could produce its effects (the argument is that of Beccaria). On all these arguments, see S. Fernandez, *Essai sur la distribution des compétences en droit pénal international, op. cit.*

37 Y. Mayaud, *Droit pénal général*, 5th ed., Paris PUF, no. 84.

38 R. Merle and A. Vitu, *Traité de droit criminel, Problèmes généraux de la science criminelle, Droit pénal général*, 7th ed., Paris, Cujas, no. 5, p. 29.

39 Arts. L. 113-6 and 113-7 of the Criminal Code. The personal jurisdiction exercised against the offender is referred to as 'active' personal jurisdiction, whereas 'passive' personal jurisdiction is that exercised on the basis of the victim's nationality, see inter alia Y. Mayaud, *Droit pénal général, op. cit.* This last possibility was opened up by the Law of 27 June 1866 in order to compensate for the principle of non-extradition of nationals, see explicitly, in the explanatory memorandum to the Law, Law of 27 June 1866, *S.*, 1866, Lois annotées, p. 39, spec. p. 42, no. 3. On this question see D. Rebut, *Droit pénal international, op. cit.*, no. 129. The criminal law may also apply by virtue of a quality or status, as in the case of the military, see *ibid.*, nos. 166 et seq.

40 Art. L. 113-10 of the Criminal Code.

41 This presentation, which has been taken up by some textbooks (Y. Mayaud, *Droit pénal général, op. cit.*, pp. 105 et seq.), is that of the Criminal Code itself, which distinguishes between offences committed on French territory (Section 1 of the chapter devoted to the application of criminal law in space) and those committed outside the territory of the Republic (Section 2 of the same chapter).

used against a limited number of offences listed by the law, personal jurisdiction is, like territorial jurisdiction, general: it can be used against all offences.[42] However, when it is exercised against a French person who has committed an offence abroad, personal jurisdiction is restricted, only in the case of offences, by a condition of reciprocity of incrimination.[43] Indeed, French criminal law will only apply if the offence in question is recognised by the legal system in which the offence took place.[44] This restriction is explained in the light of the *ratio legis* of 'active' personal jurisdiction, which is to palliate the principle of non-extradition of nationals.[45]

527. The criteria of the Market Abuse Directive. The Market Abuse Directive provides identical bases for the application of criminal law in Member States. The Directive requires Member States to establish jurisdiction where market abuse has been committed 'in whole or in part within their territory',[46] but also if it has been committed 'by one of their nationals, at least in cases where the act constitutes an offence where it has been committed'.[47] The Market Abuse Directive also allows Member States to establish, optionally, jurisdiction where 'the offender is ordinarily resident in its territory',[48] but also where 'the offence has been committed for the benefit of a legal person established in its territory'.[49] The Market Abuse Directive does not provide for Member States to establish jurisdiction where the victim is a national of the Member State. This is probably because market abuse does not have the effect of creating harm to

42 This distinction between general and special titles of jurisdiction is taken from the thesis of D. Chilstein, *Droit pénal international et lois de police*, *op. cit.*, no. 47.

43 Crimes are not subject to this restriction because of their seriousness, see D. Rebut, *Droit pénal international*, *op. cit.*, no. 138. The author adds: 'The criminal characterisation of the act in question is assessed solely according to French criminal law.' (*ibid.*) It should also be noted that certain offences are not subject to this incrimination (*ibid.*, no. 141).

44 Proof of the existence of the incrimination in foreign law must be provided, but, as this is a question of fact, it is subject to the sovereign appreciation of the trial judges. Moreover, as the incrimination does not have to be identical, some authors prefer to speak of the condition of double incrimination: see S. Fernandez, *Essai sur la distribution des compétences en droit pénal international*, *op. cit.*, no. 182.

45 Explicit in the explanatory memorandum of the law instituting personal jurisdiction, Explanatory Memorandum, Law of 27 June 1866, *S.*, 1866, Lois annotées, p. 39, spec. p. 42, no. III. On this question see H. Donnedieu de Vabres, *Principes modernes de droit pénal international*, *op. cit.*, p. 116; D. Rebut, *Droit pénal international*, *op. cit.*, no. 129.

46 Art. 10(1)(a) Market Abuse Directive.

47 Art. 10(1)(b) Market Abuse Directive.

48 Art. 10(2)(a) Market Abuse Directive. This is a departure from the Directive, because although the former Market Abuse Directive of 2003 already contained a provision on the scope of application of the criminal law of the Member States in relation to market abuse, it gave market abuse a scope of application corresponding to that of the classic territorial jurisdiction (Art. 10 of the former Market Abuse Directive). These jurisdictional criteria correspond to those of a framework decision taken at the same time (see Art. 9 of the Council Framework Decision of 13 June 2002 on combating terrorism).

49 Art. 10(2)(b) Market Abuse Directive.

particular persons, if not the market maker, but of corrupting the integrity of the price determination mechanism and the confidence of investors in it.[50]

B. The Implementation of Territorial Jurisdiction

528. The properties of the offences in question. As Professor Mayaud writes, not all offences 'are conceived on the same model, and it is necessary, in order to locate them in space, to refer to their properties, and to fix oneself in relation to what they imply in terms of originality in the way they are carried out'.[51] The originality of market abuse lies in the fact that its constituent facts (the use of privileged information, its communication, the placing of orders, or the fraudulent manoeuvres employed) are not necessarily committed on the financial market affected by the abuse.[52] Far from being an element of the offence, corruption of the financial market is its consequence. This dissociation leads to the general difficulty of rigorously establishing the territorial jurisdiction of French criminal law. It is true that French criminal law may apply on the basis of the domicile of the offender[53] on French territory, but the offenders are not necessarily located there. This is why case law has been led to artificially localise the facts constituting the offence on the territory of the market they affect. It is as if, in the field of market abuse, the theory of the result, dear to Travers, was enshrined: the legal order where 'one or more consequences of the guilty activity' occur, or where 'the profit deriving from the offence is realised', has territorial jurisdiction.[54] From this point of view, it does not matter that the offender is domiciled abroad and that the orders were placed abroad, the mere location in France of the financial market on which the instrument affected by the abuse is admitted to trading is sufficient.[55] Similarly, it does not matter that

---

50 Passive personal jurisdiction is more difficult to support as there is no real *victim* of market abuse, with the possible exception of the market manager (on this issue, see the explanations of J. Prorok, *La responsabilité civile sur les marchés financiers*, *op. cit.*) See D. Chilstein, *Droit pénal international et lois de police*, *op. cit.* no. 343: 'The effect on the market is in fact independent of the nationality of the perpetrator or "victim" of the criminal conduct or alleged criminal conduct. Moreover, the very notion of "victim" is problematic with regard to a possible application of the passive personality principle, since the incrimination tends to protect the market itself.'

51 Y. Mayaud, *Droit pénal général*, *op. cit.*, no. 86.

52 The situation is analogous to the complex torts arising from issuer liability for defective information, where the place of the damage will not always correspond to the place of the operative event, see *supra*, para. 414.

53 Passive personal jurisdiction is deactivated by the absence of a real victim, if not the market manager, see on this question closely linked to the alteration of the stock market price J. Prorok, *La responsabilité civile sur les marchés financiers*, *op. cit.*

54 M. Travers, *Traité de droit pénal international*, Paris, Sirey, 1920, t. 1, no. 27.

55 For a recent contentious application, see, on the side of administrative repression, Decision no. 3 of 2 May 2018 of the Autorité des marchés financiers, taken on the basis of price manipulation, and in which the respondent challenged the international jurisdiction of the AMF, precisely on the grounds that he was domiciled in Portugal where he had issued the disputed orders.

the transaction itself does not involve a financial instrument admitted to trading on a French market, if the underlying instrument is admitted to trading on a French market, the offence is likely to be constituted.[56] This obviously applies to price manipulation, since the offence is necessarily located 'at the place where the market is established', the price targeted being that of an instrument admitted to a financial market. The same applies to insider trading and dissemination of false information, since, as Mr Chilstein writes:

> 'If one is willing to admit, in spite of the Pechiney ruling, that the protected market can only be the French market, there is no need to question the possible extraterritoriality of the offence. The offence prosecuted is located in France even if the disclosure of the information occurred abroad, because the damage necessarily occurred on the French market.'[57]

529. Unsuitability of territorial jurisdiction. In other words, since the offence was committed in relation to a financial market located on French territory, French criminal jurisdiction would necessarily be territorial. One can see how loose such a criterion is: even if the constituent elements of the offence were not committed on the territory of the Republic, even if the place of execution of the disputed transaction was not a French financial market, its mere assignment would trigger the applicability of French criminal law. This possibility of jurisdiction of French criminal law, based on a territorial link that is in fact non-existent, is not a textbook case,[58] nor is it reserved for financial matters.[59]

The dematerialisation and internationalisation of the facts constituting the offence undoubtedly show the weakness of the operative act as a connecting factor, and this beyond the criminal sphere. We know that the connection of civil torts has evolved: the criterion of the place of commission has gradually

---

56 For a recent application from an administrative enforcement perspective, AMF Decision no. 11 of 24 October 2018. Several respondents challenged the AMF's international jurisdiction 'on the grounds that while these securities were admitted to trading on the French market, the transactions concerned did not involve their purchase or sale and were carried out in the United Kingdom' (*ibid.*, p. 5). This was a failure to understand Art. L. 621-15 of the Monetary and Financial Code, as the AMF Enforcement Committee pointed out in its decision.

57 D. Chilstein, *Droit pénal international et lois de police*, *op. cit.*

58 For the application of French law to the disclosure of inside information by a company established in the Netherlands, see AMF Decision of 27 November 2009.

59 The difficulty seems to be increasing today, see the very critical observations on French territorial jurisdiction over several offences by D. Chemla, 'Actualité et conséquences de l'extraterritorialité de la loi pénale française', *TCFDIP*, 2016-2018, pp. 85 et seq. See S. Fernandez, *Essai sur la distribution des compétences en droit pénal international*, *op. cit.*, no. 20, then nos. 81 et seq. When it is not the artificial location of constituent acts on the territory, certain offences used extensively, such as complicity, indivisibility and connexity, make it possible to achieve similar results, see *ibid.*

been replaced by that of the damage.[60] In the same way, in criminal matters, the law of the place of the damage would lead to results that are undoubtedly less artificial and therefore more predictable: in relation to market abuse, it leads to the application of the law of the financial market. From the point of view of civil liability for market abuse, it would lead to the application of the law of the market, the damage occurring on the order book of the trading platform. This convergence is perhaps an incentive to rethink the true physiology of the criminal offence. The relevant material acts were previously carried out physically at the place where the exchange itself was located, which did not necessarily make it possible to realise the true basis of the jurisdiction of the repressive law in market matters, namely that of the effects felt on the financial market itself. This observation leads to the proposal of a connecting factor independent of territorial jurisdiction and based on '*competence réelle*'.

II. The Possible Basis for 'Compétence Réelle'

530. Rather than the artificial basis of territorial jurisdiction, the application of French law would benefit from being based the '*compétence réelle*'. Indeed, the latter has the advantage of taking into account the purpose of the offence, the protection of the French market, in order to delimit a suitable scope of application in principle, but also to proceed to a welcome unilateral restriction of jurisdiction in order to avoid possible undue cumulation of criminal jurisdiction. Moreover, it is perfectly foreseeable for the perpetrator of the criminal conduct, fulfilling the requirement of criminal legality[61] (A). However, it is flawed in that it leaves a loophole in the case where the criminal conduct is committed by a French person against a foreign market. This is why it is necessary to retain personal jurisdiction (B).

A. The Coherent Basis of '*Compétence Réelle*'

531. '*Compétence réelle*' of French criminal law in cases of market abuse. '*Compétence réelle*' justifies its existence in that it allows the application of French law to offences that do not involve French victims, or whose constituent elements are not located on national territory.[62] It corresponds perfectly to the hypotheses of market abuse, where the jurisdiction of French criminal law seems

---

60 Art. 4 of the Rome II Regulation.

61 S. Fernandez, *Essai sur la distribution des compétences en droit pénal international, op. cit.*

62 The use of territorial jurisdiction in order to seize offences that would rather fall under the '*compétence réelle*' is not new. Offences threatening the sovereignty of the State were historically understood as if they were offences located on the territory of the State, see S. Fernandez, *Essai sur la distribution des compétences en droit pénal international, op. cit.*

to us to be of a 'real nature', in the doctrinal and etymological sense,[63] since the *res* (thing) affected is the French trading platform. Nevertheless, two arguments oppose the '*compétence réelle*'. Firstly, the justification for '*compétence réelle*' has long been based on the idea of protecting the interests of the State[64]; however, the financial market does not belong to the State, but to a commercial company under private law. However, this argument does not appear to be decisive. Indeed, the French legislator has replaced the notion of 'interest of the State', which traditionally formed the basis of '*compétence réelle*', with that of 'fundamental interest of the Nation', thus making clearer the offences that '*compétence réelle*' is intended to cover.[65] It is therefore easy today to consider that the protection of the French financial market, which is of considerable importance to the local economy – this is easy to see from the regime attached to the management of these platforms[66] – constitutes a fundamental national interest.

The true obstacle to the prosecution of market abuse on the basis of '*compétence réelle*' is that it is not included in the restrictive list of Article 113-10 of the Criminal Code, the seat of this jurisdiction. The principle of legality of offences and penalties requires a formal approach to '*compétence réelle*' and therefore a restrictive interpretation of this article.[67] However, such an entry is possible: in addition to offences against the 'fundamental interests of the Nation' punishable under Title 1 of Book IV of the Criminal Code[68] and against French diplomatic or consular agents and premises, '*compétence réelle*' punishes offences that must be described as economic, such as

---

63 C. Lombois, *Droit pénal international*, *op. cit.*, no. 292: 'A criminal law is said to have "*compétence réelle*" when it seizes certain offences by reason of their nature, without any consideration of the place of their commission or the nationality of their perpetrator'. On the history of '*compétence réelle*', see S. Fernandez, *Essai sur la distribution des compétences en droit pénal international*, *op. cit.*, no. 254.

64 The theoretical justification for actual jurisdiction has long been that of 'the natural right of self-defence' of the State, see H. Donnedieu de Vabres, *Les principes modernes du droit pénal international*, *op. cit.*, p. 87. The author nevertheless observes that while 'the tradition of "*compétence réelle*" is old, its theoretical justification has varied'.

65 S. Fernandez, *Essai sur la distribution des compétences en droit pénal international*, *op. cit.* As the author writes, 'the notion of "fundamental interests" is therefore certainly broader than that of "security", which is centred on issues relating to sovereignty and security' (*ibid.*, no. 259). On the circumscription of the fundamental interest of the nation, see A. Vitu, *J.-Cl. Pén*, Art. 410-1, fasc. 20: 'Atteintes aux intérêts fondamentaux de la nation', no. 7.

66 See *supra*, paras. 81 et seq.

67 Some authors argue that it is the nature of the offence committed abroad that is the basis for actual jurisdiction, see for an account of this doctrine and its criticism, S. Fernandez, *Essai sur la distribution des compétences en droit pénal international*, *op. cit.*, no. 260.

68 These include espionage, treason, attacks on the institutions of the Republic and national defence.

counterfeiting.[69] It is similar to the criterion generally used in competition law to punish offences.

532. Analogy with counterfeiting. It could no doubt be argued that the singularity of the offence of counterfeiting money is that it attacks property created and issued by the state, that is, it attacks the state itself by other means.[70] In other words, it is because the property belongs to the state that its devaluation would be repressed by the 'compétence réelle'. However, on the one hand, the prohibition remains even though the currency is no longer created by decision of the French State and, on the other hand, the existence of an administrative connecting factor of trading platforms brings the two situations closer together. Moreover, it is also possible to consider that the basis of '*compétence réelle*' here is the collective economic importance of the institution in question, and that the currency itself must be protected. Indeed, through it, it is the economic stability of the French legal order that is protected.[71] This *ratio legis* is similar to that of market abuse, which is to protect the proper functioning of the financial market. *De lege lata*, the analogy also concerns elements of the regime: in the same way that '*compétence réelle*' can be used to protect the interests of foreign States,[72] because it was considered that the counterfeiting of foreign currencies was likely to affect the French currency, the prohibition of market abuse can be aimed at

---

69 Today, other offences seem to refer to the reality system, such as Art. 662-1 of the *Code de l'entrée et du séjour des étrangers et du droit d'asile*, Art. L. 121-7 of the *Code de justice militaire*. On the hidden extension of the field of '*compétence réelle*', see S. Fernandez, *Essai sur la distribution des compétences en droit pénal international*, *op. cit.*, no. 258. For a similar, but hybrid, mechanism, as it is conditional on the nationality of the perpetrator, see Art. 113-13 of the Criminal Code (on which see *ibid.*, nos. 348–349).

70 F. Martucci, *L'ordre économique et monétaire*, *op. cit.*, no. 41, see also nos. 113–114; J.-V. Louis, *L'Union européenne et sa monnaie*, 3rd ed., Brussels, University of Brussels, 2013, pp. 263–273.

71 A. Vitu, 'Un aspect particulier du droit pénal international: la protection des intérêts publics étrangers par le droit criminel français' in *Mélanges en l'honneur du professeur Jérôme Larguier*, Grenoble, PUG, 1993, pp. 368: 'A single penal regime was indeed necessary, since, in the context of the international trade in money and the constitution of foreign currency reserves by the French Treasury, foreign coins and banknotes must arouse the same confidence as our country's monetary signs.' In other words, the interests of the foreign state are protected, because these interests are also those of the forum. It should be added here that the interest of the French legal system in the protection of foreign currency should not be overestimated. Indeed, one-off counterfeiting operations do not risk driving out good money, but simply reduce its reliability step by step. The same applies to market abuse. On the other hand, in the case of both counterfeiting and market abuse, the systematisation of the offence would lead to serious local economic difficulties by considerably reducing the confidence necessary for the functioning of the currency and the financial market.

72 See, for example, Art. L. 442-1 of the Criminal Code: counterfeiting foreign currency is also punishable under French law. The explanation adopted was also that of the representation of the affected State by the State of the place of the act, thus explaining the subsidiary regime of "competence réelle", see on this theory, and then on its incisive criticism, H. Donnedieu de Vabre, *Les principes modernes de droit pénal international*, *op. cit.*

protecting European markets.[73] Finally, the '*compétence réelle*' regime makes it possible to disregard the *ne bis in idem* principle abroad: it does not matter that a foreign judgment has already taken place, French criminal law is not thereby deactivated.[74] It should simply be noted that these last two aspects should not be cumulative: if the exclusivity of '*compétence réelle*' makes sense when it is a question of protecting a fundamental interest of the French nation, it is likely to create pathological situations of cumulation of criminal laws when it is added to the effective implementation of foreign criminal law.

533. '*Compétence réelle*'and allocation of law enforcement powers. What is true for counterfeiting foreign currency tried and convicted abroad[75] is also true for market abuse committed mainly on the foreign financial market. In the case of counterfeiting of European currency, the jurisdiction of Article 689-9 of the Code of Criminal Procedure, enacted to protect the financial interests of the European Union, is ordered by the *ne bis in idem* principle.[76] However, in our opinion, the question does not arise in the same terms in the area of market abuse: whereas the criminal protection of the European currency should be pursued by a European prosecution authority because of the uniqueness of the European currency, market abuse can occur on each of the financial markets attached to a Member State. Either there is a single market abuse, the constituent elements of which have taken place on the territory of several Member States, and criminal jurisdiction should then be exercised as a matter of priority by the Member State of the affected financial market if it is established that the existence of parallel proceedings would lead to a slowing down of the investigation; or

---

[73] See *supra*, para. 524. This prohibition of market abuse committed on foreign financial markets can be explained by the community of interests of the legal orders affected. Indeed, as the financial markets exert an influence on each other, the local market would be affected (admittedly to very different degrees depending on the markets affected), which explains the French interest in having criminal jurisdiction in this area. On the broader protection afforded to foreign public interests by French criminal law, see A. Vitu, 'Un aspect particulier du droit pénal international: la protection des intérêts publics étrangers par le droit criminel français', *op. cit.*

[74] In accordance with territorial jurisdiction and in contrast to personal jurisdiction, see D. Rebut, *Droit pénal international*, *op. cit.*, nos. 83 et seq. (for territorial jurisdiction), no. 123 (for actual jurisdiction) and no. 162 (for personal jurisdiction). See also, very explicitly, for personal jurisdiction, Art. 113-9 of the Criminal Code.
This exclusive character of criminal jurisdiction was originally doctrinal, and is now justified by the *Conseil d'État*, because the offences falling under the "competence réelle" are linked 'to the essential conditions of national sovereignty' (CE, Ass. gén., Avis no. 370-136 of 29 April 2003, see also Cons. const., 19 November 2004, Decision no. 2004-505 DC, *JORF* of 24 November, p. 19885, spec. no. 20). On this question see D. Rebut, *Droit pénal international*, *op. cit.*, nos. 81 et seq.; S. Fernandez, *Essai sur la distribution des compétences en droit pénal international*, *op. cit.*, no. 266.

[75] S. Fernandez, *Essai sur la distribution des compétences en droit pénal international*, *op. cit.*, no. 274 and references cited.

[76] See *ibid.* This jurisdiction falls within the scope of universal jurisdiction, on which see D. Rebut, *Droit pénal international*, *op. cit.*, nos. 173 et seq.

there are several market abuses which have affected different financial markets in a ubiquitous manner, in which case more than one investigation would have to be carried out.

534. In the first case, the jurisdiction of the State 'most exposed to the offence committed'[77] should be retained: this is obviously the financial market that is the subject of the offence. In the second case, which involves, for example, market abuse committed on a security listed on several financial markets, two solutions are possible. Firstly, one may wonder whether it would not be better to entrust repression to a single authority according to this same criterion. The fact that several financial markets are affected should then simply be taken into account as a factor in the seriousness of the offence, since the constituent facts are identical and the offender is the same. The designation of the competent authority could then be made *a priori* by following the method of directed dialogue, instituted inter alia in the field of counterfeiting,[78] or on the basis of the criterion of competence developed for the purposes of reporting transactions

---

[77] The expression is borrowed from J. LELIEUR-FISCHER, 'L'Union européenne face aux conflits de compétence' in *Mélanges en l'honneur du professeur Alain Fournier*, Nancy, Presse-Universitaire de Nancy, 2014, pp. 269 et seq.

[78] Compulsory but non-binding consultation has been established for offences relating to counterfeiting (Art. 7(3) of Council Framework Decision 2000/383/JHA of 29 May 2000 on increasing protection by criminal penalties and other sanctions against counterfeiting in connection with the introduction of the euro), organised crime (Art. 7(2) of Council Framework Decision 2008/841/JHA of 24 October 2008 on combating organised crime) and terrorism (Art. 9(2) of Council Framework Decision 2002/475/JHA on combating terrorism). On this method, see J. LELIEUR-FISCHER, 'L'Union européenne face aux conflits de compétence', *op. cit.*, p. 269; S. FERNANDEZ, *Essai sur la distribution des compétences en droit pénal international*, *op. cit.*
Consultation is based on an obligation to provide information, coupled, where appropriate, with direct consultations. The above-mentioned authors nevertheless note the absence of any sanction for the obligation to inform in the Framework Decision, which is reflected in the transposition into domestic law (see Art. 695-9-56 of the Code of Criminal Procedure, which merely provides for exceptions to the principle of communication). The same authors note that, even if direct consultation were to take place, its non-binding nature makes it unlikely to thwart parallel proceedings. However, it should be noted, on the one hand, that an authority will withdraw from a case all the more easily if it has been a party to the process (see already the observations of Ms Fernandez, *ibid.*, no. 539) and, on the other hand, that since the authorities have limited resources, they can benefit from the distribution of the coordinated prosecution of international crime. In addition, peer pressure, in the form of the opinion that Eurojust can give on the resolution of conflicts of jurisdiction (see *ibid.*, nos. 541 et seq.), will strengthen the incentive mechanism.
Once the principle of jurisdiction has been retained, cooperation with other Member States should be possible. The mechanism outlined here, which disregards territorial jurisdiction, has already been envisaged in the context of transboundary pollution, see the draft Convention on Transboundary Pollution between France and the Federal Republic of Germany of 1985 and, on this draft, the remarks of A. HUET, 'Réflexions sur les dispositions révolutionnaires de droit pénal international d'un projet de convention relative à la pollution transfrontière', in *Droit pénal contemporain: Mélanges en l'honneur d'André Vitu*, Paris, Cujas, 1989, p. 249.

allowing the identification of market abuse.[79] Another solution would be to allow the offence to be punished in each legal order whose financial market is affected by the abuse, and to temper the penalty imposed by taking into account the fact that it is to be paid in another country.

B. The Subsidiary Personal Jurisdiction of French Law

535. Subsidiary jurisdiction. In French positive law, '*compétence réelle*' does not replace personal jurisdiction. In other words, it is not because French criminal law would be exercised primarily through '*compétence réelle*' that it could not also have jurisdiction, subsidiarily, in the name of personal jurisdiction.[80] In the case of market abuse, personal jurisdiction is 'active': it covers offences committed by French nationals on foreign financial markets.

The subsidiarity of personal jurisdiction is manifested in two aspects of its regime: firstly, by the admission of the *res judicata* effect of the foreign criminal judgment,[81] and secondly, by the condition of double criminality. The latter subordinates the exercise of French law to the existence of a similar offence in the foreign law, and allows French public action only insofar as the foreign authority has not previously acted. In reality, here, 'French criminal law (is) ultimately intended to intervene only in the event of a repressive gap',[82] which explains the monopoly of the public prosecutor's office as regards repression.[83] In other words, if the legal order of the market affected by the abuse does not have a functional equivalent of the criminal regulation of market abuse, personal jurisdiction cannot be exercised.

The purpose of market abuse regulation nevertheless makes it possible and desirable to exercise personal jurisdiction where market abuse is committed by French nationals against other European financial markets. This is particularly the case where the reporting obligations relating to the prevention of market abuse are addressed to the financial market authority in respect of the issuer's headquarters, and the prosecuting authority is particularly well placed to carry

---

79 See *infra*, para. 543.

80 Thus, terrorism is subject to French criminal repression both in the name of personal jurisdiction and '*compétence réelle*', see Art. L. 113-12 of the Criminal Code. The advantage of the latter regime is that, compared to the former, it ignores the decision that has obtained *res judicata* abroad.

81 Art. L. 113-9 of the Criminal Code. See on this point S. Fernandez, *Essai sur la distribution des compétences en droit pénal international*, *op. cit.*, nos. 168 et seq.

82 S. Fernandez, *Essai sur la distribution des compétences en droit pénal international*, *op. cit.*

83 Art. 113-8 of the Criminal Code. Indeed, in these cases, the victim cannot be a civil party. Ms Fernandez writes in this regard that 'the monopoly of the Public Prosecutor's Office in this area is explained by the need for a "filter" to establish the seriousness of the offence, which then justifies the jurisdiction of the French authorities for an extraterritorial offence' (S. Fernandez, *Essai sur la distribution des compétences en droit pénal international*, *op. cit.*, no. 171).

out on-site inspections. On the other hand, the objective of protecting the European financial markets should lead to not retaining the jurisdiction of French law when the financial markets are foreign. However, it seems that two other arguments can be identified to support the merits of personal jurisdiction: on the one hand, the morality of the offence and undue enrichment, and on the other hand, the fact that the prosecuting authority of the place of residence of the accused persons is best placed to carry out the proceedings. This argument acquires additional force whenever the French State refuses to extradite its nationals or to implement a foreign decision depriving them of their liberty.[84]

536. Personal jurisdiction and morality. The moral basis historically justifies the personal jurisdiction of French law.[85] Such a perception is widespread in other legal orders: the United States, for example, has experienced a debate on the appropriateness of repression based on personal jurisdiction, in particular so that the American territory does not become a 'coast for barbary', a refuge for bandits. The interest of the legal system in not becoming such a refuge was weighed against the interest of not squandering the resources of American institutions in the face of the repression of offences that only have effects abroad.[86] It is not insignificant that personal jurisdiction, after having been abandoned in matters of 'registrations requirements', which essentially concern administrative obligations regarding the issue of financial securities,[87] has been elevated to the

---

84 In intra-European relations, Art. 7 of the Dublin Convention of 27 September 1996 prevents extradition from being refused on the basis of the nationality of the requested Member State, see D. Rebut, *Droit pénal international, op. cit.*

85 Thus, Faustin Hélie considered that jurisdiction 'is personal in the sense that it follows persons to regulate their moral capacity as personal status regulates their civil capacity', see F. Hélie, *Traité de l'instruction criminelle*, 2nd ed., Paris, Henri Plon, 1866, t. II, no. 659, quoted by D. Rebut, *Droit pénal international, op. cit.*, no. 128. The author criticises Mr Hélie for proceeding with a questionable alignment of civil and criminal laws.

86 'Congress would have wished the precious resources of United States courts and law enforcement agencies to be devoted to them rather than leave the problem to foreign countries', in *Bersch v. Drexel Firestone*, Inc, 519 F 2d 974, 985 (2nd Cir.), *cert. Denied sub nom.* Bersch v. Arthur Andersen & Co, 423 U.S. 1018 (1975).

87 The functional equivalent of which is the prospectus. It seems indisputable that the administrative requirements apply only to the US market: it is difficult to understand how they would apply abroad, even if the SEC initially retained their application under the personal jurisdiction of US law. Indeed, when the SEC began to question the scope of US securities regulation in the 1960s in response to the emergence of the Eurobond market, it considered that the purpose of the regulation was primarily to protect US investors, i.e. US citizens and residents (see SEC Release, no. 4708). It was only with the enactment of *Regulation* S that the SEC changed its approach and considered that the protection offered by US regulation was not, in the words of some authors, 'an American birthright, but rather as a protection provided to those participating in U.S. Capital Market', see E.F. Greene and L.C. Quinn, *Building on international convergence of the global market: a model for securities law reform*, 1281 PLI Corp 11, 53, 2001. As Ms Bédart notes: 'Although the United States may have an interest in not becoming a 'Barbary Coast' harbouring international securities pirates, they have no interest in applying U.S. registration and reporting provisions to transactions in foreign securities impacting investors in foreign securities markets. The

status of international jurisdiction in matters of 'anti-fraud' regulations, in the name of its moral basis.[88] It is as if, the closer one comes to fraudulent matters, the more admissible personal jurisdiction becomes.[89] However, in these latter cases, the American law can only be applied subsidiarily, at the risk of being rejected in terms of jurisdictional competence by the *forum non conveniens* exception.[90]

537. **Morality and self-limitation of French law.** In the French case, if personal jurisdiction corresponds in principle to a moral necessity, it is difficult to articulate such a basis with the condition of double criminality: there is something curious about considering that a rule has a moral vocation, and applying it only when it has been violated in certain places.[91] This is so true that offences that the French legislator finds truly immoral see the double criminality condition disappear.[92] Morality and legality seem to be combined here: certainly, repression is of a moral nature, but it is limited insofar as, for it to be possible, the offender must have violated a rule of the legal order affected by his behaviour, either in the commission of the offence or in its effects. Otherwise, the offender may argue that he has obeyed the rule of conduct of the place affected by his conduct. This consideration of foreign law may be seen as a reflection of the principle of the legality of offences,[93] but it does raise a certain unease in the context of market abuse, which is a sophisticated type of offence whose absence from foreign law is not the result of a liberal legislative policy but of a lack of understanding of the functioning of financial markets.

---

registration provisions are concerned solely with the deleterious effects on the US securities market; they do not embody a second regulatory interest of the harbour type, which courts have identified in the antifraud provisions.' J. Bédart, *International conflicts of Antitrust and Securities Regulations: 'It's all about effects'*, *op. cit.*, p. 175 (see also pp. 233 et seq.).

88 Precisely on behalf of the '*Barbary Coast' argument v. SEC Kasser*, 548 F.2d 109, 116, *cert. Denied*, 431 U.S. 938 (1977).

89 In addition, the American Congress considered that fraudulent practices were most often present at the time of issue, which explains its conception of the obligation to disclose: see P.-H. Conac, *La régulation des marchés boursiers par la commission des opérations de bourse (COB) et la securities and exchange commission (SEC)*, *op. cit.*, p. 47: 'The concentration of Congress on issues is an equally revealing sign of its conception of the disclosure requirement as an instrument for preventing fraud and fraudulent practices.'

90 J. Bédart, *International conflicts of Antitrust and Securities Regulations: 'It's all about effects'*, *op. cit.*, pp. 515 et seq. basing his argument on the analysis of two cases: *Robinson v. TCI/ US Westcommunication INC*, 117F.2d and *Alfadda v. Fenn*, 935 F.2d 475 (2nd Circuit 1991).

91 This is one of the reasons why this condition is criticised, see A. Fournier, 'Aperçu critique du principe de double incrimination en droit pénal international', in *Les droits et le droit, Mélanges dédiés à Bernard Bouloc*, Paris, Dalloz, 2006, p. 224.

92 This is the case, for example, of sexual abuse of minors committed abroad by a French person.

93 In this sense, see S. Fernandez, *Essai sur la distribution des compétences en droit pénal international*, *op. cit.*, no. 489.

538. Protection of foreign financial markets. The French legal system is in fact not very fond of criminal prosecution for market abuse. Adding personal jurisdiction to a little-used territorial jurisdiction was already audacious, all the more so given that the French prosecuting authority is often less well placed than the authority of the place of the affected market. It is generally added that the purpose of the French offence is not the repression abroad of such conduct, but the protection of the socio-economic framework established by the protected market.[94] This last argument leads to the retention of personal jurisdiction, which is the only basis for the prosecution of French nationals engaging in market abuse in other European financial markets. Indeed, the local authority is often in the best position to prosecute them when the constitutive acts are committed in France by French persons, and the administrative authority is moreover the receiver of the information obligations allowing their detection. Nevertheless, it seems necessary to maintain personal jurisdiction over market abuse in the financial markets of third countries, despite our observations on the objective of this regulation. The reason is related to the particularities of criminal law enforcement in international relations: by not allowing the extradition of nationals or the enforcement of foreign criminal decisions, the absence of the possible exercise of personal jurisdiction over French nationals committing market abuse in foreign countries that enforce it would lead to their criminal impunity. Personal jurisdiction continues to compensate for the principle of non-extradition of nationals.[95]

---

[94] See *ibid.*, no. 180; D. Chilstein, *Droit pénal international et lois de police*, *op. cit.*, no. 343. These reflections suggest that the 'most competent" criminal law being the law of the place of the affected market, it would undoubtedly be necessary to substitute the application of French law for that of foreign law. It would be as much a question of applying the foreign law because it is the most predictable as because the foreign legal system is the only one economically affected. In most cases it is not very effective, and rarely necessary, to apply foreign criminal law, except perhaps in those residual cases where, in the words of one author, "the law of the social roots of the offence' (R. Koering-Joulin, *L'article 693 du Code de procédure pénale et la localisation internationale de l'infraction [Article 693 of the Code of Criminal Procedure and the international localisation of the offence]*, *op. cit.*, p. 348) leads to the application of the law of the economic order of the market affected by the abuse. However, it will often be more desirable to notify the elements available to the French authority to its foreign counterpart, and to ensure the cooperation of the French authorities. Indeed, the French authority has sufficiently limited resources to devote them primarily to the surveillance of its own market (cf. the argument developed in the United States, see note under para. 538), which is ensured by the principle of opportunity for prosecution.

[95] See *supra*, para. 528.

§ 3. CONFRONTATION WITH THE CRITERIA OF ADMINISTRATIVE JURISDICTION

539. While criminal litigation on market abuse is limited to a few decisions per year, it should be noted that administrative litigation is more important.[96] Indeed, administrative enforcement has at least two advantages over judicial enforcement[97]: it is much quicker,[98] and the members of the authority, both the sanctions commission and the prosecution authority, have the expertise necessary for enforcement.[99] The AMF's jurisdictional criteria are now based

---

96 See the statistics in the report by Mr Dominique Baert, rapp. AN no. 36226 cited above: 'Between 1 January 2004 and 1 August 2014, 182 proceedings were referred by the AMF to the Paris public prosecutor's office, and to the National Financial Prosecutor's Office since February 2014: an average of 18 proceedings each year were likely to be the subject of dual criminal and administrative proceedings. The most frequent type of litigation is insider dealing. Of the 182 cases, 150 were decided by the AMF Enforcement Committee, representing 82% of the investigation reports sent to the public prosecutor. Of the criminal proceedings in these 182 cases, 131 had been completed by 1 August 2014 and 50 were under investigation or being investigated. In all, about 20% of the proceedings referred by the AMF were referred to the criminal court. The aim of the National Financial Prosecutor's Office is not to shift the balance in favour of the prosecution service as a result of the reform of procedures. It seems legitimate and efficient to it that, in the context of future preliminary consultations, about 80% of the cases should be the subject of a notification of grievances and not of the initiation of public action.' Administrative repression remains measured. In 2019, only 5 decisions out of the 13 taken over the year were taken on the basis of the repression of insider trading, of which only 4 resulted in sanctions: no. 3 of 13 March 2019, no. 4 of 17 April 2019, no. 5 of 25 April 2019 (which concerned the Illiad/T-Mobile case), no. 13 of 1 October 2019. In 2018, only 7 decisions over the year were taken on the basis of the insider trading regulation, and resulted in sanctions: decisions, no. 5 of 7 May 2018, no. 7 of 5 July 2018, no. 8 of 16 July 2018, no. 9 of 18 July 2018, no. 11 of 24 October 2018, no. 12 of 9 November 2018, no. 15 of 13 December 2018. To this should be added Decision no. 3 of 2 May 2018, taken on the basis of price manipulation, which is the only one published condemning such an abuse, and in which the respondent challenges the international jurisdiction of the AMF. Such a challenge also occurred in Decision 11 of 24 October 2018. This low occurrence is also found in other countries, such as Belgium, where there were three administrative sanctions and only one criminal sanction from 2009 to 2019 see https://www.lecho.be/les-marches/actu/general/le-combat-perdu-contre-le-delit-d-initie/10166823.html (accessed on 7 October 2019).

97 P.-H. Conac, *La régulation des marchés boursiers par la Commission des opérations de bourse (COB) et la Securities and exchange commission (SEC), op. cit.*, no. 90, p. 111. Mr Conac notes an advantage that will not be retained here, which is the unity of jurisprudence permitted by this repression. Indeed, the national jurisdiction of the national financial prosecutor's office leads to the same thing.

98 This is a considerable advantage here, as well as being in line with what is expected of a sentence: 'The more prompt the punishment, the more closely it follows the crime that has been committed, the more just and useful it will be.' C. Beccaria, *Des délits et des peines*, Paris, Flammarion, 2006, p. 108.

99 It is interesting to note that the regulatory authority initially did not want to obtain a sanctions committee, but the possibility of being able to prosecute offenders under criminal law. The legislator did not grant it the power to replace the public prosecutor's office, but allowed it to obtain, by way of compensation, this sanctions committee (Art. 9-2 of the

on '*compétence réelle*' and territorial jurisdiction. This second criterion is not convincing and would benefit from being replaced by one based on personal jurisdiction; moreover, a difficulty affects the articulation of administrative jurisdiction and criminal jurisdiction (I). The jurisdiction of the authority of the place of listing for the purposes of repression of market abuse should make it, in principle, the recipient of information provided by operators in order to detect market abuse (II).

I. The Criteria for Law Enforcement Jurisdiction

540. Credentials. Market abuse is also subject to administrative enforcement by the *Autorité des Marchés Financiers.*[100] The behaviours targeted by administrative enforcement are the same, i.e. those defined uniformly throughout the Union by the Market Abuse Regulation. The AMF has two international jurisdiction bases. The first is founded on the admission of the financial instrument that is the subject of market abuse to trading on a French financial market.[101] This can be seen as an avatar of the '*compétence réelle*' that would benefit from basing the entire repression of market abuse, administrative and criminal. The second gives the AMF jurisdiction when the offence was committed on French territory and the offence concerns another EU financial market.[102] This is the criterion of territorial jurisdiction, the traditional basis for enforcement.

The '*compétence réelle*' of the French authority deserves full approval. The virtues of this title of jurisdiction have already been shown.[103] However, the territorial jurisdiction chosen is not very convincing. Its purpose is to allow the authority to sanction market abuse committed by French residents against other financial markets. Nevertheless, the dematerialisation and internationalisation of material transactions constituting market abuse allow French residents to

law no. 89-531 of 2 August 1989 on the security and transparency of the financial market). P.-H. Conac, *La régulation des marchés boursiers par la Commission des opérations de bourse (COB) et la Securities and exchange commission (SEC)*, *op. cit.*, nos. 82-83.

100 The French system does not directly provide for the application of French administrative law, but declares the Autorité des marchés financiers competent to punish certain behaviour constituting market abuse. In other words, the market authority is competent on a basis distinct from criminal law, even if the administrative provisions are largely inspired by criminal provisions: see F. Drummond, *Droit financier*, *op. cit.* Comparative law provides other systems, in which the infringement of a regulatory provision issued by the regulator may constitute a criminal offence, for example in the United States. For a presentation of this system and its nuances, see P.-H. Conac, *La régulation des marchés boursiers par la Commission des opérations de bourse (COB) et la Securities and exchange commission (SEC)*, *op. cit.*, 101–102.

101 Art. L. 621-15(c) of the Monetary and Financial Code.

102 Art. L. 621-15(d)(4°) of the Monetary and Financial Code.

103 See *supra*, paras. 532 et seq.

escape this jurisdictional criterion.[104] The objective of territorial jurisdiction is the protection of other European financial markets, which is based on the AMF's mission to 'assist in the regulation of these markets [of financial instruments] at the European and international levels',[105] and the objective of the regulation of market abuse to protect European financial markets. The AMF should therefore have jurisdiction on a personal basis, i.e. on the basis of the perpetrator's residence on French territory. It should be limited to abuses committed on European markets: these are the ones that the market abuse regulation is intended to protect. In cases where the AMF cannot establish its jurisdiction, it is always possible to refer the case to the criminal authorities. This option for the administrative authority requires an account to be given of the relationship between repressive, administrative and criminal jurisdiction.

After a long period of tolerating a combination of administrative and criminal sanctions,[106] an *a priori* linkage is now made by the so-called referral technique, whereby the AMF decides whether it wishes to prosecute the offence itself or leave the possible prosecution to the financial prosecutor of the Republic.[107] In the first case, the authority notifies the public prosecutor of its intention, who, if he or she wishes to prosecute, may object and refer the matter to the public prosecutor of the Paris Court of Appeal for a decision.[108]

---

104 For an illustration, see AMF, Sanction 26 June 2008, *RDBF*, July 2009, comm. 142. note S. Torck. In this case, the defendants had used inside information relating to the filing of a public offer for the shares of a Danish company whose securities were listed on the Copenhagen stock exchange. However, the elements of the offence were not located in France: the purchase orders had been placed from accounts opened in institutions registered in the United Kingdom and Israel, and never from France. The Enforcement Committee therefore declared itself incompetent.

105 Art. L. 621-1 of the Monetary and Financial Code.

106 On the reasons that led the legislator to this solution, see the enlightening report by Mr Dominique Baert, rapp. AN no. 3622, registered on 30 March 2016, pp. 48 et seq. Cumulation was nevertheless ordered by one of the meanings of *ne bis in idem*: criminal proceedings could be added to administrative proceedings, and not vice versa. On this point, see J. Pradel, *Procédure pénale*, 17th ed., Paris, Cujas, 2013, no. 1023.

107 The AMF has jurisdiction over market abuse cases throughout France (Art. L. 456-1 of the Monetary and Financial Code, see also Art. 705 of the Code of Criminal Procedure). In practice, in the legislator's view, the judicial authority should deal with one case out of five: 'In total, about 20% of the proceedings referred by the AMF have been referred to the criminal court. The aim of the National Financial Prosecutor's Office is not to shift the balance in favour of the prosecution service following the reform of procedures. It seems legitimate and efficient to it that, in the context of future preliminary consultations, approximately 80% of cases should be the subject of a notification of grievances and not of the initiation of public proceedings.' D. Baert, *report*, p. 17.

108 Art. L. 465-3-6(II) of the Monetary and Financial Code - the decision is not open to appeal, see Art. L. 465-3-6(V) of the same Code. If the criminal route is chosen, the public prosecutor can still use the procedure of immediate appearance on prior acknowledgement of responsibility, which not only speeds up the procedure but also limits the criticism traditionally levelled at the criminal route for market abuse. See in this sense, D. Martin and L.-M. Savatier, 'Le critère de gravité dans la répression des abus de marché', *Revue de droit des affaires*, January 2017, pp. 32 et seq.

In the second case, the Authority voluntarily relinquishes jurisdiction to the prosecutor. One of the most apparent difficulties with this new system is the absence of a criterion for choosing between the two means of enforcement in French law.[109] Indeed, neither the directive nor the transposition law specifies how to delimit the two types of repression.[110] It is only in the recitals of the Market Abuse Directive that we find a reference to the criterion of the seriousness of the offence.[111] However, on the one hand, the seriousness of the offence needs to be characterised, which makes it difficult for litigants to foresee how the criterion should be applied; on the other hand, this criterion is not used to delimit the jurisdiction of the AMF Enforcement Committee, given the authority's ability to propose transaction (*composition administrative*) to the respondent.[112] This situation certainly benefits administrative enforcement, which in practice concentrates the means of detection and the initiative for notification.[113]

---

[109] See already in this sense A.-V. Le Fur and D. Schmidt, 'Sanctions des abus de marché: "l'aiguillage" source de déraillement', *D.*, 2015, p. 1450; T. Bonneau, 'Aiguillage et déraillement', *BJB*, 2016, p. 297: D. Martin and L.-M. Savatier, 'Le critère de gravité dans la répression des abus de marché', *op. cit.*

[110] This notion of seriousness is in fact enshrined in the *Grande Stevens* judgment of the European Court of Human Rights: 'The criminal nature of a case is subordinate to the degree of seriousness of the sanction to which the person concerned is *a priori* liable.' On this judgment, which prompted the reform of the French system, see F. Drummond, *Droit financier*, *op. cit.*, no. 169. In defence of this criterion, which should be used among others, but in a preponderant way, see D. Martin and L.-M. Savatier, 'Le critère de gravité dans la répression des abus de marché', *op. cit.* for a critique of the criterion, see T. Bonneau *et alii*, *Droit financier*, *op. cit.*

[111] Recital 10 of the Market Abuse Directive.

[112] The articulation of administrative and criminal sanctions follows another articulation, the one internal to the AMF, which allows it to offer a choice to the respondent between the traditional procedure before the '*Commission des sanctions*' and the possibility of compromise: this is the '*composition administrative*' (Art. L. 621-14-1 and Arts. R. 621-37-1 et seq. of the Monetary and Financial Code). '*Composition administrative*' is a favour to the respondent, if only because of the choice that the authority offers. The criterion used by the Authority to propose the composition is whether the legal issue has already been decided by the Enforcement Committee. As Professor Drummond points out, such a criterion moves away from the criterion of seriousness that the European system of repression of market abuse encourages, and prevents the Commission from pursuing its mission of protecting financial public order: some breaches are new without being serious, while others, repeated, may nevertheless constitute, precisely because of their seriousness, major breaches of financial public order. See F. Drummond, 'A qui profite la composition administrative?', *BJB*, November 2016, p. 449.

[113] Even though the reform of European law was set in motion because of the observation that: 'The adoption of administrative sanctions by Member States has so far proved insufficient to ensure compliance with the rules on preventing and combating market abuse.' (Recital 5 of the Market Abuse Directive).

II. The Criteria for Preventive Competence

The prevention of market abuse involves various information obligations owed to the regulator by a number of players. There are two distinct objectives for these reporting obligations in the area of market abuse: to prevent the offence from occurring, i.e. to prevent the abuse from occurring in the first place; and to facilitate enforcement.

541. Avoiding abuse. In order to avoid abuse, managers[114] are prohibited from trading directly or indirectly, for their account or for the account of a third party[115] in the issuer's shares and debt securities in the thirty days preceding the publication of a financial report, whether this is published by obligation of national law, or of market rules.[116] Moreover, the European legislator has instituted an obligation to disclose inside information which, by making it public, makes it possible to put an end to the asymmetry of information.[117] In other words, the purpose of this obligation is to protect investors through the dissemination of inside information. Nevertheless, it is possible for the issuer to defer, under its responsibility, the disclosure of inside information under certain conditions.[118] The issuer must then notify the competent authority of this deferral. Curiously, for issuers from one Member State, the competent authority

---

114 The notion of manager is not determined by the *lex societatis* but by the Regulation itself, which gives a specific definition, Art. 3(24) of the Market Abuse Regulation ('person discharging managerial responsibilities').

115 Art. 19(11°) of the Market Abuse Regulation.

116 Except in the case of exceptional circumstances and special situations, see Art. 19(12°) of the Regulation on market abuse. Similar rules have long existed in American law, see P.-H. Conac, *La régulation des marchés boursiers par la Commission des opérations de bourse (COB) et la Securities and exchange commission (SEC)*, *op. cit.*, p. 72: 'Congress instituted a confiscatory provision designed to discourage the managers of listed companies from manipulating their company's share price by disseminating false information. Indeed, it provided for the outright confiscation of profits made by the latter on the purchase and sale, or vice versa, of their company's shares over a period of 6 months.' The basis of this obligation is Section 16(b) of the *Securities Exchange Act, the* scope of which was extended in 1964 to any person registering with the SEC in order to disseminate its securities to the public, independently of any listing.

117 Even today, the Regulation specifies that in order to prevent 'insider trading and to avoid investors being misled, it is essential that issuers disclose inside information in their possession' (Recital 49 of the Market Abuse Regulation), except in the case of harm to 'the legitimate interests of the issuer', which are listed in a non-exhaustive manner in the paratext of the Regulation (Recital 50 of the Market Abuse Regulation), and possibly supplemented by the European Securities and Markets Authority (Art. 17(11°) of the Market Abuse Regulation). See already Art. 6(1°) and (2°) of the former Market Abuse Directive.

118 Art. 17(4°) of the Market Abuse Regulation. The article refers to the case where the issuer is a credit institution. Indeed, the disclosure of the information could be likely to affect the stability of the financial system, and would therefore justify deferring disclosure for credit or financial institutions (Recital 52 and Art. 17(5°) Market Abuse Regulation). The systemic importance is then assessed by the competent authority (Recital 53 and Art. 17(6°) of the Market Abuse Regulation).

is always that of the registered office, even when the issuer has exclusively admitted its securities to the trading platform of another Member State.[119] Such a criterion is not without paradox when the Commission insists that 'the single competent authority receiving the notification should be the one with the greatest interest in market supervision' and ensures 'avoidance of the exercise of discretion by the issuer'.[120] This should be the authority of the place of listing, noting that notification may be made, where appropriate, to the authority of the seat and the authority of the place of listing.

In the case of issuers from a third country, the competent authority is that of the first place of admission of the securities.[121] In the case of a first listing of securities by simultaneous multiple listing, the competent authority is the one of the 'most relevant market in terms of liquidity', i.e. depending on the financial instrument, the market on which the first admission to trading took place or the one with the largest volume of transactions.[122] This is a

---

119 This is not determined by the Regulation, which refers to a delegated act by the Commission (Art. 17(3°) Market Abuse Regulation). The Commission's delegated act (Commission Delegated Regulation [EU] 2016/522 of 17 December 2015) wants 'the single competent authority receiving the notification to be the one with the greatest interest in market surveillance and to avoid (*thus*) the exercise of discretion by the issuer' (*ibid.*, p. 8). This delegated act provides, in its Art. 6(1°): 'The competent authority [...] shall be the competent authority of the Member State where the issuer has its registered office in the following cases (a) where the issuer holds equity securities which are admitted to trading or traded with its consent, or for which the issuer has applied for admission to trading, on a trading venue in the Member State where the issuer's registered office is situated; (b) where the issuer does not hold equity securities which are admitted to trading or traded with its consent, or for which the issuer has applied for admission to trading, on a trading venue in a Member State, provided that the issuer holds other financial instruments which are admitted to trading or traded with its consent, or for which the issuer has applied for admission to trading, on a trading venue in the Member State in which its registered office is situated.' Everyone will appreciate the Commission's French translation, which oscillates between unintelligibility and misinterpretation: it is obviously not the holding of 'equity securities' that is referred to, but their issue. The latter are 'shares in companies and other securities equivalent to shares in companies, *partnerships* or other entities, as well as certificates representing shares.' (Art. 4(1°), point 44, a of the MiFID Directive, on the basis of Art. 2 of the aforementioned Delegated Regulation 2016/522).

120 Recital 17 of the Delegated Regulation (EU) 2016/522.

121 Art. 6(2°) of the above-mentioned Delegated Regulation.

122 The expression quoted is taken from Art. 6(2°), *in fine*, of the above-mentioned Delegated Regulation. The latter article refers to Art. 26(9°)(b), of the MiFID Regulation which gives ESMA the competence to determine 'the criteria for defining the relevant market', a notion used by the same article (Art. 26(1°) of the MiFID Regulation) in order to determine the authority to which investment firms must report their transactions in financial instruments. *In fine*, the Commission has devoted a regulation to this issue (Commission Delegated Regulation [EU] 2017/570 of 26 May 2016 on markets in financial instruments through technical regulatory standards relating to the determination of a market that is significant in terms of liquidity in connection with notifications of temporary trading suspensions), Art. 1 of which designates as a 'significant in terms of liquidity' market for financial instruments the first market on which the instrument has been admitted to trading (Art. 1(b) and (c) of Regulation 2017/570), with the exception of 'shares, depositary receipts, listed funds,

criterion that has been suggested by legal scholars, but whose rejection in positive law was linked to its contingency: such a market is likely to vary over time, which means that this criterion does not allow for the stability of the competent authority.[123] This criticism must be put into perspective in view of the possibility of obtaining this information by means of cooperation.

542. Facilitate enforcement. A permanent information obligation is imposed on financial market managers in order to allow the repression of market abuse and to deter its commission. Market operators must notify the authority of their registered office of any financial instrument for which an application for admission to trading has been made, and notify them again when an instrument ceases to be traded.[124] Issuers are also required to maintain a list of insiders and to provide a set of information about them.[125] The issuer's directors[126] have an obligation to disclose to the issuer and the competent authority 'transactions carried out for their own account relating to the shares or debt securities of the issuer, or to derivatives or other financial instruments related to them'.[127] The purpose of such a rule is to reveal possible conflicts of interest that could lead to market abuse.[128]

The issuer's information relating to financial instruments, or relating to insiders, must be notified to the listing authority, whose law applies to the

preference certificates and similar financial instruments' for which reference is made to Art. 4 of Commission Delegated Regulation (EU) 2017/587. The latter article considers that the relevant market is the one that 'has the highest trading volume in the Union for the financial instrument in question' (Art. 4(1°) of Regulation 2017/587, bearing in mind that the method for calculating the volume is prescribed by the same article, in its 3°).

123 See *supra*, note under para. 492.

124 Art. 4(1°) of the Market Abuse Regulation. The list of information required by the Regulation is extensive (Art. 4(3), *ibid.*)

125 Art. 18 Market Abuse Regulation. In view of the cost of the obligation for companies to disclose inside information (Recital 55 Market Abuse Regulation), small and medium-sized companies could be exempted from this obligation, but still be obliged to provide it upon (*ad hoc*) request of the competent authority (Recital 56 Market Abuse Regulation).

126 The category of managers is understood here in a broad sense, since it includes 'persons having a close link with the issuer'. This includes majority shareholders or members of the supervisory board, as well as any person on the insider list, which is a valuable evidentiary prerequisite.
This *disclosure* obligation also applies to investment and statistical recommendations. The analysts in question are legally required to present objective information, but also to mention the existence of their interests in relation to the financial instruments they comment on (Art. 20(1°) of the Regulation on market abuse).

127 Art. 19(1°)(a) Market Abuse Regulation. These transactions are listed in a non-exhaustive manner in Art. 19(7°) of the Market Abuse Regulation. Point 6° provides for the content of the notification.

128 The issuer and its managers must therefore disclose to the competent authority 'any transaction carried out for their own account and relating to the shares or debt securities of that issuer, or to derivatives or other financial instruments related to them' (Art. 19(1°) Market Abuse Regulation).

dissemination arrangements.[129] This is not the case for notification requirements for transactions carried out by persons exercising managerial responsibilities, either on behalf of the issuer or for their own account. The latter are subject to the law and authority of the registered office when the issuer has its registered office in a Member State.[130] For third country issuers, the competent authority is the one they have designated to provide the information in the Transparency Directive.[131] The latter refers to the Prospectus Directive, i.e. to the authority of the first Member State from which savings are sought.[132]

The establishment of a list of insiders directly concerns the functioning of the financial market, and justifies the competence of the financial market authority and the applicability of its law. The same is true for obligations relating to financial instruments, which enable law enforcement authorities to keep a closer eye on instruments whose trading price may have been subject to unusual variations. As the two types of information are complementary, it is also desirable that the same authority should have immediate access to all such information. More curious is the obligation for directors to inform the registered office authority of transactions.[133] This obligation is unambiguously intended to facilitate the repression of insider trading;[134] in this sense, it is surprising that the applicable law is not that of the market and, above all, that notifications are made to the authority of the registered office. The reason for this is undoubtedly that the registered office authority is in the best position to carry out on-the-spot checks in order to punish any market abuse that may have occurred. Nevertheless, it seems that, in these cases, the information would be better distributed to both authorities.[135]

543. Conclusion of the section. 'Most offences are still a matter for national laws and judges, and in criminal law, as in all other areas of private law, international life poses above all a problem of coordination and cooperation

---

129 Art. 22 of the Market Abuse Regulation.

130 Art. 19(2) Market Abuse Regulation. However, some rules are standardised: for example, the person on whom the obligation to inform rests has three working days from the date of the transaction.

131 On which see *supra*, para. 343.

132 Art. 2(1°)(m)(iii) of the Prospectus Directive is applicable because of the reference in Art. 19(2°)(2) of the Market Abuse Regulation to Art. 2(1°)(i) of the Transparency Directive, which in turn refers to Art. 10 of the Prospectus Directive concerning the competent authority for the annual obligation, the definition of which is given by Art. 2(1°)(m)(iii) of the same Directive. Art. 19(2)(2) of the Market Abuse Regulation provides for the competence of the authority of the trading platform in a subsidiary way.

133 It is not really explained by Recital 58 on the ratio of this information obligation.

134 Recital 58 of the Market Abuse Regulation.

135 This is the case even if the information is disseminated through the media. The Market Abuse Regulation recommends the use of the mechanism established by Art. 21 of the Transparency Directive on the dissemination and storage of regulated information. On this mechanism in French law, see Art. L. 621-10-2 of the Monetary and Financial Code, and the observations of F. Drummond, *Droit financier*, *op. cit.*, p. 110.

between systems'.[136] This statement by Professor Malaurie is still true. In relation to market abuse, the territorial jurisdiction of French law leads to the double pitfall of artificially linking the elements constituting market abuse to French territory, in addition to providing for the jurisdiction of French law over offences that the regulation of market abuse does not pursue. It would obviously be advantageous to base the applicability of French law on '*competence réelle*', the *res* affected by the offence always being the French trading platform. Such a jurisdictional title would make it possible to reflect more accurately, in international relations, the 'physiology' of the offences in question, but also the reasons why the place where the offence was committed is in fact irrelevant: only the harm to the financial market matters. Moreover, it incorporates the purpose of the offences, thus embracing the advantages of the unilateral conflict rules method. It explains why the scope of application of market abuse is generally that of the French markets. Moreover, retaining '*competence réelle*' makes it possible, like territorial jurisdiction, to disregard the authority of a foreign judgment that would claim to substitute for the French State in punishing the perpetrators of market abuse on the French market. Finally, from the point of view of the conditions and objectives of domestic criminal law, the use of '*competence réelle*' is predictable and respects the requirement of criminal legality, and from the point of view of international criminal law, the use of '*competence réelle*' makes it possible to rationalise and optimise the current use of jurisdictional titles. However, it will sometimes be useful to base the applicability of French criminal law on personal jurisdiction in order to prosecute French nationals who commit market abuse in foreign financial markets.

These jurisdictional criteria should apply on the same terms, whether the prosecuting authority is judicial or administrative, since the objectives of the regulation of market abuse are the same in both cases. It should be added that in administrative matters, the information to be provided by operators should always be communicated to the authority of the place of listing, since it is this authority that bears the primary burden of repression. Finally, it should be noted that the criteria for criminal jurisdiction proposed here, i.e. personal jurisdiction over nationals and "competence réelle" over foreigners, are in line with the criteria generally used by an administrative authority for financial market supervision.[137]

---

136 P. Malaurie, preface C. Lombois, *Droit pénal international*, *op. cit.*, p. VI.

137 See *supra*, paras. 9 et seq.

SECTION 2. COOPERATION BETWEEN ADMINISTRATIVE AUTHORITIES

544. The need for cooperation. In financial matters, the need for the authorities to cooperate most often arises from the difficulty they have in obtaining information from a foreign company, in particular because they can no longer use their most coercive powers directly. In such cases, cooperation enables the authority to exercise its prosecutorial function. It is particularly necessary in order to crack down on market abuse committed by foreign persons.[138] Cooperation is also necessary to ensure compliance with prudential rules.[139]

The first attempts at cooperation between administrative authorities were made in the United States. Because of the early internationalisation of the American financial markets, the SEC was the first to realise the need for cooperation, particularly because the companies in dispute were invoking banking secrecy or even blocking laws to counter its particularly intrusive evidentiary practices.[140] As the use of direct legal action or judicial cooperation was unsuccessful, it turned to administrative cooperation.[141] The former COB suffered from the same difficulties[142] and also turned to administrative cooperation, also referred to here as mutual assistance. Already present in tax [143] or competition matters,[144] cooperation between administrative authorities takes the form of requests for information between authorities, assistance with

---

138 See R. Sansonetti, *L'entraide administrative internationale dans la surveillance des marchés financiers*, Zurich, Schulthess, 1998. In the same way as cooperation in competition matters is used to enable the prosecution of infringements of competition law. It therefore seems that administrative cooperation does not have quite the same function as criminal cooperation: C. Lombois, *Droit pénal international*, *op. cit.*, no. 9: 'Extradition is a palliative for the refusal to enforce a foreign conviction; international letters rogatory are a palliative for the refusal to consider as valid in one country the preparatory investigation carried out in another country.'

139 See *supra*, para. 117.

140 One thinks in particular of the blocking laws against the practice of *pre-trial discovery*. On this point, see P.-H. Conac, *La régulation des marchés boursiers par la commission des opérations de bourse (COB) et la securities and exchange commission (SEC)*, *op. cit.*, paras. 378 et seq.

141 See the account and analysis of this phenomenon by P.-H. Conac, *La régulation des marchés boursiers par la commission des opérations de bourse (COB) et la securities and exchange commission (SEC)*, *op. cit.*, nos. 378 et seq. On the length of international mutual legal assistance, see A. Bloch, 'Dans les coulisses de l'entraide judiciaire internationale', *Dalloz Actualité*, 5 June 2020.

142 Added to this was the fact that it could not even accede to the Hague Convention of 18 March 1970 since it did not have legal personality, nor could it use the bilateral and multilateral treaties on mutual assistance in criminal matters signed by France and linking it to some fifty States, the latter being reserved for judicial authorities, see P.-H. Conac, *La régulation des marchés boursiers par la commission des opérations de bourse (COB) et la securities and exchange commission (SEC)*, *op. cit.*, no. 399.

143 See A. Kallergis, *La compétence fiscale*, Paris, Dalloz, 2018, nos. 746 et seq.

144 See *infra*, note under para. 561.

investigations, or even coordination of actions when the tortious elements are spread over the territory of several States. This cooperation is more than a powerful palliative to the plurality of authorities' territorial jurisdictions and the resulting positive conflicts[145]: instead of parallel procedures becoming obstacles, they can mutually enrich each other. Cooperation is now a necessity if the supervisory authorities are to carry out their duties properly, both because the activities carried out by the professionals under their supervision have become internationalised, and because the constituent elements of market abuse no longer always take place in the authority's territory. Cooperation is nevertheless subject to certain conditions, which borrow from the techniques of the law of recognition of foreign judgments (§ 1). In addition, it is subject to a regime that is closer to international mutual legal assistance (§ 2).

§ 1. THE CONDITIONS FOR COOPERATION

The conditions for cooperation are not perfectly identical within the European Union (I) and in international matters (II), even if the most significant difference lies more in the institutional aspect: in intra-European relations, a European authority is likely to intervene in order to resolve the difficulties caused by a lack of cooperation.

I. European Conditions for Cooperation

The European conditions for cooperation are now inspired by the law of international jurisdiction and are therefore strict. This rigidity is explained, in the law of civil jurisdiction, by the fact that a foreign judgment may, under certain conditions, be enforced in the territory of the forum, and leads to restrictions on cooperation (A). The idea underlying this restriction is inspired by the *ne bis in idem* principle, which should be challenged here. In criminal matters, a State is free to judge as it sees fit conduct that has already been punished by another State (B). The disadvantages of this solution for the defendant are tempered by consideration of the foreign penalty (C).

[145] S. Fernandez, *Essai sur la distribution des compétences en droit pénal international*, *op. cit.*, no. 26.

A. Conditions for Cooperation

545. The conditions of the obligation to cooperate. In European matters, several regulations enshrine a genuine 'obligation to cooperate'[146] for administrative authorities, which an authority can only evade in the cases exhaustively provided for by the regulation, when 'communication of relevant information could adversely affect the security of the Member State addressed', when 'complying with the request is likely adversely to affect its own investigation, enforcement activities or, where applicable, a criminal investigation', when 'judicial proceedings have already been initiated in respect of the same actions and against the same persons before the authorities of the Member State addressed' and, finally, when 'a final judgment has already been delivered in relation to such persons for the same actions in the Member State addressed'.[147]

These grounds for refusal to cooperate are reminiscent of those in the law of international civil jurisdiction, which has long been familiar with these mechanisms.[148] There is recognition of *lis pendens*,[149] *res judicata*[150] and what appears to be a restricted form of public policy.[151] The only element that might appear to be genuinely specific to the law of cooperation between authorities is the power to refuse assistance if this might prejudice the

146 This is the title of Art. 25 of the Market Abuse Regulation. See also Art. 33 of the Prospectus Regulation. For a historical perspective up to MiFID, see F. Recine, 'The new framework for cooperation between supervisory authorities in the Markets in Financial Instruments Directive', *REDBF (Euredia)*, 2004, no. 2, pp. 336 et seq.

147 Listed in Art. 25(2°) of the Market Abuse Regulation. See also the identical criteria listed in Art. 33(2) of the Prospectus Regulation and Art. 83 of MiFID 2, and the comments of B. Stoeva, *La coopération entre les superviseurs financiers dans l'Union européenne, op. cit.*, nos. 181 et seq.

148 Comp. P.-H. Conac, *La régulation des marchés boursiers par la commission des opérations de bourse (COB) et la securities and exchange commission (SEC), op. cit.*, no. 415, who considered that the reasons for refusing administrative cooperation were to be found in bilateral treaties on mutual assistance in criminal matters.

149 Art. 25(2°) c of the Market Abuse Regulation, Art. 33(2)(b) of the Prospectus Regulation; we even recognise the conditions: 'for the same and against the same persons'.

150 Art. 25(2°)(d) of the Market Abuse Regulation, Art. 33(2)(c) of the Prospectus Regulation. This condition also appeared as a refusal of judicial cooperation in other sectors, see Art. 7 of the Convention of 26 July 1995 on the protection of the European Communities' financial interests, [1995] OJ no. C316/48. This convention has been replaced by a directive (Directive [EU] 2017/1371 of the European Parliament and of the Council of 5 July 2017 on the fight against fraud affecting the Union's financial interests through criminal law) which does not lay down any positive rules in this area, but provides in its Recital 21 that 'in view of the multiple possible jurisdictions for cross-border criminal offences falling within the scope of this Directive, Member States should ensure that the *ne bis in idem* principle is fully respected in the application of national legislation transposing this Directive'.

151 Through the security of the addressed Member State, see Art. 25(2°)(a) of the Market Abuse Regulation.

ongoing investigation,[152] but it seems rather that this exception constitutes a continuation of the exception of *lis pendens* by other means.[153] In the law of international jurisdiction, the *lis pendens* exception is a coordination technique which leads to the second authority petitioned being relieved of jurisdiction in cases where there is more than one jurisdiction.[154] The basis of *res judicata* is to be found in the refusal to judge again the same situation that has already been the subject of a court decision.

546. The extension of this principle from civil proceedings to criminal proceedings, which can be seen here in the grounds for refusal to cooperate, shows the indirect penetration of the *ne bis in idem* principle into the European legal order.[155] According to this principle, 'an accused person who has been judged by a decision that is not subject to appeal may not be prosecuted again for the same act'.[156] The ground for refusal because of the prior existence of a final judgment is very clearly a variation of the *ne bis in idem* principle in international relations. This is already a ground for refusing cooperation in non-extradition mutual legal assistance agreements.[157] It also seems to be the case,

---

152 Art. 25(2°)(b) of the Market Abuse Regulation; Art. 33(2)(b) of the Prospectus Regulation. All these provisions now appear in Art. L. 632-5 of the Monetary and Financial Code.

153 This feeling is reinforced by the fact that the investigation must already have begun in order to be able to oppose cooperation. It should also be noted that European law does not recognise grounds for refusal relating to interference with the exercise of the authority's powers, or if the information requested can be obtained more easily by other means (in order to protect the authority's financial resources), as is sometimes the case, see P.-H. Conac, *La régulation des marchés boursiers par la commission des opérations de bourse (COB) et la securities and exchange commission (SEC)*, *op. cit.*, no. 442.

154 Art. 29 of the Brussels Ia Regulation.

155 The promotion of this principle in international relations appeared very early on. Donnedieu de Vabres himself promoted it, seeing it as a form of acquired right, see H. Donnedieu de Vabres, *Les principes modernes du droit pénal international*, *op. cit.*, p. 319: 'However subsidiary or very subsidiary the jurisdiction of the foreign court may be, it is no less universal. And when the factual circumstances have enabled it to exercise the former, it has given rise to an acquired right. It must be admitted that this 'natural' right attached to these persons, 'follows' them and applies independently of the legal system in which it is found.'

156 See 'non bis in idem' in *Vocabulaire Capitant*, 11th ed. The Latin maxim literally means 'not twice about the same thing'. According to the vocabulary of Capitant, it has a second, more procedural meaning, according to which 'when a material fact may fall within the scope of several incriminations, the judge may retain only one of the possible qualifications so that the offender is not punished twice for the same action'. On the history of the *ne bis in idem* rule, which evolved from a technical rule of concentration of action to a rule of general interest before being enshrined as a principle of individual protection against state interference, see F. Drummond, 'Le fabuleux destin de la règle *non bis in idem*', *BJB*, December 2014, p. 605. The principle has nevertheless been the subject of an erratic application in domestic law, see in particular in the context of the cumulation of administrative and criminal repression of market abuse H. Le Nabasque and A. Couret, *Droit financier*, *op. cit.*, nos. 1789 et seq.

157 For example, it is a mandatory ground for refusal in the convention signed by France, see Art. 4(2) of the convention with India of 20 November 2002 and 14 January 2003. On other occasions, it is an optional ground for refusal, see Art. 17(1) of the Convention of 14 January 1993 with Australia, or Art. 3§2 of the Convention of 18 April 2005 with China.

preventively, through *lis pendens*. In both cases, these grounds for refusal to cooperate benefit the person being prosecuted. Cooperation is only permitted where a single prosecuting authority exercises jurisdiction. In other words, the aim is to encourage a single international law enforcement authority. Of course, if it so wishes, the foreign administrative authority will still be able to prosecute, but it will have less evidence with which to effectively punish the offence. This is undoubtedly an ingenious technique which, without calling into question the system of criminal jurisdiction within the Union,[158] makes it possible to promote the application of the *ne bis in idem* principle in European relations[159] and, consequently, to better coordinate legal systems. However, this principle will be challenged for three reasons: first, because the *ne bis in idem* principle leads to the introduction of a chronological jurisdictional rule that disregards any link between the authority responsible for enforcement and the dispute; second, because it denies the ubiquity of the harm caused by market abuse; and third, because the basis of criminal jurisdiction differs from civil jurisdiction.

B. Critical Analysis

547. An inadequate allocation principle. In the first place, the *ne bis in idem* principle, when extended to international relations, appears above all as a chronological criterion for the *a posteriori* allocation of certain repressive jurisdictions[160] without constituting an obstacle to simultaneous proceedings. However, repression does not sit well with the exercise of a single jurisdiction.[161] *A priori*, the legal system can at best rationalise its jurisdiction in order to avoid exercising its repressive power when it is not really being infringed. *A posteriori*, it seems unreasonable to restrict the exercise of its own jurisdiction because of the *ne bis in idem* rule, which appears here as a simple principle of chronological priority, unconnected with the substance of the dispute. As Mr d'Avout puts it: 'It is rare, moreover, in international law that a simple chronological priority, disconnected from any consideration of the title of intervention of States, is

---

158 Art. 54 of the Convention on the application of the Schengen agreements provides that: 'A person who has been finally judged by a Contracting Party may not, in respect of the same acts, be prosecuted by another Contracting Party, provided that, in the event of conviction, the penalty has been imposed or is currently being enforced or can no longer be enforced under the laws of the convicting Contracting Party'. Art. 55 of the Convention nevertheless provides that the State may make an exception if 'the acts covered by the foreign judgment took place either wholly or in part in its territory.'

159 F. Lefèvre and C. Van Muylder, 'Le principe *non bis in idem* dans un contexte international', *Banque et droit*, special issue, February 2020, pp. 63 et seq.

160 See S. Fernandez, *Essai sur la distribution des compétences en droit pénal international*, *op. cit.*

161 As Mr d'Avout puts it, 'in international matters, State criminal proceedings, initiated by authority and for reasons specific to the prosecuting States, are difficult to assimilate'. L. d'Avout, *L'entreprise et les conflits internationaux de lois*, *op. cit.*, no. 255.

sufficient to produce balanced solutions to conflicts of law, jurisdiction and authority.'[162]

548. A ubiquitous offence. Secondly, the constituent elements of market abuse may be a limit to these causes of refusal to cooperate, since the same insider dealing or price manipulation may affect several financial markets, triggering the jurisdiction of several law enforcement authorities. Indeed, despite the similarity of the constituent elements, a different offence exists each time a distinct financial market has been affected. Paradoxically, in the case of market abuse, whether the identity retained by criminal law is legal or material,[163] it is the '*idem*' that is not fulfilled here. An analogy can be drawn here with competition law, where the Court of Justice has held that where the punishment of unlawful conduct has produced anti-competitive effects in the territory of several legal systems, each authority is able to punish the conduct in question without the *ne bis in idem* principle having to come into play.[164] In addition, it is often possible to reach a settlement with the administrative authority in order to extinguish proceedings.[165] Extending the *ne bis in idem* principle to relations between legal orders therefore runs the risk of giving the defendant the option of coming to an agreement with the most conciliatory authority, in order to then set the latter's decision against the others'.[166]

549. The foundations of civil and criminal jurisdiction. Thirdly, in civil proceedings, *res judicata* constitutes an obstacle to the trial and to cooperation because the concomitant exercise of international jurisdiction is likely to result in contradictory decisions for the private person.[167] The situation is not the same in criminal matters, where jurisdiction does not serve to bring justice to private individuals, but to punish those who have caused harm to society. The objective of preventing contradictory decisions is therefore subordinate to the administration of a penalty deemed appropriate by each legal system affected

---

162 L. D'AVOUT, *L'entreprise et les conflits internationaux de lois*, *op. cit.*, no. 309.

163 Whichever concept of identity is adopted, whether it is the legal identity of the offence for which the person is being prosecuted, or the material identity, i.e. the litigious conduct on which the trial is based, it will not be the same facts that are judged. On this point, see S. FERNANDEZ, *Essai sur la distribution des compétences en droit pénal international*, *op. cit.*, nos. 656 et seq. and the references cited.

164 Case C-289/04, *Showa Denko KK*, ECLI:EU:C:2006:431, paras. 53–55. This example is reported by L. D'AVOUT, *L'entreprise et les conflits internationaux de lois*, *op. cit.*, no. 309.

165 Administrative composition, inspired by the United States (see A. GARAPON and P. SERVAN-SCHREIBER, *Deals de justice*, Quadrige, Paris, PUF, 2020), now has its equivalent in criminal law with the public interest judicial agreement, see Art. 41-1-2 of the Code of Criminal Procedure.

166 See in this respect the comment by Mr d'Avout following the paper by D. CHEMLA, 'Actualité et conséquences de l'extraterritorialité de la loi pénale française', *TCFDIP*, 2016–2018, pp. 85 et seq., spec. pp. 114–115.

167 In the same way, res judicata is used in the law of jurisdiction as a ground for refusing to enforce a foreign decision in order to preserve the French internal order.

by the offending conduct. As a result, prosecution by a foreign administrative authority should not constitute an obstacle to punishment in France. Under these conditions, the existence of a prosecution in France should not constitute a reason for refusing to cooperate. As regards administrative mutual assistance, the existence in France of a final criminal judgment should not be an obstacle to French cooperation in proceedings taking place abroad. This is all the more important as the local administrative investigation will often be decisive in establishing proof of the offence. This was the case in *Ubisoft*, where the evidence gathered by the Canadian authority was the only one capable of proving insider dealing in an instrument admitted to trading on a French regulated market.[168] Moreover, the lack of cooperation does not constitute an obstacle to local administrative proceedings. So why allow a request for cooperation to be resisted on the grounds of *lis pendens* or *res judicata*, when it is considered that it will be possible for the requested legal system to judge the offence again?

C. Proposed Solutions

550. The above observations lead us to restrict refusals to cooperate, in particular by ruling out those based on a form of lis pendens or res judicata, associated with a refusal to recognise, as a matter of principle, the foreign criminal judgment. Such a refusal would not be tantamount to ignoring the foreign judgment: firstly, because of the principle of discretionary prosecution, which would allow the public prosecutor not to prosecute an offence for which a satisfactory response has been received abroad[169] and, secondly, in the case of effective prosecution when a judgment has already been handed down abroad, by taking into account the sentence imposed abroad. This solution is in line with that of the Criminal Division (*chambre criminelle*) of the Court of Cassation, according to which the provisions 'which preclude dual prosecutions for a single offence are only applicable where the two proceedings have been initiated in the territory of the same State'.[170] As Mr d'Avout writes, this position, which 'excludes neither international cooperation at the prosecution stage nor the taking into account of foreign sanctions previously applied, avoids encouraging forum shopping for the purpose of purging offences, with the person exposed to multiple prosecutions "confessing" the offence in the country of his choice, with the assurance of

---

[168] CA Paris, 29 June 2017, no. 17/02898, on this judgment see L. d'Avout, " 'Ubisoft: sursis à statuer pour cause de connexité internationale', *op. cit.*; see also AMF, comm. sanct., 28 September 2012, J.-M. Moulin, 'La coopération de diverses autorités de marché nationales permettant la poursuite et la sanction d'un manquement d'initié', *BJB*, January 2013, p. 13.

[169] However, this argument could be tempered by the filing of a civil action.

[170] Crim., 14 March 2018, no. 16-82.117, *D.*, 2018, 618; *AJ pénal* 2018. 254 obs. P. de Combles de Nayves, *Rev. Sociétés*, 2018, 459 note J.-H. Robert; *D.*, 2018, 1934, obs. L. d'Avout

being immune from sanctions everywhere else [...]'.[171] What emerges here is an effective method of coordination between authorities, well known in private international law, 'the taking into consideration' (*méthode de la prise en considération*).

551. In this case, the foreign penalty will be taken into account in the form of an imputation, i.e. by deducting the penalty imposed by the foreign decision from the penalty that it intends to impose on the investor. The object of the imputation is therefore not the foreign standard, but the concrete situation in which the litigant who is the subject of the consideration is placed. In other words, the local authority takes into consideration the foreign decision – the sentence already served abroad – in order to establish the French sentence.[172] Imputation may also be used to temper the effects of dual prosecution for both administrative and criminal offences.[173] This is a technique well known to administrative law when faced with tax law and the double taxation phenomena that it gives rise to.[174]

---

171 L. d'Avout, obs. cited above under Crim., 14 March 2018.

172 It does not seem to us that this is an autonomous 'method', but simply a variety of consideration (*comp.* I. Stibbe, *Les autorités administratives indépendantes et le droit du commerce international*, *op. cit.*, nos. 411 et seq. who considers that the method is irreducible to all the others). Admittedly, the authority may be obliged to take this pronouncement into consideration, but it is sovereign in its assessment of the foreign decision, which appears only as a factual element to be taken into account by the local authority.

173 D. Rebut, *Droit pénal international*, *op. cit.*, no. 754. In international cases, convictions may be taken into consideration on the basis of Art. 132-24, para. 1 of the Criminal Code, relating to the judge's power to set the sentence on the basis of the offender's personality. In European cases, the court is obliged to take account of convictions (Art. 132-23-1 of the Criminal Code), but this only applies to the facts of the case, not to their classification, which is a matter for the French courts to determine in accordance with French law (Art. 132-23-2 of the Criminal Code, and D. Rebut, *Droit pénal international*, *op. cit.*, no. 758).

174 In order to prevent the same income from being taxed twice in both the source State and the State of residence, States enter into tax treaties, the purpose of which is to coordinate the scope of taxation and harmonise the criteria giving rise to taxation. The rules thus established enable each State to limit the exercise of its jurisdiction (see A. Kallergis, *La compétence fiscale*, *op. cit.*, nos. 328–352). In other words, international tax law proceeds essentially by way of self-limitation of local law through the conclusion of international conventions dividing the tax according to the State of residence and the State of source (it will come as no surprise that these conventions include a large proportion of undertakings by States to *exempt* certain income from taxation where this has taken place abroad, see 'Impôt' in C. David and G. Gest, *Répertoire de droit international*, Paris, Dalloz, no. 39; A. Kallergis, *La compétence fiscale*, *op. cit.*, no. 372). However, in addition to limitation, tax law also uses the tax credit technique, also known as the imputation method (see 'Impôt' in C. David and G. Gest, *Répertoire de droit international*, *op. cit.*, no. 39). This is where the withholding tax applied by the State of origin of the income enables a tax to be collected in the event that the beneficiary does not declare the said income to his State of residence. The withholding tax constitutes a tax credit which is deducted from the tax payable by the beneficiary in his State of residence. This avoids both fraud and double taxation.

552. Imputation also makes it possible to distinguish, from an international perspective, between exemption and exoneration. Where exemption constitutes a self-limitation of the applicable law, exoneration results from the application of the law, but constitutes for the private person a discharge of the obligation normally due by reason of the factual circumstances present. In this case, the foreign tax ruling taken into consideration as a fact may result in a total exemption from the tax normally due. Similarly, the exoneration will be partial, or even total, for an investor who has already served his sentence abroad. Strictly speaking, however, there is no exemption: the law remains applicable and has been applied. This characteristic of exoneration is in fact a consequence of the method of taking into consideration. Indeed, imputation acts here in the same way as the taking into consideration of a foreign overriding mandatory rule, which may represent a ground of exoneration (force majeure) of a debtor who has refused to perform a contract.[175] Admittedly, the porosity in certain cases between the taking into account of a foreign rule and its actual application has been emphasised, with the two sometimes leading to the same result.[176] However, cases of imputation clearly highlight the applicability of the local law[177] in that, once it has exhausted the effect given to the foreign decision, the law of the forum will extend the sanction according to its own canons. In criminal matters, imputation has the advantage above all of tempering the disadvantages of the absence of the *ne bis in idem* principle in international relations, whether the punishment is administrative or criminal,[178] in order to administer a punishment proportionate to the transgression observed.

553. The solution proposed here makes it possible to formulate a comment on the conflict of laws solutions used by administrative authorities. It has

175 S. Bollée, 'La prise en considération des lois de polices étrangères dans le Règlement Rome I', *op. cit.*, no. 4.

176 *Ibid*, nos. 8 et seq.

177 This point was not lost on Mr Bollée in the context of his study, who simply observed that in certain cases relating to contractual disputes, even if the *lex contractus* retained its authority, the result was the same, whether the foreign mandatory rules were simply taken into account or applied (*ibid.*, no. 12).

178 The imputation no doubt accounts for what has been described as the reconciliation of laws (see in particular P. Glenn, 'La conciliation des lois', *RCADI*, vol. 364, The Hague, Martinus Nijhoff, 2011). Mrs Stibbe has already written along these lines: 'Conciliation is possible by agreeing to give effect to the decision of the foreign authority first spetitionedfor the same situation. The imputation method responds to a concern for coordination of legal systems which contributes to the international effectiveness of control decisions emanating from the originating authority.' I. Stibbe, *Les autorités administratives indépendantes et le droit du commerce international*, *op. cit.*, no. 401; on this question see also E. Fohrer-Dedeurwaerder, *La prise en considération des normes étrangères*, Paris, LGDJ, 2008, p. 308 on the taking into consideration of foreign repressive decisions. However, the reconciliation of laws is only possible in a matter where the conflict of laws takes the form of an accumulation of applicable laws, and not of a competition requiring the selection of a single law.

already been observed that authorities do not hesitate to use self-limitation in order to coordinate with other authorities.[179] Along with others,[180] it should be added here that consideration is another technique of choice for limiting the shortcomings of unilateralism. These two mechanisms make it possible to temper the disadvantages inherent in the two peculiarities of administrative authorities when they are confronted with the coordination of legal orders: the unilateral formulation of the scope of the rules they apply, combined with an administrative jurisdiction based on an avatar of *forum legis*. These techniques are all the more useful in that they appear to be specially adapted to the cumulation of applicable rules, a frequent situation when administrative law is applied in cross-border relations. Finally, these techniques make it possible to observe that while administrative (and criminal) law is resistant to the bilateral conflict of laws rule, the forum is not indifferent to the application of a foreign administrative or criminal law.[181] These observations also confirm the function of 'taking into consideration' (*méthode de la prise en considération*). Some authors see it as a relaxation of the conflict rule, the mechanics of which would not be able to take account of the complexity of the international law relationship.[182] This is why 'taking into consideration' (*méthode de la prise en considération*) has been presented as a 'legal technique for achieving substantive justice within the justice of conflicts'.[183]

II. International Conditions for Cooperation

554. Agreements with third countries and EU law. In principle, each authority has the power to enter into bilateral cooperation agreements with third country authorities.[184] However, an authority proposing to enter into such an agreement must notify ESMA, and the cooperation agreement should, if possible, be a

---

179 See, in particular, as regards market infrastructure, *supra*, para. 221 and marketing obligations *supra*, para. 360; 372.

180 L. d'Avout, '«L'Entreprise et les conflits internationaux de lois', *op. cit.*, nos. 317 et seq.

181 From the point of view of criminal law, see the explanations given by C. Lombois, *Droit pénal international*, *op. cit.*, nos. 10 et seq. and, more recently, but along the same lines, D. Rebut, *Droit pénal international*, *op. cit.*, no. 28. For a critique of this state of affairs, and the proposal to reason here in the terms of private international law, see, already, H. Donnedieu de Vabres, *Les principes modernes de droit pénal international*, *op. cit.*, no. 173 and Lombois's critique (note 11, p. 25 of the above-mentioned textbook).

182 E. Fohrer-Dedeurwaerder, *La prise en considération des normes étrangères*, *op. cit.*, no. 1.

183 H. Muir Watt, 'Droit public et droit privé dans les rapports internationaux (vers la publicisation des conflits de lois?)', *Archives de philosophie du* droit, 1997, p. 207; E. Fohrer-Dedeurwaerder, *La prise en considération des normes étrangères*, *op. cit.*, no. 11 and nos. 31 et seq.

184 Art. 26(1°) of the Market Abuse Regulation. In fact, in France cooperation can even take place informally and without an agreement, see on the AMF's right to cooperate outside the agreements and procedures provided for in Arts. L. 632-7 and L. 632-16 of the Monetary and Financial Code, see Cass. com., 2 October 2019, no. 17-28462, *BJB*, January 2020, p. 13,

standard document drawn up by ESMA.[185] It would therefore be up to the competent authority to report on the reasons why it has departed from ESMA's recommendations. Furthermore, agreements may only be entered into insofar as 'the information disclosed is covered by guarantees of professional secrecy at least equivalent to those provided for' by the Market Abuse Regulation.[186] In practice, this means that the EU checks the agreements concluded with third countries. Nevertheless, before the adoption of these European mechanisms, the AMF was already a signatory to a significant number of bilateral agreements,[187] and was able to make use of informal administrative cooperation.[188] In addition, the AMF is a signatory to the multilateral agreement of the International Organisation of Securities Commissions.[189]

555. The IOSCO multilateral agreement. The International Organisation of Securities Commissions (IOSCO) is an international institution with legal personality that promotes both standard-setting principles for the regulation of financial markets and instruments for cooperation between administrative authorities. IOSCO is unique in that its membership is conditional on the signing of a multilateral agreement on consultation, cooperation and the exchange of information.[190] Accession to this agreement does not render bilateral agreements obsolete, since the latter often enable closer cooperation.[191] It could no doubt be argued that the agreement's lack of binding force deprives it of any relevance.[192]

note M. Galland; see also on this judgment A.-C Rouaud, 'Efficacité de la coopération et protection des droits de la défense', special issue, *Banque et Droit*, February 2020, pp. 58 et seq., spec. pp. 59–60.

185 Art. 26(1°) para. 2 and (2°) of the Market Abuse Regulation.

186 Art. 26, 3° of the Market Abuse Regulation.

187 Available on the authority's website.

188 On which see P.-H. Conac, *La régulation des marchés boursiers par la Commission des opérations de bourse (COB) et la Securities and exchange commission (SEC)*, *op. cit.*, nos. 412 et seq.

189 R. Bismuth, *La coopération internationale des autorités de régulation du secteur financier et le droit international public*, *op. cit.*, nos. 357 et seq.

190 For the history of this agreement, see *ibid.*, no. 611.

191 P.-H. Conac, *La régulation des marchés boursiers par la commission des opérations de bourse (COB) et la securities and exchange commission (SEC)*, *op. cit.*, no. 435; A. Tenenbaum, 'À propos des abus de marché et de la coopération au sein de l'Organisation internationale des commissions de valeurs mobilières', *Banque & Droit*, no. July-August 2015, no. 162, and, by the same author, *L'application internationale du droit boursier*, *op. cit.*, pp. 654 et seq.

192 Art. 6(a) of the IOSCO Multilateral Agreement: 'The purpose of the provisions of this Agreement is not to create legally binding obligations or to supersede national laws.' This type of provision is nevertheless common in this type of agreement, and does not mean that it is devoid of legal value, see R. Bismuth, *La coopération internationale des autorités de régulation du secteur financier et le droit international public*, *op. cit.*, nos. 309–310. On this question, see also M. Audit, *Les conventions transnationales entre personnes publiques*, Paris, LGDJ, 2001, nos. 220 et seq., and P.-H. Conac, *La régulation des marchés boursiers par la commission des opérations de bourse (COB) et la securities and exchange commission (SEC)*, *op. cit.*, no. 458. The author likens these agreements to those reached in tax matters (*ibid.*, no. 460).

Yet the agreement is curiously effective, for several reasons. On the one hand, taking note of the weak imperative nature of agreements between authorities, the IOSCO agreement requires its provisions to be incorporated into national legislation in order to give it a binding force that it would otherwise lack. In other words, in order to be able to adhere to the prerogatives offered by the multilateral agreement, one must first undertake to respect it; its violation would lead to exclusion from the IOSCO. Secondly, the strength of the agreement lies in the fact that, in order to become a member, the applicant authority must first demonstrate its ability to exchange information with third-party authorities.[193]

556. The conditions for cooperation in the IOSCO agreement. The multilateral agreement nevertheless lays down conditions for cooperation. In particular, cooperation may be refused in four circumstances: if the request would oblige the requested authority to act in violation of its national legislation, if the request is not made in accordance with the provisions of the agreement, on grounds of public interest or essential national interest and, finally, on grounds of prior prosecution or conviction in the legal system of the requested authority.[194] The grounds for refusing cooperation are similar to those already examined in the European context. However, with regard to the last ground for refusal, a limit is set in the case:

> 'Where a criminal proceeding has already been initiated in the jurisdiction of the Requested Authority based upon the same facts and against the same Persons, or the same Persons have already been the subject of final punitive sanctions on the same charges by the competent authorities of the jurisdiction of the Requested Authority, unless the Requesting Authority can demonstrate that the relief or sanctions sought in any proceedings initiated by the Requesting Authority would not be of the same nature or duplicative of any relief or sanctions obtained in the jurisdiction of the Requested Authority.'[195]

This provision is useful. Both *res judicata* and the *ne bis in idem* principle are based on the *identity* of the allegations in question and of the parties to the dispute. The clarification added by IOSCO therefore makes it possible to limit the scope of these principles to material identity,[196] while offering a favourable evidentiary regime to persons prosecuted for a second breach.

---

193 This is at least the perception of the French regulator, see B. de Juvigny and F. Buisson, 'La coopération internationale entre régulateurs de marchés financiers', 'Annales des Mines - Réalités industrielles', 2015/1 February 2015, pp. 43 et seq., spec. p. 46.

194 Art. 6(e) of the IOSCO Multilateral Agreement.

195 Art. 6(e)(ii) of the IOSCO Multilateral Agreement.

196 See *supra*, no. 550.

§ 2. THE COOPERATION SYSTEM

557. Once cooperation has been accepted, it should be subject to an identical regime in European and international matters. However, there is a special feature in European matters. If the requested authority fails to act, the cooperation regime allows the requesting authority to refer the matter to ESMA which, if conciliation between authorities fails, can intervene directly.[197] Similarly, in the event of a cross-border investigation, ESMA can be called upon by the authorities to coordinate the investigation. These provisions are particularly welcome, as they show that the jurisdiction of the federal regulator is subject to the request of the national authorities, and can only be triggered once it has been established that national cooperation has failed.[198] Furthermore, the law applicable to cooperation (I) and the possible legal remedies (II) should not vary according to whether the cooperation is intra-European or international.

I. The Law Applicable to Cooperation

558. Cooperation mechanisms. In the field of market abuse,[199] the substance of cooperation is of three distinct types: the request for information between authorities,[200] the coordination of investigations when market abuse is committed on the territory of several Member States[201] and, finally, assistance with investigations.[202] The implementation of this last possibility will vary greatly depending on the requested authorities, which may, at their discretion, carry out the on-site inspection or investigation themselves,[203] or authorise the authority that submitted the request to participate in/carry out the on-site inspection or investigation itself,[204] or even instruct 'auditors or experts to carry

197 Art. 25(7) of the Market Abuse Regulation refers to Art. 19 of the ESMA Regulation. This latter art. allows ESMA to intervene directly if conciliation fails, see Art. 19(3°) of Regulation 1095/2010.

198 See our comments *supra*, para. 170.

199 Administrative cooperation between authorities is likely to vary quite widely depending on the sectors and models adopted, see L. d'Avout, *L'entreprise et les conflits internationaux de lois*, *op. cit.*, nos. 299 et seq., spec. nos. 303 (elements common to specialised international mutual assistance networks) and 304 (the forms that mutual assistance may take).

200 Art. 25(1) and (4) of the Market Abuse Regulation.

201 Art. 25(5) of the Market Abuse Regulation.

202 Art. 25(6) of the Market Abuse Regulation.

203 Art. 25(6)(a) of the Market Abuse Regulation.

204 Art. 25(6)(b) and (c) of the Market Abuse Regulation. France has chosen the maximalist option, allowing the *Autorité des Marchés Financiers* and the *Autorité de Contrôle Prudentiel et de Résolution* to go so far as to authorise the foreign authority to carry out an investigation or on-site inspection, see Art. L. 632-3 of the Monetary and Financial Code. This solution appears to be new, as Mr Conac observed: 'The procedures provided for in the agreements concluded by the *SEC* reflect a greater openness on the part of foreign authorities towards the SEC. On the contrary, in the case of agreements concluded by the COB, the applicable procedures reflect a lesser degree of cooperation. In fact, many agreements provide that *SEC*

out the on-site action or investigation'.[205] These last aspects, undoubtedly the most remarkable, merit attention in order to determine the law applicable to cooperation and, more specifically, to the resulting investigation and liability.

559. The applicable law. Determining the applicable law in the first case, where the requested authority carries out investigations at the request of another, can perhaps be resolved by analogy. In the related field of competition law, the Cour de cassation has been able to affirm the application of the law of the requested authority to an investigation carried out on its territory at the request of a foreign authority.[206] The *Cour de Cassation* has affirmed an identical solution for acts of investigation in the context of the implementation of the IOSCO cooperation agreement with the UK authority.[207] The actions of auditors and experts should also be subject to the law of the requested authority, since they act only on the basis of a delegation of administrative powers. They will therefore be subject to the provisions of local law and, in particular, may not have more prerogatives than the authority that appointed them. As far as the foreign authority authorised to take part in the on-site inspection or investigation is concerned, it is placed in a passive role and collects the information and evidence gathered by the local authority. This is why the law applicable to the status of the documents resulting from the investigation should be that of the legal system of the requested

agents may participate in procedures that take place abroad, whereas in France the COB has traditionally been reserved about the participation of agents of foreign authorities in information-gathering procedures.' (P.-H. Conac, *La régulation des marchés boursiers par la commission des opérations de bourse [COB] et la securities and exchange commission [SEC]*, *op. cit.*, no. 445).

205 Art. 25(6)(e) of the Market Abuse Regulation.

206 In competition matters, Council Regulation (EC) No 1/2003 of 16 December 2002 on the implementation of the rules on competition (hereinafter the Competition Mutual Assistance Regulation) established a European network for international mutual assistance while providing for procedures similar to those provided for in the Market Abuse Regulation, see e.g. Art. 22 of the Mutual Assistance Regulation: 'A competition authority of a Member State may carry out on its territory any inspection or other investigative measure under its national law on behalf of and for the account of the competition authority of another Member State in order to establish an infringement of Article 81 or 82 of the Treaty.' Admittedly, the wording is distinct, but it amounts to carrying out an inspection or an investigation at the request of a competent authority of another Member State. It is on the basis of this article that the Court of Cassation has had the opportunity to state that 'a competition authority that agrees to carry out an investigative measure on its territory does so by applying its national law and not that of the country of the requesting authority in the name and on behalf of which the measure is carried out', see Cass. com., 20 January 2015, nos. 13-16745, 13-16764, 13-16765 and 13-16966, *RCDIP*, 2016, p. 521 and the note by L. d'Avout. This formulation is in line with the older principles in force with regard to cooperation in criminal matters (see, in the absence of an international agreement, the principle formulated by Cass. civ. 1re, 22 May 2007, *RCDIP*, 2008, p. 278, note D. Foussard).

207 Cass. com., 1 March 2017, no. 14-26.225, *Rev. soc.*, 2017, 365, note E. Dezeuze.

authority. On the other hand, the foreign authority authorised to carry out the on-site inspection or investigation presents a definite originality.[208]

560. The special case of the foreign authority authorised to carry out the on-site inspection or investigation. From an international point of view, this possibility raises the question of the law applicable to the inspection and investigation: is it the law of the requesting authority, authorised by the requested authority to carry out the inspection itself, or the law of the place of investigation?[209] There are two possible reasons for applying local law. On the one hand, the foreign authority cannot have prerogatives that the authority that authorised it to act would not have, and on the other hand, the requested State has exclusive normative competence in matters of coercive acts. On reflection, however, none of these arguments is convincing. The foreign authority is not acting on behalf of the local authority, but on the instructions of its own legal system.[210] The legitimacy of the requesting authority's action, and its basis, does not lie in a norm – rule or decision – of the domestic country, but in its country of origin. In other words, administrative authorisation does not entail, in a causal manner, the application of the law of the authority of the requested State to the inspection or investigation of the foreign authority; at most, it may be considered that it is

---

208 Nevertheless, the procedure is not unknown in positive law, nor is it specific to European law, nor is it even recent: see Art. 19 of the Hague Convention of 18 March 1970. On the limits of this convention for certain foreign authorities, in particular the SEC, see P.-H. Conac, *La régulation des marchés boursiers par la Commission des opérations de bourse (COB) et la Securities and exchange commission (SEC)*, *op. cit.*, no. 399. See also, in relation to the stock market itself, Art. 4, entitled 'Cross-border visit' of the memorandum of understanding concerning consultation, cooperation and exchange of information relating to the supervision of covered entities in the asset management industry between the Securities and Exchange Commission of the United States of America (SEC, United States of America) and the *Autorité des marchés financiers* (AMF, France), *JORF*, no. 0219 of 22 September 2015, text no. 68. As Mr d'Avout wrote, *Sur les solutions du conflit de lois en droit des biens*, *op. cit.*, no. 164, on the basis of the State's territorial monopoly of enforcement operations: 'Enforcement procedures constitute a public service that is in principle necessary for the maintenance of good internal order, which does not mean that a State cannot delegate its management from time to time, under its control, to private actors, or even to foreign public bodies (in which case there would be genuine extraterritoriality), which would be empowered to carry out this or that act of material coercion that does not call into question the integrity of the State on whose territory the measure is to be enforced.'

209 However, a clear distinction must be drawn here between the law applicable to the investigation and the law applicable to the authority: the foregoing discussion refers only to the law applicable to the investigation, not to the question of the law applicable to liability, which is governed by other considerations.

210 The representation argument is reminiscent of that used by the realist doctrine in international criminal law with regard to '*compétence réelle*' exercised in order to protect the interests of third States, see H. Donnedieu de Vabres, *Les principes modernes de droit pénal international*, *op. cit.*, pp. 110 et seq. for the presentation, and pp. 126 et seq. for the critical examination, in particular because of the difficulty of determining the legal cause of 'representation'.
The situation of the foreign authority is therefore distinct from that of the experts, who act by delegation from the authority; in the latter case there is a genuine form of empowerment.

likely to apply to the material scope of the permission given, and therefore to the field in which the foreign authority may operate.

Secondly, the rule of public international law in question would be disfigured if it were to be interpreted as a rule prohibiting the requested State from consenting to the application of foreign rules to the procedure followed by a foreign authority on its own territory.[211] Basically, as Professor Combacau writes, the international sovereignty of the State is a freedom 'which the State has to do what is in its power',[212] which includes the power to authorise a foreign authority to carry out investigative measures on its territory.[213] Such an affirmation nevertheless makes it necessary to ensure that the freedom does not turn against itself, and that international power relations do not render the consent of the requested State illusory.[214]

561. In the end, it seems to us that the application of local law should prevail, but for reasons specific to private international law.[215] Administrative investigation and inspection measures, which are intrusive for defendants, make it necessary to protect them.[216] The law of the place where the investigation or

---

211 On this question, which is related to the question of the self-limitation of the State, and the legal freedom of the sovereign, see J. Combacau and S. Sur, *Droit international public*, Paris, Montchrestien, 10th ed., 2012, pp. 254 et seq., spec. p. 263: 'The principle is for the State to have the power to act within the limits of the residual freedom that it has reserved for itself by not self-limiting all its primitive freedom.' Some authors then speak of a 'certain "abdicative capacity" (which) may be recognised in a State that possesses both freedom in the exercise of competences and freedom to renounce the free exercise of its competences', S. Fernandez, *Essai sur la distribution des compétences en droit pénal international, op. cit.*, no. 31 (the author refers to the thesis by C. Castella, *Souveraineté et pouvoir de punir*, thesis, Université Toulouse I, 2009, nos. 18 and 19).

212 J. Combacau, 'Pas une puissance: une liberté: la souveraineté internationale de l'État', *Pouvoirs*, no. November 1995, no. 67, *La Souveraineté*, p. 51; from the point of view of criminal sovereignty, see S. Fernandez, *Essai sur la distribution des compétences en droit pénal international, op. cit.*, no. 31; from the point of view of international law, A. Pellet, 'Lotus que de sottise on profère en ton nom! Remarques sur le concept de souveraineté dans la jurisprudence de la Cour mondiale' in *Mélange en l'honneur de J.-P. Puissochet*, Paris, Pedone, 2008, p. 216.

213 See L. d'Avout, *Sur les solutions du conflit de lois en droit des biens, op. cit.*, no. 165, on the basis of the State's territorial monopoly of operations of material coercion: 'The sole function of the prohibitive rule of international law is to protect the interests of the State concerned, which is free to waive it and to allow, by courtesy or by treaty obligation, the intrusion of foreign State bodies into its territory to carry out a material activity.'

214 What would then occur in international matters would be a phenomenon already circumscribed in domestic law, on which see M. Fabre-Magnan, *L'institution de la liberté*, Paris, PUF, 2018, pp. 109 et seq.

215 Comp. L. d'Avout, *L'entreprise et les conflits internationaux de lois, op. cit.*, no. 305. The author seems to take the view that the power of direct extraterritorial enforcement by the authority of origin would be subject to the law of the legal system of origin, which would eliminate the problem of the multiplication of procedural laws.

216 See, in this regard, L. d'Avout, 'De l'entraide judiciaire internationale au contentieux civil intégré', *op. cit.*, no. 9: 'It is much more, it seems, the concern for good order in international private relations, and particularly the requirement to protect the person concerned by the measure, which explains the predominance of the point of view of the requested State.'

inspection takes place seems best able to protect them, not only because it is the law with which they are most familiar, but also because it is the most predictable for them. Added to this are the benefits of the correlation of *forum* and *jus* in a matter that can be marked by urgency.[217] This solution, adopted in the context of bilateral protocols in application of the IOSCO multilateral convention,[218] is also the one adopted in the context of non-extradition mutual legal assistance under international criminal law,[219] itself influenced by European law.[220] These developments are reinforced by international conventions. For example, the IOSCO agreement subjects the gathering of documents requested under the agreement 'to the procedures in force in the jurisdiction of the requested

217 One example is the difficulty of initiating summary proceedings on the basis of foreign law. Here, the geographical and cultural proximity of the judge is a determining factor.

218 See Art. 4(b) ('Cross-border visits') of the aforementioned protocol between the AMF and the SEC. If the foreign authority cooperates with the local authority, it is in particular to ensure that its conduct complies with local laws and regulations.

219 See, for example, Art. 10(1) of the Convention of 10 December 1998 with the United States: 'The requested State shall comply with the request to search, seize and hand over to the requesting State any object if the request contains information justifying the search under the law of the requested State.' (See in the same sense Art. 14(1) of the Convention of 14 January 1993 with Australia, or Art. 5(4) of the Convention of 15 December 1989 with Canada). In other words, as Mr Rebut writes, the taking of evidence 'can only be carried out in accordance with the fundamental rights and freedoms of the requested State' (D. Rebut, *Droit pénal international*, *op. cit.*, no. 449).

220 The field of investigative acts is the subject of Directive 2014/41/EU on investigative decisions in criminal matters, which is intended to 'apply to all investigative measures aimed at gathering evidence' (Recital 8 and Art. 3 of the aforementioned Directive).
However, the application of the law of investigation or inspection is not universal. For example, European personal data law, subject to the agreement of the originating authority, allows the requesting authority to carry out investigations itself, in application of its own law, on the territory of the requested authority (although the rule is not crystal clear, see Art. 62(3) and (4) of the RGPD). In financial matters, the American administrative authority has managed to apply its own law in an exceptional manner. In the event of misrepresentation, the SEC can ask a federal prosecutor to initiate criminal proceedings for perjury, as the territorial scope of this offence is not limited to the United States. Although this threat is theoretical, in practice it acts as a strong deterrent, as the persons charged would no longer be able to gain access to the United States, which would be very detrimental to them as financial intermediaries or bankers. On this issue, see P.-H. Conac, *La régulation des marchés boursiers par la commission des opérations de bourse (COB) et la securities and exchange commission (SEC)*, *op. cit.*, no. 446. According to Mr Conac, this is less a question of procedural imperialism than of a desire to obtain the sincere cooperation of persons interviewed under foreign law. The author notes in this regard that many agreements signed by the SEC provide that the privileges recognised exclusively by the law of the State of the requesting authority may be invoked by the person being heard. Such a provision is very protective because of the protection offered by the US Constitution against self-incrimination. However, the law applicable to the authority's liability is always the law of the requested authority: there is an indissoluble link between the authorisation of these measures and the resulting liability.

Authority'.[221] A particular feature of this agreement is that it can be supplemented by bilateral protocols between authorities that are members of the multilateral agreement, which make it possible to specify and supplement cooperation, often following the same model as that proposed.[222] For example, with regard to the status of evidence obtained, the general trend is for it to be subject to the law of the authority that obtained it; its subsequent use is therefore subject to this law.[223] In effect, this law governed the conditions under which the information was obtained: it should therefore govern its eventual dissemination, and in particular the restrictions to which such dissemination is subject. This includes both compliance with the purpose for which the information was provided, and the confidentiality to which the persons to whom the information is communicated are subject.[224]

II. Legal Remedies

562. Jurisdictional competence. The reasons of proximity justifying the application of local law to investigative measures also justify the jurisdiction of the court of the requested authority, irrespective of the person who carried out the investigation.[225] This priority given to the court of the place where the investigative acts were carried out is without prejudice to any possible appeal against the investigative measures within the requesting legal system, but nevertheless has a procedural consequence: the applicant should be precluded if he has not previously exercised this appeal at the place of the disputed investigation. This principle, which aims to concentrate litigation with the court best placed to rule on the infringement, is found in related areas such as

221 Art. 9(d) of the IOSCO Multilateral Agreement. This article has been the subject of litigation, marking the application of the law of the requested authority to proceedings carried out abroad, see Com., 1 March 2017, no. 14-26225.

222 See, for example, the aforementioned protocol between the AMF and the SEC allowing cross-border visits subject to the application of the law of the place of the investigation.

223 See Art. 6 of the aforementioned protocol between the AMF and the SEC, and Arts. 27(2) (in intra-European relations) and 29 (in relations with third countries) of the Market Abuse Regulation. If the reporting authority and the authority that obtained the evidence are separated, the applicable law should be that of the authority that obtained the evidence. As Mr d'Avout writes: 'It is possible to draw up a legal status for procedural documents. In principle, it is dictated by the law that governed the preparation of the document.' (note cited above, *RCDIP*, 2016, p. 532).

224 See on prudential matters, B. Stoeva, *La coopération entre les superviseurs financiers dans l'Union européenne*, *op. cit.*, nos. 187 et seq.

225 It seems to us that this perception can be supported by the *a contrario* interpretation of this statement by the Court of Cassation in the aforementioned judgment of the Commercial Chamber in anti-competitive matters: 'The authorisation and conduct of the investigation are governed by the national law applicable in the State to which the request for assistance is addressed, under the control of the competent courts of that State, and it is not for the French judge to authorise or control the conduct of investigative measures in territories other than its national territory.'

competition law[226] and insolvency law.[227] This principle is also explicitly found in the case law of the Court of Justice on the international jurisdiction of the European Union.[228] On the other hand, the court with jurisdiction to challenge the substantive reasons for issuing the investigative decision should be the court of the legal system that gave rise to the request. An identical solution has been adopted for judicial cooperation.[229] However, it seems to us that the court in the place where the investigation is taking place still has jurisdiction to assess whether the cooperation of the local administrative authority is justified, which will inevitably lead it to make an assessment of the purpose of the investigation.

563. Conclusion of the section. Co-operation is a necessity for the authorities responsible for supervising professionals in the sector and punishing market abuse. The function of repression is to punish the perpetrator and repair the damage to the social organism. It should be possible for this function to be exercised by each legal system which considers itself affected by the offending conduct, and cooperation should not therefore be restricted by a single objective of repression. The interests of the private individual can be safeguarded by a mechanism for taking account of foreign penalties, which is already familiar from criminal law. The system of administrative cooperation must be distinguished according to whether the applicable law or the competent jurisdiction is in question. Both the investigation and the status of the document it enables to be gathered should be subject solely to the law of the requested authority. This law will therefore apply to the conditions under which the document obtained may be communicated, and to the purposes to which its communication is subject. The court with jurisdiction to challenge

---

226 This is the case in anti-competitive matters (see *supra*, para. 561); on this question, and on the status of foreign procedural documents, see the thoughts of Mr d'Avout, in his aforementioned note under the judgment of the Commercial Chamber, *RCDIP*, 2016, spec. pp. 553 et seq.

227 In the area of insolvency, the Court of Justice has held, on the basis of European Regulation 1346/2000 on insolvency proceedings, that 'if an interested party, considering that the centre of the debtor's main interests is in a Member State other than that in which the main insolvency proceedings were opened, intends to challenge the jurisdiction assumed by the court which opened those proceedings, it is for that party to avail itself, before the courts of the Member State in which those proceedings were opened, of the remedies provided for by the national law of that Member State against the decision to open those proceedings' (Case C-341-04, *Eurofood*, ECLI:EU:C:2006:281, para. 43); the Cour de cassation has echoed this decision, see Cass. com, 27 June 2006, no. 03-19.863, *Bull. civ.*, IV, no. 149 (*Daisytek*).

228 Under the Brussels I Regulation, it is as if an infringement of Union law could not be relied on as an exception to the recognition of a judgment given by another Member State if local judicial remedies allowing the judgment at issue to be set aside had not been exhausted: Case C-681/13, *Diageo Brands BV v. Simiramida-04 EOOD*, ECLI:EU:C:2015:471, *JCP* 2015, p. 1426, note D. B. in this sense.

229 See e.g. Art. 14 of the aforementioned Directive 2014/41 on the criminal investigation order: 'The substantive grounds on which the European investigation order was issued may be challenged only by an action brought in the issuing State, without prejudice to the guarantees of fundamental rights in the executing State.'

the substantive grounds for the investigation will be that of the authority that made the request, but the court at the place of the investigation will retain jurisdiction to assess the merits of the local cooperation decision. These observations lead us to see many analogies with judicial cooperation in the international system of administrative cooperation. Nevertheless, should we be surprised that administrative cooperation borrows from the regime of the institution it replaces?

564. Conclusion of the chapter. Market abuse is a set of offences by which the legal system punishes behaviour that undermines the operation of financial markets and the confidence that investors may have in them. It is therefore logical that the criterion of jurisdiction should be based on damage to the local financial market. It has been shown that this criterion would benefit from the elimination of the criterion of the commission of the acts constituting the offence in the territory: the internationalisation and dematerialisation of the markets make it possible that these acts constituting the offence never take place in the territory where the financial market is located, and therefore make the exercise of territorial jurisdiction artificial. It would be better to retain the '*compétence réelle*': the *entity* affected is the French trading platform, which is now an indispensable instrument for the pursuit of the State's legislative and economic policy. However, personal jurisdiction should not be ruled out. In the first place, because it makes it possible to prosecute market abuse committed by French nationals on other European financial markets, and because the regulation of market abuse aims to protect all financial markets whose operator is established on EU territory. What is more, the local authority will sometimes be in the best position to crack down on market abuse, notably because it is likely to have direct access to the disputed information, and the offences will have taken place on its territory. Nevertheless, it is desirable that the information obligations incumbent on operators and the authorities in order to detect market abuse should always be communicated to the authority of the place of listing. Secondly, personal jurisdiction appears to offset the principle of non-extradition of nationals, which is likely to prevent legitimate criminal prosecution of an abuse committed on the financial market of a third country.

These jurisdictional criteria highlight the need for the authorities to cooperate in order to combat market abuse. This cooperation is necessary in the same terms for the purposes of supervising professionals in the sector. Today, it is unduly conditional on criteria that pursue the objective of a single crackdown. It would benefit from being freed from this: in law enforcement matters, each State has a legitimate right to punish offences that have affected its legal system. The interests of private individuals will be protected by taking account of sentences already served abroad. From the point of view of the system of cooperation, the law applicable to the investigation and to the status of the resulting document should be that of the requested authority, since that is the authority that presided over the coercive acts and made it possible to obtain the document. If the substantive reasons for the investigation have to be challenged before the court of the requesting authority, the court of the place where the investigation took place will always be competent to verify the merits of the local authority's cooperation with the foreign procedure, which will inevitably lead it to assess the purpose of the procedure.

565. Conclusion of the title. The relationship between investors and financial markets is truly the domain of financial market law. It is applied here with the specific aim of ensuring that the system functions properly. There are three aspects to the application of financial market law.

Firstly, this law requires market members to obtain a special status, that of investment firm, or an equivalent status. Through this status, the law of the financial market obliges members to provide a set of information obligations to market managers to enable them to establish prices, and also requires them to execute the orders they receive on trading platforms. The law of the financial market does not disregard the relationship between members and their clients: although it no longer extends its jurisdiction to the contractual relationship between members and their clients, it nevertheless imposes rules of conduct on members to protect their clients regardless of their location.

Secondly, financial market law applies to market transactions. Its purpose is to govern the terms and conditions of issuer control, which has a direct impact on price formation and the artificial alteration of the price of instruments admitted to trading. For this reason, the listing venue should be given overall jurisdiction whenever oversight of the issuer is at stake, whether in the case of a threshold crossing or a takeover bid. In the first case, the crossing of a threshold is subject to both the *lex societatis* and the *lex mercatus*, since it serves the dual purpose of informing the corporate bodies and protecting the operation of the market. In the second case, the jurisdiction of the *lex societatis* should be rejected, quite simply because the objective of the law on takeover bids is not the functioning of the corporate bodies. The *lex societatis* only has incidental jurisdiction in this case, in that it determines, for example, the conditions for the increase in the offeror's capital that is often necessary for a public exchange offer. Arguments that seek to base the jurisdiction of the *lex societatis* on corporate sanctions must be rejected, not only because the sanction of a norm does not dictate its classification, but also because it is open to the legal system to have recourse to other sanctions in order to ensure compliance with it. In the same way, the legal system of the market has the possibility of instituting rules governing the behaviour of foreign corporate bodies during a takeover bid in order to dissuade disloyal behaviour on the part of directors. Finally, there is no doubt that the regulation of share buy-backs and short selling are subject to the law of the financial market in that they have a direct influence on the disclosure of the market price.

Thirdly, the law of the financial market applies to the repression of abuses committed on the financial markets that it institutes. As the objectives of this repression are to protect the European financial markets, the jurisdiction of the criminal law is first and foremost of a '*compétence réelle*', the *res* affected being the trading platform. Territorial jurisdiction, based on the place where the acts constituting the offence were committed, leads to artificial results because of the internationalisation and dematerialisation of the markets. However, this '*competence réelle*' would benefit from being supplemented by personal jurisdiction. On the one hand, this would enable the local authority to suppress abuses committed on other European financial markets and, on the other hand, to suppress those committed on foreign financial markets when the latter have equivalent legislation, the forum refusing to extradite its nationals or to deprive them of their liberty by virtue of a foreign decision. The repression of market abuse today makes the cooperation of the administrative authorities particularly necessary, as they are the spearhead of repression. Given that it is open to each State to crack down on behaviour that has affected the integrity of its legal system, this cooperation should not be conditional on the requirement of a single crackdown. The interests of private individuals will be protected by taking account of sentences already served abroad. From the point of view of the system of cooperation, the law applicable to the investigation and to the status of the resulting document should be that of the requested authority, since this is the authority that presided over the coercive acts and made it possible to obtain the document. If the substantive reasons for the investigation have to be challenged before the court of the requesting authority, the court of the place where the investigation took place will always have jurisdiction to verify the merits of the local authority's cooperation in the foreign proceedings, which will inevitably lead it to assess the purpose of the proceedings.

566. Conclusion of the part two. The study of the field of the law of the financial market has shown that the law of the financial market applies to distinct securities depending on whether its relationship with issuers or with investors is at issue.

When it applies to issuers, its function is essentially to protect investors; its jurisdiction is then that of the law of the place of solicitation. In these circumstances, it does not seek to remove the pre-eminence of the issuer's law over the issue of securities; at most, it imposes material requirements, compliance with which is a condition of admission to trading. It does, however, attach consequences to the *negotia* represented by the securities as soon as they have an impact on the control of the issuer, and may therefore affect the operation of the company, as well as any restructuring procedure. These two aspects, which are specific to the relationship between financial market law and the issue of securities, are those in which the objectives of market operation are added to those of investor protection. Traditionally, the law governing the financial market has exclusive jurisdiction over the marketing of foreign securities on its territory, the consequence of which is to impose disclosure requirements on the issuer. The pursuit of the objective of investor protection has an influence here on the international regime of these rules: they are likely to be self-limiting whenever the company's home regulations provide for equivalent protection. They should not, however, have the consequence of limiting the jurisdiction of the local authority which remains best placed to oversee this information. The information provided should be such as to give rise to liability on the part of the issuer. The characterisation of this liability is relatively contingent and will depend, on the one hand, on the beneficial ownership of the financial instrument by the claimant and, on the other hand, on the basis of the claim. If the liability action is contractual, the applicable law will be that of the contract, and the competent court will depend on the presence of a choice of court clause or the presence of a consumer. If the liability action is in tort or delict, the legal system of the place where the tort or delict occurred should be able to have global jurisdiction, where its residents have been called upon, in order to make good the damage they have suffered; this is not yet the case as the case law of the Court of Justice stands.

When applied to investors, the law of the financial market pursues the function for which it was instituted: the proper functioning of the market. In this sense, there is a *lex mercatus*, made up of rules relating to the operation of the financial market and governed by the law of the trading platform. This body of law consists first and foremost of the obligations incumbent on the market operator and its members to encourage trading and disclose prices; it does not, however, extend to contracts concluded between members and their clients. The protection of the latter is ensured by the rules of good conduct applicable to the professional status of members, irrespective of their membership status. Secondly, the *lex mercatus* comprises the regulation of market transactions, both those relating to the control of the issuer, i.e. the law on threshold crossings and public offers, and those designed to prevent artificial price distortion, such as the rules on share buybacks and short selling. All these rules should be subject solely to the law of the financial market, rather than to an inappropriate mix with the *lex societatis*. Thirdly, the *lex mercatus* consists of the prohibition of market abuse. These rules, on the borderline between the operation of the market and the suppression of criminal behaviour, are subject to criminal law. It has been argued that market abuse should be understood in the light of the '*compétence réelle*', and should be subject to it as soon as the French trading platform is affected. Alternatively, '*compétence réelle*' can be used where a European trading venue is troubled and the French authority is best placed to act. Market abuse is nonetheless subject to the inevitable interference of international criminal law, which makes it advisable, in certain residual cases, to apply local market abuse regulations to offences committed on foreign markets in order to avoid possible impunity for the French.

PART 3.

The Status of Financial Instruments

567. The preceding discussions have shown, in particular, how market infrastructures are connected to a legal order and how the law of the financial market is deployed by relying on the connecting factor of the trading platform. The following developments extend these reflections to the status of financial instruments. The influence of the law of the central depository and the clearing house on the proprietary status of financial securities and on the law applicable to financial contracts will be shown. This influence is independent of the financial market, simply because financial instruments can be provided independently of a financial market. The use of a financial market nevertheless implies the use of the services of the clearing house and the central depository as soon as a financial contract or the exchange of a security is concluded through a trading platform.

In the case of securities, the main difficulty today lies in the connecting factor to their proprietary effect. It will be shown that these difficulties, which have their roots in the thesis of the plurality of connections, should be resolved, both in the direct and indirect holding system, by a unitary solution of the conflict of laws. In the indirect holding system, this solution should be based on the connection of the securities settlement system itself (Title 1).

From the point of view of financial contracts, the law applicable to them sometimes suffers from uncertainty when purely domestic contracts or consumer contracts are involved. The difficulty facing the status of financial contracts is, however, less related to the determination of the *lex contractus* than to its reconciliation with the laws that affect the formation of the contract and its performance. It is in this latter respect that the law of the compensation system will most often extend its realm to the entire *lex contractus* (Title 2).

TITLE 1
THE CONNECTING FACTOR OF SECURITIES' PROPRIETARY STATUS

568. Double degree of regulation of property law. The status of securities, from a proprietary point of view, is often obscured by confusions arising from property law, which justify some remarks on the bias of the developments to come. We subscribe to this school of thought, which distinguishes between two levels of regulation stemming from property law, the first relating to ownership of property and the second, isolated within the first, concerning rights over tangible things.[1] This conception of property law, which considers that the 'proprietary status' of rights is independent of their content, has several consequences.

Firstly, there is a 'primary regime'[2] of property law, applicable irrespective of the content of the relevant objects. This primary regime can be determined by reference to the domain of the applicable law. This is mainly made up of the following questions[3]: the regime of its transfer; the opposability of this transfer to third parties; the constitution and effects of conventional and legal guarantees likely to have an impact on the thing; the conflicts of competing rights, also known as priority rights. These elements make it possible to emphasise the importance of the issue at hand. The choice made by the French legislator to favour, in matters of securities, the good faith purchaser[4] is not universal: priority conflicts are not necessarily resolved in favour of the purchaser and, even when this is the case, not necessarily under the same conditions. Above all, the scope of this law extends to all the guarantees which have an impact on the security: the validity and the terms of their enforcement depend on the proprietary status to which they are attached.

---

1. L. d'Avout, 'Biens' in *Répertoire de droit international, Dalloz*, 2008, no. 1; L. d'Avout, *Sur les solutions du conflit de lois en droit des biens*, Paris, Economica, 2006, no. 10; On this perception, see recently G. Sebban, *Le bien juridique*, thesis, Université Paris II Panthéon-Assas, 2020, nos. 10 et seq.
2. L. d'Avout, *Sur les solutions du conflit de lois en droit des biens*, *op. cit.*
3. See, in relation to financial securities, the enumeration of the field of their proprietary status by H. Synvet, 'Rapport sur un projet de règle de conflit de lois portant sur les titres financiers', p. 7. One could undoubtedly add to the field of the applicable law of the primary regime the possibility of dismembering the ownership of the right, and the regime of this dismemberment, it being observed that this possibility and this regime are both likely to vary according to the subject matter.
4. Art. L. 211-16 of the Monetary and Financial Code.

The reason for this is simple: the law of guarantee is a branch of property law, if only because their enforcement always requires a form of alienation. If the links between the law of guarantee and the law of property no longer need to be demonstrated,[5] the same applies to the links between the law of guarantee and the law of insolvency,[6] not to mention the fact that the usefulness of the guarantee ultimately derives from the means of enforcement that they open up to their holder.[7] As a result, it is not surprising that these different bodies of law may have an influence on the solution of the conflict of laws. This primary regime must nevertheless be understood strictly, since many aspects of the rights regime derive from the nature and structure of the property under consideration.[8] Very few are common to all appropriable assets. Two significant limits to the field of proprietary status can be noted. On the one hand, the characterisation of the right depends not on the proprietary status, but on the *lex creationis*, i.e. the law that presided over the creation of the right. This is the *lex rei sitae* for tangible things, the *lex contractus* for certain intangible things such as claims, or the *lex societatis* for shares. On the other hand, the law applicable to the proprietary status of the security does not, in principle, extend to the validity of the assignment contract. This contract is governed by the law designated by the Rome I Regulation.

Secondly, the proprietary status will not necessarily correspond to the content and nature of the prerogatives derived from the thing. This possible disjunction is not always apparent at first sight because of the too frequent reference to the law of tangible things alone. Indeed, the law applicable to rights *in rem* is derived from the law of location; this law extends to the entire proprietary status of tangible things. This is not the case with intangible things, whose prerogatives are most often determined by the *lex creatonis*. However, the latter will not necessarily extend to the entire proprietary status; at most, it may, in certain respects, shape it, for example by making the object created non-assignable. Thus, the contract for the issue of debt securities may prohibit the transfer of the securities issued.[9] However, the proprietary status of the

5 From a French perspetive, see C. Gijsbers, *Sûretés réelles et droit des biens*, Paris, Economica, 2015.

6 From a French perspetive, see C. Favre-Rochex, *Sûretés et procédures collectives*, Paris, LGDJ, 2020.

7 From a French perspetive, see C. Séjean-Chazal, *La réalisation de la sûreté*, Paris, Dalloz, 2019.

8 M. Fabre-Magnan, 'Propriété, patrimoine et lien social', *RTD civ.* 1997, vol. 3, p. 583, spec. no. 28, p. 606: 'In particular, one does not exercise one's right of ownership in the same way on tangible things and on intangible things and, this is why, since the essence of ownership is also found in the relationship to intangible things, it is vain to want to find a similarity between the two types of ownership, that is to say, between the two types of power, at all costs.' See also in this sense L. d'Avout, *Sur les solutions du conflit de lois en droit des biens*, *op. cit.*, no. 9.

9 See *supra*, para. 303.

debt security is not necessarily subject to the law of the contract of issuance. It is therefore necessary to distinguish between the primary jurisdiction of the legal system which gave rise to the asset in question, which may itself require dissociating the law of the issuer and the law of the *negotium*, and the secondary jurisdiction which may, insofar as the law of the issuer and the law of the *negotium* allow it, apply to the proprietary regime of the asset.

569. Location of things and location of rights.[10] Ownership of property can be determined differently within each legal order and therefore depends on the legal order in which one is located. A person may be the owner of a thing in one legal order and a third party to that thing in another. It is in the latter sense that some authors refer, from an international perspective, to the ubiquity of rights.[11] In the case of tangible things, the determination of the owner is often facilitated by the international acceptance of the conflict rule, which applies the law of its geographical location to the determination of the ownership of the thing. The latter then tends to impose the location of the right, either because of the confusion between the location of things and that of rights, or because of the fiction that the right is incorporated in the thing, or because of the force that can sometimes be attached to appearance. However, this solution does not seem to be transposable as such to the location of rights in intangible things which do not have an obvious geographical location.[12] In such cases, it is necessary to determine the legal order with which the relationship in question has greater *legal* proximity. However, this can be interpreted in different ways, and several places are likely to be connected with the legal relationship. As Professor Wengler wrote:

> 'It is sometimes the territory in which the enforcement of the subjective right normally takes place, sometimes the territory in which the authorities are prepared to sanction a violation of this right or to protect it, sometimes the territory of the most effective protection, sometimes the territory in which the authorities are able to act on the holder of the right as regards its exercise or assignment.'[13]

---

[10] This title, as well as this discussion, is inspired by Wengler's article, 'La situation des droits', *RCDIP*, 1957, 185.

[11] W. Wengler, 'La situation des droits', *op. cit.* F. Rigaux, 'Les situations juridiques individuelles dans un système de relativité générale', *op. cit.*, no. 24; in the same sense, see already G. de Vareilles Sommières, 'La définition et la notion juridique de la propriété', *RTD civ.*, 1905, pp. 443 et seq.

[12] As Wengler writes ('La situation des droits', *op. cit.*, p. 186): 'As is often the case with legal concepts that derive their original meaning from everyday life or from the natural sciences, the word 'location of a right' often serves to conceal the lack of clarity or even the absence of ideas.'

[13] W. Wengler, 'La situation des droits', *op. cit.*, p. 498. This observation comes after the author has already explored each of these spaces.

Within these different possible criteria of localisation, Wengler considered that a preponderant localisation of the law within the state that grants the most effective protection should be determined. This idea of legal localisation will guide the reflections that follow. It finds a particularly strong basis in the early observations of Thaller,[14] the work of Professor Chemaly,[15] and that of Ms Maisie Ooi.[16] These authors have respectively shown, in the law of bearer securities, in the law of negotiable instruments and in the English law of securities held in indirect holding system, the impasses of the plurality of connections and the benefits of a unitary solution of the conflict of laws. We would like to generalise their comments here and show that the idea of legal localisation, combined with the need to respect the purpose of the internal institutions in question, militates in favour of the application of a single and invariable law to the proprietary status of securities.

570. The proprietary status of securities has long been dependent on the form they take. This was due, on the one hand, to the impact that the form of the securities had on the terms of their assignment and, on the other hand, to the importance attached to these terms on the solution of conflicts of law. The result was, for example, that registered shares, whose transferability was effected at the company's registered office, were subject to the *lex societatis*, whereas bearer shares, which were transferable by the hand-to-hand transfer of their paper medium, were subject to the *lex rei sitae*. Although the form of the securities is still a determining factor in the solution of the conflict of laws today, it is nevertheless for other reasons, which we shall explore. In any event, it suffices for the moment to observe that companies wishing to admit their securities to a financial market are now obliged to register them, at least in part, in bearer form, 'in the operations of a central depository'. As a result, from the point of view of bearer securities, their proprietary status is now dependent on the holding system in which they are held. Traditionally, the owner of the security held it physically, a situation referred to retrospectively as the 'direct holding system'. Today, securities are most often booked through a chain of intermediaries, a situation sometimes referred to as 'the indirect holding system'. Three solutions could have been envisaged in order to resolve the difficulties caused, on the one hand, by the intermediation of the holding of securities and, on the other hand, by the international entanglement of intermediation systems: substantial unification, analogous application of the connecting factor

14 E. Thaller, 'D'un règlement qui aurait pour objet de résoudre les conflits de lois en matière de dépossession de titres au porteur', *Ann. dr. com*, 1905, pp. 259 et seq.

15 R. Chemaly, *Conflits de lois en matière d'effets de commerce*, thesis, Paris II, 1981; 'Conflits de lois en matière d'effets de commerce', RCADI, vol. 209, The Hague, Martinus Nijhoff, p. 351.

16 M. Ooi, *Shares and other securities in the conflict of laws*, *op. cit.*; 'The ramifications of fragmentation in the choice of law for shares', *JPIL*, August 2016, pp. 411 et seq.

of third-party effect of assignment of claims or that of negotiable instruments. All three are dysfunctional, showing the need for a solution specific to securities (Chapter 1). Today, the connecting factor of bearer securities is nevertheless identical to that of the plurality of connection in force in the law of negotiable instruments. The solution to which this connection gives rise, i.e. the application of a new law to each transfer of securities, is to be proscribed, *a fortiori* within the indirect holding system within which its defects are multiplied (Chapter 2). The best solution to the conflict of laws is based on a bilateral conflict rule based on a unitary connection: that of the law of the issuer for registered securities, in accordance with legal tradition, and that of the law of the central securities depositary (CSD) for bearer securities, a solution existing in positive law, the scope of which is proposed here to be extended (Chapter 3).

CHAPTER 1
THE NEED FOR A SPECIFIC SOLUTION

571. Conflicts of laws relating to the ownership of securities most often arise in connection with their transfer.[1] The transfer of securities, like the contractual assignment of claims is, from the point of view of conflict of laws, at the intersection of three distinct laws: the law of the object transfered, the law

[1] Several documents from European or international bodies will be cited here. A distinction will be made between those issued by the Hague Conference, namely

- Hague Conference on Private International Law, *The Law Applicable to Dispositions of Securities Held in an Indirect Holding System, Report by Christophe Bernasconi*, Prel. No 1, November 2000, hereinafter *Bernasconi Report.*
- Hague Conference on Private International Law, *Hague Securities Convention, Explanatory Report by Roy Goode, Hideki Kanda and Karl Kreuzer, with the assistance of Christophe Bernasconi*, 2[e] ed., 2017, hereinafter Explanatory Report.

And those from the Commission:

- European Commission, 'Communication from the Commission to the European Parliament, the Council, the European Economic and Social Committee and the Committee of the Regions on the law applicable to proprietary effects of securities transactions', Brussels, 12 March 2018, COM(2018) 89 final, hereinafter 'Communication on the law applicable to proprietary effects'.
- European Commission, 'Commission staff working document, Impact assessment accompanying the document proposal of a regulation of the european parliament and of the council on the law applicable to the third-party effects of the assignment of claims, Communication from the Commission to the european parliament, the council, the european economic and social commitee and the committee of the regions on the aapplicable law to the proprietary effects of transactions in securities', Brussels, 28 March 2018, SWD(2018) 52 final/2, hereinafter 'Commission Impact Assessment on the Law Applicable to Proprietary Effects'.
- European Commission, 'Proposal for a Regulation of the European Parliament and of the Council on the law applicable to the perfection of assignments of receivables', COM(2018) 96 final, p. 5; hereinafter, European Commission, 'Proposal for a Regulation on the law applicable to the perfection of assignments of receivables'.

At the same time, a question of terminology needs to be clarified. In order to designate, within the chain of intermediaries, the person holding the last account in the chain of intermediation, reference will be made indistinctly to the 'ultimate account holder', a notion used by the Commission, see European Commission, 'Legislation on legal certainty of securities holding and dispositions', Brussels, DG Markt G2 MET/OT/acg D[2010] 768690, p. 3. However, we recognise that the end investor is not necessarily an investor and agree with Professor Gullifer on this issue, see 'Introduction', in *Intermediation and beyond*, Oxford, Hart, 2020, pp. 10 et seq.

applicable to the transfer and, finally, the law applicable to the third party 'effect' ('enforceability') of the transfer.

As regards the law of the object transferred, it should simply be recalled that, from the point of view of transfer transactions, the decisive aspect of the regime of securities is their negotiability. Negotiability is dependent on the form assigned to the securities, decided by the law of the issuer or the contract of issue.[2] As regards the contract of transfer, which determines the contractual relations between the transferor and the transferee, this is subject to its own law; the *lex contractus* will depend on the means by which the contract is concluded. In the context of the financial market, three cases must be distinguished. First, the transfer contract may result from the issuance of an order on the trading platform, in which case the applicable law will be that of the trading platform between the members[3] and the contract between the member and its client.[4] Secondly, in the case of a public offer of securities, the applicable law will be that designated by the offer.[5] Thirdly and lastly, in the case of an over-the-counter transfer of securities admitted to trading, the applicable law will be that determined by the transfer contract or, in the absence of choice of law, by the domicile of the seller.[6]

However, while the law applicable to the transfer contract applies to all contractual aspects of the relationship between the transferor and the transferee according to the scope of the *lex contractus* granted by the Rome I Regulation, it does not extend to the transfer of financial instruments. The reason for this is that in several legal systems,[7] the transfer of ownership of securities does not take place *solo consensus*, as in the case of claims in French law,[8] but results

---

2 See *supra*, paras. 300 et seq.

3 See *supra*, para. 442.

4 See *supra*, para. 451.

5 See *supra*, para. 495.

6 This means, for example, that in the case of a systematic internaliser, the applicable law will not necessarily be that of the intermediary, but may be that of the customer. For an in-depth discussion of the law applicable to the assignment contract, see D. Pardoel, *Les conflits de lois en matière de cession de créances*, Paris LGDJ, 1997, nos. 132 et seq.

7 On the French conception of assignment, see *infra*, paras. 733 et seq.

8 It should be noted here that subjecting the effects of the assignment contract to the law of the autonomy of the assignment contract does not mean that the transfer of the claim must also be subject to it. Thus many – Niboyet, Holleaux, Vareilles-Sommières – have argued for the application of the *lex creationis* of the assigned claim despite the abandonment of the real status of claims. On this question and the references, see D. Pardoel, *Les conflits de lois en matière de cession de créances*, *op. cit.* On the real status of claims, see the comparative perspectives of Pillet and Niboyet reported and criticised by L. d'Avout, *Sur les solutions du conflit de lois en droit des biens*, *op. cit.*

from the entry in an account.[9] A distinction must therefore be made between the contractual aspects of the assignment, which are subject to the law of the transfer contract, and the *proprietary* effects of the transfer,[10] also known as third-party enforceability. It is to this latter aspect that this study is devoted.

572. The law applicable to the transfer itself is the law that more generally governs the proprietary status of the security. Indeed, its scope extends beyond the effectiveness of the transfer, and should correspond, with a few adaptations, to the traditional scope of the law applicable to third party enforceability of an assignment of a claim and the issues arising from it.[11] The difficulty of determining a consensual connection under the aegis of the Hague Conference has pushed States towards the adoption of uniform substantive law rules. It seems to us that this unification will not solve the problems posed. Above all, the proposed substantive rules are likely to create more difficulties than they solve (Section 1). The difficulty of determining a criterion for deciding whether an assignment is effective against third parties is not specific to securities. Thus, in the related field of assignments of claims, the criterion is not uniform throughout the Union and has been the subject of contrasting analyses in France. The solutions proposed, although not applicable by analogy, may nevertheless constitute sources of inspiration (Section 2). In the same way, the study of conflict-of-laws rules for negotiable instruments makes it possible to observe the impasses to which the thesis of the plurality of connections gives rise (Section 3).

SECTION 1. THE ILLUSION OF SUBSTANTIAL UNIFICATION

Substantive unification appears to be an illusory response to the difficulties raised by the ownership of securities for two reasons. The first is to be found in the relationship between substantive unification and conflicts of laws: the latter are not likely to allow the suppression of the former (§ 1). The second reason relates to the concrete proposal of the uniform law which lies in the

---

9 However, this does not mean that the book entry is constitutive of the right: as Mr Synvet expresses it, 'to say that one becomes the owner by the book entry, or that the book entry makes the ownership pass from the seller to the buyer, are not two identical things', H. Synvet, 'La propriété des titres financiers' in *20 ans de dématérialisation des titres en France*, Revue Banque, 2001, no. 24.

10 Sometimes referred to as 'real' aspects (in the sense of *res*) see e.g. S. Laval, *Le tiers et le contrat*, Brussels, Larcier, 2016, no. 31. The expression, which sometimes leads to confusion between claims and tangible property, of which the real status of claims was an illustration, will not be used here.

11 See Art. 5, European Commission, 'Proposal for a Regulation on the law applicable to the perfection of assignments of claims'. This scope of application, with certain variations, is also retained by certain international conventions, see Art. 2(1) of the Hague Convention.

generalised introduction of 'intermediated securities', the quality of the result of which may be discussed (§ 2).

§ 1. SUBSTANTIVE UNIFICATION AND CONFLICT OF LAWS

573. International uniform law conventions. International commercial law has an ambiguous relationship with the conflict of laws rules. Most often, it makes immoderate use of them: it is known that civil and commercial contracts, associated with payment instruments, have made great use of the rule of conflict method. However, the inherent defects of this procedure sometimes lead commercial law to wish to discard it through the unification of substantive law. In the context of securities, the approach was different. Indeed, it was the poor success of the Convention resulting from the work of the Hague Conference that led to the development of a Convention on substantive rules regarding multi-intermediated securities, under the aegis of Unidroit (the so-called Unidroit Convention).[12] What these Conventions have in common is that they have had very modest success. However, the effort was not in vain, since the work leading to this Convention has resulted in a better understanding of foreign systems, as well as the adoption of a more or less common vocabulary to designate identical realities despite the disparity of the systems.

Even if the Unidroit Convention had been introduced into the substantive law of the countries that contributed to its elaboration, it would not have had the consequence of eliminating the need for conflict rules. Indeed, the law of securities is at the borderline of several disciplines: property law (proprietary status), contract law (contract of issuance), company law (relationship with the issuer), financial law (marketing conditions) and, in the case of certain legal systems, trust law.[13] Even if the proprietary status of securities, and the prerogatives they offer, can be standardised, all other issues are likely to interfere with the regime of securities, either as a preliminary matter or by influencing the qualification.[14]

---

[12] Another initiative has taken place at European level, through the Legal Certainty Group set up by the Commission, which has produced two reports, the second of which proposes a set of material solutions to the difficulties identified, see Legal Certainty Group, *Second Advice of the Legal Certainty Group, Solutions to Legal Barriers related to Post-Trading within the EU*, August 2008.

[13] H. Synvet, 'La propriété des titres financiers' *20 ans de dématérialisation des titres en France*, *op. cit.*, no. 1; M. Ooi, 'The choice of a choice of law rule' in *Intermediated securities*, *op. cit.*, p. 229.

[14] By playing on the qualification, we know that the judges in *Macmillan* thus subjected the form of the titles to the *lex fori*, and that the judges in *Secure Capital* reduced the question of the prerogatives arising from the title to the contractual question.

574. The Geneva Conventions on bills of exchange. These difficulties find a singular echo in the French history of the interaction of conflict of laws law with uniform law.[15] French law experienced a similar difficulty after introducing into its substantive law the uniform law of the International Convention on Bills of Exchange and Cheques negotiated within the Geneva Conference in the 1930s.[16] Because the law of bills of exchange was seen as a discipline receptive to uniformity of substantive law, States attempted the dual undertaking of unifying the substantive rules that could be unified, and the conflict of laws rules with respect to those aspects of the law that could not be agreed upon in substance.[17] This gave rise to the Geneva Conventions of 7 June 1930 and 19 March 1931, concluded under the aegis of the Geneva Conference and containing uniform laws, respectively on bills of exchange and promissory notes on the one hand[18] and on cheques on the other hand.[19] These laws were accompanied by two conventions on conflicts in these two areas.[20] The signatory States undertook to introduce the provisions of the Uniform Law into their national law, subject to *ad hoc* modifications as announced. The method used by the Geneva Conventions was likely to raise two preliminary legal problems which are also found in the Unidroit Convention on securities: on the one hand, the identification of the nature of the resulting norm – international law or uniform law integrated into the national legal orders – and, on the other hand, the conflicting methodology which results from it. Indeed, is it then the international law that is applied, or the national law as transposed by the Conventions? Far from being theoretical,

15 P. Malaurie, 'Loi uniforme et conflit de lois', *TCFDIP*, 1967, p. 83.

16 The Geneva Conference is an institution established under the aegis of the League of Nations which continued the work of the Hague Conference begun before the First World War, in particular on the question of the uniform law prepared by the Hague Conference (1910-1912). The Geneva Conference of 1930 and the Conventions which resulted from it are the direct heirs of this early work - a sign of the identity of the projects, the main French representative, the heart of the drafting committee, remains Professor Lyon-Caen. On the history of these conventions, see R. Roblot, *Les effets de commerce*, *op. cit.*, 44–49. The importance of the Geneva Conference declined with the drastic decrease in international commercial relations linked first to the war and then to the 1929 crisis, not to mention the fear of another war (B. Goldman, 'Les conflits de lois en matière d'instruments négociables', *op. cit.*, pp. 2–3).

17 Certain parts of the law of exchange were left outside the scope of the conventions, where the previous solutions, both in terms of conflict of laws and substantive law, remained in force. The Geneva Conflict of Laws Convention was adopted in a separate document from the Uniform Regulations in order to allow countries not wishing to accede to the Uniform Regulations to be able to ratify the Conflict of Laws Convention anyway (see *Proceedings of the Geneva Convention of 1930*, p. 345). This was aimed in particular at the United Kingdom, but the latter did not ratify, not so much because of their disagreement with the proposed rules as because they were waiting to see what the United States would decide on the reform of its own law on negotiable instruments (see the intervention of the English delegate, Guttenbridge, in the Proceedings of the *1930 Geneva Convention*, *op. cit.)*

18 *JORF*, 24 October 1936, *RCDIP*, 1935, 829.

19 *RCDIP*, 1936, 246.

20 Geneva Convention of 7 June 1930, *JORF*, 24 October 1936.

the question has arisen in several cases, the most emblematic of which is the *Hocke* judgment.

575. *Hocke* judgment. The Hocke judgment raised a question of law unified by the Uniform Act and, as such, incorporated in the same terms in the French and German regulations, but interpreted differently in the two legal orders. This difference in interpretation, which determined the resolution of the dispute on the merits, had the effect of resurrecting the conflict of laws.[21] Some eminent commercial lawyers were concerned about this, precisely because in their minds the uniform law had extinguished the conflict of laws.[22] Thus Professor Gaston

---

21 The *Hocke* judgment settles the question of the interpretation of what was at the time Art. 130 new para. 6 of the Commercial Code according to which 'the endorsement must indicate on whose behalf it is given. In the absence of this indication, it is deemed to be given for the drawer'. The simple or irrefutable nature of this presumption in favour of the drawer in the absence of an indication of the person for whom the guarantor is guaranteeing has been the subject of divergent interpretations, in particular between the Courts of Appeal and the Cour de Cassation: the courts of appeal applied a simple presumption, whereas in five censure rulings of the same day, the Court stated '[...] that such a presumption, since it constitutes the sanction of the omission of a legal formality, is not likely to be countered by evidence to the contrary' (Com., 23 January 1956, *D.*, 1956, 204). Academics were concerned by this, see for example G. Lagarde, who observes that 'faithful to the French tradition, these courts of appeal, encouraged by a part of the academics, analysed it as a presumption *juris tantum*', in G. Lagarde, 'Portée internationale d'une interprétation nationale de la loi uniforme sur la lettre de change et le billet à ordre', *Mélanges Roger Secrétan*, Montreux, 1964, p. 1.
From the point of view of the conflict of laws, the real difficulty stems from the "cross-fertilisation" that took place between the French and German courts, with the German Supreme Court, like the Court of Cassation, disavowing the lower courts and thus taking a 'liberal' approach at the same time as the French Court was taking a literal turn. Indeed, at the time the *Hocke* judgment was handed down, a symmetrical case was being heard in Germany and decided by the *Bundesgerichtshof* on 29 October 1962, which decided that the judges of the court of first instance had interpreted French law in a sovereign manner by refusing to investigate whether, despite the absence of any indication, the debtor guaranteed by the giver of the guarantee was not in fact the drawee (see the commentary by Paul Lagarde, *op. cit.*, In other words, at the same time as the Cour de cassation characterised the presumption laid down by Art. 130 para. 6 of the Commercial Code as irrebuttable, the *Bundesgerichtshof* enshrined its simple nature. In this regard, Gaston Lagarde complains that the *Bundesgerichtshof* betrays the interpretation of French law and 'notes with regret that foreign judges have had to go to great lengths to seek – and not find – the meaning of French law: their interpretation of Article 130 para. 6 of the Commercial Code betrays that of the French Court of Cassation, and no account is even taken of another provision of French law – this one alien to the uniform law – Article 156 para. 2 of the Commercial Code, under the terms of which "the forfeiture only takes place with regard to the drawer if he justifies that he has made a provision on the due date'. G. Lagarde's criticism does not, however, take into account the fact that the conflict rule only gave French law jurisdiction to designate the scope of the guarantee, and not for the consequences attached to the advance payment, which are the responsibility of the law of the issue, in combination with Arts. 5 and 6 of the Geneva Convention.

22 This question of the relationship between the uniform law and the conflict of laws was already present in the debates on the Convention. For example, the negotiators had difficulty in reaching agreement on the need for an article on the effects of exchange obligations,

Lagarde criticised the decision by comparing and then distinguishing between the provisions of the Uniform Law and those of the Civil Code after the Napoleonic conquests. In the latter case, the author observes that the regained sovereignty of these States required the French judge to apply their national law not as a uniform provision, but as a foreign national law, even though these norms stemmed from a common rigorous identity, that established by the Napoleonic Code. The same would not be true of the uniform law resulting from the Geneva Conventions, which derives from a common sovereignty resulting from different national sovereignties, and not from the national fragmentation of a common provision.[23] This is why Gaston Lagarde considers that before the question of the resolution of the conflict of laws, and thus of the application of the conflict rule designating German law here, the judge should have asked himself: 'Is the competent law the uniform law?'[24]

The demonstration is seductive, as it admirably describes the two legislative movements: firstly, the unification imposed by Napoleonic force, then fragmented by the effect of time and the rediscovered influence of the local legal culture; secondly, the diversity overcome by collective adherence to a single law. Here we recognise the two opposing movements of dominion and federalism. However, it is the nature of the uniform law that the author misunderstands: the legal nature of its articles does not derive from the convention itself. The provisions of the Geneva Convention only become applicable by virtue of their incorporation into the national legal orders, in this case French and German.[25] The competent law is therefore the national law designated by the conflict rule, in this case German law, which is in the same normative situation as Belgian or Dutch law resulting from the Napoleonic

since this question seemed to have been resolved by the Uniform Rules, see Reports on *the Geneva Convention*, pp. 358–359. Even Asser (Reports of the *Geneva Convention of 1930*, p. 358) is against such an article, fearing that it would encourage States to sign the conflict of laws convention instead of the uniform regulation. The arguments given by Mr Percerou (*Comptes rendus de la Convention de Genève de 1930*, p. 359) are convincing: some States did not intend to adhere to the Uniform Regulations, in which case this article made sense; secondly, even if States ratified both, it was possible that their parliaments would only accept the Conflict of Laws Convention; and thirdly, the reservations made this article necessary because of the concrete divergences that might arise. The author had not foreseen the possibility of divergent interpretation.

23 G. Lagarde, 'Portée internationale d'une interprétation nationale de la loi uniforme sur la lettre de change et le billet à ordr"', *op. cit.*, p. 5: 'Various articles of the original Napoleonic Code remained in force in the Rhineland countries until the implementation of the BGB, others are still in force in Belgium. Now, if a French judge is called upon to apply these texts, as German or Belgian law, he will have to concern himself with the interpretation given to them by national, German or Belgian case law, and respect it, even if it is opposed to that which applies in France.'

24 *Ibid.*, p. 7.

25 Already in this sense, P. Lagarde, 'Les interprétations divergentes d'une loi uniforme donnent-elles lieu à un conflit de lois?', *RCDIP*, 1964, p. 235, and spec. p. 247.

Code.[26] The considerations raised by the *Hocke* judgment make it possible to clarify the nature of the norm resulting from uniform laws, and consequently the essential place of the conflict of laws which, while it is presented as a last resort for the residual pockets where uniformisation has not taken place, in reality determines the true coordination of the legal orders.[27]

576. Methodology of the Geneva Conventions. The Geneva Conventions are an early example of the potential of negotiating a uniform law, as well as the limitations of the process.[28] Far from creating a community of States transformed into a form of supreme legislator, the method employed by the Geneva Conference was more modestly one of negotiation by States of a model uniform law. Uniform law is not so much an international law, external to domestic legal systems, as an *international discipline*,[29] maintained by states in order to allow coordination of their legal orders.[30] Substantive unification has the advantage of reducing conflicts of laws. These historical developments show, however, that the Unidroit Securities Convention will not be able to eliminate the importance of conflict of laws, because substantive unification, when possible, is never possible in all aspects. Moreover, when unification takes place, the divergence of rules is replaced by the divergence of their interpretation. The Geneva Securities Convention could, however, have been a welcome step towards reducing conflicts if the solution it proposed had not attracted so little support.

---

26 Far from being futile, Gaston Lagarde's analysis has one major contribution: the foreign law should have been interpreted as the foreign supreme interpreter would have done. The Court of Cassation should therefore have respected the interpretation of this provision as given by the *Bundesgerichtshof*. And only from the Supreme Court, which can be considered as the only one that can bind, from the point of view of the foreign judge, the interpretation of the provisions.

27 In this sense, we endorse the fine conclusions of Professor Paul Lagarde on this subject, reproduced as an epitaph to the introduction (*supra*, para. 1).

28 Y. Lequette, 'De l'utilitarisme dans le droit international privé conventionnel de la famille' in *Mélanges Yvon Loussouarn*, Paris, Dalloz, 1994; Y. Lequette, 'Le droit international privé de la famille à l'épreuve des conventions internationales', RCADI, vol. 246, The Hague, Martinus Nijhoff, 1995.

29 The expression is used by Dean Hamel, in J. Hamel and M. Ancel (eds.), *La convention de Genève sur l'unification du droit du chèque*, foreword by J. Hamel, Paris, Recueil Sirey, 1937, p. 18. Unlike the author who considers that 'when a State adheres to a uniform law, it substitutes for its own national sovereignty the authority of an international discipline', it seems to us more accurate to consider that the signatory State imposes an international discipline on itself in the exercise of its sovereignty. This is how we understand the expression 'international discipline' here, and this is how it seems to us to be used.

30 Nevertheless, because of the reservations it provides for, the Convention has been criticised as 'being nothing more than a mere façade, a sort of trompe-l'œil, almost a fault committed against the good faith of those who rely on the League of Nations to unify certain matters of private law' (J. Hamel, in *La convention de Genève sur l'unification du droit du chèque*, *op. cit.*, p. 17; the criticisms are not the author's own, but are reported by him). The criticism appears excessive: on the one hand, reservations are not systematic, as many parts have been agreed upon without the possibility of a reservation and, on the other hand, the publication of reservations was organized in order to be aware of foreign legislation on the issue.

§ 2. THE REJECTION OF ELECTED *SECURITY ENTITLEMENTS* BY UNIFORM LAW

The Unidroit Securities Convention explicitly chooses a functional approach.[31] It bases its entire mechanism on the creation of 'intermediated securities', a concept behind which we find the security entitlements inspired by American law.[32] Once these new objects are created in positive law, the challenge is to recreate the proprietary status of such objects, which consist in clumsily mimicking the regime traditionally attached to the ownership of securities.[33]

577. Dual function of financial securities. Two functions of securities can be distinguished.[34] The first relates to the circulation of the securities. This function, which Prof. Paech describes as a 'horizontal' aspect,[35] extends to the entire proprietary status of the security and understands the security as a medium of exchange, a means of payment as the bill of exchange once was. This first function is clearly distinguished from the second, which pursues the 'vertical' aspect of the financial instrument and confers on the holder of the security the prerogatives arising from the *negotium* against the issuer.[36] In the case of equity securities, this means the right to vote, to receive dividends and all the other prerogatives offered by the shares and the corporate regime in force; in the case of debt securities, the prerogatives offered by the contract of issue, possibly combined with the prerogatives of the law chosen by the contract of issue, or even those offered by the applicable insolvency law.[37] The horizontal aspect of the security was previously captured by the *real status* and, even today, it is from the perspective of property law that the questions it raises are most often addressed in comparative law. The vertical aspect, on the other hand, is generally perceived and characterised as a contractual issue involving the relationship between the issuer and the holder of the security. Depending on the aspect considered, the characterisation may therefore differ.[38]

---

31 Explanatory Report, nos. 2–18.

32 On which, see *infra*, para. 672.

33 It should be added here that *security entitlements* were designed to solve the liquidity problems of credit institutions in the US in the late 1980s. The global environment has changed considerably since then and, in particular, the European economic environment is not likely to fuel a liquidity problem again: the European Central Bank has been supplying credit institutions with liquidity, and there is no indication that this trend will change in the near future.

34 These two functions have been perfectly perceived by Mr Nizard in the way he approaches negotiable instruments, distinguishing in the first part 'Rights evidenced by negotiable instruments', from those which he refers to in his second part as 'Rights on negotiable instruments', see F. Nizard, *Les titres négociables*, *op. cit.*

35 These two 'horizontal' and 'vertical' sides of title ownership are borrowed from P. Paech, 'Conflict of Laws and Relational Rights', in *Intermediation and beyond*, *op. cit.*, p. 300.

36 On the distinction between *instrumentum* and *negotium*, see *supra*, para. 287.

37 See *supra*, paras. 320 et seq.

38 See the *Secure Capital* judgment *supra*, para. 399.

This parallel presentation of these two functions and the resulting characterisations is nevertheless misleading. It conceals the links between the two functions: on the one hand, in order to be the holder of the prerogatives against the issuer, it is necessary to be the holder of the securities and, on the other hand, the value of the instrument, which determines its vocation to be circulated (circulation only makes sense because of the pecuniary value granted to the security), depends largely on the prerogatives that the security offers to its holder. This is why the purpose of facilitating the circulation of financial securities is not only to increase their by facilitating their transfer and enforceability against third parties, but also to make it easier to obtain ownership of the *negotium*.[39]

578. Vices inherent to intermediated securities. Intermediated securities favour the horizontal aspect, the circulation of the security, to the point that they break the link that attaches the true shareholder (the one who bears the corporate risk) to the company, or the true bondholder to the issuer. It is this congenital infirmity of intermediated securities, associated with a certain looseness of characterisation, that gives rise to certain legal difficulties arising from the recent European litigation.[40] These difficulties are, however, much broader: the indeterminacy of the beneficial shareholder hinders the exercise of his voting right[41]; the exercise of preferential subscription rights may become an obstacle course; the payment of dividends may be captured by the intermediary, either in

---

39 Here we find two aspects already present within negotiable instruments: on the one hand, the value of the instrument depends largely on the solvency of its debtors and, on the other hand, in the same way that negotiable instruments had both a credit and a payment function, but the payment function prevailed (see *infra*, paras. 602 et seq.), of the two aspects of the financial instrument, the possibility for its holder to avail himself of the prerogatives offered by the financial instrument should prevail.

40 See especially the *Secure Capital* judgment, para. 399. The *Kolassa* judgment shows the difficulty inherent in the absence of ownership of the securities, and of the contractual relationship that such ownership makes it possible to establish with the issuer, see *supra*, para. 400.

41 From a French perspective, see C. Coupet, *L'attribution du droit de vote dans les sociétés*, *op. cit.*, nos. 162 et seq.
This system reproduces one of the vices of bearer shares, see already in this sense, H. Decugis, 'La loi du 28 février 1941 relative à la forme et à la négociation des actions', *op. cit.*, p. 130: 'The dispersion of bearer shares in the hands of innumerable small savers, who never attend AGMs and are unaware of corporate affairs and of those they were supposed to manage, has created an ever-widening gulf between them and the directors of companies. Absenteeism of shareholders has become the usual rule and legal quorums can only be obtained in most large companies by means of blank proxies given through banks, at the cost of repeated and costly convocations, especially in cases where the three-quarters or two-thirds quorum is required by law. Shareholder control is, in fact, illusory and, in many companies, boards of directors have increasingly become irresponsible oligarchies. They recruit themselves by co-option and have lost all useful contact with the unknown and changing mass of their shareholders, about whom they do not always care enough, until the day the disaster occurs.'

violation of the contract binding him to his client, or because of his insolvency; the breakdown of the ownership of the securities prevents the ultimate holder from taking advantage of the issuance contract, and in particular of the possible insurance policy issued in favour of the bondholder; this breakdown may prevent a debt restructuring because of the *quorum* rules relating to the decisions taken by the bondholders' mass;[42] drawing on their clients' securities is made all the easier as the intermediary is the sole owner of the securities, making its insolvency even more cruel for its client.

579. It is undoubtedly possible to find specific solutions to some of these difficulties. For example, threshold crossing requirements allow the issuer to know its true shareholders. However, by retaining a system that makes the ultimate account holder the owner of the security, French law has avoided a considerable number of difficulties, while protecting the person bearing the risk of the investment. Moreover, the regime of intermediated securities in its function of circulation of the security does not contribute anything: it is a question of reproducing more or less the entire property regime. Thus, the legal orders instituting intermediated securities grant an action to reclaim the underlying securities held by the intermediary, and grant the acquirer of an intermediated security protection against the defects that affect it.

Advocates of intermediated securities most often compare the advantages of this system to that of paper securities without necessarily observing that one can have an intermediation system without breaking the link between the holder of the securities and the ultimate account holder.[43] Most of the advantages mentioned by the authors are therefore valid for all intermediation systems, regardless of the nature of the *negotium* exchanged.[44] The criticism made here is not of intermediation, whose advantages are undeniable, but of the scope it is given with respect to the *negotium* exchanged.

580. Conclusion of the section. The unification of substantive rules will not extinguish the conflict of laws: the continuity of laws will be followed by the discontinuity of their interpretation. The difficulties are, however, likely to be amplified by standardisation on the model of intermediated securities, which is a false solution. It is therefore necessary to search for the relevant connecting factor; this cannot, however, be sought in the status of claims.

---

42 See for the English law of *schemes of arrangement*, J. Payne, 'Intermediation and bondholders schemes of arrangement', *op. cit.*

43 L. Gullifer and J. Payne, 'Conclusion' in *Intermediation and beyond*, *op. cit.*, p. 360.

44 See *ibid.*

SECTION 2. THE IMPOSSIBLE EXTENSION OF THE CONNECTING FACTOR OF THIRD-PARTY ENFORCEABILITY OF ASSIGNMENT OF CLAIMS TO SECURITIES

581. From the point of view of securities, the particular interest of the solutions arising from assignments of claims stems from two similarities: on the one hand, assignments of claims are also part of the context of translational transactions where the question of third parties is sometimes central; on the other hand, the assignment of claims has also suffered from the influence of the *lex situs*. The conflict-of-laws solutions regarding the enforceability of claims against third parties have reflected this latter aspect.[45] However, today, the resolution of the conflict of laws is independent of the *lex situs* (§ 1); it is moving forward the desirable application of the law of the assignor (§ 2).

§ 1. POINT OF VIEW OF THE CONFLICT OF LAWS

582. The conflict rule designating the law applicable to the third party effects of assignments of claims still depends on the national law of the Member States. Although the criterion of the assignor's habitual residence was included in the proposal for a Rome I Regulation published by the Commission in 2005,[46] it was not retained because of the diversity of opinions on the question.[47] However, the Member States offer different solutions for the resolution of this conflict. As Mr d'Avout puts it, these criteria can be classified into two distinct orders, 'geographical: place of residence of the assignor; legal and ancillary: law of the

45 Bartin himself, when he wishes to determine the law applicable to the regime of financial securities, begins by determining the law applicable to the civil claim and the promissory note, see E. Bartin, *Principes de droit international privé*, vol. III, Paris, Domat-Montchrestien, 1935, pp. 51 et seq. Indeed, the author successively attempts to assign a fictitious status to the various intangible movables, see spec. para. 374: 'The first and simplest application of this analysis of the *lex rei sitae* for intangible movables is provided by the system of ownership of the civil claim of the classic type, as opposed to the claim which is the subject of a promissory note and, even more so, by the claim which is the subject of a registered document of title or bearer document.' On the retreat of the real status of claim, see *infra*, para. 630.

46 Art. 13(3) of the proposed Rome I Regulation, published by the Commission in 2005: 'The law of the country in which the assignor or subrogator has his habitual residence at the time of the assignment or transfer governs the enforceability of the assignment or subrogation against third parties.'

47 *Impact assessment*, p. 14; T. Hartley, 'Choice of law regarding the voluntary assignment of contractual obligations under the Rome I Regulation', *International and comparative law quarterly*, 2011, pp. 29 et seq.

object assigned, law of the assignment contract'.[48] In all these cases, the debtor is excluded from the material scope of application of third-party effect of the assignment of claims. Indeed, under the Rome I Regulation, the debtor is not considered as a third party to the assignment. Therefore, the enforceability of the assignment against the assigned debtor is determined by 'the law governing the claim which is the subject of the assignment',[49] i.e. the law of the assigned claim. Two observations can be made about this state of affairs.

Firstly, a distinction can be drawn between the enforceability of the assignment against the debtor and against third parties. As a result, the question of the effectiveness of the assignment against third parties should be assessed independently of the debtor's interests, which are already protected by the application of the *lex creationis*.[50] The debtor's situation is unlikely to be aggravated by the criterion chosen for the effectiveness of the assignment against third parties.[51] The choice in favour of the *lex creationis* of the assigned claim should be made only because of the protection of the interests of third parties, and not to preserve the unity of enforceability which governs quite different interests depending on whether it is addressed to the assigned debtor or to third parties.[52] This is why it is of no importance for the

---

48 L. D'Avout, 'La loi applicable à la cession de créance ou de contrat après l'ordonnance du 10 février 2016', *D.*, 2017, 457, no. 5. The author notes that one could also resort to an international substantive rule, inspired by the internal resolution of the conflict resulting from the adage *prior tempore, prior jure*. However, as the author observes: 'It is likely that this method of dealing with disputes about priority or ownership of the assigned object would not be followed every time the dispute arose abroad, before the judge of a country whose domestic law dissociates the date on which the assignment agreement takes effect between the parties and the date on which the transfer becomes effective vis-à-vis third parties. Outside litigation, the reliability of a reasoning which universalises the French principle of the enforceability of assignments from the outset, and combines it with the *priority time* rule, is therefore not in all circumstances guaranteed.' (*ibid.*).
It should undoubtedly be added that, among the possible criteria, the *locus regit actum* rule could have been envisaged if it did not lead to such disadvantageous results, see D. Pardoel, *Les conflits de lois en matière de cession de créances*, *op. cit.*

49 Art. 14(2) of the Rome I Regulation.

50 This first observation is particularly important because, as Ms Pardoel has shown for France: 'The construction of private international law solutions in the area of assignment of claims is based on one principle: the assigned debtor must not see his situation worsen as a result of the assignment, in which he did not participate.' D. Pardoel, *Les conflits de lois en matière de transfert de créances*, *op. cit.*, no. 481.

51 Conversely, the connecting factor of the emforceability of the assignment against the assigned debtor should not influence the solution of the conflict of laws regarding enforceability against third parties.

52 See T. Hartley, 'Choice of law regarding the voluntary assignment of contractual obligations under the Rome I Regulation', *op. cit.*, p. 56. Mrs Pardoel, after having made the most detailed observations on the conflicts of laws relating to assignments of claims, finally preferred the application of the *lex creationis* of the assigned claim, expressing her preference for the unity of the connection of enforceability, without distinguishing between the assigned party and third parties, see D. Pardoel, *Les conflits de lois en matière de transfert de créances*, *op. cit.*, no. 385.

solution sought to the question of enforceability to third parties that the Rome I Regulation breaks with the French rule. The latter made the enforceability of the assignment to the assigned debtor subject to the law of his domicile.[53] In view of the above discussion, this rupture should have no consequences for the solution of the question of enforceability against third parties. As regards the application of the *lex creationis* to the enforceability of the assignment against the assigned debtor, it is undoubtedly true that it is less advantageous for the debtor than the law of his domicile, which is the one he knows best. However, the *lex creationis* is foreseeable for the assigned debtor, as well as for the assignor and the assignee, which makes it easier for the latter to know the conditions of the debtor's discharge.

Secondly, among the considerations that should motivate the selection of the connecting factor, the main requirement should be the predictability of the criterion of enforceability against third parties. In the alternative, considerations relating to the stability of the connecting factor and its compatibility with the transactions, which are frequent in practice, of assignment of the bulk of claims should be encouraged. On the other hand, rules based on the configuration of domestic law should be rejected if not to retain the objective they pursue.[54]

---

53 CA Paris, 18 November 1927, *Sinder*, *D. H.*, 1927, III, 91, *Clunet*, 1928, 972, obs. J. P.; *RCDIP*, 1934, 121, note J.-P. N. The decision is particularly rich, as Mrs Pardoel observes: 'The court is not content to declare French law applicable in order to declare the assignment of a claim unenforceable against the assigned debtor. It examines the content of French law with regard to service. And, using Article 560 of the Code of Civil Procedure as an analogy, it deduced two different rules: on the one hand, service on a foreign assigned debtor who does not live in France cannot be validly effected in France at the public prosecutor's office. On the other hand, service on an assigned debtor domiciled in France can only be validly effected by a French bailiff, either in person or at home. The first of these rules is nothing more than an affirmation of the incompetence of the French authorities to effectively effect service on a foreign assigned debtor domiciled abroad. The second is simply the assertion that the French authorities alone are competent to serve an assignment of a claim on an assigned debtor residing in France. [...] French law does indeed provide that the French authorities have exclusive jurisdiction to publicise assignments of claims', D. Pardoel, *Les conflits de lois en matière de cession de créances*, *op. cit.*

54 See from this point of view the close study by Mr d'Avout on the new internal provisions of the Civil Code determining the conflict of rights in the case of assignment of a claim, which contribute significantly to a well-founded understanding of the application of the law of the assignor's domicile to the enforceability against third parties, L. d'Avout, 'La loi applicable à la cession de créance ou de contrat après l'ordonnance du 10 février 2016', *op. cit.*, no. 6. In France, the application of the law of the place of residence of the assigned debtor to the opposability to third parties was formerly explained by the advertising formalism of the former Art. 1690 of the Civil Code, which required the debtor to be served with an authenticated document of the assignment, CA Paris, 26 March 1986. The previous solution made the former article 1690 of the Civil Code a mandatory rule, see L. d'Avout, *Sur les solutions du conflit de lois en droit des biens*, *op. cit.* Such reasoning in terms of mandatory rules, instead of a bilateral conflict rule, is always possible, but, as Mr d'Avout has said, 'this would possibly lead to casuistic solutions, even though the concrete solutions would remain explicable according to one or other of the polyvalent connecting principles presented so far', the connections in question being those also discussed here, see L. d'Avout, 'La loi

These various arguments lead to a preference for the application of legal criteria based on the law of the assigned claim or of the assignment contract, and to a preference, within the geographical criteria, for that based on the law of the assignor.

§ 2. THE DESIRABLE CONNECTION TO THE LAW OF THE ASSSIGNOR'S

It will first be shown why the assignor's domicile is the most appropriate connecting factor (I) before rejecting the exceptions recently proposed by the European Commission to the principle of its application (II).

I. Reasons for the Choice of the Assignor's Law

583. Rejection of the law of the assignment contract. The enforceability of the assignment against third parties has the function of designating *the* assignment that is enforceable against third parties in a situation where, in most cases, several competing assignments of the same claim are to be considered. To base enforceability against third parties on the law of the assignment contract makes it necessary to introduce a criterion for determining the law applicable to each of the assignments. However, as Mr d'Avout observes, 'the legal connection to the law of the act of assignment would be tantamount to enshrining the substantive principle of enforceability from the outset of valid legal acts whenever this is the solution defended by the law applicable to the earliest assignment'.[55] Such a system results in making the law applicable to enforceability unpredictable for all assignees who acquired the claim after the first assignee, who may have validly made their assignment enforceable against third parties according to the act of the assignment from which they thought they benefited. In other words,

applicable à la cession de créance ou de contrat après l'ordonnance du 10 février 2016', *op. cit.*, no. 5. Contrary to appearances, the rule in Art. 1690 of the Civil Code had mixed functions. While it was primarily intended to protect the debtor against double payment, Mrs Pardoel has shown that this rule was probably not originally indifferent to the protection of third parties: see D. Pardoel, *Les conflits de lois en matière de transfert de créances*, *op. cit.*, no. 334, and on the contemporary discussion of this protection following the entry into force of the Dailly assignment, see spec. nos. 337–338. Finally, from a contemporary perspective, following the repeal of Art. 1690 and the creation of provisions under Arts. 1323 and 1325 of the Civil Code, see L. d'Avout, 'La loi applicable à la cession de créance ou de contrat après l'ordonnance du 10 février 2016', *op. cit.*

55 L. d'Avout, 'La loi applicable à la cession de créance ou de contrat après l'ordonnance du 10 février 2016', *op. cit.*

the connecting factor penalises precisely those whom perfection against third parties is intended to protect, and must therefore be rejected.[56]

584. Rejection of the law of the assigned claim. The law of the assigned claim has better characteristics. It is considered relatively predictable in the sense that it can be discovered by reading the contract from which the claim arises. Moreover, it allows a certain stability because of its uniqueness: in the event of multiple assignments, the applicable law will always be the same. In addition, there is no risk of a possible change of connecting factor due to a possible move of the assignor or the assigned debtor. Moreover, it has the advantage of simplicity through the application of a single criterion for the enforceability of the debtor and the assignee, which may result in cost savings.[57] However, there are two difficulties with this connecting factor. The first, and most serious, relates to the foreseeability of the law of the assigned claim. Indeed, it makes it necessary for the choice of law to have been provided for in the contract. If this is not the case, it will be necessary to determine the characteristic performance of the contract in order to know whether to apply the law of the assignor or that of the assigned debtor. However, the claims likely to be assigned are of various origins, and such a search makes it considerably more difficult not only to predict the connection, but also to determine it – it is commonly known that the characteristic performance is not always easy to determine.[58] A second difficulty is that, even if a choice of law has been made, the criterion of the law of the subject-matter of the assignment does not lend itself well to transactions involving the assignment of masses of claims. Indeed, this criterion leads the assignee to seek the law applicable to the enforceability against third parties of each of the assigned claims.

585. Rejection of the criterion of the debtor's domicile. From the French point of view, the application of the law of the debtor's domicile made it possible under the old French case law to provide a unitary criterion for enforceability, whether it related to the debtor or to third parties in a French context where enforceability was not without links to legal advertising (*publicité légale*).[59]

---

56 See already in this sense, D. Pardoel, *Les conflits de lois en matière de transfert de créances*, *op. cit.*

57 These obvious qualities explain why they have attracted several Member States, such as Spain, Poland, see European Commission, *Proposal for a Regulation on the law applicable to the enforceability of assignments of claims*, p. 5. This solution also appealed to the United Kingdom, which already applied the *lex creationis* to the enforceability of the assignment, and thus proceeds from a unified approach to enforceability against third parties (see Dicey, Morris, and Collins, *The Conflict of Laws*, *op. cit.*)

58 For example, the characteristic performance of a currency swap contract is not easy to determine, see *infra*, para. 800.

59 D. Pardoel, *Les conflits de lois en matière de transfert de créances*, *op. cit.*, 368: 'Although the concepts of enforceability and publicity do not systematically overlap, the formalities prescribed by French law on the transfer of claims are based on the link between the two concepts: it is because it provides for a system for informing third parties that the assignment

Moreover, the debtor's domicile is comparatively more stable than that of the assignor: the debtor remains identical, whereas the same claim is often the subject of successive assignments.[60] Other disadvantages may relate to the determination of the debtor's domicile, and to cases of multiple debtors, but all this can easily be solved by the adoption of *ad hoc* rules.[61]

There are three main defects in the criterion of the assignor's domicile. The first is its weak legal connection with the conflict of priority between successive assignees of the claim. It is quite possible for the assignor to be located abroad and for the assignments to be subject to foreign law, or even for the debtor's assets not to be located in the country of his domicile.[62] However, even in this case, the debtor's domicile retains a link to the dispute in that it is the place of payment of the claim sought. Nevertheless, it is uncertain that this link is sufficiently preponderant to characterise the proximity of the debtor's domicile and the enforceability against third parties. This leads Mr d'Avout, for example, to consider that 'the debtor (not being) the pivot of the realisation'[63] of the assignment, it is the place of establishment of the assignor which 'therefore expresses the centre of gravity of the legal situation'.[64] However, this is not the main drawback. The fundamental defect of the assignor's domicile is that it is only apparent to *certain* third parties. In particular, it is apparent to the

---

of a claim becomes enforceable against third parties.' Ms Pardoel thus considers that the importance of publicity in the configuration of German domestic law is likely to explain the rule adopted in Germany, which in her view is not a variation of the adage *locus regit actum* (such an application could have been explained since, as the author herself expresses it: 'In our field, the difficulty arises from the relationship between the requirements of publicity and the conditions of form' (see *ibid.*, no. 422). Behind the *locus regit actum* rule is in fact the application of another rule, *auctor regit actum*, which designates the law of the bailiff competent to serve the document, see *ibid.*, nos 307 et seq. in particular no. 310. However, the author refuses to base the connecting criterion of opposability to third parties on the following reasons: 'Once it is accepted that the formalities for publicising assignments of claims are rules designed to strike a balance between the interests of third parties and of the assigned debtor, not forgetting those of the assignee, and once the French rules on publicising assignments of claims are not considered to be an expression of the French State's interest In short, since the rules on the publication of assignments of claims are intended to settle a question of priority between private interests, it is sufficient for the choice of connection to take account of the interests identified above without systematically seeking to achieve publication.' (*ibid.*, no. 378). On the discussion of the connection of publicity measures, see *ibid.*, nos. 349 et seq.

60 It is true that the debtor may move; however, this is not so frequent and the application of the law of the debtor's domicile on the day of the assignment is likely to resolve the difficulty.

61 On these difficulties, see *ibid.*

62 Comp. L. d'Avout, who considers that there are no links, except that 'only its assets constitute the basis for performance by equivalent of the assigned object and these assets may be scattered throughout the world', see L. d'Avout, 'La loi applicable à la cession de créance ou de contrat après l'ordonnance du 10 février 2016', *op. cit.*

63 *Ibid.*, no. 7.

64 *Ibid.*, no. 5.

assignee or assignees and allows a harmonious resolution of the conflict of priority when it concerns only the different assignees of the same claim. It is not so when the conflict concerns other creditors of the assignor and the assignee. Some third parties are therefore left in the dark, which makes the connecting factor structurally dysfunctional. Finally, the third disadvantage of this criterion stems from its inability to designate a single law in the case of assignments of a mass of claims.

586. The merits of the criterion of the assignor's domicile. The advantages of this criterion have already been sketched out. From a legal point of view, the assignor is the real center of gravity of the assignment.[65] From a geographical point of view, his domicile is the best known to all interested third parties, i.e. the assignees in dispute,[66] as well as to his own creditors. Its application allows a single law to be applied to an assignment of a mass of claims. Moreover, it provides a solution to the hypothesis of the assignment of future claims. Finally, it corresponds to the criterion adopted by the 2001 United Nations Convention on the Assignment of Receivables in International Trade[67] and, from the Union's point of view, is likely to support the solution adopted by the Insolvency Regulation in the event of proceedings initiated against the assignor.[68] It is therefore not surprising that this criterion has been elected as a principle by the Commission in its draft Regulation. The main disadvantage of this criterion is the possibility for the assignor to change his domicile between the two assignments of the same right. However, such a change is not frequent. Moreover, this difficulty can be solved by inserting a substantive rule which gives the right to the first assignor who has made his assignment effective against third parties according to the law of the assignor's domicile on the day of the assignment.[69] The strength of this connection and the equality it promotes for third parties explain why exceptions to this law must be carefully studied, justified and, where appropriate, strictly regulated. This is not the case with those proposed by the Commission.

---

65 See Wengler, who, in order to determine the criterion of the preponderant location of rights, considers that it must be sought within the various States that offer protection, the one that 'offers the most effective protection', and considers that in the case of an assignment of a claim, it is the State that can compel 'the one who is up to now the holder of the right, and who can compel him to make the necessary declarations of intent to ensure the assignment. To this extent, the right to assignment is located primarily at the domicile of the person who has undertaken to assign'. W. Wengler, 'La situation des droits', *op. cit.*, p. 208.

66 Mrs Pardoel has already observed that the latter is the most likely to preserve the protection of appearance, see D. Pardoel, *Les conflits de lois en matière de transfert de créances*, *op. cit.*, no. 379.

67 Art. 30 of the 2001 United Nations Convention on the Assignment of Claims in International Trade.

68 European Commission, 'Proposal for a Regulation on the law applicable to the enforecability of assignments of claims'.

69 This rule is the one retained by the draft Commission Regulation, see Art. 4(1) of the draft Regulation.

II. The Rejection of Exceptions to the Law of the Assignor

587. The exceptions to the law of the assignor's domicile proposed by the Commission. The Commission's proposal nevertheless provides, by way of exception, for the application of the law of the assigned claim in different ways. First, the law of the assigned claim will govern the enforceability of the assignment of 'cash credited to an account with a credit institution' and 'claims arising from a financial instrument'.[70] Secondly, it will be possible for the assignor and the assignee to choose, instead of the law of the assignor's domicile, the law of the claim assigned for securitisation.[71] These two exceptions have been included for different reasons, but both deserve to be rejected.

588. Exceptions subject to the *lex creationis*. In the case of claims arising from bank accounts and claims arising from financial instruments, the *lex creationis* does not apply for the same reasons. These two types of claims have in common that they are distinguished by the Commission from 'traditional claims',[72] but have nothing to do with each other.[73] Cash credited to an account with a credit institution represents 'money' issued by commercial banks and, depending on the balance of the account, will either represent a claim or a liability to the bank. In this first case, applying the *lex creationis* is tantamount to extending the law of the account agreement to third party enforceability. The Commission explains this exception by the hypothesis that the holder of the account would wish to pledge it in order to obtain a loan from another credit institution,[74] considering that in this case the application of the account agreement would be more predictable.[75] However, the selection of this criterion results in precisely the opposite result: the only third party who could know the law applicable to the account is the assignee who would have requested a copy of the account agreement. Far from protecting third parties in general, the motivation for this exception is therefore to protect only credit institutions that are beneficiaries of

70 Art. 4(2) of the draft regulation.

71 Art. 4(3) of the draft regulation.

72 European Commission, 'Proposal for a Regulation on the law applicable to the enforceability of assignments of claims', p. 7.

73 Regardless of the fact that, depending on the Member State, both may be booked, see European Commission, 'Proposal for a Regulation on the law applicable to the enforceability of assignments of claims', pp. 6–7.

74 European Commission, 'Proposal for a Regulation on the law applicable to the enforceability of assignments of claims', p. 20.

75 The Commission thus writes: 'For third parties such as creditors of the assignor and competing assignees, greater predictability is offered if the law applicable to the enforceability of the assignment of cash credited to an account opened with a credit institution is the law applicable to the cash claim. Indeed, it is generally accepted that the claim held by an account holder on cash credited to an account opened with a credit institution is governed by the law of the country where this institution is established.' See European Commission, 'Proposal for a Regulation on the law applicable to the enforceability of assignments of claims', pp. 20–21.

pledges on cash accounts. Apart from the fact that it is difficult to understand why credit institutions should enjoy such an advantage, this conflict rule amounts to subjecting the enforceability to third parties to a subjective criterion, determined by the parties alone, in contradiction with the interests of third parties.[76]

In the second case, that of claims arising from a financial instrument, the application of the law of the assigned claim is more specifically aimed not at financial instruments in general, but at financial contracts in particular.[77] The application of the *lex creationis* thus leads to the extension of the law applicable to the financial contract towards the enforceability against third parties of the balance of the financial contract, 'for example, the sum due after the calculation of the liquidation costs in the context of a derivative contract'.[78] Again, far from being a favour to third parties in general, the application of the law of the assigned claim favours certain third parties, in this case the co-contractor of the financial contract, in order to enable it, by being in the best position to know the law applicable to perfection, to take precedence over any third parties. The stated purpose of this exception is to promote the proper functioning of the financial market. The underlying idea is that by giving priority to the contracting party to the financial contract, it is possible to improve its performance and thus its efficiency. Even if this rationale for the rule were correct, it is not the proper functioning of the financial market that is aimed at, but the protection of the interests of some of its users who are parties to financial contracts. Above all, the invocation of the proper functioning of the financial markets is all the less convincing as the material scope of application of this provision is unrelated to the financial market: only financial instruments are covered. However, financial contracts can be concluded over the counter, outside any financial market.

589. The exception subject to a limited choice of law by the parties. With regard to securitisation, the reason given by the European Commission is not legal either. Indeed, the Commission simply wishes to recognise 'the practice of large operators of applying the law of the assigned claim to the enforceability of assignments of claims';[79] this in the hope that 'the flexibility provided in the conflict of laws rules applicable to securitisation will facilitate the expansion

---

76 All the criticisms relating to the *PRIMA rule* can be raised against this solution, see *infra*, para. 697.

77 The wording of this exception is particularly unfortunate. On the one hand, the notion of 'claim arising', apart from being remarkably ungainly, is frighteningly imprecise and contains within itself the promise of significant and casuistic litigation. On the other hand, why include all financial instruments when only some of them are explicitly covered by the purpose of the rule?

78 European Commission, 'Proposal for a Regulation on the law applicable to the enforceability of assignments of claims', p. 7.

79 European Commission, 'Proposal for a Regulation on the law applicable to the enforceability of assignments of claims', p. 6.

of the securitisation market through the entry of new operators on the market and the creation of new commercial opportunities'.[80] Such a motivation is disappointing.[81] Moreover, if it is truly linked to the desire of securitisation specialists to subject the enforceability against third parties of a set of claims subject to the same law, it would have been logical, as Professor Cuniberti observes, to 'limit the scope of the power to choose 'the law of the assigned claim' to cases where all the claims assigned for the purpose of a securitisation would be subject to the same law'.[82]

590. The draft regulation therefore appears inadequate whenever it attempts to exempt the enforceability of the assignment against third parties from the application of the law of the assignor's domicile. Far from constituting convincing limits to the validity of this rule, the exceptions in the draft regulation are intended to favour certain third parties to the detriment of others without any obvious justification. Rather, they appear as a further illustration of the importance of private interests in the development of EU law.[83] On the other hand, by excluding transfers of securities from its scope of application, the draft regulation deserves approval. Indeed, the application of the law of the assignor does not lead, for securities, to a harmonious resolution of the conflict of laws.

§ 3. THE IMPOSSIBLE ANALOGY TO TRANSFER OF SECURITIES

591. Frequency of transfer. Since negotiable instruments such as securities represent claims, there would be no difficulty in subsuming them within the material scope of the Regulation and, as such, making the effectiveness of their

[80] *Ibid.* See also the explanation given by the Commission, European Commission, 'Proposal for a Regulation on the law applicable to the enforceability of assignments of claims', p. 21.

[81] Mr Cuniberti considers that this is probably due to the influence of the Securitisation Regulation adopted shortly before, even if, in the words of the author, 'this Regulation, however, does not contain any conflict of laws rules, so that the influence it has exerted here hardly seems rational', see G. Cuniberti, 'La proposition de règlement de la Commission sur la loi applicable à l'opposabilité de la cession de créance', *RCDIP*, 2016, p. 793. This securitisation regulation would nevertheless be able to compensate for the absence of a definition of the concept of securitisation in the draft regulation.
Basically, precisely because it concerns third parties, it should not be possible for the law applicable to the enforceability of the assignment of a claim to be altered by a subjective location, still less the law chosen by the parties to the assignment. Moreover, the law of the assignor's domicile seemed perfectly suited to resolving the conflicts of law arising from securitisation.

[82] G. Cuniberti, 'La proposition de règlement de la Commission sur la loi applicable à l'opposabilité de la cession de créance', *op. cit.*

[83] See already our comments *supra*, para. 23 and the report on the Financial Collateral Directive *infra*, para. 753.

transfer against third parties subject to the law of the transferor's domicile.[84] However, such an analysis would ignore the rationale of the particular form of certain shares, claims or units in collective investment undertakings. Negotiable instruments, and subsequently financial instruments, were created in order to avoid the particularly cumbersome formalities for the perfection of the assignment of civil claims. The enforceability of these instruments was therefore facilitated by the techniques of endorsement for the former, and by tradition (in the Roman meaning of tradition *i.e.* hand-to-hand transfer) and then transfer within securities accounts for bearer securities. The particularity of the tradition of bearer securities is that it was valid both as a transfer and as an enforceability to third parties, except in the case of theft.[85] The function of these rules is to allow securities to be exchanged very frequently. However, this is the weakness of the application of the law of the assignor, which triggers the application of a possibly different law to each assignment, and therefore multiplies the defects that may affect the assignment. This weakness is insurmountable in the sense that it negates the function of commercial law through the regime attached to the negotiability of securities, which is precisely to give commercial transactions a speed and security that they would otherwise lack.[86] To this first weakness are added two others, the first one linked to the exchange of securities through a financial market, the second one specific to the modern holding structure of securities. These two weaknesses are nevertheless linked, because of the influence of the admission to trading on the proprietary status of securities.

---

84 Ms Pardoel excludes securities from her study because the interests involved are not the same. Indeed, while the purpose of the assignment of a claim is to 'ensure that the assigned debtor is not obliged twice for the same claim, unless he is mistaken', and to 'ensure that the assignment of a claim does not undermine the solvency of the assignor with regard to his successors', these interests would not be paramount in the context of the circulation of securities (D. Pardoel, *Les conflits de lois en matière de cession de créances*, *op. cit.*, no. 32). Only the first argument is really convincing because of the holding structure of the securities, which allows reliable identification of the holder (and not because 'securities represent long or very long term claims for which payment does not appear to be the first priority', see *ibid.*). The second argument appears less relevant. Indeed, it is difficult to see why the circulation of securities should allow a debtor to fleece his creditors: the protection of the third party purchaser is not systematic.

85 On this aspect, see *infra* para. 639.

86 As Dean Hamel wrote: 'First, if it is true that the function of law is to provide frameworks for the phenomena of social life, commercial law is specialised in the organisation and systematisation of the phenomena of economic life; it determines how the production and circulation of wealth should be organised in a given society. It cannot be denied that these phenomena can only be included in legal frameworks if these frameworks have certain characteristics that are adapted to the subject matter they are intended to cover. Let us recall only two of these characteristics, which demonstrate the necessary autonomy of commercial law: the speed of commercial operations and the pre-eminent place of credit.' J. Hamel and G. Lagarde, *Traité de droit commercial*, Paris, Dalloz, vol. I, 1954, p. III. Gaston Lagarde will explain in his preface to volume II that this preface is the almost exclusive work of Dean Hamel (G. Lagarde, 'In Memoriam' in *Traité de droit commercial*, vol. II, Paris, Dalloz, 1966, p. VII).

592. The influence of admission to trading on the proprietary status of securities. The function of securities was originally to facilitate the assignment of the *negotia* issued. Today, their regime has more in common than the mere question of transfer: the notion of securities allows for the application of identical marketing rules.[87] However, the ease with which the security can be transferred remains of fundamental importance in the interest of these securities, and conditions their very possibility of being admitted to trading on a financial market.[88] Moreover, the platform constituting the financial market has the effect of making the parties to the assignment anonymous.[89] The application of the law of the assignor will therefore be impossible to determine for the assignee. The other effect of the financial market is to require that the securities be deposited with a central depository. This has the effect of significantly altering the *ratio legis* of the law of the assignor's domicile, by shifting the legal centre of gravity of the assignment from the assignor to the securities settlement system managed by the central depository, which is known to all third parties.

593. Conclusion of the section. Walh considered that 'the history of the bearer bond can be seen as a chapter in the history of debt assignments'.[90] The statement is correct and it is for this reason that one should look to these solutions whenever the assignment of title is conceived by reference to a simple tripartite transfer operation, without taking into account the rationale of the negotiability of the securities, or the effects that the existence of a financial market has on the issue at hand. However, the application of the law of the assignor's domicile ignores, on the one hand, the high frequency with which securities are transferred and, on the other hand, the holding structure in which the securities fit. This makes it necessary to develop a specific rule that takes these characteristics into account. With the help of the solutions developed in the neighbouring area of the law on negotiable instruments, it will now be shown that these characteristics should not be sought in the thesis of the plurality of connections, but in a unitary solution of the conflict of laws.

---

87 With the exception of shares and units in collective investment schemes, which may be subject to separate rules.

88 See *supra*, para. 308.

89 See *supra*, para. 41.

90 A. Wahl, *Traité théorique et pratique des titres au porteur*, Rousseau, 1891, vol. I, p. 13, no. 13.

SECTION 3. LESSONS FROM THE LAW OF NEGOTIABLE INSTRUMENTS

594. Interest of the study. It is legitimate to wonder about the interest of a development on the solutions of conflicts of laws in the area of bills of exchange: if these techniques have not totally disappeared, they are nevertheless losing significant ground.[91] It should be added that neither the bill of exchange nor the 'savings bond' (*bons du trésor*) are financial instruments,[92] and do not *a priori* fall within the scope of this study. It seems to us, however, that despite the evolution of payment and credit techniques, their purpose has not only remained relatively stable, but is above all partly common with that of financial securities.[93] This is why the regulation of these first negotiable instruments and their mechanisms still serves as a model for financial instruments;[94] this is also why it is necessary to observe the possible pathologies of solutions that may appear in the past, but whose vigour still irrigates positive law. In fact, the peculiarities of securities have most often given rise to a solution of the conflict of laws based on what has been called the thesis of the plurality of connections.[95] This thesis has been enshrined in the conflict-of-laws solutions for negotiable instruments. It refers to two realities: on the one hand, the disaggregation of the various aspects of the economic operation of the bill of exchange (issue, validity, effects of the exchange obligations, transmission of the provision by the instrument, etc.) and, on the other hand, the use of a connection leading to the application of a different law to each transfer of the bill. The latter solution is the most damaging; it is this solution which is the main subject of the critical discussion which follows.

---

91 In 2013, bills of exchange and promissory notes accounted for 981 million euros of daily payments in France, i.e. 4.65% of payments, compared with 18.9% for cheques and 51.45% for credit transfers, which are therefore by far the most common means of payment, see Insee, *Les tableaux de l'économie française*, 2015, p. 185 (data collected in 2013).

92 Art. L. 211-1 of the Monetary and Financial Code.

93 This can be seen from the fact that the ECB considers the security to be a monetary aggregate that can be substituted for money when cash is given as collateral, see *supra*, para. 287.

94 Negotiable instruments and bearer securities are sometimes considered together by certain foreign conflict rules, see for example in English law, Dicey, Morris, and Collins, *The Conflict of Laws*, *op. cit.*, rule 241, no. 33-387. However, these solutions, which give pride of place to the local law, *lex loci actus* or *lex rei sitae*, continue to condition the conflict of laws: to be convinced of this, it is sufficient to observe that certain European conflict of laws rules relating to securities are still entitled '*lex rei sitae*' (see Art. 24 of the Winding Up Directive, reproduced and studied *infra*, para. 685).

95 R. Chemaly, 'Conflits de lois en matière d'effets de commerce', *op. cit.*, p. 391.

§ 1. DEAD ENDS OF THE PLURALITY OF CONNECTIONS IN NEGOTIABLE INSTRUMENTS LAW

595. Origin and function of the bill of exchange.[96] As the main instrument of the law of exchange and born in the cross-border commercial practice of the Middle Ages,[97] the bill of exchange dominated internal commercial relations for a long time[98] before being abandoned during the 20th century in favour of other techniques, in particular that of the bank transfer.[99] During this same period, the bill of exchange returned to the field where it had originated: international relations.[100] The function of the bill of exchange has evolved over the centuries and is a hybrid instrument. Thus, in its early days, the exchange and its instrument of implementation, the bill of exchange, were decried as serving 'to disguise usurious practices'.[101] The evolution of practice has given a specificity to the bill of exchange, which is due as much to its nature as an instrument of credit and payment,[102] as to

---

96 In addition to the bibliography indicated by R. Libchaber, 'Effet de commerce et chèques', *Répertoire de droit international*, Paris, Dalloz, see the considerable references to French and foreign conflict law provided by R. Roblot, *Les effets de commerce*, Paris, Sirey, 1975, no. 653, p. 566, fn. 1.

97 The bill of exchange was originally part of the contract of exchange, before being gradually separated from it in order to allow a form of interest-bearing loan, officially proscribed by the Doctors of the Church. On this subject see 'Effet de commerce et chèques' in R. Libchaber, *op. cit.*, no. 7; R. de Roover, *L'évolution de la lettre de hange. XIVe-XVIIIe siècles*, Paris, Armand Collin, 1953, spec. the first part. The latter author, echoed by Roblot (R. Roblot, *Les effets de commerce*, *op. cit.*, no. 15, p. 14), notes, however, that the Church had to fight for several centuries against the *cambium siccum*, in which bankers invented false differences in place in order to be able to charge interest on the sums loaned. This shows that the favour of international relations, which manifests itself in the creation of material rules, was already susceptible to misuse and to affect the social order of the forum.

98 The importance acquired by the bill of exchange can be measured by what Begouen, orator of the Corps Législatif, said of it: 'The bill of exchange was invented. This event, which forms an epoch in the history of commerce almost comparable to the discovery of the compass and America, has done away with all these obstacles. The bill of exchange freed movable capital, facilitated its movement and disposal, and created an immense amount of credit: from then on, trade knew no other limits than those of the world.' Locré, *Législation*, vol. XVIII, p. 140, quoted by H. Lévy-Bruhl, *Histoire de la lettre de change en France aux XVIIe et XVIIIe siècles*, *op. cit.*, pp. 32–33.

99 Insee, *op. cit.*; R. Libchaber, 'Effet de commerce et chèques', *op. cit.*

100 *Ibid*, no. 7.

101 H. Lévy-Bruhl, *Histoire de la lettre de change en France aux XVIIe et XVIIIe siècles*, *op. cit.*, p. 24; R. Szramkiewicz and O. Descamps, *Histoire du droit des affaires*, *op. cit.*

102 In French law, the bill of exchange is both an instrument of transfer of rights, which is manifested by the provision according to which the bearer of the bill of exchange acquires the claim arising from the provision, and an instrument of payment: the presentation of the bill of exchange enables a debt to be extinguished. This dual function is historical: 'Of the two functions that we recognise today in this instrument of commerce, that of remittance from place to place and that of instrument of credit, it is the first that plays the most important role. Without doubt, the bill of exchange, especially when the practice of endorsement became widespread, served from then on powerfully to circulate wealth and played more and more the role of an auxiliary fiduciary currency; this point of view was

the particular efficiency of the payment it grants.[103] This dual function, combined with its regime, explains why the bill of exchange was able to compete with money itself as a means of payment,[104] as the credit granted was so secure.[105] It is therefore not surprising that merchants wanted to avail themselves of the benefits of the bill of exchange in international relations. However, the diversity of conflict of laws rules and the substantive regulations governing them were an obstacle. It was against this background that the first international conventions began to be negotiated, and the Geneva Conventions of 7 June 1930 and 19 March 1931 on uniform laws for bills of exchange and promissory notes on the one hand and cheques on the other were born. These laws were accompanied by two conventions on the conflict of laws in these two areas.[106]

596. The mechanism of the bill of exchange. Today, negotiable instruments constitute a heterogeneous category consisting mainly of the bill of exchange, the promissory note and the cheque. Thus, while some instruments have more of a payment function, such as the cheque, others can also have a credit function, such as the bill of exchange. In contemporary commercial relations, the operation of the bill of exchange consists of a creditor, known as the drawer, issuing a bill of exchange based on a claim he has against his debtor, known as the drawee, obliging the latter to pay the beneficiary of the bill, most often the bearer of the

---

gradually confirmed during the 13th century.' H. Lévy-Bruhl, *Histoire de la lettre de change en France aux XVIIe et XVIIIe siècles*, *op. cit.*, p. 22. The author notes just before: 'The bill of exchange, in its structure, was already at that time (17th and 18th centuries) what it is today. Its technique has changed relatively little. On the contrary, its function has changed. The bill of exchange, in our old law, is essentially the method of execution of the exchange contract.'

103 This effectiveness is manifested by the sanction of which its non-payment is the object: once the protest is drawn up, the intervention of the public authorities is triggered and the judicial liquidation is, so to speak, already recorded.

104 Commercial bills are traditionally defined as 'any security that is commonly received in payment in commercial transactions in place of money, without however having the attributes of money' (R. Roblot, *Les effets de commerce*, *op. cit.*, no. 4, p. 2), a formula taken up by Art. 29 of the 1967 Act (*Ibid.).*

105 Thus, in order to prosper, Law's 'system' had to put in place a prohibition on bills of exchange by an edict of May 1716, the official reason for which was to combat usury. As Lévy-Bruhl writes: 'Moreover, in the first third of the 18th century, Law's "system" had a serious influence on the bill of exchange, at least on its form. In order to develop the circulation of the notes of the newly founded Royal Bank as much as possible, and to hinder the competition with bills of exchange, considered this time as an instrument of credit, a royal declaration of March 1716 prohibited the use of bearer bills of exchange. This prohibition was brought back in January 1721, after the failure of the system', H. Lévy-Bruhl, *Histoire de la lettre de change en France aux XVIIe et XVIIIe siècles*, *op. cit.*, p. 24; The objective appears all the more fallacious as immediately after the fall of Law's system, a new royal declaration of 1721 abolished the prohibition, see *ibid.*, p. 210. On Law's system, see also the influence it had on the stockbrokers themselves, *supra*, para. 39 and references.

106 See *supra*, paras. 575 et seq.

bill of exchange.[107] The latter may in turn endorse the bill of exchange in favour of another person. The bill of exchange is subject to a number of particularities as regards its conditions of formation, especially because of a certain confusion of the elements of form and substance. The bill of exchange also has a unique regime, in that it is subject to conditions of facilitated transmission, and all those who endorse the bill are guarantors of its payment. From an international perspective, three series of difficulties specific to this operation have made it difficult to choose the law applicable to the bill of exchange: the confusion between the instrument and the obligations entered into by means of a bill of exchange ('exchange obligations'); the effects of the exchange obligation on the obligation arising from the original contract; and, finally, the effects of each signature on the exchange obligation.

597. The plurality of connections. These characteristics led the authors of the Geneva Convention to adopt the so-called plurality of connections thesis.[108] It is not certain that this thesis still incurs the same criticism in its two aspects of disaggregation and applying a plural connection to their transfer. Indeed, the general disaggregation of the bill is not necessarily problematic: traditional claims, and even financial securities, are subject to different laws depending on whether one is talking about the conditions of their validity, their transfer or their enforceability. The finesse of Mr Chemaly's criticism of the thesis of the plurality of connections lies not in the principle of disaggregation, but in the fact that this would not have been necessary because of the primary purpose of the bill of exchange, payment, which allowed the application of the law of payment to all these aspects. However, this criticism is not necessarily convincing. To convince oneself of this, one can take the example of capacity, which is subject to the personal status in the Geneva Convention.

598. The function of personal status in the Geneva Convention. Although personal status may seem outdated in commercial matters today, it has had considerable influence in the field of negotiable instruments. Indeed, in the 17th and 18th centuries, the personal law could prevail over the law of payment (i.e. the domicile of the drawee) in order to determine the jurisdiction of the courts, at a time when

---

[107] Or taker. In principle, the operation is tripartite: there is a drawer, a drawee and the taker of the bill of exchange. If one were to compare these three legal positions with an assignment under common law, the drawer would be the equivalent of the assignor. The drawee, i.e. the person on whom the bill was drawn (the expression appeared late in French law, see H. Lévy-Bruhl, *Histoire de la lettre de change en France aux XVIIe et XVIIIe siècles, op. cit.*, p. 8) would be the assigned debtor, and the taker of the bill of exchange would be the assignee. Doctrinal writers have made numerous comparisons between the law of bills of exchange and common law, see the summary by F. Nizard, *Les titres négociables, op. cit.*

[108] See the defence of the plurality of connections by P. Lescot and R. Roblot, *Les effets de commerce*, vol. 2, Rousseau, 1953, nos. 1069 and seq.

this was not unconnected with the applicable law.[109] The importance of personal law has undoubtedly diminished, but retains a role in the Geneva Convention. First, the Convention traditionally provides that national law governs capacity, while providing in a second sentence that 'if that national law declares the law of another country competent in the matter, this latter law shall be applied'.[110] This is a technique that allows the criterion of domicile to be respected for countries that have chosen it in personal matters. The Convention then proceeds to a more original arrangement. Firstly, it provides that any incapacity resulting from personal law may be overridden by the law of the place of the act.[111] Secondly, the Convention makes it possible for one of the signatory States not to recognise an undertaking validated by the law of the place of the act, but which would be null and void under the personal law of the person affected.[112]

The application of the law of the place of the act to capacity is not unknown in the US.[113] On the one hand, this may be seen as a reflection of the importance given to appearance, which was also seen in France in the *Lizardi* judgment,[114] but above all as a favour given to the validity of the bill of exchange and its payment. The Italian delegation did not take well the possibility, defended by the German and French delegations, for a signatory State to refuse the application of the *lex loci actus*, considering this to be a 'fraud on trade'.[115] The result of this dual provision is undoubtedly legal instability, the very thing that

---

109 See on this hypothesis H. Lévy-Bruhl, *Histoire de la lettre de change en France aux XVIIe et XVIIIe siècles*, *op. cit.*, p. 296. Nevertheless, this was perhaps more of a one-off exception than a rule, without it being known whether jurisdiction was granted solely on the grounds that the drawee was French, or whether it was the combination of several connecting factors (nationality of the drawee, nationality of the bearer of the bill of exchange, issue in France of the bill) to France that justified this connection. The competent court was already at that time the court of the debtor.

110 Art. 2 of the Geneva Convention, para. 1.

111 The incapable person according to his or her State of origin will be 'validly bound, if the signature has been given in the territory of a country under whose law the person would have been capable' (Art. 2, para. 2 Geneva Convention).

112 Art. 2(3) of the Geneva Convention.

113 B. Goldman, 'Les conflits de lois en matière d'instruments négociables', Report to the International Bar Association, 4th Conference (London 1950), The Hague, p. 7: 'In the United States "the law of the place of conclusion of the contract determines the contractual capacity of the parties" (Restatement of the law of conflict of laws of the American Law Institute, Art. 333); in England, the solution is controversial, but especially in the case of "mercantile contracts", considerable authors discard personal law in favour of the *lex loci contractus* (Dicey) or the law of the contract (Cheshire).' However, capacity was governed at the time of the Convention by the '*lex loci contractus*', the theory of domicile being excluded in all commercial matters, see Guttenbridge intervention, *Proceedings of the 1930 Geneva Conference*, p. 346.

114 Y. Lequette and B. Ancel, *Les grands arrêts de la jurisprudence française de droit international privé*, *op. cit.*, comm. no. 5; R. Chemaly, 'Conflits de lois en matière d'effets de commerce', *op. cit.*, p. 381.

115 *Proceedings of the 1930 Geneva Conference*, pp. 350–351. This article provoked heated debate, with the Italian delegation stating that it 'will not be able to sign the Convention if the Conference adopts Article 3 in its present form, as it would be inadmissible to enshrine

the conflict rules were intended to prevent. This is undoubtedly why Professor Berthold Goldman,[116] like the *International Bar Association*, simply wanted to set aside personal law as the principle for settling questions of capacity.[117]

599. Such a decision, favourable to the validity of the bill of exchange and to the trade that it allows, nevertheless appears inappropriate. Indeed, the basis of incapacity, at least in French law,[118] is not to favour trade, nor even to protect a weak party in the sense that certain provisions of the Rome I Regulation[119] now do, i.e. to increase the protection of all persons in a weak position in a given legal relationship. The function of incapacity is to protect a *category of persons*, namely the most vulnerable in a society, those nationals who are least able to express their free will, regardless of the situation.[120] This very residual category of persons deserves special treatment, and it would be surprising, to say the least, to dismiss the jurisdiction of the country that is supposed to protect them, on the altar of a favour to trade or payment.[121] Indeed, the *lex loci actus*, like the law of payment,

---

fraud in international trade'. Art. 3 will eventually correspond to Art. 2, and the Italians ended up signing the Convention without reservation. Moreover, France did not make use of this option in the end.

116 Followed by R. Chemaly, 'Conflits de lois en matière d'effets de commerce', *op. cit.*, p. 370.

117 B. Goldman, «æes conflits de lois en matière d'instruments négociables', *op. cit.*, p. 7. The author is in favour of the *lex loci actus* in matters of capacity, as this would make it possible to 'unify the solution of all conflicts concerning the validity and effectiveness of the creation and circulation of the instrument'. The author comes close to an English approach to capacity.

118 Mr Lequette has summed it up admirably: 'Capacity is an aptitude, a potential subjective quality. It is therefore only realised in connection with other legal institutions, especially contracts. This connection implies that capacity, or its opposite, incapacity and the related protection regime, can be understood either as a quality proper to the person or as a constituent element of any act. By focusing on one or the other aspect, incapacity and the protection regime are oriented towards unity or diversity. In private international law, depending on the approach adopted, capacity and protection of incapacitated persons will either be the subject of an autonomous category or attached to the regime of acts. It is the second conception that tends to prevail in *common law* countries', in Y. Lequette, *Protection familiale et protection étatique des incapables*, Paris, Dalloz, 1976, no. 52, p. 30. See on the English and French perceptions of capacity, H. Glenn, *La capacité de la personne en droit international privé français et anglais*, Paris, Dalloz, 1974.

119 These are two very different issues, as the Rome I Regulation also states that questions of capacity do not fall within the scope of the law designated by the conflict-of-laws rules it contains.

120 In the area of bills of exchange, the protection of the most vulnerable of a regime which in certain respects is particularly cruel to the debtor, is manifested by Art. L. 511-5 of the Commercial Code which prescribes the nullity of the exchange obligations arising from the signature of the bill of exchange by a minor, an incapable person, or 'for any other reason, cannot bind the persons who signed the bill of exchange, or in whose name it was signed'. The commitments of the other signatories remain intact according to the same provision.

121 It may be argued that the law of payment is perhaps just as capable of protecting them, but it is undeniable that this would lead to solutions in which a legal system protecting its most vulnerable nationals through incapacity could see its legislation set aside in favour of another, possibly less favourable, law. However, there is a particular legitimacy of the community of origin, whether determined by nationality or domicile, to protect the people who come from it.

does not have an unlimited field of application: its basis is that of the favour done to payment. One of its boundaries must at least be that protection of the most vulnerable which a society is intended to protect.[122] The argument in favour of payment is all the more flimsy because it is a category that is numerically very small, but symbolically too important to allow for any compromise.

It therefore appears that the defect in the thesis of the plurality of connections stems essentially from the fact that it leads to a multiplication of the laws applicable to the assignment of the bill of exchange and thus contravenes the payment function of the bill of exchange. This function therefore explains why, on the one hand, it is illusory to wish to base the thesis of the plurality of connections on the internal characteristics of the bill of exchange (I) and, on the other hand, the cumulative system of applicable laws assigned to the assignment of the bill deserves vigorous condemnation (II).

I. The Contradiction of the Geneva Convention System with the Function of the Bill of Exchange

600. Distinction between title and exchange obligation. Many authors often confuse a title (*instrumentum*) and an obligation under a contract of exchange (*negiotum*), not only because of the representation of obligations under a contract of exchange by a title, but also because of the particular evidential importance of the title for the transmission of the obligation. However, the distinction between a document of title and an exchange obligation is easily tested: it is sufficient to note that the disappearance of the document of title[123] does not lead to the extinction of the exchange obligation.[124] The law therefore provides for a mechanism enabling the holder to prove his exchange obligation by a means other than the presentation of the bill of exchange. The owner of the bill of exchange is the holder of the exchange obligation, irrespective of the presentation of the original

---

122 Percerou summed up the issue perfectly when he stated during the negotiations, in relation to this particular question of the possibility of limiting the *lex loci actus*, that there was 'a conflict between the interest of credit and the interest of protecting the incapable'.

123 The loss of the bill of exchange does not in any event affect theoriginal contract, which can be proved by any means. Otherwise there would be a risk of the drawee being unjustly enriched and, therefore, there would be a quasi-contractual basis on which the dispossessed owner of the bill of exchange could sue the drawee. This scheme is also used in other legal systems, for example in Germany, see R. Rodière, *Droit commercial*, 5th ed., Paris, Dalloz, no. 90 p. 85. This action does not, however, make it possible to prove the existence or not of the exchange obligation.

124 Indeed, the holder of the exchange obligation who has been dispossessed of his bill of exchange may in this case turn to his immediate endorser. The latter is then 'obliged to lend him his name and care' and thus to go back step by step, 'from endorser to endorser', through the whole chain of endorsements to the drawer of the bill (Art. L. 511-36 of the Commercial Code; the legislator has provided for the protection of the bearer in good faith with whom the payment discharges the drawee). See R. Roblot, *Les effets de commerce*, *op. cit.*, nos. 452 et seq.

bill of exchange that was drawn up.[125] The existence of the title should therefore not be sought as a justification for the thesis of the plurality of attachments of the bill of exchange.

In the same way, it is sometimes the exclusion of exchange obligations from the category of contractual obligations that explains the separate treatment they receive in conflict-of-laws rules. However, if one looks at the reasons given, one is hard put to convince oneself of this as far as French law is concerned. Confusion is maintained in this respect by three questions: the relationship between title and obligation, the abstract nature of the exchange obligation, and the scope of form in the creation of exchange obligations. It is often in the name of these three arguments that local law has been applied to exchange obligations: application of the *lex rei sitae* to the obligation 'contained' in the document of title; exclusion from the law of the obligation of what was too far removed from a contractual obligation; or application of the *lex loci actus* to the effects of the exchange obligation created by the formalism of the document of title (a phenomenon which has been described as the absorption of substance by form). We shall endeavour to show that the thesis of the plurality of connections cannot be sought in the characteristics of the bill of exchange either (A). In reality, it stems from a confusion as to the relationship between the rules of domestic law and conflict of laws (B).

A. Function of the Characteristics of the Bill of Exchange

601. It is argued that the specificity of the law of exchange is that, in this area, the forms create obligations. Therefore, the law traditionally applicable to the form of the acts should determine the effects of the exchange commitments[126] since the form would be the source of the obligation. However, even if the forms were truly obligation-creating, the argument would not be decisive since the form serves the substance, which is to enable payment. In other words, the importance given to form in domestic law is absolutely subordinate to the payment of the obligation. In addition, the presupposition about the function of the formalism of the

125 This is further confirmed by another legislative provision: even in the event that the holder of the bill of exchange obligation is unable to establish a 'next' in the terms of the law (i.e. a form of duplicate of the first), 'he may request payment of the lost bill of exchange and obtain it by order of the judge by proving its ownership by his books and by giving security', see Art. L. 511-34 of the Commercial Code. The ruthlessness of the regime of bills of exchange for the debtor makes equivalent protection necessary (protection which is manifested by the rule according to which the debtor under the regime of bills of exchange is only obliged to pay on presentation of the bill of exchange), which requires a particularly high degree of proof of the obligation: if it is not the drawer, only a judicial decision can provide such proof. In other words, only a court decision can establish an equivalent degree of protection.

126 It is important to distinguish this allegation from that of *formalism*: the creative effect of forms consists in imputing the creation of obligations to particular forms, whereas formalism lies in subjecting the creation of obligations to solemnities.

exchange is incorrect: the formalism of the exchange has primarily a function of protection of the debtor and secondarily of protection of the payment (1), whereas the function of the exchange regime is entirely directed towards payment (2).

1. *The Function of Exchange Formalism and Protection of the Debtor*

602. Protection of the debtor. If the non-presentation of a bill of exchange does not prevent the payment of the exchange obligation from being sought in court, it is clear that the exchange obligation exists independently of the title and therefore, *a fortiori*, independently of any handwritten inscriptions on it. Admittedly, Article L. 511-1(II) of the French Commercial Code seems to affirm the contrary when it states: 'A document of title in which one of the statements indicated in I is missing is not valid as a bill of exchange, except in the cases determined in III to V of this article.' However, it should already be noted that the law compensates for some of the absences of the formalities that are nonetheless said to be 'compulsory',[127] so that it would be excessive to say that they are all compulsory. Within the so-called obligatory formalities, only the absence of those relating to the drawee's consent leads to the disqualification of the bill of exchange and its possible conversion by reduction.[128] The first function of formalism appears here: the protection of the exchange debtor against a commitment which he cannot escape in the name of the exceptions

[127] Thus, of the eight formalities made mandatory by Art. L. 511-1(I) of the Commercial Code, three absences are remedied by the law, which establishes the meaning of their absence in Art. L. 511-1(III), (IV) and (V) of the Commercial Code.

[128] In this sense, it is not insignificant that the law does not make up for the absence of the denomination of the bill of exchange from the instrument, as well as the most basic indications to *prove* that there is an exchange relationship between the potential holder of the obligation and its debtor.
It was highly desirable for the legislator to subject these exchange obligations to special evidential mechanisms, just as Art. 1359 (formerly 1341) of the Civil Code subjects claims for sums of money above a certain amount to special evidential conditions. These two rules have the same function, and no-one has ever thought of asserting that civil obligations are contained in their *instrumentum*, or created by it, or that a title determines their existence (even Professor Flour, in his classic article in the Capitant series, simply observes that form seems to have an influence which may have been neglected; in reality, in order for consensualism to produce the effects which we expect from the freedom which it offers to individuals, it is still necessary for the latter to be ordered: This is the end of the rules of form in French private law). These two rules stemming from Art. 511-1(II) of the Commercial Code and 1359 of the Civil Code only diverge as to their degree because of the seriousness of the exchange undertaking which makes a greater degree of proof necessary. This same seriousness of the commitment explains the prohibition of the use of bills of exchange in matters where the regime imposed by the law of exchange seems too strict, see for example the legislative prohibition of bills of exchange in consumer credit transactions (Law no. 78-22 of 10 January 1978, Art. 17), or in the area of real estate credit (Law no. 79-596 of 13 July 1979, Art. 35).

to payment arising from the general law of contract.[129] These formalities do not therefore create the exchange obligations; they merely make it possible to prove them. Where the legislator considers that the document does not make it possible to establish the existence of a bill of exchange, the *instrumentum* can still be used as *prima facie* evidence in writing of a debt under ordinary law.[130] This is why the formalism of the bill of exchange, which makes the validity of the commitments entered into subject to strict rules of form, is not an obstacle to their affiliation to contractual obligations, in the same way that the formalism of contracts for the sale of real estate[131] or contracts of guarantee or insurance,[132] which nevertheless determine the validity of the commitment entered into, does not deprive these commitments of their contractual character.[133]

603. Protection of payment. The second function of the formalism of the exchange is to ensure that the obligation will be paid, which is rather similar to the payment function of the bill of exchange and is found within the regime of the exchange obligation. The aim here is to protect the exchange obligation itself. This is shown by the importance attached to the signature, which is a condition of the exchange obligation. Therefore, the signature should probably not be seen

129 The regime of the exchange is indeed draconian and, in order to be able to refuse the other party the benefit of the opposability of the exceptions to payment, or to condemn him to penal sanctions in the event of non-payment, it is fortunate that the law provides for *a minimal degree of proof* allowing to account for the fact that the drawee, the endorsee or the guarantor actually intended to enter into an exchange relationship.

130 See in particular Cass. com., 17 October 1995, no. 93-18.642.

131 Of course, the comparison can always be criticized, since the real estate sales contract remains valid between the parties before the reiteration by authentic instrument, but is simply not enforceable against third parties, whereas in the case of the exchange obligation, it is the absence of certain conditions for the formation of the legal acts that are not enforceable against the bearer of the bill of exchange.

132 Art. L. 112-3 para. 5 of the Insurance Code. The Court of Cassation has traditionally interpreted this provision as a rule of evidence, and recently the High Court stated that "if the insurance contract constitutes a perfect consensual contract from the moment the wills of the insurer and the insured meet, its proof is subordinate to the drawing up of a written contract", to censure a decision by a court of appeal which had accepted the proof of a modification of the insurance contract by tacit admission, "whereas it noted that the insured had not signed any rider making it possible to prove that he had accepted the restriction of cover issued by the insurer" (Cass. civ. 2e, 17 March 2011, no. 10-16.553). On this text and its interpretation, see the comments of H. Synvet, *D.*, 2017, 2176.

133 See F. Chénedé, *Les commutations en droit privé*, *op. cit.*, 409: 'The word source evokes both the idea of birth and the idea of origin. The two meanings do not overlap. While the first focuses on the *appearance of* the commitment, the second evokes the *origin of* the obligation. If one adopts the first meaning, the source can indeed be defined as the fact that generates the obligation. It is indeed *at the moment of* the realisation of this fact that the obligation comes into being. On the other hand, if one adopts the second definition, one is led to ask a different question: one no longer wonders what event is the *source of the* obligation, but rather the *origin of* the obligation.

as the source of the exchange obligation.[134] Rather, the particular effects of the signature should be seen in the context of the special function of commercial law in general and of the law of the exchange in particular with regard to the certainty of the commitment. Indeed, for traders, the signature has a very intense psychological importance which marks a certain commitment.[135] Rather than being a 'creative form', it would therefore seem appropriate to present the signature as the only manifestation of will by which such a commitment can be made.[136] This is all the more true as the drawee can raise the exception of forgery against the legitimate bearer of the bill of exchange.[137] Above all, the protection afforded to payment appears even more clearly in the regime of the exchange.

2. *Function of the Exchange Regime and Protection of Payment*

604. The exchange regime and the protection of payment. The most original aspect of the regime of the exchange obligation is also the one which best shows the importance attached to payment: the 'abstract' character of the exchange obligation. Abstraction is the characteristic of obligations which exist without consideration (in the sense of what was known in French law as 'cause'),[138] the

---

134 The fact that in the event of loss of the bill of exchange the existence of the exchange obligation can be proven by other means does not affect the value attached to the signature: in the event of loss, it is precisely by other means that the signature is proven to have been affixed.

135 The particular significance given to the signature, and the consequences it entails, confirm the idea that it is the exchange obligation and its validity that one wishes to preserve: the aim is to ensure that the letter is as reliable as possible, which means disqualifying it if it does not meet a sufficient degree of certainty.

136 In other words, here the signature removes any ambiguity in the manifestation of the will. See V. Malassigné, *Les titres représentatifs*, *op. cit.*, nos. 183–185.

137 In the light of 'Articles 1324 of the Civil Code, 287, 288 of the New Code of Civil Procedure and 121 of the Commercial Code, now Article L. 511-12', the Court of Cassation states that 'in the case where the accepting drawee denies the authenticity of his signature on a bill of exchange, for the purposes of acceptance, and thus intends to exclude having entered into an exchange obligation, it is up to the judge to proceed with the verification of the contested document in the light of the elements available to him, after having, if necessary, enjoined the parties to produce all useful comparison documents', see Com., 5 December 2000, no. 97-20236. This is the application of an age-old principle, see V. Malassigné, *Les titres représentatifs*, *op. cit.*, fn. 461, see in particular. CA Rouen, 26 April 1893, *Recueil de jurisprudence commerciale et maritime du Havre*, 1893, II, p. 169; CA Lyon, 20 February 1954, *Bq.* 1954, p. 520, note X. Marin; Cass. com, 2 December 1997, *Bull. civ.* IV, no. 96; *D.*, 1998, *I.R.*, p. 13; See also for a promissory note: CA Paris, 25 May 1990, *D.*, 1990, *I.R.*, p. 157.

138 H. Capitant, *De la cause des obligations*, Paris, Dalloz, 1923, p. 13: 'Finally, there is one last question which must necessarily attract and hold our attention, and that is the validity or possibility of the abstract juridical act. If every obligation created by the will is closely dependent on cause and cannot live without it, it is nevertheless conceivable that this link may be broken, that the obligation may be detached from its cause, either because the parties want it to be, or because the needs of legal commerce require it.' In contemporary literature, see M. Fabre-Magnan, *Droit des obligations*, vol. 1, *op. cit.*, p. 444, fn. 5, who considers that the hypothesis of abstract obligation is only valid because of the particular purposes of commercial

absence of consideration being revealed by the unenforceability of defences.[139] Indeed, the debtor of an exchangeable obligation cannot raise defences inherent in the debt[140] or those relating to the person of the creditor.[141] At the most, the exchange debtor could invoke a possible incapacity.[142] In other words, defects of consent will not constitute an exception to the payment of the bill of exchange, in order to facilitate exchanges.[143] In these circumstances, abstraction has caused

---

law, where 'the needs of commerce and the security of transactions have sometimes led to the admission that an act is valid without the debtor being able to raise against the creditor any exception, that is to say, any defence based on their relations prior to the drawing up of the act, in particular that the act is devoid of cause'. Comp. P. Malaurie, L. Aynès and P. Stoffel-Munck, *Droit des obligations*, *op. cit.*, 347 for whom abstraction means that 'the obligation is valid by the sole consent of the debtor [...]. The debtor is obliged because he has willed it; he cannot escape by invoking the absence of cause'. The authors quote the German textual basis (BGB, 'the promise which by itself is the basis of the obligation'.
Some authors have denied the abstraction of the exchange obligation, seeing it only as a favour done to appearance, given that the three elements which make it possible to found an obligation on such a cause are united, see M. Vivant, 'Le fondement juridique des obligations abstraites', *D.*, 1978, chron., p. 39. However, G. Friedel had already envisaged and refuted this hypothesis, see G. Friedel, *De l'inopposabilité des exceptions en matière d'effets de commerce*, Rousseau, 1951, no. 69, pp. 94–95: 'The role of the apparent regularity of the document and of good faith is not, in fact, absolute. Certain defences based on defects, even if not apparent, have always been declared enforceable, even against a holder acting in good faith: the incapacity of the debtor, and a false signature. The case of forgery defeats all the rules: one cannot be held liable for it. But it would have to be decided that the incapable person must be held, since after all he has signed a document in which there is nothing to reveal the circumstance which he will invoke to free himself. We must therefore find an explanation other than appearance if we want to justify the rule that exceptions cannot be enforced.'

139 V. Delaporte, *Recherches sur la forme des actes juridiques en droit international privé*, Université Paris I Panthéon-Sorbonne, 1974, no. 17: 'Obligations created in this way are most often described as abstract obligations, because their essential character is that they are detached from their causes.' It should be borne in mind that it is because the exceptions arising from theoriginal contract are unenforceable against the creditor of the exchange obligation that commercial paper is said to be *abstract*, and not the other way round. The defences in question are those which the debtor may raise against the *payment of* the obligation, which in this case takes the form of a *payment of* money. In positive law, the article enshrining the unenforceability of defences to payment is Art. L. 511-12 of the Commercial Code.

140 Although the example of the arbitration clause may lead one to put this into perspective.

141 Art. L. 511-12 of the Commercial Code. It is because he cannot oppose what is personal in the contractual relationship from which the obligation arises, in other words the contractual 'bond', that the obligation is said to be *abstract*, because it is disembodied from the circumstances which gave rise to it. This is what may have facilitated the comparison with real rights, see e.g. Mr Haftel who would like to subject the transmission of trade bills to Art. 2276 of the Civil Code, B. Haftel, *La notion de matière contractuelle en droit international privé*, Université Paris II Panthéon-Assas, 2008, no. 383.

142 This shows once again that the will is not absent from the exchange relationship, that the form alone is not sufficient to create legal effects.

143 As Dean Hamel writes: 'In order to facilitate trade, which is the very basis of commerce and one of the essential factors of the economy, commercial law admits that, in the areas in which it triumphs - tangible movables and currency claims - legal science, with its subtleties and its desire for fairness, is replaced by a much simpler system devoid of nuances', see J. Hamel, preface to the thesis by G. Friedel, *De l'inopposabilité des exceptions en matière d'effets de commerce*, *op. cit.*, p. XII.

some confusion, as it could lead to the belief that, since the will is no longer the principle of the transaction, the forms have become so. This is why one could speak of 'creative forms'[144] of law. These forms could undoubtedly be described as creative if the conditions for the formation of legal acts were all set aside. This is not the case here.[145] The use of the concept of *non-enforceability* is indicative of the underlying legal reality: the validity of the exception is not denied, it is simply not allowed any effect vis-à-vis the holder in good faith.[146] This is a consequence of the favouring of payment within the regime of the exchange obligation. This makes it possible to realise that the bill of exchange is as much an instrument of credit as an instrument of payment.

605. Formalism and the regime of the exchange obligation. Within the regime of the exchange, one will also find the answer to the argument that the formalities of the exchange constitute the source of the obligation. Indeed, it is from the unenforceability of exceptions that it has been deduced that the forms of the instrument had a 'creative effect'.[147] As the originality of the document of title was not manifested between the parties to the original contract, since the ordinary law obligation supplants the effects of the exchange obligation between them,[148] the authors were able to consider that the originality of the document of title and its "creative force" was manifested between the subscribers and the bearer.[149] Basically, the strength of the argument that the forms of the bill of exchange are the source of the exchange obligations stems from the fact that the

---

144 V. Delaporte, *Recherches sur la forme des actes juridiques en droit international privé*, *op. cit.*

145 Even if, unquestionably, an exchange commitment wrung by a vitiated consent or without any cause (this is the hypothesis of a non-existent provision) still produces its effects for the benefit of the holder in good faith - and only in this hypothesis, which restricts the limits assigned to the will within narrow boundaries, in the manner of acquisitive prescription (in the sense of such a comparison see J. Hamel in his preface to the thesis by G. Friedel, *De l'inopposabilité des exceptions en matière d'effets de commerce*, *op. cit.*, p. XI).

146 It is in this sense that these exceptions *to payment* are *unenforceable*. However, these defences remain enforceable against the original creditor, i.e. the drawer in the case of the drawee, or its author in the case of any of the endorsers of the bill of exchange.

147 And not anything strictly related to form, see V. Delaporte, *Recherches sur la forme des actes juridiques en droit international privé*, *op. cit.*

148 This was very clearly stated in a decision of the Paris Court of Appeal on 16 December 1986, *D.*, 1987, IR 12, the operative part of which is limpid: 'This rule [of Art. L. 511-12 of the Commercial Code, which provides that defences are not enforceable, is not applicable in cases where the drawer is sued by the drawee or by the original beneficiary of the bill of exchange which he received from the drawer in exchange for consideration given in cash, goods, accounts or otherwise; In these two cases, the exchange debt remains conditional on the pre-existing relationship which serves as its cause and, if this relationship is extinguished as a result of a payment or set-off, the exchange relationship which is based on it also disappears.' See also J. Hamel, G. Lagarde and A. Jauffret, *Traité de droit commercial*, vol. II, *op. cit.* no. 1431-2; P. Lescot and R. Roblot, *Les effets de commerce*, vol. I, *op. cit.*, no. 316.

149 In this sense, the subscriber cannot, for example, refuse to pay the holder because of a defect in his consent when signing.

endorsee who does not really adhere to the instrument cannot rely on his lack of will when he apparently adheres to the exchange obligation: this is the principle of the unenforceability of exceptions. However, the latter, while preventing the debtor from relying on an absence of consent, does not in principle allow obligations to be created: the unenforceability of defences is only a consequence of the exchange regime.[150] If abstraction corresponded in Rome to a 'need for simplification natural to primitive legislations',[151] it is indisputable here that it is linked to the safety of commercial transactions. The regime of the exchange obligation, if it influences the conditions of its formation, is therefore not such as to exclude it from contractual matters.[152]

B. Rejection of Exchange Characteristics as an Explanation for the Plurality of Attachments

606. Independence of signatures and plurality of connections. Above all, the well-established idea of some commercialists lawyer that negotiable instruments cannot be subject to a single law stems from a misunderstanding of private international law.[153] The Geneva Conventions originated at a time when Bartin's particularist ideas had gained considerable momentum in legal thought. Thus, the fundamental characteristics of the rules of domestic law were to be found in the conflict of laws rules. However, in order to facilitate payment, the law of exchange adopted a principle which is said to be an exception to the fundamental rule of civil law according to which one cannot transmit more rights than one has received (*Nemo plus juris ad alium transferre potest quam ipse habet*),[154]

---

150 See G. Friedel, *De l'inopposabilité des exceptions en matière d'effets de commerce*, *op. cit.*

151 It is enlightening to quote Henri Capitant *in extenso* here: after observing that 'in Rome, certain contracts constitute abstract acts, such as *expensilatio* or stipulation', the author remarks: 'They generate obligations without there being any need to investigate whether they correspond to the will of the person who commits himself [...]. In stipulation, which is the most common form of obligation, the cause of the promise is not even stated; the promisor is content to respond affirmatively to the request for a commitment addressed to him by the stipulator. It is the abstract act par excellence. [...] It was not, as in certain contemporary legislations, the concern to develop and make commercial transactions more secure which determined the Romans to adopt it, but the need for simplification natural to primitive legislations' in H. Capitant, *De la cause des obligations*, *op. cit.*, 96–97.

152 See also, considering the commercial paper as a contract, V. Malassigné, *Les titres représentatifs*, *op. cit.*

153 Curiously, it is taken up by Mr Haftel to help explain the exclusion of contractual matters, see B. Haftel, *La notion de matière contractuelle en droit international privé*, Paris, Université Paris II Panthéon-Assas, 2008, no. 385.

154 *Nemo plus juris ad alium transferre potest quam ipse habet.* Roland and Boyer note in their work on the adages of French law that the hypothesis where 'the successor in title receives more than his author had [...] is generally explained by the need for security in legal relationships which would be compromised if *Nemo plus juris...* continued to apply'. Then the authors analyse the exception, which is not an exception in their view: 'Moreover, on closer examination, the adage is in reality irrelevant; it is not the author of the agreement

and which is formulated in a well-known principle of exchange: that of the independence of signatures.[155] This principle states that a signature on the title is equivalent to a commitment to exchange, regardless of whether the other signatures are invalid, including the first, or even the drawee's signature, which is the basis of the original contract.

This rule stems from a very clear legal policy: to allow the bearer of the bill of exchange to be paid, since his debtor cannot oppose him on the basis of the original contract, or even the lack of validity of his own undertaking.[156] However, some professors of commercial law[157] thought that the projection of this rule of independence of signatures should be materialised at the international level by the independence of the law applicable to the latter. It was therefore logical, in their view, to subject each signature to its own law, so that they would be truly independent of each other.[158] This was not to understand the purpose of the rule by looking only at its technical aspect, its internal dynamics; rather, it should have been noted that it is part, if not of a legislative whole, at least of a more general mechanism. The *purpose* of the independence of signatures is to favour payment, to guarantee that the bearer will actually be paid thanks to the bill of exchange, to make the bill of exchange a particularly certain means of being "fulfilled of his rights". However, by multiplying the laws applicable to signatures through the theory of multiple connections, the opposite is precisely the case. The most flagrant paradox is undoubtedly that Bartin himself observes that subjecting the forms of the obligation to the law of form means failing to understand that the rules of form actually absorb substantive provisions.[159] In other words, for Bartin,

---

who will pass on more than he has; it is the law or the virtue of an *ad hoc* adage which will mean that the beneficiary will receive more.' H. ROLAND and L. BOYER, *Adages du droit français*, 4th ed., Paris, Litec, no. 259, p. 508.

155 In fact, even in the law of exchange this is not an exception to the rule. The independence of signatures means above all the independence of obligations: the exchange obligation of which the signatory is a debtor is simply independent of the others, whether they arise from theoriginal contract or from the exchange obligations of which the other signatories are debtors. It would be less inappropriate to say that the unenforceability of defences fulfils this function, but we have seen that this is not the case.

156 Except, as we have seen, if the carrier is the drawer.

157 See among others P. LESCOT and R. ROBLOT, *Les effets de commerce*, vol. II, *op. cit.*

158 This idea, despite its obvious practical disadvantages, spread to several European countries. During the negotiation of the Convention, the Italians were intransigent on the scope of this principle in private international law, see e.g. *Comptes rendus des travaux de la Conférence de Genève de 1930*, p. 361, where the representative of the Italian delegation produces one of the longest and most unfortunate pleas in favour of the independence of exchange obligations as a basis for the plurality of connections, any other conflict of laws rule being 'contradictory'.

159 This is why he pronounces *in fine* for the application of the law of payment to the effects of exchange obligations (BARTIN, *Principes*, vol. 2, para. 354, p. 479). One might think that for Bartin, it is not so much the purpose of the institution in question (to allow payment) as some of the characteristics of the 'document of title' (the need to be able to circulate) which

it is because the obligation to pay must circulate that the law of payment must intervene: a single law, objectively defined and easily identifiable, is more likely to allow the legal security of circulation, i.e. the security of transactions,[160] in order to preserve the interests of future purchasers.

II. The Impasse of the Plurality of Connections

607. One of the peculiarities of the bill of exchange is that it can be both a mechanism for the transfer of the claim that gave rise to it and an instrument for the creation of exchange obligations. However, the value of the bill of exchange is all the more certain as the number of exchange debtors is large; it is therefore this latter aspect that should be particularly preserved by the application of a unitary and stable law. One must observe that it is precisely the opposite that occurs: the translative effect of the instrument is subject to the unitary law of issue. This law does not, however, constitute the legal centre of gravity of the transaction, which would have been better placed under the law of payment (A).

---

explain why the law of payment must intervene. In this sense it would be close to the theory criticised here, which sees in the characteristics of the instrument a need for a plurality of connections. The divergence of the conclusions reached with the commercialists cited would perhaps be due to the fact that Bartin analyses the legal institution more finely, and no doubt unconsciously analyses it in the light of their true purpose. However, this is not the case, and if Bartin refers to 'the circulation of the title' in this way, it is because he thinks that this is its purpose, in the manner of a currency *(ibid.)*. However, circulation for circulation's sake, like Sisyphus tirelessly pulling up his stone, is meaningless; precisely circulation has an end: payment. It is precisely because payment is assured that the title can circulate, that the obligation can be transmitted. It is therefore the trust placed in the obligations evidenced by the document that gives the bill of exchange its force. Because Bartin rises above the technical considerations of domestic law, but interprets these mechanisms in the light of their purpose, he detects in them the need for an objective determination of the applicable law, and rejects the contractual analysis in this sense: it is precisely because the purpose is to circulate that future purchasers must be protected, which convinces the author to reject the place of the will in the order of conflict of laws (Bartin, *Principes*, vol. 2, para. 354, p. 476). Bartin perfectly perceived that the circulation of the title involves third parties in another way. He also perceived that the law of payment, the law of the drawee, inscribed on the instrument itself, allows for an easily identifiable law, not subject to the vagaries of the will of the parties, without observing, however, that this law has the additional advantage of imposing itself on the debtor with particular force (*ibid.*, p. 478). These words could be transposed as they stand to financial securities: the circulation of the security requires the protection of third parties, who are better protected by an objective criterion, determined independently of the parties to the transfers of the security.

160 It is on this same basis that Bartin develops the application of the rule resulting from the status in rem, which he will develop in a more debatable way by assigning a status in rem to claims. On this subject, see the presentation of the opposition between Bartin and Niboyet set out, with criticism, by L. D'Avout, *Sur les solutions du conflit de lois en droit des biens*, *op. cit.* The author concludes, after setting out Bartin's point of view: 'This is where this theory of the real status of the claim asserted as such leads: obviously too far, because of the artificial separation made between the obligational content of the claim and its property regime, which could lead one to believe that the law applicable to the content of the right has no say in the terms of its assignment. [...]'

The second aspect, both from the point of view of the creation of the exchange bonds and their effect, is governed by the law of the geographical location of the paper security, causing a new law to be applied to the transfer each time the security is transferred to a new legal order. It is this second aspect of the system adopted by the Geneva Convention that deserves the most severe criticism (B).

A. The Translative Effect of the Instrument

608. Depending on each State's understanding of the bill of exchange, the hand-to-hand transfer of the bill will or will not entail the transfer of the provision. In French law, such a transfer is linked to the acceptance of the bill by the drawee: if the drawee has accepted, the transfer of the bill of exchange will entail the transfer of the underlying provision. However, this acceptance by the drawee is subject to the law of the original claim, whereas the translative effect of the bill is subject to the law of creation of the instrument. Both aspects are open to criticism. In the first case, the aim is both to ensure that the claim is transferable and to protect the drawee who is not obliged to accept the bill of exchange. The law of payment would nevertheless have protected the drawee and guaranteed the effectiveness of the payment (1). In the second case, the application of the law of the issuer corresponds to the conflict of laws rule in contractual matters: the drawer of the bill of exchange is indeed the debtor of the characteristic performance of the bill of exchange. However, the debtor of the provision is the drawee, who is the real centre of gravity not only of the provision, for which he ensures payment, but also of the final burden of the debt of the exchange transaction (2).

1. *Acceptance by the Drawee Subject to the Law of the Original Claim*

609. Application of the law of the original contract to acceptance. Unlike the exchange obligation,[161] the original claim is subject to the Rome I Regulation. The law of the original contract is the *lex contractus*, i.e. in principle the law of autonomy[162] and, failing that, the law of the habitual residence of the debtor of the characteristic performance,[163] which may vary according to the type of contract. In a field where the exchange obligation is intended to be profoundly independent of the basic obligation,[164] it may seem paradoxical that the law of the original claim should play any role in the regulation of the exchange obligation.

---

161 The exchange obligation is excluded from the scope of application of the Rome I Regulation on the basis of two separate articles: on the one hand, the exclusion of obligations arising from negotiable instruments in Article 1(2)(d)), and on the other hand on the basis of Article 25(1) relating to international agreements previously formed. On these two questions, see *infra*, para. 624.

162 Art. 3 of the Rome I Regulation.

163 Art. 4(2) of the Rome I Regulation.

164 Recall of the underlying and the financial contract see *infra*, paras. 770 et seq.

However, the law of the original contract regulates the obligation or not of acceptance of the drawee,[165] which determines the possibility of transferring the provision into the hands of the bearer.[166] The application of the law of original contract to acceptance is criticised. Mr Chemaly considers, for example, that 'the drawee, although a debtor of the drawer and while being willing to pay the debt it owes to the latter, may have perfectly legitimate reasons for not committing itself by way of exchange'.[167] The author therefore favours the law of payment in order to ensure better protection of the drawee. However, such a proposal seems to presume that the law of payment will be more favourable than the law of the contract, by not leaving the drawee the option of refusing the exchange undertaking, a presumption that no element supports.[168] Nevertheless, the real basis for the application of the law of payment is the protection of the drawee insofar as this law coincides with that of his domicile.

610. The application of the law of the original contract stems from the fact that, since the exchange contract has its cause in the original obligation, the obligation of acceptance should also be subject to it.[169] The other reason for the

---

165 The question is nevertheless contested and would, according to some, be better left to the law of payment. On this point, see R. Chemaly, 'Conflits de lois en matière d'effets de commerce', *op. cit.*, p. 405.

166 It may seem that it is not for the law of the original contract to determine the translative nature of the bills of exchange drawn on this claim. This presentation does not necessarily imply that the assignability of the claim is determined by the law of the issue. It may be accepted that the law of the issue determines the translative nature of the provision in the assignment of a bill of exchange, while recognising that the assignability of the original claim depends on the law of the original claim. In this case, the law of the original claim could paralyse the law of the issue, since once the claim is unassignable, it can by definition no longer be transferred. However, once declared assignable, it is up to the law of issue to determine the validity of the transfer of the provision, which is binary: either it takes place with the assignment of the exchange obligation, or the issue of a bill of exchange has no influence on the ownership of the provision. The problem we are dealing with may be compared to the distinction made by Mr Lequette in relation to capacity, who, after a discussion setting out the difficulties of the classical approaches, shows that a distinction in terms of the principle of protection and the realisation of that principle makes it possible to resolve most of the problems of adaptation of the matter, see Y. Lequette, *Protection familiale et protection étatique des incapables*, *op. cit.*, p. 23. Here the distinction leads to equally happy results: the principle of transmission is always authorised by the law of the original claim, whereas its realisation is authorised by the law of the exchange obligation.

167 R. Chemaly, 'Conflits de lois en matière d'effets de commerce', *op. cit.*, p. 405.

168 Mr Chemaly's other arguments, while often numerous and often vigorous in favour of the law of payment, do not seem convincing here. To state that the contract is distinct in order to refuse to see the law of the first contract applied to questions concerning the others is to ignore the fact that the purpose of the exchange contract is not only to create exchange obligations, but also to transfer the provision, and it is logical that the law applicable to the transferred obligation should determine its assignability, with the result that the drawee's right of acceptance is subject to it.

169 In favour of the application of the original contract, see P. Arminjon, *Droit international privé*, *op. cit.*, no. 171, p. 327; P. Lescot and R. Roblot, *Les effets de commerce*, *op. cit.*, vol. II, no. 1080.

application of the law of the original contract lies in the fact that the exchange bill is also a form of assignment. Not all claims are capable of being accepted by the drawee, in particular because not all claims are capable of being assigned; the law applicable to the original contract, without being the driving force of the transfer, may in any case paralyse it.[170] In other words, the law of the original contract has a principled jurisdiction as to the transferability of the claim for a reason of effectiveness.[171] This is also the reason why the law applicable to the drawee's obligation to accept or not the bill of exchange is, because of the effects it has on the transfer of the provision, closely linked to the existence of the provision.[172] This question is not settled by the Geneva Convention: at one time governed by the law of the issue,[173] the existence of the provision is now subject to that of the payment. While Professor Arminjon defended the application of the law of the original contract,[174] Mr Chemaly is opposed to the application of this law, because 'it may be objected that the possibility for the creditor (here, the drawer) to draw a draft on his debtor (here, the drawee) is not implied *ipso facto* and in a necessary manner by the agreement (the 'original contract') entered into between them'.[175]

It may be added that the law applicable to the acceptance will also govern its effects, and in particular the enforceability of defences which the drawee

170 See *supra*, paras. 291 et seq.

171 The function of the law of the original contract with regard to the assignability of the provision is comparable to that of the assigned claim in the transfer relationship under ordinary law. However, two particularities affect the original contract. In contrast to assignments under ordinary law, it is not the sole object of the bill of exchange contract, which also has the effect of creating an obligation under the bill of exchange on the part of each assignor, and the influence of the number of obligees under the bill of exchange as guarantors on the reliability of the bill of exchange is well known. Moreover, other legal systems do not necessarily recognise the effect of a transfer by way of exchange on the original claim, which is why Art. 6 of the Geneva Convention provides that the law of the issuing State shall determine this question.

172 The existence of the provision here goes hand in hand with the date on which the provision must exist.

173 Cass., 6 February 1900, *S.*, 1900, 1, p. 161, note Lyon-Caen. The other decisions cited in support of this opinion do not provide a clear solution. For the doctrine, see in particular A. Pillet, *Traité pratique*, vol. 2, no. 758; Lyon-Caen and Renault, *Traité*, vol. 4, no. 643, all cited by R. Chemaly, 'Conflits de lois en matière d'effets de commerce', *op. cit.*, p. 422. The law of the issue was the transposition of the solution in contractual matters, which saw the law of the place of conclusion of the contract apply in the absence of a choice of law at the beginning of the 20th century.

174 In favour of this solution, P. Arminjon, *Traité de droit international privé*, 1947, no. 178.

175 R. Chemaly, 'Conflits de lois en matière d'effets de commerce', *op. cit.* p. 422. The author justifies his position by stating that 'the issue of the bill of exchange constitutes an autonomous act, even if the cause is to be found in a previous agreement and even if it does not entail novation of the claim generated by this agreement. It follows that the existence of the provision of the draft (is it necessary? if so, on what date?) is itself an autonomous problem whose centre of gravity, one might say, is more on the side of the instrument itself than on the side of the prior agreement.' (*ibid.*)

may raise against the exchange creditor,[176] who should be subject to the law of payment, as these defences have little to do with the obligation founding the provision. In the end, it seems essential above all to apply a single law to the obligation of acceptance and to the regime of the provision (its existence, transfer and consistency) because of the systematic links between these rules. If one considers it necessary to protect the drawee when the acceptance occurs, and to apply the law of payment to him, one must necessarily apply this law to the existence of the provision.

2. *The Translative Effect of the Instrument on the Provision Subject to the Law of the Issue*

611. The provision. While the creation of a bill of exchange has the effect of creating a new obligation, of the exchange type, at each endorsement, for the benefit of the drawer, the bill of exchange also has the effect of transferring, under certain conditions, the provision due by the drawer to the drawee, in the manner of a contract of assignment. In both cases, the law of the place of creation of the instrument is that of the domicile of the drawer, which corresponds to the assignor. The function of the transfer of the provision to the bearer is to facilitate the payment of the bill of exchange. In international relations, payment is facilitated by a criterion designating a single law. Indeed, a connecting factor that could designate different laws for each transfer would have the unfortunate consequence of interrupting the chain of transfer of the provision in the event that the law designated by the conflict rule did not attach the transfer of the provision to the delivery of the instrument.[177]

612. The application of the law of issue to the transfer of the provision. The law of issue, also called the law of creation of the instrument, corresponds in the bill of exchange system to the law of the drawer. Its function in the Geneva Convention is to determine the law applicable to the question of whether or not the delivery of the bill of exchange to the bearer entails the transfer of

---

176 As we have seen, these exceptions have been reduced to a trickle, but we should mention one from the famous *DS* judgment: the arbitration clause included in the fundamental report may be invoked against the drawer who has become the bearer again (Colmar, 24 February 1965, 1966, p. 544, note by P. B., *Revue critique*, 1967, p. 152, note G. Lagarde). The law of payment may also be applied to questions of unjust enrichment against the drawee in the event of prescription of the exchange action or negligence (Y. Loussouarn and J.-D. Bredin, *Droit du commerce international*, *op. cit.*, no. 479 - the authors report the solution proposed by Lescot and Roblot); R. Chemaly, 'Conflits de lois en matière d'effets de commerce', *op. cit.*

177 Such a result can undoubtedly be put into perspective because of the joint and several liability of the holder of the exchange obligation, which allows the holder of the exchange obligation to sue for payment, *in fine*, any of the endorsees, all of whom are debtors of an exchange obligation and obliged to pay. The drawer himself is a guarantor of payment, see Art. L. 511-6 of the Commercial Code.

the provision.[178] Indeed, not all legal systems accept that the transmission of the exchange obligation produces this effect.[179] This is why the Geneva Convention[180] stipulates that 'the law of the place of creation of the instrument determines whether the bearer of a bill of exchange acquires the claim which gave rise to the issue of the instrument'.[181] This is a good solution in that it designates a unitary criterion. It would have been even more so if the law of payment had been applicable. Indeed, the debtor of the provision is the drawee: he is the real centre of gravity not only of the provision, for which he ensures payment, but also of the final burden of the debt of the exchange transaction. This is all the more true because it would then have been possible to subject the time limits for the exercise of the recourse action to the law of payment, rather than to the law of creation of the instrument, so as to allow better respect for the legislative body constituted by the bill of exchange.

---

178 The concept of provision is used exclusively in French law, which is why the wording was not taken up by the Geneva Convention, in particular because of the criticism of the German representatives who also wished to delete this provision. See on this point the explanations in the *Comptes rendus des travaux de la Conférence de Genève de 1930*, p. 364.

179 This is the case in French law. Art. L. 511-7 of the Commercial Code, in its para. 3, provides that 'ownership of the provision is transferred by right to the successive holders of the bill of exchange'.

180 The question of the applicability of the Geneva Convention could have been discussed. In fact, the transfer of the provision does not constitute an obligation arising from the negotiability of the bill of exchange; it is well known that this characteristic was set up as a criterion for excluding negotiable instruments from the scope of the Rome I Regulation by its Art. 1(2)(d). However, Art. 25(1°) of the Rome I Regulation, which in substance takes up Art. 21 of the Rome Convention, imposes compliance with international conventions previously concluded, including in the contractual matter covered by these European instruments. It could no doubt be objected that Art. 25(2°) of the Rome I Regulation provides for a derogation, but this is not applicable here since the Geneva Convention was signed by non-EU Member States. It is therefore within the Geneva Convention on the conflict of laws that the solution must be sought.

181 Art. 6 of the Geneva Convention. The wording of the provision does not make it clear what is meant by the acquisition of the claim. In the absence of precision, it is as if the law of the creation of the instrument governed both the questions of opposability to the assigned debtor and opposability to third parties; in fact, the assignability of the claim is reserved for the law of the assigned claim, whose competence is necessary both from the logical point of view and to ensure its effectiveness. Indeed, in practice, the alleged drawee may base his refusal to pay on the prohibition, made by the law of the original claim, of its transmission. This Art. 6 was the subject of intense debates between the signatories, particularly on the appropriateness of such an article given, on the one hand, the discussions on the connecting factor, with the German delegation contesting the appropriateness of applying the law of payment to this question, and, on the other hand, the very interest of such a provision, as this question had given rise to only one judicial decision in Germany in the fifty years preceding the drafting of this Convention. See Reports on the *1930 Geneva Convention*, p. 364. Finally, the solution enshrined in the Geneva Convention is similar to that adopted by the Rome I Regulation, which applies to the validity of the transfer of a claim, in the absence of a choice of law in the assignment contract, the law of the domicile of the debtor of the characteristic performance, i.e. the law of the domicile of the assignor (Art. 14(1°) of the Rome Regulation). On the links between this Art. 6 and the Rome Convention, see D. Pardoel, *Les conflits de lois en matière de cession de créances*, *op. cit.*

613. The application of the law creating the title to the time limits for bringing an action for review.[182] The fact that the law creating the bill determines the time limits for bringing an action for recourse may seem surprising. The explanation lies in the application of the *lex loci actus* to the effects of the exchange undertaking. The application of the law of the place of the deed would have led to the recourse action being subject to the law of the place of each signature, with the result that, depending on the debtor concerned by the bill of exchange, some actions would be extinguished and others existing. The need to select a predictable criterion offering a certain permanence gave the choice between the law of creation of the instrument and the law of payment. The choice in favour of the law of creation of the bill may lie in the idea that, since the law of issue has created the exchange bond, it is up to it to manifest its longevity, to declare the time during which an action concerning it may be received. However, the application of the law of payment would have been preferable. The latter has the advantage of coinciding with the law of the drawee, whose court has jurisdiction in most cases. Thus, the application of the law of payment would have allowed the application of the *lex fori* in matters at the borderline of substance and procedure. Moreover, given that it is precisely an action *for payment* that is envisaged here, or an exception against payment, such a solution would have favoured respect for the body of law normally determined by the law of payment, *a fortiori* if one takes into account that the sanctions provided for in the event of refusal of payment will be administered by the legal order of the drawee, i.e. the legal order of the place of payment.

B. The Application of Local Law to the Obligations Entered into by Means of a Bill of Exchange ('Exchange Obligations')

Obligations entered into by means of a bill of exchange are governed in their entirety by the *lex loci actus*: not only the formal requirements, which are of particular importance here (1), but also their effects (2).

1. *Formal Requirements Subject to the* Lex Loci Actus

614. The application of the *lex loci actus* to formal requirements. The Geneva Convention applies to 'the form of any contract arising out of a bill of exchange [...] the laws of the territory in which the contract has been signed'.[183] It is traditional that the law of the place of the act governs the formal requirements. There are several reasons for this. The first is that, like the real status, the

[182] Art. 5 of the Geneva Convention.

[183] Art. 3 para. 1 of the Geneva Convention.

legitimacy of the law of the place of the act is explained by the predictability and strength of the appearance.[184] As Professor Louis-Lucas observed:

> 'The *Locus regit actum* rule is easily accepted as referring to the fairly obvious differentiation that can be made between the object of the operation and the way in which it is carried out. And it is said that, limited to this technicality, local law draws the two reasons for its competence from the convenience and practicality of using the law of the country in which one undertakes to act.'[185]

In addition to these first reasons, the law of the place of the act does not constitute a favour granted, in principle, to one of the parties: the weight of internationality weighs on the party moving.

615. Unsuitability of local law. All these reasons remain valid in the context of foreign exchange, but they are countered by the particularity of the exchange contract, which is that it can be extended to a large number of parties because of the circulation of the instrument. In order to preserve the circulation, a rule of conflict of favour on payment specifies precisely that:

> 'If, however, the obligations entered into by means of a bill of exchange or promissory note are not valid according to (*the law of the place of the act*), but are in conformity with the laws of the territory in which a subsequent contract has been entered into, the circumstance that the previous contracts are irregular in form does not invalidate the subsequent contract.'[186]

It is clear from this correction to the initial conflict rule that the authors of the Convention were influenced by the principle of the independence of signatures in the law of exchange. It is known that, according to this principle,

---

184 This is what Dean Batiffol taught about 'the persistent favour of real status', H. Batiffol, *Aspects philosophiques de droit international privé*, *op. cit.*, no. 115, p. 254.

185 P. Louis-Lucas, «'La distinction du fond et de la forme dans le règlement des conflits de lois' in *Mélanges offert à Jacques Maury*, t. 1, *Droit international privé et public*, Paris, Dalloz/Sirey, La distinction du fond et de la forme dans le règlement des conflits de lois», *Mélanges Maury*, t. 1, p. 175, spec. p. 177. Among the aspects mentioned by the author, convenience corresponds to the appearance, and practicality to the predictability of seeing the forms of an act governed by the law of the place where it was concluded.

186 Art. 3 para. 2 Geneva Convention. It would also have been possible to subject the formal requirements to the law of the place of issue. Admittedly, at the time of the issue of the bill of exchange, the two will most often coincide: the law of the place of the document corresponds to the law of the issue, i.e. the law of the drawer's domicile. However, as each exchange commitment gives rise to a new exchange obligation independent of the others, it was not unreasonable to subject all obligations to 'the local law, the law of issue of the instrument' at a time when the contract was subject to the law of the place of its conclusion. In fact, if there are new obligations with each exchange commitment, they are merely added to a single contract, that of the exchange, which pre-exists them and on which they are based. Nevertheless, it will be seen that this law is not that of the issue of the instrument, but that of the payment. See already in this sense E. Bartin, *Principes*, t. 2, para. 354, p. 478.

the nullity of one of the signatures does not affect the validity of those that follow it, which is an exception to the *nemo plus juris* rule. The function of this rule of independence of signatures is of course to increase the reliability of payment.[187] However, this is favoured by the application of a single law, the law of payment, rather than by the baroque system provided for by the Convention. The solution is all the more surprising in that at the same time the Geneva Convention on the conflict of laws in respect of cheques, which also recognises the principle of independence of signatures, opted for the law of payment, the *lex loci solutionis*.[188]

616. In the area of bills of exchange, it should also be noted that applying the conditions of form the law of the place of the act is of particular importance in that it will dictate the characterisation of the obligation that may be in dispute, in particular in order to determine whether it is negotiable. Admittedly, the Geneva Convention does not explicitly mention the law applicable to the negotiability of the security, which in France is traditionally subject to the law of the issuer.[189] However, the application of the law of the issuer leads here to two difficulties. On the one hand, it does not correspond to the law of payment (the drawee is likely to be domiciled in a State other than the drawer), and deprives itself of one of its major advantage, effectiveness, in the context of the exchange where the question of payment is the central object of the mechanism. On the other

187 In this respect, it should be noted that, within the formal requirements, the preparatory debates for the Convention concentrated, in particular, on the law applicable to the signature. The dilemma was whether to apply the law of the place where the signature took place or the law of the place where the bill of exchange indicates that it took place. During the negotiations, the German delegation was in favour of the place indicated on the bill of exchange, regardless of whether it was fictitious. This was in line with the principle of domestic law that the statements on the bill of exchange are legally binding. Above all, from an international point of view, it strengthened faith in the bill of exchange: as some negotiators had pointed out, 'the security of circulation also requires that each bearer of a bill of exchange should be able to consider as correct all the indications of place inserted in the bill of exchange' (see *Minutes of the Geneva Conference of 1930*, p. 352; the amendment of the German delegation will apparently be rejected for a fiscal reason – see *ibid.*, p. 355).

188 This difference might be related to the univocal purpose of the cheque, which is exclusively related to payment and never to credit. This is the reason why separate conventions have been enacted for different instruments. While instruments of 'pure' payment can easily be grouped together and subjected almost entirely to the law of payment, the same cannot be said for instruments of 'credit' such as the bill of exchange and the promissory note, which, while subject to an identical regime in domestic law, are in reality closer to mechanisms of assignment of rights. This is very clear in domestic law, for example, in the French rule that a provision must be made when the cheque is *issued*, whereas in the case of a bill of exchange, the *provision* can wait until the moment when the instrument is presented to the drawee. The first rule shows that the cheque is exclusively a means of payment, whereas the bill of exchange is a transfer of right, which allows payment. In this sense, the bill of exchange can be compared to contemporary financial instruments: the latter can also enable payment. This is the case, for example, with the payment of dividends by portfolio shares.

189 R. Chemaly, 'Conflits de lois en matière d'effets de commerce', *op. cit.*, p. 412; on this submission, see *supra* nos. 291 et seq.

hand, it results in dissociating the law applicable to the obligations entered into by means of a bill of exchange and the law applicable to negotiability, whereas the former should dictate the latter: this is the logical solution to the conflict of laws.[190] Nevertheless, the application of the *lex creationis* is fraught with difficulties because of the dysfunctional connection of the obligations entered into by means of a bill of exchange, which is not only removed from the legal centre of gravity of the transaction but, above all, because of the mechanism of the bill of exchange, which multiplies the exchange obligations, leads to the application of as many laws as there are different places where these obligations have been entered into.

2. *The Effects of the Obligations Entered into by Means of a Bill of Exchange Subject to the Law of the Place of Signature*

617. Application of the law of the place of the act to the effects of the bill of exchange commitment. The Geneva Convention applies the law of payment to the effects of the obligations of the acceptor of the bill of exchange. Nevertheless, it subjects 'the effects produced by the signatures of the other parties to a bill of exchange [...] to the law of the place where these instruments are payable'.[191] However, in the case of the acceptor, the latter corresponds not to the law of the place of payment (his domicile), but to the place where he accepted the bill. The application of the law of the place where the deed was concluded to the effects of other persons bound by the exchange relationship reflects the protection which it was intended to give to signatories, so that they are bound by the law which they are most likely to know, that of the place where they signed the deed. Added to this is the desire of the authors of the Convention to allow the parties a certain amount of freedom in determining the law applicable to the form.[192]

---

190 Admittedly, compared to submission to the *lex fori* (advocated for example by certain English judges, see *supra* para. 300), which would result in the negotiability of the security being qualified according to criteria different from those that guided the parties, the law of the issue nevertheless had the advantage of permanence and of not being able to be manipulated by the parties.

191 Art. 4, paras. 1 and 2 of the Geneva Convention. This rule is consistent with Art. 8, which applies the law of the place of the act to the preservation of Cambodian rights.

192 Some negotiators felt that: 'This solution corresponds to the principle that, in the first instance, the declarations made on the bill of exchange should be legally taken into account. It is also in the interest of the circulation of bills of exchange, as it gives the parties concerned the possibility to determine the applicable law. If the circulation of bills of exchange is to be facilitated, the difficulties involved in producing evidence must be avoided as far as possible. The security of circulation also requires that each bearer of a bill of exchange be able to consider as correct all the indications of place inserted in the bill of exchange.' R. Roblot, *Les effets de commerce*, *op. cit.*, no. 666. This was also the opinion of the German delegation. The latter will be keen to take account of the signatory's will in determining the applicable law, whether for the law applicable to the form of the bill of exchange, the law of the form by the place indicated by the parties rather than the actual place of signature (*Comptes rendus des travaux de la Conférence de Genève de 1930*, p. 354), or the effect of

618. Unsuitability of local law. This rule is nevertheless particularly unfortunate, for at least three reasons: the law of the place of the act does not fit in well with the permanence of the connection sought in commercial matters and *a fortiori* in matters of payment; it completely breaks the respect for the body of law constituted by the law of the exchange; and it stems from a misunderstanding of the role of the will in domestic law and in private international law. Firstly, the most obvious drawback of subjecting the effects of an exchange undertaking to the law of the place of the act is its particularly contingent nature, which causes two difficulties. On the one hand, the signing of the deed does not necessarily take place at the domicile of the signatory, which means that the law of the place of the deed is not only not necessarily the most protective for the signatory, but is not even necessarily the one he knows best. The argument that the law of the place of signature protects the author of the commitment is therefore unsatisfactory; if it were correct, the domicile of the signatory would have been chosen as the connecting factor anyway. Moreover, as the various signatures may take place in very different countries, all the exchange commitments are then subject to as many different laws, which results in the scope of the commitments made being unknown.

Secondly, the uncertainty as to the law applicable to each commitment does not help to strengthen confidence in the instrument, since it is not known which laws may be applicable to the commitments which the final creditor of the exchange obligations hopes to invoke. This is all the more so because the radical nature of the regime governing bills of exchange is not only to be understood in the light of commercial law, which also uses assignments under ordinary law, but also because of the historical purpose of the bill of exchange, which is to be an instrument of credit *and* payment. Consequently, compliance with this body of law would have been better ensured by subjecting it to a single law, that of payment.[193] Finally, giving the parties the choice of determining the applicable law is not in the interest of the circulation of bills of exchange. Indeed, the *lex loci actus* risks changing with each signature depending on the place indicated by the parties. The objective of strengthening confidence in the bill of exchange would have been better pursued by a permanent criterion subjecting not only all forms of the bill of exchange, including the validity

---

the signature governed by the place indicated by the parties, again because 'the signatory's will must indeed be taken into account' (*ibid.*, p. 357). This question of will is also found in the law applicable to the transfer of the provision: again, the German delegation criticises the choice of the law of payment, because: 'Here it is not the intention of the parties, but the place where the bill of exchange is payable that must be considered. Nevertheless, this place is generally of no value in determining the intention of the parties. It could be quite accidental and appear simply for reasons of convenience, as in the case where the bill is payable at a place other than the domicile of the drawee' (*ibid.*).

193 See on this point R. Chemaly, 'Conflits de lois en matière d'effets de commerce', *op. cit.*, p. 452.

of signatures and their effects, to the same law. It would also have rendered obsolete the rule that commitments subsequent to an invalid commitment are valid according to the requirements of the local law applicable to the form of the commitment,[194] which is only there to alleviate the significant drawbacks of the *lex loci actus*.[195]

619. Conclusion of the paragraph. It is usual to present negotiable instruments as credit instruments. The study of the bill of exchange shows that the purpose of credit is here subordinated to its purpose of payment, both from a historical point of view and in its regime. Thus, the plurality of purposes does not exclude their hierarchy. This conclusion is valuable from the point of view of financial securities, where the monetary/proprietary function of securities tends to supplant their primary function, which is to place the owner of the financial security in the community of shareholders or creditors and in a direct personal relationship with the issuer. From the point of view of conflict of laws, several general points should be stressed. The plurality of connections thesis has a number of significant disadvantages, foremost among which is its inability to respect the coherence of the bodies of law it governs and to pursue its function in international relations. With the exception of capacity, the thesis of legislative unity should prevail in principle, for several reasons. Firstly, it is neither necessary nor desirable to apply local law to the effects of the signature, i.e. to subject the transmission of the exchange obligation to the law of the place of the act. A single law capable of governing all transfers is likely to enable the obligation transmitted to be enforced. Secondly, the importance of the purpose of internal institutions in resolving conflicts of laws: rather than basing them on rules that are understood in isolation, it is necessary to understand what function these rules, taken together, serve. Thirdly, although the study of the internal legal technique of the institutions is indispensable in order to enact a good conflict-of-laws rule, the latter must not be based on them. The study of the latter makes it possible to detect the purpose of a legislative body; it is this purpose that must guide the author of the conflict rule. Fourthly, behind the same connecting factor, in this case the law of payment, there may be several issues: fulfilment of the purpose of the internal institution, to allow payment, or international protection of the

---

194 Art. 3 para. 2 of the Geneva Convention.

195 Finally, it should be noted that the article was largely controversial at the time, as the Italian delegation voted against it, and the English representative states that he 'is obliged to confess that this article leaves him in great uncertainty; but he has come to the conclusion that he does not wish to tire his colleagues by exposing his doubts; he will endeavour to dispel them himself'. (*Proceedings of the 1930 Geneva Conference*, p. 355). This is probably related to the fact that the English, at the time of the Geneva Convention, included the form of the bill of exchange within the scope of the law of issue (Guttenbridge speech, *Proceedings of the 1930 Geneva Conference*, p. 346). While the latter was perhaps not as suitable as the law of payment, it did have decisive advantages in terms of permanence and predictability, which the *lex loci actus* lacks.

debtor. Finally, it should be noted that the thesis of the plurality of connections has given the *lex loci actus* not only a disproportionate and inappropriate scope, but also an imperativeness which it had never known before.

§ 2. THE SOLUTION OF THE LAW OF PAYMENT FOR THE BILL OF EXCHANGE

620. Despite the longevity of the Geneva Convention, there is nothing in the solutions it contains that is indicative of an inescapable trend towards conflict of laws in respect of bills of exchange, or even commercial and financial matters; they are merely the contingent solutions of a community of lawyers who, being too close to their object, have lost sight of its significance.[196] The disinterest of the bill of exchange is not only linked to the competition of more efficient technologies, it is also due to the concrete consequences of international bill of exchange practice, despite its own efforts to limit its uncertainty.[197] The bill of exchange would have greatly benefited from being subject to a single law, that of payment, the merits of which we would like to summarise before outlining the modalities of its implementation.

621. The foundations of the law of payment. The thesis of legislative unity is the one which best ensures the community of function of the bill of exchange, through the priority importance given to the payment of the bill, and the only one capable of accounting for the legislative whole constituted by the rules of the exchange.[198] In order to select the applicable law, the doctrine hesitates between two laws,[199] which often coincide in practice: the law of the creation of the exchange obligation,[200] and the law of its extinction, i.e. the law of payment. Since the purpose of the credit granted by the bill of exchange is payment, the

---

196 This is an illustration that leads to qualify Dean Batiffol's analysis according to which: 'We are probably faced here with one of the classic difficulties of the legal method - and of thought in general: the search for intelligibility must not ignore the complexity of reality. A persevering attitude on the part of men of action, which at first sight is difficult to explain, is often the sign, in its unanalysed constancy, of a reality that speculation must discover', see H. Batiffol, *Aspects philosophiques*, *op. cit.*, p. 254.

197 On these practices, see P. Bloch, *Les lettres de change et billets à ordre dans les relations commerciales internationales*, Paris, Economica, 1986.

198 In this sense, see H. Batiffol, *Aspects philosophiques*, *op. cit.*, pp. 19–20: 'The idea that private international law works to constitute a systemic order implies that each domestic private law constitutes a system; their coordination, moreover, poses problems only because of this systematic character. But this character is not immediately apparent […].'

199 R. Chemaly, 'Conflits de lois en matière d'effets de commerce', *op. cit.*, p. 386; R. Libchaber, 'Effet de commerce et chèques', *op. cit.*

200 The expression is reminiscent of Maisie Ooi's *lex creationis*, which is manifested in financial securities by the law of the issue. Here, it is the law of the *place* where the security was created, the reference to a topographical situation bringing this law closer to the law of the situation.

law of payment can claim a particularly serious basis, since it is ultimate and it would not be unreasonable to order all the effects of the instrument. The law of issuance can be seen as the law of autonomy of the exchange relationship,[201] allowing the wills of the parties to be expressed at the time of the creation of the instrument, while also guaranteeing the permanence of the connection. The law of payment nevertheless has several advantages which, combined, appear to be decisive: it takes into account the purpose of the bill of exchange; it truly constitutes the seat of the legal relationship – the legal centre of gravity of the exchange transaction;[202] it is known to the drawee and all the signatories at the time they sign; finally, it coincides with the law of the country of realisation of the sanctions.[203] It is therefore no coincidence that, prior to the Geneva Convention, French law chose the law of payment.[204]

---

201 In this sense, see R. LIBCHABER, 'Effets de commerce et chèques', *op. cit.*, no. 32.

202 The signatories of the bill of exchange, the drawer, the endorsee and the guarantor, on the other hand, are all aware of the drawee's domicile and have signed the bill with a view to being paid by him (even in the absence of acceptance by the drawee, since even in this case the drawee is not the final debtor of the exchange mechanism). The law of payment is therefore known to all signatories at the time they sign, which is not the case for other signatories. The other signatories can only be sued once the formalities of the protest have been completed, as these formalities make it possible to prove the insolvency of the drawee. It is only once these formalities have been completed that they can be sued, and it therefore does not seem extraordinary to apply to them the law of the person who *should have* paid the bill of exchange. Especially in the light of the favourable treatment of payment which characterises the whole regime of the bill of exchange and which must be reflected in the resolution of the conflict of laws.
Finally, it should be added that if the bill of exchange and the promissory note can be considered in domestic law as instruments of credit (in this sense, see the presentation given by the manuals on the subject, e.g. R. BONHOMME, *Instruments de crédit et de paiement*, 10th ed., Paris, LGDJ, p. 5), it is possible to consider that its function in international relations is that of an instrument of payment, given the certainty that attaches to its settlement, the latter being subject to the same exchange regime as payment instruments.

203 Indeed, the domicile of the drawee is the most important place for the realisation of the claim, not only because of the number of assets likely to allow payment, but also because it is the 'psychological' seat of the debtor.

204 Lévy-Bruhl notes, in his history of the bill of exchange, that 'in principle, payments made abroad were subject to the law of the place where the payment was to be made and, sequentially, protests obeyed the law applicable to the domicile of the drawee for their drafting and time limits' (H. LÉVY-BRUHL, *Histoire de la lettre de change en France aux XVIIe et XVIIIe siècles*, *op. cit.*, p. 239) The application of the law of payment to these two questions is probably based on two very different grounds. Thus Pothier (*Traité du contrat de change*, Paris et Orléans, Debure et Rouzeau-Montaut, 1773, no. 155) justifies the law applicable to the protest by an ancestor of *lex loci actus*. In reality, it seems that the protest is irreducible to the other questions opened up by the bill of exchange, so much so that it is a sanction which intimately concerns local public policy, with the criminal sanctions which were attached at the time to the insolvency of the drawee having accepted a bill of exchange. The law of the drawee also has a special influence in relation to recourse actions by the bearer, which for Savary must apply, whereas Boullenois applies the law of the drawee to all guarantors and not that of the guarantor (*Traité des statuts personnels et réels*, t. I, p. 372, quoted by H. LÉVY-BRUHL, *Histoire de la lettre de change en France aux XVIIe et XVIIIe siècles*, *op. cit.*, p. 283). This perception of Boullenois is confirmed by two

622. The exclusion of negotiable instruments from the category of contractual obligations in positive law. Negotiable instruments, which include bills of exchange, are excluded from the Rome I Regulation. This exclusion dates from the Rome Convention. In his report on the draft convention, Dean Batiffol considers that 'this subject is indeed heterogeneous to contract law; it was also the subject of the Geneva Conventions of 1931, which already achieved a unification that went beyond the framework of the European Economic Community, and it would have been doubly inadvisable to take up this subject again'.[205] In fact, since the Geneva Convention produced an easily perfectible result, there would have been no point in taking up the conflict-of-laws rules that they may have laid down; it was rather the pain that the debates had caused that led the authors to concentrate on other obligations.

In French law, the affirmation of the non-contractual nature of negotiable instruments is relatively recent. Niboyet, for example, considered a trade to be a contract,[206] and was part of a long tradition since Pothier himself supported this position.[207] More recently, some authors have taken up the argument of

rulings of the 'Conservation de Lyon' (Tribunal de la Conservation des privilèges royaux des foires de Lyon, a court of exception in Lyon): a sentence of 5 August 1664 and a ruling of 28 February 1668 (reported by La Serra, cited *ibid.*, p. 235, fn. 5). From the doctrinal point of view, Pothier himself was already in favour of the law of payment (R.-J. Pothier, *Traité du contrat de change*, *op. cit.*, no. 155) and the internationalists, at least since Bartin, have been in favour of it: Batiffol, Goldman and above all Chemaly, speak out in favour of it. The application of the law of payment is advocated by Batiffol's study of conflicts of laws in contract law, when he observes that American case-law applies the law of reimbursement which coincides with the law of negotiable instruments; for Batiffol, according to the observation of American case-law, this is the law of payment, see H. Batiffol, *Les conflits de lois en matière de contrat*, *op. cit.* The representatives of the practice were also in favour of subjecting the effects of a contract to the law of payment, as shown by the draft resolution of the *International Bar Association* to this effect (B. Goldman, 'Les conflits de lois en matière d'instruments négociables', *op. cit.*), and this position was partially defended by the Polish delegation during the negotiations of the Geneva Convention (*Comptes rendus de la Convention de Genève de 1930*, p. 358).

205 H. Batiffol, 'Projet de convention C.E.E. sur la loi applicable aux obligations contractuelles', *RTDEur*, 1975, p. 182 (a few decades earlier, the author included conflicts of laws in the area of exchange law in the section on 'contractual obligations' in his annual overview of the law of conflicts of laws, see e.g. *RCDIP*, 1937, p. 434). Similarly, Professors Giuliano and Lagarde consider in their report on the Rome Convention that the inclusion of these matters would have required special conflict rules, that the Geneva Conventions already regulate most of the problems, and that these obligations are considered non-contractual by some Member States, see M. Giuliano and P. Lagarde, 'Report on the Convention on the law applicable to contractual obligations', [1980] OJ C 282/11.

206 Thus the eminent author takes offence, in a note under a judgment of 28 February 1935, at the fact that the Paris Court of Appeal applied to a question of formation of the contract the law of payment and not the classic solutions of conflict of laws in contractual matters designating the law of the contract, see CA Paris, 28 February 1935, critical note by Niboyet, *RCDIP*, 1935, p. 748.

207 R.-J. Pothier, *Traité du contrat de change*, *op. cit.*

the non-contractual character of the negotiable instrument in French law.[208] The author explains the exclusion by certain characteristics of the bill of exchange. The latter would be marked by 'an abstraction and a formalism absolutely irreducible to the contract'.[209] We have already seen that neither the formalism[210] nor the abstraction[211] was such as to exclude the obligations entered into by means of a bill of exchange from contractual matters.

Some authors also considers that the bill of exchange departs from the contractual model because it has the originality of establishing a plurality of commitment which cannot be subject to a single law, but which are necessarily governed by the law of the place of payment or the law of the place of each declaration.[212] However, it seems to us that there is a confusion here between the choice of the authors of the Convention to favour the thesis of the plurality of connections, and the nature of exchange obligations. It is perfectly possible to subject all the foreign exchange obligations evidenced by a document of title to a single law, for example that of payment.[213] Finally, some authors try

---

208 B. Haftel, *La notion de matière contractuelle en droit international privé*, *op. cit.*, no. 382. The author specifies that in his mind this statement does not apply as much to promissory notes as to other negotiable instruments.

209 *Ibid.* In addition to this first argument based on the characteristics of the promissory note, the author presents a second argument relating to the interests of third parties, which is not convincing: the successors in title of the cambia creditor are not really more interested in the note than in any other obligation present in the patrimony of their debtor. As for the future bearers of the bill of exchange, who are then third parties to the exchange obligation, they are likely to be interested in the very subject-matter of the contract; taking them into account is not likely to qualify as a categorical exclusion.

210 See *supra*, para. 604.

211 See *supra*, para. 606.

212 *Ibid.* The assertion is incorrect. Art. 4 of the Geneva Convention states that 'the effects of the obligations of the acceptor of a bill of exchange and of the subscriber to a promissory note are determined by the *law of the country in which these instruments are payable*'. For there to have been an acceptor, there must still have been an acceptance, a question which therefore clearly does not fall within the scope of this Art. 4 designating the law of payment. The drawee's obligation to accept, which is not dealt with by the Geneva Convention, has been subject in French law to the law of the issue, whereas doctrine has subsequently tended to favour the law of the original contract. The solutions are certainly open to criticism (see Y. Loussouarn and J.-D. Bredin, *Droit du commerce international*, *op. cit.*, p. 556), but they have been adopted by the majority of authors. The law of payment retains within its scope the delimitation of the obligations of the acceptor, the examination of the relationship with the drawer and the consequences of the prescription of the instrument. In other words, within the category 'bill of exchange', the law of payment governs only the effects of a bill of exchange which has been accepted, the other effects of the bill of exchange concerning the drawee's obligation to accept are controversial and there has been some hesitation between the law of the original contract and the law of payment, whereas for the presentation for acceptance the hesitation is between the law of issue and the law of payment.
On this point and the resulting discussion, see R. Chemaly, 'Conflits de lois en matière d'effets de commerce', *op. cit.*, pp. 403 et seq.

213 This criterion is used by Art. 1(2°)(d) of the Rome I Regulation, taking over Art. 1(c) of the Rome Convention. For Mr Haftel, the argument relating to third parties seems to explain the plurality of connections; but there is no doubt that the submission of the effects

to demonstrate that the criterion of excluding negotiable instruments from the contractual category is specific to negotiability.[214] This notion would allow to delimit the scope of the exclusion.[215] However, those same authors observe themselves that the explicit exclusion of negotiable instruments was unnecessary for two reasons. Firstly, because the application of Article 12 of the Rome Convention already led to the same result as the Geneva Convention with regard to negotiable instruments.[216] On the other hand, because of Article 1(2°)(e) of the Convention which allows the *lex societatis* to take precedence over the *lex contractus* for 'other negotiable instruments'.[217] It is indeed because they constitute contractual obligations of a particular type that they had to be explicitly treated separately.

The solutions of the Rome Convention and, subsequently, the Rome I Regulation are not identical to those of the Geneva Convention. They would have the advantage of putting an end to the disproportionate influence of the law of form, by subjecting the conditions of form to the law designated by the contract, or to the law of the drawee's domicile.[218] However, this law will also regulate the effects of the exchange obligation, except for certain aspects of the transfer of the provision, in particular its assignability, which will remain subject to the law of the original contract.[219] A single law, the law recorded on the document of title or, failing that, the law of the drawee's domicile, would therefore be applicable to the essential aspects of the exchange obligation; at most, the drawee's obligation to accept could be excluded. The conflict rules in contractual matters are therefore likely to resolve the conflicts of laws relating to bills of exchange.[220]

623. Conclusion of the section. In the law of negotiable instruments, the rule of plurality of connections leads to a dead end: it breaks the legal certainty

of the transfer to a single and permanent law would make it possible to provide much greater security for third parties: it is obviously the subjective and contingent nature of the connection criterion that is harmful to them.

214 B. Haftel, *La notion de matière contractuelle en droit international privé*, *op. cit.* The Rome I Regulation makes negotiability the exclusion criterion.

215 *Ibid.*, no. 384.

216 See already in this sense, *ibid.*

217 *Ibid.*, no. 385.

218 As the law of the domicile of the debtor of the characteristic performance. Indeed, the latter is the payment.

219 Art. 14(1°) of the Rome I Regulation, which clarifies the terms of Art. 12(1°) of the Rome Convention, keeping its spirit.

220 Admittedly, the thesis of the plurality of connections would risk resurfacing in favour of the law of payment, because, as is the strength of the negotiable instruments, each endorsement gave rise to a new exchange obligation, creating a new possible payer. The consequence of this would be that both the validity and the effects of the exchange obligation would always be subject to the law of the habitual residence of the person who signed it. Such an analysis appears to be unfruitful, in particular because if payment can, in certain cases, be claimed from each signatory, the final burden of the debt falls on the drawee.

which is necessary for instruments whose negotiability implies multiple transfers and which make the application of a single law desirable. This is obvious in the law of negotiable instruments, where the argument of the plurality of connections constitutes an obstacle to the payment of the bill of exchange, which is nevertheless the very purpose of the instrument. The choice of this connection stems from a misunderstanding of the articulation of the function of domestic rules in the international order. It could usefully have been replaced by the law of payment, which allows the application of a unitary, predictable law, which is moreover the one which has the closest legal links with the instrument in question.

624. Conclusion of the chapter. Financial securities are still those '*richesses nouvelles*' of which Ripert said that it was an 'invention almost as marvellous as joint-stock companies'.[221] Because they constitute wealth, securities are the preferred instrument of exchange, facilitated by the qualities attached to the form they take. This aspect should not, however, obscure the fact that securities always represent a *negotium*. This is why substantive unification based on intermediated securities should be rejected. This is also the reason why solutions arising from contractual assignments of claims could have found an analogous application. This finds a particularly secure basis in the application of the law of the assignor's domicile to the enforceability of the assignment against third parties. However, this solution does not take into account the particularity of claims when they take the form of a negotiable instrument. In such cases, on the one hand, the right is made to circulate and requires a unitary criterion and, on the other hand, its insertion within an intermediation structure multiplies the number of potential assignors. These observations have led to a shift in focus towards conflict of laws solutions in the law of negotiable instruments, from which solutions applicable by analogy could have been derived. Unfortunately, the plurality of connections thesis that is in force there produces results that contradict the very function of the instruments in question.

---

[221] G. Ripert, *Aspects juridiques du capitalisme moderne*, *op. cit.*

CHAPTER 2
CRITIQUE OF THE PLURAL CONNECTION OF BEARER SECURITIES

Securities in bearer form have long been materialised on a paper medium and thus subject to the lex situs. The latter reproduced the impasses of the thesis of the plurality of connections, whereas a unitary solution of the conflict of laws based on the law of the issuer was possible (Section 1). Paper documents, although still in use in some jurisdictions, have been replaced by book-entry securities. This method of representing securities is based on intermediation. However, on the one hand, intermediation has different effects in different legal systems and, on the other hand, intermediation chains are often international, resulting in their entanglement (Section 2). Such a situation makes the plurality of connections particularly inappropriate, although it is envisaged both by the rules of the European Union and by the Hague Securities Convention (Section 3).

SECTION 1. THE IMPASSES OF THE *LEX SITUS* FOR TRANSFERS OF BEARER SECURITIES

625. The rule resulting from the plurality of connections exists in the same terms within bearer securities representing shares or claims. The cumbersome heritage of the *lex situs* of securities (leads to the application to their transfer of the law of the location of the *instrumentum* (§ 2). However, it would have been preferable to apply the law of the issue (§ 3).

§ 1. THE CUMBERSOME LEGACY OF THE *LEX SITUS* TO SECURITIES

626. Since the *Kantoor de Maas* judgment,[1] French law is 'solely applicable to proprietary rights in movable property situated in France'.[2] If the influence of the lex situs has been so persistent on securities while claims have been released from it, it is because of the metaphor of the incorporation of the right into the security. The purpose of this metaphor, however, was never to subject securities to the law of situation of the certificate, but to facilitate the transmission of securities. In view of this masterpiece of confusion, we should remember that in France the lex situs was not originally intended to apply to movable property, nor was it intended to apply to transfer transactions.[3] It is not by chance that intangible movables have progressively moved away from it (I); on the other hand, it is a misfortune that securities are still subject to it (II).

I. Reversal of the Lex Situs to Claims

627. Incorporation within the lex situs. For a long time, the formulation of the applicable law to third-party enforceability was obscured by the general influence of the lex situs over claims. The latter has been the subject of controversy over the centuries, the main points of which will simply be recalled here.[4] From the point of view of the conflict of laws, the fundamental question is that of the solution of principle between their submission to the rule resulting from the status in rem, by way of an analogy with tangible property, and the applicability of the *lex creationis*. However, the formulation in these terms only occurs in the 20th century with Niboyet. Initially, at the time of the statutists, the debate was about the consequences of the territoriality of the laws of succession and the search for the unity of the succession. Since movables were then subject to *mobilia sequuntur personam* and to the last domicile of the deceased,[5] claims, characterised as movables, followed this movement[6] at a time when the lex situs was a residual category: what did not belong to personal law fell under

1 Req. 24 May 1933, S. 1935. 1. 253, note Batiffol, *RCDIP*, 1934, 132, note J.-P. Niboyet.

2 See the justifications for this application by the commentators of the major judgments under the *DIAC* judgment, B. Ancel and Y. Lequette, *Les grands arrêts de la jurisprudence française de droit international privé*, *op. cit.*, comm. no. 48.

3 On the origin of the *lex situs* in France, a territorial custom whose original function is the preservation of property in families, see L. d'Avout, *Sur les solutions du conflit de lois en droit des biens*, *op. cit.*

4 For details, see in particular D. Pardoel, *Les conflits de lois en matière de cession de créances*, *op. cit.*, nos. 105 et seq.; L. d'Avout, *Sur les solutions du conflit de lois en droit des biens*, *op. cit.*, nos. 81 et seq.

5 On the origin and evolution of this principle see L. d'Avout, *Sur les solutions du conflit de lois en droit des biens*, *op. cit.*, nos. 108 et seq. and references.

6 D. Pardoel, *Les conflits de lois en matière de cession de créances*, *op. cit.*, no. 107.

the lex situs.[7] However, as Lainé later notes, it is still necessary to determine whether claims should be 'located' in the domicile of the debtor or the creditor. In this context, Lainé observes that ancient professors – Guy Coquille and Simon d'Olive – had developed the localisation of the claim at the domicile of the debtor, because:

> 'It is there that the creditor will have to go to seek his claim or to claim it in court. Similarly, it is the debtor's behaviour that will determine the value of the claim, depending on his probity, honesty and the favourable or unfavourable circumstances prevailing at the debtor's home.'[8]

Here a number of factors point to the debtor's domicile: the inherently enforceable nature of any claim;[9] the importance of the debtor's person in determining the value of the claim; the importance of the political and economic context of the country in which the debtor is located. Another argument in favour of the debtor's domicile was taken up by Arminjon and Jitta: that of enforcement, according to which it is the authorities of the debtor's domicile that will oblige him to pay and therefore justify the legislative competence of the debtor's domicile.[10]

628. The gradual detachment of claims from the lex situs. Once the debtor's domicile has been chosen as the connecting principle in the name of the lex situs, the law of the claim becomes specialised with two types of distinction which, coming from the law of property, nevertheless contribute to freeing it from the logic of the lex situs. Firstly, there is the distinction between *ut singuli* and *ut universi* transmissions, and secondly the distinction between the law applicable to the *inter partes* relationship and the law applicable to the enforceability to third parties.[11] In order to determine the applicable law, the purpose of the laws involved as a criterion of location appears.[12] It is in this context that, as Mrs Pardoel writes, 'detached both from the attraction of the patrimony and

7 In this sense, B. Ancel and Y. Lequette, *Les grands arrêts de la jurisprudence française de droit international privé*, *op. cit.*, comm. no. 3, *Stewart*, p. 25. The authors note that d'Argentré had been described as a 'deep-rooted feudal' by Niboyet (*S.* 1940.1.49). The eminent author approved in his note the decision of the Cour de cassation to have chosen the law of the last domicile of the deceased as the law applicable to the movable succession.

8 Guy Coquille (Questions et réponses, Question CCXXXVII cited by Lainé in *Introduction au droit international privé*, t. II, p. 263, note 3) and Simon d'Olive (Questions notables du droit décidées par divers arrest de la Cour du parlement de Toulouse, ch. 22 [Œuvre de Simon d'Olive, Lyon, 1650] cited by Lainé *op. cit.*) These authors are quoted by D. Pardoel, *Les conflits de lois en matière de cession de créances*, *op. cit.*

9 According to these authors, when what is now Art. 1342-6 of the Civil Code (formerly 1247) considers that payment is enforceable, it is merely stating a rule derived from the nature of things, in the manner of the principle of jurisdiction of the defendant's domicile.

10 See W. Wengler, 'The situation of rights', *op. cit.*, p. 193.

11 D. Pardoel, *Les conflits de lois en matière de cession de créances*, *op. cit.*, nos. 118 and 119.

12 *Ibid.*, no. 120.

from the place where the formalities of publicity must be carried out, the law of the assigned claim can finally take on a new meaning',[13] giving Niboyet the means to reject the old law and to propose the modern formulation of the conflict of laws. The author rejects the analogy of claims with tangible property subject to the lex situs, and consequently rejects the wording of the debate 'locating' claims in the domicile of the debtor or the creditor. He then proposes to attach claims to their *lex creationis* because of their specific nature,[14] giving rise, in the words of Ms Pardoel, 'for the first time in French private international law (to) an abstract attachment of the claim without geographical consideration'.[15] Unfortunately, bearer securities were not so lucky because of the metaphor of the incorporation of the right into the security.

II. The Continuing Influence of Lex Situs *on Securities*

629. The metaphor of the incorporation of the right into the security is not a figure of speech, or an abuse of language, but a voluntary and teleological legal fiction in order to make the personal right evidenced by the security a tangible movable property.[16] Its function was to enable the claim thus "incorporated" to escape the rules governing the assignment of claims in the law of obligations, subject to the formalities of Article 1679 of the Civil Code, which were deemed too cumbersome for commercial exchanges.[17] By characterising the right, once incorporated in the security, as a tangible movable, it is possible to bring into play Article 2276 of the Civil Code (formerly 2279), according to which 'possession is

13 *Ibid.*, no. 121.

14 J.-P. Niboyet, *Traité de droit international privé*, t. IV, *op. cit.*, p. 670.

15 D. Pardoel, *Les conflits de lois en matière de cession de créances*, *op. cit.*, no. 121.
Bartin will remain opposed to Niboyet, who would have confused the intangible movable claim with the legal relations of which it was the consequence or the object, *Principes*, 1935, vol. III, no. 375, pp. 36 et seq. On the opposition between Bartin and Niboyet, see L. d'Avout, *Sur les solutions du conflit de lois en droit des biens*, *op. cit.*, no. 81. It may be thought that Niboyet's intervention was decisive in many respects in the development of French doctrine as regards the status of intangible property, whereas, for example, English doctrine remained, at least until Maisie Ooi's thesis, trapped under the influence of the lex situs. To be convinced of this, it is sufficient to observe the successive editions of Dicey, Morris and Collins from the 12th edition onwards.

16 Metaphor is a trope, i.e. 'a happy change of meaning of a word or phrase' (C. Perelman and L. Olbrechts-Tyteca, *Traité de l'argumentation*, Brussels, Ed. Université Libre de Bruxelles, 2008, no. 87, p. 534), which constitutes a form of analogy, particularly condensed, going far beyond a comparison between the terms of the theme and those of the phore. The metaphor results, more than from a rigorous identification, from a real fusion between an element of the theme and an element of the phore (*ibid*). This is why metaphor has precisely the effect, by its very nature of merging terms, of confusing the notions employed (*ibid*: 'Metaphor does not only influence the argument for which it is created. In particular, it can contribute to the confusion of notions.')

17 On the history of representation, which began with goods and extended to shares and claims, see V. Malassigné, *Les titres représentatifs*, *op. cit.*

equivalent to ownership'. Tradition (*traditio*, hand-to-hand transmission of the thing) is then worth presumption of ownership of the security, and especially of the ownership of the right represented.[18] What appeared to be a metaphor to explain the particular regime of bearer securities, a regime that had been selected to facilitate transmission, has turned into a genuine theory according to which the *negotium* has been incorporated into the *instrumentum*, and the two are now one.[19]

630. Far from being interested in the function of this metaphor, the authors retained only the result, which led to the characterisation as movable the claims evidenced by the securities. Characterised as movable by domestic law, bearer securities were also characterised as such by private international law, which applied to the property regime of the security the law of its geographical location. In this context, the enforceability of documents of security against third parties was subject to the lex situs, but, curiously, not the translative relationship itself. Thus, at the beginning of the 20th century, it was customary to distinguish between what concerns the transfer of ownership between the parties and vis-à-vis third parties.[20] As between the parties, the authors do not see the need to apply the *lex situs* because it is 'not a question of organising ownership or safeguarding public credit, but simply of assessing the effect of an agreement'.[21] On the other hand, the transfer of ownership to third parties 'concerns the public credit' and is therefore subject to the *lex situs*.[22] In 1930, Bartin also adopted the metaphor and its consequences in private international law,[23] while subsequently noting

---

18 As some authors write: 'Their transmission was subject to the legal regime of the sale of a tangible movable: the security sold was delivered by *traditio*, the sale was enforceable to third parties by the sole effect of the agreement, the operation of Article 2279 of the Civil Code paralysed the nemo plus juris rule and prohibited in principle the assertion of a claim against the purchaser in good faith', T. Bonneau and F. Drummond, *Droit des marchés financiers*, *op. cit.* F. Drummond, *Droit des marchés financiers*, *op. cit.*, no. 91-1.
This metaphor can probably be compared to the notion of *jus in re* in Roman law. *Jus* was not a subjective right, but an incorporeal thing, which could be incorporated into a corporeal thing, giving *jus in re*, cf. M. Villey, 'Du sens de l'expression *jus in re* en droit romain classique', *Revue internationale des droits de l'Antiquité*, 1949, p. 421 and p. 431. Here the mechanism was similar: the claim - share, bond or unit of a collective investment scheme - was incorporated into the security, the sheet of paper.

19 This particularity gave rise to the theory of the incorporation of the right into the security, according to which the *negotium* would have been incorporated into the *instrumentum*, and the two would become one. On this theory and its denial in domestic law, see V. Malassigné, *Les titres représentatifs*, *op. cit.*, no. 176 et seq.

20 F. Despagnet, *Précis de droit international privé*, 5th edition by C. de Boeck, Paris, Sirey, 1909, no. 395, p. 1136; In the same vein, significantly, as he is considered an expert on this question in relation to securities, J. Bezard-Falgas, 'Des modes de transmission de la propriété des titres nominatifs d'actions et d'obligations', *Revue de législation professionnelle*, 1911.

21 F. Despagnet, *Précis de droit international privé*, *op. cit.*, no. 1138.

22 *Ibid.* no. 395, p. 1138.

23 E. Bartin, *Principes de droit international privé*, t. I, *op. cit.*, p. 247.

the difficulties to which this presentation leads.[24] This analysis is still relevant in the second half of the 20th century.[25] Significantly, Professors Loussouarn and Bredin follow this metaphor, which can truly be said to have flourished: 'In particular, in the case of bearer securities, the claim being incorporated into the security, it is the material holding of the *instrumentum* that confers on the shareholder or bondholder his right in the company.'[26] This does not fail to make the eminent authors uncomfortable, in view of the consequences that this perception of the security entails in terms of the application of the lex situs so that they finally propose the application of the law of the claim.[27] Such a choice is easily explained: rights evidenced by securities are basically debt rights.[28] The only function of the form that these claims take is to give them negotiability. Rather than turning to property law, whose solutions were not designed for intangible property, it would have been better to turn to solutions similar to contractual assignments of claims; these were not much more satisfactory, however.[29]

§ 2. THE IMPASSE OF THE *LEX SITUS* RULE

631. There are several reasons why a detailed study of the conflict of laws solutions to paper-based bearer securities is necessary, even though they are now dematerialised. The first is that these solutions still condition the perception of the problem today.[30] The second is that exchanges of financial securities often

---

24 E. Bartin, *Principes de droit international privé*, t. III, *op. cit.*, p. 56: 'This analysis, the subtlety of which it is all too easy to criticise, fortunately does not raise any difficulties in the area of domestic civil or commercial law. The same is not true, as is well known, in the area of conflict of laws, where irony is not enough to disentangle the respective application of the *lex situs* to the fictitious situation of the share or obligation, an incorporeal movable, and to the material situation of the bearer instrument, a tangible movable into which the share or obligation has been incorporated. Nevertheless, it is possible, with some difficulty, to take sides, subject, as we have seen in Volume I, to the intervention of the always arbitrary concept of international public policy [...].' Public order, which by its use not in a single instance, but chronically, shows that the problem is systemic, and inherent in a presentation that is nonetheless not critisised. The doctrine is all the more unoriginal in that Bartin is merely repeating on this question the observations of A. Weiss, *Traité théorique et pratique de droit international privé*, Paris, Sirey, 1912, p. 214.

25 Professor Larguier's thesis is perhaps the best known *La notion de titre en droit privé*, Paris, Dalloz, 1951.

26 Y. Loussouarn and J.-D. Bredin, *Droit du commerce international*, *op. cit.*, p. 405.

27 *Ibid.*, p. 405: 'Despite the incorporation of the claim into the security, should not the solution of legislative competence be sought by reference to the conflict rule of the law of obligations, since the law of the claim is the most suitable to govern the security?'

28 H. Le Nabasque, 'Les actions sont des droits de créance négociables', *op. cit.*

29 See *supra*, paras. 593 et seq.

30 It is sufficient to note that Art. 9 of the Financial Collateral Directive concerning the conflict of laws applicable to the ownership of collateral securities is ensecurityd '*lex situs*'.

take place across borders and that some of the main foreign systems, including US law, still have paper-based bearer securities. They have therefore retained the conflict-of-laws rules applicable to their transfer, or even apply them as they stand to securities held by an intermediary. The third reason relates to the continuity of the position of the conflict of laws problem, which is posed yesterday as today in an identical manner: who to favour between the dispossessed owner and the third-party purchaser in good faith? This question, which is answered by the lex situs designated by the conflict rule, leads to an impasse, which is reflected both in the conflict of security in English law (I) and in the difficulties which dispossession has caused in French law (II).

I. The Impasse of Priority Over Security in English Law

632. The facts of the *Macmillan* case.[31] In English law the conflict of laws rule comes from the *Macmillan* judgment. Its facts deserve to be detailed, but first two rules from US law must be specified. Firstly, US law allows shares which are registered in a register to be the subject of a form of "right to transfer" evidenced by a bearer certificate.[32] Rights are then issued, evidenced by certificates, the presentation of which by their *bona fide* owner to the issuer grants the owner of the certificate the registered transfer of the share, and purges any defects in the ownership of the security.[33] The advantages of the operation lies in the fact that, since registration is a source of administrative and fiscal cost, the creation of these special rights, evidenced by a certificate, allows for a cheaper exchange of share ownership. From the issuer's point of view, however, only its shareholders are the persons registered in the share register. In practice, simply holding the certificate is an effective financial guarantee: if the registered shareholder transfers the share certificate, the banker need only hold it without registering with the issuer.[34] The difficulty with this practice, however, is that these certificates are

---

31 *Macmillan Inc v. Bishopsgate Investment Trust plc* (No 3) [1995] EWCA Civ 55, [1996] WLR 387. On the analysis of *Macmillan*, see, among others, M. Ooi, *Shares and other securities in the conflict of laws*, *op. cit.*, nos. 1. 01 et seq.; M. Ooi, 'The ramifications of fragmentation in the choice of law for shares', *op. cit.*, no. 411.

32 These are the '*certificated securities*' from Art. 8 of the former New York Uniform Commercial Code. Today, there is a single Commercial Code for the entire United States. The existence of these *certificated securities* is linked to the transfer taxes collected by the US tax authorities each time a shareholder changes his or her name in the registered share register in the context of a legal system that imposes the registered form on shares. As the same causes produce the same effects, it should be noted that the obligation to register shares in a register in registered form has led to the appearance of a similar technique in Belgian and Dutch law through the certification of shares, see V. Malassigné, *Les titres représentatifs*, *op. cit.*

33 On this issue, see the summary by Slaughton LJ, *Macmillan*, *supra*, point 460.

34 In the event of default, the banker may register by name. Scottish law requires the registration of shares in the name of the guarantor, see M. Ooi, 'The ramifications of fragmentation in the choice of law for shares', *op. cit.*, p. 411 et seq., commenting on the leading case *Enviroco v. Farstad Supply A/S* (2011) 3 ALL ER 451 at 455.

sometimes confused with the shares themselves.[35] Secondly, these certificates are sometimes deposited with a centralising body, the depositary trust company, which then holds the certificates on behalf of its clients. In this case, only the name of a trustee is recorded in the securities accounts of the depositary trust company, which holds the certificates on behalf of its own clients.

633. *Macmillan* is a US subsidiary of a UK group of companies, *Maxwell Communication Company plc*. The company has offered some of its shares to the public, but remains owned by its founder, Robert Maxwell, and his family. *Macmillan* owns the majority of the shares of *Berlitz Inc*, a New York registered company, which it entrusts to a trustee, *Bishopsgate Invesment Trust*. The latter was registered as a shareholder in the register of *Bertliz Inc*. At the same time, an agreement was drawn up under which *Bishopgate* acted only as a nominee, under the orders of the real shareholder, *Macmillan*.[36] However, *Bishopgate*, in breach of the trust obligations, transferred a large portion of the certificated securities to the New York central depository, while the other portion of the certificates was sent to London. The practice of the central depository was to request that the name of its agent, *CEDE*, be entered in the *Berlitz* registers. However, *CEDE* only holds the shares on behalf of an intermediary (Morgan Stanley Bank), which in turn holds these powers on behalf of a company owned by *Bishopgate*. The ultimate investor is therefore *Bishopgate*. Subsequently, *Bishopgate* took out several loans with three London finance companies, secured by the claims on the *Berlitz Inc.* share transfer certificates. Nevertheless, each of these companies did not obtain the certificates in the same way: one of them received the certificates already in London, while the others had a security interest transferred to the accounts of the central depository.

634. Position of the problem and reasoning of the Court of Appeal. The legal question put to the Court is basically an issue of priority, that of the ownership of the *Berlitz* shares, while the holding of the securities is the result of a chain of transmission using a central securities depository. However, the question, posed in the form of the law applicable to the bona fide third party purchaser, led the London Court of Appeal, by a sinuous reasoning, to decide the priority conflict as if it were a direct holding system.

The Court of Appeal held that the law applicable to negotiability was English law,[37] and therefore characterised the shares as registered because

[35] See in this sense, M. Ooi, 'The ramifications of fragmentation in the choice of law for shares', *op. cit.*, p. 431: 'The difficulty with certificates accompanied by registrable transfers is that they have by extensive commercial usage come to be regarded by the securities and financial markets as the shares themselves.'

[36] 'Mr Maxell signs a nominee agreement in which Bishopsgate acknowledged that it held the shares as nominee for the account and benefit of Macmillan, and had "no power or right to take any action with respect thereto without the express consent of *Macmillan*".'

[37] On this issue, see *supra*, para. 300.

of the presence of a register. For this reason, the *Macmillan* judges applied a conflict of laws rule to the direct holding system in this case, despite the presence of a central depository in the holding pattern. In considering that the priority conflict related to registered shares, these judges applied the conflict rule specific to registered shares: the application of the law of the place of registration, i.e. New York law. US law resolves priority conflict in favour of the holder of the certificate, whose possession purges the defects affecting the ownership of the security. In other words, under New York law, *Macmillan* could no longer argue that the invalidity of *Bishopgate's* transfer of the shares nullified, by implication, the subsequent transfers.

635. Critical analysis of the *Macmillan* solution. The reasons why the form of the securities should have been subject to the *lex creationis* and not the local law have already been given.[38] The difficulty with this solution does not lie in the application of the American law, but in its unpredictability when the form of the securities is subject to the *lex fori* or the *lex loci actus*, the latter of which can give rise to heterogeneous solutions depending on the conception of the place of the act. This is the first impasse reached by the solution in Macmillan. A more rigorous solution should have led to the application of the law of the issuer to the form of the securities, i.e. to the American law which considers that the prerogatives evidenced by the certificate are distinct from the share and negotiable under the law of the issuer. However, the English conflict rule for negotiable, i.e. bearer, instruments points to the law of the place where the instrument is located.

It turns out that this second conflict rule applicable to bearer securities leads to a second impasse, which Ms Maisie Ooi has demonstrated on several occasions.[39] Indeed, in the presence of a certificate granting its holder the right to register as a shareholder, English law characterises the legal issue as relating not to the ownership of the shares, but to the ownership of the *instrumentum*. Consequently, English judges apply the *lex loci actus*, i.e. the law of the place where the last transaction giving rise to the delivery of the bearer securities took place, in order to determine who is the owner of the instrument, and therefore of the share.[40] As Ms Maisie Ooi puts it, whether there is a transfer certificate or not, the actual question of law that should be the subject of the characterisation lies in the ownership of the shares.[41] The

---

38 See *supra*, paras. 301 et seq.

39 M. Ooi, *Shares and other securities in the conflict of laws*, *op. cit.*; M. Ooi, 'The ramifications of fragmentation in the choice of law for shares', *op. cit.*

40 This rule may refer to the law of the place of registration, held at the place of the registered office, as the situation of registered shares appears to judges to be analogous to that of tangible movables (M. Ooi, 'The ramifications of fragmentation in the choice of law for shares', *op. cit.*, p. 431; Auld LJ, (1996) 1 WLR 387, 411–412)

41 M. Ooi, 'The ramifications of fragmentation in the choice of law for shares', *op. cit.*, p. 431, p. 434.

same applies whether the share represented is the subject of a bearer share certificate or whether it is registered. It is true that priority will be determined by the form of the share. However, this form must first be determined by the *negotium* which is represented.[42] It is this law which will determine both the form taken and the resulting regime as to the ownership of the *negotium* represented.[43]

636. Critical analysis of the basis of the lex situs. The reasoning is doubly obscured in English law in that it continues to refer to the *lex situs*. In the manner of the ancient French doctrine, the authors attribute a fictitious situation to the *negotia*. Thus, the 15th edition of *Dicey and Morris* continues to present shares as 'things in action', which depend on 'the law of property', and to which a *situs* must be assigned. This type of reasoning is not necessarily harmful in terms of the solutions deployed. Indeed, assigning a fictitious *situs* to the shares at the place of the issuer's seat amounts to applying the law of the issuer. At most, it can be observed that the *lex situs* does not help. However, on the one hand, it most often causes notorious difficulties when it is necessary to check the chain of transmission of the securities in order to ensure the absence of defects affecting their ownership and, on the other hand, it is likely to obscure the relationship between the *negotium* represented and its support. This was the case for bearer securities. This is still sometimes the case with the role given by certain authors to book entries and, above all, by positive law.

II. The Impasse of the Dispossession of Securities in French Law

637. Law applicable to the transmission of bearer securities. While the metaphor of the incorporation of the right into the security was internationally shared, it nevertheless came up against the theft or loss of bearer securities. More precisely, the dispossession itself does not generally lead to a divergence of solutions in the different legislations. Indeed, the ownership of the dispossessed person is not contested – i.e. it can be successfully claimed – as long as the thief of the security keeps it. Similarly, the legal systems converged on the possibility for the dispossessed owner to lodge a stop payment instruction with the issuing institution on the lost or stolen document.[44] The institution had to refrain from paying the person presenting himself with the lost or stolen document once it had received the objection. The stumbling block appeared at the later stage, in the event that the lost or stolen document was subsequently sold. In this case,

---

42 See *supra*, paras. 301 et seq.

43 See *supra*, paras. 301 et seq.

44 See in this sense E. Thaller, 'D'un règlement qui aurait pour objet de résoudre les conflits de lois en matière de dépossession de titres au porteur', *op. cit.*, pp. 250–252. The author notes that this convergence on the admissibility of the opposition and the interruption of the service of the security by the issuer was not immediate, with Belgian case law opposing it for a time.

some systems favoured, under certain conditions, the dispossessed owner, while others purged the ownership of the bona fide third party purchaser of its defects. French law thus grants protection to the *verus dominus*, subject to opposition by the dispossessed person, whereas some foreign laws prefer to protect the bona fide purchaser.[45] It is on this issue that the 'schism of laws'[46] erupts and that conflicts of laws relating to the dispossession of bearer securities develop.

638. The case of dispossession: the law of 15 June 1872. The desired consequence of assimilating bearer securities to tangible movables was to facilitate the transmission of securities. It also had the effect of allowing the bearer in good faith to have his property purged of its previous defects. Since civil law provided for opposition in the event of theft, the dispossessed owner could nevertheless recover ownership of the security in return for compensation to the bona fide third party purchaser of the price of his acquisition.[47] As Thaller already observed, such a system was in practice similar to foreign systems refusing to claim against the bona fide third party purchaser, because 'if the victim has to pay back a purchase price to regain possession of the value, he will prefer not to claim it: the sacrifice would be equal to the remuneration'.[48] However, if the dispossessed owner does not recover his security, the opposition notified to the issuer is in vain: without the security, he will not be able to recover payment and, correlatively, the holder in good faith is likely to obtain, *in fine*, his due. By failing to offer a more effective opposition regime than the ordinary law does, the dispossessed owner is deprived of any action, except against his thief. The fundamental relationship, from which the entire opposition regime derives, including vis-à-vis the issuer, is that of the dispossessed owner and the third party purchaser.

639. Observing a consequence that it had probably not intended, the French legislator enacted in 1872 a law instituting a special opposition regime when a document of security had been lost or stolen, in order to 'ensure that dispossessed bearers are protected in a way that the rules of civil law do not provide'.[49] The 1872 law provided for a twofold opposition system: on the one hand, the victim's opposition to the document of security with the Chambre syndicale des agents de change,[50] which prohibited the negotiation of the lost or stolen

45 The question is identical in contemporary litigation, see the question of law in the *Macmillan* judgment *infra*, paras. 634 et seq.

46 The expression comes from E. Thaller, 'D"un règlement qui aurait pour objet de résoudre les conflits de lois en matière de dépossession de titres au porteur', *op. cit.*

47 This system has been retained in Belgium.

48 E. Thaller, 'D'un règlement qui aurait pour objet de résoudre les conflits de lois en matière de dépossession de titres au porteur', *op. cit.*, p. 253. The author rightly adds: 'It is only in the rather exceptional case where a significant increase has occurred in the meantime that it would be in the interest of the company to avail itself of the right to take it back.'

49 Y. Loussouarn and J.-D. Bredin, *Droit du commerce international*, *op. cit.*, no. 355.

50 See *supra*, nos. 41 et seq.

document of security, and on the other hand, the opposition with the issuer, which no longer allowed the holder of the document of security to exercise the prerogatives attached to the *negotium* represented (payment, right to vote).[51] As Thaller observes, the linchpin of this organisation is the first opposition, which, by publicising the dispossession, enables the dispossessed owner to recover the security as soon as it is traded again, while the third-party purchaser in good faith has a liability action against the intermediary who sold him a security whose origin he could and should have verified.[52] The determination of the spatial scope of application of this law has been a source of difficulty. Two distinct theories have been defended: the theory of the lex situs, to which the name of Niboyet[53] is attached, and which leads to an impasse, and a second theory, defended by Thaller, which has not received the support it deserves despite its indisputable accuracy, and which we will refer to here as the theory of the personal status of the security ('*statut personnel du titre*').

640. The case law position and the characterisation of the mandatory rule. The theory known as the lex situs of security aimed to apply the 1872 Act to all French and foreign securities located in France. Two criteria could be envisaged: the application of the 1872 Act to securities located in France (French law applicable under the *lex situs*), and those whose transfer operation took place in France (French law applicable under the *lex loci contractus* because the transfer contract was concluded in France). In the first case, the connecting factor is therefore solely the geographical location of the security. The major disadvantage is, of course, that it is sufficient for the third party purchaser to move the security to a country that protects it from such a claim to render the law ineffective. This is why the case law has extended the application of the 1872 law to all securities whose *traditio* took place in France. It can already be observed that the theory of the lex situs of the security pays no heed to, in its two variants, the origin of the issuing authority, and focuses on the location of the *instrumentum* or transfer. Nevertheless, this situation had the disadvantage of leaving 'the French holder of French securities totally defenceless, when the thief had negotiated the security in

51 *Ibid.* This system of opposition was criticised for being too broad: 'By the extreme ease with which oppositions are exercised and prolong their effects without the need to justify their merit, the law gives a real premium to blackmail. This right of opposition should be kept within narrower limits.' (E. Thaller, 'D'un règlement qui aurait pour objet de résoudre les conflits de lois en matière de dépossession de titres au porteur', *op. cit.*)

52 E. Thaller, 'D'un règlement qui aurait pour objet de résoudre les conflits de lois en matière de dépossession de titres au porteur', *op. cit.*

53 J.-P. Niboyet, *Les conflits de lois relatifs à l'acquisition de la propriété sur les meubles corporels à titre particulier*, Paris, Sirey, 1912, pp. 305 et seq., pp. 451 et seq.; *Traité*, t. IV, no. 1304, p. 691. On this question, see also A. Pillet, *Traité pratique de droit international privé*, t. 1, 1923, nos. 372 et seq., pp. 765 et seq.; See 'Titres au porteur perdus ou volés' in J. Bezard Falgas, *Rép. Lapradelle-Niboyet;* Y. Loussouarn and J.-D. Bredin, *Droit du commerce international*, *op. cit.*, nos. 347 et seq.; L. d'Avout, *Sur les solutions du conflit de lois en droit des biens*, no. 85, p. 120.

a foreign country, and the foreign law of the country of negotiation did not allow the possibility of a claim'.[54] The case law then decided that 'the opposition made in France to the Chambre syndicale des Agents de change prevented any valid negotiation of the security, even abroad'[55] and then allowed the victim's claim against the third party holder who had acquired the security in foreign territory. This was to adopt, at least in part, the theory of the personal status of the security, which was intended to protect securities issued by French companies.

This '*urbi et orbi*' application[56] of the 1872 law confused the doctrine before it was qualified as an overriding mandatory law (*loi de police*),[57] unilaterally determining its scope of application. The choice made by the case law apparently maximises the application of the 1872 law. In reality, it has the disadvantage of being ineffective. Indeed, when the foreign security left French territory to be negotiated again abroad, the Law of 1872 lost all hope of application: French law was then no longer designated to resolve the relationship between the third party purchaser and the dispossessed owner. In addition, the foreign issuing institution had no reason to submit to the application of the 1872 law and could ignore the French opposition.[58] These two elements indicate impasse to which the theory of the *lex situs* leads, whereas the theory of personal status appeared to be more respectful not only of foreign laws, but also of the international harmony of solutions.

641. The impasse of the theory of the lex situs of the security. Niboyet[59] considers that 'bearer securities are, by definition, tangible movables'[60] and must be subject to the *lex situs*.[61] The author categorically rejects the idea of subjecting the terms of transmission of securities to the *lex debitoris*, i.e. the

---

54 Y. Loussouarn and J.-D. Bredin, *Droit du commerce international*, *op. cit.*, no. 358.

55 *Ibid.*

56 The expression comes from a commentator of the time, see L. d'Avout, *Sur les solutions du conflit de lois en droit des biens*, *op. cit.*, p. 120.

57 Y. Loussouarn and J.-D. Bredin, *Droit du commerce international*, *op. cit.*, no. 358.

58 See already in this sense, E. Thaller, 'D'un règlement qui aurait pour objet de résoudre les conflits de lois en matière de dépossession de titres au porteur', *op. cit.*

59 At the same time, however, Weiss was already saying that: 'The fact that it was in France that the transmission of this security took place is enough to place it under its authority. This law (Weiss refers to the law of 1872) is in a way the lex situs of the security' in A. Weiss, *Traité théorique et pratique de droit international privé*, *op. cit.*, p. 217. The author is nevertheless much less critical than Niboyet as regards the conclusions of the Institut de droit international, p. 222.

60 J.-P. Niboyet, *Des conflits de lois relatifs à l'acquisition de la propriété et des droits sur les meubles corporels à titre particulier*, *op. cit.*, p. 305.

61 He is not unaware of the other perception which refuses, in his own words, 'to equate bearer securities and chattels in general, bearer securities being fictitious chattels, and symbols'. However, he very clearly teaches that: 'The jurisdiction of the law of the situation is admitted for all tangible movables. Thus, bearer securities, which are tangible property and which currently constitute one of the most important economic forms of movable property, obey this law.' J.-P. Niboyet, *Cours de droit international privé*, *op. cit.*

lex societatis, because, according to the author, 'it is not admissible that, after having given it bearer form, it should be subject to the regime of intangible movables, i.e. claims'.[62] In order to defend the application of local law, the theory of the lex situs benefits, alongside the *lex situs*, from a second relay: the *lex loci contractus*, applicable to the conclusion in France of the assignment contract. Now, the application of the *lex situs* of the security at the time when the assignment contract took place and the application of the law of the place where the assignment contract took place will result in the designation of the same law since the transfer of the security takes place hand-to-hand. However, because of the links between the regulation of these second relationships and the first, adopting such a conflict rule means subjecting the entire enforceability regime to the law of the place where the security is located. Indeed, the ownership of the foreign security ultimately determines the success of the enforcement against the issuer. This is why the application of the lex situs means that the 1872 Act is inapplicable when a document lost or stolen in France is subsequently traded on a foreign market. In other words, it is deactivating French law in international relations.[63] We can see where the twofold excess of the theory of incorporation of the law into the security, on the one hand, and of the systematic application of the law of the situation, on the other leads. The most appropriate solution to the conflict of laws here would have been to apply the law of the issuer.

§ 3. THE ISSUER'S LAW SOLUTION FOR BEARER SECURITIES

642. The theory of the personal status of security was first advocated by Thaller.[64] The author favours a conflict rule based on the law of origin of the security[65] (*lex creationis*), which should determine the effects of the negotiation

---

[62] J.-P. Niboyet, *Des conflits de lois relatifs à l'acquisition de la propriété et des droits sur les meubles corporels à titre particulier*, *op. cit.*, p. 307. Niboyet is not isolated: Bartin develops similar ideas, and declares that 'bonds and shares are still incorporeal movables, whose constitution and transmission can depend equally only on the *lex situs*', E. Bartin, *Principes de droit international privé*, t. III, *op. cit.*, para. 378.
However, the author excludes from the scope of the *lex situs* 'everything that concerns the establishment and operation of the company to which these securities correspond' (*ibid.*)

[63] As Thaller writes: 'The day when this precept of international law prevails, no thief will ever again commit the stupidity of selling his frustrated securities on a French stock exchange; he will divest himself of them on a foreign market, which he will choose wisely from among the States provided with legislation favourable to him, and he will thus consolidate his theft and make its effects irrevocable. We shall only have to repeal our law of 1872, for this international concession will have forcibly rallied us to the regime which excludes the claim.' E. Thaller, 'D'un règlement qui aurait pour objet de résoudre les conflits de lois en matière de dépossession de titres au porteur', *op. cit.*, p. 262.

[64] E. Thaller, 'D'un règlement qui aurait pour objet de résoudre les conflits de lois en matière de dépossession de titres au porteur', *op. cit.*

[65] *Ibid.*, no. 1.

of the latter.[66] From the point of view of domestic law, Thaller observes that the central issue is that of the relationship between the dispossessed owner and the bona fide third party purchaser, since this is, from a substantive point of view, the one that will govern the solution of the possible dispute with the issuing institution. Secondly, from an international perspective, Thaller first notes that no author attempts to subject the relationship between the issuing institution and the dispossessed owner to a law other than that of the issuer. However, the author has already observed that, because of the configuration of the legal problem, the law of the issuer can only record the solution designated by the law applicable to the relationship between the dispossessed owner and the third-party purchaser.[67] Thaller observes that the applicability of the 1872 law to these relationships does not pose any difficulty as long as the issuing institution is located in France. Indeed, even if a third party purchaser who has obtained his security on a foreign market obtains a judgment from a foreign court in his favour, in order to be applicable to the French seat of the issuer, this judgment would have to receive the *exequatur*, which the third party will not obtain if the 1872 law has been evaded.[68]

643. It could be said that the theory of the personal status of the security does too much or too little. It would do too much in that it creates an obligation on the foreign intermediary to check the French stop payment notice every time he sells a French security. It would do too little by excluding French holders of foreign securities from the protection offered by French law. The first criticism can be tempered in that the theory of the personal status of the security does not directly impose any obligation on the foreign intermediary. At most, its liability may be engaged according to the canons of the foreign law, which is likely to take into consideration the French opposition regime, and to impose itself the respect of the prescriptions of the law of the foreign security in order to guarantee its effectiveness.[69] The second criticism comes down to questioning the objectives of the 1872 law, which, according to Thaller, are less to protect French residents than the securities themselves. Such an argument is not fully convincing, since the aim is not to protect issuers against thieves, but to protect dispossessed French owners. Rather than giving such an interpretation to the objectives of the 1872 legislator, it is better to observe, soberly, that through the mechanism created by the 1872 law, the French legislator has international leeway only when the issuer's seat is in France. It is a common reason for respecting the domain of

---

66 *Ibid.*, no. 2. Unlike Niboyet, who does not exclude it *ab initio*, the author quickly dismisses the jurisdiction of the *lex fori*, because this would lead to obvious *forum shopping*. The case law position will be similar to Niboyet's suggestion: this law will only be applied when the French court is petitioned.

67 *Ibid.*, no. 8.

68 *Ibid.*, no. 14.

69 Thaller rightly observes that the opponents of the opposition regime are the intermediaries, as its existence is likely to engage their responsibilities, *ibid*, p. 267.

the issuer's foreign law, combined with the principle of effectiveness, that dictates the scope of application given by the theory of the personal status of the security. On the other hand, the protection of French holders of foreign securities can be ensured by the topical rules of their marketing in France: for example, by a system of centralisation of the support of foreign securities when the foreign legislation attributes to the bearer form the effects known to it as regards the transfer of the represented *negotium*. It is then sufficient to create a certificate granting ownership of the foreign security, which is subject to French law. This practice of domiciling securities in France[70] is reminiscent of the contemporary practice of certificates representing foreign shares, more commonly known as depositary receipts.[71]

644. Nevertheless, the disadvantage of this system is that it does not allow for the application of a single law to a security interest in a portfolio of securities held in the same place. However, the disadvantage appears to be less than the advantages offered by the law of the issuer. Indeed, in retrospect, one cannot but be attracted to Thaller's perception. Despite the unfortunate anthropological analogies,[72] which undoubtedly slowed down the propagation of the underlying ideas, the theory developed by Thaller is the only one to propose a harmonious solution to the conflict of laws, while respecting the effectiveness of French law. The modernity of the author's argument is undoubtedly due to the fact that he understood, before others, that one could not reason in the same way for tangible and intangible movables.[73] It should also be added here that, from the point of view of the proposed connection, the effectiveness of Thaller's system is based on the correspondence between the law of the place of issue and that of payment. This is why this system, because of the creation of an organisation centralising bearer securities,[74] is still able to inspire solutions to the conflict of laws, both in France and abroad. In fact, it corresponds to the solutions arising from the law applicable to registered securities, which have always been the subject of consensus.

---

70 Y. Loussouarn and J.-D. Bredin, *Droit du commerce international, op. cit.*, no. 360, p. 421. The authors criticise the system because it does not provide sufficient protection for the victim in the event of the acquisition of foreign securities 'located' or traded in France.

71 On this practice, see V. Malassigné, *Les titres représentatifs, op. cit.*, no. 17 and especially nos. 481 et seq.

72 '*Personal* status' of the security, even 'nationality' of the security.

73 Thus, the eminent commercialist writes: 'As soon as the agreement relates to intangible movables, to stock exchange securities, one ceases to be able to discuss in the same way. Such movable property has a legal attachment to the place where the issuing establishment is located, and this place is known to the public; the mere designation of the debtor of the security reveals it to anyone who comes across it', see E. Thaller, 'D'un règlement qui aurait pour objet de résoudre les conflits de lois en matière de dépossession de titres au porteur', *op. cit.*, p. 267.

74 See *infra*, paras. 648 et seq.

645. Conclusion of the section. Among the difficulties caused by the extension of the lex situs, the most remarkable is that, as Dean Savatier wrote, 'the law of situation is disappointing for all intangible movables, which have no concrete situation'.[75] This explains in particular why intangible property is not subject, in principle, to the lex situs. However, the tentacles of the lex situs have, for a time, seized claims because of their movable nature. Unfortunately, the backlash against the lex situs of claims did not extend to securities because of their questionable characterisation in international relations as tangible movables. Based on the rule resulting from the lex situs, the plurality of connections finds its foundation in the metaphor of the incorporation of the right into the security. This fiction, which is useful in the domestic order to extend the scope of the rules facilitating transfer under property law, is clearly toxic in international relations. Far from facilitating transfer, it constitutes a particularly serious obstacle to it. The application of the lex situs rule is in fact unfounded and should be rejected: it leads to unsatisfactory results, whereas the application of the law of the issuer would allow the application of a single, predictable law to the chain of transmission of securities. Intermediation, which could have put an end to these difficulties, has instead multiplied them.

SECTION 2. INTERMEDIATION SYSTEMS

There is not one intermediation system for holding securities, but several. We will trace the evolution of the French system (in order to understand what the entanglement of intermediation systems in international relations means (§ 2)

§ 1. THE EVOLUTION OF THE FRENCH SYSTEM

The evolution of the French intermediation system is closely linked to the relationship between the centralising institution, which in France was the CCDVT, the SICOVAM and now Euroclear France, and the French regulation of financial securities themselves. For this reason, we will distinguish two periods: the first, from the creation of the CCDVT to the dematerialisation of securities (I), an event that marks the creation of the contemporary system composed of Euroclear and the services it offers (II).

75 R. Savatier, *Cours de droit international privé*, *op. cit.*, no. 409.

I. *From CCDVT to Dematerialisation of Securities*

The foundations of the contemporary system are all already present in the precursor system of the CCDVT (A). From this retrospective point of view, the system created with the SICOVAM appears to be a parenthesis that closed with the 1981 dematerialisation law, but of which certain after-effects, of doctrinal origin, nevertheless persist (B).

A. The Precursor System of the CCDVT

646. The creation of the CCDVT. In France, changes in the form of securities led to the creation of a centralising body.[76] The Act of 28 February 1941,[77] motivated by a variety of reasons,[78] requires French shares traded on a market[79] to be in registered form. As for shares in foreign companies, the law commands that they 'may only be delivered to purchasers in the form of registered certificates, the conditions for the establishment, form and method of transfer of which shall be determined by an order of the Secretary of State for Finance'.[80] The bearer

---

76 'The idea of having an entity that centralises deposits and allows securities to appear in the form of an account item was in fact not new. The mechanism of the central depository which allows circulation by transfer was developed in Germany and Austria in the second half of the 19th century under the name of *Kassenverein* [on this system, see J. Escarra, E. Escarra and J. Rault, *Principes de droit commercial*, t. 6, Paris, Sirey, 1936, nos. 994 et seq.] The 1941 reform merely transposed the system to France.' P. Didier and P. Didier, *Les sociétés commerciales*, t. 2, Paris, Economica, 2011, no. 1172.

77 *JORF*, 5 March 1941, pp. 1015 et seq.

78 Professor Paul Didier sees in the motivations of this law 'the concern of the public authorities to reduce the number of bearer securities', and 'that of the banks to lighten their management'; *ibid*, p. 61. The public authorities had a more equivocal desire, linked to the resolution to 'curb speculation to protect the franc, perhaps also to monitor overly rapid enrichment, and especially the acquisition of shares by Germans or on their behalf', A. Tunc, 'La représentation des actions par la comptabilité de la Caisse centrale de dépôts et virements de titres', *JCP*, 1947, I, 659, no. 1. Finally, some authors see behind this law the action of the tax authorities: H. Decugis, 'La loi du 28 février 1941 relative à la forme et à la négociation des actions', *op. cit.*, p. 129: 'At the beginning, only tax concerns guided the supporters of this measure. They sought only to strengthen administrative control over the collection of both the global tax and the income transfer tax in the event of death or inter vivos donation.'

79 Art. 1 para. 1 of the law of 28 February 1941: 'The shares of French companies, negotiated on a market, may only be delivered to purchasers in registered form.' The Act of 3 February 1943 subsequently extended the obligation to deposit shares to all shares of French companies. This second law, which appeared to be a complement to the first, actually has a distinct international scope (it does not apply to foreign shares), and seems to amend the objectives of the first, see H. Rousseau, 'La forme des actions et la caisse centrale de dépôts et de virements de titres', *JCP*, 1944, I, 410, no. 1-2.

80 Art. 1 para. 2 of the Act of 28 February 1941. The wording of the provision is misleading: the share is not delivered at all. It is precisely to avoid delivery that the registered certificate is provided instead of the share. The latter is similar, in a form of invertedsymmetry, to the bearer certificate for American registered shares, see *supra*; para. 634.

form could nevertheless be used 'on condition that they remain on deposit in banks or stockbrokers' companies'.[81] This meant that the withdrawal of shares had the implication of making them registered.[82] As Professor Paul Didier writes: 'Customers remained the owners of their shares. But they no longer had possession of them.'[83] This law, while increasing the costs of the institutions, allowed them in return to establish 'one or more limited companies'[84] which would allow them to transfer securities by compensation and account transfer.[85]

647. This limited company was created by the law of 18 June 1941 on the creation of a central securities deposit and transfer fund ('CCDVT').[86] According to the 1941 law, the purpose of this fund is 'to receive all deposits of securities on behalf of stockbrokers and banks whose membership it has accepted, and to facilitate, by means of account-to-account transfers, the circulation of these securities'.[87] Such a system presupposes the fungibility of securities, which is enshrined in the law,[88] but does not call into question the previous rules on transfer. As Professors Paul and Philippe Didier write: 'The legal significance of *traditio* was given to the book-entry transfer. Like the *traditio*, the entry in the account was a formality of delivery and enforceability.[89] The significance of this postponement also stems from the fact that the bearer securities deposited with the CCDVT were perforated and were no longer intended to circulate.[90]

---

81 Art. 2 of the law of 28 February 1941. The article added: 'The registration of the shares of French companies and the conversion into registered certificates of the shares of foreign companies thus deposited shall only be compulsory at the time of withdrawal by the depositor.'

82 This is explicitly stated in Art. 2 of the law of 28 February 1941: 'The registration of shares of French companies and the conversion into registered certificates of shares of foreign companies thus deposited shall only be compulsory at the time of withdrawal by the depositor.'

83 P. Didier, *Droit commercial*, t. 3, Paris, PUF, 1993, p. 61.

84 Art. 3 of the law of 28 February 1941.

85 P. Didier, *Droit commercial*, t. 3, *op. cit.*, p. 62.

86 It was set up as a limited company 'with the Banque de France, the main banks in Paris and the provinces, and the Compagnie des agents de change de Paris as shareholders', see *ibid.*

87 Art. 1 of the law of 18 June 1941.

88 Art. 2 of the law of 18 June 1941. See on this Article, S. Torck, *Essai d'une théorie générale des droits réels sur choses fongibles*, *op. cit.*, nos. 409–410.

89 P. Didier and P. Didier, *Les sociétés commerciales*, t. 2, *op. cit.*, no. 1174.

90 This perforation was caused by a lack of organisation on the part of the CCDVT: the latter could not keep the securities, so when it received them from the affiliated institutions, it perforated them before sending them back to the institution that had sent them, due to lack of space. From the time of the perforation, as Mr Tunc writes, 'the security is definitively immobilised. It will remain in the vault where it is, despite all the negotiations of the law. Its coupons will not be detached for presentation to the company. It will never be returned to anyone. Even if the shareholder prefers his right in registered form, it will not be returned to the company, but the company will only be credited to the account it has with the CCDVT'. As Mr Torck puts it: 'The old perforated securities were no longer used to justify the total amount of shares of the same category registered in an account', S. Torck, *Essai d'une théorie générale des droits réels sur choses fongibles*, *op. cit.*, no. 409. Mr Tunc already considered that

Newly issued bearer securities are no longer subject to the creation of paper securities. The only real evidentiary instrument that is authentic is therefore the accounts held by CCDVT. This prevalence of CCDVT's accounts stems from the fact that only CCDVT's accounts make it possible to establish the number of shares deposited with it and subsequently put into circulation. As Professor Torck puts it:

> 'Only the accounts kept by the Fund gave an accurate account of the number of shares deposited, and therefore likely to be traded in the share current account, in particular because it knew, unlike the affiliated institutions, the total number of bearer shares issued by the issuing companies and whose deposit was mandatory.'[91]

648. This predominance of CCDVT's accounts was expressed when a CCDVT member was placed in receivership, and a discrepancy was observed between its accounts and those of CCDVT. Indeed, as Professor Tunc already mentioned:

> 'The representation of shares in the accounts of the CCDVT and its members entails a theoretically very serious danger: the possibility of creating fictitious shares in the accounts. Just as banks create money through their bookkeeping, and sometimes in a dishonest manner, CCDVT and its members can irregularly create shares.'[92]

The law then provided that the shares held by the member in the CCDVT would be divided among the customers in proportion to the shares in their account. The clients would then only have a liability claim against the member.[93] That is, the relevant securities accounts were those maintained by CCDVT. Despite

---

the 'old securities' had become 'simple accounting justifications', A. Tunc, 'La représentation des actions par la comptabilité de la Caisse centrale de dépôts et virements de titres', *op. cit.*, no. 12.

91 S. Torck, *Essai d'une théorie générale des droits réels sur choses fongibles*, *op. cit.*, no. 410. The author continues: 'The same was not true of the accounts kept by the affiliated institution for its clients. In this respect, one could not rule out the risk of drawing on the mass of shares deposited with CCDVT, while maintaining the amount of the entries in the clients' accounts (drawing on the mass) with the consequence that there could be a large difference between the (fictitious) amount of the shares entered in the clients' accounts and the (real) amount of the shares entered in the accounts of the Caisse centrale in the name of the affiliated institution.' In fact, drawing on the mass was encouraged since the COB's hostility was only belated, see P.-H. Conac, *La régulation des marchés boursiers par la commission des opérations de bourse (COB) et la securities and exchange commission (SEC)*, *op. cit.*, p. 272; T. Bonneau *et al.*, *Droit financier*, *op. cit.*
See already on this question H. Rousseau, 'La forme des actions et la Caisse centrale de dépôts et de virements de titres', *op. cit.*, no. 22.

92 A. Tunc, 'La représentation des actions par la comptabilité de la Caisse centrale de dépôts et virements de titres', *op. cit.*, no. 9. The author considers that fraud by the central body is unlikely, because of the close supervision it is subject to by the administration, and that the error would be promptly rectified. However, the hypothesis of fraud by a member appears less unlikely.

93 Art. 3 of the law of 18 June 1941.

the considerable advantages for intermediaries,[94] the CCDVT was dissolved by the Act of 5 July 1949.[95] The creation of the CCDVT by the Vichy regime, combined with the holders' taste for the material detention of paper securities[96] and the very high cost of custody fees (i.e. account management), overrode the laws that governed the creation of the CCDVT and the regime of securities deposited there.[97]

B. The SICOVAM and the dematerialisation law

We will first present the parenthesis opened by the creation of the SICOVAM in 1949 and closed by the law on the dematerialisation of bearer securities in 1981 (1) before drawing up a critique of the doctrinal analysis of this law (2).

1. *The Creation of SICOVAM and the Law on the Dematerialisation of Bearer Securities*

649. The creation of SICOVAM. The decree of 4 August 1949, taken in application of the law of 5 July 1949, re-established the old rules relating to the form of

94 Mr P. Didier notes that this system 'reduced storage costs. It eliminated delivery, transfer and insurance costs. It eliminated all risks of loss and theft and removed the obligation to proceed with oppositions and their verification in accordance with the procedure of the law of 15 June 1872. It made the payment of coupons remarkably easy'. P. Didier, *Droit commercial*, t. 3, *op. cit.*, p. 62; see already in this sense F. Goré, 'Le nouveau régime des valeurs mobilières', *op. cit.*, no. 7.

95 Art. 26 para. 1 of the law no. 49-874 of 5 July 1949 on various economic and financial provisions.

96 As expressed by Mr Goré, 'Le nouveau régime des valeurs mobilières', *op. cit.*, no. 7: 'Above all, holders of securities rejected the institution because it resulted in dispossessing them of their securities. Their rights were no longer asserted except by illegible slips, which were easy to misplace and of questionable legal value, or statements of account that were open to dispute. Represented by a few lines of writing, investments had become immaterial. This was a notion that French savers, who had a long tradition of keeping track of their investments, could not easily accept. No doubt foreign examples of collective deposits were invoked, in particular the German *Kassenverein*; but the mentality of French holders of securities is not the same as that of foreign holders, for whom, moreover, recourse to these organisations is optional.' Indeed, as Mr Decugis points out, the bearer security 'was the democratic security par excellence, suitable for the most modest savers as well as for wealthy capitalists'. The author considers that 'it had developed considerably in France during the 19th and early 20th centuries, far more than in other countries', H. Decugis, 'La loi du 28 février 1941 relative à la forme et à la négociation des actions', *op. cit.*

97 *Ibid.*, p. 62. See in the same sense, F. Drummond, 'La société, l'actionnaire et le dépositaire central', *op. cit.* On the reasons for the creation of SICOVAM, see also L. Avéran-Horteur, *De la C.C.D.V.T. à la Sicovam, Le compte courant d'actions*, Paris, Dalloz, 1959, pp. 24–30; F. Goré, 'Le nouveau régime des valeurs mobilières', *JCP*, 1951, I, 948, nos. 1 to 15, spec. nos. 3–4: 'It is the particularly onerous nature of the management of securities [...] which was the origin of these various measures. It is the consequence of the monetary depreciation and the creation of the CCDVT. The monetary depreciation did not spare securities [...]. It reduced their real value while the cost of securities transactions continued to rise.'

securities: shares may be issued in registered form or in bearer form; the same decree created the '*Société Interprofessionnelle de Compensation des Valeurs Mobilières*' ('SICOVAM').[98] The latter operates on a model similar to that of the CCDVT: all bearer shares can be deposited with the SICOVAM through an affiliated institution,[99] which has the effect of making them fungible and transferable only by transfer to the SICOVAM accounts.[100] Two fundamental differences nevertheless distinguish the SICOVAM from the CCDVT. On the one hand, the choice of depositing the securities in the current account is always *ultimately* up to the owner of the securities.[101] Even when the holder has the option of depositing them in the SICOVAM's current accounts, he/she retains the possibility of withdrawing them, in which case he/she will simply be given a security of the same nature.[102] Whether the security has been deposited in the SICOVAM's accounts, or is kept with the intermediary, when the owner withdraws his security, it is indeed a paper security that is returned to him.[103] On the other hand, the paper security is kept and not centralised at the level of the SICOVAM: the affiliated organisations sometimes keep them in their own safes. It was not until the 1981 law on the dematerialisation of securities that the system set up by the SICOVAM was identified with that of the CCDVT.

650. The 1981 dematerialisation law. The coercive nature of the Finance Act of 30 December 1981[104] is reminiscent of the Act establishing the CCDVT. Once again, it contains a provision requiring registered shares, but this time for all

---

98 Decree no. 49-1105 of 4 August 1949 taken for the application of Art. 26 modified of the law of 5 July 1949 and relating to the system of securities as well as to the modalities of liquidation of the central fund of deposits and transfers of securities (C.C.D.V.T.)

99 F. Goré, 'Le nouveau régime des valeurs mobilières', *op. cit.*, no. 123; J. Hamel and G. Lagarde, *Traité de droit commercial*, Paris, Dalloz, 1956 no. 527, p. 647.

100 Art. 7 para. 1 of the aforementioned decree: 'The affiliated establishments may only deliver to each other the securities paid into their current accounts or likely to be paid into them by means of a transfer made by the interprofessional body.' On this question, see S. Torck, *Essai d'une théorie générale des droits réels sur choses fongibles*, *op. cit.*, nos. 407 et seq.

101 This freedom is nevertheless restricted: the legislator, anxious to promote current accounts, presumes that the deposit of securities with an institution allows the latter to deposit them in a current account with the SICOVAM. It is therefore necessary for the depositor to expressly stipulate, when depositing the securities, that 'shares of the same nature without identity of number be returned to him', Art. 10 of the decree of 4 August 1949, on which see F. Goré, 'Le nouveau régime des valeurs mobilières', *op. cit.*, no. 128.

102 Such a prerogative is reminiscent of the prerogative of holders of current accounts with credit institutions. Indeed, on the face of it, the customer can withdraw the money he or she holds in his or her current account from an ATM. However, the analogy is only apparent. In reality, the customer has only a claim on his bank and the scriptural money he receives on his account is not real money. On the other hand, when he withdraws, the bank repays his claim with real money, namely the central bank's money.

103 F. Goré, 'Le nouveau régime des valeurs mobilières', *op. cit.*, no. 12: 'A special form of fungible deposit has been created, "en compte courant d'actions", which is optional: depositors can withdraw their shares at any time in bearer form, but without any number identity.'

104 Loi no. 94-11 of 30 December 1981

companies whose shares are not admitted to trading.[105] The purpose of this registration is still to be monitored by the authorities, but this time it is the tax authorities.[106] A second provision requires the 'dematerialisation' of securities, which must then be represented by an entry in accounts held by the issuing legal person or by an authorised intermediary.[107] We find here the elements that had presided over the foundation of the CCDVT: the SICOVAM is then the central depositary in the sense that the CCDVT had been. Indeed, all bearer securities issued by French companies are deposited with the SICOVAM, which records them in its issue accounts. At the same time, it verifies the correspondance between the number of securities registered in the accounts opened in the name of its affiliates and the number of securities registered in its issue accounts.[108] The dematerialisation law, which should have led to the adoption of the CCDVT's analyses, has nevertheless given rise to very different approaches.

651. Doctrinal analysis of dematerialisation. This change of regime was mainly analysed from the point of view of the nature of securities accounts, the regime of these new book entries, or the change in nature of fiduciary securities into 'book-entry securities'.[109] Transposing the regime of the securities held by the SICOVAM, part of the doctrine proceeds to an analysis that can be summarised in several steps. The premise is to consider that dematerialisation does not affect the ownership of the security, which remains attributed to the ultimate investor. The first step is to deduce that the security registered in the owner's name is the equivalent of the paper security. Mr Paul Didier expresses this idea perfectly. 'The book-entry security,' he writes, 'consists of an inscription on an account. This inscription belongs to the holder whom it designates. He is in a way the owner, just as the holder of a bearer bond was the owner of his bond.'[110]

The desire to replicate the regime for paper bearer securities leads to a desire to recreate a direct holding relationship. It is therefore considered that the book entry representing the security *is* the security, the ownership of which belongs to the holder of the securities account. This is the second stage. This desire for identity between the previous regime and the modern regime has an important consequence on the nature of the securities account that the owner opens with his immediate intermediary. Indeed, since the true

---

105 Art. 94-1 of the 1981 Act.

106 An instruction from the General Tax Directorate dated 4 June 1982 (*JCP*, 1981, III, 7392) explicitly states that: 'Article 94-2 is part of a set of provisions intended to combat tax fraud. It improves knowledge of assets and increases the effectiveness of income control. It also makes it possible to improve the supervision of transfer duties.'

107 Art. 94-2 of the 1981 Act.

108 What Paul Didier calls 'the watertightness of the system', P. Didier, *Droit commercial*, t. 3, *op. cit.*, p. 66. The expression is often used, see for example F. Drummond, 'La société, l'actionnaire et le dépositaire central', *op. cit.*, p. 201.

109 See, for example, P. Didier, *Droit commercial*, t. 3, *op. cit.*, pp. 65 et seq.

110 P. Didier, *Droit commercial*, t. 3, *op. cit.*, p. 65.

security is registered in the securities account held by the owner with the intermediary, only the latter is the 'true' securities account. All other securities accounts in which the same financial instrument would be allocated are merely tracking accounts, or accounts of a different nature.[111] This second step of the reasoning leads to inverting the location of the securities within the chain of intermediation: where it was previously linked to the accounts of the CCDVT, or of the register kept by the issuer, it is now linked to the securities account opened by the owner of the security.

2. *Critique of the Doctrinal Analysis of the 1981 Law*

652. A correct premise. The analysis set out above is based on a perfectly accurate premise in French law: the investor at the end of the chain is the holder of the financial securities. Under French law, neither dematerialisation nor the intermediation system had the purpose or effect of conferring ownership of securities on intermediaries: a French investor who acquires a share in a French company whose shares are admitted to trading in a securities settlement system is the owner of his share.

653. The mistake is to try to recreate the system used by the SICOVAM in 1949, which starts 'from the bottom', with the securities deposited by their owners with their intermediaries, who themselves sometimes deposit them in the SICOVAM's accounts. The authors want to reconstitute this pattern whereby the owners deposit their securities in the securities account held by their direct intermediary, and that the latter then registers these securities in the superior account that it holds with another intermediary or the central depository, the latter account being only a reflection of the one held in the name of the final investor.[112] Such a desire to mimic the pre-1981 SICOVAM system, which some authors believe is linked to the influence of the theory of incorporation of the right into the security,[113] prevents us from seeing that the most important effect of the dematerialisation law is not to have abolished paper securities, but to have concentrated issuance with a centralising body. The most coercive aspect of the 1981 law was not to alter the form of bearer securities, but, through this alteration, to force the concentration of securities in the accounts of the central depository. Like the Athenians, who were stunned that Alcibiades had cut off his dog's tail and did not question him about his treachery towards the Spartans, the

[111] This analysis continues to be defended by the most eminent doctrine, T. Bonneau and F. Drummond, *Droit des marchés financiers*, *op. cit.* no. 86-1; F. Drummond, 'La société, l'actionnaire et le dépositaire central', *op. cit.*, no. 205; F. Drummond, *Droit financier*, *op. cit.*

[112] See very clearly in this sense, F. Drummond, *Droit financier*, *op. cit.*, p. 873, note 2.

[113] See in this sense V. Malassigné, *Les titres représentatifs*, *op. cit.*, no. 11.

doctrine, focused on a means (the dematerialisation of securities[114]), forgot the purpose: the concentration of the deposit of securities with the SICOVAM and the monitoring of the French people's assets that it allows.[115]

654. Thus, the freedom to issue securities has undergone this twofold movement of expansion of the *negotia* that can be represented,[116] and of restriction of the forms by which they are represented: issuers can only issue registered securities, centralised in a register, or bearer securities, centralised in the issue accounts of the central depository.[117] It is these registers that determine the existence of securities. The particularity of registered securities is that this register also determines the allocation of the security, which is not the case for the issue account of the CSD.[118] The other accounts of the central securities depository make it possible to attribute the holding of these securities to its affiliates, without these accounts determining the true attribution of the security. This is one of the functions of the account held by the ultimate investor with his intermediary, to determine, within the securities held by him with the central depository, the securities of which he is the holder. This function of the securities account held by the ultimate investor with his intermediary explains why it is considered that the entry in the securities account of the intermediary in the name of the owner may have a 'possessory' function, i.e., the entry in the account puts the owner in 'possession' so as to enable him to transfer the represented *negotium*.[119] It is in this sense that the intermediary exercises control over these securities since it has, vis-à-vis the holder of the securities, the only means of

---

114 It is known that there have been intense debates on the nature of the book entry, which would always constitute the security in the same way as the paper security constituted the share (on this theory and its refutation, see V. Malassigné, *Les titres représentatifs*, *op. cit.*, nos. 157 et seq.), or that the book entry would create the *negotium*.
It should simply be noted that if this were true, the loss of the bearer security would have extinguished the right represented, and the disappearance of the book entry would have extinguished the right. This is not the case, see *supra*, paras. 640 et seq. for the loss of securities represented on a paper medium. As for the disappearance of the register, this does not entail the disappearance of the rights represented: the ownership of the latter can then be proven by any means, see Cass. com, 5 May 2009, no. 08-18.165.

115 Thus, one of the conditions of admission for issuers to the Euroclear France system is 'to comply at all times with the provisions of Article 1672 of the General Tax Code' (Art. 2.3.2 of the Euroclear operating rules); Art. 1672 of the General Tax Code is the one providing for withholding tax on sums paid to beneficiaries of income from movable capital, which must therefore be 'declared and paid to the Treasury by the person established in France who ensures the payment of the income' (Art. 1672(2°) of the General Tax Code).

116 F. Drummond, 'Un nouveau principe: la liberté d'émettre toutes valeurs mobilières', *RDBF*, September-October 2004, p. 361, H. Le Nabasque, 'La liberté d'émettre "toutes valeurs mobilières"' in *Mélanges Paul Le Cannu*, Paris, Dalloz, 2014, p. 325.

117 On which see *infra*, para. 664.

118 In order to do so, it would need the owners of the financial securities to open a securities account directly with it, a hypothesis which is not purely theoretical, see prospectively F. Drummond, 'La société, l'actionnaire et le dépositaire central', *op. cit.*

119 V. Malassigné, *Les titres représentatifs*, *op. cit.*, nos. 257 et seq.

gaining access to them. This is why, in French law, the attachment takes place on this account, whether it is the relevant account for the purpose of pledging, or whether the custodian is the relevant person to make the holder's tax declaration.

655. The difficulty lies in the fact that the two perceptions of the chain of intermediation (location of the security within the immediate securities account of its intermediary, or in the accounts of the central depository) make it possible to account for the regime granted to book entry. This is what allows Mr Paul Didier, for example, to consider that:

> '[The ownership of the account entry] is even so strong that in the event of judicial reorganisation of the financial intermediary holding the account, it can have all its rights transferred to an account held by another financial intermediary or by the issuing legal person, without the creditors of the debtor in reorganisation being able to object.[120]'

Rather, it appears that it is because the actual securities are located at the central depository that the movement order can be made to an intermediary *that is affiliated with the same central depository*. If the theories adopted by academics as to the relevant securities account were correct, one could transfer the securities registered in an account with one's direct intermediary to the accounts of any other authorised intermediary. This is not the case, as such book entries are only valid if the intermediary holds the securities in the accounts of the central depository.[121] The most striking proof of this is that if the intermediary does not hold as many securities in its account with the central securities depository as its clients have booked with it, the latter will, in the event of the intermediary's insolvency giving rise to an action to reclaim their shares, only have a corresponding proportion of securities. The true location of the securities is not clear as long as the intermediary is *in bonis*; the collective proceeding initiated against the intermediary then appears to be the moment of truth.

In these circumstances, what significance should be attached to the owner's book entry with the intermediary? The intermediary is normally a custodian. However, the contract concluded by the custodian-account holder and its client is generally described as a complex contract, since it combines the regimes of a depository contract and a mandate contract.[122] Under these conditions, the custodian-account holder is therefore a securities depository, with the securities

---

120 P. Didier, *Droit commercial*, t. 3, *op. cit.*, p. 65. This provision has become Art. L. 211-10 of the Monetary and Financial Code.

121 The activity of custody account keeper consists of keeping the assets corresponding to account registrations, which requires 'for the custody of assets corresponding to financial securities' to open 'one or more accounts with the central depository', Art. 322-3 of the AMF General Regulations.

122 V. Malassigné, *Les titres représentatifs*, *op. cit.*, nos. 283 et seq.

materialising through the crediting of the intermediary's account in the books of the central depository.[123] The securities account opened by the custodian-account keeper for its client appears to be the instrument for individualising the securities held by it with the central depository, but also the means for the account holder to dispose of the securities.[124] Since then, the situation has not fundamentally changed, despite the acquisition of SICOVAM by Euroclear and the advent of a European regulation on central depositories.

II. The Pre-Eminence of the Accounts of the Central Depository

656. Euroclear. As a result of a European merger of market operators, several central securities depositories merged to create a group of companies, the holding company of which is registered in Brussels and which has a subsidiary in several countries, including France.[125] In France, the activities of SICOVAM were therefore taken over by Euroclear France, a limited company under French law. From the point of view of sources, the central depository is now subject to the European CSD Regulation. French law has only two legislative provisions that clearly distinguish between central depositories, their operating rules and the settlement system for the securities they manage. The central depository, like the SICOVAM and the CCDVT before it, is subject to approval by the AMF after consultation with the *Banque de France*.[126] As a sign of the depositary's importance, the AMF may substitute a provisional administrator appointed by it in the event of the depositary's malfunctioning or violation of the applicable prudential regulations.[127]

657. The operating rules of the central securities depository must be approved by the AMF.[128] These operating rules govern the relationship between issuers and the central depository, as well as the relationship between members of the securities settlement system and the central depository.[129] In order to be able to admit its securities to the central depository, the issuer must first

---

123 See also in this sense *ibid*, no. 284.

124 For this reason, the procedure for seizure of securities must be carried out with the custodian account holder, and not with the central depository, see Art. R. 232-1 of the Code of Civil Enforcement Procedures. A similar *ratio* explains why, in the case of administered registered securities, the attachment must take place with the intermediary mandated to manage the account of the ultimate holder, see Art. R. 232-3 of the Code of Civil Enforcement Procedure.

125 On the monitoring of this group, see *supra*, para. 119.

126 Art. L. 441-1 of the Monetary and Financial Code. Changes to the constituent parts of the authorisation require prior authorisation from the AMF.

127 Art. L. 441-2 of the Monetary and Financial Code.

128 Art. L. 441-1 of the Monetary and Financial Code.

129 See in this sense Art. 2.2 of the Euroclear operating rules. These rules are therefore perfectly distinct from the statutes of the central depository as a limited company.

apply to Euroclear France to become a participant.[130] The rules of the securities settlement system operated by the depository must also be approved by the AMF.[131] This system is also subject to a set of legislative rules[132] resulting from the transposition of the Finality Directive.[133] The system set up by Euroclear is called ESES France[134] and is designed to settle securities admitted to the central depository. Its participants are the financial intermediaries that hold the securities on behalf of third parties or for their own account.[135]

European law, which has standardised the status and methods of central securities depositories in Europe, distinguishes between three 'basic services' of the central securities depository.[136] The first, a so-called 'notary service', is intended for issuers. The other two, a 'centralised maintenance service' and a settlement service, are intended for intermediaries. These three services, which do not, however, exhaust the scope of its possibilities,[137] must be provided by the central depository and are in fact interrelated. It will be shown here that, in accordance with the system of the CCDVT and the SICOVAM from the 1981 law onwards, the particular competence granted to the accounting of the central depository with regard to the location of bearer securities lies in the fact that it is both the one with whom the securities issued by the issuer are registered, but also the one who keeps the accounts of the persons who hold them, on their behalf and that of others. It is from this pre-eminence of the accounts of the central depository that the preponderant place given to its securities settlement system is deduced.

---

130 Art. 2.3.3.2 of the Euroclear Operating Rules.

131 Art. L. 441-1 I and II of the Monetary and Financial Code. In practice, the same decision approving a depository authorisation also approves Euroclear's operating rules, which include the rules of the securities settlement system, see AMF, Decision of 16 April 2019 on the authorisation of Euroclear France SA as a central securities depository and approval of its operating rules. The rules cited are those approved and reproduced by this decision.

132 Art. L. 330-1 of the Monetary and Financial Code.

133 On the notion of system see *supra*, paras. 227 et seq.

134 For the history of this system, see P. Didier, *Droit commercial*, *op. cit.*, pp. 225 et seq. F. Drummond, *Droit des marchés financiers*, *op. cit.*, no. 872, and for an exhaustive presentation, A.-C. Muller, *Droit des contrats et droit des marchés financiers*, *op. cit.*, nos. 314 et seq.

135 The list of persons authorised to be participants in the system is given in Art. 2.1 of the Euroclear Operating Rules.

136 Section A of the Annex to the CSD Regulation. Also commenting on these functions, see V. Malassigné, *Les titres représentatifs*, *op. cit.*, nos. 279–282.

137 The European regulations provide a non-exhaustive list of services that the central depository may also offer, depending on the function in question (see Section B of the Annex to the CSD Regulation). With regard to the securities settlement system, it can also: organise securities lending between participants, manage participants' collateral, or even the transactions themselves. As far as the centralised maintenance of securities accounts is concerned, the CSD can also offer to take care of the entire issuance operation: from the maintenance of shareholder registers to the processing of corporate actions to the holding of general meetings, see the complete list in Section B of the Annex to the CSD Regulation.

658. The 'notary' service of bearer securities. Euroclear's operating rules make a clear distinction between participation in Euroclear France and participation in the ESES France system.[138] Participation in Euroclear France corresponds to what is referred to in the European Regulation as the 'notary service', i.e. the service provided by Euroclear to issuers. The issuer is free to apply for admission to any central depository established in the Union[139]; conversely, the central depository may refuse an application for admission.[140] Once its application for admission has been accepted,[141] the issuer, or its agent, may have its securities admitted to Euroclear,[142] which determines the conditions of admission and de-listing.[143] Once the securities are admitted, Euroclear then provides the so-called 'notary service', i.e. the service whereby the central depository performs the 'initial registration of securities in a book-entry system'.[144] This means that the depository registers all securities issued by a participant[145] on a specific account,[146] commonly called 'issue accounts'; each registered financial instrument is then assigned a unique identifier.[147] The provision of such a service in another Member State therefore requires compliance with the rules governing the issuance of securities, which are usually governed by local company law.[148] This is why, in the event that an issuer uses a central depository established in another Member State,[149] the CSD Regulation itself provides that: 'The corporate or similar law of the Member State under which the securities are constituted shall continue to apply.'[150] This is merely a matter of respecting the pre-eminence of the jurisdiction of the issuer's law over the issue.[151]

---

138 See Art. 2.1 of the Euroclear operating rules. Some confusion is created by the fact that the securities, Euroclear France, designate both the ESES France system and the admission by issuers to the Euroclear France notary service.

139 Art. 49 CSD Regulation.

140 In which case an appeal is possible to the competent authority of the CSD (Arts. 33(3°) and 49(4°) of the CSD Regulation). The procedure is detailed in Art. 1 of the CSD Delegated Regulation 2017/392. Under French law, there is no special channel for appealing to the AMF. However, as Professor Drummond observes: 'the reporting of the challenge to the refusal decision would require the AMF to take up the matter for the purpose of ordering, where appropriate, the central depository to provide access to the participant or issuer', on the basis of Arts. L. 621-14 and L. 621-15 of the Monetary and Financial Code, see F. Drummond, *Droit financier*, *op. cit.*, no. 1047.

141 On the conditions of admission, see Arts. 2.2 et seq. of the Euroclear Operating Rules.

142 Art. 3.4 of the Euroclear Operating Rules.

143 See Arts. 3.1 et seq. of the Euroclear Operating Rules.

144 Section A(1°) of the Annex to the CSD Regulation.

145 Art. 560-1 *bis* of the AMF General Regulation; Art. 4.1.1 of the Euroclear operating rules.

146 Art. 560-1 of the AMF General Regulation.

147 F. Drummond, *Droit financier*, *op. cit.*

148 From a French perspective, see *supra*, paras. 304 et seq.

149 On the conditions to which the free provision of market infrastructure services is subject, see *supra*, paras. 124 et seq.

150 Art. 49(1) CSD Regulation. On the implementation of this article, see HCJP, Report on Central Depository Passports, 25 September 2020.

151 See *supra*, paras. 291 et seq.

659. Registered securities. In the case of registered securities, the company may allow the central depository to manage the register, or it may decide to keep the securities accounts of its registered shareholders in parallel with the central depository. In this case, the shareholder will have an account with an administrator account holder. This account will 'duplicate the securities accounts maintained by the company' and will be 'administered by the account holder on the instructions of the shareholder'.[152] The custodian-account keeper, who is the only one habilitated to receive orders from the holder for the securities, then draws up a registered reference slip when the holder of the administered registered security changes,[153] and sends it to the issuer via the central depository, which then has the function of circulating the registered reference slips.[154] In the case of registered securities, admission to the operations of a central depository does not necessarily mean that the issuer abandons the determination of its shareholders.[155]

660. Services offered to participants. Under the ESES France rules, Euroclear actually offers two separate services, identified by European regulations as the 'centralised maintenance service' and the 'securities settlement' service. These two services are aimed at what Euroclear refers to as 'ESES participants', i.e. all intermediaries that provide the custodian account-keeping service, either on behalf of others or for themselves. Like issuers wishing to have their securities admitted, ESES participants must apply for admission.[156] Once accepted,[157] they

---

152 F. Drummond, 'La société, l'actionnaire et le dépositaire central', *op. cit.*, no. 10. In this case, the author seems to consider that the authentic account is the one held by the issuer. We know that the same author considers, in the case of bearer securities, that the authentic account is precisely that of the custodian, because of its direct link with the owner.

153 Art. 322-54 AMF General Regulation.

154 Art. 322-57 AMF General Regulation. The AMF General Regulation delegates to the operating rules of central depositories the 'technical standards' for the composition of slips and the organisation of their circulation (*ibid.*). More curiously, while the AMF General Regulation establishes the deadlines within which issuers and custodian-account holders must make book entries (Arts. 322-55 and 322-56 AMF General Regulation), as well as the starting point for any penalties (Art. 322-59 of the AMF General Regulation), it delegates to the central depository the discipline of custodians and issuers, since the central depository's operating rules are responsible for establishing 'the penalties to which intermediary custodians and issuing legal entities that do not draw up registered reference slips within the required timeframe are subject' (Art. 322-58 of the AMF General Regulation).

155 See for a recent illustration A. Gaudemet, 'Comptabilité des titres financiers en rétention et droit de participer aux assemblées générales d'actionnaires', *op. cit.*

156 Art. 2.3.3.1 and Arts. 2.3.4 et seq. of the Central Depository Rules.

157 The contractual characterisation of the relationship between the depository and the participant has been contested, see A. Tunc, 'La représentation des actions par la comptabilité de la Caisse centrale de dépôts et virements de titres', *op. cit.*, no. 16, who considered it to be a legal regime from which the 'consensuality' is nevertheless not absent. The relationship between the central depository and the participants appears to us to be contractual as it stands, for reasons identical to those governing the contractual characterisation of the relationship between a market member and the financial market manager, see *supra*, paras. 248 et seq. It is therefore not surprising that the legislator specifies that persons

can open an account with the central depository in order to hold the securities that have been admitted to its operations, this is the service provided by the centralised account keeping, but also to make transfers of securities: this is the service provided by the securities settlement system.

The persons who may participate in the system are listed exhaustively in the law.[158] Central securities depositories themselves may be participants of other central securities depositories in order to provide their own participants with access to securities registered by other depositories.[159] Such links between CSDs 'amplify the risks to which they are exposed and add new risks, such as the legal risk arising from conflicts of law governing the linked systems'.[160] In an attempt to address these difficulties, the CSD Regulation sets out a prudential procedure prior to the establishment of a link. First, the CSD Regulation requires a specific authorisation from the competent authority of the requesting CSD.[161] Second, it requires that the contract between the CSDs 'provide for an unambiguous choice of law that govern each aspects of the link's operations'.[162] Finally, the CSD Regulation lays down certain substantive rules, including the obligation not to transfer securities before the first transfer is definitive.[163]

661. The 'centralised maintenance service'. The 'centralised maintenance service' consists of the central depository grouping together in its books the securities accounts[164] of all custody account keepers participating in its operations. Accounts opened in the name of participants are kept according to the principle of segregation. This principle requires that, within the accounts held by the central depository on behalf of custodians, the account holder's own accounts are distinguished from the accounts of its clients.[165] 'Collective segregation of

eligible to be participants in a settlement or delivery system may be indirect participants by concluding a contract with a direct participant in the system, provided that they are known to the system operator (Art. L. 330-1(II) of the Monetary and Financial Code). Such a contract does not, of course, affect the direct participant's liability for orders that it enters on behalf of the indirect participant (*ibid.*)

158 The persons who may participate in a settlement system are listed in Art. L. 330-1(II) of the Monetary and Financial Code.

159 F. Drummond, *Droit financier*, *op. cit.*

160 *Ibid.*

161 Art. 47(2) CSD Regulation

162 Art. 48(3) CSD Regulation.

163 Art. 48(4) CSD Regulation.

164 This qualification is given by the CSD Regulation itself, see explicitly Section A(2°) of the Annex to the CSD Regulation. It is not surprising to observe that the authors who fight against the localisation of securities at the level of the central depository challenge the European qualification, see F. Drummond, *Droit financier*, *op. cit.*, no. 1059. However, the authors are at a loss to explain the true securities account when the custodian account holders are themselves the owners of the securities. They admit that the relevant securities account is the one held with the central depository, see *ibid.*

165 Art. 38(2) CSD Regulation.

clients' occurs when the participant's account distinguishes its securities from those of all its client accounts[166] and 'individual client segregation' occurs when the participant's account distinguishes the securities of each of its clients.[167] If the participant must offer its client a choice between the two types of segregation,[168] the cost of individual segregation for the client, while it has the advantage of dissuading the intermediary from disposing of its securities without its consent, will sometimes be dissuasive.[169]

662. Rationale for the pre-eminence of the central depository's accounts. It is from this centralised maintenance service that the depositary derives its name of *central* depository. It is also from this service, associated with the notary's service, that the central depository's accounts derive their vocation to apprehend the securities issued. Indeed, the recording of securities deposited by the issuer in what are sometimes referred to as 'issue accounts' is coupled with Euroclear's ongoing verification that 'for each issue, the total number of financial securities recorded in the specific accounts [...] is equal to the total number of financial securities recorded in the accounts of its participants, taking into account outstanding securities transactions'.[170] This verification, which is sometimes referred to as a 'system tightness' verification, is only possible because of Euroclear's maintenance of issue accounts and the centralisation of the accounts of central securities depositories. In other words, because, on the one hand, Euroclear keeps records of the issuer's securities and therefore knows the exact number of securities issued and, on the other hand, Euroclear centralises all the accounts of the intermediaries participating in its system, it can match the number of securities initially issued with the number of securities recorded in the accounts of its members.[171]

---

166 Art. 38(3) CSD Regulation.

167 Art. 38(4) CSD Regulation.

168 Art. 38(5) CSD Regulation.

169 As Mr Malassigné observes: 'It should be noted that if the accounts kept by the central securities depository had only a purely accounting scope, as is generally taught, so much care would perhaps not have been taken to achieve this individualisation at this level and this individualisation would perhaps not have been reinforced by the European regulation on central securities depositories', V. Malassigné, *Les titres représentatifs*, *op. cit.*, no. 284.

170 Art. 4.1.1 of the Euroclear Operating Rules.

171 See Art. 37 'Integrity of the issue' of Regulation CSD, in particular 1° 'The CSD shall take appropriate accounting reconciliation measures to verify that the number of securities that make up an issue or part of an issue entrusted to it is equal to the sum of the securities recorded in the securities accounts of the participants in the securities settlement system that it operates and, where applicable, in the accounts of holders that it maintains. These accounting reconciliations shall be performed at least daily.' See in the same sense Art. 550-1(4°) of the General Regulation, and Arts. 4.1.4 and 4.1.5 of the Central Depository Rules. See also F. Drummond, *Droit financier*, *op. cit.*, no. 1060: 'The keeping of these dual accounts – issue accounts and accounts of the participants holding the custodian accounts – enables the central depository to control the integrity of each of the issues admitted to trading.'

Therefore, as Professor Drummond writes, by admitting its securities to the operations of a central depository, the company 'relinquishes to the central depository control over the integrity of its issues'.[172] It is from this surrender that the pre-eminence of the settlement system operated by Euroclear is derived. This pre-eminence is very similar to the pre-eminence generally recognised to the issuer in the framework of its internal organisation. More than a resemblance, it is an identity: by admitting its securities to a central depository, the issuer entrusts it with the competence to determine the ownership of the financial securities admitted,[173] and will correlatively refuse to recognise a holder who cannot prove the ownership of his security within the settlement system of the central depository.[174] The issuer nevertheless retains the prerogatives it holds on behalf of the issue. For this reason, the depository only admits the issuer's securities to its operations if the issuer guarantees their existence, as well as certain characteristics: the securities 'must be validly issued, fully paid up if they are equity securities, and freely negotiable'.[175] The pre-eminence of the accounts of the central depository is verified both in the existence of the securities and in the modalities of their transfer and even in the exercise of the prerogatives of the securities.[176] It explains the decisive

The obligation to verify the correspondence between the number of securities issued and the number of securities registered in its accounts is maintained in the case of financial securities for which it does not keep an account of the issue, see Art. 37 of the CSD Regulation, and Art. 4.1.5 of the Euroclear operating rules.

172 F. DRUMMOND, 'La société, l'actionnaire et le dépositaire central', *op. cit.*, no. 10. This explains, as the author writes, that 'the company is no longer obliged to keep the securities accounts of its shareholders itself'.

173 This is why the central depository, when it accepts securities issued on the basis of foreign laws, holds them 'according to the practices of the place of origin' (Art. 4.1.4 of the Euroclear operating rules), which, in the case of physical bearer securities, means that it will hold them 'physically in its vaults' (*ibid.*), and that it will 'periodically carry out verifications in its vaults' (Art. 4.1.5).

174 On the basis of this competence and the freedom it offers, see *supra*, paras. 291 et seq.

175 F. DRUMMOND, 'La société, l'actionnaire et le dépositaire central', *op. cit.*, no. 7. The author relies on the Euroclear operational manual.

176 Mr Malassigné has thus shown that the exercise of preferential subscription rights or the payment of dividends depended on these securities accounts, see V. MALASSIGNÉ, *Les titres représentatifs*, *op. cit.* The same author already saw in the system of delivery of securities the true place of their location, see *ibid.* See also in this sense, S. TORCK, *Essai d'une théorie général des droits réels sur chose fongible*, *op. cit.* The distinction made by Mr Jeantet in relation to the CCDVT can be used here. The author distinguished between the existence and the attribution of the security, the existence being established by issue accounts, while the attribution would fall under the central depository's securities settlement system: 'The collective deposit of bearer securities at the Caisse centrale de dépôt et de virement de titres.', *op. cit.*, pp. 187–188: 'As a result of the deposit, a sort of unblocking takes place (') depending on whether the question is whether the rights exist or who is ensecurityd to them. The existence of the rights depends on the existence of the numbered securitys in the estate [...]. But the attribution (ownership in the broad sense) of rights no longer depends on the

importance of its system, which can be compared to the payment system, with which we have seen that it must be closely linked.[177]

663. Similarities and dissimilarities in payment and securities settlement systems. The structure of the payment and settlement systems is clearly similar. Both systems have a pyramid structure, with a single institution at the head of the system with a public service mission for the ECB, and a public service-like mission for the central depository.[178] Both structures are based on chains of accounts, and the accounts held by the lead institution are the ultimate authoritative ones: primary money is used only on accounts held by the ECB; the existence of securities is guaranteed only by accounts held with the central depository.

664. These similarities help to explain part of the regime for current accounts or securities accounts held by system operators. Indeed, in the case of a transfer made between the accounts of the same bank, the bank decreases the balance of the account that makes the transfer, while crediting the one that receives it. As an author writes, 'these balances are modified without being transmitted'.[179] In contrast, whenever the transfer takes place between the accounts of two different banks, the bank whose customer makes the transfer will have to pay the amount of the transfer in central bank money to the bank of the customer receiving the transfer. This payment takes place in the accounts of the central bank, which carries out this movement.[180] Only central bank money is liberating vis-à-vis the banks. In the same way, a transfer of securities between the securities accounts of the same custodian is truly carried out: it is sufficient to reduce the balance of the transferor's securities account and to increase the balance of the account of the recipient of the transfer. On the other hand, whenever the transfer is to be made to the securities account of another custodian, the former will have to make a transfer to the accounts held by the central depository.

---

securities in the pool. It depends on the transactions between members, recorded by the Fund.' F.-C. Jeantet, 'Le dépôt collectif de titres au porteur à la Caisse centrale de dépôt et de virement de titres', *op. cit.*

177 On the articulation of payment and settlement systems, see *supra*, paras. 237 et seq.

178 This is the basis for its disciplinary prerogatives. Such a comparison therefore prompts one to abandon the idea that the central depository is simply another capitalist company, even if it is closely regulated. It could be seen as a company entrusted with the public service of centralising securities. This idea, already put forward by Mr Tunc in relation to the CCDVT, was developed by Mr Barban in relation to the market firm. It could usefully be extended to the clearing house. In fact, in the case of the clearing house and the central depository, there is also a de facto, or even de jure, monopoly, which contributes to the idea that the profits resulting from this activity should probably be attributed to the community rather than to shareholders. Above all, since the bankruptcy of these establishments entails the certain realisation of the systemic risk, their bail-out by public funds is certain, so that the absence of risk taken by their shareholders probably does not justify a remuneration.

179 V. Malassigné, *Les titres représentatifs*, *op. cit.*, no. 838.

180 See the pedagogical explanation by V. Malassigné, *Les titres représentatifs*, *op. cit.*

665. These structural similarities should not, however, mask profound differences. The first of these is the objects exchanged at the level of the centralising body: securities are issued by a multitude of different issuers, representing distinct *negotia*, whereas the central bank's currency is unitary in its *negotium* and in its origin. The second is institutional: there is no Eurosystem for central depositories,[181] despite the presence of a group of companies carrying out this activity. The existence of this group does not alter the fact that there are as many securities settlement systems as there are central depositories. It is true that there are as many payment systems as there are national central banks; however, the currency issued is always that of the Eurosystem. Above all, how can we fail to see that the very existence of the Eurosystem considerably standardises practices, both because of its regulatory power over payment systems,[182] and because of the mechanisms necessary for the interoperability of exchanges, as well as the informal relations between its members? The third major difference stems from an element of the regime specific to securities, and which lies in the action offered to their owners. Indeed, the holder of a current account with a bank can, in the event of bankruptcy, only declare his claim to the collective procedure.[183] On the other hand, the owner of the financial instrument benefits from an action to *claim the securities* registered in the account. Only this prerogative really distinguishes the holder of a securities account from the holder of a current account, and imposes a different treatment of the scope of the registration in an account of a sum of money and a financial instrument in French law.

§ 2. THE ENTANGLEMENT OF INTERMEDIATION SYSTEMS

666. Since the existence in France of an organisation centralising securities deposits, the solution to cross-border acquisitions of securities has always been for the real investor to register in the name of his intermediary. This was true for the French investor who wished to purchase foreign securities under both the CCDVT and the SICOVAM. Indeed, the share current accounts opened by the SICOVAM for the benefit of its affiliated institutions can only record bearer shares issued by companies having their registered office in France or in the French Empire, which are admitted to a listing.[184] Foreign securities, even those admitted to listing in France, cannot therefore be entered in the current accounts of the SICOVAM. However, Article 19 of the Decree of 4 August 1949 created

181 On the Eurosystem, see *supra*, paras. 61 et seq.

182 See *supra*, para. 244.

183 However, in all cases where his current account did not have a balance of more than one hundred thousand euros, the customer will be reimbursed by the deposit guarantee fund set up for this purpose, see *supra*, para. 158.

184 Art. 4 of the above-mentioned decree of 4 August 1949.

an original mechanism, apparently inspired by a practice of the CCDVT,[185] according to which:

> 'Owners of foreign securities which are essentially registered may have their securities registered in the name of the professional body referred to in Article 5 above (i.e. the SICOVAM). The latter then exercises all the rights attached to these securities vis-à-vis the issuing companies, but in this case it only acts as agent for the real owners who exercise their ownership rights through it, in particular with regard to voting rights, the collection of all proceeds or reimbursements and the exercise of subscription rights. The beneficial owners may at any time have the securities in question registered in their name.'[186]

This mechanism, which was already in place under the CCDVT, has not fundamentally changed, but has simply become more sophisticated. As a result, the existence of national intermediation chains (I) gives rise to their entanglement in international relations (II).

I. Intermediation Chains

667. The first level of intermediation. The institution of a central securities depository is a phenomenon that has appeared in all legal systems where transactions in securities have developed.[187] However, the causes for the emergence of these systems are different. In the United States, for example, the creation of the *depositary trust company* is linked to a paperwork crisis,[188] which was resolved by two techniques, depending on whether the rights

---

185 F. GORÉ, 'Le nouveau régime des valeurs mobilières', *op. cit.*, no. 159.

186 Art. 19 of the decree of 4 August 1939. This procedure is reminiscent of the one known in English and American law, which allows the creation of a certificate of transfer of securities, see *supra*, para. 634.

187 The authors of the Explanatory Report consider that the widespread establishment of CSDs seems to have spread to almost all countries of the world since the publication of the Group of Thirty report in 1989 on national clearing and settlement systems (Group of Thirty, 'Clearance and settlement in the World's Securities Market', New York & London, March 1989, see Explanatory Report, p. 9).

188 In this respect, Mr Conac observes that 'the *broker-dealers*, who were still handling paper share certificates, had not put in place procedures capable of absorbing the growth in the volume of orders, which had led to the disorganisation of transactions and the loss of many certificates representing securities. In response to this crisis, intermediaries created the *depositary trust company*, where most share certificates are deposited, and clearing *corporations*, which allow account-to-account transfers to be made with minimal paper handling'. P.-H. CONAC, *La régulation des marchés boursiers par la commission des opérations de bourse (COB) et la securities and exchange commission (SEC)*, *op. cit.*, no. 210. On the evolution of the indirect holding system in the United States, see K. KETTERING, 'Repledge Deconstructed', (1999) 61 *U. Pitt. L. Rev.*, pp. 45 et seq. On the risk created by the US intermediation system see S.L. SCHWARCZ, 'Intermediary risk in a Global economy' (2001) 50 *Duke L. J.*, pp. 1541 et seq.

represented are exclusively bearer or require registration. In the case of bearer securities, in particular bonds, the technique consists of issuing a single security representing all the *negotiable securities* issued (*global note* for debt securities or *jumbo certificate* for equity securities), which is immobilised with the central depository.[189] In the case of registered shares, all shares are in the name of the same *nominee*, *Cede&Co*, which represents the central depository and constitutes the first level of intermediation.[190] In both cases, it is the accounts of the central depositories that are then used as proof. In France,[191] as in the EU, the central depository constitutes the first level of intermediation.

668. The second level of intermediation. This first level of intermediation may be complemented by another. The final investor rarely has direct access to the centralising body.[192] In the same way that the investor must call upon a market member to purchase financial instruments on his behalf through the trading platform, the investor must most often call upon an intermediary who is a member of the settlement system for securities managed by the centralising body. With the exception of cases where the member of the settlement system buys financial securities on its own behalf, there are always at least two levels of intermediation: that of the centralising body, and that of the intermediary member of the system managed by this body.

However, this second level of intermediation may be multiplied where the intermediary to whom the ultimate investor has turned is not a member of

---

More generally, transfers of paper securities had to be carried out by physical delivery of the paper securities and the transfer instruments, which increased the cost of the transfers and the time of delivery. Mr Bernasconi summed up the difficulties of the old system perfectly: 'These operations also presented high risks, because the physical securities had to be transported and, as a result, could be lost, mislaid, stolen or falsified. The costs of protecting the vouchers against these risks and the costs of transporting them over long distances made the transfer of vouchers in a direct holding system expensive. Moreover, during the transport from the old to the new owner, the securities could neither be used nor invested. This created a liquidity risk for the securities.' *Bernasconi Report*, p. 2.

189 For the use of such a system, see the *Secure Capital* judgment supr,a para. 399. This technique is also used in Swiss law under the security of 'global certificate' (see Art. 973 b of the Swiss Code of Obligations and, for its presentation, V. Malassigné, *Les titres représentatifs, op. cit.)*
In English law, the chain of intermediation can take place through the initial issuance of a paper security representing the entirety of the *negotia* issued and held by a central depository, or through an initial issuance directly registered in the central depository's issue accounts, see L. Gullifer, 'Ownership of Securities' in *Intermediated Securities*, Hart, Oxford, 2010, p. 2. When registered in the accounts of the central depository, the latter acts as a registry, see V. Dixon, 'Legal nature of intermediated securities' in *Intermediation and beyond*, *op. cit.*, p. 63.

190 For an illustration, see the *Macmillan* judgment. On this question, see V. Malassigné, *Les titres représentatifs*, *op. cit.*

191 Where the institution of the central depository surprisingly does not stem from a crisis, but from the administration's desire to control the system, see *supra*, para. 648.

192 The rise of the *blockchain* is nevertheless likely to change this state of affairs, see *supra*, para. 137.

the securities settlement system, and asks another intermediary to access it on his behalf. This will often be the case when the investor's direct intermediary is resident in the same country as the investor, but the security has been issued with a foreign central securities depository, whose direct intermediary is not a member of the securities settlement system.[193] The investor's direct intermediary will then turn to an intermediary that is a member of that settlement system in order to acquire a share. It is in this context that chains of intermediation can develop and that three difficulties arise from a factual reality: the different intermediaries are not always located in the same legal order.

The first difficulty is related to the divergent structure of securities accounts held by intermediaries. Indeed, depending on the legal system, intermediaries have very different professional obligations to segregate their accounts. Some intermediaries must keep the securities they hold on behalf of their clients in separate accounts, not only in their own accounts but also in the accounts they hold at the upper tier. Other legal orders allow intermediaries to have only one account with the upper-tier intermediary in which not only its securities, but also all securities it holds for its clients, are recorded. In the latter case, the account is called an *omnibus* account or fungible account.[194] These two types of accounts may also coexist within the same legal system, depending on the situation, in which case the internationalisation of intermediaries only accentuates an already existing difficulty. The second difficulty lies in the intermediary's lack of knowledge of the composition of the chain of intermediation leading to its own holding of the security, and it will often be very difficult to trace this chain of intermediation. This is referred to as the *no look-through principle*.[195] Finally, the third and most significant difficulty stems from the fact that the prerogatives exercised by the investor at the end of the chain against his immediate intermediary are not necessarily the same depending on the legal system. As Professor Benjamin writes, 'finance is global, but financial law is fragmented'.[196]

---

193 L. Gullifer, 'Introduction' in *Intermediation and beyond*, *op. cit.*, p. 9; G. Morton, 'Historical introduction' in *Intermediation and beyond*, *op. cit.*, p. 25. The latter author believes that this is either because of practical issues or because of the local structure of security holding.

194 See *Bernasconi Report*, p. 10. These two systems may also coexist within the same legal order depending on the situation.

195 On this principle,see J. Benjamin and L. Gullifer, 'Stewardship and collateral: the advantages and disadvantages of the no look through system' in *Intermediation and beyond*, *op. cit.*

196 J. Benjamin, 'The Oxford colloquium on collateral and conflict of laws: overview', *op. cit.*

II. The Nature of the Right Exercised Against the Intermediary in Foreign Intermediation Systems

669. The investor at the end of the chain as the owner of the financial instrument.[197] Some legal systems consider the ultimate account *holder* as the owner of the financial instrument, i.e. the person at the end of the intermediation chain who generally bears the risk of the financial instrument issued.[198] This intermediation system corresponds, for example, to the French domestic system in which the person acquiring a security issued by a French company from a French central depository, through a French intermediary, is the owner of the security.[199] This system is in force in France and in several EU countries. In contrast to this system, it is possible to imagine that the investor at the end of the chain holds only a simple contract with the intermediary, and the intermediary's client then has only contractual prerogatives against him. This system does not seem to be used in any legal system, presumably because of the risk that this situation poses to the client in case of insolvency of the intermediary.[200] In fact, when one tries to classify the other types of rights exercised by the investor at the end of the chain, one can distinguish, probably roughly, between those who have a *sui generis* right against their intermediary, those who have a right arising out of a chain of *trusts*, and those who have a co-ownership right in the securities held by their intermediary.[201]

670. The investor at the end of the chain has a *sui generis* right against his intermediary: US law. This system of intermediation only grants the ultimate investor, on whom the risk of the acquisition falls, a *sui generis* right against his intermediary, who in turn only has a claim against his own intermediary, right up to the beneficial owner of the security. The latter will sometimes be the central depository, or an intermediary in the chain. In this system, the ultimate investor cannot go back up the chain of intermediation (*no look-through principle*), simply because, fundamentally, the issuer of the *negotium* recorded in the intermediary's accounts is not the issuer of the original security, but the intermediary itself.

US law was the first to create this type of right of the ultimate investor against his direct intermediary, which could almost be likened to a *sui generis*

---

197 Among an extensive literature, see among others F. Drummond, 'Les titres intermédiés. Regard sur un nouveau concept en droit financier' in *Mélanges Paul Didier*, Paris, Economica, 2008, pp. 147 et seq.; see also by the same author, 'Intermediated securities: reflections on a new concept in French financial markets law'(September 2007) *Law and Financial Markets Review*, p. 435.

198 On this aspect of the split between ownership and uncertainty, see C. Coupet, *L'attribution du droit de vote dans les sociétés*, *op. cit.*

199 Art. L. 228-1 of the Commercial Code.

200 See in this sense, *Bernasconi Report*, p. 20.

201 This is also the approach taken by the preliminary work of the Hague Conference (see *Bernasconi Report*, p. 20, and by the Unidroit Legislative Guide, see Unidroit Legislative Guide on Intermediated Securities, pp. 18 et seq.)

debt security issued by the intermediary for the benefit of his client.[202] The intermediary is defined as a clearing organisation, or as 'a person, including a bank or broker, who in the ordinary course of business maintains securities accounts on behalf of other persons and acts in that capacity'.[203] The context in which this right was created is important. For a long time, US law had as many commercial codes as it had member states; in 1952 it instituted a *Uniform Commercial Code*, which has since been regularly reformed. Following the 1987 stock market crash, the US regulator observed that one of the difficulties that caused the crash was a liquidity crisis, in particular because the banks themselves could not obtain credit because they did not have enough collateral to offer. Indeed, while they could deposit as collateral the monetary funds deposited by their clients, the same could not be said of the securities, the ownership of which remained with their clients. It is in this context that the reform that gave rise to Articles 8 and 9 of the *Uniform Commercial Code*,[204] which came into force in 1994, was conceived. Article 8, entitled *Investment securities*, is subdivided into six parts relating respectively to general provisions, the issuer and the issue, the transfer of securities, whether or not they are certificated, the registration of registered securities, *security entitlement*, and transitional provisions. Article 9, entitled *secured transaction*, relates to financial collateral.

Article 8 of the *Uniform Commercial Code* establishes security entitlement, i.e. a set of personal and real rights of an investor towards his intermediary and his property.[205] Personal rights include the right to require the intermediary to hold an equivalent number of security entitlements and underlying securities, to pay dividends on the shares attached to the security entitlement, or to exercise voting rights in accordance with the intermediary's instructions.[206] Property

[202] For a US presentation, see J. Rogers, 'Toward international harmonization of the commercial law of the modern securities holding and transfer system: some reflections from the United States Article 8 Revision Project' in *Capital Market Forum discussion paper no. 6*, International Bar Association, 1996. For an analysis from the English point of view, see M. Ooi, *Shares and other securities in the conflict of laws*, *op. cit.*, no. 11.08. From the point of view of French law, see V. Malassigné, *Les titres représentatifs*, *op. cit.*, nos. 542, 544 and 547. According to Mr Malassigné, the presence of a real right within the prerogatives enjoyed by the holder of the debt security is not such as to allow for a complete assimilation, see *ibid.*, no. 548.

[203] Art. 8-102(a)(14): '"Securities intermediary" means:
(i) a clearing corporation; or
(ii) a person, including a bank or broker, that in the ordinary course of its business maintains securities accounts for others and is acting in that capacity.' Translation is from the *Bernasconi Report*, p. 45.

[204] On this issue,see H. de Vauplane, 'Cadre juridique des garanties financières', *RDBF*, January 2007, pp. 82 et seq.

[205] A confusion between English and American law arises from the fact that the notion of '*security interest*' is used in American law to designate a security interest (Art. 1-201(37) of the UCC) whereas the notion of '*interrest in securities*' designates in English law the interest in securities.

[206] Art. 8-506 of the *Uniform Commercial Code.*

interests[207] constitute a pro rata right to financial assets.[208] The latter are not considered to be the property of the intermediary,[209] and as such are protected from the actions of the intermediary's creditors.[210] These financial assets may, under certain conditions, be the subject of an action by the security entitlement holder against the bona fide purchaser.[211] Swiss law has been largely inspired by US law by creating a modified form of intermediated securities. The latter are also issued by intermediaries, and 'have both certain characteristics of claims and of things';[212] their characterisation is nevertheless more delicate than the US intermediated securities because of the regime attached to them.[213]

671. The investor at the end of a chain of *trusts*. English law[214] also has an equivalent of intermediated securities through a *trust* system, at the end of which *securities' interests* are transmitted, i.e. intangible rights distinct from the initial securities, but which grant prerogatives on the latter. In the English holding chain, ownership of the original securities is vested in the participant

207 Art. 8-503 of the *Uniform Commercial Code.*

208 Art. 8-503(b) of the *Uniform Commercial Code.*

209 Art. 8-503(a) of the *Uniform Commercial Code.*

210 *Ibid.*

211 Art. 8-503(d) *Uniform Commercial Code.* As Professor Rogers, the official reporter on Art. 8, puts it: 'A security entitlement is not a claim to a specific identifiable thing; it is a bundle of rights that a person can enforce through and against securities. The rules of the amended Article 8 relating to the indirect holding system make no allowance for any concept that separate objects can be traced into the hands of different persons. Rather, the fundamental principle underlying these rules is that the intermediary has an obligation to ensure that all pecuniary and corporate rights relating to the securities held are passed on to the entitlement holders and that, therefore, those entitlement holders look only to the intermediary for performance of the obligations. The entitlement holder cannot enforce its rights directly against other persons, such as other intermediaries through whom the intermediary holds the assets.' J.S. Rogers, 'Policy Perspectives on Revised U.C.C. Article 8' (1996) 43 *U.C.L.A. L. Rev.*, pp. 1456–1457. The translation is that of the *Bernasconi Report*, pp. 24–25. See also J.S. Rogers, 'Towards International Harmonization of the Commercial Law of the Modern Securities Holding and Transfer System: Some Reflections from the United States Article 8 Revision Project' in R. Guynn (ed.) *Capital Markets Forum*, International Bar Association, 1996, pp. 59 et seq.

212 F. Drummond, 'Les titres intermédiés. Regard sur un nouveau concept en droit financier', *op. cit.* V. Malassigné, *Les titres représentatifs*, *op. cit.*, no. 557 evokes 'a *sui generis* asset at the confluence of personal and real rights'.

213 See the difficulties raised by the analysis of this singular intermediated security, V. Malassigné, *Les titres représentatifs*, *op. cit.*, nos. 553 et seq.
On the state of Swiss law before the reform incorporating the *security entitlement* into domestic law, see *Bernasconi Report*, pp. 56 et seq.

214 Dixon points out that the laws of Australia, Ireland and Hong Kong can be compared to English law, see V. Dixon, 'Legal nature of intermediated securities', *op. cit.*, p. 63.
On English law, see J. Benjamin, *Interest in securities: a propriatery analysis of the International Securities Markets*, Oxford, OUP, 2000, pp. 3 et seq.; Financial Markets Law Committee, 'Property Interests in Investment Scurities', July 2004 and, more recently, Mr Justice Briggs' analysis based on the most recent judgments, Mr Justice Briggs, 'Has English Law coped with the Lehman collapse?' (2013) *Butterworth Journal of International Banking and Financial Law*, pp. 131 et seq.

in the securities settlement system.[215] All intermediaries downstream of the intermediary participating in the securities settlement system have only an *equitable interest*, referred to as a *securities interest*.[216] The latter are capable of being booked and transferred in the same way as securities. According to English law, they constitute a 'beneficial interest under a trust or sub-trust'.[217] The characterisation of the nature of this *beneficial interest* has changed over time and English doctrine, based on the most recent judgments, holds that it consists of a right in the co-ownership of the entire pool of financial securities held by the intermediary.[218] Indeed, trust law is sufficiently flexible to allow the beneficiary of a sub-trust (resulting from a successive chain of trusts) to hold a real right through the chain of intermediation.[219] This overview shows that English law, through the trust technique, is probably closer to another category of prerogatives, those resulting from an analysis based on co-ownership.

672. The investor has a real right of co-ownership in the securities held by the intermediary. Several European legal systems[220] grant the investor at the end of the chain a right *in rem* ('*droit réel*') over all of the securities held by his intermediary. One example is Luxembourg law, which provides as follows:

> 'The depositor shall have a right in rem, of an intangible nature, to all securities and other financial instruments of the same kind received in deposit or held in account

215 V. Dixon, 'Legal nature of intermediated securities', *op. cit.*, p. 63.

216 B. Macfarlane and R. Stevens, 'Interests in securities: practical problems and conceptual solutions', *Intermediated securities, op. cit.*, p. 33.

217 *Ibid.*, pp. 39 et seq.; L. Gullifer and J. Payne, 'Introduction', *Intermediation and beyond, op. cit.*, p. 14; V. Dixon, 'Legal nature of intermediated securities', *op. cit.*, pp. 63 et seq.

218 'A co-ownership interest in relation to the entire pool of securities held by the intermediary', V. Dixon, 'Legal nature of intermediated securities', *op. cit.*, p. 65. The judgments in question are all related to the Lehman Brothers bankruptcy, see e.g. *Re Lehman Brothers International (Europe) (in administration), Pearson v. Lehman Brothers Finance SA* (*RASCAL*) (2010) EWHC 2914 (Ch), upheld by the London Court of Appeal, (2011) EWCA Civ 1544.

219 R. Goode, 'Security Ensecurityments as Collateral in the Conflict of laws', *Butterworth journal of international banking and financial law*, special supplement, 1998, p. 23; J. Benjamin, *Interests in securities: a proprietary law analysis of the international securities market*, Oxford, OUP, 2000, chaApter 7; G. Morton, 'Historical introduction', *op. cit.*, p. 30.

220 Ms Dixon thus brings together Germany, Belgium, Luxembourg, Austria, the Netherlands, Slovakia and Mexico, see V. Dixon, 'Legal nature of intermediated securities', *op. cit.*, p. 67. On these systems, see *Bernasconi Report*, p. 21.
However, in Belgian and Dutch law, there is another category of securities that must be distinguished. These legal systems have introduced certificates which allow an intermediary (in Dutch law, an 'administratiekantoor') to own and manage the shares and to issue a certificate representing a right of claim at the end of which the holder of the certificate receives the sums paid by the company issuing the certified shares and can demand that the certificate be converted into shares under certain conditions (see V. Malassigné, *Les titres représentatifs, op. cit.*) However, the particularity of these share certificates is that they can only be issued in respect of shares of companies domiciled in the same legal order. This is why they no longer constitute depository receipts within the meaning of MiFID 2 (Art. 4(1)(45)), and as such can no longer be included among financial securities (*ibid.*, no. 575).

by its depositary, to the extent of the number of securities and other financial instruments registered in its account.'[221]

In these systems, as Ms Drummond writes, 'the book entry is therefore not the original security, nor is it the proof of the account holder's ownership of the original security'.[222] However, after having distanced the direct relationship between the depositor and the security, Luxembourg law reinstates the regime: thus the depositor is deemed to have retained the same rights as if the securities had remained in his hands.[223] The legal systems offering a right of co-ownership to the investor at the end of the chain are in line with those that have already been described: whatever right is exercised against the intermediary, the regime attached to it has the function of 'acting as if' the person were the owner of the initial security.[224] This can be seen from two elements. On the one hand, the prerogatives of the security must be exercised in accordance with the will of the ultimate investor, i.e. dividends must be paid to him and the intermediary must follow the voting instructions of the ultimate investor. On the other hand, in the event of investor insolvency, the ultimate investors all have a functional equivalent of the reclamation action and, in the event of insufficient financial securities in the intermediary's accounts, the securities are distributed *pari passu*. These provisions, which are undoubtedly effective in domestic law, become less effective when confronted with certain international situations, as shown by the *Secure Capital* case where the Luxembourg investor at the end of the chain, not being the owner of the disputed debt security, was not a contracting party within the meaning of the contract of issue subject to English law.[225] The other difficulty, illustrated by the *Macmillan* judgment, is to decide on the priority issue that may arise between the end investor and the bona fide third party purchaser.[226]

673. Meaning of the entanglement of intermediation chains. As Professors Drummond and Malassigné observe, when referring to the intermediated holding

[221] Art. 6 of the Act of 1 August 2001 on the circulation of securities and other fungible instruments.

[222] F. Drummond, 'Les titres intermédiés. A look at a new concept in financial law', *op. cit.*, p. 151. The author specifies that what guided these legal systems to exclude the direct relationship of the investor at the end of the chain with the initial security is the fungibility of these securities.

[223] The law is drafted in these terms in Luxembourg law (Art. 6 of the above-mentioned Luxembourg law).

[224] This technique exists in the regime of other mechanisms of representation: for Mr Malassigné, the regime of securities which, according to the author's distinction, "imperfectly represent" goods are precisely intended to act *as if* the holder of the security in question were placed in full possession of the good, V. Malassigné, *Les titres représentatifs*, *op. cit.* The author also sees such a purpose behind the money of commercial banks, *ibid.*, no. 845.

[225] See *supra*, para. 399.

[226] See *supra*, para. 634.

system, two very distinct realities are evoked according to the legal orders.[227] In the French case, intermediation refers to the holding of securities, not their ownership; in the foreign cases mentioned, it is the ownership itself that no longer belongs to the ultimate investor, but to the intermediary. This characteristic is sometimes revealed by the identification of the issuer of the security, which is the intermediary itself. While the chain of intermediation is similar, the *negotium* represented by the book entry therefore diverges drastically. This means that whenever a French investor wants to buy a share issued in the accounts of a foreign custodian registered in a system where the ultimate investor is not the owner of the securities, he can never be. His French intermediary will acquire the equivalent of a *security entitlement* from an intermediary participating in the system of the central depository where the securities were issued. More generally, whenever the intermediation chain uses an intermediary established in a foreign legal system where the investor is not the owner of the security acquired on his behalf, he risks acquiring not the desired security, but a set of rights against his intermediary. It is in this context that the question arises as to what solutions conflict of laws can offer.

Section conclusion. This discussion has shown the fundamental importance, in France, of the central depository: it is its accounts that record the issuance of securities, and it is the accounts it keeps for the participants in its settlement system that are authentic. The evolution of the French intermediation system shows that this has not always been the case, especially during the parenthesis from the creation of SICOVAM to the 1981 dematerialisation law. Furthermore, the great heterogeneity of intermediation systems was observed and, consequently, the difficulties that their entanglement in the international order creates. It was then shown that these difficulties lie less in the structure of intermediation, which is most often based on a central depositary, than in the diversity of the rights exercised with intermediaries. This observation already points the way to a balanced solution of the conflict of laws, which should not be based on the accounts held by the intermediaries, but on the common element of the intermediation structures: the presence of an original registration with a central depositary. Unfortunately, contemporary conflict rules rely on the "relevant" intermediary to locate securities. Such rules lead to a renewal of the plurality of connections, but in a form that further increases its shortcomings.

227 F. Drummond, 'Les titres intermédiés. Regard sur un nouveau concept en droit financier', *op. cit.* V. Malassigné, *Les titres représentatifs*, *op. cit.*, no. 538.

SECTION 3. IMPASSE OF CONFLICT RULES BASED ON THE 'RELEVANT' INTERMEDIARY

674. The previously dominant conflict rules, by applying the law of the issuer or the law of the paper security as to the proprietary status of the security, had the advantage of preserving both functions of the security.[228] This is not the case with modern rules, and particularly with the so-called PRIMA rule,[229] which is partially in force in Europe and is supported by the Hague Securities Convention in one of its variants. This rule is intended to take over from the lex situs previously applicable to securities, and therefore applies to the proprietary status of the security. Its scope is nevertheless variable depending on the rules envisaged. However, it generally covers at least some of the aspects that Professor Synvet identified when he proposed the PRIMA rule in French law, such as:

> 'The determination of the rights attached to the book entry, the enforceability of these rights against third parties, the regime of their transmission, the conditions of the reclamation of the securities, the constitution and the conventional effects on securities, the legal interest likely to encumber them, the conflict of competing rights relating to the same financial securities.'[230]

We shall endeavour here to show the origin of the PRIMA rule (before highlighting its shortcomings, both in its version based on an objective location criterion derived from European legislation (§ 2), and in its subjective version based on a subjective location criterion in the Hague Securities Convention (§ 3).

§ 1. THE AMERICAN ORIGIN OF THE PRIMA RULE

675. The origin of the rules based on the relevant intermediary can be found on the other side of the Atlantic. The PRIMA criterion was instituted by the US legal system at the same time as it reformed its financial securities law and created the security entitlements.[231] It is therefore in contemplation of the configuration of these particular securities that the PRIMA connection was

---

228 The 'vertical' function of the relationship with the issuer, and the 'horizontal' function relating to the transmission of the security, see *supra*, para. 579. See already P. Paech, 'Conflict of laws and relational rights' in *Intermediation and beyond*, *op. cit.*

229 For 'Place of the Relevant Intermediary Approach'.

230 H. Synvet, 'Report on a draft conflict of laws rule on financial securities', *op. cit.*, p. 7.

231 On which, see *supra*, para. 692.

developed by Article 8-110 of the Uniform Commercial Code.[232] Indeed, these documents of security are issued by the intermediary for the benefit of its client, and give rise to prerogatives only against the intermediary. Whether one applies to these securities the *lex creationis*, the law of the debtor of the characteristic performance, the law of the place of payment, or the law of the place of the original account, all these factors converge in any event towards the application of the law of the intermediary. Within all these criteria, it seems to be on the basis of the law of the issuer that the PRIMA rule applies. However, US law actually applies this test only to security entitlements, not to original financial securities. In order to convince ourselves of this, we will successively study the conflict rules applicable to initial securities (I), before turning to those relating to security entitlements (II).

I. The Law Applicable to Financial Securities under US Law

676. Application of the law of the issuer.[233] Section 8-110 of the Uniform Commercial Code deals with all conflicts of laws relating to financial securities. With respect to original securities, Section 8-110(a) gives principle jurisdiction to the local law of the issuer's jurisdiction. This law is determined by the place of the issuer's registered office. If the place of organisation of the issuer so permits, the issuer may decide to apply to its securities the law designated by it, except for the validity of the security,[234] which remains subject to the law of the issuer. This choice of law option offered by some States to the issuer will allow, inter alia, the application of the law of the registry in case of dissociation between the place of the registry and the seat of the issuer. The conflict of laws rule is therefore liberal: it leaves open the possibility, if the federal state so wishes, of allowing the issuer to obtain a genuine choice of law for the entire proprietary status, with the notable exception of the validity of the security. It is then only by exception, in the absence of choice of law, that the law of the issuer's registered office will be applicable.

677. Scope of the issuer's law. The scope of the issuer's law then concerns the proprietary regime of the security: the determination of the validity of the security, the rights and obligations of the issuer with regard to compliance with the registration and transfer of the security, the effectiveness of the transfer, the duties of the issuer with regard to a person claiming ownership of a security and, finally, the resolution of the conflict of law in the case of acquisition *a non*

---

232 In this sense, although *ISDA* may have wished to extend this criterion, it does not seem to us that it was at the origin of it as some authors believe, see e.g. A. Riles, *Collateral knowledge*, *op. cit.*, p. 171.

233 The translations given here are those adopted by the Hague Conference, see *Bernasconi Report*, pp. 52–53.

234 Art. 8-110(d) of the *Uniform Commercial Code*.

domino.[235] A cut-off to the law of the issuer is provided for in the case where the security is represented by a paper security. In this case, the conflict of laws and the enforceability against third parties of the transfer of a paper security *certificate* are governed by the law of the location of the certificate at the time of the transfer.[236]

II. The Law Applicable to Securities Entitlement

678. The connecting factor for security entitlements, based on the place of business of the intermediary, is designed as an offshoot of the application of the law of the issuer, and appears in Section 8-110(b) of the Uniform Commercial Code. However, the two rules are perfectly independent, simply because the security entitlement is distinct from the original security.[237] Consequently, US conflict of laws very explicitly refuses to locate the security entitlement by reference to the original security.[238]

679. Law applicable to security entitlement. US law provides for a succession of cascading conflict rules to determine the applicable law.[239] The first provides that if an agreement between the security entitlement holder and the intermediary specifically provides for the application of the law of the intermediary under Article 8 of the Uniform Commercial Code, that law will apply. Otherwise, the law of the contract between the intermediary and the security entitlement holder will apply. In the absence of a choice of law agreement between those parties, if there is an express agreement as to the place where the account for the original securities is to be maintained, the law of that place will apply to the security entitlement. In the absence of such an agreement, the competent law is the law of the place of the institution maintaining the account of the holder of the security entitlement. Finally, if such an institution cannot be identified, the applicable law is that of the administrative headquarters of the intermediary. The conflict rule under US law is therefore based, in principle, on the parties' choice of law. Only by exception does the law of the registered office of the intermediary prevail. The domain of the designated law is the proprietary status of the security entitlement. The main difference with the area of the law applicable to the security is the validity of the instrument. In the case of a security entitlement, the issue is rather the validity of the acquisition of a security entitlement from the relevant intermediary. This is how US law itself puts it.[240]

---

235 Art. 8-110(a) of the *Uniform Commercial Code.*
236 Art. 8-110(c) of the *Uniform Commercial Code.*
237 See *supra*, para. 672.
238 Art. 8-110(f) of the *Uniform Commercial Code.*
239 Art. 8-110(e) of the *Uniform Commercial Code.*
240 Art. 8-110 (b) of the *Uniform Commercial Code.*

680. Extension to financial collateral. US law applies to financial collateral the law applicable to the proprietary status of the security issued. In other words, where the security is a paper security, the law of the location of the certificate applies to the security. Where the security is registered, the law of the issuer, or the law designated by the issuer if it has been able to make such a choice, will apply to the financial collateral. In the same way, the law applicable to the security entitlement extends to the collateral to which it may have been subject. However, in the case of financial collateral there are two intermediaries: the intermediary who lends the money and receives the collateral securities, and the intermediary who receives the money and lends the collateral securities. The application of the law of the intermediary who receives the collateral securities could be based on the idea that he can obtain control over them through the perfection mechanism, which aims at the enforceability of the collateral against third parties.[241] One method of perfection against third parties is perfection by control.[242] However, the transfer of securities is not an effect of the security interest and is even less its mode of creation: it is a mode of enforcement. This is why the law applicable to financial collateral is always the law of the account where the security entitlement is initially located, i.e. the law of the intermediary of the collateral provider.[243]

From a logical point of view, it is normal that the law applicable to ownership of the security, conflict of rights and enforceability against third parties, is also the law applicable to the security interest of which the security may be the subject. Indeed, the enforcement of the security interest leads precisely to the appropriation of the securities, which will give rise to a priority issue and even of perfection against third parties whenever the person who provided the securities was not the owner.[244] It is therefore fortunate and consistent that a unitary rule has been introduced.

681. Analysis. It can be seen that the PRIMA rule was developed in the United States in contemplation of the security entitlement regime, and not for initial securities. It is nevertheless inspired by the rule applicable to registered securities, with some American states allowing the issuer to subject the proprietary status of

---

[241] See in this sense *Bernasconi Report*, p. 8.

[242] Art 9-314 of the *Uniform Commercial Code*. A *security interest* is a form of *investment property*, see Art. 9-102(49) *Uniform Commercial Code*. The control argument is noted by M. Ooi, *Shares and other securities in the conflict of laws*, *op. cit.*, no. 11.24. Art. 9 of the *Uniform Commercial Code* is at the origin of the very notion of *collateral*, conceived in contemplation of the commercial practices observed in the 1950s, see A. Riles, *Collateral knowledge*, *op. cit.*

[243] The rejection of the control argument isdefended by M. Ooi, *Shares and other securities in the conflict of laws*, *op. cit.* Comp. V. Malassigné, *Les titres représentatives*, *op. cit.*, no. 1086, who considers that it is less a question of the law of the issuer than of the law of the source; here, however, the two agree.

[244] This is why these questions are, in our opinion, part of the "primary regime" of economic rights, see *supra*, para. 570.

the registered security to foreign law. The liberalism of the rule is obvious in that the designated a law which does not necessarily have to be that of the register. It is therefore easy to understand why, inspired by the law applicable to initial securities, the PRIMA rule is a variation of the issuer's law – it is always a question of identifying the seat of the securities intermediary – but a variation marked by the liberalism of the connecting factor designed for the issuer's law. Above all, the application of the law of the intermediary as the law of the issuer is explained by the nature of the security entitlement: all the prerogatives it gives rise to can only be enforced against the intermediary and the securities it holds. Finally, it can be observed that the connecting factor resulting from the structure of the security entitlement is attached to a rational and unitary domain, consisting of the entire proprietary status of the security and extending from the ownership of the securities to the guarantees to which it may be subject. Unfortunately, European law has a much less coherent law to assert. Having no uniform, or even harmonised, substantive law on which to base its conflict of laws rules for securities, European law has introduced an avatar of the PRIMA rule.

§ 2. THE EUROPEAN APPROACH BASED ON OBJECTIVE LOCATION

682. European law has not given securities a homogeneous regime, yet it developed the PRIMA rule at the same time as the Uniform Commercial Code came into force. The PRIMA rule first appeared in 1998, in the Finality Directive, before its scope was extended by the Financial Collateral Directive. However, at the time of its appearance in the Finality Directive, the PRIMA rule was originally competing with another conflict-of-laws rule, that of the law of the securities settlement system. Indeed, the introduction of the PRIMA rule into European law is inseparable from the heterogeneous instruments that gave rise to it. However, the rule is part of directives whose objective implies the elaboration not only of rules applicable to the proprietary status of securities when the parties are solvent, but also when they become insolvent and the *lex concursus* can then paralyse securities transactions. Nevertheless, the *lex concursus* regime, because of the singular substantive rules attached to it, associated with a specific conflict rule, deserves its own analysis.[245]

683. Conflict of laws rules. The intermediary-based securities localisation rules are derived from three European directives which will be set out in order of entry into force: the Finality Directive, which relates to payment and securities settlement systems, the Winding-up Directive, which aims to prevent bank insolvency, and the Financial Collateral Directive, which harmonises the regime

[245] See *infra*, paras. 745 et seq.

of certain security interests in financial instruments within the Union. The Finality Directive is the first to introduce a conflict of laws rule for the purpose of locating securities and determining the law applicable to collateral security interests in book-entry securities held for the benefit of participants in a system, or central banks of Member States, by participants in the system. Article 9(2) of the Finality Directive reads as follows:

> 'Where securities (including interests in securities) are provided as collateral for the benefit of participants and/or central banks of the Member States or the future European Central Bank, as referred to in paragraph 1, and their interest (or that of any nominee, agent or third party acting on their behalf) in the securities is legally recorded in a register, account or centralised deposit system located in a Member State, the determination of the rights of those entities as holders of the collateral in respect of those securities shall be governed by the law of that Member State.'[246]

Article 24 of the Winding-up directive states:

> 'The exercise of rights of ownership in instruments or other rights in such instruments, the existence or transfer of which requires registration in a register, account or centralised deposit system held or located in a Member State, shall be governed by the law of the Member State in which the register, account or centralised deposit system in which such rights are registered is held or located.'[247]

Article 9 of the Financial Collateral Directive contains a similar rule, applying to:

> 'It defines the relevant account as "the account - which may be maintained by the collateral taker - in which the entries by which financial instruments are delivered as collateral to the collateral taker are made.'[248]

All three rules have in common that they are based on the objective location of the relevant intermediary, which amounts to a continuation of the impasse of multiple connections in the indirect holding system (I). Moreover, the implementation of these three rules is made difficult because of their distinct scope of application and the differences in the field of the designated law and

246 The provision has been transposed into Art. L. 330-2(IV) of the Monetary and Financial Code. Some Member States have, however, considerably extended the rule of Art. 9(2) to all account entries. For example, Germany has transposed the article in the following terms, see Art. 17a of the *Depotdesetz*, translation *Bernasconi Report*, p. 49, note 152. On the different transpositions, see *Impact Assessment*, pp. 103 et seq.

247 Transposed into Art. L. 613-31-8 of the Monetary and Financial Code.

248 Art. 2(1)(h) of the Financial Collateral Directive. The article excludes the reference. This rule was first transposed in Art. L. 431-7-4 of the Monetary and Financial Code, and is now included in Art. L. 211-39 of the Monetary and Financial Code.

the equivocality of the criterion they use. Nevertheless, it is possible to adopt an interpretation that can remedy, in part, the uncertainties of these rules (II).

I. The Impasse of the Rules Based on the Objective Approach of the Intermediary

684. There are three reasons for the impasse in European rules. The first stems from the combination of two methodological difficulties: on the one hand, the importation into the Union of a rule that was designed for a different purpose than the one assigned to it in European law and, on the other hand, precisely because of the rule traditionally adopted in the Member States of the Union (A). The second reason for the dead-end impasse is specific to the deleterious effects of the PRIMA rule where a chain of intermediaries is involved: the criterion used leads to the multiplication of applicable laws and their fragmentation (B). Finally, the third reason is related to another effect of the PRIMA rule. It applies the law of the assignee to the transfer transaction, i.e. the one which, of the three possible criteria, is the least predictable for third parties (C).

A. The Methodological Impasse

685. A surprising transplant. The PRIMA rule is undoubtedly one of the most curious examples of legal transplant.[249] Designed in US law in contemplation of security entitlement, it was imported into Europe at a time, not yet past, when the European regime for securities was neither standardised nor harmonised. Initially confined to the systems of the Finality Directive, it was extended through intensive lobbying.[250] However, the graft has taken hold and, curiously, there is now a genuine European conception of the PRIMA rule.[251] Basically, if the graft has taken, it is because it has led to a replication of the previous system based on the law of situation. Indeed, from a European perspective, the PRIMA rule is presented as an avatar of the *lex situs*, which would make it possible to adapt the rule resulting from the *lex situs* to the dematerialisation of property. This is

---

249 On this notion, see A. Watson, *Legal Transplants: an approach to comparative law*, Athens, University of Georgio Press, 1993.

250 H. de Vauplane, 'Cadre juridique des garanties financières', *op. cit.* The role of *ISDA* is asserted as instrumental, as is the case in most state reforms of netting see A. Riles, *Collateral knowledge*, *op. cit.*, pp. 198 et seq.

251 This example reflects Professor Teubner's idea that transplants from a foreign legal order do not fit into a new system as such, but are gradually reconditioned by the host system, which by a reciprocal movement is itself altered by the reception of the transplant, see G. Teubner, 'Legal irritants: Good faith in British Law or how unifying law ends up in new divergences' 61 *Modern Law Review*, p. II-32. See already in this sense the *Hocke* judgment, *supra*, para. 577.

how the doctrine presents the rule,[252] but this is also how the European legislator has called it.[253] Two remarks are in order at this stage, concerning the basis of the *PRIMA* rule in European law, and concerning the evils of the *lex situs* in the field of securities.

686. Confusion about the basis of PRIMA. On the one hand, the PRIMA rule was never originally conceived as an avatar of the *lex situs*, but as a variation of the law of the issuer. This is undoubtedly the case in US law, but also in English law, where intangible things did not have a location precisely because they were intangible. They began to be given an artificial geographical connection in order to enable them to be taxed, and this was fixed at the place where these rights could be enforced, i.e. at the place of payment which designates the debtor's seat.[254] However, in the English perspective of the chain of trusts, if there are rights *in rem*, it is nevertheless primarily from the perspective of the enforcement of rights against the intermediary that the PRIMA rule is supported. Professor Goode writes as follows:

> 'Whichever of the two approaches – *lex situs* or direct rule – is adopted, the fact that the investor has a personal right to delivery against the securities intermediary which survives the latter's bankruptcy reinforces the case for applying to the rights of the parties the law of the place of the intermediary, *where is where those rights are enforceable*.'[255]

It is therefore clear that European law is deeply confused in its attempt to attach a rule specific to the issue of securities to property law. In addition, the PRIMA rule was designed for *negotia* issued by each intermediary and not by a system based on the actual securities regime. In other words, if the PRIMA rule was *ultimately* about property (in the patrimonial sense where a claim can be considered as property), this property was singular and its regime profoundly different from that of securities in the different European countries. Admittedly, the confusion between security entitlements and securities could be understood because of the identity of the regime attached to the form of these goods: the presence of a book entry, the possibility of simplified transfer, the negotiability attached to the represented *negotium*. However, these questions of form, while

252 See e.g. H. de Vauplane and P. Bloch, 'Loi applicable et critères de localisation des titres multi-intermédiés dans la Convention de la Haye du 13 décembre 2002', *op. cit.*, no. 4; H. Le Nabasque, A. Couret *et al.*, *Droit financier*, *op. cit.*, no. 1552; D. Robine and S. Praicheux, 'Garanties Financières', *Etudes Joly Bourse*, 2018, no. 96.

253 Heading of Art. 24 of the Winding up Directive, recital 8 Financial Guarantee Directive.

254 J. Benjamin, 'Oxford Colloquium on Collateral and Conflict of Laws: an Overview', *Special Supplement to Butterworths Journal of International Banking and Financial Law*, p. 2; Dicey, Morris, and Collins, *The Conflict of Laws*, *op. cit.*

255 R. Goode, 'Oxford Colloquium on Collateral and Conflict of Laws', *op. cit.*, p. 27, emphasis added. The author reserves the application of the foreign law to the modalities of perfection to third parties in the case of liquidation, see *ibid.*, p. 28.

undeniably important in financial law, are not decisive. The structure of the asset itself is the only decisive factor; it is this structure which gives it its value. However, the prerogatives resulting from a security entitlement and a dematerialised financial instrument, whether French or German, held through an intermediary are very different.[256] Here, the desire to force categories is reminiscent of the technique used by Procrustean.[257]

687. The harms of the *lex situs* in the area of securities. It seems curious to wish to give additional longevity to the extension of the rule resulting from the *lex situs* securities when it was already struggling, under the reign of paper securities, to propose satisfactory solutions.[258] It is true that it was shared by all European and US legal systems. Moreover, it was based in these various countries on a relatively fungible domestic law: in the various legal systems, the bearer form materialised by a sheet of paper went hand in hand with the negotiability regime which, on the one hand, facilitated the methods of transmission by making them subject to the real tradition and, on the other hand, resolved priority in favour of the third party purchaser in good faith.[259] However, there is no international fungibility of the regime for securities held with an intermediary. The only advantage of the *lex situs is* no longer available. On the other hand, its disadvantages remain: it is recalled that the *lex situs* caused a mobile conflict as soon as the paper materialising the security was transferred to another legal order. The law of goods of the latter State was then likely to decide the conflicts arising from the ownership of the security in a different sense.[260] It is not surprising in these circumstances that the PRIMA rule, conceived by Europeans as an avatar of the *lex situs*, raises the same difficulties. In addition, there is a problem relating to the account retained by the conflict rule: it is not that of the assignor, but of the assignee.

B. Unpredictability of the Law of the Assignee for Third Parties

688. Assignment. Assignment involves two persons, i.e. two securities accounts, and two intermediaries. If the rule is allusive as to the identification of the

---

256 The authors and defenders of the Hague Convention fail to convince when they allege that it is a 'myth' that the Convention was designed to work only with American substantive law, see H.C. Sigman and C. Bernasconi, 'Myths about the Hague Convention debunked' (2005) *International financial law review*, pp. 31 et seq. This may not have been the desired result, but the rule adopted by the Convention corresponds well to the American rule and produces dysfunctions for countries with a continental tradition, which is not the same as saying that the European regime is satisfactory.

257 It is known that the latter offered travellers to stay with him. He would then force them to throw themselves on a bed, cutting off the limbs that protruded from it, while stretching the feet of those who were too small.

258 See *supra*, para. 643.

259 See *supra*, para. 640.

260 See *supra*, para. 643.

securities account whose law is applied, it will unfortunately most often be the law of the transferee's securities account, which in practice is the one where the securities are registered at the time priority issue arises.[261] In this context, the PRIMA criterion misses the relevant securities account by selecting that of the transferee. This is a location criterion that cannot be foreseen by third parties: solutions in the field of contractual assignment of claims have already shown this.[262] The example of a French investor who undertakes to sell his securities to an English investor will serve as proof. Before delivering the securities, the same investor provides a financial guarantee on his securities to a Dutch credit institution. The latter then obtains the transfer of the collateral securities to an account held by it in the Netherlands. The PRIMA rule, as it has emerged from European law, will apply Dutch law to the resolution of the conflict of laws. However, the application of this law was completely unpredictable for the English buyer. It is also open to manipulation by the parties, as a simple transfer of the securities to an intermediary located in another legal system can circumvent the application of the law of the assignor.

689. Law of the transferee and interest of third parties. The application of the law of the assignee is not a neutral choice. It was the choice made by the drafters of the Hague Convention, for example. They considered that the interests of the collateral taker deserved greater protection than other creditors.[263] The treatment of third party interests does not depend on the legal culture, common law or civil law.[264] The only reason why the law of the assignee was selected is to protect the interests of the collateral takers. Such a rationale is perhaps understandable when these collateral takers are national central banks, or participants in a securities settlement system of reported systemic importance. It is less understandable

261 It is therefore inaccurate to state that through 'the *PRIMA* connecting factor of the place of the intermediary [...] one would thus find the idea of the law of the assigned debtor, since one considers that it is the right against the relevant intermediary that is assigned' (S. Laval, *Le tiers et le contrat*, *op. cit.*, no. 29). On the one hand, in French law, and in most European laws, it is not rights against the intermediary that are exercised, but real rights. On the other hand, even if the assertion were correct, the law selected is not that of the assigned debtor.

262 See *supra*, paras. 584 et seq.

263 See very clearly in this sense, H.C. Sigman and C. Bernasconi, 'Myths about the Hague Convention debunked', *op. cit.* pp. 33–34. It would appear to be inaccurate to assert, as the Conference experts do, that the Convention is neutral in its impact: there is a question of legal policy, which is that of protecting certain interests rather than others.

264 Professor Roy Goode, commenting on the solutions adopted by American law, himself observes that: 'What is surprising to me, and is no doubt due to my ignorance of the background, is that it should be competent to parties to a private agreement to determine the law which is to apply to the proprietary rights and priorities of third parties who have not participated to that agreement and have no means of discovering its terms. The law thus selected may have no relationship to the securities intermediary or the place of record, either of which would be a natural place by the law of which third parties might reasonably expect to be governed.' R. Goode, 'Oxford Colloquium on Collateral and Conflict of Laws', *op. cit.*, p. 27.

when, as is the case within the Financial Collateral Directive, any financial entity can benefit from such a rule.[265] In cases under the Financial Collateral Directive, there is no doubt that the interests of third parties are best taken into account by the application of the law of the assignor, and should only be rejected here because of the fragmentation and multiplication to which the PRIMA rule structurally leads.

C. Fragmentation and Multiplication of Applicable Law

690. Multiplication of transfers. Just as the *lex situs* rule multiplies the laws applicable to the transfer of bearer securities, the PRIMA rule multiplies the laws applicable to the transfer of book-entry securities. This phenomenon was already known from the application of local law under the negotiable securities regime, and can be referred to as *fragmentation*, since the criterion used leads to the application of a separate law to each transfer. However, the PRIMA criterion stands out because of the chain of intermediation of the securities, which gives rise to a second multiplication, even in the presence of a single economic transaction consisting of a single transfer. Indeed, behind the appearance of a single transfer between the transferor and the transferee, a multitude of transfers actually take place in each transaction. Based on the account, the PRIMA criterion leads to the view that there is a new transfer for each securities account credit in the various accounts in the chain linking the transferor's intermediary to the central depository and then to the chain linking the central depository to the transferee's intermediary.[266] This is the multiplication of loaves, PRIMA version. A single economic and legal transaction of sale or guarantee with transfer of ownership thus corresponds to a plurality of transfers of securities. It is difficult to understand why the question of the effectiveness of a transfer of securities against third parties should depend on the cumulative applicability of the laws of intermediaries' accounts, which are merely mirror accounts and whose sole purpose is to contribute to the net crediting of the security in the account of the final holder.[267]

691. Fragmentation of the applicable law. Because of the multiplicity of transfers involved in a single transaction, the PRIMA criterion results in the fragmentation of the applicable law. Indeed, the applicable law will be different for each credit of securities made within the accounts of the various intermediaries involved in the intermediation chain. The fragmentation no longer results from the transfer

---

265 See *infra*, para. 898.

266 Except where the transferor and transferee have the same intermediary, in which case there is no need to go back to the central depository: the intermediary will make the transfer to its own accounts since it is solely responsible for doing so.

267 See already in this sense, M. Ooi, 'The Hague Securities Convention: a critical reading of the road map' (2005) (4) *Lloyd's maritime and commercial law quarterly*, pp. 467 et seq., spec. p. 487.

chain, but from the intermediation chain, and is therefore multiplied even though the same economic transaction is involved. This reality has been perfectly summarised by the authors of the Explanatory Report on the Hague Convention, applicable here as regards the effects of the PRIMA criterion:

> 'The rules of the Convention apply separately in respect of each securities account (in other words, to each relationship between an account holder and its relevant intermediary). Thus, where there is a chain of intermediaries between an account holder and the issuer or between an account holder making a transfer and the counterparty to that transfer, there is no single law, such as the law of the place of incorporation of the issuer, that would govern all matters [in the area of proprietary status of the security] in respect of all securities accounts maintained by intermediaries standing between the account holder and the issuer or between the account holder and its counterparty. Such a result would be inconsistent with the fundamental principle underlying the Convention, according to which the applicable law must be that which is based on the relationship between a particular account holder and its relevant intermediary.'[268]

The multiplicity of laws applicable to what is nevertheless the same economic transaction is detrimental to the legal certainty of the transfer: as long as the credit to the securities account is not obtained, the applicable law will be that of the intermediary to whose account the security is registered. The difficulty is increased by the existence of general or omnibus accounts within which there is no individual segregation of securities. Moreover, the application of the PRIMA rule leads to absurdities and impossibilities that go far beyond the determination of the status of a security:[269] how to provide, for the transferee, the law applicable to each transfer?

692. Multiplication of applicable laws. The PRIMA rule is all the more problematic in a context where the transferred *negotium* will not be the same depending on the legal system of the relevant intermediary. For example, whenever a French share is held through an English intermediary, the ultimate account holder will not have a property right but an *interest in securities*; in the presence of a German intermediary, the account holder will only have a co-ownership right. By multiplying the laws applicable to the transfer, the PRIMA rule creates the risk of blocking the transferred *negotium* at the level of the intermediary whose legal order does not transfer ownership, but only an ersatz

268 Explanatory Report, nos. 4–11.

269 Using the terms impossibilities and absurdities to qualify the method that would claim to rely on the location of securities to determine the applicable law, see J.S. Rogers, 'Of normalcy and anomaly: thoughts on choice of a law for the indirect holding systems' (September 1998) *Butterworth journal of international banking and financial law*, pp. 47 et seq. It will be seen that such a method, which is not advocated here, leads to less complex reasoning.

ownership. In order to ensure that the transfer of ownership has taken place, it is therefore necessary to apply *cumulatively* all the laws in presence between the central depository and the ultimate account holder.[270] This observation serves as a reminder that while book entry has a 'possessory function', 'possession' *ultimately* depends on the book entry, within the chain of intermediaries, of the one who originally holds the rights of the central depository.[271]

The additional vice of the multiplication of applicable laws within the intermediation chain is that it can derail it by causing 'draws on the mass', not by the effect of the dishonesty of intermediaries, but by the effect of the law itself. This has been referred to as 'double liability', 'double responsibility' or double interest. Indeed, as the application of the law of the transferee does not necessarily correspond to the law applicable between the account holder and its intermediary, it is possible that the transfer has validly taken place under the law of the transferee, but is considered invalid by the law of the transferor's securities account.[272] In the latter case, both securities accounts of the two intermediaries will record a book entry of the security, whereas only one of these book entries corresponds to an existing security in the securities settlement system. In this case, the intermediary is not relieved of its custody obligation towards its client and will have to bear the redemption risk.[273]

693. These characteristics are independent of the subjective or objective method of account location. They are specific to the criterion of the location

[270] Coming to the same conclusion from the point of view of the incidental question, see M. Ooi, 'The Hague Securities Convention: a critical reading of the road map', *op. cit.*, p. 481.

[271] This is why Mr Synvet's observation that the institution of the PRIMA rule in the Financial Collateral Directive has the effect of 'making effective, in France, collateral put in place abroad on financial instruments located there', H. Synvet, 'Les garanties financières', *RDBF*, January 2007, pp. 81–82, should be nuanced. Indeed, the rule seems to give a bilateral twist to Art. 29-1 of Law 83-1 of 3 January 1983 on the development of investments and the protection of savings, which applied French law to 'pledges of financial instruments registered in an account, whether French or foreign' (on this Art., see H. de Vauplane and S. Mouy, 'La réforme du nantissement des titres dématérialisés', *Banque et droit*, 1996, no. 48, p. 3). However, this bilateralisation does not make it immediately clear that the foreign financial instrument does not necessarily correspond to the French financial instrument.

[272] The authors of the Explanatory Report to the Hague Convention (Explanatory Report, nos. 4–48) put the difficulty in these terms: 'In the more complex (but more realistic) situation where the two accounts are governed by different laws but maintained by separate intermediaries, and where there is a chain of intermediaries between A's account and C's account, either A's intermediary or C's intermediary, or another intermediary standing between A and C, would bear a double liability (in the sense that its transfer to C would not relieve it of its continuing obligation to A) in the absence of provisions in its account agreements with the relevant account holder redistributing the risk of that double liability to the account holder or spreading it over all the *intermediary*'s account holders.' On this issue, see also M. Ooi, 'The Hague Securities Convention: a critical reading of the road map', *op. cit.*, pp. 484 et seq.

[273] For the options left to the intermediary, see Explanatory Report, no. Int-30, note 17.

of the account and thus to the triggering of the conflict rule by a credit. Thus, the Explanatory Report to the Hague Convention, after observing that the same translative transaction 'raises questions as to the law that governs the respective rights of different persons', states that 'the autonomous application of the Convention in respect of each securities account means that the rights of a person resulting from a credit of securities to a particular securities account will be governed by the law of the Convention determined in respect of that account'.[274] However, the European rules have a peculiarity: they do not even allow for the certainty of designating an applicable law.

II. The Shortcomings of the European Rules

European rules suffer from two different pathologies. The first is contingent and stems from the diversity of their sources. Depending on the origin of the conflict rule, it has a different scope of application and the area of the law designated varies (A). The second, more structural and more serious, lies in the criterion used, which is unable to designate a law with certainty (B).

A. Inconsistencies

694. Divergent scopes of application.[275] The Finality Directive justifies its existence by the will of the European legislator to reduce systemic risk and, to this end, establishes a rule in favour of European central banks and participants in payment and securities settlement systems.[276] The scope of application of Article 9(2) of the Finality Directive is limited due to the function of this directive: it relates only to systems.[277] It is first of all limited *rationae personae:* the collateral must be placed by a participant in a Finality Directive system,[278] towards another participant. It is also limited *rationae materiae*, on the one hand geographically because of the location of the relevant registry, and on the other hand because of the instruments involved. For the conflict rule to be applicable,

---

274 Explanatory Report, nos. 4–45.

275 On the substantive scope of application of these three rules, see *Impact Assessment*, p. 114 (the authors nevertheless mix the substantive scope of application of the conflict rule with the field of the designated law).

276 See already in this sense *Bernasconi Report*, p. 49.

277 On which see *supra*, para. 231.

278 Some authors have argued for a broader application of the conflict rule in Art. 9(2) of the Finality Directive, which would be independent of Art. 9(1), in view of which it was clearly conceived. The idea was to apply this conflict rule to all systems (and not only to the systems of the Finality Directive), as well as to indirect participants in these systems, see R. Potok, 'Legal certainty for securities held as collateral' (1999) *International financial review*, p. 12 and M. Ooi, *Shares and other securities in the conflict of laws, op. cit.*, no. 12.10.

the instrument registering the security must be located in a Member State.[279] The purpose of this limitation is to allow the conflict rule to designate only the law of a Member State.[280] Where one of these elements is missing, the conflict rule in Article 9(2) will not apply. Moreover, the instruments referred to are in fact not limited to securities. Indeed, contrary to appearances, the definition given by the Directive to the notion of security is made by reference to the entire section C of Annexe I of the MiFID. The latter includes all financial instruments, securities and contracts.[281]

695. The scope of application of the Financial Collateral Directive is precisely to extend the scope of application of the Finality Directive to all financial collateral, including that which is not concluded within a system, including if the account is not located within a Member State. Indeed, *rationae personae*, the Directive applies to financial institutions subject to prudential supervision, public authorities, central banks[282]; *rationae materiae* the financial collateral must be constituted by cash, financial instruments or credit claims,[283] and its proof must be in writing, i.e. any 'durable medium'.[284] Finally, the law designated is no longer limited to that of a Member State. The scope of application of the Winding-up Directive is similar to that of the Finality Directive in one respect: geographically, the designated law can only be that of a Member State. On the other hand, materially, the scope of the rule is limited to the effects of the reorganisation or winding up of the credit institution on the rights in rem of third parties in respect of financial instruments.[285] The latter are understood as those of MiFID.[286]

696. Divergent transpositions. The limited scope of application of these rules means that when an international situation does not fall within the scope of European rules, national rules will apply. This is all the more true since the difference in the scope of application of the directives is compounded by the difference in the scope of application of the transpositions, which may moreover

---

279 If it is in a third State, the rule will not apply, see M. Ooi, *Shares and other securities in the conflict of laws, op. cit.* On the uncertainties related to the scope of application of this rule, see the author's discussion, nos. 12.14 et seq.

280 This is one of the postulates of the bilateral conflict rule: in order to function, it must be applied within a community of law, and it is precisely the work of the directive to contribute to this by harmonising the substantive rules relating to the systems.

281 Art. 2(h) of the Finality Directive refers the definition of securities to the list established by Annex I Section C of the MiFID.

282 Art. 1(2) of the Financial Collateral Directive, transposed in Art. L. 211-36 of the Monetary and Financial Code.

283 Art. 1(4)(a) of the Financial Collateral Directive. It is not clear whether this embryonic definition of financial securities would cover financial contracts, but Art. L. 211-36 II° of the Monetary and Financial Code includes them.

284 Arts. 1(5) and 2(3) of the Financial Collateral Directive.

285 Art. 20(c) of the Winding-up Directive.

286 Art. 2 of the Winding-up Directive.

prove to be untrue.[287] From a material point of view, Member States have not always allowed all financial instruments listed in MiFID to be registered in a securities account.[288] However, registration in an account is a condition for falling within the scope of the conflict rule. As a result, the same financial instrument will be subject to the European conflict rule in State A, but will fall under the national conflict rule in State B. From the point of view of personal scope, some states have extended the scope of the Directives to natural persons and private investors. Finally, from a geographical point of view, some states have restricted the application of the rules of the Directives, either by excluding countries from the European Economic Area in the case of the Finality and Winding-up Directives, or by restricting the designated law to the laws of the Member States in the case of the Financial Collateral Directive.[289] In addition to these differences in scope, there are also differences in the scope of the designated law.

697. The heterogeneity of the field of applicable law. Within the Finality Directive, the scope of the designated law is unclear due to the elliptical nature of the provision, which applies the designated law to 'the determination of the rights of those entities as holders of the security interest in those securities'. It may be inferred that the designated law will govern the characterisation of rights arising from the security interest, the resolution of priority conflicts in the securities, and the rules of perfection of any transfer of ownership arising from the enforcement of the security interest.[290] Some authors believe that the law designated by Article 9(2) will extend to the regime of these interests in the event of insolvency.[291] It is known that collateral arrangements are traditionally at the crossroads of several laws: the *lex contractus*, applicable to the financial collateral arrangement, the law of the collateral – *lex situs* for tangible things, most often the *lex creationis* for intangible things – and, finally, the *lex concursus*,

---

287 See from the point of view of the Financial Collateral Directive, D. Robine and S. Praicheux, "Garanties Financières", *op. cit.*, no. 114.

288 Indeed, the Commission's impact study shows that while securities are registered in securities accounts in almost all Member States, this is not the case for other financial instruments, see the summary table in the *Impact Study*, pp. 117–118. From the point of view of French law, Art. 322-2 of the AMF General Regulation, when referring to custody account keeping, refers to 'the custody account service for financial instruments'. However, Ms Drummond considers that: 'Only financial securities take the form of a book entry in a securities account. When the asset is other, the activity does not fall under custody account keeping; it is then referred to as "position keeping" or "record keeping"', F. Drummond, *Droit financier*, *op. cit.*, no. 437.

289 *Impact assessment*, p. 120.

290 See already in this sense, see M. Vereecken, 'Reducing systemic risk in payment and securities settlement systems (1998) *Journal of financial regulation and compliance*, pp. 107 and seq., spec. p. 125; M. Ooi, *Shares and other securities in the conflict of laws*, *op. cit.*

291 M. Ooi, *Shares and other securities in the conflict of laws*, *op. cit.* The question appears less central since Art. 9(1) precisely restricts the effects of collective proceedings with regard to the holder of the security.

possibly applicable in the event of insolvency proceedings of the collateral taker or beneficiary. Of these three aspects, Article 9(2) of the Finality Directive seems to address only the second: the Finality Directive is not intended to interfere with the details of the parties' contractual arrangements; the validity of the contract will therefore be subject to the *lex contractus*. The scope of the rule under the Financial Collateral Directive merely clarifies the scope of the Finality Directive. Indeed, the designated law will apply both to the legal nature and proprietary effects of the collateral and to the requirements relating to 'the perfection of a financial collateral arrangement', which includes, inter alia, the modalities of its enforceability against third parties, conflicts of law relating to the financial instruments provided as collateral, and the enforcement of the collateral.[292]

In contrast, the scope of the conflict rule in the Winding-up Directive is particularly broad. Its function is to 'safeguard the confidence of third party purchasers in the contents of registers or accounts in respect of certain assets which are the subject of entries in those registers and accounts'.[293] Therefore, it applies beyond the sole issue of pledging financial securities to the entire proprietary status of securities. In fact, its scope extends to the contractual aspects of a transfer of securities: the validity of the disposition is subject to the law of the registry, account or custody system.[294] The narrow material scope of the Wingind-up Directive is thus matched by a broad scope of the designated law.

B. The Equivocal Interpretation of the Criterion Used

What the conflict rules have in common is that they have a particularly uncertain connecting factor (1) which leaves room for interpretation (2).

1. *The Ambiguity of the Criterion Used*

698. State of the difficulties. All the European rules have in common that they localise securities in order to designate the law applicable to their property status. To do this, the location criterion used is that of the account where the securities are registered. This criterion gives rise to several uncertainties. The first relates

292 Art. 9(2) of the Financial Collateral Directive.

293 Recital 29 of the Winding-up Directive.

294 It is therefore not surprising that the Winding-up Directive provides that reorganisation or winding-up measures do not affect security interests in property situated on the territory of another Member State, see Art. 21(1) of the Winding up Directive. The article has a broad understanding of the rights that may constitute such guarantees, see Art. 21(2) of the Winding up Directive. In other words, when the Winding-up Directive is euphemistic, its recital 26 specifies that it 'does not call into question the provisions of Directive 98/26/EC according to which insolvency proceedings must not have any effect on the enforceability of orders validly entered into a system, or on collateral provided for a system'. Far from calling into question the conflict rule of the Finality Directive, it expands its scope of application.

to the purpose of the localisation: it may be the account or the intermediary providing the securities account. The second uncertainty stems from the legal issue to be resolved. Indeed, the localisation of the security is most often done in order to designate the law applicable to the enforceability of a transfer, which implies several intermediaries and securities accounts; and the designation of the relevant account is neither clear nor intuitive. Finally, the location criterion itself is awkward[295] and above all uncertain.

699. Uncertainty as to the relevant intermediary in the case of a transfer of securities. Another difficulty lies in determining the relevant intermediary in the event of a transfer between several securities accounts. In reality, there are always at least two accounts at the time of the transfer, most often held by two different intermediaries: the transferor's and the transferee's. Let us take the example of a person who, in need of liquidity, takes out a loan and in exchange provides financial collateral in securities held in an account with his intermediary. In need of more liquidity, the person approaches another lender, registered in a separate legal order, which requests in exchange a financial collateral with transfer of ownership of the securities placed as collateral. The person complies. Which law will apply to priority, the law of the first or the second intermediary? The European conflict rules answer this question by the place of book entry, which makes the law applicable to the proprietary effects of the collateral depend on whether or not there is a transfer of the securities when they are given as collateral. Such an answer is however insufficient. It all depends on the book entry to be considered, between the one appearing before the transfer (in which case the transferor's account entry) or the one appearing after the transfer (i.e. the transferee's account entry). The rules of the Finality and Winding-up Directives do not provide an answer to this question. The Financial Collateral Directive provides a possible answer by defining the relevant account as: 'the account – which may be maintained by the collateral taker – in which the entries by which financial instruments are delivered as collateral to the collateral taker

---

295 The wording of the three rules, which seek to localise the account by attributing a location to it, is indeed awkward. The account would have deserved to be mentioned as a connecting factor if, following the example of American law, the intention had been to apply the law of the relevant securities account to the financial collateral regime. However, the European rules, by referring to the *location of* the account, choose an objective location approach to property law, which will therefore consist in locating the intermediary to whom the location of the account is attributed. Either the location is objective, and the intermediary providing the securities account maintenance service must be located, or the location is subjective, and the law of the account agreement must be applied to the proprietary status of the securities held in the account. There is no 'hybrid' route based on the artificial attribution of a status to an account.

are made'.[296] In the case of a transfer of collateral securities, the relevant account is that of the transferee's intermediary.

700. The tangle of criteria used. The criterion for determining the applicable law adopted by the European rules appears, at first sight, to be simple. It means, for example, that when a registered share held in France is pledged as collateral by a participant for the benefit of another participant in the system, French law will apply to the regime of the financial collateral granted, or to the effects of the reorganisation or winding-up measure as regards the rights in rem held by third parties; if the security is registered in a securities settlement system ('centralised deposit system'), the law of the system will apply. In both cases, there is in fact a unitary register. On the other hand, the third hypothesis, that of the 'account', is more ambiguous for two reasons.

701. First, the ubiquity of securities registrations poses two types of difficulties. The first is the multitude of securities accounts recording the security: there are as many book entries as there are intermediaries in the intermediation chain. The difficulty can, however, be resolved in light of the interpretation of the Financial Collateral Directive, which holds that the relevant account is the one where the securities are delivered as collateral, i.e. the ultimate securities account. The second is linked to the intertwining of the account criterion with the other two criteria. Indeed, a security is registered in a securities settlement system as well as in the securities account maintained by the intermediary for the ultimate account holder; similarly, when a registered security is 'administered', there will be an administration securities account and a register. As the authors of the Commission's impact assessment observe:

> 'The wording of the Finality and Winding-up Directives leaves open the question of which registry is relevant when the book entry is simultaneously recorded in a "registry, account, or central depository system".'[297]

The two difficulties mentioned are not symmetrically resolved. Where an administration account exists, it is generally considered to be a mere management tool and not a securities account, not only within the meaning

[296] Art. 2(1)(h) of the Financial Collateral Directive. This indeterminacy of the rule in the Finality Directive was noted by the ECB itself when asked about the Financial Collateral Directive: 'The ECB supports the establishment of legal certainty regarding the cross-border use of book-entry assets by introducing a single clear rule for determining the location of such assets, further developing and clarifying the principles in the Settlement Finality Directive.' See ECB Opinion CON/2001/13, para. 6.

[297] *Impact assessment*, p. 20.

of domestic law,[298] but also within the meaning of the conflict of laws rule.[299] Only the register of names counts. On the other hand, where a securities settlement system exists, the application of its law seems to be limited to the transfers of securities between the participants in the system, and not to the subsequent transfers within the intermediation chain, each of which is subject to its own law.[300] This interpretation is consistent with the logic of the PRIMA rule, which is to subject each transfer in the intermediation chain to its own law.

702. Secondly, the abstraction of the account raises another difficulty. The account is an abstraction materialised by an accounting system resulting from an account agreement,[301] subject to the law designated by this agreement. An account therefore has no geographical location, other than that of the computer servers on which it is registered. These servers will not always coincide with the intermediary providing the securities account maintenance service. However, it is easy to see that the location of the account held by the intermediary is not the same as the location of the technical means used to hold the account.[302] The focus should therefore be on the location of the account holder's immediate intermediary. However, the rule does not give any indication as to the criterion to be used to locate the intermediary. It is not overly critical to observe this, and to conclude that the rule adopted is profoundly clumsy: did not the Commission itself recognise that 'the conflict of laws provisions contained in the three directives do not clearly define how to determine the place where the securities account is located or maintained'[303]?

2. *The Possibilities of Interpretation*

703. The Commission's interpretation. The Commission wished to add to the Rome I Regulation a conflict-of-laws rule relating to the enforceability against third parties of the assignment of claims, making it subject to the law of the assignor's domicile. This proposal was accompanied by a Communication on

---

298 Ms Drummond thus considers that 'the activity of the service provider who administers a client's securities account can be considered as position keeping; he does not keep the securities, which are in the account opened by the issuer, but keeps a register', F. Drummond, *Droit financier*, *op. cit.*, no. 437.

299 This is, for example, what the Hague Securities Convention provides.

300 Otherwise, the securities account held for the ultimate holder would never be relevant, since in order to hold its client's assets, the custodian must open 'one or more accounts with the central depository, or […] with another custodian or a foreign entity with equivalent status' (Art. 322-3(2°) AMF General Regulation).

301 D.R. Martin, 'De l'idée de compte' in *Mélanges AEBDF-France II*, Banque éditeur, 1999, p. 285: 'Basically, the idea of an account evokes that of a table, in the form of an accounting diptych, where arithmetic values relating to the patrimonial situation of a given person are traced in credit and debit.'

302 See already in this sense, *Bernasconi Report*, p. 40.

303 *Communication from the Commission*, p. 5

the law applicable to the proprietary effects of securities transactions, preceded by an impact study on the conflict rule relating to the enforceability against third parties.[304] This Communication clarifies several elements. Firstly, the Commission states that, despite the different meanings used in the various translations of the Finality, Winding-up and Financial Collateral Directives, the terms used have an identical meaning.[305] Secondly, the Commission considers that the common basis of the law for the proprietary effects of a transfer of security is to be based on the *lex situs*, which was already retained in recital 8 of the Financial Collateral Directive. However, the Commission notes that:

> 'Many Member States, when transposing the provisions of the Settlement Finality Directive and the Winding-up Directive, have not included additional criteria in their national legislation that would prescribe how to determine the country where the account or register is located.'[306]

Moreover, where Member States have included criteria specifying the applicable law, these may lead to divergent results. The Commission specifies that three approaches are possible: the place where custody services are provided; the account agreement; the place of the usual activity of managing securities accounts according to the Hague Convention, i.e. the place where securities account entries, payments and securities transactions are monitored. However, of these three criteria, the one based on the account agreement appears to be incompatible with the text of the various directives.

704. Incompatibility of subjective criteria with the guidelines. It seems contradictory to want to rely on an objective approach to location while relying on the account agreement, a *fortiori* once it is observed that location is based on the rule derived from the *lex situs*. This statement deserves some elaboration on the relationship between the role of the will and the connecting factor of the *lex situs*. Indeed, some authors consider that the European approach would also result from a criterion based on will.[307] However, this perception seems to us to

304 The Committee preferred the Communication to legislative intervention because of the diversity of views on the criterion to be taken into account from both the Member States' and stakeholders' perspectives, see *Impact Assessment*, p. 69.

305 Indeed, in order to locate the securities account, the first two directives used the term "maintained", while the Financial Collateral Directive used the term 'located'

306 *Communication from the Commission*, p. 6.

307 Mr de Vauplane and Ms Bloch thus affirm that 'Community law links the choice of applicable law as resulting from the will of the parties to the existence of a securities account in the country of choice of law, an approach known as *PRACA* ("The Place of the Relevant Account Approach") as opposed to *PRIMA*', H. de Vauplane and P. Bloch, 'Applicable Law and Criteria for the Location of Multi-Intermediated Securities in the Hague Convention of 13 December 2002', *op. cit.*, no. 51. Such an approach can be claimed by the most eminent authors. Thus, Savigny himself considered that: 'This voluntary submission to a local law appears to us in different forms and to different degrees: sometimes one takes as a rule

stem from a confusion as to the role of the will in that it dictates human behaviour and constitutes the instrument of international connection. Thus, when a person *wishes* to acquire real estate, this is the result of his will; consequently, he *must* submit to the *lex situs*.[308] It is specious to say that this person wanted to submit to such a law: he had to submit, because he wanted to acquire. It is therefore not a difference in degree that distinguishes the will as a connecting factor from the application of a law localised by an objective criterion, but a difference in kind. If the European rules had been more ambiguous about the desired location, it might have been disputed that they were based on an objective approach, and one might have wanted to replace the approach taken with a subjective criterion based on the will of the parties. However, it is clear that the European rules are based on an objective locational approach. Therefore, a subjective interpretation of the chosen criterion, however obscure, constitutes a violation of the Directive.

705. It is therefore questionable to assert, as the European Commission does, that a transposition of the Directive that bases the proprietary effects of the transfer of securities on the law designated by the account agreement is valid. Similarly, the use of a legal identifier designating the entity providing the custodian account service among the different institutions of the custodian account holder does not appear to be consistent with the objective approach.[309] The authors of the impact assessment argue that this is simply a matter of defining the wording of the Finality Directive more clearly.[310] This is not the case: such a criterion actually amounts to subverting the *ratio legis*, since it leaves the choice of applicable law to the parties. Indeed, since the activity of custody account holder is most often carried out by companies established in several legal systems, it will be possible for the parties to designate the law of any of the countries in which the intermediary has an establishment. This is not the case for the other two criteria proposed by the Commission, which are similar: the place where custody services are provided, and the place where the monitoring

---

a given local law, while one could just as well choose another; this is what happens in particular in the field of obligations, where the freely chosen local law must be considered as an integral part of the contract. In other cases this voluntary submission results from the very acquisition of a right, for example, a person who acquires a building situated in the domain of a foreign law was free not to acquire it, but by the very fact of the acquisition, he accepts the local law which governs the building.' F.-C. von Savigny, *Traité de droit romain*, vol. VIII, *op. cit.*, p. 109.

308 See Savigny quote in previous note.

309 This solution was already proposed in the preparatory work of the Hague Conference, and has been the subject of attention in the doctrine, see for a recent analysis P. Paech, 'Conflict of Laws and Relational Rights', in *Intermediation and beyond*, *op. cit.*

310 Referring to the costs of such an approach, the authors of the impact assessment write:'The costs of compliance with this option are likely not to be excessive, given that it stays close to the current wording of the Financial Collateral Directive (the law of the state where the account is maintained) but defines this concept more clearly to avoid differing national interpretations.'

of securities account entries, the management of payments and securities transactions is carried out.[311]

706. The location of the provision of custody services. Custodial services consist of the monitoring of securities account entries, as well as the management of payments and securities transactions.[312] By locating the custodian by the service it provides, this criterion has the advantage of neutrality: the collateral taker is not, *a priori*, privileged compared to other creditors.[313] It also has the advantage of avoiding the pitfall of localisation by the intermediary's registered office when the service would in fact be provided by a branch present at the investor's domicile. The attractiveness of this criterion is undoubtedly increased because it corresponds to the subsidiary rule of the Hague Securities Convention, and has the possible advantage of international adherence.[314] However, it should be noted that the main rule of the Hague Convention is the freedom of choice of law; therefore, the subsidiary rule is based on the rule applicable to the location of *contracts*. Indeed, the provision of the securities account service corresponds precisely to the characteristic performance of the contract, for which the debtor is the intermediary.

However, this criterion is not suitable for the location of the securities account for the purpose of applying it to the proprietary effects of a securities transfer. Indeed, the place of supply of services is not apparent. It is difficult to know the country from which the securities are booked, or who handles the payments. Each of these operations can be carried out from any of the countries from which the intermediary operates: the account holder only needs a computer to carry out the provision of the service. This observation leads to a second difficulty: the place of supply of this service is not stable. It should be noted here that the conflict-of-laws rule in contractual matters is not based on the characteristic service, which is merely the means of identifying the party whose law is to be applied to the *place of* the debtor of that service.

707. The place of the intermediary's registered office. Under these conditions, it could probably be considered that the service of custody account keeping could be deemed to be provided at the intermediary's registered office. However, this criterion may appear artificial because of the liberalism that characterises the registered office today, which is not corrected here by an administrative

---

311 See already the criteria proposed by T. Cremers, 'La localisation d'un compte d'instruments financiers', *Banque et droit*, 2008, no. 119, pp. 11 et seq.

312 Art. 322-3 of the AMF General Regulations states that custody account keeping consists of: '1° Recording financial securities in a securities account in the name of the holder, i.e. recognising the holder's rights to said financial securities. […] 2° Holding the corresponding assets. […] 3° To process the events occurring in the life of the financial securities held in custody.'

313 It is in fact so by the simple fact that whenever the collateral taker transfers securities to its securities account, the localised intermediary will be its own, not that of the transferee.

314 See *infra*, paras. 711 et seq.

authorisation.[315] Indeed, EU law does not consider the activity of custody account holder as an investment service, but as a service ancillary to investment services.[316] As a result, the exclusive provision of a custody account-keeping service does not require specific authorisation. However, authorisation plays an important role in the stability of an intermediary's location, not only by requiring the overlapping of the registered office and the headquarters, but also because of the joint supervision exercised by the home authority and the host authority.[317] As a result, the registered office can only have a very remote connection with the legal relationship in question. Moreover, whenever the account maintenance service is provided by a branch, in particular one that may be active at the investor's domicile, the head office criterion will not allow for the actual localisation of the legal relationship.

708. Proposed solution. Consideration could be given to introducing a system similar to that developed by the EU for the location of investment services.[318] The intermediary would be located at its branch when it has established one at the investor's domicile and, in other cases, where it was acting under the freedom to provide services, it would be located at its registered office. In order to ensure the stability of the criterion, in particular in the case where the branch is subsequently closed, the moment of characterisation would be the moment of opening the securities account.[319] In order to give the criterion an even clearer appearance, a legal identifier would be included in the account agreement and will appear on the security of the securities account.

The solution can then be summarised as follows:

- as a matter of principle, the securities account is deemed to be maintained at the registered office of the account holder;
- by way of exception, if the intermediary has a branch in the legal order of the account holder at the time of opening the account, the account is deemed to be maintained at the place of that branch;
- the account keeper must record the designated law within a visible legal identifier on the securities account and in the account agreement.

Such an interpretative solution minimises the risk of artificiality of the connection retained, and gives it a certain permanence. In order to make it more apparent to third parties, the account holder should be obliged to

315 On the correction administered by the administrative authorisation to the jurisprudential interpretation of the freedom of establishment, see *supra*, paras. 81 et seq.

316 French law has nevertheless chosen to require an authorisation, see Art. L. 542-1 of the Monetary and Financial Code and, on this question, see F. Drummond, *Droit financier*, *op. cit.*, nos. 432–433.

317 See *supra*, para. 120.

318 See *supra*, para. 142.

319 This criterion is suggested by the impact study, but is not retained by the Commission. Indeed, the study considers that it is too far from international standards and requires a change in Member States' practice, see *Impact Assessment*, p. 64.

mention a legal identifier which would appear both in the various elements of the securities account and on the account agreement. On the other hand, the addition of an exception rule that would allow French law to be applied in contradiction with the objective criterion, for example based on the appearance of account keeping in another legal system, appears unreasonable from the point of view of legal certainty, unless it can be shown that the account holder had fraudulent intent.

However, the disadvantage of this solution is that it leaves the problem of a custodian acting exclusively under the freedom to provide services, i.e. without a branch, unresolved, while its registered office is artificially located in a legal system unrelated to securities account keeping.[320] This disadvantage can be tempered by the fact that, as already observed by Mr Cremers, 'the geographical location and service offering in a given market are part of the account holder's business strategy'.[321] In other words, an account holder wishing to develop a real clientele in a given place will establish a branch there. De *lege ferenda*, in order to perfect the criterion, it would be possible to subject custodian account holders to a separate authorisation, the justification for which would lie in the importance of this service for the protection of public credit, in particular because of the submission of an entire part of the patrimonial regime of the security to its location.[322]

§ 3. THE SUBJECTIVE APPROACH OF THE HAGUE CONVENTION

709. Introduction. The Hague Securities Convention is an international convention negotiated under the auspices of the Hague Conference, the negotiations of which ended on 13 December 2002.[323] It took several years for the text agreed upon by the Conference to be signed on 5 July 2006 by only two countries, the United States of America and Switzerland. On 24 April 2008, Mauritius also signed the Convention. However, such an instrument only enters into force when at least three countries have ratified it. While Switzerland and Mauritius did so quickly, the United States did not do so until 15 December 2016.

---

320 It does not seem advisable to use the criterion of solicitation, applying the law of the place of domicile, since this is in these conditions completely unforeseeable for third parties. Another solution has been proposed which would lead to the use of tax and accounting obligations as a means of identification, see C. Kessedjian and M. Germain, 'La loi applicable à certains droits sur des titres détenus auprès d'un intermédiaire', *RCDIP*, 2004, pp. 49 et seq.

321 T. Cremers, 'La localisation d'un compte d'instruments financiers', *op. cit.*, p. 16.

322 Such an authorisation would also make it possible to impose a sanction for the failure to record a legal identifier on each securities account, which could go as far as withdrawing the authorisation.

323 On the history of the negotiations, see Explanatory Report, no. int-6 et seq., pp. 5–7.

The European Union, following the ECB's advice on this point, never ratified the Convention.[324] Switzerland and the United States are two legal systems that have introduced *security entitlements* into their domestic law,[325] which largely explains their adherence to the conflict rules of the Convention. This Convention is also based on the PRIMA rule, except that it is a rule that is closer to the American modalities allowing the parties to extend the law applicable to their securities account agreement to the enforceability against third parties of a transfer.[326]

710. Rationale for the PRIMA rule within the Hague Convention. The application of the PRIMA rule to proprietary aspects is based on the desire to 'develop a new method that takes into account the existence of the indirect holding system and respects the legal principle that the law applicable to proprietary issues is the law of the place where the security is held and where, consequently, judgments relating to ownership are enforceable'.[327] Thus, the identification of the intermediary as a connecting factor stems from the fact that 'the books of the direct intermediary in which the entries relating to pledges or transfers of ownership by way of security are made play an essential role'.[328] This is why 'the location of the intermediary is the most likely 'location' of the pledged or transferred interest'.[329] This is also the reason why, according to the authors of the Convention, it does not matter 'whether *PRIMA* is merely an improved version of the *lex situs* principle in order to adapt it to the new market realities, or whether it should be considered as a new concept'.[330] The scope and coverage of the Convention will be examined first (I) before the connecting factor is explained (II).

I. Area and Scope

711. The domain of the designated law: the proprietary status of the security. The Hague Convention gives a broad scope to the law it designates through its Article 2(1) and applies to two distinct aspects of the proprietary status of the security.[331] First, this law governs the legal nature and effects, as against an intermediary, of rights resulting from the credit of securities to a securities

324 On the ECB's opinion, see *infra*, para. 724.

325 See *supra*, para. 672.

326 See *supra*, paras. 678 et seq.

327 *Bernasconi Report*, p. 29.

328 *Bernasconi Report*, p. 30.

329 *Ibid.*

330 *Ibid.* The author refers to Roy Goode, the chairman of the Conference's expert group, who preferred not to reason about the attribution of status to securities, see 'Oxford Colloquium on Collateral and Conflict of Laws', *op. cit.*, p. 27.

331 The Convention deals in the same article with its scope and its field of application. The two should nevertheless be distinguished. This seems to be an Anglo-Saxon practice, see C. Kessedjian and M. Germain, 'La loi applicable à certains droits sur des titres détenus auprès d'un intermédiaire', *op. cit.*

account or a transfer of securities held with an intermediary. Secondly, this law applies to the legal nature and effects against third parties of rights resulting from such a credit or transfer, including 'whether a person's interest in securities held with an intermediary has the effect of extinguishing or overriding the interest of another person'.[332] While the designated law is intended to deal broadly with the proprietary status of the security, it does not apply to the contractual aspects of the transfer, governed by the transfer agreement, nor to the contractual aspects of the relationship with the intermediary, governed by the securities account agreement.[333] In other words, the validity of the transfer agreement is subject to its own law, just like the securities account agreement between the client and his intermediary. Similarly, the Hague Convention excludes its own application to the relationship between the issuer, or the registrar, and the holder of the rights in the securities.[334]

The material scope of the Convention is limited to securities held with an intermediary.[335] This notion refers, according to the Convention, to 'the rights of an account holder resulting from the credit of securities to a securities account'.[336] The use of this concept is central to the Convention's operative provisions, not only because it determines the scope of application (A), but also because it constitutes the criterion for determining the applicable law (B).

A. The Material Scope of Application

712. Notion of securities and limitation of the material scope of application. The notion of securities held with an intermediary limits the scope of application of the Convention for two reasons: first, the nature of the securities and, second, the notion of intermediary. Indeed, the notion of securities held with an intermediary makes the Convention inapplicable to registered securities, or to securities that continue to be issued in paper form. In particular, when a *jumbo certificate* or a *global note* is issued, the initial relationship between the issuer and the central depository will therefore not be subject to the Convention.[337] Moreover, by basing the characterisation not on the relationship between the

---

[332] The wording is borrowed from the ECB, see ECB, *op. cit.*, no. 4.

[333] Art. 3(3)(a) and (b) HagueConvention; on the exclusion of contractual relationships arising out of the relationship between the account holder and its intermediary, see Explanatory Report, nos. 2-4 and 2-7: the law designated by the Convention 'does not cover issues such as the content and frequency of account statements, the standard of care to be exercised by the intermediary in the maintenance of securities accounts, the risk of loss, the cut-off time for the issuance of instructions and the like'. (*ibid.*)

[334] Art. 3(3)(c) Hague Securities Convention.

[335] Art. 2(1) Hague Securities Convention.

[336] Art. 1(f) Hague Securities Convention.

[337] As the authors of the Explanatory Report observe (no. I-16): the Convention 'does not apply to rights held directly from the issuer by a person who is the holder of securities registered in records maintained by or for the issuer who is the physical holder of certificates

intermediary and its client, but on the apparently technical, accounting and objective characterisation of 'credit of securities to a securities account', the notion of securities held with an intermediary makes it possible to disregard the national diversity of the characterisation adopted with respect to the legal nature of the security (ownership, co-ownership, contract, *sui generis* right…). Indeed, this nature will be determined by the law designated by the Convention.[338]

713. Risk of recharacterisation. This solves, *a priori*, the difficulty of characterising the disputed legal relationship. The latter could have rendered the use of the Convention in international relationships illusory because of the diversity of domestic characterisations of securities held by an intermediary for its client. Moreover, this unitary characterisation also allows the parties to foresee the risk of recharacterisation[339] to which certain securities transactions, and in particular repurchase agreements, are subject.[340] In international relations,[341] the issue will arise in practice where collective proceedings are initiated against

representing the securities. Thus, until the first credit of securities to a securities account, which brings them into the intermediated system, the Convention does not apply to those securities'.

It has already been seen that this may raise a difficulty as to whether the investor at the end of the chain can rely on the contract of issuance or the articles of association, since from the point of view of the issuer who has issued a paper security, the owner of the *negotia* issued is the person who owns the security, i.e. the central depository, see *supra*, para. 399.

338 Art. 2(a) of the Hague Securities Convention; see also Explanatory Report, nos. 2-5 and 2-12.

339 That is to say, the risk that the competent forum does not use the same characterisation as that of the parties to the transaction. On this risk, see J. Benjamin, 'Recharacterisation Risk and Conflict of Laws', in *Oxford Colloquium on Collateral and Conflict of Laws, Special Supplement to Butterworths Journal of International Banking and Financial Law*, September 1998, pp. 29–37, and R. Fentiman, 'Cross-Border Securities Collateral: Redefining Recharacterisation Risk', *ibid.*, pp. 38–46. The latter author considers that the notion of 'recharacterisation' improperly refers to the difficulty constituted by the divergence between the initial characterisation of the transaction by the parties and the subsequent characterisation by the forum; according to the author, this is essentially a conflict between a subjective characterisation (that of the parties) and an objective one (that of the Court), see *ibid.*, p. 39. In our view, such a presentation is misleading, since the so-called subjective characterisation will most often correspond to the one adopted by the contractual forum, and has been thought of as such. The risk of re-characterisation is linked to the particular competence of the *lex concursus* judge.

340 As M. Bernasconi writes: 'A *repurchase agreement*, also known as a repo, RP or buyback agreement, is a contract under which one party sells securities and agrees to buy back equivalent securities at a specified time and price. A repurchase agreement can be settled at different times: *intraday*, *overnight*, *open* or *forward*. In the first case, the transaction matures at the latest on the day it was concluded. A one-day repo matures on the day following the initial date of its conclusion. An open-ended repo has an indefinite maturity date, so either party can terminate the transaction at first request. A term repo matures on a fixed date longer than one day. Finally, a *reverse repo* is a repo from the buyer's perspective.' *Bernasconi Report*, pp. 6–7.

341 The risk of recharacterisation is not specific to international relations, but may arise in domestic law. It is simply less frequent there. See for recharacterisation of interests in English domestic law, J. Benjamin, 'Recharacterisation and conflict of laws', *op. cit.*, p. 31.

the collateral provider and the liquidator wishes to recover the collateral provided to the foreign collateral taker.[342] In such a case, the liquidator, in requesting the application of the law of the proceedings to the foreign collateral, will seek a recharacterisation as another collateral known to the *lex concursus*, the enforceability requirements of which will not have been complied with and which will therefore be unenforceable against the proceedings. The Convention does not eliminate the risk of re-characterisation, since it does not harmonise the substantive laws of the States Parties to the Convention, but by making the law designated to the transaction foreseeable, it allows the parties to anticipate the influence of the designated law on the contemplated transaction.[343]

714. Notion of intermediary and limitation of the material scope of application. The scope of application of the Convention is also limited by the concept of intermediary that it adopts, which 'means any person who, in the course of a business or other regular activity, maintains securities accounts for others or both for others and for its own account and acts in that capacity.[344] In order to remove any form of ambiguity, Article 1(3) of the Convention excludes from the notion of intermediary persons who act: '(a) as registrar or transfer agent of an issuer of securities or (b) (make) entries in their own books relating to securities held in a securities account maintained by an intermediary in the name of other persons for whom they are acting as manager, agent or otherwise in a purely administrative capacity.'

These two hypotheses concern the management of registered securities and therefore contribute to excluding their managers from the scope of application of the Convention.[345] On the other hand, the Convention aims to cover as broadly as possible all intermediation channels for bearer securities. It therefore explicitly includes within the notion of intermediary the central securities depository,[346] whether it acts as such or not,[347] 'in order to benefit from the legal certainty resulting from the Convention'[348]. However, central securities depositories have different roles in different jurisdictions: the provision is perfectly understandable for the US central securities depository, whose *nominee* is the first level of intermediation. It is less understandable for

342 See for an explanation of this case, *ibid.*
343 Explanatory Report, no. 2-19.
344 Art. 1(c) Hague Securities Convention.
345 In the first case, this means excluding the person who may have been mandated by the issuer to keep its register, in the second case, excluding the manager of administered registered securities accounts, see Explanatory Report, nos. I-33 to 35. See also C. Kessedjian and M. Germain, 'La loi applicable à certains droits sur des titres détenus auprès d'un intermédiaire', *op. cit.*, no. 14.
346 Art. 1(4) Hague Securities Convention.
347 For example, whenever it is registered as an intermediary in the accounts of a foreign custodian in order to give its members the benefit of ownership of foreign securities.
348 Explanatory Report, no. I-36.

the English and Irish central depository, *CREST*, which, although not a transfer agent, keeps the register of rights holders.[349] The situation can be compared with the issue accounts of the French central depository.[350] Therefore, when the 'books [of the system operator] constitute the primary record of the rights in such securities vis-à-vis the issuer', the Convention provides that 'the Contracting State under whose law those securities are constituted may, at any time, make a declaration that the person which operates that system shall not be an intermediary for the purposes of this Convention'.[351]

The notion of primary registration shows that the authors of the Convention have perceived the singularity of the pyramid structure of the intermediation chain. The equivalent of the primary registration, if any, is the jumbo certificate, or global note, held by the central depository. It is known that the relationship between the holder of the certificate and its issuer is also excluded from the Convention. This exclusion is explained by the primacy of the *lex creationis*. The Convention in fact only applies to reflections of the primary registration, and applies a new law to each new registration. It can already be seen here that it would have been a better method, rather than excluding the primary registration from the Convention, to extend its applicable law to all secondary registrations resulting from it in the mirror securities accounts.

715. Relationship of the Convention with the *lex concursus*. The Convention provides that the law designated by it will apply to all matters within its scope, to the extent that those matters 'relate to any event occurring prior to the commencement of these proceedings'.[352] However, the law designated by the Convention does not encroach on the scope of the *lex concursus*, which remains applicable to 'the ranking of categories of claim or the avoidance of a disposition as a preference or a transfer in fraud of creditors', and to 'the enforcement of rights after the opening of an insolvency proceeding'.[353] This rule, which preserves the validity of rights acquired prior to the insolvency proceedings by leaving them subject to the law under which they were constituted, is also the one retained by the European Insolvency Regulation.[354]

349 It is in contemplation of this particular custodian that the provision was adopted, see Explanatory Report, no. 1-37. On the *CREST* system, see M. Yates 'UK settlement', in M. Blair, G. Walker and S. Willey (eds.), *Financial Markets and Exchanges Law*, 2nd ed., Oxford, OUP, 2012, nos. 12.01 et seq.

350 See *supra*, para. 664.

351 Art. 1(5) Hague Securities Convention.

352 Art. 8(1) Hague Securities Convention.

353 Art. 8(2) Hague Securities Convention.

354 Art. 8 of the Insolvency Regulation.

B. Criteria for the Applicability of the Convention

716. The applicability of the Convention is triggered by the credit of securities to a securities account, which is functionally defined by the Convention as 'an account maintained by an intermediary to which securities may be credited or from which securities may be debited'.[355] The authors of the Explanatory Report consider that 'the term "securities account" should be interpreted broadly to include any form of book entry and transfer, *whether or not the operator designates it as an account*'.[356] By focusing on the account, the drafters of the Convention are forced to make the notion of credit to a securities account the trigger for the application of the Convention,[357] in particular in order to avoid the diversity of characterisations.[358] However, the credit to a securities account will not always have the same meaning depending on the account in question within the intermediation chain. Sometimes it is a simple accounting entry on behalf of its client in French law, sometimes it represents a right in the analysis of a chain of *trusts* in English law, and the very notion of credit to a securities account also presents, *in fine*, divergences in characterisation. These differences will resurface with each credit to the chain that arises from each transfer of a financial instrument in the contemporary system of indirect holding. The lack of a conceptual basis for the notion of credit, combined with the desire for a functional approach on the part of the authors of the Convention, is already showing its first limits here. As Dean Vedel wrote: 'Functional notions are generally destined to disappear by being absorbed at least in part into a higher synthesis of a conceptual nature.'[359]

II. Connecting Factor

717. Connection to the law chosen by the parties in the account agreement. The connecting factor used by the Hague Convention is the law designated for this purpose by the account agreement itself. The parties may therefore provide in the account agreement for the application of one law to all proprietary aspects of the Hague Convention security. This law does not have to be identical to the law chosen by the parties to govern the contractual aspects of the relationship between the account holder and his intermediary.[360] However, in the absence

---

355 Art. 1(b) Hague Securities Convention.
356 Explanatory Report, no. 1-6. Italics added.
357 See, *inter alia*, Explanatory Report, no. 2-3. The authors of the Explanatory Report make it clear that the Convention applies from the first credit to a securities account (no. 2-13).
358 See *supra*, para. 715.
359 G. Vedel, 'La juridiction compétente pour prévenir, faire cesser ou réparer la voie de fait administrative', *JCP G*, 1950, I, 851.
360 Even if no law is provided for the contractual aspects of the account agreement, the law designated to govern the proprietary aspects of the securities will apply, see Explanatory Report, no. 4-1.

of an explicit specification in the account agreement, the law applicable to the contractual aspects of the account agreement will then extend to the proprietary aspects governed by the Hague Convention.

718. Oversight of the choice made. The parties do not, however, have absolute freedom when choosing the law applicable to the proprietary aspects of book-entry securities. The parties still have to designate the law of a 'compliant' establishment,[361] i.e. an establishment whose activity is consistent with the purpose of the Convention. This is the main difference between the rule in the Convention and that in Article 8 of the *Uniform Commercial Code.* A place of business, within the meaning of the Hague Convention, means the 'place of business where one of the activities of the intermediary is carried on',[362] it being understood that it cannot be a temporary activity. However, the law designated by the parties must, at the time of the conclusion of the securities account agreement, comply with a condition relating to the status of the institution in order for it to be declared compliant. The Hague Convention provides for two possibilities.[363]

First, the parties may only designate the law of a State in which the intermediary has an establishment which, alternatively:

> 'i) effects or monitors entries to securities accounts;
>
> ii) administers payments or corporate actions relating to securities held with the intermediary; or
>
> iii) is otherwise engaged in a business or other regular activity of maintaining securities accounts'[364]

Each of the first two activities is relevant to the compliance of the institution whose law is designated. In particular, the Convention provides that an institution may be declared compliant if it carries out its securities account-keeping activity 'otherwise'. In order to avoid a liberal assessment of this third possibility, which would render illusory the limits within which the authors

361 The concept of 'compliant institution' does not appear in the Convention, but in the Explanatory Report, nos. 4-9 and 4-21 et seq. The compliance of the institution is assessed at the time of the conclusion of the account agreement: if it loses this status afterwards, this does not affect the validity of the choice of law made. Conversely, if the institution is not compliant at the time of the conclusion of the account agreement, but becomes compliant thereafter, the designated law will not be applicable and reference will have to be made to the subsidiary connections, see Explanatory Report, no. 4-27.

362 Art. 1(1)(j) Hague Securities Convention.

363 The alternative nature of these conditions is only mentioned in the explanatory report (no. 4-38).

364 Art. 4(1a) Hague Securities Convention.

of the Convention wished to place freedom of choice of law, the Hague Convention excludes certain elements which would be likely to retain an extensive conception of the activity of custodian-account keepers.[365]

Secondly, an institution is declared compliant if it can be 'identified by an account number, bank code, or other specific means of identification as maintaining securities accounts in that State'.[366] The first criterion aims at ensuring that the institution whose law is designated is actually engaged in the business of maintaining securities accounts and is not an artificial institution or one whose purpose is unrelated to the maintenance of securities accounts. The second criterion is designed to identify the precise institution designated by the account agreement. The most original aspect of the oversight is undoubtedly that it does not require a link between the securities account and the compliant institution. An institution may be compliant under Article 4 of the Convention even though it has no connection with the maintenance of the securities account designated by the account agreement.[367] This refusal to establish a link is justified, according to the authors of the explanatory report, by the multiplicity of institutions from which securities account maintenance operations can be carried out.[368]

719. Connecting factor in the absence of a choice. If no choice is made, or if the choice made does not comply with the conditions set out in the Convention, Article 5 provides for several cascading solutions which have in common that they are based on the location of the intermediary. The first solution is to apply the law of the institution with which the account agreement was concluded. To do so, the account agreement must be in writing and it must be 'expressly and unambiguously' clear[369] that the agreement was entered into with a particular institution of the relevant intermediary and that this institution is 'compliant'.

The second solution is to apply the law of the registered office of the intermediary.[370] Finally, if the intermediary is not a legal person, or does not have an organisation allowing it to locate its registered office, the third solution is to apply the law of the principal place of business of the intermediary at the time of the conclusion of the written account agreement, or, if there is

365 Art. 4(2) of the Hague Securities Convention.

366 Art. 4(1)(b) Hague Securities Convention.

367 This point is also made by the authors of the Explanatory Report, no. 4-23.

368 Explanatory Report, no. 4-24.

369 Art. 5(1) of the Hague Securities Convention. In order to assess the express character and the absence of ambiguity, the Convention specifies some of the elements that cannot be taken into consideration by the judge.

370 According to Art. 5(2) of the Hague Securities Convention: 'The law in force in the State [...] whose law governs the constitution or, failing that, the organisation of the relevant intermediary at the time of the conclusion of the written account agreement, or, in the absence of such an agreement, at the time of the opening of the securities account.' The use of the notion of organisation is intended to cover groups without legal personality, see Explanatory Report, no. 5-8.

none, at the time of the opening of the securities account.[371] In order to avoid the application of criteria not mentioned in the Convention, the Convention itself excludes certain elements, in particular the registered office of the issuer; the location of the certificate representing the securities; the location of the registry or of another intermediary than the relevant intermediary.[372] These last two approaches nevertheless lead to the following contradiction: the law of an establishment declared non-compliant under the principal connection may be applicable under the connection in the absence of a choice.[373]

720. Determining the relevant account in a transfer. However, when there is a transfer of securities, whether by reason of a sale, financial collateral or other securities transaction, at least two accounts are involved in the transaction. The Hague Convention invites to consider among them the 'relevant intermediary', i.e. the one designating within the chain the immediate intermediary of the client.[374] Both the transferor's and the transferee's agreement may be considered relevant. However, from the point of view of predictability of the applicable law, the law of the transferor is the one that appears most central to the transaction.[375] Despite its importance, the determination of the relevant intermediary, curiously, is not given by the Hague Convention. It is in the Explanatory Report that the solution, discussed in the application of the Convention to third party enforceability, appears[376]:

> 'When securities are transferred, the transferee's rights and all the other Article 2(1) issues, remain governed by the Convention law determined with respect to the transferor's securities account for so long as the securities are credited to that account, but once the securities are credited to the transferee's securities account, the transferee's rights, and all the other Article 2(1) issues, are governed by the Convention law determined with respect to the transferee's securities account.'[377]

In other words, when a security is transferred, the law applicable to its proprietary status is that of the transferee. Such a connection has the apparent advantage of simplicity. Indeed, the relevant securities account is very easy to locate for the transferee: it is the one on which the securities are registered.

---

371 Art. 5(3) Hague Securities Convention.
372 Art. 6 Hague Securities Convention.
373 This somewhat paradoxical solution is noted by the authors of the Explanatory Report, who are not moved by it, see Explanatory Report, no. 4-9.
374 Explanatory Report, no. I-17.
375 See in this sense our comments on the law applicable to the opposability to third parties of the contractual assignment of a claim, *supra*, paras. 584 et seq.
376 Or, in the words of Art. 2(e): 'The obligations, if any, of an intermediary to a person other than the account holder who asserts competing claims to securities held with that intermediary against the account holder or another person.'
377 Explanatory Report, no. 2-26. For an illustration with concrete hypotheses, see Explanatory Report nos. 4-12 to 4-51.

The transferee need only transfer the securities to an account subject to an applicable law whose perfection rule is favourable to it in order to ensure the ownership of the securities. Paradoxically, we find here a solution close to the one resulting from the *lex situs*.[378]

721. However, the authors of the Convention seem to have made an exception to this principle when the transfer of securities takes place between the securities account of a client and that of its own intermediary in favour of the latter. This is the case, which is common in practice, of an intermediary which is a credit institution acting both as custodian and as beneficiary of a financial collateral or pledge over its client's securities obtained in return for a loan. In which case, the Convention states that: 'a) that intermediary is the relevant intermediary; b) the account agreement between the account holder and that intermediary is the relevant account agreement; c) the securities account for the purposes of Article 5(2) and (3) is the securities account to which the securities are credited immediately before the disposition'.[379] In the case of a transfer of securities between the intermediary and its customer, the applicable law is that of the transferor. The authors of the Explanatory Report consider that 'this makes sense because it is the account holder's interest with its (lower-tier) intermediary and not the account held in the intermediary's books at the upper-tier that is pledged or transferred'.[380]

Without this provision, 'the fact that the disposition was recorded in an account maintained by the upper-tier intermediary might have led to the conclusion that this was the relevant intermediary and the account it maintained was the relevant account'.[381] The analysis is reminiscent of that of the French authors who make the securities account of the final investor the place of location of the securities, and are therefore faced with an aporia as soon as the securities account holder becomes the owner of the securities; this inevitably leads them to change their analysis in this case.[382] The drafters of the Convention are faced with a similar difficulty in private international law and are therefore forced to apply the law of the transferor, as the transferee's securities account plays no role in localisation. There is no reason for the

[378] On which see *supra*, paras. 643 et seq. Noting this already, M. Ooi, 'The Hague Securities Convention: a critical reading of the road map', *op. cit.*, pp. 475–476. The author nevertheless observes that the law of the location of the tangible object applies as the law applicable to the proprietary aspects of a disposition. In the case of securities, the transfer takes place when the securities are still in the transferor's securities account, whose law should therefore apply. One can only be surprised at the similarity of this solution, whereas the chairman of the group of experts who helped to draw up the Hague Convention, and author of the Explanatory Report, argued precisely that the PRIMA rule should be regarded as a connection quite distinct from the *lex situs*.

[379] Art. 4(3) Hague Securities Convention.

[380] Explanatory Report, no. 4-41.

[381] *Ibid.*

[382] See *supra*, note under para. 663.

duality of the conflict rules. It does, however, have the advantage of showing the overabundance of weaknesses in the connecting factor envisaged, that of a credit to a securities account.

III. Criticisms of the Subjective Approach

The Hague Convention approach is as open to criticism as the objective approach: the methodological impasse is identical, the dual application of the law of the transferee leads to the same defects and, above all, the effects of the multiplication of applicable laws are similar.[383] In addition to these inherent flaws of the PRIMA test, there are other flaws, identified by the ECB, which ultimately led to its rejection by the European Union.

722. The ECB's criticisms. As the Hague Convention affects the systems of the Finality Directive, the ECB was able to issue an opinion on the Convention.[384] The ECB criticised several aspects of the Convention, arguing that ratification of the Convention required a prior impact assessment of the Convention on Community and Member State legislation.

The ECB's first criticism relates to the Convention's influence on securities settlement systems. Indeed, the material scope of application of the Convention encompasses securities held within a system. The choice of law made by the Convention therefore leads to the application of different laws within the same securities settlement system. However, the ECB considers that 'the application of the laws of a multitude of legal systems within a system increases legal complexity and may affect systemic stability',[385] whereas the application of the law of the system ensures 'legal certainty and transparency" and precisely avoids "systemic risk'.[386] The main disadvantage of the multiplicity of applicable laws concerns the finality of the settlement.[387]

---

383 The Convention has nevertheless attracted some authors, A. Gaudemet, *Les dérivés*, *op. cit.*

384 On the relationship between the ECB and these systems see *supra*, para. 244.

385 ECB, cit., no. 10.

386 ECB, cit., no. 11.

387 As the ECB writes: 'If these laws are not harmonised, the effects of such diversity on settlement finality, in particular where the law(s) chosen in the account agreement do not offer protection comparable to that offered by the Settlement Finality Directive, are likely to undermine the soundness of the entire system and lead to systemic risks', *ibid.*
The Hague Conference, through the voice of those who prepared it, considers that the PRIMA criterion does not prevent the competent authorities from imposing the choice of law on operators, see H.C. Sigman and C Bernasconi, 'Myths about the Hague Convention debunked', *op. cit.*, It is clear that supervisory authorities are, in the exercise of their authority, free to prohibit intermediaries from choosing any governing law, or choosing a particular governing law, or choosing a governing law other than the law specified by the authority, or from taking any of these courses of action in a specified class of transactions.'
The ECB observes, however, that 'there can be no guarantee that this will in fact be the case if the Convention is signed and ratified', ECB, cit., no. 12.

The ECB's second criticism lies in the treatment of third party rights. In fact, the ECB makes two distinct criticisms here. First, the ECB regrets the disjunction produced by the Convention between the law applicable to the resolution of the priority conflict between third parties, and the court competent for the purposes of attachment and enforcement of securities. In practice, the law applicable to the priority of the seizing creditor's interest in the securities and the intermediary's obligations to that creditor will be determined by the law designated by the Convention.[388] However, this law will not coincide with the law of the connection and enforcement judge, which will, for example, be a source of difficulty in the case of statutory liens. Secondly, and more significantly, the ECB notes that it will be very difficult for third parties to know the law applicable to the proprietary status of the security,[389] and that this difficulty is increased by the choice of freedom of contract.[390]

The third criticism relates to the methodology of the Hague Conference, which is based on the harmonisation of the conflict of laws rule, whereas the ECB believes that it should also concern certain aspects of substantive law.[391]

The fourth criticism relates to the Convention's power to apply third-party laws on the basis of public policy or overriding public order. The ECB seems to consider that, contrary to what the authors of the report allege, the application of mandatory rules will not take place in 'situations of exceptional rarity',[392] but will take place whenever a securities settlement system is affected by a third party law if a State deems it necessary to protect its market infrastructure.[393] In the same vein, the ECB is concerned that various laws, the scope of which is excluded from the Hague Convention, and which make the location of securities a presupposition of their application, nevertheless interfere with the conflict rule laid down by the Hague Convention by instituting a location distinct from that provided for by the Convention.[394]

723. Criticism of the connection test. To these criticisms, all of which are correct, we must add one specific to the criterion used, which oscillates between freedom of contract and the reality test. The result is not convincing, precisely

388 Art. 2(1)((c) and d Hague Securities Convention.

389 ECB, cit., no. 14.

390 The ECB thus writes: 'Although it is not always easy for third parties to establish where their debtors' book-entry securities accounts are maintained under a conflict of laws regime based on the location of the account (sic), it follows from the Convention's regime of contractual freedom that the law applicable to book-entry securities for the purpose of exercising competing rights of third parties, for example by way of attachment, will depend on and vary according to the subjective criterion of the law chosen in the account agreement, which is often confidential, and the account agreement may even be amended so as to change that law (Article 7, paragraph 1, of the Convention)', *ibid.*

391 ECB, cit., no. 15.

392 Explanatory Report, no. 11-1.

393 ECB, cit., no. 16.

394 ECB, cit., no. 17.

because it calls into question the possibility of determining with certainty the law designated by the Convention. In order to be able to prove that the choice of law in the account agreement does not correspond to a compliant establishment, the third party would have to establish that the intermediary did not have a branch in the legal order whose law was selected. However, this proof is not only close to a negative proof, but also appears to be subject to various interpretations. Above all, the correlative application of a law that was not foreseen by the parties calls into question all the predictions based on this choice. If the legal policy is indeed to designate an apparent and stable law, it would have been better to choose a truly objective criterion.[395]

724. The possibility of a different interpretation. Ms Maisie Ooi considers that an interpretation other than the one adopted by the explanatory report is possible. Inspired by the changes in the English interpretation of the *lex situs*, she proposes to disregard the PRIMA rule and to apply the law of the transferor by displacing the characterisation.[396] This solution is far preferable to the one adopted by the Explanatory Report. We have already studied its advantages in relation to the assignment of claims, which can be transposed here[397]; it was observed at the time that its shortcoming lay in the instability of the criterion, since the applicable law will change with each transfer,[398] as it did when bearer securities were subject to lex situs. It is remarkable that the PRIMA criterion constitutes such a regression that one would be pleased to return to the less dizzying impasses of the rules of the direct holding system.

725. Theoretical aspects of private international law. The most interesting aspect of the Hague Convention is nevertheless to get rid, once and for all, of the cumbersome legacy of the *lex situs*. The selection of the law of autonomy corresponds to a long-standing proposal made by Professor Gaudemet-Tallon in his note under the *DIAC* judgment,[399] often taken up since,[400] and contributes to further extending the hold of the individual will on the connecting criteria of conflict of laws.[401] The subsidiary criterion chosen, which corresponds to the criterion of the domicile of the characteristic performance, will naturally appeal

395 See in this sense, our proposal *supra*, para. 584. Compare this criticism with that made by Mr Lequette on utilitarianism, see Y. Lequette, 'De l'utilitarisme dans le droit international privé conventionnel de la famille', *op. cit.*

396 M. Ooi, *Shares and other securities in the conflict of laws*, *op. cit.*; nos. 13.32 et seq.; M. Ooi, 'The Hague Securities Convention: a critical reading of the road map' *op. cit.*

397 See *supra*, paras. 584 et seq.

398 See *supra* for the disappointing results of this solution for negotiable instruments and paper-based bearer securities.

399 Civ. 1re, 8 July 1969, see B. Ancel, Y. Lequette, *Grands arrêt de la jurisprudence française de droit international privé*, *op. cit.*, no. 48.

400 See lastly, but in different terms, L. d'Avout, *Sur les solutions du conflit de lois en droit des biens*, *op. cit.*

401 D. Bureau, 'L'influence de la volonté individuelle sur les conflits de lois', in *L'avenir du droit - Mélanges en hommage à François Terré*, Paris, Dalloz, 1999, pp. 285 et seq.

to those who have already come out in favour of it.[402] However, we do not share the enthusiasm for these criteria.

The law of autonomy allows for effects that are at odds with some of the purposes of the ownership rules where the rights of third parties are central. This is why the hierarchy of priorities accorded to different creditors should not be left to the discretion of the parties, simply because there is, it seems, an overriding legal policy behind an order, and one that should not be altered by a choice of law. This legal policy is based on the reality that for a creditor the debtor is not the main adversary; the creditor's hell is the other creditors.[403] However, the law of autonomy makes it possible to select laws that simply give priority to the fastest creditor, or to the one who first appropriated the security. In addition, the application of the law of the transferee allows the transferee to easily override all third parties by transferring the disputed security to a securities account subject to a law giving priority to the first 'controlling' creditor.

The characteristic performance test has the advantage of objectivity. However, this criterion was developed in order to determine the law applicable to contractual relationships, the location of which was thought to be based on the socio-economic aspects of the contract, as determined by the characteristic performance.[404] However, the contractual relationships envisaged are most often bilateral and, when they are multilateral, they often proceed from a central party having contracted with a plurality of other parties. Relations with third parties are of a different order. Thus, behind the rule deciding a possible conflict of priority lies an ordering of the legitimacy of third parties. The legal centre of gravity of the relationship with third parties, if it were to be objective, would therefore not necessarily be linked to the characteristic performance of the contract. This is singularly not the case with the proprietary status of securities, whose legal centre of gravity is based on the system of settlement of securities to which they have been admitted. This is, moreover, the criterion used by the *lex concursus*, which the study will show could usefully be extended to the entire proprietary status of securities.

726. Conclusion of the section. In intermediation-based systems, the thesis of the plurality of connections leads to even more disastrous results than when securities were materialised on paper. The proposed solutions are not only out

---

402 S. LAVAL, *Le tiers et le contrat*, *op. cit.*, no. 56.

403 As has been written: 'The purpose of the security interest is not to invest its holder with all or part of the utilities of the encumbered asset, but rather to protect him against the patrimonial loss that could result from the debtor's default, by shifting the burden of his insolvency onto the assets of his other creditors and successors.' C. GIJSBERS, *Sûretés réelles et droit des biens*, Paris, Economica, 2015, no. 19.

404 See in particular the account given by Mr Lequette on the hesitations on the connecting factor in contractual matters, Y. LEQUETTE, '*Les mutations du droit international privé: vers un changement de paradigme?*', *op. cit.*

of step with the holding structure, which gives a central place to the accounts of the central depository, but are in fact likely to make the transfer of securities difficult by imposing the cumulative compliance with an incalculable number of laws whose application is difficult to predict. In addition, the criterion used in European law is notoriously obscure; the determination of the relevant account would benefit from being inspired by the solutions known in European investment services law.

727. Conclusion of the chapter. The thesis of the plurality of connections leads to results as unfortunate in the area of financial securities as those already observed in the law of negotiable instruments. Its fundamental flaw is that it multiplies the laws applicable to the transfer, whereas it would be appropriate, on the contrary, to provide for the application of a single law that is objective, predictable and has a strong link with the security. The thesis of the plurality of connections was based on an undue extension of the lex situs in order to justify its application to the law of bearer securities, leading to the paradoxical result of making the transfer of securities difficult in the international order. Transposed to situations where securities are book-entry securities within intermediation systems, the plurality of connections thesis leads to even more unsatisfactory results through the cumulative application of a prohibitive number of laws to the transfer, in addition to relying on inconsistent and deeply dysfunctional conflict rules.

CHAPTER 3
PROPOSAL FOR A UNITARY SOLUTION TO THE CONFLICT OF LAWS

728. The preceding discussion has shown the impasse to which the plural connection of the proprietary status of bearer securities leads. A unitary solution to the conflict of laws is desirable. It already exists in the law of registered securities: it is the law of the issuer, which would benefit from being extended to securities registered within a blockchain (Section 1). In fact, a unitary solution already exists for book-entry securities within a chain of intermediaries. This is the law of the securities settlement system, applicable to the proprietary status of securities held by the insolvent participant. It will be shown here that this connecting factor to the law of the securities settlement system should be generalised to all bearer securities registered in the accounts of a central depository (Section 2).

SECTION 1. THE CONNECTION TO THE LAW OF THE ISSUER OF REGISTERED SECURITIES

The proprietary status of registered securities has always been subject to a single law: the *lex societatis*. The solution, which originated from academics, nevertheless remains ambiguous today as to the jurisdiction of the *lex societatis* in the event of dissociation between the place where the register is kept and the registered office of the company. It seems to us that this difficulty can be resolved by relying on the objective of the registered form in French law, which dictates the application of the *lex societatis*, independently of the location of the possible registrar (§ 1). The appearance of securities registered on a blockchain extends to the possible modes of representation of registered securities, without changing the function assigned to the registered form or the solutions it promotes (§ 2).

§ 1. SOLUTIONS ARISING FROM THE LAW APPLICABLE TO REGISTERED SECURITIES

729. It has already been observed that French law allows a foreign law to be applied to the form of securities.[1] It was then observed that if the issuer's law is sovereign as to the characterisation of the form it intends to impose on the securities issued by the companies it governs, this sovereignty allows, at least in French law, the election of a third law – that of the *negotium* – to the form assumed by the claim in question. Thus, a French company should be able to submit the claims it issues to a form governed by American law, to which the issue contract would also be subject. Such a choice of law makes it possible to recreate the legislative unity of the *negotium* and the *instrumentum*, subject to the prohibitive rules relating to the terms of the issue, which remain subject to the law of the issuer. The question studied here is different and consists of examining, for securities issued by French companies and subject to French forms – registered or bearer –, the scope of this choice of form from the point of view of the law applicable to their proprietary status. The dysfunction resulting from the bearer form has already been studied. It remains to observe the consequences of the nominative form from the point of view of the applicable law. It will first be shown that the French *lex societatis*, when it proposes or imposes the registered form, then also dictates its application to the proprietary status of the shares (I). This solution should be extended to the localisation of registered shares in the context of the insolvency of the holder (II).

I. *The* Lex Societatis *Rule*

730. At first glance, one might wonder how the transfer of registered shares could give rise to any conflict of laws or jurisdictions. Article L. 211-3 of the Monetary and Financial Code clearly states that the issuer must keep the share register itself when the shares are registered. In this case, there can be no doubt: the law of the issuer applies to the ownership of registered shares. This law will apply to the enforceability against third parties of any transfer, seizure or pledges to which the registered share may be subject. The solution is all the more clear since, in this case, all the material acts of enforcement will take place with the issuer;[2] it is the issuer who will be liable for the causes of the seizure if he does not comply with the enforcement measures.[3] In other words, there is here a

[1] See *supra*, paras. 291 et seq.

[2] Art. L. 211-20 of the Monetary and Financial Code; Art. R. 211-2 of the Code of Civil Enforcement Procedures.

[3] Art. L. 123-1 of the Code of Civil Enforcement Procedures states that a third party who evades the obligations to which he is legally bound by law 'may be compelled to fulfil them, if necessary under penalty of a fine, without prejudice to damages', but may also 'be ordered to pay the causes of the seizure, unless recourse is taken against the debtor'.

welcome convergence of the law applicable to the property regime and the law applicable to the modalities of its enforcement.

However, the solution is less obvious in the event that the issuer has 'entrusted the keeping of the register which is its responsibility'[4] to an agent, who may be located abroad. This freedom offered by the legislator makes it possible to refine the understanding of contemporary French law (A) Indeed, the solutions to the conflict of laws are still today of case law and academic origin and were developed at a time when the regime attached to the form of securities was different. However, the objective pursued by company law today, when it imposes the registered form, unambiguously militates in favour of the application of the *lex societatis*, irrespective of the place where the register is kept (B).

A. The Regime Attached to the Form of the Securities

731. Rationale for the contemporary regime. The form of the shares has long had a determining influence on the terms of their transfer.[5] If the share was a bearer share, Article 2276 of the Civil Code protected the purchaser in good faith; if the share was a registered share, the ordinary law of sale applied: the existence of a defect in the chain of transmission of the share was likely to cancel successive transfers by application of the *nemo plus juris* rule. This era is now over: all shares issued by *sociétés par actions* (i.e. the majority of limited companies) are securities, regardless of the form they take.[6] Now, shares all benefit from the negotiability regime by virtue of Articles L. 211-15 and L. 211-16 of the Monetary and Financial Code, i.e. they offer the considerable advantage for the purchaser in good faith of purging the defects that could affect the ownership of their author.

With these provisions, the Monetary and Financial Code settles a question traditionally devolved to property law: that of knowing who to favour between the dispossessed owner or the purchaser in good faith. The answer provided by civil law is based on a distinction between movable and immovable property; it was conceived in a social and economic context in which immovable property

4 Art. R. 211-3 of the Monetary and Financial Code.

5 H. Synvet, 'La propriété des valeurs mobilières en droit français', in *20 ans de dématérialisation des titres en France*, Paris, Revue banque édition, 2005, pp. 37 et seq.

6 Art. L. 228-1 of the Commercial Code. The implication of the former was that the holder of a bearer security registered in an account could have his ownership challenged because of the nullity of any contract in the chain of transmission. This consequence of the application of civil law was all the more distressing because the search for the origin of ownership of the security is impossible for the future purchaser and, as Professor Paul Didier puts it: 'It would be an obstacle to any stock market if it were made necessary in securities trading. Thus, since they first appeared, securities have been considered, like tangible movables, as negotiable rights, i.e. as rights that escape the *nemo plus juris* rule.' P. Didier, *Droit commercial*, t. 3, Paris, PUF, 1999, pp. 132–133.

constituted a singularly important class of property from both the symbolic and pecuniary points of view.[7] In these circumstances, it appeared as if the *bona fide* purchaser was protected in transactions involving low-value property, while in truly significant property the *verus dominus* took precedence over the purchaser, even if he was bona fide.[8] In fact, historical studies show that regardless of the value of the property, security of transactions was already central to the protection of the purchaser in the old law, at least in some traditions; as a result, the action for recovery of property, where possible, was nevertheless difficult to enforce.[9]

This means that the advent of joint-stock companies and the considerable importance of such wealth has not given Article 2276 of the Civil Code a truly new *ratio legis*: when it applied to bearer securities materialised on a paper medium, the protection of purchasers in good faith was always aimed at the speed and security of transactions, including for certain goods of considerable value.[10] The relevant criterion justifying the protection of purchasers in good faith is therefore no longer the d of the property in question, but the pragmatism of the solutions[11] in the face of what constitutes for some authors the very social utility of movable property: its circulation.[12] The economic policy inherent in this legal function is nevertheless, as is often the case in civil relations, limited by a rule with a moral basis: only the purchaser in *good faith*[13] may avail himself of acquisition *a non domino*. This limitation of the scope of the rule, which assigns it an evidential and not an acquisitive function,[14] has three consequences.

First, proof of bad faith on the part of the third-party purchaser may remove the presumption established by Article L. 211-16 of the Monetary

---

7 J.-L. Halpérin, *Histoire du droit des biens*, Paris, Economica, 2008, pp. 90 et seq.

8 It should be noted in this respect that in certain traditions, the old law sometimes considered, from the point of view of their transmission, shares in companies as real estate without it being known whether this was because of the size of the company's share or the company's object (see the example of the Toulouse mills reported by J.-L. Halpérin, *Histoire du droit des biens*, *op. cit.*)

9 On the nuanced history of the conditions of the property claim, *ibid.*, pp. 102–103.

10 The contentious issue was, it seems, not so much the application of these rules designed for tangible movables, but rather the qualification of the shares, which varied between a share of a co-ownership, that of the capital, and a right of claim against the company. This means that the contemporary qualification of shares in UCIs has ancient roots...

11 The expression is used by *Histoire du droit des biens*, *op. cit.* p. 103.

12 'Circulation is to furniture what productivity is to real estate: the basis of its social utility.' A.-M. Patault, *Introduction historique au droit des biens*, Paris, PUF, 1989, no. 246, p. 291.

13 As has been written, 'when the owner is divested by theft (or loss), the requirements of trade bow to public policy' (A.-M. Patault, *Introduction historique au droit des biens*, *op. cit.*, p. 292). We find here the traditional dialectic of morality and economics in the basis of the rules governing relations between private persons, see M. Fabre-Magnan, *De l'obligation d'information dans les contrats*, *op. cit.*

14 P. Berlioz, 'La cession des droits sociaux', *Revue des sociétés*, 2015, pp. 14 et seq.

and Financial Code and allow the share to be claimed under the conditions of ordinary law. In the event of successive transfers of the same registered share, such a mechanism will allow, for example, the first transferee to obtain ownership of the share even if the registration of the third-party purchaser in bad faith has already taken place. The *verus dominus* can therefore always prevail over the acquirer *a non domino*. Secondly, the evidentiary function of Article L. 211-16 of the Monetary and Financial Code also explains why, in the event of the disappearance of the register, the ordinary law of proof of ownership applies again.[15] Thirdly, the presumption of Article L. 211-16 of the Monetary and Financial Code is irrebuttable only with respect to third parties acting in good faith; the registered person benefits only from a simple presumption with respect to its author, and without any impact on the possible defect affecting not the ownership of the share, but the prerogatives attached to it by the issuer.[16]

This, in a nutshell, is the legal policy of the French legislator. Its balance lies between the objective of guaranteeing the security and speed of transactions relating to securities, and the need not to grant undue protection to purchasers in bad faith. Although property law shows here, as in the past, its concern for third parties, the real justification for the solution adopted is nevertheless to be found outside of it: it is closely linked to the singularity of shares from joint-stock company ('*action*') in the field of particular assets that are company shares ('*parts sociales*'), and shows in certain respects the perenniality of the distinction between partnership ('*société de personnes*') and capital companies ('*société de capitaux*').[17] Indeed, the rule previously attached to registered shares was that of partnerships, whose shares are not negotiable, precisely because the person of the partner takes precedence. On the other hand, the transfer of shares should be facilitated in capital companies, regardless of their form, since the quality of the contribution takes precedence over that of the partner.[18]

732. The continued importance of the form of securities. However, it would be misleading to think that the form of registered shares no longer has any positive influence: it still leads to the application of a specific system for their administration. In the case of registered shares, it is the issuer's responsibility

15 Cass. com., 5 May 2009, pourvoi no. 08-18.165. The decision was handed down under the pre-2004 legislation; the solution it promotes should not be altered by the new provisions.

16 Art. L. 228-28 Commercial Code: failure to pay up the contribution is enforceable against the transferee. On this question, see F. Drummond, *Droit financier*, *op. cit.*

17 It has been observed that it was eroding as the distinction between types of company became less clear, D. Bureau, 'L'altération des types sociétaires' in *Mélanges en l'honneur de Paul Didier*, Paris, Economica, 2008, pp. 57 et seq.

18 Regretting this division of the modalities of the transfer of membership rights between partnerships and others, M. Caffin-Moi, *Cession de droits sociaux et droit des contrats*, Paris, Economica, 2009, pp. 212 et seq.

to keep the register in which the registered shares are represented[19] by book entry.[20] Article R. 211-3 of the Monetary and Financial Code nevertheless allows the issuer to entrust the keeping of this register to an agent. In this case, the legislator does not restrict the mandate to professionals who manage securities accounts. It may be, for example, another company, which is a 'frequent case in groups'.[21] Nor does the legislator restrict it in terms of space: the agent may be established abroad. Whether the shares are registered in a register kept by the issuer or its agent, they are said to be 'pure' registered shares: there is only one element contributing to the possession of the share, the registration in the register.

Nevertheless, it is possible, especially when neither the law nor the issuer imposes the method of holding the share, that the holder of registered shares decides to use an administration account held by an intermediary.[22] In this case, the registered shares are said to be "administered" in the sense that they benefit from an administration account through which the shareholder can exercise his transfer orders. However, the shareholder will only be able to exercise his orders through this medium, giving it a possessory function without it being a determining factor in the ownership of the share: only the entry in the register kept by the issuer or its agent[23] is authentic. The aim is to bring the status of administration accounts for registered shares closer to that of securities accounts for bearer shares. Indeed, the presence of an administration account is frequent when registered shares are admitted to trading on a financial market. In such cases, there may be a time lag between trading on

[19] The issuer, when it has made a public offering, acquires the status of custodian, see Art. L. 542-1 of the Monetary and Financial Code and Art. 322-49-1 of the AMF General Regulation.

[20] The register in question is the one that the issuer must keep on the basis of Art. L. 211-3 of the Monetary and Financial Code, which records the registration of the registered share in a securities account. This is not the register of securities movements. In the event of a discrepancy between these two registers, i.e. if the securities account register is not updated in relation to the securities movement register, academics divided on which register is authentic. Professor Drummond considers that the letter of Art. L. 211-17 of the Monetary and Financial Code does not allow the register of securities movements to be considered authentic (F. Drummond, *Droit financier*, *op. cit.*, no. 282), while the ANSA (ANSA, Comité juridique, 7 February 2018, no. 18-007) and Professor Coupet give the shareholder's entry in the register of share movements a greater scope (C. Coupet, 'Société par actions – Notion d'inscription en compte et transfert de propriété', *Dr. Sociétés*, October 2018, comm. 169).

[21] *Sociétés commerciales*, Memento Series, Brussels, Ed. Francis Lefebvre, 2022, no. 62240.

[22] Art. L. 211-6 of the Monetary and Financial Code. On this option, see F. Drummond, *Droit financier*, *op. cit.*, no. 277.

[23] This reality is sometimes obscured by Art. R. 232-3 of the Code of Civil Enforcement Procedure, according to which: 'If the holder of registered securities has entrusted an authorised intermediary with the management of his account, the is carried out with the latter.' The explanation is that the here is only of the securities account to which the holder has access, see *supra*, para. 656. For a detailed analysis from a property law perspective, see V. Malassigné, *Les titres représentatifs*, *op. cit.*

the market and the transfer of ownership resulting from the transmission of the transfer form by the seller's custodian to the central depository and then to the issuer. Such a time lag may create significant difficulties, especially when a general meeting is in preparation and the purchaser, who is not registered until the seller's transfer form reaches the issuer, cannot be considered as a shareholder.[24]

In the case of bearer shares, on the other hand, an intermediation regime is necessarily put in place whereby the holder only possesses its shares through a securities account held by a custodian.[25] This difference has consequences, for example, as to who is required to contribute to the realisation of the security interest, or the actual basis of the security interest. Indeed, in the case of registered shares, the addressee of the notification of the pledge is the issuer or its agent, whereas in the case of bearer shares, it is the custodian account holder. Above all, the basis of the security interest is not quite the same: in the case of registered shares, it is unquestionably the share that is the subject of the pledge,[26] whereas in the case of bearer shares, it is apparently the securities account that is encumbered.[27] Even today, the form of shares is therefore not entirely irrelevant to certain aspects of their proprietary regime.

Nevertheless, it is from the point of view of private international law that the form of securities obtains the most remarkable elements of regimes. Indeed, when it comes to determining the law applicable to the proprietary aspects of shares, the conflict of laws solutions still diverge, as in the past, depending on whether registered or bearer shares are involved. Although the form of the securities constitutes a criterion of distinction here, the permanence of which may appear, at first sight, to be in contrast with its relevance, this difference is in fact explained by the asymmetry of the mode of administration of securities according to their form and the importance that these modalities have in the perspective of property law. Bearer securities have already been studied, with the dysfunctions noted. We would now like to give an account of private international law solutions for registered shares at a time when the legislation governing them is also changing. On the one hand, the legislator allows limited companies to entrust the keeping of their register to a foreign agent in a context where book entry has now become a central element of the opposability of the transfer of shares to third parties. In addition, the legislator

24 A. Gaudemet, 'Comptabilité des titres financiers en rétention et droit de participer aux assemblées générales d'actionnaires', *Bull. Joly. Sociétés*, June 2020, pp. 6 et seq. The author stresses the need to force the seller's custodian to send the registered form in order to obtain an effective transfer of ownership.

25 See *supra*; para. 656.

26 On this point, we refer to the well-known demonstration of H. Synvet, 'L'objet du gage du compte d'instruments financiers' in *Études offertes à Jacques Béguin*, Paris, Litec, 2005, pp. 719 et seq.

27 Although the solution is not consistent, see *ibid.*

now allows registered shares to be represented by registration in a blockchain. Can these legislative developments have an influence on the solution of the conflict of laws? The answer is no, but leads to a review of the basis for the application of the *lex societatis*.

B. The Application of the *Lex Societatis*

For a long time, it was thought that the form of securities was exclusively linked to the transfer of ownership that it entailed. Private international law has therefore made this difference in regime the cornerstone of the solution to the conflict of laws. Today, it is easier to see the futility of this reasoning because of the identity of the transfer regimes and the permanence of the duality between registered and bearer forms. Fundamentally, this reasoning is hampered above all by ignorance of the objective pursued by French company law when it imposes the registered or bearer form, which dictates, in our view, the application of the *lex societatis* to the registered share (1). If there is any doubt as to the applicability of the *lex societatis* to registered shares in the event that the register is entrusted to a foreign agent, it is less because of property law than because of the law of enforcement; the latter is nevertheless not an obstacle to the exclusivity of the *lex societatis* in this area (2).

1. *The Reasons for the Application of the* Lex Societatis

733. The traditional reasoning. The idea that the way in which one conceives the transfer of ownership of shares was decisive for the solution of the conflict of laws was very clearly formulated by professors Loussouarn and Bredin.[28] These authors considered that the consensual conception of the transfer of ownership of registered shares made it impossible to set up a register of transfers outside the registered office, since the formalities necessary to make the transfer effective against third parties had to be carried out at the time at the debtor's domicile.[29] Therefore, 'the courts of the country in which the register of transfers was established must bow to the requirements of the *lex societatis* and consider the establishment of the register of transfers as null and void'.[30] If, on the other hand, the *lex societatis* had had an autonomous conception of transfer and allowed for the dissociation of the contract of assignment from the transfer of ownership, and the country of the register of transfer also, 'the law applicable to the transfer of securities would be that of the country in whose

[28] J.-D. Bredin and Y. Loussouarn, *Droit du commerce international*, Paris, Sirey, 1969, no. 350.

[29] *Ibid.*

[30] *Ibid.*

territory the transfer office was established'.[31] In relation to current legislation, this perception of the conflict of laws has a very clear consequence: the transfer of registered shares, whether pure or administered, is subject to the law of the place where the registrar has its registered office.[32]

This analysis deserves to be discussed. The authors seem to draw an analogy between the mechanism in force for bearer securities – the transfer took place by the handing-over of the security – and the mechanism for registered shares – the opposability of the transfer took place by the fulfilment of the formalities of Article 1690 of the Civil Code, which are carried out at the debtor's registered office. In their minds, it was as if, in the same way as the share, when stipulated as a bearer share, was 'incorporated' into the security and subject to Article 2276 of the Civil Code in the domestic order, and to the *lex rei sitae* in international relations, the law applicable to the transfer of registered shares should also be determined according to the terms and conditions of the transfer of ownership. However, it is not enough for the terms of the transfer of ownership to change for the connecting factor to be altered. On the one hand, because of the position of the problem, which gives a singular jurisdiction to company law as the law presiding over both the creation of the right in question and determining the forms it may take.[33] On the other hand, by focusing on the mechanism of transfer of ownership rather than on the objective pursued by company law when it allows or imposes certain forms on the shares issued by the entities it governs, the analysis in question ignores, in our view, the decisive aspects of the selection of the relevant criterion and confines itself to elements of its implementation.

734. From a corporate law perspective. It will be recalled here that the ownership of shares is fundamentally governed by company law, simply because it determines membership of a corporate body. French conflict of laws law thus holds that the *lex societatis* alone is competent to attribute shareholder

31 *Ibid.* The authors note, however, that Batiffol seemed to rule out the jurisdiction of the law of the country where the company had established a register of transfer, since he wrote: 'Since the transfer must necessarily obey, in substance, the law governing the title, its formalism, i.e. the link between substance and form, prevents the *locus regit actum* rule from being taken into account, which is optional, in the exceptional case, no doubt, that the register is not kept in the country whose law governs the title.'

32 The property status of 'administered' registered shares, i.e. those for which an administration account has been set up, would not really change. Indeed, in this case, the decisive proof of ownership is the entry in the register held by the issuer or the agent to whom it has been entrusted. The administration account maintained by the intermediary, while it has an impact on certain procedures for the creation of security interests or attachments under French law because of the possessory effect attached to it, will not prevail over the register. See A. Gaudemet, 'Comptabilité des titres financiers en rétention et droit de participer aux assemblées générales d'actionnaires', *op. cit.*

33 See *supra*, paras. 291 et seq.

status.[34] The solution is easily explained: the status of shareholder is central to determining the persons authorised to participate in the AGM, the central organ of the functioning of French companies. The jurisdiction of the *lex societatis* does not mean that the *lex societatis* is insusceptible of designating the law of another State, better placed, to recognise its shareholders. This is well known to be the case for bearer securities.[35] However, it is not certain that the analogy with bearer securities is convincing here, because of the different functions attached to each form.

The original purpose of the bearer form was to facilitate the circulation of the represented security, and this function is still relevant today. In the past, it was manifested by the submission of paper securities to the former Article 2279 of the Civil Code and the submission of the latter to the law of the place where the paper evidencing the action is located. Today, one might question the permanence of this function given that registered shares are subject to the same transmission regime as bearer shares. However, the identity of the transfer mechanism is only intended to unify the regime of corporations;[36] the two forms retain their singularity because of their mode of administration and the regime attached to it.

The bearer form can, in principle, only be used when the company wishes to admit its securities to a financial market.[37] Indeed, in this case, the French company will have to admit its securities 'to the operations of a central depository', and such admission, when the securities are traded on a financial market, presupposes that at least part of the securities in question have been stipulated in bearer form. By this decision, the French company necessarily leaves to another entity the task of recognising, if not its shareholders, at least the person registered in the account. From the point of view of the financial market, the advantage is multiple. Firstly, this admission allows the settlement of securities and their payment to coincide because of the coordination between the securities settlement system and the payment system.[38] Secondly, this admission is also likely to speed up the transactional process: between the moment a transaction takes place and the moment of settlement, there cannot be more than two days.[39] Thirdly, a 'final' character is attached to the transactions in question: the insolvency of one of the parties is not likely to call

[34] Civ. 1re, 17 October 1972, *Royal Dutch*, *Bull. civ.*, I, no. 204, *JDI*, 1973, 716, note B. Oppetit, *RCDIP*, 1973, 520, note H. Batiffol.

[35] See *supra*, paras. 685 et seq.

[36] See *supra*, para. 733.

[37] Art. L. 212-3 of the Monetary and Financial Code.

[38] See *supra*, para. 240.

[39] Art. L. 211-17(III) of the Monetary and Financial Code, Art. 570-2 of the AMF General Regulation, and Art. 5 of Regulation (EU) No 909/2014 of the European Parliament and of the Council of 23 July 2014 on improving securities settlement in the European Union and on central securities depositories.

into question the transaction.[40] The bearer form regime promotes the speed and security of transactions. It is also a regime that favours the marketing of the securities in question abroad. On the one hand, a foreign intermediary is allowed to be a member of the French central depository's securities settlement system, so that its clients can benefit from the securities registered there. On the other hand, French custodians may also join the settlement system of a foreign custodian to facilitate the supply of foreign securities in France. In many respects, the existence of a securities intermediation system, independent of the issuer, is likely to facilitate the international marketing of the securities deposited therein.

The objective of the registered form is distinct. Firstly, this form aims to enable the issuer to know, immediately, its shareholder base. It is true that the issuer of bearer securities may, in the end, know the identity of its shareholder. However, this knowledge is always obtained through the intermediation chain: it must ask the central depository, in return for a fee, for the identity of the shareholders,[41] whereas the company need only ask the person registered as a registered shareholder who the true holder is, and he is required to provide this information.[42] The difference is not benign. Secondly, the use of this form is intended to increase the personal involvement of the shareholders in question by associating them with the operation of the company. This is particularly apparent in the case of companies whose securities are admitted to trading. These companies are thus obliged to use the registered form if they wish, for example, to offer some of their shareholders a double voting right.[43] In the latter case, the registered form is the instrument for retaining shareholder loyalty; it is likely that this form will not decrease in a context where European company law now aims to promote long-term shareholding.[44] This observation makes it possible to realise that the form taken by the share, if it has an impact on the proprietary regime, also has an impact on the *negotium* itself.

However, these objectives of the registered form are not modified by the fact that French stock company law offers issuers the option of entrusting an agent with the keeping of the register of registered shares. In fact, this option is only a derogatory measure:[45] the rule of principle is that the issuer must

---

40 See *infra*, paras. 746 et seq.

41 Arts. L. 228-2, L. 228-3-1 and L. 228-3-7 of the Commercial Code. If the true shareholder refuses to disclose, he may be deprived of his voting rights and the payment of his dividends may be deferred until the situation is remedied, see Art. L. 228-3-3 of the Commercial Code.

42 On pain of losing the advantages of the registered form, see Art. L. 228-3 of the Commercial Code.

43 Art. L. 225-123 of the Commercial Code.

44 This is, for example, the explicit objective of Directive 2017/828 of the European Parliament and of the Council of 17 May 2017 on long-term shareholder engagement.

45 Art. R. 211-3 of the Monetary and Financial Code.

keep the register itself.[46] This relationship between principle and exception has consequences. Firstly, the maintenance of the register by the trustee is precarious: in the event of dissatisfaction, the issuer is quite free to take over the maintenance of the register at any time. Second, the Monetary and Financial Code's characterisation of the issuer's relationship with its agent as a mandate must be taken seriously. On the one hand, this means that the issuer, and not the agent, is deemed to act. On the other hand, the issuer is still responsible for keeping the register; any fault of the agent in keeping the register may be imputed to the issuer. This is the difference with the bearer form: when the issuer entrusts the maintenance of the bearer shares it issues to a central depository, it wishes to facilitate the marketing of the securities, especially abroad. The central depository does not act here as a mere agent, but provides, in its own name, a genuine notary service:[47] it is indeed the central depository that registers the securities issued, it alone that moves the securities of the intermediaries that are members of its system, and it alone that guarantees the watertightness of the system.[48]

Why did the French legislator offer French companies the option of outsourcing their registry? There are several intertwined reasons.[49] Firstly, it avoids a director's stranglehold on the register in a context where the register is of crucial importance for the ownership of shares. For example, the transfer may be made difficult if the shareholder who has been ousted is also the manager, or if the transferee has the clear intention of removing him from office. It is well known that relations between shareholders can be the subject of punctilious agreements, the sanction of which sometimes lies in the transfer of shares. Secondly, this task, which is crucial from a legal point of view, is nevertheless a costly administrative burden for some companies; it may therefore be attractive to either outsource it to a specialist or, for groups of companies, to concentrate the keeping of all registers in the hands of one of the companies in the group.

In short, it is excessive to infer from Article R. 211-3 of the Monetary and Financial Code a promotion of a conflicting liberalism that would result in disabling French law as regards proof of ownership of registered shares issued by French companies. However, such a solution is not unthinkable. It would be possible, in particular, if the keeping of the register by a foreign agent were part of an operation to market registered securities abroad and, in this context, to

[46] Art. L. 211-3 of the Monetary and Financial Code.

[47] As used in Section A of the Annex to Regulation (EU) No 909/2014 of the European Parliament and of the Council of 23 July 2014 on improving securities settlement in the European Union and on central securities depositories.

[48] V. Malassigné, *Les titres représentatifs*, *op. cit.*, nos. 278 et seq.

[49] Art. R. 211-3 of the Monetary and Financial Code originates from Art. 3 of Decree 83-359 of 2 May 1983 on the dematerialisation of securities.

facilitate the transfer of securities to their holders. However, the relevant form would not be registered shares, but bearer shares, as the latter would allow such a scheme.[50] This is all the more true since, although registered shares are the only shares that can, in principle, be issued by unlisted companies, the latter may, by way of exception, issue shares whose registered holder is not the beneficial shareholder, but an intermediary acting on behalf of non-resident shareholders.[51] This is tantamount to instituting the bearer form for foreign holders: the ownership of the share depends on the information provided by the registrant, not on the registration itself.

2. *The Absence of an Obstacle to Property Rights or Enforcement*

735. The internationalist doctrine, when it states that the mode of transfer of ownership is the criterion for the applicable law, is in fact based less on company law than on property law. More precisely, by making registration the criterion of transfer, the authors consider that there is a legal policy choice here with consequences for the designation of the applicable law. This possibility is nevertheless accompanied, for these authors, by a limit: the application of the law of the place where the transfer of ownership takes place is only possible if this legal system itself has an identical conception of the transfer.[52] Such a condition, which conveniently allows the exclusion of renvoi,[53] nevertheless raises a doubt: if the substantive foreign law is designated only insofar as it corresponds exactly to French law, is it really the foreign law that is applied? Shouldn't it rather be the application of French law, which is based simply on a material element – the proof of the entry in the account – located abroad?

This questioning is all the more legitimate since French law itself does not give the evidence from the register absolute probative force. The latter is bound by two important limits: on the one hand, the good faith of the purchaser[54] and, on the other hand, the necessary existence of the register.[55] These two

---

50 It is not exclusive of registered administration: the foreign depositary of bearer shares is perfectly likely to issue registered certificates. The reverse is also possible: a bearer certificate may be issued which grants ownership of a registered share when addressed to the depositary. This is the case in American law, see *supra*, para. 634. On this question, see also J.-P. Niboyet, *Traité de droit international privé*, t. IV, *op. cit.*, no. 1304, p. 692.

51 Art. L. 211-4 para. 3 of the Monetary and Financial Code.

52 J.-D. Bredin and Y. Loussouarn, *Droit du commerce international*, *op. cit.*, no. 350.

53 To take account of the registry law's conception of transfer of ownership - for example, a consensual one, which would make the transferring contract the event giving rise to the transfer - would be to contradict the substantive choice made by the issuer's law to give a particular scope to registration in the registry. Referral would not be an instrument of coordination of legal orders, but rather an obstacle to it; in any event, it would run up against the legal policy pursued by French law.

54 See *supra*, para. 733.

55 If the register disappears - either because the paper burns or is lost, or because the computer medium malfunctions - the ordinary law of proof of ownership comes back to its application.

limits are derived from the rules of the legal system of the issuing company's registered office. These observations make it possible to realise that, if the ownership of the registered share is made dependent on the foreign register, it is always because of the evidential value that *French law* wishes to give, under certain conditions, to the aspect. As Niboyet wrote in a related case, the presence of the agent abroad is a 'mere material and de facto temporary displacement of the company's various services'.[56]

This assessment is not contradicted by the law on security interests. European law makes the validity and enforceability against third parties of financial collateral in respect of financial securities dependent on 'the law of the country where the relevant account is located':[57] in the case of registered shares, the relevant account is the shareholder's account, which the issuer is deemed to hold even if it entrusts the management of the account to an agent. At the same time, the validity of a pledge of a securities account for registered shares is not subject to notification to the registrar,[58] so that the location of the pledge in this context does not appear to be particularly significant.[59] Therefore, the foreign agent will be bound by Article L. 211-20 of the Monetary and Financial Code on pledges of financial securities, irrespective of how the legal system of its registered office views the status to be given to foreign security interests. If the location of the agent is important, it is actually less for the validity of the security interests than for their enforcement. It is in this respect that the notification of the pledge to the registrar is relevant. If the advantage of security interests lies in the constraint exercised on the debtor and in the specific means of enforcement offered to the creditor,[60] then it must be admitted that the difficulty inherent in the presence abroad of the agent to whom the register is entrusted does not really lie in property law, but in the law of enforcement.

736. From an enforcement law perspective. If one senses an interference of the law of the agent's registered office in the proprietary status of the security, it is in fact less because of the geographical location of the register and the appearance attached to it – there is no application of the *lex situs* here as in the past in the case of bearer securities[61] – but because by instituting a presumption of ownership

---

56 J.-P. Niboyet, *Traité de droit international privé*, t. IV, *op. cit.*, note 1, pp. 692–693. The author refers to the hypothesis of the transfer of the Belgian National Bank to France in 1939.

57 Art. 9 of the Financial Collateral Directive.

58 Art. L. 211-20 of the Monetary and Financial Code.

59 H. Synvet, 'L'assiette du gage de comptes d'instruments financiers', *op. cit.*

60 C. Séjean-Chazal, *La réalisation de la sûreté*, *op. cit.*

61 The application of the law of the registry or of the issuer is sometimes presented as an application of the *lex rei sitae* (this perception is shared in other legal systems, see *Bernasconi Report*, p. 3), even though some authors observe that 'the attribution of a place of location (*situs*) to registered securities has a more marked artificial character' (*ibid.*, p. 27). This

based on simple entries in a register, French law places the registry administrator in a position to control the ownership of shares. However, only the legal system of its place of establishment can materially constrain it. It seems to us, however, that this argument of material constraint should not be overestimated in the search for the connecting factor.

Firstly, from the point of view of French enforcement law, this law states that the entry must be made by the agent in charge of the securities' accounts, it being understood that the French issuing company must inform the bailiff of the name of the agent in charge of keeping its accounts.[62] The servicing of the document abroad by the bailiff does not, as such, pose any practical impossibility. The same does not apply to the need for a possible constraint on the foreign agent. However, this is not an obstacle: it is possible to obtain the cooperation of foreign bodies - especially within the Union - for a means of enforcement designed by French law.[63]

Secondly, even if one takes the sole view of the necessary constraint that should be exerted on the foreign agent, it seems to us that the proceeding should still produce its effects because of the presence in France of the true debtor, who is not the agent, but the issuer. The issuer can therefore be compelled to instruct its agent to amend the entries in the register. The company is in fact responsible for keeping the register and should therefore be able to be held

assertion must be rejected here. If the law of the register applies, it is not in the name of the law of location, which has never been extended to registered securities, but because the register constitutes an apparent geographical element with a significant legal link to the property regime of financial securities. Not every geographical location process necessarily means the application of the law of location, *a fortiori* when it is only one element of the reason for the selected criterion. Nevertheless, there is a common feature of the law of the register and the law of location, which lies in their relationship with the law of the issuer. Indeed, just as the law of location is only effective to the extent that the issuer's law has recognised the negotiability of the security and the regime attached to it, the validity of the transactions carried out on the register is only effective to the extent that it is recognised by the issuer's law. This is why the rule proposed by Mr Synvet is supported: 'Financial securities registered on a register or in an account maintained by the issuer are governed by the law of the issuer or, by reference thereto, by the law of the State in which the register or account is maintained', H. Synvet, Draft on a report on conflict of laws rules for financial securities, 2008.

62 Art. R. 232-2 of the Code of Civil Enforcement Procedures.

63 Here, the analogy with the seizure of a foreign bank account does not hold because it is based on the coincidence between the account holder and the debtor, whereas a shareholder's account held by an agent shows a dissociation between the debtor, who is the issuer, and the register holder, who is his agent. The latter merely holds a securities account whose evidentiary function is exercised against another. The bank account and the securities account do not therefore form part of the same concept of account: they do not allow the same *negotium to be* represented. In other words, under an identical title there are two different concepts, which is clearly seen when the regime for one does not lead to satisfactory solutions for the other, as is the case with pledges, see H. Synvet, 'L'assiette du gage de comptes d'instruments financiers', *op. cit.*

liable for the causes of the proceeding,[64] i.e. paying the debt, under the same conditions as if it kept the register. The reason for proceeding against the agent is to prevent proceedings against the shareholder-manager.[65] The latter could be tempted by fraudulent behaviour, even if this is likely to be countered by the good faith necessary for the validity of the transfer.[66] In any event, there is no difficulty in applying French law to a civil enforcement procedure which basically takes place against a debtor located in France.[67]

This discussion, based on current French law, does not mean that the law of the register is, in absolute terms, insusceptible of determining the proprietary status of the rights represented by the entries recorded in it. This will be the case, firstly, when the entries in question constitute a right. This may also be the case, secondly, where the registrar provides a service of a notarial nature, i.e. where the evidence he provides engages his own responsibility and not that of the issuer of the securities represented. This is the case with the central securities depository when it is entrusted with an issue of bearer securities.[68] If, in this case, positive law today shifts the applicable law from the central depository to the custodian account holder, it is solely because of the interest of the latter; the law of the central depository, which is competent under the law of the settlement system to govern the proprietary status of the bearer security when the account holder affiliated to it fails to do so, would in fact benefit from being the only law applicable in these cases.[69]

It should also be added that, irrespective of the objective assigned to the registered form by company law, the register is not a promising connecting factor. It is true that, like the issuer's registered office, it is a unitary criterion: the register designates the same law to all transfers of ownership. However, it has two disadvantages. On the one hand, it is not necessarily as apparent as the issuer's registered office, especially if the choice to entrust the maintenance of the share register is not public. On the other hand, the stability of the location of the register depends on the issuer's decision not to revoke the proxy holder

64 Art. L. 123-1 of the Code of Civil Enforcement Procedures, on which see *supra*, note under para. 732.

65 R. Perrot and P. Théry, *Procédures civiles d'exécution*, 3rd ed., Paris, Dalloz, 2013, no. 705.

66 The dubious circumstances of a transaction are sufficient to characterise the absence of good faith, see F. Drummond, *Droit financier*, *op. cit.*, no. 287.

67 It should nevertheless be added that the law of enforcement is not impervious to the internationalisation of situations; it is not inconceivable – even less so within the Union – not only that a foreign State agrees to carry out an enforcement procedure ordered abroad, but also that foreign law be taken into consideration, or even applied, to the content of the enforcement procedure thus ordered from abroad. This question goes beyond the scope of this study, and we refer here to the demonstration of L. d'Avout, 'La portée internationale des voies d'exécution civiles' in *Mélanges en l'honneur du professeur Philippe Théry*, Paris, LGDJ, pp. 49 et seq.

68 See *supra*, para. 660.

69 See *infra*, paras. 757 et seq.

or to change its registered office. Finally, if the register disappears, an aporia arises. This leads to the law of the issuer being given back the jurisdiction it has relinquished, and to reference being made to its ordinary law of evidence.

II. The Absence of Interference of the Lex Concursus

The rule of private international company law can be challenged by the rules of insolvency law, which provides for separate localisation rules depending on the form of the securities. These rules determine not only the allocation of registered shares between the main and secondary proceedings, but also the validity of the security interests that may be attached to them and their enforceability in the proceedings. It seems to us that the latter have no impact on the location of the registered share.

737. The first Insolvency Regulation (No 1346/2000), applicable to proceedings against a person whose centre of main interests is situated in the territory of the Union, already provided for a rule on the location of securities, according to which:

> '"the Member State in which assets are situated" shall mean, in the case of:
>
> — tangible property, the Member State within the territory of which the property is situated,
>
> — property and rights ownership of or entitlement to which must be entered in a public register, the Member State under the authority of which the register is kept'

In practice, however, this rule has proved to be insufficiently precise, and the recast of the Insolvency Regulation has made it possible to improve it. Today, from the point of view of financial securities, Article 2(9) of the Insolvency Regulation No 848/2015 provides that:

> '"the Member State in which assets are situated" means, in the case of: (i) registered shares in companies other than those referred to in point (ii), the Member State within the territory of which the company having issued the shares has its registered office;
>
> (ii) financial instruments, the title to which is evidenced by entries in a register or account maintained by or on behalf of an intermediary ("book entry securities"), the Member State in which the register or account in which the entries are made is maintained'

The combination of the rules in Article 2(9)(i) and (ii) creates a clear distinction: if the evidence of ownership of the financial instrument is derived from an entry in a register or an account maintained by an intermediary, the law of the registered office of the issuer ceases to apply and the law of the registered office of the account holder or registrar applies. However, it is helpful in interpreting these rules to clarify their purpose.

In the context of the Insolvency Regulation, these rules for locating intangible assets have a dual function.[70] The first is to allocate these assets between the legal orders of the main insolvency proceedings and the secondary proceedings.[71] The second relates to the application of Article 8 of the Insolvency Regulation 848/2015, which subjects the rights in rem of third parties to the law of the 'location' of the assets rather than to the *lex concursus*. The solution chosen is therefore not insignificant: on the one hand, it determines the possibility of opening secondary proceedings within the State where the registered shares are located, i.e. for certain creditors to avail themselves of rules that are more favourable to them than those of the main proceedings. On the other hand, this solution allows creditors who have pledged registered shares located in another Member State than the one of the main or secondary collective proceedings to realise their pledge without having to suffer from the *lex concursus*.

These two functions are, in some respects, antinomic. Where the purpose of the location of the registered share is to distribute the assets between the main and secondary proceedings, it allows the registered shares to be subject to the assets distributed by the effect of the secondary proceedings if it is located in that country. The function of this location is simply to determine which *lex concursus*, that of the main or secondary proceedings, is competent to govern the distribution of the shares among the creditors concerned. On the other hand, when the localisation of the registered shares occurs from the perspective of Article 8 of the Insolvency Regulation, its objective is to take the registered share out of the scope of the creditors' competition, out of the scope of the *lex concursus*. The hypothesis is that of a creditor who has, for example, validly pledged a registered share located in a Member State other than the State in which the main or secondary proceedings are opened. Article 8 of the Insolvency Regulation allows him to enforce his pledge without having to face the competition of other creditors on what is nevertheless an asset of the debtor like any other.

In any event, it follows from these rules that if the registered share is entered in a register maintained by the issuer itself, Article 2(9)(i) of the Insolvency Regulation applies and the registered share is located at the registered office

---

[70] F. Garcimartin, 'The situs of shares, financial instruments and claims in the Insolvency Regulation Recast', *IPrax* 2015, 489.

[71] Recital 39 of the Insolvency Regulation.

of the issuer.[72] If the issuer has entrusted the maintenance of its register to an agent, the applicability of Article 2(9)(ii) of the Insolvency Regulation may be questioned. Indeed, the proof of ownership of the registered share results from the register that the agent keeps, and the agent can be characterised as an intermediary. Although the Insolvency Regulation does not define the latter concept, private international treaties generally understands the agent as an intermediary.[73] There are several arguments to avoid this characterisation, which has the disadvantage of depriving registered shares of a unitary location. Firstly, it can be argued that if a proxy holder is entrusted with the registration of registered shares, the proxy holder performs a function of the corporate body that he represents and therefore does not act as an intermediary.[74] Secondly, the material act relates to the internal functioning of the company, so that the agent is pursuing a function devolved to company law: to enable the issuer to recognise its shareholders; to enable the purchasers of shares to obtain title to their rights. Thirdly and above all, the objective pursued by these rules, whether it is a question of the distribution of assets between the *lex concursus* or the limitation of the *lex concursus* vis-à-vis the law of the location of the intangible property, relates to the predictability of the solution for the creditors of the shareholder. However, the most apparent location of a registered share is that of the issuer, which is public, not that of an agent who is known only to the company and can be dismissed at any time. It is therefore to be expected that the solution of the conflict of laws in European insolvency matters has no real influence on the location of the registered share, even when the register is entrusted to a foreign agent.

These elements show, in our opinion, the considerable importance that private international law still attaches to the form of shares today. This means that the renewal of registered shares through blockchain technology is, at first sight, not insignificant in this context; its scope has nevertheless been reduced by the French legislator itself.

§ 2. EXTENSION TO THE BLOCKCHAIN

The registration of securities in a blockchain is now a legal reality made possible by the development of distributed registers, and in particular those based on *blockchain* technology (I). This new mode of representation, which is

72 The presence of an administration account is an irrelevant circumstance here since it does not alter the proof of ownership, which always results from the register.

73 This is the case in the context of the Hague Convention on the Law Applicable to Agency Contracts of 14 March 1978.

74 Art. 3(a) of the Hague Convention on the Law Applicable to Agency Contracts of 14 March 1978.

currently restricted to registered shares, should nevertheless, as the law stands, have no impact on the solution of conflict of laws: only the form of the security matters (II).

I. Registration of Financial Securities in a Blockchain

738. Blockchain technology. Blockchain technology is generally defined as 'a technology for storing and transmitting information that is transparent, secure, and operates without a central controlling body'.[75] It was initially designed to allow the creation of electronic money without recourse to a central bank or any other centralising mechanism. The designer of the blockchain wanted to eliminate any trusted third parties.[76] Although there had already been attempts to create an electronic currency, the innovative character of blockchain technology stems from the fact that it prevents double payment, understood as the ability of the same person to use the same payment unit for two separate transactions. This prevention is made possible by the succession of several operations.[77]

Firstly, the blockchain is based on the creation of a 'block', i.e. a time-stamped electronic medium recording a transaction. Each block has an identifier that allows it to be linked to previous and subsequent blocks in the transaction chain,[78] thus creating a chain of blocks. Secondly, the addition of one block to another, and the transaction it records, is subject to a set of rules, called consensus rules. These authorise the transaction after verification, with several blockchains, that the seller actually owns the object he intends to transfer.[79] This verification, which is costly, is carried out by certain users (the 'miners'). The latter may be remunerated by the object for which the blockchain is the medium, i.e., in the context of electronic money, by this currency; in other contexts, they may be remunerated by the users.[80] Thirdly, the verifications made by these users are then transmitted to the registry holders, called 'nodes', which continuously update the various registries. One of the most fundamental features of the blockchain is the duplication of registers, combined with the possibility of self-monitoring of the system by its users, which allows its

---

75 See the blockchain France website.

76 S. Nakamoto, 'Bitcoin: A Peer-to-Peer Electronic Cash System', 2008.

77 See also the summary presentation by X. Vamparys, *La blockchain au service de la finance*, Paris, RB éditions, 2018, pp. 28 et seq.

78 Office parlementaire d'évaluation des choix scientifiques et technologiques, Notes no. 4 'Comprendre les *blockchains*', April 2018, p. 2.

79 This verification principle is not, in itself, revolutionary: the T2S settlement platform is also based on an identical mechanism, where a verification of the seller's and buyer's accounts is carried out before proceeding with the transaction, see *supra*, para. 239.

80 T. Cremers, 'The blockchain and financial securities: back to the future', *BJB*, June 2016, no. 114j7, p. 271.

decentralisation. These elements make it very difficult to hack the blockchain itself, since it would require corrupting a majority of the registers.[81]

This presentation of the blockchain is the one generally used when dealing with electronic currencies and, in particular, bitcoin. It is generally referred to as a public or open *blockchain* precisely because it is self-monitoring and open to anyone: any user can attempt to read or write a block. However, blockchain technology can be organised in a less decentralised way, and the verification of transactions, or even access to the transaction, can be restricted to certain authorised members, or even be organised by a central authority. In the latter case, the blockchain is said to be closed or private. While there are several nuances between a public and a private blockchain,[82] it should be noted that, in the case of a blockchain that is not purely public, the institution of a regulatory authority will most often be necessary in order to authorise members. In other words, in cases where the blockchain is not purely open, a trusted third party will inevitably be instituted.[83] From the users' point of view, whatever the type of blockchain, access to the assets recorded by the blockchain is conditioned by the knowledge of two codes, called public and private keys. The public key allows the other party to the transaction to identify itself. The private key gives access to the electronic address that makes it possible to dispose of the goods recorded by the blockchain. The private key is therefore particularly essential[84]; its loss can lead to the loss of the assets registered in the blockchain.

Blockchain technology has expanded beyond electronic money. Its registry function allows it to replace other media for the representation of financial securities and, in particular, the book entry. In this case, the blockchain *is* no longer intended to be a medium for electronic money, but for financial securities.

739. Digital security and legal security. The blockchain is the legislative name for *blockchain* technology.[85] This designation was intended to be 'broad and neutral with respect to the various processes so as not to exclude further

81 The absence of piracy should nevertheless be tempered: on the one hand, corruption of a paper register is not common either and, on the other hand, theft of the private key is quite possible. This second hypothesis is already the subject of litigation, see *D.*, 2022, 1773 and obs. A. Gridel.

82 The La Raudière and Mis report distinguishes four ways in which *blockchains* operate, see Information Report AN no. 1501 (XVth legislature) on *blockchains*, December 2018. See also 'Introduction', no. 7, in V. Magnier and P. Barban (eds.), *Blockchain et droit des sociétés*, Paris, Dalloz, 2019; See 'Blockchain' in D. Legais, *J.-Cl. Com.*, fasc. 534, no. 12.

83 Here we return to the very model that the designer of *blockchain* wanted to get rid of.

84 See on the importance of the private key, H. de Vauplane, '*Blockchain* and Conflict of Laws', *RTDF*, 2017, p. 50 and, in English perspective, S. Green and F. Snagg, 'Intermediated Securities and Distributed Ledger Technology' in *Intermediation and beyond*, *op. cit.*

85 We sometimes speak of distributed registry technology, a broader category to which *blockchain* belongs, see 'Blockchain' in D. Legais, *J.-Cl. Com.*, fasc. 534, no. 11.

technological developments. This name covers the main characteristics of blockchain: its registry function and its shared nature'.[86] The registry function of the blockchain enables the representation of securities.[87] The material scope of the securities that can be registered is limited only to those not admitted to trading, i.e. those in registered form.[88] From the point of view of registered shares, the notable development is that here the blockchain acts as a securities movement register, within which it would nevertheless be possible to identify shareholder accounts. The advantage of this type of record-keeping is therefore the systematic correspondence between the securities register and the shareholder accounts. This is made possible by the equivalence of the scope of the entries and their administration.

The equivalence set out in Article L. 211-3 of the Monetary and Financial Code means that the entry in a register, even if it is electronically shared, provides proof of ownership of the security.[89] However, the issuer or its authorised representative are always the only administrators. The use of the blockchain has two advantages for the issuer: on the one hand, the identity of the entries in the securities register and the securities accounts, and on the other hand, the reduction of the risks of material corruption of the entries in the register. However, this second advantage should not be overestimated. It is always possible for the registrar to make entries that are not supported by any

---

86 Report to the President of the Republic on the ordinance on the use of a blockchain for the representation and transmission of financial securities (no. 2017-1674 of 8 December 2017).

87 M. Julienne, 'L'inscription des titres financiers en *blockchain*', *BJB*, March 2019, no. 118d2, p. 58, no. 4.

88 This restrictive scope is explained by the European CSD Regulation, which makes book-entry with a central depository mandatory if securities are admitted to trading. If the possibility of registering financial securities admitted to trading in a blockchain were to be extended, the same need for a central authority would arise. This is not a problem, since one already exists: the central depository. *Blockchain* would have the advantage of creating a direct link between the central depository and the holder of the financial instrument. However, such a system would have a disadvantage from the point of view of the settlement platform. Indeed, the payment of financial securities is made in central bank money by an intermediary, and a new platform would have to be created in order to link the *blockchain* transaction to a platform, see V. Malassigné, 'Le principe d'équivalence de l'inscription en compte et de l'inscription dans un dispositif d'enregistrement électronique partagé' in V. Magnier and P. Barban (eds.), *Blockchain et droit des sociétés*, Paris, Dalloz, 2019, nos. 26 and 27.

89 This principle of equivalence is based on two analogies: on the one hand, registration in a blockchain provides a durable medium of identification when recording the transaction relating to a security and, on the other hand, it allows the control of the security, cf. V. Malassigné, 'Le principe d'équivalence de l'inscription en compte et de l'inscription dans un dispositif d'enregistrement électronique partagé', *op. cit.*, nos. 7 and 8. However, there are as many types of *blockchain* as there are consensus rules, which determine both the integrity of the system and the type of governance of the register. As Professor Malassigné has shown, 'a large part of the regime of financial securities was conceived in consideration of the existence of a person holding the securities account, and therefore of a person materially managing the instrument of representation of a financial security' (*ibid.*, no. 19).

legal act. However, the only blockchain that the law allows French companies to use is based on a private blockchain.[90] a single private key, which is not entrusted to the holder of the right represented by the entry, but only to the registrar. As a result, it is mainly an administrative gain for the issuer, not any legal security. The protection of Article L. 211-16 of the Monetary and Financial Code can always be set aside if the purchaser *a non domino* acts in bad faith. A rectification of the entry will have to be made. There is no necessary identity between technological and digital security and legal security, unless the blockchain is a register constitutive of rights rather than an instrument for representing rights to which a specific evidentiary regime is attached. In the latter case, however, the security obtained will be in defiance of the limits that the legislator has so far wished to include in the law.[91]

Moreover, the blockchain used by the issuer must be capable of offering the same advantages as traditional account registration: the need to individualise the account in order to allow the exercise of the prerogatives arising from registered shares, and control of the movement of securities in order to allow holders of security interests in registered shares to exercise their prerogatives.[92] By making the effective equivalence of the blockchain a condition for its use, the legislator has brought this new form of administration into line with the old ones: they pursue the same objectives as when the registered share is represented by a book entry.

II. Solutions to the Conflict of Laws

The above observations explain why the law applicable to the proprietary status of registered shares is unchanged by their representation by a blockchain From the point of view of private international company law, there is no reason to change the jurisdiction of the issuer's law. The law of the issuer will therefore apply to the transfer of ownership of registered shares, to the conflict of priorities between successive transferees, to the validity of the chain of transfer of ownership or to the security interests that may be attached to them. The enforcement of the pledge of registered shares registered in a blockchain can

---

[90] This is apparent from the conditions set out in Art. R. 211-9-7 of the Monetary and Financial Code. Indeed, an administrator is needed to identify the owners of financial securities, to carry out securities transactions, to draw up the updated business continuity plan, or to implement the anti-money laundering and anti-terrorist financing regulations, cf. Art. R. 228-8 of the Commercial Code, R. 211-2 and 3 of the Monetary and Financial Code. Mr Malassigné considers that the exclusion of public *blockchain* is not express, but is evident from the wording of the articles. Comp. M. Julienne, 'L'inscription des titres financiers en blockchain', *op. cit.*, nos. 21–22, who observes that a public *blockchain* can be used, and that the securities regime can then be managed by the issuer's intervention.

[91] See *supra*, para. 732.

[92] Art. R. 211-9-7 of the Monetary and Financial Code.

be done independently of the location of the possible agent: it is sufficient to exert a constraint on the issuer so that it prescribes its agent to correct the registration. The coercive mechanisms of civil enforcement law remain relevant. In the same way, the application of the insolvency regulation leads to the same solutions as when the registered share is represented in an account. This is true both when the registered share represented in a blockchain is located in the context of the distribution of assets between main and secondary proceedings and in the context of the limit placed on the *lex fori concursus* by Article 8 of the Regulation. Although the solution is obvious at this stage, we will nevertheless try to explain the reasons for rejecting the solutions based on general connections, which are specific to any use of blockchain and are intended to cover all applications of blockchain (A), and those reserved for the registration of securities in a blockchain (B).

A. The General Connecting Criteria

740. Rejection of the general criteria test. Several criteria have been proposed to resolve conflicts of law arising from blockchain: the effects test and the private key test.

The effects criterion, traditionally used to link certain competition law infringements to a territory, has been used by the Monegasque legislator. Indeed, Article 5 of Law No. 237 of 21 December 2017 on blockchain provides that Monegasque law applies 'to blockchains […] which produce effects on the territory of the Principality of Monaco'. Such a conflict rule, applicable indiscriminately to all functions that may be pursued by the use of blockchain, appears remarkably undesirable. Applied to the registration of financial securities in a blockchain, the effects test could, for example, lead to the application of Monegasque law whenever an investor resident in Monaco acquires French shares represented by a registration in a blockchain. However, the effects test appears dysfunctional because it does not allow for the designation of a precise law: while the effects of anti-competitive behaviour can be circumscribed and linked to a territory, the same cannot be said of the use of the blockchain.[93] It is therefore necessary to add to the effects criterion a real connection criterion, considering, for example, that the blockchain is deemed to produce effects in Monaco when the issuer of securities represented by a blockchain has its registered office there, or that the manager of the blockchain, if there is one, is located there.[94] The effects criterion alone is therefore of no use.

---

93 See already in this sense, M. Audit, 'Blockchain and private international law' in M. Behar-Touchais (ed.), *La Blockchain saisie par le droit*, Paris, IRJS, 2019, p. 117.

94 M. Audit, 'Blockchain and private international law', *op. cit.*, p. 118.

Some authors have argued for the application of the law of the place of the receptacle of the private key.[95] It is known that the private key is the means by which the user disposes of the assets that the blockchain supports. This solution has two advantages: on the one hand, it is based on the importance, within the blockchain, of the private key. The private key is, if not the instrument of possession of digital assets, at least the necessary means of their use.[96] On the other hand, the private key is the common point between all uses of blockchain. Nevertheless, localisation through the private key causes several critical disadvantages. First, the location of the key is likely to vary according to the use of the blockchain. Indeed, depending on the case, the key can be accessed by two means: either by a ledger, a kind of USB key that allows it to be located, or by holding the key with an intermediary. This first uncertainty as to the location of the key inevitably gives rise to a second uncertainty insofar as the applicable law will not be easy to determine for third parties. Above all, in cases where the private key is located by a physical ledger, its location is likely to vary according to the geographical location of the medium.[97] In relation to the registration of securities in a blockchain, this solution appears particularly undesirable. Indeed, it reiterates the impasse reached by the *lex situs* for paper securities: each transaction will change the law applicable to the proprietary status. Such fragmentation is precisely what is sought to be avoided. Moreover, in the event of loss of the private key, it creates an aporia if one wishes to introduce a key recovery mechanism: what mechanism should be applied to the dispossession regime if the location of the key was supposed to determine it?

More generally, the temptation to make proprietary rules depend on the form of the rights represented rather than on their substance should be resisted. A claim is not transferred in the same way as a patent or a registered share. Similarly, the security interests that can be attached to these different objects are not identical. The means of enforcement to which they may be subject are dissimilar. The general solutions therefore seem to us to be based on an inaccurate premise: the method of representation of intangible property is not the decisive instrument for its apprehension by property law; it is difficult to understand why it should be. What do a registered share in a French company

---

95 See H. de Vauplane, 'Blockchain and Conflict of Laws', *RTDF*, 2017, p. 50; S. Green and F. Snagg, 'Intermediation and distributed leger technology', *op. cit.*, p. 357. The authors do not, however, give a method for locating the private key, but observe, no doubt with some humour, that: 'It is true that it would require a rule for identifying the location of the key/key-holder, and that this could be a complicated question. It is submitted, however, that it is likely to be no more difficult than identifying the location of the relevant account under PRIMA.'

96 Insisting on this aspect, see H. de Vauplane, 'Blockchain and Conflict of Laws', *op. cit.*, p. 50.

97 M. Audit, 'Blockchain and private international law', *op. cit.*, p. 117.

registered in a blockchain, a bitcoin and a non-fungible token have in common? Except for the medium of their representation, not much.

At the same time, we must also resist the utilitarian temptation to make the law of autonomy the criterion for attaching the proprietary status of the rights represented by the entries in a blockchain. This would give this criterion a scope unknown until now in European and French law. There is a misunderstanding here of the function pursued by the rules relating to proprietary aspects, which is not to provide a rule that is solely foreseeable for co-contractors, but for third parties. We would fall back into the mischief of the Hague Securities Convention, except that this time the absence of intermediation would avoid falling into the mirage of the securities account.[98] The result is that, unsurprisingly, the law of autonomy does not seem particularly satisfactory, not so much because it would not be predictable (it is likely to be if the author of the blockchain makes it public, and if a legal identifier is attached to the blockchain in question or the digital asset in question), but because it amounts to selecting a connecting criterion that bears no relation either to the objectives pursued by the legislation on proprietary aspects or to the legal and geographical proximity of the substantive elements.[99]

When blockchain is used to represent a registered share of a French company, there is no reason to deactivate the conflict rule from private international company law. The method of representation, by an account or by a blockchain, is irrelevant to the purpose of the registered form. This is not to deny the economic importance of the underlying technology, or to consider that it is politically (or even morally) neutral, but rather to consider that its use in the context of the representation of securities is subordinate to the *legal* effects it hopes to produce. The law ensures its effectiveness here by making compliance with its rules the condition for the use of the technology.[100]

In short, *substantive* characterisation remains central, even when rights are represented in a blockchain. To see this, one need only consider a hypothesis close to the one for which the blockchain was designed: the support of a payment currency. When the blockchain is used to represent central bank digital money, it has the effect of allowing everyone to hold and use the money it issues. Indeed, today it is mainly commercial banks that use 'central bank money'. Central bank money is represented by an entry in the books kept by

[98] On which, see *supra*, paras. 711 et seq.

[99] Moreover, as has been observed, blockchains very rarely report a choice of state law, having been developed in opposition to the state model: M. Lehmann, 'Private International Law in the Proposal by the UNIDROIT Working Group on Digital Assets', *European Association of private international law blog*, 1 February 2023, available at: https://eapil.org/2023/02/01/private-international-law-in-the-proposal-by-the-unidroit-working-group-on-digital-assets/.

[100] See significantly the conditions set out for the use of technology by Art. R. 211-9-7 of the Monetary and Financial Code.

the central bank; accounts with commercial banks do not represent money, but a claim on the bank.[101] The creation of these central bank digital currencies would allow everyone to use a currency issued by the central bank, as is fiat money. However, this will not necessarily result in true disintermediation as commercial banks are likely to continue to hold this central bank digital currency on behalf of their customers, in the same way that custodians hold financial securities on behalf of their customers. The most remarkable effects of this creation are elsewhere. From the point of view of monetary law, they lie in the competition that this money induces for commercial banks, whose ability to create 'money' would be less attractive than today. However, it is not certain that central bank digital money will displace commercial bank 'money'; their coexistence is the most likely outcome. From the point of view of proprietary law, the effects are to be seen in terms of the possible claim of the owner of central bank digital money against the commercial bank that administers them on its behalf, in the manner of the claim of the holder of securities against the bankrupt custodian account holder. In any event, in these monetary cases, the conflict rule applicable to payment systems remains relevant. It should, in our view, lead to the application of the law of the central bank to the transfer of funds insofar as the central bank has designed the payment system in question.[102] In blockchain matters, as in general law, everything remains a matter of characterisation.[103]

Beyond the undesirable effects of these solutions, it is the very principle of a conflict rule applicable to all uses of the *blockchain* that seems undesirable.[104] There are two reasons for this. The first reason was set out by Professor Matthias Audit.[105] In his view, since blockchain is not yet generally regulated in national laws, a conflict rule cannot arise in the absence of a common law. The second reason is to consider that the function pursued by the technology is likely to vary considerably not only according to the way it is designed (among other things, the consensus rules chosen, the question of whether it will be a private or public blockchain), but also according to the way it is used: it is not the same thing to represent a store of value that would like to be assimilated to a non-state electronic currency, and to represent the shares of a French company. In these two cases, blockchain pursues very different purposes, and

[101] This can be seen from the fact that the bankruptcy of the bank leads to a declaration of the depositors' claims in the collective proceedings. For this reason, funds are set up to guarantee customer deposits up to one hundred thousand euros.

[102] See also B. Yüksel Ripley, 'Cryptocurrency Transfers in Distributed Ledger Technology-Based Systems and Their Characterisation in Conflict of Laws', July 2022, available at SSRN: https://ssrn.com/abstract=4336222.

[103] *Ibid.*

[104] See also Financial Market Law Committee, 'Distributed Ledger Technology and Governing Law: Issues of Legal Uncertainty', March 2018, no. 7.1.

[105] M. Audit, 'Blockchain and private international law', *op. cit.*, pp. 118–119.

it seems illusory to try to bring them under the same rule of conflict. It is therefore to specific criteria, inspired by solutions for the desirable localisation of the proprietary rights of securities, that we must now reflect.[106]

B. The Particular Connecting Factor

741. Rejection of criterial other than the law of the issuer for registered securities. Several criteria can be considered here: localisation by the *lex creationis*,[107] by the registered office of the issuer, or the registrar.

The application of the *lex creationis* does not seem desirable. Indeed, while it has the advantage of stability, the *lex creationis* has the disadvantage of not always allowing the identification of the law applicable to debt securities. The latter are dependent on the law of an issuing contract which is not necessarily public. Moreover, this solution leads to an increase in the number of laws whose application is necessary for securities transactions, and the search for solutions that they promote, where the application of the law of the central registry authority allows the application of a single law, whatever the origin of the security. While not a desirable solution, the *lex creationis* also lacks a textual basis. However, some authors believe that Article 211-3 of the Monetary and Financial Code could form the basis of the conflict rule relating to the proprietary status of the security.[108] However, this article refers to the issuance of financial instruments and not to their proprietary regime. It cannot, as such, be the basis for locating the proprietary regime of financial securities registered in a blockchain just as it has never been the basis for locating the proprietary regime of securities represented by a paper medium or registered in an account. This is precisely why the draft order provided for the institution of an Article L. 211-3-2 in the Monetary and Financial Code, worded as follows:

> 'Rights in securities registered in a blockchain [blockchain] are governed by French law where the registered office of the issuer is located in France or the issue is governed by French law.'

This article extended the dual criterion of the registered office and the choice of law applicable to the issue to the proprietary status of securities.[109] Such a

---

106 See also X. Vamparys, *La blockchain au service de la finance*, *op. cit.*, p. 56 where the author considers that it is possible to approach *blockchain* through its uses. However, the author believes that only international material regulation is likely to govern *blockchain* (*ibid.* p. 57).

107 It should be recalled here that the *lex creationis* of the security is not necessarily that of the issuer: debt securities may have their source in an issue contract subject to a foreign law – see *supra*, para. 302.

108 M. Julienne, 'L'inscription des titres financiers en blockchain', *op. cit.*, no. 10.

109 On this double criterion, see *supra*, para. 304.

unilaterally formulated provision is paradoxical. This article prevents a French issuer from placing its securities under the auspices of a law that is more permissive as to the form of its securities; yet, it precisely allows foreign issuers selecting French law in their contract of issue to subject their proprietary status to French law.[110] The rationale for such a rule is probably to favour French law, which is therefore sufficiently attractive to be offered to foreign issuers, but not sufficiently attractive to let French issuers choose another.

Above all, extending the convoluted choice of law from the form of securities to their proprietary status confuses the purpose of the designated law's domain, which is no longer merely to promote trade, but, once trade has taken place, to protect purchasers and third parties. Because it allows a choice of law, the *lex creationis* does not seem desirable. It seems to us that it would be better to choose between the two criteria in favour of the law of the issuer:[111] this is susceptible to bilateralisation, and is more objective than the law of the contract of issue.[112] We have seen that the objectives of the registered form contribute to the application of this law.

On the other hand, the use of bearer form should lead to the application of the law of the registered office of the central administrator of the blockchain The pre-eminence of the central administrator in this case, where one exists, even prompted the authors of the HCJP report, who were in favour of applying the law of the issuer, to propose that the legislator require French issuers to use only the services of an administrator established on French territory.[113] However, it seems possible for the central administrator to subject its blockchain system to a law other than that of its registered office. The Financial Market Law Committee therefore proposes to subject the proprietary status of financial securities to the law of the system selected by the central administrator.[114]

---

110 It is well known that in the event that the law of the foreign issuer prohibits such a solution, such an article is doomed to ineffectiveness, see *supra*, para. 303 on the need to respect the mandatory requirements of the legal system of the registered office.

111 The *Haut Comité juridique de la Place de Paris* proposed very early on to apply the law of the issuer to the proprietary status of the financial security represented in a blockchain, HCJP, Response to the public consultation of the Direction Générale du Trésor on the draft legislative and regulatory reforms relating to the *Blockchain*, 18 May 2017, pp. 21–22.

112 Even though organisations have a choice of location within the EU and the possibility of changing their location, these changes are cumbersome and infrequent.

113 *Ibid.*: 'It could be argued that the law of the State in which the operator of the system used is established should apply to the rights in the securities and the modalities of their transfer. In order to alleviate this possible difficulty (the HCJP) is in favour of requiring issuers of unlisted securities to use a DLT established on national territory, provided that this limitation is not contrary to European principles.'

114 Financial Market Law Committee, 'Distributed Ledger Technology and Governing Law: Issues of Legal Uncertainty', *op. cit.*, no. 6.4 for the proposed system, awkwardly entitled 'elective situs'. The authors consider that this is an application of the *PRIMA* rule in its subjective aspect (on which see *supra* no. 711 et seq.) The assertion appears to be incorrect since PRIMA is based on a chain of intermediation, whereas the application of the law

Such a solution amounts to taking over the conflict of laws solution applicable to the systems of the Finality Directive, on which the system of settlement of securities depends. The conflict of laws rule applicable to these systems is based on a choice of law restricted to the registered offices of the various participants and provides for the publication of the designated law.[115] It should be noted, however, that while choice of law is possible under the Finality Directive, it was only made possible because of the harmonisation brought about by the Finality Directive. Above all, in practice, the systems have always borrowed the law of their manager, so that rather than providing for a sophisticated mechanism to restrict the choice of law after it has been granted, it would be better to simply subject the system to the law of the manager's registered office. It will still be possible for them to set up a subsidiary in another EU legal order if they wish to avail themselves of another legal system.

Conclusion of the section. The conflict-of-laws rule derived from the law of registered securities shows the way forward as regards the connection of securities in general: by providing for the application of the law of the issuer, it gives a unitary, apparent, objective and stable solution to the conflict of laws, moreover based on the objective pursued by the registered form. The existence of a new mode of representation – – the blockchain – is not likely to change the relevance of this rule.

SECTION 2. CONNECTING BEARER SECURITIES TO SECURITIES SETTLEMENT SYSTEM LAW

742. The benefits of a unitary solution to the conflict of laws, which would apply the same law to the proprietary status of securities, allowing third parties as well as parties to determine the rule according to which the ownership of the security must be assessed, are largely apparent through the impasses to which the plurality of connections leads. It will be shown here that such a solution is also possible when bearer securities are intermediated. In these cases, the solution to the conflict of laws can be based on the pyramid structure of intermediation of the holding, which is common to all intermediation systems. Indeed, it is always possible to apply to the proprietary status of all securities the law of the settlement system in which they are registered. This solution is already in force

of the DLT system binds all members to the same system, and is therefore similar to a securities settlement system from which the final account holders have left. See also *ibid.*, no. 7.1 for the favouring of this choice. Also in favour of the application of the law of the electronic platform used by the security holder, P. Paech, 'Securities, intermediation and the blockchain: an inevitable choice between liquidity and legal certainty?', *Uniform Law Review - Revue de droit uniforme*, 2016, no. 4, pp. 612 et seq.

115 See *supra*, paras. 277 et seq.

within the *lex concursus*, in a dynamic where financial market law tries to restrict the disruption caused by insolvency law (§ 1). However, this connecting factor could be generalised to the entire proprietary status of securities registered in the systems of a central depository (§ 2).

§ 1. THE LIMITATION OF THE *LEX CONCURSUS*

743. *Ratio legis* of the limitation of the *lex concursus*. The failure of an intermediary and the resulting risk of non-payment are likely to disrupt the functioning of the financial market, or, more precisely, that of payment and securities settlement systems, and even contribute to systemic risk by triggering a bankruptcy of the counterparties of the insolvent person. Such a disruption is not a textbook hypothesis. For example, the bankruptcy on 26 June 1974 of one of the largest private German banks, *Bankhaus I.D Herstatt*, caused a systemic risk in the US foreign exchange market where US banks had settled Herstatt before receiving payment from the counterparty.[116] This event, coupled with the failure of the US Franklin National Bank in May 1974, resulted in the creation of the Basel Committee.[117] It revealed the need for protection of SSSs, which the Eurosystem reports on by recalling the large amounts of money flowing through its payment systems.[118] The large amounts involved and the interdependence between the participants in the system mean that the insolvency of one of the participants would be likely to jeopardise transfer operations that have already given rise to other transfers.[119] This would make further transfer orders impossible, 'in a systemic chain reaction'.[120] It is because of this risk that the Finality Directive protects payment systems against the insolvency of one of the participants in the

116 BIS, *History of the Basel Committee and Its Membership*, https://www.bis.org/publ/bcbsc101.pdf, March 2001, p. 1; FB Bourse, 'La faillite de la banque Herstatt en 1974', http://www.fb-bourse.com/faillite-banque-herstatt-en-1974, 15 July 2012 and G. Galati, 'CLS Bank et le risque de règlement dans les opérations de change', BIS Quarterly Report, December 2002, pp. 1 and 2; C. Feunteun, *Insturments hybrides et Accords de Bâle*, Paris, University of Paris II Panthéon-Assas, Paris, no. 4.

117 *Ibid*, nos. 4 et seq.

118 To get an idea of this, Professor Pascale Bloch wrote as early as 1999 that 'the risks attached to large-value payments between banks, the volume of which represents in a few days the amount of the gross domestic product of the industrialised countries'. P. Bloch, 'La directive 98/26/CEE concernant le caractère définitif du règlement dans les systèmes de paiement et de règlement des opérations sur titre' in *Mélanges AEBDF* II, 1999, pp. 49 et seq. The author relies on the *Banque de France*'s information note, 1997, no. 104.

119 D. Devos, 'La protection juridique des systèmes de paiement en cas de défaillance d'un participant', *RD Bancaire et Bourse* 1997, no. 59, p. 11; see also in this sense P. Bloch, 'La directive 98/26/CEE concernant le caractère définitif du règlement dans les systèmes de paiement et de règlement des opérations sur titre', *op. cit.*, spec. p. 51.

120 D. Servais (ed.), *L'intégration des marchés financiers*, *op. cit.*, no. 1030.

system.[121] This first reason is undoubtedly supplemented by a second, which lies in the protection of the financial markets themselves, since, as Professor Robine writes, 'protection [of the creditor] against the insolvency of the debtor is one of the conditions for the success of these financial markets'.[122]

The challenge is therefore to limit the disruption created by the intervention of the *lex concursus*. This is the meaning of the solutions developed within the European Union. These are based on two aspects, material and conflictual, which, combined, considerably limit the *lex concursus*. From the material point of view, the original limitation of the Finality Directive allows to preserve the integrity of systems, which is necessary to protect against systemic risk. The extension of the limitation of the *lex concursus* to all financial collateral was done on the same basis, which appears nevertheless more questionable (I). From a conflict perspective, the criterion selected to govern the proprietary status of the security is the law of the securities settlement system (II).

I. *The Material Limitation of the Lex Concursus*

The *lex concursus was* originally limited by the Finality Directive (1). The material scope of this limitation was considerably extended by the Financial Collateral Directive in the name of systemic risk (2). This rationale appears questionable, which is best illustrated by studying the resolution of credit institutions, where transactions taking place through systems governed by the Finality Directive are preserved in the name of systemic risk, unlike financial collateral (3).

A. The Original Limitation from the Finality Directive

744. The Finality Directive. The Finality Directive was drawn up by the Commission at the same time as the revision of Articles 8 and 9 of the *Uniform Commercial Code*. Indeed, as early as 1993, the European Commission studied the legal framework for intra-Community cross-border payments and set up a group of national experts to study the 'systemic' aspects linked to the failure of a participant.[123] This group of experts developed two directives: one on cross-

---

121 This justification can be compared with that given by Dean Hamel to the non-opposability of defences in the area of negotiable instruments. The author wrote that on this aspect, the break with civil law 'does it not coincide with the notion of this rigid and strict Commercial Law, which is not afraid to sacrifice particular interests to the general interests of economic life?' J. Hamel, preface to the thesis by G. Friedel, *De l'inopposabilité des exceptions en matière d'effets de commerce*, *op. cit.*, p. XI.

122 D. Robine, *La sécurité des marchés financiers face aux procédures collectives*, *op. cit.*

123 On the draft Finality Directive [1997] OJ C375/34, see D. Devos, 'La protection juridique des systèmes de paiement en cas de défaillance d'un participant', *RD Bancaire et Bourse*, 1997, no. 59, p. 11; P. Bloch, 'La directive 98/26/CEE concernant le caractère définitif du règlement dans les systèmes de paiement et de règlement des opérations sur titre', *op. cit.*;

border credit transfers[124] and the other on settlement finality, proposed in 1995 by the European Council. The Finality Directive is prophetic in that, having come into force in 1998, it bases its application on the 'systemic risk inherent in payment systems'[125] and therefore considers that 'the reduction of systemic risk requires in particular the finality of settlement and the recovery of collateral'.[126] The two sides of the directive are already apparent: the issue of finality on the one hand, and the recovery of collateral on the other.

Firstly, the issue of finality makes it possible not to call into question a transaction that has taken place through a payment or securities settlement system. To this end, the Directive establishes both conflict of laws rules and substantive rules which, taken together, make it possible to deactivate the *lex concursus* by excluding from its scope the rights of participants in systems.[127] Secondly, central banks have a special interest in the issue of financial collateral: they are the beneficiaries. Indeed, central banks may provide credit to participants either in order to facilitate the settlement of transactions in the system or in the context of the implementation of monetary policy operations.[128] However, any credit from a national central bank implies the pledging of assets, including financial securities.[129] This is the origin of the special protection enjoyed by holders of financial collateral within the Purposes Directive, who also benefit from protective substantive and conflicting rules.

D. Devos, 'La directive européenne du 19 mai 1998 concernant le caractère définitif du règlement dans les systèmes de paiement et de règlement des opérations sur titre', *Euredia*, 2/1999, p. 149.

124 Which gave rise to Directive 97/5 of the European Parliament and of the Council of 27 January 1997 on cross-border credit transfers.

125 Recital 1 of the Directive Purpose.

126 Recital 9 of the Finality Directive. However, if the basis of the systemic risk constitutes in retrospect the particular strength of the directive, and undoubtedly the main objective of the directive (in this sense M. Vereecken, 'Reducing systemic risk in payment and securities settlement systems' (1998) *Journal of financial regulation and compliance*, pp. 107 et seq. The recitals of the directive refer to the contribution to the completion of the internal market, to the free movement of capital and services, to the achievement of economic and monetary union and to the contribution to the efficient functioning of payment systems. The heterogeneity of the objectives pursued has already been noted, see D. Servais (ed.), *L'intégration des marchés financiers*, *op. cit.*, no. 1010.

127 These rules have been transposed into Art. L. 330-1(II) *in fine*, (III) and (IV).

128 On this point, see *Bull. Banque de France*, no. 46, October 1997; P. Bloch, 'La directive 98/26/CEE concernant le caractère définitif du règlement dans les systèmes de paiement et de règlement des opérations sur titre', *op. cit.*, p. 66; D. Servais (dir.), *L'intégration des marchés financiers*, *op. cit.*, no. 1038.

129 Banque de France, 'Remise d'actifs en garantie des opérations de refinancement de l'Eurosystème' in *Cadre opérationnel de la politique monétaire*, Banque de France website, available at https://www.banque-france.fr/politique-monetaire/cadre-operationnel-de-la-politique-monetaire/remise-dactifs-en-garantie-des-operations-de-refinancement-de-leurosysteme (accessed on 15 August 2021).

745. The substantive rules for protection against the insolvency of a participant. In order to protect the system from the insolvency of a participant, Article 3(1) of the Finality Directive states:

> 'Transfer orders and netting shall be legally enforceable and, even in the event of insolvency proceedings against a participant, shall be binding on third parties, provided that transfer orders were entered into a system before the moment of opening of such insolvency proceedings.'[130]

Collective proceedings cannot therefore call into question orders already issued and entered into a system before the opening judgment, and the moment of entry of a transfer order is governed by the operating rules of the central depository.[131] To ensure the effectiveness of this measure, the Finality Directive neutralises the possible retroactive effect of the opening judgment at 'zero hour' of the day on which it is pronounced, by stating that 'the moment of opening of insolvency proceedings shall be the moment when the relevant judicial or administrative authority handed down its decision', and by holding that 'insolvency proceedings shall not have retroactive effects on the rights and obligations of a participant arising from, or in connection with, its participation in a system earlier than the moment of opening of such proceedings'.[132]

In addition to this first rule for the protection of transactions governed by the system, there is a second rule for the protection of holders of financial

---

130 Art. 3(1)(of the Finality Directive. Paragraph two allows an order entered and executed on the day of the opening judgment to also be preserved from the collective proceedings if the central depositary was not aware of the insolvency. However, such negative proof may be difficult to establish. Professor Pascale Bloch nevertheless observes that such proof may 'result in some cases from differences in the operating hours of systems in different countries', P. Bloch, 'La directive 98/26/CEE concernant le caractère définitif du règlement dans les systèmes de paiement et de règlement des opérations sur titres', *op. cit.*
French law has extended this protection from the moment the order becomes irrevocable, see Art. L. 330-1(III) of the Monetary and Financial Code. Already observing this extension, H. Synvet, 'The exclusion of certain creditors from the law of collective proceedings' in W.-G. Ringe, L. Gullifer and P. Théry, *Current issues in European Financial and Insolvency Law*, Oxford, Hart Publishing, 2009, p. 172.

131 Art. 3(3) of the Directive Finality. The protection is granted to the system independently of the interposition of the clearing house. This clarification is important because it distinguishes the protection granted to the clearing system within the Finality Directive from other hypotheses of protection where it is the interposition of the clearing house which justifies the protection, in a particular form of application of contractual clearing in case of insolvency, see for example the hypothesis of the airline clearing house, *British Eagle International Airline Ltd v. Cie National Air France*, [1975] 1 WLR 758, HL and *International Air Transport Association v. Ansett Holdings Ltd*, [2008] HCA 3. On these cases, see M. Bridge, 'Clearing Houses and Insolvency'(2008) *Law and Financial Markets Review*, p. 418, M. Bridge and J.P. Braithwaite, 'Private Law and Financial crisis' (October 2013) *Journal of Corporate Law Studies*, pp. 361 et seq.

132 Art. 6(1) and (7) of the Finality Directive, on which see D. Servais (ed.) *L'intégration des marchés financiers*, *op. cit.*, no. 1035.

collateral. This protection follows an identical pattern. Indeed, the Finality Directive adopts a broad definition of the notion of collateral,[133] and through Article 9, 1, immunises "the rights of a participant in respect of collateral provided to it in connection with a system" from insolvency proceedings against the participant who provided the collateral.[134] As the Directive makes clear, such collateral 'may be realised for the satisfaction of these rights'.[135] The benefit of such collateral has been extended by the Financial Collateral Directive.

B. The Extension by the Financial Collateral Directive

As part of the Commission's Financial Services Action Plan,[136] the Financial Collateral Directive harmonises the collateral provided between financial institutions. In addition, it extends the scope of application of the conflict rule on financial collateral from the Finality Directive.[137] Financial collateral is a mechanism that is all the more effective (1) as it is resistant to collective proceedings (2).

1. *The Mechanism of Financial Collateral*

746. Constitution and enforceability of financial collateral. The possibility of entering into financial collateral arrangements is limited to certain professionals.[138] The assets that may be subject to a financial collateral arrangement are 'financial instruments, bills, creditors, contracts or money'.[139] The agreement may provide for the creation of such assets as security, or for their transfer to the lessee as full ownership.[140] In both cases, the agreement, by providing financial security for the

133 Art. 2(m) of the Finality Directive.

134 Art. 9(1) of the Finality Directive. As regards financial collateral, the Finality Directive goes even further by immunising financial collateral pledged for the benefit of central banks outside a system, see *ibid.*

135 Art. 9(1) of the Finality Directive.

136 Recital 2 of the Financial Collateral Directive; European Commission, Implementing the framework for financial services: Action Plan, Brussels, 11 May 1999, COM (1999) 232 Final, p. 7.

137 Recital 1 of the Financial Collateral Directive. However, the Financial Collateral Directive is not really based on the reduction of systemic risk. Indeed, the objective of establishing a common financial collateral regime is to promote 'the integration and cost-effective functioning of the financial market and the stability of the Community's financial system, and thus the freedom to provide services and the free movement of capital in a single market for financial services'. (Recital 3 of the Financial Collateral Directive). In reality, the scope of the Directive goes far beyond the financial markets.

138 Art. L. 211-36 of the Monetary and Financial Code.

139 Art. L. 211-38 of the Monetary and Financial Code.

140 Art. 1(a), (b) and (c) of the Financial Collateral Directive. The field of financial guarantees also extends to netting, see in particular H. Le Nabasque, A. Couret *et al.*, *Droit financier*, *op. cit.*, no. 1512.

benefit of the lessee, gives him possession or control.[141] However, the Directive does not provide any criteria for determining what constitutes possession or control of the intangible collateral. The Court of Justice has clarified that the acquisition of possession or control of the collateral by the collateral taker occurs 'only on condition that the collateral provider is prevented from disposing of it'.[142] French law does not require any additional formality: the financial collateral must be in writing and dispossession is the only requirement for the collateral to be enforceable against third parties.[143] In practice, as far as securities are concerned, this dispossession can be ensured by transferring the securities to a securities account opened in the name of the beneficiary of the collateral.[144]

Since the financial collateral arrangement grants the collateral taker control over the collateral deposited, it is easy to understand why the collateral taker acquires the right to 're-use' the financial collateral, i.e., possibly to dispose of it, on condition that it 'replaces the financial instruments originally provided as collateral no later than the date fixed for the performance of the financial obligations covered by the arrangement'.[145] This singular regime does not lead to a delimitation of the rights of each of the parties, but to a real superposition,[146] which places the party providing the collateral in a weak

141 Art. 2(2) of the Financial Collateral Directive provides: 'Any reference in this Directive to financial collateral being "provided" or to the "provision" of financial collateral means its settlement, transfer, holding, registration or other treatment which results in the collateral taker or the person acting on its behalf acquiring possession or control of that financial collateral.' The reference to 'control' is reminiscent of the test for third party enforceability in the US system (*priority by control*, see *supra*, para. 682). Mr de Vauplane sees this as a further sign of American influence, see H. de Vauplane, 'Cadre juridique des garanties financières', *op. cit.*

142 The Court ruled on the qualification of collateral relating to funds deposited in a bank account, and in particular on the question of whether a pledge relating to funds deposited in a bank could constitute a collateral see Case C-156/15, *'Private Equity Insuranc Group' SIA v. 'Swedbank' AS*, ECLI:EU:C:2016:851, para. 42. On this judgment, see J. Morel-Maroger, *Banque et droit*, January 2017, pp. 43–44; T. Bonneau, *RDBF*, March 2017, p. 82; A. Bouverresse, *Europe*, January 2017, pp. 20–21; P.-E. Paetsch and T. Evans, *RTBF*, April 2017, p. 151 (the authors criticise the formal interpretation given by the Court, as the provision of the collateral would imply a form of dispossession).

143 Art. L. 211-38(I). On this question, see H. Le Nabasque, A. Couret *et al.*, *Droit financier*, *op. cit.* D. Robine and S. Praicheux, 'Garanties Financières', *op. cit.*

144 This observation supports the possessory function of book entry, on which see V. Malassigné, *Les titres représentatifs*, *op. cit.*

145 Art. 5(2) of the Financial Collateral Directive, transposed in Art. L. 211-38(III) of the Monetary and Financial Code. The instruments must be replaced by equivalent goods or rights, which is strictly assessed, see *ibid.* For a critical analysis, see C. Gijsbers, *Sûretés réelles et droit des biens*, *op. cit.*

146 A. Riles, *Colleteral knowledge*, *op. cit.*, p. 165. The author thus considers that the rights of the parties 'are entangled, not delineated', and that it is therefore, in the sense of property law, an anti-common: 'There are two hands on the baton, so to speak, each with legitimate claims that can either chill the other from using the collateral, or encourage each to exploit it as much as possible in the short-term to the detriment of long-term use.' The author sees this, *in fine*, *as* a legal fiction, see *ibid.*, p. 172.

position: he loses control of the property given until the end of the contract.[147] On the other hand, and this is undoubtedly its real justification, this regime is particularly advantageous for the beneficiary of financial guarantees. Indeed, it allows institutions that use it to considerably increase their liquidity by being able to dispose of the assets that have been deposited as collateral.[148]

747. The area of the proprietary status of the collateral. It is known that due to the PRIMA criterion of Article 9(2) of the Financial Collateral Directive, this transfer will also have the effect of subjecting its applicability to the law of the registered office of the intermediary with whom the account is maintained.[149] While this rule does not determine the law applicable to other assets that may be subject to collateral,[150] its scope makes it possible to decide, at least from the point of view of collateral, and more specifically of assets subject to the PRIMA rule, whether the characterisation of collateral depends on the proprietary status of the collateral or on the collateral arrangement.[151] Indeed, Article 9(2) of the Financial Collateral Directive makes the property status of the collateral eligible for registration subject to 'the legal nature and proprietary effects of the

---

147 Ms Riles considers that: 'Collateral is fundamentally a hierarchical relationship: the debtor-pledgor is in a position of structural weakness vis-à-vis the credit-pledgee [...]. Posting collateral is an act of sacrifice.' (*ibid.*)

148 On the assets that can be assigned to a collateral, see H. Gourdy, *La couverture sur les marchés financiers*, Paris, Université Paris II Panthéon-Assas, 2019, nos. 332 et seq.

149 See *supra*, paras. 684 et seq.

150 It only covers financial instruments that can be booked. Observing already this duality, D. Robine and S. Praicheux, 'Garanties Financières', *op. cit.*, no. 117.

151 The question has often arisen from the point of view of the retention of title clause, see, in doctrine, P. Mayer, 'Les conflits de lois en matière de réserve de propriété après la loi du 12 mai 1980', *JCP*, 1981, 1, 3019; Y. Loussouarn, 'Les conflits de lois en matière de réserve de propriété' in *Études offertes à Roger Houin, Problèmes d'actualités posés par les entreprises*, Paris, Dalloz, 1985, p. 275; J.-P. Scarano, 'Opposabilité ou inopposabilité de la clause de réserve de propriété', *RTD. com.*, 1990, 533; see 'Faillite' in H. Synvet, *Répertoire de droit international*, *op. cit.*, no. 64.
This conflict of qualification may be compared to that of the qualification of property situated outside the territory, on which see M.-C. de Lambertye-Autrand, *La distinction des meubles et des immeubles en droit international privé*, Paris, Université Paris I Panthéon-Sorbonne, 2001, spec. chapter 1. The author sees behind the *lege causae* qualification of immovables the principle of effectiveness, see no. 48: 'Indeed, it seems to us that by distinguishing according to whether the disputed question concerns movable or immovable property, the forum has taken a stand on the place that should be given to considerations of effectiveness in the elaboration of its rules of private international law. It has taken the view that for property which it regards as immovable, the concern to give a decision which can be enforced at the place where the property is situated justifies reserving jurisdiction to the law (or the court) of the State where the property is situated. On the contrary, in the case of property which it considers to be movable, it has set aside these considerations of effectiveness, considering that they are not such as to determine the choice of applicable law or the criteria of jurisdictional competence.'; see also in this sense, L. d'Avout, *Sur les solutions du conflit de lois en droit des biens*, *op. cit.* On this question, see more generally Y. Lequette, 'Le renvoi de qualifications' in *Mélanges dédiés à D. Holleaux*, Paris, Litec, 1990, pp. 249 et seq.

collateral'. However, it is possible that the law of the insolvency proceedings imposes a different characterisation.

2. *Collective Proceedings*

748. Extension of immunity from the scope of collective proceedings. The second remarkably advantageous aspect of financial collateral is that it is immune from the effects of collective proceedings. The financial collateral arrangement 'may not be declared invalid or void or be reversed on the sole basis that the financial collateral arrangement has come into existence, or the financial collateral has been provided: (a) on the day of the commencement of winding-up proceedings or reorganisation measures, but prior to the order or decree making that commencement; or (b) in a prescribed period prior to, and defined by reference to, the commencement of such proceedings or measures or by reference to the making of any order or decree or the taking of any other action or occurrence of any other event in the course of such proceedings or measures'.[152] From the French point of view, this immunity is ensured when the insolvency proceeding is opened in France, since Articles L. 211-38(I) and L. 211-40 of the Financial Monetary Code provide for the enforcement of the collateral 'even when one of the parties is subject to one of the procedures provided for by Book VI of the Commercial Code'.[153] The issue does not arise in the same way when the proceedings are opened abroad. The bodies of the foreign proceedings may then try to dispossess the beneficiary of the guarantee, in particular by re-characterising it.[154]

749. Proceedings opened in the territory of the Union. If the proceedings are initiated within the territory of the Union, the legal system of the State of initiation will have similar rules excluding financial collateral from the scope of the proceedings. The harmonisation of substantive law by the Directive makes it possible to achieve a less disparate characterisation of financial collateral within the European Member States.[155] However, the risk of divergent characterisation is not non-existent, on the one hand because the Directive leaves room for

---

152 Art. 8(1) of the Financial Collateral Directive. The Directive was initially transposed in Arts. L. 431-7 et seq. of the Monetary and Financial Code, and is now included in Arts. L. 211-38 et seq. of the same Code. The question arose as to whether the Financial Collateral Directive created a new type of collateral. On this debate, which was settled by the author insofar as the rules resulting from the Financial Collateral Directive would simply add to the ordinary law of securities, see H. Gourdy, *La couverture sur les marchés financiers*, *op. cit.*, paras. 326 et seq.

153 See nevertheless the residual hypotheses noted by D. Robine and S. Praicheux, 'Garanties Financières', *op. cit.*, no. 103.

154 See J. Benjamin, 'The Oxford colloquium on collateral and conflict of laws: overview', *op. cit.*, pp. 2–3.

155 Since all Member States are familiar with this particular guarantee, the risk of certain aspects of the regime of these guarantees being classified differently depending on the forum petitioned is reduced. On the risk of recharacterisation, see *supra*; para. 715.

manoeuvre to the Member States when transposing it into national law and, on the other hand, because the Member States may transpose the Directive incorrectly into their national law.[156] It is therefore necessary to know whether the characterisatin of financial collateral should be subject to the *lex concursus*, or to property law.

In favour of the law of the *lex concursus*, two arguments can be made. Firstly, the scope of the law of the proprietary effect of collateral under the Financial Collateral Directive does not include the issue of insolvency. In other words, the law applicable to the proprietary effect of collateral would only apply as long as the parties to the collateral are *in bonis*.[157] Secondly, the purpose of the *lex concursus* is, in particular, from a legislative point of view, to adopt a coherent system for organising creditor competition, which justifies the application of a single law. Indeed, the bankruptcy law applies in order to 'determine the scope of the principle of equality of creditors and the exceptions that may be applied to it',[158] so that it is competent to 'decide on the effectiveness of a guarantee, in the broad sense, invoked by a creditor'.[159]

In favour of the law of property, it can be argued that the *ratio* of the Financial Collateral Directive is to preserve financial stability, and that this preservation would be futile if the enforcement of the collateral could be paralysed by a disqualification of the law of the proceeding. Furthermore, a strong argument is provided by Article 8 of the Insolvency Regulation, which specifically preserves 'the rights in rem of third parties of a creditor or a third party in respect of assets [...] belonging to the debtor which are situated within the territory of a Member State at the time of the opening of the proceedings'. Such a rule constitutes a strong preference for the law of the property, which should prevail as regards classification. The risk of recharacterisation is

156 These two hypotheses correspond, for example, to the French and German transpositions, see D. Robine and S. Praicheux, 'Garanties Financières', *op. cit.*, no. 115.

157 This reading is reinforced by the distinction made by the Finality Directive, which provides for a different law to the rights of participants depending on whether the participant in the system is solvent or not.

158 Y. Loussouarn, 'Les conflits de lois en matière de réserve de propriété', *op. cit.*

159 J.-P. Rémery, note under Cass., 1re civ., 8 January 1991, no. 89-16741, *Bull. civ.*, I, no. 9; *D.*, 1991, p. 276. The judgment under review concerned a retention of title clause inserted in a contract subject to German law. The beneficiary of the clause wished to claim the property. While there was no doubt that the claim was subject to the law of the insolvency proceedings, the law applicable to the validity of the retention of title was in dispute, and was *ultimately* subject to the law of the proceedings in the following terms: 'The conditions under which goods sold with retention of title may be claimed are, in the event of the purchaser's insolvency, determined by the law of the insolvency proceedings, irrespective of the law governing the validity and enforceability, in general, of the retention of title clause.' On this judgment, see also the observations of H. Synvet, see 'Faillite' in *Répertoire de droit international*, *op. cit.*, nos. 64 et seq. The possible analogy with financial collateral, already observed by D. Robine and S. Praicheux, 'Garanties Financières', *op. cit.*, no. 119.

therefore ruled out when the judge declaring the opening judgment is from a Member State of the Union.

750. Proceedings opened in the territory of a third State. It is therefore especially in the case of insolvency proceedings opened in the territory of a third State that the financial collateral may not be protected, not only because the risk of recharacterisation is greater, but also because the law of the foreign insolvency proceedings will not grant it specific protection.[160] In the latter case, the fate of the collateral will largely depend on two factors. Firstly, it will depend on the concept of bankruptcy held by the court of the place where the asset is located, and in particular on whether, as in France, it will refer to the *lex concursus* the task of determining the effects of the bankruptcy, including with regard to the disputed asset which is the subject of the collateral.[161] Secondly, the fate of the collateral will depend on whether the *forum concursus* is aware of the effects of the bankruptcy and on its understanding of rights relating to assets located outside its territory.[162]

C. The Test of Resolution

751. The actual basis of the Financial Collateral Directive. The Financial Collateral Directive was designed with the same objective as Articles 8 and 9 of the *Uniform Commercial Code*. As Mr de Vauplane writes, 'some intermediaries felt that it was inefficient not to use this pool of securities – their own, but also those of their clients – in their accounts for which they provided custody or deposit'.[163] The reasons that motivated the adoption of the American reform of financial securities[164] are recognised. It is therefore rather the interests of certain financial institutions, combined with the desire to enhance the value of the European

---

160 Even if it is so qualified, the *lex concursus* will not necessarily exclude it from the scope of the procedure, see already in this sense D. Robine and S. Praicheux, 'Garanties Financières', *op. cit.*, no. 121.

161 See Y. Loussouarn and J.-D. Bredin, *Droit du commerce international*, *op. cit.*, no. 713; See 'Faillite' in H. Synvet, *Répertoire de droit international*, *op. cit.*, no. 57.

162 See, in French perspective, the observations of D. Robine and S. Praicheux, 'Garanties Financières', *op. cit.*, no. 122.

163 H. de Vauplane, 'Cadre juridique des garanties financières', *op. cit.*, no. 10.

164 See *supra*, no. 672. See A. Gaudemet, *Les dérivés*, *op. cit.*, no. 561, who sees here the penetration into French law of foreign considerations remarkably favourable to certain creditors. On the insolvency protection rules of *close-out netting* and financial collaterals in American law, see C. Mooney, 'The Bankruptcy Code's Safe Harbors for Settlement Payments and Securities Contracts: When is Safe too Safe?'(2014) 49 *Tex Int'l Law Journal*, pp. 247–251. This preferential treatment has been the subject of an extensive critical literature in the United States, see the references given by P. Paech, 'The value of Financial Market Insolvency Safe Harbours' (2016) 36(4) *Oxford Journal of Legal Studies*, p. 858, note 16.

financial centre[165] by increasing the liquidity of the sector,[166] which seems to be the basis for the regulation. For this reason, neither the European legislator nor the Court of Justice are convincing when they say that the Financial Collateral Directive was enacted to protect against systemic risk.[167] As Professor Antoine Gaudemet has already observed, this was the only basis that allowed for a derogation from the collective procedure to be granted.[168] This is apparent from the scope of the Directive itself, but also from the scope of the Resolution Directive.

752. The scope of the Financial Collateral Directive. In order to protect the financial system from systemic risk, as financial institutions are interdependent, it was desired to protect the fulfilment of the commitments of these actors from the impact of collective proceedings. Indeed, although the protection already granted to the participants in a system was necessary, it does not cover all the relationships that could trigger the systemic risk. This argument appears specious for several reasons. First, as Mr Synvet observes, if it were correct, the Financial Collateral Directive should have restricted its scope to financial collateral between financial institutions,[169] and not extended it to anyone entering into a financial collateral arrangement with one of these institutions.[170] Secondly, if the desire to prevent systemic risk was the basis of this directive, it would have been sufficient to oblige financial institutions entering into contracts requiring the provision of financial collateral to do so through a clearing house. Finally, it is not certain that the rules of exclusion from the scope of collective proceedings allow the fight against systemic risk. Firstly, because their existence may encourage operators to take more risk because of this protection, which is sometimes referred to as *moral hazard*.[171]

165 D. Robine and S. Praicheux, 'Garanties Financières', *op. cit.*, no. 4.

166 Demonstrating that the real purpose of the rules stemming from the Financial Collateral Directive is to increase market liquidity, see P. Paech, 'The value of Financial Market Insolvency Safe Harbours', *op. cit.*

167 Recital 1 of the Financial Collateral Directive. See also *ibid.* The authors rely on the judgment of the Court of Justice that the difference in treatment of financial collateral compared to other collateral is "based on an objective criterion which is related to the legitimate aim of Directive 2002/47, which is to enhance the legal certainty and effectiveness of financial collateral in order to ensure the stability of the financial system", see Case C-156/15, *'Private Equity Insurance Group' SIA v. 'Swedbank' AS*, ECLI:EU:C:2016:851, para. 51.

168 A. Gaudemet, *Les dérivés*, *op. cit.*, no. 513. This explains why it was possible to write, in a retrospective analysis, that 'the foundation of the prevention of 'systemic risk' [...] will end up becoming to financial law what the cream pie is to the circus school', A. Caillemer du Ferrage, 'L'impact de la résolution sur le netting', *RDBF*, October 2013, file 38.

169 The term should be understood as all the institutions designated by Art. 1(2) of the Financial Collateral Directive.

170 H. Synvet, 'The exclusion of certain creditors from the law of collective proceedings', *op. cit.*, p. 179. See also the observations of C. Boillot, 'Droit bancaire et financier et procédure collective: exception ou contradiction?' *D.*, 2003, pp. 2741 et seq., spec. p. 2748; A. Gaudemet, *Les dérivés*, *op. cit.*, no. 555.

171 On this argument, see P. Paech, 'The value of Financial Market Insolvency Safe Harbours', *op. cit.*; p. 873 and references.

Secondly, because the termination-compensation mechanisms associated with the seizure of collateral accelerate the collapse of the entity in difficulty.[172]

753. The scope of application of the Resolution Directive. These remarks are supported by the comparison of the exclusion of systems and financial collateral from the *lex concursus* and the law of resolution. The demonstration is simple and consists in observing that if the Resolution Directive limits the powers of the resolution authorities with regard to payment and securities settlement systems, it does not do the same with financial collateral in general, proof that the protection of the latter has less to do with systemic risk than it seems.

The first limitation of the resolution power appears with regard to the suspension of payment and settlement obligations. Indeed, Article 69(1) of the Resolution Directive gives resolution authorities the power to 'suspend any payment or settlement obligation arising out of a contract to which an institution subject to resolution proceedings is a party'. However, the same article specifies that these suspensions do not apply to payment obligations to Finality Directive systems, European and recognised third country clearing houses and central banks.[173] This limitation is explained precisely by the European legislator's awareness that the preservation of these systems is necessary to prevent systemic risk. The second limitation of the Resolution Directive is the power given to resolution authorities 'to restrict the right of secured creditors of an institution subject to resolution proceedings to enforce security interests in the assets of that institution'.[174] However, again, this power cannot be exercised against collateral held by Finality Directive systems, or against central counterparties or central banks.[175] Indeed, the legislator considered that beneficiaries of financial collateral did not deserve to be protected from resolution powers, simply because financial collateral does not address systemic risk.

Finally, a third limitation on resolution powers concerns transfers of assets, and contractual changes to which the institution subject to resolution proceedings is a party, whether by virtue of the terms or the substitution of the very status of party to the contract. Again, the exercise of these resolution tools 'shall not affect the functioning and regulation of the systems covered by Directive [Finality]'.[176] The Directive specifies that nothing should be done to affect the finality of transactions concluded within a payment or securities settlement system.[177]

---

172 *Ibid.*, p. 876.
173 Art. 69(4) of the Resolution Directive.
174 Art. 70(1) of the Resolution Directive.
175 Art. 70(2) of the Resolution Directive.
176 Art. 80(1) of the Resolution Directive.
177 Art. 80(2) of the Resolution Directive.

754. This preservation of the Finality Directive's systems, based on the prevention of systemic risk, sheds light on both the relationship between resolution and market infrastructures and the protection afforded to financial collateral. First, it means, from the perspective of the European Union, that the stability of the systems constituting market infrastructures is more important than banking stability, or rather that it is a condition for it. This statement explains why the use of resolution instruments is most often conditional on the consideration of their effects on financial markets.[178] Secondly, it allows for the perception that the protection of beneficiaries of financial guarantees is excessive. Robine and Praicheux consider that 'financial guarantees, like all legislation relating in particular to securities, attempt a delicate acrobatic exercise between the interests of the creditor, the debtor and the market ('third parties' in the broadest sense of the term)'.[179] In fact, it seems to us that they are rather an instrument to promote the financial contracting industry, and in particular credit institutions and investment firms which are the main beneficiaries of these provisions. Systemic risk protection rules should not be based on insolvency exemption rules, but on prudential rules combined with institutional supervision and possibly a specific resolution regime.[180]

II. The Application of the Law of the System to Securities of Insolvent Participants

755. The application of the law of the system to the rights and obligations of an insolvent participant. The *lex concursus* is traditionally that of the forum of the judgment opening the collective proceedings,[181] nowadays determined by the main centre of interests of the debtor. However, as regards the rights and obligations arising from the insolvent debtor's participation in the payment or securities settlement system, Article 8 of the Finality Directive modifies the connection by substituting the law of the system for the competent *lex fori concursus*:

> 'In the event of insolvency proceedings being opened against a participant in a system, the rights and obligations arising from, or in connection with, the participation of that participant shall be determined by the law governing that system.'

---

178 See e.g. the instrument of internal bail-in, Art. 43 of the Resolution Directive, or the need to take into account the impact on financial markets of an authority's ability to suspend payment or settlement obligations of the institution subject to resolution, Art. 33a(5) of the Resolution Directive.

179 D. Robine and S. Praicheux, 'Garanties Financières', *op. cit.*, no. 4.

180 See already in this sense, P. Paech, 'The value of Financial Market Insolvency Safe Harbours', *op. cit.*, pp. 879 et seq.

181 On this question, see L. d'Avout, 'Sens et portée de la *lex fori concursus*', *op. cit.*

This originality is confirmed by the Insolvency Regulation[182] which states that 'only the law applicable to the system or market concerned should apply to such transactions'.[183] This rule does not in itself mean that rights arising from the payment system are excluded from the scope of the *lex concursus*, but merely that the *lex concursus* applicable to such rights is that of the law applicable to the system.[184] In other words, it extends the scope of the law of the system to the treatment of transactions where one of the participants is insolvent. There may be a difficulty with the articulation of the law of the system, applied as *lex concursus*, and the financial guarantees to which the rights of the participants may have been subject. In reality, the articulation is simple insofar as the designated law will be the same, since the Finality Directive then submits the 'determination of the rights of these entities as collateral holders' to the central deposit system. These observations call for several remarks: from the point of view of the *lex concursus*, the law of the system, and the proprietary status of the security.

756. From the point of view of the *lex concursus*. From the point of view of the *lex concursus*, this rule already shows, before the introduction of the Insolvency Regulation, that it is possible to separate the law applicable to the insolvency of the court competent for the opening of proceedings from the law applicable to creditors' rights in insolvency.[185] This rule on the application of the law of the system is not unique: other elements within the Insolvency Regulation are subject to their own law.[186] In the latter cases, 'only the Law of the Member State so designated may apply and it applies in full, including its insolvency law'.[187] As Mr d'Avout writes:

> 'The rationale behind these bilateral micro connecting rules in Europe is that of a special bankruptcy law, chosen for its greater convenience. For reasons of substance, practicality of the law and protection of certain category interests, the legislator has deemed it appropriate to subject the effects of bankruptcy on employment contracts, rights traded on a regulated market, real estate contracts, etc., to a law with exclusive jurisdiction: the one that normally governs the civil institution in question and which is extended to cover insolvency law issues.'[188]

---

182 See Art. 9 of Regulation 1346/2000, and Art. 12 of Regulation 2015.
183 Recital 27 of Regulation 1346/2000 and Recital 71 of Regulation 2015.
184 On the determination of the law applicable to the system, see *supra*, paras. 277 et seq.
185 L. d'Avout, 'Sens et portée de la *lex fori concursus*', *op. cit.*, p. 44.
186 The same applies to rights in rem in immovable property or employment contracts, see Arts. 11 and 13 of the Insolvency Regulation.
187 M. Virgos and E. Schmit, *Report on the Convention on insolvency proceedings*, doc. EC no. 6500/96, nos. 118 et seq.
188 L. d'Avout, 'Sens et portée de la *lex fori concursus*', *op. cit.*,p. 52.

In the particular case of systems covered by the Finality Directive, the special derogation granted to the law of the system should be read in conjunction with the substantive rules established by the Finality Directive, which aim at excluding transactions carried out by a system from the scope of the *lex concursus*. While it is therefore apparently a special law of bankruptcy, the application of the law of the system is in fact aimed at avoiding the disruption of any *lex concursus*, in particular foreign *lex concursus*, resulting from the insolvency of a participant in the system whose main centre of interests is located in a non-EU State.

757. From the point of view of the law of the system. From the point of view of the law of the system, its scope exceeds that traditionally given to the *lex contractus*, on which its applicability is however based.[189] Applicable to transactions within its system, it extends to the proprietary status of securities between system participants, but also to the effects of the insolvency of a participant on transactions and on the status of securities. This derogatory rule of conflict, together with the substantive rule limiting the effect of the procedure on the rights and obligations of the debtor in difficulty in the system, fully protects the systems of the Finality Directive. The unity of the law applicable to all transactions makes it possible to unify the regime of the rights and obligations of the participants, including in the event of collective proceedings: this is an indisputable stabilising element.[190] The application of this rule is all the more welcome as its scope of application is strictly limited to system participants: the insolvency of an indirect participant will therefore not be subject to the law of the system nor that of the downstream person in the intermediation chain. Moreover, only the effects of the insolvency relating to the rights and obligations of the system are subject to the law of the system; the other aspects of the insolvency of the participant remain subject to the *lex concursus*.[191]

758. From the point of view of the proprietary status of securities. Of course, the main reason for the derogation from the *lex concursus* is to allow the proper execution of transactions carried out by the financial markets and, incidentally, to protect the category interests of certain creditors. A deeper reason, however, is

---

189 See *supra*, para. 277.

190 See already in this sense P. Bloch, 'La directive 98/26/CEE concernant le caractère définitif du règlement dans les systèmes de paiement et de règlement des opérations sur titres', *op. cit.*, p. 72.

191 This is the meaning of Recital 17 of the Directive: 'This Directive also aims to determine, in the event of the opening of insolvency proceedings against a participant in a system, which insolvency law is applicable to the rights and obligations of that participant arising from its participation in a system.' Despite this clarification, the field of the designated law is not always limited in this way in foreign law, e.g. in English law, which applies the law of the system to all aspects of the insolvency ('any questions relating to the rights and obligations arising from, or in connection with, the participation'), see M. Ooi, *Shares and other securities in the conflict of laws, op. cit.*

the location of the securities and the principle of effectiveness. Indeed, securities are closely linked to the securities settlement system of the central depository with which they have been admitted. In the event of a discrepancy between the accounts of the central depository and those of other intermediaries, the accounts of the former will always be authoritative. The central depository is the recipient of a competence which belongs to the issuer, and which is vested in it by the issuer.[192] The legal centre of gravity of securities is constituted by this settlement system; it is therefore desirable that the latter extends its law to their proprietary status. This preponderant location of securities in the settlement system can also be based on the principle of effectiveness, since the issuer will only be liable to the owners of the securities determined by the central depository.[193] This is consistent with trading systems, whose law applies to contracts concluded within them; similarly, the law of the securities settlement system should apply to the proprietary status of securities located there.[194] The only difference should be the nature of the criterion, which would be objective and no longer subjective, since it is not a question of contractual relations between the parties, but vis-à-vis third parties.

Moreover, and even more importantly, the law of the system has the three qualities sought for the law applicable to the proprietary status of the security: unity, since transfers of the same security will always be subject to the same law; stability, since the system's connection is not subject to change; and accessibility, insofar as it is known to the participants. It is the law chosen by the participants, usually chosen by the central securities depository and notified by the Member State where the depository is located to the ESMA.[195] These virtues encourage extending the scope of the law of the system to the entire proprietary status of securities admitted to a securities settlement system.

---

192 See *supra*, para. 664.

193 This means that the assertion that, in the case of transfers of securities, the issuer constitutes the centre of gravity of the transfer must be qualified (S. Laval, *Les tiers et le contrat*, *op. cit.*, no. 29).

194 Already drawing such an analogy, M. Ooi, 'The choice of a choice of law rule', *op. cit.*, p. 232: 'An analogy could be drawn from transactions through a stock exchange, where market expectations would be that the laws regulating the exchange in question would determine entitlement to the securities traded through the exchanges.'

195 See *supra*, para. 277.

§ 2. APPLICATION OF THE LAW OF THE SYSTEM TO THE PROPRIETARY STATUS OF THE SECURITIES

The virtues of the law of the system have just been explained. Nevertheless, we will identify the basis for the application of the law of the system to the proprietary status of the security (I) before observing that there is no obstacle to the generalisation of the criterion to the whole proprietary status of securities deposited in the accounts of a central depository (II).

I. The Basis of the Law of the System

759. ***Vox clamans in deserto.*** The generalisation of the application of the law of the system to the entire proprietary status of the security is not a new idea. It was already proposed by Professor Joanna Benjamin in the context of the application of the *lex situs*, the author rightly considering that the securities settlement system was the true location of securities.[196] However, it is to Ms Maisie Ooi that we owe the most attractive demonstration of why the law of the system appears to be the most appropriate. The author has had the opportunity to regularly recall its virtues, which can be appreciated by contrast with each new English judicial decision. However, the author's demonstration comes close to a voice crying in the wilderness: the Commission's impact study on the proprietary effects of title transfer does not even consider this possibility. It is true that the '*travaux préparatoires*' and the explanatory report of the Hague Convention mention a possibility close to the law of the system, called 'Super-PRIMA', which 'would consist in applying the same law in respect of each securities account with each intermediary standing between an account holder and the issuer or in respect of each securities account involved in a transfer of securities effected by book entry along a chain of intermediaries'.[197] The drafters of the Convention rejected this approach because it would result in the perfection test being determined only *ex post*, once the security has been credited to the transferee's account.[198] This statement is correct, but no longer applies if one substitutes the securities settlement system for the ultimate holder's securities account.

760. The basis of the law of the system. Maisie Ooi bases part of the applicability of the law of the system on the *lex creationis*, the law of the source, that which governs the creation of the law. The author considers that in the English system, the admission of securities to a central depository changes the nature of what

[196] See already in this sense, J. Benjamin, 'Determining the situs of interests in immobilized securities' (1998) 47(4) *International and comparative law quarterly*, pp. 923 et seq. and, by the same author, 'The Oxford colloquium on collateral and conflict of laws: overview', *op. cit.*

[197] *Explanatory Report*, no. 4-63.

[198] M. Ooi, *Shares and other securities in the conflict of laws, op. cit.*, nos. 13–24.

is traded. This means that the book entry in the securities settlement system does not represent the financial instrument, but a separate object, issued by the central depository itself. The law of the system therefore applies to the *lex creationis*, the law of the object transferred, in the same way that the law of the US intermediary applies to the *security entitlement*. Maisie Ooi's analysis can, however, be tempered by two elements.

Firstly, Ms Maisie Ooi focuses on the distinction between the financial security issued by the issuer and the *res* exchanged within the securities settlement system. However, in Ms Maisie Ooi's thinking, there is still some uncertainty as to the origin of what is exchanged: is it a *res* created by the central depository, or by the securities settlement system? The question may appear theoretical since the law of the system is, in practice, most often subject to the seat of the central depository. However, as European law stands, this correlation is not a necessity.[199] If it is the CSD which creates a new *res* after the deposit of the genuine securities in its issue accounts, it must be assumed that it is the originator of the rights issued and traded in its system. In the latter case, the law of the system is applicable only to the extent that it corresponds to the law of the central depository; if the depository creates a system subject to a foreign law, the law of the system will not apply to the proprietary status of the rights traded in it. The nature of the *res* alone will determine whether it is a matter of successively exercised personal rights or a right in rem. In continental systems, it is rather rights in rem that are traded on the securities settlement system.

Secondly, the nature of the *res* does not necessarily change by its registration within a securities settlement system. French law is an eloquent example, where the *res* exchanged on the securities settlement system is indeed the financial security itself. In the latter case, the application of the *lex creationis* would refer to the *lex societatis* or the law of the contract of issue, which does not necessarily coincide with the law of the system. Such a solution seems to us unsatisfactory in that it does not allow the unification of the proprietary status of financial securities of all securities admitted to the same central depository. Moreover, the latter is most often the only one to determine the ownership of securities. It therefore seems appropriate to dissociate the law of the system from the *lex creationis* and to consider that the law of the system does not apply as *lex creationis*, but on its own basis. Indeed, the securities settlement system is the predominant legal location of the proprietary status of securities, which stems from the fact that it is the space where the protection of rights is most effective since it is from there that the original registration originates. Moreover, this law designates a unitary, stable and predictable law. Finally,

199 See *supra*, para. 277.

all book-entry securities within an intermediation chain are always originally registered in such a system.

II. *The Absence of Obstacles to Generalisation*

761. Application to foreign *negotia*. It may be considered that this law does not correspond to systems which, precisely, follow a logic where the rights resulting from an account registration are exercised against the direct intermediary, in the manner of *security entitlements*. However, the application of the law of the system allows for harmonious solutions. Two hypotheses allow for this. The first is where a security admitted to the systems of the French depositary is registered in an account with an authorised American intermediary, for the benefit of a French account holder. In this first case, the application of the law of the system allows the account holder to benefit from French law and not to see his ownership vitiated by the chain of intermediation. The second case is where a French account holder asks its French intermediary to acquire a security admitted to the US securities settlement system. The account holder will then only have a *security entitlement*. Again, it should be noted that the PRIMA rule does not lead to anything else, simply because the intermediary itself would have had only a *security entitlement* against the US intermediary, a party to the US securities settlement system, from which it would have acquired the security on behalf of its client.

The application of such a law is even more satisfactory for legal systems based on the co-ownership of securities. These systems, refusing to recognise the possibility of rights in rem in fungible things, seek to recreate the regime of ownership of securities. However, we have observed that this regime could be disqualified when the forum applied its *lex fori*, rather than the law of the system, to the determination of title. The application of the law of the system to any security deposited with a central depository makes it possible, precisely, to recreate the coherence of a category that English private international law jurisprudence has sought to break down.[200]

762. There is no doubt that it is better, as the ECB observed, to agree on certain substantive elements in order to create the conditions for a unitary conflict rule. Nevertheless, some of this agreement already exists, which explains why the law of the system is so effective. Indeed, intermediation chains all have in common their pyramid structure, headed by a securities settlement system managed by a central depository. Although the modalities of these systems differ, they always have in common that they are the first element allowing the existence of an intermediation chain based on securities accounts. They also have in common, when acting as a central depository, that they are then linked

---

200 See *supra*, para. 399.

to a securities registration service. This is also why the argument of the opacity of the intermediation chain sometimes used against the application of the law of the system does not seem particularly relevant.[201]

763. Transparency of the intermediation chain. The transparency argument is powerful because it is based, in essence, on the aspect and predictability of the criterion used. However, it must be challenged. Indeed, it is easy to know the settlement system in which securities are admitted. It is not necessary to go back up the chain of intermediation, but simply to know the origin. This information is usually available on the issuer's website or in the prospectus, and it should be possible to make the provision of this information mandatory in both media. Finally, it would be possible to accompany the book-entry security with a legal identifier that would designate the relevant settlement system.

764. Nature of the securities account. Another argument that is sometimes used relates to the nature of the securities account. Indeed, it is based on the idea that the link between the registration in the investor's account at the end of the chain and the ownership of the security is sometimes impossible to establish. This would be the case whenever the entry takes place in the accounts of an intermediary using an *omnibus* account. This is, however, to misunderstand the influence of the distinction between securities accounts that individualise the securities and omnibus securities accounts, at least from the point of view of French law. This distinction is especially relevant in case of insolvency of the intermediary, where it allows the clients of the securities account holder to explicitly claim the segregated securities, whereas in case the account is omnibus and the securities are disposed of, they will only have a pro rata right. However, where the securities account holder is *in bonis*, the securities do belong to the ultimate account holder.

765. Plurality of laws applicable to securities accounts. Finally, a last argument comes from the plurality of laws applicable to securities account pledges. This argument is stronger: it is in fact the only reason to adopt PRIMA. The PRIMA rule has the advantage for the intermediary of subjecting the pledge of a securities account to only one law, that of the relevant intermediary, i.e. its own, whereas the application of the law of the securities settlement system results – when there are securities admitted to the systems of several securities settlement systems within the account – in the need to look at the conditions of application of each of these laws. However, the argument seems to be overstated. On the one hand, the number of securities settlement systems is very limited, at most one or even two per country and sometimes none at all. The rules of enforceability are, moreover, less remote than claimed, due to the harmonisation achieved by the Financial Collateral Directive for EU

[201] See *Bernasconi Report*, p. 28.

Member States and due to the reciprocal influence of financial legislation in foreign states.[202] The cost of complying with the different modalities of pledge enforceability should therefore not be overestimated. On the other hand, from a legal policy point of view, this cost is much lower than the significant risks posed by the PRIMA test.

However, the personal interests of account managers have prevailed over the rule subjecting the proprietary status of securities admitted to the settlement system to the law of the settlement system, which was initially included in Article 46 of the draft CSD Regulation, and which explains the presence of Recital 57 in the same Regulation. The latter explains that 'this is a horizontal issue which goes beyond the scope of this Regulation and could be dealt with in future Union legislative acts'. This is a further illustration of the overweighting of certain private interests in the development of state rules, which financial law is apparently accustomed to.

766. Conclusion of the section. There is a unitary, objective, predictable and apparent solution to the conflicts of laws arising from the proprietary status of bearer securities registered within an intermediation chain. This solution lies in the application of the law of the securities settlement system. This connection, already used when one of the participants becomes insolvent, is based on the element common to all intermediation structures: the existence of an original tier, which is the only one able to verify the correspondence between the securities registered in its issue accounts and those circulating within the securities settlement system. The law of its system is truly the one that constitutes the centre of gravity of the proprietary status of securities, because of the strength that attaches to the probity of the entries in its system, which are the only ones able to prevail.

767. Conclusion of the chapter. When securities are intermediated, there is a solution to the conflict of laws based on the application of a unitary, predictable law that corresponds to the legal centre of gravity and the function of the institutions involved. This law has long existed for registered securities: it is the law of the issuer. This solution would benefit from being extended to securities registered in the blockchain. Where there is a central depository, the law applicable to the proprietary status of the securities should be that of its securities settlement system. This solution already exists to determine the law applicable to the securities of a member of the settlement system in case of insolvency; it should be extended to all those whose original registration is in the system of the central depository.

---

202 Whether through the influence of stakeholders, international institutions such as UNCITRAL, or IOSCO.

768. Conclusion of title. The difficulties to which the law applicable to the proprietary status of the title gives rise stem from a misunderstanding of the scope to be given to the rules of domestic law in international law. Their projection into the international order should not result in replicating their technical mechanisms, but the function for which they were designed. The authors would then have more easily realised the inappropriateness of a conflict-of-laws rule that leads to a multiplication of the laws applicable to the transfer of securities, whereas a unitary solution is necessary for the legal security of cross-border relationships. This could moreover be found in the analysis of the institutions involved. In the case of bills of exchange, it was the law of payment; in the case of bearer securities, the law of the issuer; and, finally, when the securities are registered in securities accounts within an intermediary chain based on a central depository, the law of the latter's securities settlement system.

TITLE 2
LAW APPLICABLE TO FINANCIAL CONTRACTS

769. Concept of financial contract. Financial contracts constitute, alongside securities, the other component of financial instruments. Positive law does not provide a criterion for distinguishing between the two, but their function and regime make it possible to distinguish them. Unlike securities, financial contracts do not have a financing purpose,[1] are not issued or represented by a security, and do not benefit from the negotiability regime; their circulation is ensured by other techniques.[2] Financial contracts are therefore fundamentally contracts. However, their definition by enumeration shows different varieties of contracts.[3] Different typologies of financial contracts have therefore been developed, depending on their economic purpose, the nature of the risk taken, the obligations entered into, the underlying, the settlement or the negotiation methods.[4] However, this enumeration has the disadvantage of not allowing a spontaneous conceptual understanding of the notion.[5] A financial contract can be defined as a contract in which a person undertakes to pay a sum of money or to deliver goods according to the evolution of the value of an underlying asset, with performance being postponed to a later date.[6] This discrepancy between the date of conclusion of

---

1 See however the exception of derivative securities which do not have a financing purpose, T. Bonneau *et al.*, *Droit financier*, *op. cit.*, nos. 778 et seq.; A. Couret, H. Le Nabasque *et al.*, *Droit financier*, *op. cit.*, nos. 1136 et seq.

2 P. Pailler, *Le contrat financier, un instrument financier à terme*, *op. cit.* On the refutation of the idea that financial contracts are negotiable, see also A. Couret, H. Le Nabasque *et al.*, *Droit financier*, *op. cit.*, no. 1240.

3 This definition, developed by the European legislator, is included in Art. D. 211-1(A) of the Monetary and Financial Code, by reference to Art. L. 211-1(III) of the Monetary and Financial Code. The enumerative technique was already in force before the transposition of the MiFID, see A. Couret, H. Le Nabasque *et al.*, *Droit financier*, *op. cit.*, no. 1220. For some authors, this is a sign of the disparity of financial contracts, see P. Pailler, *Le contrat financier, un instrument financier à terme*, *op. cit.*, no. 2.

4 A. Gaudemet, *Les dérivés*, *op. cit.*, nos. 98 et seq. A. Couret, H. Le Nabasque *et al.*, *Droit financier*, *op. cit.*, no. 1225; P. Pailler, *Le contrat financier, un instrument financier à terme*, *op. cit.*, no. 2; R. Dambre, *Les contrats financiers sur actions*, *op. cit.*, no. 2.

5 This may also have been intended to avoid a disadvantageous qualification for financial contracts, see P. Cornut St-Pierre, *La fabrique juridique des swaps*, Paris, Presse de SciencesPo, pp. 139 et seq.

6 See also A. Couret, H. Le Nabasque *et al.*, *Droit financier*, *op. cit.*, no. 1220; R. Dambre, *Les contrats financiers sur actions*, *op. cit.*, no. 33: 'It is essentially a question of transferring to another party the risk of the evolution of the value of a thing over time.'; A. Gaudemet, *Les dérivés*, *op. cit.*, no. 95, who considers that derivatives 'are contracts whose purpose is to

the contract and its execution is one of the most distinctive features of financial contracts, allowing the parties to take opposing positions on the change in the value of the object taken into consideration by the contract, referred to as the underlying. Two observations must be made here.

Firstly, the time lag between the conclusion of the contract and its execution appears to be central, to the extent that it was previously included in the very title of the concept when it was described as a *futures* instrument.[7] This time lag is in fact likely to allow the speculative[8] and

---

abstract the value of an underlying thing to allow the parties to expose their hopes or fears about the future'; see also H. GOURDY, *La couverture sur les marchés financiers*, *op. cit.*, no. 3. From an American perspective, see A. RILES, *Collateral Knowledge*, *op. cit.* S. HENDERSON, *Henderson on Derivatives*, 2nd ed., Paris, LexisNexis, 2009. It should be noted here that the title of the concept, which is of legal origin, does not perfectly describe the mechanism at stake. The contract may be considered financial in that it involves the payment of a sum of money and is concluded professionally by 'financial' entities, i.e. investment service providers.

7 The title was nevertheless misleading because, as Mr Gaudemet writes, it gave the impression that 'all the contracts designated under this name use the suspensive term procedure, which is not legally correct' (A. GAUDEMET, *Les dérivés*, *op. cit.*, no. 163), whereas it is possible to use the unilateral promise to contract. On the contractual implementation of this time lag, see *ibid.*, chapter 1; R. DAMBRE, *Les contrats financiers sur actions*, *op. cit.* Moreover, the term of the financial contract does not correspond to the term as understood within the general regime of obligations, see P. PAILLER, 'Le rôle du terme et du sous-jacent dans la formation du prix', *Revue de jurisprudence commerciale*, September-October 2013, no. 5, p. 383.

8 Some authors distinguish between two types of speculation (see T. BONNEAU *et al.*, *Droit financier*, *op. cit.*, no. 835): the traditional one, which is linked to the notion of gambling, and a second one, which is referred to as financial arbitrage. It is known that the qualification of a gamble is likely to obstruct the performance of the contract, which has long focused the attention of doctrine (Art. 1965 of the Civil Code, see A. Gaudemet, *Les dérivés*, *op. cit.*, no. 179; R. DAMBRE, *Les contrats financiers sur actions*, *op. cit.*, no. 57; and from the French historical point of view, N. HISSUNG-CONVERT, *La spéculation boursière face au droit 1799-1914*, *op. cit.*), without the Court of Cassation giving this rule of public policy an international dimension (Cass., civ. 1re, 16 March 1999, no. 96-21, 794, note P. DELEBECQUE, *Defrénois*, 15 December 1999, p. 1324). The question has also arisen in English law, see J. BRAITHWAITE, *The Financial Courts: Adjudicating Disputes in Derivatives Markets*, Cambridge, CUP, 2021, p. 29. Indeed, the Court of Cassation refused to qualify the exception of international public policy gambling in order to undermine the execution of a financial contract subject to English law, considering that 'the contractual mechanism put in place was intended to guarantee the stability of the exchange rates to the company de Loisy et Gelet, and deduced exactly that the execution, in France, of this agreement, did not offend international public policy.. If the solution deserves approval, the formula of 'contractual mechanism intended to guarantee the stability of prices' appears imprecise. As Professor Delebecque observes in his above-mentioned note, 'the expression is not very happy in a field where the essential element must be that of uncertainty'. The Court of Justice itself has considered that the prohibition of transactions on the futures market was not contrary to the freedom to provide services, see Case 15/78, *Société générale alsacienne de banque SA v. Walter Koestler*, ECLI:EU:C:1978:184, Rec. 1871.

Arbitrage 'consists of taking advantage of inefficiencies revealed in the formation of prices on the markets by playing on the differences in quotations between the different financial centres'. R. DAMBRE, *Les contrats financiers sur actions*, *op. cit.*, no. 32. Other authors

insurance functions[9] traditionally pursued by financial contracts[10] to be fulfilled, and which have always been the subject of controversy. These two functions make it possible to account for the purpose of the financial contract, which is to transfer a risk.[11]

Secondly, another gap allowed by the financial contract arises from its very purpose. This is the distance between the reciprocal commitments of the parties and the underlying asset taken into consideration by the contract in order to establish these commitments. This discrepancy constitutes the core of the financial contract technique. It is at the origin of the name sometimes attributed to it of derivative. However, while all financial contracts are derivatives, in the sense that the commitments made by the parties to the contract depend on ('derive'[12]) the underlying asset, some derivatives take the form of financial securities, and in particular debt securities.[13] The technique of 'derivation' is most often referred to as abstraction.[14] It is the common feature of all

consider that arbitrage does not have a speculative function and make it a third function pursued by certain financial contracts, especially *swaps*, as not all contracts lend themselves to arbitrage (see *ibid.*).

9 The insurance function of the financial contract is sometimes referred to as hedging (which covers distinct realities – see *infra*, para. 864). However, a distinction must be made between the obligation to hedge against a risk, which leads to the conclusion of a financial contract and moves the obligation to hedge, and the obligation to hedge, which may refer to the obligation to compensate for the financial contract. The insurance function of the contract refers to the ability of one of the parties to hedge against the occurrence of a risk. The difference lies, however, in the nature of the risk against which one is hedged: thus, the insured risks are statistically predictable and can therefore be modelled (see X. Lagarde, 'Le droit des marchés financiers présente-t-il un particularisme?' *JCP G*, no. 44, November 2005; P. Pailler, *Le contrat financier, un instrument financier à terme*, *op. cit.*, nos. 307 et seq.), whereas the financial contract, and in particular the credit derivative, can insure against risks whose predictability is less obvious.

10 On these two functions, see T. Bonneau *et al.*, *Droit financier*, *op. cit.*, nos. 835 et seq. A. Couret, H. Le Nabasque *et al.*, *Droit financier*, *op. cit.*, no. 1224; P. Pailler, *Le contrat financier, un instrument financier à terme*, *op. cit.*, nos. 252 et seq.; R. Dambre, *Les contrats financiers sur actions*, *op. cit.*, nos. 31 et seq.

11 Thus Mr Gaudemet shows, in the first part of his thesis, that derivatives are 'an instrument of risk transfer'; see also R. Dambre, *Les contrats financiers sur actions*, *op. cit.*, no. 27. This risk transfer function explains the presentation often made of financial contracts as a simple risk management tool for the parties using them. However, it seems that the uses of financial contracts go beyond this presentation, see P. Cornut St-Pierre, *La fabrique juridique des swaps*, *op. cit.*, pp. 177 et seq.; J. Braithwaite, 'Standard Form Contracts as Transnational Law'(2012) *Modern Law Review*, pp. 779 et seq.

12 The term derivatives comes from an anglicism, the English referring to the notion as *derivatives*.

13 T. Bonneau *et al.*, *Droit financier*, *op. cit.*, no. 762, and on derivative securities, no. 778; A. Couret, H. Le Nabasque *et al.*, *Droit financier*, *op. cit.*, nos. 1136 et seq. A. Gaudemet, *Les dérivés*, *op. cit.*, nos. 105 et seq.

14 Abstraction here takes on a meaning quite distinct from that which it has had in civil law, or in the law of exchange.

derivatives,[15] allowing them to capture ever more diverse underlyings; the main ones today are exchange and interest rates, commodities, equities and credit risk.[16] The objective of the parties here is to abstract the financial contract from the underlying, in order to make their bilateral commitments independent of the underlying. In other words, while the economic amount of the commitments depends on the underlying, the derivative is intended to be legally independent of the underlying. As Professor Antoine Gaudemet writes:

> 'The autonomy rule is the most direct manifestation of the abstraction principle. It requires that derivatives follow their own law, independently of the underlying thing on which they are based: if the commitments of the parties to a derivative are determined by reference to the value of an underlying thing, they are nevertheless independent of that thing in legal terms.'[17]

770. The autonomy rule is relevant to the regime of the financial contract. First, it explains why the payment of the obligation arising from the financial contract, sometimes referred to as unwinding, is independent of the delivery of the underlying. Indeed, while the financial contract may provide for the delivery of the thing at the end of the term when there is one,[18] it may also provide for an unwinding based on the payment of a sum of money equivalent to the price of the delivery of the underlying,[19] or other unwindings as well.[20] The key is not the method of settlement but the transfer of risk. Secondly, the autonomy rule helps to explain the relationship of the contract to the underlying, which is for the former to replicate the utilities of the latter without transferring the asset. Indeed, the financial contract transfers the utilities of the underlying, usually transferred by ownership.[21] Thirdly, in the case where the financial contract does not provide for the delivery of the underlying, the autonomy

---

15 A. Gaudemet, *Les dérivés*, *op. cit.*, no. 95. Some authors compare this abstraction with abstract obligation (on which see *supra*, para. 606), P. Cornut St-Pierre, *La fabrique juridique des swaps*, *op. cit.*

16 On the diversification of underlyings and their understanding by ISDA, see *ibid.*, pp. 128 et seq. One of the reasons why the financial contracts sector grew considerably from the end of the 1970s onwards was mainly due to the development of exchange rate *swap* contracts, made necessary by the end of the dollar's indexation to gold on 15 August 1971.

17 A. Gaudemet, *Les dérivés*, *op. cit.*, no. 221.

18 R. Dambre, *Les contrats financiers sur actions*, *op. cit.*, no. 66.

19 *Ibid.* no. 71.

20 *Ibid.* no. 76.

21 By concluding a financial contract, Mr Dambre considers that 'one of the parties contractually obtains the economic attributes of property, without the property itself', *ibid.* no. 94. For the author, such an 'economic replication of legal property then creates a form of *synthetic property* for the benefit of one of the parties', *ibid.* The notion of synthesis must be understood here in its chemical sense of 'artificial production of a substance usually produced by cells or living organisms', see 'Synthesis', *Trésor informatique de la langue française*.

rule allows for financial contracts based on purely hypothetical underlyings. For example, some financial contracts are based on a 'notional amount', which 'refers to the theoretical amount to which the calculation of the *quantum of* the parties' obligations applies'.[22] The notional amount is thus specific to financial contracts that are based on a theoretical underlying: for example, a theoretical loan constructed from different loans made by a set of representative issuers.[23] The concept also allows for an assessment of the sums at stake for the sector.[24]

Finally, from the point of view of conflict of laws, the autonomy rule explains the independence in principle of the law of the financial contract from that of the underlying, in the same way that a collateral agreement, if linked to the main contract, may be subject to a separate law. The following discussion will show, however, that the autonomy rule is likely to be undermined whenever the law of the underlying intervenes, either to prevent the formation of financial contracts, to interfere with their regime or to punish the contracting parties. This observation from the law of conflict of laws shows that, of all the classifications made of financial contracts, those relating to the underlying is undoubtedly the most relevant, since it forms the basis, alongside the general regime for financial contracts, of a genuine special regime applicable according to the underlying.

771. How financial contracts are negotiated. Financial contracts can be concluded on a financial market or over-the-counter; the choice will depend on various economic and legal factors.[25] In both cases, the contracts have been standardised and subjected to the same substantive regime to facilitate their circulation.[26] However, certain differences remain, depending on the hypothesis considered, and ultimately determine the law applicable to the contract. In the first case, financial contracts are drawn up by the financial market operator, which provides the model as part of the service it offers to market members.[27] In the second case, OTC financial contracts are subject to a contractual architecture that needs to be clarified. Indeed, OTC financial contracts have been

---

22 R. Dambre, *Les contrats financiers sur actions*, *op. cit.*, no. 77.

23 A. Couret, H. Le Nabasque *et al.*, *Droit financier*, *op. cit.*, no. 1264.

24 The notional amount is thus valued every six months by the Bank for International Settlements.

25 H. Synvet, 'Libres propos d'internationaliste sur les obligations d'intermédiation et de concentration', *op. cit.* no. 18: 'OTC has the advantages of flexibility. Regulated markets offer greater legal certainty (thanks to clearing houses, del credere), as well as reliable settlement systems. These are the qualities that can tip the balance, not a monopoly that has become largely illusory.'

26 In the French perspective, this transferability is facilitated by Arts. L. 211-37 and 38 of the Monetary and Financial Code.

27 T. Bonneau *et al.*, *Droit financier*, *op. cit.*, no. 882.

subject to an advanced standardisation,[28] operated by a specialised association, the International Swaps and Derivatives Association, known as ISDA.[29] This association has been active since the 1980s and has drawn up a standard contract,[30] which is particularly widespread[31] and is used for various financial contracts, such as futures, options and swaps. The documentation is divided into two types: on the one hand, the definition codes and the user guide,[32] and on the other hand, the models. The ISDA code provides definitions of the concepts used in the different contract templates, while the user guides provide guidance to the parties so that they can use the ones that best suit them.[33] The model contracts consist of three elements: the *Masters agreement*, amendments to the contract, called schedules, and implementation contracts, called confirmations.[34] In reality, of these three documents, only the implementation contracts constitute financial contracts, the other documents being supports for the conclusion of implementation contracts.[35] Finally, OTC financial contracts have often been subject to English law and English courts, making this legal system the reference for their interpretation.

772. These observations on the way OTC contracts are traded lead to several remarks. The first is to recall the distinction between the legal concept of financial market, i.e. the multilateral trading facility, and the 'economic'

---

28 P. Pailler, *Le contrat financier, un instrument financier à terme*, *op. cit.*, no. 33; R. Dambre, *Les contrats financiers sur actions*, *op. cit.*, no. 10; J. Gavriloff, *Les méthodes du conflit de lois à l'épreuve du produit dérivé*, *op. cit.*, no. 61.

29 ISDA is incorporated in New York State but has a presence in many countries. On the origin, functioning and evolution of ISDA, see S.M. Flanagaan, 'The Rise of a Trade Associations: Group interactions Within the International Swaps and Derivatives Association' (2001) 6 *Harvard Negotiation Law Review*, pp. 212 et seq.; P. Cornut St-Pierre, *La fabrique juridique des swaps*, *op. cit.* pp. 98 et seq.

30 On the qualification of a standard contract, see P. Pailler, *Le contrat financier, un instrument financier à terme*, *op. cit.*

31 The contracts offered by ISDA enjoy a wide dominance within the industry. According to ISDA, ninety percent of the transactions concluded, see J.P. Braithwaite, 'Standard Form Contracts as Transnational Law', *op. cit.*, p. 784, note 46; P. Cornut St-Pierre, *La fabrique juridique des swap*, *op. cit.*, p. 99. This domination is also explained by the staggering concentration of the OTC financial contracts sector, as only fourteen 'dealers were responsible for approximately 82 per cent of the global swap markets by total national amount outstanding', see J. Braithwaite, *The Financial Courts: Adjudicating Disputes in Derivatives Markets*, *op. cit.*, p. 23. According to the same author, the legal reasons for the domination of ISDA contracts lie in *netting* (see *infra*, para. 896) and the collateral provided for in the contract (see *ibid.*, pp. 37 et seq.).

32 These two sources of ISDA documentation are crucial to the interpretation of ISDA contracts by English courts, see *ibid.*, p. 114.

33 P. Cornut St-Pierre, *La fabrique juridique des swaps*, *op. cit.*, p. 108.

34 P. Wood, *Set-off and netting, Derivatives, Clearing system*, London, Sweet&Maxwell, 2007, pp. 217 et seq.; J. Braithwaite, 'Standard Form Contracts as Transnational Law', *op. cit.*, p. 787; P. Cornut St-Pierre, *La fabrique juridique des swaps*, *op. cit.*, p. 109

35 *Ibid.* See also P. Pailler, *Le contrat financier, un instrument financier à terme*, *op. cit.*

concept of financial market, which designates a sector of activity,[36] in this case the financial contracts sector.[37]

The second is to refute the claim that ISDA contracts provide an 'autonomous normative order […] whose practices and standard clauses in themselves actually constitute the regulation […] of the global financial market'.[38] The claim appears excessive.[39] If this were true, ISDA would not so much seek to influence state legislation. The practices and standard clauses of their contracts do not constitute an autonomous normative order, nor even the only applicable regulation. This is easy to see: the contracts drawn up by ISDA are most often subject to a state jurisdiction and, for European institutions, this was almost always that of London until Brexit.[40] This jurisdiction justifies the necessary references to English solutions.[41] Moreover, this can also be seen from the point of view of conflict of laws, since, on the one hand, it is indeed the English conception of contracts that underlies their validity, the terms of their performance or their interpretation[42] and, on the other hand, numerous

[36] Internationalist doctrine sometimes seems to confuse the two, see e.g. H. Muir Watt, 'La gouvernance privée des marchés financiers: les enjeux de la *lex contractus*' in H. Muir Watt *et al.*, *Le tournant global en droit international privé*, *op. cit.*, pp. 355 et seq., spec. p. 358; G. Cuniberti, 'Choix de la loi dans les contrats internes: vers un droit d'accéder aux marchés financiers étrangers' in H. Muir Watt *et al* (ed.), *Le tournant global en droit international privé*, Paris, Pedone, 2020, p. 547.

[37] On this sector and its considerable evolution since the 1980s, see J. Braithwaite, *The Financial Courts: Adjudicating Disputes in Derivatives Markets*, *op. cit.*

[38] H. Muir Watt, 'La gouvernance privée des marchés financiers: les enjeux de la *lex contractus*', *op. cit.*, p. 358; M. Audit, 'Les dérivés de crédit à l'ombre du contrat sans loi' in *TCFDIP*, Paris, Pedone, 2016, p. 85.

[39] Nevertheless, it seems to correspond to the project pursued by certain ISDA councils, see P. Cornut St-Pierre, *La fabrique juridique des swaps*, *op. cit.*, p. 103 and p. 218. This perception may have been fuelled by the political difficulty, experienced in the United States, of subjecting the OTC financial contracts sector to the supervision of a regulatory authority, see B. Carruthers, 'Economy and Law', *op. cit.*, pp. 133–134.

[40] These have the advantage of being able to establish a uniform and predictable interpretation of financial contracts, where arbitral decisions are not binding, see J. Braithwaite, 'Standard Form Contracts as Transnational Law', *op. cit.* Disputes are nevertheless rarely resolved in courts, but often informally, see A. Riles, *Collateral Knowledge*, *op. cit.*, p. 56.

[41] The Anglo-Saxon conception underlying the development of the ISDA contract sometimes makes it unsuitable for certain legal systems where the OTC financial contracting sector is structured differently, see for example the Japanese example reported *ibid.*, pp. 50–51.

[42] M. Penadès Fons, 'Commercial Choice of Law in Context: Looking Beyond Rome' (2015) *Modern Law Review*, pp. 241 et seq. The author shows that the English judge's reasoning on the choice of law clause varies greatly if certain sectors of activity are concerned, and in particular those governed by maritime and insurance law, whose importance for the country justifies both the judge's jurisdiction and gives him 'progressive accumulation of jurispudential wealth in business activity' (*ibid.*, p. 273). It is therefore not surprising that English maritime and insurance law, which are highly developed, have influenced, among other things, the interpretation by the English judge of financial contracts, see J. Braithwaite, *The Financial Courts: Adjudicating Disputes in Derivatives Markets*, *op. cit.*, pp. 62–67 and 105–107; on the English interpretation of the ISDA contract, see *ibid.*, pp. 76 et seq.

laws foreign to the *lex contractus* govern the conclusion and performance of financial contracts concluded by mutual agreement. The third point is to refute the prevailing analysis of the international development of financial contracts as a *lex mercatoria.* Since the persons entering into financial contracts are not part of a 'community of merchants',[43] the content of the law of the state legal orders involved in the relationship will influence the decision made. Moreover, this depends essentially on factors outside the realm of *lex contractus*, but provided for by state law: the intervention of state courts in the event of a dispute; the interference of state rules from insolvency law.[44] In short, *ISDA* is not the Hanseatic League: on the contrary, it relies on state law and state courts.

773. Unquestionably, this distinction according to the mode of negotiation of the contract has long determined the law applicable to the financial contract. Indeed, the resolution of conflicts of law arising from financial contracts and financial markets may have been relatively simple: either financial contracts were concluded through the multilateral trading system, in which case the law of the financial market applied to all aspects of the financial contract; or financial contracts were concluded over-the-counter, and their very frequent internationality allowed the application of a foreign law regardless of the existence of a financial market. It should no doubt be noted that, if it did not apply as the law of the financial market, local law was always likely to apply to the financial contract as the law of the consumer's habitual residence (Chapter 1). Nevertheless, the protective provisions of consumer law are usually of no use to the consumer if the information obligations have been properly provided and he is already bound by the contract.

Such a presentation could lead one to think that if financial market law makes compliance with it the condition for its use, the reciprocal is also true: its lack of use allows the parties to evade the public order that it wished to establish. This presentation of positive law is now wrong, not only because of the nature of the financial contract, but also because of the functions assigned to financial market law. As far as the nature of the financial contract is concerned, the autonomy rule that characterises it allows it to affect its underlying, in particular its price when it is admitted to trading, without using the financial market.[45] It is therefore possible for the financial contract to disrupt the trading system without using it. In this case, it should be noted that the financial market is unable to respond without

---

43 As Professor Braithwaite has already shown, see 'Standard Form Contracts as Transnational Law', *op. cit.*, p. 798.

44 It is better to consider, following Professor Wautelet, that these models have rather acquired a 'quasi-customary status', see P. Wautelet, 'Réglementation étatique et marchés financiers: entre autonomie et relativité', *op. cit.*

45 See already in this sense, A. Gaudemet, *Les dérivés*, *op. cit.*

the help of the legal order in which it is embedded, as it is difficult for the law of the trading platform to paralyse transactions that harm the financial market without using it, or to impose any obligations on persons outside the financial market.

Moreover, this presentation ignores the functions assigned to financial market law, which are not limited to the protection of the trading system, but may pursue, as part of the financial law of which it is a part, two other functions: on the one hand, the protection of residents and, on the other, the stability of the financial system in general and the prevention of systemic risk in particular. These objectives, pursued by heterogeneous bodies of law, have one common feature: they interfere with the formation and execution of the financial contract without, however, intervening in the field of *lex contractus*.[46]

At the time of contract formation, the protection of residents could have been effectively based on capacity if the latter did not lead to the infantilization of residents and the promotion of their bad faith when paying. This is why the protection of residents takes place through rules applicable prior to the very formation of contracts. These are, on the one hand, rules relating to the marketing of financial contracts, and in particular those arising from the regime of banking and financial canvassing and, on the other hand, professional rules arising from the status of investment firms, the only ones authorised to conclude financial contracts on a regular basis. The stability of the financial system, like that of the underlying asset, is also likely to hinder the formation of the financial contract, by making its content illegal, or by engaging the professional responsibility of those who conclude them. The interference of the financial contract on the price of its underlying asset justifies here, in a form of reciprocity, the disturbance of the underlying asset on the very ability to conclude a financial contract (Chapter 2).

At the time of contract execution, the stability function of the financial system was for a long time ensured by the law of the market in that it obliged its users to execute the contract at a clearing house. However, the possibility offered to parties to conclude their financial contracts over the counter made clearing with a clearing house optional. This prudential obligation is now independent of the method of negotiation and is imposed, for financial contracts likely to be subject to clearing, by reason of the institution's presence in the EU. The consequence of this prudential obligation is that the market infrastructure in question, the clearing house, is responsible for designating the *lex contractus* of the contracts it clears. In the majority of cases, this law will be that of the clearing system itself; in other cases, it will be necessary to

46 This is why the statement that 'since private international law methods fail to grasp financial instruments, it is the structures specific to the markets that must ensure their security and stability', J. Gavriloff, *Les méthodes du conflit de lois à l'épreuve du produit dérivé*, *op. cit.*

delimit precisely what is the service provided by the clearing house, subject to the law of the clearing system, and what falls within the domain of the law of the contract (Chapter 3).

CHAPTER 1
THE LAW APPLICABLE TO THE FINANCIAL CONTRACT

774. Mode of negotiation and connection. As a financial contract is a commercial contract, it falls within the material scope of the Rome I Regulation. In order to ensure that the parties' choice of law is respected, the contract must be international. If the contract is concluded through a financial market, it will necessarily be concluded by its members. Internationality will not pose any difficulty since the law applicable to the financial contract will most often be the law of the trading platform;[1] this connection is nevertheless not really decisive since the contract is then recorded with the clearing house.[2] On the other hand, if the financial contract is concluded over-the-counter, the internationality of the financial contract needs to be characterised. This characterisation is fundamental insofar as it conditions, on the one hand, the very possibility of relying on a choice of law in an area where the law of the contract is likely to determine the enforceability of contractual guarantees, in particular those relating to set-off in the event of insolvency, and, on the other hand, the possibility of relying on a set of legal benefits depending on the applicable law.[3] According to the criteria of the Rome I Regulation, the internationality of the financial contract is characterised, as it is most frequently concluded in an international situation (Section 1). From the point of view of connection, internationality allows the parties, through the selection of a given law, to attribute jurisdiction to the legal system most favourable to the possible contentious enforcement of the contract. This choice is all the more important as in practice the possible interference of the derogatory rule of the Rome I Regulation specific to consumer contracts is rare: it requires, in addition to the characterisation of consumer, the existence of a solicitation by the professional (Section 2).

---

1 Either because the contract standardised by the system operator expressly provides for it (on this standardisation, see P. Pailler, *Le contrat financier, un instrument financier à terme*, *op. cit.*, p. 442. The question of internationality may nevertheless arise if the market operator proposes the conclusion of contracts subject to a law foreign to its system. However, in this residual case, the application of the foreign law will most often be explained by the foreignness of the underlying asset, as is the case for contracts relating to credit risk, which is likely to characterise the internationality of the financial contract (see *infra*, para. 786).

2 See *infra*, para. 884.

3 In particular the services that ISDA can provide in relation to credit derivatives, see *infra*, para. 891.

SECTION 1. INTERNATIONALITY

775. Condition of internationality. In order to benefit from the option of choice, it is traditionally held that the contract must be international, simply because 'for conflict of laws, internationality acts as a signal and triggers the application of the conflict rule'.[4] However, internationality also has the function of triggering the application of substantive rules. This distinction between these two functions of internationality has an echo in positive law: in order to determine internationality within the meaning of the conflict rules, French case law relied rather on legal criteria which are based on the links of the contract with more than one state,[5] whereas in order to determine the internationality allowing to avail oneself of a regime specific to international relations it uses rather an economic criterion.[6]

---

4 J.-M. Jacquet, 'L'internationalité. Rapport introductif', *Revue Lamy de droit des affaires*, 2002, supplement, no. 46.

5 From the time of the adoption of the Rome Convention, legal writers were in favour of such an interpretation, see e.g. P. Mayer, 'La délocalisation du contrat' in *La relativité du contrat, Travaux de l'Association Henri Capitant*, Colloque de Nantes, Paris, LGDJ, 1999, 2000, pp. 123 et seq., spec. p. 129, and, by the same author, 'Réflexions sur la notion de contrat international' in *Mélanges en l'honneur de Pierre Tercier*, Zurich, Schulthess, 2008, p. 873. Nevertheless, it is within German doctrine that one finds the most elaborate mechanisms, described in these terms by Professor Witz: 'German doctrine generally teaches that this connection with the foreign country must be of sufficient intensity to justify that the parties can escape the mandatory rules of the normally applicable law. Some German authors, under the Rome Convention, concretise the density of this connection and distinguish between strong and weak foreign ties. A strong foreign connection always exists when the parties have their habitual residence or place of business in two different states. The same would apply if the place of performance of at least one obligation is abroad. A weak foreign connection would be constituted by the place of conclusion abroad or the foreign nationality of one of the parties, as soon as these connections are not supplemented by other elements', C. Witz, 'L'internationalité et le contrat', *Revue Lamy de droit des affaires*, 2002, supplement, no. 46.

6 The distinction made here was first made by Lerebours-Pigeonnière, and has been frequently taken up since, see P. Lerebours-Pigeonnière, 'A propos du contrat international', *JDI*, 1951, 1; D. Bureau, *Les sources informelles du droit dans les relations privées international*, thesis, Paris II, 1992, nos. 1032 et seq.; C. Witz, 'L'internationalité et le contrat', *op. cit.*
The initial use of an economic criterion is the result of case law in the context of the application of the rules on international payments, where it was necessary, in order to rely on it, for the contract to characterise 'an ebb and flow movement' across borders according to the formula of the Attorney General Matter, Cass., civ., 17 May 1927, *Pélissier du Besset*. The case law has since been confirmed, see the references given by B. Audit and L. d'Avout, *Droit international privé, op. cit.*, no. 1069, note 157. The legislator has followed this trend: thus, in order to determine the international character of an arbitration, the economic transaction must 'involve the interests of international trade', Art. 1504 of the Code of Civil Procedure.
However, it is not certain that the economic criterion is really appropriate to account for positive law simply because the Vienna Convention on the International Sale of Goods, which is the most successful example of international substantive rules, uses a legal criterion based on the place of establishment of the parties (Art. 1 of the Vienna Convention).

In practice, the criteria have proved difficult to systematise[7] without necessarily being a cause for concern: it is possible to lend them a functional character.[8]

776. In the context of private international contract law,[9] the function of internationality is to grant a regime that favours those who conclude it, by granting them freedom of choice of law and the possibility of determining the competent court.[10] The criterion used was formulated by Dean Batiffol in these terms: 'The departure between domestic and international contracts results from the existence of links to several systems, however secondary one of them may be.'[11] As Professor Mayer writes, the fact that any foreign element can characterise the internationality of the contract is undoubtedly regrettable, whereas it is now accepted that when the contract is international, the parties can choose a law that has no connection with the dispute,[12] and allows them 'to set aside the laws that do not suit them', so that 'giving them this power presupposes a serious justification'.[13] To this first difficulty is added a second specific to the field of choice of law: it allows the designation of a law unrelated to the contract, and therefore diminishes the idea that the volition merely indicates the location of the contract.[14] This observation is decisive from the point of view of financial

---

On this question, see P. Mayer, 'La notion de contrat international', *op. cit.*, no. 4. The author proposes to distinguish between rules aimed at increasing contractual freedom in international trade, and those adopted with a view to harmonising the law.

7 V. Heuzé, *La réglementation française des contrats internationaux*, Paris, GLN éditions, 1990, no. 269.

8 P. Mayer, 'La notion de contrat international', *op. cit.* As Mr Synvet had already written, 'there is no decisive reason to adopt a unitary conception of the international contract. There is no international contract per se. The criterion chosen must be adapted to the use made of the concept', H. Synvet, comments under CA Toulouse, 26 October 1982, *JDI*, 1983, p. 603, spec. p. 609.

9 In the case of international substantive rules based on an economic criterion, it is difficult to see the link between the criterion selected and the aim pursued, which no doubt confirms Professor Mayer's suggestion for a distinction, see P. Mayer, 'La notion de contrat international', *op. cit.*, nos. 5–7.

10 *Ibid.*, no. 1.

11 H. Batiffol, note under judgment, *RCDIP*, 1956, 683.

12 This is the element that explains the difference in viewpoint between Batiffol and Mayer: the former saw the choice of law as a means for the parties to designate, within the legal systems with which their situation was linked, the one that seemed most appropriate to them.

13 P. Mayer, 'La notion de contrat international', *op. cit.* The author tries to substitute three criteria for internationality: the establishment of the parties in different countries, the presence of acts of material performance abroad, and the inclusion of the contract in a group of contracts (*ibid.*, no. 9).

14 This European choice is not especially widespread in foreign law. Indeed, the *Restatement Second* of American law provides that the choice of law cannot take place if the country has no substantial relationship to the parties or the transaction or there is no other reasonable basis for the parties' choice ('the chosen state has no substantial relationship to the parties or the transaction and there is no other reasonable basis for the parties' choice', *Restatement Second on the Conflict of Laws*, 1971, § 187(2)(a)).

contracts, where the law and the competent court selected are not necessarily linked to the contract.[15]

777. It should nevertheless be noted that the Rome Convention and the Rome I Regulation still echo the criterion described by Dean Batiffol. Thus, the Rome I Regulation provides for its applicability 'in situations involving a conflict of laws'.[16] This provision must be read in conjunction with Article 3(3) of the Rome I Regulation, which states:

> 'Where all the other elements of the situation are located, at the time of that choice, in a country other than that whose law is chosen, the choice of the parties shall not affect the application of provisions which the law of that other country does not permit to be derogated from by agreement.'

Recital 37 of the Regulation specifies that the concept of 'provisions which cannot be derogated from by agreement' is not limited to mandatory rules alone, but includes all local, non-delegable provisions.[17] This article, which is already present in the Rome Convention, allows two clarifications regarding the material scope of the Rome I Regulation. First, it applies to purely internal situations where a choice of law has been made, but limits its scope by applying to the contract the provisions that cannot be derogated from by agreement.[18] Secondly, in order for Article 3(3) of the Rome I Regulation to be applicable, all the 'elements of the situation', with the exception of the choice of law clause, must be located in the same country. The notion of 'element of the situation', applied to financial contracts, raises at least two types of difficulties. The first, which is not specific to financial contracts, is whether the "elements of the situation" must be assessed in the light of the subsidiary connecting factors traditionally used by the contractual conflict-of-laws rules and, in particular, those used by the Rome I Regulation. A negative answer has been given by the English case law in cases relating to financial contracts (§ 1). The second

15 On the reasons for this choice, see *infra*, para. 798.

16 Art. 1(1) of the Rome I Regulation. This reading is supported by Art. 3(3) of the same Regulation according to which 'the choice of the parties shall not affect the application of provisions which the law of that other country does not permit to be derogated from by agreement', and Art. 3(4) which provides for a similar provision when the elements of the contract are located in a Member State and the designated law would evade the mandatory provisions of Union law. See B. Audit and L. d'Avout, *Droit international privé*, *op. cit.*, no. 1028.

17 On this question see also *ibid.*

18 As Mr d'Avout writes: 'The parties entered by artifice into the field of conflict of laws (Art. 1, § 1); the law of conflict of laws practically took them out of it by restoring the ordinary imperative of the national law that had been ousted on the contractual transaction in question (Art. 3, § 3).' L. d'Avout, 'Le contrat artificiellement internationalisé devant la Cour de justice (un naufrage juridique)', *JCP G*, 2017, 1655.

question is, when Article 3(3) is applied to financial contracts, what are the relevant elements for assessing the international character of the contract (§ 2).

§ 1. THE NOTION OF ELEMENTS OF THE INTERNATIONAL SITUATION

English case law has successively adopted several conceptions of the concept of 'elements of the situation'. The first, which is restrictive, assimilates the elements of the situation to the connecting factors provided for by the Rome I Regulation in the absence of a choice. The second takes a broader view of the concept of relevant factors. The third abandons the view of the location of the contract and is thus clearly a substantive rule offering the parties the option of choosing a foreign law.

778. 'Other elements of the situation' and connecting factors in the absence of choice. The 'other elements of the situation' may refer to connecting factors, such as those mentioned for example in the absence of a choice of law, such as the habitual residence of the debtor of the characteristic performance or the place of performance of the contract. According to this view,[19] if the subsidiary connecting factor is local law, the contract must be regarded as purely internal. This approach has several advantages: on the one hand, it makes it possible to define precisely the relevant elements for availing oneself of the choice of law option and, on the other hand, it appears to be consistent with Article 1 of the Rome I Regulation, which provides for its applicability to situations involving a conflict of laws. It nevertheless has two disadvantages. The first is that it is not certain that each of these criteria is such as to allow the internationalisation of the contract: thus the nationality of one or other of the parties does not appear relevant in this respect.[20] The second is not to characterise as international certain sets of contracts which nevertheless deserve it. This is particularly the case for groups of contracts which constitute a single transaction between the parties and whose internationality by virtue of their connectedness should be retained.[21]

779. However, this view was affirmed in a 2015 *Dexia Crediop* judgment of the London High Court.[22] The court held that all the elements of the situation

---

19 Inspired by the German doctrine, on which see *supra*, para. 776.

20 See already in this sense, P. Mayer, 'La notion de contrat international', *op. cit.*

21 See already in this sense, *ibid.*

22 *Dexia Crediop v Comune di Prato* (2015) EWHC 1746 (Comm), hereinafter *Dexia* Judgment of 1st instance.

were internal in a case where a swap agreement[23] subject to English law had been concluded between an Italian municipality and an Italian bank. The municipality argued that in Italy that both parties were incorporated, that it was where they had communicated with each other, that it was where the swaps were entered into, and that it was where the obligations under the swaps had to be performed.[24] In other words, all the connecting factors applicable in the absence of a choice under the Rome I Regulation pointed to Italy. In order to characterise the internationality of the situation, the Italian bank considered that certain elements of the situation were not located in Italy, not only because of the international origin of the elaboration of the content of the contract, which was based on an ISDA model agreement, but also because the swap contract concluded with the Italian municipality was part of a set of contracts that it had itself concluded, some of which were with parties located abroad.[25] At first instance,[26] the English judge agreed with the Italian municipality and considered, on the one hand, that the international origin of the content of the contract was not such as to induce the foreignness of the situation between the parties[27] and, on the other hand, that the conclusion by *Dexia* of international contracts linked to this transaction, but concluded with other parties, was not relevant either in order to characterise the foreignness of the situation.[28] More fundamentally, the High Court considered that the connecting factors of the

---

23 The *swap* contract is 'the contract by which the parties agree to exchange assets (in the case of currencies) or interest flows linked to an underlying transaction, according to a determined schedule', A. Couret, H. Le Nabasque *et al.*, *Droit financier*, *op. cit.*, no. 1031.

24 *Dexia* judgment of 1st instance,, *supra*,para. 209.

25 For each of the *swap* contracts at issue, the Italian bank 'entered into a back to back hedging swap with a bank outside Italy in the international market using the same industry standard documentation.' *Dexia* judgment of 1st instance, *supra*, para. 210.

26 On appeal, the Court of Appeal had delivered the *Banco Santander* judgment detailed below, the solution of which extended to the *Dexia* judgment when the latter was submitted to the Court of Appeal, see *Dexia Crediop* [2017] EWCA Civ 428 (15 June 2017), hereinafter Dexia judgment of 2nd instance. The latter judgment has been described by practitioners as 'relief to banks', see Dentons, 'Court of Appeal upholds consistent interpretation of ISDA Master Agreement', 16 January 2018.

27 *Dexia* judgment of 1st instance, cit., no. 211: 'As to the master agreement, it is true that it is an international standard form, but it does not follow from this that it is an "element in the situation" which is connected to a country other than Italy. It is of course designed to promote certainty, but that does not give it a connection to a country other than Italy. Nor does the significance and global nature of ISDA. Even if the standard form itself were shown to have a connection with another country, that would not in the present case be an "element relevant to the situation" as it existed at material times. Throughout the relevant period everything relevant to the use of the form happened in Italy.'

28 *Dexia* judgment of 1st instance, cit., no. 211: 'As to Dexia's decision in each case to choose a non-Italian counterparty for its back-to-back hedging swap, that does not appear to me to be an element relevant to the situation as between Prato and Dexia. Whether or not Dexia entered into a hedging swap is a matter for Dexia alone: to Prato it is immaterial. There was no contemplation that a non-Italian entity would take over obligations of either party. Dexia's choice to use a non-Italian counterparty is something which is completely external to "the situation" at the time that choice of law was agreed.'

contract led exclusively to the application of Italian law. However, the London Court of Appeal overturned this judgment in *Banco Santander*.

780. The 'elements of the situation' and consideration of the social and economic environment. The 'other elements of the situation' can be assessed according to the social and economic environment in which the contract is situated. This second perception of the elements of the situation was retained by Judge Blair in a judgment of the Financial List, a specialised chamber of the High Court, and confirmed by the Court of Appeal in London in a 2016 judgment.[29] In that judgment, the facts were similar to those in *Dexia*: a swap contract had been concluded between Portuguese transport companies and a Portuguese bank, and executed in Portugal. The London Court of Appeal nevertheless considered that the contract was indeed international since, on the one hand, the swap contract was necessarily part of the international 'market' (in the sense of a sector of activity[30]) of swaps because of the contracts that it was likely to create for one of the parties[31] and, on the other hand, in this case, the Portuguese subsidiary of the bank had been associated with its Spanish parent company in the elaboration of the price of the swap contract. According to this analysis, the 'elements of the situation' must be assessed not only in terms of the connecting factors applicable in the absence of choice, but according to the elements of the social and economic environment in which the parties operate. This view is based on the idea that if the authors of the Rome Convention had wished to limit internationality to contracts that could rely on a connecting factor applicable in the absence of a choice designating a foreign law, they would not have used the expression 'element of the situation' but rather 'connecting factors'. In the absence of such an indication, it must therefore be considered that not only can elements other than the connecting factors of the contract in the absence of choice be taken into account in order to assess the internationality of the situation, but also, for the English judges, that elements other than the relationship between the parties alone make it possible to characterise internationality.

781. Choice of law and location of the contract. However, another argument is at work in the *Banco Santander* decision, which is based on a third perception,

---

29 *Banco Santander* (2016) EWCA Civ. 1267, upholding the first instance judgment *Banco Santander* [2016] EWHC 465 (Comm). On this judgment, see G. Cuniberti, 'Choice of law in domestic contracts: towards a right to access foreign financial markets', *op. cit.*, p. 547. On the *Financial List*, see J. Braithwaite, *The Financial Courts: Adjudicating Disputes in Derivatives Markets*, *op. cit.*, p. 10.

30 The use of the expression international *swaps* 'market' in the following discussion, justified by its frequent use, is to be understood in the sense of a sector of activity. This use of the concept of market, which is similar to the sector of activity, or even to the concept of relevant market from competition law, is somewhat confusing and not in the sense of financial markets, which is not the case in *Banco Santander*, since it concerns an OTC contract.

31 *Banco Santander* (2016) EWCA Civ. 1267, no. 63.

very distinct from the other two, because it is free of the notion of localisation. This third view is inspired by English conflict of laws jurisprudence and is more like a substantive rule offering a subjective right to choose the applicable law.[32] In English law, for the choice of law to be valid, it must be legal and made in good faith (*bona fide*).[33] The internationality of the situation would therefore not be a relevant element of the validity of the choice of law. However, this view was rejected by the authors of the Convention. The concept of 'elements of the situation' is precisely the result of a compromise between the maximalist perception limiting internationality to the mere presence of foreign laws designated by the connecting factors of the contract in the absence of choice, and the English perception making the choice of law a subjective right granted by the legal order designated as competent.[34] Even if it is incompatible with both the very text from which it is derived,[35] and the intention of its authors, this third conception has already been favoured by the Court of Justice.[36] However, it is to be hoped that the incisive criticism of this case law on the Insolvency Regulation will lead the Court of Justice to a more orthodox assessment of the

---

32 Analysing the law of autonomy independently of this third perception, V. Heuzé, *La réglementation française des contrats internationaux*, *op. cit.*

33 As the London Court of Appeal observed in *Banco Santander*: 'English conflict of laws jurisprudence was firmly in favour of the right of the parties to select the law of the contract, provided their intention was bona fide and legal.' The basis given for the rule is *Vita Food Products Inc v. Unus Shipping Co Ltd* [1939] AC 277, 290 (PC).

34 The Giuliano-Lagarde report (spec. p. 15) indicates that this solution was the result of a compromise between 'on the one hand, the desire of certain experts to limit the freedom of choice of the parties enshrined in this article by a corrective which would make it clear that the choice of a foreign law would not in itself suffice to allow the application of that law if the situation at the time of the choice did not involve another foreign element, on the other hand, the concern of other experts, in particular British experts, that such a remedy might have excessively hampered the freedom of the parties even in situations where their choice appeared justified, made in good faith and capable of satisfying interests worthy of protection. These experts, in particular, argued that derogations from the principle of the parties' freedom of choice should only be allowed in exceptional circumstances, such as in the case of the application of mandatory rules of a law other than the law chosen by the parties; they also gave several examples in which the parties' choice of a foreign law was fully justified, although the situation did not seem to present any other foreign element.
The group recognised the validity of the above concern, while maintaining the principle that the parties' choice of a foreign law, where all other elements of the situation are located at the time of the choice in a single country, cannot affect the mandatory provisions of the law of that country.'

35 P. de Vareilles-Sommières, 'Autonomie substantielle et autonomie conflictuelle en droit international privé des contrats' in *Mélanges en l'honneur du Professeur Pierre Mayer*, Paris, Lextenso, 2015, pp. 869 et seq.

36 Indeed, the Court has already had occasion to consider, in the context of a similar provision of the Insolvency Regulation, that the choice of law option could 'be validly invoked where the parties to a contract, who are domiciled in one and the same Member State, in whose territory all the other relevant elements of the situation concerned are also located, have designated the law of another Member State as the law applicable to the contract', Case C-54/16, *Vinyls Italia*, ECLI:EU:C:2017:433, para. 56. This proposal had already been supported by Professor Claude Witz, who considered that 'two contracting parties residing

internationality requirement.[37] In any event, it is the second interpretation of the elements of the situation that must be adhered to since it is in line with the letter and spirit of the Rome Convention and the Rome I Regulation. This second interpretation requires, in order to be applicable, to circumscribe the relevant elements allowing, in the case of financial contracts, to characterise internationality.

§ 2. CIRCUMSCRIBING THE INTERNATIONAL ELEMENTS OF A FINANCIAL CONTRACT

782. The circumscription of the international elements of a financial contract may be the decisive element of the dispute: in these two judgments, the London Court of Appeal itself notes that the application of local law would have led to the annulment of the contracts concluded by the Italian municipality, or to the characterisation of the bad faith of the banker.[38] When attempting to define the international elements of a financial contract within the meaning of the Rome I Regulation, several aspects deserve to be discussed, including, in the first place, the moment of characterisation of the internationality of the contract. This moment is determined by the very text of Article 3(3) of the Rome I Regulation, which provides that the assessment of internationality is made at the moment when the parties make this choice.[39] This is why the argument developed by Judge Blair in *Banco Santander* that the possibility for the contract to be assigned to a foreign party would characterise the internationality of the contract should be rejected.[40] Secondly, the relevant elements of internationality must be defined. The most relevant and indisputable element is the establishment of the parties in different countries. As regards the others, a discussion appears necessary between those relating to the content of the contract (I), and those relating to the environment in which the contract is situated (II).

---

or established in one of the countries of the Union should be able to submit their contract in its entirety to the law of one of the countries of the Union, even if that contract has no foreign element', C. Witz, 'L'internationalité et le contrat', *op. cit.*

37 On these criticisms, see, among others, L. d'Avout, 'Le contrat artificiellement internationalisé devant la Cour de justice (un naufrage juridique)', *op. cit.*; S. Bollée, obs. *D.*, 2017, 2054.

38 See respectively *Dexia Crediop* (2017) EWCA Civ 428, no. 158; *Banco Santander* (2016) EWCA Civ 1267, no. 75.

39 On this article, see L. Stark, *L'internationalité en droit international privé*, thesis Université Bourgogne Franche-Comté et Université Johannes Gutenberg de Mayence, 2020, pp. 385 et seq.

40 See already in this sense G. Cuniberti, 'Choix de la loi dans les contrats internes: vers un droit d'accéder aux marchés financiers étrangers', *op. cit.* On the other hand, the parties may, by means of an assignment, change the law applicable to the contract.

I. International Elements and Content of the Financial Contract

783. Origin of the content of the contract. It is necessary to distinguish the origin of the content of the financial contract from the content itself. With regard to the origin of the content, the *Banco Santander* judgment held that the use of an ISDA contract was such as to characterise the internationality of the contract.[41] This argument is hardly convincing. The drawing up of a standard contract abroad is irrelevant to the internationality of the contract: ISDA is not a party to the contract and merely designs its normative architecture, without intervening in the situation between the parties.[42] This argument distorts Article 3(3) of the Rome I Regulation, and in fact aims to systematically allow the selection of English law.[43] Presumably, as the English judgment itself observes, the use of a foreign language is not such as to characterise the internationality of the contract.[44] On the other hand, the content of the contract may characterise internationality. ISDA has developed several types of contracts: one, entitled 'Local Currency-Single Jurisdiction', has not been used by the parties, while the second, entitled 'Multicurrency-Cross Border Jurisdiction', is precisely the one that has been chosen. The latter choice has an impact on the content of the contract, which allows, more than the intention of the parties, to characterise its internationality.[45] Two elements of the content of the financial contract

---

41 *Banco Santander* [2016] EWHC 465, no. 399. The argument was confirmed by the Court of Appeal in *Dexia Crediop* [2017] EWCA Civ 428, no. 132.

42 It has a similar role to that of the market operator when it offers financial contracts on its trading system, and acts only as a service provider. The international origin of the content of the contract can be taken into consideration in the context of the international environment in which the financial contract is embedded, see *supra*, para. 782.
Similarly, the inclusion of one of the parties in a group of companies, and the involvement of the parent company of one of the parties in advising on the pricing of the contract obligations, should be irrelevant to the characterisation of the internationality of the contract. *Contra Banco Santander* [2016] EWHC 465, No. 409(5)(i).

43 J. Braithwaite, *The Financial Courts: Adjudicating Disputes in Derivatives Markets*, *op. cit.*, p. 321. Similarly, the use of the intention of the drafters of the contract should not override the intention of the parties. It is true that ISDA has been able to intervene in the English courts on the interpretation of the contract, see *Lomas & ors (together the Joint Administrators of Lehman Brothers International (Europe) (in administration)) v. JFB Firth Rixson, Inc & ors* (2010) EWHC 3372 (Ch). However, English law is also not very receptive to a uniform interpretation of financial contracts, even those drawn up by ISDA, as Briggs J noted: 'the 1992 Master Agreement has come to be incorporated into a bewildering variety of different types of derivative transactions, so that caution needs to be exercised against a slavish assumption that the meaning of a particular provision of the Master Agreement in one type of transaction is necessarily to be transported lock stock and barreal as its precise meaning in some very different type of transaction', *Anthracite Rated Investments (Jersey) Ltd* no. 115. On this question in English law, see J. Braithwaite, 'Standard Form Contracts as Transnational Law', *op. cit.* pp. 801 et seq.; see in French the comments by P. Cornut St-Pierre, *La fabrique juridique des swaps*, *op. cit.*, pp. 217 et seq.

44 *Banco Santander* [2016] EWHC 465 No 399.

45 Comp. G. Cuniberti, 'Choix de la loi dans les contrats internes: vers un droit d'accéder aux marchés financiers étrangers', *op. cit.*

should be of a nature to characterise its internationality: the currency in which the monetary obligations are settled, and the underlying itself.

784. Foreign currency and internationality of the contract. In *Banco Santander*, the judge had the opportunity to state that the payment of the monetary obligation in a foreign currency allowed the internationality of the contract to be characterised. This solution is explained by the fact that the monetary obligations undertaken by the parties are often the essential commitment of the financial contract. Indeed, the characteristic performance of the contract lies in the payment of a monetary obligation. It is therefore not insignificant that the payment of these obligations takes place in a currency other than that of the parties' registered office; such a foreign element appears sufficiently significant to characterise the foreignness.[46]

785. Foreign underlying and internationality of the contract. The assertion that the reference to an underlying subject to foreign law allows the internationality of the contract to be characterised is likely to make it particularly easy,[47] and therefore raises a certain amount of suspicion. Moreover, some authors consider that the underlying is only a means of calculating the price of the monetary obligation to be paid at the end of the derivative contract and should not be considered as an element of the situation to be taken into account, except in the case where the 'derivative contract is a hedging contract'.[48]

786. On the contrary, it seems to us that the speculative or insurance nature of the contract should have no impact on the characterisation of foreignness. Similarly, the indication in the financial contract that the underlying may be delivered should be irrelevant. Both of these attempts to limit the choice of law option seem to us to deny the international character of a financial contract that explicitly refers to a foreign underlying. The clearest evidence of the internationality of a contract concluded between two persons established in the same country, but basing their contract on an underlying subject to a foreign law, is that the latter may interfere with the regime of the financial contract, or even penalise the parties to the contract.[49] There are two other arguments in favour of this. Firstly, if the purpose of the financial contract is not to transfer ownership of property, but the mere payment of monetary obligations, these

---

46 For some authors, it would even constitute an element that would make it possible to determine the law applicable to the dispute, proof of its importance see *infra*; para. 801.

47 A. Gaudemet, *Les dérivés*, *op. cit.*, no. 569.

48 J. Gavriloff, *Les méthodes du conflit de lois à l'épreuve du produit dérivé*, *op. cit.*

49 On these aspects, see *infra*, paras. 844 et seq. It should be noted here that all underlying elements that can be described as foreign or international should be capable of characterising the internationality of the contract, including those that cannot be appropriated, such as indices. An index is a 'measure which expresses a relationship between two prices of the same item' F. Drummond, 'Le contrat comme instrument financier', *op. cit.*, p. 665. On the notion of index, see P. Didier, *Droit commercial*, t. 3, Paris, PUF, 1993, p. 284. Comp. J. Gavriloff, *Les méthodes du conflit de lois à l'épreuve du produit dérivé*, *op. cit.*, no. 95,

obligations are based on the evolution of an object located abroad.[50] Secondly, the purpose of the financial contract may be to protect one of the parties against the local consequences of events triggered abroad. As a result, only financial contracts concluded between two persons established in the same country and whose underlying object is not foreign to that country should be considered purely domestic. However, their inclusion in a contractual package makes it possible to consider this contract as international.

II. International Elements and the Contract Environment

787. The term 'contract environment' is not unequivocal. A distinction will be made here between the immediate environment of the contract, i.e. the contractual grouping in which it is included, and the wider environment of the contract, which is sometimes referred to as the international 'market'[51] for financial contracts, and which would be likely to characterise an inherent internationality in the conclusion of such contracts.

788. Contractual grouping and internationality of the contract. Three types of contractual groupings can be distinguished here. The first is the financial contract and the transaction it covers.[52] In this case, the question arises as to whether the foreignness of the main contract is such as to enable the financial contract concluded as a hedge to be characterised as international. The answer here should be positive, because if the contracts are independent of each other, the notion of "element of the situation" should allow the assessment to be extended to the economic whole in which the transaction between the parties is embedded.[53] The second type of contractual grouping corresponds to the normative architecture of ISDA contracts. The question is then whether the future conclusion of international confirmation contracts allows the framework agreement to be qualified as international and, conversely, whether, insofar as the framework agreement has been validly subject to a foreign law, the

who considers that considering the underlying as an element of the situation which makes it possible to characterise the internationality of the contract would lead to an artificial internationalisation.

50 A currency *swap* contract should therefore be such as to allow the foreignness of the contract to be characterised by reference to a foreign currency. Comp. G. Cuniberti, 'Choice of law in domestic contracts: towards a right of access to foreign financial markets', *op. cit.*

51 On the polysemy of this notion, see our comments *supra*, para. 2.

52 See from the point of view of domestic law, P. Pailler, *Le contrat financier, un instrument financier à terme*, *op. cit.*, no. 46.

53 This is not necessarily the case, however, if the financial contract is concluded with a party other than that of the main contract. However, in the latter case, the foreignness of the underlying will allow internationality to be characterised. The difficulty is even greater from the point of view of jurisdiction if the main contract and the financial contract are subject to separate judges, see J. Braithwaite, *The Financial Courts: Adjudicating Disputes in Derivatives Markets*, *op. cit.*

implementation contracts can take advantage of the foreignness of the framework agreement to also be subject to that law. The answer should be in the affirmative in order to ensure the coherence of the contractual whole, given that the situation between the parties is, overall, international in nature.

789. A third type of contractual package can be considered. This is the case where one of the parties, in order to limit the risks taken by the conclusion of a financial contract with a party established in its own country on a local underlying, concludes another financial contract with a foreign party, either in order to transfer the risk taken by the conclusion of the initial contract or in order to reduce it. This practice, known as hedging,[54] is common. The question arises whether, on the one hand, the foreignness of the initial contract can be considered as an element of the situation of the subsequent contracts transferring the risk taken and, on the other hand, whether the foreignness of these subsequent contracts can allow the initial contract to be qualified as international. The answer should be negative in both cases. Indeed, this contractual ensemble does not tend to a single transaction, but to a succession of hedging transactions aimed at the protection of one of the parties. The opposite solution leads to an excessive dilution of the notion of "element of the situation", which should be limited to the relationship between the parties or to the hedging transaction envisaged,[55] unless one considers that the conclusion of financial contracts is necessarily part of an international situation.

790. The internationality inherent in the conclusion of financial contracts. Some arguments can be made for the view that internationality is inherent in financial contracts today. Firstly, this would be explained by the ease with which these contracts circulate.[56] Not only do most national legal systems have a special statutory regime facilitating transmission,[57] but also the presence of standardised model contracts actually facilitates such transfer. Secondly, it is often argued that the swaps "market" would necessarily be international,[58] which would have several consequences. Firstly, it would demonstrate the internationality of

54 In reference to building a hedge in one's garden, i.e. a form of protection.

55 Comp. *Banco Santander* [2016] EWHC 465, no. 409 where the judge takes this element into account in determining the internationality of the situation.

56 Demonstrating that financial contracts are designed to circulate as easily as a financial security, P. Pailler, *Le contrat financier, un instrument financier à terme*, *op. cit.*

57 See, from the French point of view, Arts. L. 211-37 and L. 211-38(I) of the Monetary and Financial Code, on which see T. Bonneau *et al.*, *Droit financier*, *op. cit.*, nos. 878 et seq.. On the circulation of financial contracts, see more generally P. Pailler, *Le contrat financier, un instrument financier à terme*, *op. cit.*, nos. 137 et seq.

58 See in this sense, *Banco Santander* [2016] EWHC 465, nos. 397–398; C. Kleiner, 'L'élection de for en matière bancaire et financière: entre clauses asymétriques, clauses modèles et quasi-réglementaires', *op. cit.*, p. 61; J. Braithwaite, *The Financial Courts: Adjudicating Disputes in Derivatives Markets*, *op. cit.*, p. 318. The latter author suggests that the desire to maintain the effectiveness of choice of law clauses stems from the desire of English courts to give full effect to the financial contract, see *ibid.*, p. 12.

financial contracts, since, on the one hand, these contracts would necessarily be transmitted to parties across borders and, on the other hand, the financial contract by which one party can temper the result to which another financial contract leads would most often be concluded with a foreign party. Secondly, the unitary legislative and jurisdictional response made possible by the conjunction of choice of law and choice of jurisdiction clauses would contribute to the international uniformity of solutions.

791. However, these arguments are not convincing. Indeed, as regards the arguments relating to circulation, neither the presence of a standardised contract nor that of a facilitating regime granted by a legal order have the consequence of making the institution they govern international in themselves. In the absence of a special provision, the situation referred to in Article 3(3) of the Rome Convention and the Rome I Regulation is necessarily that which is *concretely* understood *between the parties*.[59] Secondly, if the 'relevant' market is necessarily international, it would first be necessary to obtain an empirical study of all OTC contracts,[60] as well as of contracts concluded within the same legal order, in order to go beyond the stage of mere allegation.[61] In reality, this argument must be rejected as its sole purpose is to create a presumption of internationality. Neither the Rome Convention nor the Rome I Regulation was intended to create such a presumption. This is all the less the case since, on the one hand, the content of the financial contract itself and the immediate contractual grouping in which it forms part will most often make it possible to characterise the internationality of financial contracts and, on the other hand, the substantive law of the Union provides that it is always possible for a party

[59] The thesis aiming to characterise the internationality of the contract 'abstractly' between certain 'types of participants' is a technique aiming to give priority to the interest of certain parties (here certain investment firms) over the collective interest, see P. Cornut St-Pierre, *La fabrique juridique des swaps*, *op. cit.*, pp. 216–220.

[60] The sociological approach, apart from the fact that it should be conducted in different territories, does not appear to be sufficient to characterise the internationality of the contract, as suggested by C. Avasilencei, 'L'internationalité des contrats-financiers: une «co-production «entre le texte juridique et le contexte économique' in H. Muir Watt *et al.* (eds.) *Le tournant global en droit international privé*, Paris, Pedone, 2020, pp. 537 et seq.

[61] What is a necessarily international business for one Member State is not necessarily so for another. The existence of identical model contracts drawn up by ISDA, even though they are subject to different jurisdictions (the United States, the United Kingdom and France), at least shows that ISDA considers that the existence of different national models is likely to satisfy their clients.
It seems to us that at the stage of contract interpretation, consideration should be given to the worldwide use of a contract with identical provisions (this is the case in the United Kingdom, see J. Braithwaite, *The Financial Courts: Adjudicating Disputes in Derivatives Markets*, *op. cit.*, p. 199), in particular by observing the interpretations of foreign courts (as the New York courts have been able to do with English judgments, see *ibid.*, p. 212). In the latter case, the international context is useful so that the interpreter has as much access to the 'micro' aspects, i.e. the aspects specific to the dispute, as to the 'macro' aspects, i.e. the sector of activity in which the contract is situated, see in this sense *ibid.*, p. 216.

wishing to conclude a financial contract to go through a financial market located in another Member State.

792. Conclusion of the section. At the end of this discussion, it may be considered that the financial contract will almost always be considered as international. This is true, but simply because the financial contract *is* most often an international contract, either because the parties are established in different legal orders, or because its content is based on monetary obligations denominated in a foreign currency or whose valuation is based on a foreign underlying, or because of the immediate environment of the contract. However, the idea that the financial contract would necessarily be international should be rejected, as the OTC financial contract sector would be ontologically international. The conflict-of-laws regulation of contracts does not have the effect of deactivating the choice of law, but of limiting the creation of artificial international situations. Whenever the contract is not subject to artificial internationalisation, its choice of law should be respected. In the very residual cases where the contract is purely domestic, Article 3(3) of the Rome Convention and the Rome I Regulation should apply.

793. The solution that this situation leads to would not be fully corrected by a narrower conception of internationality than that adopted by the Rome I Regulation, which would eliminate certain internationalisation factors such as the foreignness of the underlying. This would undoubtedly make it possible to avoid the artificial internationalisation of certain situations, but this correction would be superficial since the factors of internationality would remain numerous. The origin of the difficulty is the European conception of the law of autonomy, which allows the parties to give jurisdiction to a legal order without any link with the contract, and therefore without any link with the predominant socio-economic environment in which the legal relationship is embedded.[62] The law of autonomy, which has been stripped of the idea of location, is therefore less and less a rule of conflict and more and more a substantive rule. It is therefore difficult to adapt to the limits traditionally assigned to the application of foreign law, and special connections are not likely to correct this difficulty of principle.

62 This conception has given the English legal system a virtual monopoly on the contractual interpretation of financial contracts concluded over the counter, and some English judges believe that they have been the true *stewards* of these contracts: 'English law has more or less done its stuff in relation to its stewardship of the ISDA agreement, for all those who have chosen it', Lord Justice Briggs, 'How has English law Coped with the Lehman Collapse?' in D. Faber and N. Vermunt (eds.), *Bank Failure: Lessons from Lehman Brothers*, Oxford, OUP, 2017, p. 121, see also J. Braithwaite, *The Financial Courts: Adjudicating Disputes in Derivatives Markets*, *op. cit.*, pp. 50 et seq. The latter author considers that this competence of the English judge has brought his function of contractual interpretation closer to the role of a real macro prudential regulator, without necessarily having the tools to do so, see *ibid.*, pp. 71 et seq.

SECTION 2. CONNECTING FACTORS

794. The law applicable to the financial contract is the one agreed by the parties. This choice is most often made by the professional organisation that drew up the contract, which selects the applicable law not so much because of the perfection of the foreign contractual regime as because of the specific characteristics of the legal system designated as competent. This is why the absence of choice of law is rare (§ 1). The choice of law is all the more important because, in practice, even where one of the parties is considered a consumer for the purposes of the Rome I Regulation, the derogatory conflict rule specific to consumer contracts will only come into play in cases where there has been a solicitation by a professional, thereby reducing its interference with the law chosen by the parties (§ 2).

§ 1. THE MAIN CONNECTING FACTORS

795. After reporting the reasons for the parties' choice of law (I), the applicable law in the absence of choice will be studied (II).

I. The Choice of Law

796. The principle of choice of law. Where the parties have chosen the law, the designation of the applicable law will in the vast majority of cases be the result of an express provision in the Masters agreement. In practice, since Masters agreements are standardised, they systematically provide for the applicable law and the competent court in the event of a dispute. In the case of ISDA, this is most often US or English law, and the authors of the Masters agreement then designate as competent the court whose law is applicable. The withdrawal of the United Kingdom from the European Union is nevertheless likely to give a certain vigour to the ISDA convention under French law since the decision rendered by the French court is now the only one to benefit from the recognition regime granted by the Brussels I *a* Regulation.[63]

797. The reasons for choice of law. The freedom of choice of law offered to the parties and the predominance of the ISDA conventions within the standard contracts used in the OTC market place the American association in a singular situation of hegemony with regard to legal systems. It is not our intention here to

---

[63] HCJP Report, 'Préconisation sur la mise en place à Paris de chambres spécialisées pour le traitement du contentieux international des affaires', 3 May 2017; D. Bureau and H. Muir Watt, 'L'avenir du contentieux international des affaires en Europe' in *Mélanges en l'honneur du professeur Bertrand Ancel*, pp. 315 et seq.

comment on the principle of legislative competition.[64] However, we will make an observation about the *scope* of this competition. Indeed, the law of autonomy is criticised as a symptomatic element of a neo-liberal regime that would allow legislative competition between countries in order to offer, if not to the powerful, at least to creditors, a particularly favourable regime.[65] This criticism of the autonomy law criterion would be admissible if the competition had as its object the validity of the contract, or its regime. However, while it is true that the parties seek to ensure the validity of the contract,[66] most legal systems already give effect to such contracts. One of the generally accepted limits to the validity of the financial contract is precisely outside the realm of *lex contractus*, namely the capacity of the contracting party.[67] This observation makes it possible to state that competition is not concerned with legal issues that are within the domain of the law of contract. Therefore, the criterion of party autonomy is, at least for financial contracts, indifferent to the increase in legislative competition.

798. From a legislative point of view, the actual field of competition is specific to the insolvency law of the registered office of the contracting party.[68] This is particularly noticeable in ISDA's practice of developing synoptic tables on netting-friendly jurisdiction.[69] From a jurisdictional point of view, two elements appear to be relevant: the specialisation of judges, and the ease with which the judgment rendered can be recognised in States where the other party has assets. In this sense, more than the reform of contract law,[70] the creation of

---

64 On this issue, see R. Sefton-Greren and L. Usunier, *La concurrence normative. Mythes et réalités*, Société de législation comparée, 2014; see lastly, from the point of view of financial contracts, J. Gavriloff, *Les méthodes du conflit de lois à l'épreuve du produit dérivé, op. cit.*, nos. 32 and 57.

65 The favouring of English law by ISDA is said to be due to the fact that it is more favourable to creditors, see A. Gaudemet, *Les dérivés, op. cit.*, no. 564. This favouring of creditors would be most noticeable at the time of clearing, see P. Wood, *Set-off and netting, Derivatives, Clearing system, op. cit.*, no. 1-001. However, the choice of the English legal system also, if not primarily, stems from its experience with international standardised contracts, in particular thanks to its pre-existing expertise in maritime and insurance law, see *supra* note under para. 774.

66 As Professor Gaudemet observes, 'in the presence of an international derivative, the parties first seek a law which ensures the validity of their contract', A. Gaudemet, *Les dérivés, op. cit.*

67 See *infra*, paras. 818 et seq.

68 As Professor Gaudemet writes, the parties 'then agree to conclude only if the law applicable to the insolvency proceedings possibly opened against the other party guarantees the enforceability of the termination-compensation mechanism and collateral agreements', A. Gaudemet, *Les dérivés, op. cit.*, nos. 568 and 571.

69 That is to say, of a legal nature giving very favourable treatment to the close-out netting mechanism in case of default of one of the parties. There are now more than 40 of them, see P. Paech, 'Close-out netting, Insolvency and Conflict of Laws' (October 2014) *Journal of Corporate Law Studies*, pp. 419 et seq., spec. p. 431.

70 From a contract law perspective, French law provides the same advantages as English law, see A. Downe, 'La nouvelle convention-cadre ISDA de droit français', *RDBF*, November 2020, study 20; HCJP, Rapport contrat-cadre ISDA 2002 (droit français), 5 November 2020.

an international chamber within the Paris Court of Appeal, as well as the eviction of the United Kingdom from the recognition regime provided for by the Brussels Ia Regulation, appear to be the most decisive elements of the attractiveness of French contract law, despite its reform, but of the French legal order as a whole.[71] Where financial contracts are intended to cover the risk arising from a main contract with which it is closely linked, the parties are nevertheless likely to designate the same judge as in the main contract in order to avoid the splintering of litigation.[72]

II. The Applicable Law in the Absence of Choice

799. No choice and characteristic performance. In the absence of choice of law, the designation of the applicable law will depend on the characteristic performance provided,[73] which is specific to each type of financial contract.[74] However, the characteristic performance criterion will not identify the law applicable to contracts in which the parties' mutual obligations are identical.[75] It is nevertheless possible to identify the characteristic performance outside the obligations of the parties, in particular because of the quality of the investment service providers of one of the contracting parties.[76] If this quality is shared by them, Professor Gaudemet considers that it is then possible to identify the characteristic service by reference to the party who 'documents' and 'structures the contract', 'or even who will keep the accounts where the clearing balances will be debited and credited at successive intervals'.[77] If none of these elements allows the identification of a characteristic performance, then the closest connection test must be applied.[78]

---

71 See already in this sense, A. Caillemer du Ferrage, 'L'impact du Brexit sur les infrastructures de marché', *RDBF*, November 2017, no. 6, file 37.

72 On this risk, see C. Kleiner, 'Les risques d'éclatement du contentieux en raison de la dualité de clauses d'élection de forum dans un contrat de financement et le contrat de swap (*High Court BNP Paribas SA v. Trattamento Rifiuti Metropolitani SPA* [2020] EWHC 2436 [Comm])', *RDBF*, April 2021, p. 25.

73 Art. 4(2) of the Rome I Regulation.

74 Thus, for financial contracts analysed as option contracts, the characteristic performance is that provided by the promisor (A. Gaudemet, *Les dérivés*, *op. cit.*, no. 167), for alternative derivatives, the characteristic performance is that of the debtor of the alternative obligation (*ibid.*, no. 169).

75 See already in this sense, B. Sousi-Roubi, 'La Convention de Rome et la loi applicable aux contrats bancaires', *D.*, 1993, chron., pp. 183 et seq. A. Gaudemet, *Les dérivés*, *op. cit.*, no. 170.

76 *Ibid.*, no. 171.

77 *Ibid.*, no. 170.

78 Art. 4(4) of the Rome I Regulation. This criterion can also be used when there is a lack of choice of law in a Masters Agreement or in a Confirmation. From the point of view of conflict of laws, the question arises whether the choice of law in a masters Agreement extends, as a matter of principle, to Confirmations. If the parties' choice of law in the Confirmation is assumed, the answer must be negative. Indeed, the contracts are autonomous

800. Lack of choice and closest connection. Some authors consider in this case that, for want of anything better, the currency of settlement of obligations should identify the applicable law,[79] or, alternatively, that the law of the underlying asset should be applied to the financial contract, if there is one.[80] Both solutions must be rejected. Firstly, if the use of a foreign currency is likely to allow, within English case law, the establishment of the international nature of the contract,[81] it should not be able to determine the applicable law, for at least two reasons. Firstly, if the designated currency is common to several countries, such as the euro, then it is not possible to identify an applicable law. On the other hand, the settlement currency may have a remote link to the contract. Secondly, with regard to the extension of the law of the underlying to the financial contract itself, the underlying is not necessarily an asset subject to a law, and will therefore not necessarily allow for the designation of an applicable law. Moreover, in cases where there is an underlying that is an asset subject to a law, the latter may have a very distant relationship with the contract: this is the very principle of the autonomy rule, which is the basis of the concept of financial contract.[82]

801. In order to determine the applicable law in the absence of a choice of law for a financial contract whose characteristic performance cannot be determined, a distinction must be made between financial contracts which are subject to clearing and others. For the former, the performance of obligations at the clearing house may constitute a legal proximity of such a nature as to manifest the closest links. Indeed, in these cases, the hedging obligation is considered essential to the financial contract.[83] Therefore, the law applicable to the clearing system should be applied as the law of the financial contract in the absence of a choice.[84] For the latter, in cases where there is no netting and the characteristic performance cannot be identified, a casuistic analysis of the situation is required, weighing up the respective importance and possible combination of the location of the parties, the country of the solicited party, the currency of settlement and

---

from each other, and it is open to the parties to select a separate law in their Confirmation. The question is different in the case where there is no choice of law in the Confirmation. In this case, the characteristic performance criterion is likely to designate a law different from the one selected by the Masters Agreement. However, it would then be possible – and desirable in order to ensure a consistent application of these contracts – to consider that, as a Confirmation, it has manifestly closer links with the Masters Agreement, and to apply to it the law of the Masters Agreement on the basis of Art. 4(3) of the Rome I Regulation (see also in this sense, *ibid.*). On this issue, see S. Corneloup, 'Choix de loi et contrats liés', *op. cit.*; D. Sindres, 'Le contrat cadre en matière internationale', *AJ contrat* 2017, p. 107.

79 A. Gaudemet, *Les dérivés*, *op. cit.*, no. 173.

80 J. Gavriloff, *Les méthodes du conflit de lois à l'épreuve du produit dérivé*, *op. cit.*, nos. 62 and 343.

81 See *supra*, para. 785.

82 See *supra*, paras. 770 et seq.

83 P. Pailler, *Le contrat financier, un instrument financier à terme*, *op. cit.*, no. 341.

84 On the determination of this law, see *supra*, para. 277.

the underlying. Such a solution is unsatisfactory; it can be put into perspective by its very residual character.[85]

§ 2. THE CONSUMER CONTRACT EXCEPTION

802. In EU law, as in French law, the protection of lay parties to a contract is most often achieved through consumer legislation. This is one of the reasons why consumer contracts are subject to a derogatory rule in Article 6 of the Rome I Regulation, allowing the law of the consumer's habitual residence to apply to the contract. However, the applicability of this conflict rule to financial contracts is doubly uncertain, firstly because of the exclusion of financial instruments and the inclusion of investment services in the material scope of this rule (I). Secondly, even if the law of the consumer's habitual residence applies in respect of the provision of an investment service, the personal scope of application is likely to be an obstacle, since the person must still be characterised as a consumer and must have been solicited (II).

I. Material Scope of Application

803. Criticism of the exclusion of financial instruments. As a preliminary remark, it should be noted that the possible interference of consumer status is not likely to come into play with regard to the contract concluded by the multilateral trading facility since market members cannot be consumers.[86] It is therefore within OTC contracts that the question of consumer contracts specifically arises. Article 6 of the Rome I Regulation provides for a specific conflict rule relating to consumer contracts. However, certain matters are excluded from the material scope of the rule and, in particular, it is inapplicable to 'rights and obligations which constitute financial instruments'.[87] The *ratio* of this exclusion is given by Recital 28 of the Rome I Regulation, according to which:

> 'It is important to ensure that rights and obligations which constitute a financial instrument are not covered by the general rule applicable to consumer contracts, as that could lead to different laws being applicable to each of the instruments issued, therefore changing their nature and preventing their fungible trading and offering. Likewise, whenever such instruments are issued or offered, the contractual

---

85 On the one hand, as financial contracts are standardised, it is very unlikely that such a fundamental element as the designation of the applicable law will be forgotten, on the other hand, financial contracts for which it is impossible to designate a characteristic benefit remain a minority and, finally, the latter should not be subject to set-off, thus making them even more residual.

86 On the status of market members, see *supra*, parasno. 435 et seq.

87 Art. 6(4)(d).

relationship established between the issuer or the offeror and the consumer should not necessarily be subject to the mandatory application of the law of the country of habitual residence of the consumer, as there is a need to ensure uniformity in the terms and conditions of an issuance or an offer.'[88]

It is therefore clear that the European legislator wanted to enable the offeror of financial securities to guarantee the uniqueness of the law applicable to the offer, despite the fact that the addressees, even if they are consumers, are located in very different States.[89] In other words, it is the public nature of the offer, combined with the multiplicity of countries in which the addressees may be located, which justifies the exclusion of the Article 6 rule and the correlative application of a single law selected on the basis of Article 3 of the same regulation.

However, this justification is difficult to extend to financial contracts, whose configuration is different: on the one hand, there is no public offer of financial contracts and, on the other hand, financial contracts are not issued in such a way as to allow their dispersion. Under these circumstances, it is difficult to understand why the exclusion of financial instruments has been extended to all financial instruments and, de *lege ferenda*, it would be appropriate to restrict the inapplicability of this provision to financial securities only. It is in the light of this initial inconsistency that the inclusion of investment services in the scope of Article 6 of the Rome I Regulation should be interpreted.

804. Investment services and financial contract. At first sight, the inclusion of investment services within the scope of Article 6 of the Rome I Regulation is not such as to allow the application of the law of the consumer's habitual residence to the financial contract. Indeed, Recital 26 of the Rome I Regulation explicitly provides for the application of Article 6 to 'financial services such as investment services and activities and related services provided by a professional to a consumer and referred to in Sections A and B of Annexe I to Directive 2004/39/EC (*MiFID*) and contracts for the sale of units of common funds'.

The scope of the reference made by this recital carefully excludes financial instruments, which appear only in Section C of Annex I of MiFID. Indeed, Sections A and B refer only to investment and ancillary services. The exclusion of financial instruments requires a distinction between the provision of the investment service and the provision of a financial instrument. This distinction

88 The legislator adds that: 'The same principle should apply in respect of multilateral systems covered by Article 4(1)(h), where it should be ensured that the law in force in the country of habitual residence of the consumer will not interfere with the rules applicable to contracts concluded within such systems or with the operator of such systems.'

89 On the application of this provision to an offer of financial securities, see *supra*, para. 370.

is explicitly formulated by Recital 26 of the Rome I Regulation in relation to financial securities.[90]

805. The distinction between investment services and public offer of securities is clear; when it comes to distinguishing an investment service and financial contracts it can be more problematic. Indeed, in relation to financial contracts, this distinction means that the contract for the provision of the investment service should be subject to the material scope of application of Article 6 of the Rome I Regulation, while the financial contract itself should be excluded. The distinction appears to be workable in certain configurations.[91] However, the situation is more difficult where the investment service provided is proprietary trading. This is an investment service defined by Article D. 321-1(3) of the Monetary and Financial Code as 'concluding transactions in one or more financial instruments by committing one's own capital'.[92] In this case, the terms investment service and financial contract overlap: the conclusion by an investment service provider of a financial contract with its client is precisely the purpose of the investment service. In other words, whenever the provider acts as counterparty for his client, he is providing an investment service.[93]

806. In these circumstances, two interpretations of the application of Article 6 of the Rome I Regulation to financial contracts concluded between an investment service provider and its client are possible. The first interpretation gives precedence to the letter of Article 6, which is a provision, over Recital 26,

---

90 According to the latter: 'Where reference is made to the terms and conditions of the issue or offer to the public of negotiable securities, or the subscription and redemption of units in unit trusts, this reference should encompass all aspects linking the issuer or offeror to the consumer, excluding those relating to the provision of financial services.' This helps to show that the exclusion of financial instruments from Art. 6 of the Regulation was only intended for securities.

91 Thus, where an investment service provider concludes an investment advice contract relating to the conclusion of a financial contract, or negotiates on behalf of the client a financial contract with another counterparty, there can be no doubt that these contracts, which constitute investment services (Arts. 3 and 5 of Section 1 of Annex A of MiFID), fall within the material scope of Art. 6, while any financial contract concluded will be subject to its own law.

92 This definition of proprietary trading is a more precise variation of the definition provided by Art. 4.1.6 of MiFID 2. However, as Professor Drummond observes, this definition 'is less comprehensive than the one previously set out in the former Article 312-3 of the AMF General Regulation. The latter provided that "any authorised provider that buys or sells financial instruments for its own account", but supplemented the proposal by specifying that this activity constituted an investment service only when it was carried out by the provider outside of its treasury or equity transactions', see F. Drummond, *Droit financier*, *op. cit.*, no. 419, note 5.

93 As Caillemer du Ferrage and Duhamel wrote: 'The definition of investment services, mainly proprietary trading, order execution for third parties and order reception and transmission for third parties, covers in practice all possible interventions in the derivatives market', A. Caillemer du Ferrage and A. Duhamel, 'Monopoly of investment services providers and OTC derivatives', *Banque et droit*, 2001/76, p. 3, spec. p. 4.

which, as a recital, only provides guidelines for interpretation, or even objectives to be achieved, but is not binding on the courts.[94] The second interpretation is teleological, and amounts to the observation that the legislator did not intend to exclude financial contracts from the material scope of Article 6, but clearly wished to include investment services. This second interpretation should be retained. Indeed, it allows this provision to accomplish the purpose for which it was designed, and to correct the unjustified blanket exclusion of financial contracts from the material scope of Article 6.[95] However, even in those cases where the conclusion of a financial contract by a provider can be characterised as an investment service, in order for it to trigger the rule of Article 6 of the Rome I Regulation, the contract must be concluded with a consumer, and the consumer must have been solicited.

II. Personal Scope

807. The personal scope of application of Article 6 of the Rome I Regulation depends on two criteria. First, the client of the investment service provider must qualify as a consumer. In the case of a financial contract, the notion of consumer under the Rome I and Brussels I *a* Regulations could have been inspired by the European financial law provisions, which subjectively assess the status of the parties in order to protect them. Here, however, the characterisation of consumer is independent of the contract concluded and is assessed objectively (A). Secondly, the service provider must have solicited his client (B).

A. The Notion of Consumer under the Rome I Regulation

808. Article 6 of the Rome I Regulation states that a consumer contract is 'a contract concluded by a natural person for a purpose which can be regarded as being outside his trade or profession (the consumer) with another person acting in the exercise of his trade or profession (the professional)'. Two criteria stand out from the notion of consumer: only natural persons can be characterised as consumers; in order to be characterised as a consumer, the natural person must act outside his or her trade or profession. In order to define this second criterion, the question arises as to whether this characterisation of consumer in the sense of

---

94 In this case, the non-application of Art. 6 does not necessarily leave the consumer without protection, because the rules on solicitation and the rules of good conduct are applicable irrespective of the law designated by the *lex contractus* (see *infra*, paras. 830 et seq.). On the relationship between the recitals and the articles, see S. Lemaire, 'Interrogations sur la portée juridique du préambule du règlement Rome I', *D.*, 2008, 2157.

95 See already in this sense, Mr Chacornac, who commenting on the *Petruchova* judgment where a financial contract was at issue, considers that it was a provision of investment services falling 'within the scope of the protection rule of the Rome I Regulation', 'La double autonomie de la notion de consommateur dans le règlement Bruxelles I bis en matière financière', *RCDIP*, 2020, 300.

conflict of laws law overlaps with the characterisation already known in financial law and with the characterisation in the law of international jurisdiction in the Brussels Ia Regulation.[96]

809. Consumer status and substantive financial law. European financial law distinguishes between two types of protection, depending on whether the issue is the marketing of financial securities by means of a prospectus[97] or the provision of an investment service, which may include the conclusion of a financial contract.[98] In the first case, the Prospectus Regulation distinguishes between qualified and non-qualified investors, while in the second case, MiFID distinguishes between professional and retail clients. However, the Prospectus Regulation has aligned the notion of qualified investor with that of professional client. As an author writes, this is because:

> 'These two bodies of law, Prospectus and MiFID [...] share a common logic, profoundly different from consumer law, which consists in varying the scope of protection according to the investor's skills, i.e., ultimately, according to 'subjective' considerations.'[99]

Indeed, the protection enjoyed by the individual in financial law is entirely based on the knowledge of the risks taken by the contractor.[100] As an author writes, the reason for this is that:

> 'Investment has a singular dimension compared to the act of consuming goods or services in that, apart from the fact that it does not directly satisfy any need, it confronts the investor with a risk linked to the object on which his act is based rather than to his situation of relative weakness. The issue is not one of contractual equilibrium, but of controlling a risk.'[101]

---

96 This 'double autonomy' has already been explored from the point of view of conflict of jurisdictions by J. Chacornac, 'La double autonomie de la notion de consommateur dans le règlement Bruxelles I bis en matière financière', *op. cit.*

97 See *supra*, para. 805.

98 The provision of an investment service goes beyond the mere conclusion of a financial contract, but contains it: see *supra*, para. 805.

99 J. Chacornac, 'La double autonomie de la notion de consommateur dans le règlement Bruxelles I bis en matière financière', *op. cit.*; on this question, see also, by the same author, *Les fonctions de l'information en droit des instruments financiers*, *op. cit.*

100 The protection offered by substantive financial law is nevertheless criticised because of the indeterminacy of the objective of protection, and its content, see A. Tehrani, *Les investisseurs protégés*, *op. cit.*, first part. See from the English perspective N. Moloney, 'The investor model underlying the EU's investor protection regime: consumers or investors?' (2012) 13 *European Business organization Law Review*, pp. 169 et seq., spec. pp. 173 et seq.; N. Moloney, *How to protect investors*, Cambridge, CUP, 2010, p. 30.

101 *Ibid.* As Professors Drummond and Bonneau have already written, 'it is against market risks that investor protection is organised', T. Bonneau and F. Drummond, *Droit des marchés financiers*, *op. cit.*, no. 453. See, in the same sense, Professor Daigre who considered that 'the investor is not an ordinary consumer and does not deserve the same degree of protection.

Therefore, the protection of financial law takes into account the subjective knowledge of risk-taking, which is not the practice of consumer law: the latter usually takes an objective assessment.[102] In particular, the rule of Article 6 of the Rome I Regulation is applicable because of the objective characterisation of the notion of consumer, which ignores the actual knowledge of the person.

810. Consumer status under international jurisdiction law. The Brussels Ia Regulation also contains, by way of exception, consumer protection rules which allow, under certain conditions, the court of the consumer's domicile to have jurisdiction.[103] In application of these rules, the case law adopts an objective assessment of the notion of consumer 'referring to the position of that person in a given contract, in relation to the nature and purpose of that contract, and not to the subjective situation of that person'.[104] The consequence of this interpretation is that:

> 'To consider that the consumer status of a co-contractor may depend on the knowledge and information he possesses in a given field, and not on whether the contract he has concluded is intended to satisfy his personal needs, would be to refer to the subjective situation of that contract.'[105]

This approach explains why the Court of Justice considers that taking into account the personal expertise of the contractor would be tantamount to adding a condition which the jurisdictional rule does not provide for.[106] However, the interpretation of the concept of consumer within the meaning of these jurisdictional rules can be extended to the interpretation of Article 6 of the Rome I Regulation.[107] Indeed, these rules pursue identical aims and the

---

While everyone must be able to consume everyday products in complete safety, no one is obliged to risk his or her money on the stock market. Everyone should know that a stock exchange, like a casino, is not the equivalent of a supermarket. Moreover, what allows for unexpected financial gains is the risk of making losses' (see J.-J. Daigre, 'La responsabilité du banquier en matière de prestation de services d'investissement', *RDBF*, November 2006, no. 6, file 30, no. 12).

102 On the growing influence of consumer law on financial law, see N. Moloney, 'The investor model underlying the EU's investor protection regime: consumers or investors?', *op. cit.*

103 Art. 18 of the Brussels Ia Regulation.

104 Case C-208/18, *Petruchova*, ECLI:EU:C:2019:825; see especially para. 41 of the *Petruchova* judgment, which is part of the Court's well-established case law (see the judgments cited by the Court). The judgment was confirmed by Case C-500/18, *Reliantco investments*, ECLI:EU:C:2020:264, spec. paras. 67–71.

105 Para. 56 of the *Petruchova* judgment.

106 Para. 54 of the *Petruchova* judgment.

107 In its *Petruchova* judgment, the Court of Justice nevertheless had the opportunity to affirm the independence of the rule of international jurisdiction and the domain of the conflict-of-laws rule. However, there are two reasons for observing the concept of consumer retained by the Court of Justice in relation to international jurisdiction. On the one hand, the decision in *Petruchava was intended to* avoid extending the exclusion of financial instruments under Article 6 of the Rome I Regulation to the rule on jurisdiction over consumer contracts

conditions for triggering the rule are similar. Moreover, the legislative policy pursued by these derogation rules is identical, and makes it necessary to have a uniform interpretation of the notion of consumer.[108] As a consequence, the subjective assessment of the risk taken should be set aside in order to qualify the consumer for the purposes of Article 6 of the Rome I Regulation. The reason for such an approach at European level may be the wide disparity in knowledge and experience of retail investors,[109] so that the subjective approach was likely to lead to an overly fragmented and casuistic application of the Regulation. It is also due to the interpretation policy of the Court of Justice, which does not necessarily take into account substantive European law in order to interpret the Brussels I*a* Regulation.[110]

811. This approach deserves approval. Admittedly, it has the consequence, both from the point of view of international jurisdiction and conflict of laws, of doing too much or too little: too much, because it risks allowing a natural person who is perfectly aware of his risk to avoid the law normally applicable to the contract,[111] too little, because it will not allow the protective rule to come into play in the case of an inexperienced legal person who will not necessarily be aware of the risk taken.[112] However, knowledge of the financial risk taken is not the same as knowledge of the legal risk, in particular that of having to litigate at the domicile of the contracting party,[113] or of being subject to foreign contract

(even though Article 6 of the Rome I Regulation would not have been applicable if financial services had been classified as such in this case). This exclusion was therefore linked to the material scope of Article 6 of the Rome I Regulation, and not to its personal scope of application. As far as the personal scope is concerned, the two rules should therefore contribute to the same notion of consumer in the name of the European legislator's desire for consistency. Secondly, because the purpose of the rules converges since they both contribute, both from the point of view of determining the internationally competent court and the applicable law, to derogating, by way of exception, from the rule of principle in order to protect the consumer, subject to the same conditions.

108 Recital 7 of the Rome I Regulation.

109 N. Moloney, 'The investor model underlying the EU's investor protection regime: consumers or investors?' *op. cit.*

110 This follows from the *Falco* (Case C-533/07, ECLI:EU:C:2009:257) and *Car Trim* (Case C-381/08, ECLI:EU:C:2010:90) cases. The Court of Justice refused to take account of substantive European law in the former case in order to define the provision of services, whereas it did so in the latter. On this question see H. Gaudemet-Tallon and M.-E. Ancel, *Compétence et exécution des jugements en Europe*, *op. cit.*, no. 198 and references.

111 Described as *robust risk-takers*, as opposed to *prudent savers*, see N. Moloney, 'The investor model underlying the EU's investor protection regime: consumers or investors?'.

112 Comp. A.-C. Rouaud, 'L'investisseur, un consommateur comme les autres? A propos de l'application des règles de compétence internationales issues du Règlement Bruxelles I *bis*', *RISF*, 2020/2, pp. 3–5.

113 As Mr Chacornac writes: 'Thus, it must undoubtedly be recognised that the imperative of protection, in terms of jurisdiction, can emancipate itself from the imperative of substantive protection, based on the technical mastery of the subject matter of a legal relationship

law.[114] Nevertheless, the characterisation of consumer is not sufficient to allow the application of Article 6 of the Rome I Regulation: the consumer still has to prove the existence of a solicitation by a professional.

B. The Existence of a Solicitation by a Professional

812. In relation to financial contracts, the determination of professionals does not pose any difficulty: the existence in European law of an authorisation for investment firms makes it possible to define them precisely. However, it is not enough for the contract to be concluded with a professional for Article 6 of the Rome I Regulation to apply. Two additional conditions must be met which, while not entirely within the personal scope of application, are closely related in that they are justified by the conduct of the professional. Indeed, not only must the contract be concluded in the context of his professional activity,[115] but there must also be a solicitation on his part. The notion of solicitation does not appear in the text of Article 6 of the Rome I Regulation. However, it can easily be deduced from Article 6(1) of the Rome I Regulation, according to which the professionnal must: '(a) pursue his commercial or professional activities in the country where the consumer has his habitual residence, or (b) by any means, direct such activities to that country or to several countries including that country.'

---

in civil and commercial matters, especially in view of the absence of a specific forum of protection in financial matters.' J. Chacornac, 'La double autonomie de la notion de consommateur dans le règlement Bruxelles I bis en matière financière', *op. cit.*

114 This last remark may be tempered in the light of the protection afforded to protected investors under financial law, which is independent of the law applicable to the contract. These will be, on the one hand, the regulations relating to the marketing of financial services and, on the other hand, the professional information obligations on the investment firm, which will be applicable regardless of the law applicable to the financial contract. In addition to these two sets of rules, there are those resulting from the transposition of Directive 2002-65 of 23 September 2002 concerning the distance marketing of consumer financial services, on which see *infra*, para. 840.

115 It is possible for an investment service provider to conclude contracts outside his professional activity, i.e. the provision of investment services. This is true for all professionals, which makes it necessary to distinguish the qualification as a professional from the two additional conditions required by Article 6 of the Rome I Regulation: on the one hand, the conclusion of the contract at issue in the course of the professional activity of the person qualified as such and, on the other, the characterisation of a causal link between the contract at issue and the professional activity. The first condition can be presumed by considering that the qualification of professional should be reserved for 'one who acts in the course of his professional activity'. See 'Rome I Regulation: Contractual obligations', in S. Francq, *Répertoire de droit international, op. cit.*, no. 119. On the second condition relating to the causal link, see Recital 25 of the Rome I Regulation, P. Lagarde and A. Tenenbaum, 'De la Convention de Rome au règlement Rome I', *RCDIP*, 2008, pp. 727 et seq. See 'Rome I Regulation: Contractual obligations', in S. Francq, *Répertoire de droit international, op. cit.*, no. 112.

813. In the context of investment services, the condition of Article 6(1)(a) will be deemed to be met whenever the professional has an establishment in the consumer's Member State.[116] This condition is limited to the provision of investment services under the freedom to provide services. It is here that the second condition, that of Article 6(1)(b) of the Rome I Regulation, makes it possible to characterise the solicitation. This characterisation should be inspired by Article 42 of MiFID 2.[117] Such a unitary approach, which is based on active solicitation, makes it possible, on the one hand, to circumscribe it precisely and, on the other hand, to give a coherent approach to European financial regulation.

814. In practice, this interpretation means that the condition of Article 6(1)(b) of the Rome I Regulation is deemed to be fulfilled if the investment firm from another Member State or from a third country sends a paper or electronic letter to the client, or calls him. Similarly, targeted advertising via social networks or a search engine constitutes a solicitation. More generally, unsolicited communications[118] lead to the fulfilment of this condition. The characterisation of solicitation is more casuistic in the context of the setting up of a website by the investment firm.[119] In this case, as Professor Synvet and Ms Tenenbaum write, 'the use of the Internet will be considered as an active solicitation if the site is specifically aimed at investors residing in France'.[120] Otherwise, it would seem excessive to deduce from the mere fact that a website is online that the professional is seeking to direct his activity towards a country.[121] This assertion,

---

116 See 'Rome I Regulation: Contractual obligations', in S. Francq, *Répertoire de droit international*, *op. cit.*, no. 112, with the exception of the case where the contract was concluded with a company of the same group established abroad and not operating in the consumer's country of residence.

117 See *supra*, para. 208. Recall the definition of the act of banking and financial canvassing proposed in French law by Art. L. 341-1 of the Monetary and Financial Code: 'any unsolicited contact, by whatever means, with a natural person or a specific legal entity, with a view to obtaining an agreement on the part of that person or entity on' a set of strictly defined transactions (including the conclusion of investment services, see spec. Art. L. 341-1(3°)) constitutes an act of canvassing. On canvassing, see *infra*, paras. 830 et seq.

118 On this, see Art. 10 of the Financial Services Marketing Directive.

119 Without this being the subject of an advertising reference on a search engine. In this case, the characterisation of solicitation should be retained.

120 H. Synvet and A. Tenenbaum, 'Financial instruments', *op. cit.*, no. 138. In this case, it will be necessary to deduce from the wording of the site's pages the existence of a solicitation, which can be deduced from the presence of several indicators, such as hypertext links designating national sites, a set of national cultural references, or even by the presence of a national legal reference. Some authors add the 'means of access to the Internet' (see *ibid.*). The same authors note that this method of bundling indices is shared internationally, see *ibid.* Language, like currency, is nevertheless not a relevant index, see Recital 24 of the Rome I Regulation. Professor Francq lists several additional criteria, see 'Rome I Regulation: Contractual obligations', in S. Francq, *Répertoire de droit international*, *op. cit.*, nos. 123–124.

121 This was the view of the Court of Justice when interpreting Art. 15(1)(c) of the Brussels I Regulation (Case C-190/11, *Mühlleitner*, ECLI:EU:C:2012:542), see also F. Ragno, 'The Law Applicable to Consumer Contracts under the Rome I Regulation' in F. Ferrari (ed.)

based on the idea of 'focus',[122] is supported by the assertion of the Court of Justice in the context of the interpretation of the Brussels I Regulation according to which: 'It must be held that, in order for Article 15(1)(c) of Regulation No 44/2001 to be applicable, the trader must have manifested its intention to establish commercial relations with consumers from one or more other Member States, including that of the consumer's domicile.'[123]

815. Section conclusion. The configuration of the financial contract, which is most often drawn up by specialised professional associations, explains, on the one hand, that the applicable law is most often already selected by the parties and, on the other hand, that this choice is paradoxically the result of factors that are generally exogenous to contract law. However, the law chosen by the parties does not have total control and could be undermined by the characterisation of a financial contract constituting an investment service where the provider actively solicits the consumer residing in France.

816. Chapter conclusion. The financial contract is most often an international contract, either because of the location of the parties in different states, or because of its content based on the payment of a monetary obligation denominated in a foreign currency, or whose valuation is based on a foreign underlying, or because of the immediate environment of the contract. On the other hand, financial contracts are not intrinsically international because of an industry that is structurally international. This frequent internationality has led to the development of model contracts drawn up by specialised professional associations, first and foremost ISDA, which most often select English law for reasons which, contrary to appearances, are not based solely on contract law. This choice of law is nevertheless likely to be contradicted whenever the financial contract will constitute an investment service. In this case, which overlaps with proprietary trading, the law of the consumer's habitual residence will apply to the contract if it is actively solicited by the professional.

Rome I Regulation, Paris, Selliers, 2015, no. 31. A final situation arises at the borderline of the two conditions of Article 6(1)(a) and (b) of the Rome I Regulation: where a contract is concluded between a consumer and a foreign trader who has not made any active solicitation, but has an establishment in the consumer's legal system which has not been involved in either the formation or performance of the contract. In this case, a literal application of Art. 6a would probably lead to its application, but the teleological application of the article leads to its rejection. The latter interpretation should prevail, see already in this sense F. Garcimartin Alférez, European Legal Forum 2008, I.73, No 59, quoted by S. Francq, 'Rome I Regulation: Contractual Obligations', *op. cit.*, no. 122.

122 Proposed in France by O. Cachard, *La régulation internationale du marché électronique*, Paris, LGDJ, 2002. On this method, see D. Bureau and H. Muir Watt, *Droit international privé*, t. 2, *op. cit.*, no. 1017; V. Pironon, 'Dits et non-dits sur la méthode de la focalisation dans le contentieux contractuel et délictuel du commerce électronique', *JDI* 2011, October 2011, var. 4.

123 Joined Cases C-585/08 and C-144/09, *Peter Pammer*, ECLI:EU:C:2010:740, para. 75.

CHAPTER 2
DISRUPTIONS RELATED TO THE FORMATION OF THE CONTRACT

817. Defects of consent are part of the general protection afforded to contracting parties in French law. These conditions of validity are subject by the Rome I Regulation to the *lex contractus*.[1] However, the formation of the contract is likely to be disrupted by the application of certain rules traditionally excluded from the domain of the law of contract, either in order to protect the persons concluding financial contracts or in order to protect the underlying asset affected by the conclusion of the financial contract. These rules can be divided into two sets. The first set consists of legislation on the capacity of persons.[2] In French law, however, these do not interfere much with the conclusion of financial contracts, as the enactment of an incapacity regime has more disadvantages than advantages (Section 1). This is why French law favours a second set of rules, relating to the marketing of financial contracts, to ensure the protection of its residents (Section 2). The rules relating to the protection of the underlying are intended to prevent the financial contract, thanks to the rule of autonomy which characterises it, from constituting for the parties an instrument for circumventing the rules applicable to the underlying (Section 3).

SECTION 1. THE CAPACITY

On the face of it, French law provides for a measured regime of incapacity that tends to promote the hedging function of the financial contract while preventing it from being used for speculative purposes; on reflection, however, the criterion of speculative intent appears dysfunctional (§ 1). In relation to financial contracts, the enactment of an incapacity regime is tantamount to an incapacity of enjoyment (*incapacité de jouissance*), not of exercise (*incapacité d'exercice*): when applicable to legal persons, the regime should be aimed at the ability to contract (§ 2).

---

1 Art. 10(1) of the Rome I Regulation.

2 One should probably add here the case of lack of consent, which is likely to be governed by the law of the investor's domicile, see Art. 10(2) Rome I Regulation.

§ 1. A MEASURED REGIME OF INCAPACITY IN FRENCH LAW

818. The French regime. French law does not provide for any specific restriction on the conclusion by a natural person of a financial contract. As Professor Gaudemet has already pointed out, the protection of natural persons is not established by an incapacity regime, but by 'the existence of extensive pre-contractual information and, secondarily, by the sanctioning of defects of consent'.[3] Similarly, French case law, by qualifying the conclusion of derivative contracts as a management operation, favours the validity of financial contracts concluded by legal persons,[4] which does not exclude a corporate action for liability if the articles of association explicitly provide for the prohibition of concluding financial contracts.[5] As an exception, the French legal system limits the capacity of certain legal persons. The legislator has thus expressly restricted the capacity of UCITS and insurance companies.[6] The question has also arisen as to whether the French legal system allows its local authorities to enter into financial contracts insofar as they can only act for a reason of general interest.[7] Although the case law has never held that such contracts are null and void,[8]

---

3 A. Gaudemet, *Les dérivés*, *op. cit.*, no. 279; see also in this sense R. Dambre, *Les contrats financiers sur actions*, *op. cit.*, nos. 116–117.

4 This follows from the *Savour Club* decision, Cass. Com., 7 April 1998, no. 96-13373, on which see A. Gaudemet, *Les dérivés*, *op. cit.*, no. 293, T. Bonneau *et al.*, *Droit financier*, *op. cit.*, nos. 765 et seq. and references, R. Dambre, *Les contrats financiers sur actions*, *op. cit.*, nos. 118–119.

5 A. Gaudemet, *Les dérivés*, *op. cit.*, nos. 299–300. The author observes that it is then possible to act with a social action *ut universi* or *ut singuli*. An action on the basis of mismanagement is also possible, as opposed to an action based on the violation of a clause limiting powers mentioned in the body of the text.

6 For UCITS, see Arts. L. 214-20,(I)(5°) and R. 214-15 et seq. of the Monetary and Financial Code, for insurance undertakings, see Arts. R. 332-45 to R. 322-58 of the Insurance Code. On these articles, see T. Bonneau *et al.*, *Droit financier*, *op. cit.*, nos. 864 et seq., R. Dambre, *Les contrats financiers sur actions*, *op. cit.*, no. 124.

7 A. Gaudemet, *Les dérivés*, *op. cit.*, nos. 282 et seq.; T. Bonneau *et al.*, *Droit financier*, *op. cit.*, no. 772; R. Dambre, *Les contrats financiers sur actions*, *op. cit.*, nos. 121 et seq. This is also the case in foreign law where local authorities have been the subject of an identical dispute which gave rise to a much criticised judgment in English law, *Hazell v. Hammersmith & Fulham LBC* [1992] 2 A.C. 1 HL. This judgment, which found in favour of the local authorities, was so intensely criticised by the industry that a legislative response *ultimately* granted general jurisdiction to the local authorities, see J. Braithwaite, 'Thirty years of ultra vires: local authorities, national courts and the global derivatives markets' (2018) 71(1) *Current Legal Problems*, p. 369; J. Braithwaite, *The Financial Courts: Adjudicating Disputes in Derivatives Markets*, *op. cit.* In a recent perspective, see the *Dexia Crediop* and *Bando Santander* judgments mentioned above, but also the numerous references from the different Member States on which see E. Wymeersch, 'Regulation and Case Law Relating to Financial Derivatives', *RDBF*, 2013, pp. 1 et seq.; J.P. Braithwaite, 'Thirty years of ultra vires: local authorities, national courts and the global derivatives markets', *op. cit.*

8 *Ibid.* Investment service providers were condemned under their warning obligations. Nullity has been upheld in foreign law, notably in English law, see J. Braithwaite, 'Thirty years of ultra vires: local authorities, national courts and the global derivatives markets', *op. cit.*, pp. 369 et seq.

the legislator has nevertheless intervened, making the conclusion of a financial contract conditional on the presence of specific contractual clauses,[9] so that the ability to conclude such contracts is restricted here if their purpose was not to cover a credit risk.[10]

819. Analysis. The incapacity regime enacted here, which is far removed from the gambling exception,[11] is tailor-made: it is not a general incapacity, but an incapacity to enter into *certain* financial contracts, i.e. those whose purpose is not to cover a risk, but which in themselves constitute the taking of a risk. In fact, the French legislator is pursuing two distinct purposes here. In the case of insurance companies and UCITS, they have in common that they are professional institutions whose investment risks must be limited. The French legislator therefore ensures that the aforementioned entities avoid operations which are lucrative but too risky and therefore unsuited to their status. The function pursued by these rules is the protection of the subscribers of these funds. The objective pursued in the case of local authorities is both similar and different. Similar, because, as an English judge has held, the purpose of incapacity is 'the use or misuse of the council's funds':[12] the protection of the subscribers is replaced by that of the taxpayer. However, the aim is different because, unlike insurance companies and UCITS, local and regional authorities

---

9 Art. L. 1611-3-1 of the General Code of Local Authorities. This question must be distinguished from the interference of rules relating to the expression of consent of public persons, on which see M. Audit, S. Bollée and P. Callé, *Droit du commerce international et des investissements étrangers, op. cit.*

10 R. Dambre, *Les contrats financiers sur actions, op. cit.*, no. 122; A. Gaudemet, 'Compétence pour conclure des opérations financières spéculatives', *RDBF*, 2012, comm. 166.

11 In some respects, the enactment of a regime of personal incapacity is reminiscent of the configuration of the gambling exception, which *ultimately* promoted bad faith on the part of those who could benefit from it: either they lost at the end of the contract, in which case they refused to pay and could not be compelled to do so thanks to the gambling exception, or they won and took their winnings, see *supra*, para. 456. This is the reason why incapacity may appear unsuited to the protective purpose pursued, since it leads to the infantilisation of residents, whether public or private, whereas the information obligations of professionals make it possible, on the contrary, to enlighten investment decisions, irrespective of whether a person is a natural or legal person.
However, such an observation would miss two significant differences with the gambling exception regime. The first is that the gambling exception regime did not lead to the enactment of a regime of incapacity, but simply deprived the beneficiary of a bet of his recourse to payment. Now, incapacity, in that it always leads to the nullity of the contract, appears to be an effective deterrent to the conclusion of the contract, without any premium for bad faith (insofar as the latter is foreseeable, which is not necessarily the case, see from the point of view of the English law, J. Braithwaite, 'Thirty years of ultra vires: local authorities, national courts and the global derivatives markets', *op. cit.*) The second difference is that it is not a general incapacity, but an incapacity to enter into *certain* financial contracts, i.e. those whose purpose is not to hedge a risk, but to take a risk.

12 *Hazell v. Hammersmith and Fulham London Borough council* (1990) 2 QB 697 (CA), 776 (Sir Stephen Brown P) cited in J. Braithwaite, 'Thirty years of ultra vires: local authorities, national courts and the global derivatives markets', *op. cit.*, p. 372.

are relatively inexperienced persons who need to be protected so that they are not seduced by contractual proposals that are in fact disadvantageous. The legislator's requirements appear here as protective measures.[13] Nevertheless, it is questionable whether the criterion set up is really operational, for two reasons.

820. The first is that this criterion requires a particularly detailed analysis in order to determine whether the party whose capacity is restricted has entered into the contract for speculative purposes or not. It may be considered sufficient to show the existence of the initial contract that the financial contract seeks to cover. However, the litigation caused by this criterion reveals its foreseeable difficulties.[14] Firstly, the financial contract may have been concluded for a mixed purpose, and does not necessarily have the sole function of hedging the original contract. In such cases where the functions are mixed, it will be very difficult to delineate what is speculative and what is not.[15] Indeed, the hedging function may depend on factors external to the contract, such as the overall strategy, the interaction of the instruments, or the inclusion of the financial contract in the hedging of the group of companies in which the party is involved.[16] Secondly, the initial financial contract may have been entered into with the primary objective of hedging the initial risk, but subsequently be the subject of riders, or linked contracts, which are, in turn, entered into with the exclusive objective of making profits.[17] In practice, the distinction between hedging and speculative functions is most often seen as a primary difference of degree. As expressed by the London Court of Appeal:

> 'The dichotomy [...] between hedging and speculation is to some extent illusory, in the sense that the two shade into each other [...]. We are not surprised that the

13 It is perhaps surprising that this protective regime has not been extended to all natural and legal persons who are not specialised in providing investment services. However, it should be noted that this regime has been reserved, on the one hand, for private persons whose proper function is the pooling of risks and diversified investment in order to limit risks and, on the other hand, for public persons whose financial management must not lead to speculation. Such a restriction is welcome, as the other solutions excessively restrict the exercise of residents' contractual freedom, which can be clarified by *ad hoc* information obligations and the limitation of offerors to regulated professionals.

14 These have been contentiously illustrated in several judgments, see in particular *Titan Steel Wheels Ltd v. The Royal Bank of Scotland plc* (2010) EWHC 211 (Comm); *Standard Chartered Bank v. Ceylon Petroleum Corporation* (2012) EWCA Civ 1049; *Credit Suisse International v. Stichting Vestia Groep* (2014) EWHC 3103 (Comm). On these cases, see J. Braithwaite, *The Financial Courts: Adjudicating Disputes in Derivatives Markets*, *op. cit.*, pp. 331–332 and references.

15 As the Court of Appeal expressed it in the above-mentioned *Standard* judgment (see point 9), this classification cannot be applied 'solely objectively'.

16 These observations are taken from the remarks of the above-mentioned judges, summarised by J. Braithwaite, *The Financial Courts: Adjudicating Disputes in Derivatives Markets*, *op. cit.*, p. 332.

17 This was for example the case in *Titan Steel Wheels Ltd v. The Royal Bank of Scotland plc* (2010) EWHC 211 (Comm).

experts in this case [...] were divided in their opinion. We consider on the whole that hedging may come in more or less speculative forms, and that speculation may come in more or less hedged or risk averse forms.'[18]

The Court concluded that the only relevant question was whether the contracts could be concluded by the disputed entity, and no longer ventured into the subjective analysis.[19]

821. The second difficulty with this criterion is specific to the very notion of capacity into which it fits, for two reasons: foreign law does not always use the same notion of capacity; the consequences of nullity are governed by the law of the contract. Firstly, the concept of capacity may be understood very differently in different countries. Nevertheless, it is known that thanks to the technique of adaptation, the local concept of capacity can be given foreign law meanings which are not qualified in the same way in foreign law, but which nevertheless pursue the same purpose. However, adaptation may lead to unsatisfactory results, as shown by the *Haugesund Kommune* judgment.[20] In this judgment, Norwegian municipalities had concluded an ISDA-type financial contract with an Irish bank, which was subject to English law and London jurisdiction. The question was whether Norwegian municipalities were entitled to enter into such contracts.[21] The concern is that Norwegian law does not treat the difficulty in terms of capacity, but rather sees it as a form of relative nullity depending on the law of the contract. The English court, however, considered that the function pursued by the Norwegian legal institution was the functional equivalent of capacity. It therefore resorted to this characterisation, and consequently annulled the contracts. A dissenting voice in the Court observed that this 'bizarre result'[22] meant that contracts, which would have been valid if Norwegian law had been applicable to them, or if the Norwegian party had been English, were nullified by

18 *Standard Chartered Bank v. Ceylon Petroleum Corporation* (2012) EWCA Civ 1049, no 15. The judges further state: 'the question of hedging and speculation is, at any rate, in the context of an issue of capacity, a false question' (*ibid.*, no. 22).

19 *Ibid.*, no. 23. The solution has since been confirmed, see J. Braithwaite, *The Financial Courts: Adjudicating Disputes in Derivatives Markets*, *op. cit.*, p. 333. The English courts had already been confronted with the difficulties of the subjective approach in their domestic order, see J. Braithwaite, 'Thirty years of ultra vires: local authorities, national courts and the global derivatives markets', *op.* cit.

20 *Haugesund Kommune v. Depfa ACS Bank* [2009] EWHC 2227 (Comm); *Haugesund Kommune v. Depfa ACS Bank* [2010] EWCA Civ 579; *Haugesund Kommune v. DEPFA ACS Bank (No 2)* [2011] EWCA Civ 33.

21 Legislation restricting the circumstances under which Norwegian municipalities could borrow money, see *Haugesund Kommune v. Depfa ACS Bank* (2009) EWHC 2227 (Comm) no. 10.

22 See Etherthon LJ, *Haugesund Kommune v. Depfa ACS Bank* [2010] EWCA Civ 579, no. 144. This situation is not new in private international law, and may arise when a legislative package is carved up, see already in succession law Y. Lequette, 'Ensembles législatifs et droit international privé des successions', *TCFDIP*, Paris, Pedone, 1985, pp. 163 et seq.

the cumulative application of the two laws. This shows the limits inherent, if not in resolving the conflict of laws, at least in dissecting the different aspects of the contract. Secondly, even if the adaptation makes it possible to adopt a welcoming conception of foreign capacity, the law of the contract remains competent to determine restitution. It is therefore quite possible that the law of the contract does not really lead to the results that the law of incapacity attaches to nullity.

822. One possible solution would be to abandon this criterion and grant general jurisdiction to residents.[23] This could then be tempered by the enactment of mandatory local rules, on the one hand, in the field of solicitation, by simply prohibiting the solicitation of certain inexperienced persons[24] and, on the other hand, in the field of professional obligations, by maintaining a high standard of obligation to advise and warn. Violation of these obligations then makes it possible, in the field of tort,[25] to obtain the full jurisdiction of the affected legal order, which can then restore the balance that the legal order designated by the contract is likely to ignore.

§ 2. THE CONNECTION OF THE INABILITY TO CONCLUDE A FINANCIAL CONTRACT

823. Capacity in the Rome I Regulation. Questions of capacity are, in countries with continental traditions, subject to personal status, which is still linked to the nationality of persons. This is why Article 1(2)(a) of the Rome I Regulation provides for the exclusion of matters relating to 'questions involving the status or legal capacity of natural persons, without prejudice to Article 13'. Article 13 limits this exclusion by providing that:

> 'In a contract concluded between persons who are in the same country, a natural person who would have capacity under the law of that country may invoke his incapacity resulting from the law of another country, only if the other party to the contract was aware of that incapacity at the time of the conclusion of the contract or was not aware thereof as a result of negligence.'

This rule is intended to promote the validity of the contract by limiting the application of the incapacity provided for by the national law of the contracting party to the case where the other party was aware of it or where his ignorance was due only to 'negligence'. However, this rule is only applicable when the two

---

23 This was the English solution, see J. Braithwaite, 'Thirty years of ultra vires: local authorities, national courts and the global derivatives markets', *op. cit.*, p. 374.

24 Including a non-exhaustive list of such persons.

25 In the contractual field, the resources of English law are not very conducive to engaging the liability of service providers, see J. Braithwaite, *The Financial Courts: Adjudicating Disputes in Derivatives Markets*, *op. cit.*

persons are in the same country. In relation to financial contracts, Article 13 of the Rome I Regulation will have little effect, either because the parties are not in the same country or because, as a regulated professional with a monopoly on the provision of investment services, the negligence of the investment firm may be established where it fails to verify the capacity of its contracting partner under its national law.[26] The key question is whether a possible inability to conclude financial contracts falls within the scope of the exclusion provided for in Article 1(2a) of the Rome I Regulation. In order to answer this question, a distinction must be made between incapacity to enjoy and exercise rights on the one hand and incapacity to represent and capacity to contract on the other.

824. Distinction between incapacity to enjoy and exercise. The first question is whether a possible incapacity to conclude financial contracts constitutes an incapacity of 'enjoyment' or of exercise. Professors Audit and d'Avout consider that 'special disabilities of enjoyment are likely to fall under personal law, when they are enacted on the basis of a characteristic of the person concerned',[27] but more often than not 'a disability of this kind is aimed at a given type of act for a reason of general interest rather than the personal characteristics of those involved in it, and must therefore be applied on the basis of the environment of the act and not on the basis of the personal law'.[28] On the other hand, the incapacities of exercise are those, sometimes referred to as natural incapacities, which 'are inherent to man; it will always be necessary to protect individuals either from the lack of maturity or inexperience due to youth, or from psycho-physical deficiencies',[29] and as such fall under personal status, allowing for the continuity of status.[30] The desire to protect individuals when entering into financial contracts is more related to an incapacity of 'enjoyment', since it is aimed at a given type of act, for a reason of general interest. However, the application of the law of the act would most often result in the incapacity regime being rendered ineffective because the contract is very often subject to foreign law which does not provide for this type of protection. This observation makes it possible to refine the understanding of an incapacity regime relating to financial contracts. It is explained first of all by the dangerousness of the act,

---

26 See already in this sense, A. Gaudemet, *Les dérivés*, *op. cit.*, no. 289. This search is undoubtedly a burden for the investment firm, and even if it can be simplified by the professional asking his co-contractor to prove his capacity to contract according to his national law, it will always require the professional to check the canons of the foreign law.

27 B. Audit and L. d'Avout, *Droit international privé*, *op. cit.*, no. 726.

28 *Ibid.* The topical example, cited by the authors, being the incapacity of the doctor to receive from the person whose last illness he treated (Art. 909 of the Civil Code). The English law of conflict of laws echoes this distinction, by subjecting capacity to the cumulative law of the act and of the person (see Rule 162 of *Dicey, Morris & Collins*, cited above). Such a rule, pragmatic in its essence, reflects the idea that the protection of persons is done according to legal orders.

29 Y. Lequette, *Protection familiale et protection étatique des incapables*, *op. cit.*, no. 1.

30 On this argument, see B. Audit and L. d'Avout, *Droit international privé*, *op. cit.*

which is not felt at the time of the contract, except by the initial deposit of a sum of money. However, this sum will be out of all proportion to the amount that the person concerned may have to pay. The incapacity regime is also explained by the difficulty of fully perceiving the stakes of the risk taken for anyone who is not a knowledgeable professional.[31] The singularity of this incapacity regime is therefore likely to extend to all persons, natural and legal, except for those who can be shown to have mastered the risk taken. Such incapacity therefore relates more to incapacity to exercise a profession and should be subject to personal status in order to ensure the effectiveness and continuity of protection.

825. Distinction between powers of representation and capacity to contract. Ability to contract is traditionally referred to as capacity for natural persons.[32] Its function is to protect the incapable natural person, or his contracting partners, by hindering the conditions for the validity of the contract. In the case of legal persons, there are two distinct issues behind capacity. The first, which is resolved by the rules on powers of representation, is the question of which body within the company or administrative organisation is competent to contract.[33] It is in this sense that the notion of competence for public persons is sometimes used. However, this first question is distinct from capacity, as understood for natural persons, which refers to the actual ability to contract. This is traditionally restricted since legal persons are subject to the principle of speciality.[34] This is why, if the most frequent contentious hypothesis is that of the validity of a contract concluded by a legal person capable of contracting, but whose director did not have a valid power of representation, it is also possible that a director has a valid power of representation, but that the disputed act does not fall within the scope of the capacity of the legal person.[35] Similarly, a member of

---

31 See for an illustration, P. Cornut St-Pierre, *La fabrique juridique des swap*, *op. cit.*, p. 1.

32 Arts. 1128 and 1145 of the Civil Code.

33 See also B. Audit and L. d'Avout, *Droit international privé*, *op. cit.*, no. 724: 'Unlike capacity, *power* is not aimed at protecting the person exercising rights, but at protecting the rights in question; power is in fact the right attributed to a person to manage the interests of others. It is therefore necessary to turn to the law applicable to the institution in question. For legal persons [...], the capacity to enjoy is governed by the law of the State of incorporation, the capacity to exercise is governed by the law of the State of the *siege réel*.'

34 Although the legal speciality of companies and the corporate object are linked, they are not confused, see 'Objet social' in Y. Chaput, *Répertoire droit des sociétés*, nos. 8–10. In French law, the role of the corporate object is less to limit the capacity to use the legal person than to verify that it is indeed a company. In this case, the corporate object makes it possible to determine the civil or commercial nature of the company and possibly to limit the powers of the directors. Depending on the situation, the corporate purpose will then make it possible to engage the liability of the directors in the internal order, and for partnerships to make the corporate purpose enforceable against third parties see *ibid.*, nos. 60 et seq. The restrictions linked to the corporate purpose have all disappeared in English law following the criticism of the latter, see J. Braithwaite, 'Thirty years of ultra vires: local authorities, national courts and the global derivatives markets', *op. cit.*, pp. 375–376.

35 The legitimate ignorance of the third party will sometimes render this act enforceable, see B. Audit and L. d'Avout, *Droit international privé*, *op. cit.*, no. 600.

the government, a central administration or a local authority may have a valid power of representation, without the law or the constitution having made them capable of contracting in all areas. The concept of capacity of legal persons used here retains these two aspects of powers of representation and ability to contract.

826. Applicable law. The Rome I Regulation also excludes from its application the question of whether "an organ of a companý, association or legal person may bind that companý, association or legal person towards third parties".[36] This question, which in the perspective of the Rome I Regulation falls within the broader field of powers of representation,[37] is traditionally subject in France to the law which established the legal person, i.e. in the case of companies, the *lex societatis*.[38] The *lex societatis* is therefore applicable to the representation of companies by their organs, which is in any case a matter of the internal organisation of the company and was therefore excluded on another basis.[39] The law of the registered office of the legal person should also apply to the question of capacity to contract, since it is for the legal system which has granted legal personality to determine the conditions under which it may enter into commitments. It should be possible to extend this rule to public persons.[40]

---

36 Art. 1(2)(g) of the Rome I Regulation.

37 See for example, for a presentation in this sense, see 'Rome I Regulation: Contractual obligations', in S. Francq, *Répertoire de droit international*, *op. cit.*, no. 39.

38 However, the latter, applicable to the question of whether the company is bound by the acts of its representative, will not necessarily be applicable, where appropriate, to the civil liability of the director where the *lex damni* is likely to prevail.

39 Art. 1(2)(f) of the Rome I Regulation.

40 The capacity of public persons is not subject to a specific exclusion within the Rome I Regulation. Since public bodies can conclude civil and commercial contracts falling within the scope of the Rome I Regulation, it can nevertheless be assumed that the law applicable to their capacity is the law of their registered office, by virtue of the analogous application of the provisions relating to legal persons governed by private law (see for an example from English case law under the Rome Convention applying the law of its seat to a public company, see *Banco Santander* [2016] EWHC 465 nos. 247 et seq.) In the same way, the law which established the collective is also applicable as regards its capacity to contract.
The question arises in an analogous way in the context of international arbitration, see M. Audit, S. Bollée and P. Callé, *Droit du commerce international et des investissements étrangers*, *op. cit.* However, in these cases, the conflicting reasoning on the jurisdiction of public entities is sometimes contested in doctrine, because 'a sovereign State is free to make the commitments it wants in the international order, notwithstanding the provisions enacted for the internal order. The principle of good faith prevents anyone from going back on a commitment made'. (B. Audit and L. d'Avout, *Droit international privé*, *op. cit.*) The argument does not meet with complete approval. On the one hand, the competence of public persons exceeds that of the State understood as the government and the central administration. On the other hand, there may be some confusion between the legal order and the state. Indeed, the very competence of the State to contract depends on an enabling norm established by the legal order, which therefore does not necessarily depend on the State itself, so that good faith is not necessarily at stake. Indeed, it is possible for a state official to be unaware of, in good faith, the limitation of his or her ability to bind the state due to, for example, constitutional or statutory restrictions.

This exclusion from the Rome I Regulation continues in the field of international jurisdiction[41] without the provisions in question having identical objectives: it is quite possible to consider that an issue is excluded from the Rome I Regulation without falling within the scope of Article 24(2) of the Brussels I a Regulation. This is why the question of the capacity to contract of legal persons should not necessarily be dealt with outside contractual litigation. The Court of Justice had the opportunity to state this in a *BVG* judgment of 12 May 2011.[42] In this decision, a German public entity considered that the conclusion of the financial contract at issue exceeded its capacity to contract, a matter which should be subject to the exclusive jurisdiction of the courts of its registered office. However, the Court of Justice, following the English courts,[43] held that the provision of the Brussels Ia Regulation on exclusive jurisdiction in corporate matters was not applicable, because:

> 'In a dispute of a contractual nature, questions relating to the contract's validity, interpretation or enforceability are at the heart of the dispute and form its subject-matter. Any question concerning the validity of the decision to conclude the contract, taken previously by the organs of one of the companies party to it, must be considered ancillary. While it may form part of the analysis required to be carried out in that regard, it nevertheless does not constitute the sole, or even the principal, subject of the analysis.'[44]

This is an orthodox interpretation of the function of the exclusive jurisdiction recognised in the courts of the registered office.[45] Above all, the judgment thus reasoned puts an end to what could be described as 'ultra vires torpedo', a litigation strategy aimed at destabilising the jurisdiction clause by invoking its lack of capacity.

827. Section conclusion. French law makes sensible use of the incapacity regimes it enacts, on the one hand, by limiting them to those who need them and, on the other hand, by still allowing financial contracts to be concluded when they allow a risk to be covered. The criterion used to govern incapacity is, however, difficult to implement. This regime of incapacity to conclude certain financial contracts is part of the incapacity to exercise one's rights and should be subject to personal law, whether for natural persons or legal persons. The regime adopted by French law, which is liberal in inspiration, is also explained by the existence of marketing rules to which financial contracts are subject.

---

41 Art. 24(2) of the Brussels Ia Regulation.

42 Case C-144/10, *BVG v. JP Morgan Chase*, ECLI:EU:C:2011:300.

43 On the decisions of which J. Braithwaite, *The Financial Courts: Adjudicating Disputes in Derivatives Markets*, *op. cit.*, pp. 294–298.

44 Case C-144/10, *BVG v. JP Morgan Chase*, ECLI:EU:C:2011:300, para. 38.

45 On which see *supra*, para. 90.

SECTION 2. MARKETING

828. The main objective of the regulation of the marketing of financial contracts in France, as in the case of securities, but in a different way, is the protection of residents.[46] This regulation stems from three types of rules, whose international scope of application is not homogeneous, but which have in common that some of them fall outside the domain of the law of the contract and therefore apply regardless of the law designated by the Rome I Regulation. The first type of rule is the monopoly on investment services. Indeed, these rules reserve the conclusion of such contracts on a regular basis to European investment firms only,[47] considering that the conclusion of a financial contract would necessarily be part of the provision of an investment service.[48] These investment firms are subject to pre-contractual obligations to provide information, advice and warnings in their dealings with their clients as part of their professional obligations, and this is one of the conditions of their authorisation. These rules of conduct have already been studied. It will be recalled here that, within the Union, their submission to local law now depends on the provision of investment services under the freedom to provide services or on the existence of a branch within the client's country and, secondly, that their violation is likely to give rise to civil liability on the part of the firm.[49]

The second type of rules consists of regulating the activity of canvassing in relation to financial services: firstly, by reserving the possibility of canvassing to certain authorised persons, secondly, by imposing a set of rules of conduct on them and, thirdly, by simply prohibiting canvassing for certain products. These rules are not specific to financial contracts or even to financial instruments. Moreover, they have the particularity of being of national origin.[50] Based on

---

46 The protection appears all the more important as the acquisition of financial securities by residents only allows them to lose the amount committed, whereas the conclusion of financial contracts is likely to result in much greater losses than the initial deposit deposited for the hedgeing. Such a difference makes the conclusion of financial contracts dangerous.

47 Art. L. 531-10 of the Monetary and Financial Code. The provision of an investment service without authorisation is punishable under criminal law, see *supra*, para. 455. On the monopoly of investment firms in the conclusion of financial contracts, see A. Caillemer du Ferrage and A. Duhamel, 'Monopole des prestataires d'investissement en matière de conclusion de contrats financiers'. *op. cit.*, A. Gaudemet, *Les dérivés*, *op. cit.*, nos. 450 et seq, P. Pailler, *Le contrat financier, un instrument financier à terme*, *op. cit.*, nos. 101 et seq, R. Dambre, *Les contrats financiers sur actions*, *op. cit.*, nos. 126 et seq.

48 See *supra*, para. 805.

49 See *supra*, paras. 138 et seq.

50 Canvassing is excluded from the scope of MiFID regulation, see Recital 38 of the MiFID Directive taken up by Recital 101 of the MiFID 2 Directive. The regulation is therefore the result of Law no. 2003-706 of 1 August 2003, known as the Financial Security Act, see Arts. 341-1 et seq. of the Monetary and Financial Code. However, the influence of Directive 2002-65 of 23 September 2002 on the distance marketing of consumer financial services should be noted here. Indeed, the regulation of canvassing stems from Law no. 2003-706 of 1 August 2003, known as the Financial Security Act, which partially transposes

both the act and the activity of direct marketing, these rules have an original scope of application, which is also independent of the law of the contract, and which would benefit from being applied under the professional obligations of direct marketers (§ 1).

A third type of rules, applicable only to financial contracts concluded at a distance with a consumer, establishes a special regime for financial contracts concluded with the consumer, which is fully within the domain of the *lex contractus*[51] (§ 2).

§ 1. BANKING AND FINANCIAL CANVASSING

829. Scope of application of direct marketing of banking and financial services. The regulation on direct marketing of banking and financial services is based on the act of direct marketing of banking and financial services. This is defined as 'any unsolicited contact, by whatever means, with a natural person or a specific legal entity, with a view to obtaining an agreement' relating to a set of transactions listed in Article L. 341-1 of the Monetary and Financial Code. The latter includes the conclusion of investment services.[52] However, the material scope of application of canvassing is limited in certain cases, particularly when certain recipients are involved, such as qualified investors listed in Article L. 411-2 of the Monetary and Financial Code.[53] In contrast to this limitation on canvassing, Article L. 341-10(1°) of the Monetary and Financial Code excludes the possibility of canvassing in order to provide certain products, in particular 'products for which the maximum risk is not known at the time of subscription or for which the risk of loss is greater than the amount of the initial contribution'.[54] Some financial contracts may fall into this category. For this reason, the same article provides an exception for 'products which form part of a normal hedging transaction, provided that such products are offered exclusively to legal persons'.[55]

The persons authorised to carry out canvassing are strictly defined by Article L. 341-3 of the Monetary and Financial Code[56] and are subject

this directive. However, the regulation has undergone some specific modifications, see E. Jouffin, 'Démarchage et vente à distance de produits et services financiers: principes généraux', *D.*, 2006, 1534.

51 Art. L. 121-20-8 of the Monetary and Financial Code.

52 See spec. Art. L. 341-1(3°) of the Monetary and Financial Code.

53 Art. L. 341-2(1°) of the Monetary and Financial Code.

54 The foreignness of the instrument can also be a cause of exclusion, see 'Financial instrument' in H. Synvet and A. Tenenbaum, *Répertoire de droit international*, *op. cit.*, no. 149.

55 This includes the possibility of entering into certain financial contracts only in the context of a hedging operation.

56 Art. L. 341-3 of the Monetary and Financial Code.

to rules of good conduct.[57] All persons authorised to canvass have the particularity of being able to carry out their activity only after having obtained an administrative authorisation, most often a licence. Consequently, sanctions relating to banking and financial canvassing can be administered by the competent national authorities: the Autorité de contrôle prudentiel et de résolution for credit institutions, and insurance companies and the Autorité des marchés financiers for investment firms.[58]

830. The international application of the rules on direct marketing of banking and financial services. Firstly, it will be shown that the rules on banking and financial canvassing unquestionably apply to persons canvassing persons residing in France, and are often provided with effective protection independent of the law applicable to the financial contract[59] (I). Secondly, it will be shown that the French regulation of banking and financial canvassing, whose primary function is to protect French residents, is likely to be able to protect foreign residents in a subsidiary way when the latter are solicited by French canvassers, and that such a solution is likely to reinforce the international harmony of solutions (II).

I. Canvassing of French Residents by Persons Established Abroad

The issue under consideration here is the application of the rules on canvassing to a foreign company that solicits a French resident to propose the conclusion of transactions covered by the French concept of banking and financial canvassing. French law does indeed allow certain foreign persons to canvass French residents, but in such cases it provides for the application of rules of conduct to them (A), failure to comply with which, on the one hand, allows the person canvassed to incur civil liability on the part of the canvasser (B) and, on the other, leads to the application of administrative and criminal penalties on the part of the canvasser (C).

A. Determining who is Entitled to Canvass

Since the rules on direct marketing are intended to protect French residents, they certainly apply regardless of the establishment of the person making the request. This means that the list of persons authorised to canvass established

[57] Arts. L. 341-11 et seq. of the Monetary and Financial Code. In the event of a mandate, these rules are also binding on the persons mandated. Indeed, authorised persons may mandate persons to make enquiries on their behalf, see Art. L. 341-4 of the Monetary and Financial Code.

[58] Art. L. 341-17 of the Monetary and Financial Code.

[59] These rules, which are aimed at the protection of residents, could therefore be integrated into a unilateral conflict rule outlined in relation to the protection of residents and triggered by the criterion of solicitation, see *supra*, para. 282.

by Article L. 341-3 of the Monetary and Financial Code is internationally applicable. However, this provision states that 'equivalent institutions and companies authorised in another EU Member State and authorised to operate on French territory' may conduct direct marketing. This inclusion makes it necessary to specify who are the persons authorised to canvass, as well as the regime attached to them.

831. Delimitation of authorised persons. With regard to the foreign persons entitled to canvass, three observations must be made here. Firstly, the spatial scope of authorised persons clearly excludes, on the one hand, persons from third countries and, on the other, persons from the European Economic Area. The latter are therefore not eligible for authorisation to market under French law.[60] Secondly, the equivalence of establishments and firms authorised in another Member State does not pose a problem. Indeed, this equivalence should be determined by reference to the authorisation harmonised by the European regulation.[61] However, equivalent foreign institutions are subject to the same restrictions as French institutions and may not market to French residents for transactions that are not covered by their authorisation.[62]

832. Regime for authorised persons. The regime applicable to authorised foreign persons is, however, that derived from French law. The rules of conduct applicable to canvassing are independent of those relating to the provision of an investment service and, since their primary function is the protection of residents, they are applicable to the canvassing of French residents. This point is reinforced by the independence of the conditions for authorising investment firms and those for authorising direct marketers, and by the existence of separate conduct of business rules with their own sanction regime.

---

60 See already in this sense, 'Instruments financiers' in H. Synvet and A. Tenenbaum, *Répertoire de droit international*, *op. cit.*

61 On which see *supra*, para. 120.

62 See *supra*, para. 130. This equivalence should, however, be limited to institutions that have obtained an authorisation allowing the freedom to provide services, i.e. those with a legal personality. This means that a branch of a third country established in another Member State cannot be considered as equivalent to an institution under Art. L. 341-3 of the Monetary and Financial Code. The notion of authorisation to operate on French territory may, at first glance, appear to be a mysterious additional condition. In reality, it refers to the need for investment firms established and authorised in another Member State to be notified by their head office authority to the French authority, i.e. the Autorité des marchés financiers, of their desire to provide investment services or to carry on business on French territory, as well as the programme of operations they intend to carry on in France, see Art. 34(2) and (3) of MiFID 2, transposed in Arts. L. 532-18 et seq. and R. 532-17 et seq. of the Monetary and Financial Code. On this issue, see *supra*, para. 131. For credit institutions, see Art. L. 511-22 of the Monetary and Financial Code.

B. The Civil Consequences of the Violation of the Rules

As regards the civil consequences of the violation of the rules on canvassing, two aspects have to be considered: the civil liability of canvassers and the nullity of the acts concluded as a result of the canvassing.

833. The tort liability of canvassers. The civil liability of canvassers may be engaged[63] by the persons canvassed.[64] In particular, there are two elements that may give rise to liability on the part of the direct canvasser: the violation of legal rules of good conduct to which he is subject and the unlawful nature of the canvassing. These two transgressions constitute a fault, causing damage to the person canvassed, thereby enabling the latter to incur civil liability. In order to determine the nature of the liability, it will be necessary to follow the methodology indicated by the case law of the Court of Justice according to which it must be determined whether the obligation breached is imposed independently of the conclusion of the contract.[65] As professional rules, the rules of good conduct of Articles L. 341-11 et seq. of the Monetary and Financial Code for direct marketers are obligations applicable by virtue of the status of direct marketers, independently of the conclusion of any contract, in the manner of the rules of good conduct of investment firms.[66]

This classification as a tort or delict nevertheless makes it necessary to determine whether certain rules of conduct, in particular those which constitute pre-contractual information obligations,[67] do not constitute 'dealings prior to the conclusion of a contract' within the meaning of Article 12 of the Rome II Regulation and as such subject to the law of the contract. It is undeniable that these information obligations concern elements at the heart of the contractual field. However, it seems to us that such an interpretation should be rejected because of the purpose of the rules on canvassing, which is not to establish a special contract law, but to protect residents. However, the contractual characterisation of these provisions would have the consequence that they could be deactivated by subjecting the contract to a foreign law. Under private international law, the violation of these provisions should therefore engage the tort liability of the canvasser,[68] in addition to any administrative liability.

---

63 More specifically, two types of persons may be held liable: on the one hand, the persons who themselves carried out the contentious canvassing activities and, on the other hand, the persons who may have mandated them under Art. L. 341-4 of the Monetary and Financial Code.

64 The possibility of engaging the civil liability of the canvasser explains the latter's obligation to take out insurance, see Art. L. 341-5 and, already in this sense, see 'Démarchage bancaire ou financier' in H. Aubry, *Répertoire de droit des sociétés*, Paris, Dalloz, no. 148.

65 On this case law, see *supra*, para. 397.

66 On which, see *supra*, paras. 137 et seq.

67 For example, those arising from Art. L. 341-12 of the Monetary and Financial Code.

68 Comp. 'Démarchage bancaire ou financier' in H. Aubry, *Répertoire de droit des sociétés,op. cit.*, no. 147.

In the case of canvassing, the damage should be deemed to take place at the domicile of the person canvassed for three reasons. Firstly, the damage is due to the fact that one would not have contracted if the canvassing had taken place in accordance with the rules of good conduct or if it had not taken place because of its unlawful nature. Secondly, the burden of internationality should not fall on the person canvassed but on the canvasser. Finally, it is up to the legal order that has been affected by the damage to ensure reparation; this legal order is here the one whose residents have been unduly solicited.

834. Nullity of contracts. In rulings handed down under the law prior to the Financial Security Act,[69] the case law, approved by academics, was able to declare null and void deeds signed in the context of illegal canvassing, considering that 'agreements concluded following prohibited and criminally sanctioned canvassing are illegal as contrary to public policy'.[70] Professor Aubry now states: "Even if no case law has been found under the Financial Security Act, it can be said with almost certainty that even today a transaction concluded following unlawful canvassing by a bank or financial institution must be cancelled".[71] This nullity would therefore apply on the basis of the unlawfulness of the contract concluded in disregard of the rules on canvassing.[72] By the same token, the author's assertion should probably be restricted to cases where the financial contract is subject to French law.[73] Indeed, the subject matter of the contract, as a condition of substantive validity, is in principle subject to the law of the contract.[74]

Admittedly, the characterisation of this law as a mandatory rule would allow for derogation from the law that may be applicable. However, two reservations should be made. Firstly, the generality of Article 6 of the Civil Code, according

69 Loi no. 2003-706 of 1 August 2003 on financial security, *JORF*, no. 177 of 2 August 2003.

70 Cass., civ. 1re, 20 July 1994, no. 92-12.431, *Bull. civ.*, I, no. 261, *D.*, 1995. 279, obs. F. Magnin; 4 February 1997, no. 94-19.059; 15 May 2001, no. 99-12.498, *Bull. civ.*, I, no. 139, *D.*, 2001; *AJ*, 1879, obs. A. Lienhard.

71 See 'Démarchage bancaire ou financier' in H. Aubry, *Répertoire de droit des sociétés*, *op. cit.*, no. 153. The author cites several converging doctrinal references.

72 The situation here is therefore quite different from the violation of the rules of conduct of investment firms, which rarely results in the nullity of the disputed act, but rather in the liability of the service provider (see *supra*, para. 137), unless the investment firm's behaviour constitutes fraudulent concealment (Cass., com., 15 September 2009, no. 08-14398). It seems to us that this distinction can probably be explained by the applicable rules of conduct: those relating to pre-contractual information obligations or marketing bans make it possible to characterise obstacles to the formation of the contract (whether they affect the integrity of consent or the illegality of the subject matter of the contract), whereas rules of conduct such as the '*best execution* obligation relate to the performance of the contract and therefore only engage the liability of the service provider.

73 Or to a foreign law which the judge would agree to take into consideration in the context of the unlawfulness of the subject matter of the contract.

74 Art. 10 of the Rome I Regulation. See 'Rome I Regulation: Contractual obligations', in S. Francq, *Répertoire de droit international*, *op. cit.*, no. 155. See already under the Rome Convention, see 'Convention de Rome' in P. Lagarde, *Répertoire de droit international*, Paris, Dalloz no. 110.

to which: 'No derogation may be made, by means of special agreements, from laws which concern public policy and morality', is not such as to allow the identification of a mandatory rule within the meaning of private international law. Even if one were to consider that it is a question of safeguarding the country's economy, one would come up against the nature of the sanction, which is of jurisprudential origin: the law does not provide for the specific nullity of contracts concluded as a result of canvassing acts.[75] In order to be effective, it would therefore be necessary to extend the characterisation of a mandatory rule to the case law sanctions that follow from it, making these sanctions even less predictable for the person affected. Secondly, even if a mandatory rule could be identified in order to nullify a contract subject to a foreign law, the consequences of the nullity of this contract would remain subject to the *lex contractus*.[76] These observations lead to the conclusion that the rules on canvassing will have difficulty in obtaining, on the basis of mandatory rules, the nullity of the act;[77] if they do, they will not govern the consequences.

The situation would be different if the law explicitly provided for the nullity of acts concluded in violation of the rules on canvassing. This nullity would then have to be compared with the freedoms of movement and in particular with Article 56 of the TFEU on the freedom to provide services. This provision thus allowed the condemnation of a Croatian law which provided for the nullity of acts concluded with residents by non-authorised credit institutions,[78] including contracts concluded before its entry into force. However, there are several key differences between the two situations. Firstly, in the context of canvassing, it is not necessarily a question of annulling acts because of the absence of the professional status required to conclude them, but because of the violation of the rules of conduct applicable under that status.[79] Secondly, the Croatian law may have aroused particular hostility because of its retroactivity to foreign providers only.[80] Finally, the rules on canvassing do not originate in EU law, but in French law. However, as Mr d'Avout observes in his note to the judgment, it is 'up to the law that has enacted a condition to govern

---

75 With the exception of the specific steps referred to in Art. L. 341-2(7°) of the Monetary and Financial Code. Observing this gap, see 'Démarchage bancaire ou financier' in H. Aubry, *Répertoire de droit des sociétés*, *op. cit.*, no. 153. As to the impact of consumer law, see *infra*, paras. 840 et seq.

76 Art. 12(1)(e) of the Rome I Regulation.

77 Recall the sanctioning of the late stockbrokers' monopoly, *supra*, para. 454.

78 Case C-630-17, *Milivojević*, ECLI:EU:C:2019:123, *JDI*, October 2020, chron. 10, no. 2, obs. L. d'Avout.

79 The rules on canvassing specifically provide for the assimilation of other EU entities to the required status, see *supra* no. 832.

80 *Milivojević* judgment, no. 62.

the consequences of its violation'.[81] French law may have some leeway here, which has become rare in financial law, in order to enact civil sanctions to the administrative law it has instituted.

C. Criminal and Administrative Sanctions

835. French regulations on direct marketing of banking and financial services were designed from an administrative perspective. It is therefore not surprising that the sanctions provided for in Article L. 341-17 of the Monetary and Financial Code are primarily disciplinary in nature. This allows them to be imposed quickly and to have a definite dissuasive effect, since the competent administrative authority can go so far as to withdraw the licence of the offending operator, which amounts to preventing him from carrying on his business. Such a system of sanctions, which is extremely effective in the domestic order, is much less effective when the authority is confronted with foreign entities whose authorisation is granted by another authority.[82] Some of these difficulties have been resolved by prohibiting companies from third countries from canvassing French residents. On the other hand, when the canvassing is carried out by an investment firm authorised in another Member State, sanctioning it is more difficult. However, the Monetary and Financial Code provides that the French regulatory authority – the AMF – has the power to impose administrative sanctions on providers from other Member States.[83] Among the sanctions that the authority can administer, two are likely to be easily applicable: the one relating to 'the temporary or permanent prohibition of the exercise of all or part of the services provided' and the one consisting of 'a financial penalty, the amount of which may not exceed 100 million euros'.[84] The Monetary and

---

81 Note cited above under the *Milivojević* judgment. The author then recalls Cass., civ., 6 March 1956, *Moreau*, B. Ancel and Y Lequette, *Les grands arrêts de la jurisprudence française*, *op. cit.*

82 See the observations of Professor Synvet on the difficulty of coordinating an administrative regime designed for domestic law with the international order, see H. Synvet, 'Les conséquences du transfert du siège d'une SE immatriculée en France sur les porteurs d'obligations et de valeurs mobilières donnant accès à son capital', *op. cit.*

83 Art. L. 341-17 refers to Arts. L. 612-39, L. 621-15 and L. 621-17 of the Monetary and Financial Code for the sanctioning of breaches of obligations relating to direct marketing by authorised persons. Art. L. 612-39 relates to sanctions administered by the ACPR (its personal scope of application is determined by reference to Art. L. 612-2 I of the Monetary and Financial Code), while Arts. L. 621-15 and L. 621-17 relate to sanctions imposed by the AMF. With regard to investment service providers, the AMF's jurisdiction is established by a reference in Art. L. 621-15 to Art. L. 621-9(II), which provides for its jurisdiction over 'investment service providers [...] authorised or operating freely in France' (Art. L. 621-9(II)(1)), as well as over 'persons authorised to carry out direct marketing as referred to in Articles L. 341-3 and L. 341-4'.

84 Art. L. 621-15(III)(a) of the Monetary and Financial Code. The exercise of the AMF's jurisdiction to ban an authorised firm from another Member State appears to be compatible with the freedoms of movement, and in particular with the freedom to provide services.

Financial Code also provides for criminal sanctions for canvassing offences.[85] In this case, the application of the French criminal law[86] should be triggered by the transgression of the rules on canvassing, and the applicability of the criminal law should be made by reference to the international scope of application of these same rules.[87]

II. Canvassing by French Persons of Foreign Residents

836. The applicability of French law. From the point of view of public international law, the application of the regulation on canvassing to persons established in France but soliciting foreign residents is possible.[88] Nothing prevents the French legislator from extending the protection it wishes to offer to French residents to foreign residents. It is in fact legitimate for the French legislator to be concerned about the behaviour of institutions established on its territory.[89]

837. Compatibility with the freedom to provide services. Within the EU, the Netherlands has extended the prohibition on direct marketing by authorised intermediaries to foreign residents. The compatibility of this provision with the freedoms of movement, and in particular with the freedom to provide services, was the subject of a preliminary question before the Court of Justice in the *Alpine Investments* judgment. At issue was the practice of cold calling, a canvassing technique whereby an intermediary contacts a person by telephone in order to sell him a financial futures contract on goods. The intermediary argued that: 'the prohibition of cold calling by the Netherlands Government is unnecessary

Indeed, the Court of Justice has had the opportunity to state that the freedom to provide services 'does not preclude national legislation which, in order to protect investors' confidence in national financial markets, prohibits the practice of making unsolicited telephone calls to potential customers residing in other Member States with a view to offering them services relating to investment in commodity futures contracts', Case C-384/93, *Alpine Investment*, ECLI:EU:C:1995:126, para. 56. For an illustration of a sanction prohibiting an investment firm authorised abroad from operating in France, see Comm. sanct. AMF, 29 July 2016, reported by A. Tenenbaum, 'Les autres sources du droit européen des contrats: incidence du droit matériel européen des sociétés et des marchés financier', *Revue des contrats*, March 2017, no. 3, p. 149.

85 Art. L. 353-1 of the Monetary and Financial Code.

86 Determined by Art. L. 113-2 of the Criminal Code, on which see *supra*, para. 527.

87 On the application of criminal law in situations with a foreign element, see *supra*, paras. 526 et seq.

88 On the other hand, it would be contrary to international law to apply French law to foreign persons soliciting foreign residents, as such a situation has no connection with France.

89 This concern is shared by many countries. For example, the United States regularly hesitates to apply its own legislation on canvassing to operators who, from US territory, solicit foreign residents, in particular for fear that their country might become *a coast for barbary.* For such hesitation, see *SEC v. Kasser*, 548 F.2d 109, 116, *cert. Denied*, 431 U.S. 938 (1977). This argument is often contrasted with the need not to expend the resources of the United States see *supra*, para. 538 and note.

because the Member State of the provider should rely on the control carried out by the Member State of the recipient'.[90] The Court of Justice replied:

> 'This argument must be rejected. Indeed, the Member State from which the telephone call is made is best placed to regulate cold calling. Even if the host State wishes to prohibit cold calling or make it subject to certain conditions, it is not in a position to prevent or control telephone calls from another Member State without the cooperation of the competent authorities of that State.'[91]

838. The application of French law to persons canvassing foreign residents. There is no explicit legislative criterion relating to the international application of the regulation of French persons soliciting foreign residents. Under the legislation prior to the Financial Security Act, the Cour de cassation was able to approve a court of appeal in convicting a German company offering French clients transactions on the US markets.[92] The criterion suggested by this case law is that of residence,[93] which would make French regulation of canvassing inapplicable to French persons canvassing foreign residents. While this old solution is not inconsistent,[94] the connection of the regulation could be shifted from the residence of the persons solicited to the persons at the origin of the solicitation. Three arguments can justify such a change.

The first is the French text itself. Although the law and its explanatory memorandum are silent on the international scope of application that the legislator intended to give it,[95] it is nevertheless possible to deduce this scope from the definition of the act of canvassing that it proposes, as well as

---

90 *Alpine Investment*, para. 47. See in the same sense, H. Muir Watt, 'L'entrave à la prestation transfrontière de services' in *Mélanges Béguin*, Paris, LexisNexis, pp. 545 et seq. On this judgment, see also by the same author *Aspects économiques du droit international privé, op. cit.*

91 *Alpine Investment*, para. 48.

92 Cass. crim., 11 May 2000, no. 99-84.362. On this judgment, see 'Instruments financiers' in H. Synvet and A. Tenenbaum, *Répertoire de droit international, op. cit.*, no. 58.

93 See already in this sense, *ibid.*

94 There are at least three reasons for this long-standing case law. Firstly, it is the responsibility of the State whose residents are sought to protect them. Secondly, the modalities of this protection are better ensured by the State that knows the psychology of its residents. Thirdly, as this protection is likely to mobilise the resources of the public authorities, the use of these resources for the protection of foreign residents is likely to offend the taxpayer and create some confusion about the function of the local authorities.

95 It should nevertheless be noted that the press release of the Council of Ministers of 5 February 2005 stated that: "The objective of this important reform is to consolidate the credibility of the *French* financial markets, to reassure shareholders and investors, to improve the business environment and thus to stimulate the country's growth in an international context marked in recent months by financial scandals.' (Italics added). However, it is not certain that the legislator is referring to canvassing when he speaks of the 'credibility of the French financial markets', but rather to the establishment by this law of the Autorité des marchés financiers, whose mission is more precisely in line with this objective.

from the recipients that it excludes. The act of canvassing is defined as 'any unsolicited contact [...] with a natural or legal person'.[96] As this definition does not indicate any spatial limitation relating to residence, limiting it to French residents only would be tantamount to adding a condition which the law does not provide for.[97]

The second argument relates to the location of the solicitation. As the Court of Justice pointed out in the above-mentioned passage of the *Alpine Investment* judgment, the State of the establishment from which the solicitation originates constitutes the legal centre of gravity of the canvass, for at least two reasons. Firstly, it is the State of the authorised person from which the act of soliciting originates, and it is from that person that the solicitation originates. Secondly, from the French point of view, French regulation is entirely centred on the person authorised to canvass, who is closely defined, subject to a specific regime, and is the subject of administrative sanctions in the event of a breach of his canvassing obligations.[98] Just as the conduct of business rules for investment firms are applicable regardless of the client's domicile in the EU, the rules on canvassing should apply, as professional rules, regardless of the domicile of the person canvassed.[99]

The third argument lies in the effectiveness of the regulations on canvassing. Indeed, in this area, sanctions are best administered by the State of origin

96 Art. L. 341-1 of the Monetary and Financial Code.

97 This is all the more true since the criterion for limiting the application of the rules on canvassing adopted by Art. L. 341-2 of the Monetary and Financial Code, when certain addressees are involved, does not concern the residence of the addressees, but their character as qualified investors, regardless of their residence. This is a recognition of the criterion relating to the person's knowledge of the risk taken, which already guides the international applicability of European financial law (see *supra*, para. 810), and which should be retained.

98 This is why it is necessary to qualify the assertion of certain authors who believe that it is the 'determination of the addressees of the contact that is at the heart of the act of canvassing', see 'Instruments financiers' in H. Synvet and A. Tenenbaum, *Répertoire de droit international,op. cit.*, no. 147.

99 It may be objected that such a location ignores the idea that the State of residence of individuals is the best judge of the psychology of its residents, and therefore the best able to defeat the techniques by which they may be solicited. However, this argument needs to be qualified. Indeed, the techniques of solicitation are increasingly standardised, so that the methods for their substantial regulation are converging. Moreover, it is possible for the State of residence to institute its own protection regime which would apply cumulatively, except in cases where the protection provided by the country of solicitation appears sufficient. Far from being a textbook case, this measured position, based on a self-limitation of the rules, was adopted by the American courts in a case where the law applicable to the contract was deemed to contain sufficient protection measures deemed equivalent, see Bonny v The Society of Lloyd's, 3 F 3d 156 [7th Cir. 1993], cert. denied, 114 S. Ct. 1057 [1994], quoted by H. Synvet and A. Tenenbaum, 'Financial instrument' in *Répertoire de droit international, op. cit.*, no. 147.

of the canvassing.[100] This is why it can be considered that the international effectiveness of solutions would be better ensured by the application of French law to canvassing carried out from France.[101] These observations on the international applicability of the status of canvassers are similar to those on the professional rules applicable to investment firms.[102] These arguments are partly transposable to the rules of conduct of other regulated professionals. The latter most often benefit from being applicable, regardless of the law applicable to the act in question, or the location of their clients.

§ 2. FINANCIAL CONTRACTS CONCLUDED AT A DISTANCE WITH CONSUMERS

839. The special regime for financial contracts concluded at a distance with consumers. The transposition of Directive 2002-65 of 23 September 2002 concerning the distance marketing of consumer financial services has made it possible to establish a special regime for financial contracts concluded at a distance with consumers.[103] This regime is applicable when French law is designated by the financial contract, or when the conditions of Article 6 of the Rome I Regulation are met. However, one may wonder whether these rules, at least in part, would not be applicable as a matter of mandatory rule or as a matter of tort. The answer to both questions is no.

840. Mandatory Rules and the special contractual regime for financial contracts. Firstly, the question arises whether, even if the financial contract is subject to a foreign law, certain provisions of consumer law could not be applied under overriding mandatory rules (*lois de police*), such as the central provision of the special regime allowing the consumer to avail himself of a 'period of fourteen completed calendar days in which to exercise his right of withdrawal, without

[100] This is echoed from the French perspective by the Autorité des marchés financiers, see in this sense 'Financial instrument' in H. Synvet and A. Tenenbaum, *Répertoire de droit international*, *op. cit.*, no. 150. This second argument can undoubtedly be qualified in that it would be possible to create a favourable regime for the reception of foreign administrative convictions made on the basis of equivalent regulations. The same authors temper the appropriateness of applying French legislation to foreign residents because this could be to the detriment of French institutions (*ibid.*, no. 146).

[101] The argument relating to the resources and function of the local authority may then be raised. However, it should be noted, on the one hand, that the global allocation of state resources is better used by the application of local regulations and, on the other hand, that disciplinary sanctions cost the local authority little and are likely to be profitable. As regards the function of the authority, it should be noted that it is no longer only to prosecute French breaches, see Art. L. 621-1 of the Monetary and Financial Code.

[102] See *supra*, paras. 137 et seq.

[103] Art. L. 121-20-8 of the Monetary and Financial Code.

having to give any reason or incur any penalty'.[104] Such an application of consumer law under mandatory rules must be rejected for at least three reasons. The first reason is an express derogatory provision in the Rome I Regulation for consumer contracts. The non-application of this provision should therefore lead to respecting the choice of law made by the parties.[105] In addition, in order to fall outside the conditions of Article 6, the consumer must himself have requested the professional to make the contract subject to the foreign law. To describe the provisions of the Consumer Code as overriding mandatory rules would therefore mean applying them to situations where it would be the consumer who would have to bear the burden of internationality, because of the request he made.

The second reason for rejecting their application as overriding legislation is simply that it is not clear that the consumer provisions, which constitute a special contractual regime, constitute overriding legislation. Indeed, consumer protection is already ensured by several sets of legislation, the one relating to the status and obligations of investment firms, and the one relating to canvassing.[106] Under these conditions, it seems excessive to consider that these provisions are necessary to safeguard the economic organisation of the country.

The third reason lies in the harmful consequences of such a characterisation, which is indifferent to the law designated by the conflict rule. However, it is quite possible that the law designated by the conflict rule provides for an equivalent provision, *a fortiori* if it designates the law of another Member State: these rules are in fact derived from a European directive. It is undoubtedly possible that the divergent transposition of the directive will lead to the application of the foreign law being set aside in favour of the law of the forum;[107] however, the effect of the directives is precisely to harmonise the laws, making such cases residual.

841. Law applicable to pre-contractual obligations. The Distance Marketing of Consumer Financial Contracts Directive provides for a set of pre-contractual information obligations on the person providing the service. Such obligations can be qualified as tortious obligations on the basis of Article 12 of the Rome II Regulation. However, this provision applies the law of the contract to these obligations, whether or not the contract was ultimately concluded, insofar as these obligations arise 'out of dealings prior to the conclusion of a contract'. These obligations relate precisely to such dealings since they require the supplier to communicate, in certain forms,[108] a set of information relating to the supplier,

---

104 Art. L. 121-20-12 of the Monetary and Financial Code.

105 See already in this sense the reflections of H. Synvet and A. Tenenbaum, 'Financial instrument' in *Répertoire de droit international*, *op. cit.*, no. 140; Y. Loussouarn, P. Bourel and P. de Vareilles-Sommières, *Droit international privé*, 10th ed., Paris, Dalloz, 2013, no. 584; B. Audit and L. d'Avout, *Droit international privé*, *op. cit.*, no. 1044.

106 See respectively *supra*, paras. 137 et seq.; 830 et seq.

107 Case C-184/12, *Unamar*, ECLI:EU:C:2013:663, *Europe*, 2013.

108 Art. 4 of the Distance Marketing Directive.

the financial service, the distance contract, and the possible remedies,[109] and will therefore be subject to the *lex contractus*.[110]

842. Conclusion of the section. This section has shown that the violation of French regulations on canvassing of banking and financial services will make it possible to engage the civil liability of the canvasser according to the canons of French law; the consequences for the acts concluded will depend on the competent judge and his or her desire to take into consideration the unlawfulness of the subject matter of the contract under French law. Moreover, the administrative and criminal sanctions that this legislation provides for are likely to dissuade operators from proposing the conclusion of financial contracts without being subject to it. These developments have also shown that the connecting factor for the rules on banking and financial canvassing (distinct from the professional obligations arising from the provision of an investment service, but also applicable to financial contracts) is the residence of the persons canvassed. Nevertheless, it should not be inferred, *a contrario*, that they do not apply to French persons canvassing residents abroad, on the one hand, because positive law supports such an interpretation and, on the other hand, because such an application contributes to the international harmony of solutions.

SECTION 3. THE UNDERLYING

843. The formation of a financial contract may be hindered by the application of the law of the underlying, not so much for the protection of the parties as for the underlying itself. It is common to classify financial contracts according to their underlying, and to distinguish between them according to their appropriability. In the case of shares and securities admitted to trading, the interference of the law of the underlying is independent of its appropriability. In the case of shares, its application is most often the result of the unlawful hedging of the risk inherent in the social hazard.[111] In the case of admission to trading, the application of the law of the underlying is linked to the influence that the financial contract is likely to have on the underlying, and in particular on its price.[112] In relation

109 Art. 3 of the Distance Marketing Directive.

110 For a critical analysis of the solution provided by Art. 12 of the Rome II Regulation, see A. Gridel, 'A case for a restrictive conception of contractual characterisation', *op. cit.*

111 See already A. Gaudemet, *Les dérivés*, *op. cit.*, C. Coupet, *L'attribution du droit de vote dans les sociétés*, *op. cit.*, nos. 208 et seq.; R. Dambre, *Les contrats financiers sur actions*, *op. cit.*, nos. 244 et seq.

112 As Professor Pailler writes about financial contracts on commodities: 'Financial contracts also fulfil a function of revealing the price, the extent of which is not known exactly on the physical market. Hence the following question: if the underlying and the term unquestionably play a role in the formation of the price of the financial contract, do not financial contracts also play a role in the formation of the price of the underlying?' P. Pailler, 'Le rôle du terme

to the field studied here, some authors have deduced that the financial contract is influenced by the law of listed companies on financial contracts.[113] It will be attempted to show that, on the contrary, company law, when it wishes to prohibit the conclusion of financial contracts interfering with the internal functioning of companies, does so independently of the admission to trading of the company's shares (I). On the other hand, when financial market law prohibits the conclusion of certain financial contracts on securities admitted to trading, it is not in order to correct a disturbance that the admission to trading causes in the company's operation, but in order to guarantee the proper functioning and stability of the financial market (II).

§ 1. THE INFLUENCE OF THE *LEX SOCIETATIS*

844. As the risk of partnership is consubstantial with the qualification of partner, the financial contract, by allowing the partner to cover the risk of partnership that he is supposed to bear, blurs the boundaries and may be opposed, it seems, to the mandatory rules of the partnership.[114] The latter is likely to allow the contract to be annulled, and to engage the liability of those who have recourse to it. This is because, in certain cases, the share-based financial contract leaves the domain of the law of contract to interfere with a problem traditionally subject to the *lex societatis*: the internal functioning of the company. Two examples from French law will be given: the first, from common company law, is the prohibition of leonine clauses; the second, from special company law, is the remuneration of directors.

845. Leonine clauses. Article 1844-1 paragraph 3 of the Civil Code provides that:

> 'A stipulation attributing to a partner all the profits made by the company or exempting him from all the losses, or excluding a partner entirely from the profits or charging him with all the losses, shall be deemed unwritten.'

However, such unfair terms may be stipulated in a contract subject to foreign law, which will often be the case if they are crowded out in a financial contract.

et du sous-jacent dans la formation du prix', *op. cit.* In the case of commodities, which is beyond the scope of this study, it should simply be noted that the law of the underlying is then the law of the situation that is likely to intervene, either by prohibiting the conclusion of financial contracts on the underlyings, or by making it conditional (see in particular on this question, A. Gaudemet, 'Les limites de position sur les marchés dérivés de matières premières agricoles en quête de légitimité', *RDBF*, May 2013, comm. 109).

113 R. Dambre, *Les contrats financiers sur actions*, *op. cit.*, nos. 325 et seq.

114 *Ibid.*, nos. 180 et seq. and C. Coupet, *L'attribution du droit de vote dans les sociétés*, *op. cit.*, nos. 127 et seq. On the difficulties of this dissociation, see also K. Vanneste, 'Decoupling economic rights from voting rights: a threat to the traditional corporate governance paradigm' (2014) 15 *European Business Organization Review*, pp. 59 et seq.

However, it is not certain that such clauses fall within the scope of the law of the contract. Indeed, the prohibition of ineffective clauses relates both to the relationship between the partner and the company and to the status of the shareholder; both relate to the internal organisation of the company and as such fall within the exclusive domain of the *lex societatis*.[115] The question is therefore that of the material criteria that French company law imposes in relation to the prohibition it provides for, and these are currently very limited, making any attempts to apply the *lex societatis*[116] residual.

846. Remuneration of corporate directors. The remuneration of company directors is nowadays increasingly carried out, at least in part, through the allocation of shares.[117] Such a mechanism allows the convergence of the interests of directors with those of shareholders. Although there is no general

---

115 See our comments on shareholders' agreements *supra*, para. 503.
In this sense, it is of little importance that the sanction for unfair terms results from the fact that they are deemed unwritten, which is undoubtedly better able to surgically paralyse the aspect of the contract that runs counter to corporate public policy: in this case, the main norm whose violation is alleged is of a corporate nature, and is part of the common law of corporate public policy. In the same way, the evolution of case law validating what are similar to leonine clauses when the contract is concluded by a financial backer providing a financial service or a simple co-contracting partner is not such as to call into question this qualification. On this case law, see C. Coupet, *L'attribution du droit de vote dans les sociétés*, *op. cit.*

116 These criteria are now restricted by three aspects. Firstly, only clauses which have the effect of completely exonerating the partner from losses are likely to be qualified as leonine, so that the existence of a slight hazard in the contract is such as to make it escape the sanction (see R. Dambre, *Les contrats financiers sur actions*, *op. cit.*, no. 199). Secondly, the prohibition does not apply if the disputed clause is part of a broader economic transaction aimed at transferring the shares; if the contract provides for the possibility of delivery of the underlying, it will not be subject to the prohibition (*ibid.*). Finally, as Mr Dambre observed, the evolution of the case law on carry agreements, which deactivates the prohibition depending on whether the contracting party is a financial backer or a mere partner, is likely to be transposed to the parties to a financial contract, in particular to the financial institution acquiring shares for the purpose of hedging its position under the financial contract (*ibid.*). This last aspect, which emphasises the quality of the contracting party, should not lead to the qualification of the rule on ineffective clauses as contractual. It simply constitutes a self-limitation of the applicable law by taking into account, at the substantive level, the configuration of the legal relationship. Mr Dambre wishes to extend this limitation of the law on unfair terms to all financial contracts, including those which do not provide for the delivery of shares (in the manner of *total return equity swap* contracts), on the basis of the idea that: 'The parties to the contract do not envisage the substitution of one for the other in the company contract by a transfer of company rights, but essentially organise an exchange of economic flow.' (*ibid.*, no. 200) It seems to us that the argument is unconvincing, precisely because it is opposed to the *ratio legis* of the prohibition of ineffective clauses, which is to allow the partnership to function by ensuring that its partners always have a common interest: that of possibly contributing to losses. It is precisely for the same reason that the author admits the application of company law in order to paralyse a financial contract which frees the shareholder-manager from the possibility of incurring losses, see *ibid.*, no. 209.

117 For the theoretical foundations of economic risk alignment, see *ibid.*

prohibition on financial contracts that prohibits directors/partners from entering into such contracts, the special company law applicable to credit institutions, transposed from the CRD IV Directive, has regulated the terms and conditions of remuneration, not only of directors, but of a group of persons involved in the management of the company.[118] In particular, they are prohibited from "using individual hedging or insurance strategies in relation to remuneration or liability in order to limit the application of the provisions of this sub-section",[119] the provision being therefore a matter of public policy.[120] This rule makes it possible to hold the director liable for misconduct if he enters into a financial contract which limits his losses as a shareholder. From the point of view of French contract law, this provision also makes it possible to characterise the unlawfulness of the content of the financial contract thus entered into and therefore allows its cancellation.

847. The difficulty is, however, to preserve this possibility of annulment when the financial contract is subject to a foreign law. It is true that the foreign law is likely to have an identical prohibition, and this will be the case in particular if it is the law of another Member State. However, as this provision is of a corporate nature, it will not fall within the scope of the foreign law of the contract; at the same time, the French provision will struggle to apply under company law precisely because it relates to the content of the contract, which is governed by the foreign *lex contractus*. In order to resolve this conflict of laws, two solutions are possible.[121]

Firstly, the provision may be qualified as an overriding mandatory rule (*lois de police*). The French court will then impose its application. If the court of another Member State is petitioned, it may take the rule into consideration under the *Nikiforidis* case law,[122] which will lead it to declare the content of the contract unlawful under the foreign *lex contractus*.[123] Finally, the court of a third country is likely to have an identical mechanism for taking into account or applying foreign mandatory rules, especially when the link with the dispute is so strong. However, this solution comes up against the characterisation of overriding mandatory rules: this provision, although it is part of the internal

118 See the list provided by Art. L. 511-71 of the Monetary and Financial Code.

119 Art. L. 511-85 of the Monetary and Financial Code, transposing Art. 94(1)(p) of the CRD IV.

120 This clarification comes from the French transposition, as the directive only provides for a commitment on the part of directors.

121 A third solution, consisting in retaining the incapacity of the director to conclude such contracts, is rejected from the outset: on the one hand, it could not apply to foreign directors of French companies and, on the other hand, the provision clearly does not apply to capacity, the purpose of which is very different, see *supra*, para. 820.

122 Case C-135/15, *Nikiforidis*, ECLI:EU:C:2016:774.

123 S. Bollée, 'La prise en considération des lois de polices étrangères dans le Règlement Rome I', *op. cit.*

public policy of company law, is not necessarily such as to characterise a genuine overriding mandatory rule. It is not the safeguarding of the economic organisation of the country that is targeted, but the internal functioning of French credit institutions.[124]

Secondly, it is possible to consider that since the financial contract has the effect of exonerating the shareholder-manager from his losses, it relates to the internal functioning of the company and is therefore excluded from the scope of the Rome I Regulation. This rule, which is part of a section of the Monetary and Financial Code relating to the governance of credit institutions and finance companies, is part of a body of legislation explicitly aimed at preventing conflicts of interest within the companies in question.[125] This second reasoning, based on the international characterisation of the provision, seems preferable. It leads to more certain solutions and is based on a better analysis of the legal relationship envisaged, reflecting its true centre of gravity, which is company law and not contract law. Moreover, this reasoning can be extended to all cases where company law prescribes identical rules, either because of the activity carried out or because of the admission to trading of the securities.

848. The two examples reported therefore only paralyse share-based financial contracts concluded by a shareholder in specific cases. It is regrettable that these rules are so fragmented, whereas company law is capable of adapting contracts that are likely to thwart the objective it promotes: the functioning of the companies subject to it. This is all the more true in companies whose securities are admitted to trading, where the existence of a market price is likely to facilitate the drawing up of the financial contract. De *lege ferenda*, as proposed by Mr Dambre, a mandatory reporting regime for loss-limiting financial contracts could be introduced.[126] This would apply to the status of partner in the company and would be sanctioned by the suspension of voting rights whenever, at the end of the financial contract, the partner would profit in the event of a decrease in the value of the shares. Such a regime would effectively correct the consequences of the conclusion of financial contracts on the organisation of the company.

§ 2. THE INFLUENCE OF THE *LEX MERCATUS*

849. The influence of the *lex mercatus* on the financial contract is exercised in two ways: either because the underlying is a financial instrument admitted

124 It may be considered that, given the importance of these establishments for the country, their operation is of particular significance, but it is doubtful whether this is sufficient to characterise a mandatory rule.

125 Art. L. 511-71 para. 2 of the Monetary and Financial Code.

126 R. Dambre, *Les contrats financiers sur actions*, *op. cit.*, nos. 269 et seq.

to trading, in which case the financial contract will be covered under the regulation of market transactions, or because the financial contract constitutes market abuse. In the latter case, the influence of the underlying asset appears to be quite intuitive because of the criminal nature of market abuse and the very broad criteria for the international application of French criminal law.[127] However, the constituent elements of the offence are indifferent, on the one hand, to the submission of the contract to a foreign law and, on the other hand, to the existence or absence of delivery of the underlying. In these circumstances, a financial contract that constitutes insider dealing or market manipulation on a European trading system is subject to French law. While it is possible that the commission of such an offence may invalidate the contract on the basis of the illegality of its content,[128] the application of French law will not automatically invalidate the contract. It is above all through administrative sanctions, and according to a distinct international mode of enforcement, that the *lex mercatus* is applied.[129] The reason for its application is to be found in the effect that the financial contract has on the formation of the price of the underlying admitted to trading.[130] The purpose of the law of the financial market is to prevent the financial contract from being an instrument for circumventing the regulations on thresholds or takeover bids (I) or short sales (II) through the mechanisms for replicating the utilities of the underlying asset that it permits.

I. Threshold Crossing and Takeover Bids

850. Financial contracts and threshold calculation. The material applicability of the law on threshold crossing and takeover bids is conditional on the crossing of a single threshold.[131] The link with financial contracts arises in the calculation of this threshold. Indeed, the threshold is determined by the direct or indirect ownership of shares representing a certain percentage of the voting rights.[132]

---

[127] See *supra*, paras. 526 et seq.

[128] In French law, the fact that the contract contributes to, or even constitutes, an offence will not necessarily lead to its annulment. On this issue, see A. Valoteau, *La théorie des vices du consentement et le droit pénal*, Aix-en-Provence, PUAM, 2006; A. Dadoun, *La nullité du contrat et le droit pénal*, Paris, LGDJ, 2011; E. Raschel, *La pénalisation des atteintes au consentement dans le champ contractuel*, Paris, LGDJ, 2014.

[129] For an illustration where the AMF declared itself competent to deal with a market manipulation caused by a financial contract subject to German law, but whose underlying asset was admitted to trading on a French financial market, see Comm. sanct. AMF, Decision no. 9 of 28 May 2021, *Global Derivatives Trading GmbH*, *Banque et Droit*, July 2021, p. 61, note J. Chacornac.

[130] Professor Antoine Gaudemet already wrote that financial contracts had a '*price discovery* function', A. Gaudemet, *Les dérivés*, *op. cit.*, no. 245; P. Pailler, 'Le rôle du terme et du sous-jacent dans la formation du prix', *op. cit.*, no. 24; see our comments on the obligation to negotiate, *supra*, para. 438.

[131] See *supra*, para. 483.

[132] Art. L. 233-7 of the Commercial Code, on which see *supra*, paras. 472 et seq.

In other words, certain financial contracts, regardless of the law applicable to them, are assimilated to these shares, as they fall within the material scope of the legislation. This is the case, for example, according to Article L. 233-9(4°) of the Commercial Code, for 'shares already issued' that can be 'acquired on one's own initiative, immediately or in the future, under an agreement or a financial instrument mentioned in Article L. 211-1 of the Monetary and Financial Code'.[133] This provision makes it possible to assimilate share options and, more generally, any financial contract that may give rise to a settlement in shares. Such a provision deserves approval in that these contracts directly increase voting power:[134] they already offer, through the exercise of an option, the possibility of being a shareholder.[135]

851. The regulation of threshold crossing, which has been perfected by successive extensions of its material scope,[136] also assimilates shares or voting rights, on the basis of Article L. 233-9(4° *bis*) of the Commercial Code, to shares already issued:

> 'In respect of which any agreement or financial instrument referred to in Article L. 211-1 of the Monetary and Financial Code which has for that person or any of the persons referred to in 1° and 3° an economic effect similar to the possession of those shares, whether that agreement or financial instrument entitles the holder to a physical settlement or to a cash settlement.'

The regulation here covers financial contracts, most often in the form of equity swaps or total return equity swaps,[137] which do not provide for the delivery of shares, but allow for the replication of the share price and the taking of a position with respect to it. Here, the mere reference to an underlying admitted to trading will trigger the applicability of the law of the market, regardless of the law applicable to the contract. Such a scope of application appears excessive in that it shifts the criterion for the application of the regulation from the admission to trading of the underlying to a criterion of the effect on the underlying admitted to trading. Financial contracts on shares undoubtedly have an effect on the share price even if delivery is not foreseen. However, only the effect on voting power, and not on the share price, should be taken

---

133 Art. L. 233-9(I)(4) of the Commercial Code.

134 On this notion, developed by Mr Chacornac, see *supra*, para. 473.

135 F. Barrière, 'Les prises de participation rampante à l'heure des *swap*' in *Mélanges en l'honneur du professeur Philippe Merle*, Paris, Dalloz, 2012, pp. 27 et seq.

136 See the transcript of this improvement, A. Couret, H. Le Nabasque *et al.*, *Droit financier*, *op. cit.*, nos. 1252 et seq.

137 On these contracts, see A. Couret, H. Le Nabasque *et al.*, *Droit financier*, *op. cit.*, nos. 1347 and 1346, and R. Dambre, *Les contrats financiers sur actions*, *op. cit.*, nos. 17 and 84 et seq.

into account.[138] Of course, it is possible for a party to enter into a financial contract that does not provide for delivery, and to draw up an amendment when the term approaches, but it is from the day of insertion of a delivery clause that the contract should be assimilated to shares for the purpose of calculating the threshold. It may be argued that the future purchaser need only insert the amendment at the last moment in order to gain access to the capital surreptitiously. However, such manoeuvres are then likely to fall under the heading of price manipulation, since they have the effect of concealing the purchaser's intention and deceiving the market so that the price of the coveted share does not rise.[139]

852. From the point of view of the financial contract, the application of the law of the market in respect of threshold crossings will have little effect, but a distinction must be made between cases where the threshold crossing does or does not entail the obligation to file a takeover bid. In the first case, where the threshold for a takeover bid has been crossed, the violation of this regulation does not invalidate the contract or paralyse its performance, even where it provides for the delivery of securities. At most, if the financial contract actually results in the delivery of the shares, the *lex societatis* may restrict, for a time, the voting rights of the delivered shares and thus paralyse the effects that the acquirer wished to obtain. On the other hand, from the point of view of the parties to the contract, the law of the market may be much more restrictive, since

[138] Either these financial contracts actually provide for the delivery of the underlying, in which case the assimilation to shares is legitimate because the voting power is affected, or such delivery is not provided for, and as long as it is not provided for, the financial contract cannot be assimilated to shares. These observations are in line with the analyses of domestic law, which advocated a limited extension of the scope of the regulation of threshold crossing to financial contracts offering a potential acquisition of the underlying securities, and not a broad extension to financial contracts providing exclusively for a cash settlement, see A. Couret, H. Le Nabasque *et al.*, *Droit financier*, *op. cit.*, no. 1254.

[139] On this offence see F. Drummond, *Droit financier*, *op. cit.*, p. 522.

the violation of this regulation may engage the administrative[140] and criminal[141] liability of their authors.

853. Financial contract and obligation to file a takeover bid. In the case where the crossing of the threshold entails the obligation to file a takeover bid, again, the regulation has little effect on the financial contract itself. The main effect is on the party crossing the threshold. The latter may be obliged by an administrative injunction from the AMF to file a bid.[142] A certain ambiguity remains in the event that the bidder resists the injunction. In such a case, the AMF chairman may appeal to the court to put an end to the irregularity or remove its effects.[143] However, if the financial contract at issue does not provide for delivery of the underlying shares and is subject to US law by parties based in the United States, it will be difficult for this decision to be enforced without the cooperation of the parties. The AMF could try to obtain the exequatur of the decision in the United States, or even ask the American judge to declare the financial contract unlawful because of its purpose, taking into account French public policy rules. Such a procedure, if possible, remains long and uncertain;[144] its legitimacy is doubtful as long as the intention to acquire is not evaded by the financial contract.

854. This illustration shows how difficult it is for the law of the financial market to apply to private law relationships as long as the use or disturbance of the trading system has not been proven. As soon as the operators wish to acquire the securities, it is possible for the law of the financial market, based on an agreement with the country of the issuer's registered office, to paralyse

---

140 In these cases, information is due to the AMF (Art. L. 233-7 of the Commercial Code and L. 223-14 of the AMF General Regulation), which makes it inevitable that in the event of a breach of this disclosure obligation, the investor will be liable to the authority. However, the administrative liability of an investor who fails to report is not explicitly provided for in the texts. It is, however, part of the AMF's more general jurisdiction over any 'failure to protect investors or to ensure the proper functioning of the market' (Art. L. 621-14(II) of the Monetary and Financial Code, to which Art. L. 621-15(II)(c)(4°) of the same Code). On this broad application of the combination of these two articles, see R. Elineau, 'Fasc. 2131, Franchissement de seuil', *J.-Cl banque-crédit-bourse*, nos. 150–151, and R. Vabres and S. Maouche, 'Fasc. 1511: Autorité des marchés financiers. – Pouvoir de sanction', *J.-Cl banque-crédit-bourse*, no. 4. As Professor Conac writes, 'the absence of a threshold crossing declaration or an inaccurate declaration could be considered as a failure to provide ongoing information if the concealed fact, if made public, would be likely to have a significant impact on the price of the financial instruments concerned', P.-H. Conac, 'Franchissement de seuil' in *Répertoire de droit des sociétés*, Paris, Dalloz, no. 171.

141 Art. L. 247-2(I) of the Commercial Code.

142 On the basis of Art. L. 621-14(II) of the Monetary and Financial Code. For an illustration, see the *Sacyr-Eiffage* case on which see H. Synvet, 'Propos désenchantés sur l'affaire Sacyr-Eiffage', *op. cit.*; T. Bonneau *et al.*, *Droit financier*, *op. cit.*, no. 1166.
Another case recently arose in which the person had attempted to acquire the capital without filing a public offer, see Comm. Sanct. AMF, decision no. 20 of 31 December 2019.

143 Art. L. 621-14(III) of the Monetary and Financial Code.

144 This was the experience of the SEC, which encouraged the authority to develop administrative cooperation (see *supra*, para. 546).

the prerogatives – pecuniary, political – of the security that the persons wished to possess.[145] However, if the parties to the financial contract never wished to acquire securities, the connection with the financial market is virtually non-existent, unless it can be proved that the existence of this contract undermines the integrity of the market, and is therefore likely to constitute market abuse. This last hypothesis clearly shows that the effects test should be reserved for criminal and administrative law.

II. Short Selling

855. Short selling and contract validity. Financial contracts whose underlying assets are admitted to trading may be subject to certain conditions if they fall under the Short Selling Regulation. This regulation aims at the stability of the financial markets and therefore prohibits financial contracts when they move away from their hedging function and become a pure means of speculation.[146] The regulation then provides for administrative sanctions for operators who try to do so. However, it is questionable whether the prohibitions set out in the Short Selling Regulation could characterise the unlawfulness of the purpose of the financial contract under French law. Indeed, this regulation focuses on protecting the very ability of public authorities to avoid the negative spirals that can result from short selling and credit risk swaps.[147] This allows these prohibitions to be enshrined in the domestic public policy.[148] It will be up to each *lex contractus* to determine the civil consequences of the prohibition under the EU Regulation. The question arises, however, whether the prohibition rule can be extended to financial contracts subject to a non-European law. An affirmative answer is possible, but a distinction must be made here according to whether the competent court is established in the Union or outside the Union.

856. In the first case, the competent court is likely to characterise the prohibition of mandatory rules and apply it by virtue of the Rome I Regulation since it constitutes, by the effect of the legislative nature of the European Regulation, a law of the forum. However, this characterisation raises a twofold difficulty: on the one hand, because this characterisation is not included in the Regulation itself and, on the other hand, because the Regulation does not provide for the nullity of contracts concluded. The first difficulty can undoubtedly be

145 On this proposal in the context of takeover bids, see *supra*, para. 510.

146 See *supra*, para. 515 et seq.

147 Recitals 1 and 2 of the Short Selling Regulation.

148 Either under public policy relating to the State when the short sale takes place on securities issued by the French sovereign, or under economic public policy, as the prohibition of short selling may be part of both the public policy of direction and protection, on these notions, see F. Terré *et al.*, *Droit civil. Les obligations*, *op. cit.*, nos. 490 and 495 et seq. See also from the point of view of cause P. Pailler, *Le contrat financier, un instrument financier à terme*, *op. cit.*

overcome in that the prohibitions stemming from the Short Selling Regulation are part of the protection of the economic organisation not only of the State, but of the Union, so that the characterisation as an overriding mandatory rule can be established by the court itself. The second difficulty, however, is that the application of the regulation, even under the heading of overriding mandatory rules, does not achieve the desired result since it does not envisage the nullity of the contract. It is to the mechanism of taking into consideration that one must turn in order to obtain such a nullity. Indeed, the court petitioned may, by application of foreign contract law, take into consideration this Short Selling Regulation in order to characterise the unlawfulness of the content of the contract.[149] It is true that foreign law may not recognise as unlawful a contract concluded in violation of a foreign prohibition, even if this prohibition was introduced to protect the foreign economic organisation. However, the EU court may then, alternatively, disregard the application of the foreign law under the exception of international public policy and subject the contract to the law of the forum, or apply European law as mandatory rules as regards the characterisation of the unlawfulness and the *lex fori* as regards the sanctioning of the unlawfulness.

857. In the second case, where the court petitioned is established outside the Union, it is possible that the prohibition rule would also apply under consideration of the foreign law, since the mandatory rules method would lead to identical dead ends. Consideration would allow the foreign court to find that the subject matter of the contract, or the concept that constitutes its functional equivalent, is unlawful in that it infringes a prohibition enacted by the legal order of the place where the underlying is traded. Again, the foreign court may consider that it is not part of its public contractual order to annul contracts concluded in violation of European regulations, even if they are so important. Its judgment will nevertheless be subject to refusal of enforcement if the person ordered to pay the contract is only established in the Union.

858. Section conclusion. From the point of view of financial contracts, this discussion helps to show that, among the many classifications of financial contracts, the one based on the underlying asset is likely to dominate the others. From a legal point of view, a truly special regime for financial contracts has emerged.[150] Indeed, the nature of the underlying may condition the validity of the financial contract, the obligation to be cleared with a clearing house, the

[149] Or the equivalent concept that has the function attributed to the content of the contract in French law. In our view, therefore, there is no real application of the law of the underlying, as suggested by certain authors, see J. Gavriloff, *Les méthodes du conflit de lois à l'épreuve du produit dérivé*, *op. cit.*, no. 298. In the same way, the laws of the underlying of financial contracts are not necessarily mandatory rules: they only rarely intervene in order to paralyse the formation or performance of the financial contract.

[150] This is echoed in the specialisation of works on financial contracts, see e.g. A. Gauvin, *Droit des dérivés de crédit*, Paris, Revue Banque Édition, 2003; R. Dambre, *Les contrats financiers sur action*, *op. cit.*

guarantee mechanisms to which it is subject, will interfere with the execution of the financial contract. From the point of view of private international law, this analysis has shown the tension that exists between the need for the *lex mercatus* to apply according to the effects test to ensure the achievement of the ends it pursues, and the obstacle it encounters when the parties have made the contract subject to a foreign law, which can only be imperfectly limited in practice, if not by the administrative and criminal sanctions against the parties.

859. Chapter conclusion. The law of the financial contract has certain limitations as to the conditions of its formation. These depend on at least three other legal systems, those of personal status, the residence of the parties, and the underlying subject matter of the contract. From the point of view of the financial contract, these three systems have in common that they often protect the persons concerned by making the possibility of concluding a financial contract conditional on its pursuit of a hedging, and not speculative, purpose, with the exception of the *lex societatis* applicable to financial contracts on shares, which is precisely aimed at preventing the hedging of the risk inherent in the social hazard. The regime applicable to marketing is unique in that it offers greater protection to residents, on the one hand, by restricting the persons entitled to make enquiries and, on the other hand, by imposing on the latter a set of information obligations to be provided to their prospects. Finally, from the point of view of private international law, this chapter has shown that the selection by the financial contract of a foreign law is an obstacle neither to the protection of residents nor to the regulation of the function pursued by the financial contract.

CHAPTER 3
DISRUPTIONS IN THE PERFORMANCE OF THE CONTRACT

860. Functions of set-off. Once a contract is formed, the regulation of collateral and set-off can disrupt its performance. As the former have already been studied,[1] it is the set-off that will be studied here. Set-off, whether contractual or legal in origin, is defined as 'the simultaneous extinction of reciprocal obligations between two persons'.[2] Its primary function of payment[3] is widespread in both civil law and *common law* systems.[4] However, as Professor Jérôme François writes, set-off 'is an institution whose extinctive function does not reveal its full richness. It also fulfils a guarantee function and may even, in certain cases, represent the best of guarantees for the party who is in a position to invoke it'.[5] This evolution of the function of set-off, from payment to guarantee of payment, is especially perceptible when one of the parties to the contract is subject to collective proceedings. In this context, the regime which may be attached to set-off will allow 'the creditor to appropriate the debtor's claim against himself without having to fear any competition'.[6]

861. This distinction in the function of set-off depending on whether the parties are in good standing or whether one of them is subject to collective proceedings has a particular echo in financial law,[7] but also in conflict of laws: it explains why the law applicable to set-off is not the same when the parties are in

---

1 See *supra*, paras. 748 et seq.

2 Art. 1347 Civil Code.

3 Some authors consider that it is more precisely a 'shortened payment', see J. François, *Les obligations, Régime général*, 5th ed., Paris, Economica, 2020, no. 64. The author considers that although set-off has an economic function close to that of payment, it is nevertheless distinct from it in that it allows only indirect satisfaction of the creditor (*ibid.*). However, one may wonder if, in the context of financial contracts where the obligations consist exclusively of the payment of sums of money, set-off cannot be assimilated to payment.

4 P. Pichonnaz and L. Gullifer, *Set-off in Arbitration and commercial transactions*, Oxford, OUP, 2014, no. 2.61.

5 J. François, *Les obligations, Régime général*, *op. cit.* See already in this regard, G. Duboc, *La compensation et les droits des tiers*, Paris, LGDJ, 1989, no. 5: 'Set-off thus appears to be both a method of payment and a technique of guarantee. These two aspects are inherent to the institution and intimately linked' quoted by A. Couret, H. Le Nabasque *et al.*, *Droit financier*, *op. cit.*, no. 1512.

6 F. Terré *et al.*, *Droit civil, Les obligations*, *op. cit.*, no. 1678.

7 See *infra*, nos. 950 et seq.

good standing and when one of the parties is subject to collective proceedings.[8] Before examining this question, it should be noted that the law applicable to netting now depends on whether the financial contract is subject to the clearing obligation, i.e. the obligation to hedge with a clearing house. This is laid down in the EMIR regulation, the scope of which must first be defined (Section 1). In the event that the clearing obligation is applicable, the intervention of the clearing house leads to the application of a double original regime: on the one hand, it alters the law applicable to the financial contract and, on the other hand, it allows the financial contract to escape the law of collective procedures and resolution (Section 2). If the financial contract is not subject to the clearing obligation, the EMIR Regulation requires the contracting parties to mitigate their counterparty risk. This translates into a derogation regime allowing it to ensure the execution of the guarantees provided for in the contract, including in the event of insolvency of one of the parties, or reorganisation measures of the credit institution. On the other hand, unlike the contracts executed with the clearing house, these guarantees can be paralysed by the resolution of one of the parties to the contract (Section 3).

SECTION 1. THE CLEARING OBLIGATION

862. The clearing obligation stems from the EMIR Regulation, which 'lays down clearing and bilateral risk-management requirements for over-the-counter ("OTC") derivative contracts, reporting requirements for derivative contracts'.[9] In particular, clearing is defined by Article 2, 3 of EMIR as 'the process of establishing positions, including the calculation of net obligations, and ensuring that financial instruments, cash, or both are available to cover the exposures arising from those positions'. By using the verb 'to cover' in its definition, the Regulation recalls the origin of this obligation; by referring to this process as clearing, the Regulation also refers to the mutation of the functions to which this obligation has been subjected (§ 1). This change explains the evolution of its scope, which is now independent of the *lex contractus* (§ 2).

---

8 Comp. P. Pichonnaz and L. Gullifer, *Set-off in Arbitration and commercial transactions*, *op. cit.*, nos. 4.65-4.66 who believe that the change of applicable law is explained rather by the procedural aspect of set-off in the context of collective proceedings. It seems to us rather that behind the procedural aspect of insolvency there is a substantive issue, governed by the law applicable to the creditor's contest, determined by the centre of the debtor's main interests.

9 Art. 1(1) of the EMIR. In addition to providing, from a market infrastructure perspective, for 'uniform obligations regarding the conduct of business of central counterparties and trade repositories' (*ibid.*) on which see *supra*, nos. 81 et seq.

§ 1. THE EVOLUTION OF THE FUNCTION

863. Original function. The 'clearing obligation' of the EMIR regulation is the European name for an obligation that is well known in France under the term 'couverture'.[10] In French law, the notion of '*couverture*' is somewhat ambiguous.[11] It may first refer to the insurance function of financial contracts, known as *hedging*, which allows a financial contract to be concluded in order to avoid a risk.[12] It may also refer to the hedging and risk-spreading ratios imposed on investment services providers by their prudential obligations.[13] The term '*couverture*' may also refer to the guarantees set up to protect against a risk, which are part of the EMIR clearing obligation. In order to distinguish between them, we will refer to the hedging function in the first case, the hedging ratio in the second case and the notion of clearing obligation in the third case, it being understood that this refers to the clearing obligation with the clearing house.[14]

864. The clearing obligation was first conceived in practice: it was a custom of stockbrokers[15] to ensure their own protection. This practice was therefore part of the contractual domain.[16] This obligation, imposed by French stockbrokers but shared internationally, consisted, on the one hand, of an initial deposit and, on the other hand, of a margin call, i.e. the regular deposit of a sum whose amount is correlated to the fluctuations of the price of the underlying asset. This practice of stockbrokers, which already made it possible to 'provide the contracting party with protection adapted to a variable counterparty risk',[17] was

---

[10] The notion of 'clearing' is used by the decree of 7 October 1890 relating to the stock exchange, and was still used when this decree was abrogated by law no. 88-70 of 22 January 1988 (see e.g. Art. 62), and the correlative entry into force of the general regulations of the Conseil des bourses de valeur. On this development, see H. Gourdy, *La couverture sur les marchés financiers*, *op. cit.*

[11] See already in this sense, P. Pailler, *Le contrat financier, un instrument financier à terme*, *op. cit.*, no. 291, H. Gourdy, *La couverture sur les marchés financiers*, *op. cit.*, nos. 11 et seq.

[12] On the practice of *hedging*, see *supra*, para. 833.

[13] Art. L. 533-2 of the Monetary and Financial Code, see *supra*, para. 100.

[14] The clearing obligation, in its broader sense, can refer to any risk mitigation technique, including collateral for contracts that cannot be cleared. The clearing obligation is sometimes referred to as a central clearing obligation (see e.g. M. Roussille, 'Mutations des pouvoirs de l'AMF à l'occasion de l'entrée en vigueur d'EMIR', *op. cit.*). The adjective 'central' recalls the name of the central counterparty chamber. From an international perspective, the choice was made to focus on the hedging function rather than on the institutional mechanism through which it is deployed.
Similarly, the clearing obligation is sometimes referred to as 'hedging on the financial markets' (see, for example, Ms Gourdy's thesis cited above). However, the clearing obligation is nowadays deployed independently of the conclusion of the contract by a financial market.

[15] H. Gourdy, *La couverture sur les marchés financiers*, *op. cit.*, no. 23.

[16] However, behind the protection of the solvency of foreign exchange agents, it was the stability of the financial system that was undoubtedly protected, see *supra*, paras. 41 et seq.

[17] H. Gourdy, *La couverture sur les marchés financiers*, *op. cit.*, no. 72. For the author, this is the nature of the clearing obligation.

given legislative authority by the decree of 7 October 1890 on the stock exchange. Hedging was then made mandatory by a decree of 14 October 1960, not only in the relationship between the principal and the intermediary, but gradually between intermediaries and clearing members and then between members and the chamber.[18] As Ms Gourdy writes: 'Hedging was then the subject of a sort of chain 'transmission' to the clearing house, since each intermediary in this chain was simultaneously the beneficiary of a hedge and obliged to establish another one with the next intermediary.'[19] A special regime was attached to the collateral, providing for the transfer of ownership of the collateral deposits to the clearing house as soon as they were created.[20] This regime is now[21] defined by reference to the financial collateral regime of Article L. 211-38 of the Monetary and Financial Code.[22] This reference to financial collateral, designed to limit systemic risk,[23] shows the evolution of the function of the clearing obligation: it has moved from protection against counterparty risk, which is the characteristic of all collateral, to prevention of systemic risk.

865. Contemporary function. In fact, the system risk prevention function of the clearing obligation has not so much replaced as added to the counterparty risk protection function. This development was caused by the realisation that financial contracts can contribute, through their risk transfer function, to the development of system risk.[24] The subprime crisis was a clear manifestation

---

18 P.-H. Conac, *La régulation des marchés boursiers par la commission des opérations de bourse (COB) et la securities and exchange commission (SEC)*, *op. cit.*, p. 203.

19 H. Gourdy, *La couverture sur les marchés financiers*, *op. cit.*, no. 26.

20 This regime was enshrined in Art. 9-1 of the Law of 17 June 1987 and extended by Arts. 49 and 52 of the Law on the modernisation of financial activities, see *ibid.* This provision is now included in Art. L. 440-7 of the Monetary and Financial Code. However, this does not mean that the Chamber has a right of ownership over these deposits, as Art. L. 440-7 para. 2 of the Commercial Code provides that neither the member nor the chamber may 'claim any right whatsoever over these deposits even on the basis of Title I or Title II of Book VI of the Commercial Code', relating to the prevention of business difficulties and safeguarding. However, it is possible that the chamber or clearing member uses these deposits to cover itself under another financial contract. The situation is similar to that of drawing on the estate (see already on this comparison, P.-H. Conac, *La régulation des marchés boursiers par la commission des opérations de bourse [COB] et la securities and exchange commission [SEC]*, *op. cit.*, p. 272). From the point of view of deposits, the question arises as to their status, and in particular whether the transfer of deposits is valid.

21 Since the Law on the Separation and Regulation of Banking Activities of 26 July 2013, which, under the influence of the European regulation on OTC products, designs the clearing obligation regime.

22 On which see our developments *infra*, para. 940 and the references.

23 On this questionable basis see *supra*, para. 753.

24 This phenomenon was observed by Professor Gaudemet in part 2 of his thesis, A. Gaudemet, *Les dérivés*, *op. cit.* Today, this function explains that the prevention of system risk can justify the suspension of the clearing obligation in certain cases, see Art. 6 *bis*(1)(c) of the EMIR regulation, and Recital 82 of the CCP resolution regulation.

of this.[25] This development was accompanied by the introduction of trading and reporting requirements. The rationale for these obligations requires a more in-depth look at the functions of the clearing house.

866. The clearing of financial contracts with a clearing house, in addition to avoiding the counterparty risk for the contracting parties and the realisation of the systemic risk, also presents a third advantage, which explains a subsidiary function of the clearing obligation. Indeed, by imposing a central counterparty, it is possible to improve market transparency since, as Mr Gaudemet writes, 'the clearing house has knowledge of the exposure of all clearing participants and can communicate this exposure to the regulatory authorities for the exercise of their mission'.[26] However, the pursuit of this function is not only ensured by the clearing obligation: it cannot cover all financial contracts.[27] In these cases, full knowledge of the contracts entered into by operators is ensured by the trading and reporting obligations of investment firms. It should be noted, however, that the general knowledge of contracts concluded by operators serves two distinct purposes: the first, fulfilled by the trading and reporting obligations arising from the MiFID Regulation, is to enable the multilateral trading facility to provide the most accurate price possible,[28] and the second, fulfilled by the reporting obligation arising from the EMIR Regulation, is to know the total exposure of operators to financial contracts in order to measure the state of system risk.[29] The latter, also known as the reporting requirement, is subject to the same scope as the clearing obligation.

867. Finally, the institution of the clearing obligation makes it possible to nuance the assertion that clearing houses are a private initiative whose function, within international relations, is to reduce the legal risk inherent in cross-border relations.[30] If this were true, the OTC derivatives market would not have developed to such an extent and there would be no need to impose the

---

25 The ability of clearing houses to hedge default risks was the main reason for the enactment of the hedging requirement in the OTC regulation, see J. Braithwaite and D. Murphy, 'Central counterparties (CCPs) and the law of default management' (2016) *Journal of Corporate Law*, pp. 291 et seq.; J. Braithwaite, *The Financial Courts: Adjudicating Disputes in Derivatives Markets*, *op. cit.* Chambers may even have been called *unlikely* heroes in the context of the *Lehman Brothers* bankruptcy, see P. Norman, *The risk controllers*, Chichester, Wiley, cited by J.P. Braithwaite, 'The dilemma of client clearing in the OTC derivatives market' (2016) *European Business Organization Law Review*, p. 355. Financial contracts could already have been an instrument for the bankruptcy of other actors. This was the case, for example, in the bankruptcy of the *Long Term Capital Management* (LTCM) fund, on which see B. Carruthers, 'Economy and Law', *op. cit.*, p. 135.

26 A. Gaudemet, 'Les obligations de négociation et de compensation', *op. cit.*, no. 5.

27 See *infra*, para. 912.

28 On these obligations, see *supra*, para. 441.

29 The existence of these two distinct purposes explains why it is probably excessive to consider that the obligation to negotiate is an extension of the obligation to compensate.

30 See in this sense, J. Basedow, *The Law of Open Societies*, *op. cit.*, no. 141.

use of clearing houses. In fact, in cross-border relationships, the clearing house has exactly the same function as in domestic relationships, i.e. to limit the counterparty risk and, consequently, the system risk.

§ 2. THE INTERNATIONAL SCOPE OF APPLICATION

The evolution of the function of the clearing obligation has had little impact on its regime.[31] However, it has led to an expansion of its scope of application, not only in material terms, i.e. on the financial contracts subject to the clearing obligation (I), but also in personal and international terms, since the EMIR Regulation applies to any person established on the territory of the Union, regardless of the law applicable to the financial contract (II).

I. The Material Scope of Application

868. Contracts subject to the clearing obligation. The financial contracts subject to the clearing obligation are listed in a register maintained and updated by ESMA.[32] These are currently financial basis swaps classes, fixed and floating interest rates, credit risk,[33] or overnight indexed rates, and forward rate agreements.[34] Inclusion in this list is either initiated by ESMA or requested by a clearing house when the contracts are deemed to be eligible for clearing.[35] As it has been written:

> 'The difficulty faced by the drafters of the EMIR regulation was to reconcile two contradictory factors: on the one hand, a desire to include as many derivative contracts as possible in the clearing obligation; on the other hand, the need not to

---

[31] This was already based, by reference to Art. L. 440-7 of the Monetary and Financial Code, on the use of financial guarantees, developed to prevent systemic risk. Here the means seem to have preceded the full perception of the end.

[32] The register is available on its website.

[33] The obligation to clear financial contracts relating to credit risk was the main objective of the authorities after the 2008 crisis, see European Central Bank/Eurosystem, 'Credit Default Swaps and Counterparty Risk', August 2009, pp. 76 et seq.

[34] See ESMA's *Public Register for the Clearing Obligation under EMIR*, 2 March 2021, available on the authority's website. Comp. financial contracts subject to mandatory clearing in the United States, *Clearing requirement determination under section 2(h) of the CEA*, 17 C.F.R. § 50.5 (2012) and *Clearing requirement determination under section 2(h) of the CEA for Interest Rate Swaps*, 81 Fed. Reg. 39506 and 71202 (2016). At the end of 2013, ISDA estimated that 65% of financial interest rate contracts were cleared (see ISDA, *Size and Uses of the Non-Cleared Derivatives Market: an ISDA study*, April 2014, p. 3) while the Bank for International Settlements noted that one-third of credit derivatives were now cleared, Bank for International Settlements, *Statistical realease: OTC Derivatives Statistics at End December 2015*, Basel, May 2016, p. 2.

[35] T. Bonneau *et al.*, *Droit financier*, *op. cit.*, no. 657.

impose on CCPs, managed by private companies, the obligation to clear contracts that they would not be able to clear.'[36]

In particular, certain material aspects of the financial contract itself may constitute an obstacle to its clearing and have been listed in Article 4.4 of the EMIR Regulation. The three criteria used, standardisation, liquidity, and price valuation of the financial contract[37] are identical to those conditioning the negotiability of the financial contract on a multilateral trading facility, and show the kinship of the institutions. Like the multilateral trading facility, the clearing system requires a minimum number of persons using it for the same type of transaction in order to be functional and profitable. In addition to these three aspects, there is the type of risk transferred.

869. Margin call and credit risk. Some authors believe that the complexity of the structuring of the contract and, consequently, the causal difficulty in establishing the risk transferred and the correlative price, is the reason for the difficulty in clearing the financial contract.[38] In fact, it seems to us that the structure of the risk may in itself constitute an obstacle to clearing. Indeed, the clearing obligation regime is essentially based on the margin call technique,[39] and this does not necessarily allow the risk transferred by the contract to be correctly apprehended, even if standardisation is possible, and the amount due at the foreseeable maturity. Margin calls are effective when there is volatility in the underlying asset, the value of which may move up or down over time, i.e. when there is 'variable counterparty risk'.[40] However, the variability of this counterparty risk, also referred to as the volatility of the underlying, is not uniform. The assumption on which the clearing obligation was based, and the risk it sought to minimise, was that of continuous variability over time, which

---

36 A. Couret, H. Le Nabasque *et al.*, *Droit financier*, *op. cit.*, no. 1235.

37 The third criterion will be facilitated if the other two are already fulfilled: players will be able to communicate their price evaluation software, see J. Hull, 'OTC derivatives and central clearing: can all transactions be cleared?', *Revue de Stabilité Financière*, July 2010, p. 81.
These three criteria have been criticised. Indeed, standardisation is carried out by professional associations in a non-transparent way, and the qualification of a contract meeting the standardisation requires a legal analysis. Moreover, non-standardised contracts can be offset. Finally, by obliging the clearing of standardised contracts, the clearing houses are deprived of their ability to choose whether or not to clear certain contracts depending on the risk that this entails for them. On these criticisms, see J.P. Braithwaite, 'The inherent limits of "legal devices": lessons for the public sector's central counterparty prescription for the OTC derivatives markets' (2011) 12 *European Business Organization Law Review*, p. 87, pp. 107 et seq.

38 J. Hull, 'OTC derivatives and central clearing: can all transactions be cleared?', *op. cit.*

39 Ms Gourdy considers that this is the essence of the clearing obligation, and makes it the criterion for its identification, see H. Gourdy, *La couverture sur les marchés financiers*, *op. cit.*, no. 236; for a detailed description of the margin call mechanism, see *ibid.*, no. 244.

40 *Ibid.*, no. 194.

could change every day in either direction. This assumption is particularly accurate when the underlyings are interest rates or foreign exchange, which are the most traditional underlyings of financial contracts. However, the movement towards diversification of underlyings has led to the emergence of objects for which the notion of variability or volatility is not appropriate, because the risk does not lie in the evolution of the underlying, but in the occurrence of an event. This is the case in particular for financial contracts relating to a credit risk,[41] where the underlying is the occurrence of a credit event, linked to an entity, referred to as the reference entity. The credit event is most often characterised by a payment default, the bankruptcy of the reference entity, or the restructuring of one of its debts. There are only two possibilities: either the reference entity does not experience difficulties, in which case the margin call is not necessary, or the reference entity gets closer to the credit event, in which case the entire amount covered by the credit derivative becomes due.[42]

870. This lack of risk progression and its sudden realisation usually render the margin call technique ineffective and, therefore, the clearing obligation difficult to implement.[43] This is all the more true because although the technique of having the same credit derivative cover different defaults may give the impression that a certain diversification of risks would reduce them,[44] this is only an illusion. Indeed, the multiplication of credit events does not create a fluctuation in value, because the risk taken is always binary: either the credit event occurs or it does not. The most appropriate solution is then to provide for a high initial collateral deposit.[45] Where the financial contract relates to a single reference entity (*Single Name*), this solution may prevail. However, it

---

41 Financial contracts relating to credit risk are those by which 'a protection buyer hedges against a credit event in return for the payment of a periodic premium, with the protection seller obliging itself to pay the contingent part of the *swap in the event of the* occurrence of a credit event', A. Caillemer du Ferrage and C. Saudo, 'Une chambre de compensation pour les dérivés de crédit', *BJB*, January 2010, no. 1, p. 58.
On the typology of credit derivatives, see A. Gauvin, *Droit des dérivés de crédit*, *op. cit.*, pp. 83 et seq.; F. Drummond, *Droit financier*, *op. cit.*, no. 366; A. Couret, H. Le Nabasque *et a.l*, *Droit financier*, *op. cit.*, nos. 1349 et seq. See 'Instruments financiers à terme', in S. Praicheux, *Répertoire de droit des sociétés*, Paris, Dalloz, no. 52

42 Observing already this singularity, A. Gaudemet, 'Les obligations de négociation et de compensation', *op. cit.*

43 See already in this sense, *ibid.*, no. 10 on the singularity of credit derivatives and the weakness of margin calls in this case.

44 This is similar to what is at the heart of the practice of certain investment funds such as UCITS.

45 As Messrs Caillemer du Ferrage and Saudo write (A. Caillemer du Ferrage and C. Saudo, 'Une chambre de compensation pour les dérivés de crédit', *op. cit.*): 'The risky nature of CDSs stems mainly from the possibility of correlation risk and "Jump to Default" risk, i.e. the risk that a default will occur before the market has been able to assess the existence of this risk. High initial margins paid by clearing members cover the existence of the latter risk.' The traditional deposit is on average 5% of the nominal amount of the contract, see A. Couret, H. Le Nabasque *et al.*, *Droit financier*, *op. cit.*, no. 1229. On the details of the

is possible that the financial contract relates to the realisation of credit events relating to several reference entities, and it is then much more difficult to provide for the appropriate amount of the initial deposit, and therefore to clear them with a chamber.[46] In these cases where the financial contract cannot be cleared, EMIR requires the development of techniques to minimise the risks.[47] These techniques include the provision of financial guarantees proportionate to the risk incurred.[48] Failure to comply with these risk mitigation techniques may also result in administrative liability for the so-called financial counterparties.[49]

II. The Personal and International Scope of Application

871. Personal criterion. Article 1(2) of the Derivatives Regulation states that:

> 'This Regulation shall apply to central counterparties (CCPs) and their clearing members, to financial counterparties and to trade repositories. It shall apply to non-financial counterparties and trading venues where so provided.'

The Regulation defines financial counterparties as most entities engaged in financial activities and subject to authorisation.[50] Non-financial counterparties are defined as 'an undertaking, other than the entities referred to in points (1) and (8), established in the Union',[51] i.e. any entity established in the Union. In other words, EMIR is applicable to all persons domiciled within the Union. This remarkably broad scope of application has, however, been limited by the intervention of a material criterion: the clearing threshold.[52] This threshold

margin call and the methodology used, see *LCH.Clearnet*, 'Instruction no. IV.2-2 relating to the clearing obligation on derivatives markets', 4 December 2020, available on the chamber's website.

46 Especially since in these cases, the lack of liquidity makes it difficult to clear them in any case. This particular type of financial contract relating to credit risks, known as *building blocks*, is considered to have played an instrumental role in the 2008 financial crisis, see J.P. Braithwaite, 'The inherent limits of "legal devices": lessons for the public sector's central counterparty prescription for the OTC derivatives markets', *op. cit.*

47 Art. 11 of the EMIR.

48 Art. 11(3) and (4) of the EMIR.

49 For an illustration, see AMF, Dec., 24 January 2020, no. 1, SAN-2020-02.

50 Such as investment firms, insurance companies, reinsurance companies, UCITS and management companies, occupational pension institutions, AIFs and their managers, and credit institutions.

51 Art. 2(9) EMIR.

52 This limitation applies only to the clearing obligation, and not to the other obligation instituted by the Regulation: the reporting obligation. This obligation obliges the parties to a financial contract, whether or not it is subject to the clearing obligation, to declare its characteristics to a central repository whose function is to list all financial contracts so that system risk can be monitored. The characteristics to be declared are quite detailed, and the formalism attached to the declaration is strictly assessed, see for an illustration AMF decision, dec., 24 January 2020, cit..

is set according to the notional amount of all financial contracts, below which non-financial counterparties are no longer subject to the clearing obligation.[53] The rationale behind this limitation is to balance the reduced risk of financial contracts with low notional amounts with the benefits of entering into financial contracts for any person wishing to protect themselves against the realisation of a risk related to one of their economic transactions.[54] Initially confined to non-financial parties, this material limitation has been extended to 'small' financial counterparties, albeit under a stricter regime.[55]

872. Despite its self-limiting nature, the Regulation's application criterion means that any person established in the territory of the Union is likely to be subject to EMIR, and in particular to the clearing obligation that it imposes. This criterion also implies that the location of the other party to the financial contract on the territory of a third country does not deactivate the clearing obligation, which is fortunate. Indeed, the generally international nature of financial contracts means that they may frequently be concluded with companies from third States. Therefore, in the same way that its inclusion in the *lex contractus* would make it easy to evade, the clearing obligation would be emptied of its substance and unable to reduce systemic risk if it were sufficient to avoid triggering it by concluding the contract with a party from a third State. Conceived as a prudential obligation whose function is independent of the regime of the financial contract since its purpose is to fight systemic risk, the clearing obligation is therefore applicable by virtue of the presence of one of the parties to the contract on the territory of the Union.[56]

873. Direct, substantial and foreseeable effect test. The Regulation nevertheless provides for the application of the OTC Regulation's obligations to contracts concluded solely by third country entities in the event that these entities:

This function of the reporting obligation explains why its scope is perfectly identical to that of the Regulation: the reporting obligation applies to any person established on the territory of the Union who concludes a financial contract.

53 This threshold is currently determined by Art. 11 of the Commission Delegated Regulation no. 149/2013, and is set at EUR 3 billion in gross notional value for OTC interest rate derivatives contracts. On the notion of notional amount, see *supra*, para. 814.

54 This means that, as Mr Gaudemet writes, behind the submission of non-financial counterparties, there is a question of legal policy, see A. Gaudemet, 'Les obligations de négociation et de compensation', *op. cit.*; T. Bonneau *et al.*, *Droit financier*, *op. cit.*

55 Art. 4a of the EMIR Regulation, see T. Bonneau *et al.*, *Droit financier*, *op. cit.*, no. 656.

56 On the applicability of other prudential requirements due to the location of their headquarters in the EU, see *supra*, para. 101; 205. The link between the activity carried out and the registered office is more apparent here (see already our comments *supra*, para. 89). However, the clearing obligation differs from the other prudential obligations in that the latter constitute a special corporate law, affecting the capital structure of certain companies, whereas the clearing obligations are of a purely financial nature, and affect all entities that incur a systemic risk.

> 'The Commission considers that such contracts would be subject to these obligations if they were established in the Union, provided that such contracts have a direct, substantial and foreseeable effect in the Union or where such an obligation is necessary or appropriate in order to prevent circumvention of a provision of this Regulation.'[57]

This criterion has been defined by a Commission Delegated Regulation according to which the direct, substantial and foreseeable effect is retained 'when at least one third country entity benefits from a guarantee provided by a financial counterparty established in the Union covering all or part of its commitment under that OTC derivative contract'.[58] However, not all guarantees are covered, but only those of a certain size, assessed in absolute and relative terms.[59] The connection is therefore not made solely on the basis of the effect of the contract, but also by the involvement of a person established in the territory of the Union in the economic operation of the financial contract, and on whom the risk of the contract may ultimately be borne. In other words, the clearing obligation is applicable by virtue of the presence of one of the parties, or their guarantors, in the territory of the European Union. However, the scope of application may be extended where the parties attempt to 'circumvent' the rules or obligations of the Regulation.[60] Such a provision reactivates the corrective mechanism, well known from the conflict of law methodology, of *fraude à la loi*.

874. The effects test employed here does not have quite the same function as that known from competition law, or that used by criminal law to govern market abuse.[61] In the latter two cases, the function of the effects test is to give the broadest possible scope to the legislation in order to ensure that the

57 Art. 11(12) EMIR.

58 Art. 2(1) of the Commission Delegated Regulation (EU) No 285/2014 of 13 February 2014 supplementing Regulation (EU) No 648/2012 of the European Parliament and of the Council with technical regulatory standards concerning the direct, substantial and foreseeable effect of contracts within the Union and the prevention of circumvention of rules and obligations. This criterion of direct, substantial and foreseeable effect of the financial contract concluded by third country entities is also the one used to apply the MiFID trading obligation to entities that are not subject to it by virtue of the connecting factor retained by the Regulation. The criterion used is identical, Arts. 1 and 2 of the Commission Delegated Regulation (EU) 2017/579 of 13 June 2016 supplementing Regulation (EU) no. 600/2014 of the European Parliament and of the Council on markets in financial instruments with technical regulatory standards regarding the direct, substantial and foreseeable effect of derivative contracts in the Union and the prevention of circumvention of rules and obligations.

59 Art 2(1) of the above-mentioned Delegated Regulation.

60 Art. 3 of the Delegated Regulation. According to this article, the Regulation is applicable to all OTC derivatives to arrangements which have as their 'principal objective [...] to defeat the object, spirit and purpose of a provision of the Regulation'.

61 See *supra*, para. 527.

prosecuting authority can act.[62] Such a criterion has a comminatory function vis-à-vis foreign companies that would register their activity vis-à-vis the European market. In the case of the clearing obligation, the effects test probably also has this function. However, there is, in addition, a diplomatic function, to ensure that the United States would participate in multilateral negotiations on the development of its own clearing obligation. This function is in line with the methods developed in the prudential field to disseminate European legislation. These observations lead to the rejection of two analyses that have been made of the international scope of the clearing requirement, which consider it to be a mandatory rule, or a law with extraterritorial scope.

875. Rejection of the mandatory rule analysis. The analysis of the clearing obligation as a *loi de police* has the advantage that it clearly shows the link between the function pursued by the clearing obligation and its international scope of application. However, such a link does not necessarily make it a *loi de police*, as unilateral and bilateral conflict-of-laws rules take into account the purpose of the legislation in question in order to establish their connecting factor. In fact, the characterisation as a overriding mandatory rule is based on the premise that this obligation is a mode of performance of the financial contract, and that its application therefore derogates from the *lex contractus*.[63] However, this analysis comes up against a major obstacle: the purpose of the clearing obligation is not the performance of the financial contract and it does not fall within the scope of the law of contract. Its purpose is not to interfere with the regime of the financial contract, but to reduce systemic risk by reducing counterparty risk.[64] There is ample evidence of this, including the following two. First, the very limits that EMIR has set on this obligation show this. Indeed, if it were truly an obligation relating to the performance of the contract, the conclusion of the contract by two parties belonging to the same group of companies should not affect it. However, intra-group transactions are not subject to the netting obligation precisely because, as they are concluded between members of the same group subject to the same consolidation scope, they do not affect the systemic risk.[65] Secondly, if the clearing obligation were part of the performance of the contract, its violation would lead to a contractual sanction. However, the EMIR

---

62 What these criteria have in common, however, is that they combine this broad material scope with self-limiting assumptions; they do not, however, concern situations of internationality.

63 This relationship between mandatory rules and conflict rules has been formulated in these terms by Professor Mayer: 'To give the definition a completely general character, it is sufficient to say that mandatory rules are those which, according to the law of the country from which they emanate, are applicable whatever the law designated by the conflict rule of that country.' See 'Lois de police' in P. Mayer, *Répertoire de droit international*, no. 1; see also, P. Mayer, V. Heuzé and B. Rémy, *Droit international privé*, *op. cit.*, no. 123.

64 On the evolution of this function, see *supra*, paras. 907 et seq.

65 This exception is referred to in Art. 2(19) of the EMIR Regulation, and explained in Recital 38 of the Regulation.

Regulation itself specifies that the non-fulfilment of the obligation does not lead to the nullity of the contract or to legal compensation for the other party, but provides for the possibility of administrative sanctions.[66] Admittedly, the parties may attach consequences to this failure to liquidate positions *ex officio*, but this apprehension has no bearing on the very nature of the clearing obligation.[67]

876. Rejection of the extraterritorial characterisation. It may seem excessive to state that the clearing obligation 'has an extraterritorial scope'.[68] Indeed, the connection with the territory of the Union is not tenuous: the financial entities necessarily have their statutory and real seat in the Union because of the authorisation to which they are subject.[69] Even though the Regulation promotes the deployment of the effects criterion, which is likely to characterise a potentially looser link with the European territory, it *ultimately* uses a personal criterion that makes use of the seat of the guarantor of the financial contract. As an author writes, 'the European regulation "EMIR" is not an extraterritorial text; or if it is, it is reluctantly, as if "backwards"'.[70] The connection of the clearing obligation to the registered office of entities that enter into financial contracts deserves approval: the prudential nature of the obligation dictates the connection to the registered office insofar as it designates the social and economic environment affected by the realisation of the risk that this obligation intends to avert. Even if the financial contract is concluded with an entity from a third State, the insolvency of the latter is likely to spread to the entity established in the territory of the Union and, therefore, to affect the environment of the head

66 Art. 12(3) of the EMIR. From a French perspective, see the dual jurisdiction exercised by the ACPR (Art. L. 612-1(II)(1) and (2) of the Monetary and Financial Code) and the AMF (Art. L. 621-18-6 of the Monetary and Financial Code). Aware of this overlap, the authorities issued a joint press release detailing how these powers are organised, see *Dr. Sociétés*, 2013, Alert 57; *Bull. Joly Bourse*, 2013, no. 9, p. 387. On this superposition, see from an internal point of view M. Roussille, 'Mutations des pouvoirs de l'AMF à l'occasion de l'entrée en vigueur d'EMIR', *op. cit.*. See also our comments *supra*, paras. 55 et seq., 57. Making the obligation to hedge a condition of validity of the financial contract had however been proposed in doctrine, see A.-C. Muller, *Droit des marchés financiers et droit des contrats, op. cit.* In the same sense, this would sanction the idea according to which hedging would be the essential obligation of the financial contract, see P. Pailler, *Le contrat financier, un instrument financier à terme, op. cit.*

67 See already in this sense, P. Pailler, *Le contrat financier, un instrument financier à terme, op. ci.t*, no. 356. The author, while observing the importance of compulsory liquidation for the originator which 'intervenes as a form of forced execution', considers that 'if it does not reduce to nothing its indisputable regulatory dimension, it shows that the obligation to hedge is essential', *ibid.*

68 F. Drummond, *Droit financier, op. cit.*, no. 996; T. Bonneau, *Régulation bancaire et financière européenne et internationale, op. cit.*, p. 22.

69 See *supra*, para. 84.

70 A. Caillemer du Ferrage, 'Les enjeux de l'extraterritorialité du droit financier', *op. cit.* The drafters of the EMIR regulation precisely intended to avoid this reproach, see M. Barnier, 'Coordination internationale: la condition du succès sine qua non de la réforme des marchés de dérivés négociés de gré à gré', *Revue de stabilité financière*, April 2013, pp. 47 et seq.

office in a predominant way. In other words, the clearing obligation falls within the category of prudential law and contributes to the development of the field.[71]

877. Conclusion of the section. This section has shown that the international scope of application of the clearing obligation is now based on the presence of one of the parties or its guarantor in the territory of the Union, but that this broad criterion is limited by a material criterion relating to the risk taken. This solution, which is balanced, corresponds to the evolution of the function of the clearing obligation which, from contractual origin, has become prudential and thus allows the protection of the social and economic environment in which the persons bearing the risk of the financial contracts are predominantly involved. In light of this conclusion, we can see how the function of the clearing system is distinct from that of the trading system. If they were linked for a long time in that the use of a financial market made the intervention of the clearing house necessary, by an obligation stemming from the market rules themselves, this link has now been weakened by the evolution of the function of hedging, which today makes the clearing house indifferent to the origin of the contracts it clears. This statement is probably less apparent when the conditions for clearing financial contracts are identical to those for trading them, and when the use of the clearing obligation can appear as a means of developing the financial markets themselves. However, this indifference is more perceptible when it has made it necessary to enact a body of rules autonomous from the law of the contract in order to protect residents, a protection traditionally provided by the law of the financial market.

SECTION 2. THE INTERVENTION OF THE CLEARING HOUSE

878. Intermediation. Where financial contracts fall within the material scope of the clearing obligation, the parties must initiate a clearing process with the clearing house. Like access to multilateral trading facilities, access to clearing systems is restricted to clearing members. Only clearing members can admit their contract to the clearing system and, if the parties to the financial contract are not themselves clearing members, they will each have to use a person who is. The role of the clearing member, like that of the market member, can be conceived in two models.[72] First, the clearing member may simply represent

---

[71] On the linkage of prudential law, see *supra*, paras. 100 et seq.

[72] On these models, see H. Euké and L. Vincent, 'Utilité et périmètre des avis juridiques relatifs à la compensation centrale des contrats dérivés OTC: les premières ISDA Client Clearing Opinions', *RDBF*, January 2015, study no. 1, nos. 7 et seq; E. Dwyer and R. Tredgett, 'OTC Derivatives: Client Clearing Agreements – A Piece in the Clearing Jigsaw' (October 2014) 9, *Capital Market Law Journal*, pp. 343 et seq.; P. Cornut St-Pierre, *La fabrique juridique des swaps*, *op. cit.*, pp. 251 et seq.

the principal and act in its name and on its behalf: this is the model sometimes referred to as agency, which simply requires the conclusion of an agency agreement.[73] Secondly, the clearing member may itself interpose itself between the originator and the clearing house, a model described as principal to principal. This second model, used in France and the most widespread in the Union,[74] has two consequences: on the one hand, a financial contract must be concluded between the clearing member and its client and, on the other hand, the clearing house will only deal with the member. It is according to this scheme that the French clearing house intervenes with respect to the financial contract (§ 1). However, the obligations resulting from its intervention will not necessarily be subject to the law of the clearing system (§ 2).

§ 1. CHANGE OF CONTRACTOR

879. The intervention of the clearing house. The intervention of the clearing house has long been the subject of controversy amongs academics, with some authors perceiving this intervention as an interposition between the contracting parties leading to the novation of the initial contract into two separate contracts with each of the parties.[75] Others believe that there has never been an initial contract and that the contract concluded by a financial market is always concluded only with the clearing house and never by the matching of orders in the central book.[76] Still others refuse to see the clearing house as a party to the contract, but at most as a provider of accounting services granting a performance guarantee to the transaction.[77] This ambiguity of the clearing house's role was reinforced, on the one hand, by its different names, clearing house or central counterparty and, on the other hand, by the silence of the legislative texts.

880. Nevertheless, it seems to us that these different analyses can be reconciled by considering that the clearing house pursues two purposes, which correspond moreover to the two functions of clearing, and which are revealed by its two names of clearing house and central counterparty. Firstly, it can act as a provider

---

73 On which see, from the point of view of the conflict of laws, *supra*, paras. 451. 454 et seq. This model is for example in force in the United States, see J.P. Braithwaite, 'The dilemma of client clearing in the OTC derivatives market', *op. cit.*

74 From a comparative perspective, see the different systems reported by M. Yates, 'UK settlement' in M. Blair and G. Walker (eds.), *Financial Markets and Exchanges Law*, Oxford, OUP, 2007, pp. 321 et seq.

75 The thesis of novation was for the first time, it seems, raised in 1906 by the fundamental work of Haristoy, on which see M. Roussille, *La compensation multilatérale*, *op. cit.* The renewal of this analysis is due to Mrs Riassetto, see I. Riassetto, *Les garanties des contrats à terme négociés sur le MATIF*, thesis, University of Strasbourg III, 1999, nos. 276 et seq.

76 A.-C. Muller, *Droit des marchés financiers et droit des contrats*, *op. cit.*

77 M. Roussille, *La compensation multilatérale*, *op. cit.*, nos. 157 et seq. For a summary, see T. Bonneau *et al.*, *Droit financier*, *op. cit.*

of accounting services to facilitate payment.[78] Secondly, it can interpose itself between the parties to the original contract in order to guarantee the proper completion of the transactions submitted to it, and by becoming the central counterparty to financial contracts.[79] The analysis is undoubtedly obscured by the inversion of these two functions: the original and preponderant function of the clearing house was at one time that of providing accounting services, which explained in particular its role in interbank relations,[80] whereas this function is now subsidiary. In fact, the obligation imposed on operators to admit their financial contracts to a clearing system is designed to ensure that the clearing house guarantees these transactions. This duality of functions is now enshrined in the EMIR regulation.[81] This regulation defines a central counterparty as 'a legal person that interposes itself between the counterparties to the contracts traded on one or more financial markets, becoming the buyer to every seller and the seller to every buyer'.[82] However, this first function attached to the clearing house is distinct from the definition of clearing, which refers to the provision of an accounting service enabling clearing.[83]

881. The law of the conflict of laws supports this analysis. Indeed, when the clearing house intervenes as an accounting service provider, which includes the material acts performed for the purpose of the short payment, it provides a service subject to the clearing rules, i.e. to the clearing system[84] resulting from

---

78 As Professor Drummond writes, the clearing house 'had as its sole purpose the simplification of payments' (F. Drummond, *Droit financier*, *op. cit.*, no. 994). The author then observes that 'the idea of the interposition of a central counterparty splitting the contractual relationship in order to secure transactions came only at a later stage' (*ibid.*) and is closely linked to the futures markets.

79 In the Finality Directive, both terms, clearing house and CCP, were used.

80 On this aspect, see M. Roussille, *La compensation multilatérale*, *op. cit.*
This double distinction between the title of the institution and the obligation is also found in English law. The latter sometimes refers to *clearing houses* or *central counterparties* to designate clearing houses, whereas clearing in the sense of the law of obligations is expressed by the notion of *set-off*, the obligation to register the contract with the clearing house is expressed by the *clearing obligation*. It should be noted, however, that the clearing obligation is broader, as it refers to risk mitigation, and thus goes beyond the *clearing obligation*.

81 And consequently, in French law. Moreover, Art. L. 440-1 of the Monetary and Financial Code now states that 'clearing houses are the central counterparties defined' by the EMIR regulation.

82 Art. 2(1) of the EMIR regulation. This perception, which has now become established, had been heavily criticised by some authors, who saw in the chamber's service a provision of accounting services, see M. Roussille, *La compensation multilatérale*, *op. cit.*, nos. 265 et seq.

83 Art. 2(3) EMIR, reproduced *supra*, para. 864.

84 It should be recalled here that the clearing system within the meaning of the Finality Directive is constituted by the clearing rules, whereas the clearing rules, when they define the clearing system within them, designate the computer system, which is in fact an asset belonging to it and enabling it to provide its service. On the nature of the systems and their international connection, see *supra*, paras. 227 et seq.

the Finality Directive.[85] On the other hand, when the clearing house interposes itself and pursues its function of central counterparty, the resulting obligations are not necessarily subject to the law of the clearing system. Thus, where the clearing house interposes itself between two participants who have entered into an over-the-counter financial contract relating to a credit event, developed by ISDA and subject to English law, the obligations arising from the interposition will be subject to English law. In order to explain this second aspect, it is necessary to focus on the analysis of the change of contractor resulting from the interposition of the chamber.

882. The change of contracting party. For a long time, there was ambiguity as to the mechanism by which the clearing house, which is initially a third party to the financial contract, becomes the counterparty of the two participants.[86] Today, the texts state that this change of contracting party takes place by novation. Indeed, the recording of the transaction in the clearing system would be the trigger for a novation of the initial contract, whether it was concluded by a multilateral trading system or by OTC. This initial contract, extinguished, would be novated into two new contracts binding each of the parties with the clearing house, and justifying its designation as central counterparty. This analysis is the one adopted by LCH's clearing rules, which stipulate:

> 'Upon registration, there is novation. As a result of this novation, LCH SA becomes the counterparty of the Clearing Member and becomes the holder of the rights and obligations resulting from the Transaction registered in the name of the Clearing Member.'[87]

This analysis, which is also suggested by the EMIR Regulation, which mentions novation as one of the conditions of the clearing obligation,[88] has been heavily criticised in the literature.[89] Without calling into question the lucidity of the critics, we will simply observe here that the characterisation of novation,

---

85 This choice is not subject to change in that the service provided is then constitutive of the notion of a system within the meaning of Art. 2(a) of the Finality Directive, i.e. 'a formal agreement between three or more participants [...] containing common rules and standardised procedures for the execution of transfer orders between participants'. Or rather, if the choice is likely to vary, then a new system would have to be notified. The issue is nevertheless sensitive, as the activity carried out by the clearing house is justified by the derogation granted to Finality Directive systems.

86 This ambiguity has given rise to a copious analysis of the institution in question through most of the techniques of contract law and the general regime of obligations, see M. Roussille, *La compensation multilatérale*, *op. cit.*

87 Art. 1.3.2.1 of the clearing rules.

88 The notion of novation appears in Arts. 4(1)(b), 4a(1)(c), 10(1)(c) of EMIR.

89 A.-V. Delozière-Le Fur, *La compensation dite multilatérale*, Paris, Édition Panthéon-Assas/LGDJ, 2003 no. 99, D. Robine, *La sécurité des marchés financiers face aux procédures collectives*, *op. cit.*, no. 348. M. Roussille, *La compensation multilatérale*, *op. cit.*, nos. 157

unsatisfactory from the point of view of French law,[90] appears today to be marked by the seal of approval of positive law, and that it has important consequences in terms of private international law, both when the contract has been concluded through a financial market and OTC.

§ 2. THE LAW APPLICABLE TO NOVATED OBLIGATIONS

Novated obligations are subject to the law designated by the rules of set-off. However, the rules are not identical for all types of contracts. Indeed, the French clearing house, LCH, provides for two distinct bodies of clearing rules, which contain different conflict rules that will be detailed here. The first are applicable to financial contracts concluded by a financial market, and to traditional financial contracts concluded over the counter (I). The latter are applicable to financial contracts concluded over the counter relating to a credit risk (II).

I. The Traditional Rules of Set-Off

883. The traditional set-off rules apply to all financial contracts concluded through a multilateral trading facility, but may also apply to contracts concluded over the counter. With respect to these contracts, the law applicable to netting governs the novated obligations incurred, which results from the Clearing rules.[91] The application of French law may pose difficulties in certain cases where the initial contract was subject to a foreign law. Indeed, novation entails the extinction of the obligations arising from the contract initially concluded by the offsetting participants. This means that the law applicable to the initial obligations, whether it is the law of the financial market where it was traded if the initial contract was the result of the matching of their orders by the trading system, or the law designated by the parties in the case of OTC trading, will not necessarily be the same as the law applicable to the new obligations. Indeed, trading platforms are independent of clearing systems, so that a contract traded

---

et seq.; A.-C. Muller, *Droit des marchés financiers et droit des contrats*, *op. cit.*, nos. 382 et seq.; P. Pailler, *Le contrat financier, un instrument financier à terme*, *op. cit.*, no. 190. For a synthesis, see T. Bonneau *et al.*, *Droit financier*, *op. cit.*, nos. 1318 et seq.

90 Novation is the mechanism retained by the rules of set-off under English law. It is suggested here that, in addition to the thesis of Madame Riassetto, the French qualification of novation was undoubtedly inspired by the English qualification, because of its identity of title and the common Roman origin of the institution, without, however, corresponding perfectly to it. On the application of novation when registering a transaction with an English chamber, see J. Braithwaite, 'The inherent limits of "legal devices": lessons for the public sector's central counterparty prescription for the OTC derivatives markets', *op. cit.*, p. 105.

91 Art. 1.3.5.1 of the Clearing Rules: 'In the absence of explicit indication to the contrary, the Clearing Rules shall be governed by and interpreted in accordance with French law.'

on a Belgian financial market may be cleared on a French system.[92] This situation may cause difficulties when the legal system of the financial market wishes to impose particular constraints, for example on the timing of the transfer of rights. Admittedly, it is then possible, from a litigation perspective, to consider that laws relating to the transfer of ownership of goods traded through financial markets are overriding mandatory rules. However, if one wishes to ensure a permanent coordination of legal systems, it is still preferable to provide for the applicability of foreign civil law relating to the transfer of ownership through the rules of netting when the novated contract has been concluded on a foreign financial market.[93]

884. What is true for contracts concluded on the financial markets is equally true for those concluded over-the-counter where the parties use English or American law, which does not prevent them from wishing to clear them through a French system. However, it should be borne in mind that only the contract concluded by the clearing members is novated, and that the contract between the principal and the clearing member is separate: it is not registered by the clearing house, is not subject to novation, and may be subject to a different law from the one applicable between the members and the clearing house.[94] Nevertheless, in these cases, in particular those relating to financial contracts on interest rates, the decorrelation between the initial contract and the novated contract does not lead to a misalignment of the price of these contracts, or of the sums due under them. As Mr Caillemer du Ferrage writes: 'The transition to post-novation French law in the (*CCP*), imposes no identified reorganisation costs or burdens on market participants'.[95] This application of the law of clearing rules to contracts resulting from the novation operated by the recording of the transaction in the clearing computer system is not, however, systematic. This is clearly not the case for financial contracts relating to credit risk, which constitute a particular segment of the financial contract market known as CDS (Credit Default Swap) and are subject to their own rules.

---

92 On the independence of the financial market and the clearing house, and the links they nevertheless maintain, see *supra*, para. 44.

93 Thus, Art. 1.3.2.13 of the LCH Clearing Rules states: 'The general provisions of Belgian civil law concerning the determination of the moment of transfer of ownership of Financial Instruments bought, sold or exchanged as a result of a Transaction are applicable.'

94 The situation here is the same as when a principal approaches a market member to conclude a contract on the trading system, see *supra*, paras. 449 et seq.

95 A. Caillemer du Ferrage, 'L'impact du Brexit sur les infrastructures de marché', *op. cit.* The author also considers that 'For a long time in the equity derivatives market, ISDA OTC transactions on listed French underlyings have been hedged against positions concluded on French futures markets, without this having caused any difficulty for the development of the market', *ibid.*

II. *The Case of OTC Financial Contracts for Credit Risk*

885. Disjunction of the law applicable to the clearing system and the novated obligations. In this particular segment, there is a body of rules applicable in principle, the CDS segment rules,[96] to which must be added two bodies of special rules, the CDS Clearing supplement and the FCM CDS Clearing Regulation.

The body of rules of principle, drafted in English by LCH, provides, on the one hand, that the application of French law will be limited solely to the rules relating to the provision of accounting services and to the admission contract[97] and, on the other hand, a distributive application of English and American law to the transactions concluded.[98] Indeed, English law applies to the special rules (CDS Clearing Supplement),[99] to the ISDA definitions of credit derivatives and to the transactions concluded. In addition, the CDS segment rules also provide for the application of US law to the FCM CDS Clearing Regulation. These relate to transactions with futures commission merchants (FCMs),[100] a category of intermediary subject to regulation by the Commission Futures Trade Commissions (CFTC),[101] the regulatory authority for financial contracts in the United States.

These two bodies of specific rules aim to apply to novated obligations the same regulation as that applied to pre-novation obligations arising from the original contract. In particular, two types of contracts are covered: ISDA contracts subject to English law and those subject to US law.[102] In the case of ISDA contracts subject to English law, the CDS Clearing Supplement recreates the contractual documentation of the three different contracts covered, and the same is true for transactions subject to US law. It would therefore be simplistic to consider that this law applies only to novated obligations, since it governs the entire area subject to the law of the contract.[103] Thus, in the case of transactions with FCMs, the special regulation applies both to novated obligations and to the provisions governing the execution of collateral techniques specific to

96 CDS is the acronym for Credit Default Swap. The acronym CDS will be used here because of its use by the applicable clearing rules.

97 Art. 1.2.14.1 of the CDS Clearing Rules.

98 At the same time, certain agreements between clearing participants and the clearing house relating to the transfer of financial collateral under a regime known to Belgian law are subject to Belgian law, see Art. 1.2.14.3 of the clearing rules for the CDS segment.

99 Art. 1.2.14.2 of the CDS Clearing Rules.

100 Art. 1.2.14.3 of the CDS Clearing Rules.

101 Art. 1.3(p) of the CFTC rules.

102 This is explicitly stated in the special rulebooks, see CDS Clearing supplement, pp. 1 et seq.

103 As the authors of the HCJP Opinion on the legal feasibility of developing a clearing offer for interest rate derivatives in Paris of 17 October 2017 write (p. 40), the 'CDS Clearing Supplement is intended to determine the contractual framework applicable to cleared credit derivatives (terms and conditions, payment and delivery obligations, management of the occurrence of a credit event, unwinding of the transaction)'.

these obligations: on the one hand, the account technique and the rules on the segregation of clients' accounts, on the other hand, collateral in the broad sense (collateral, security interest) and the transfer of assets. Nevertheless, because of their character as specific rules, the clearing house, which did not intend to give them a wider scope, explicitly mentions that the law applicable to these bodies of specific rules does not extend to the other services provided by the clearing house.[104]

886. Private international characterisation and intervention of the clearing house. The law of conflict of laws can shed light on the nature of the intervention of the clearing house in financial market law, and particularly in financial contract law. Professor Roussille is responsible for the analysis according to which multilateral netting is independent of the intervention of a clearing house: it is a liquidation technique that can be found in other branches of private law. Moreover, this author considers that the intervention of a clearing house does not lie in its interposition between the parties, but in the provision of an accounting service, likely to facilitate multilateral clearing by transferring securities and cash, coordinating with the payment system and securities settlement systems, recording transactions in its system, and calculating margins.[105] Moreover, the clearing house will occasionally provide an additional service consisting of what has long been referred to in French law as a 'performance guarantee'.[106] It seems to us that this analysis has not lost its accuracy, but that this second service has now become at least as central, because it is almost systematic. These two services, which correspond to the two identified functions of clearing,[107] may be subject to two different laws: the provision of the accounting service will always be subject to the law of the clearing system as long as the clearing house wishes to continue to benefit from the Finality Directive in order to guarantee payment, whereas the interposition itself, which is independent of it, may see its terms and conditions subject to another law, like any private law transaction.[108] In the case of financial contracts relating to credit risk, such a separation is not only possible, it would seem necessary.

887. Origin and reasons for the separation. There are historical and legal reasons for this separation. From a historical point of view, until the subprime

---

104 *FCM Clearing Regulations*, p. 1.

105 M. Roussille, *La compensation multilatérale*, *op. cit.*

106 On this institution, see T. Bonneau *et al.*,. *Droit financier*, *op. cit.*, no. 1382.

107 See *supra*, para. 904. The comparison cannot be total in that multilateral clearing is not a sum of bilateral clearing and has its own regime; however, it has an identical function: the facilitation of payment. In favour of the qualification of simplified payment processing, see also A.-V. Delozière-Le Fur, *La compensation dite multilatérale*, *op. cit.*

108 A difficulty remains, however, if the designated *lex contractus* does not recognise the singularity of the regime accorded to contracts made through a set-off system, and in particular the finality of the latter. For this reason, it seems to us that the rules of set-off will not designate a contract law that ignores such a regime.

crisis, CDSs were not subject to any clearing offer by a clearing house. Indeed, the singularity of the risk taken linked to the occurrence of a credit event,[109] combined with a lack of fungibility of the contracts and therefore of their liquidity, made them unsuitable for clearing. They were therefore concluded solely over-the-counter.[110] Following the subprime crisis, the legislator nevertheless encouraged clearing houses to find ways of clearing these contracts,[111] while at the same time wanting to be able to monitor the contracts concluded by operators on its territory. The difficulties have been overcome[112] by applying the law of origin of the financial contract relating to a credit risk, while reducing as much as possible the risks arising from this separation,[113] the interpretation of which is left to an arbitration tribunal.[114] This question requires a review of the risk transferred by the credit derivative and the application of US law.

888. We have already observed that when the underlying is the realisation of a credit risk of a reference entity, the risk taken is not similar, and the margining technique will not necessarily be able to reduce the risk transferred.[115] This specificity of the risk transferred is also reflected in the legal framework. In the case of financial contracts involving credit risk, the realisation of the risk depends on the occurrence of a credit event. The latter is a *legal* event, determined

---

109 See *supra*, para. 913.

110 On the conditions of set-off relating to the financial contracts themselves, see *supra*, para. 870, 912

111 See in particular. H. de Vauplane, 'Les propositions du G20 en matière de sécurité sur produits dérivés', *Banque*, January 2009, p. 83; H. Boucheta, 'Compensation des Credit Default Swaps: quels enjeux?', *BJB*, 2009, p. 158, no. 24; and 'Marché des Credit Default Swaps, La régulation est en marche': *Banque*, May 2009, p. 93; A. Couret, H. Le Nabasque *et al.*, *Droit financier*, *op. cit.*, no. 1232.

112 On this aspect, see A. Caillemer du Ferrage and C. Saudo, 'Une chambre de compensation pour les dérivés de crédit', *BJB*, January 2010, pp. 58 et seq.

113 As some authors write: '(a) the content of documents governed by law other than French Law was reduced to the strict minimum necessary; (b) no ISDA master agreement, whose provisions could have conflicted with the provisions of the clearing rules subject to French Law, was put in place between clearing members and LCH SA (with the exception of transactions entered into for hedging purposes in the context of default management); (c) a strict hierarchy of the different documents constituting the clearing rules has been put in place, in order to manage the residual risk of inconsistencies between these documents, and to ensure that in the event of a conflict between several documents, the principles relating to the management of clearing members' defaults by LCH SA,and then the remaining provisions of the *CDS Clearing Rule Book* will prevail over the provisions of the other documents (except in respect of any conflicts relating to the determination of the existence and/or amount of payment and delivery obligations in respect of cleared transactions, in which case the provisions of the documents governed by English Law will prevail to the extent permitted by law).' HCJP Opinion on the legal feasibility of developing a Paris interest rate derivatives clearing offer of 17 October 2017, p. 41.

114 This procedure is referred to in the *CDS Dispute resolution Protocol*, a non-public document, the provisions of which are partly reported by the HCJP Opinion on the legal feasibility of developing a clearing offer for interest rate derivatives in Paris of 17 October 2017, pp. 41–42.

115 See *supra*, para. 913.

differently in each legal order. In other words, if the parties have concluded a financial contract relating to a credit event, the occurrence of the event[116] will not be analysed in the same terms depending on whether it is assessed under French law or English law.[117] However, the legal terms and conditions of this occurrence condition the entire financial contract, and in particular its price, but also, for the clearing house, the terms and conditions for valuing the clearing obligation. This means that if the novation has the effect of changing the *lex contractus* from English law to French law, this change of applicable law may considerably alter the very interest of using a clearing house. As Mr Alban Caillemer du Ferrage has written:

> 'What triggers a payment obligation under a *CDS* is therefore not a statistical variable, the price of an asset, the level of an interest or exchange rate or any objective and observable data, but a legal concept/notion. The question of its intellectual content, its qualification, the case law and doctrine that develop around it is therefore essential to the market since it is around these notions and their interpretation that these instruments are valued. The stability, uniformity and predictability of their interpretation are prerequisites. The *OTC CDS* market is dominated by the use of market documentation published in English and New York law by the *International Swaps and Derivatives Association* (*ISDA*).'[118]

889. The author's observations can nevertheless be nuanced. Firstly, it is as much the intellectual content of English law as its substantial liberalism that is sought by the parties.[119] Thus, English contract law does not prevent the characterisation of the occurrence of the credit event from being subject to a criterion chosen by the parties and, in this case, from referring the occurrence to a decision of the Credit Derivatives Determination Committee.[120] These committees, set up by the ISDA, decide on the occurrence of the credit event, independently of the 'content' of

---

116 That is, a default by the reference entity, its bankruptcy or the restructuring of one of its debts, to which may be added, in certain circumstances, a change in the reference entity itself (e.g. by merger or absorption), see *supra*, paras. 871, 913 et seq.

117 The interpretation of default is, along with payment itself and termination of the contract, one of the three most contentious issues in the English courts. This is notoriously the case with section 2(a)(iii) of the 1992 *ISDA Master Agreement* on counterparty default, and in particular the question of whether the payment obligation of the non-defaulting party is suspended or extinguished upon the occurrence of an event of default by its counterparty, see J. Braithwaite, *The Financial Courts: Adjudicating Disputes in Derivatives Markets*, *op. cit.*

118 A. Caillemer du Ferrage, 'L'impact du Brexit sur les infrastructures de marché', *op. cit.*

119 Recall what Professor M. Audit seemed to express, 'Les dérivés de crédit à l'ombre du contrat sans loi', *op. cit.*, p. 85.

120 Incorporated in the definition of 'credit event' in the clearing rules: 'In respect of any Cleared Transaction, as defined under the terms of such Cleared Transaction incorporating the ISDA Credit Derivatives Definitions.' On these committees, see J. Braithwaite, *The Financial Courts: Adjudicating Disputes in Derivatives Markets*, *op. cit.*, pp. 93 et seq.

the law designated by the contract,[121] even though they have the disadvantage of not having the required independence: their members are interested in the occurrence of the event.[122] The binding force of their opinion is nevertheless only ensured by their recognition in the contract. In other words, it is possible for the law of the contract to impose, as a matter of public policy resulting from a specific regime for financial contracts, the qualification of the occurrence of a credit event. It is in this sense that 'this distancing from state law'[123] is only possible insofar as it is permitted by state law.[124]

---

121 However, one's legal understanding of the question of interpretation (textual, i.e. literal, teleological or taking into account contextual factors) is necessarily that of a certain legal culture: the law then necessarily comes back, but masked - see the examples reported *ibid.*, p. 95. The issue has been decided by ISDA in favour of the contextual approach (ISDA, 'The ISDA Credit Derivatives Determinations Committees', May 2012, available on the ISDA website), which is also the case for English law (see J. Braithwaite, *The Financial Courts: Adjudicating Disputes in Derivatives Markets, op. cit.)* The question of interpretation by the *Determination Committee* has nevertheless been the subject of some controversy in the case of the Greek sovereign default, *ibid.*, p. 96; A. Gelpherm and M. Gulati, 'CDS Zombies' (2012) 13 *European Business Organization Law Review*, pp. 347 et seq.; M. Audit, 'Les dérivés de crédit à l'ombre du contrat sans loi', *op. cit.*, pp. 88–89. The latter author considers that the function of these committees illustrates 'ISDA's project' which would be 'undeniably to allow its contractual model to be used throughout the world, and to avoid that national laws or, above all, decisions of state courts are likely to drive a wedge into this universality, by instilling a certain legal relativity', see M. Audit, 'Les Credit Default Swaps comme miroir des dérives de l'endettement public' in H. Gherari (ed.), *Les dérèglements économiques internationaux: crise du droit ou droit des crises?*, Paris, Pedone, 2014, p. 81 (on this question, see also S. Praicheux, 'Instruments financiers à terme' in *Répertoire de droit des sociétés, op. cit.*, no. 68).
It seems to us that Professor Audit's statement needs to be nuanced. The ISDA project is to draw up contracts whose implementation will minimise litigation, which is always a costly factor for the parties. If the aim is to minimise the interference of the judiciary, the authors of the ISDA conventions are aware that the contracts they draw up will be susceptible to interpretation by a state judge and this is why the selection of the latter is one of the aspects guiding the law applicable to the contract (see *supra*, para. 841). As Professor Wautelet has already observed: 'The interference of the judiciary in the agreements of the parties did not, however, thwart their expectations. The existence of a residual power of control on the part of the judiciary is indeed part of the constraints accepted by the operators. The intervention of the judiciary does not constitute an unforeseeable accident. On the contrary, it is part of the normal course of events', P. Wautelet, 'Réglementation étatique et marchés financiers: entre autonomie et relativité', *op. cit.*, p. 348. See A. Riles, *Collateral Knowledge, op. cit.*, p. 16. On this question, see in particular J. Braithwaite, 'Standard Form Contracts as Transnational Law', *op. cit.*

122 D. Awrey, 'The limits of private ordering within modern financial markets' (2014) 34 *Review of Banking and Financial Law*, pp. 183 et seq., spec. p. 183 and pp. 249 et seq. The composition of these committees, which include individuals representing some of the most exposed institutions, shows the limits of the private ordering model, according to the author.

123 M. Audit, 'Les dérivés de crédit à l'ombre du contrat sans loi', *op. cit.*, p. 90.

124 See A. Riles, *Collateral knowledge, op. cit.*, p. 43, referring to the difficulties of private international law: 'Robert Wai terms these thorny doctrinal problems "touchdown points" in the relationship between global private governance and national law - points which the efforts of private organisations such as ISDA to achieve "liftoff" from national regimes comes to rest on national law itself.' This is undoubtedly what tempers the idea according to

This discussion already shows that the 'autonomy rule' developed from the perspective of the financial contract regime in domestic law cannot be transposed as it stands to conflict of laws. Indeed, if it is possible, and frequent in practice, for the law of the financial contract to be distinct from the law of the underlying, the underlying is likely to influence the choice of the applicable law. The example is all the stronger in that the underlying is not the risk of volatility of an asset subject to its own law, but the occurrence of a credit risk, the characterisation of which is, eventually, also dependent on a state law, even if it is substantially liberal.[125]

Secondly, the model adopted by central clearing within the Union, according to which the clearing member interposes itself between its client and the clearing house, has the consequence that there are always at least two other contracts in contemplation of which the clearing was requested: those binding the two clients and their clearing member reciprocally. However, these contracts have not been novated and are still subject to the same law, that elected by the ISDA model agreement subject to English or American law. This makes it necessary to subject all of these contracts to the same law in order to respect what ultimately constitutes a contractual whole, despite the novation.[126] Here, the plurality of applicable laws would constitute a diriment obstacle to the realisation of the transfer of risk, i.e. the very object of the financial contract.[127] The disjunction between the law applicable to the rules of set-off and the law applicable to the novated obligation has the effect of allowing the latter to be subject to the same law as the one under which it was initially constituted.

---

which, on the one hand, the financial contract could constitute a form of contract without law, including in its renovated version (see M. Audit, 'Les dérivés de crédit à l'ombre du contrat sans loi', *op. cit.*, p. 85) and, on the other hand, that the financial contract could constitute a form of contract without law, including in its renovated version (see M. Audit, 'Les dérivés de crédit à l'ombre du contrat sans loi', *op. cit.*, p. 85) and, on the other hand, the more general one, according to which, as Professor Libchaber writes, the new business contracts seek 'to give the contractual enterprise a specific normative support that escapes any State legal order, while being sufficiently precise to face the course of its existence', R. Libchaber, *Le contrat au XXIe siècle*, Paris, LGDJ, 2020, no. 43. The same author nevertheless considers, not without some paradox, that such a statement 'does not mean, moreover, an absence of choice of law', but that this 'hardly has any consequences' (*ibid.*, note 6). Such a statement seems excessive: even within financial contracts, despite the fact that a model contract has been drawn up by a dedicated professional association which monitors all the decisions on state enforcement of its models, the choice of law appears to be decisive, if only because it conditions the validity of the choice of law clause.

125 It may be added here that the modification of the reference entity, for example by merger or absorption, is likely to affect the derivative.

126 No doubt one can see here an additional limit to the qualification of novation, on which see *supra*, para. 881.

127 See also A. Caillemer du Ferrage, 'L'impact du Brexit sur les infrastructures de marché', *op. cit.* who considers that 'the transactions themselves and their market price would have been intrinsically modified'.

890. Conclusion of the section. This section has shown that, from the point of view of financial contracts, the intervention of the clearing house was decisive since it resulted in the novation of the obligations arising from the contract concluded by the clearing members, regardless of whether the contract was formed by the use of a financial market or over-the-counter.[128] The law of conflict of laws confirms this analysis, applying a new law to the novated obligations. This will often be the law designated by the rules of set-off, with the occasional application of the law of the earlier contract to certain aspects of the new contract. On the other hand, where the financial contract relates to a credit risk, the Clearing rules apply to the novated obligations the law of the contract under which the financial contract was originally made.

SECTION 3. CONTRACTUAL SET-OFF IN INSOLVENCY

891. Contractual netting of financial contracts follows the more general trend of set-off: a mechanism to facilitate payment when the parties are solvent, it becomes a guarantee when one of the parties becomes insolvent, derogating from the principle of prohibition of payments after the opening judgement. Although it is often combined with financial collateral[129] to reduce counterparty risk, contractual netting is in itself the most effective technique for reducing counterparty risk.[130] Determining the law applicable to the set-off when they are solvent is less difficult.

892. Law applicable to the set-off where the parties are solvent. Where the parties have not provided for a law applicable to their netting agreement,[131] and one of the parties intends to take advantage of the statutory set-off, the applicable

[128] See already in this sense, the observations of Professor A.-C. Muller, *Droit des contrats et droit des marchés financiers*, *op. cit.*

[129] The provision of collateral in the context of financial contracts is carried out by means of financial guarantees, whose regime and the resolution of the conflicts of law they give rise to have already been studied, see *supra*, paras. 748 et seq. At most, it can be recalled here that, as a derogation from insolvency law in the name of the preservation of systemic risk, financial collateral is nevertheless subject to the application of the law of resolution. It is therefore not surprising that the netting of financial contracts is subject to an identical international regime when one of the parties becomes insolvent.

[130] EMIR requires parties entering into financial contracts that are not subject to clearing with a clearing house to have 'due diligence [...] procedures and arrangements to measure, monitor and mitigate the operational and credit risk of the counterparty', see Art. 11(1)(b) of EMIR. These techniques include the adoption of netting and collateral, but also the adoption of rules of behaviour, and the institution of 'formalised, robust and resilient procedures' to resolve disputes, monitor price movements and the risk of the financial contract, see Art. 11(1)(a) and (b), and Art. 11(2) of EMIR. The regulation sets out six techniques, on the details of which see A. Gaudemet, 'EMIR 2/5: les techniques d'atténuation des risques', *RDBF*, January 2015, comm. 22.

[131] Or to the provisions on compensation within the framework contract.

law must be determined. Where the obligations to be set off arise from the same contract, or from contracts subject to the same law, the law applicable to the set-off is that of the source of the obligation (*lex creationis*), i.e. the law designated by the contract. When the parties' reciprocal obligations arise from contracts subject to different laws, several solutions have been envisaged: the cumulation of the laws of the two obligations,[132] the application of the *lex fori*,[133] or the law of one of the obligations, *a priori* that of the obligation against which the set-off is invoked. This last possibility is retained by Article 17 of the Rome I Regulation. Applicable when no contractual set-off is provided for,[134] this article favours legal set-off, which is made possible even if one of the laws of the claims to be set off opposes it.[135]

893. With respect to financial contracts, the set-off operates according to the common law of conflict of laws, which depends on the implementation of the contractual set-off: either the set-off is the object of a contract whose sole purpose is the set-off of a part or all of the contractual relations, or the set-off agreement is integrated into a master contract.[136] In the latter case, it is possible to provide for a breakdown of the contract and the application of a separate law

---

132 This was for a long time, among others, the French position, see already H. BATIFFOL, *Les conflits de lois en matière de contrat*, *op. cit.*, no. 250. Professors Pichonnaz and Gullifer explain this position in that it reflects the position of the domestic law of countries where set-off is automatic, *ipso jure*, see P. PICHONNAZ and L. GULLIFER, *Set-off in Arbitration and commercial transactions*, *op. cit.*, no. 4.11. This position was favoured by the Court of Justice under the Rome Convention, see Case C-87/01, *Commission v. CCRD*, ECLI:EU:C:2003:400. On the solutions adopted prior to the entry into force of the Rome I Regulation, see M.-N. JOBARD BACHELIER, 'Obligations', *Répertoire de droit international*, Paris, Dalloz, nos. 70 et seq.; D. PARDOËL, *Les conflits de lois en matière de cession de créances*, *op. cit.*, 'Instruments financiers' in A. TENENBAUM, *Répertoire de droit international*, *op. cit.* no. 188; G. MINNE, 'Les règles de conflit de lois en matière de compensation dans le secteur financier', *Bulletin Droit et Banque*, Apr. 2011, no. 47, spec. nos. 7 et seq.

133 Professors Pichonnaz and Gullifer observe that this position is frequent in *common law* countries, where it can be explained in order to limit the costs of proceedings. It is probably also related, on the one hand, to the procedural nature that set-off may have had for a long time and, on the other hand, to the fact that set-off is often raised during collective proceedings and that the law of the forum then corresponds to the *lex concursus*, see P. PICHONNAZ and L. GULLIFER, *Set-off in Arbitration and Commercial Transactions*, *op. cit.*, nos. 2. 18 et seq.

134 See 'Rome I Regulation: Contractual obligations', in S. FRANCQ, *Répertoire de droit international*, *op. cit.*, no. 179; P. PICHONNAZ and L. GULLIFER, *Set-off in Arbitration and commercial transactions*, *op. cit.*, nos. 4.24-4.26.

135 Inspired by the German concept of set-off by declaration (*ibid.*, no. 4.23), this rule avoids the cumulative application of laws, which could prevent set-off, or the application of the *lex fori*, and the uncertainty that accompanies it. The connecting factor used is consistent with the objective of set-off, which is to facilitate payment under certain conditions. Indeed, payment is facilitated through the application of the law of the contract from which the obligation sought to be paid arises, and compliance with the conditions which it lays down cannot therefore be evaded.

136 G. MINNE, 'Les règles de conflit de lois en matière de compensation dans le secteur financier', *op. cit.*

for the netting agreements alone; in the absence of such a choice, the law of the master agreement will apply. If a netting agreement has been concluded on a stand-alone basis, the law designated in that agreement will apply; in the absence of a choice of law, the absence of a genuine characteristic performance leads to the application of the law of the closest connections, which designates the law of the master agreement.[137] If no netting agreement is provided for, statutory netting will take over since, from a substantive point of view, a regime facilitating netting has been established.[138]

894. The contractual organisation of the netting of financial contracts in case of insolvency. The singularity of the netting of financial contracts is especially appreciated in the case where one of the parties becomes insolvent, because of the mechanisms put in place in financial contracts. These mechanisms were conceived from the perspective of English law, due to its use by the *ISDA* conventions, but were the subject in 2013 of an attempt at substantial harmonisation under the aegis of Unidroit,[139] which adds to the project already developed by *ISDA* for national legislators.[140] In English law, French 'compensation' corresponds to the set-off.[141] It can take different forms. When it is contractual in origin, it is referred to as netting and corresponds, according to English academics, to 'the process that replaces countervailing obligations between contracting parties with a single net sum'.[142] Several forms of netting can be distinguished.

---

137 *Ibid.*, no. 41; Comp. J. Gavriloff, *Les méthodes du conflit de lois à l'épreuve du produit dérivé*, *op. cit.*, no. 545, who considers that without a choice of law, it is very difficult to designate a law applicable to the netting contract.

138 On which see *infra*, para. 940.

139 Institute for the Unification of Private Law, *Principles on the Applicability of Termination-Compensation Clauses*, Rome, 2013. The principles do not contain conflict of laws rules, due to a flip-flop of the negotiators, see P. Paech, 'Close-out netting, Insolvency and Conflict of Laws', *op. cit.*, pp. 419–420.

140 This is the framework for a significant number of legal orders. On ISDA's efforts to bring its model to fruition, see J. Braithwaite, *The Financial Courts: Adjudicating Disputes in Derivatives Markets*, *op. cit.*, p. 28; A. Riles, *Collateral Knowledge*, *op. cit.*, p. 188 et seq.

141 Professors Pichonnaz and Gullifer define *set-off* as follows: 'A mode of discharging the obligations of the debtor and the creditor towards one another, as far as they are coextensive, if the requirements of the applicable law are fulfilled.' P. Pichonnaz and L. Gullifer, *Set-off in Arbitration and commercial transactions*, *op. cit.*
The assertion that 'there is no equivalent in English law to our general concept of "netting"', A. Caillemer du Ferrage, 'Le rêve familier du global netting à la française', *op. cit.*, no. 3, must be tempered.

142 M. Bridge and J. Braithwaite, 'Private Law and Financial Crisis', *op. cit.* Recall the definition given by P. Pichonnaz and L. Gullifer, *Set-off in Arbitration and commercial transactions*, *op. cit.*, no. 2.12: 'several open accounts are joined into one consolidated account.' The latter authors specify that *netting* 'is not a legal term' (*ibid.*). Indeed, there are specificities distinguishing *close-out netting* from *set-off* (P. Wood, *Set-off and netting, Derivatives, Clearing system*, *op. cit.*, nos. 1-003 et seq.; R. Goode, *Principles of corporate insolvency law*, 4th ed., London, Sweet&Maxwell, 2011, no. 9-09; O. Boger, 'Close-out

The first is settlement netting,[143] sometimes referred to as set-off arrangements or reciprocal netting agreements.[144] The latter, provided for in section 2(c) of the *ISDA Master Agreement*, is defined by the Resolution Directive as 'an arrangement under which two or more claims or obligations owed between the institution under resolution and a counterparty can be set off against each other'.[145] The function of settlement netting is to reduce settlement risk,[146] to improve its efficiency, to allow for a greater volume of transactions and to reduce the pressure on market infrastructures.[147]

The second is called default netting or close-out netting, which is usually translated as termination-netting or netting agreement.[148] It is most often the form taken by the set-off in the event of certain events, including the insolvency of one of the parties.[149] It is now[150] defined by the Resolution Directive:

> 'An arrangement under which a number of claims or obligations can be converted into a single net claim, including close-out netting arrangements under which, on the occurrence of an enforcement event (however or wherever defined) the

netting provisions in private international law and international insolvency law (Part I)', *op. cit.*, pp. 235–236), which correspond to the differences between the close-out netting mechanism and netting in French law.

143 When the financial contract provides for the delivery of fungible underlyings, settlement netting takes the form of delivery netting.

144 Name used in Art. 2(98) of the Resolution Directive.

145 Art. 2(99) of the Resolution Directive. On this form of *netting*, see M. Bridge and J. Braithwaite, 'Private Law and Financial Crisis', *op. cit.*, p. 389 and in particular the English judgment *Pioneer Freight Futures company Ltd* (2011) EWHC 1888 (Comm).

146 Also called 'Herstatt risk', after the bankruptcy of the eponymous bank, see *supra*, para. 97.

147 See in this sense J. Benjamin, *Financial Law*, Oxford, OUP, 2007, no. 45 quoted by M. Bridge and J. Braithwaite, 'Private Law and Financial Crisis', *op. cit.*, p. 390.

148 See in particular Art. 2(98) of the Resolution Directive, which therefore distinguishes it from the notion of reciprocal netting agreements for *settlement netting*. Indeed, *close-out netting* is unique in that it allows the extinguishment of obligations arising from transactions of a different nature, of which only the negative balance will be the subject of a payment. See also in this sense, P. Wautelet, 'Réglementation étatique et marchés financiers: entre autonomie et relativité', *op. cit.*, p. 344, and the English decision *Commissioners for Her Majesty's revenue & Customs v Enron Europe Ltd* (2006) EWHC 824 (Ch), (2006) BCC 953, no. 20.

149 See in this sense M. Bridge and J. Braithwaite, 'Private Law and Financial Crisis', *op. cit.*, p. 390; P. Pichonnaz and L. Gullifer, *Set-off in Arbitration and commercial transactions*, *op. cit.* O. Boger, 'Close-out netting provisions in private international law and international insolvency law (Part II)', *op. cit.* Some authors consider in the same sense that 'if one were trying in two words the nature of close-out netting, "extended" set-off would probably be an adequate term', P. Paech, 'Close-out netting, Insolvency and Conflict of Laws', *op. cit.* In French doctrine, see A. Caillemer du Ferrage, 'Le rêve familier du global netting à la française', *Banque et Droit*, September-October 2001, no. 79, p. 3.
However, the credit event must be distinguished from other events that may cause the termination of the contract ('Termination event'), as they do not give access to the same contractual regime, see J. Braithwaite, 'Standard Form Contracts as Transnational Law', *op. cit.*

150 On the origin of *netting*, see A. Riles, *Collateral knowledge*, *op. cit.*

obligations of the parties are accelerated so as to become immediately due or are terminated, and in either case are converted into or replaced by a single net claim.'[151]

This description of the close-out netting mechanism, which corresponds to the one traditionally used in English law,[152] gives it the function of reducing 'the financial exposures arising from outstanding contracts where one of the parties to those contracts becomes insolvent before their maturity'.[153] This function is particularly crucial insofar as the parties to financial contracts do not simply participate in an isolated transaction, but conclude financial contracts with a multitude of operators.[154] As an author points out, from the point of view of French law, even if it is most often translated by the notion of '*résiliation-compensation*', the close-out netting mechanism is less similar to set-off than to a contract termination clause, associated with a contractual indemnification clause.[155] It is only at a later stage that the balance resulting from this compensation will be extinguished, as far as possible, by offsetting, through the global netting mechanism, which is most often included in the

---

151 Art. 2(1)(98) of the Resolution Directive. Comp. the definition given by the *Unidroit Principles* (*Unidroit Principles*, cit., spec. principle 2, p. 25): 'A "termination-compensation clause" means a contractual clause on the basis of which, upon the occurrence of an event predefined in the clause concerning one party to the contract, the obligations of the parties to each other which are covered by the clause, whether or not they are due at that time, shall, automatically or by choice of a party, be reduced to, or replaced by, a single net obligation, whether by novation, termination or otherwise, representing the aggregate value of the combined obligations, which is then due from one party to the other party.'

152 Indeed, the English doctrine describes *close-out netting* as follows: 'This is where obligations, one or both of which may not be for the payment of money, and one or both of which may be executory on a particular trigger such as default or insolvency, are valued, accelerated, and rescinded. They are either then replaced by obligations to pay their monetary value, which are set off against each other so that only the balance is payable, or by a single new obligation calculated as the net balance is due. All other obligations are extinguished. Such close-out netting could be considered a conditional anticipatory agreement to set-off if set-off operates automatically, which is normally the case', P. Pichonnaz and L. Gullifer, *Set-off in Arbitration and commercial transactions*, *op. cit.*, P. Wood, *Set-off and netting, Derivatives, Clearing system*, *op. cit.*, no. 1-005.
In English insolvency law, however, the validity of *close-out netting* was not originally established by statutory rules, but by case law, see in this sense *Lomas v JFB Firth Rixson* (2012) EWCA 419, see O. Boger, 'Close-out netting provisions in private international law and international insolvency law (Part II)', *op. cit.*, p. 534; J. Braithwaite, *The Financial Courts: Adjudicating Disputes in Derivatives Markets*, *op. cit.*

153 A. Caillemer du Ferrage, 'Le rêve familier du global netting à la française', *op. cit.*. See also in this sense, Model Law on Netting and ISDA Guide 2018 no. 1.2.

154 P. Wautelet, 'Réglementation étatique et marchés financiers: entre autonomie et relativité', *op. cit.*

155 The termination results in a 'close-out amount' that allows for compensation. This perception of *close-out netting* is internationally shared, see for example from the Japanese point of view, A. Riles, *Collateral knowledge*, *op. cit.*, p. 209. On the calculation of compensation, see P. Cornut St-Pierre, *La fabrique juridique des swaps*, *op. cit.*, pp. 117–119 and pp. 212 et seq.

framework contract. This is notably the case with ISDA master agreements,[156] for which netting has been described as the 'ethos'.[157]

895. It is through this last mechanism that the substantive regime applicable to the netting of financial contracts interferes with the insolvency regime. Indeed, the close-out netting clause allows its beneficiaries to escape not only the prohibition of payments of the insolvent party, but above all the competition of creditors.[158] While it should be noted that the netting, even if it is global, will not necessarily suffice to extinguish all financial obligations,[159] it will nevertheless allow the extinction of the essential part of the reciprocal claims,[160] the remainder being able to be paid by the assets given as collateral.[161] This is probably why it is the most widely used mechanism in all financial transactions.[162] This means that the conflict of laws rules instituted in favour of set-off in the case of insolvency are truly determining. However, they are heterogeneous and give rise to divergent interpretations.

Some authors believe that the termination-compensation mechanism should be subject to the *lex contractus* in order to respect the parties' expectations.[163] It seems to us that this statement is incorrect and leads to a dead end. Indeed, the mechanism of close-out netting, if it is contractual in its origin, is triggered

---

156 On the different stages of the termination-compensation mechanism, see lastly R. Dambre, *Les contrats financiers sur actions*, *op. cit.*, nos. 143 et seq.

157 *Pioneer Frreight Futures Company Ltd v. TMT Asia Ltd* (2011) EWHC 1888 (Comm), no. 44. The same judgment considers that this is the 'commercial purpose' of the contract.

158 As Professors Bridge and Braithwaite put it perfectly: 'In practice, close-out netting means that insolvency practitioners cannot cherry-pick favourable transactions from the bundle of deals that may be open under the parties' Master Agreement. It also means that the Non-defaulting Party avoids having to pay into the insolvent's estate for out-of-the-money transactions, while having to prove for the in-the-money transactions as an unsecured creditor', M. Bridge and J. Braithwaite, 'Private Law and Financial Crisis', *op. cit.*

159 It is true that the appropriation of the assets given through the financial collateral will enable the creditor to get paid. However, this will not always be enough to extinguish the claim resulting from the balance of the netting. In this case, the creditor will have to declare his residual claim to the collective proceedings and will find himself subject to the law of the contest.

160 The Bank for International Settlements estimates that parties' mutual exposure is reduced by 80%, see Bank for International Settlements, 'OTC Derivatives Statistics at End-June 2020', 9 November 2020.

161 A. Riles, *Collateral Knowledge*, *op. cit.*, p. 99.

162 Both by central banks, central counterparties and any party to a financial contract. As Mr Paech writes: 'It is probably fair to say that close-out netting is *the* commercial law mechanism underlying the major part of modern wholesale financial transactions, together with collateralization', P. Paech, 'Close-out netting, Insolvency and Conflict of Laws', *op. cit.*, p. 427. See also in this sense M. Bridge and J.P. Braithwaite, 'Private Law and Financial Crisis' (2013) *Journal of Corporate Law Studies*, pp. 361 et seq., spec. p. 364: 'Given the absence of collection and enforcement cost, it is even more effective than proprietary security in the event of the obligor's insolvency.'

163 See e.g. in this sense O. Boger, 'Close-out netting provisions in private international law and international insolvency law (Part II)' (2013) *Uniform Law Review*, p. 560.

mainly when the counterparty becomes insolvent, and is therefore not part of the *lex contractus*, but of the insolvency. We will try to show here that international harmonisation would be better ensured by applying the law of insolvency, which is the centre of gravity of the relationship in question, and which alone has the right to decide on the limits of the mechanism of close-out netting. This will be demonstrated by first looking at the way in which the crowding-out of the beneficiaries of close-out netting clauses is currently organised (§ 1), before observing its limits (§ 2).

§ 1. THE CROWDING-OUT OF THE COMPETITION

The protection of the mechanism of close-out netting is the work of the substantive law of insolvency (I). It is reinforced, in terms of conflict, by a set of rules favourable to the exercise of set-off (II).

I. Substantive Protection

896. The contractual netting of financial contracts is subject to substantial protection in the event of insolvency of one of the parties. This protection was instituted by Article 7 of the Financial Collateral Directive[164] and transposed into Articles L. 211-36 et seq. of the Monetary and Financial Code.[165] The French regime is based on the concept of 'financial obligation', which is derived from the Financial Collateral Directive and is not defined by the Monetary and Financial Code.[166] The qualification of a financial obligation nevertheless appears to depend on two criteria listed in Article L. 211-36 of the Monetary and Financial Code, the first relating to the contract from which the obligation arises, the second to the quality of the parties to the contract. Indeed, obligations arising from 'any contract giving rise to a cash settlement or delivery of financial instruments or goods represented by a storage receipt ["*reçu d'entreposage*"]',[167]

164 This states: 'Member States shall ensure that a close-out netting clause can produce its effects in the manner it provides:
(a) notwithstanding the commencement or continuation of winding-up proceedings or reorganisation measures in respect of the collateral provider and the collateral taker or either of them;
(b) notwithstanding any purported assignment, seizure, judicial or otherwise, or other disposition of or in respect of the rights concerned.'

165 On this transposition, see A. Couret, H. Le Nabasque *et al.*, *Droit financier*, *op. cit.*

166 'Garanties Financières' in D. Robine and S. Praicheux, *Etudes Joly Bourse*, *op. cit.*, nos. 28 et seq.

167 Art. L. 211-36(I)(2°) of the Monetary and Financial Code.

and concluded by parties of which at least one is a financial or similar entity,[168] can be qualified as financial obligations. These two aspects are fundamental as they constitute the conditions under which the privilege of the close-out netting is granted. They may differ from one legal order to another.[169] Once the qualification of a financial obligation has been established, a particular regime is attached to the contract from which it arises, and to the guarantees to which it may be subject.[170] This regime provides in particular for the possibility of close-out netting,[171] its enforceability to third parties[172] and, above all, immunity from collective proceedings. Article L. 211-40 of the Monetary and Financial Code states that:

> 'The provisions of Book VI of the Commercial Code [i. e. insolvency law], or those governing any equivalent judicial or amicable proceedings initiated on the basis of foreign law, shall not preclude the application of the provisions of this Section.'.[173]

---

168 More specifically, according to Art. L. 211-36(I)(1°) of the Monetary and Financial Code, 'a credit institution, a finance company, an investment service provider other than a portfolio management company, a public institution, a local authority, an institution, a person or entity benefiting from the provisions of Article L. 531-2 of the Monetary and Financial Code, a clearing house, a non-resident institution with a comparable status, an international financial organisation or body of which France or the European Union is a member'. This article contains the two stages of the close-out netting process identified by Mr Caillemer du Ferrage, see *supra*, para. 896.

169 Report, *supra*, para. 715.

170 In French law, the qualification of set-off as financial collateral is debated. Thus, some authors consider that 'set-off is a financial guarantee [...] without being a "guarantee of financial obligations" as referred to in Article L. 211-38 of the Monetary and Financial Code' (A. Couret, H. Le Nabasque *et al.*, *Droit financier*, *op. cit.*, no. 1512. Others emphasize 'that, on the one hand, from a formal point of view, set-off does not appear among the securities dealt with by the Civil Code, and that, on the other hand, although set-off undeniably has a guarantee effect, it does not constitute a security because it does not result in the satisfaction of the creditor by the realization of the asset [which would be, in this case, a claim] assigned as a guarantee by the debtor, but rather by the liquidation of the debt without payment of the debt itself. Moreover, Article 2(1)(a) of the Financial Collateral Directive envisages only two categories of financial collateral: security interests based on a transfer of ownership, and other collateral [pledges in particular]', see 'Garanties Financières' in D. Robine and S. Praicheux, *Etudes Joly Bourse*, *op. cit.*, no. 20.

171 Art. L. 211-36-1(I) of the Monetary and Financial Code: 'Agreements relating to the financial obligations referred to in Article L. 211-36 may be terminated, and the debts and claims relating thereto may be set off between all parties. The parties may provide for the establishment of a single balance, whether these financial obligations are governed by one or more agreements or master agreements.'

172 Art. L. 236-36-1(2°) of the Monetary and Financial Code.

173 There are other possible legislative techniques to enable *close-out netting to* be carried out in the event of insolvency and to become a 'netting-friendly' legal system: German law provides that *netting* benefits from the legal set-off that is automatically applicable when insolvency proceedings are opened, Belgian law provides for the inapplicability of certain principles of insolvency proceedings to the close-out netting mechanism, while English law, which is comparable to French law, simply declares close-out netting *enforceable* in spite of the opening of insolvency proceedings, see P. Paech, 'Close-out netting, Insolvency and Conflict of Laws', *op. cit.*, p. 430. The particularity of the English model is that the protection

This provision has two meanings. Firstly, where the collective proceedings are opened in France, i.e. where the insolvent party has its centre of main interests in France. This article limits the scope of the collective proceedings and excludes financial contracts. As a result, the regime of set-off under ordinary law, applicable when the parties are *in bonis*, is identical when one of the parties is subject to collective proceedings. In French law, the substantial protection therefore consists in extending the favourable regime known when the parties are solvent to the case where one of them becomes insolvent.[174] Secondly, the awkward wording of Article L. 211-40 of the Monetary and Financial Code seems to indicate its application to foreign collective proceedings. In fact, it should be understood that, in the event that the foreign law designates French law as applicable to the close-out netting mechanism under the law of the contract, Article L. 211-40 of the Monetary and Financial Code also provides for the application of Articles L. 211-38 et seq.

This gloss of Article L. 211-40 of the Monetary and Financial Code shows the profound ambiguity of the law applicable to the set-off of financial contracts in the event of insolvency, which seems to apply both under the *lex concursus* of one of the parties to the contract and under the *lex contractus* of the financial contract itself. This uncertainty is explained by the applicable conflict rules.

II. The Applicable Conflict Rules

Parties to financial contracts, when they become insolvent, may be subject to different instruments depending on their status. Indeed, the Insolvency Regulation is not applicable to credit institutions, investment firms, insurance companies and UCITS.[175] Credit institutions and certain investment firms are covered by the Winding up Directive, while insurance undertakings are covered by the Solvency II Directive.[176]

---

regime for *close-out netting* is based on case law. For the American model, see J.-B. Mojuyé, *Le droit des produits dérivés financiers (Swaps, Options, Futures...) en France et aux États-Unis*, Paris, LGDJ, 2005, nos. 1151 et seq.; see also the American trace and criticisms of this protection, P. Cornut St-Pierre, *La fabrique juridique des swaps*, *op. cit.* For an overview of most countries that have introduced *netting*, see P. Wood, *Set-off and netting, Derivatives, Clearing system*, *op. cit.*; pp. 140 et seq.

174 As Mr Gaudemet has written: 'The law of enforcement procedures, the law of insolvency procedures and the law of collateral interests were set aside when they were in the way', A. Gaudemet, *Les dérivés*, *op. cit.*, no. 513.

175 Art. 1(2) of the Insolvency Regulation.

176 This means that UCITS and investment companies not covered by the Winding up Directive are subject to French common international insolvency law (see T. Mastrullo, 'Entreprises en difficulté: droit international et européen' in, *Répertoire de droit des sociétés*, Paris, Dalloz, 2018, no. 249; P. Paech, 'Close-out netting, Insolvency and Conflict of Laws', *op. cit.*, pp. 436–437). We will only look at the European rules here, as they are likely to influence French case law solutions, because as Professors Audit and d'Avout write about the

897. The law applicable to set-off in the Insolvency Regulation. Article 7(2) of the Insolvency Regulation provides for the application of the *lex concursus* to 'the conditions for the effectiveness of the set-off', to 'the rights of creditors who have been partially satisfied after the opening of the insolvency proceedings by virtue of a right in rem or by the effect of a set-off', as well as to 'the rules relating to the nullity, annulment or unenforceability of legal acts detrimental to the general body of creditors'.[177] This application of the principle is subject to two exceptions designed to facilitate set-off. The first is not specific to offsetting and consists in the case where the debtor has an establishment in another Member State whose law is more favourable to offsetting, to request the opening of secondary proceedings in that State. In this case, Article 28 of the Regulation provides that 'the law applicable to the secondary insolvency proceedings shall be that of the Member State within the territory of which the secondary insolvency proceedings are opened'.[178] The second exception is provided for in Article 9(1) of the Regulation which states:

> 'The opening of insolvency proceedings shall not affect the right of creditors to demand the set-off of their claims against the claims of a debtor, where such a set-off is permitted by the law applicable to the insolvent debtor's claim.'[179]

898. This provision makes the Insolvency Regulation an even more favourable instrument for set-off than the Rome I Regulation is for legal set-off, since in the event of insolvency, set-off is permitted as long as it is made possible by one of the two laws involved, that of the party in collective proceedings, or that of

Insolvency Regulation: 'The solutions it introduces, which are more precise and modern, are undoubtedly bound to influence common law in the field that is still its own', B. Audit and L. d'Avout, *Droit international privé*, *op. cit.*, no. 1247.

177 Respectively Art. 7(2)(d)(i) and (m) of the Insolvency Regulation.

178 Already observing this possibility, F. Mélin, 'La loi applicable à la compensation dans les procédures communautaires d'insolvabilité', *JDI*, 2007, var. 4, no. 15; P. Pichonnaz and L. Gullifer, *Set-off in Arbitration and commercial transactions*, *op. cit.*, no. 4.93.

179 The rule thus formulated has been qualified by some authors as a 'rule of substantial favour', which would only take into consideration the law of the claim (see D. Bureau, 'La fin d'un îlot de résistance: le règlement du Conseil relatif aux procédures d'insolvabilité', *RCDIP*, 2002, 613; B. Audit and L. d'Avout, *Droit international privé*, *op. cit.*, no. 1283). Nevertheless, it seems that here the concepts of taking into account and applying a foreign law lead to identical results (as is the case in other areas, see *supra*, para. 554; 891). The Virgos-Schmidt report itself argues in conflicting terms about this rule, see Report on the Insolvency Convention (1996), No 108. This is why, as Mr Mélin writes, 'if such an approach is attractive on the theoretical level, its subtlety is perhaps excessive, so that it would probably be preferable to retain that it is up to the law applicable to the debtor's claim to decide on the possibility or impossibility of the set-off', F. Mélin, 'La loi applicable à la compensation dans les procédures communautaires d'insolvabilité', *op. cit.*, no. 18. In the same sense, J. Gavriloff, *Les méthodes du conflit de lois à l'épreuve du produit dérivé*, *op. cit.*

the disputed claim.[180] The Solvency II Directive also contains a conflict rule in Article 288[181] which states:

> 'The opening of reorganisation measures or winding-up proceedings shall not affect the right of creditors to demand the set-off of their claims against the claims of the insurance undertaking, where such a set-off is permitted by the law applicable to the claim of the insurance undertaking.'

This rule can be likened to the mechanism of Article 9, 1 of the Insolvency Regulation[182]: either the law of the insolvency allows set-off, in which case there is no difficulty, or it does not, in which case the law designated by the claim may apply to allow set-off. Finally, the Winding up Directive contains two rules on netting, the first in Article 23, which is identical to the one used in the Insolvency Regulation and the Solvency II Directive, and the second in Article 25,[183] which states:

> 'Without prejudice to Articles 68 and 71 of Directive 2014/59/EU, netting agreements shall be governed exclusively by the law applicable to the contract governing such agreements.'

In the English version, the notion of '*accord de compensation*' in this Article 25 is translated as 'netting' whereas the '*compensation*' referred to in Article 23 is translated as 'set-off'. The rule is therefore different from that of the Insolvency Regulation and appears to be both more precise and more favourable than the insolvency law. More precise, because it designates exactly the law designated

---

180 See clearly in this sense Recital 70 of the recast Insolvency Regulation. In a way, we find ourselves in the opposite situation to that of the cumulation of applicable laws, since here it is sufficient for one of the two laws in question to be favourable to the set-off for it to take place.
This rule is often justified on the grounds that the opposite solution would thwart the parties' expectations (see, among others, G. Minne, 'Les règles de conflit de lois en matière de compensation dans le secteur financier', *op. cit.*, no. 51) and would oppose the guarantee function that netting would play in an international (*ibid.*, and the author quotes in this sense M. Virgòs and F. Garcimartín, *The European Insolvency Regulation: Law and Practice*, Kluwer Law International, 2004, no. 179). The argument is not convincing. The law of insolvency is foreseeable for the parties, since it will most often be the statutory registered of, and it is quite possible for the parties to foresee that in the event of the insolvency of the other party, the set-off will be governed by this law, which is the only one capable of governing the contest and therefore the only one likely to add conditions to the set-off. If the registered office of the other party changes, it is sufficient to provide for this in the contract and to include a revision clause in the contract.

181 This article is a repeat of the former Art. 22 of Directive 2001/17 of the European Parliament and of the Council of 19 March 2001 on the reorganisation and winding-up of insurance undertakings and transposed into Art. L. 326-25 of the Insurance Code.

182 From which it also borrows the limit on prejudicial acts, see Art. 288(2) of the Solvency II Directive.

183 Transposed in Arts. L. 613-31-5(4°) and L. 613-31-6 of the Monetary and Financial Code.

by the netting agreements. More favourable, because Article 25 of the Winding up Directive does not contain a reservation allowing acts detrimental to creditors, including those subject to foreign law, to be annulled under the nullity of the suspect period.[184] However, these conflict rules in Article 9(1) of the Insolvency Regulation, Articles 23 and 25 of the Winding up Directive and Article 288 of the Solvency II Directive are all ambiguous as to which rules they refer to.[185]

899. The designated law. The first uncertainty is whether Article 9(1) of the Insolvency Regulation is applicable to the close-out netting mechanism. The argument in favour of its non-application lies in the existence of a specific rule on *close-out netting* within the Winding up Directive, which is not the case of the Insolvency Regulation.[186] Some authors deduce that the mechanism would escape the Insolvency Regulation and be governed by the Rome I Regulation. This argument must be rejected. The existence of a specific rule in the Winding up Directive is not sufficient to exclude the close-out netting mechanism from the scope of Article 9(1), which must be understood in the light of the purpose of the Insolvency Regulation itself and of the institution at issue. Since the purpose of the latter is ultimately to offset claims arising from contracts where one of the parties is insolvent, there is no doubt that the mechanism of close-out netting falls within the scope of Article 9(1) of the Insolvency Regulation.[187] Above all, the mechanism of close-out netting, if it does not fall within the scope of Article 9(1) of the Insolvency Regulation, would risk being subject not to the *lex contractus*, but to the *lex concursus* in respect of ongoing contracts,[188] which

---

184 On these rules, see *infra*, para. 955. It is true that, under this article, the creditor will not be able to rely on the law of the insolvency if it is more favourable to the set-off, but the parties will have already chosen the law that is more favourable to the effectiveness of the set-off in the collective proceedings. The rule does not, however, mean that the *lex fori concursus* is set aside, as it remains competent for the purpose of qualification (see already in this sense A. Caillemer du Ferrage, 'Close-out netting and international bankruptcy', *RDBF*, 2007, no. 1, p. 37, spec. no. 15). In particular, the *lex concursus* may disqualify a close-out netting mechanism that is not concluded between entities that are entitled to do so (See also P. Paech, 'Close-out netting, Insolvency and Conflict of Laws', *op. cit.*, p. 457, note 127).

185 See already in this sense, the comments of F. Mélin, 'La loi applicable à la compensation dans les procédures communautaires d'insolvabilité', *op. cit.*, nos. 23 et seq.

186 A. Caillemer du Ferrage, 'Close-out netting and international bankruptcy', *op. cit.*, no. 12; O. Boger, 'Close-out netting provisions in private international law and international insolvency law (Part I)', *op. cit.*, no. 260 and the foreign law references cited in note 155.

187 This solution seems all the more certain as the Commission's proposal to insert a special article in the Insolvency Regulation applying the law of the contract in the manner of the Winding up Directive was precisely rejected, see Art 6a, European Commission, *Proposal for a European Regulation of the European Parliament and of the Council amending Council Regulation (EC) No 1346/2000 on insolvency proceedings*, 12 December 2012, COM (2012) 744 final.

188 F. Garcimartin, 'The review of the insolvency regulation: Hybrid Procedures and Other Issues' (2011) *International Insolvency Law Review*, pp. 321 et seq.

would then easily contradict the very purpose of the termination-compensation mechanism.

The second uncertainty relates to the question of whether, in the case of a choice of law in a netting agreement, the rule in Article 9(1) refers to the law of the netting agreement, or whether it refers to the law of the claim of the debtor who is the object of the netting. Mr Mélin considers that the formula of 'the law applicable to the claim of the insolvent debtor' in Article 9(1) 'does not accord with the proposal to take into account the law governing the set-off agreement'.[189] The statement is correct, but should be qualified in that it leads to a paradoxical solution which is to thwart the expectations of the parties who have made a choice of law for their contractual set-off agreement, even though the rule in Article 9(1) was designed to respect the parties' expectations. It therefore seems preferable to consider that Article 9(1), when applied to a contractual netting, designates the law provided for in the netting agreement.[190]

900. The rules designated by Article 9, 1 of the Regulation. Article 9(1) of the Insolvency Regulation contains another ambiguity insofar as two interpretations are possible as to the designation of the rules of 'the law applicable to the claim of the insolvent debtor'. Indeed, unless there is a specific regime, it may be the law of the general system of obligations or the law of collective proceedings.

In favour of the application of contract law, i.e. the law of set-off when the parties are *in bonis*, it can be considered that the 'law applicable to the claim of the insolvent debtor' of Article 9(1) is the *lex contractus* in which the set-off is made, designated by the rules of the Rome I Regulation, and that this regulation has as its domain contract law. This interpretation is the one adopted by the English ISDA Council[191] in the context, analogous here, of a reorganisation or liquidation procedure of a credit institution. The latter considers:

> 'In the event of an *ISDA* master netting agreement governed by English law between a solvent counterparty and a credit institution subject to insolvency proceedings in a Member State of the European Economic Area other than the United Kingdom, English law would apply to the enforcement of that master netting agreement,

189 *Ibid.*, no. 28.

190 Recital 70 of the Insolvency Regulation. This is also the meaning of the interpretation of the Virgos-Schmidt report: 'That in the case of an agreement on the contractual set-off of various claims between two parties, the law of the Contracting State applicable to that agreement will govern the set-off of claims covered by the agreement and arising prior to the commencement of the insolvency proceedings', Report on the Insolvency Proceedings Convention (1996), No 16. This report accompanied the 1996 Insolvency Convention, from which the Insolvency Regulation is largely derived. See also in this sense, Mr Virgos Soriano and F. Garcimartin Alférez quoted by F. Mélin, 'La loi applicable à la compensation dans les procédures communautaires d'insolvabilité', *op. cit.*

191 Allen & Overy is the 'main representative of ISDA for all its European business', see P. Cornut St-Pierre, *La fabrique juridique des swap*, *op. cit.*, p. 103.

without regard to the insolvency law of the home Member State. Since it is not possible under the Winding up Directive to open insolvency proceedings in the UK in respect of a European credit institution which is subject to insolvency proceedings in another Member State, English insolvency law would not apply to the question of the enforcement of the master close-out netting agreement, which would instead be governed by other principles of English law, principally English contract law.'[192]

901. These arguments are not convincing. Firstly, they are based on the idea that English substantive insolvency law is inseparable from its application by the English court, and that it cannot be applied by another court, even though it has jurisdiction over insolvency. However, in this case, as in the more general case of the *lex concursus*,[193] it is necessary to distinguish the international jurisdiction of the court (the *forum concursus*) from the law applicable to the guarantees if this were to differ from that of the *lex concursus*.[194] In this sense, the argument relating to the particularity of the Winding up Directive, which would not allow the institution of a secondary procedure, does not appear to be relevant, since the applicability of the rules can be dissociated from the competent forum.[195] Secondly, the function of the designation of English law in the Netting Agreement is not to grant the English legal system any jurisdiction over the insolvency proceedings, but to identify the category within which the applicable rules fall.[196] The consequences of the function of netting as a guarantee when one of the

---

192 Allen & Overy, 'Validity and Enforceability under English Law of Close-Out Netting under the 2002, 1992 and 1987 ISDA Master Agreement', 12 December 2011, cited by A. Gaudemet, 'Close-out netting – Proposal for a Resolution Directive: an opportunity to do away with Articles 25 and 26 of the Directive of 4 April 2001 on the reorganisation and winding-up of credit institutions', *RDBF*, May 2013, comm. 108. The author seems to agree with this view. See already in this sense, A. Caillemer du Ferrage, 'Close-out netting and international bankruptcy', *op. cit.*, no. 16.
In the same sense, a French specialist had already considered that 'it seems that since English law has no vocation to govern the bankruptcy of these French entities and because the DALEC (the Winding up Directive), contrary to the European Regulation, even prohibits the opening of secondary proceedings in another Member State, it is the general principles of English contractual law that should determine the conditions of opposability', A. Caillemer du Ferrage, 'Close-out netting and international bankruptcy', *op. cit.*, no. 16.

193 On the distinction between the applicable law and the competent court in insolvency matters, see *supra* no. 758 and *infra* no. 956.

194 The statement appears all the more inaccurate as English law provides for cases where the English judge is obliged to apply foreign insolvency law, see for example section 426 of the Insolvency Act, designed by the British legal system so that its courts can assist the courts of its colonial empire, see O. Boger, 'Close-out netting provisions in private international law and international insolvency law (Part II)', *op. cit.*, p. 536. On this question of the relationship between *forum* and *jus* in insolvency law, see *supra*, para. 758 and *infra*, para. 956.

195 See on this issue our comments *supra*, para. 758.

196 See already in this sense, P. Wood, *Set-off and netting, Derivatives, Clearing system, op. cit.*, no. 6-015.

parties is insolvent must be drawn here:[197] the centre of gravity of netting shifts from the law of the contract to the law of the insolvency.[198] It may be considered that once the law is designated by Article 9, it is up to that law to designate the body of rules applicable to the situation. However, it is at least logical that the possible designation of a law other than that of the debtor's seat should have as its object, within this foreign law, the substantive rules relating to insolvency rather than those arising from the general law.[199]

Moreover, the reasoning that refers to the ordinary law leads to extending the benefit of the favour to all cases of set-off, which can be invoked with much greater ease since the set-off of solvent parties is easier to invoke outside the context of collective proceedings.[200] These arguments explain why this interpretation was favoured by the circular on the entry into force of Regulation (EC) No 1346/2000 of 29 May 2000 on insolvency proceedings, which states that 'the term "applicable law" refers to the insolvency law of the State whose

---

197 Explicitly mentioned by Recital 70 of the Insolvency Regulation.

198 See also P. Paech, 'Close-out netting, Insolvency and Conflict of Laws', *op. cit.*, p. 420: 'Enforceability of close-out netting is primarily a matter of insolvency law.'

199 Since one of the parties is insolvent, it is difficult to see why the latter rules should not be designated, even though they were designed precisely for such cases. See in this sense, O. Boger, 'Close-out netting provisions in private international law and international insolvency law (Part I)' (2013) *Uniform Law Review*, p. 256, and the numerous references in this sense in footnote 139; recall the already known difficulty when the centre of the debtor's main interests does not correspond to the statutory seat, see in particular Case C-594/14, *Kornhaas*, ECLI:EU:C:2015:806.
Some confusion is undoubtedly created in this respect by the preferential rule in Art. 8 of the Insolvency Regulation concerning the rights in rem of third parties. The latter is interpreted, in the light of Recital 68 of the Regulation, as an immunity of the security interest in certain assets located abroad, so that it is enforced according to the ordinary law on security interests of the Member State where the asset is located, 'as if' the grantor were not subject to collective proceedings (on this question, see B. Audit and L. d'Avout, *Droit international privé, op. cit.*, no. 1283). However, if the rule of Art. 9(1) of the Insolvency Regulation is also a preferential rule relating to a guarantee, the Regulation does not indicate such an analogous treatment, and there is therefore no reason to ignore the existence of collective proceedings opened against the debtor, see already in this sense, F. Mélin, 'La loi applicable à la compensation dans les procédures communautaires d'insolvabilité., *op. cit.*, no. 31. Comp. B. Audit and L. d'Avout, *Droit international privé, op. cit.*, no. 1283, who consider that Art. 9 should be treated 'in a similar spirit' to Art. 8 of the same Regulation.

200 As Mr Mélin writes: 'To admit a reference to the general provisions of this law alone would lead to giving the exception provided for by Article 6 (now Article 9) too wide a scope. It is true that this article aims to protect the legitimate expectations of the parties, by removing them from the control of the law of the State where the proceedings are opened. However, by referring to the law applicable to the debtor's claim, Article 6 makes no distinction between the general provisions of that law and those specific to collective proceedings, so that there is no particular reason to set aside the latter.' F. Mélin, 'La loi applicable à la compensation dans les procédures communautaires d'insolvabilité', *op. cit.*

general law governs the claim.'[201] This interpretation applies in the same terms to the Reorganisation and Solvency II Directives.[202]

§ 2. THE LIMITS OF THE CROWDING-OUT OF THE COMPETITION

902. Interference of close-out netting with insolvency law. Among the mandatory rules of insolvency law, the cardinal rule, which explains the very institution of a procedure, gives its name to the *lex concursus*, and justifies the legislative competence of the place where the procedure is opened, is that of the competition of creditors. The purpose of the latter is to allow for an equal distribution of the debtor's assets among the unsecured creditors,[203] after payment of preferential claims. It also explains several rules. The first is the method of distribution of the bankrupt debtor's assets, which includes the ordering of priorities of preferential claims in the competition[204] and concentrates the most imperative part of the legislative policy pursued by the forum. The contest also explains why the bankruptcy law determines 'the assets that form part of the insolvency estate',[205] but also why the *lex concursus* will try to reconstitute the debtor's assets when acts detrimental to the creditor's estate have been established,[206] or determines 'the effects of the insolvency proceedings on outstanding contracts to which the debtor is a party'.[207]

However, the regime granted to the netting mechanism has the particularity of thwarting all of these rules: it deprives the other creditors of a significant part of the debtor's assets by extinguishing them through netting; it upsets the order of preferences by making the beneficiary an even more privileged creditor than the others; and it prevents the financial contract from continuing. Under these conditions, if a large part of the legal systems, and in particular the European legal systems, agree on the principle of *netting*, it is not surprising that they differ on its modalities. This explains the main limitation of the avoidance

---

201 *JORF*, 30 July 2003, p. 12939, spec. no. 3.3.2.

202 It may be argued that the rules are redundant since all EU countries have transposed the Financial Collateral Directive and the Member State initiating the procedure will in all cases accept the netting of financial collateral. The statement is correct, but as the Financial Collateral Directive has not been transposed in the same terms in all States, the more or less liberal transposition of the opening State will affect the possibility of netting. The benefit of Art. 9(1) of the Insolvency Regulation and its equivalents is therefore not superfluous for the parties if they have designated in their netting agreement a more favourable law than the opening law.

203 This explains the name sometimes given to the *pari passu* competition.

204 Art. 7(2)(e) of the Insolvency Regulation.

205 Art. 7(2)(b) of the Insolvency Regulation.

206 Art. 7(2)(m) of the Insolvency Regulation.

207 Art. 7(2)(e) of the Insolvency Regulation.

of competition, which lies in the place where the insolvency proceedings are opened (I). To this is added a second limit, of a substantial nature: the case of resolution (II).

I. The Place where the Procedure is Initiated

The seemingly unique place of initiation of the procedure actually conceals two types of difficulties: the difference in protection of each place of initiation, and the multiplicity of places of initiation.

903. The difference in protection. Two different hypotheses must be considered. The first concerns the absence of protection for close-out netting. It is possible that the forum in which the proceedings are initiated does not have any rules in favour of set-off in general, and the mechanism of close-out netting in particular, either from a substantive or conflictual point of view. This may be the case when the proceedings are initiated in the territory of a third State. In this case, the creditor will inevitably have to declare its claim to the proceedings, since the *lex concursus* will be difficult to circumvent: the debtor's assets are most often located there; proceedings initiated at the seat of secondary establishments and whose law is likely to be favourable to the set-off of financial contracts may recognise the principle jurisdiction in this matter of the law of the main proceedings.

The second hypothesis relates to differences in the conditions of protection. Although legislations most often grant protection to close-out netting clauses, they do not all do so under the same conditions. The main limitation will most often be differences in the delimitation of the scope of application due to the many countries granting a privilege to beneficiaries of close-out netting clauses. These differences may occur whether the place of opening is within or outside the EU. This concerns, on the one hand, the persons eligible for protection[208] and, on the other hand, the contracts that may be used. In the latter case in particular, the Financial Collateral Directive left a significant margin of manoeuvre to the Member States, in particular by allowing them, if they so wished, to restrict the benefit of the protection granted to the close-out netting mechanism when the solvent party knew, or should have known, that its counterparty was going to be imminently insolvent.[209] In addition to this

[208] The persons who can benefit from *close-out netting* are not the same: some legal systems require that both parties be financial entities, while in others the status of one of the parties is sufficient to make the protection regime applicable.

[209] See Recital 15 of the Financial Collateral Directive. The United Kingdom, for example, has seized this option, whereas Belgium has abandoned it, see P. Paech, 'Close-out netting, Insolvency and Conflict of Laws', *op. cit.*, p. 442; see also the German transposition scheme reported by A. Caillemer du Ferrage, 'L'impact de la résolution sur le netting', *op. cit.*

difference in protection, there is, in practice, the multiplicity of places where proceedings are initiated.

904. The multiplicity of places of initiation. The multiplicity of places of initiation may arise from several aspects which have their source in the difficulty of determining *a priori* the centre of main interests of the counterparty. This will be the case, for example, where the contract is concluded with a branch of a counterparty whose foreign registered office does not correspond to its actual seat, or where the contract is concluded with a subsidiary of a group whose decisions are always taken by the parent. In these cases, the registered office might not be the centre of the insolvent debtor's main interests, which would deprive the parties of the foresight necessary for the conclusion of such contracts. This difficulty is compounded by the possibility of multiple proceedings since the Insolvency Regulation allows for proceedings to be opened not only at the place of each subsidiary but also at each branch office.[210] Combined with the different ways in which local law governs the mechanism of close-out netting, the multiplicity of places of initiation is a source of uncertainty.[211] However, this presentation can be nuanced. In the case of financial entities, the authorisation requires the correspondance of the statutory registered office and the actual seat, making the registered office indicated for the counterparty reliable. Moreover, the development of a universal and coordinated procedure at the level of the parent company's registered office for credit institutions, insurance companies and certain investment companies further reduces this difficulty.[212]

---

210 Art. 3(1) and (2) of the Insolvency Regulation.

211 P. Paech, 'Close-out netting, Insolvency and Conflict of Laws', *op. cit.*, pp. 444–448. The most important illustration was the bankruptcy of *Lehman Brothers* bank, which culminated in the *Belmont* judgments handed down by the English courts (see most recently *Belmont Park Investments Pty Ltd and others v. BNY Corporate Trustee Services Ltd and another*, UKSC, 38, 2011) and the New York court, which was petitioned after the judgment handed down by the London Court of Appeal, but before that of the Supreme Court (*Lehman Brothers Special Financing Inc v. BNY Corporate Trustee Services Ltd*, case no. 09-01242, Bank. SDNY, 25 January 2010). Both courts took jurisdiction over the interpretation of the clause at issue and issued conflicting decisions. At issue was a complex dispute ('of purgatorial complexity' according to Lord Mance, see *Belmont, supra*, para. 138) relating to a bond issue entitled *Dante*. The dispute centred on the enforceability of a clause reversing the order of priorities on financial guarantees in the event of default by one of the parties (the so-called 'flip' clause). The New York courts held that this clause was prohibited by insolvency law as constituting an act prejudicial to creditors, while the English courts gave it enforceability. For an overview of these two judgments, see J. Braithwaite, *The Financial Courts: Adjudicating Disputes in Derivatives Markets*, *op. cit.*, pp. 302 et seq. and P. Wautelet, 'Réglementation étatique et marchés financiers: entre autonomie et relativité', *op. cit.*, and H. Muir Watt, 'La gouvernance privée des marchés financiers: les enjeux de la *lex contractus*', *op. cit.* The two positions were *ultimately* reconciled in a later New York decision, see G. Moss QC, 'Anti-deprivation, flip clauses, ipso facto rules and the Dante inferno' (2017) *Insolvency intelligence*, pp. 24 et seq.

212 On these see *supra*, paras. 152 et seq.; see also P. Paech, 'Close-out netting, Insolvency and Conflict of Laws', *op. cit.*, p. 450.

II. *Resolution and Limits of Protection*

905. Quality of the parties and applicable regime. If the quality of the parties conditions the favourable regime granted to the netting of financial contracts,[213] it is more fundamentally in the event of the triggering of a resolution measure that this appears to be decisive. Indeed, resolution is a regime applicable to investment firms and credit institutions, the triggering of which is capable of paralysing the netting clauses contained in financial contracts.[214] There are two types of rules in this sense. The first one is automatic, and provides that the close-out netting mechanism cannot be triggered by the mere occurrence of a resolution measure.[215] A second rule allows the resolution authority, in the event of resolution and under certain conditions, 'to suspend the termination rights of any party to a contract concluded with a subsidiary of an institution subject to a resolution procedure'.[216] However, these rules on the neutralisation of close-out netting clauses are limited by the need for the party subject to resolution to continue to perform the essential obligations under the contract.[217]

906. Resolution measures and contract law. Some authors, based on the contractualist thesis of the close-out netting mechanism, consider that these measures have an extraterritorial reach without necessarily having the means to do so, i.e. without being able to ensure their effectiveness. According to these authors, resolution measures would only be enforceable if the law of the contract recognises them as applicable.[218] In this case, the possibility of suspending close-out netting clauses would be conditional on the applicability of the law of a Member State, but would be inoperative if the law of a third country was designated by the contract. The argument of this contractualist thesis is all the stronger because it seems to be supported by two elements of the Resolution Directive itself, as well as by the behaviour of ISDA. Firstly, the Resolution Directive characterises as "overriding legislation" the provisions of its Article 68, which neutralise the close-out netting clauses in the event of a

---

213 See *supra*, para. 940.

214 The resolution authority has other types of prerogatives in relation to derivatives, see Art. 49 of the Resolution Directive.

215 The latter 'shall not in itself be considered, by virtue of a contract concluded by that entity, as an enforcement event within the meaning of Directive 2002/47/EC (*the Financial Collateral Directive*) or as insolvency proceedings within the meaning of Directive 98/26/EC (*the Finality Directive*)' Art. 68(1) of the Resolution Directive. The measure extends to intra-group contracts.

216 Art. 71(2) of the Resolution Directive.

217 In other words, if the party subject to termination ceases to perform the contract, it is possible for the other party to rely on the close-out netting clause.

218 See in this sense, A. Caillemer du Ferrage, 'L'impact de la résolution sur le netting', *op. cit.*, no. 18; A. Kannan, 'ISDA 2014 Resolution Stay Protocol and suspension of close-out netting agreements: towards an extraterritorial recognition of resolution measures', *RDBF*, May-June 2015, no. 8.

resolution measure. Such a characterisation is based on a double presupposition: the neutralisation measures fall within the domain of the law of the contract; they will be applied by the *forum contractus*. Secondly, the Resolution Directive requires Member States to compel institutions subject to the Directive:

> 'Include in any financial contract which they enter into and which is governed by third-country law, terms by which the parties recognise that the financial contract may be subject to the exercise of powers by the resolution authority to suspend or restrict rights and obligations under Articles 33a, 69, 70, and 71 and recognise that they are bound by the requirements of Article 68.'[219]

This obligation is extended to subsidiaries of institutions from third countries, as part of the parent's establishment within the EU, in order to facilitate resolution at group level.[220] Finally, ISDA has established a protocol allowing parties who wish to adhere to it to modify their financial contracts, in order to recognise the applicability of resolution measures under the law of the contract: the inclusion of the close-out netting mechanism within the domain of the law of the contract is thus definitively characterised.[221] Thus, some authors write in this regard that 'the tendency of the resolution is not to impose the law of the State in which the proceedings are initiated on the law of the contract, but to ensure its recognition. Cooperation seems to have been preferred: ISDA ensures through protocols the effectiveness of resolution measures'.[222]

907. Critical analysis of the contractualist thesis. We would like to propose here an alternative reading of the contractualist thesis. First of all, the notion of cooperation is inappropriate in that it corresponds to a form of horizontal coordination, between equals. Indeed, the presence of these obligations in the Resolution Directive is likely to *impose* these rules on ISDA, whose standard agreements could no longer be used by their European clients.[223] This is all the more true as contractual recognition is not a condition for the authority to benefit from its resolution powers, which are still applicable from the Union's point of view.[224]

---

219 Art. 71a(1) of the Resolution Directive.

220 Art. 71a(2) of the Resolution Directive; on this aspect, see *supra*, paras. 151 et seq.

221 A first *ISDA 2014 Resolution Stay* Protocol was developed, before being replaced by a second, *ISDA 2015 Universal Resolution Protocol.*

222 J. Gavriloff, *Les méthodes du conflit de lois à l'épreuve du produit dérivé*, *op. cit.*

223 This is why the statement that 'by a sort of reversal of history, the efficiency of state law in prudential matters is ensured by contract, and this on the basis of a decision adopted and implemented by *ISDA*, i.e. a private power', M. Audit, 'Les dérivés de crédit à l'ombre du contrat sans loi', *op. cit.*

224 Art. 71a(4) of the Resolution Directive.

Secondly, the objective of the resolution is not to ensure its recognition, which is only a means, but its effectiveness.[225] This is not in doubt as long as the persons and assets affected are within the EU. It is only when an institution is established in a third country that it is necessary to ensure that the resolution measures are recognised. In reality, the only limits to resolution are those provided for by the Commission: either in cases where it observes the limits of the effectiveness of the measures it wishes to institute, in particular in the case of the resolution of groups of institutions located in the territory of a third country,[226] or where it deems it legitimate to maintain certain contractual positions. Two examples are given here which limit the power of the resolution authority to suspend the close-out netting mechanism in the case of a crisis prevention or management resolution measure.[227]

Firstly, the power offered to the resolution authority to suspend the close-out netting mechanism is only possible if 'the substantive obligations under the contract, including payment and delivery obligations and the provision of collateral, continue to be performed'.[228] Here we find a limit similar to the one known for ongoing contracts under the traditional regime of collective proceedings, but which is original in the case of resolution. Indeed, this condition can be lifted in the case where the suspension takes place on the basis of Article 33a of the directive, which provides for certain short-term suspensions.[229]

Secondly, when the resolution authority uses resolution instruments, the termination mechanism can be preserved. This is the case when the authority uses an internal bail-in instrument that depreciates derivatives in particular: on the one hand, the latter can only be depreciated when they are liquidated, which makes it necessary to trigger the close-out netting mechanism[230] and, on the other hand, the order of depreciation is strictly regulated by the Resolution

225 See already in this sense our comments on the resolution and the establishment in third countries, *supra*, para. 201.

226 On this aspect, see our comments *supra*, para. 201.

227 The 2008 financial crisis has shown that the close-out netting mechanism can be 'an aggravating factor precipitating the bankruptcy of institutions in difficulty', see C. Louisfert, 'Les conséquences de la loi de séparation et de régulation des activités bancaires sur le mécanisme de résiliation compensation (close out netting)', *BJB*, November 2013, no. 110t3, p. 546.

228 Art. 68(1) of the Resolution Directive.

229 Art. 68(5) of the Resolution Directive. However, this article is only applicable to financial contracts concluded over the counter. It does not apply to financial infrastructure, see Art. 33a(2) of the Resolution Directive. In this case, the exercise of this power must take into account its impact on the financial markets, 'the powers of supervision and jurisdiction and the rights of creditors and the equal treatment of creditors in normal insolvency proceedings', Art. 33*bis*(5) of the Resolution Directive.

230 Art. 49(2) of the Resolution Directive.

Directive, limiting the discretion of the resolution authority.[231] These two examples illustrate the international limits that the legislator intended to assign to resolution versus netting, and which are contained in the substantive law of resolution. Moreover, these examples show that the law applicable to the netting of an institution in resolution is not the law of the netting agreement, but the law of resolution.

908. Resolution measures and insolvency law. The argument that netting agreements are subject to the law of the contract in the event of termination is based on a double confusion. The first is the belief that the law of set-off when the parties are *in bonis*, *i.e.* the law of the contract, continues to apply when one of the parties enters into insolvency proceedings. The second is that this argument seems to ignore the fact that resolution law is a specific law of insolvency, applicable in respect of the failure of certain institutions. In other words, in the event of the failure of an institution subject to the Resolution Directive, the *lex fori concursus* is the law of the competent authority under resolution. There is therefore no doubt that when the mechanism of close-out netting is invoked in the context of a resolution, it is not the conditions of compensation of ordinary law that are applicable, but those resulting from insolvency law and, in this case, those resulting from resolution law. This means that the law applicable to the set-off of a contract concluded by an institution in resolution is that of the seat of the institution in resolution.[232] A certain confusion is maintained, on the one hand, by the conflict rule of the Winding up Directive which applies the law of the contract to the close-out netting mechanism and, on the other hand, because a special unitary regime has been established in the field of close-out

231 This is also the case when the resolution authority decides on a partial transfer of assets, in which case the Resolution Directive provides that 'Member States shall ensure appropriate protection of the following arrangements and counterparties to such arrangements' (Art. 76 Resolution Directive) including *netting* and *set-off arrangements* and financial collateral (Art. 76(2)(b), (c) and (d) Resolution Directive), irrespective of the law applicable to them (Art. 76(3)(b) Resolution Directive). In addition, there are two specific provisions relating to the protection of financial collateral arrangements and netting agreements, which require Member States to provide 'that [...] close-out netting agreements are adequately protected so as to prevent the transfer of some, but not all, of the rights and obligations protected by [...] a netting agreement between the institution and another person' (Art. 77 of the Resolution Directive). As Professor Gaudemet writes, without this provision, the contractual forecasts would be ruined: 'This risk, assuming it were true, would be the pure and simple ruin of the contractual forecasts of the counterparties of the defaulting financial institution which will have determined themselves in consideration of the existence of a netting agreement and will generally have adjusted their "collateral" to the amount of the potential netting balance of this agreement.' See A. Gaudemet, 'Suspension of the execution of close-out netting agreements concluded by a defaulting credit institution or investment firm', *RDBF*, January 2013, comm. 27.

232 If the two institutions are in resolution, it would then be necessary to rehabilitate the doctrine of cumulation of law applicable to set-off in order to allow it to finally find a legitimate basis. On this doctrine, which was unduly applied when the parties were *in good standing*, see *supra*, para. 894.

netting, applying indiscriminately depending on whether the parties are *in bonis* or whether one of them is subject to insolvency proceedings. However, this preferential rule and special regime are exorbitant and exceptional. They do not alter the centre of gravity of the set-off in the context of collective proceedings, which is the seat of the debtor in difficulty. These observations should not, however, lead to the conclusion that the ISDA protocol is useless, given the international divergence of characterisations and the possibility for a foreign legal system to retain a contractual characterisation of a netting agreement, even when one of the parties is insolvent.[233]

909. Rejection of the characterisation as overriding mandatory rules. The characterisation of resolution measures as overriding mandatory rules is only of residual use here: on the one hand, it is not necessary within the framework of the Union, since the measures are recognised by virtue of the Resolution Directive and, on the other hand, for third countries which retain a contractual characterisation, they will only be applied according to the goodwill of the competent court. This characterisation is, however, the inevitable temperament of all authors who want to substitute an objective criterion for that of the law of autonomy,[234] most often alleged in order not to thwart the legitimate expectations of the parties. This scheme, which is intended to be subtle because it allows for the adoption of tailor-made solutions by mandatory rules, is to be avoided.

Firstly, because it is based on the idea that the law of insolvency is, if not unforeseeable, at least unexpected by the parties. But this is a specious assertion: all the parties know that insolvency triggers a specific law, which the mechanism of close-out netting is precisely trying to avoid. Moreover, this right is perfectly foreseeable, since in the vast majority of cases it will be the counterparty's registered office. The difficulty arises less from the unpredictability of insolvency law than from the combination of two factors:

---

233 It is quite possible that a third country, for example the country of the seat of the counterparty, or of an asset of the institution in resolution, or of any secondary collective proceeding established at the seat of a subsidiary or branch of a third country, will retain a contractual qualification of the law applicable to the termination-compensation, and choose to ignore the mandatory rules of third countries. This situation is not a textbook case given the mostly international nature of institutions subject to resolution. In this case, the ISDA protocol, applicable under the contractual prescriptions, is likely to counter the desire of the locally competent judge to ignore the prescriptions of the *lex concursus*. However, the persons concerned must adhere to the ISDA protocol, which is not compulsory, and whose adherence may engage the liability of the person who adheres to it vis-à-vis its shareholders. See already in this sense, A. Kannan, 'ISDA 2014 Resolution Stay Protocol and suspension of close-out netting agreements: towards an extraterritorial recognition of resolution measures', *op. cit.*, no. 15.

234 See on the subject of *close-out netting*, O. Boger, 'Close-out netting provisions in private international law and international insolvency law (Part II)', *op. cit.*

the plurality of competent fora and the diversity of the fields of protection, which make it more difficult to predict the applicable law.[235]

Secondly, the legitimacy of a privilege as exorbitant as that granted to close-out netting[236] can only be assessed by the law of the seat of the insolvent debtor's interests. To be convinced of this, one must recall the political source of the jurisdiction of the *lex fori concursus*. Indeed, this law is that of the legal order that bears the main socio-economic effects of the insolvency: the employees who work there lose their jobs, the local social bodies that will have to compensate for some of the consequences of the bankruptcy,[237] the public authorities that lose tax resources, local suppliers that lose an outlet,[238] to which must be added the local registration of the majority of the creditors. It is an understatement to say that the *lex concursus* is best able to assess who can be protected from the effects of insolvency. In this sense, the justification of the contractual characterisation, which is based on the idea of legal certainty of the parties, appears to be particularly inappropriate in that it leads to the ordering of preferences being subject to a law other than the *lex concursus*, moreover by creating an additional and hidden privilege.[239]

Thirdly, the proposed solution leads to a disastrous result: nothing is more unpredictable than the characterisation of a mandatory rule, *a fortiori* in an area where the imperative nature of the law is so strong that there are many provisions that can claim such a characterisation.

910. For an application of the law of insolvency. It would be better to promote convergence of the international characterisation of the guarantees of persons subject to insolvency proceedings,[240] which would begin with an effort to ensure the internal coherence of Union law, by making set-off, security interests and all guarantees subject to the *lex fori concursus*. It would then be up to this law to decide on the one hand on the persons and contracts eligible and on the other

---

235 As Mr Paech writes: 'it is not the multiplicity of fora alone that forms the greatest source of legal uncertainty; rather, it is the combination of that multiplicity with a heterogeneous set of largely substantive avoidance rules that renders the enforceability of close-out netting so unpredictable', P. Paech, 'Close-out netting, Insolvency and Conflict of Laws', *op. cit.*, p. 452.

236 As one author has written about the equivalent protection enjoyed by the *close-out netting* of financial contracts under US law: 'No other financial instruments receive such favourable treatment under the Bankruptcy Code', see B. Faubus, 'Narrowing the Bankruptcy Safe Harbor for Derivatives to Combat Systemic Risk' (2010) 59 *Duke Law Journal*, 823, quoted by M. Bridge and J. Braithwaite, 'Private Law and Financial Crisis', *op. cit.*, p. 391.

237 For example, in France the AGS for the wage guarantee scheme.

238 Whether it is the wage guarantee bodies or the unemployment bodies.

239 As Mr Paech put it perfectly: 'most jurisdictions would not welcome an extension of insolvency privileges through the backdoor of private international law. This means that changes to the fragmented conflict-of-laws framework cannot be justified by the promise of increased legal certainty alone', P. Paech, 'Close-out netting, Insolvency and Conflict of Laws', *op. cit.*, p. 449.

240 English law itself considers that payment after the commencement of collective proceedings is governed solely by the *lex concursus*.

hand on the protection regime. These two aspects can usefully be influenced by the European harmonisation of substantive measures,[241] which is a condition for the unification of the conflict rule.[242] This perception of the close-out netting mechanism is not a theoretical view. It was also defended in these terms by the English judicial system in the context of a dispute relating to the field of the choice of court clause when one of the parties, a Canadian, was insolvent.[243] The solvent party considered that the English judiciary, exclusively designated by the clause, was the only one competent to determine the amount of the payment due under the close-out netting mechanism, and requested an *anti-suit injunction.* The injunction was refused, precisely because the English judge was of the opinion that these matters should be decided by the court of the place of initiation,[244] which could nevertheless comply with the contractual interpretation of the clause under English law, which the English judge was willing to give.[245]

---

[241] See already in this sense, A. Gaudemet, 'Close-out netting – Proposal for a Resolution Directive: an opportunity to put an end to Articles 25 and 26 of the Directive of 4 April 2001 on the reorganisation and winding-up of credit institutions', *op. cit.*: 'Today, priority can no longer be given to the legal certainty of the parties to netting and novation agreements, or to repo agreements, over the effectiveness of the powers of resolution, reorganisation or winding-up of the national administrative and judicial authorities. It seems inconceivable that the powers of resolution, reorganisation or liquidation of credit institutions by national authorities could be thwarted, even partially, by the application of a foreign law to certain agreements concluded by these institutions. This is the whole ambition of the proposed Resolution Directive: to invest national authorities with effective powers to resolve the difficulties of their credit institutions. And it is hard to see why this ambition should be limited to the resolution powers of national authorities and not also concern their powers of reorganisation or winding up.'

[242] See already in this sense, P. Paech, 'Close-out netting, Insolvency and Conflict of Laws', *op. cit.*, pp. 449 et seq.

[243] *AWB (Geneva) SA v. North America Steamship Ltd* (2007) EWCA Civ 739.

[244] The development of the English judge deserves to be reproduced: 'Those proceedings are part of insolvency proceedings and the issues that arise within them are governed by Canadian law. The issues encompassed within insolvency proceedings are wide. AWB and Pioneer accepted that those included questions of whether claims should be recognised and admitted in the insolvency, the relative priority among creditors, avoidance of pre-insolvency transfers as preferences and fraudulent transfers. In my view, the scope of the insolvency proceedings extends to the present claim for relief in Canada as it is relief sought within the proceedings. AWB is a creditor and Pioneer is, at present, a contingent creditor. They are therefore within the potential jurisdiction of the insolvency proceedings and accept that the Canadian Court can, in relation to certain insolvency issues, exercise its jurisdiction. It is, in my view, a matter for the Canadian Court to decide on the relief that it is prepared to grant within the scope of those proceedings as it is concerned with issues of insolvency and not with issues that relate to the contractual obligations under the agreement. The application in relation to the exercise of its insolvency jurisdiction is therefore not within the clause.' *AWB (Geneva) SA v. North America Steamship Ltd* (2007) EWCA Civ 739, no. 27.

[245] *AWB (Geneva) SA v. North America Steamship Ltd* (2007) EWCA Civ 739, no. 37. On this issue, see J. Braithwaite, *The Financial Courts: Adjudicating Disputes in Derivatives Markets*, *op. cit.*; pp. 300 et seq.

911. Mr Paech proposes to temper this solution by subjecting the voidness of detrimental acts to the law of the act.[246] Several arguments militate in favour of this application: its foreseeability for the parties; the fact that the *lex contractus* already governs the other causes of nullity and the restitutions which result from them[247]; the safeguarding of the legislative policy of the forum by the application of the *lex concursus* to the conditions for the protection of close-out netting. However, this is already the state of positive law. Indeed, if the voidness of the detrimental acts are governed by the *lex concursus*, and can prevent the compensation of an act that is prejudicial to creditors,[248] Article 16 of the Insolvency Regulation provides that:

> 'Point (m) of Article 7(2) [related to the voidness of the detrimental acts] shall not apply where the person who benefited from an act detrimental to all the creditors provides proof that:
>
> (a) the act is subject to the law of a Member State other than that of the State of the opening of proceedings; and
>
> (b) the law of that Member State does not allow any means of challenging that act in the relevant case.'

This provision thus allows a close-out netting mechanism subject to a law other than the insolvency law not to be set aside even if it is considered by the *lex fori concursus* as an act prejudicial to all creditors, to the extent that the designated law would not have allowed it to be set aside.[249] This provision is said to have been established 'with a view to equity" and to "protect the validly acquired rights of a third party whose legitimate expectations should not be misled'.[250] The argument is not convincing for material and conflicting reasons. From the material point of view, equity is determined by the legislative policy of the *lex fori concursus* and the *ratio legis* of the voidness of detrimental acts is precisely to challenge *illegitimate* acts, in order to reconstitute the debtor's assets.[251] As the Court of Justice itself wrote in relation to a related rule of German

---

246 *Ibid.*, p. 452.

247 Art. 10(1) and 12(1)(e) of the Rome I Regulation.

248 Art. 9(2) of the Insolvency Regulation which states that Art. 9(1) 'shall not preclude actions for voidness, voidability or unenforceability referred to in Article 7(2)(m)'. This limitation also applies to the Solvency II Directive, but not to the Winding up Directive.

249 The regime of this article was clarified in the *Lutz*, *Nike* and *Vinyls Italia* judgments, see 'Entreprises en difficulté: droit international et européen' in T. Mastrullo, *Répertoire de droit des sociétés*, *op. cit.*, nos. 509–515.

250 *Ibid.*, no. 509.

251 If, as a matter of principle, private law techniques do not have to subject their validity to a purpose considered objectively legitimate, the voidness of detrimental acts is the exception, see in this sense M. Bridge and J. Braithwaite, 'Private Law and Financial Crisis', *op. cit.*

insolvency law, the voidness of detrimental acts 'contributes to the achievement of an objective which is intrinsically linked, *mutatis mutandis*, to all insolvency proceedings, namely the prevention of possible reductions in the estate before the opening of insolvency proceedings with a view to the equal satisfaction of creditors'.[252] From a conflictual point of view, the application of a single law to all acts detrimental to creditors is the result of the very effectiveness of the *lex concursus*: the competition of creditors must be on an equal footing in order to be legitimate, and there is no reason to derogate from this equality by virtue of the application of a third law.[253] This is why, *de lege ferenda*, it would be beneficial to withdraw Article 16 of the Insolvency Regulation.

912. Unity and applicability of the *lex concursus*. These observations allow us to add two remarks on the applicability of the *lex concursus*. The first relates to the basis for its unitary character. Professors Audit and d'Avout distinguish two reasons justifying the legislative competence of the *lex concursus*: the multilateral nature of the procedure, making it 'necessary for the procedure to be uniformly subject to an "umbrella" law, establishing a link between the relations, including international relations, concerned with insolvency', and 'the particular imperative of the law in this area',[254] consisting of economic mandatory rules. This twofold statement, which is very lucid, can be clarified on its second side. Indeed, if it were a traditional overriding mandatory rule, its limitation could take place unilaterally, and there would not necessarily be any difficulty in admitting the self-limitation of local law in a number of cases. In particular, it would be possible to make the various acts concluded by the debtor subject to the law of the contract, the latter designating, as from the opening judgment, the insolvency law of the legal system covered by the act. However, it seems to us that if such self-limitation cannot take place, it is because the purpose of insolvency proceedings is to establish competition between creditors in order to

---

252 Case C-594/14, *Kornhaas*, ECLI:EU:C:2015:806. Recall the statement by Professors Bridge and Braithwaite that: 'The tension here is between legitimate self-help and distributive fairness' (*ibid.*, p. 366). The law of insolvency is best able to determine the balance of this tension.

253 It may well be argued that these are two distinct rules, the purpose of the rules on the concurrence of creditors being to distribute the debtor's assets in accordance with the order provided for by the forum, whereas the purpose of the rules on the voidness of detrimental acts is to reconstitute the debtor's assets (see M. Bridge and J. Braithwaite, 'Private Law and Financial Crisis', *op. cit.*, pp. 367–368, clearly distinguishing the two rules in English law and showing the importance of this distinction in domestic law because of the substantive regime associated with the interpretation of each of these rules). However, it should be noted that their functions are closely linked: the purpose of reconstituting the bankrupt debtor's assets is to enable them to be distributed to creditors. This is why their internal coherence makes it necessary to subject them to the same law.

254 B. Audit and L. d'Avout, *Droit international privé*, *op. cit.*, no. 1255, see already in this sense, L. d'Avout, 'Sens et portée de la *lex fori concursus*', *op. cit.* On this question, see also F. Mélin, 'L'application d'une loi étrangère devant les procédures européennes d'insolvabilité', *op. cit.*

distribute the bankrupt's assets among them. Nevertheless, this distribution does not bear the interference of a third party law, which is inevitably likely to call into question the legislative policy pursued by the forum, and whose superior legitimacy to the other legal orders involved in the relationship makes it the centre of gravity of all the bankrupt debtor's relationships.[255]

The second remark is specific to the mode of application of the *lex concursus*. When it is applied to the contract in order either to annul it or to compel its continuation, it apparently has the characteristics of a mandatory rule. Because of the importance of the legislative policy it pursues, it derogates from the law normally applicable. However, this presentation is not fully satisfactory. The law designated by the contract is applicable only through the conflict rule resulting, in the European perspective, from the Rome I Regulation. However, this choice only applies to the area of the law of the contract, defined by the Regulation. The latter no longer necessarily applies where one of the parties is insolvent: most legal systems have insolvency law before which certain contractual provisions stop. In other words, the insolvency law in such cases does not derogate from the contract law designated by the act, but is the only law applicable.[256] The question is rather whether the insolvency law is that of the legal system designated by the contract or that of the seat of the bankrupt debtor. For the reasons given, there is no doubt that it is the latter.

913. Section conclusion. This section has described how the law on conflict of laws assists domestic law in crowding out the creditor's contribution to a financial contract from the *lex concursus*, but also the limits of this crowding out. These observations have shown that the enforceability of the termination-compensation mechanism should be subject to the *lex concursus* of the bankrupt debtor, which is the only one able to determine the extent of the possible protection granted to this mechanism.

914. Chapter conclusion. The performance of the financial contract is dependent on the clearing obligation. The evolution of the clearing obligation towards a prudential function explains why its connection is made through the seat of the parties to the contract, or their guarantors, on whom the risk borne ultimately falls. Such a connection, measured and based on the purpose of the obligation in question, deserves approval. For the parties subject to it, the

---

[255] As Professors Bureau and Muir Watt write: 'The diversity of the applicable laws [involved in the settlement of the bankruptcy], beyond the complexity it creates in the course of the procedure, also disturbs the internal balance of the latter by forcing it to deal with heterogeneous rules, even though unity would be a much better vector of coherence.' D. Bureau and H. Muir Watt, *Droit international privé*, *op. cit.*, no. 1003.

[256] As the Court of Cassation has stated, 'the annulment, revocation or unenforceability, pronounced at the request of the organs of a collective procedure, of acts passed by the debtor before the opening of the procedure and considered prejudicial to the creditors is a consequence of the procedure and, as such, falls within the scope of the law governing it', Cass., com., 2 October 2012, no. 10-18.005, (2 judgments).

clearing obligation implies clearing the financial contract with a clearing house. The intervention of the clearing house causes, by means of novation, a change of contracting party and makes the clearing house the central counterparty of the financial contract. As a consequence, the novated obligations will be subject to the law designated by the clearing rules which, depending on the financial contract, will not necessarily be the law applicable to the clearing rules themselves. It is perhaps surprising that the execution of the clearing obligation, when executed at a clearing house, can have such an impact on the law applicable to the contract entered into by the clearing participants. However, the clearing rules are careful to ensure that such a change only occurs where it does not affect the transaction itself. When the financial contract cannot be offset, the European legal order protects the parties to the financial contract against the insolvency of one of them by giving a preferential regime, both in terms of conflict of laws and in terms of substance, to the creditor of the financial contract. However, this preferential regime struggles sometimes to convince from a private international point of view in that it leads to the *lex concursus* being deprived of questions which fall within its domain. Moreover, it has its own limitations due to the internationalisation of insolvency proceedings or to the existence of a resolution measure. These limits, unknown to the clearing house, are additional arguments in favour of the latter.

915. Conclusion of title. At the end of this discussion, it is now clear that if financial contracts concluded by mutual agreement allow in the majority of cases the selection of a foreign law, the financial contract remains very dependent on other legal systems, which, without intervening in the field of the *lex contractus*, can hinder its validity or paralyse its execution. Thus, the personal status of the parties, the place of their residence or the law of the underlying itself are all rules, independent of the law of the contract, which are likely to prevent its validity either in order to protect one of the parties or to protect the underlying. With regard to their enforcement, financial contracts benefit from a protective regime which makes the collateral they benefit from, the set-off and the assets given as financial collateral, immune from the competition of creditors inherent in the insolvency of one of the parties. This protective regime can be deactivated in the event of a resolution, unless the netting takes place with a clearing house.

It is here that the financial market, after having been ousted for a long time in favour of OTC contracts, reappears. Although the ability to conclude a financial contract is in principle independent of the financial market, the latter has reintroduced its necessity thanks to the clearing houses. By imposing the clearing of many OTC financial contracts with a clearing house, the conditions were created for the introduction of an obligation to trade these contracts on a financial market. The obligations related to the clearing obligation follow its scope of application, notably international, based on the establishment in the territory of the Union of one of the parties or its guarantor in the territory of the Union. From the point of view of the transactions concluded, the application of the clearing obligation will often be decisive since the clearing house's clearing rules may modify the law of the contract concluded between the clearing members.

916. Conclusion of the third part. Financial market law does not apply to the status of financial instruments, but forces it to submit to infrastructures that will govern many aspects of it. In the case of financial securities, it has been shown that by requiring issuers to deposit their securities with a central depository, financial market law paradoxically renders their proprietary connection unstable. Indeed, the latter is now subject to criteria that have the effect of multiplying the laws applicable to their transfer. We have seen that these criteria, which arose under the influence of the direct holding system, which was not necessary, were clearly harmful, whereas it was possible and highly desirable to subject financial securities to a unitary law, that of the issuer's registered office or the central depository's securities settlement system.

The status of financial contracts, for its part, responds to the dynamics of domestic contract law, between contractual freedom and public policy. However, when projected into the international order, public policy follows different methodological paths depending on the interests involved. Firstly, it restricts freedom of choice of law to truly international contracts, and excludes it in the presence of a consumer. Secondly, it intervenes to protect residents against contracts whose stakes are often beyond the comprehension of neophytes. It acts in French law not through the enactment of an incapacity regime, but through the professional rules to which direct marketers and investment firms are subject and which are applicable independently of the *lex contractus*. Moreover, financial contracts have the particularity of being able to disrupt the functioning of companies and financial markets; the laws governing their functioning are then likely, in a form of reciprocity, to disrupt the formation or performance of these contracts. However, they will most often fail to apply to the contract itself, and will rather benefit from sanctioning the persons who enter into them. It is nevertheless in order to protect the entire legal system that public policy is most intense, and justifies the submission of financial contracts to prudential rules. These are applicable according to the location of the parties involved, and require the intervention of a clearing house, whose operation conditions the very possibility of choice of law. They expand the field of the prudential category outlined in the study of the status of infrastructure managers.

GENERAL CONCLUSION

In stating our intention to reconcile the rules of financial law and the rules of conflict of laws, we wanted to take advantage of the resulting synthesis to make a diagnosis of the discipline and possibly reveal its deficiencies. Two of them can be highlighted: the contradiction of the objectives of financial law and a complex relationship with common law. A general solution to these difficulties consists in precisely delimiting the interactions of financial law with the various branches of common law in order to account for the reasons why a specific objective justifies the enactment of a special rule. In this delimitation exercise, the methodology of private international law can provide valuable assistance. At the same time, it is intended to show the undeniable contributions of the international application of financial law to the theory of private international law.

Contradictory objectives. The tension that financial law rules are subject to is first of all exacerbated by the sometimes contradictory nature of the objectives they pursue, between the liberalism to which the matter aspires and the protection of investors that it requires. The implementation of commercial operations requires speed and security, which we agree justify the existence of derogatory solutions. However, these solutions may come up against the objective of investor protection, which is not necessarily satisfied with the freedom-responsibility pairing created by this first objective. In this respect, the current point of balance lies in the abundance of information that financial law requires issuers to provide in order to market their securities; it is not certain that this abundance truly allows for the protection of investors by enlightening their consent, unless, precisely, they are investment specialists. This is all the more true since only the latter are in a position to engage the civil liability of issuers who disseminate defective information by proving the causality between the latter and their investment decision or their investment advice. This means that other investors will be better protected by imposing rules of conduct on intermediaries to protect clients, together with prudential rules to ensure their solvency and integrity. The protection of the financial market itself, where financial instruments are admitted to it, is in principle ensured by the administrative and criminal liability of issuers and investors.

Moreover, the influence of related disciplines may interfere with the objectives of financial law. This is particularly true of European Union law and the fundamental ambiguity of its objectives: unification of the internal market does not necessarily mean protection of investors. The balance to which the discipline aspires has not yet been found; it is hoped that this book has proposed solutions that could contribute to it.

Relationship with ordinary law. This contradiction of objectives is compounded by the paradox that financial law has become specialised, in the sense that few authors today master all aspects of this discipline, even though it touches on all branches of law, to which it makes exceptions in order to pursue its objectives. The need for versatility in the whole of private law and beyond makes it difficult to grasp the financial phenomenon in its entirety. How can one understand market abuse law without studying repressive law? How can one grasp the singularity of financial securities transactions without recalling the fundamental mechanisms of property law? How can one understand the law of market transactions without a precise knowledge of the functioning of commercial companies? And since each of these derogations has links with the others, in particular because of their common objectives and the means of achieving them, it is easy to understand the particular problem raised by the study of financial law. Several pitfalls are therefore possible: underestimating the derogations necessary for the objectives pursued by this law; denying the singularities resulting from the collective structure of a financial market; overemphasising the special nature of the discipline in order to give its players undue advantages. Financial law is therefore advancing like a tightrope walker.

Ordering of financial law. In a discipline as rich as financial law, private international law helps to distinguish between the different branches of this field, particularly the law of financial instruments and the law of financial markets, but also to untangle the interactions it has with the branches of law that are related to it. It seems to us that the law of conflicts of laws in particular shows that the law of financial instruments is a discipline that has, in fact, two aspects: external and internal.

It is by its external aspect that the law of financial instruments justifies its existence, by grouping together within the same category operations which have in common, for the parties, to present a risk (i.e. a hazard) whether it is a question of the supply of securities or financial contracts, and explain the need for a body of rules protecting investors. This protection takes the form, firstly, of a binding administrative status for professionals who habitually provide financial instruments and, secondly, of information obligations triggered by the provision of financial instruments. The effectiveness of this protection is ensured by two means: the supervision by an administrative authority of professionals' compliance with these rules, and the assumption of administrative and civil liability for professionals who violate these obligations.

The hypothesis of the insolvency of the professional, which would make compensation of clients by tort law illusory, is tempered by the existence of guarantee funds. In this first aspect, the law of financial instruments is thus confronted with administrative law and tort law; it must therefore submit to the logic of these disciplines: we have seen that its international application reflects this.

In its internal aspect, however, the law on financial instruments presents a profound asymmetry between financial securities and financial contracts. Financial securities, because they are issued, are first of all connected to the group from which they originate, and then subject to the contract that binds the holder of the security to the issuer, articles of association for shares, an issue contract for bonds, and a fund settlement contract for UCITS. The rationale behind these sets of laws, which mainly concern the issuer and the purchaser of the security and bring the law of financial instruments closer to the rationale of company law and contract law, does not, however, eliminate the difficulties. Indeed, because financial securities are intangible assets, their transmission causes difficulties specific to the property law, within which the relevant solutions to the difficulties they give rise to should be sought, while taking into account the sometimes decisive interferences caused by the holding structure and negotiability of the securities. As for financial contracts, they obey the traditional logic of contract law, between contractual freedom and *ordre public*. The massive standardisation to which they have been subjected, the frequent internationality of their contracting parties and of the economic operations they are intended to carry out, combined with their risk-transfer function, make them undeniably original contracts. This explains the intrusion of other bodies of law than contract law, both as regards their formation and their execution. In particular, the influence that these contracts can exert on the realisation of a system risk explains why prudential law, by imposing a clearing obligation, most often obliges the parties that resort to it to use a clearing house.

Financial market law is unquestionably based on the law of financial instruments, since its function is to allow their trading; it differs, however, in that its own objective is to ensure the proper functioning of the mechanism it institutes and which is contained by the trading platform. The objective is to ensure, on the one hand, the liquidity of the market, i.e. the existence of a minimum number of transactions allowing for the establishment of a stable price, and on the other hand, to establish trading rules that allow for the establishment of the most reliable price possible for the instruments admitted to it: this is where the law on market operations finds its *raison d'être*. This objective also requires it to ensure the legal organisation of the persons who manage this market, both by enacting a statute for the managers of the financial market to prevent the conflicts of interest that its particular situation generates, and by instituting obligations on the market members.

On the side of private international law. The study of the international application of financial law is subject to the same complaint of ultra-specialisation as that which has been made about it in domestic law; it is not, however, unique to it. With a few exceptions, it has indeed become rare for internationalists to know both the competent court for the dissolution of the matrimonial regime and the exceptions to the application of the *lex concursus*. The authors meet again on the private international law of obligations, through the Brussels I bis, Rome I and Rome II regulations which constitute today the new grammar of the discipline; it is without surprise that the internationalist doctrine generally approaches financial law through these regulations. The institution of these regulations, while it has had the considerable advantage of making the regulation of private international relations accessible, while most often perfecting the rules themselves, has the disadvantage of cutting them off from the intellectual source of the solution they promote: substantive law. This difficulty is compounded by a curious subversion: the anteriority of European private international law over any common private law, to which is added the threefold refusal of the Court of Justice to take into consideration the objectives of the national law at issue in the preliminary question, to take into account the substantive law, even though it was established by the European legislator, or sometimes even the links between the various private international law regulations. Solutions in financial matters are not exempt from these criticisms, but they have an additional dimension because of the lack of understanding of the configuration of legal relationships governed by financial law. The topical example is that of the judge with jurisdiction over the civil liability of issuers for the dissemination of defective information: the analysis cannot ignore the reasons for the obligation to draw up a prospectus, the procedures for its dissemination, or the actual harm that the investor is complaining about. The current headlong rush, first towards a futile localisation of securities, now towards a bundle of clues where casuistry has become king without necessarily making it possible to obtain the most basic solutions, is indicative in many respects of the inadequate analysis of the substantial disputes involved.

Although it is not unique in this respect, this study nevertheless reveals several original features at a time when private international law is considered to be undergoing a paradigm shift: the strength of the method of the rule of conflict of laws; the resilience of objective location criteria; the resistance of local law to the penetration of foreign norms; the importance of administrative authorities in the coordination of legal orders. More generally, this coordination often involves deference to an entire legal order when it enjoys indisputable preponderance, sometimes established through the use of a market infrastructure. Third party legal orders are therefore faced with a binary situation: recognise the foreign organisation, in its various components, or prohibit its use by its nationals. The pivotal role of the administrative authorities within this coordination is no longer in question: the idea that they would necessarily apply their own law is incorrect; their recourse to methodologies borrowed from private international law is obvious, particularly in the case of the mutual assistance required for international investigation procedures. The clearest manifestation of the penetration of private international law within this administrative coordination is perhaps in the context of the equivalence method which, if it is based exclusively on administrations, obeys the dialectic of the objectives of private international law, between coordination of legal orders and protection of the social order of the forum.

The latter objective has reached a particularly high standard in financial matters. Local protection rules are difficult to avoid, either because they are established at EU level or because they are outside the scope of contract law and therefore have a strong link with the domestic order due to their objective connection. The introduction of prudential legislation is likely to tighten the grip of local administration and legislation on the players, while professional rules take care of consumer protection. The big absentee is the *lex contractus*, whose scope is ever more restricted: the *lex societatis* ousts it as soon as the functioning of the companies it has created is at stake, the *lex mercatus* imposes itself when the functioning of the financial market is at stake, and the *lex damni* is superimposed when the contractual breach also constitutes a breach of a professional rule. This last aspect is particularly important in relationships where the protection of the contracting party, or even the performance of the contract, is often governed by the professional status itself. To this must be added, on the one hand, the link between the legislation protecting savings and the domicile of the persons solicited and, on the other hand, the preponderant jurisdiction of the country where the damage occurred in a matter that is conducive to criminal behaviour. In any event, the existence of organisations, even contractual ones, shifts the connecting factor from the law of autonomy to the seat of the organisation. By giving a particularly strong anchor point to a legal order, which grants protection to the organisation formed, local law will then often extend to operations between private persons permitted by this organisation. The submission of market organisations to state rules nevertheless has as a corollary the influence that the former attempt to exert, with undeniable success, on the latter in order to make their own interests prevail.

In financial matters, private international law appears to be far removed from family matters, where public policy is sometimes stripped of its substance. However, it would be simplistic to attribute this only to the prerogatives that individuals derive from the interpretation of Article 8 of the European Convention on Human Rights, which is most often irrelevant to the legal relationships studied here. This difference in the intensity of protection of the domestic order stems above all from a more profound evolution of the local interests that seem to merit protection. In other words, the domestic order is more readily protected in financial matters simply because today the French and European legal orders attach more importance to the money of their residents than to a family model they wish to preserve or promote.

We will conclude by summarising the various proposals of this research, which follow the path of the thesis put forward: it consists of affirming that market infrastructures are the object of a singular connection to the State and that this connection makes it possible to found the operations between private persons who make use of them (I). On the one hand, such a connection makes it necessary to delimit the proper scope of financial market law (II). On the other hand, this connection makes it possible to establish the connecting factor of financial instruments: the securities settlement system would provide a particularly secure connecting factor to the proprietary status of the securities admitted to it, while the clearing system already constitutes the connecting factor of the vast majority of financial contracts that use it (III).

PROPOSALS

I. CONNECTING FACTOR OF MARKET INFRASTRUCTURES

THE CONFIGURATION OF THE INFRASTRUCTURE CONNECTING FACTOR

1) The financial market today is based on four infrastructures: trading platforms, clearing systems, securities settlement systems and payment systems. These four infrastructures have in common that they are made up of a legal element, the rules of the system, and a material element, the IT tool.[1]
2) In France, the various market infrastructures, as well as their supervision, were for a long time managed by the corporation of stockbrokers (*agents de change*), whose administrative status dictated the international connecting factor of the French stock exchanges.[2]
3) The growing sophistication of financial markets has led to a distinction being made between infrastructures, and to their management being entrusted to specialised legal persons who have in common the form of a commercial company under private law, with the exception of payment systems which are managed by the national central banks as soon as they use the central bank's currency; yet, the connecting factor of the manager is of decisive importance to that of the infrastructure.[3]
4) The institutional evolution of market infrastructure supervisors creates new interactions between the European and national legal orders, according to supervisory and decision-making models that are not comparable to each other. Nevertheless, they have in common that, in order to avoid conflicts of authorities and laws, it is necessary, on the one hand, to distinguish between the concepts of power and competence and, on the other hand, to have a division of competences between national

1 *Supra*, para. 31.
2 *Supra*, paras. 37 et seq.
3 *Supra*, paras. 41 et seq.

and European administrative authorities that is reminiscent of that known from the law of international jurisdiction.[4]

A. *Connecting Factor of Managers*

1. The Connecting Factor of European Managers

5) Like all legal persons, these infrastructure managers are subject to the legislation of their registered office. Their particularity is, however, that they are linked to their head office (*siege reel*) and that this dictates the application not only of local company law, but also of a so-called prudential law and a special insolvency prevention law, that of resolution.[5]

6) From the point of view of company law, the function of the head office connecting factor is not to protect third parties, whose protection can be ensured by substantive rules or by tort law, but to link the rules of organisation and management of the company to the place where the effective management is ensured.[6]

7) Prudential law is most often concerned with rules relating to the organisation of the legal person in order to make it more suitable for the pursuit of its activity: its primary aim, however, is to prevent the insolvency of the person it governs in order to protect the economic and social order within which it operates.[7]

8) As it stands, only the clearing house is necessarily subject to resolution law because of the systemic risk it carries by interposing itself between its clients; but the other market managers would benefit from being subject to it because of the systemic risk that would be caused by the effect of their bankruptcy, if the systems they manage were to be interrupted.[8]

9) Resolution law applies the law of the seat of the company in a remarkably universalist way: it tempers it, in particular, when confronted with certain systems constituting market infrastructure, those of the Finality Directive.[9]

10) The management of a market infrastructure is subject to an administrative authorisation, which is associated with a monitoring of compliance with the conditions under which the authorisation is given, all of which constitutes a real administrative connecting factor of the manager.[10]

---

[4] *Supra*, paras. 59 et seq.
[5] *Supra*, paras. 84 et seq.
[6] *Supra*, paras. 86 et seq.
[7] *Supra*, paras. 94 et seq.
[8] *Supra*, paras. 103 et seq.
[9] *Supra*, paras. 109 et seq.
[10] *Supra*, paras. 112 et seq.

11) The seat of the manager is traditionally the criterion for designating the national competent administrative authority for the purposes of its supervision, which is the basis for a European distribution of administrative competences, coordinated through the mutual recognition of approvals.[11]
12) Nevertheless, infrastructure managers are obliged by both primary and secondary EU law to offer a right of access to the infrastructure they manage to European investment firms.[12]
13) Decentralised administrative supervision requires bilateral or even multilateral cooperation under the aegis of agreements between authorities and colleges of authorities, where the European Supervisory Authorities can provide binding mediation.[13]
14) Under this decentralised system, access to the territory of another Member State is subject to a procedure for notifying the intention to carry on business there, the implementation of which was inspired by the criterion of private international contract law. The latter appeared to be singularly irrelevant; the proposed criterion of solicitation is more conducive to the balance sought by the objectives of unifying the internal market and protecting investors pursued by the European legislator.[14]
15) The object of mutual recognition is here not only the foreign administrative decision, but also the supervision and control of the foreign authority, which explains its original regime, and in particular the drastic limitation of local administrative action.[15]
16) Under this decentralised regime, the designation of rules of conduct applicable to investment firms acting cross-border has been based on different criteria of objective location of the investment service in question. The common feature of these criteria is that they are irrelevant in situations where the selection of rules should be based on the mode of access to the territory of the other Member State.[16]
17) This designation should be used to characterise the place of the event giving rise to the damage in the context of Article 17 of the Rome II Regulation if the extra-contractual liability of the investment firm is engaged.[17]

---

[11] *Supra*, paras. 115 et seq.
[12] *Supra*, paras. 126 et seq.
[13] *Supra*, paras. 117 et seq.
[14] *Supra*, paras. 130 et seq.
[15] *Supra*, paras. 134 et seq.
[16] *Supra*, paras. 139 et seq.
[17] *Supra*, para. 148.

18) This decentralised model of administrative supervision extends in the same way to resolution, where a particularly broad competence is given to the authority of the seat of the possibly defaulting legal person.[18]

19) When a banking licence is granted to the infrastructure manager, the decentralised model ceases to be applicable: the administrative decision is then centralised in the hands of the European Central Bank, which is likely to deconcentrate the execution of supervision to local authorities, making it necessary for national and European authorities to interact constantly.[19]

20) The ECB's administrative jurisdiction does not entail the application of uniform European legislation: it must therefore deal with the national law applicable to the institution it supervises[20]; this dissociation appeared all the more fortunate[21] as the alleged reasons for this extension of the ECB's jurisdiction are not fully convincing.[22]

21) In the context of the determination of jurisdiction for the purpose of challenges to ECB acts, this dissociation between administrative decision-making authority and applicable law should be the basis for a *forum legis*, or at least for the establishment of a reverse preliminary ruling mechanism between the Court of Justice and the national supreme court to determine the relevant interpretation of the applicable national law.[23]

22) The centralised model of administrative supervision extends in the same way to resolution, with the exception that the resolution decision is not taken by the administrative authority, but by the political authority.[24]

2. Relations with Third Country Managers

23) As a matter of principle, third country operators wishing to provide access to market infrastructure must comply with EU legislation; by way of exception, they may benefit from an exemption, distinct according to the infrastructure in question, based on the equivalence method.[25]

24) Third country investment firms do not have to comply with EU legislation if they have only responded to a request from an EU client; they may, however, be granted national authorisation for their branch for the local

18 *Supra*, paras. 149 et seq.
19 *Supra*, paras. 180 et seq.
20 *Supra*, paras. 177 et seq.
21 *Supra*, paras. 182 et seq.
22 *Supra*, paras. 168 et seq.
23 *Supra*, paras. 186 et seq.
24 *Supra*, paras. 193 et seq.
25 *Supra*, paras. 204 et seq.

market only, which gives significant control to the country of the place of establishment.[26]

25) The equivalence method is based on the equivalence of foreign legislation and administrative supervision, incorporating an individual registration decision and binding the foreign entity with its own regime.[27]
26) Within the various infrastructures, foreign regulated markets are treated in a special way, with two equivalence mechanisms, one national and one European: they should be conflated.
27) The equivalence method appears, in certain respects, to be a projection of the mutual recognition method with third countries; it differs, however, in that it does not presuppose the reciprocity inherent in mutual recognition, and in that the decision on equivalence, entrusted to the Commission, is also taken on political grounds.[28]
28) The equivalence method follows the dialectic of the objectives of private international law: it allows the coordination of legal orders and, therefore, the development of cross-border private relationships; in order to preserve the domestic order, it is nevertheless liable to be crowded out or competed with when it contradicts the objectives of the legislative bodies of the forum whose equivalence is sought.[29]

B. The Connecting Factor of Systems

29) The connecting factor of systems is based on the characterisation of this concept, the source of which is to be found, for trading platforms, in the MiFID 2 Directive, and for payment, clearing and securities settlement systems in the Finality Directive.[30]
30) The characterisation of trading platforms, and especially of regulated markets, entails the application of the Transparency, Takeover and Market Abuse Directives, and as such imposes obligations on those who make use of the financial market. The Finality Directive also attaches a special regime to transactions that make use of the systems it governs. For this reason, the connecting factor of the system is likely to constitute the proper connection of the transactions that make use of it.[31]

---

[26] *Supra*, paras. 205 et seq.
[27] *Supra*, paras. 209 et seq.
[28] *Supra*, paras. 219 et seq.
[29] *Supra*, paras. 218 et seq.
[30] *Supra*, paras. 227 et seq.
[31] *Supra*, paras. 227 et seq.

1. The Notion of a System

31) Each of the systems has a function independent of the others[32]; the functioning of the financial market nevertheless requires international coordination between systems subject to different laws, which is achieved in particular through private law contracts concluded between the managers of the securities settlement systems and the national central banks.[33]

32) The multilateral, i.e. collective, nature of the system gives rise to an interest in the system itself, distinct from the sum of the interests of the bilateral contracts with its members.[34]

33) The ECB is responsible for the supervision of payment systems; it has claimed that it is also responsible for the supervision of securities clearing and settlement systems. This claim has been rejected by the Court of Justice: the supervision of the latter systems is the responsibility of their operators, who are themselves subject to their own administrative supervision.[35]

34) There is a controversy as to the nature of system rules, and especially the rules of regulated markets; the view defended here is that these rules are all contractual, with the contract in question being entered into, on the one hand, by the members of the system and its manager, and on the other hand, where appropriate, by the issuers and the manager.[36]

2. The Applicable Conflict Rules

35) The contractual nature of the rules does not, however, imply the application of the law of autonomy: MiFID 2 thus applies to regulated market rules the law of the seat of their managers, whereas it does not provide for any rule for other financial markets; the law of the seat of their manager should apply by analogy.[37]

36) The law of autonomy is not necessarily the most suitable for governing organisations, even contractual ones, and *a fortiori* organisations that are of crucial interest to the country in which they are predominantly located.[38]

37) The Finality Directive uses a conflict rule based on a limited choice of law for the systems it governs; this criterion, which has so far only resulted in

32 *Supra*, paras. 231 et seq.
33 *Supra*, paras. 240 et seq.
34 *Supra*, paras. 242 et seq.
35 *Supra*, paras. 244 et seq.
36 *Supra*, paras. 248 et seq.
37 *Supra*, paras. 267 et seq.
38 *Supra*, paras. 271 et seq.

the application of the law of the seat of the operator, would benefit from being replaced by the law of the seat of the operator.[39]

II. THE SCOPE OF FINANCIAL MARKET LAW

38) If the connection of trading platforms is the basis for the international application of capital markets law, it is still necessary to determine the cases where the law of the financial market actually applies in order to protect the operation of the trading platform. This is the case only where it applies to investors; where it applies to issuers, the law of the financial market applies, in the vast majority of cases, as the law of the place of solicitation in order to protect investors.[40]

A. Relationships with Issuers

39) In its relationship with issuers, the law of the financial market could be presented as a unilateral conflict rule, whose application would be based on the criterion of solicitation and which would be self-limited where the law of the issuer offers equivalent protection. While this idea governs in an underlying way the international applicability of the rules relating to the marketing of securities and the resulting liability, independently of the admission of the securities to a financial market, it does not fully account for the pre-eminence of the law of the issuer in relation to the issuance of securities.[41]

1. The Issue

40) From an international perspective, issuance must be strictly distinguished from marketing, which begins with the delivery of the security to the first beneficiary. The laws governing these two sets of legislation are not always the same: they follow different rationales and objectives that do not always converge.[42]

41) In the case of securities, the law of the issuer has primacy, not because it is the law under which the represented *negotium* was originally constituted, which is true only in the case of shares, but because it is at the origin of the issue itself; this primacy does not mean, however, that the law

---

39 *Supra*, paras. 277 et seq.

40 *Supra*, paras. 282 et seq.

41 *Supra*, paras. 282 et seq.

42 *Supra*, paras. 290 et seq.

of the issuer must be applied to all aspects of the security, but that its prescriptions cannot be contradicted.[43]

42) The law of the issuer applies to the conditions of the issue, i.e. in the first place to the ability to create financial securities, and may, to a certain degree, extend to the determination of the consideration required for the granting of the *negotium*, in particular by making the ownership of the share conditional on the performance of certain acts.[44]

43) On the other hand, the application of the law of the issuer to the form of the securities is not a necessity: the *lex creationis* of the *negotium* – the *lex societatis* for shares, the law of the contract of issue for claims – would be preferable.[45]

44) The *lex mercatus* does not directly interfere with the law applicable to the form of the securities, but it conditions the admission of securities to trading on compliance with the substantive solutions it promotes.[46]

45) The reason for the invariable competence of the *lex societatis* with regard to shares is to be found in a principle of substantive law, the principle of equal treatment of shareholders, and in a principle of conflict of laws: the shareholders constitute the founding group of the company, and the need for legislative unity in the organisation of the company is all the more important when a legal person is involved.[47]

46) The *lex mercatus* does not interfere with the share regime, but conditions the applicability of some of its regulations – those on threshold crossings and takeover bids – on the prerogatives offered by their ownership, even if only in power.[48]

47) The *negotia* represented by debt claims are subject to the law of the contract of issue, the scope of which must be circumscribed and articulated with the *lex societatis* as soon as the *negotium* gives access to capital.[49]

48) Restructuring clauses in the issue contract that are subject to foreign law and jurisdiction do not fall under private international contract law, but private international insolvency law: it is the latter that must assess their validity and scope,[50] while the law of the contract remains applicable only to the adjustment of the debt between the creditors and the company.[51]

---

43 *Supra*, paras. 294 et seq.
44 *Supra*, paras. 297 et seq.
45 *Supra*, paras. 303 et seq.
46 *Supra*, paras. 311 et seq.
47 *Supra*, paras. 314 et seq.
48 *Supra*, para. 317.
49 *Supra*, paras. 318 et seq.
50 *Supra*, paras. 324 et seq.
51 *Supra*, para. 332.

49) The shares of the collective investment undertaking are subject to the *lex societatis,* whereas the units of the unincorporated undertaking should be subject to the law of the fund rules; in the latter case, where administrative supervision exists, it may informally interfere with the choice of law.[52]

2. Marketing

50) The rules on the marketing of financial securities have the function of protecting residents and are therefore naturally subject to the law of the place of solicitation. The admission of financial securities to trading on a market is a particularly intense form of solicitation of residents; the law of the financial market is therefore likely to intervene, as the law of the place of solicitation, in order to govern the marketing rules.[53]

51) The law of the place of solicitation has the particularity of being self-limiting when the law of the issuer provides for equivalent protection. This idea has penetrated the European legal order so well that, in intra-European relations and after harmonising the rules in question, the country of the issuer's registered office has usually been given jurisdiction in principle.[54]

52) It is unfortunate that the legislative competence given to the law of the issuer's registered office with regard to marketing rules in these circumstances extends to administrative competence for the approval of marketing documents, which should remain with the authority of the place of solicitation.[55]

53) The coordination of administrative authorities in international relations frequently takes place by means of self-limitation, which most often takes the form of a decision to exempt the foreign entity. This technique, which owes its success to the advantageous situation in which it places the authority, sometimes appears to be a last resort, making it possible to adjust a scope of application that is unsuited, if not to the legislative policy pursued, at least to the pursuit of that policy in international relations.[56]

54) Marketing acts are not, in principle, subject to the law of the financial market, but to the law designated by the act. However, the trading rules of the platform on which the securities are admitted are indirectly applicable to all marketing activities by imposing certain constraints on the issuer

52 *Supra*, paras. 333 et seq.
53 *Supra*, paras. 340 et seq.
54 *Supra*, paras. 340 et seq.
55 *Supra*, paras. 353 et seq.
56 *Supra*, paras. 362 et seq.

under the membership agreement, the violation of which may lead to the delisting of its securities.[57]

55) Listing and delisting are unsurprisingly subject to the *lex mercatus*, except in the case where delisting is initiated by the shareholder of the issuer whose securities are listed. In the latter case, the *lex societatis* is applicable without any particularly satisfactory basis: delisting should be governed solely by the law of the financial market.[58]

56) The law applicable to the public offer of financial securities, in the absence of a choice of law, should be the law of the place of business of the offeror in order to preserve the legislative unity of the transaction, either in respect of the sale or in respect of the characteristic performance. On the other hand, the scope of this law, which cannot be set aside by the special rule for consumers, cannot exceed that granted to the *lex contractus.*[59]

57) The rules of the financial market, when the financial securities offered to the public are admitted to trading, nevertheless impose their application to the transaction by obliging the issuer *a priori* to comply with them under the membership agreement concluded with the market operator, at the risk, otherwise, of having the securities delisted.[60]

3. Responsibility

58) The issuer's liability for the information it disseminates on the basis of the marketing of the securities has several particularities, the most significant of which is that of the harm it may cause to the investor: the alteration of his decision to invest.[61]

59) As the case law of the Court of Justice stands, the nature of the issuer's liability is marked by a certain contingency depending on whether the claimant's action is based on contract or tort.[62]

60) The action may in fact be contractual on the basis of the contract of issue or public offering; if it can be characterised as tortious, it is most often because the plaintiff, while bearing the risk inherent in the disputed investment, is not necessarily the owner of the security and cannot, therefore, rely on one of these contracts.[63]

61) If the issuer's liability is characterised as contractual, the law of the contract will be the one he selected and the presence of a consumer is not

57 *Supra*, paras. 366 et seq.
58 *Supra*, paras. 367 et seq.
59 *Supra*, paras. 370 et seq.
60 *Supra*, paras. 370 et seq.
61 *Supra*, paras. 378 et seq.
62 *Supra*, paras. 383 et seq.
63 *Supra*, paras. 383 et seq.

likely to alter it; however, the determination of the competent jurisdiction is subject, on the one hand, to the interference of the consumer contract and, on the other, to the interference inherent in the current disorder relating to the validity and enforceability of jurisdiction clauses.[64]

62) From the point of view of tort, the damage suffered – the alteration of the investment decision – is necessarily located at the investor's seat. From the perspective of the Brussels Ia Regulation, such a solution establishes a *forum actoris*, and should therefore be tempered by the localisation of the damage according to the event giving rise to it, the local dissemination of the contentious information, in order to respect the objective of predictability of the Regulation. The notification of the prospectus to the local administrative authority is likely to characterise this solicitation.[65]

63) According to the case law of the Court of Justice, it is expected that a *forum actoris* may be established if it is not disputed that the issuer intentionally misled investors by the information it disseminated.[66]

64) The admission of securities to trading on a financial market constitutes a form of solicitation and should therefore give jurisdiction to local courts for civil liability claims; it should not, however, preclude the jurisdiction of other countries where the disputed information was intentionally disseminated.[67]

65) The admission to trading of securities should not lead to the enactment of a specific solution in the field of applicable law: ordinary law produces particularly satisfactory results by allowing the legal system disturbed by the damage to obtain compensation, while taking into account the rules of conduct of the place of the event giving rise to the damage.[68]

B. Relations with Investors

66) The purpose of the rules triggered by admission to trading allows them to be grouped together in a bilateral conflict-of-laws rule according to which: 'Rules relating to the operation of the financial market are subject to the law of the trading venue.'

67) The scope of such a rule covers those relating to the obligations of market members towards the financial market, the regulation of market transactions, and the law of market abuse, even though as the law stands,

64 *Supra*, paras. 405 et seq.
65 *Supra*, paras. 415 et seq.
66 *Supra*, paras. 426 et seq.
67 *Supra*, paras. 428 et seq.
68 *Supra*, paras. 430 et seq.

part of the regulation of market transactions is still unduly subject to the law of the seat of the target company.[69]

1. Relationships with market members

68) Market members enter into relationships with three types of people: their clients, other market members and the market manager. In the past, the law of the financial market applied indiscriminately to the different relationships of market members, their clients, other members and the manager; today it has been withdrawn from the relationship between market members and their clients, and retains its applicability to others.[70]

69) The obligations of the market member to the manager are subject to the *lex mercatus* by virtue of their status as market members; the relationship between members, when arising from transactions entered into through the use of the trading platform, is subject to the law of the market by virtue of the Rome I Regulation.[71]

70) The law applicable to the relationship between market members and their clients is now governed by the rules of the 1978 Hague Convention on the law applicable to agency, which allows the parties to designate the applicable law. However, this does not affect the effect of the rules of conduct of market members, which are applicable by virtue of their investment firm status and are indifferent to the law applicable to the contract.[72]

2. Market Operations

71) The regulation of trading, whether it is concerned with the supervision of the issuer or the artificial alteration of price, pursues the objective of a well-functioning market: as such, it is in principle subject to the *lex mercatus*.[73]

72) However, there is an ambiguity in the rules governing supervision of the issuer. On the one hand, the rules on shareholding thresholds also serve the purpose of the proper functioning of the issuer and are therefore legitimately subject to the *lex societatis* in a cumulative manner.[74]

69 *Supra*, paras. 436 et seq.
70 *Supra*, paras. 437 et seq.
71 *Supra*, paras. 437 et seq.
72 *Supra*, paras. 449 et seq.
73 *Supra*, paras. 459 et seq.
74 *Supra*, paras. 470 et seq.

73) On the other hand, some of the rules on takeover bids are unduly removed from the sphere of capital market law and made subject to the legal system of the registered office of the company to which the bid is made, without any satisfactory explanation: neither the argument of equal treatment of shareholders nor the use of a corporate sanction can justify an exclusively corporate characterisation of the rules on exemptions from the obligation to file a bid, on the percentage of voting rights that gives control, on defences against takeover bids, or on shareholders' agreements that restrict share transfers.[75]
74) The contract resulting from the acceptance of the takeover bid would benefit from an objective connection to the law of the place of listing.[76]
75) In the case of takeover bids, the legal system of the place of listing should be given overall jurisdiction, making compliance with its provisions by the legal system of the issuer's registered office a condition for the issuer's listing.[77]
76) There can be no doubt that the market legal order has overriding jurisdiction over the rules on artificial price distortion, both as regards the rules on short selling and share buybacks.[78]

3. Market Abuse

77) The international application of the regulation of market abuse is subject to the interference of the jurisdictional criteria of French criminal law. The latter are unsatisfactory: French territorial jurisdiction leads to artificial solutions for offences whose constituent elements have largely been dematerialised.[79]
78) The objective of market abuse law is to protect the integrity of European financial markets: whenever the transaction constituting market abuse corrupts the mechanism of the French or European trading platform in question, French criminal law should have jurisdiction.[80]
79) This legislation would therefore benefit from being subject to '*competence réelle*', which has the advantage of taking into account the purpose of the rules in question, while guaranteeing the predictability of their application: to this end, let the use or allocation of the trading platform be the criterion for their international application.[81]

---

75 *Supra*, paras. 481 et seq.
76 *Supra*, paras. 500 et seq.
77 *Supra*, paras. 509 et seq.
78 *Supra*, paras. 516 et seq.
79 *Supra*, paras. 533 et seq.
80 *Supra*, paras. 525 et seq.
81 *Supra*, paras. 536 et seq.

80) The personal jurisdiction of French law must nevertheless be retained in order to avoid a repressive gap in the event that certain French nationals commit market abuse within foreign legal systems in which they are not prosecuted or extradited.[82]
81) The conditions for administrative cooperation in the enforcement of market abuse are largely based on the general law of international jurisdiction.[83]
82) This extension of the principles of civil proceedings to criminal proceedings appears questionable from the point of view of the authority accorded to *res judicata* abroad, since it amounts to applying the *ne bis in idem* principle in international relations, whereas in criminal matters, the State should be free to judge those who have caused such a serious breach of its social order.[84]
83) Coordination in criminal matters should not take place through a principle of a *priori* division of competences, moreover based on a temporal criterion, but, on the one hand, through the existence of a discretion of the public prosecutor's office as to the appropriateness of the prosecution and, on the other hand, through an imputation of the penalty imposed and served abroad at the time of the execution of the locally administered criminal sanction.[85]
84) For reasons of private international law, the regime of cooperation of administrative authorities should give an important part to the local law, either as the law of the requested authority or as the law of the place of investigation, both as regards cooperation, investigative measures, the resulting liability or the status of the evidence thus obtained.[86]
85) The court of the place where the investigative measures are carried out should have jurisdiction irrespective of who actually investigated the case, and without prejudice to a possible appeal against the measures taken in this respect within the legal system of the requesting authority.[87]

III. THE STATUS OF FINANCIAL INSTRUMENTS

86) The influence of the central depository on the proprietary status of financial securities and of the clearing house on the law applicable to financial contracts can be manifested independently of the use of the

[82] *Supra*, paras. 540 et seq.
[83] *Supra*, paras. 552 et seq.
[84] *Supra*, paras. 549 et seq.
[85] *Supra*, paras. 552 et seq.
[86] *Supra*, paras. 560 et seq.
[87] *Supra*, paras. 564 et seq.

financial market, since recourse to these infrastructures can also take place for OTC transactions.[88]

87) The relationship between these infrastructures and the status of the instruments they admit into their system is asymmetrical: where the law of the central depository system does not necessarily apply to the proprietary status of the security admitted into it, even though this application would make it possible to resolve most of the related difficulties, the law of the clearing system already applies to the vast majority of the contracts that use it.[89]

A. *The Proprietary Status of Securities*

88) The proprietary status of securities is often obscured by confusions arising from property law: it would be preferable to use the notion of ownership rather than that of property in order to recall that, although intangible property is susceptible to appropriation, the prerogatives that it offers cannot be assimilated to those arising from tangible property.[90]

89) Securities are now held through a chain of intermediaries, which makes the still existing plurality of connections thesis, according to which a potentially separate law should apply to each transfer, even more dysfunctional; the persistence of this thesis, in contrast to its misdeeds, is a real curiosity when a unitary solution to the conflict of laws is possible: it is based on the system of settlement of securities.[91]

1. Position of the Problem

90) Substantial unification of the prerogatives offered by book-entry securities will not resolve conflicts of law; the one proposed by Unidroit, which is based on *security entitlement*, will only increase them.[92]

91) If the *negotia* represented by financial instruments are fundamentally claims, and if the law of the transferor now proposed to govern the enforceability of their transfer against third parties is indisputably correct, it is nevertheless futile to seek solutions to the conflict of laws relating to financial instruments within their statute; it is necessary to consider the negotiability attached to securities and the objective which it pursues, which militates in favour of a unitary solution to the conflict of laws.[93]

---

88 *Supra*, paras. 569 et seq.
89 *Supra*, paras. 569 et seq.
90 *Supra*, paras. 570 et seq.
91 *Supra*, paras. 571 et seq.
92 *Supra*, paras. 574 et seq.
93 *Supra*, paras. 583 et seq.

92) Lessons can usefully be drawn from the law of negotiable instruments, where thesis of the plurality of connections, which had no substantive basis in domestic law, had the effect of frustrating the objectives pursued by these instruments in international relations, whereas a unitary solution was possible and based on the law of payment.[94]

2. Critique of the Plural Connection of Bearer Securities

93) Financial securities in bearer form have long been materialised by a paper medium and as such subject to the *lex situs*; the latter, however, reproduced the impasses of the thesis of the plurality of connections in the law of negotiable instruments, whereas a unitary solution of the conflict of laws based on the law of the issuer could be envisaged.[95]

94) Today, securities are registered in an account with an intermediary, which is most often part of an intermediation chain that goes as far as the central depository, whose accounts are the only ones that can be used as proof of the existence and integrity of the securities that the issuer has registered with its services; the accounts of the central depository[96] are thus pre-eminent.

95) From an international perspective, the singularity of this intermediation is twofold: on the one hand, national systems of intermediation are intertwined in international relations and, on the other hand, the book entry of securities allows the exercise of different rights with the intermediary depending on the legal system.[97]

96) The conflict rule currently in force in the European Union, known as PRIMA, which makes the relevant intermediary the connecting factor, originated in the United States, where it was designed as a variation of the issuer's law for secondary securities issued by the intermediaries themselves, and not for primary securities.[98]

97) The *PRIMA* rule, as established in the European Union, is based on a methodological confusion, which has led to the validity of the transfer of securities being multiplied by all the laws of the intermediaries in the chain of intermediation, not to mention the fact that it uses the law of the seat of the transferee in each case, i.e., of the three criteria that could be envisaged – the transferor, the transferred security and the transferee – the one that is the least foreseeable.[99]

---

94 *Supra*, paras. 596 et seq.
95 *Supra*, paras. 628 et seq.
96 *Supra*, paras. 648 et seq.
97 *Supra*, paras. 668 et seq.
98 *Supra*, paras. 677 et seq.
99 *Supra*, paras. 684 et seq.

98) In addition to confirming the thesis of multiple connections, a defect for which no absolution is possible, the implementation of the *PRIMA* rule within the Union suffers from two pathologies: the first stems from the diversity of its sources, which modifies its material scope of application and its domain depending on the case; the second lies in the criterion it uses, which is incapable of designating with certainty a law.[100]

99) The solution to this uncertainty as to the criterion used is to retain, as a matter of principle, the application of the law of the registered office of the account holder; by exception, if the intermediary has a branch within the legal system of the account holder at the time of its opening, it should on the other hand be deemed to be held at the place of that branch. This solution could usefully be supplemented, on the one hand, by requiring the account keeper to include an apparent legal identifier on the title of the securities account and on the account agreement and, on the other hand, by subjecting custodian-account keepers to approval.[101]

100) The PRIMA rule, as implemented by the Hague Convention, differs from the European rules in that it makes it possible to base the property status of the security not on the objective location of the intermediary, but on the choice of law made by the parties in the account agreement; the criticisms it incurs are therefore even more important.[102]

3. Proposal for a Unitary Solution of the Conflict of Laws

101) The argument of the plurality of connections has never been uncontested: the connection of the law of registered securities to the law of the issuer thus gave the conflict of laws a unitary, predictable and harmonious solution, based on the objective pursued by company law when it imposes the registered form.[103]

102) This solution would benefit from being extended to securities registered in a shared electronic recording device based on *blockchain* technology, as long as they are in registered form.[104]

103) In the context of securities registered with an intermediary, the *PRIMA* rule also originally suffered from a particular handicap: the competition of the law of the securities settlement system in case of insolvency of the member, in a dynamic where financial law tries to limit the disruption caused by bankruptcy law.[105]

---

100 *Supra*, paras. 696 et seq.
101 *Supra*, paras. 705 et seq.
102 *Supra*, paras. 711 et seq.
103 *Supra*, paras. 733 et seq.
104 *Supra*, paras. 740 et seq.
105 *Supra*, paras. 744 et seq.

104) From a substantive point of view, this limitation of the *lex concursus*, while of indisputable relevance when it concerns the systems of the Finality Directive, has no relevance in the context of financial collateral for OTC transactions: this is even more apparent when one of the contracting parties is subject to the resolution regime.[106]

105) From a conflictual point of view, the application of the law of the settlement system to the proprietary status of the securities registered therein is fully supported; the virtues of this law are such that it should govern the entire proprietary status of securities deposited in the accounts of a central depository, thus definitively purging the law of securities of the thesis of the plurality of attachments.[107]

B. *The Status of Financial Contracts*

106) The rule of autonomy, which makes it possible to abstract the financial contract from its underlying, is likely to account for the regime attached, in domestic law, to this contract; from the international point of view, the scope of this rule is limited: the law of the underlying may intervene either to prevent the formation of financial contracts, or to interfere in their regime, or to punish the contractors.[108]

107) The massive standardisation of financial contracts under the aegis of the *ISDA*, and the importance of the procedures that this association has implemented, does not make it possible to characterise a *lex mercatoria*, nor to detach these contracts from the state legal orders.[109]

1. The Law Applicable to the Financial Contract

108) Financial contracts are not characterised by an intrinsic internationality of the sector of activity in question, but are most often international because of the presence in different countries of the parties to the contract, the foreignness of the underlying asset whose risk they are trying to avoid, or the contractual grouping within which they are embedded.[110]

109) The law chosen by the parties, which is frequently that selected by the professional association that drew up the contract, is usually chosen independently of the substantive content of the *lex contractus*: on the one hand, because of the insolvency law of the designated legal order, and on the other hand, because of the court chosen by the contract, whose

---

[106] *Supra*, paras. 745 et seq.
[107] *Supra*, para. 761 et seq.
[108] *Supra*, paras. 813 et seq.
[109] *Supra*, paras. 815 et seq.
[110] *Supra*, paras. 819 et seq.

choice is closely linked to membership of a regional and international system that favours the recognition of decisions taken.[111]

110) Financial contracts, as investment services, are subject to Article 6 of the Rome I Regulation.[112]

2. Disruptions Related to the Formation of the Contract

111) While certain rules, which protect the integrity of the underlying, may affect the validity of the financial contract in question, defects in consent are, in principle, governed by the *lex contractus*. As a result, from an international perspective, the protection of residents against the risks inherent in the conclusion of financial contracts takes place through the legislative packages relating to the capacity and marketing of financial contracts.[113]

112) On the face of it, French law provides for a measured regime of incapacity that tends to promote the hedging function of the financial contract while preventing it from being used for speculative purposes. On reflection, the criterion of speculative intent nevertheless appears dysfunctional: it should be preferred to the enactment of mandatory local rules, on the one hand, in the field of canvassing, by purely and simply prohibiting the solicitation of inexperienced persons, and on the other hand, in the field of the status of professionals, by the creation of advisory obligations.[114]

113) For natural persons, the incapacity laid down by French law is analysed as an incapacity to act and is therefore subject to personal status. For legal persons, the incapacity in question, which is not a question of the power of representation of the corporate officer, but of the legal person's ability to contract, is a matter of company law, which does not mean, from the point of view of jurisdiction, that it falls within the scope of the exclusive jurisdiction laid down for the *forum societatis*.[115]

114) The marketing of financial contracts to residents is governed by the French regulation on canvassing: its international application should be based on the status of the professionals of the persons to whom it applies and should apply regardless of the residence of the contracting parties; the specific regime applicable to financial contracts concluded with a consumer, on the other hand, should only apply under the *lex contractus*.[116]

---

[111] *Supra*, paras. 840 et seq.
[112] *Supra*, paras. 846 et seq.
[113] *Supra*, paras. 861 et seq.
[114] *Supra*, paras. 862 et seq.
[115] *Supra*, paras. 867 et seq.
[116] *Supra*, paras. 873 et seq.

115) Where the underlying contract is a share in a company and one of the contracting parties is a shareholder or manager, the financial contract may interfere with company law, which will usually find it difficult to oppose the validity of such a contract, unless the contract in question is itself subject to the *lex societatis* because it falls within its domain.[117]

116) Where the underlying is admitted to trading, the *lex mercatus* will not necessarily invalidate a contract that disturbs the functioning of the market; it therefore provides for administrative or even criminal sanctions against the contracting parties themselves where the contracts violate the regulations on public offers, short selling or market abuse.[118]

3. Disruptions in the Performance of the Contract

117) The purpose of the clearing obligation has evolved from protection against the risk of insolvency of the contracting party to prevention of systemic risk; its international scope of application reflects this and now provides for its applicability in respect of the domicile of one of the parties, or their guarantors, in the territory of the Union.[119]

118) The compulsory intervention of the clearing house between the participants has the effect of novating the contracts by subjecting them to the law designated by the system itself; if this does not correspond to the law of the system itself, a distinction must be made between the contract concluded, subject to the *lex contractus*, and the accounting service offered by the clearing house, which remains subject to the law of the clearing system.[120]

119) OTC financial contracts most often provide for a close-out netting mechanism, which benefits from a favourable regime in the event of insolvency, aimed at extracting its beneficiaries from the competition with the bankrupt party's other creditors.[121]

120) The contractualist analysis of the close-out netting mechanism, which claims to subject it to the *lex contractus* alone, even in the event of the contractor's resolution, must be rejected; the insolvency law, of which resolution is only a special variation, is the only legitimate one to decide on the principle and the extent of the favour to be reserved for close-out netting clauses subscribed by the bankrupt party.[122]

---

117 *Supra*, paras. 888 et seq.
118 *Supra*, paras. 893 et seq.
119 *Supra*, paras. 906 et seq.
120 *Supra*, paras. 922 et seq.
121 *Supra*, paras. 935 et seq.
122 *Supra*, paras. 941 et seq.

BIBLIOGRAPHY

Handbooks

ANCEL (B.) and LEQUETTE (Y.), *Les grands arrêts de la jurisprudence française de droit international privé*, 5th ed, Paris, Dalloz, 2006.

ATIAS (C.), *Droit civil, Les biens*, 11th ed., Paris, LexisNexis, 2011.

AUDIT (B.) and D'AVOUT (L.), *Droit international privé*, 8th ed., Paris, LGDJ, 2018.

AUDIT (M.), BOLLÉE (S.) and CALLÉ (P.), *Droit du commerce international et des investissements étrangers*, 3th ed., Paris, LGDJ, 2019.

BARTIN (E.), *Principes de droit international privé selon la loi et la jurisprudence française*, t. 1, 2 and 3, Paris, Montchrestien, 1935.

BÉZARD-FALGAS (J.), *Traité théorique et pratique du contentieux des transferts d'actions et obligations nominatives*, 3th éd, Paris, LGDJ, 1924.

BONHOMME (R.), *Instruments de crédit et de paiement*, 10th ed, Paris, LGDJ.

BONHOMME (R.) and ROUSSILLE (M.), *Instruments de crédit et de paiement*, LGDJ, 13th ed., 2019

BONNEAU (T.),

- *Droit bancaire*, 13th ed, Paris, LGDJ, 2019.
- *European and International Banking and Financial Regulation*, 5th ed, Brussels, Bruylant, 2020.

BONNEAU (T.) and DRUMMOND (Fr.), *Droit des marchés financiers*, 3th ed, Paris, Économica, 2010.

BONNEAU (T.), PAILLER (P.), ROUAUD (A.-C.), TEHRANI (A.) and VABRES (R.), *Droit financier*, Paris, LGDJ, 1st ed. (2017) et 2th ed. (2019).

BOURASSIN (M.) and BRÉMOND (V.), *Droit des sûretés*, 7th ed., Paris, Sirey, 2019.

BREDIN (J.-D.) and LOUSSOUARN (Y.), *Droit du commerce international*, Paris, Sirey, 1969.

BRUN (P.), *La responsabilité civile extracontractuelle*, 5th ed., Paris, LexisNexis, 2018.

BUREAU (D.) and H. MUIR WATT (H.), *Droit international privé*, 4th ed., Paris, PUF, 2017, 2 volumes.

COMBACAU (J.) and SUR (S.), *Droit international public*, 10th ed., Paris, Montchrestien, 2012.

COURET (A.), LE NABASQUE (H.), COQUELET (M.-L.), GRANIER (T.), PORACCHIA (D.), RAYNOUARD (A.), REYGROBELLET (A.) and ROBINE (D.), *Droit financier*, Paris, Dalloz, 2019.

DESPAGNET (F.), *Précis de droit international privé*, 5th ed. by C. DE BOECK, Paris, Sirey, 1909.

DEVÈZE (J.) *et al*, *Lamy Droit du financement*, Paris, Lamy, 2015.

DICEY, MORRIS and COLLINS, *The Conflict of Laws*, 15th ed, London, Sweet&Maxwell, 2012.

DICKINSON (A.), *The Rome II Regulation*, Oxford, OUP, 2008.

DIDIER (P.),

- *Droit commercial*, t. 3, Le marché financier, Les groupes de sociétés, Paris, PUF/Thémis, 1993.

- *Les sociétés commerciales*, t. 2, Paris, Economica, 2011.

Drummond (F.), *Droit financier*, Paris, Economica, 2020.

Escarra (J.), Escarra (E.) and Rault (J.), *Principes de droit commercial*, t. 6, Paris, Sirey, 1936.

Fabre-Magnan (M.), *Droit des obligations*, t. 1, 5th ed., t. 2, 4th ed., Paris, PUF, 2019.

Favoreu (L.) and Philip (L.), *Les grandes décisions du Conseil constitutionnel*, 18th ed., Paris, Dalloz, 2016.

François (J.), *Les obligations, Régime général*, 5th ed, Paris, Economica, 2020.

Gaudemet Tallon (H.),

- *Compétence et exécution des jugements en Europe*, 5th ed., Paris, LGDJ, 2015.
- and Ancel (M.-E.), *Compétence et exécution des jugements en Europe*, 6th ed., Paris, LGDJ, 2018.

Gauvin (A.), *Droit des dérivés de crédit*, Paris, Revue Banque Edition, 2003.

Gullifer (L.) and Payne (J.), *Corporate finance Law: principles and policy*, 2nd ed, Oxford, Hart, 2015.

Hamel (J.) and Lagarde (G.), *Traité de droit commercial*, Paris, Dalloz, 1956.

Hamel (J.), Lagarde (G.) and Jauffret (A.), *Traité de droit commercial*, t. 1, Paris, Dalloz, 1954.

Hilaire (J.), *Introduction au droit commercial*, Paris, PUF, 1986.

Lalande (A.), *Vocabulaire technique et critique de la philosophie*, 3th ed, Paris, PUF, 2010.

Le Cannu (P.) and Dondero (B.), *Droit des sociétés*, 8th ed., Paris, LGDJ, 2019.

Lepage (A.), Maistre du Chambon (P.) and Salomon (R.), *Droit pénal des affaires*, 5th ed., Paris, LexisNexis, 2018.

Lescot (P.) and Roblot, (R.) *Les effets de commerce*, t. 1 et 2, Paris, Rousseau et cie, 1953.

Lombois (C.), *Droit pénal international*, Paris, Dalloz, 1971.

Lucas (F.-X.), *Droit de la faillite*, 3th ed., Paris, PUF, 2021.

Malaurie (P.), Aynès (L.) and Stoffel-Munck (P.), *Droit des obligations*, 11th ed., Paris, LGDJ, 2020.

Marcadé and Pont, *Explication théorique et pratique du Code civil*, t. 8, Paris, Delamotte et Fils, 1877.

Mayaud (Y.), *Droit pénal général*, 5th ed., Paris, PUF, 2015.

Mayer (P.), Heuzé (V) and Rémy (C.), *Droit international privé*, 12th ed., Paris, LGDJ, 2019.

Mazeaud (H. and L.), *Traité de la responsabilité civile*, t. 3, 4th ed.

Mémento Sociétés Commerciales, Francis Lefebvre, 2017.

Menjucq (M.), *Droit international et européen des sociétés*, 5th ed., Paris, LGDJ, 2018.

Merle (P.), Fauchon (A.), *Sociétés commerciales*, 24th ed., Paris, Dalloz, 2020.

Merle (R.) and Vitu (A.), *Traité de droit criminel, Problèmes généraux de la science criminelle, Droit pénal général*, 7th ed., Paris, Cujas, 2000.

Niboyet (J.-P.), *Traité de droit international privé*, vol. 3 and 4, Paris, Sirey, 1948.

Partsch (P.-E.), *Droit bancaire et financier européen, t. 1, Cadre général - Les établissements de crédit*, 2nd ed., Brussels, Larcier, 2016.

Pellet (R.)

- *États et marchés financiers*, Paris LGDJ, 2017.
- *Droit financier public*, t. 1, Series 'Thémis', Paris, PUF, 2018.

Pillet, *Traité pratique de droit international privé*, vol. 1, 1923.

POTHIER, *Traité du contrat de change*, Paris/Orléans, Debure/Rouzeau-Montaut, 1773.

REBUT (D.), *Droit pénal international*, 3th ed., Paris, Dalloz, 2015.

RIASSETTO (I.) and STORCK (M.), *Les organismes de placement collectif*, t. 1, 2th ed., Paris, Joly Editions, 2016.

RIPERT (G.) and ROBLOT (R.), *Traité élémentaire de droit commercial*, t. II, Paris, LGDJ, 1964.

ROBLOT (R.), *Les effets de commerce*, Paris, Sirey, 1975.

RODIÈRE (R.), *Droit commercial*, 5th ed., Paris, Dalloz, 1970.

ROLAND (H.) and BOYER (L.), *Adages du droit français*, 4th ed, Paris, Litec, 1999.

SAVIGNY (F.C.), *Traité de droit romain*, t. VIII, trans. C.GUÉNOUX, Paris 1860.

SZRAMKIEWICZ (R.) and DESCAMPS (O.), *Histoire du droit des affaires*, 2th ed, Paris, LGDJ, 2013.

TERRÉ (Fr.), LEQUETTE (Y.), SIMLER (P.) and CHÉNEDÉ (F.), *Droit civil : les obligations*, 12th ed., Paris, Dalloz, 2018.

THALLER (E.), *Traité élémentaire de droit commercial à l'exception du droit maritime, t. I et II*, 8th ed. revised and updated by J. Percerou, Paris, 1931.

VAUPLANE (H. DE) and BORNET (J.-P.), *Droit des marchés financiers*, 3th ed., Paris, Litec, 2001.

VIANDIER (A.), *OPA OPE et autres offres publiques*, 5th ed, Paris, Francis Lefebvre, 2014.

VINEY (G.), JOURDAIN (P.) and CARVAL (S.), *Les conditions de la responsabilité*, 4th ed, Paris, LGDJ, 2013.

Monographs

ADALID (S.), *The European Central Bank and the Eurosystem*, Brussels, Bruylant, 2015.

ANCEL (B.), *Les conflits de qualifications à l'épreuve de la donation entre époux*, Paris, Dalloz, 1977.

ANCEL (B.), *Éléments d›histoire du droit international privé*, Paris, Édition Panthéon-Assas, 2017.

ANCEL (M.-E.), *La prestation caractéristique du contrat*, Paris, Economica, 2002.

ARCHINARD-GREIL (B.), *Lois de police et conflits de juridictions (Essai sur la coordination des systèmes à l'aide de la notion d'ordre juridique prépondérant)*, thesis, Université Lyon III, 2017.

ARSOUZE (C.), *Procédures boursières*, Paris, Editions Joly, 2008.

AUDIT (B.), *Le caractère fonctionnel de la règle de conflit (sur la 'crise' des conflits de lois)*, *RCADI*, t. 186, 1984.

AVÉRAN-HORTEUR (L.), *De la C.C.D.V.T. à la SICOVAM - Le compte courant d'actions*, Paris, Dalloz, 1959.

D'AVOUT (L.), *Sur les solutions du conflit de lois en droit des biens*, Paris, Economica, 2006.

D'AVOUT (L.), *L'entreprise et les conflits internationaux de lois*, *RCADI*, t. 398, Leiden, Brill, 2019.

BARBAN (P.), *Les entreprises de marché, Contribution à l'étude d'un modèle d'infrastructure de marché*, Paris, Institut Universitaire Varenne, 2015.

BARRIÈRE (F.) (av. propos), *Le traitement des difficultés des établissements bancaires et institutions financières*, Paris, LexisNexis, 2017.

BASEDOW (J.), *The Law of Open Societies*, *RCADI*, t. 360, The Hague, Martinus Nijhoff, 2013.

BATIFFOL (H.), *Les conflits de lois en matière de contrats - étude de droit international privé comparé*, Paris, Sirey, 1938.

BATIFFOL (H.), *Aspects philosophiques du droit international privé*, Paris, Dalloz, 1956.

Baxi (U.), *Mass torts, multinational enterprise liability and private international law*, RCADI, t. 176, The Hague, Martinus Nijhoff, 1999.

Beaud (O.), *Théorie de la Fédération*, 2th ed., Paris, PUF, 2009,

Beccaria (C.), *Des délits et des peines*, Paris, Flammarion, 2006.

Bédart (J.), *International Conflicts of Antitrust and Securities Regulation: It's All About Effects*, thesis, Columbia University, 2006.

Behar-Touchais (M.) (ed.), *La Blockchain saisie par le droit*, Paris, IRJS, 2019.

Benjamin (J.), *Interests in securities: a proprietary law analysis of the international securities market*, Oxford, OUP, 2000.

Bézard (P.), *Les offres publiques d'achat*, Paris, Masson, 1982.

Bismuth (R.), *La coopération internationale des autorités de régulation du secteur financier et le droit international public*, Brussels, Bruylant, 2011.

Bloch (P.), *Les lettres de change et billets à ordre dans les relations commerciales internationales*, Paris, Economica, 1986.

Blumann (C.) and Dubouis (L.), *Droit institutionnel de l'Union européenne*, Paris, LexisNexis, 2019.

Bode (M.), *Le groupe international de sociétés*, Brussels, Peter Lang, 2012.

Boissière (G.), *La Compagnie des agents de change et le marché officiel à la Bourse de Paris*, Paris, Rousseau, 1908.

Bonifay (E.), *Le principe de reconnaissance mutuelle et le droit international privé*, Paris, Institut Universitaire Varenne, 2017.

Bonneau (T.) (ed.), *La modernisation des activités financières*, Paris, GLN-Joly, 1996.

Boskovic (O.), *La réparation du préjudice en droit international privé*, Paris, LGDJ, 2003.

Boucobza (X.), *L'acquisition internationale de société*, Paris, LGDJ, 1998.

Bourel (P.), *Les conflits de lois en matière d'obligations extracontractuelles*, Paris, LGDJ, 1961.

Bourel (P.), *Du rattachement de quelques délits spéciaux*, RCADI, t. 214, Laiden, Martinus Nijhoff,1989.

Bouthinon-Dumas (H.), *Le droit des sociétés et le marché boursier: étude des conditions juridiques de la détermination de la valeur de la société par le marché boursier*, Paris, LGDJ, 2006.

Bradford (A.), *The Brussels Effect, Oxford*, OUP, 2020.

Braithwaite (J.), *The Financial Courts: Adjudicating Disputes in Derivatives Markets*, Cambridge, CUP, 2021.

Bureau (D.), *Les sources informelles du droit dans les relations privées internationales*, thesis, Université Paris II Panthéon-Assas, 1992.

Canivet (G.), Martin (D.) and Molfessis (N.) (dir.), *Les offres publiques d'achat*, Paris, LexisNexis, 2009.

Capitant (H.), *De la cause des obligations*, 3th ed, Paris, Dalloz, 1927.

Carreau (D.), *Souveraineté et coopération monétaire et internationale*, Paris, Cujas, 1970.

Chacornac (J.), *Essai sur les fonctions de l'information en droit des instruments financiers*, Paris, Dalloz, 2014.

Chemaly (R.), *Conflits de lois en matière d'effets de commerce*, thesis, Université Paris II Panthéon-Assas, 1981.

Chemaly (R.), *Conflits de lois en matière d'effets de commerce*, RCADI, t. 209, The Hague, Martinus Nijhoff, 1988.

Chénedé (F.), *Les commutations en droit privé, Contribution à la théorie générale des obligations*, Paris, Economica, 2008.

CHILSTEIN (D.), *Droit pénal international et lois de police - essai sur l'application dans l'espace du droit pénal accessoire*, Paris, Dalloz, 2003.

International colloquium on the private international law of corporate groups, Schweizerische Beiträge zum Europarecht, Geneva, 1974.

Compagnie des agents de change, *Manuel des agents de change: banque, finance et commerce, contenant les lois, règlements et actes officiels qui régissent et intéressent l'exercice de leurs fonctions*, 5th éd, Paris, 1914.

CONAC (P.-H.), *La régulation des marchés boursiers par la commission des opérations de bourse (COB) et la securities and exchange commission (SEC)*, Paris, LGDJ, 2002.

CORNELOUP (S.), *La publicité des situations juridiques - Une approche franco-allemande du droit interne et du droit international privé*, Paris, LGDJ, 2003.

CORNUT ST-PIERRE (P.), *La fabrique juridique des swaps*, Paris, Presse de SciencesPo, 2019.

COUPET (C.), *L'attribution du droit de vote dans les sociétés*, Paris, LGDJ, 2015.

CRAIG (W.L.), *La société sous contrôle étranger*, thesis, Université Paris II Panthéon-Assas, 1981.

DAMBRE (R.), *Les contrats financiers sur actions*, Brussels, Larcier, 2016.

DECKERT (K.), *La sollicitation publique des investisseurs en droit communautaire, français et allemand*, thesis, Université Paris I Panthéon-Sorbonne, 2009.

DELAPORTE (V.), *Recherches sur la forme des actes juridiques en droit international privé*, thesis, Université Paris 1 Panthéon-Sorbonne, 1974.

DELOZIÈRE-LE FUR (A.-V.), *La compensation dite multilatérale*, Paris, Panthéon-Assas, 2003.

DEVAUX (C.), *La fabrique du droit du commerce international - Réguler les risques de capture*, Brussels, Larcier, 2019.

DEXANT - DE BAILLIENCOURT (O.), *Les pactes d'actionnaires dans les sociétés cotées*, Paris, Dalloz, 2012.

DIETHELM (M.-B.), *Le droit des offres publiques d'achat : une approche internationale*, thesis, Université Paris II Panthéon-Assas, 1992.

DONNEDIEU DE VABRE (H.), *Les principes modernes de droit pénal international*, Paris, Sirey, 1928, republished by Ed. Panthéon-Assas, 2004.

FABRE-MAGNAN (M.), *De l'obligation d'information dans les contrats*, Paris, LGDJ, 1992.

FABRE-MAGNAN (M.), *L'institution de la liberté*, Paris, PUF, 2018.

FARNOUX (É.), *Les considérations substantielles dans le règlement de la compétence internationale des juridictions - Réflexions autour de la matière délictuelle*, thesis, Université Paris I Panthéon-Sorbonne, 2017.

FENET (P.-A.), *Recueil complet des travaux préparatoires du Code civil*, t. 15, Paris, 1827.

FERNANDEZ (S.), *Essai sur la distribution des compétences en droit pénal international*, Paris, Fondation Varenne, 2016.

FERNÁNDEZ ARROYO (D.), *Compétence exclusive et compétence exorbitante dans les relations privées internationales*, RCADI, t. 323, The Hague, Martinus Nijhoff, 2006.

FERRAN (E.), *Building an EU securities* market, Cambridge, CUP, 2004.

FEUNTEUN (C.), *Instruments hybrides et Accords de Bâle*, thesis, Université Paris II Panthéon-Assas, 2019.

FOHRER-DEDEURWAERDER (E.), *La prise en considération des normes étrangères*, Paris, LGDJ, 2008.

FRANCESCAKIS (P.), *La théorie du renvoi et les conflits de systèmes en droit international privé*, Pais, Sirey, 1957.

FRIEDEL (G.), *De l'inopposabilité des exceptions en matière d'effets de commerce*, Paris, Rousseau, 1951.

GARAPON (A.) and SERVAN-SCHREIBER (P.), *Deals de justice*, Series 'Quadrige', Paris, PUF, 2020.

GARCIMARTIN ALFEREZ (F.), *Cross-border listed companies*, RCADI, t. 328, The Hague, Martinus Nijhoff, 2007.

GASPARD (R.), *La reconnaissance mutuelle en droit bancaire et financier*, Paris, Fondation Varenne, 2019.

GAUDEMET (A.), *Les dérivés*, Paris, Economica, 2008.

GAVRILOFF (J.), *Les méthodes du conflit de lois à l'épreuve du produit dérivé*, thesis, Université Paris X Nanterre, 2020.

GIJSBERS (C.), *Sûretés réelles et droit des biens*, Paris, Economica, 2015.

GLENN (P.), *La conciliation des lois*, RCADI, t. 364, The Hague, Martinus Nihjoff, 2011.

GOLBERG-DARMON (M.), *Les aspects juridiques de l'introduction en bourse*, thesis, Université Paris II Panthéon-Assas, 2000.

GOODE (R.), *Principles of corporate insolvency law*, 4th ed, London, Sweet&Maxwell, 2011.

GOURDY (H.), *La couverture sur les marchés financiers*, thesis, Université Paris II Panthéon-Assas, 2019.

GRANIER (C.), *Les sources du droit financier*, thesis, Université Lyon III, 2018.

GREENE (E.F.), BELLER (A.L.) *et al*, *U.S. Regulation of the International Securities and Derivatives Markets*, 12th ed., Wolters Kluwer.

GLENN (H.), *La capacité de la personne en droit international privé français et anglais*, Paris, Dalloz, 1974.

GULLIFER (L.) and PAYNE (J.), *Intermediated Securities*, Oxford, Hart, 2010.

GULLIFER (L.) and PAYNE (J.), *Intermediation and beyond*, Oxford, Hart, 2020.

HAFTEL (B.), *La notion de matière contractuelle en droit international privé - Étude dans le domaine du conflit de lois*, thesis, Université Paris II Panthéon-Assas, 2008.

HÄKER (B.), *Consequences of Impaired Consent Transfers: A Structural Comparison of English and German Law*, Oxford, Hart, 2013.

HAMEL (J.) and ANCEL (M.) (dir.), *La convention de Genève sur l'unification du droit du chèque*, Recueil Sirey, Paris, Sirey, 1937.

HARDY (G.), *L'européanisation de la surveillance bancaire*, thesis, Université Paris II Panthéon-Assas, 2021.

HENDERSON (S.), *Henderson on Derivatives*, 2nd ed., Paris, LexisNexis, 2009.

HEUZÉ (V.), *La réglementation française des contrats internationaux - étude critique des méthodes*, Paris, GLN édition, 1990.

HEYMANN (J.), *Le droit international privé à l'épreuve du fédéralisme européen*, Paris, Economica, 2010.

HISSUNG-CONVERT (N.), *La spéculation boursière face au droit 1799-1914*, Paris, LGDJ, 2009.

HOLLEAUX (D.), *Compétence du juge étranger et reconnaissance des jugements*, Paris, Dalloz, 1970.

JAULT-SESEKE (F.) and ROBINE (R.) (eds.), *Le nouveau règlement Insolvabilité : quelles évolutions*, Paris, Joly Editions, 2015.

JOBARD-BACHELLIER (M.-N.), *L'apparence en droit international privé – Essai sur le rôle des représentations individuelles en droit international privé*, Paris, LGDJ, 1984.

KAHN (P.) *La vente commerciale internationale*, Paris, Sirey, 1961.

KALLERGIS (A.), *La compétence fiscale*, Paris, Dalloz, 2018.

KLEINER (C.), *La monnaie dans les relations privées internationales*, Paris, LGDJ, 2010.

Koering-Joulin (R.), *L'article 693 du Code de procédure pénale et la localisation internationale de l'infraction. Essai sur le règlement des conflits de loi pénale dans l'espace,* thesis, University of Strasbourg, 1973.

Kronke (H.), *Capital Markets and Conflict of Law*, RCADI, t. 286, The Hague, Martinus Nijhoff, 2000.

Lambert (S.), *L'application internationale du droit financier,* thesis, Université Paris II Panthéon-Assas, 2021.

Lambertye-Autrand (M.-C. de), *La distinction des meubles et des immeubles en droit international privé*, thesis, Université Paris I Panthéon-Sorbonne, 2001.

Larguier (J.), *La notion de titre en droit privé*, Paris, Dalloz, 1951.

Laval (S.), *Le tiers et le contrat - Étude de conflit de lois*, Brussels, Larcier, 2016.

Le Bos (Y.-E.), *Renouvellement de la théorie du conflit de lois dans un contexte fédéral*, Paris, Dalloz, 2010.

Legrand (Y.), *Actions contractuelles en droit financier et compétence internationale*, Master 2 thesis, Université Panthéon-Assas, 2017.

Lehmann (P.-J.), *Histoire de la bourse de Paris*, Paris, PUF, 1998.

Lequette (Y.), *Protection familiale et protection étatique des incapables*, Paris, Dalloz, 1976.

Lequette (Y.), *Le droit international privé de la famille à l'épreuve des conventions internationales*, RCADI, t. 246, The Hague, Martinus Nijhoff, 1994.

Lequette (Y.) *Les mutations du droit international privé : vers un changement de paradigme ?*, RCADI, t. 387, The Hague, Martinus Nihjoff, 2017.

Lévy (L.), *La nationalité des sociétés*, Paris, LGDJ, 1984.

Lévy-Bruhl (H.), *Histoire de la lettre de change en France aux XVIIe et XVIIIe siècles*, Paris, Sirey, 1933.

Libchaber (R.), *Recherches sur la monnaie en droit privé*, Paris, LGDJ, 1992.

Libchaber (R.), *L'ordre juridique et le discours du droit*, Paris, LGDJ, 2013.

Libchaber (R.), *Le contrat au XXIème siècle*, Paris, LGDJ, 2020.

Louis (J.-V.), *L'Union européenne et sa monnaie*, 3th ed., Brussels, Université de Bruxelles, 2013.

Lucas (F.-X.), *Les transferts temporaires de valeurs mobilières*, Paris, LGDJ, 1997.

Magnier (V.) and Barban (P.) (eds.), *Blockchain and company law*, Paris, Dalloz, 2019.

Marcadé and Pont, *Explication théorique et pratique du Code civil*, t. 8, Paris, Delamotte et fils, 1967.

Martin (D.), *et al*, *Les abus de marché*, Paris, LexisNexis, 2013.

Martin Laprade (F.), *Concert et contrôle*, Paris, Joly sociétés, 2007

Martucci (F.) (ed.), *L'Union bancaire*, Brussels, Bruylant, 2016.

Mayer (P.), *La distinction entre règles et décisions en droit international privé*, Paris, Dalloz, 1973.

Mayer (P.), *Le phénomène de la coordination des ordres juridiques étatiques en droit privé*, RCADI, t. 327, The Hague, Martinus Nijhoff, 2007.

Méadel (J.), *Les marchés financiers et l'ordre public*, Paris, LGDJ, 2007.

Mojuye (J.-B.), *Le droit des produits dérivés financiers (swaps, options, futures, etc.) en France et aux États-Unis*, Paris, LGDJ, 2005.

Mollot, *Bourses de commerce, agents de change et courtiers*, t. I, 3rd ed., Paris, 1853.

Moloney (N.), *How to protect investors*, Cambridge, CUP, 2010.

Moloney (N.), Ferran (E.), Payne (J.) (eds.), *The Oxford Handbook of Financial Regulation*, Oxford, OUP, 2017.

Moreau-Bourles (M.-A.), *Structure du rattachement et conflits de lois en matière de responsabilité civile délictuelle*, thesis, Université Paris II Panthéon-Assas, 1985.

Morel-Maroger (J.), *Les opérations de banque en droit international privé*, thesis, Université Paris I, 2003.

Motulsky (H.), *Principes d'une réalisation méthodique du droit privé – La théorie des éléments générateurs des droits subjectifs*, Paris, Dalloz, 1948, reprinted 2002.

Muir Watt (H.), *Aspects économiques du droit international privé (Réflexions sur l'impact de la globalisation économique sur les fondements des conflits de lois et de juridictions)*, RCADI, t. 307, The Hague, Martinus Nijhoff, 2004.

Muller (A.-C.), *Droit des marchés financiers et droit des contrats*, Paris, Economica, 2007.

Neau-Leduc (P.), *La réglementation de droit privé*, Paris, Litec, 1998.

Niboyet (J.-P.), *Des conflits de lois relatifs à l'acquisition de la propriété et des droits sur les meubles corporels à titre particulier. Etude de droit international privé*, Paris, Sirey, 1912.

Niboyet (J.-P.), *Les doubles impositions du point de vue juridique*, *RCADI*, t. 31, The Hague, Martinus Nijhoff, 1931.

Nizard (F.), *Les titres négociables*, Paris, Revue Banque édition/Economica, 2003.

Ooi (M.), *Shares and other securities in the conflict of laws*, Oxford, OUP, 2003.

Pailler (P.), *Le contrat financier, Un instrument financier à terme*, Paris, IRJS Éditions, 2010.

Pardoël (D.), *Les conflits de lois en matière de cession de créance*, Paris, LGDJ, 1997.

Parrot (K.), *L'interprétation des conventions de droit international privé*, Paris, Dalloz, 2006.

Payne (J.), *Schemes of arrangement: Theory, Structure and Operation*, Cambridge, CUP, 2014.

Peltier (F.), *Marchés financiers & droit commun*, Paris, Revue Banque édition, 1997.

Perelman (C.) and Olbrechts-Tyteca (L.), *Traité de l'argumentation*, Brussels, Université Libre de Bruxelles, 2008.

Picone (P.), *La méthode de la référence à l'ordre juridique compétent en droit international privé*, RCADI, t. 197, The Hague, Martinus Nijhoff, 1986.

Picone (P.), *Les méthodes de coordination entre ordres juridiques en droit international privé*, RCADI, t. 276, The Hague, Martinus Nijhoff, 1999.

Pietrancosta (A.), *Le droit des sociétés sous l'effet des impératifs financiers et boursiers*, thesis, Université Paris I Panthéon-Sorbonne, 1999.

Pistor (K.), *The Code of Capital*, Princeton University Press, 2019.

Praicheux (S.), *Les sûretés sur les marchés financiers*, Paris, Revue Banque édition, 2004.

Quéguiner (J.-S.*), Qualification et détermination de la compétence spéciale : l'exemple de la matière contractuelle*, thesis, Université Lyon III, 2012.

Riassetto (I.), *Les garanties des contrats à terme sur le MATIF*, thesis, Strasbourg, 1999.

Rigaux (F.), *Les situations juridiques individuelles dans un système de relativité générale*, *RCADI*, t. 213, The Hague, Martinus Nijhoff, 1989.

Riles (A.), *Collateral knowledge: Legal Reasoning in the Global Financial Markets*, Chicago University Press, 2011.

Ringe (W.), Gullifer (L.) and Théry (P.), *Current issues in European Financial and Insolvency Law*, Oxford, Hart, 2009.

Ripert (G.), *Aspects juridiques du capitalisme moderne*, 2th ed, Paris, LGDJ, 1951.

Robine (D.), *La sécurité des marchés financiers face aux procédures collectives*, Paris, LGDJ, 2003.

Roblin (L.), *Les offres publiques d'achat*, Paris, Dunod, 1969.

Romano (R.), *The advantage of Competitive Federalism for Securities Regulation*, AEI Press, 2003.

ROMANO (S.), *L'ordre juridique*, Paris, Dalloz, 1975.

ROOVER (R. de), *L'évolution de la lettre de change. XIVe-XVIIIe siècles*, Paris, Armand Collin, 1953.

ROSA (F.), *Les actes de réglementation privée*, thesis, Université Paris I Panthéon-Sorbonne, 2011.

ROUAUD (A.-C.), *Contribution à l'étude de l'opération de marché, étude de droit des marchés financiers*, Paris, IRJS, 2010.

ROUSSILLE (M.), *La compensation multilatérale*, Nouvelle Bibliothèque de thèses, Paris, Dalloz, 2006.

SAAD (M.), *La notion de titre de capital*, thesis, Université Paris I Panthéon-Assas, 2016.

SABY (F.), *La notion de contrôle en droit comptable*, Master 2 thesis, Université Panthéon-Assas, 2019.

SANSONETTI (R.), *L'entraide administrative internationale dans la surveillance des marchés financiers*, Zurich, Schulthess, 1998.

SAVIGNY (F.-C.), *Traité de droit romain, vol. VIII*, reprinted in Panthéon-Assas, 2002.

SCHMITTHOFF (C.), *Agency in international trade*, RCADI, t. 129, The Hague, Martinus Nijhoff, 1970.

SEBBAN (G.), *Le bien juridique*, thesis, Université Paris II Panthéon-Assas, 2020.

SERVAIS (D.) (ed.) *L'intégration des marchés financiers*, Brussels, Université de Bruxelles, 2007.

SEUROT (L.), *L'autorisation administrative*, thesis, Université de Lorraine, 2013.

SOTIROPOULOU (A.), *Les obligations d'information des sociétés cotées en droit de l'Union européenne*, Brussels, Larcier, 2012.

SPITZ (N.), *La réparation des préjudices boursiers*, Paris, Revue Banque Edition, 2010.

STARK (L.), *L'internationalité en droit international privé*, thesis, Université Bourgogne Franche-Comté and Université Johannes Gutenberg de Mayence, 2020.

STIBBE (I.), *Les autorités administratives indépendantes et le droit du commerce international*, thesis, Université Paris II Panthéon-Assas, 2001.

STOEVA (B.), *La coopération entre les superviseurs financiers dans l'Union européenne*, thesis, Université du Luxembourg and Université Paris II Panthéon-Assas, 2013.

SYNVET (H.), *L'organisation juridique du groupe international de sociétés*, t. II, thesis, University of Rennes, 1979.

SYNVET (H.), *Accès à la cote et retrait de la cote*, Cours Inédit, 2018.

TEDJANI (M.), *Takeover bids: the international application of Swiss law*, Zurich, Schultess, 2015.

TEHRANI (A.), *Les investisseurs protégés en droit financier*, Paris, LexisNexis, 2015.

TENENBAUM (A.), *L'application internationale du droit boursier*, thesis, Université Paris I, 2000.

THALLER (E.), *De la faillite des agents de change et de la liquidation de leur charge*, Imp. Larose et Forcel, 1883.

TORCK (S.), *Essai d'une théorie générale des droits réels sur choses fongibles*, thesis, University of Paris II, 2001.

TRÉBULLE (F.-G.), *L'émission des valeurs mobilières*, Paris, Economica, 2002.

VABRES (R.), *Comitologie et services financiers*, Paris, Dalloz, 2009.

VAMPARYS (X.), *La blockchain au service de la finance*, Paris, Revue Banque Edition, 2018, pp. 28 et seq.

VERHEIJ (D.J.), *Credit rating agency liability in Europe. Rating the combination of EU and national law in rights of redress*, Eleven International Publishing, 2020.

VIRGÒS (M.) and GARCIMARTÍN (F.), *The European Insolvency Regulation: Law and Practice*, Kluwer Law International, 2004.

Vocabulaire Capitant, 8th ed, Paris, PUF, 2007.

Wahl (A.), *Traité théorique et pratique des titres au porteur*, t. I, Paris, Rousseau, 1891.

Watson (A.), *Legal Transplants: an approach to comparative law*, University of Georgio Press, 1993.

Weiss (A.), *Traité théorique et pratique de droit international privé*, Paris, Sirey, 1912.

Wood (P.), *Set-off and netting, Derivatives, Clearing system*, London, Sweet&Maxwell, 2007.

Articles

Adalid (S.), 'Le MSU, nouveau sous-système de droit de l'Union européenne', *RAE*, 2017, No. 2., pp. 363 et seq.

d'Ambra (D.) and Frison-Roche (M.-A.), 'La résolution bancaire entre droit commun des procédures collectives et droit commun de la régulation' in *Mélanges en l'honneur de Jean-Luc Vallens*, Paris, Lextenso, 2017, pp. 293 et seq.

Amieux, see 'Agent de Change' and 'Bourse (opérations de)', *Répertoire Niboyet-Lapradelle*, Paris, Sirey, 1929.

Ancel (M.-E.), 'Le champ personnel des clauses d'élection de for', *Les clauses attributives de juridiction : de la prévisibilité au désordre*, Paris, Ed. Panthéon-Assas, 2021, pp. 121 et seq.

Annunziata (F.), 'European Banking Supervision in the Age of the ECB', *European Business Organization Review*, January 2020, pp. 545 et seq.

Armour (J.), 'Making Bank resolution credible' in N. Moloney, E. Ferran and J. Payne (eds.), *The Oxford Handbook of Financial Regulation*, Oxford, OUP, 2017, pp. 453 et seq.

Arranz (L.), 'Level playing field: towards a more uniform application of banking legislation' in *ECB Legal Conference*, 6 October 2016, pp. 260 et seq.

Aubry (H.), see 'Démarchage bancaire ou financier', *Répertoire de droit des sociétés*, Paris, Dalloz.

Audit (M.),

- 'L'interprétation autonome du droit international privé communautaire', *JDI*, 2004, pp. 789 et seq.
- 'Les Credit Default Swaps comme miroir des dérives de l'endettement public' in H. Gherari (ed.) *Les dérèglements économiques internationaux : crise du droit ou droit des crises?* Paris, Pedone, 2014, pp. 81 et seq.
- and Bismuth (R.), Mignon-Colombet (A.), 'Sanctions et extraterritorialité du droit américain : quelles réponses pour les entreprises françaises ?', *JCP G*, 12 January 2015, pp. 37 et seq.
- 'Les autorités de régulation et le droit international privé' in *Mélanges en l'honneur du professeur Pierre Mayer*, Paris, LGDJ, 2015, pp. 43 et seq.
- 'Les dérivés de crédit à l'ombre du contrat sans loi', *TCFDIP*, Paris, Pedone, 2016, pp. 85 et seq.
- 'Does the French State get into debt by contract? A la recherche de la nature juridique des obligations assimilables du Trésor (OAT)', *Revue des contrats*, September 2018, pp. 462 et seq.
- 'Blockchain et droit international privé' in M. Behar-Touchais (ed.), *La Blockchain saisie par le droit*, Paris, IRJS, 2019, pp. 117 et seq.

Avasilencei (C.), 'L'internationalité des contrats-financiers : une "co-production" entre le texte juridique et le contexte économique' in H. Muir Watt *et al* (eds.), *Le tournant global en droit international privé*, Paris, Pedone, 2020, pp. 537 et seq.

d'Avout (L.):

- see 'Property', *Répertoire de droit international*, 2008.

- 'Sens et portée de la *lex fori concursus*', *Annuaire sud-américain de droit du commerce international (DeCITA)*, 2009, pp. 40 et seq.
- 'De l'utilité résiduelle du droit commun en matière de transfert d'actions et autres titres financiers', *D.*, 2010, pp. 123 et seq.
- 'Les quotas face au conflit international des lois', *Revue Lamy de droit des affaires*, 1 January 2011, no. 56, pp. 93 et seq.
- 'De l'entraide judiciaire internationale au contentieux civil intégré' in E. Pataut, S. Bollée, L. Cadiet and E. Jeuland (eds.), *Les nouvelles formes de coordination des justices étatiques*, Paris, IRJS, 2013, No. 9.
- 'Les directives européennes, les lois de police de transposition et leur application aux contrats internationaux', *D.*, 2014, pp. 60 et seq.
- 'La reconnaissance dans le champ des conflits de lois', *TCFDIP*, Paris, Pedone, 2014-2016, pp. 215 et seq.
- 'Le traitement des groupes de sociétés : entre formalisme et réalisme' in F. Jault-Seseke and D. Robine (dir.), *Le nouveau règlement Insolvabilité : quelles évolutions*, Paris, Joly Editions, 2015, pp. 129 et seq.
- 'Suites de la jurisprudence *Centros*: les sociétés *off shore* rattrapées par le droit local de l'insolvabilité', *JCP G*, 2016, pp. 519 et seq.
- 'Commentaire comparé' in *Les Grands Arrêts de la jurisprudence de l'Union européenne*, Paris, PUF, 2016, no. 60.
- 'La loi applicable à la cession de créance ou de contrat après l'ordonnance du 10 février 2016', *D.*, 2017, pp. 457 et seq.
- 'La transmission de l'obligation en droit international privé' in C. Larroumet and R. Ibarra Garza (eds.), *La transmission de l'obligation*, Paris, Ed. Panthéon-Assas, 2017, pp. 123 et seq.
- 'Les phénomènes collectifs et l'analyse macro en droit international privé' in *Mélanges en l'honneur du professeur Bertrand Ancel*, Paris, LGDJ, 2018, pp. 151 et seq.
- 'L'articulation des droits et des procédures dans un espace fédéralisé', *Banque et Droit*, special issue February 2020, pp. 17 et seq.
- 'Commercialisation de titres financiers et compétence internationale de proximité', *D.*, 2015, pp. 770 et seq.

Awrey (D.), 'The limits of private ordering within modern financial markets' (2014) 34 *Review of Banking and Financial* Law, pp. 183 et seq.

Aymeric (N.), 'La résolution bancaire - Aspects transfrontières' in *Le traitement des difficultés des établissements bancaires et institutions financières*, Paris, LexisNexis, 2017, pp. 195 et seq.

Barban (P.):
- 'The concentration principle under MiFID 2', *RISF*, 2015/3, pp. 47 et seq.
- 'Market infrastructures and competition', *RISF*, 2019/2, pp. 17 et seq.

Barnier (M.), 'International coordination: the condition for the sine qua non success of the reform of OTC derivatives markets' *Financial Stability Review*, April 2013.

Barrière (F.), 'L'Union bancaire, une œuvre inachevée' in *Mélanges en l'honneur de Jean-Patrice et Michel Storck*, Paris, Dalloz, 2021, pp. 133 et seq.

Barrière (F.), 'Les prises de participation rampantes à l'heure des swaps' in *Mélanges en l'honneur du professeur Philippe Merle*, Paris, Dalloz, 2012, pp. 27 et seq.

Batiffol (H.),
- 'La nationalité des sociétés', *TCFDIP*, 1970, pp. 79 et seq.

– 'Draft E.E.C. Convention on the law applicable to contractual obligations', *RTD eur*, 1975, pp. 182 et seq.

Beaud (O.), 'La répartition des compétences dans une Fédération. Essai de reformulation du problème', *Jus Politicum*, no. 16, pp. 190 et seq.

Benjamin (J.),

– 'The Oxford colloquium on collateral and conflict of laws: overview' in 'Oxford Colloquium on Collateral and Conflict of Laws', *Special Supplement to Butterworths Journal of International Banking and Financial Law*, September 1998.

– 'Recharacterisation Risk and Conflict of Laws', in 'Oxford Colloquium on Collateral and Conflict of Laws', *Special Supplement to Butterworths Journal of International Banking and Financial Law*, September 1998, pp. 29 et seq.

– 'Determining the situs of interests in immobilized securities' (1998) 47(4) *International and comparative law quarterly*, pp. 923 et seq.

– and Gullifer (L.), 'Stewardship and collateral: the advantages and disadvantages of the no look through system' in *Intermediation and beyond*, Oxford, Hart, 2020, pp. 215 et seq.

Bernardi (O.) and Feunteun (C.), 'L'externalisation sera-t-elle un cheval de Troie britannique ?', *RISF*, 2019, no. 3-4, pp. 119 et s.

Bezard-Falgas (J.),

– 'Des modes de transmission de la propriété des titres nominatifs d'actions et d'obligations', *Revue de législation professionnelle*, 1911.

– 'Bearer securities lost or stolen' *Lapradelle-Niboyet Rep.*

Bialard (A.), 'L'offre publique de contrat', *RTD civ.* 1971, pp. 750 et seq.

Bismuth (R.), 'L'Union bancaire ou les imperfections de la fédéralisation de la régulation financière au sein de l'Union européenne. Quelques réflexions à l'aune d'une comparaison des modèles fédéraux américain et canadien' in *L'Union bancaire*, Brussels, Bruylant, 2016, pp. 57 et seq.

Bloch (P.), 'La directive 98/26/CEE concernant le caractère définitif du règlement dans les systèmes de paiement et de règlement des opérations sur titres' in *Mélanges AEDBF-France II*, Revue Paris, Revue Banque Edition, pp. 49 et seq.

Block-Lieb (S.), 'Fishing in Muddy Waters: Clarifying the Common Pool Analogy as Applied to the Standard for Commencement of a Bankruptcy Case' (1993) 42 *The American University Law Review*, pp. 337 et seq.

Boger (O.),

– 'Close-out netting provisions in private international law and international insolvency law (Part I)' (2013) *Uniform Law Review*, pp. 256 et seq.

– 'Close-out netting provisions in private international law and international insolvency law (Part II)' (2013) *Uniform Law Review*, pp. 560 et seq.

Boillot (C.), 'Droit bancaire et financier et procédure collective: exception ou contradiction?', *D.*, 2003, pp. 2741 et seq.

Bollée (S.),

– 'La responsabilité extracontractuelle du cocontractant en droit international privé' in *Mélanges en l'honneur du professeur Bernard Audit*, Paris, LGDJ, 2014, pp. 119 et seq.

– 'La prise en considération des lois de polices étrangères dans le Règlement Rome I' in *Mélanges en l'honneur du professeur Bertrand Ancel*, Pars, LGDJ, 2017, pp. 203 et seq.

Bonneau (T.),

– 'De l'inutilité du droit contractuel pour assurer le respect des règles de marché', *RTD com*, 1999, pp. 257 et seq.

- 'De la notion de place dans les textes législatifs contemporains' in *Mélanges AEBDF II*, Paris, Banque éditeur, pp. 83 et seq.
- 'Législation financière et droit communautaire' in *Le Code de commerce, 1807-2007*, Paris, Dalloz, 2007, pp. 707 et seq.
- 'Control of the Euronext group', *RDBF*, November 2010, No. 6, comm. 236.
- 'Third-country companies and the European banking and financial market', *RDBF*, May-June 2013, pp. 11 et seq.
- 'European banking union. Introductory remarks', *RDBF*, July-August 2014, pp. 62 et seq.
- 'Le traitement administratif des entreprises bancaires et financières', *RDBF*, November 2014, pp. 77 et seq.
- 'Financial markets - Extraterritoriality, open markets and democracy', *RDBF*, January 2015.
- 'La norme prudentielle', *RDBF*, May 2015, pp. 36 et seq.
- 'L'adaptation de la France aux directives Résolution bancaire et Garantie des dépôts par l'ordonnance du 20 august 2015', *JCP E*, 2015, pp. 1434 et seq.
- 'Difficultés financières', *RDBF*, January 2015, comm. 27.
- 'Recovery, resolution and market infrastructures', *RDBF*, January 2016, benchmark 1.
- 'Union bancaire et Autorité européenne des marchés financiers' in *L'Union bancaire*, Brussels, Bruylant, 2016, pp. 223 et seq.
- 'Switching and derailment', *BJB*, 2016, pp. 297 et seq.
- 'Notion de marché équivalent', *RDBF*, May 2017, comm. 142, pp. 77 et seq.
- 'The precise nature of Inside information in European and French case law', *RTDF*, 2015, No. 3.

Bornet (J.-P.), 'La notion de marché dans la Directive Européenne sur les Marchés d'instruments financiers – "MIF" – du 21 avril 2004' in *Mélanges Dominique Schmidt*, Paris, LGDJ, 2005, pp. 77 et seq.

Boskovic (O.), 'Réflexions sur le dommage en tant que facteur de rattachement en droit international privé' in *Mélanges en l'honneur de Bertrand Ancel*, Paris, LGDJ, 2018, pp. 263 et seq.

Boucard (J.-P.), "Supervision of smaller institutions: Articulation of the competences of the ECB and national competent authorities", *RDBF*, July 2017, no. 4.

Boucheta (H.),
- 'Compensation des Credit Default Swaps : quels enjeux ?', *BJB*, 2009, pp. 158 et seq.
- 'Credit Default Swaps, Regulation is on the way', *Banque*, May 2009, pp. 93 et seq.
- 'MiFID 2: microstructure and transparency, the price discovery mechanism in question', *BJB*, June 2015, pp. 279 et seq.

Boucobza (X.),
- 'La loi applicable à l'offre publique d'acquisition', *BJB* 1997, pp. 3 et seq.
- 'L'offre publique transfrontière' in *Mélanges AEBDF I*, 1997, pp. 53 et seq.

Braithwaite (J.),
- 'The inherent limits of "legal devices": lessons for the public sector's central counterparty prescription for the OTC derivatives markets' (2011) 12 *European Business Organization Law Review*, pp. 87 et seq.
- 'Standard Form Contracts as Transnational Law' (2012) *Modern Law Review*, pp. 779 et seq.
- 'The dilemma of client clearing in the OTC derivatives market' (2016) *European Business Organization Law Review*, pp. 355 et seq.

- 'Thirty years of ultra vires: local authorities, national courts and the global derivatives markets' (2018) 71(1) *Current Legal Problems*, pp. 369 et seq.
- and MURPHY (D.), 'Improving resolvability: partial property transfers and central counterparties' (2019) 14(4), *Capital Markets Law Journal*, pp. 431 et seq.
- and MURPHY (D.), 'Central counterparties (CCPs) and the law of default management' (2016) *Journal of Corporate Law*, pp. 291 et seq.

BRÉHIER (B.), 'Les nouveaux législateurs : OICV, Comité de Bâle, FSB, G20', *RDBF*, May 2015, pp. 31 et seq.

BRESCIA MORRA (C.), 'Nature and role of the AboR', *ECB Legal Conference 2019*, pp. 335 et seq.

BRIDGE (M.),
- 'Clearing Houses and Insolvency' (2008) *Law and Financial Markets Review*, pp. 418 et seq.
- and BRAITHWAITE (J.), 'Private Law and Financial crisis' *Journal of Corporate Law Studies*, October 2013, pp. 361 et seq.

BRIGGS (Lord Justice),
- 'Has English Law coped with the Lehman Collapse?' (2013) *Butterworth Journal of International Banking and Financial Law*, pp. 131 et seq.
- 'How has English law Coped with the Lehman Collapse?' in D. FABER and N. VERMUNT (eds.), *Bank Failure: Lessons from Lehman Brothers*, Oxford, OUP, 2017, p. 121.

BUCCI (V. DI), 'Quelques questions concernant le contrôle juridictionnel sur le mécanisme de surveillance unique' in *Liber amicorum A. Tizzano, De la Cour CECA à la Cour de l'Union, Le long parcours de la justice européenne*, Turin, G. Giappichelli editore, 2018, pp. 316 et seq.

BUISSON (J.), 'Les compensations entre agents de change', Chronique de la Bourse, *Banque* 1947, pp. 50 et seq.

BURBIDGE (P.), 'British Bankruptcy Tourism. L'Angleterre comme paradis de la faillite et les propositions de réforme du Règlement 1346/2000 sur les procédures d'insolvabilité' in *Mélanges Paul Le Cannu*, Paris, Dalloz, 2013, pp. 587 et seq.

BUREAU (D.),
- 'L'influence de la volonté individuelle sur les conflits de lois' in *L'avenir du droit - Mélanges en hommage à François Terré*, Paris, Dalloz, 1999, pp. 285 et seq.
- 'La fin d'un îlot de résistance : le règlement du Conseil relatif aux procédures d'insolvabilité', *RCDIP*, 2002, pp. 613 et seq.
- and MUIR WATT (H.), 'L'avenir du contentieux international des affaires en Europe' in *Mélanges en l'honneur du professeur Bertrand Ancel*, Paris, LGDJ, 2018, pp. 315 et seq.

CABOTTE (J.-C.), 'Aspects de compétences des différentes autorités en matière de gestion de crises bancaires' in *Le traitement des difficultés des établissements bancaires et institutions financières*, Paris, LexisNexis, 2017, pp. 151 et seq.

CAILLEMER DU FERRAGE (A.),
- 'Close-out netting and international bankruptcy', *RDBF*, 2007, no. 1, pp. 37 et seq.
- 'The impact of the resolution on netting', *RDBF*, October 2013, file 38.
- 'Les enjeux de l'extraterritorialité du droit financier', *RDBF*, November 2015, pp. 95 et seq.
- 'The impact of Brexit on market infrastructures', *RDBF*, November 2017, no. 6, dossier 37.
- and DUHAMEL (A.), 'Monopole des prestataires de services d'investissement et produits dérivés négociés de gré à gré', *Banque et droit*, 2001/76, pp. 3 et seq.

– and Saudo (C.), 'A clearing house for credit derivatives', *BJB*, January 2010, no. 1, pp. 58 et seq.

Cardon (C.), Durand (Q.) and Faugérolas (L.), 'Offre au public et admission aux négociations de titres financiers sur un marché réglementé', *Etudes Joly Bourse*, Lextenso, 2019.

Carreau (D.) and Létréguilly (H.), 'Offres publiques : OPA, OPE, OPR', *Répertoire de droit des sociétés,* Paris, Dalloz.

Carruthers (B.), 'Economy and Law' in P. Aspers and N. Dodd (eds.), *Re-imagining Economic Sociology*, Oxford Scholarship Online, 2015, pp. 137 et seq

Cazenave (N.), 'La perspective d'une autorité nationale de supervision', *Banque et droit*, special issue February 2020, pp. 26 et seq.

Chacornac (J.), 'La double autonomie de la notion de consommateur dans le règlement Bruxelles I bis en matière financière', *RCDIP*, 2020, pp. 300 et seq.

Chaput (Y.), see 'Objet social', *Répertoire droit des sociétés.*

Chemaly (R.), see 'Bourses (de valeurs et de marchandises)', *Répertoire de droit international*, 1st éd., Paris, Dalloz, 1968.

Chemla (D.), 'Actualité et conséquences de l'extraterritorialité de la loi pénale française' *TCFDIP*, Paris, Pedone, 2016-2018, pp. 85 et seq.

Cohen (D.), 'La responsabilité civile des dirigeants en droit international privé', *RCDIP*, 2003, pp. 585 et seq.

Combacau (J.),

– 'Pas une puissance : une liberté : la souveraineté internationale de l'État', *Pouvoirs*, 1995, no. 67, La Souveraineté, p. 51.

– 'Conclusions générales', in Société française de droit international, *Les compétences de l'État en droit international*, Paris, Pedone, 2005, pp. 314 et seq.

Conac (P.-H.),

– see 'Franchissement de seuil', *Répertoire de droit des sociétés*, Paris, Dalloz.

– 'La fusion de la COB et du CMF', in *Mélanges AEBDF-France III*, Paris, Banque Editeur, 2001, pp. 59 et seq.

– and Caillat (V.), 'De CESR à l'ESMA : le Rubicon est franchi', *BJB*, 2010, pp. 500 et seq.

Corneloup (S.),

– 'Choix de loi et contrats liés' in *Le règlement communautaire 'Rome I' et le choix de loi dans les contrats internationaux*, Paris, Litec, 2011, pp. 289 et seq.

– 'La place du règlement Rome II dans la régulation globale des marchés financiers', *Cahier de droit de l'entreprise*, November 2012, dossier 30.

– 'Vers une réforme du règlement Rome II : la réparation des dommages causés par une violation du droit des marchés financiers nécessite-t-elle une règle de conflit spéciale' in M. Douchy-Oudot and E. Guinchard (dir.), *La justice civile européenne en marche*, Paris, Dalloz, 2012, pp. 63 et seq.

Couret (A.), 'La notion juridique de conversion' in *Mélanges P. Vigreux*, Toulouse, Université des sciences sociales de Toulouse I, 1981, pp. 219 et seq.

Cox QC (R.), 'Are warranties in an Immobilised Bearer Note Enforceable?' in L. Gullifer and J. Payne (eds.), *Intermediation and beyond*, Oxford, Hart, 2020.

Cremers (T.),

– 'La localisation d'un compte d'instruments financiers', *Banque et droit*, 2008, no. 119, pp. 11 et seq.

– 'Blockchain and financial securities: back to the future', *BJB*, June 2016, no. 114j7, pp. 271 et seq.

CRÔNE (R.), 'La loi applicable aux pouvoirs des dirigeants de sociétés étrangères', *TCFDIP*, 1998-2000, pp. 243 et seq.

CUNIBERTI (G.),

- 'La proposition de règlement de la Commission sur la loi applicable à l'opposabilité de la cession de créance', *RCDIP*, 2016, pp. 793 et seq.
- 'Choice of law in domestic contracts: towards a right of access to foreign financial markets', in H. MUIR WATT *et al* (eds), *Le tournant global en droit international privé*, Paris, Pedone, 2020, pp. 547 et seq.

CUSSET (P.-J.), 'Les succursales de pays tiers dans le cadre du Brexit', *RISF*, 2019/1, pp. 19 et seq.

DAIGRE (J.-J.),

- 'Conséquences du transfert d'un marché réglementé à l'égard des professionnels', *JCP* E 2002, pp. 958 et seq.
- 'La fin des bourses', *RDBF*, 2003, No. 2, pp. 83 et seq.
- 'De la sélection discrétionnaire des investisseurs lors d'une introduction ou d'une émission en bourse' in *Mélanges AEBDF IV*, Paris, Revue Banque, 2004.
- 'L'évolution de la notion de marché financier' in *Liber amicorum Jacques Malherbes*, Brussels, Bruylant, 2006, pp. 233 et seq.
- 'Commentaire des aspects de droit des marchés financiers de la loi pour la confiance et la modernisation de l'économie du 26 juillet 2005', *Rev. Sociétés*, July 2006, pp. 461 et seq.
- 'La responsabilité du banquier en matière de prestation de services d'investissement', *RDBF*, 2006, no. 6, dossier 30.
- and FRANÇOIS (B.), 'Commentaire de l'ordonnance du 22 janvier 2009 relative à l'appel public à l'épargne', *Revue des sociétés*, 2009, pp. 1 et seq.
- and FRANÇOIS (B.), 'La société par actions simplifiée, une société pouvant faire appel au marché?', *Rev. Soc.* 2010, pp. 11 et seq.
- and PAILLER (P.), 'Commentaire de l'ordonnance n° 2009-15 du 8 janvier 2009', *Rev. sociétés* 2009, pp. 3 et seq.

DAVID (O.), 'Du marché réglementé au marché équivalent : quand la loi Pacte ouvre la boîte de Pandore', *RISF*, 2019/3-4, pp. 88 et seq.

DAVID (C.) and GEST (G.), see 'Impôt', *Répertoire de droit international, Paris,* Dalloz.

DECUGIS (H.), 'La loi du 28 février 1941 relative à la forme et à la négociation des actions', *Journal des sociétés*, 1941, pp. 133 et seq.

DÉGUÉE (J.-P.), 'La directive 2001/24/CE sur l'assainissement et la liquidation des établissements de crédit : une solution aux défaillances bancaires internationales ?', *Euredia*, 2001-2002, no. 1, pp. 247 et seq.

DEVOS (D.),

- 'La protection juridique des systèmes de paiement en cas de défaillance d'un participant', *RD Bancaire et Bourse* 1997, pp. 11 et seq.
- 'The European Directive of 19 May 1998 on settlement finality in payment and securities settlement systems', *Euredia*, 2/1999, pp. 149 et seq.

DIDIER (P.), 'Brèves notes sur le contrat organisation', in *Mélanges en l'honneur de François Terré*, Paris, Dalloz, 1999, pp. 636 et seq.

DIXON (V.), 'Legal nature of intermediated securities' in L. GULLIFER and J. PAYNE (eds.), *Intermediation and beyond*, Oxford, Hart, 2020.

DOUVRELEUR (O.), 'Le nouveau compartiment professionnel du marché réglementé' in *Mélanges AEDBF – France,* 1 December 2008.

DOWNE (A.), 'La nouvelle convention-cadre ISDA de droit français', *RDBF*, November 2020, study 20.

DRUMMOND (F.),

- 'Le contrat comme instrument financier' in *Mélanges François Terré*, Paris, PUF, 1991 pp. 661 et seq.
- 'Un nouveau principe: la liberté d'émettre toutes valeurs mobilières', *RDBF*, September-October 2004, pp. 361 et seq.
- 'L'information des actionnaires et des investisseurs' in *Entreprise : information et rumeur, RJ. Com*, 2005, special issue, pp. 15 et seq.
- 'Code de commerce et Code monétaire et financier ou l'enchevêtrement des Codes' in *Le Code de commerce, Livre du bicentenaire*, Paris, Dalloz, 2007.
- 'Les titres intermédiés. Regard sur un nouveau concept en droit financier' in *Mélanges Paul Didier*, Paris, Economica, 2008, pp. 147 et seq.
- 'La société, l'actionnaire et le dépositaire central' in *Mélanges Philippe Merle*, Paris, Dalloz, 2012, pp. 199 et seq.
- 'Who benefits from administrative composition?', *BJB*, November 2016, pp. 449 et seq.
- 'Loi PACTE et actifs numériques', *BJB*, July 2019, no. 118 m3, pp. 60 et seq.

DWYER (E.) and TREDGETT (R.), 'OTC Derivatives: Client Clearing Agreements - A piece in the Clearing Jigsaw' (2014) 9 *Capital Market Law Journal*, pp. 343 et seq.

EIDENMÜLLER (H.),

- 'Contracting for a European insolvency regime'(2017) 18 *European Business Organization Law Review*, pp. 273 et seq.
- 'What is an insolvency proceeding?' (2018) *American Bankruptcy Law Journal*, pp. 92 et seq.

ELINEAU (R.), 'Franchissement de seuil', *J.-Cl banque-crédit-bourse*, Fasc. 2131.

ESCUDERO (M.-L.), 'Le contrôle juridictionnel de la Cour de justice dans le domaine de l'Union bancaire', *Cahiers de droit européen*, April 2020, pp. 549 et seq.

EUKÉ (H.) and VINCENT (L.), 'Utilité et périmètre des avis juridiques relatifs à la compensation centrale des contrats dérivés OTC : les premières ISDA Client Clearing Opinions', *RDBF*, 2015, no. 1, study no. 1.

FABRE-MAGNAN (M.), 'Propriété, patrimoine et lien social', *RTD civ.*, 1997, vol. 3, pp. 583 et seq.

FADLALLAH (I.), 'Point de vue sur l'affaire Péchiney. La localisation du délit d'initié', *RCDIP*, 1996, pp. 626 et seq.

FAUGÉROLAS (L.) and CARDON (C.), 'Premier bilan du compartiment professionnel après quatre ans d'existence', *BJB*, March 2012, pp. 112 et seq.

FENTIMAN (R.), 'Cross-Border Securities Collateral: Redefining Recharacterisation Risk', *Special Supplement to Butterworths Journal of International Banking and Financial Law*, September 1998, pp. 38 et seq.

FERNANDEZ-BOLLO (E.), 'L'impact de l'Union bancaire sur la coopération en matière de contrôle bancaire', *Banque et droit*, special issue February 2020, pp. 12 et seq.

FERRAN (E.), 'Institutional Design for Financial Market Supervision: The Choice for National Systems', *University of Cambridge Faculty of Law, Legal Studies Research Paper Series 14-15*, 15 April 2014.

FEUNTEUN (C.), 'Refonte du régime prudentiel européen des entreprises d'investissement', *RDBF*, November 2019, comm. 211.

FLANAGAAN (S.M.), 'The Rise of a Trade Associations: Group interactions Within the International Swaps and Derivatives Association' (2001) 6 *Harvard Negotiation Law Review*, pp. 212 et seq.

FOURNIER (A.), 'Aperçu critique du principe de double incrimination en droit pénal international' in *Les droits et le droit, Mélanges dédiés à Bernard Bouloc*, Paris, Dalloz, 2006, pp. 224 et seq.

FRANCESCAKIS (P.), 'Lois d'application immédiate et droit du travail: l'affaire du comité d'entreprise de la Compagnie des Wagons-lits', *RCDIP*, 1974, pp. 273 et seq.

FRANÇOIS (B.), 'Appel public à l'épargne', *Répertoire de droit des sociétés*, Paris, Dalloz, 2006.

FRANCQ (S.), 'Rome I Regulation: Contractual Obligations', *Répertoire de droit international.*

FRISON-ROCHE (M.-A.), 'Réguler les "entreprises cruciales"', *D.*, 2014, pp. 1556 et seq.

FYON (M.) and WAUTELET (P.), 'Le champ d'application, les questions de droit international privé et le prospectus' in *La réforme de la réglementation sur les offres publiques d'acquisition*, Kluwer, 2007, No. 32.

GARCIMARTIN ALFEREZ (F.),

- 'New Issues in the Rome I Regulation: The Special Provisions on Financial Market Contracts' (2008) *Yearbook of PIL*, pp. 245 et seq.
- 'The Rome I Regulation: Exceptions to the Rule on Consumer Contracts and Financial Instruments' (2009) *Journal of Private International Law.*
- 'The law applicable to prospectus liability in the European Union' (2011) *Law and Financial Market Review*, pp. 449 et seq.
- 'The Rome I Regulation: Exceptions to the Rule on Consumer Contracts and Financial Instruments' (2009) *Journal of Private International Law*, pp. 85 et seq.
- 'The review of the insolvency regulation: Hybrid Procedures and Other Issues' (2011) *International Insolvency Law Review*, pp. 321 et seq.

GARGANTINI (M.), 'Prospectus Liability. Competent Courts of Jurisdiction and Applicable Law' in D. BUSCH, G. FERRARINI and J.P. FRANX (eds.), *Prospectus Regulation and Prospectus Liability*, Oxford, OUP, 2020.

GAUDEMET (A.),

- 'System risk: a historical perspective', *RTDF*, July 2010, pp. 97 et seq.
- 'Competence to enter into speculative financial transactions', *RDBF*, 2012, comm. 166.
- 'Suspension of the execution of close-out netting agreements entered into by a defaulting credit institution or investment firm', *RDBF*, January 2013, comm. 27.
- 'Trading and clearing obligations', *RDBF*, January 2013, pp. 65 et seq.
- 'Les limites de position sur les marchés dérivés de matières premières agricoles en quête de légitimité', *RDBF*, May 2013, comm. 109.
- 'Le risque de système' in A. SUPIOT (ed.), *Face à l'irresponsabilité, la dynamique du principe de solidarité*, Paris, Collège de France, 2018, pp. 161 et seq.
- 'La loi PACTE et le droit des offres publiques', *BJB*, July 2019, pp. 40 et seq.
- 'Comptabilité des titres financiers en rétention et droit de participer aux assemblées générales d'actionnaires', *Bull. Joly. Sociétés*, June 2020, pp. 6 et seq.
- and BOUCHETA (H.), 'Reform of the OTC derivatives markets in the United States and the European Union: the new structure requirements', *BJB*, May 2011, no. 5, pp. 339 et seq.

GAUDEMET-TALLON (H.), 'Autorisation des cautionnements, avals et garanties dans les contrats internationaux : pour une "ignorance excusable de la *lex societatis*"', in *Le Code de commerce 1807-2017, Livre du bicentenaire*, Paris, Dalloz, 2007, pp. 751 et seq.

GELPHERM (A.) and GULATI (M.), 'CDS Zombies' (2012) 13 *European Business Organization Law Review*, pp. 347 et seq.

GIRARD (O.), 'Une brève histoire des clauses d'équivalence ou l'Union européenne comme rouage clé de la régulation financière mondiale' in *Liber amicorum Blanche Sousi*, Paris, Revue Banque Edition, 2016, pp. 124 et seq.

GIZARD (B.) and DESCHANEL (J.-P.), 'Déontologie financière et pouvoir disciplinaire' in *Mélanges AEBDF III*, Paris, Banque Éditeur, 2001, pp. 157 et seq.

GOLDMAN (B.),
- 'Rapport sur la nationalité des sociétés dans la C.E.E.', *TCFDIP*, Paris, 1970, pp. 215 et seq.
- 'Les conflits de lois en matière d'instruments négociables', *International Bar Association*, The Hague, Martinus Nijhoff, 1950, Appendix 1.

Goode (R.), 'Security Entitlements as Collateral in the Conflict of laws' (1998) *Butterworth journal of international banking and financial law*, special supplement, pp. 23 et seq.

GORÉ (F.), 'Le nouveau régime des valeurs mobilières', *JCP*, 1951, I, pp. 948 et seq.

GOSSET-GRAINVILLE (A.), 'Coopération et souverainetés', *Banque et Droit*, February 2017, special issue, pp. 71 et seq.

GOURIO (A.) and GILLOUARD (M.), 'Les options ou discrétions nationales en matière prudentielle', in *Liber Amicorum Blanche Sousi*, Paris, Revue Banque Editions, 2016, pp. 77 et seq.

GREEN (S.) and SNAGG (F.), 'Intermediated Securities and Distributed Ledger Technology' in *Intermediation and beyond*, Oxford, Hart, 2020.

GRIFFITH (S. J.), 'Substituted Compliance and Systemic Risk: How to Make a Global Market in Derivatives Regulation' (2014) *University of Minnesota Law Review*, pp. 1291 et seq.

GUERCHOUN (F.), see 'Jeu-Pari', *Répertoire de droit civil*, Paris, Dalloz.

GUILLARD, 'La bourse: les agents de change et les opérations de bourse dans les législations étrangères', *Journal de droit international privé*, 1877, pp. 307 et seq.

GUILLAUME (E.) and COUDRAY (L.), 'Autorités de régulation' in *Répertoire du contentieux administratif*, Paris, Dalloz, 2010.

GUINAUDEAU (D.), 'Succursales: loi applicable et supervision au titre de la directive concernant les Marchés d'instruments financiers (MIF)' in *Mélanges AEBDF V*, Paris Revue Banque Editions, 2008, pp. 231 et seq.

GULLIFER (L.),
- 'Ownership of Securitie', in *Intermediated Securities*, Oxford, Hart, 2010.
- 'Introduction' in *Intermediation and beyond*, Oxford, Hart, 2020.
- and PAYNE (J.), 'Conclusion', in *Intermediation and beyond*, Oxford; Hart, 2020, pp. 360 et seq.

GUTMANN (D.), 'Du matériel à l'immatériel dans le droit des biens' in *Archive de philosophie du droit*, t. 43, 1999, pp. 65 et seq.

GUYON (Y.) and BUCHBERGER (M.), 'Responsabilité civile des dirigeants', *JCl. soc.*, June 2017, Fasc. 132-10.

HAENTJENS (M.) and VERHEIJ (D.), 'Finding Nemo: Locating Financial Losses after Kolassa/ Barclays Bank and Profit', *JIBLR*, 2016-6.

HAFTEL (B.), 'Les normes auto-limitées en droit international privé' in *Mélanges en l'honneur du professeur Bertrand Ancel*, Paris, LGDJ, 2018, pp. 864 et seq.

HARTLEY (T.), 'Choice of law regarding the voluntary assignment of contractual obligations under the Rome I Regulation' (2011) *International and comparative law quarterly*, pp. 29 et seq.

HEUZÉ (V.), 'La loi applicable aux actions directes dans les groupes de contrats', *RCDIP*, 1996, pp. 243 et seq.

HEUZÉ (V.), 'De quelques infirmités congénitales du droit uniforme : l'exemple de l'article 5.1 de la Convention de Bruxelles du 27 septembre 1968', *RCDIP*, 2000, pp. 595 et seq.

Hopt (K.-J.), 'European takeover reform of 2012/2013 – time to re-examine the mandatory bid' (2014) 15(2) *European Business Organization Review*, pp. 143 et seq.

Howell (E.), 'Regulatory Intervention in the European Sovereign Credit Default Swap Market' (2016) 17 *European Business Organization Law Review*, pp. 319 et seq.

Hull (J.), 'Produits dérivés de gré à gré et compensation centrale : toutes les transactions peuvent-elles faire l'objet d'une compensation ?', *Revue de Stabilité Financière*, July 2010, pp. 81 et seq.

Jackson (H.-E.), 'Substituted compliance: The Emergence, Challenges, and Evolution of a New Regulatory Paradigm' (2015) *Journal of Financial Regulation*, pp. 169 et seq.

Jacquet (J.-M.), 'L'internationalité. Rapport introductif', *Revue Lamy de droit des affaires*, supplement, no. 46, 1 February 2002.

Jeantet (F.-C.), 'Le dépôt collectif de titres au porteur à la Caisse centrale de dépôt et de virement de titres', *Journal des sociétés*, 1945, pp. 161 et seq.

Jeantin (M.), 'Le droit financier des biens' in *Prospectives du droit économique, Dialogues avec Michel Jeantin*, Paris, Dalloz, 1999, pp. 3 et seq.

Jobard Bachellier (M.-N.), 'Obligations', *Répertoire de droit international*, Paris, Dalloz.

Jouffin (E.), 'Démararchage et vente à distance de produits et services financiers : principes généraux', *D.*, 2006, pp. 1534 et seq.

Julienne (M.), 'L'inscription des titres financiers en blockchain', *BJB*, March 2019, no. 118d2, pp. 58 et seq.

Juvigny (B. de) and Buisson (F.), 'La coopération internationale entre régulateurs de marchés financiers', *Annales des Mines - Réalités industrielles*, February 2015.

Kannan (A.), 'ISDA 2014 Resolution Stay Protocol and suspension of close-out netting agreements: towards extraterritorial recognition of resolution measures?', *RDBF*, May-June 2015, No. 8.

Keller (C.), 'Regulation of payment systems - some reflections on article 22 of the statute of ESCBÆ, *Euredia*, 2001-2002, no. 3, pp. 459 et seq.

Kessedjian (C.) and Germain (M.), 'La loi applicable à certains droits sur des titres détenus auprès d'un intermédiaire', *RCDIP*, 2004, pp. 49 et seq.

Kettering (K.), 'Repledge Deconstructed' (1999) 61 *U. Pitt, L. Rev.*, pp. 45 et seq.

Kleiner (C.), 'L'élection de for en matière bancaire et financière : entre clauses asymétriques, clauses modèles et quasi- réglementaires' in M. Laazouzi (ed.), *Les clauses attributives de juridiction : de la prévisibilité au désordre*, Paris, Ed. Panthéon-Assas, 2021, pp. 49 et seq.

Kleinschmidt (J.), 'Agency and Authority Agent' in *Encyclopedia of Private International Law*, Cheltenham, Edward Elgar, 2017, pp. 29 et seq.

Knestch (J.), 'La réparation du dommage extracontractuel en droit international privé' in *Mélanges en l'honneur du professeur Bertrand Ancel*, Paris, LGDJ, 2018, pp. 979 et seq.

Kokkola (T.) (ed.), *The payment system*, Frankfurt am Main, ECB, 2010, pp. 151 et seq.

Kornezov (A.), 'The Application of National Law by the ECB - A Maze of (Un)answered Question', *ECB Legal Conference 2016*, 6 October 2016, pp. 242 et seq.

Kovar (J.-P.),

- 'La BCE et les autorités nationales de surveillance' in *L'Union bancaire*, Brussels, Bruylant, 2016, pp. 236 et seq.
- 'Les autorités européennes de surveillance : Organes des régulateurs nationaux, agences européennes ou autorités européennes de régulation', *RDBF*, July-August 2011, no. 4.
- and Lasserre Capdeville (J.), 'Clarification par le Tribunal de l'UE de la répartition des compétences au sein du Mécanisme de surveillance unique', *Revue Banque*, July-August 2017, no. 810, pp. 86 et seq.

KRONKE (H.), see 'Liability, Capital Markets' in J. BASEDOW, G. RUHL, F. FERRARI and P. DE MIGUEL ASCENCIO (eds.), *Encyclopedia of Private International Law*, 2017, pp. 1135 et seq.

KUIPERS (J.-J.), 'Schemes of arrangement and voluntary collective redress: a gap in the Brussels I Regulation' (2012) *Journal of Private International Law*, pp. 225 et seq.

LAGARDE (G.), 'Portée internationale d'une interprétation nationale de la loi uniforme sur la lettre de change et le billet à ordre' in *Mélanges Roger Secrétan*, 1964, pp. 1 et seq.

LAGARDE (P.),

- 'Les interprétations divergentes d'une loi uniforme donnent-elles donner lieu à un conflit de lois', *RCDIP*, 1964, pp. 235 et seq.
- 'La Convention de La Haye sur la loi applicable aux contrats d'intermédiaires et à la représentation', *RCDIP*, 1978, pp. 21 et seq.
- and TENENBAUM (A.), 'De la Convention de Rome au règlement Rome I', *RCDIP*, 2008, pp. 727 et seq.

LAGARDE (X.), 'Le droit des marchés financiers présente-t-il un particularisme?', *JCP G*, November 2005, No. 44.

LANGLOIS (P.), 'Droit boursier et droit du travail' in G. CANIVET, D. MARTIN and N. MOLFESSIS (eds.), *Les offres publiques d'achat*, pp. 153 et seq.

LARDEUX (G.), 'La loi applicable à la représentation conventionnelle', *RCDIP*, 2014, pp. 513 et seq.

LE CANNU (P.),

- 'Obligations remboursables en actions: les enseignements de l'arrêt Métrologie International', *BJB*, 1995, para. 50, pp. 251 et seq.
- 'Réflexions sur l'apport de la loi du 2 juillet 1996 au droit des sociétés', *Bull. Joly*, 1996, pp. 796 et seq.
- 'Public offers, the new general regulations', *BJB*, 1997, p. 2.

LEFÈVRE (F.) and VAN MUYLDER (C.), 'Le principe non bis in idem dans un contexte international', *Banque et droit*, special issue February 2020, pp. 63 et seq.

LEFRANC (T.), 'Offres publiques d'acquisition', *J.-Cl. Soc.*, fasc. 2133, 4 April 2014.

LE FUR (A.-V.) and SCHMIDT (D.), 'Sanctions des abus de marché : "l'aiguillage", source de déraillements', *D.*, 2015, pp. 1450 et seq.

LEGAIS (D.), see 'Blockchain', *J.-Cl. Com.*, fasc. 534.

LEHMANN (M.),

- 'Where does economic loss occur?' (2011) 7(3) *Journal of private international law*, pp. 523 et seq.
- 'Proposal for a special rule in the Rome II Regulation for financial crimes', *RCDIP*, 2012, pp. 485 et seq.
- 'Prospectus liability and private international law - assessing the landscape after the CJEU's Kolassa ruling (Case C-375/13)' (2016) 12(2) *Journal of Private International Law*, pp. 318 et seq.
- 'Single Supervisory Mechanism Without Regulatory Harmonisation? Introducing a European Banking Act and a "CRR Light" for Smaller Institutions', *EBI Working Paper Series*, 2017, pp. 8 et seq.
- and ZETZSCHE (D.), 'How does it feel to be a third country? The consequences of Brexit for Financial market Law' in E. LEIN and O. FITZGERALD (eds.), *Complexity's Embrace*, Center for International Governance Innovation, 2018, pp. 105 et seq.
- 'Le législateur allemand face au Brexit', *RDBF*, September 2019, No. 5, dossier 45.

– 'La coopération avec les États tiers en matière bancaire et financière : la confiance n'exclut pas le contrôle', *Banque et droit,* special issue February 2020, pp. 35 et seq.

Lelieur-Fischer (J.), 'L'Union européenne face aux conflits de compétence' in *Mélanges en l'honneur du professeur Alain Fournier*, Nancy, Presse-Universitaire de Nancy, 2014, pp. 269 et seq.

Lemaire (S.), 'Interrogations sur la portée juridique du préambule du règlement Rome I', *D.*, 2008, pp. 2157 et seq.

Le Nabasque (H.),

– 'Les actions sont des droits de créance négociables' in *Mélanges Yves Guyon*, Paris, Dalloz, 2000.

– 'La fin de la connexion apports/capital' in *Quel avenir pour le capital social*, Colloque CRDF Paris I, Dalloz, 2004, pp. 103 et seq.

– 'La liberté d'émettre toutes valeurs mobilières' in *Mélanges Paul Le Cannu*, Paris, Dalloz, 2014, pp. 325 et seq.

Lenhof (J.-B.), 'Les règles de marché à l'épreuve du temps' in *Mélanges en l'honneur du professeur Paul Le Cannu*, Paris, LGDJ, pp. 181 et seq.

Leplat (F.), 'Marchés financiers. Comment les libertés communautaires renforent le rôle propre des autorités nationales, chron. de droit européen n° III - Le rôle conféré par le droit communautaire aux droits nationaux des États membres (2e partie)', *Les Petites Affiches*, 2003, no. 100, pp. 3 et seq.

Lequette (Y.), 'Le renvoi de qualifications' in *Mélanges dédiés à D. Holleaux*, Paris, Litec, 1990, pp. 249 et seq.

Lerebours-Pigeonnière (P.), 'A propos du contrat international', *JDI*, 1951, pp. 1 et seq.

Le Tourneau (P.), 'Responsabilité : généralités' in *Répertoire de droit civil*, Paris, Dalloz, 2009.

Libchaber (R.), 'Effet de commerce et chèques' in *Répertoire de droit international*, Paris, Dalloz.

Lokiec (P.), 'Vers un nouveau droit du travail', *D.*, 2017, pp. 2109 et seq.

Lo Schiavo (G.), 'The ECB and its application of national law in the SSM' in G. Lo Schiavo (ed.), *The European Banking Union and the Role of Law*, Cheltenham, Edward Elgar, pp. 177 et seq.

Louis (J.-V.), 'Coopération rapprochée, un nouveau mode de coopération renforcée?' in *L'identité du droit de l'Union européenne, Mélanges en l'honneur de Claude Blumann*, Series 'Droit de l'Union européenne', Brussels, Bruylant, 2015, pp. 216 et seq.

Louis (J.-V.),

– 'L'Union bancaire, un processus incomplet?' in *Liber Amicorum Blanche Sousi*, Paris, Revue Banque Edition, 2016 pp. 153 et seq.

– 'Conclusion' in *L'Union bancaire*, Brussels, Bruylant, 2016, pp. 248 et seq.

Louisfert (C.), 'Les conséquences de la loi de séparation et de régulation des activités bancaires sur le mécanisme de résiliation compensation (close out netting)', *BJB*, November 2013, no. 110t3, pp. 546 et seq.

Louis-Lucas (P.), 'La distinction du fond et de la forme dans le règlement des conflits de lois' in *Mélanges Maury*, t. 1, *Droit international privé et public*, Paris, Dalloz/Sirey, pp. 175 et seq.

Loussouarn (Y.),

– 'L'œuvre de Lerebours-Pigeonnière', *JDI*, 1954, pp. 892 et seq.

– 'Les conflits de lois en matière de réserve de propriété' in *Études offertes à Roger Houin, Problèmes d'actualités posés par les entreprises*, Paris, Dalloz, 1985, pp. 275 et seq.

- and Bourel (P.), 'La Convention de La Haye sur la loi applicable aux contrats d'intermédiaires et à la représentation', *RTD com*, 1979, pp. 166 et seq.

Lucas (F.-X.),

- 'La distinction des titres de capital et des titres de créance' in A. Couret, H. Le Nabasque (eds.), *Quel avenir pour le capital social*, Dalloz, 2004, pp. 21 et seq.
- and Poracchia (D.), 'L'expropriation de l'associé qui ne finance pas la restructuration de la société en redressement judiciaire' in *Etudes en la mémoire de Philippe Neau-Leduc*, Paris, LGDJ, 2018, pp. 629 et seq.

Macfarlane (B.) and Stevens (R.), 'Interests in securities: practical problems and conceptual solutions' in *Intermediated Securities*, Oxford, Hart, 2010.

Malabat (V.), 'Libres propos sur les conflits de lois en matière pénale' in *Droit répressif au pluriel, Liber amicorum in honour of Renée Koering-Joulin*, Limal, Anthemis 2015, pp. 527 et seq.

Malassigné (V.), 'Le principe d'équivalence de l'inscription en compte et de l'inscription dans un dispositif d'enregistrement électronique partagé' in V. Magnier and P. Barban (eds.), *Blockchain et droit des sociétés*, Paris, Dalloz, 2019.

Malaurie (P.), 'Loi uniforme et conflit de lois', *TCFDIP*, 1967, pp. 83 et seq.

Marais (B. du), 'Crise de la régulation ou capture du régulateur?' in A. Mérieux (ed.), *Rapport moral sur l'argent dans le monde*, 2009.

Martin (D.),

- 'Le coût de la cotation' in *L'entreprise multinationale dans tous ses états*, Archive de philosophie du droit, Paris, Dalloz, 2003.
- 'La compétence internationale de l'autorité des marchés financiers en matière d'offre publique', *RTDF*, 2006, pp. 37 et seq.
- and Haas (F.), 'La compétence internationale de l'autorité des marchés financiers en matière d'offre publique', *RTDF*, 2006, pp. 37 et seq.
- and Molfessis (N.), 'Offres publiques d'acquisition – Les défenses anti-OPA' in G. Canivet, D. Martin and N. Molfessis, *Les offres publiques d'achat*, pp. 573 et seq.
- and Savatier (L.-M.), 'Le critère de gravité dans la répression des abus de marché', *Revue de droit des affaires*, January 2017, pp. 32 et seq.

Martin (D.-R.), 'De l'idée de compte' in *Mélanges AEBDF-France II*, Paris, Banque Editeur, 1999, pp. 285 et seq.

Martin Laprade (F.),

- 'Crossing a threshold' in *Dictionnaire Joly Bouse*, Paris, Joly, 2012, no. 018-028.
- 'Critical assessment of the AMF's public consultation on IPOs', *BJB*, January 2015, pp. 14 et seq.
- 'Contentieux boursiers : abus de marché et autres manquements', *Répertoire de droit des sociétés*, Paris, Dalloz, 2017.

Martucci (F.),

- 'Les pouvoirs de l'Autorité européenne des marchés financiers à l'épreuve du droit constitutionnel de l'Union', *Revue des affaires européennes*, 2014, pp. 19 et seq.
- 'Union bancaire, la méthode du "cadre": du discours à la réalité', in *L'Union bancaire*, Brussels, Bruylant, 2016, pp. 13 et seq.
- 'European System of Central Banks – European Central Bank and Eurosystem – Organisation', *JCl. Europe*, 2019, fasc. 243.
- Martucci (F.) and Vabres (R.), 'Rapport sur la faisabilité de la consécration par le législateur de l'Union d'une procédure de forbearance faisant intervenir l'Autorité européenne des marchés financiers', *RTDF*, 2018, no. 4, pp. 3 et seq.

MASTRULLO (T.), see 'Entreprises en difficulté: droit international et européen' in *Répertoire de droit des sociétés*, Paris, Dalloz.

MATHEY (N.), 'Regulator: status of the ACPR', *RDBF*, March-April 2017, comm. no. 46.

MAYER (P.),

- 'Droit international privé et droit international public sous l'angle de la notion de compétence', *RCDIP*, 1979, pp. 1 et seq., pp. 349 et seq. and 537 et seq., reprinted in *Choix d'articles de Pierre Mayer*, 2015, pp. 21 et seq.
- 'Les conflits de lois en matière de réserve de propriété après la loi du 12 mai 1980', *JCP* 1981, 1, pp. 3019 et seq.
- 'La délocalisation du contrat' *in La relativité du contrat, Travaux de l'Association Henri Capitant*, Colloque de Nantes 1999, Paris, LGDJ, 2000, pp. 123 et seq.
- See 'Police Laws' in *Répertoire de droit international.*
- 'Réflexions sur la notion de contrat international' in *Mélanges en l'honneur de Pierre Tercier*, Zurich, Schulthess, 2008, pp. 873 et seq.

MAZEAUD (H.), 'Conflits de lois dans le domaine de la responsabilité civile délictuelle et quasi-délictuelle', *RCDIP*, 1934, pp. 376 et seq.

MÉLIN (F.),

- 'La loi applicable à la compensation dans les procédures communautaires d'insolvabilité', *JDI*, 2007, var. 4.
- 'L'application d'une loi étrangère devant les procédures européennes d'insolvabilité' in *Mélanges en l'honneur de Jean-Luc Vallens*, Paris, Lextenso, 2017, pp. 331 et seq.

MEROVACH (I.) and WALTERS (A.), 'The Characterization of Pre-insolvency Proceedings in Private International Law' (2020) 21 *European Business Organization Law Review*, pp. 855 et seq.

MINNE (G.), 'Les règles de conflit de lois en matière de compensation dans le secteur financier', *Bulletin Droit et Banque*, April 2011, No. 47.

MOLONEY (N.), 'The investor model underlying the EU's investor protection regime: consumers or investors?' (2012) 13 *European Business organization Law Review*, pp. 169 et seq.

MOONEY (C.), 'The Bankruptcy Code's Safe Harbors for Settlement Payments and Securities Contracts: When is Safe too Safe?' (2014) 49 *Tex Int'l Law Journal*, pp. 245 et seq.

MORTON (G.), 'Historical Introduction' in *Intermediation and beyond*, Oxford, Hart, 2020.

MOSS (G.) QC, 'Anti-deprivation, flip clauses, ipso facto rules and the Dante inferno' in *Insolvency intelligence*, 2017, pp. 24 et seq.

MOULIN (J.-M.), 'La coopération de diverses autorités de marché nationales permettant la poursuite et la sanction d'un manquement d'initié', *BJB*, January 2013, pp. 13 et seq.

MOURLON-DRUOL (E.), 'History of an incomplete EMU' in F. AMTENBRINK and C. HERMANN (eds.), *The EU law of Economic and Monetary Union*, Oxford, OUP, 2020, nos. 2.1 et seq.

MUIR WATT (H.),

- 'Droit public et droit privé dans les rapports internationaux (vers la publicisation des conflits de lois ?)', *Archives de philosophie du droit*, 1997, pp. 207 et seq.
- 'La globalisation et le droit international privé' in *Mélanges Pierre Mayer*, Paris, LGDJ, 2015, pp. 591 et seq.
- 'La gouvernance privée des marchés financiers : les enjeux de la *lex contractus*', in H. MUIR WATT *et al*, *Le tournant global en droit international privé*, pp. 355 et seq.

MULLER (A.-C.),

- 'Premier bilan après un an d'application de la MIF', *RDBF*, March-April 2009, pp. 59 et seq.

- 'La sécurisation du secteur bancaire et financier', *RDBF*, 2014, pp. 66 et seq.
- 'Regards sur la directive Résolution', *BJB*, December 2015, no. 112z0, pp. 579 et seq.
- 'New Prospectus Regulation: progress delayed until July 2019', *Revue Lamy Droit des affaires*, 2019, no. 132, pp. 16 et seq.

Muniesa (F.), 'Contenir le marché, la transition de la criée à la cotation électronique à la bourse de Paris', *Sociologie du travail*, vol. 47, October-December 2005, pp. 485 et seq.

Nakamoto (S.), 'Bitcoin: A Peer-to-Peer Electronic Cash System', 2008.

Neau-Leduc (P.), 'A propos de la réglementation des marchés financiers' in *Mélanges Michel Cabrillac*, Paris, Dalloz/Litec, 1999.

Niboyet (J.-P.), 'Notice biographique de Pillet' in *Mélanges Pillet*, Paris, Recueil Sirey, 1929, pp. 13 et seq.

Nuttens (J.-D.), 'La "comitologie" et la conférence intergouvernementale', *RMCUE*, 1996, no. 397, pp. 314 et seq.

Ooi (M.),
- 'The Hague Securities Convention: a critical reading of the road map' (2005) (4), *Lloyd's maritime and commercial law quarterly*, pp. 467 et seq.
- 'The choice of a choice of law rule' in *Intermediated Securities*, Oxford, Hart, 2010, pp. 229 et seq.
- 'Intermediation and its effects on investors rights' (2015) *The Law Quarterly Review*, pp. 536 et seq.
- 'The ramifications of fragmentation in the choice of law for shares' (2016) *Journal of private international law*, august 2016, pp. 411 et seq.
- 'Re-enfranchising the investor of intermediated securities' (2020) 16 *Journal of private international law*, pp. 69 et seq.

Oppetit (B.), 'Les tendances régressives dans l'évolution du droit contemporain' in *Mélanges dédiés à Dominique Holleaux*, Paris, Litec, 1990 pp. 315 et seq.

Paech (P.),
- 'Close-out netting, Insolvency and Conflict of Laws' (2014) *Journal of Corporate Law Studies*, pp. 419 et seq.
- 'Securities, intermediation and the blockchain: an inevitable choice between liquidity and legal certainty?' (2016) (4) *Uniform Law Review - Revue de droit uniforme*, pp. 612 et seq.
- 'The value of Financial Market Insolvency Safe Harbours' (2016) 36(4) *Oxford Journal of Legal Studies*, pp. 855 et seq.
- 'Conflict of Laws and Relational Rights' in *Intermediation and beyond*, Oxford, Hart, 2020, pp. 300 et seq.

Pailler (P.), 'Le rôle du terme et du sous-jacent dans la formation du prix', *Revue de jurisprudence commerciale*, September-October 2013, no. 5, pp. 383 et seq.

Parléani (G.), 'La localisation des services financiers' in *Mélanges en l'honneur de Jean Stoufflet*, Paris, LGDJ, 2001, pp. 279 et seq.

Partsch-Bobricheff (O.), 'Analysis of the current legal framework for clearing and settlement services in the European union', *Euredia*, 2005/1, pp. 46 et seq.

Pataut (E.), 'Relire "Compagnie des Wagons-lits" La représentation collective des salariés dans l'espace international' in *Liber amicorum en hommage à Pierre Rodière*, Paris, LGDJ, 2019, pp. 387 et seq.

Payne (J.),
- 'Intermediated securities and the right to vote in the UK' in *Intermediated Securities*, Oxford, Hart, 2010, pp. 187 et seq.

- 'Schemes of arrangement, takeovers and minority shareholder protection' (April 2011) *Journal of corporate law*, pp. 67 et seq.
- 'The regulation of short selling and its reform in Europe' (2012) 13 *European Business Organization Law Review*, pp. 413 et seq.
- 'Cross-border schemes of arrangement and forum shopping' (2013) *European Business Organization Law Review*, pp. 563 et seq.
- 'Intermediation and Bondholder schemes of arrangement' in *Intermediation and beyond*, Oxford, Hart, 2018, pp. 175 et seq.

Pazzola (A.), 'The Role of the European Central Bank in the Single Supervisory Mechanism: A New Paradigm for EU Governance' (2018) 43(1), *European Law Review*, pp. 3 et seq.

Peltier (F.),
- 'L'agrément et le contrôle prudentiel' in *La modernisation des activités financières*, Paris, GLN Joly, 1996.
- 'À propos la nature juridique de la créance présentée par l'ORA. Reply to P. Le Cannu', *BJB*, 1996, para. 3, pp. 23 et seq.

Pellet (A.), 'Lotus que de sottise on profère en ton nom! Remarques sur le concept de souveraineté dans la jurisprudence de la Cour mondiale' in *Mélange en l'honneur de J.-P. Puissochet*, Paris, Pedone, 2008, pp. 216 et seq.

Penadès Fons (M.), 'Commercial Choice of Law in Context: Looking Beyond Rome' (2015) *Modern Law Review*, pp. 241 et seq.

Pertriaux (A.), 'Clearing houses: between sovereignty and the market', *Revue Banque*, April 2020, pp. 34 et seq.

Pietrancosta (A.),
- 'International jurisdiction of the AMF to approve prospectuses', *Étude Joly Bourse*.
- 'Law 2006-837 of 31 March 2006 on takeover bids: French "options"', *RTDF*, June 2006, pp. 5 et seq.
- and Prat (J.-F.), 'Offres publiques et droit des sociétés' in G. Canivet, D. Martin and N. Molfessis (eds.), *Les offres publiques d'achat*, Paris, LexisNexis, 2009, pp. 143 et seq.
- and Maraud des Grottes (A.), 'La notion de «placement privé» abolie par le Règlement Prospectus du 14 june 2017?', *BJB*, January 2018, pp. 60 et seq.

Pillet (A.), 'La loi de conclusion du contrat dans les marchés à terme', *Annales de droit commercial* 1910, repr. *Mélanges Pillet*, Paris, Recueil Sirey, 1929, t. II, pp. 67 et seq.

Pironon (V.), 'Dits et non-dits sur la méthode de la focalisation – dans le contentieux contractuel et délictuel - du commerce électronique', *JDI*, 2011, October 2011, var. 4.

Pistor (K.), 'Host Dilemma: Rethinking EU Banking Regulation in Light of the Global Crisis', *ECGI Finance WP n° 286/2010*, 28 June 2010.

Poracchia (D.), 'Remarques sur la titularité du droit de convertir des obligations en action', *RTDF*, 1/2-2015, pp. 107 et seq.

Potok (R.), 'Legal certainty for securities held as collateral' (1999) *International financial review*, pp. 12 et seq.

Poulle (J.-B.), 'Les entreprises de pays tiers', *RDBF*, November-December, 2014, no. 9.

Praicheux (S.), see 'Instruments financiers à terme' in *Répertoire de droit des sociétés*, Paris, Dalloz.

Prek (M.),
- 'Mutual judicial deference? The delineation of the (interpretative) competence of European and national courts in the judicial review of ECB acts based on national law' in *ECB Legal Conference*, December 2019, pp. 129 et seq.

– and Lefèvre (S.), 'Le contentieux de la surveillance prudentielle des établissements de crédit devant le tribunal de l'Union européenne', *Journal de droit européen*, 2019, pp. 99 et seq.

– and Lefèvre (S.), 'The EU Courts as "national" courts: National law in the EU judicial process' (2017) 54(2) *Common Market Law Review*, pp. 369 et seq.

Prüm (A.),

– 'Le nouveau cadre européen du traitement des faillures à vol d'oiseau', *RDBF*, 2014, no. 6, pp. 94 et seq.

– 'L'Union bancaire européenne et les autorités de surveillance nationales', *RDBF*, July-August 2014, pp. 74 et seq.

Racine (J.-B.), 'Les clauses d'élection de for asymétriques' in *Mélanges en l'honneur du Professeur Bertrand Ancel*, Paris, LGDJ, 2018, pp. 1323 et seq.

Ragno (F.), 'The Law Applicable to Consumer Contracts under the Rome I Regulation' in F. Ferrari (ed.), *Rome I Regulation*, Paris, Selliers, 2015.

Recine (F.), 'The new framework for cooperation between supervisory authorities in the Markets in Financial Instruments Directive', *REDBF (Euredia)*, 2004, no. 2, pp. 336 et seq.

Reynier (H.), 'Les offres publiques internationales : répartition géographique de compétences', *RTDF*, 2006, no. 3, pp. 96 et seq.

Riassetto (I.), 'Pour une commercialisation transfrontalière sans entrave des fonds d'investissement européen', *BJB*, November 2018, pp. 60 et seq.

Robine (D.),

– 'L'effet international de la faillite : la solution des directives relatives à l'insolvabilité des établissements de crédit et des entreprises d'assurance' in *L'effet international de la faillite*, Paris, Dalloz, 2004, pp. 37 et seq.

– 'The creation of resolution mechanisms under the influence of the financial crisis', *BJB*, October 2015, no. 112v4, pp. 481 et seq.

– and Praicheux (S.), 'Garanties Financières', *Etudes Joly Bourse*, 2018.

Roe (M.), 'Clearinghouse Overconfidence' (2013) (101) *California Law Review*, pp. 1641 et seq.

Roeges (L.), 'Quelques réflexions sur le cadre légal pour la libre prestation de services bancaires et financières', *REDBF (Euredia)*, 2000, no. 2, pp. 149 et seq.

Rogers (J.),

– 'Toward international harmonization of the commercial law of the modern securities holding and transfer system: some reflections from the United States Article 8 Revision Project' in *Capital Market Forum discussion paper no.* 6, International Bar Association, 1996, pp. 59 et seq.

– 'Policy Perspectives on Revised U.C.C. Article 8' (1996) 43 *U.C.L.A. L. Rev.*, pp. 1431 et seq.

– 'Of normalcy and anomaly: thoughts on choice of law for the indirect holding system', *Butterworth journal of international banking and financial law*, September 1998, pp. 47 et seq.

Rouaud (A.-C.),

– 'The provision of investment services in the EU by third-country firms under MiFID II and the PACTE Law', *RTDF*, October 2019, No. 3, pp. 24 et seq.

– 'Efficacité de la coopération et protection des droits de la défense', *Banque et Droit*, special issue February 2020, pp. 58 et seq.

– 'Is the investor a consumer like any other? À propos de l›application des règles de compétence internationales issues du Règlement Bruxelles Ibis', *RISF*, 2020/2, pp. 3 et seq.

– 'L'accès des pays tiers au marché européen bancaire et financier' in *Mélanges en l'honneur du professeur Gilbert Parléani*, Paris, IRJS, 2021, forthcoming.

Rousseau (H.), 'La forme des actions et la caisse centrale de dépôts et de virements de titres', *JCP*, 1944. I, pp. 410 et seq.

Roussel Galle (P.) and Douaoui-Chamseddine (M.), 'Les défaillances bancaires et financières, un droit spécial?', *RDBF*, November 2014, pp. 64 et seq.

Roussille (M.), 'Mutations des pouvoirs de l'AMF à l'occasion de l'entrée en vigueur d'EMIR', *RDBF*, January 2014, comm. 23.

Roussille (M.), Bréhier (B.), Pailler (P.), Rouaud (A.-C.) and Boucheta (H.), 'MiFID 2: what transparency at any price could cost', *BJB*, November 2012, pp. 496 et seq.

Salter QC (R.), 'Enforcing Debt Securities' in L. Gullifer and J. Payne (eds.), *Intermediation and beyond*, Oxford, Hart, 2020.

Samin (T.) and Torck (S.), 'Rejection by the General Court of the EU of the appeal brought by a German bank against the ECB's decision classifying it as a large entity', *RDBF*, September 2017, no. 5, pp. 31 et seq.

Scarano (J.-P.), 'Opposabilité ou inopposabilité de la clause de réserve de propriété', *RTD com.*, 1990, pp. 533 et seq.

Schammo (P.), 'Marchés financiers - Emetteurs – Prospectus et admission à la négociation sur un marché réglementé (fasc. 1025)' in *JCl. Europe Traité*, Paris, LexisNexis, 2014.

Schiller (S.) and Cremers (T.), 'Effectivité de la représentation et de la transmission des titres financiers non cotés par une blockchain ainsi que des minibons', *JCP G*, 2019, 92, I, A.

Schneiberg (M.) and Batley (T.), 'Regulating or redesigning finance? Market architectures, normal accidents, and dilemmas of regulatory reform' in M. Lounsbury and P. Hisrh (eds.), *Markets on trial: the economic sociology of the U.S. financial crisis*, Research in the sociology of organizations, Emerald Press, 2010, pp. 281 et seq.

Schwarcz (S.L.), 'Intermediary risk in a Global economy' (2001) 50 *Duke L. J.*, pp. 1541 et seq.

Segain (H.), Devaux (S.), 'Defenses anti-OPA au sein des sociétés françaises du CAC 40 et du CAC NEXT 20. Panorama 2017/2018', *RTDF*, 2018, no. 2/3, pp. 22 et seq.

Sigman (H.C.) and Bernasconi (C.), 'Myths about the Hague Convention debunked' (2005) *International financial law review*, pp. 31 et seq.

Simler (P.), 'Pour en finir avec le débat sur la nature juridique de la clause de ducroire' in *Mélanges en l'honneur de Jean-Philippe et Michel Storck*, Paris, Dalloz, 2021.

Sindres (D.), 'Le contrat cadre en matière internationale', *AJ contrat*, 2017, pp. 107 et seq.

Smith (W.H.), 'Le champ d'application territorial de la réglementation des offres publiques', *Rev. CMF*, 1997, no. 4, pp. 25 et seq.; *Rev. CMF*, 1998, no. 6, pp. 22 et seq.; *Rev. CMF*, no. 7, pp. 9 et seq.

Smits (R.), 'The ECB and the rule of law', *ECB Legal Conference 2019*, pp. 350 et seq.

Solomon (S.D.), 'Rhetoric and reality: a Historical Perspective on the Regulation of Foreign Private Issuers' (2010) *University of Cincinnati Law Review*, pp. 619 et seq.

Sotiropoulou (A.),

– 'Reflections on proposed CCP resolution tools', *RTDF*, 2018, no. 2/3, pp. 62 et seq.

– 'Le contrôle juridictionnel des décisions du Conseil de résolution unique', *BJB*, November 2020, pp. 57 et seq.

Sousi (B.),

– 'La Convention de Rome et la loi applicable aux contrats bancaires', *D.*, 1993, chron., pp. 183 et seq.

– 'La reconnaissance mutuelle, victime collatérale de l'Union bancaire', *D.*, 2012, pp. 2531 et seq.
– 'L'harmonisation européenne des services financiers et le juge national' in *Le juge et le droit de l'économie, Mélanges en l'honneur de Pierre Bézard*, Paris, Montchrestien, 2002, pp. 200 et seq.

Spitz (N.), 'MiFID 2: la recomposition des lieux d'exécution', *RDBF*, November 2014, pp. 12 et seq.

Storck (M.), 'Vers une amélioration de la distribution transfrontalière des organismes de placement collectif', *Revue Lamy de droit des affaires*, November 2019, pp. 14 et seq.

Storck (M.) and Riassetto (I.), 'La règle des quatre yeux en matière bancaire et financière' in *Mélanges en l'honneur de Jean-Jacques Daigre*, Paris, Lextenso, 2017, pp. 783 et seq.

Suire (L.), 'La nouvelle réglementation européenne de la distribution transfrontalière de fonds d'investissement', *RISF*, 2020/2, pp. 56 et seq.

Susset (E.),
– 'De quelques particularités de la résolution des groupes transfrontaliers', *RDBF*, November 2014, pp. 106 et seq.
– 'Le régime français de prévention et de gestion des crises bancaires après la transposition de la directive sur la résolution bancaire' in *Le traitement des difficultés des établissements bancaires et institutions financières*, Paris, LexisNexis, 2017, pp. 91 et seq.

Synvet (H.),
– 'The investment services directive: first reading', *BJB*, 1993, pp. 545 et seq.
– 'La réforme du droit français à la lumière de la directive sur les services d'investissement', *LPA*, 8 May 1996, No. 56, pp. 18 et seq.
– see 'Faillite' in *Répertoire de droit international*, Paris, Dalloz, 1998.
– 'Libres propos d'internationaliste sur les obligations d'intermédiation et de concentration' in *Mélanges en l'honneur de Michel Vasseur*, Paris, Banque Edition, 2000.
– see 'Société' in *Répertoire de droit international*, Paris, Dalloz, 2004.
– 'La propriété des valeurs mobilières en droit français' in *20 ans de dématérialisation des titres en France*, Paris, Revue Banque Edition, 2005, pp. 37 et seq.
– 'Objet du gage de compte d'instruments financiers' in *Études J. Béguin*, Paris, Litec, 2005, pp. 719 et seq.
– 'Les garanties financières', *RDBF*, January 2007, pp. 81 et seq.
– 'L'internationalisation du droit des affaires', in *Le Code de commerce 1807-2007, Livre du bicentenaire*, Paris, Dalloz, 2007, pp. 727 et seq.
– 'The exclusion of certain creditors from the law of collective proceedings' in W.-G. Ringe, L. Gullifer and P. Théry (eds.), *Current issues in European Financial and Insolvency Law*, Oxford, Hart, 2009, pp. 172 et seq.
– 'Propos désenchantés sur l'affaire Sacyr-Eiffage' in *Mélanges en l'honneur de Philippe Merle*, Paris, Dalloz, 2012, pp. 669 et seq.
– 'Law and financial markets', *BJB*, November 2014, pp. 517 et seq.
– 'European banking union – Presentation', *RDBF*, 2014, No. 4, dossier 24.
– 'Summary report. The extraterritoriality of law in banking law', *RDBF*, July 2015, pp. 41 et seq.
– 'Summary report', *RDBF*, July 2015, No. 4, pp. 41 et seq.
– 'La place de la décision administrative en droit bancaire' in *Mélanges en l'honneur du professeur Pierre Mayer*, Paris, LGDJ, 2015, pp. 845 et seq.

- 'Les conséquences du transfert du siège d'une SE immatriculée en France sur les porteurs d'obligations et de valeurs mobilières donnant accès à son capital' in *Mélanges Hervé Hovasse*, Paris, LexisNexis, 2016, pp. 187 et seq.
- 'Principe de légalité et résolution bancaire' in *Mélanges en l'honneur de Jean-Jacques Daigre*, Paris, Lextenso, 2017.
- 'Propos impertinents sur l'activisme actionnarial', *RDBF*, November 2020, pp. 75 et seq.
- and FERRAND (P.-N.), 'L'accueil en France des *schemes of arrangement* de droit anglais', *RDBF*, January-February 2014, pp. 10 et seq.
- and TENENBAUM (A.), 'Instruments financiers' in *Répertoire de droit international*, 2008.

TENENBAUM (A.),

- 'Réflexions sur la Convention de La Haye du 13 décembre 2002 sur la loi applicable à certains droits sur des titres détenus auprès d'un intermédiaire', *Revue des sociétés*, 2004, pp. 835 et seq.
- 'La compétence internationale des autorités de surveillance des marchés financiers en matière d'offre publique', *RCDIP*, 2006, pp. 557 et seq.
- 'Retombées de l'affaire Madoff sur la Convention de Lugano', *RCDIP*, 2012, pp. 45 et seq.
- 'L'Autorité européenne des marchés financiers: une autorité nouvelle au service d'une mutation de l'ordre juridique européen?' in *Mélanges en l'honneur du professeur Pierre Mayer*, Paris, LGDJ, 2015, pp. 847 et seq.
- 'La disparition de l'exigence de territorialité en matière de compétence des autorités de contrôle à l'épreuve du droit des marchés dérivés?', *RDBF*, July 2015, pp. 74 et seq.
- 'À propos des abus de marché et de la coopération au sein de l›Organisation internationale des commissions de valeurs mobilières', *Banque & Droit*, July-August 2015, No. 162.
- 'Les autres sources du droit européen des contrats : incidence du droit matériel européen des sociétés et des marchés financiers', *Revue des contrats*, March 2017, pp. 149 et seq.

TEUBNER (G.), 'Legal irritants: Good faith in British Law or how unifying law ends up in new divergences' (1998) 61 *Modern Law Review*, pp. 2 et seq.

THALLER (E.), 'D'un règlement qui aurait pour objet de résoudre les conflits de lois en matière de dépossession de titres au porteur', *Ann. dr. com*, 1905, pp. 259 et seq.

TOCQUEVILLE (J.-G. DE), BONZOM (A.) and FEUNTEUN (C.), 'Focus sur la réforme CRR2', *RDBF*, November 2019, study 15.

TOMASI (A.), 'Les conflits de lois en matière de représentation conventionnelle et l'opportunité d'une convention internationale', *RCDIP*, 1958, pp. 651 et seq.

TOMASI (M.), 'Vers un renouveau de la lutte contre les manipulations de cours' in *Mélanges AEBDF-France IV*, pp. 444 et seq.

TORCK (S.), 'Le rachat par les sociétés cotées de leurs propres actions', *BJB*, 2002, pp. 509 et seq.

TRICOT (B.), 'L'agrément administratif des institutions privées', *D.*, 1948, pp. 25 et seq.

TROCHU (M.),

- 'Les offres publiques d'achat', *RTD com*, 1967, pp. 695 et seq.
- 'Le triomphe du capitalisme sauvage, ou BSN contre Saint Gobain', *D.*, 1969, pp. 222 et seq.

TRÖGER (T.H.), 'The Single Supervisory Mechanism – Panacea or Quack Banking Regulation?' (2015) 15 *European Business Organization Review*, pp. 449 et seq.

TUNC (A.),

- 'Aspects de droits étrangers' in M. VASSEUR (ed.), *Les autorités boursières créatrices de droit*, ENAJ, 1981, pp. 147 et seq.

– 'La représentation des actions par la comptabilité de la Caisse centrale de dépôts et virements de titres', *JCP*, 1947, I, pp. 659 et seq.

Usunier (L.),

– 'Conflits de lois et de juridictions et jeux en ligne' in M. Behar-Touchais, J. Rochfeld and A. Guillenchmidt-Guignot (eds.), *Les jeux en ligne en France et en Europe : quelles réformes trois ans après l'ouverture du marché*, Société de législation comparée, 2013, pp. 530 et seq.

– 'La dématérialisation du jeu en ligne et la territorialité de la loi française' in G. Julia (ed.) *Jeu, argent et droit*, Paris, Dalloz, 2013, pp. 157 et seq.

Vabres (R.),

– 'L'influence des comités européens des régulateurs sur le droit des services financiers', *REDBF (Euredia)*, 2007/2008, no. 3, pp. 294 et seq.

– 'Establishment of the European Securities and Markets Authority and development of technical standards', *RTDF*, 2010, No. 3, pp. 64 et seq.

– 'The Board of Appeal of the European Supervisory Authorities', *BJB*, January 2012, pp. 4 et seq.

– 'Le système européen de supervision : état des lieux et perspectives', *RDBF*, January 2020, study 3.

– 'Autorité bancaire européenne et Union bancaire' in *L'Union bancaire*, Brussels, Bruylant, 2016, pp. 192 et seq.

– 'Les plans (préventifs) de résolution' in *Le traitement des difficultés des établissements bancaires et institutions financières*, Paris, LexisNexis, 2017, pp. 163 et seq.

– and Maouche (S.), 'Autorité des marchés financiers. - Pouvoir de sanction', *J-Cl. Banque-crédit-bourse*, fasc. 1511.

Vallens (J.-L.), 'La défaillance des établissements de crédit et le recours au juge', *RDBF*, 2014, pp. 91 et seq.

Vanneste (K.), 'Decoupling economic rights from voting rights: a threat to the traditional corporate governance paradigm' (2014) 15 *European Business Organization Review*, pp. 59 et seq.

de Vareilles Sommières (G.), 'La définition et la notion juridique de la propriété', *RTD civ.*, 1905, pp. 443 et seq.

de Vareilles-Sommières (P.), 'Autonomie substantielle et autonomie conflictuelle en droit international privé des contrats' in *Mélanges en l'honneur du Professeur Pierre Mayer*, Paris, Lextenso, 2015, pp. 869 et seq.

de Vauplane (H.),

– 'Les notions de marché', *Revue de droit bancaire et de la bourse*, March-April 1993, No. 36, pp. 62 et seq.

– 'Cadre juridique des garanties financières', *RDBF*, January 2007, pp. 82 et seq.

– 'The G20 proposals on derivatives security', *Banque*, January 2009, pp. 83 et seq.

– 'Blockchain and Conflict of Laws', *RTDF*, 2017, p. 50 et seq.

– 'Des titres papiers aux titres digitaux' in V. Magnier et P. Barban (dir.), *Blockchain et droit des sociétés*, Paris, Dalloz, 2019, pp. 32 et seq.

– and Daigre (J.-J.), 'Directive Prospectus. Présentation générale', *Banque et droit*, August 2003, pp. 47 et seq.

– and Bloch (P.), 'Loi applicable et critères de localisation des titres multi-intermédiés dans la Convention de la Haye du 13 décembre 2002', *JDI*, 2005, pp. 3 et seq.

– and Mouy (S.), 'La réforme du nantissement des titres dématérialisés', *Banque et droit*, 1996, no. 48, pp. 3 et seq.

Vedel (G.), 'La juridiction compétente pour prévenir, faire cesser ou réparer la voie de fait administrative', *JCP G*, 1950, I, pp. 851 et seq.

Vereecken (M.), 'Reducing systemic risk in payment and securities settlement systems' (1998) *Journal of financial regulation and compliance*, pp. 107 et seq.

Viandier (A.), 'Offres publiques et droit des sociétés', *Gaz Pal*, 3 May 1988, doctr. pp. 247 et seq.

Villey (M.), 'Du sens de l'expression jus in re en droit romain classique', *Revue internationale des droits de l'Antiquité*, 1949, pp. 421 et seq.

Vitu (A.), 'Un aspect particulier du droit pénal international : la protection des intérêts publics étrangers par le droit criminel français' in *Mélanges en l'honneur du professeur Jérôme Larguier*, Grenoble, PUG, 1993, pp. 368 et seq.

Wahl (A.), 'Les jeux de bourse en droit international', *JDI*, 1898, pp. 234 et seq.

Wautelet (P.), 'Réglementation étatique et marchés financiers : entre autonomie et relativité' in H. Muir Watt *et al* (eds.), *Le tournant global en droit international privé*, Paris, Pedone, 2020, pp. 341 et seq.

Wei (T.-B.), 'The Equivalence Approach to Securities Regulation' (2007) 2 *Northwestern Law Journal of International Law and Business*, pp. 255 et seq.

Wengler (W.), 'La situation des droits', *RCDIP*, 1957, pp. 185 et seq.

Witte (A.), 'When Does National Law Transpose a Directive' in *ECB Legal Conference* 2016, 6 October 2016, pp. 247 et seq.

Witz (C.), 'L'internationalité et le contrat', *Revue Lamy de droit des affaires*, 1 February 2002, supplement, no. 46.

Wymeersch (E.),

- 'Les défenses anti-OPA après la treizième directive' in *Mélanges en l'honneur de Jean Stoufflet*, Paris, LGDJ, 2001, pp. 397 et seq.
- 'Regulation and Case Law Relating to Financial Derivatives', *RDBF*, 2013, pp. 1 et seq.
- 'The Single Supervisory Mechanism or 'SSM', Part One of the Banking Union', *European Corporate Governance Institute (ECGI) – Law Working Paper No. 240/2014*, 21 February 2014.

Yates (M.), 'UK settlement' in M. Blair, G. Walker and S. Willey (eds.), *Financial Markets and Exchanges Law*, 2nd ed., Oxford, OUP, 2012, Nos. 12.01 et seq.

CASE LAW OBSERVATIONS

Affaki (G.)
Banco Santander [2016] EWHC 465 (Comm) *Banque et Droit*, No 167, May-June 2016, 45.

Ancel (B.)
ECJ, 2 October 2008, *Hassett*, Case C-372/ 07, *RCDIP.* 2009. 71.

Ancel (M.-E.)
Cass. com., 2 October 2012 (2 rulings), *Droit et patrimoine*, january 2013, 69.

Aubry (H.)
ECJ, 3 October 2019, Case C-208/18, *Petruchova, D.*, 2020, 624.
ECJ, 2 April 2020, Case C-500/18, *Reliantco investments, D.*, 2021, 594.

Audit (B.)
Cass., civ. 1re, 1 June 1976, *JDI* 1977, 91.
CA Paris, 27 September 1984, *D.*, 1985, somm. 178.
Cass., civ. 1re, 10 October 1995, *D.*, 1996, 171.

d'Avout (L.)
Cass., com., 5 May 2009, no. 08-18165, *D.*, 2010, 123.
Cass., com., 2 October 2012 (2 judgments), *D.*, 2013, pan., p. 2293.
ECJ, 7 February, 2013, Case C-543/10, *Refcomp, D.*, 2013, 2301.
United States of America v. BNP Paribas SA, D., 2014, 1967.
Cass., com., 7 January 2014, no. 11-24.157, *D.*, 2014, 1969.
Cass., com., 20 January 2015, no. 13-16745, 13-16764, 13-16765, 13-16966, *RCDIP*, 2016, 521.
ECJ, 28 January 2015, Case C-375/13, *Harald Kolassa v. Barclays Bank plc, D.*, 2015, 770.
ECJ, 21 May2015, Case C-352/ 13, *Cartel Damage Claims (CDC), D.*, 2015, 2031.
ECJ, 7 April 2016, Case C-483/ 14, *KA Finanz, D.*, 2016, 2025.
ECJ, 16 June 2016, Case C-12/15, *Universal Music, D.*, 2016, 2025.
Cass., com., 20 April 2017, no. 15-16.922, *D.*, 2017, 2054.
ECJ, 8 June 2017, Case C-54/16, *Vinyls Italia, JCP G*, 2017, 1655.
ECJ, 7 March 2018, Case C-560/16 *E. ON Czech Holding*, no. 31, *D.*, 2018, 1934.
Cass., crim., 14 March 2018, no. 16-82.117, *D.*, 2018, 1934.
ECJ, 12 September 2018, Case C-304/17, *Löber, JDI*, October 2019, p. 1445.
ECJ, 14 February, 2019, Case C-630-17, *Milivojević, JDI*, October 2020, chron. 10, no. 2.
Cass., com., 15 January 2020, no. 17-22.295, *D.*, 2020, 1970.
ECJ, 12 May 2021, Case C-709/19, *Effectenbezitters, RCDIP*, 2021, 536.

Avout (L.) and Borga (N.)
Cass., com., 13 September 2011, no. 10-25.533, *D.*, 2011, 2518.

Barban (P.)
AMF, 4 December 2015, *Sociétés Euronext Paris-Vertu Financial Europe LTD*, SAN-2015-21, *BJB*, 2016, 164.
ECJ, 16 November 2017, Case C-658/ 15, *BJB*, March 2018, 112.

Barbiéri (J.-F.)
Cass., com., 21 December 1987, *JCP*, 1988, II, 21230.
Barrière (F.)
AMF, 4 December 2015, *Sociétés Euronext Paris-Vertu Financial Europe LTD*, SAN-2015-21, *BJB*, 2016, No. 4, p. 143.
CE, 19 May2017, *BJB*, 2017, no. 5, p. 322.
Batiffol (H.)
Cass., req., 24 May 1933, *S.*, 1935, 1, 253.
Cass., civ., 25 May 1948, *RCDIP*, 1949, 89.
Cass., civ., 21 June 1950, *RCDIP*, 1950, 609.
Cass, civ. 1re, 17 October 1972, *RCDIP*, 1973, 520.
Berlioz (P.)
ECJ, 7 February 2013, Case C-543/10, *Refcomp*, *RJ com.*, 2013, 498.
Bollée (S.)
ECJ, 12 May2011, Case C-144/ 10, *D.*, 2011, 2434.
Cass., com., 13 September 2011, no. 10-25.533, *D.*, 2331.
ECJ, 7 February 2013, Case C-543/10, *Refcomp*, *D.*, 2013, 1110.
ECJ, 28 January 2015, Case C-375/13, *Harald Kolassa v. Barclays Bank plc*, *D.*, 2015, 2031.
Cass., com., 1 March 2017, no. 14-25 426, *D.*, 2017, 2054.
ECJ, 8 June 2017, Case C-54/ 16, *Vinyls Italia*, *D.*, 2017, 2054.
ECJ, 15 June 2017, Case C-249/ 16, *D.*, 2017, 2054.
Bonneau (T.)
Cass., com., 6 April 2001, *Popovici c/Sté des bourses françaises*, now Euronext Paris, *RDBF*, March 2002, study 100016.
ECJ, 22 March 2012, Case C-248/11, *BJB*, 2012, para. 111, p. 248.
ECJ, 16 June 2015, Case C-62/ 14, *RDBF*, 2015, comm. 109.
ECJ, 10 November 2016, Case C-156/15, *Swedbank*, *RDBF*, March 2017, 82.
ECJ, 16 November 2017, Case C-658/ 15, *RDBF*, May 2018, comm. 85.
Boskovic (O.)
ECJ, 16 June 2016, Case C-12/ 15, *Universal Music*, *D.*, 2016, 2156.
Bourel (P.)
Cass., civ. 1re, 30 May 1967, *RCDIP*, 1967, 728.
ECJ, 30 November 1976, *Mines de potasse d'Alsace*, *RCDIP*, 1977, 563.
Bouveresse (A.)
ECJ, 10 november 2016, C-156/15, *Swedbank*, *Europe*, January 2017. 20.
Brignant (J.-M.)
AMF, 4 December 2015, *Sociétés Euronext Paris-Vertu Financial Europe LTD*, SAN-2015-21, *RSC*, 2016, 310.
Brill (J.-P.)
Cass., com., 21 December 1987, *D.*, 1989, 122.
Bureau (D.)
Cass., civ. 1re, 28 October 2003, n° 00-18.794 and n° 00-20.065, *RCDIP*, 2004, 83.
Cass., com., 2 October 2012 (2 rulings), *RCDIP*, 2013, 201.
ECJ, 7 February 2013, Case C-543/10, *Refcomp*, *RCDIP*, 2013, 710.
Cass., civ. 3e, 16 January 2013, no. 11-13.509, *RCDIP*, 2013, 620.
Cass., com., 20 April 2017, no. 15-16.922, *RCDIP*, 2017, 542.
ECJ, 7 March 2018, Case C-560/16 *E.ON Czech Holding*, *RCDIP*, 2018, 633.

ECJ, 3 October 2019, Case C-272/18, *VfK v. TVP, RCDIP*, 2020, 349.

Capitant (H.)
Cass., civ., 17 May 1927, *D.P.*28.1.25.

Carval (S.)
Cass., com., 3 May2006, no. 04-12683; *RDC*, 2006/4, 1227.

Chabas (Fr.)
Cass., civ. 1re, 1 June 1976, *JCP G*, 1979, II, 19082.

Chacornac (J.)
AMF, dec., 4 December 2015, *Sociétés Euronext Paris-Vertu Financial Europe LTD*, SAN-2015-21, *RDBF*, 2016, No. 1, No. 45.
ECJ, 7 April 2016, Case C-483/14, *KA Finanz, D.*, 2016, 1404.
ECJ, 3 October 2019, Case C-272/18, *VfK v. TVP, D.*, 2020, 378
ECJ, 3 October 2019, Case C-208/18, *Petruchova, Banque et droit*, May-June 2020, no. 191, 65.
ECJ, 17 December 2020, Case C-316/ 19, *Banque et droit*, January 2021, 61.

Clavel (S.)
Cass., com., 15 January 2020, no. 17-22.295, *D.*, 2020, 951.

Clavel-Thoraval (J.)
ECJ, 2 April 2020, Case C-500/18, *Reliantco investments, BJB*, July 2020.

Combet (M.)
ECJ, 7 February 2013, Case C-543/10, *Refcomp, RLDA*, March 2013, 4510.

Comble de Nayves (P. de)
Cass., crim., 14 March 2018, no. 16-82.117, *AJ pénal*, 2018, 254.

Corneloup (S.)
Cass., com., 7 January 2014, no. 11-24.157, *RCDIP*, 2014, 432.
ECJ, 20 April 2016, Case C-366/13, *Profit investment Sim, R.I.S.F.*, 2016/3.

Courbe (P.) and Chanteloup (H.)
ECJ, 10 June 2004, Case C-168/ 02, *Kronhofer v. Maier and others, D.*, 2004, 1192.

Couret (A.)
Cass., com., 13 June 1995, *Bull. Joly sociétés*, 1995, 855, para. 305.

Cremers (T.) and Boucheta (H.)
AMF, dec., 24 January 2020, no. 1, SAN-2020-02, *BJB*, September 2020, no. 119f9, 20.

Daigre (J.-J.)
T. Com. Paris, 16e ch., 14 September 2012, *BJB*, April 2013, 192.
AMF, dec., 4 December 2015, *Sociétés Euronext Paris-Vertu Financial Europe LTD*, SAN-2015-21, *Banque & Droit, 2016*, No. 166, 40.

Decoopman (N.)
CA Paris, 28 March 1988, *D.*, 1989, jurispr. 116.

Delebecque (P.)
Cass., civ. 1re, 16 March 1999, no. 96-21 794, *Defrénois*, 15 December 1999, p. 1324.

Dezeuze (E.)
Cass., com., 1 March 2017, *Rev. soc.*, 2017, 365.

Didier (P.)
Cass., com., 13 June 1995, *Rev. Sociétés*, 1995, 736.

Diener (P.)
CA Paris, 27 September 1984, *JDI*, 1985, 664.

Droz (G.)
ECJ, 30 November 1976, *Mines de potasse d'Alsace*), *D.*, 1977, 613.

Dubertret (M.)
Cass., com., 5 May 2009, no. 08-18165, *Revue des sociétés*, July 2009, 580.

Duranton
Cass., ass. plén., 21 December 1990, *Roval*, *RCDIP*, 92, 70.

Esmein (P.)
Cass., civ., 17 May 1927, *S.*, 27.I.289.

Fages (B.)
Cass., com., 13 September 2011, no. 10-25.533, *RTD civ.*, 2012, 113, and 116.

Farnoux (E.)
ECJ, 12 September 2018, Case C-304/17, *Löber*, *D.*, 2019, 1946.
ECJ, 3 October 2019, Case C-272/18, *VfK v. TVP*, *D.*, 2020, 1970.
ECJ, 2 April 2020, Case C-500/18, *Reliantco investments, D.* 2020. 1970.

Ferrier (D.)
ECJ, 21 may2015, case C-352/ 13, *Cartel Damage Claims (CDC)*, *D.*, 2016, 964.

Foussard (D.)
Cass., civ. 1re, 22 May2007, *RCDIP*, 2008, 278.

Francescakis (P.)
Cass., civ. 1re, 17 June 1958, *RCDIP*, 1958, 705.

Galland (M.)
Cass., com., 2 October 2019, no. 17-28462, *BJB*, January 2020, 13.

Gaudemet-Tallon (H.)
Cass., com., 13 September 2011, no. 10-25.533, *D.*, 2012, 1228.
Cass., com., 3 June 2014, no. 12-18012, *D.*, 2015, 1056.
ECJ, 7 April 2016, Case C-483/14, *KA Finanz*, *D.*, 2017, 1011.

Gazin (F.)
ECJ, 22 March 2012, Case C-248/11, *Europe*, 2012, no. 5, comm. 193.

Germain (M.) and Frison Roche (M.-A.)
Cass., com., 13 June 1995, *RDBB*, 1995, 148.

Goldman (B.)
CA Paris, 3 October 1984, *JDI*, 1986, 156.

Guez (P.)
ECJ, 7 February 2013, Case C-543/10 *Refcomp*, *JCP*, 2013, no. 516.

Guinchard (E.)
ECJ, 12 May2011, Case C-144/10, *RTD eur.* 2011, 477.
ECJ, 28 January 2015, Case C-375/13, *Harald Kolassa v. Barclays Bank plc*, *RTD eur.*, 2015, 374.
ECJ, 16 June 2016, Case C-12/15, *Universal Music*, *RTD eur.*, 2016, 805.

Guyon (Y.)
Cass., com., 8 March 1982, *Rev. soc.*, 1983, 573.
Cass., com., 13 June 1995, *JCP E*, 1995, I, 712.

Haftel (B.)
ECJ, 28 January 2015, Case C-375/13, *Harald Kolassa v. Barclays Bank plc*, *RDC*, 2015, 547.

Hamel (J.)
Cass., civ., 21 June 1950, *D.*, 1951, 749.

Heuzé (V.)
Cass., civ. 1re, 10 October 1995, *RCDIP*, 1996, 332.

Houin (R.)
CA Paris, 2 December 1963, *RTD com*, 1964; 642.

Hovasse (H.)
Cass., com., 3 January 1996, *JCP E*, 199, II, 808.
Cass., com., 5 May 2009, no. 08-18165, *Droit des sociétés*, July 2009, 21.

Huet (A.)
ECJ, 30 November 1976, *Mines de potasse d'Alsace*, *JDI*, 1977, 728.

Idot (L.)
ECJ, 19 September 1995, Case C-364/ 93, *Marinari*, *Europe*, November 1995, no. 408.
ECJ, 2 October 2008, Case C-372/07, *Hassett*, *Europe*, 2008, comm. 342.
ECJ, 7 February 2013, Case C-543/10, *Refcomp*, *Europe*, 2013, comm. 194.
ECJ, 17 October 2013, Case C-184/12, *Unamar*, *Europe*, 2013, comm. 2.
ECJ, 21 May2015, Case C-352/13, *Cartel Damage Claims (CDC)*, *RTD eur.*, 2015, 807.
ECJ, 24 November 2020, Case C-59/19, *Wikingerhof GmbH*, *Europe*, 2021, comm. 39.

Jacquet (J.-M.)
ECJ, 17 October 2013, Case C-184/12, *Unamar*, *JDI*, 2014, comm. 7.

Jault-Seseke (F.)
ECJ, 12 May2011, Case C-144/ 10, *D.*, 2012, 1228.
Cass., com., 2 October 2012 (2 judgments), *D.*, 2013, 62.
ECJ, 21 May 2015, Case C-352/13, *Cartel Damage Claims (CDC)*, *D.*, 2015, 1045.
ECJ, 28 January 2015, Case C-375/13, *Harald Kolassa v. Barclays Bank plc*, *D.*, 2015, 1056.
Cass., civ. 1re, 13 November 2013, no. 13-13586, *D.*, 2014, 1059.
ECJ, 7 February 2013, Case C-543/10 *Refcomp*, *D.*, 2013, 1509.
ECJ, 2 April 2020, Case C-500/18, *Reliantco investments*, *D.*, 2021, 923.
ECJ, 12 September 2018, Case C-304/17, *D.*, 2019, 1016.

Jobard-Bachellier (M.-N.)
CA Paris, 26 March 1986, *RCDIP*, 1987, 351.

Kleiner (C.)
ECJ, 24 October 2013, Case C-85/12, *Landbanski*, *D.*, 2014, 249.
ECJ, 20 April 2016, Case C-366/13, *Profit investment*, Sim, *JDI* 2017, 585.
ECJ, 12 September 2018, Case C-304/17, *Löber*, *JDI*, April 2019, 503.
ECJ, 3 October 2019, Case C-208/18, *Petruchova*, *RDBF*, chr. 1, no. 44.
ECJ, 2 April 2020, Case C-500/18, *Reliantco investments*, *RDBF*, September 2020, 23.
High Court BNP Paribas SA v. Trattamento Rifiuti Metropolitani SPA [2020] EWHC 2436 (Comm), *RDBF*, April 2021, 25.

Kovar (J.-P) and Lasserre Capdeville (J.)
ECJ, 16 June 2015, Case C-62/14, *Bank*, 2015, 91.

Lagarde (G.)
CA Colmar, 24 February 1965, *RCDIP*, 1967, 152.

Lardeux (G.)
Cass., civ. 1re, 28 October 2003, n° 00-18.794 and n° 00-20.065, *Bull. civ.*, I, no. 219, *JCP*, 2004, II, 10006.

Le Cannu (P.)
CA Paris, 13 July 1988, *D.*, 1989, jur. 160.

Légier (G.)
Cass., civ. 1re, 28 October 2003, n° 00-18.794 and n° 00-20.065, *JDI*, 2004, 499.

Legrand (V.)
ECJ, 7 February 2013, Case C-543/10, *Refcomp*, *LPA*, 10 April 2013, 6.

Le Nabasque (H.)
Cass., com., 10 February 2015, no. 13-14778, *Bull. Joly sociétés*, 2015, 182.

Lerebours-Pigeonnière (P.)
Cass., civ., 25 May 1948, *D.*, 1948, 357.

Lévy (J.-P)
Cass., civ., 21 June 1950, *JCP*, 1950, II, 5812.

Libchaber (R.)
Cass., civ. 1re, 28 October 2003, n° 00-18.794 and n° 00-20.065, *Defrénois*, 2004, 37894.
Cass., com., 5 May 2009, no. 08-18165, *Bulletin joly sociétés*, December 2009, 1065.

Loussouarn (Y.)
CA Paris, 2 December 1963, *RCDIP*, 1966, 40.
Cass., com., 13 February 1967, *Bull civ.*, no. 67, *RCDIP*, 1968, 52.

Lyon-Caen (C.)
Cass., 6 February 1900, *S.*, 1900, 1, 161.

Malaurie (P.)
Cass., civ. 1re, 30 May1967, *D.*, 1967, 629.

Malaurie-Vignal (M.)
ECJ, 24 November 2020, Case C-59/19, *Wikingerhof GmbH, Contrats Concurrence Consommation*, 2021, comm. 4.

Marmisse-d'Abbadie d'Arrast (A.)
ECJ, 2 October 2008, Case C-372/07, *Hassett*, *JCP*, 2009, I, 107.
ECJ, 12 May2011, Case C-144/10, *RTD com.*, 2011, 814.
ECJ, 7 February 2013, Case C-543/10, *Refcomp*, *RTD com.*, 2013, 381.
ECJ, 7 March 2018, Case C-560/16, *E. ON Czech Holding*, *RTD com.*, 2018, 517.
ECJ, 8 May2019, Case C-25/18, *Kerr*, *RTD com.*, 2019, 789.
ECJ, 3 October 2019, Case C-272/18, *VfK v. TVP*, *RTD com.*, 2020, 211.

Martin-Laprade (F.)
Sanct. AMF, 24 November 2005, *Allianz AG and Société Euroclear France*, *BJB*, April 2006, 470.
AMF, dec. N° 211/C/0024 of 7 January 2011, *Rev. Sociétés*, 2011, 364.

Martin-Serf (A.)
Cass., com., 13 September 2011, no. 10-25.533, *RTD com.*, 2011, 801.

Mathey (N.)
CE, Assemblée, 21 March 2016, *Société Fairvesta International GMBH et autres*, no. 368082, *RDBF*, 2016, comm. 108.

Mélin (F.)
Cass., com., 2 October 2012 (2 rulings), *JCP*, 2012, 1246.
ECJ, 3 October 2019, Case C-208/18, *Petruchova*, *Dalloz actualité*, 22 October 2019.

Menjucq (M.)
ECJ, 7 March 2018, Case C-560/16, *E. ON Czech Holding*, *Bull. Joly*, July-August 2018, 417.

Mestre (J.) and Mestre-Chami (A.-S.)
Cass. com. 3 june 2014, no. 12-18012 *Revue Lamy droit des Affaires* november 2015. 47.
Michel (V.)
EGC, 6 May2019, Case T-281/18, *ABLV Bank v. BCE, Europe*, July 2019, comm. 266.

Moille (C.) and Pellegrini (C.)
Cass., com., 13 September 2011, no. 10-25.533, *RTD eur.*, 2012, 522.

Morel-Maroger (J.)
ECJ, 16 June 2015, Case C-62/14, *Banque et Droit*, May-June 2015, 65.
ECJ, 10 November 2016, Case C-156/15, *Swedbank*, *Banque et droit*, January 2017, 43.
Cass., com., 1 March 2017, no. 14-25 426, *La Gazette du Palais*, 13 June 2017, 85.

Muir Watt (H.)
ECJ, 10 June 2004, Case C-168/02, *Kronhofer v. Maier and others*, no. 19, *RCDIP*, 2005, 326.
ECJ, 12 September 2018, Case C-304/17, *Löber*, *RCDIP*, 2019, 135.

Muller (A.-C.)
CA Paris, 13 February 2013, no. 10/17571, *RDBF*, January 2014, no. 1.
ECJ, 16 November 2017, Case C-658/15, *Droit et patrimoine*, December 2018, 286.

Niboyet (J.-P.)
Cass., civ., 21 June 1950, *S.*, 1952, 1, 1.
Cass., civ., 25 May 1948, *S.*, 1949, 1, 21.
CA Paris, 18 November 1927, *RCDIP*, 1934, 121.
Cass., req., 24 May 1933, *RCDIP*, 1934, 132.
CA Paris, 28 February 1935, *RCDIP*, 1935, 748.

Nourrissat (C.)
ECJ, 7 February 2013, Case C-543/10, *Refcomp*, *Procédures*, 2013, comm. 104.
ECJ, 24 November 2020, Case C-59/19, *Wikingerhof GmbH*, *JCP G*, 2021, 132, no. 7; *Procédures* 2021, comm. 68.

Pailler (P.)
CE, ass., 21 March 2016, *Société Fairvesta International GMBH et autres*, no. 368082, *RDBF*, 2016, comm. 144.
CE, 19 May2017, *RDBF*, no. 5, 2017, comm. 226.
Cass., com., 7 March 2018, no. 16-15821, *BJB*, May 2018, no. 117m8, 160.

Parléani (G.)
ECJ, 15 October 2009, Case C-101/08, *Audiolux*, *Rev. Sociétés*, 2010, 45.

Partsch (P.-E.) and Evans (T.)
ECJ, 10 November 2016, Case C-156/15, *Swedbank*, *RTBF*, April 2017, 151.

Petit (J.)
CE, 14 January 1998, *Syndicat départemental Interco*, *AJDA*, 1999, 164.

Pietrancosta (A.)
Cass., crim., 1 April 2020, no. 19-82223, *BJB*, May 2020, p. 21.

Pignarre (P.-E.)
ECJ, 16 June 2015, Case C-62/14, *Constitutions*, 2015, 371.

Pingel (I.)
ECJ, 17 December 2020, Case C-316/19, *JDI*, April 2021, var. 3.

Pironon (V.)
Cass., com., 20 April 2017, no. 15-16.922, *AJ Contrat*, 2017, 289.
Cass., com., 15 January 2020, no. 17-22.295, *RCDIP*, October 2020, 814.

Poillot-Peruzzetto (S.)
CA Grenoble, 11 January 1996, *RCDIP*, 1998, 483.

Prorok (J.)
ECJ, 2 April 2020, Case C-500/18, *Reliantco investments*, *Banque et droit*, June 2020.

Quéguigner (J.-S.)
ECJ, 20 April 2016, Case C-366/13, *Profit investment*, *JDI*, 2017, 1585.
ECJ, 7 March 2018, Case C-560/16, *E. ON Czech Holding*, *JDI*, 2019, 1462.
ECJ, 3 October 2019, Case C-208/18, *JDI*, October 2020, chron. 10.

Querleux (K.) and Beaumont (S.)
Cass., com., 15 January 2020, no. 17-22.295, *Revue Lamy de la concurrence*, 2020, no. 95, 35.

Rémery (J.-P.)
Cass., com., 13 September 2011, no. 10-25.533, *RCDIP*, 2011, 870.

Rémy-Corlay (P.)
ECJ, 7 February 2013, Case C-543/10, *Refcomp*, *RTD civ.*, 2013, 338.

Revet (T.)
Cass., com., 5 May 2009, no. 08-18165, *RTD civ.*, 2010, 136.

Riassetto (I.)
Comm. sanct. AMF, 2 July 2019 (SAN-2019-10), *BJB*, September 2019, no. 5, p. 12.

Robert (J.-H.)
Cass., crim., 14 March 2018, no. 16-82.117, *Rev. Sociétés*, 2018, 459.

Rondu (J.)
ECJ, 19 December 2018, Case C-219/17, *Berlusconi*, *RTD eur.*, 2019, 853.

Rontchevsky (N.)
CE, ass., 21 March 2016, *Société Fairvesta International GMBH et autres*, no. 368082, *RTD com*, April 2016, 298.

Rouaud (A.-C.)
ECJ, 19 December 2018, Case C-219/17, *Berlusconi*, *RISF*, 2019/1.

Schlumberger (E.)
ECJ, 7 April 2016, Case C-483/14, *KA Finanz*, *Droit des sociétés*, January 2017, 17.

Seiller (B.)
CE, ass., 21 March 2016, *Société Fairvesta International GMBH et autres*, no. 368082, *La Gazette du Palais*, 14 June 2016, 27.

Sexer (Y.)
CA Paris, 13 July 1988, *BJB*, 1988, 715.

Simon (D.)
ECJ, 16 June 2015, Case C-62/14, *Europe*, 2015, study 5.

Synvet (H.)
CA Toulouse, 26 October 1982, *JDI*, 1983, 603.
CA Paris, 3 October 1984, *RCDIP*, 1985, 526.
Cass., com., 21 December 1987, *Revue des sociétés*, 1988, 398.
Goldman Sachs International v. Novo Banco, Queen's Bench Division, Commercial Court, 7 August 2015, [2015] EWHC 2371 (Comm), *D.*, 2015, 2145.
ECJ, 16 June 2015, Case C-62/14, *D.*, 2015, 2147.
CE, ass., 21 March 2016, *Société Fairvesta International GMBH et autres*, no. 368082, *BJB*, December 2016, 212.
ECJ, 19 December 2018, Case C-219/17, *Berlusconi*, *D.*, 2019, 2009.

Tenenbaum (A.)
Cass., com., 7 January 2014, no. 11-24.157, *RCDIP*, January 2012, 45.
Cass., com., 3 June 2014, no. 12-18012, *BJB*, September 2014, 400.
AMF dec. of 29 July 2016, *Roderer Limited*, *Banque et Droit*, September 2016, 39.
Cass., com., 1 March 2017, no. 14-25 426, *Banque et Droit*, May 2017, 50.
ECJ, 3 October 2019, Case C-208/18, *Contract Review*, 2020/1.

Torck (S.)
AMF, sanct., 26 June 2008, *RDBF*, July 2009, No. 4, comm. 142.
ECJ, 22 March 2012, Case C-248/11, *Dr. Sociétés*, 2012, no. 106, p. 27.

Treppoz (E.)
ECJ, 12 May 2011, Case C-144/10, *RCDIP*, 2011, 922.

Vabres (R.)
AMF, dec., 4 December, 2015, *Sociétés Euronext Paris-Vertu Financial Europe LTD*, SAN-2015-21, *Dr. sociétés*, no. 5, 2016, comm. 86.
ECJ, 16 November 2017, Case C-658/15, *Dr. Sociétés*, March 2018, comm. 50.

Vallens (J.-L.)
Cass., com., 13 September 2011, no. 10-25.533, *RTD com.*, 2011, 801.

Vasseur (M.)
CA Paris, 26 March 1986, *D.*, 1986, 374, 2nd esp.

Vauplane (H. de) and Mattout (J.-P.)
ECJ, 20 April 2016, Case C-366/13, *Droit et patrimoine*, September 2017, 84.

Von Coester (S.)
CE, ass., 21 March 2016, *Société Fairvesta International GMBH et autres*, no. 368082, *Revue française de droit administratif*, May 2016, 497.

Zabala (B.)
ECJ, 22 March 2012, Case C-248/11, *Option finance*, 2012, no. 1172, p. 27.

Zekkoui (N. B.)
Court of Appeals, No. 11-397-cv (2 d Cir. August 15, 2014), *Parkcentral Global Hub Ltd. v. Porsche Automobil Holdings SE*, *BJB*, January 2015, p. 19.

CASE LAW

FRENCH CASE LAW

CONSTITUTIONAL COUNCIL

Cons. const., 17 January 1989, DC no. 89-248.
Cons. const., 28 July 1989, DC no. 89-260.
Cons. const., 12 August 2004, DC no. 2004-504.
Cons. const., 5 August 2015, DC no. 2015-715.

COUNCIL OF STATE (CONSEIL D'ÉTAT)

CE, 29 June 1973, *RCDIP*, 1974, 344.
CE, 14 January 1998, *Syndicat départemental Interco.*
CE, ass., 21 March 2016, *Société Fairvesta International GMBH et autres*, no. 368082.
CE, 19 May2017, *BJB*, 2017, no. 5, p. 322.

COURT OF CASSATION

Civil chambers

Cass., civ., 6 February 1900, *S.*, 1900, 1, 161.
Cass., civ., 17 May 1927, *Gaz. Pal*, 27, 2, 153.
Cass., civ., 25 May 1948, *RCDIP*, 1949, 89.
Cass., civ., 21 June 1950, *Messagerie Maritime*, *RCDIP*, 1950, 609.
Cass., civ. 1re, 17 June 1958, *RCDIP*, 1958, 705.
Cass., civ. 1re, 30 May 1967, *RCDIP*, 1967, 728.
Cass., civ. 1re, 17 October 1972, *Bull. civ.*, I, no. 204.
Cass., civ. 1re, 1 June 1976, *JDI*, 1977, 91.
Cass., civ. 1re, 20 July 1994, no. 92-12.431, *Bull. civ.*, I, no. 261.
Cass., civ. 1re, 10 October 1995, *RCDIP*, 1996, 332.
Cass., civ. 1re, 16 March 1999, no. 96-21 794.
Cass., civ. 1re, 28 October 2003, no. 00-18.794 and n° 00-20.065.
Cass., civ. 1re, 22 May2007, *RCDIP*, 2008, 278.
Cass., civ. 2^{e}, 17 March 2011, no. 10-16.553.
Cass., civ. 3^{e}, 16 January 2013, no. 11-13.509.
Cass., civ. 1re, 13 November 2013, no. 13-13586.
Cass., civ. 1re, 1 March 2017, no. 14-25.426.

Commercial Chamber

Cass., com., 23 January 1956, *D.*, 1956, 204.
Cass., com., 13 February 1967, *Bull civ.*, no. 67, *RCDIP*, 1968, 52.
Cass., com., 8 March 1982, no. 79-10.412, *Bull. civ.*, IV, no. 92.
Cass., com., 21 December 1987, pourvoi no. 85-13.173, *RCDIP*, 1989, 344.
Cass., com., 13 June 1995, *Bull. civ.*, IV, no. 181, p. 168, *Rev. Sociétés*, 1995, 736.
Cass., com., 17 October 1995, no. 93-18642.
Cass., com., 3 January 1996, *JCP E*, 199, II, 808.
Cass., com., 7 April 1998, no. 96-13373.
Cass., com., 5 December 2000, no. 97-20236.
Cass., com., 6 April 2001, *RDBF*, March 2002.
Cass., com., 20 May 2003, no. 99-17.092, *Bull. civ. IV*, no. 84.
Cass., com., 3 May 2006, no. 04-12683.
Cass., com., 19 December 2006, no. 04-18888.
Cass., com., 5 May 2009, no. 08-18165.
Cass., com., 9 March 2010, nos. 08-21.547 and 08-21.793.
Cass., com., 15 March 2011, no. 09-72027.
Cass., com., 13 September 2011, no. 10-25.533.
Cass., com., 2 October 2012, no. 10-18.005.
Cass., com., 7 January 2014, no. 11-24.157.
Cass., com., 3 June 2014, no. 12-18012.
Cass., com., 20 January 2015, nos. 13-16745, 13-16764, 13-16765, 13-16966.
Cass., com., 10 February 2015, no. 13-14778.
Cass., com., 1 March 2017, no. 14-25.
Cass., com., 1 March 2017, no. 14-26.225.
Cass., com., 20 April 2017, no. 15-16.922.
Cass., com., 7 March 2018, no. 16-15821.
Cass., com., 16 May 2018, no. 16-20.684.
Cass., com., 2 October 2019, no. 17-28462.
Cass., com., 15 January 2020, no. 17-22.295.

Social Chamber

Cass., soc., 25 September 1991, *Bull. V*, no. 381.

Criminal Chamber

Cass., crim., 30 June 1885, *D. P.* 1886.1.839.
Cass., crim., 2 March 1978, no. 76-92008.
Cass., crim., 14 March 2018, no. 16-82.117.
Cass., crim., 1 april 2020, no. 19-82223.

Assemblée Plénière and Chambre des requêtes

Req., 24 May 1933, *S.*, 1935, 1, 253.
Ass. plén., 21 December 1990, *Roval*, *JCP*, 91, II, 21640.
Ass. plén., 13 January 2020, no. 17-19.963.

COURT OF APPEAL

CA Paris, 18 November 1927, *D. H.*, 1927, III, 91.
CA Paris, 28 February 1935, *RCDIP*, 1935, 748.
CA Paris, 2 December 1963, *D.*, 1965, 377.
CA Colmar, 24 February 1965, *RCDIP*, 1966, p. 544.
CA Toulouse, 26 October 1982, *JDI*, 1983, 603.
CA, 27 September 1984, *D.*, 1985, somm. 178.
CA Paris, 3 October 1984, *RCDIP*, 1985, 526.
CA Paris, 26 march 1986, *D.*, 1986, 374, 2nd esp.
CA Paris, 28 March 1988, *D.*, 1989, jurispr. p. 116.
CA Paris, 13 July 1988, *D.*, 1989, jur. 160.
CA Paris, 2 November 1989, *Rev. Sociétés*, 1990.
CA Grenoble, 11 January 1996, *RCDIP*, 1998, 483.
CA Paris, 30 June 2006, RG no. 04/06308.
CA Paris, 30 March 2010, no. 2009/12248.
CA Paris, 4e ch., 13 February 2013, RG no. 10/17.571.
CA Paris, 2 October 2014, no. 2012/20580.

COMMERCIAL COURT

T. com., Paris, 16e ch., 14 September 2012, *BJB*, April 2013, 192.

FINANCIAL MARKET AUTHORITIES

AMF, Enforcement Committee, 24 November 2005, *Allianz AG and Société Euroclear France*, *BJB*, April 2006, 470.
AMF, Enforcement Committee, AMF dec. of 26 June 2008, *RDBF*, no. 4, July 2009, comm. 142.
AMF, Enforcement Committee, AMF dec. of 27 November 2009.
AMF, Enforcement Committee, AMF dec. no. 211/C/0024 of 7 January 2011, *Rev. Sociétés*, 2011, 364.
AMF, Enforcement Committee, AMF dec. of 28 September 2012.
AMF, Enforcement Committee, 4 December 2015, *Sociétés Euronext Paris-Vertu Financial Europe LTD*, SAN-2015-21.
AMF, Enforcement Committee, AMF dec. no. 3 of 2 May 2018.
AMF, Enforcement Committee, AMF dec. no. 5 of 7 May 2018.
AMF, Enforcement Committee, AMF dec. no. 7 of 5 July 2018.
AMF, Enforcement Committee, AMF dec. no. 8 of 16 July 2018.
AMF, Enforcement Committee, AMF dec. no. 9 of 18 July 2018.
AMF, Enforcement Committee, AMF dec. no. 11 of 24 October 2018.
AMF, Enforcement Committee, AMF dec. no. 12 of 9 November 2018.
AMF, Enforcement Committee, AMF dec. no. 15 of 13 December 2018.
AMF, Enforcement Committee, AMF dec no. 3 of 13 March 2019.
AMF, Enforcement Committee, AMF dec. no. 4 of 17 April 2019.
AMF, Enforcement Committee, AMF dec. no. 5 of 25 April 2019.
AMF, Enforcement Committee, dec. of 2 Kuly 2019 (SAN-2019-10), *BJB*, September 2019, no. 5, p. 12.
AMF, Enforcement Committee, AMF dec. no. 13 of 1 October 2019.

AMF, Enforcement Committee, AMF dec. no. 20, 31 December 2019.
AMF, Enforcement Committee, AMF dec. no. 1 of 24 January 2020, SAN-2020-02.
AMF, Enforcement Committee, AMF dec. no. 9 of 28 May 2021.

EUROPEAN CASE LAW

EUROPEAN GENERAL COURT

Case T-496/11, *United Kingdom v. ECB*, ECLI:EU:T:2015:133.
Case T-733/16, *Banque Postale v. ECB*, ECLI:EU:T:2018:477
Case T-133/16, *Caisse régionale de crédit agricole mutuel Alpes Provence v. ECB*, ECLI:EU:T:2018:219
Case T-281/18, *ABLV Bank v. ECB*, ECLI:EU:T:2019:296.
Case T-149/18, *Arkéa Direct Bank and Others v. ECB*, ECLI:EU:T:2020:393.

EUROPEAN COURT OF JUSTICE

Case 21-76, *Mines de potasse d'Alsace*, ECLI:EU:C:1976:166.
Case 15/78, *Société générale alsacienne de banque SA v/Walter Koestler*, ECLI: ECLI:EU:C:1978:184.
Case 133/78, *Gourdain v. Nadaler*, ECLI: ECLI:EU:C:1979:49.
Joined Cases C-143/88 and C-92/89, *Zuckerfabrik Süderdithmarchchen and others*, ECLI:EU:C:1991:65.
Case C-214/ 89, *Powell*, ECLI: ECLI:EU:C:1992:115.
Case C-384/93, *Alpine Investment*, ECLI:EU:C:1995:126.
Case C-364/93, *Marinari*, ECLI:EU:C:1995:289.
Case C-465/93, *Atlanta Fruchthandelsgesellschaft and others*, ECLI:EU:C:1995:369.
Case C-55/94, *Gebhard*, ECLI:EU:C:1995:411.
Case C-212-97, *Centros*, ECLI:EU:C:1999:126.
Case C-11/00, *OLAF*, ECLI:EU:C:2003:395.
Case C-87/01, *Tetra Pak*, ECLI:EU:C:2003:400.
Case C-168/02, *Kronhofer v. Maier e.a.*, ECLI:EU:C:2004:364.
Case C-341/04, *Eurofood*, ECLI:EU:C:2006:281.
Case C-289/04, *Showa Denko KK*, ECLI:EU:C:2006:431.
Case C-372/07, *Hassett*, ECLI:EU:C:2008:534.
Case C-210/06, *Cartesio*, ECLI:EU:C:2008:723.
Case C-533/07, *Falco*, ECLI:EU:C:2009:257.
Case C-189/08, *Zuid-Chemie*, ECLI:EU:C:2009:475.
Case C-101/08, *Audiolux*, ECLI:EU:C:2009:626.
Case C-381/08, *Car Trim*, ECLI:EU:C:2010:90.
Joined Cases C-585/08 and C-144/09, *Peter Pammer*, ECLI:EU:C:2010:740.
Case C-144/10, *BVG*, ECLI:EU:C:2011:300.
Case C-248/11, *Nilas*, ECLI:EU:C:2012:166.
Case C-190/11, *Mühlleitner*, ECLI:EU:C:2012:542.
Case C-370/12, *Thomas Pringle*, ECLI:EU:C:2012:756.
Case C-543/10, *Refcomp*, ECLI:EU:C:2013:62.
Case C-184/12, *Unamar*, ECLI:EU:C:2013:663.
Case C-85/12, *Landbanski*, ECLI:EU:C:2013:697.

Case C-9/12, *Cormans-Collins*, ECLI:EU:C:2013:860.
Case C-270/12, *ESMA*, ECLI:EU:C:2014:18.
Case C-548/12, *Brogsitter*, ECLI:EU:C:2014:148.
Case C-375/13, *Harald Kolassa*, ECLI:EU:C:2015:37.
Case C-352/13, *Cartel Damage Claims (CDC)*, ECLI:EU:C:2015:335.
Case C-62/14, *Gauweiler*, ECLI:EU:C:2015:400.
Case C-681/13, *Diageo Brands*, ECLI:EU:C:2015:471.
Case C-594/14, *Kornhaas*, ECLI:EU:C:2015:806.
Case C-483/14, *KA Finanz*, ECLI:EU:C:2016:205.
Case C-366/13, *Profit investment*, ECLI:EU:C:2016:282.
Case C-12/15, *Universal Music*, ECLI:EU:C:2016:449.
Case C-196/15, *Granarolo*, ECLI:EU:C:2016:559.
Case C-135/15, *Nikiforidis*, ECLI:EU:C:2016:774.
Case C-156/15, *Swedbank*, ECLI:EU:C:2016:851.
Case C-54/16, *Vinyls Italia*, ECLI:EU:C:2017:433.
Case C-249/16, *Kareda*, ECLI:EU:C:2017:472.
Case C-658/15, *Robeco Holland*, ECLI:EU:C:2017:870.
Case C-560/16, *E. ON Czech Holding*, ECLI:EU:C:2018:167.
Case C-304/17, *Löber*, ECLI:EU:C:2018:701.
Case C-219/17, *Berlusconi*, ECLI:EU:C:2018:1023.
Case C-630/17, *Milivojević*, ECLI:EU:C:2019:123.
Case C-450/17 (T122-15), *Landeskreditbank*, ECLI:EU:C:2019:372.
Case C-25/18, *Kerr*, ECLI:EU:C:2019:376.
Case C-208/18, *Petruchova*, ECLI:EU:C:2019:825.
Case C-272/18, *VfK v. TVP*, ECLI:EU:C:2019:827.
Case C-500/18, *Reliantco investments*, ECLI:EU:C:2020:264.
Case C-59/19, *Wikingerhof GmbH*, ECLI:EU:C:2020:950.
Case C-316/19, *Commission v. Slovenia*, ECLI:EU:C:2020:1030
Case C-709/19, *Effectenbezitters*, ECLI:EU:C:2021:377.
Case C-911/19, *FBF.* ECLI:EU:C:2021:599.

ENGLISH CASE LAW (ALPHABETICAL ORDER)

aWB (Geneva) SA v. North America Steamship Ltd (2007) EWCA Civ 739.
Banco Santander [2016] EWHC 465.
Banco Santander (2016) EWCA Civ. 1267.
Belmont Park Investments Pty Ltd and others v. BNY Corporate Trustee Services Ltd and another, UKSC, 38, 2011.
BNP Paribas SA v. Trattamento Rifiuti Metropolitani SPA [2020] EWHC 2436 (Comm).
British Eagle International Airline Ltd v Cie National Air France [1975] 1 WLR 758, HL.
Credit Suisse International v Stichting Vestia Groep (2014) EWHC 3103 (Comm).
Dexia Crediop v Comune di Prato (2015) EWHC 1746 (Comm).
Dexia Crediop [2017] EWCA Civ 428 (15 June 2017).
Haugesund Kommune v. Depfa ACS Bank [2009] EWHC 2227 (Comm).
Haugesund Kommune v. Depfa ACS Bank [2010] EWCA Civ 579.
Haugesund Kommune v DEPFA ACS Bank (No 2) [2011] EWCA Civ 33.
Hazell v. Hammersmith and Fulham London Borough council (1990) 2 QB 697 (CA), 776.
Hazell v Hammersmith & Fulham LBC [1992] 2 A.C. 1 HL.

International Air Transport Association v Ansett Holdings Ltd [2008] HCA 3.
Lomas & ors (together the Joint Administrators of Lehman Brothers International (Europe) (in administration)) v JFB Firth Rixson, Inc & ors (2010) EWHC 3372 (Ch).
Macmillan Inc v Bishopsgate Investment Trust plc (No 3) [1995] EWCA Civ 55, [1996] WLR 387.
Re DAP Holding NV [2005] EWHC 2092 (Ch); [2006] BCC 48.
Re Harvard Securities Ltd (in liq.) & Anor (1998) B.C.C.
Re Lehman Brothers International (Europe) (in administration), Pearson v Lehman Brothers Finance SA (RASCAL) (2010) EWHC 2914 (Ch).
Re Lehman Brothers International (Europe) (in administration), Pearson v Lehman Brothers Finance SA (RASCAL) (2011) EWCA Civ 1544.
Re Real Estate Development Co [1991] BCLC 210.
Re Rodenstock GmbH [2011] EWHC 1104 (Ch); [2012] BCC 459.
Secure Capital SA v Credit Suisse AG [2017] EWCA Civ 1486.
Standard Chartered Bank v Ceylon Petroleum Corporation (2012) EWCA Civ 1049.
Titan Steel Wheels Ltd v The Royal Bank of Scotland plc (2010) EWHC 211 (Comm).
Vita Food Products Inc v Unus Shipping Co Ltd [1939] AC 277, 290 (PC).

AMERICAN CASE LAW (ALPHABETICAL ORDER)

Bersch v. Drexel Firestone, Inc, 519 F 2d 974, 985 (2nd Cir.), cert. Denied sub nom. *Bersch v. Arthur Andersen & Co*, 423 U.S. 1018 (1975).
Bonny vs The Society of Lloyd's, 3 F 3d 156 [7 th Cir. 1993], cert. denied, 114 S. Ct. 1057 [1994]
Europe and Overseas Commodity Traders, SA v Banque Paribas London 147 F 3d 118, 129 (2 d Cir 1998).
Parkcentral Global Hub Ltd. v. Porsche Automobil Holdings SE, Court of Appeals, No. 11-397-cv (2 d Cir.) August 15, 2014.
SEC V. Kasser, 548 F.2d 109, 116, cert. Denied, 431 U.S. 938 (1977).
United States District Court, Southern District of New York, *US v. BNP*, Statement of Facts, 28 june 2014.

INSTITUTIONAL REPORTS

The Hague Conference on Private International Law,
- *La loi applicable aux actes de disposition de titres détenus dans le cadre d'un système de détention indirecte*, Report by Christophe Bernasconi, Doc. Prel. No. 1, November 2000.
- *Hague Securities Convention, Explanatory Report* by Roy Goode, Hideki Kanda and Karl Kreuzer, with the assistance of Christophe Bernasconi, 2nd ed, 2017.

Commission of the European Communities,
- 'The completion of the internal market', COM (85 final), Brussels, 14 June 1985.
- 'Implementing the framework for financial services: action plan', COM (1999) 232 final, Brussels, 11 May 1999.

European Commission,
- Communication from the Commission to the European Parliament, the Council, the European Economic and Social Committee and the Committee of the Regions on the law applicable to property consequences of securities transactions, Brussels, 12 March 2018, COM (2018) 89 final.
- Commission staff working document, Impact assessment accompanying the document proposal of a regulation of the european parliament and of the council on the law applicable to the third-party effects of the assignment of claims, Communication from the Commission to the european parliament, the council, the european economic and social commitee and the committee of the regions on the applicable law to the proprietary effects of transactions in securities, Brussels, 28 March 2018, SWD(2018) 52 final/2.

Deletré (B.), Azoulay (J.) and Dugos (P.), 'Rapport de la mission de conseil sur le contrôle du respect des obligations professionnelles à l'égard de la clientèle dans le secteur financier', July 2009.

ESMA, 'Questions and answer on MiFID II and MiFIR market stuctures topics', 14 November 2018, ESMA70-872942901-38.

Financial Market Law Committee, 'Distributed Ledger Technology and Governing Law: Issues of Legal Uncertainty', March 2018.

HCJP,
- Recommendations on setting up specialised chambers in Paris to handle international business litigation, 3 May 2017.
- Response to the Treasury's public consultation on the draft legislative and regulatory reforms relating to Blockchain, 18 May 2017.
- Opinion on the legal feasibility of developing a clearing offer for interest rate derivatives in Paris, 17 October 2017.
- Report on the accessibility of the French market by UK banking and financial institutions in a post-Brexit environment, 7 November 2017.
- Report on the collateral effects of extending the European concept of public offer of financial securities, 25 March 2019.
- Report on central depository passports, 25 September 2020.
- Report on the 2002 ISDA master agreement (French law), 5 November 2020.
- Report on the reattachment of companies, 31 March 2021.

GIULIANO (M.) and LAGARDE (P.), 'Report on the Convention on the law applicable to contractual obligations' [1980] OJ *OJEC* 1980, C282/11.
Group of Thirty, 'Clearance and settlement in the World's Securities Market', New York/London, March 1989.
European Group for Private International Law, *Draft law applicable to company law*, Milan, 2016.
JENARD, 'Jenard Report', [1979] OJ C59/1.
LAROSIÈRE (J. DE) (ed.), 'The High-Level group on Financial supervision in the EU', report, Brussels, 25 February 1999.
LYON-CAEN (C.), 'Rapport à l'Institut de droit international', *Annuaire de l'Institut de droit international*, vol. 5, 1906-1911.
Office parlementaire d'évaluation des choix scientifiques et technologiques, Notes No. 4 'Understanding blockchains', April 2018, p. 2.
IOSCO and BIS, *Principles on financial markets infrastructures*, April 2012.
PÉROUSE (M.), *La modernisation des méthodes de cotation, d'échange et de conservation du marché des valeurs mobilières*, Paris, La Documentation française, 1980.
Final report of the Committee of Wise Men, *The Regulation of European Securities Markets*, 15 February 2001, available on the AMF website.
SYNVET, (H.), *Report on a draft conflict of laws rule for financial securities*, 2008.
VIRGOS (M.) and SCHMIDT (E.), *Report on the Convention on insolvency proceedings*, doc. CE no. 6500/96.

INDEX